JEWISH LATIN AMERICA

*Ilan Stavans, series editor*

**Titles Available in the University of New Mexico Press Jewish Latin America Series:**

Mestizo: A Novel by Ricardo Feierstein

The Jewish Gauchos of the Pampas by Alberto Gerchunoff

Cláper: A Novel by Alicia Freilich

The Book of Memories by Ana María Shua

The Prophet and Other Stories by Samuel Rawet

The Fragmented Life of Don Jacobo Lerner by Isaac Goldemberg

Passion, Memory, and Identity: Twentieth-Century Latin American Jewish Women Writers, edited by Marjorie Agosín

King David's Harp: Autobiographical Essays by Jewish Latin American Writers, edited by Stephen A. Sadow

The Collected Stories of Moacyr Scliar by Moacyr Scliar

Sun Inventions and Perfumes of Carthage by Teresa Porzecanski

Losers and Keepers in Argentina by Nina Barragan

The Martyr: Luis de Carvajal: A Secret Jew in Sixteenth Century Mexico by Martin Cohen

Like a Bride and Like a Mother by Rosa Nissán

The Algarrobos Quartet by Mario Goloboff

Yiddish South of the Border: An Anthology of Latin American Yiddish Writing, edited by Alan Astro

Unbroken: Testimony of a Holocaust Survivor in Buenos Aires, by Charles Papiernik, translated from the Spanish by Stephen A. Sadow

The Letters That Never Came by Mauricio Rosencof, translated from the Spanish by Louise B. Popkin

Pomegranate Seeds: Latin American Jewish Tales by Nadia Grosser Nagarajan

The Entre Rios Trilogy: Three Novels by Perla Suez, translated from the Spanish by Rhonda Dahl Buchanan

*Secrecy and Deceit*

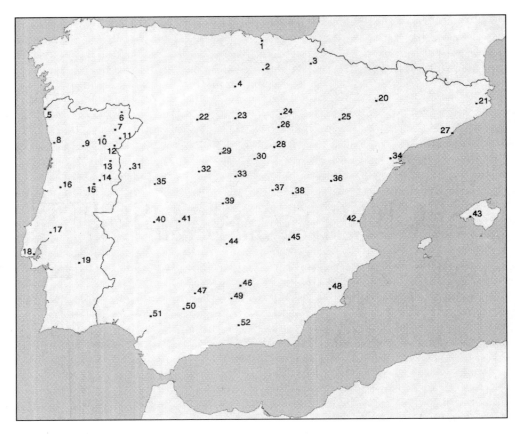

Principal locations of converso communities discussed in the text

1  Bilbao
2  Miranda de Ebro
3  Pamplona
4  Burgos
5  Caminha
6  Bragança
7  Carção
8  Porto
9  Lamego
10 Rebordeio
11 Vilariinha
12 Lagoaça
13 Pinhel
14 Belmonte
15 Covilhã
16 Coimbra
17 Santarem
18 Lisboa
19 Evora
20 Barbastro
21 Gerona
22 Valladolid
23 Aranda de Duero
24 Soria
25 Zaragoza
26 Almazán
27 Barcelona
28 Sigüenza
29 Segovia
30 Huete
31 Ciudad Rodrigo
32 Avila
33 Madrid
34 Tortosa
35 Hervás
36 Teruel
37 Huete
38 Cuenca
39 Toledo
40 Trujillo
41 Guadalupe
42 Teruel
43 Palma
44 Ciudad Real
45 Garcimuñoz
46 Baeza
47 Córdoba
48 Murcia
49 Jaén
50 Ecija
51 Sevilla
52 Granada

# SECRECY AND DECEIT

## The Religion of the Crypto-Jews

*David M. Gitlitz*

*Introduction by Ilan Stavans*

University of New Mexico Press
Albuquerque

© 1996 by David M. Gitlitz
© 2002 for the introduction by Ilan Stavans
Published by arrangement with the author
First University of New Mexico Press edition 2002
All rights reserved.
Originally published in 1996 by the
Jewish Publication Society, ISBN 0-8276-0562-5

10 09 08 07 06    2 3 4 5 6
ISBN-13: 978-0-8263-2813-7
ISBN-10: 0-8263-2813-X

**Library of Congress Cataloging-in-Publication Data:**
Gitlitz, David M. (David Martin)
Secrecy and deceit : the religion of the Crypto-Jews / David
M. Gitlitz ; introduction by Ilan Stavans
p. cm. — (Jewish Latin America)
Includes bibliographical references (p. ) and index.
ISBN 0-8263-2813-x (pbk. : alk. paper)
1. Jews—Spain—History.
2. Marranos—Religious life.
3. Spain—Ethnic relations.
I. Title. II. Series.
DS135.S7 G58 2002
946'.004924—dc21          2001059015

He said that he does not know how to reply to trivial accusations that would evoke laughter if they were not the cause for so many tears that they would extend unto the fifth generation.

*Dixo que no sabe qué responder a chanzas que eran buenas para reydas sino fueran causa de tantas lágrimas que llegaran hasta la quinta generación.*

> Francisco Vergara responds to accusations put to him by Inquisitors, Lima, Peru, July 1636 (García de Proodian, *Los judíos en América* 433)

# Contents

Preface / x
Introduction by Ilan Stavans / xvi
*Converso* Chronology / xix

**Part I  Historical Introduction / 1**
Chapter I      Conversions and *Conversos* through 1492 / 3
Chapter II     *Conversos* after 1492 / 35
Chapter III    The Major Points of Controversy / 73

**Part II  The Religious Customs of the Crypto-Jews / 97**
Chapter IV        The Crypto-Jewish Belief System / 99
Chapter V         Attitudes toward Christian Beliefs / 135
Chapter VI        Superstitions / 183
Chapter VII       Birth Customs / 199
Chapter VIII      Education / 217
Chapter IX        Marriage and Sex / 243
Chapter X         Ritual Purification and Hygiene / 271
Chapter XI        Death and Funeral Customs / 277
Chapter XII       Sabbath Customs / 317
Chapter XIII      Holidays / 355
Chapter XIV       Books / 425
Chapter XV        Crypto-Jewish Ritual and Prayer / 443
Chapter XVI       Oaths / 501
Chapter XVII      Communal Organizations, Synagogues, Rabbis / 507
Chapter XVIII     Clothing and Ceremonial Items / 523
Chapter XIX       Food and Dietary Laws / 531
Chapter XX        Conversion / 563
Chapter XXI       The Social Contexts of Crypto-Judaism / 587

Appendix—Edict of Faith / 625
Works Cited / 629
Index / 653

# ❧ Preface

The history of Jews on the Iberian Peninsula spans three thousand years. The beginnings are obscure, but may go as far back as Solomon's trade with Andalusian Tarshish (1 Kings 10:22) or the Phoenician coastal trading settlements of Iberia in the tenth century BCE. Jews undoubtedly traded along the Spanish coasts during the periods of Greek and Carthaginian domination of the Mediterranean, even though the first tangible archaeological evidence of Jewish Iberians dates only from Roman times. For the next fifteen hundred years the fortunes of Iberian Jews followed those of the Romans, Visigoths, Moslems, and Christians who successively controlled the Peninsula. On the whole Jews fared better when the dominant culture's religion was not fundamentalist in character or conversionist in policy. Jewish low points occurred when the Roman (312 CE) and then Visigothic states (589 CE) became Christian or when the puritanical Moslem Almoravids (1090) and later the Almohads (1147–60) purged Andalusian Islam. The high point was undoubtedly the florescence of Jewish culture in Moslem Andalucia during the tenth through the twelfth centuries. When Christian dominance over the Peninsula was finally assured in the mid-thirteenth century, Jews played a crucial role in cultural transmission and in the financial and political administration of the Christian kingdoms. Eventually this too turned sour, and on March 31, 1492, the Catholic Monarchs Fernando and Isabel signed an order giving the Jews four months to be Christian or be gone. From August 1, 1492, until the late nineteenth century there were legally no Jews in Spain. The fifteen thousand or so Jews who live there today are almost entirely recent immigrants.

Documentary evidence suggests that from at least Christian Roman times there had been many converts from and a few converts to Judaism. Those provisions of the separatist laws of the Council of Elvira (c. 300 CE), the Visigothic code (654–81), the Islamic Pact of Omar (ninth century), and medieval Christian legislation such as Alfonso X's *Siete partidas* (1265) which are aimed at hindering conversions from Christianity to Judaism would not have been necessary if sporadic conversions had not been taking place.[1] Numbers are impossible to estimate but, to judge from the scarcity of other documentation dealing with neophyte Jews, conversions to Judaism must have been rare. Other provisions of these laws encouraged conversion to the dominant religion, and evidence suggests that the number of Jews becoming Moslem or Christian was far greater than the number of converts to

Judaism. We know of many Jews who were forced to accept Islam by the Almoravid and Almohad fundamentalist rulers of Andalucia, but on the whole those converts emigrated at the first opportunity and took up Judaism again outside Iberia.[2] There were not sufficient numbers of converts from Judaism in either Moslem or Christian Spain to constitute a separate class of people until the 1391 riots suddenly forced tens of thousands of Jews in Christian Spain to accept baptism. As a result of the discouraging events of the next century many other tens of thousands of Jews converted to Christianity, and the 1492 Expulsion from Spain and the 1497 Expulsion from Portugal produced additional waves of converts. Prior to the Expulsions these *conversos* lived side by side with Jewish neighbors and family members. Following the Expulsions they and their descendants lived as a recognizable subgroup among the Christian populace of the Iberian world until they died, emigrated, or assimilated.

The converts from Judaism constituted a recognizable class of people, or, as the Spanish historian Américo Castro termed them, a *caste*.[3] Whether on the Iberian Peninsula or in the far-flung provinces of the Spanish and Portuguese empires, the new-Christians recognized themselves as a group (or groups) and were stigmatized as such by their old-Christian neighbors. The dozens of epithets coined to identify them frequently suggested both the circumstances of their conversion and their degree of adherence to Judaism. Hebrew-speaking Jews called them *anusim* (forced converts), *meshumadim* (willing converts), or *goyim gemorim* (full gentiles).[4] Spanish old-Christians called them *conversos* or *confesos* (converts), *cristianos-nuevos* (new-Christians) or *novells*,[5] *judaizantes* (Judaizers), *Marranos*, or just plain *judíos* (Jews). The Portuguese had their own versions of these terms and also called them people of the *Nação* (Nation). From the mid-fifteenth to the mid-seventeenth centuries, as a group the converts were so economically successful that Spain and then Portugal instituted so-called "purity-of-blood" laws explicitly to exclude them from a variety of professions. As a group the *conversos* were the butt of satire, the target of persecution, and a perennial subject of debate both within Spain and without. Even though individual *conversos* manifested the widest conceivable variations in lifestyle and belief, their coherence as a caste merits their treatment as a group. It permits certain kinds of generalizations about their religious customs and beliefs as well as their strategies for assimilating into Christianity or for holding on to their Jewish culture. These topics and the examples that substantiate them are the principal subject of this book.

While the converts shared many traits, they were by no means homogeneous in their practices or beliefs. Those *conversos* who wished to meld into the Christian mainstream did all they could to shed their Jewish practices and cover up their Jewish ancestry. Those who successfully assimilated tended to disappear from view. Other converts labored to preserve as much of their Jewish heritage as they could, but within the obsessively Christian milieu of the Iberian world their Judaism soon became idiosyncratic. Before long the "crypto-Jewish religion" was in many significant ways different from traditional Jewish practice. In spite of the will of many *conversos* to preserve their Jewish heritage, by the end of the seventeenth century the vast majority of these Judaizing converts had disappeared from Iberia and her possessions. The meager remnants who have surfaced in the twentieth century are the exceptional few, not the rule.

In part because clandestine societies are inherently fascinating, and in part because so many significant institutions and historical events depend on a clear understanding of who the converts were, over the years the crypto-Jews of Iberia have attracted a good deal of scholarly attention.[6] Likewise, the secrecy of the Spanish and Portuguese Inquisitions and the more violent aspects of their procedures have appealed to the popular, sensationalist, and sometimes prurient imaginations. Over the years the objectivity of much writing about the Expulsion, the Inquisition, and the *conversos* has been tainted both by the anti-Catholic biases of some Protestant historians and by the chauvinistic religious agendas of some Jewish and Spanish Catholic historians. Until very recently it has been necessary to approach with a degree of skepticism any summary writing about the subject.[7]

While a vast literature is available on Spanish Jews, on the Spanish Inquisition, and increasingly on the new-Christians, relatively less attention has been paid to the religious and social customs of the *conversos*. The principal exceptions are Roth (1931–2; 1932a); Domínguez Ortiz (especially 1955a; 1992); Caro Baroja (1961); Révah (1968); Liebman (especially 1970); Beinart (especially 1983); and Blázquez Miguel (especially 1988). These works tend to deal extensively with the political and economic aspects of the *converso* world but, with the exception of Roth's 1931–2 article, they concern themselves less centrally with the religious and social customs of the *conversos*. Moreover, their analysis of what Roth and Révah have called the "religion of the Marranos" is often fragmentary or contradictory and sometimes contentious.[8] Often the relationships between crypto-Jewish practices and the observances of normative Judaism are glossed over, as are the syncretisms between crypto-Judaism and Christian beliefs and practices. This book is intended to fill these gaps by presenting a comprehensive, well-documented picture of crypto-Jewish religious customs.

The book is in two parts: an introductory history of the crypto-Jews and an ethnographic survey of their religious customs. The first part summarizes the history of conversions from Judaism in Iberia up through the cataclysmic events of the late fifteenth century; it then characterizes the history of the converts in nine major historical periods from before the 1391 riots and first mass conversions up to the present day. The first part closes by reviewing four of the major points of controversy in *converso* studies: the problem of quantification, the reliability of the documents, the distinguishing characteristics of crypto-Judaism, and the historical typology of the *conversos*.

The second part of the book details and documents a wealth of crypto-Jewish customs, beliefs, and attitudes. The chapters are organized by theme, beginning with basic beliefs and attitudes, the life cycle (birth, education, puberty, courtship, marriage, death), Sabbath and festival observances, prayer and religious organizations, ceremonial items, dietary customs, and the social relationships that characterized the world of the crypto-Jews. Brief bibliographical references in the text are keyed to full bibliographical information at the end of the book.

An inhibiting factor for anyone wanting to learn more about the religious customs of Iberian crypto-Jews is the relative rarity and difficulty of access of many primary and secondary sources, as well as the fact that source materials are in a variety of languages. Sources for this book include almost every published transcription of Inquisition material, with some additional unpublished material from the Spanish and Mexican historical archives and corroborative material such as contemporary historical chronicles, Jewish *responsa* literature, autobiographies, and contemporary apologetic or polemical works. Because this work is intended for both scholarly and lay audiences, citations of source materials in Spanish, Portuguese, Catalán, Latin, Hebrew, French, and Italian are given in the notes, whereas English translations are used in the text proper.

This book would not have been possible without the assistance of a number of good friends and colleagues. I owe thanks to Norman Stillman, Len Gerber, Guy Matalon, and Rabbi Jacob Hurwitz for assisting me in locating traditional sources for crypto-Jewish practices. Manuel de Costa Fontes shared with me his collection of modern Portuguese Judaizing prayers and Gregory McNab assisted me with some of the Portuguese translations. I am thankful for the expert help of the University of Rhode Island's interlibrary loan staff, particularly Vicki Burnett and Marie Rudd, and acknowledge the kind assistance of numerous librarians at U.C.L.A., Harvard, Yale, Duke, Creighton, the universities of North Carolina, South Carolina, Florida, Nebraska, Tennessee, and Indiana University, and various Spanish and Mexican archives. Peter August and the Geographic Information Systems group at U.R.I. prepared the map of crypto-Jewish communities. Discussions with Constance Rose, Michael McGaha, and my brother John Gitlitz helped clarify a point or two. Greatest gratitude goes to my wife, Linda Davidson, for her sharp editor's eye and her unflagging enthusiasm for, and patience with, this project.

# Notes

1. Sections of these laws relevant to the Spanish Jews are found in Marcus 1938.
2. The most well known of the Almohad converts was Maimonides, who after his forced conversion in 1151 abandoned Andalucia for the Kingdom of Fez. For other evidence of Jewish conversions to Islam see Ashtor 1984, 191–2.

3. Castro defines *caste* as a status which depends on a person's mere existence, as opposed to *class*, which depends on what a group does or what it possesses. Caste in Spain was determined by one's religious affiliation and led to a worldview dominated by one's own self-consciousness rather than by things or ideas. In the evolution of this caste system most professions and aspirations, as well as certain values associated with them, tended to be distributed according to caste. In Castro's vision not only did the Jews, and after 1391 the *conversos*, dominate the fields of commerce and administration, but those fields became psychologically off limits for members of the Christian caste (1954b, 607–15; 1971, 48–63). The long and bitter controversy provoked among Spanish historians by Castro's ideas is reviewed in Gómez-Martínez 1975. See also Márquez Villanueva 1965.

4. Netanyahu 1966, 62, 70–1, 76. Edwards prefers to think of them as "Jewish Christians" who have a complex relationship with both Christianity and Judaism (1985, 39). For converts this book uses the terms *converso* and "new-Christian," which tend to be the most neutral of these labels, and "crypto-Jews" for the subset of *conversos* who continued to identify themselves primarily as Jews.

5. *Hom vulgarment appella novells* [Valencia 1413] (Hinojosa Montalvo 1993, 17).

6. Pioneering studies for Spain include Amador de los Ríos 1875; Menéndez Pelayo 1880–1, whose principal interest was the literary manifestations of *converso* concerns, and H. C. Lea's 1906–8 monumental study of the Inquisition. In Portugal the pioneer was Herculano 1854–9, whose work was continued by J. Azevedo 1921.

7. Through World War II orthodox Spanish historians considered Spain to be a fundamentally Roman-Christian society that during the Middle Ages had harbored Semitic cultures whose impact had been important but not transcendental. But in 1948 Castro's *España en su historia* offered a radically new interpretation of Spanish history, claiming that Spaniards spring from the early medieval clash, and amalgam, of Christian, Jewish, and Moslem cultures. Over the next two decades Hispanic scholarship was enlivened by Castro's bitter debates with the traditionalist Sánchez Albornoz, who argued that "there is nothing of the essence of the spirit, of the emotions, of the feelings, of the ideals, of the appetites, of the hopes, of the mechanism of the intellect, of the processes of conscience, of the style of life, of the temperamental make-up of the Hebrews that has left traces among the Spaniards" (1975, 769). Eventually Castro's views to the contrary came to prevail.

Because so much information pertinent to any understanding of the *conversos* is contained in documents related to the Inquisition, serious study must begin there. Fundamental to any study of the Inquisition, despite their occasional flaws, are the pioneering historical surveys of Llorente 1817, although the numbers he estimates are very high, and especially Lea 1906–7, whose encyclopedic vision is still valid despite his having had only second-hand access to the documentation; and J. Azevedo and Baião (each 1921), comprehensive overviews of the Portuguese Inquisition. Since World War II, and even more intensively since Franco's death in 1975, Spanish historiography has occupied itself repeatedly with the Inquisition. The most balanced and accessible treatments of the subject in English are still Kamen 1965 and Baron 1969. Basic to any understanding of Jewish life in Spain in the years preceding the Expulsion are Baer 1966 and Neuman 1942. The key work on the purity-of-blood laws remains Sicroff 1960.

Among Catholic apologists for the Inquisition are Llorca, Marcu, Menéndez y Pelayo, Pinta Llorente, Walsh, and to some extent Domínguez Ortiz. As Baron 1969, 317, 324 points out, historians as diverse in perspective as Amador de los Ríos, Castro, and Sánchez Albornoz have all in one way or another blamed some attitudes or procedures of the Inquisition on Spanish Jews or *conversos*. Both Castro 1971, 68–9 and Sánchez Albornoz 1975, 863–5 go overboard in arguing that the Inquisition and purity-of-blood laws derive from essentially Jewish attitudes and institutions, arguments ably refuted by Baer 1966, 2:444–5 and Sicroff 1960. Prominent among the Jewish historians who level rhetorical broadsides at the Inquisition is Roth. Sensationalistic exaggerations of the Inquisition's use of torture can be found in writers from Edgar Allan Poe ("The Pit and the Pendulum," 1843) right up to the present, where the television comedy group Monty Python has turned British fear of the Spanish Inquisition into black humor.

8. The major points of contention are analyzed here in the third chapter of the Historical Introduction. Important review articles of *converso* studies are Márquez Villanueva 1965, Domínguez Ortiz 1965, Nahon 1977, and Lorence 1982.

# ❧ Introduction
## Ilan Stavans

*Ils s'acheminérent vers un château immense, au frontispice duquel on lisait: "Je n'appartiens à personne et j'appartiens à tout le monde. Vous y étiez avant que d'y entrer, et vous y serez encore quand vous en sortirez."*

—Diderot

David Gitlitz's encyclopedic volume is a tour through the palace thus described by Diderot in *Jacques Le Fataliste et son Maître*: a magisterial citadel—from the French locution *citadelle*: "a city within a city"—made of tortuous alleyways, where no passerby ever finds his way across.

The palace, of course, is a metaphor for the identity of crypto-Jews. Gitlitz offers a detailed catalogue of their manners: their hygiene, their birth customs, their liturgical rituals, their sexual interaction, their dietary laws and superstitions. These manners have been passed along from one generation to the next, with a sole purpose is mind: the concealment of truth. Their dishonesty isn't reprehensible; instead, it is a strategy of survival. For these crypto-Jews, the reader is made to understand, are consummate actors; on the surface they appear to be average citizens, but really they are part of a clandestine club that enables them to exist in a parallel universe. The degree of furtiveness varies from generation to generation. It isn't improbable, for instance, that for some of its members the club might be so secret an entity they might not be aware of their membership in it. In any case, for them Hamlet's question, "To be or not to be?," is turned, unapologetically, into an affirmation: "To be *and* not to be."

Gitlitz took some fifteen years of his adult life to build the catalogue, a task he came to rather circuitously. He traveled to a myriad of libraries and also found himself equipped with the inquisitive tape-recorder, hoping to seize the confession that hid another key to the enigma. From the route his mind travels it is evident that he enjoys jigsaw puzzles, and that he is an archaeological aficionado. In his youth he was in Lima, excavating sites with a team from the Universidad Católica. Then, in graduate school, he oscillated toward the orbit of peninsular luminaries such as Stephen Gilman, Raimundo Lida, and Francisco Márquez, whose erudition kept him focused on the context of literature, an aspect often ignored by hyped theorists in the field. Gitlitz reacted antagonistically to the study of the Spanish Golden Age at the time, which he found tacitly anti-Semitic, saturated with rumors and innuendoes. Still, as his curiosity piqued, he asked himself: How ought one find out more about a people whose culture flourished in eclipse? What inner and outer challenges did the crypto-Jews face? How did they manage to retain a sense of integrity amidst the seduction of assimilation by a society that refused to go beyond the racial jingoism of *la pureza de sangre*, the concept of "purity of blood"? The effort paid off: *Secrecy and Deceit*, released in a hardbound edition in 1996, was awarded the National Jewish Book Award, as well as the Lucy Dawidowicz Prize. In the arena of Sephardic culture its appearance is an event as significant, and as controversial, as William of Moerbeke's Latin translations of Aristotle in the thirteenth century. A handful of Gitlitz's critics picked up on the restrained numbers of his printed sources and on the parsimony of tête-à-tête interviews, while others portrayed him as unsuited for a task that requires a classically-trained Orthodox Jewish authority conversant in the *Talmud* and *Mishna,* and in Hebrew *responsa* in general; his endorsers, on the other hand, praised not only the overall breadth of his scholarly approach—I've already used the adjective *encyclopedic* to describe the catalogue and now add *exhaustive, plenteous,* and *inclusive*—but also the well of his anecdotes and the stunning precision in the art of evaluating crypto-Jewish religious practices over time.

Harold Bloom once exposed an inherent contradiction in Gershom Scholem's oeuvre: How is it that so intelligent a scholar devoted his entire career to deciphering and popularizing an esoteric literature when to survive that literature needs to be kept away from the masses? A similar contradiction, I'm convinced, also inhabits *Secrecy and Deceit:* Isn't the labor itself an aggression of sorts targeted on the keepers of that shrouded truth, for the moment one delves into its pages the secrets assembled evaporate, instantaneously becoming measurable facts? The answer, of course, is that there is no intellectual exercise that isn't, at its core, a form of falsification. Gitlitz's endeavor sheds light on the mysteries of identity. It is a response to the dilemma of American Jews attracted by the idols of cosmopolitanism. Proof that it is an inescapable product of its age is the fact that, almost from the start, it became a kind of template among descendants of *conversos,* especially in the Southwest, northern Mexico, and Central America. To them it is a mirror that validates a suspicion. *Suspicion,* by the way, is defined in the *Oxford English Dictionary* as "a feeling or state of mind."

I cannot think of a better way to end this introduction than to invoke an uncanny story told to me without the slightest hint of perplexity in Toledo by a financier from Greece. Part of his family lived in Istanbul, the rest in his hometown Salonika. His parents, his sister, and he—an eight-year-old Ladino speaker—were arrested in 1943 and eventually shipped to Bergen-Belsen. Prior to their departure, his father buried a treasure box under the olive tree in the backyard and hid the key and directions to the location of the box in a secret place beneath the rooftop. Only a few relatives knew the secret, but not where the key was placed. He and a cousin survived the Holocaust. Upon his return to Salonika, he was told about the secret. He looked for the key but was unsuccessful. Years went by in which he became obsessed by the whereabouts of the box. Soon he found himself married. His wife gave birth to five children. Upon fixing a leak in the house, one of them accidentally came across a folded map with directions to the treasure. The key was nearby. The financier rushed to the place beneath the olive tree and began to dig. What he found frightened him at first, then overwhelmed him with emotion: the box contained neither jewels nor real-estate documents, as he expected, but a photo-album with pictures—yellowed by time—of him, his wife, and children, all surrounding his aged parents, seated in relaxed posture under the olive tree.

# ❧ *Converso* Chronology

The nine periods in this table coincide with the phases of *converso* history discussed in the Introduction.

PRESSURE MOUNTS

| | |
|---|---|
| 1238 | Papal Inquisition established in Aragon. |
| 1290 | Expulsion of the Jews from England. |
| 1306 | Expulsion of the Jews from the kingdoms of France; many enter Aragon. |
| 1321 | Conversion of Abner of Burgos. |
| 1378 | Jews protest anti-Semitic preaching of Ferrand Martínez of Ecija; protests repeated in 1384, 1389. |

CONVIVENCIA FALLS APART

| | |
|---|---|
| 1391 | Riots in Seville and other Andalusian cities result in the destruction of the Jewish quarters and many forced conversions. |
| 1408 | Castile and Aragon oblige Jews to live within the Jewish quarters of the cities and to wear distinguishing marks on their clothing. |
| 1412 | Fray Vicente Ferrer preaches conversion of the Spanish Jews. Valladolid laws require Jews to live only within the *aljamas*. |
| 1413–4 | Disputations of Tortosa. |
| 1415 | Bull of Antipope Benedict XIII supports converting the Jews. |
| 1435 | Death of Pablo de Santa María, *converso* Bishop of Burgos. Conversion of the Jews of Majorca. |
| 1449 | Riots in Toledo, Ciudad Real, and elsewhere destroy Jewish districts and lead to more conversions. |
| 1460 | Fray Alonso de Espina's *Fortalitium fidei* urges conversion of the Jews. |
| 1462 | Anti-*converso* riots in Carmona (Seville). |
| 1467 | Anti-*converso* riots in Toledo. |
| 1473 | Riots in Andalucia; persecution of Jews in Valladolid and *conversos* in Córdoba. |

THE COMING OF THE INQUISITION

| | |
|---|---|
| 1478 | Bull of Pope Sixtus IV establishes the Castilian Inquisition. |
| 1480 | Castilian Cortes prohibits relations between Jews and *conversos*. |

| | |
|---|---|
| 1481 | First Edict of Grace published in Seville and thousands of Castilian Jews and *conversos* come forward to testify. |
| | First *auto de fe* held in Seville. |
| 1482 | Tomás de Torquemada named Chief Inquisitor in Castile. |
| 1483 | Inquisition tribunal established in Ciudad Real. |
| | Torquemada named Inquisitor General. |
| 1484 | Inquisition tribunal established in Valencia. |
| | Pedro de Arbués named Inquisitor in Aragon. |
| 1485 | Arbués assassinated. |
| 1487 | Aragonese Inquisition established in Sicily. |
| 1488 | New Spanish Inquisition begins work in Majorca. |
| 1491 | Alleged ritual murder incident in La Guardia (Toledo). |

THE EXPULSION GENERATION

| | |
|---|---|
| 1492 | January 2: Granada captured by the Christians, ending 800-year war of reconquest. |
| | March 31: Edict of Expulsion is signed giving the Jews 4 months to depart or convert. |
| | July 31: Jews are required to be gone from Castile and Aragon. |
| | August 2: Some *conversos* set sail with Columbus. |
| 1496 | Expulsion order signed in Portugal. |
| 1497 | Conversion of the Jews of Portugal. |
| 1499 | Expulsion of the Jews from Navarre. |
| 1504 | Inquisition established in the Canary Islands. |
| 1507 | Cardinal Jiménez de Cisneros appointed Inquisitor General. |
| 1513 | Inquisition established in Navarre. |
| 1520–1 | *Comunidades* war in Castile involves many *conversos*. |
| 1528 | Execution of first two men accused of Judaizing in New Spain (Mexico). |

CONVERSO CULTURE ACROSS THE EMPIRE

| | |
|---|---|
| 1539 | Inquisition established in Portugal. |
| 1540 | First Portuguese *auto da fe*. |
| 1547 | Papal bull recognizes an independent Portuguese Inquisition. |
| 1570 | Inquisition established in Peru. |
| 1571 | Inquisition established in New Spain (Mexico). |

THE PORTUGUESE DIFFUSION

| | |
|---|---|
| 1580 | Portugal annexed to Spain: Inquisition activity increases. |
| 1604 | Papal general pardon for Judaizing activity in Iberia is briefly in effect; Portuguese crypto-Jews disperse through Hispanic world. |
| 1624 | Dutch capture Bahia in Brazil. |

| 1625 | Spain retakes Bahia. |
| 1628 | Felipe IV grants Portuguese *converso* merchants the right to trade freely. |
| 1630 | Dutch capture Recife and crypto-Jews begin to practice openly. |
| 1640 | Portugal separates from Spain. |
| 1654 | Brazilian "New Holland" retaken by the Portuguese; Jews must leave. |
| 1679 | Violent persecution of the Majorcan *chuetas*. |
| 1680s | Peak of Spanish Inquisition persecution of Portuguese Judaizers. |

## Sweeping up the Crumbs

| 1707–13 | Last major wave of Inquisition trials against Judaizers in Brazil. |
| 1722–5 | Last major wave of Inquisition trials against Judaizers in Spain. |
| 1773 | King José I of Portugal voids legislation discriminating against new-Christians. |
| 1782–8 | Elimination of discriminatory laws against the Majorcan *chuetas*. |
| 1804 | Jewish resettlement of Portugal begins; first Jewish tombstones in Lisbon cemetery. |
| 1812 | Spanish Cortes suppresses Inquisition in Spain and the colonies. |
| 1814 | Spanish King Fernando VII reestablishes the tribunals. |
| 1820 | Spanish Inquisition permanently suppressed. |

## Apparatus of Oppression Dismantled

| 1821 | With independence, Mexican Inquisition abolished. Inquisition abolished in Portugal. |
| 1834 | Spanish Inquisition formally abolished. |
| 1865 | Isabel II abolishes purity-of-blood as a requirement for state positions. |
| 1892 | Portuguese decree affirms freedom of worship. |

## Rediscovery of Iberian Sephardic Roots

| 1917 | Samuel Schwarz discovers remnant crypto-Jews in Belmonte, Portugal. |
| 1940 | Arias Montano Institute for Sephardic Research established in Madrid. |
| 1964 | Franco signs order establishing Sephardic Center and Museum in Toledo. |
| 1966 | Spanish law guarantees religious freedom. |
| 1968 | Dedication in Madrid of first modern public synagogue. Expulsion Decree revoked. |
| 1992 | Quincentennary of Expulsion from Spain celebrates Sephardic culture. |

# PART I

Historical Introduction

# CHAPTER I

# Conversions and *Conversos* through 1492

## JEWS AND CONVERSOS IN SPAIN BEFORE 1391

By the middle of the thirteenth century Castile, Aragon, and Portugal, the three major Christian kingdoms in the Iberian Peninsula, had essentially won the centuries-old war of reconquest against the Moslem kingdoms of the south. For the two hundred fifty years until January 2, 1492 only the diminutive kingdom of Granada, high in the fortress of the southern mountains, remained under Moslem control. Almost all of the descendants of the Iberian Jews who had tasted the glory of Judaism's tenth- to twelfth-century Golden Age in Moslem Andalucia now found themselves living under Christian jurisdiction. As long as the issue of the final control of the Peninsula was in doubt, the Christian ruling classes had tended to deal benevolently with their Jewish subjects as useful cultural and financial intermediaries and potential enemies. For example, Fernando III of Castile (1230–52)[1] styled himself monarch of three religions, and a spirit of *convivencia*, or cultural interdependence, prevailed. However, once the balance of power had definitively shifted in the early thirteenth century to the kingdoms of Christian Spain, the precarious tolerance of *convivencia* was gradually replaced by a nationalism that adopted religious exclusivity, not diversity, as one of its defining characteristics.

Continuing earlier trends, in the thirteenth and fourteenth centuries Spain's Jews tended to cluster within the developing cities in tight-knit Jewish districts called *aljamas* (Port. *judarias*). The largest and strongest communities, each consisting of from 100 to 200 Jewish families, were in Toledo, Burgos, Zaragoza, Huesca, and Barcelona. Other towns with large Jewish populations included Cuenca, Segovia, Avila, Medina del Campo, Valladolid, Carrión de los Condes, Soria, Tudela, Pamplona, and Palma de Majorca. Jewish-related royal documents and legislation of the period concern themselves principally with the various kingdoms' financial administrators and moneylenders, but these high-profile Jews were the minority of the Jewish population. Most Jews were small farmers, wine merchants, smiths and saddlers and shoemakers, the proprietors of small shops, or artisans in leather and pottery, textiles and jewels; a few were physicians or druggists. In the port cities many were engaged in trade.[2]

Since proselytizing is central to the Christian vision of exclusive truth, it is natural that from its earliest days and down through the ages Christianity had attracted some converts from Judaism.[3] In the thirteenth century European Christendom directed new attention to policies affecting conversion. The Fourth Lateran Council, convened in 1215 to address problems of heresy that were plaguing the Church in southern France and elsewhere, among its other accomplishments established a legal framework for encouraging conversions through the systematic debasement of the Jews. European Catholicism increased its pressure on the Jews through economic strictures, localized expulsions, attacks on the Talmud, and preaching campaigns led by the new mendicant orders, particularly the Dominicans and to a somewhat lesser extent the Franciscans. The Iberian Peninsula, with its long history of coexistence among the three major religions, to a degree resisted the extremist pressures emanating from the papacy and the mendicant orders, but it was not entirely immune. As early as 1263 the Aragonese King Jaime I authorized a debate in Barcelona that pitted Saint Raymond of Penyafort and the convert Pablo Christiani against the renowned Jewish rabbi Moshe ben Nachman in a discussion of the alleged unreliability of the Talmud. Although the Barcelona disputation did not produce large numbers of converts, it established the principle that the Dominicans could go into the synagogues to preach conversion to the Jews, and that the Jews had to listen (Suárez Fernández 1991, 80–7). By 1297 there were enough converts that a law protecting their inheritance rights against Jewish interference had to be passed (Suárez Fernández 1991, 127).

In the fourteenth century the number of conversions grew from a trickle to a small stream. There were many reasons for this, ranging from the religious skepticism of many Jewish intellectuals to a variety of physical, economic, and social pressures applied by Christians, for whom the conversion of the Jews was becoming an increasingly important policy issue. Many converted Jews, particularly those who because of their views or conduct had clashed with the Jewish authorities, themselves became the most aggressive conversionists.

Perhaps the most important convert of the fourteenth century was the learned Jewish physician Abner of Burgos. After decades of religious inquiry, and visions in which Christian icons were prominent, Abner became Christian in 1321 (Baer

1966, 1:327–54) and, as Alfonso de Valladolid, devoted the rest of his life to conversionist activities. These included publishing several books, both in Hebrew and in Spanish, urging his former coreligionists to join him in apostasy. His work was very influential. The principal tenets of his reasoning were repeated in the conversionist debates of the next 160 years and bear some direct responsibility for the violent events of 1391 and what followed. Abner's strongest arguments were philosophical: he believed that classic Jewish texts implicitly supported the basic doctrines of Christianity such as the Incarnation, the Trinity, and personal salvation through the intervention of the Messiah. He rejected the philosophical rationalism of the school of Maimonides, which dominated Jewish religious thinking of his day, in favor of faith in the Christian mysteries, which he related to the Kabbala. His philosophy of history, which was highly deterministic, highlighted the favored status of Christianity and the debased state of Judaism, which he attributed to the Jews' obduracy in rejecting Jesus as the Messiah. The specifics of his polemic attacked Jewish beliefs, liturgy, holidays, and other practices in great detail. He argued that Christians had the obligation to confront Jews, to convert as many as possible, and to eliminate the rest. Although several Jewish rabbis formulated counter-arguments and counter-proofs (Baer 1966, 1:357–8), they proved unsuccessful in diminishing Abner's influence.

Jewish attempts to reintegrate converts into orthodox Judaism were universally condemned by Christian theologians and politicians. The persecutions of Jews in southern France and their expulsion in 1306 had driven many French forced converts to Christianity to take refuge among the Jewish communities of Cataluña and Aragon, where they were encouraged to return to Judaism. The French Dominican Inquisition crusaded against these "false" converts and against the Jewish abettors of heresy, the *fautores haereticorum*, who assisted them. Aragon's King Jaime II, relatively benign in matters concerning the Jews, could not permit his Jews to undermine the Catholicism of converts, and through the 1320s the offending individuals and communities were severely punished by the Aragonese Inquisition.[4] The early fourteenth century saw increasing pressure against the Jews in the kingdoms of Aragon and Navarre. Because of an alleged ritual murder on the Aragonese island of Majorca, extraordinary fines were levied against its Jewish community in 1309. In 1320–1 the French "Shepherds' revolt" spilled over into Navarre and sacked the *aljamas* of Jaca and Monclús (Suárez Fernández 1980, 163–6). Anti-Jewish riots, once rare, became increasingly common in the unsettled environment of late medieval Spain. Whenever instability was at flood or royal authority was at ebb, such as periods of interregnum,[5] or during plague years,[6] or when civil wars raged,[7] the *aljamas* trembled. Each civil disturbance caused some Jews to convert.[8]

The movement to Christianity intensified toward the end of the fourteenth century, even before the 1391 riots. The most prominent convert of this period was Solomon Halevi, chief rabbi of Burgos, who around 1389 took the name Pablo de Santa María and at Avignon Antipope Benedict XIII's request returned to Burgos as bishop, where he engaged in conversionist activities.[9] Some prominent Jews who seemed to have perceived the coming crisis arranged their conversion with very favorable terms. One example is Isaac Golluf, the son of the Jewish director of the treasury for King Juan I's wife Violante, who apostatized as Juan Sánchez de Calatayud in 1389 with the stipulation that he would nonetheless inherit his Jewish father's estate.[10] His conversion sparked that of a number of followers. This group of converts appears to have been motivated by neither coercion nor religious conviction, but rather by political or economic opportunism (Baer 1966, 2:92–4).

As the fourteenth century wore on, the Christian kingdoms imposed increasingly severe strictures on Spain's Jewish communities. Kings Felipe III (Navarre), Alfonso XI (Castile), and Jaime II (Aragon) intermittently defended the Jews, but with an eye toward their substantial financial contributions to the royal exchequer. In 1348 Castile's Jews were prohibited from lending money at interest, but there is no evidence that the law was enforced, and in 1351 it was repealed by the Cortes, which feared it would strangle the economy (Baer 1966, 1:360–2). While some Jewish communities prospered and erected splendid new synagogues, such as that built by Pedro I's chief treasurer Samuel Halevi in Toledo in 1357,[11] and Christian nobles continued to rely on their Jewish advisors and fiscal administrators, conditions overall continued to deteriorate for Spain's Jews. Both religious and class antagonisms were converging against the Jews; the outbreaks of violence these antagonisms occasioned were sometimes spontaneous and sometimes orchestrated. The lower classes—heavily taxed, frequently in debt, tending to identify the Jews with the forces they felt were oppressing them—could be set off by the slightest spark. Meanwhile those with influence and power increasingly used the negative feelings against the Jews as a tool to consolidate or extend their power and preserve their privileged status (Monsalvo Antón 1983, 91).

There were sporadic outbreaks of violence in a number of cities. In 1328 rioters in Navarre killed many Jews and destroyed Jewish property. In Seville in 1354 Jews were attacked for allegedly desecrating a host.[12] When the Castilian prince Enrique of Trastamara overthrew his brother Pedro in 1366, he based his campaign in part on purging Pedro's "Jewish administration," and in the civil wars of the late 1360s thousands of Castile's Jews were killed as cities were taken and retaken. From early times an anti-Semitic vein had run through Christian popular literature in Castile as in the rest of Europe, but it gathered new strength in the 1370s. In Aragon popular anti-Semitism was somewhat less strong, Jews were somewhat less central in royal administration and sentiments against Jewish usury did not run as high as in Castile, but Aragonese municipalities too attempted to relegate their Jewish inhabitants to activities of lower economic and social status.[13]

# 1391

Jewish-Christian relations in Andalucia plummeted in the summer of 1378 in Seville, when the popular Archdeacon Ferrand Martínez began to preach a holy war against the Jews and called for the destruction of Seville's twenty-three synagogues. The Jewish community repeatedly petitioned King Juan I to restrain the Archdeacon from "preaching evil and untrue things" about the Jews, from usurping jurisdiction over their legal affairs, from threatening to excommunicate municipal officials who did not utterly segregate the Jewish communities, and from inciting civil unrest. The King, who viewed Martínez's rabble-rousing as an affront to his personal jurisdiction over Jewish affairs and as a threat to the financial benefits he derived from the Jews, three times responded with letters of injunction (Suárez Fernández 1980). Martínez, taking license in what he called the higher authority of the Christian Gospels, as well as the protection of the Pope, persisted in his preaching. Juan I acceded to a variety of anti-Jewish demands such as prohibiting Jews from living in Christian neighborhoods and working on days of Christian festivals. That was the state of affairs when Juan I died in 1390.

The new Castilian King Enrique III (1379–1406) was still a minor and a weak interregnal regime was established. Martínez and his followers seized the opportunity to put their invective into action. There is no question that economic antagonisms between the nascent Christian burgher class and the well-established Jewish merchant community were one element that motivated the mobs. But the precipitating factor was the inflammatory preaching of Martínez, which fanned long-smoldering popular anti-Semitism into a riot. In June of 1391 rioters swept into the Jewish quarter of Seville, burning, raping, looting, destroying fiscal records, and forcibly converting as many Jews as they could to Catholicism. Within days the prosperous Jewish community of Seville lay in ruins. Within a week or two the same fate had befallen most of the rest of Andalucia's Jews, as the rioters pillaged through Montoro, Andújar, Jaen, Ubeda, and Baeza. When the rioters turned north the disorder spread to the cities of central and northern Castile. In Toledo the splendid synagogues now known as the Tránsito and Santa María la Blanca were turned into churches. In Cuenca municipal authorities rang the church bells to summon the rioters to action (Baer 1966, 2:97). The Castilian government issued strict orders to citizens to refrain from looting, but these were almost entirely ignored. Overnight the ancient Jewish communities of Ciudad Real and Burgos entirely disappeared (Suárez Fernández 1980, 208). In each community many Jews were killed. Still larger numbers were forcibly converted to Catholicism either by the clergy who accompanied the mobs in their pillaging or in the charged atmosphere of the days following the riots. When the choice was between conversion or death, most Jews chose conversion.[14]

In Aragon the riots followed the same pattern as in Castile as the rioters made their way from town to town. Early in July the Valencian Jewish community was destroyed.[15] Although the King ordered the mobs to cease and prohibited further forced conversions, the riots spread to smaller towns and many Jewish communities in the Kingdom of Valencia were converted in toto to Catholicism. In the Balearic Islands, Gerona, and Barcelona, despite the government's half-hearted preventative measures, riots broke out in early August, with the by now familiar pattern of murder, pillage, and forced conversion. Although sporadic rioting continued for nearly a year, the worst was over within the space of three months, during which Castile and Aragon induced the largest group of forced converts Judaism had known up to that time.[16] The converts came from all social classes, including the wealthy and politically advantaged. One-fourth of the 60 Barcelona Jews who served on the Jewish community's governing council toward the end of the fourteenth century were baptized in 1391 (Baer 1966, 2:37).

In the aftermath of the events of 1391 the dispirited and much weakened Castilian and Aragonese Jewish communities tried to recuperate. But it was very hard going. The Aragonese monarchs took steps to reestablish the major urban Jewish communities of Barcelona, Valencia, and Majorca, but they were fought every step of the way by the Christian burghers. More progress was made in smaller cities such as Tarragona, Gerona, Sagunto, Cervera, and Lérida. Jews now feared the crowded cities and tended to disperse among small towns in communities that were themselves small; before long there were 36 separate Jewish communities in Aragon and 216 in Castile (Suárez Fernández 1991, 204). Under such conditions Jewish intellectual life was effectively stifled. The Jewish leadership suffered still more defections to Christianity and Christian legislation increasingly attempted to make the lives of the Jews miserable in order to induce them to convert. The most important of these laws, the laws of Ayllón (1412), which turned the *aljamas* into ghettos, required Jews to wear a distinctive badge,[17] and barred them from a variety of their habitual professions, were so rigorous they could not be fully implemented. The kings, chief prelates, and principal nobles continued to engage some Jewish advisors and be attended by Jewish physicians, but after 1408 most of these posts were held instead by *conversos*.

The existence of a large and widespread group of forced converts was something new for both European Jews and Christians. Whereas before 1391 Christians could welcome converts individually, and relapsed converts might be castigated on an exceptional case basis, after the 1391 mass conversions several issues were forced into the realm of policy. How to deal with the converts, now generally referred to as *conversos* or new-Christians, constituted a major problem for Christians and Jews alike. How to behave as converts—What was permitted, or politic, or dangerous? What was vital and what was trivial?—became important issues for individual *conversos*. In the aggregate, *converso* behavior became a matter of policy for both the Jewish and Christian leadership.

Jewish policy-makers agonized between principles of tolerance and exclusion. Which would more readily assure the return to Judaism of the *conversos* and which would deter further conversions? Should Jews shun *conversos* as apostates who had accepted an idolatrous religion rather than sanctify the Divine Name by accepting martyrdom? Or should they apply the Maimonidean principle that forced conversion is permissible as long as the convert takes the first opportunity to revert to Judaism, usually through emigration (Levi 1982, 20)? Should they make every, or for that matter any, effort to woo them back to Judaism, even though this was expressly prohibited by Christian law and punishable by death, or should they leave the *conversos* alone to make their own decisions? The dilemma was particularly sharp because frequently families had been divided along religious lines when in the chaos of the riots some members, trapped in the Jewish quarter, had been forced to convert, while others escaped baptism. A 1391 letter from Maestre Astruc Rimoch of Fraga (Cataluña), to a friend whose father and brothers had converted but whose mother remained Jewish, poignantly relates the personal anguish of those difficult times:

> Regard the misfortune of your [brother who] has left the fold never to return! . . . Look about you! Everywhere brother is divided against brother and kin against kin. . . . As for your poor, regal mother, I can inform you that she is living in bitterness in her husband's house and continues to abide by the [Jewish] Law and act decorously; and although many are her tormentors and would-be converters, her one reply is that she would die before going over. But now, thanks be to God, nothing hinders her from making her way daily to the *judería*, and when she visits the House of God, the women there inquire of one another that she should not have to walk alone, and the good souls among them accompany her up to the gate of the quarter. . . . In regard to her departure, it would appear to be your father's intention not to permit her to leave the city until he takes another wife.[18]

Christians too faced legal and moral dilemmas in dealing with the *conversos*. Moderate Christians were likely to consider forced conversion reprehensible, but at the same time they held the benefits of baptism to be irreversible and the jurisdiction of the Church over the converts to be inviolable. Thus the governments issued injunctions against the emigration of *conversos* under the assumption that once they had safely crossed to France or Africa they would revert to Judaism. Similarly, numerous legal measures were taken to inhibit reversion by forbidding *conversos* to associate socially with Jews. Both sets of laws were inconsistently administered at both the national and the municipal levels.[19] Concerned long-time Christians also felt an obligation to instruct the new-Christians in the rudiments of their adopted faith,[20] but little money or effort was invested in support of this principle, the authorities trusting that, while the first generation would seldom be thoroughly Catholicized, subsequent generations would assimilate as a matter of course.[21] Instead, Christian energies were invested in efforts to achieve more conversions. Recognizing that a welcoming climate was essential for motivating voluntary conversions, Church and government officials repeatedly but ineffectively forbade mistreatment of the *conversos*.[22]

## Early Fifteenth Century: Disputations

The two decades following the riots were characterized by intense debates and disputations between the intellectual leaders of the Christian and Jewish communities about the superiority of Christianity over Judaism. In truth these "debates" were theatrical catechistic exercises (Suárez Fernández 1991, 218) designed to induce conversions. The impetus for the disputations came from Christian conversionists, who counted among their number many recently baptized Jews. Jews entered the lists only because Christian authorities compelled them to debate, yet in the course of the disputations their internal religious doubts or concerns with the theological consequences of contemporary history led them to question their commitments to Judaism.

One of the earliest and most thoughtful debates was the exchange of letters between Pablo de Santa María (formerly Solomon Halevi of Burgos) and his friend Joshua Halorki of Alcañiz. After his baptism in 1390 or 1391, Pablo went to Paris to study Christian theology; from there he corresponded with many of his former coreligionists to explain his motives and to encourage them to join him. When he claimed to have concluded that Jesus had fulfilled the Messianic predictions of the classic Jewish texts, Halorki wrote to him enumerating the four factors that in his view were the cause of so many conversions. The first was careerism, "lust after riches and honors," which is to say the increased social mobility that conversion offered to Jews. The second was Averroism, the philosophical inclination to value reason over faith and science over tradition, which fostered secularism and led Jews to be open to the possibility of conversion.[23] The third was contemplation of recent history, which led to the conclusion that God had switched allegiance from Judaism to Christianity. The fourth was that Christian doctrine, as foreshadowed in the Torah and the Prophets, as revealed in the New Testament and elucidated by the Fathers of the Church, was true. Because Halorki considered Halevi one of the great Jewish intellects of the age, and therefore largely immune to the first three, he accepted Halevi's espousal of the fourth reason as convincing evidence. He was fortified in this belief by the preaching of the Valencian Dominican Friar Vicente Ferrer (1350–1419; canonized in 1455). It is not surprising that Halorki also eventually converted and, as we will see in a moment, became an ardent Christian propagandist (Baer 1966, 2:142–50, 171). Jewish writers of this period, such as Profet Duran (*Kelimath ha-Goyim* [*The Confusion of the Gentiles*] c. 1391?) and Hasdai Crescas (*Or Adonai* [*The Light of the Lord*] 1410), worked hard to counter the eroding influence of the Christian polemicists, but on the whole the tide was against them.

The conversionist debates, which had intensified after the 1391 riots, peaked in the years 1412–6, spurred by the silver tongue of Fray Vicente Ferrer, who toured the cities of the Mediterranean coast and Castile preaching against the Jews, converting synagogues to churches, and baptizing new-Christians. Although Ferrer's sermons eschewed violence and urged that Jews be brought to the baptismal font through persuasion alone, all contemporary accounts of his preaching crusades suggest that they were conducted in an atmosphere in which violence was just below the surface.[24]

The debates were abetted by a variety of governmental policies. In these years the conversionist agenda was constantly in the ears of the young new kings of both Castile and Aragon. Ferrer himself was a principal advisor of King Fernando I of Aragon, who had assumed the throne in part through Ferrer's influence, while Pablo de Santa María, now Bishop of Burgos, advised Castilian King Juan II. In short order a number of new anti-Jewish policies were announced, culminating in the Valladolid legislation of 1412. In the urban areas Jews were required to move into special districts, often in the least attractive parts of the city. They were forced to wear the Jew badge. They were prohibited from exercising almost all of their traditional professions. And they were barred from any social intercourse with Christians (which included, of course, the new-Christians who often formed part of their extended families). The intent of these regulations was transparent: Jews must be debased to a point where conversion became an attractive option. For a variety of political and economic reasons these laws were only sporadically enforced, but they constituted a clear sign to the Jews that for them conditions in Castile and Aragon were rapidly deteriorating.

One of Vicente Ferrer's most important converts was the Joshua Halorki who had years before corresponded with the newly converted Pablo de Santa María. The Avignon Pope Benedict XIII (formerly Pedro de Luna, a Spaniard who had befriended Pablo de Santa María during their student days in Paris) at this time, as the schismatic Pope, needed successes in Spain to bolster his fight for the Roman papacy. At his behest Halorki, with the Christian name Jerónimo de Santa Fe, presided over a great debate staged in the Aragonese city of Tortosa in 1413–4. Each Jewish community in Aragon was required to send a minimum of two prominent scholars to Tortosa to be instructed in the Christian faith. The disputation began in January of 1413 with a statement from the Pope himself, who reiterated his purpose: this was not to be a debate between equals, but rather a demonstration to the recalcitrant Jews that the principal tenets of Christianity had been accurately foretold in the Talmud. For well over a year the disputation examined the fine points of messianic doctrine, and then for several months it discussed the "errors, heresies, abuses and reviling of the Christian religion in the Talmud" (Baer 1966, 2:224).[25]

While most of the religious leaders remained firm in their Jewish convictions, others—including fourteen rabbis—converted, persuaded by the theological arguments or overwhelmed by the coercive atmosphere of the disputation or motivated by one of the other reasons enumerated by Halorki twenty years before. Some, such as the Caballería (formerly Bonafos) family, were financially and politically prominent; within a year several of the new-Christian Caballerías had become the principal financial advisors and administrators of the Aragonese crown. Others, such as the poet Francisco de San Jordi (formerly Astruc Rimoch), dedicated themselves to conversionist propaganda. Each conversion of a highly visible Jew brought many others in its wake. In addition, Fray Vicente Ferrer continued to travel among the towns of Aragon inciting conversions. From 1412 to 1416, when King Fernando I died and Benedict XIII was stripped of his papal authority, thus depriving Ferrer of his own base of power, a large portion of Castile's Jews and an even larger portion of Aragon's were converted to Christianity.[26]

## THE SOCIAL AND ECONOMIC LIFE OF FIFTEENTH-CENTURY CONVERSOS

The precipitous down-slide in the fortunes of Spain's Jews that had begun with the events leading up to the 1391 riots and culminated in the Disputations at Tortosa slowed for a time when Fernando I and Benedict XIII departed the political scene. Although the great Jewish communities of Valencia and Barcelona were no more and the other Jewish communities of the Kingdom of Aragon had been greatly reduced, a fragile and intermittent truce in Jewish-Christian relations held sway. The new king of Aragon, Alfonso V (1416–58), turned his attention from religious matters to building his economic and political base and to the affairs of the Kingdom of Sicily, which he had inherited. Juan II of Castile (1406–54) was similarly more occupied with affairs of state than with those of religion. Castile had lost the ancient prestigious Jewish communities of Toledo, Burgos, and Seville, but during this period the Jewish populations of other cities and medium-sized towns showed modest natural growth.

Spain's late medieval Jewish communities were largely middle class. Although a handful of important Jewish financiers and royal advisors figure prominently in contemporary political documents and modern histories, most Jews were artisans or small businessmen. The royal chronicler Andrés Bernáldez describes them in his early sixteenth-century *History of the Catholic Monarchs.*

> They were all merchants and retailers, tax farmers and collectors of fines and administrators of estates, cloth-shearers, tailors, shoemakers, tanners, leather dressers, weavers, spice merchants, peddlers, silk merchants, silversmiths and other similar professions. None of them tilled the soil, or was a laborer, or carpenter or mason.[27]

Some Jews did own or manage vineyards or pasturages[28] and some were physicians, but on the whole Bernáldez's description is accurate in its emphasis on artisanry and small trade. Both in Spain and in Portugal the converted Jews continued in these professions as well as entering Church and municipal administration in large numbers.[29]

As Bernáldez indicates, the Jewish upper classes tended to administer estates and farm taxes.[30] About two-thirds of Castile's indirect taxes were farmed by Jews (Baer 1966, 2:250). Under Juan II, Abraham Bienveniste of Soria was the chief tax collector; under the next King, Enrique IV, Joseph ibn Shemtob held the post.

*Converso* families like the Bienvenistes, the Abravanels, and the Seneors held these posts for generations. Often, as in the case of Abraham Bienveniste, one man served as chief tax collector of the kingdom and chief rabbi and judge of the Jewish community.

Additional Jews converted to Catholicism during this period, but in numbers not nearly so great as in the preceding decades. By the 1430s it was exceedingly common among Spain's Jewish communities for there to be families some of whose members were Jews and some *conversos*. Last testaments of the time frequently divide estates among Christian and Jewish children.[31] While logic suggests that most of the 1391 forced converts (whom the Jews termed *anusim*) would continue to identify themselves as Jews and to maintain as much Jewish practice as possible, and that the willing converts (*meshumadim*) would attempt to assimilate as quickly as possible, in reality matters were not that simple. The fact that so many families included members of different religions vastly complicated matters. Despite repeated attempts to keep them separate,[32] by the mid-fifteenth century the Jews and *conversos* tended to form a single extended community. Some *conversos* had only recently come to the baptismal font. Others were the now aged veterans of the 1391 disturbances, together with their children and grandchildren who had been raised as Christians, or as Jews, or as both. Some *conversos* had entered the Church as professional clergy, while their siblings continued to celebrate the Sabbath and buy their meat from the local kosher butcher. Most *conversos* regularly attended mass; some also celebrated Yom Kippur, donated oil for the synagogue lamps, and gave alms for the maintenance of the Jewish poor. In cities where the Jewish community had been totally obliterated, such as Gerona, Barcelona, and Burgos, *conversos* tended to assimilate rather quickly. But in cities where a remnant Jewish community remained strong, such as Ciudad Real, Segovia, Toledo, Teruel, and Lérida, *conversos* continued to interact with it. Not surprisingly, these Judaizing *conversos* themselves as well as their old-Christian neighbors continued to characterize them as Jews.

The *conversos* tended to remain in the same sorts of economic activities as they had been engaged in formerly as Jews. The majority were minor businessmen, merchants, and artisans, the makers and sellers of small goods. In the years prior to the Expulsion, extended families of *converso* artisans frequently provided apprenticeship opportunities for young *converso* men with an eye to keeping them in the business and in the religion. For many *conversos* the professional milieu replaced the former social milieu of the *aljama* and was a strong factor in helping them maintain their crypto-Jewish identity.[33] Nevertheless, once the young men had established their own shops and were no longer dependent on the crypto-Jewish network, many of them became thoroughly Catholic (Haliczer 1990, 216–7).

*Conversos* from wealthy or prestigious families often found spouses from among the great noble old-Christian families. Assimilationist urban middle-class *conversos* commonly intermarried with the lower nobility, who sought thereby to improve their material fortunes, to such an extent that by mid-fifteenth century nearly every Castilian and Aragonese noble family had some formerly Jewish members. Over the next hundred years several muckraking pamphlets were published detailing the Spanish nobility's Jewish ancestry. The most popular, the *Libro verde de Aragon* and the *Tizón de la nobleza de España*, went through numerous editions (Kamen 1965, 28–30). Since Visigothic times Spain's Jews had never been peasants; *conversos* did not intermarry with the rural agricultural poor. Since male Jews had to be able to read and discuss Torah in order to fulfill their religious obligations, while their Christian counterparts needed only to hear mass, Spain's male Jews were almost 100 percent literate and Christian literacy rates were low. The *conversos* carried forward this tradition of literacy, which in the rapidly developing urban centers made them attractive candidates for mid-level positions in financial, legal, and government administration that were formally barred to Jews. In the highest circles increasingly *conversos* took positions formerly held by Jews. The new-Christian Caballería family came to dominate financial life in Aragon, while in Castile the *converso* Diego Arias de Avila and later his son Pedro served as managers of the royal accounts.

Popular antipathy toward the Jews in most respects had been transferred to the *conversos*. Interfaith relations were increasingly strained by the tensions of economic competition.[34] Old-Christian peasants and burghers were paying their taxes to Jewish or *converso* tax farmers, agents of the ruling classes who performed the unpopular work of tax collection. Their courts and municipal offices were largely in the hands of *conversos*. Old-Christian business ventures had to compete with *converso* shops up and down the street. What is more, popular wisdom held that the ubiquitous *conversos* were secret Jews whose practices maligned the Christian sacraments and risked bringing God's wrath down upon the Christian populace. The offspring of fear and envy was militant animosity. For the lower classes the fact that the crown seemed to favor the Jews just made them more odious. We see signs of the strife in repeated municipal legislative attempts to restrict the freedoms of Jews and *conversos*[35] and in repeated royal claims that Jewish matters were a royal prerogative and no affair of the towns.[36] Growing conflicts between the crown and the municipalities targeted Jews and *conversos*, as did the intensifying conflicts between the peasantry and the burghers and the peasantry and the crown. Since throughout the fifteenth century popular anti-Semitism considered Jews and Judaizing *conversos* to be a single, indivisible group, all these conflicts were stoked by the increasing attention given in sermons, pamphlets, and the courts to the traditional anti-Jewish calumnies of host desecration, ritual murder, and the slaying of Christians by Jewish doctors.

It is not surprising that these tensions sometimes flared into violence. One of the worst outbreaks occurred in Toledo in 1449. Old-Christian burghers attacked the property of a *converso* tax farmer who was trying to collect a new royal tax levied by the hated prime minister Alvaro de Luna. Several other prominent *con-*

*versos* who were arrested by Pedro Sarmiento, the commander of the city's castle, were tortured into confession, and burned at the stake as relapsed heretics who were secretly practicing Jews. What followed had aspects of a class war. Sarmiento accused the *conversos* of having infiltrated the administrative structure of the city in order to impoverish the old-Christians over whom they had gained power. He issued edicts banning *conversos* from holding most public offices or from testifying in the courts. Although King Juan II eventually apprehended Sarmiento and revoked the exclusionary laws—often considered Spain's first purity-of-blood laws[37]—these events firmly underscored the popular conviction that *conversos* were secret Jews and that their heresy was appropriately punishable by both Church and civil authorities.

## THE CONSOLIDATION OF THE SPANISH STATE

During the reign of Castile's King Enrique IV (1454–74) anti-*converso* rhetoric grew much more intense. In 1460 the King's own confessor, the Franciscan Friar Alonso de Espina, began writing *Fortalitium fidei*, in which he recounted and embellished all the anti-Jewish and anti-*converso* arguments up until his day, exemplified by a horrific series of cautionary anecdotes.[38] Cogently, and for the first time, Espina offered a solution to Spain's religious strife: an inquisition to extirpate the heretical backsliding of the *conversos* and the expulsion of Spain's remaining Jews. During the 1460s Espina preached this program in the palaces and plazas of Castile, aided by the head of the Jeronymite order Friar Alfonso de Oropesa. In 1464 local Church-sponsored inquisitions in both Toledo and Valencia punished several flagrantly Judaizing *conversos*. The interrogators were not entirely off base in their concerns about Jewish proselytizing to the *conversos*, for during this period some Spanish Jewish communities, such as that of the Aragonese city of Huesca, actively sought to reintegrate *conversos* into Judaism, even going so far as to circumcise converts in semi-public ceremonies of great solemnity (Baer 1966, 2:294–9).

These events must be considered in light of the civil war that raged in Castile throughout the 1460s. Complex dynastic concerns pitted Enrique IV and his putative daughter Juana against Enrique's teenage half-siblings Alfonso (1452–68) and Isabel. In 1465 a contingent of old-Christians led by Alfonso de Oropesa petitioned Enrique to permit an inquisition against recalcitrant *conversos*. But that same year a large faction of the kingdom attempted to depose Enrique in favor of Alfonso. For a time Castile had two warring kings. When rumors swept the *converso* communities that Alfonso intended to curry old-Christian favor by establishing an inquisition, many *conversos* switched their allegiance to Enrique's faction. Politicians lobbied both sides. When Alfonso's troops entered Toledo in 1467 passions flared into open war. The old Jewish quarter, now the *converso* district, went up in flames. Although some of the perpetrators were punished, the issue was still a tinderbox. When Alfonso was slow to answer the city leaders' demands that he endorse their anti-*converso* regulations, they threatened to defect to Enrique. Alfonso acceded, and the desires of the extremists became state policy. When the young prince-king died the following year, his seventeen-year-old sister Isabel picked up the reins and carried the anti-*converso* passion into her marriage with fifteen-year-old Prince Fernando of Aragon in October of 1469.

By then it was reasonably clear that Isabel's party would win the Castilian war. Thus she and Fernando were supported by leading Jews and *conversos*, who were well aware that their fortunes depended on their Monarchs' good will. The *converso* Caballería family of Aragon even assisted Fernando in the marriage preparations. A century of unremitting conflict had proved to the Jews and *conversos* that in times of strife they were likely to become targets. The royal newlyweds' platform of law and order won out over concern about the Monarchs' religious fanaticism.

But not even the throne's intermittent attempts to keep a tight lid on insurrection succeeded in preventing anti-*converso* violence from welling up. Riots in 1473 throughout Andalucia burned *converso* neighborhoods and sent the surviving *conversos* scurrying for safe havens. The Monarchy, which always felt threatened by any sort of civil disturbance, took some measures to quell the violence. When the Marquis of Villena took advantage of the 1473 riots to take control of the city of Segovia, the *converso* and Jewish leadership assisted in turning the city, with its castle and resources, over to Isabel, and in trying once again to make peace between her and her half-brother Enrique. Once again Jews and *conversos* were caught in the middle. In the aftermath of the 1473 disturbances the laws requiring Jews to reside inside the walled *juderías* were much more strictly enforced.[39] Some cities restricted Jewish commercial ventures to certain times and places. New versions were issued of older laws requiring Jews (and Moslems) to wear distinctive clothing. Christians and Jews were again repeatedly forbidden to mix at meals and in a variety of other social circumstances. In addition, the municipalities passed laws barring *conversos* from holding a variety of civic offices. That same year local inquisitions in Córdoba and Ciudad Real investigated their *converso* populations' Jewish practices.

When Enrique finally died in 1474 Isabel became the undisputed queen of Castile. She ruled with Fernando until her death in 1504. Fernando inherited his own crown of Aragon on the death of his father in 1479. Thenceforth they ruled a united Castile and Aragon. With what has often appeared to be a single will, the self-styled Catholic Monarchs consolidated power in the crown at the expense of the anarchic nobility and brought peace, based on foundations of law and justice, to kingdoms long wracked by war. One of their principal devices was to revive the centuries old war of reconquest, marshaling the Castilian and Aragonese factions in a united effort to eliminate the Moslem political presence in the Peninsula. In doing so, they put unity of religion at the core of their definition of the nascent modern state. Under their rule Catholic Spain would soon be purged of Moslems, Jews, and, they thought, heretics.[40]

There is no question whatsoever about the directions in which Fernando's and Isabel's policies were leading, and yet the behavior of the Catholic Monarchs and of many of the leading *converso* and Jewish courtiers of the period often seems strangely ambivalent. The major outlines of Castile's and Aragon's Jewish policies were clear by mid-century. With respect to practicing Jews, the goal was to physically isolate, politically and economically restrict, and socially degrade them to such an extent that they would be moved to convert to Catholicism.[41] With respect to *conversos*, by far the more thorny problem since as Christians the *conversos* were theoretically welcome in the majority society, the goal was to use external pressure to compel them to religious orthodoxy while at the same time to circumscribe their social and economic mobility in ways that would prevent them from allegedly dominating their old-Christian competitors (Domínguez Ortiz 1992, 19). Strong elements in the Church and the municipalities took the lead in agitating in these directions. The Monarchy followed two political courses. It jealously guarded its financial rights over the Jews and acted with vigor against any physical or commercial threat that might affect royal income and control; in other matters related to the social status or religious privilege of the Jews, it sided with the forces of restriction and persecution.

Fernando's and Isabel's personal behavior reflected this duality of approach. They were not rabid anti-Semites in the Hitlerian mold. In fact, during the early years of their reign they were remarkably evenhanded in dispensing justice to Jews and Christians alike. Both groups were obliged to pay numerous taxes, to quarter royal troops, and to defend their cities in time of need. Moreover, in the face of increasingly violent threats to the Jews the Catholic Monarchs vigorously protected them as members of the Monarchs' personal household. Documents attest to numerous instances where the Catholic Monarchs interceded on Jews' behalf. In 1475 they forced the village of Medina de Pomar to grant access to Jewish businessmen. In 1476 they deposed the mayor of Trujillo for abusing the Jews (Suárez Fernández 1991, 265). In 1490 they required the city of Bilbao to allow Jewish merchants to spend the night inside the city so they might be protected from robbers.[42] Up until the point when the Catholic Monarchs accepted the inevitability of the Expulsion of the Jews, they were protective of them.

The royal courts were filled with Jews and *conversos* who enthusiastically lent their talents in support of the emerging nation of Spain. In Castile the Jews Abraham Seneor, Rabbi Meir Melamed, Vidal Astori, Samuel Abulafia, and various members of the Abarbanel family assisted the Queen in her political and financial affairs. A host of other Jewish tax officials continued in their positions. In Aragon Fernando's *converso* retinue included several Caballerías (Jaime, who accompanied Fernando to Naples; Alfonso, Vice Chancellor of Aragon; Martín, commander of the Majorcan fleet) and members of the Sánchez family (Luis, the Chief Justice;

Gabriel and Guillén, each in turn the Chief Treasurer; Alfonso, the Deputy Treasurer), Francisco Gurrea (the governor of Aragon), Miguel de Almazán (his private secretary), and others (Madariaga 1893, 24). The Caballería family had been instrumental in helping young Fernando with his marriage plans. The Santángel family played a crucial role in arranging the financial backing for Columbus. Even while Jewish physicians were no longer officially welcome in the royal court, both the King and Queen were frequently attended by Jewish physicians. There seems to have been no ironclad policy of excluding Jews or *conversos* from other roles, even in the late 1470s as planning for the Inquisition accelerated, or in the early 1490s as the Expulsion was being contemplated. Hernando de Pulgar continued as royal chronicler. Lope de Conchillos and Miguel Pérez de Almazán continued advising the King and Queen. It is as if the Monarchs, and for that matter the leading Jews and *conversos* themselves, were able to divorce their personal behavior from official policies, as if they were blind to the inevitable outcomes of those policies and the effect they would have on their lives.

## THE COMING OF THE INQUISITION[43]

In 1478 Pope Sixtus IV granted Fernando's and Isabel's request that the Spanish crown be permitted to appoint Inquisitors to attack the heresy they said was rife in Andalucia. Simultaneously they revived the laws of 1412 that required the physical separation of Jewish and Moslem living quarters from those of Christians. By January of 1481 forced relocations were taking place throughout the Peninsula and the Inquisition had begun hearings in Seville. The early targets were almost exclusively *conversos,* most of them people who had fled Seville to escape the rumored threats of the Inquisition. And they were preponderantly from the empowered classes, including numbers of municipal and court officials. In Aragon Fernando reactivated the Inquisitorial tribunals that had previously existed, coordinating them with those of Castile. The initial feeble resistance to the establishment of the Inquisition was quickly crushed.[44] Because the non-assimilation of *conversos* was seen to be strongest in Andalucia, the early Inquisition was most active there. The royal chronicler Andrés Bernáldez estimated that in its first eight years of operation in Seville alone the Castilian Inquisition burned 750 men and women (Baer 1966, 2:327). Additionally, in 1483 all Jews were required to leave Andalucia, ostensibly to deny them influence over the *conversos* there.

Much has been written about the Spanish Inquisition, and it is not my purpose here to review that vast literature—much of it sensationalistic—or to relate its history or to discuss its procedures in any depth. Yet a basic understanding of what it was and how it operated is fundamental to understanding the 250-year survival of crypto-Jewish culture in Spain. The Inquisition impelled crypto-Judaism to develop strategies of secrecy. It influenced the choice of which Judaic customs would survive and which would quickly atrophy. In many ways it helped to create the very culture it was dedicated to eradicate. And its methodical procedures left copious records from which have been gleaned the bulk of the data for this book.

In its organization the Inquisition was hierarchical and bureaucratic. During the whole of its history it was administered by monks; during the first two centuries a large percentage of them were Dominicans. The Pope appointed the Inquisitor General, but at the behest of the King. Other appointments were at the discretion of the Inquisition itself. The first and second Inquisitors General were Fray Tomás de Torquemada and Fray Diego de Deza, both Dominicans and both *conversos*. The governing body was a council, the Consejo de la Suprema y General Inquisición, appointed by the King. Although the ultimate power derived from the papacy, from its inception the Spanish Inquisition was in essence a tool the Spanish monarchy used to consolidate and then maintain power in the throne.

During the early years tribunals were convened and dissolved as need arose, that is, when a center of crypto-Judaism was identified and until it was eradicated. By the mid-sixteenth century there were standing tribunals, twelve in Castile and four in Aragon. Each of the district tribunals was headed by two Inquisitors who were the examining judges. Each had an *asesor* who combined the duties of legal advisor and defense attorney, a prosecuting attorney called a *fiscal*, bailiffs called *alguaciles*, and a coterie of scribes. During most of the Inquisition's existence it also employed networks of paid informers called *familiares*, but it relied more heavily on voluntary informants, whom Jews and *conversos* stigmatized with the Hebrew term *malsin*.[45] Operating methods were standardized in accord with centrally authorized manuals of procedures.[46] The Inquisition was sustained financially by confiscations.

The Holy Office had jurisdiction over the spiritual transgressions of all Catholics. After the Expulsion, when officially there were no longer any non-Christians in Spain, this meant that its jurisdiction was universal. Before 1492 its jurisdiction was limited to all those who had been baptized and to those Jews and Moslems who blasphemed against Christianity or in any way impeded an individual's conversion to Christianity.[47]

In function the Inquisition was quasi-judicial. When the Inquisitors formally entered a particular city, the first event would be the public reading to the assembled populace of an Edict of Grace (later called an Edict of Faith).[48] The entire populace would be in assembly, for not to attend would call attention to oneself, and in matters of heresy any attention was potentially dangerous. The Edict of Grace required people who considered they might be guilty of some heretical practice or thought to come forward during a "grace period" of some finite number of days to confess and be assigned penance, warning that any heresy later discovered in those who did not voluntarily come forward would be severely punished. It also required information from anyone who knew of someone else's heretical behavior, or even who knew that someone else might know. To aid parishioners in properly identifying heresy, the Edict of Grace included a list of customs considered suspicious. By 1514 the Edicts of Grace enumerated these customs in great detail; later Edicts of Grace, which repeated them with little change, not only kept the Christian populace alert to signs of heresy but also ironically provided crypto-Jews with a kind of instruction manual in the basic concepts and practices of their faith.[49] Leniency was offered to those who came forward of their own volition and severity promised to those who had to be called because of other people's denunciations. Whether from a desire to unburden themselves of their secrets, or as an attempt to court leniency, or out of fear of third-party denunciation, in the early years of the Inquisition large numbers of *conversos* turned themselves in. People were encouraged to report any indication of potential heresy, no matter how trivial.[50] At the interview specific follow-up questions were asked and detailed notes taken. As will be seen, this book relies heavily on such testimony, for its very triviality and minuteness provide, in the amalgam, a comprehensive portrait of crypto-Jewish practices and alleged practices over some two hundred fifty years.

During the period of grace, and sometimes beyond, the Inquisitors took testimony from voluntary and coerced witnesses. The well-known Inquisition policy of not revealing the names of witnesses encouraged denunciations and hampered any serious defense. After information was gathered, it was culled, sifted, and cross-indexed. When evidence was deemed sufficient to suspect heresy, individuals would be arrested, usually at night, and whisked away to solitary confinement in an Inquisition prison. There they were asked to contemplate their past behavior and prepare a confession of any acts of heresy of which they might be guilty or of which they might have knowledge. Since the Inquisition recognized the temptation to give false testimony to settle personal scores, it gave accused heretics the opportunity to disqualify denunciations from their personal enemies by allowing them to make a list of people who might have grievances against them, with details about the grievance and witnesses to it.[51] The lonely imprisonment, with the burden of constructing a believable but not overly incriminating version of one's life, often wreaked havoc with the minds of the *conversos* awaiting trial.[52] At some appropriate moment they would be called to testify before an Inquisitor and the data of their lives would be taken down by scribes. If the information did not closely match what the Inquisition had received from other sources, the accused might be subjected to torture in order to "ratify" their confessions.[53] These sessions too were duly recorded. After the depositions were taken the Inquisitors would mull over the facts of the case. Often additional witnesses were called and more testimony was added to clarify details of the case.

Eventually—occasionally after many years[54]—the Inquisition would render a decision. Sometimes accused Judaizers were set free for insufficiency of evidence to convict. These were not acquittals but merely suspensions of the case, which could be reopened at any time if new evidence came to light. Even those who were eventually released without formal penalty paid a price in temporary loss of freedom, damage to reputation, and in some cases loss of health. The financial burden was great as well, since from the moment of arrest all assets of the accused would be attached to use for the maintenance of the prisoner and for court costs.

Those convicted of heresy, of course, paid a far greater price. Penance was assigned according to the severity and circumstances of the infraction. For relatively light offenses of first-time offenders, penance might include a small fine, house arrest, a certain number of prayers, or attendance at church on specified days. Frequently it compelled the guilty party to wear in public a special penitential garment, called a *sambenito*,[55] on which the guilty person's name and heresy had been written. When the sentence had been completed, these *sambenitos* would be hung in the parish church in perpetuity as a reminder to the guilty person, and his or her family and neighbors, that the family was tainted with heresy and must be scrutinized forever for any sign of relapse. For more major offenses the penalties could include confiscation of goods, imprisonment, flogging, or exile. In the second half of the sixteenth century convicted heretics were even sent to row in the royal galleys. The most serious offenders or repeat offenders might be handed over, or in the jargon of the Inquisition "relaxed," to the secular authorities (*brazo seglar*) for execution: strangling and then burning for repentant offenders and burning alive for the unrepentant. Because of the social nature of heresy, which allegedly could affect a family for generations, and because the Inquisition was entitled to a portion of the confiscated property of convicted heretics, even cases against the already deceased were prosecuted to the fullest, with the bones of the departed sometimes exhumed for public burning.

Penances would be meted out at a public ceremony designed to make vivid to all and sundry the majesty of the Church sitting in judgment and the exemplary debasement of the convicted heretic. This ceremony, called an Act of Faith (Sp: *auto de fe*; Port: *auto da fe*), was held periodically with the utmost pomp. On the appointed day the entire populace, old-Christians and *conversos* alike, would gather in the city's principal plaza. As with the reading of the Edict of Grace, not to attend would cast suspicions on the family. The accused prisoners, who had not yet been informed about the extent of their guilt, or the sentence, were marched in their penitential garments before the high tribunal of Church officials. The *auto* might well be the first glimpse in years that the family had of a loved one. With great solemnity each name was called, the litany of offenses was read, and the penance imposed. At day's end some walked away with minor punishments, some returned to prison, and some went to the stake.

In theory the chief aim of the Inquisition was the salvation of Christian souls by discovering heresy, promoting recantation, and imposing penance. Its punishments were designed to be exemplary; that is, their principal purpose was to demonstrate the consequences of heresy so as to encourage orthodoxy of belief and practice in both the convicted sinner and the general public. Whenever possible, sinners found guilty of minor heresies were "reconciled" back into the Catholic faith. Capital punishment was reserved for the unrepentant, or for repeat offenders, and in practice only a small percentage of convictions merited the ultimate penalty.[56]

All this was in theory. In practice the Inquisition pursued not only religious goals but also political, social, and economic ends in the name of religion. The very first wave of trials in Seville singled out *conversos* who occupied positions of administrative or economic influence. As much as it was a religious crusade, Inquisition activity was a sustained attack on the Iberian *converso* middle class.[57] Over the Inquisition's long history its judges did not always evaluate evidence with the same thoroughness or equanimity, or sense of fairness.[58] At times it seemed that punishment was more important than reconciliation, and that the governing motive was the extirpation of the caste of *conversos*. This was particularly true of the trials of the 1480s and 1490s, in which convictions were based on relatively slim testimony, few witnesses were disqualified, and the maximum penalty was levied with alarming frequency.

Prior to the establishment of the Inquisition *conversos* ranged along a continuum from observant Jew to observant Catholic, with innumerable gradations and inconsistencies along the way. Most *conversos* belonged to extended families in which some members identified themselves as crypto-Jews (and sometimes openly as Jews) while others were assimilationist.[59] Some *conversos* wavered between the two religions. Some practiced them sequentially; some tried to practice them concurrently. For the most part children could be reared in an atmosphere of choice. While *conversos* incurred some danger in continuing to practice Judaism, the odds were not great that the consequences would be mortal. Many, perhaps most *conversos* lived in the gray world at the intersection of the two religious cultures.

But all this changed radically in the 1480s with the coming of the Inquisition. As can be imagined, the effect on the *converso* communities at the time was devastating. The substantial number of *conversos* who continued to identify themselves as Jews and to practice Jewish customs fled for their lives at the first hint of the Inquisition's commencing hearings in their town. Trial records of the 1480s in both Castile and Aragon vividly communicate the sense of panic that overtook *converso* communities with the coming of the Inquisition. Some crypto-Jews rushed to emigrate, fleeing to nearby Christian countries, North Africa, or, with a sense of messianic immediacy, to the Holy Land in Ottoman Turkey (Baer 1966, 2:338, 381). Crypto-Jews learned from the Andalusian excesses, so that large numbers of them bolted when they learned that the Inquisition was on the way. The numbers tell the story. In the first two years of operation in Ciudad Real, 52 Judaizers were executed, and another 220 who had fled were burnt in effigy. In Barcelona in 1491, three Judaizers were burned alive and 139 in absentia (Kamen 1965, 55). In Lérida in 1487–8, 123 Judaizers were condemned, all but five in absentia (Domínguez Ortiz 1992, 35–6). Many of those who did not flee sought to protect themselves by responding to the promise of leniency offered in the Edicts of Grace. In the early moments of the Inquisition many *conversos* rushed to confess or to denounce their neighbors.

Judaizers were not the only ones who were afraid, for suspicion tended to fall on the entire caste of new-Christians. *Conversos* who were attempting to assimilate quaked in fear that some vestigial Jewish custom—even something so trivial as a physical aversion to eating pork—would brand them as heretics. What had been gray now suddenly became black and white. Assimilationist *conversos* were now compelled to shun any association with Judaism or with family members who continued to Judaize. It had been enough for them to be scrupulously Catholic in the present; now they had to find ways to mislead eyes prying into their pasts, to cover up any period of ambiguity in their family's history of becoming Catholic. Judaizing *conversos*, on the other hand, were now clearly outlaws who had to hide to survive. Prior to 1480 both groups' biggest dilemmas were which religion to choose, how to ease the transition between the two, and how to preserve family cohesiveness in an atmosphere of religious division. After 1480 both groups' biggest challenge was how to hide, how to fabricate and live a "cover story," how to become proficient in the art of the low profile. Public pressure shaped private behavior, for, as Stephen Gilman has shown, "to be a *converso* is not just a way of being to oneself; it is more importantly a way of being with others."[60]

At first some *conversos* conspired to impede the Inquisition. The most successful were the *conversos* of Teruel, who for nearly a year in 1484–5 managed to delay the establishment of the Holy Office in that city. Others plotted to assassinate the Inquisitors who were assigned to their districts, and in September of 1486 the Aragonese Inquisitor Pedro de Arbués was in fact murdered in Zaragoza. In these attempts to thwart the Inquisition *conversos* did not always act alone; many liberal intellectuals and old-Christian burghers detested the violence and coercive methods of the Holy Office, or feared that the new institution would result in additional power being concentrated in the throne and the Church, or feared that persecution of the *conversos* would bring economic ruin on their cities. Even within the royal government and the Inquisition itself there were a few voices that argued for the tolerant re-education of minor heretics and their re-acceptance into the good graces of the Church. But the voices were not heeded, the protests were ineffectual, and the few desperate acts were like walls of sand against an incoming tide. Long before the Expulsion, organized resistance to the Inquisition had ceased (Baer 1966, 2:239, 360–7, 389–90).

Coupled with Inquisition activity was an intensification of the propaganda campaign that portrayed Jews as the perpetrators of ritual crimes against Christians. Until the mid-fifteenth century Spain had been relatively free of the stream of accusations of ritual crimes that flowed in northern European anti-Semitic propaganda, beginning with the ritual murder accusation in Norwich in 1144. But in 1435 a Majorcan Jew was accused of having crucified a Moslem slave. As a result four Jews were burned in Palma, even though the bishop's investigation found that the slave in question was still alive. In 1454 the Franciscan Alonso de Espina accused some Jews of Tavara (Valladolid) of having ritually crucified a Christian child. After torture, several Jews confessed to the crime, even though a royal investigation found that the child had been killed by common thieves who wanted to steal a gold chain from his neck. After a similar unproved accusation in Sepúlveda in 1468 the town's rabbi and several other Jews were burned.

The anti-Jewish propagandists of the late fifteenth century, particularly Fray Alonso de Espina, whose 1460 *Fortalitium fidei* circulated widely during those decades, bear substantial responsibility for the Expulsion. The political strategy of these lobbyists—Franciscan and Dominican monks for the most part—was to bring pressure on the throne to convert as many Jews as possible to Christianity, to ensure the orthodoxy of the converts, to expel the Jews who would not convert, and to extirpate any converts who were not exclusively faithful to the new religion. Their pamphlets, which highlighted the diabolical interpretation of the Jews' activities, gave voice in Spain to libels that were current north of the Pyrenees: Jews poison wells; Jews spread disease; Jewish doctors murder Christian patients. Whether from ignorance or malice, these propagandists conceived of Jewish worship only in Christocentric terms. They ignored *halakhah*: for them the central tenet of Judaism was its rejection of the divine Christ as the Messiah. Thus Jewish worship was said to exalt the anti-Christ. And Jewish ritual was said to feature anti-Christian acts: parodies of the crucifixion, parodies of the mass, and violent mistreatment of Christian cult objects from consecrated hosts to crucifixes and images of the saints.[61] Espina was particularly encyclopedic in his recycling of these northern European myths.[62] He fanned the flames in both the Valladolid and Sepúlveda incidents. Accusations brought in the La Guardia case all but summarize the legendary libels Espina catalogued in his *Fortalitium fidei*.

Critical literature on the La Guardia case is copious, and I do not want to rehash it here.[63] But it will be useful for what follows if we devote some brief attention to the known facts and how authorities handled them. The facts: In 1490 in Astorga some drunks accused Benito García, a new-Christian of La Guardia (Toledo), of having stolen a consecrated host. García was arrested and after suffering 200 lashes and the water torture confessed that two or three years previous he and some Jews and *conversos* from La Guardia had ritually crucified a Christian child and had stolen some hosts in order to concoct a potion with which to poison all true Christians in the region. Under duress he named names. Despite protest by the court-appointed defense attorney, the trial was held in Segovia—residence of both Torquemada, the first Inquisitor General, and Fray Espina—not in Toledo, which should have had jurisdiction. The attorney protested that he could not prepare an adequate defense because the vague charges included neither the places or times when the alleged events occurred nor the names of all the perpetrators, their accomplices, or even the victim. The protest was ignored and the main suspect, a seventeen-year-old named Yucé Franco, was imprisoned for over a year and subjected to a variety of stresses until he eventually confessed to every accusation that was put to him.[64] A large number of arrests were made and, in due course, these suspects too confessed to most of what was put to them.

Although testimony in the case was riddled with contradictions and inconsistencies, the court seems to have ignored them. No investigation was made in La Guardia. No child's corpse was ever found. No child was declared missing. There were no grieving parents. The formal documents are short on facts and long on derogatory epithets about the Jewish and *converso* blasphemers and perpetrators of outrages against Christianity. Young Yucé and his alleged accomplices were burned to great fanfare in the first great *auto de fe* held in Avila in November of 1491 (Despina 1979, 59–64). Public outcry made it ever more difficult for the Catholic Monarchs to resist the pressures to expel the Jews and to curb the upstart, sacrilegious *conversos*.

## THE EXPULSION

The Edict of Expulsion that was signed in the newly conquered city of Granada on March 31, 1492, and promulgated to Castile and Aragon in late April, gave the two kingdoms' Jews until July 31 to depart or become Christian. The decision emerged from the political philosophy that had shaped the conduct of the Granada war. Fernando's and Isabel's decision to intensify the war against Granada, the sole surviving Islamic kingdom in Iberia, was among other things a stratagem to induce Spanish nobility to channel their aggression against the Moslems (whom the Spaniards called Moors) instead of against each other or their sovereigns. That is, it was designed to unite in common cause enemies who were veterans of the twenty-year civil wars of succession in the two kingdoms. Nonetheless the Granada war was billed as a crusade, an effort to put an end to the affront to Iberian Christianity that the existence on the Peninsula of a Moslem state represented. Thus the Catholic Monarchs' triumphant entry into Granada on January 2, 1492, vividly demonstrated that nationhood was achieved when a political force imposed upon a geographic entity a commonalty of faith. The decision to expel the Jews, which had been brewing for decades, was a logical next step. It was signed into law in Granada only eighty-eight days after the city's capture.

The text of the Expulsion order says straightforwardly that the purpose was to prevent Jews from further impeding the Christianization of Spain's *converso* community. It accurately reports the lack of effectiveness of the three major steps already taken: the attempts to isolate the Jewish communities by requiring Jews to live in separate Jewish districts; the Expulsion of the Jews from Andalucia, where large numbers of *conversos* had made little attempt to Christianize; and the establishment of the Inquisition to encourage orthodox Christian behavior and punish Judaizers. Almost from its founding the Inquisition had argued that its job was impossible because of the close relationships between the new-Christians and the Jews. These were not the only reasons for the Expulsion; historians have demonstrated economic, political, and nationalistic concerns as well.[65] But in this watershed attempt at social engineering the principal causes were religious: to banish the Jews, whose presence was increasingly deemed an insult to practicing Christians, and thus to respond to the demands of popular anti-Semitism, some of it carefully orchestrated, which had brought hatred of the Jews to a fever pitch; to separate Jews from *conversos*; and, in accord with the philosophy of conversionism that had run strongly through Spanish policy since the late fourteenth century, to encourage more Jews to become Catholic.[66]

It was reasonably effective in achieving this last aim. While some measures were taken to facilitate emigration,[67] the particulars of the Expulsion order imposed great hardships on those Jews who might choose to leave. For many the order meant financial ruin. Christians were required to allow the Jews to sell their property under equitable terms, but at the same time Jews were forbidden to take with them any precious metals or jewels. The appearance of so much Jewish property on the market at the same time depressed prices of real estate and other immovable goods.[68] Exile meant inflated transportation costs and exposure to the very real physical dangers of the road. Exile meant leaving behind one's language, climate, customs, and friends. Exile often meant leaving behind one's *converso* family members and the graves of one's ancestors. Exile was a step into the unknown.

For Jews staunch in their religious convictions, or persuaded of the inevitability of persecution in Spain and their eventual ruin, the choice to leave was simple. But for large numbers of half-assimilated Jews, Jews from divided families, and Jews financially entangled or skeptical about the duration of these hard times the choice was much harder. For these Jews the acceptance of baptism might seem a rather trivial price to pay for security, even the very problematic security of an Inquisition-dominated environment. Some converted with the intent to continue to Judaize behind closed doors, to liquidate their property at a convenient pace that would ensure a maximum price, and eventually to emigrate at their leisure.[69] Others converted with the intention of waiting out the storm, confident that before long they might begin to practice Judaism again openly. Some converted because the pull of their Catholic loved ones, their possessions, their home towns, or the opportunity for social mobility as Christians was stronger than the weak attraction of their Judaism. Others were caught up in the enthusiasm of the missionaries who went door-to-door in the Jewish districts inviting conversion. Some were attracted by the financial incentives that were occasionally offered to new converts.[70] Still others converted because they interpreted the Expulsion as final evidence that Christianity had truly replaced Judaism as God's favored religion. Some followed the example of their political and spiritual leaders, for the most noteworthy conversions were deliberately made highly visible. When on May 31 Rabbi Abraham de Córdoba converted he was sponsored by no less than the Primate of Spain, Cardinal Mendoza, together with the Papal Nuncio. Fifteen days later in Guadalupe the most exalted Jew in the kingdom, Abraham Seneor, and his son-in-law Meir

Melamed were sponsored in their conversion by the Catholic Monarchs themselves. Seneor, renamed Fernando Núñez Coronel, within days become a Councilman of Segovia, member of the Royal Council, and treasurer of the Crown Prince (Suárez Fernández 1991, 326). Many of the wealthy and powerful stayed behind to protect their interests; the bulk of the émigrés were middle-class artisans and merchants. All in all, for whatever reason or mixture of reasons, about half of Spain's remaining Jews converted during those four months.[71]

The new Diaspora followed the compass points. Half of the exiles—some 100,000—went west to Portugal, thinking no doubt that this neighboring country, whose language and climate and customs seemed almost homelike, would allow them easy return to Spain when the troubles had passed. At the Portuguese border they were charged an exorbitant fee for an eight-month visa. Twenty-five boats left Cádiz for the Algerian port of Oran but, fearful of the reception the refugees would find there, returned to Spain, from where the majority also went to Portugal (Amador de los Ríos 1875, 737). Still others crossed to Morocco, where they were so poorly received by the Jewish inhabitants of Fez that many of them, too, returned to Spain.[72] Some Jews from the northern *aljamas* went to England, France, and Flanders. Others crossed into Navarre[73]—not yet part of unified Spain—and from there by safe-conduct down the Ebro River to Catalán ports, from where they sailed to Italy and to the Turkish Balkans.

## NOTES

1. Fernando III's epitaph in the Cathedral in Seville is written in four languages: Latin, Castilian, Arabic, and Hebrew (Castro 1971, 59).

2. The social, economic, political, philosophical, and literary aspects of their lives have been treated in modern times by Baron, Baer, Beinart, Neuman, and others. Baer cites even a Jewish keeper of lions and a bullfighter (1966, 1:198–205; 2:37, 47, 56).

3. There were prominent medieval Spanish converts to Christianity as early as 1106, when Moshe de Huesca, who later as Pedro Alfonso wrote the influential *Disciplina clericalis*, was sponsored at the baptismal font by King Alfonso "el Batallador" (Suárez Fernández 1981, 44). Marcus 1960 gives excerpts from legal documents relating to the early Spanish conversions. Central to the entire Christian legal system was the concern that conversion be only a one-way street leading to but never from Christianity. For example, according to a municipal code in thirteenth-century Soria, Christian men could legitimize the offspring they had with Jewish women provided they "Christianized" the child (Dillard 1984, 131).

4. Baer (1966, 2:11–4). In the aftermath of the 1391 riots in Valencia, Judaizing *conversos* were harassed by the Inquisition, which "submitted them to economic extortion (*ad extorquendum peccunias*) instead of instructing them in the doctrines of Christianity" (Hinojosa Montalvo 1993, 119).

5. An example is the Navarrese riots of 1328. The Castilian interregnum in 1390 permitted the flaunting of royal authority that erupted into those riots.

6. When plague surged, so did the old accusation that the Jews were poisoning the water supply; with this pretext Barcelona's *aljama* was attacked in 1348 and Lérida's two years later (Baer 1966, 2:25).

7. An example is the long war that brought the Trastámara King Enrique II to the throne of Castile in 1369. One of the charges leveled against assassinated King Pedro I was that he favored the Jews. During the war the *aljamas* of Toledo, Briviesca, Aguilar de Campóo, Segovia, Avila, and Valladolid were sacked (Suárez Fernández 1980, 183–5, 197–8).

8. Contemporary documents hint at some mass conversions prior to the 1391 riots. One example is in Cadreita (Navarre) in 1328, where for the first time a mob, led by a Franciscan ideologue, followed a policy of "conversion or death" (Suárez Fernández 1991, 152). Another is Baeza, where in 1369 "the Jews turned Christian" (Domínguez Ortiz 1992, 17).

9. Pablo de Santa María later became tutor to the infant Castilian King Juan II. The extensive writings of Cantera Burgos and Serrano about the Santa María family are cited in the bibliography.

10. The conversion provoked a family crisis: Isaac's wife actually demanded a divorce, and there were rumors of a family plot on Isaac's life.

11. This is now the Sephardic museum in Toledo. Halevi's mansion across the street is today labeled "El Greco's house."

12. Host desecration trials were held in Barcelona in 1367, Teruel and Huesca in 1377, and Lérida in 1383 (Baer 1966, 2:89–91).

13. Baer 1966 is particularly good for this period; see 1:362; 2:17, 85.

14. Although the overall number of Jews who were killed is unknown, in Seville alone some 4,000 died (Suárez Fernández 1980, 207). Contemporary accounts agree that the number of Jews converted exceeded the number murdered (Suárez Fernández 1991, 190, 202).

15. Vivid accounts are given in Baer 1966, 2:100; Dánvila 1886; Hinojosa Montalvo 1993, 22–66.

16. Although Baer 1966, 2:117 considers that the Castilian-Jewish communities were destroyed "chiefly by their own moral deterioration" and not exclusively due to external instigation, most historians assign the principal cause to Church sanctioned popular anti-Semitic violence.

17. The Jew badge had been sporadically required throughout Europe; for example, in Rome in 1215 and 1227, Aragon in 1228, Navarre in 1234, Santiago in 1235, Barcelona in 1268 and 1397, Portugal in 1325, and Castile in 1263, 1371 and 1405 (Bofarull y Sans 1910, 33–4; Kamen 1965, 23).

18. Baer 1966, 2:131–2. Matrimonial issues were particularly thorny in mixed families. Both Christian and Jewish legal documents of the time refer repeatedly to questions of dowry, divorce, and release from the obligation of levirate marriage (*halizah*) (Baer 1966, 2:133; Netanyahu 1966, 54–7, 70–1; Levi 1982).

19. For example, the restrictive laws promulgated by Fernando I of Aragon and Pope Benedict XIII in 1413 were largely reversed by their successors, King Alfonso V and Pope Martin V, by 1419 (Hinojosa Montalvo 1993, 19).

20. For details of the debate about how to educate the *conversos*, see Beinart 1981a, 8–9. See also Hinojosa Montalvo 1993, 18. In Extremadura one early decree ordered new converts to attend all the appropriate Church festivals and to march one behind the other in religious processions praying with all the devotion they could muster (*manda asistir a la igle-*

*sia todas las fiestas de guardar* and also *todos vayan en procesión uno tras otro e rezando en la mas devoçion que pudieran*) (Sanabria Sierra 1984, 163).

21. Benito Ruano cites the Catholic Monarchs' chronicler Fernán Pérez de Guzmán as saying that "the first ones will not be such good Catholics, but the second and third generations will be Catholics firm in their faith" (*puesto que los primeros [conversos] no sean tan buenos cristianos, pero a la segunda e tercera generación serán católicos firmes en la fe*) (1987, 256).

22. For example, in 1390 the Cortes of Soria decreed punishment for anyone who insulted the converts by calling them *Marranos* or *tornadizos* (Benito Ruano 1987, 155). A 1449 bull of Pope Nicholas V threatened to excommunicate anyone who injured a *converso* in word or deed, or barred one from access to any profession or honor (Domínguez Ortiz 1955a, 15).

23. Averroes was a twelfth-century Islamic philosopher from Córdoba whose popularity among medieval Jewish philosophers was enormous. He and Maimonides knew each other's work on Aristotle and were similar in their stress on reason over revelation. Suárez Fernández points out that the so-called Averroism berated by medieval orthodox Christians and Jews alike had little to do with the philosophy of Averroes, but rather was an "extreme rationalism which tended to be identified with agnosticism or pantheism" (1991, 51).

24. Ferrer has been seen by Jewish historians as a major villain. To cite just one example, a hundred years after the events Usque wrote that Ferrer "led an aroused mob through the cities of Spain, carrying a crucifix in his hands and a scroll of the law in his arms. In loud and fearsome tones he called upon the Jews to gather under the cross of Christianity and convert. His gang, armed with spears and swords, would attack and kill those who refused" (M. Cohen 1965, 194).

25. These arguments are thoroughly reviewed in Baer 1966, 2:174–208, 224–9. Fundamental documentation about the Disputations is given in Palacios López 1957.

26. For Suárez Fernández the disputations and forced conversions had the ironically unintended effect of strengthening the remaining Jews in their faith (1991, 224).

27. Bernáldez 653a. Ladero Quesada's study of late fifteenth-century documents concerning 316 new-Christians in Baena and Sanlúcar de Barrameda found that 53 percent worked in the textile and leather trades, with only 16 percent in finance and public service (1984, 48–9). Suárez Fernández concludes that "económicamente, los judíos del siglo XV . . . significaban ya muy poco; los contados ricos que llegaron a producirse se convierton con facilidad" (1980, 238). Historians like Kamen, on the other hand, emphasize how the roles played by the rich and powerful Jews excited popular animus against them (1965, 24–5).

28. Jews owned land despite sporadic legal prohibitions such as the Valladolid laws of 1293. See Cantera Burgos 1970; Baer 1966, 2:247; Suárez Fernández 1980, 235.

29. For Domínguez Ortiz "the *conversos* are, quite simply, the urban bourgeoisie" (1965, 68). See Gómez Mampaso 1980; for professions of late fifteenth-century Jews in Ciudad Rodrigo see Sierro Malmierca 1990, 30; for Portugal see Saraiva 1969, 28–9. These trends continued in the next century: Kamen points out that every one of the 231 Badajoz *conversos* convicted by the Inquisition between 1493 and 1599 were engaged in commerce or the professions (1965, 26).

30. A tax farmer bid a job by promising the king or noble a certain amount up front, to be paid in fixed installments. He was then entitled to keep everything he collected, which presumably would give him a good profit margin over his original investment.

31. Baer 1966, 2:271–2 cites the cases of Tolosana Benveniste, who in 1443 left money to her Christian sons Gonzalo and Juan and her three Christian and two Jewish daughters; of the widow of Hasdai Halevi, who left money for dowries for poor Jewish girls and to her two Christian brothers whose new names she did not know; and of the widow of Salomon Shalom of Gerona, who in 1470 requested that her Christian daughter Margarita and her Jewish son Vidal live in peace with one another. See Hinojosa Montalvo 1993, 96.

32. Documents as early as a 1403 Valencian decree require Jews to leave the city three days prior to the major Jewish festivals in order to keep them from tempting the new-Christians to join their celebrations (*Item, que qualsevol juheu en qualsevol de les lurs festes judayques següents, la festa de la lur Pasqua del pa alis, e en la festa de la lur Pasqua de Cinquagesima, e en la lur festa de lur capdany, e en la festa de lur dejuni major, appellat dels perdons, e de lurs cabanyelles, que tres dies abans de cascuna de les dites festes cascun del dits juheus sia tengut buydar la dita ciutat e tots los termens vells de aquella . . .*) (Hinojosa Montalvo 1993, 115).

33. For others, the university milieu served this purpose (Révah 1968, 332–3).

34. Haliczer 1990, 210. Historians like Haliczer and Kamen find in the *conversos'* rapid rise to economic and administrative prominence a cause of the virulent popular anti-Semitism grounded in envy and fear of competition.

35. After the 1449 riots in Toledo the city adopted a *Sentencia-estatuto* barring *conversos* from holding any municipal position. Although it was denounced by the Pope as un-Christian, it was adopted nationally by King Juan II two years later. In the 1460s the laws were reiterated by Enrique IV and over the next two centuries the so-called purity-of-blood laws became a veritable mania in Spain. Sicroff (1960) remains fundamental.

36. These early attempts to restrict *converso* economic freedom were generally fought by the Monarchy and the Church as a disincentive to further Jewish conversion. See for example the 1449 Bull of Pope Nicholas V: "It is prohibited under penalty of excommunication that anyone who has converted to our Holy Catholic faith be injured in word or deed, or be barred from honors or positions, Church or civil, to which other Christians have access" (*prohibiera so pena de excomunión que a los convertidos a nuestra santa fe católica se les hiciera injuria de palabra o de obra, o se les apartara de los cargos y dignidades tanto eclesiásticas como civiles, a que los demás cristianos tienen acceso*) (Domínguez Ortiz 1955a, 15).

37. In their origin, purity-of-blood requirements were not official state policy, but rather were adopted by a wide variety of local organizations that wanted to limit membership to old-Christians. As early as the thirteenth century certain religious-military orders had exclusionary membership provisions. In 1414 the College of San Bartolomé, at Salamanca, required that members be *ex puro sanguine*. In 1437 the city government of Lérida required officials to be of pure lineage. But the Toledo laws of 1449 were the first to attract wide attention, and they were soon imitated all across Spain (Sicroff 1960, 88; Domínguez Ortiz 1992, 139).

38. Espina's book was not published until 1471 in Strasbourg. After several other European editions, the first Peninsular edition appeared in Burgos in 1479. Netanyahu argues convincingly that Espina was definitely not a new-Christian (1976, 109). Espina may well have taken his inspiration from Saint Juan de Capistrano and Bernardino de Feltre, two Franciscan anti-Jewish polemicists of great renown in the mid-fifteenth century (Despina 1979, 51). Other major anti-Jewish polemical works that appeared in Spain during this period were Alfonso de Valladolid (Abner of Burgos), *Mostrador de Justicia*; Pedro de la Caballería, *Zelus Christi contra Judaeos, Sarracenos et Infideles*, Pablo de Santa María, *Scrutinium Scripturarum*; Alonso de Cartagena, *Defensorium unitatis christianae*; and Juan de

Torquemada, *Tractatus contra madianitas et ismaelitas*. See Amador de los Ríos 1875, 12; Caro Baroja 1961, 2:393–400. Some of these books circulated in Portugal as well, augmenting the native Portuguese polemical literature against the Jews that had begun as far back as Friar João de Alcobaça's thirteenth-century *Speculum hebraeorum* (Pimenta Ferro Tavares 1987, 70).

39. These laws caused endless legal squabbling with regard to real estate. See Suárez Fernández 1963, 15.

40. As Castro pointed out (1954a, 136, 198; 1959, 3), indicative of the uniquely high esteem in which their immediate posterity held these goals is the inscription on the catafalque of Fernando and Isabel in the royal chapel in Granada, which commemorates them exclusively for their successes in stamping out religious diversity: "This marble tomb holds Ferdinand of Aragon and Isabel of Castile, called the Catholic Monarchs, who ruled with a single spirit, who vanquished the Moslem sect and extinguished perverse heresy" (*Mahometice secte prostratores / et heretice pervicacie extinctores / Fernandus Aragonum et Helisabetha Castelle / vir et uxor unanimes / Catolice appelati / marmoreo clauduntur hoc tumulo*).

41. During this period a variety of municipal laws denied the Jews recourse to justice, restricted their commerce, voided loans deemed to be usurious, relegated Jews to crowded, unsanitary residential districts, and so forth (Cantera Montenegro 1987, 108–10; Suárez Fernández 1991, 288–90).

42. Suárez Fernández 1963, 15; 1991, 266–7.

43. A good bibliographical survey of the Spanish Inquisition is Pérez/Escandell 1993.

44. See, for example, Cascales Ramos 1986; Llorca 1948; Rábade Obradó 1990a, 98–108.

45. In the 1480s even Jews were compelled to bring forward testimony against Judaizing *conversos* (Kamen 1965, 164–6; Bofarull 1911–2; Kaufman 1895–6).

46. For the most influential Spanish manual see Eimeric 1973. The first Portuguese manual was issued in 1552 and revised in 1613 and 1640 (Saraiva 1969, 57–8).

47. It also claimed jurisdiction over sorcerers and witches, no matter what their religious affiliation (M. Cohen 1972, 284).

48. Edicts of Grace, which derived from the thirteenth-century practices of the Roman Inquisition, were part of the Iberian Inquisition procedures from the first moment (Lea 1906, 2:92). Subsequently the Edicts of Faith replaced the carrot of the grace period with the stick of excommunication for those who did not come forward to denounce heresy. Their reliability as a guide to Judaizing practices is discussed below.

49. The first, a model for all to follow, was issued in Seville in 1481. Because of the importance of the Edicts of Grace to crypto-Judaism, I have included a translation of a typical Edict as an appendix to this book. Inquisitors had numerous "checklists" of Jewish—or allegedly Jewish—customs. One of the first and most widely used was the compilation of Alonso de Espina in his *Fortalitium fidei*.

50. The powerful effect of the Edicts of Faith is patent in the hundreds of reports like that of Barbara Castellana [São Vicente, Brazil 1593], who explained that she was coming forward now to testify because "only when she heard the Edict read did she remember these events or learn that they were indicative of Judaizing" (*jnda ora espois de entrar a Santa Inquisição nesta terra ouvindo leer o Editto da fee lhe lembrarão as ditas cousas, e entendeo serem judaicas*) (Furtado de Mendoça 1929, 101).

51. For an English version of a late fifteenth-century enemies list from the Toledo Inquisition, see Gilman 1972, 245–51.

52. One result was that *conversos*, never knowing when they might be called to account, became hyper-aware of their own behavior and how it might appear to others. In effect large numbers of them became autobiographers, perpetually monitoring themselves as they lived on the fragile border between self-awareness and schizophrenia. No wonder the most talented among them grew adept at projecting themselves into the souls of fictional characters and, giving vent to their angst with their pens, became the generation of prose fiction writers that produced what later developed into the modern novel.

53. Henningsen, in the most thorough survey of Spanish Inquisition proceedings to date, finds that torture was used in only about 10 percent of the cases (1984, 221).

54. Despite the popular impression, Lorence argues that "arbitrary arrest and long imprisonment without trial were exceptions" (1982, 33).

55. The name is probably a corruption of *saco bendito* (holy garment), although it is frequently ascribed to the garment's resemblance to the habit of the order of Saint Benedict (*San Benito*).

56. The 49,092 cases between 1540 and 1700 that Henningsen recorded included some 5,007 (10.2%) accusations of Judaizing. Despite the "Black Legend," which held that accusation was tantamount to execution, the 49,092 trials resulted in 1,483 people (3%) condemned to be burned, 776 in person and 707 in effigy (1984, 221).

57. The many purposes of the Inquisition have been given varying weights by historians. Lea and his followers emphasize the element of religious intolerance. Baer and Beinart focus on the socio-religious nature of the problems associated with the assimilation of a mass of new-Christians. Netanyahu and Saraiva, among others, give great importance to economic and social motives; for these historians "the aim of the Inquisition . . . was not to eradicate a Jewish heresy from the midst of the Marrano group, but to eradicate the Marrano group from the midst of the Spanish people" (Netanyahu 1966, 4). Kamen terms the Inquisition a "class weapon, used to impose on all communities of the Peninsula the ideology of one class—the lay and ecclesiastical aristocracy" (1965, 17). For Novinsky it was a political device for "reinforcing and legitimating power" (1982, 8). In point of fact, the Inquisition was driven by all these motives as well as the need—like that of most bureaucracies—to perpetuate itself. For a review of these controversies see Beinart 1981a, Márquez Villanueva 1965, and especially Lorence 1982.

58. Several scholars have documented what Liebman calls the sporadic "notorious excesses and improprieties" of the Inquisition (1970, 279).

59. Around 1468 the Jew Abrahén Memé said of Ysabel Arias that she was *muy christianada*, to which her father replied that she *era buena judía en su boluntad* (Carrete Parrondo 1986, 57).

60. "With varying degrees of intensity, suspicion, and anguish every soul born in the Peninsula shared a common dilemma: having to represent a social role and to exist at the same time" (1972, 19, 28). The Jesuit Juan de Mariana, writing in the early sixteenth century about the impact of the Inquisition, grieved that because of it "people were deprived of the liberty of listening and talking to one another, for there were in the cities, towns, and villages special persons to give warning of what was happening, a practice which some regarded as like a servitude most onerous and on a par with death." Cited by Castro 1954b, 534.

61. The charge of deicide was leveled infrequently against the Jews in medieval Spain (Roth 1992, 380), although there are some examples such as Aragonese King Alfonso V's 1427 letter charging *Ihesu Christi, quem perfidi et stollidi iudei inhumaniter crucifixerunt* (Hinojosa Montalvo 1993, 162).

62. Espina's rendering of the Hugh of Lincoln alleged ritual murder case surfaced years later, when it was copied by Diego de Espés in his concoction of the Dominguito del Val legend (Despina 1979, 68).

63. Singerman has compiled the extensive bibliography on the La Guardia case (1975, 84–6; 1993, 197–9). The essential documents were compiled by Fita y Colomé 1887. Baer's analysis of the case remains fundamental (1966, 2:398–423). See also Fita y Colomé 1887 and Suárez Fernández 1991, 314–8.

64. At one point Franco reputedly said explicitly that torture had made him confess to things which were not true: *Con los tormentos avia dicho más de lo que había, fasta que le fiziera conoscer con que le quemen* (Fita y Colomé 1887, 13).

65. Kamen, for example, sees the Expulsion as "an attempt by the feudalistic nobility to eliminate that section of the middle classes—the Jews—which was threatening its predominance in the state" (1965, 17), even though it was principally the nobles who relied on the Jews to administer their estates. Haliczer, in contrast, saw the Monarchs courting favor with the urban merchant patricians (1973, 35–58), even though the Catholic Monarchs consolidated their power by severely restricting the rights of the cities, largely with the support of the nobility. More recent historians such as Suárez Fernández see the Catholic Monarchs' support coming principally from the nobility, the Church and Inquisition hierarchies, and a handful of key new-Christian jurists and financial administrators (1991, 303–4). Almost all agree that the case of the Holy Child of La Guardia was a precipitating factor in galvanizing governmental resolve to expel the Jews, in spite of the fact that the Expulsion Decree itself makes no mention of the incident.

66. It may be argued that the Expulsion ironically failed to achieve its broadest ends. Motis Dolader sums up the argument neatly: "They wanted to eradicate a belief, not a people, although the edict produced the opposite result: Judaism remained in the form of crypto-Judaism, while the Jews went into exile" (1985, 77; translation mine). Official contemporary history, of course, reached the opposite conclusion.

67. For example, departing Jews were declared exempt from road taxes and tolls, and many were given letters of safe conduct.

68. Bernáldez's famous description of this economic chaos is accurate: "There were Christians who acquired their property and fine houses and lands for very little money, and they even had to go begging to find buyers, for there was no one who would buy them. And they sold a house for a donkey, and a vineyard for a little cloth" (1962, 652b). Motis Dolader gives vivid examples of this economic ruin, including an instance in Magallón where several houses were sold for an eight-ounce silver cup, a piece of cloth, and a black donkey (1987, 233–7). And at least one *conversa*, trying to persuade Inquisitors of her anti-Jewish feelings, bragged that she "bought houses from them so below their value that she hardly paid any money at all" (*tomandoles sus casas a menos presçio e syn dineros*) (Cantera/Carrete 1975, 159). Nevertheless, on the whole the government fulfilled its promises to expedite the Jews' departure. Petitions to the crown were rapidly acted on with rulings that facilitated converting property to cash. In many areas auctions were held to speed the disposal of property. Some debts were assigned to *conversos* who were staying behind so that they might be liquidated and forwarded when times permitted. Other debts, particularly those involving Christians and Jews, were adjudicated under royally sanctioned procedures by a committee of two judges, one nominated by the debtor and one by the creditor, who evaluated the debt and arranged settlement (Suárez Fernández 1991, 331–4).

69. Examples of these and other reasons offered as explanations for conversion are given in Chapter 20.
70. The Jews of the Condado de Luna, for example, were released from a debt of 700,000 marevedis when they converted (Suárez Fernández 1991, 326).
71. For a discussion of the issues involved in quantification see Chapter 3 of this Introduction.
72. For details of the Moroccan debacle see Ortega 1919, 95–105.
73. For the impact of the Expulsion on Navarre see Gampel 1989.

## CHAPTER II

## *Conversos* after 1492

The departure of the Jews changed the world for the Spanish and Portuguese new-Christians. On July 31, 1492, the last legal Jews were to have left Spain. Thereafter the new-Christians were largely on their own, left to their own devices to assimilate into the Catholic mainstream or to preserve as much as they could and cared to of their Judaism. It is tempting to speak of the new-Christians as if they were a homogeneous group, but aside from a few broad truths it is difficult and to a large extent specious to generalize very much. The contexts were too varied. The political, social, legal, and religious conditions under which the Iberian *conversos* lived their lives were constantly in flux and likely to be very different from one century or even decade to the next, and from one geographic region to another. We must also not lose sight of the fact that there were differences between dense *converso* communities, which tended to be found in major urban centers where critical mass permitted a degree of communal reinforcement of Judaizing practices, and cities or villages thinly settled by *conversos*, where Jewish customs tended to atrophy quickly (Baer 1966, 2:273). It is tempting to speak only of individuals or particular villages or specific historical moments. Yet the perils of generalization remain, for the relevant contexts even for individuals may vary from one moment to the next, for example, when a member of one's family or close circle of friends suddenly came to the attention of the Inquisition. Nevertheless, in order to make sense of history we must summarize the sorts of large-scale distinctions that make the aggregate of individual records most meaningful.

When generalizing about the *conversos* it is useful to make some geographical distinctions. As will be seen shortly, the history of conversions and of the new-Christians is sufficiently different in Spain and Portugal to require that the two countries be considered separately. These differences begin in the pre-Expulsion history of the Jews in Portugal and the Spanish kingdoms and continue through the mass conversions, the establishment of the Inquisitions, the 1580–1640 period when Portugal and Spain were combined, and into modern times with the striking differences between remnant crypto-Judaism in the two countries. The differences extend into the two countries' overseas possessions. Thus Portuguese Brazil and the Spanish colonial empires will be considered in separate sections within this introduction. There are also important differences among the *converso* experiences in the various territories of the Spanish overseas empire—say between Mexico, where crypto-Jewish culture flourished, and the Río de Plata region or the Andean countries, where it sputtered. But overall the similarities outweigh the differences and so some meaningful generalizations can be made about *converso* life in the Spanish colonies.

Similarly, it is useful to consider some temporal distinctions that correspond to the major historical events that shaped the new-Christian experience. Thus I discuss *conversos* during (1) the century and a half while the pressure was mounting that led to the mass conversions of 1391; (2) the following century, prior to the establishment of the Inquisition, while *convivencia* was falling apart; (3) the decade and a half between the founding of the Inquisition and the Expulsion from Spain;[1] (4) the forty years that marked the passing of the Expulsion generation, the last with personal knowledge of openly Jewish culture; (5) the middle years of the sixteenth century, when *converso* culture diffused throughout the Empire; (6) the century following the 1580 Spanish annexation of Portugal, which saw the spread and then the eradication of the Portuguese Judaizers; (7) the eighteenth-century sweep-up of nearly all the remaining active centers of Judaizing; (8) the nineteenth-century dismantling of the structures of oppression; and (9) the present century with its rediscovery of Sephardic roots.

The *converso* experience in countries outside the immediate sphere of Iberian influence merits separate treatment. For example, although some countries sometimes permitted converts to revert to Judaism (e.g., Turkey, the Low Countries, parts of Italy), nonetheless some Judaizing *conversos* continued to choose to live there as Christians. In other countries, even though Judaizing *conversos* were not permitted to revert openly to Judaism, at least they were sometimes free of the threat of the Iberian Inquisitions (e.g., France, England, some of the German and Italian states). This is a vast subject that lies beyond the scope of this book. *Conversos* outside the Iberian world will be considered here only insofar as they influence what was happening within the Iberian orbit.

## Conversos in Spain

The *converso* experience in Spain can be examined usefully in the nine periods noted above, each bounded by specific events and each having its own general characteristics. The first three periods have been discussed in the first section of this Introduction.

### Period 1: Pre-1391. Before That Summer's Riots and Mass Conversions

Prior to 1391 there was no appreciable crypto-Judaism in Spain. This period is characterized by sporadic, individual, religiously motivated male conversions to Christianity. I have not found incidences of Jewish women who apostatized in Spain during the centuries of *convivencia* prior to 1391. The new converts often became churchmen and sometimes Christian propagandists.

### Period 2: 1391–1478. Before the Establishment of the Inquisition in Andalucia

Beginning in the summer of 1391 and over the next eighty- seven years, there were large numbers of conversions, some by force, as a result of riots directed against the Jewish quarters of cities (e.g., 1391, 1449), others of a voluntary nature, as a result of the Disputation of Tortosa (1413–4), and constant other pressures to convert. Religiously, these *conversos* covered the whole spectrum from proselytizing Christians, to practicing Jews in all but name, to (insofar as the times permitted it) people whose aversion to or skepticism about religion approached agnosticism or even atheism. During this period *conversos* had access to synagogues, Jewish education, ritual objects, and kosher food, so that crypto-Judaism tended to be very close to normative Judaism in practice and belief. In both Spain and Portugal Jews and new-Christians of this period often formed a single extended family, with Jews generally treating Judaizing new-Christians as if they were still Jews[2] and frequently shunning the Christianized *conversos* as apostates. Wealthy assimilationist new-Christians easily intermarried with old-Christians. New-Christians figured prominently among royal financial and political advisors and dominated the nascent urban middle class of businessmen and artisans.

### Period 3: 1478–August 1492. Before the Expulsion Order Took Final Effect

With the advent of the Inquisition Judaizing became dangerous so that increasingly crypto-Jews went underground. The Inquisition directed its initial attention to the cities where large numbers of crypto-Jews practiced most openly: Seville, Ciudad Real, Toledo, Teruel, Zaragoza, and Palma de Majorca. As a matter of policy Spain promoted measures to separate Jews from *conversos*: physically by requiring the segregation of the *aljamas* and culturally by punishing any social interaction that could be interpreted as Judaizing. These included activities such as *converso* attendance at Jewish family life-cycle events like circumcisions or funerals or visits to family members or friends during the Jewish festivals. Because of the increasing difficulty of accessing Jewish culture directly, crypto-Judaism began to emerge as a separate culture.[3] Purity-of-blood laws attempted to bar *conversos* from corporate power structures such as the civil service and certain religious and military orders. Increasingly *conversos* thought of themselves as a class; old-Christians became reluctant to intermarry with *conversos* and endogamy among *conversos* became the rule.

### Period 4: 1492–c. 1540. Through the Disappearance of the Generation with Personal Knowledge of the Time before the Expulsion

This group of *conversos* included people who had personally experienced the coming of the Inquisition and the events leading up to the Expulsion. Some of them, of course, were third and fourth generation Catholics whose strongest desire was to blend in, to be left alone, to escape the stigma of their Jewish ancestry. Others were first generation: they had themselves faced the agonies of choice, and when they converted and remained in Spain they had watched their family members or friends depart, never to be seen again. This generation of *conversos* was shaped by vivid memories of traumatic experiences like those of Juan de Salzedo, who in 1502 recalled to Inquisitors in Soria the gut-wrenching spring of 1492:

> He said that the year that Their Majesties ordered the Jews to leave Castile, he spent Passover with the Jews at the home of Isaac the Portuguese . . . teaching one of Isaac's sons to read [the holy books]. While they were reading, old Fernando de Guernica, the pot maker . . . , who was a great friend of Isaac, came in and said: "What are you doing? Misfortune take you! You are wasting time. You read, you read! And even this fellow, alas, thinks he is doing something useful!" He was referring to me. "You would do better, festival or not, [to spend your time] thinking how you are going to liquidate your property, and how you are going to depart. Some people say that you should become Christian, but may God ruin my holiday if I advise it. The reason is that once you have become Christian they will figure out a way to shove your face in the fire. . . . Even more reason is the belief, as I believe, that you are only born to die, and there is nothing else in this world but birth and death. For after God created the world, He left everyone with their own fortune, good or bad. . . ." This is what Fernando said to Isaac . . . and his wife and his mother-in-law and me. And they all went to Portugal and never came back.[4]

The harshness of the Expulsion itself was a factor in the decision of many Judaizing new-Christians to remain in Spain after 1492. They had all heard about the rigors of the journey. They may have seen with their own eyes along the roadsides the bodies of Jews eviscerated for the gold they had allegedly swallowed to try to smuggle it out of Spain. They had heard about how the King of Portugal had forcibly torn apart immigrant Jewish families, sending the children to be raised as Catholics in the remote São Tomé Islands, and about the criminally inhospitable Jewish community in Fez and the bitter fate the Spanish exiles had met there during the winter of 1492–3.[5] They heard many of these stories from the returnees, who were permitted to buy their own property back for the selling price if they would accept baptism.[6] The lives of these early sixteenth-century *conversos* were scarred with trauma, with indelible experiences still vivid to us after five hundred years.

One of the things that emerges from the documentation is a portrait of a generation riddled with fear, self-doubt, nostalgia, and guilt. This is true even for the assimilators, but it is strongest among the Judaizers. Those crypto-Jewish *conversos* who stayed behind, whether for love or money, whether from inertia or fear of the unknown, frequently dreamed about fleeing the Iberian Peninsula or about a messiah who would lead them to a homeland in the East. In private they grumbled about the foolhardiness of their decision to exchange one perfectly good religion for another that they did not find so hospitable. They railed against the Inquisition. They expressed doubts or outright scorn for Christian dogma and ceremony. They worried about their departed relatives. And they wrestled with how much Judaism they should try to retain, how they could disguise it, and how they could pass it on to their children. Each successive life-cycle event forced them to choose anew.

Conditions made it inevitable that with each passing year the surviving crypto-Jewish communities became more clannish. They continued to be defined by old-Christians as a distinct group that was enemy to both the Catholic religion and the state.[7] Although old-Christian outsiders frequently considered them to be more homogeneous and cohesive than they were in fact, *conversos* during these years indeed fell into common patterns as they grappled with how to recognize each other for communal worship, how to retain important aspects of ceremony, and how to transmit their religion to their offspring. The key was in having a circle of family and friends who could be relied upon. To the familial bond of blood relationships was added the mutual dependency of outlaws who would be in mortal danger if they revealed each other's secrets. New-Christians still recognized each other personally from pre-Expulsion days, but it became increasingly difficult for them to know with confidence which new-Christians Judaized. Thus Judaizing *conversos* invented strategies for acknowledging each other. Judaizing families apprenticed their children to Judaizing master artisans and developed *converso* business networks, often within extended families.[8] They practiced rigorous endogamy in seeking mates for their children. They developed secure procedures for indoctrinating their children into the family crypto-Jewish practices. Because of the central role of women in early childhood education and in managing the ceremonial life of the household, *conversa* mothers and sisters often became the principal transmitters and sustainers of crypto-Judaism.[9]

It was during these years that crypto-Judaism in Spain began to evolve its distinctive forms. After August 1, 1492, Judaizing new-Christians rapidly began to lose touch with traditional Judaism. Now *conversos* no longer had available to them Jewish religious institutions like synagogues, *mikvahs* (ritual baths), or schools or religious functionaries like rabbis, cantors, or *mohels* (circumcisers). Once the Jews were gone, possession of any Jewish artifacts (such as Torahs, mezuzzahs, amulets, Hanukkah lamps) incurred mortal risk, so that Jewish regalia disappeared almost overnight.[10] Most importantly, Jewish books ceased to be available to *conversos*, with the result that the entire post-Biblical rabbinic tradition became inaccessible.[11] As a result, crypto-Judaism came to rely almost exclusively on three other sources for religious knowledge:

(1) Oral tradition. When Hebrew prayer books disappeared, only the most fundamental and frequently repeated Hebrew prayers remained in the communal consciousness: the affirmation of the oneness of God (the *Shema*); the daily blessings; and recurrent portions of daily, Sabbath, and festival prayers such as the *Kaddish*, the *Amidah*, and a number of blessings and hymns. Those prayers which were not already firmly committed to memory disappeared almost instantly.

(2) The Old Testament, still readily available as part of the Christian Bible. Those parts of the Old Testament which had formerly been part of the liturgy remained. In addition, Biblical passages that had the aura of prayer, such as the Psalms and portions of Exodus and the Prophets, were adopted for liturgical use. The Bible was generally available in Latin, from which some learned member of a *converso* prayer group might translate orally into Spanish. By the middle of the sixteenth century it was difficult to find Bibles in the vernacular: Church censorship authorities considered them dangerous because they were thought to give lay Catholics unmediated access to doctrine. With the loss of the Talmud, Mishnah, and other Hebrew religious texts, Judaizing *conversos* rapidly lost touch with the traditions of rabbinical Judaism, which had evolved substantially since Talmudic times. Increasingly crypto-Jews sought religious authority in the raw text of the Old Testament, reinterpreting in their own fashion the dictates of Leviticus and Deuteronomy.

(3) The Inquisition's Edicts of Grace. Because these public documents contained detailed lists of customs by which citizens might recognize their Judaizing neighbors, and because the Edicts varied little over the centuries in their description of Jewish belief and practice, they became a stable guide for the *conversos*. In large measure they defined Jewish practice for both the Christian public and the crypto-Jewish practitioners.

Still, even with these sources of knowledge available, the Jewishness of crypto-Judaism rapidly attenuated. Even those *conversos* who wanted to believe and who yearned to express their belief through practice found themselves putting more emphasis on intent than delivery as their knowledge about how to be Jewish became shallower and their fear of discovery grew greater. A typical example is the deposition of Mayor Alvarez, who testified in Toledo in 1527 about her brand of Judaism: "The things I did not do was because I did not know when the festivals were, or what things I was supposed to do. Sometimes I omitted doing them because I was afraid. But I did them in my heart, and I would have done more if I had known more, because I know that my salvation depends on it."[12] Several of the sentences handed down by the Coimbra Inquisition in the late sixteenth century suggest that some crypto-Jews thought that they could acquit themselves of the burden of observance through acts of charity. Leonor Nunes [1568] was accused of giving alms when she could not keep the entire Purim fast. Isabel Lopes [1583] gave alms in lieu of keeping the Yom Kippur fast. Branca Gomes, of Montemor-o-Velho, in 1568 was accused of giving alms when she was too sick or had too much work to keep the Monday/Thursday fast. Similarly, giving charity salved the conscience of Luzia Cardosa when she could not keep the Sabbath.[13]

Through the mid-sixteenth century the Inquisition conducted intense campaigns against the Judaizers. The tapering off of trials of Judaizers after the first third of the century suggests that the old-Christian establishment perceived the threat to be largely over. By this time those *conversos* who remained most overtly committed to Judaism had in the main either emigrated or lost their lives and property to the Inquisition. Both rabbinical and Inquisition evidence suggests that by 1540 most remaining *conversos* had been absorbed into the culture of Spanish Catholicism.[14] While accurate numbers or precise proportions are extremely hard to estimate, it is reasonable to conclude that by 1540 crypto-Judaism in Spain was beginning to wane.

During this period, as before the Expulsion, most *conversos* lived in the cities and towns, and most were small businessmen, professionals, or middle rank government officials of one sort or another. Some made careers in the clergy. A few amassed great wealth or attained positions of wide influence, both of which were threatening to the traditional old-Christian elites and the emerging urban middle class. The reaction to these alleged threats and the broad socio-economic goals of the Catholic Monarchs and the early Hapsburg Kings are revealed in the prominence given to the purity-of-blood laws in their reigns. What had begun in the fifteenth century as an attempt by certain municipalities and military and religious orders to exclude recent converts from their ranks—ostensibly to reduce the risk of heretical contagion, but also for reasons ranging from fear of economic or political dominance to racial snobbism—in the sixteenth century became firmly entrenched as a state policy enthusiastically supported by the masses.[15] Fernando decreed in 1501 that the children and grandchildren of any heretic condemned to death were disqualified from holding public office. After his death and during the four-year interregnum before the Hapsburg Carlos V took the throne in 1520, powerful *conversos* lobbied the incoming government to repeal the *limpieza* laws.

To an extent the purity-of-blood laws kept many *conversos* from corporate memberships or from public service in government or the Church. But for others ingenuity prevailed, and they successfully forged documents or found other ways to circumvent the system to become lawyers, magistrates, tax officials, or other sorts of administrators. A handful of prominent *conversos* reached positions of power or wealth and attracted considerable attention from the Inquisition, but most *conversos* bought and sold or produced goods on a small scale. This was true of the whole range of *conversos*, from the most ardent crypto-Jews to the most committed assimilationists. To a remarkable extent the *conversos* had become the new urban middle class.[16] When this group felt itself threatened it reacted strongly, as it did in 1520 in the so-called *Comunidades* rebellion that opposed the accession to the Spanish throne of the Hapsburg prince Charles V. *Conversos* played an active role in this rebellion, but they did so as urban bourgeoisie, not by articulating any clear *converso* agenda.[17] Indeed, the *conversos* were so diverse in their religious convictions and assimilationist strategies that they had no common political goals, except, perhaps, to urge the Christian power structure to take seriously the doctrine of equality inherent in the miracle of the eucharist.

Equality as Spaniards before the law and fair treatment as Christians were the principal political themes of the early sixteenth-century assimilationist *conversos*. It is for that reason that so many *converso* intellectuals played important roles in sixteenth-century Church reform movements.[18] Large numbers of them as well felt compelled to write about their experiences and concerns. Despite their great diversity of purpose, style, and approach, their writings contain common targets of antipathy: they tended to detest ecclesiastical organization, imperial policy, forced conversions, the Inquisition, the purity-of-blood statutes, and anything else that smacked of beliefs coerced by force rather than induced by education (Márquez Villanueva 1965, 328).[19]

Many intellectual assimilationist *conversos*, frustrated by a society that hemmed them in and a bureaucracy that seemed to wait perpetually in ambush, gave vent to their angst in literature. It is not at all surprising that the literature of escapism and alienation[20] as well as the theater of social protest of the early Spanish Renaissance[21] flowed largely from *converso* pens. In most of this literature one senses a profound dissatisfaction with the surface pieties of Spanish Catholicism and a concern for the moral rot perceived to be at the heart of Spanish society. Weary of being categorized and stigmatized as a group, *converso* writers tended to stress personal motivation and the responsibility of the individual. They of course almost never wrote about Judaism or crypto-Judaism and rarely criticized the Inquisition directly. These topics were not only forbidden, they were largely irrelevant to their main agenda. In the words of Márquez Villanueva, "the intimate tragedy of the important *conversos* was not that they felt to be Jews amidst a gentile society, but in the painful experience to be submitted to injustice and suspicion by a religion and by a society which seemed to them not to be sufficiently Christian" (1965, 320).

PERIOD 5: C. 1540–1580. BEFORE SPAIN'S ANNEXATION
OF PORTUGAL

By now the generation of *conversos* with sharp first-hand memories of normative Judaism had largely passed away. The ancestors of some *conversos* had become Christian as much as 150 years earlier. By the mid-sixteenth century the vast majority of Spanish new-Christians had assimilated quietly into the Spanish Catholic mainstream. Some new-Christians falsified their genealogy or suborned the system to obtain the certificates of purity-of-blood that facilitated their economic and social mobility. For the Inquisition, by mid-century crypto-Judaism was of less importance than the growing Protestant threat, wayward clerics, aberrant mystics, blasphemers, and such.

During these years crypto-Judaism was taking its definitive shape, and examination of contemporary sources reveals a wide range of practices. No single crypto-Jew ever observed the full gamut of crypto-Jewish customs. Individual religious practice varied in accord with *conversos'* family traditions, the habits of the crypto-Jewish local community of which they were a part, the degree of vigilance over *conversos* in their community, and their personal predilections. A study of any local set of Inquisition cases highlights the differences among individuals and, in the aggregate, permits some tentative conclusions. To cite just one of many possible examples, Bel Bravo's analysis of the trials of the 86 Judaizers sentenced in the 1593 *auto de fe* in Granada suggests that fasting was far and away the most widespread custom among these crypto-Jews (reported for 93% of the men and 89% of the women), followed by some adherence to the Jewish dietary laws (47% of the men, 58% of the women) and observance of the Sabbath (33% of the men, 48% of the women). The most frequently observed holidays were Yom Kippur (33% of the men, 28% of the women) and the Fast of Esther (20% of the men, 25% of the women). A little more than half of the people in this *auto* (53% of the men, 51% of the women) had professed belief in a unitary God rather than the triune God of the Catholics (1988, 78).

Building from local studies such as these, some generalized conclusions can be formulated about the state of crypto-Judaism in the Iberian world toward the end of the sixteenth century. Marranized Christian concepts such as belief in Moses as the key to personal salvation had supplanted many traditional Jewish beliefs. Crypto-Judaism was increasingly defined less by adherence to *halakhah* than by skepticism about or outright rejection of Christian beliefs and practices. Jewish customs decreased in number and became less complex in character. Fasts became more important than traditional feasts. The central tenets of Judaism were reduced to three: belief in one God; belief that the Messiah is yet to come; and belief in personal salvation through belief in the law of Moses. For all but the most knowledgeable, Jewish practice generally was reduced to keeping the Sabbath and three holy days: Yom Kippur, Passover, and the Fast of Esther. The complex Jewish dietary laws were essentially reduced to abstinence from pork and sometimes rabbit or scaleless fish. Among the life-cycle observances, certain Jewish funerary customs retained their importance.

Many new-Christians emigrated to the Iberian colonies, mainly for economic reasons. As in Spain, in the Spanish colonies the majority of *conversos* were assimilationist. But some strong communities of crypto-Jews remained, particularly in Mexico City. By contrast, in Brazil as in Portugal a substantial percentage of the new-Christians were crypto-Jews, and Judaizing communities thrived, particularly in the northeast. A few crypto-Jews emigrated to other parts of the Iberian empire. During this period the Inquisition was established in the colonies to combat crypto-Judaism, Lutheranism, and other heresies, as well as sexual improprieties.

### Period 6: 1580–c. 1700. Up through the Absorption or Eradication of the Portuguese Judaizers

With the 1580 merger of Spain and Portugal, and with high Inquisition activity in Portugal and relatively low activity in Spain, substantial numbers of Portuguese Judaizers emigrated to Spain and her colonies. Overnight the term "Portuguese" was understood to mean Judaizer. The influx of aggressive Portuguese Judaizers triggered an intensification of Inquisition activity in Spain and her colonies. In Spain the overwhelming majority of people accused of Judaizing during the early part of this period had clear Portuguese antecedents (Kamen 1965, 217). This was particularly true in Andalucia, Madrid, and the cities bordering Portugal, but even extended to regions like La Mancha and Spain's overseas possessions.

In 1598 Philip III ascended the throne, quickly surrounding himself with ministers who would license almost anything for a price. The Portuguese community experienced a surge of optimism; they brought their financial and political resources to bear both in Spain and in the Vatican to try to achieve a general pardon for prior acts of Judaizing. Large sums were delivered; even larger sums were promised. With the agreement of the Spanish government, Pope Paul V's 1604 order granted a general amnesty and freedom of movement. Imprisoned Judaizers throughout the Spanish empire were set free, even though almost instantly the Inquisition began to prosecute "new" cases of Judaizing. With the general pardon and a second, bribe-induced relaxation of travel restrictions in 1628, many *conversos* took advantage of the liberalized conditions to relocate to northern Europe or to the Iberian colonies. But the window of opportunity opened only briefly. In response to considerable public outcry about the government's philo-Semitic policies, and when the promised moneys were not forthcoming, in 1610 the concessions were revoked (Domínguez Ortiz 1992, 78–89).

In the 1620s and 1630s under Philip IV's prime minister Gaspar de Guzmán, the Count-Duke of Olivares, who was himself well known to have some *converso* ancestry, policies were again liberalized. Olivares recognized that the financial health of Spain depended in large measure on the strength of the business community, while that in turn required a certain tolerance for *converso* businessmen. While such tolerance was never formally stated, the highest circles of Olivares's government turned a blind eye toward the old exclusionary laws, which, while they remained on the books, were often quite aggressively circumvented. The Inquisition, now strapped for funds, would for a price sometimes "rehabilitate" a "tainted" family. In fact for wealthy new-Christians the combination of persistence, influence, and gradual accumulation of honors could even lead to an appointment as *familiar* to the Holy Office itself (Haliczer 1990, 238).

At the same time, however, the Inquisition continued to prosecute Portuguese Judaizers with rigor, especially after the fall of Olivares in 1643, which initiated a purge of *cristão novo* businessmen that largely eliminated Spain's community of financiers (Kamen 1965, 221). To judge from the biographies of people tried during the latter two-thirds of the seventeenth century, Judaizing traditions were maintained almost exclusively by the Portuguese while the native Spanish crypto-Jews had all but disappeared. Judaizers were regularly identified in the major Andalusian cities right through the end of the seventeenth century, and occasional family groups were found in other regions of Spain as well.[22] By the end of the century most of the Portuguese crypto-Jews had been eliminated too. The last *auto de fe* attended by a Spanish monarch was held in 1680 in Madrid (Domínguez Ortiz 1992, 99). In the American colonies communal crypto-Judaism had been extirpated by the 1660s (Uchmany 1991, 123).

Majorcan crypto-Jewish history is a little different in that there was very little Portuguese immigration to the Balearic Islands. Majorca's Jewish community had been converted in its entirety in 1435. Up through 1535 more than eight hundred Majorcan *conversos* were tried for Judaizing, but for the next century and a half the remaining *conversos* lived in fragile equilibrium with their surroundings. For reasons having to do with the economic vitality of Majorca, the authorities tended to leave the *conversos* pretty much alone, even though the popular animus against them remained strong.[23] The *conversos*, who by the mid-seventeenth century were known as *chuetas*, were by law clustered in the Sagell district, where they continued to exercise their traditional occupations. Although many of them were sincerely Christian and had assimilated to the extent that the Majorcan circumstances allowed, another segment continued to Judaize. This group came to the attention of the Inquisition in 1675. Over the next twenty years nearly three hundred *chuetas* were convicted by the Inquisition of Judaizing, which put an effective end to crypto-Judaism in the islands. It was not until 1782–8 that legal discriminations against the *chuetas* were eliminated, and de facto discrimination continued well into the twentieth century.[24]

This period in Iberian history was also characterized by increasing dissatisfaction with the principles and deleterious effects of the traditional exclusionary laws.

The presence or absence of crypto-Judaism, the alleged economic and political influence of the *conversos,* or, for others, the marginalization of new-Christians became important themes.[25] By the end of this period three processes—Inquisition efficiency, emigration to "freer" parts of Europe or the eastern Mediterranean, and assimilation—all but eliminated active crypto-Judaism from the Iberian world.

### Period 7: c. 1700–c. 1820. Before the Emergence of Liberalism and the Independence of Most of the Iberian Colonies

By the advent of the Bourbon dynasty in 1700, few active Judaizers remained. After this date the handful of crypto-Jews who fell into the public record—largely Inquisition cases—exhibited little knowledge of Judaism. As early as 1705 in an *auto da fe* a Portuguese bishop berated the Judaizers about to be reconciled for their paltry knowledge of Judaism and the scorn in which they were held by Jews elsewhere (Liebman 1970, 290). The principal characteristic of these Judaizers was their self-identification as Jews. Unable or unwilling to engage in visible observances, they formulated a philosophy that claimed, as Kaplan put it, that "inner psychological identification with the Jewish religious and national heritage was more important than observance of the commandments of Jewish law" (1991, 146). Some affirmed the three key crypto-Jewish beliefs (one God; Messiah not yet come; salvation through belief in the Law of Moses). Some defined their Jewishness as negativism toward things Christian. Traces remained of the observance of the Sabbath, abstinence from pork, fasting, and Jewish funeral customs. Although few Judaizers were left, nonetheless at the beginning of the century there was an intensification of Inquisition activity, which reached a high point in Cuenca in 1718–25 and in Madrid in 1721–7.[26] There were several reasons for these trials: the Portuguese War of Succession brought a second wave of Portuguese immigrants; the Inquisition was experiencing economic pressures that might be alleviated by increased confiscations; and the new chief Inquisitors were particularly zealous. Domínguez Ortiz points out that, in spite of the large number of trials during these years, the fact that most of the accused were of advanced age and the limited scope of their Judaizing indicated that the crypto-Judaism was rapidly dying out.[27] After 1750 the accusations of Judaizing are both few and trivial.[28] Of the 5,000 Inquisition cases between 1780 and 1820, only sixteen were for Judaizing: ten of those involved foreigners (Kamen 1965, 228).

### Period 8: c. 1820–1917. Before the Discovery of the Remnant Portuguese Crypto-Jews

During this period crypto-Judaism disappeared from public view. With the advent of nineteenth-century liberalism, Spain and Portugal abolished their Inquisitions. With independence, so did the former colonies. In small numbers Ashkenazi Jews emigrated to Spain and Portugal. Toward the end of the nineteenth century, which was characterized by massive European migration to the New World, large numbers of Jews, mainly Ashkenazis, emigrated to Latin America, particularly to Mexico, Brazil, and the Río de Plata region of Argentina and Uruguay. In a variety of ways they began to Hispanicize and to form a "neo-Sephardic" culture.

## Period 9: 1917–Present

Traditional crypto-Judaism was presumed dead in Iberia until 1917, when a Polish mining engineer named Samuel Schwarz, on a visit to the remote Beira region in northeast Portugal, stumbled onto several groups of villagers who still clung to a few vestigial Jewish customs. While their practices descended from those of crypto-Judaism as defined in Period 5 above, their practices were fewer, shallower, and more Christianized than those of their ancestors. An exception was the large number of "Jewish" prayers preserved in their oral tradition. Schwarz's findings were widely publicized in the scholarly and popular press, causing some members of the group, like Artur Carlos de Barros Basto, openly to espouse Judaism, and attracting Jewish "missionaries" from Britain who brought a modern Jewish education to the region.

Toward mid-century, many unverified legends of remnant crypto-Jews surfaced throughout Latin America and southwestern United States. Often the details of these legends suggest that the self-labeled Marranos are not cultural descendants of the seventeenth-century crypto-Jews. In the 1970s a strong case for vestigial crypto-Judaism was made for the Hispanic community of New Mexico,[29] and in the 1990s some attention is being given to traces of crypto-Judaism among the Azorean community of southeastern Massachusetts and Rhode Island.[30] These sorts of vestiges—termed "cultemes" by Jiménez Lozano (1984), who found them reasonably common among informants from Castilla-León toward the end of the Franco era—may well point to a broad assimilation, popularization, and ultimate trivialization of customs that in former times were explicit indicators of crypto-Judaizing. They may also indicate a reintroduction of Judaizing customs from recent Ashkenazi models at hand into communities that either have some vestigial memories of their remote *converso* ancestry or appropriate the history and myths of crypto-Judaism as a way of rationalizing their particular community's brand of anti-Catholicism.

The *chuetas* of Majorca are often considered a remnant crypto-Jewish community, but they really are not, for they preserve no vestiges of Jewish practice. Today there are still about three hundred families identified by Majorcans as *chuetas*. Although religiously they are firm Catholics, until very recently they continued to marry endogymously, to engage in traditional *converso* trades, particularly metalsmithing and jewelry making, to inhabit the former Jewish quarter of Palma, and to suffer discrimination at the hands of the island's other Catholics (Braunstein 1936, 122, 130).

Today most Spaniards and Portuguese will admit openly, frequently with pride, that they and all modern Iberians inevitably have some Jewish ancestry. Family legends, buried for centuries or invented in the recent past, recount specific Jewish roots. Some stories hinge on a dramatic revelation of Judaizing practices or include the finding of long hidden artifacts. But most stories are unverified and reside principally in the domain of folklore.[31] Remote villages identified in the popular mind as Jewish towns, such as Hervás (Cáceres),[32] have rediscovered (or re-imagined) the sites of former Jewish monuments and are courting the Jewish tourist trade.

Since World War II official Spain has begun to celebrate her Sephardic past. Even as the war raged, and with Spain allied with the Axis powers, Franco's government established and funded the Arias Montano Sephardic Seminar as part of the National Research Institute (CSIC). In 1964 the Sinagoga del Tránsito was renovated as a museum of Sephardic culture. In recent years literally hundreds of scholars and students in Spain and abroad have dedicated their energies to understanding Spain's Sephardic past. While philo-Sephardism has not yet shown itself to a similar degree in Portugal, there, too, new attention has been given to Sephardic studies. In Spain, Portugal, and the former colonies the last half decade has seen an outpouring of books on Jewish history, the Inquisition, and the crypto-Jews.

## THE PORTUGUESE EXPERIENCE

The Jewish and *converso* experience in Portugal was in broad strokes similar to that of Spain, but the details tended to differ significantly.[33] By the time Portugal had established itself as an independent kingdom in the thirteenth century, there were strong urban Jewish communities in Lisbon, Oporto, Santarem, and a number of other cities. Under the license and protection of the crown, the *aljamas* were corporate entities with rabbis and judges royally appointed and salaried by the king. As in the Spanish kingdoms, the fortunes of the Jews fluctuated with the designs of the monarch. While on the whole Jews were heavily taxed, constrained as to their living quarters, and occasionally forced to wear the Jew badge, at the same time they were allowed to prosper both politically and economically and in fact tended to enjoy rights unparalleled in the rest of Europe. Unlike the situation in Spain in the fifteenth century, in Portugal there was no large *converso* class and no gradually emerging crypto-Jewish culture. The Jewish refugees from the Spanish 1391 riots and later disturbances tended to integrate themselves wholly into the Portuguese Jewish communities. Although there were occasional riots, the worst of which murdered many Lisbon Jews in 1449, on the whole the level of anti-Jewish violence was lower than in Spain.[34] But as the fifteenth century drew to a close urban citizen groups in Portugal too demanded that Jewish "freedoms" be curtailed and that new-Christians from Spain be denied entry to Portugal (Pimenta Ferro Tavares 1987, 21). Still, unlike Spain, Portugal did not experience waves of violently forced conversions at the end of the fourteenth century or the disputation-induced conversions of the early fifteenth century.[35] In the spring of 1492 Portugal's relatively small Jewish population lived in tenuous peace with their

Christian neighbors, and Portugal's *converso* population—who tended to be assimilators rather than crypto-Jews—was negligible.[36] By late summer of 1492 all had changed.

In 1492 perhaps half of the émigrés from Spain went to Portugal.[37] For the most part these people were more firmly committed to their Jewish identity than were those who had stayed behind in Spain. They chose emigration to Portugal rather than to Africa, Italy, Turkey, or France for reasons we can only surmise, but prime among them must have been the fact that Portugal was still Iberian: the language, landscape, foods, and social climate were all familiar. Portugal was near Spain; the journey was relatively simple and inexpensive; they could maintain easy contact with those they had left behind; and if things changed they could easily go home. The Spanish Jews knew that the Portuguese had no significant history of forcing conversions and that Portugal did not have a national Inquisition.[38] This does not mean that the exiled Jews were warmly welcomed by the Portuguese. The immigrants paid dearly in gold for their right to remain in the country and to remain Jews. King João II (1481–95) charged wealthy families one hundred *cruzados* to be able to reside permanently. Poorer Jews were charged eight *cruzados* for visas that enabled them to remain for eight months. If they had not departed by then, they were claimed by the King as slaves. In an appalling act of coercion designed to increase the number of converts, King João II forcibly separated from their parents seven hundred Jewish children and sent them to be raised as Christians on the Portuguese African island of São Tomé.[39]

His successor Manoel I (1495–1521) went several steps further. As a condition of his marriage with the daughter of Fernando and Isabel of Spain he was required to expel Portugal's Jews. The Expulsion order was issued in 1496, but when Manoel took cognizance of the economic loss Portugal would suffer with the Expulsion he reversed his decision, resolving instead to prohibit emigration and to take drastic measures to convert the Jews. Early in 1497 most Jewish children were seized and baptized in an attempt to persuade their parents to remain. When this had little effect, twenty thousand of the prospective émigrés were assembled in Lisbon and in a surprise move were baptized and welcomed to Portugal as new-Catholics. Thus Portugal had instantly created what she had previously avoided: an enormous block of forced converts. When a substantial number of these new-Christians tried to emigrate, exit visas were denied. Although some continued to seek ways to leave, many of the rest settled in, relying on King Manoel's promise not to permit investigation of their internal life for twenty years and thinking that in the Inquisition-free ambiance of Portugal they could continue to Judaize with relative impunity. To his credit, King Manoel for several years promoted policies to foster the integration of the new-Christian community into the Portuguese mainstream: purity-of-blood statutes were discouraged; attempts were made to mix old- and new-Christians in the former Jewish neighborhoods; and attempts were made to immobilize new-Christians by restricting their rights to sell property or to emigrate. In recognition of the importance of endogamous marriage in the transmittal of crypto-Judaism to the next generation, converts were even prohibited from marrying other converts. Nevertheless these policies were almost wholly unsuccessful (Pimenta Ferro Tavares 1987, 41–7). Both old-Christians and the new-Christians themselves continued to think of the recent converts as Jews. The fact that they were almost exclusively forced converts, together with the lack of a national Inquisition and the King's promise not to poke into their religious lives for twenty years, gave them little incentive to try to assimilate to Portuguese Catholicism.

One has to bear in mind the fundamental difference in degree of commitment to Judaism between those who converted in Spain and those who converted in Portugal. In Spain, except for the blocks of forced converts during the 1391 and sporadic fifteenth-century riots, most *conversos* converted willingly, for reasons that ranged from careerism to love, from disillusionment with Judaism to conviction that Christianity was the true religion. Some even converted with the illusory hope that soon, when things got better, they would be able to come out of the closet and practice their Judaism openly once again. And in 1492 for the most part the staunchest Jews among the Spaniards did not convert, choosing to emigrate rather than to abandon their ancestral religion. Most of the willing converts who stayed behind were aggressively assimilationist. Although there are many dramatic individual examples to the contrary, in Spain within a generation or two the majority of the *conversos* had melted into the general Catholic populace.

Most Portuguese conversions were directly coerced; most Spanish conversions were "voluntary," even though they came about in a repressive environment that blurred the meaning of that term. Unlike the Spaniards, the Portuguese *cristãos novos* were much more likely to be crypto-Jewish than assimilationist. Prior to the 1497 mass conversion decreed by King Manoel I, for the most part Portuguese Jews had not been put through the crucible of riots, disputations, and successive waves of conversion. The Portuguese had not known a period in which large numbers of converts lived in close proximity with unconverted Jews. Moreover, after 1492 Portuguese Judaism had been swelled by Jewish refugees from Spain, refugees who were precisely that segment of Spanish Jewry most committed to their ancestral religion. In addition, the Portuguese Inquisition did not begin work until 1536, a full generation after the forced conversions.[40] Due to this combination of factors, the *cristão novo* community in Portugal had time to establish itself and create a crypto-Jewish lifestyle of some depth and complexity, a lifestyle that proved to have a much greater resilience than that of the remnant community in Spain. In the words of Yerushalmi, the key difference was the fact that in Portugal "the community itself was converted, *in toto*, whereas in Spain the [Jewish] community had remained throughout, even though eroded and diminished in number, outside the pale of conversion" (1971, 5–6). Portugal never experienced debilitating tensions between Jews and converts. Jewish families were not divided but were converted intact to Catholicism. Portuguese *cristãos novos* had no Jewish neighbors to be different from; thus their concept of themselves as Jews was not eroded by any sense of "otherness" but rather strengthened by their solidarity as a corporate group.[41] Portuguese Judaizers differed from their Spanish brethren not in the nature of their religious beliefs or practices but in the degree to which they adhered to them.

After the massive forced conversions it did not take long for matters to turn sour. As in Spain, the old-Christian urban population felt itself economically threatened by the well-educated, prospering *cristão novo* caste, which had been swelled by the Spanish immigrants. Riots broke out in Evora in 1505; in 1506 in Lisbon some two thousand *cristãos novos* were killed. In the wake of these riots King Manoel, realizing that some of the forced converts would never assimilate, permitted emigration, and many of the staunchest crypto-Jews, like the chronicler Ibn Verga, fled the Peninsula.[42] Some assimilationist new-Christians tried to escape the stigma of their origin by moving to small cities in the Portuguese interior where they hoped not to be recognized. However, most of the crypto-Jews stayed put, waiting for times to get better. Increasingly there was pressure on the King to follow the Spanish model in dealing with the Judaizing new-Christians, pressure that grew violent when the great 1531 earthquake was interpreted in Lisbon's pulpits as divine punishment for Portuguese tolerance of the *cristão novo* heretics. A Portuguese Inquisition largely on the Spanish model was authorized by the papacy in 1536, and held its first *auto da fe* in 1540. The half century of experience in neighboring Spain had shown the Portuguese crown how useful a political tool, and what an effective source of income, the Inquisition could be. Tellingly, the early debates about its establishment hinged on whether it should have the power of confiscation. The *cristão novo* community even sent an emissary to Rome to lobby against the confiscatory power, but without much success. The economic motives of the Portuguese Inquisition were dual: to enrich the Inquisition and the crown through confiscations and to eliminate the new-Christians as effective economic competitors (Saraiva 1969).

With the coming of the Inquisition to Portugal and the widespread adoption of purity-of-blood statutes,[43] crypto-Jewish religious life became much more circumspect. Most of the overt symbols of Judaism (circumcision,[44] prayer books, Torahs, Jewish ritual items such as the tallit or the mezuzzah) disappeared, as did some of the most easily observed practices such as the Festival of Booths (*Sukkot*) and the ritual slaughtering of animals. Portuguese *conversos*, especially the wealthy, took whatever protective measures they could. Some forged documents that demonstrated the ancient Christian roots of their families. Some used their relative economic well-being to contract marriage with powerful, if financially disadvantaged, Portuguese old-Christians, a practice that continued through the seventeenth century despite the restrictive environment of the purity-of-blood laws (Saraiva 1969, 132–3). Some *cristãos novos* managed to reach the Portuguese territories in the New World. Although the right of emigration was sporadically denied to them, many *cristãos novos* departed for Europe north of the Pyrenees or for Turkey, beginning a steady out-flow that lasted for over two hundred and fifty years. Others left the cities for villages in the interior of the country, particularly the Beira Alta and Trás-os-Montes regions.

With the leadership vacuum following the 1578 death of Portuguese King Sebastão and a large portion of the Portuguese nobility on a military expedition to Morocco, in 1580 Portugal was annexed to Spain. By that time the Inquisition in Spain had largely succeeded in eradicating the most blatant nuclei of Judaizing *conversos* and had turned its attention instead to rooting out Lutherans, sodomites, randy priests, and other undesirables. By contrast, the autonomous Portuguese Inquisition was at the peak of its persecution of the *cristãos novos*, holding more than fifty *autos da fe* in the last twenty years of the sixteenth century.[45] This anti-*cristão novo* campaign was sustained well into the seventeenth century, when attacks on the new-Christian middle class, as manifested in purity-of-blood laws and an incessant propaganda barrage, became a kind of national psychosis and turned the *cristãos novos* into pariahs.[46] It is not surprising that as soon as the possibility of travel was offered to the *cristãos novos* they flocked to Spain,[47] flooding major cities like Madrid and Seville[48] to such an extent that the term "Portuguese" instantly became synonymous with "Judaizer." The Portuguese immigrants gave new life to the remnant Spanish Judaizing groups and Spain once again had to deal with its so-called "Jewish problem."

After Portugal regained her independence in 1640, the Portuguese Inquisition's practice of confiscating the capital of the nation's leading new-Christian merchants became increasingly criticized for its negative impact on the economy, to such an extent that the 1647 royal charter of the Brazilian Trading Company (*Companhia Geral do Comércio do Brasil*) exempted its members from confiscations (Novinsky 1972b, 51). Liberal elements in the mercantile world and the clergy, many of them sincere Christians of Jewish descent, increased their opposition to the Inquisition, charging corruption from the highest to the lowest levels. Nonetheless the hunt for Judaizers continued until the middle of the eighteenth century with ever diminishing returns. By the 1760s the Portuguese Inquisition, like its Spanish cousin, turned its attention principally to questions of licentiousness, witchery, and liberal philosophy. The last outdoor public *auto da fe* was held in 1765; the last *auto da fe* of any sort was held in 1791. In 1773 the formal distinction between old- and new-Christian was abolished, and the Inquisition, after several temporary suspensions of activity, was formally disbanded in 1821. Unlike the case in Spain, however, where by the 1760s most Judaizing families had successfully assimilated or, if they were among those who continued to Judaize, emigrated, in Portugal crypto-Judaism persisted in a variety of remote villages around Braganza and the Douro region on the border of Spain. Entirely cut off from normative Judaism, in villages on the whole too small and too poor to allow a strong intellectual life, their religious customs developed even more idiosyncratically than those of other crypto-Jews. On the whole their villages recognized them and stigmatized them as *judeus*. Many of them suffered during the Napoleonic wars when their neighbors accused them of collaborating with the French (J. Azevedo 1921, 358). With the advent of liberal governments, Jews were permitted to return to Portugal openly even before the formal abolishment of the Inquisition. By 1813 there was a synagogue in Lisbon serving a small community in which North African Jews were prominent (Caro Baroja 1961, 3:223). The crypto-Jews in the mountains had little contact with the immigrant city-Jews. The crypto-Jews had not disappeared,[49] but neither did they attract the world's attention until the second decade of this century.

In 1917 Samuel Schwarz, a Polish-Jewish mining engineer, discovered a remnant crypto-Jewish community in Belmonte, the Trás-os-Montes region of the Beira Alta, in central Portugal along the border with Spain.[50] Eventually two crypto-Jewish communities with somewhat different practices came to light. The *judeus* around Belmonte and Covilhã abstained from pork only on Saturday, although they avoided at all times rabbit, fish without scales, and anything made with blood. They lit Sabbath candles inside clay pitchers. Preceding mass they would mumble a prayer expressing their disbelief in bread (the host) and stone (Church images). Jewish holidays were celebrated late to avert scrutiny. Their religious services were generally led by women. In the Braganza region and Carção the *judeus* did not distinguish between clean and unclean animals. Their men and women prayed separately, generally in services held in the open air away from town. They set their festival calendars by the new moon and celebrated the major life-cycle events both at church and at home. Both groups gave more attention to fasting than to feasting, and both groups preserved a large number of prayers, including scraps of Hebrew (Caro Baroja 1961, 3:230–3). The discovery attracted wide attention in the Portuguese and Jewish press, and in the following years many members of the Belmonte community were re-introduced to normative Jewish practices, sometimes with Ashkenazi rather than Iberian Sephardi models.[51]

## Conversos in the Spanish Territories

The Spanish colonies in America sustained a large *converso* population, many of whom, particularly in Mexico and to a lesser extent in Peru, were active crypto-Jews. In many ways the American crypto-Jewish experience mirrors that of Spain. But the events of the discovery, the vastness of the American territories, and the blending of cultures in the New World introduced a few significant differences. Even more so than in Spain, the *converso* experience in the Americas has been subjected to a number of romantic misconceptions, many of which have to do with the role of crypto-Jews in the discovery, conquest, and colonization, and the persistence of remnant crypto-Jewish groups into the twentieth century.

## Discovery and Conquest

With regard to the discovery and conquest, four questions are most frequently asked:

(1) Was Columbus Jewish (i.e., a Judaizing new-Christian)? No, but he most likely had Jewish ancestry. Madariaga's biography of Columbus remains the best analysis of this question.[52] Columbus was Genoese, probably of Catalán or Majorcan new-Christian ancestry, possibly of people who fled the anti-Jewish riots of the late fourteenth century. His father was a weaver, a trade much practiced among new-Christians. He was evidently raised in a Spanish-speaking ambiance, for he read and wrote Castilian as his preferred language even before setting foot on the Iberian Peninsula. Madariaga claims that even his Latin was defective in the ways common to Spanish speakers. His maritime education at the hands of people like Abraham Zacuto and Joseph Vecinho was almost entirely within Jewish or *converso* circles. In Spain his principal backers were Jews and *conversos* like Abraham Seneor, Isaac Abravanel, and the Santángel family. There is absolutely no evidence that Columbus ever thought of himself as a Judaizer or practiced any Jewish customs, and in fact his writings continually affirm his commitment to spreading Catholicism as one of the purposes of his voyages.

(2) Were there Judaizing new-Christians among his crew? Possibly. There were recent converts among the crew, but there is no solid evidence of Judaizing. Luis de Torres, a Murcian Jew who accepted baptism in 1492, was recruited for the trip as interpreter because he could speak Hebrew and Arabic and reputedly could read Aramaic and Chaldean. Eventually he became a farmer and slave holder in Cuba. Several other members of the crew, including Mestre Bernal the physician, Marco the surgeon, and crew members Rodrigo Sánchez de Segovia and Alonso de la Calle, had Jewish ancestors, but there is no evidence that any of them engaged in Judaizing practices.

(3) Were any of the conquistadors Judaizing new-Christians? Possibly, but not probably. The soldiering trades attracted few of the early generations of *conversos*, but there is evidence that a small number of Judaizers were among the pioneering generation. Two of them, Hernando de Alonso, whose ranch supplied meat to Mexico City, and Gonzalo de Morales were burned in Mexico in 1528, ostensibly for Judaizing but more likely for political reasons having to do with their involvement in Cortes's squabbles with his lieutenants.[53] Pedrarias Dávila, the conqueror and first governor of Nicaragua, came from a prominent Segovian new-Christian family, but there is no evidence that he Judaized in the New World (Cantera Burgos 1971).

(4) Were any of the colonizers Judaizing new-Christians? Yes, and in hefty numbers.[54] They were strongest in Brazil and Mexico and to a somewhat lesser extent in Peru and Chile (Böhm 1984, 20–1), but were also represented in smaller numbers throughout the other colonies. Data from New World Inquisition records are a major source for this book.

## Mexico

During its nearly three-hundred-year operation, the Mexican Inquisition tried thousands of cases on charges that ran from blasphemy to witchcraft, from bigamy to sodomy, from priests soliciting women in the confessional to Lutheranism and crypto-Judaism. Of the 1,500 cases that concerned crypto-Jews, fewer than 100 resulted in executions (*Enc. Jud.* 11:1455).[55] From surviving records in these cases a good deal can be gleaned about the social, economic, and religious life of Mexico's Judaizing new-Christians.[56]

The repeated attempts to ban new-Christians from emigration to the New World were, to judge from later Inquisition records, not very successful.[57] Even before 1510 the bishops of Puerto Rico and Cuba were complaining about the numbers of new-Christians—whom they called Jews or Hebrews—coming into the Indies (Liebman 1970, 47). The New World colonizing monks and later the bishops were from the very first granted Inquisitorial powers. At least two new-Christians accompanied Cortes in 1521 and were burned in 1528. From then until 1543 the nineteen Judaizers who surface in the records of the Mexican Inquisition were a ragtag lot who scattered themselves across the colony. Given the relatively small size of the European community at that time, it is not surprising that most of these *conversos* knew each other. Their Judaism was largely a matter of sporadic fasting, abstinence from pork, and occasional brief religious services in someone's home (Liebman 1970, 120–1).

The handful of new-Christians who followed close on the heels of the conquering armies were supplanted by substantial new-Christian immigration to Mexico during the second half of the sixteenth century and again in the first half of the seventeenth. The first wave was made up largely of Spaniards, artisans, and small-time merchants, who came not principally for religious freedom but for economic opportunity. There is no reason to believe that more than a small minority of these early *converso* immigrants continued to practice some form of crypto-Judaism (M. Cohen 1972, 285). Most of them, as in Spain, were fairly well assimilated into Spanish Christian life. A number of new-Christian clergy achieved prominence in New Spain, among them Bernardino de Sahagún and Diego de Durán (Liebman 1970, 124–5). That Judaizers were relatively inconspicuous can be seen in the fact that, of the 105 penitents who appeared in the first two Mexican *autos de fe* conducted by the Inquisition, which was finally established in New Spain in 1571, not a single Judaizer appeared. But by 1574 the Inquisition had turned its attention to the crypto-Jews, and from then to the end of the century there are numerous trials. The intensification of the Peninsular Inquisitions in the early 1600s and the tapering off of Mexican Inquisition activity at the same time appeared to offer a Mexican haven to beleaguered Peninsular Judaizers, largely Portuguese, and the silver boom offered prospects for economic opportunity. Both the first and second waves of immigrants centered in Mexico City, with smaller satellite communities in

Guadalajara, Oaxaca, the entry port of Veracruz, and the silver mining cities of the north: Guanajuato, Querétaro, Zacatecas, and San Luis Potosí.[58]

Trials beginning in the late 1570s reveal a well-established, well-networked, observant (in their fashion) Judaizing community centered in Mexico City. In 1579 Luis de Carvajal, a thoroughly assimilated new-Christian adventurer, was given a royal patent to exploit and govern a vast area called Nuevo León, which is now the entire northeast corner of the country of Mexico. Among his family were several clergymen and a Portuguese captain-general. Also among the many dozens of extended family members who accompanied him were some active crypto-Jews. Attracted to the Carvajal group, perhaps because the royal patent for exploration and settlement of this region omitted the requirement that immigrants present a certificate of purity-of-blood, were many other crypto-Jews from Spain, Portugal, and other parts of Europe. This large group formed the backbone of late sixteenth-century Mexican crypto-Judaism.[59] Their trials during the 1580s and 1590s constitute our best window on colonial crypto-Judaism at that time. The governor, Luis de Carvajal the Elder, who was found guilty not of Judaizing but of abetting heresy, died in disgrace. His nephew Luis de Carvajal the Younger, the mystic visionary, poet, and fervently observant Judaizer, was tried in 1589 and 1595–6 and eventually burned as an unrepentant heretic.[60]

As a result of the Inquisition trials of 1590, 1596, and 1601, the vast majority of the Judaizers among Mexico's new-Christians were imprisoned, executed, or deported.[61] The community as a whole was ruined financially and ceased to have any political influence to speak of. Any surviving Judaizers went into deep cover; occasionally one surfaced in trials a half century later.[62] The thoroughness of the eradication of the first wave can be seen in the fact that, when news of the 1604 general pardon reached the New World, Mexican Inquisition jails held only one accused Judaizer, Francisco López Enríquez, who was duly released (Wiznitzer 1962a, 224). Between 1601 and 1635 only nine trials of Judaizers were held, with most of the activity between 1625 and 1635.

The second wave of Mexican immigrants, which occurred in the early seventeenth century, was somewhat different from the first. A large number of them were Portuguese or the Spanish-born children of the Portuguese who had migrated into Spain after the 1580 unification of the two countries. Like their sixteenth-century predecessors, the majority were engaged in the commercial trades, although a wide variety of other professions were represented.[63] Although many of these immigrants exhibited the attenuated knowledge of Jewish practice typical of people who had been cut off from normative Judaism for several generations, others had traveled widely in Europe prior to coming to the Americas and could speak knowledgeably about the synagogues of Amsterdam, Leghorn, or Salonica.[64] The arrival in Mexico of a number of crypto-Jews who had spent time among Europe's openly practicing Jewish communities provided the Mexican crypto-Jews who had escaped the first purges with a source of fresh information, including some

Hebrew prayers the newcomers taught to the American-born *criollos*. Mexico's seventeenth-century crypto-Jews were comparatively knowledgeable in normative Judaic practices, due both to the northern European immigrants and the strong influence of the Portuguese.[65] But even with these advantages Mexico's new-Christians relied on the more traditional sources for their knowledge of Judaism: the Old Testament, usually in Latin, or other Christian religious books in Latin or Spanish with an emphasis on the Old Testament; the Inquisition's Edicts of Grace (Alberro 1988, 201); and their own weakening oral traditions, which included a number of original prayers composed by Mexican Judaizers (M. Cohen 1973, 94). Even the most learned "Jews," such as Don Francisco Rodríguez de Matos, the father of Luis de Carvajal, knew by rote only one prayer, the *Shema*, and that probably without comprehending the words (M. Cohen 1973, 96).[66]

Thus on the whole the Jewishness of these seventeenth-century Mexican crypto-Jews did not differ significantly from that of their counterparts in the Peninsula. The Mexican innovations were a product of the New World social and physical environment. For example, some Mexican new-Christians and their children, similar to other European immigrants and *criollos*, kept African or Indian servants or slaves. The offspring of *conversos*' sexual liaisons with African or Indian women were occasionally introduced to crypto-Jewish practices. The Portuguese Judaizer Pedro López Morales, for example, was accused in 1647 of planning to send his half-Indian daughter back to Spain to be raised as a Jew. Francisco López Blandón, who had wed a mulatta woman, reportedly circumcised their son. The new-Christian Esperanza Rodrígues was born in Seville of a Portuguese merchant and a Guinean black. Esperanza married an old-Christian German sculptor, emigrated with him to Mexico, and raised their three daughters as crypto-Jews. The four women were punished by the Inquisition in 1646 (Wiznitzer 1962a, 226, 240–2).

From time to time Mexican crypto-Jews made use of local products for their rituals. For example, crypto-Jews in the provinces who were unable to obtain *matza* for their Passover *seder* sometimes substituted the locally produced unleavened corn tortillas. When wine was unavailable for the *Kiddush*, they substituted the ubiquitous Mexican festive drink: chocolate.

Despite the vast distances of the New World, Mexican crypto-Jewish society of the seventeenth century was fairly tightly organized.[67] Like most immigrants everywhere who share a minority ethnic status, they formed networks to help each other. Often newcomers would be directed to the safe house in Veracruz of the crypto-Jew Fernando Rodríguez (Liebman 1970, 255–6), who would pass them along to other families in Mexico City. Antonio Váez (executed 1649) served the Mexico City community as a kind of rabbi, visiting the sick and conducting communal Passover *seders* in his home. His son Simón Váez Sevilla maintained the tradition of using his home as a religious center. He set up a number of crypto-Jews as his commercial sales agents throughout the Mexican hinterland. The most able soon established their own shops but continued to pass news of the provincial Judaizers back to the capital. Simón Váez and his friend Tomás Treviño de Sobremonte, who were the wealthiest crypto-Jews in the community, kept and promulgated the calendar of Jewish festivals for the new-Christian community.[68] Other Judaizers took other roles. Margarita de Rivera routinely helped prepare the deceased crypto-Jews for burial. Miguel Tinoco distributed *matza* for the community on Passover. Most of Mexico's crypto-Jewish community were rigorously endogamous, so that almost everyone was related to everyone else.[69] They gathered in each other's homes regularly on the Sabbath and principal festivals and for major life-cycle events like weddings and funerals.

One peculiarity of Mexican crypto-Jews was their fervent belief that the Messiah would be born into their own community. In the second quarter of the seventeenth century certain women who were considered to be particularly virtuous and faithful in their Jewish observance were venerated as potential mothers for the Messiah. Juana Enríquez (mother of the Váez Sevillas), María Gómez (the wife of Tomás Treviño de Sobremonte), Blanca Juárez, and Ynés Pereira were such women (Wiznitzer 1962a, 267; Liebman 1970, 230).

The early seventeenth-century Mexican crypto-Jewish immigrants were purged in another spate of trials in the 1640s.[70] After 1650 crypto-Judaism gradually withered in Mexico. Over the next fifty years only thirty new-Christians were tried for Judaizing, of whom three were burned. Unlike most earlier Mexican crypto-Jews, who had lived an intense communal life, these people tended to Judaize alone rather than in groups (Israel 1970, 129). The old focal points had become too dangerous, so the Judaizers tended to leave Mexico City and Guadalajara for smaller provincial towns. Their abandonment of Veracruz meant a diminished involvement in foreign trade (Liebman 1970, 277). By the time the Bourbons took power in Spain in 1700, Mexican crypto-Judaism was perceived to be so weak a threat that the Inquisition did not even routinely follow up on cases brought to its attention (Liebman 1970, 284). The last identified Judaizer was imprisoned in 1788, accused of having been circumcised and of wanting to be buried as a Jew (Liebman 1970, 295). By the beginning of the nineteenth century, Mexican crypto-Judaism was essentially dead.

Other Spanish Colonies

*Central America.* Crypto-Jews seem to have been little attracted to Central America. For example, according to Chinchilla Aguilar, only twenty-six Nicaraguans or Guatemalans were tried as Judaizers by the Mexican Inquisition from 1572, the date of the first case, until 1778, the date of the last. He identifies half of the accused as being of Portuguese origin. There is not a single instance of an organized crypto-Jewish religious community or even of a so-called "rabbi" or dogmatizer. The extent of the Guatemalans' Judaizing customs was minimal. Two were accused of washing their dead in warm water. One removed the sciatic vein from a leg of lamb before roasting it. The last of the accused, the priest Rafael Gil Rodríguez, was convicted of having circumcised two of his prison acquaintances (Chinchilla Aguilar 1953, 179–85).

*Peru.* Spain's other major sixteenth-century colony, Peru (including what are now Bolivia and Ecuador), attracted many fewer *conversos* than did Mexico. Although an Inquisition was established in Lima in 1570, it was relatively inactive against Judaizers until 1635, when suspicions of a *converso* plot to wrest independence for the colony precipitated a flurry of activity resulting in what is called the "great" *auto de fe* of 1639. By the end of this spate of activity eighty-four people had been tried for Judaizing. Given the fact that so many more men than women emigrated to the colonies, it is not surprising that eighty-one of the trials were of men. Sixty-two of the accused were of Portuguese extraction. Only four of the cases involved people born in the Americas, three of them people of mixed blood who had been instructed by their Judaizing father (Castañeda/Hernández 1989, 431). This Inquisition pressure forced many Peruvian Judaizers north into Colombia and Mexico. To judge from the paucity of references to Judaizers in Lima trials after that date, crypto-Judaism seems to have all but disappeared.

*Colombia, Venezuela.* In the early to mid-seventeenth century some crypto-Jews fleeing Brazil ended up in the Venezuelan and Colombian coastal cities. A few others came for reasons of economic opportunity. From 1610 Cartagena had its own Inquisition tribunal. On the whole the Judaizers tried there were people undistinguished in rank, accomplishment, or the depth of their Judaism (Tejado Fernández 1950, 58–69). Testimony in 1625 revealed connections between Colombian Judaizers and a Dutch association called *La cofradía de los judíos de Holanda*, the purposes of which included helping Holland acquire the Iberian possessions in the Americas (Liebman 1982, 170, 221). On the whole, crypto-Judaism did not take deep root in Colombia and Inquisition tribunals there devoted most of their attention to the pursuit of witches.

*Argentina, Uruguay, and Paraguay.* The Río de Plata cattle-ranching regions of Argentina, Uruguay, and Paraguay likewise attracted very few *conversos* in colonial times, with the exception of refugees from the Brazilian troubles (1590–1654), when some families escaped to the south. The Río de Plata region was on the whole inhospitable to the refugees. In 1603 twenty-five Portuguese new-Christians were expelled from Buenos Aires; in 1628 an attempt was made to prohibit local people from marrying the "Portuguese" (Saban 1991, 71, 189).[71] Many of the Río de Plata refugees eventually made their way north along the Pacific coast, some settling in Lima and some even reaching Mexico. The Río de Plata region was under the jurisdiction of the Lima Inquisition. The most notable trial was that of Francisco Maldonado de Silva, of Tucumán, in 1639 (Böhm 1984; Lewin 1954; Medina 1899a).

*Philippines.* Because Manila was the major Far Eastern trading center for the Spanish overseas empire, it is not surprising that a crypto-Jewish community established itself there as early as the 1580s. Philippine affairs were handled administratively through Mexico, and Mexican Inquisition files contain sporadic references to the Asian colonies. When the Carvajal family was purged in 1589, Luis de Carvajal's brother-in-law Antonio Díaz fled to Manila and Macao. Manuel Gil de la Guarda, reconciled in Mexico in 1601, had been arrested in the Philippines. In fact, Philippine crypto-Jewish activity was reported from time to time over the next hundred years. Because of incomplete records we do not know whether any Judaizers appeared in Manila's first *auto de fe* in 1580, but three Judaizers were actually burned there in 1649, and up to the end of the seventeenth century at least eight Philippine crypto-Jews were shipped to Mexico for trial (Liebman 1970, 171, 198, 231, 266, 283).

## Conversos in the Portuguese Territories

Brazil's colonial crypto-Jewish history is somewhat different from that of the Hispanic colonies, due both to Portugal's intermittent policy of encouraging new-Christian emigration to the Indies and to the Dutch occupation of part of the country in the mid-seventeenth century. At least one known new-Christian accompanied Cabral on his voyage of discovery in 1500. Two years later a consortium of Portuguese new-Christians was granted a concession to market Brazil wood in Portugal. From 1502 to 1570 a considerable number of crypto-Jews sought to make their fortunes in Brazil. In addition, from 1548 right into the eighteenth century the Portuguese tribunals intermittently deported reconciled Judaizers to Brazil (Roth 1932a, 283, 393). In the last quarter of the sixteenth century, when word of the economic prosperity of northeast Brazil spread through Portugal, the numbers of new-Christian immigrants increased even more. As is typical of any immigrant population, old-time resident *cristãos novos* helped the newcomers get established. In seventeenth-century Bahia *cristãos novos* may have amounted to 20 percent of the 10,000 or so European inhabitants (Novinsky 1972a, 144–5).

On the whole, new-Christians formed an integral part of Brazilian colonial life. From the very first, they played a crucial role in the establishment of Brazil's sugar industry. The center of Brazilian economic life was the plantation-factory-town known as the *engenho*, or sugar mill. By the year 1600 there were 120 of these *engenhos*, a large number of them owned or administered by new-Christians (Wiznitzer 1960; *Enc. Jud.* 4:1322). Brazilian colonial society consisted mainly of two classes: the slaves who did the work and the landholders, plantation and municipal administrators, and mill owners who controlled the economy. Unlike the situation in the Spanish colonies, where the crypto-Jews with rare exceptions formed part of the urban middle class and rarely amassed significant fortunes, many seventeenth-century Brazilian new-Christians were among those in control. Prestige in Brazil came from the ostentatious display of possessions, and the *engenho* owners, no matter what their origins, tended to have the wherewithal to presume to top status. The *converso* slave owners often married old-Christian women and, like their old-Christian colleagues, did not hesitate to sire children with their slaves.

Brazilian society was stratified according to color; although the purity-of-blood laws continued to bar new-Christians from a variety of professions, the fact that Portuguese new-Christian immigrants were as white as the other Europeans facilitated their integration into the mainstream. Both the *engenho* elite and the petty merchants and artisans assimilated quite thoroughly. Although the urban middle class in Brazil was small, it included many new-Christians who prospered in commerce and were teachers, administrators, and clergy. Legally they were nearly as disqualified from the professions as were the blacks, but in practice they got around the rules. It was mainly the middle-class bourgeoisie who tended to resist assimilation, and when the Inquisition became active they were its principal targets.[72]

From 1570 to 1630, however, a series of anti-*converso* measures and the intensified activity of the Portuguese Inquisition pulled in the welcome mat for Brazil's crypto-Jews. Although a tribunal of the Inquisition was never established in Brazil, which always came under direct jurisdiction of the Portuguese courts, in 1579 the Bishop of Salvador was granted Inquisitorial powers and Portuguese Inquisition "visitors" were sent to look into matters in Bahia and Pernambuco (1591–5), Olinda (1599), and Salvador (1610). To judge from the numbers, the principal concerns of the Brazilian Inquisition at this time were sodomy and blasphemy. During the "investigations" of this period only 21 percent of the denunciations were for Judaizing (207 of 950), and only 8.2 percent (40 of 486) of the convictions were for Judaizing (Siqueira 1978, 227–8). In the first half of the seventeenth century only seventeen Judaizers were accused and returned to Lisbon for trial; in the second half of the century only eight were extradited.

No overview of *converso* history in Brazil is complete without mention of the Dutch occupation. In the early seventeenth century the Dutch West India Company, many of whose stockholders were Iberian refugees, had eyes on the rich sugar lands of northeast Brazil. A Dutch military expedition took Bahia in 1624, only to lose it the following year.[73] In 1630 they took Recife, with some assistance from the local crypto-Jewish population,[74] and controlled most of the northeast until 1654. Under the Dutch occupation many crypto-Jews began to practice their Judaism openly and many European Jews migrated to Brazil seeking economic opportunity. There were synagogues in Recife and Maurícia with rabbis imported from Amsterdam, as well as numerous other less formal congregations. Perhaps half the civilian population of Dutch Brazil was Jewish. Jews participated fully in the Dutch administration of the colony and even formed a company of militia. When the Portuguese retook the colony in 1654, anyone identified as a Jew had to abandon not only the Dutch territories in the northeast, but all of Brazil. The emigration of Jews and crypto-Jews lasted through the end of the century (*Enc. Jud.* 4:1323–4).

In Bahia the most significant Inquisition event of the seventeenth century was the *Grande Inquiração* conducted in 1646 under the direction of the bishop Pedro da Silva, in which some 118 people were investigated, the majority for second-hand allegations that they were new-Christians and bad Catholics. The investigations revealed that a large part of Bahia high society had Jewish ancestry. The testimony tended to be vague about incidences of Judaizing and revealed a continuity of certain myths about *cristãos novos* more than hard facts about their observances. Still, certain patterns emerge: the Bahian Judaizers tended to avoid pork, to abstain from work on the Sabbath, to have secret Jewish names in addition to their Christian names, to congregate at "certain times" to perform "certain ceremonies," and to show disrespect for Christian icons. Some of the accused had been arrested previously; most of them had relatives in Portugal who had also been in trouble with the Inquisition (Novinsky 1972b, 130–7). On the whole their attachment to Judaism was light, as was their concern for any religious observance, Jewish or Catholic, an attitude Novinsky believes characterized Brazilian crypto-Jewish society in general in the mid-seventeenth-century, with the exception of those who professed openly during the Dutch occupation (1972b, 143). We have seen how Portuguese *cristãos novos* tended to be more orthodox in their Judaizing than their Spanish counterparts, but the most orthodox of them remained in Europe. The *cristãos novos* who went to the Portuguese Indies seem to have been assimilationists or the sorts of skeptics who did not care much for any brand of religion.

In the eighteenth century Brazil's new-Christians were active in commerce, particularly the diamond trade (Roth 1932a, 393). The last great wave of trials began in 1707, when a girl from Olinda went to the Inquisition in Lisbon and denounced fifty-five guests who had attended a crypto-Jewish wedding in Rio de Janeiro some years before. A thirty-year period of intense activity was unleashed in which several hundred Brazilian Judaizers were tried. Over Brazil's entire colonial history about four hundred Judaizers were tried; eighteen of them were executed, only one burned alive.[75] By the end of the eighteenth century Brazil's crypto-Jewish community had for all intents and purposes assimilated, emigrated, or been eradicated (Falbel 1974, 11–2).

## Conversos in Other American Colonies

*Curaçao, Surinam, Jamaica, Barbados.* The colonies most preferred by Jews and *conversos* during the seventeenth and eighteenth centuries were those controlled by the Dutch, whose commitment to religious tolerance was well known. During the eighteenth century their second preference was for colonies of the British, who were somewhat less supportive of religious diversity than the Dutch but substantially more so than the Spaniards or Portuguese. Thus Curaçao (which the Dutch took from Spain in 1634),[76] Surinam,[77] Jamaica,[78] and Barbados[79] became major

New World Jewish centers. Frequently crypto-Jews banned from Mexico ended up in the Islands, and before long many openly practicing Jews in the British or Dutch colonies had networks of crypto-Jewish relatives on the Spanish-American mainland (Liebman 1970, 275–6). There is even evidence that some Mexican crypto-Jews used to attend Jewish services openly when visiting Jamaica or Barbados.[80]

## Conversos in Other European Countries

As Chapter 20 will make clear, many Judaizing *conversos* dreamed of emigrating to lands where they could practice their religion openly. This yearning was especially strong among the generation of converts who experienced the Expulsion and the rigors of the Inquisition's first round of attempts to exterminate crypto-Judaism. At various times North Africa, the Italian states, Turkey, Holland, and England[81] beckoned to the Iberian converts; Turkey offered strong financial incentives for Jewish settlers. Over the one hundred fifty years following the 1492 Expulsion thousands of *converso* refugees slipped out of the Iberian Peninsula in order to resettle in those and other lands. The study of *converso* life and the re-emergence of Judaism in countries beyond the Iberian orbit is outside the scope of this book.[82]

Paradoxically, during the two centuries following the Expulsion substantial numbers of Judaizing *conversos* also chose to remain in the Iberian kingdoms. There were several reasons for this. For some two hundred years emigration restrictions made leaving the Iberian Peninsula difficult (although never impossible). More important were the host of economic and personal reasons for staying behind. Investments were often hard to liquidate and difficult to relocate.[83] Family members and friends were hard to abandon. Crypto-Judaism, although difficult and risky, seems to have satisfied the religious needs of many. For many half-assimilated *conversos* the benefits of their social and economic mobility as Christians outweighed the inconveniences and risks of having to mask their true religious beliefs. And there was always the hope—false only with hindsight—that things would get better. In fact, even in those Christian lands where it would have been easy to revert to Judaism, many *conversos* chose to continue to live as Christians. Pullan questions whether these crypto-Jews left Spain "out of religious zeal and at the first opportunity, or . . . because security had been utterly destroyed and because excellent opportunities were opening up for them in the Ottoman empire, [where they chose to] temporize as long as possible before taking any irrevocable step" (1983, 204). What was true of Constantinople was even truer of Venice and Ferrara and of Amsterdam and Bruges: it was easier to travel and to conduct business as a Christian than as a Jew,[84] a fact that thoroughly annoyed the local rabbis.[85] One cannot escape the conclusion that, for a substantial segment of the *converso* communities in Europe in the sixteenth and seventeenth centuries, business opportunities outweighed the imperatives and risks[86] of crypto-Judaism. For business as well as family and religious reasons, a number of crypto-Jews even returned to Iberia after having emigrated to the relatively safe cities of Northern Europe (Kaplan 1985, 198).[87]

In the mercantile Renaissance world *converso* businessmen traveled a great deal. The Mendes family, which included such notables as Doña Gracia Mendesia and João Migues, who became the Duke of Naxos, is a well-studied but in terms of travel not atypical example.[88] New World Inquisition records indicate that *conversos* came to the Americas from almost every country in Europe and from the Far Eastern trading centers as well. Captain Estevan de Ares de Fonseca, a Portuguese informer who in 1635 gave early warning to the Inquisition about Dutch plans to invade Brazil, testified to having visited Spain, France, Belgium, Holland, Italy, and Turkey (Caro Baroja 1961, 332–6).

One result of all this travel was that news circulated quickly. Former Spaniards and Portuguese were hungry for information about the friends and family they had left behind. Knowledge about arrests and *autos de fe* was avidly repeated.[89] Crypto-Jews who were burned, especially those who had reaffirmed their Judaism with some bravado before going to the stake, were widely celebrated as martyrs.[90] A second result was that the practices of individual groups of Iberian crypto-Jews were from time to time reauthenticated with information about Jewish practices outside the Peninsula.

Captain Fonseca's testimony also makes clear that openly practicing Jews, or strongly Judaizing crypto-Jews, frequently attempted to persuade traveling *conversos* to reassert their Jewish identity.[91] The responsibility the Jewish communities of Europe felt for their Iberian brethren showed itself in a variety of missionary endeavors. *Conversos* who left Iberia were aggressively proselytized by European Jews.[92] Sometimes a *mohel* would be sent to the Peninsula to circumcise those crypto-Jews who were willing.[93]

Printing presses throughout Europe produced religious material—generally in Spanish or Portuguese—for the religious edification of Iberia's *conversos*.[94] These materials appealed mainly to those *conversos* who strongly identified as Jews and who accepted the risks inherent in overt practice. They were most likely to reach the better organized crypto-Jewish groups. But they seem to have had little impact on the majority of Iberian crypto-Jews whose beliefs and practices were increasingly Christianized, and who were destined before long to be absorbed into the Iberian Catholic mainstream.

# Notes

1. These three periods, which were treated in the first part of this Introduction, will be only briefly summarized below.
2. For Portuguese examples see Pimenta Ferro Tavares 1982, 477, n 357.

3. This was perceived clearly by some contemporary Jews, such as the anonymous chronicler who wrote around 1498 that the *anusim* "had made a new law for themselves" (Marx 1908, 256).

4. *Dixo quel año que Sus Altezas mandaron salir los judíos de Castilla, estando este testigo vn día de pascua del pan çençeño de los judíos en casa de Ysaque el portugués . . . enseñando a vn fijo del dicho Ysaque a meldar, vio que estando asy entró Fernand de Guernica, el Viejo, calderero . . . que hera mucho amigo del dicho Ysaque, e dixo: "¿Qué hazes? Duelos os vengan. Gastáys tienpo en mal. Melda, melda. ¡Y avn este otro, dolorido, piensa que algo faze!" lo qual dixo por este testigo, "faríades mejor de entender avnque sea pascua o sea nada, en cómo avés de poner cobro en vuestra hazienda e cómo vos avés de yr, que aunque algunos os dizen que os tornes christianos, mala pascua me dé Dios sy yo os lo aconsejo. El por qué es que, acabado que seáys cristianos, luego buscarán por dónde den con vosotros de rostros en el fuego. . . . Quánto más que creo, como yo creo, que nace para morir, que no ay otro en este munco syno nasçer e morir, que después que Dios crió el mundo e cada vna dexó con su dicha, buena o mala. . . ." Lo qual todo susodicho desya el dicho Fernando el calderero a Ysaque . . . e a su muger e a su suegra del dicho Ysaque e a este testigo. Los quales se fueron a Portugal e nunca boluieron* (Carrete Parrondo 1985a, 155).

5. Even old-Christian chroniclers of the time recorded the pathos of the Expulsion. For a host of vivid examples from both Jewish and Catholic contemporary sources translated into English, see Raphael 1992.

6. Cantera Burgos has documented the relatively high numbers of returnees in his studies of the small city of San Martín de Valdeiglesias in the Province of Madrid (1964), as has Cantera Montenegro for Torrelaguna (Madrid) (1982). The sixteenth-century chronicler Bernáldez claims that so many Jews returned to become Christian that the priests had to spray holy water on them with a hyssop; he says that a hundred Jews returned to his own village of Palacios, and that he personally baptized ten or twelve returning rabbis (Chapters 110, 113). Motis Dolader 1987, 252 considers that, while most Aragonese Jews emigrated rather than convert, the combination of the hardships of exile and the possibility of recovering their property in Spain led substantial numbers of them to return between 1492 and 1497. Netanyahu, on the other hand, estimates the number of returnees to have been very small, overall some 6,000–7,000 (1966, 248).

7. For example, in the 1572 trial against the Renaissance humanists Gaspar de Grajal and Fray Luis de León, the Inquisitor Diego González said that "because Grajal and Fray Luis were new-Christians, they had to be committed to eclipsing our Catholic faith and returning to their own Law" (*Siendo notorio que Grajal y Fray Luis eran cristianos nuevos, tenían que estar interesados en oscurecer nuestra fe católica y en volver a su ley*) (Castro 1963, 182).

8. Révah 1968, 332–3; Caro Baroja 1961, 3:332–6.

9. Révah 1968, 333; Roth 1931–2, 11; Levine 1982. Women appear to have been more conservative in their adherence to traditional Judaism. Motis Dolader points out that in Aragon many more men converted than women (1987, 246). Melammed notes that in trials of Judaizing women in Toledo between 1492 and 1520 74 percent of the identified teachers were women (1985, 93).

10. In addition, some ritual items were confiscated by Church or Inquisition officials at the time of the Expulsion. See Cabezudo Astraín 1970, 352 for the confiscation of the library of Ejea's Jewish community and Motis Dolader 1987, 225–6 for other examples from Aragon.

11. The Church's campaign to eradicate formal Jewish learning must be considered a success, for after 1492, despite a modest trade in smuggled material, books written in Hebrew

rarely surface in the hands of *conversos* in Spain. See Chapter 12. Cohen found not one single Mexican Judaizer with significant knowledge of post-Biblical Judaism (1972, 291).

12. *E lo que dexe de fazer fue por no saber quando eran fiestas e que cosas se avia de fazer a las vezes por miedo las dexe de fazer pero en mi coraçon las fize e fiziera mas sy supiera pensando que en ello me avia de salvar* (Blázquez Miguel 1989, 186). The Christian-like belief in personal salvation is discussed in my Chapter 4.

13. *Jejuava cada anno o jejum da Rainha Esther e por ser fraca e mal deposta nam jejuava mais que o primeira dia e nos outros dous dava esmolas pollos nam poder jejuar. . . . Quando não podia jejuar dava esmolas. . . . Quando os nam podia jejuar por ser mal deposta e ter muito trabalho, dava esmolas. . . . Guardava os sabados na vontade e por os nam poder guardar na obra dava huma esmola* (Azevedo Mea 1982, 92, 448, 46, 76).

14. Netanyahu 1966, 205; M. Cohen 1972, 280.

15. Novinsky has argued how the "myth of purity-of-blood" together with the "myth of honor" consoled the common folk, who thought that these principles bound them to the highest classes in a seamless front against the hated new-Christian bourgeoisie (1972b, 45).

16. Kamen estimates the size of the middle class in the 1480s to be some 500,000 souls, most of whom were Jewish or *converso* (1965, 26).

17. Debate continues to rage on the question of the extent and motives of the new-Christian involvement in the *Comunidades* revolt. See Domínguez Ortiz 1965, 71. See also Kamen 1965, 71–2; Gutiérrez Nieto 1964; Baron 1969, 13:74.

18. A few prominent examples are the Carmelite reformer and mystic Saint Teresa of Avila; the Augustinian mystic, poet, essayist, and university professor Fray Luis de León (who was imprisoned for five years for his allegedly heterodox views); Fray Diego de Estella; Beatus Juan de Avila.

19. For example, Alonso de Oropesa, the *converso* head of the Jeronymite order, argued that to divide Christians into Old and New was to divide the body of Christ (Haliczer 1990, 211). The *conversos* always found some allies among old-Christian writers who were willing to express their profound revulsion for the abuses of contemporary religious politics. See, for example, the attack on purity-of-blood laws in Fray Domingo de Baltanás's 1556 *Apologia* (Domínguez Ortiz 1992, 65–6).

20. Examples include Fernando de Rojas, *La Celestina* (1499) and the picaresque as well as more "escapist" genres like the chivalric and pastoral novels, all of which achieved great popularity in the sixteenth century.

21. Themes such as the trauma of conversion and assimilation, the unfairness of the purity-of-blood laws when compared to the ideal equality of all Christians before the sacraments (or before death), and the exaggerated significance given to lineage in the Iberian concept of personal worth (or honor) appear in the works of early sixteenth-century playwrights such as Gil Vicente, Diego Sánchez de Badajoz, Torres Naharro, Lucas Fernández, and Miguel de Carvajal. Irony is their most common rhetorical strategy. Carvajal, by way of illustration, in his *Courts of Death* presents a group of Jews who have chosen to return to Spain and become Christian rather than perish in Morocco. Saint Augustine exhorts them to convert because Christianity "is a divine law of love, without stain or error," but then threatens them with fire (of Hell? of the Inquisition?) if they do not convert (*Deja ya de ser judíos, / pues no esperais sino brasa*). They accept baptism but one of them, Don Faraón, laments about how difficult it is to abandon every cultural vestige of Judaism: "If under the weight of all this the little Christian Judaizes just a little bit, the knife is at his throat" (*Y si acaso el cristianillo / según lo siente, y le pesa, / judaizar viese un poquillo, / luego al pescuzo el cuchillo*) (1872, 32).

22. By Roth's count, in the last half of the seventeenth century the highest percentage of Inquisition convictions was still for Judaizing: 324 of 399 cases in Córdoba, 556 of 855 in Toledo, 78 of 85 in Valladolid (1932, 85).

23. From 1535 to 1645 only ten Majorcan *conversos* were executed for Judaizing (Kamen 1965, 225).

24. See Braunstein 1936; Forteza 1966; Moore 1976; Domínguez Ortiz 1992, 100–2; 121–5.

25. See the works of Mateo Alemán, Francisco de Quevedo, and Miguel de Cervantes, inter alia.

26. The trials that resulted from the 1720 discovery of a clandestine synagogue in Madrid resulted in 824 arrests and 75 executions (Lea 1906–7, 3:308–9).

27. Domínguez Ortiz 1992, 107–10. For a capsule biography of the tobacco merchant Simón de Alarcón, tried in Valencia in 1721, see Haliczer 1990, 233–4.

28. For Kamen the last wave of *converso* trials "shows clearly that they were unable as a body to become assimilated into society." Yet much of his own information suggests the contrary. For example, during the century and a half from 1645 to 1794 the Toledo tribunal tried only some 659 people for Judaizing, with trials exceedingly rare after 1730 (1965, 184, 214, 228), which suggests that by then most *conversos* had successfully assimilated. Uchmany 1991, 123 suggests that by the eighteenth century the Inquisition was combating only the memory of Jews.

29. The most balanced review of arguments for and against the colonial origin of the New Mexican crypto-Jews is Tobias (1991, 9–21). See also Fierman 1987, 15–6; Hordes 1991, 213–5.

30. In 1991 Alvin Rubin, Ronald Schneider, Carolina Matos, and members of the southeastern New England academic and lay communities founded the Aristides Sousa Mendes Society to encourage the exchange of information about this group.

31. Some of these stories have found their way into print. See Anon. 1989; Cardoza 1989; Kurzweil 1980, 311–7; Fierman 1987, xi–xii; Beller 1969, 273–80; Prinz 1973, 3–6. Especially persistent are legends of keys to the ancestral estates, such as this one, recalled by an anonymous contributor to *Avotaynu* in 1989: "A Spanish friend of mine, who is Christian, told us of an exiled Sephardic Jew in Poland who traveled to Madrid, knocked on the gate of a house there and showed the owner of the house . . . an ancient key. The owner let the Jew try the key in the gate lock and it worked! Then he asked if he could be allowed to excavate a little hole in the patio; his ancestors had buried something there. He was permitted to do so and dug up a leather pouch with some parchments in it!" (Anonymous 1989, S5).

32. Atienza (1978, 174–6). Historically other towns have been characterized as "Jewish." One example is Hellín (Murcia), which in the eighteenth-century Macanaz trial was said to be "infected with Jews" (*Dicha villa es la más notada de infección de judíos que hay en todo aquel reino*) (Martín Gaite 1970, 271).

33. Despite Portugal's rich archives, Judaism in that country has not yet been as thoroughly investigated as in Spain, as Baer 1966, 1:187, Baron 1965, 10:157, Novinsky 1972b, 23, and others have pointed out.

34. The handful of major anti-Jewish disturbances, such as the 1383 and 1449 Lisbon riots, did not result in large numbers of converts (Saraiva 1969, 31).

35. Pimenta Ferro Tavares 1970, 75–6. Humberto Moreno documents how Portugal was not entirely free from anti-Jewish agitation during this period (1985).

36. Despite its relatively small size, the pre-1492 *converso* community was not wholly exempt from discrimination or persecution. To cite just one example, the city of Oporto in 1485 refused resident permits to new-Christians (Pimenta Ferro Tavares 1987, 21).

37. *Enc. Jud.* 13:921 gives the number who entered Portugal as 150,000. For more conservative estimates see p. 75. There were strong *cristão novo* communities in Lisbon, Oporto, Setúbal, Guarda, Santarém, Faro, Evora, and Portalegre, as well as minor communities in dozens of other small cities and villages (Saraiva 1969, 27).
38. Local inquisitions were functioning sporadically in several Portuguese cities, but executions of crypto-Jews, such as João de Niebla who was burned in Santarém around 1487 (Pimenta Ferro Tavares 1987, 21), were rare.
39. Baron presents an excellent bibliography of contemporary descriptions of this outrage (1969, 13:327–8).
40. Portugal had tribunals in Evora and Coimbra as well as in Lisbon, which also had jurisdiction over the colonies.
41. This analysis follows Yerushalmi 1971, 5–8. See also Pullan 1983, 201, and Lewin 1946, 24.
42. The decree of 1507, which reversed the 1499 legislation that prohibited new-Christian emigration, was also an attempt to incorporate the skills and capital of *crisãos novos* in bolstering the Portuguese economy. It granted them the right to trade freely with Christian countries in Portuguese ships and extended them ample protections under the law. In Rivkin's view these conditions spurred the new-Christian contributions to the extraordinary development of Portuguese entrepreneurial capitalism at the time (1971, 142–4).
43. On the whole, the history of the purity-of-blood statutes in Portugal parallels that in Spain (Saraiva 1969, 113–9).
44. New World crypto-Jews, particularly in Mexico, continued to practice circumcision well into the seventeenth century. Uchmany observes that 98 percent of the men cited as Judaizing in the Mexican *autos de fe* of the 1650s had been found by the Inquisition's medical examiners to have been circumcised (1991, 135).
45. During its nearly three centuries of operation the Portuguese Inquisition in 750 *autos da fe* sentenced some 30,000 people, of whom 1,200 were executed and another 600 burned in effigy (*Enc. Jud.* 13:924).
46. The terms are Novinsky's. She also presents a good summary of what things *cristãos novos* were prevented from doing (1972b, 41, 47–8).
47. Domínguez Ortiz points out that, as Portugal lost her dominance in the Atlantic to Holland and England, many Portuguese *cristãos novos* were also attracted by the expanded commercial opportunities offered by Spain's immense empire (1991, 78).
48. In 1630 as much as 25 percent of Seville's population was Portuguese (Novinsky 1972b, 42).
49. Caro Baroja documents nineteenth- and early twentieth-century contacts with these crypto-Jews (1961, 3:225–6).
50. Schwarz's book about that discovery is reviewed and contrasted with that of several contemporaries by Caro Baroja (1961, 3:229–34).
51. These communities have been studied in detail in the intervening years. See Canelo 1987; da Cunha e Freitas 1952; Paulo 1985; "Tradições Cripto-Judaicas" 1928; Vasconcelos 1958.
52. Madariaga 1940, chapter 11. A river of ink has flowed on this question of Columbus's alleged Jewish roots and Jewish participation in the discovery and conquest. For basic bibliography, see Singerman 1975, 93–7; 1993, 207–14.
53. For a study of these cases see Conway 1928.
54. Liebman calculates that by 1545 at least 25 percent of the immigrants to Mexico were Jews (by which he means new-Christians) and estimates that in Mexico City there may

have been more new-Christians than old-Christians (1970, 42). He concludes that "Jews [i.e., *conversos*] swarmed to the shores of New Spain after the conquest of 1521" (1970, 18). I agree with Martin Cohen's caveats on this point: "Evidence presently available does not permit the conclusion that crypto-Judaism embraced a majority or even a large plurality of the New Christians in New Spain in either the sixteenth or seventeenth centuries. . . . They fail to show the existence of appreciable numbers of crypto-Jews in the eighteenth century" (1972, 286).
55. For much smaller estimates see Wiznitzer 1962a, 268.
56. The best overview of Mexican crypto-Judaism remains Liebman 1970, despite the confusions introduced by his referring to most new-Christians undifferentiatedly as Jews.
57. Fernando and Isabel issued the first ban in 1501; Carlos V repeated it in 1522; it formed part of the Law of the Indies (Book 9:26–15) in 1523 (Liebman 1970, 46).
58. Israel 1970, 126 calculates that roughly half of the people accused of Judaizing lived in Mexico City, with another third in Guadalajara and Veracruz. In the late 1620s the Inquisition in Mexico City received reports about Judaizers in Michoacán, Sinaloa, Zacatecas, Trujillo, Guadiana, and Taxco, as well as from Guatemala and from Cartagena, which is now part of Colombia (Liebman 1970, 219).
59. The circle of the Carvajals has been studied by a number of historians: M. Cohen 1973; Liebman 1967; 1970; Toro 1932.
60. Liebman calls him "God-intoxicated" and concludes that his liturgical writings "attest a Divine inspiration" (1970, 160).
61. For a concise summary in English of the accusations leveled against the thirty-nine Judaizers who appeared in the 1601 *auto* see Wiznitzer 1962a, 222.
62. For example, Ana de León Carvajal, Luis's sister, who was reconciled in 1601 at age 19 and then 48 years later was executed in the *auto de fe* of 1649 as a relapsed Judaizing heretic (Wiznitzer 1962a, 225).
63. Liebman surveyed 300 Inquisition cases over the entire colonial period involving males. He found 24 shopkeepers, 21 merchants, 20 priests and monks, 17 government officials, 16 brokers, 6 soldiers, 6 miners or mine owners, 5 silver- and gold-smiths, 5 doctors, 4 musicians or actors, 4 grocers, 4 importers-exporters, 4 peddlers, 3 tailors, 2 pharmacists, 2 carpenters, 2 tavern-keepers, 2 soap and candle manufacturers, 2 barbers, 2 university students, 1 dueling master, 1 sword maker, and 1 dye manufacturer. Six of these people were also identified as "rabbis" (1970, 301).
64. Trials of the late 1640s included those of Pedro Fernández de Castro (who had lived in Ferrara, Genoa, Leghorn), Jorge Jacinto Bazán (Marseilles, Florence, Pisa, Leghorn, Salonica), and Rafaela Enríquez (Amsterdam, Leghorn, Pisa) (Wiznitzer 1962a, 242–4). The Portuguese Manuel Fonseca, tried in Lima in 1608, had been circumcised in Leghorn on his way to America. About the same time in Lima Domingo López said that he suspected that his family was new-Christian, since his brother had married a Jewish woman in Turkey (Castañeda/Hernández 1989, 436, 450).
65. Liebman concludes that this Mexican generation "not only lived as Jews in the fullest sense of the word, but they were accepted as Jews in other lands where Judaism was openly professed and practiced" (1970, 254).
66. Rodríguez de Matos was certain that what he practiced was the authentic, immutable Judaism observed throughout the ages. But, as M. Cohen has shown, his "was a pathetically atrophied form of Judaism. It was a shadowy caricature of the tradition of Judaism as it was being practiced in Constantinople, Salonica, Safed, Ferrara, and the great centers of Jewish life in Ashkenazi Europe in the sixteenth century" (1973, 94).

67. Liebman speaks of three groups of extended families within each of which the members knew each other very well. There was also some communication across groups and considerable antipathy between them. According to Liebman, the Treviño family clan tended to be religiously "traditional and punctilious" in their adherence to religious formalism. The Váez Sevilla clan tended to accommodate their Judaizing to their commercial interests. The Vaz Acevedo group was integrationist, or assimilationist, often intermarrying with old-Christians. In addition to these three groups there were a number of "unaffiliated" Judaizers (1970, 230, 302–3).

68. Treviño merits an entire chapter in Liebman 1970, 237–51.

69. Exogamous marriage was likely to be a strategy consciously employed by those Mexican *conversos* eager to assimilate into the Catholic mainstream (Alberro 1988, 203).

70. These trials are discussed in some detail in Liebman 1970, 217–66. Although during the first half of the seventeenth century trials of Judaizers in Mexico were the minority of the cases heard by the Inquisition, these seem to have received the severest sentences, and Israel's conclusion that crypto-Jews were the principal target of the Inquisition at that time is justified. Israel argues that "Judaism alone aroused violent feelings because, of Spain's traditional religious enemies, only the Jews had slipped, by means of disguise, into the mainstream of Spanish life, and only the Jews were evident to any significant extent in seventeenth-century Spanish America" (1970, 125). The report of the May 8, 1646 *auto de fe* in Mexico City that was sent to Spanish investigators by Pedro de Estrada y Escovedo hyperbolizes the Jewish threat to colonial Mexico: "Perfidious Judaism, in ancient times rebellious against the divine empire, never bound by its miraculous benefits, always self-motivated to express its haughty ingratitude, today the fertile mother of unheard-of sacrilege, in all regions cruel stepmother to perversely misguided people, where has it not reached with its irreligious daring? . . . This Holy Tribunal, unmistakably informed of the large throng of secret Jews, in its solemn deliberations and prudent regulations has begun to deal with an effective remedy to such exorbitant harm" (*La perfidia judaica, antiguamente rebelde al Imperio Divino, nunca obligada de milagrosos beneficios, siempre ocasionada de sí misma a indignas ingratitudes, hoy fecunda madre de sacrilegios inauditos, en todas partes madrastra cruel de la gente que protervamente engaña, ¿hasta dónde no ha llegado con la impiedad y con el atrevimiento? . . . Conocida pues, con infalibles noticias, por este Santo Tribunal, la numerosa muchedumbre de disimulados judíos, empezó a tratar, en sus graves juntas y en sus prudentes acuerdos, del eficaz remedio de tan exorbitantes daños*) (García 1910, 15, 21).

71. In 1619 an Inquisition official named Francisco de Trexo wrote to Spain complaining about the numbers of so-called Jews flocking into Argentina: "They are fleeing Brazil. This next year we are certain that many Jews fleeing from Spain and Brazil are going to come here. . . . With this information you can consult the Lord Viceroy; for certainly a remedy must be found for the ease with which Jews enter and leave this Port. It cannot be helped for they are all Portuguese who hide each other. I will keep watch with careful vigilance" (*An benido uyendo del brasil para el año Biene tenemos por cierto que a de benir mucha gente uyda judios despaña y del brasil. . . . V.s. sirbiendose la pueda consultar al Señor Virrey que cierto pide remedio la facilidad conque entran y salen judíos en este Puerto sin que se pueda remediar que como son todos portugueses se encubren unos a otros yo estoy con muy grande cuidado y vijilancia*) (Saban 1991, 158).

72. Novinsky 1972b, 61. Novinsky's studies suggest that about 36 percent of the Brazilian *cristãos novos* were merchants, 32 percent were in the professions, 20 percent were associated with agriculture, mainly sugar, and 12 percent were artisans or sailors (102). She also

points out that from 1624 to 1654 not one single new-Christian *engenho* owner was tried by the Inquisition (70).
73. The loss and recapture were celebrated by Lope de Vega in his 1625 play *El Brasil restituído*.
74. The extent of crypto-Jewish assistance has been vigorously debated. The arguments are reviewed in Novinsky. She concludes that the Jews were used by Portuguese politicians as scapegoats: that many old- and new-Christians backed the Dutch invaders, largely for economic rather than religious or political reasons, and that, similarly, many new-Christians remained loyal to Portugal and assisted in Bahia's defense (1972a, 154).
75. Wiznitzer 1960, 145–8, 165.
76. Brazilian and Dutch Sephardis flocked to Curaçao after 1650, and by the middle of the eighteenth century perhaps half of Curaçao's white inhabitants were Jews. See Huisman 1986, 67; Karner 1969; Liebman 1970, 179–85.
77. The Dutch and Italian crypto-Jews who went to Surinam in 1639 were joined by Brazilian refugees in 1664. Most ran sugar plantations. See Huisman 1986, 69; Liebman 1982, 185–8.
78. See Liebman 1982, 177–8; Holzberg 1987, 9–24.
79. See Liebman 1982, 174–7; Beller 1969, 96–104; Shilstone n.d., xvi-ix. In 1656 Jews on the Island were granted full protection of the British laws (Roth 1932a, 289).
80. This is the case of Agustín de Espinola, who was accused of this by the Mexican Inquisition around 1712 (Liebman 1970, 290, 295).
81. Wolf 1893–4, 57 argues that soon after the Expulsion a small group of crypto-Jews settled in England: "Crypto-Jews in Spain and Portugal had learnt to regard London as a place of refuge where they could observe the rites and ceremonies of Judaism without being molested, provided they did not invite public attention to their heresy."
82. For a good overview see Yerushalmi 1980.
83. Szajkowski describes dozens of early seventeenth-century instances in which recent Jewish immigrants to the French district of Gironde signed powers of attorney to their new-Christian relatives or agents remaining in Spain for the purpose of liquidating their properties or collecting their dowries or debts (1960, 71–3).
84. Bloom concludes that in the battles for the Low Countries in the 1590s many *conversos* "remained Marranos either for business reasons or because they feared that, in the event of Spanish victory over the United Provinces, their lot as Jews would be intolerable" (1937, 7). Faced with the realities of their environment, Turkish rabbis even went so far as to rule that it was permissible for the former Christians to continue to use their Christian names for purposes of trade (Roth 1932a, 202). For rabbinical opinion on this point and on other problems related to the reincorporation of the *conversos* into orthodox Judaism, see Levi 1982, 46 passim. For the implications for Dutch Jewish identity see Kaplan 1991.
85. One rabbi noted that "in order not to attract attention the Jews assumed names common in Holland. . . . In the synagogue, however, they were addressed by their Jewish appellations. In consequence of this, the Jews living here conduct themselves like Christian merchants in matters of business, wills and donations" (Bloom 1937, 14). Kaplan 1991 documents a number of these cases.
86. Venice was typical of most European Catholic countries in that it was rarely aggressive in its prosecution of Judaizing new-Christians (Pullan 1983, 201). Wherever international trade prospered in the Protestant trading cities of northern Europe, Sephardic business communities took root (Roth 1932a, 220). Many of these *converso* communities, and the

openly Jewish communities as well, traded actively with groups of crypto-Jews remaining in the Iberian Peninsula (Szajkowski 1960).

87. The most famous example is undoubtedly the playwright Antonio Enríquez Gómez, who after a successful career in Amsterdam returned to Spain under the alias Fernando de Zárate and was in due course arrested by the Inquisition.

88. See Roth 1947; 1948.

89. This was just as true for the Americas as for the Iberian Peninsula. Boats coming to Brazil, for example, always brought news of Portuguese or Spanish *conversos* who had been caught, tried, and released, punished, or executed (Novinsky 1972b, 110).

90. See, for example, Antonio Enríquez Gómez's poem in honor of Judá Creyente (Oelman 1982, 177–203).

91. Fonseca said that in Bayonne a Portuguese crypto-Jew called Don Nicolás López Villareal tried to persuade him to be a Jew. He was also proselytized by Doctor Duarte Enríquez and his new-Christian friends in Bordeaux, his cousins in Amsterdam (where he allowed himself to be circumcised), and the Sarabia brothers in Antwerp (Caro Baroja 1961, 332–6). For proselytization of crypto-Jews in southern France see Roth 1932b.

92. Levi 1982, 37–52; Yerushalmi 1980.

93. For example, in 1635 Isaac Farque went to Spain from Amsterdam at the behest of the *cristão novo* community of Madrid to perform circumcisions (Caro Baroja 1961, 1:421). Cf. Liebman (1970, 209). In the early 1640s the Mexican *converso* Gabriel de Granada said that he had been circumcised by a visiting rabbi (G. García 1910, 54).

94. Many such works are catalogued in Kayserling 1890.

# CHAPTER III

# The Major Points of Controversy

## THE PROBLEM OF QUANTIFICATION

From the distance of more than half a millennium, and with only incomplete and imprecise documentation at hand, it has proven impossible to quantify precisely the demography of the Sephardim at significant moments in their Iberian history. How many Jews lived in each of the Iberian kingdoms before the 1391 riots? How many converted then, or during the disputations, or during the later fifteenth-century riots? In 1492 how many chose conversion over exile? How many went to Portugal? How many returned to Spain? How many *conversos* were tried by the Inquisition? And most difficult to estimate of all: how many of the *conversos* were crypto-Jews and how many were assimilationists? Historians and polemicists have wrestled with these questions from the late fifteenth century until today, basing their calculations on a variety of available data: sketchy census reports, tax rolls, confiscations, Inquisition documents, and estimates by participants in the events. Many read the data or shaped their conclusions to fit their political agendas. It is beyond the scope of this book to try to resolve these polemics, but a review of the principal arguments and some tentative conclusions will give the reader some perspective on the matters being discussed.

- The total population of Spain and Portugal in 1491.

    Spain: 7,000,000–9,000,000.[1] Caro Baroja estimates 7 to 8 million (1961, 1:188); Kamen (1965, 15) and Netanyahu (1966, 245) put the number at around 9 million.

    Portugal: 1,000,000–1,500,000 (Marques 1972, 1:166).

- The Jewish population of the Spanish kingdoms in 1491.

    125,000–200,000. Estimates by historians of only twenty years ago have been revised downward in recent years. Suárez Fernández, looking at tax rolls at the end of the thirteenth century, estimated a Jewish population at that time of 372,000 (1961, 96),[2] a number consistent with Kamen's estimate of a Spanish pre-Expulsion middle class of some 500,000 souls, most of whom were Jewish (1965, 26). The most widely cited estimate for the 1492 population is that of Andrés Bernáldez, the chronicler of the Catholic Kings, who estimated the number of Jews living in Castile at the time of the Expulsion as some 335,000, to which must be added some 30,000 Aragonese Jews, for a total of 365,000.[3] Domínguez Ortiz considers 200,000–250,000 a much more reasonable estimate (1992, 13, 141). Gampel calculates that in the 1490s approximately 10 percent of Navarre's 100,000 inhabitants were Jews (1989, 20). Beginning with Baer, however, many historians have argued, I believe convincingly, that these numbers exaggerate the Jewish presence in pre-Expulsion Spain, which because of the events of the fourteenth and fifteenth centuries had dropped substantially since its high-water mark in the late thirteenth century. Bernáldez and other contemporaries reckoned by households, numbers that they and modern historians like Caro Baroja somewhat arbitrarily argued should be multiplied by five. Most recent demographers suggest 3.5 as a more accurate estimate of average family size. Suárez Fernández's most recent estimate, based on an analysis of tax records from 1482–8 and the fact that we now know with considerable confidence the exact size of certain *aljamas*,[4] concludes that 100,000 is the maximum credible estimate for the number of Jews in the Spanish kingdoms in 1491 (1991, 337–8).

    Portugal: 10,000–20,000. Based on tax rolls, Pimenta Ferro Tavares (1987, 23) establishes probable ranges for the pre-1492 Jewish population of the four largest cities: Lisbon (3,700–14,800), Evora (2,000–8,000), Oporto (835–3,340) and Coimbra (514–2,056), but the higher figures are improbable in light of the Spanish numbers.

- The number of *conversos* (i.e., converts and descendants of converts) pre-1492.

    Spain: 225,000. Netanyahu estimates the number of Jews converted subsequent to the 1391 riots as 200,000, and that there were some 600,000–700,000 *conversos* by 1480 (1966, 248). Domínguez Ortiz's estimate of some 225,000 seems much more reasonable (1992, 43).

    Portugal: very few.

- The number of Jews expelled from Spain in 1492.

    100,000–160,000. Among contemporary chroniclers and pre-modern historians, estimates of the numbers of Jews expelled in 1492 vary widely, from a low of 40,000 to a high of more than a million. Caro Baroja's (1961) and Baer's (1966) best estimate is 160,000. Suárez Fernández estimates 100,000 (1980, 98). Kamen estimates that some 25,000 of the expellees died en route (1965, 32).

- The number of Spanish Jews converted in 1492.

    25,000–50,000. Caro Baroja estimates the number of the newly converted in 1492 who remained behind at 240,000, strikingly higher than Kamen's estimate of 50,000 (1965, 32), or Domínguez Ortiz's estimate of 20,000–30,000 (1992, 43). For Caro Baroja, most Spanish Jews chose to convert and remain. Suárez Fernández (1980, 270) argues to the contrary, based on his perception that we have so little hard evidence of specific conversions in 1492.

- The number of expelled Jews who went to Portugal.

    50,000. Kamen (1965, 215) and Saraiva (1969, 33), following Zacuto's contemporary estimates, put the number at 120,000. The Portuguese historian Marques sets the number at closer to 50,000 (1989, 1:211).

- The number of expelled Jews who returned to Spain and converted in the decade following 1492.

    5,000–8,000. Netanyahu puts the number who returned to the two kingdoms at some 6,000–7,000 (1966, 248). This number may be high. Suárez Fernández has discovered the names of some 177 returnees, many of whom indicated that they came back with groups of Jews. Motis Dolader, who has studied the Aragonese Expulsion, does not give a number but argues that, although most Aragonese Jews left the kingdom in 1492, a large percentage of them returned over the next five years, pushed by the harsh conditions of exile and drawn by the opportunity to recover their property (1987, 252).

- The number of crypto-Jews in the Iberian colonies.

    40,000. Lewin estimates that there were some 30,000 crypto-Jews in the Spanish American colonies, and 10,000 in Brazil (1987, 185). Presumably the number of assimilationist new-Christians was much higher.

- The number of Judaizers tried by the Inquisition.

    Spain: 25,000–50,000. Although there are sporadic good data for local tribunals, overall the available data do not permit even a good guess as to the total number of Judaizers tried, or convicted, or executed by the Inquisition over its 350-year history.[5] Caro Baroja estimates the number tried during the first fifty years of the Inquisition to be 50,000; Domínguez Ortiz estimates half that number (1992, 43). Kamen's numbers, based upon the few precise figures that exist for local tribunals in Spain, are substantially lower (1965, 281). There were periods and places in which the Inquisition mainly pursued crypto-Jews and periods and places Judaizers were on the margins of the Inquisition's efforts. They were clearly the main focus in Spain during the first forty years of the Inquisition. A good example of local temporal variation is Valencia. During the first forty years of Inquisition operation 91.6 percent of the cases were for Judaizing.[6] This number represents 2,160 Judaizers tried, of whom 909 were condemned to death. From 1540 to 1820 only 100 Judaizers were tried, 55 of them between 1701 and 1730; of the 100 only seven were executed. Clearly

Valencia, unlike much of the rest of Spain, was relatively unaffected by the Portuguese influx at the beginning of the seventeenth century (Haliczer 1990, 223).[7] The best attempt at establishing a global overview is that of Henningsen, who tabulated all the hard data he could find, by tribunal. His numbers show that, in ten Aragonese tribunals from 1539 to 1791, 25,773 cases were registered, of which 940 (3.6%) were people accused of Judaizing. In eleven Castilian tribunals from 1547 to 1695 16,441 cases were registered, of which 3,495 (21.3%) were people accused of Judaizing. The last concerted wave of trials of Judaizers occurred in the early 1700s; in the 64 *autos de fe* held on the Peninsula from 1721 to 1727, some 820 Judaizers appeared (Haliczer 1990, 233). Over the full range of Inquisition cases that Henningsen tabulated, which include those of the American tribunals, some 10.5 percent were of people accused of Judaizing. Of the accusations of Judaizing, 3.48 percent resulted in sentences of death (1.83% in person, 1.65% in effigy) (1977, 564).[8]

Portugal: 30,000. Aaron Lichtenstein estimates that overall as many as 30,000 Judaizers were sentenced at *autos da fe* in Portugal, of whom some 1,200 were executed (*Enc. Jud.* 13:924). Based on census data, Marques concludes that in 1542 there were more than 60,000 *Cristãos novos* in Portugal, with some 30,000 remaining in 1604 (1989, 1:287).

Colonies: 4,000. Lewin estimates that some 3,000 Judaizers were tried in the Spanish American colonies and 1,000 in Brazil (1987, 185).

There is little agreement as to whether the number of Judaizers tried by the Inquisition represents a large or small percentage of the number of new-Christians who actually Judaized. Among those who believe the trials are a small fraction of the total are Cohen (1972, 280) and Liebman (1970, 288–9). On the other hand, my reading of the records of many local Spanish tribunals suggests that by the end of the sixteenth century the Inquisition had likely identified almost all the Spanish crypto-Jews, who at that time tended to cluster in networks of extended families, and that during the seventeenth century a large proportion of the Portuguese crypto-Jews were identified. This issue is related to the question of the representativeness of the documents, treated below.

- The number of *conversos* who were crypto-Jews and the number who assimilated.

    The incompleteness of the data, coupled with the fact that successful assimilators disappeared from view, means that precision is impossible; in fact even relative percentages are unachievable. Nevertheless, all the available data suggest that assimilationist new-Christians substantially outnumbered those who continued to identify as Jews.[9]

THE RELIABILITY OF THE DOCUMENTS

Three issues are generally raised regarding the evidence from which a portrait of the lives and beliefs of the new-Christians can be drawn. Since one of the main sources for such a portrait is Inquisition documents, the first question is the accuracy or credibility of such documents. The second, related to the first, is the representativeness of such documents. The third is the nature and reliability of other evidence to supplement or temper the Inquisition material.

Given the prominence of Inquisition documents in almost all the historiography of the new-Christians, the first issue is vital. Simply stated, the question about Inquisition documents—Edicts of Grace, indictments, depositions, transcripts of testimony, summations of findings, reports of *autos de fe*, and correspondence—is whether they tell the truth or whether they exaggerate, misrepresent, or falsify outright their reports of the new-Christian experience. My answer is qualified confidence in the documents: most of what they report is mostly accurate, and while occasional individual records may be suspect, in the aggregate the portrait of crypto-Jewish life that they reveal is reasonably truthful. There are several reasons why this is so.

Inquisition scribes were well-trained and adept at speed writing. There is no reason to doubt that the verbatim records are generally accurate transcripts of what was actually said. The documents record information introduced by three sorts of people—Inquisitors, informers, and the accused—all of whom had both reasons to lie and reasons to tell the truth. Inquisition officials were invariably churchmen whose professional sense of fairness and accuracy has to be considered within the context of their commitment to eradicate heresy. They tended to report the truth as they saw it, but the lenses through which they perceived their truth induced an astigmatism of bias.[10] For most Inquisitors, Judaizing was Devil-induced heresy, pernicious and dangerous. They were predisposed to react to it emotionally and with severity. They interpreted what they saw and heard against a template of preconceptions about crypto-Judaism which they acquired both from their formal education and from popular mythology, and which were handily codified in the Edicts of Grace and their own manuals of interrogation. They were much less likely to write down objective observations than they were to record statements that corroborated their preconceptions. Although there are many instances of people freed for insufficient evidence, on the whole the Inquisitors were inclined to see in the testimony more guilt rather than less. For the more serious the menace of Judaizing was, the more their own profession was justified. And the more convictions the Inquisition obtained, the greater were its confiscations of property.

With all this taken into account and allownce made for the occasional instance of out-and-out lying, the facts stated by Inquisitors (on April 15, 1585, "María Pérez baked and distributed *matza*") still appear to be reliable. On the other hand, their statements of conclusions ("María Pérez was a dogmatizer and fomenter of heresy") or their summations of testimony generally contain some kernels of truth but need to be deconstructed by the critical reader.

Inquisition protocols recognized the fact that informers might be tempted to fabricate accusations for reasons of personal animus. The Inquisition took two measures to guard against this: they allowed the accused to draw up a list of personal enemies whose testimony against them should be discounted, and they severely punished perjurers. It is also true that some testimony was coerced.[11] And the tribunals admitted a good deal of hearsay evidence that frequently recounted unsubstantiated rumors or repeated hoary stereotypical libels against the Jews and *conversos*. Some of the hearsay testimony must be interpreted as evidence of common myths, rather than as evidence of particular practices. But a large portion of informer testimony has the ring of truth about it. Many informers reported events they claimed to have seen with their own eyes. Often the event had other witnesses, whom the informers listed by name and whose subsequent testimony confirmed the circumstances. The probability of being caught at perjury in such cases was very high and not to be risked lightly. Thus on the whole I am inclined to believe the actions reported in eyewitness testimony.[12]

In some ways the most problematic of all Inquisition materials are the words of the accused themselves. They, too, risked perjury, but the risks they and their families might incur by their telling the truth could be infinitely greater. Three very human tendencies muddy confessional data. The first is the instinct for self-protection. Sometimes witnesses confessed trivialities and omitted damaging events. They neglected to mention an uncle who was burned thirty years ago or "forgot" who was present at some family ceremony. They frequently lied about their own activities, even in the face of sometimes overwhelming evidence to the contrary. Sometimes they invented stories to throw the Inquisitors off the track or to convince them that they were insane and therefore could not be responsible for their actions. Similarly, even when their hopes of personal acquittal had been dashed, some people lied to protect loved ones or to try to preserve the family possessions from confiscation. Second, people reacted unpredictably to the threat or fact of physical coercion. Some told one story in the audience chamber and quite another in the torture chamber. Under duress, people were likely to tell the Inquisitors what they wanted to hear to make them stop inflicting pain. Sometimes people would confess to lesser crimes that they had not committed in the hope of avoiding torture or in the hope that interrogation would cease before some more serious transgressions were revealed.[13] Third, some of the accused courted martyrdom, confessing to Jewish beliefs and practices in great detail in the belief that their virtue would thereby increase. For all these reasons the records must be read with caution.

Yet, as with the informers, most testimony of those accused of Judaizing smacks of the truth. The accused, too, narrated events in which they had personally played a part. They gave the names of witnesses who could, and did, corroborate their stories. They often described events in great detail, repeating those details in testimony given sometimes years later and even sometimes under torture. It is true that their stories were often guided by the Inquisitors' leading questions, but it is also true that frequently their stories took off in idiosyncratic directions, revealing unusual, non-standard events, practices, or details.

There is some concern about whether the many thousands of preserved cases that deal with new-Christians are truly representative of the scope of new-Christian lifestyles. Clearly a bias is introduced by the fact that the more blatant Judaizers were more likely to have been caught, while the more successfully assimilated were, tautologically, less likely to have come to the notice of the Holy Office. Over the first two hundred years of its history the Inquisition pursued Judaizers with intermittent zeal. By the seventeenth century the most egregious Judaizers, for reasons having to do with endogamy and with the need for group safety, tended to try to preserve their secret existence by functioning as tightly-knit extended family clans. Large groups were almost impossible to keep hidden for long periods of time because when the Inquisition identified one member the trail quickly led to the others. Detailed studies of particular towns, such as Beinart's work on Trujillo and Guadalupe, suggest that the Inquisition had called to account the bulk of the region's Judaizing community. Historians can therefore be fairly confident that by the late seventeenth century a large percentage of the more orthodox crypto-Judaizers in Spain, Portugal, and their possessions are documented in the Inquisition records.[14] On the other hand, there is no reliable way to estimate the number of the more assimilated new-Christians, the casual Judaizers whose heterodoxy might be expressed by an avoidance of pork or an occasional skeptical remark about some aspect of Catholic dogma or disrespect for some Christian icon. These people appear with great frequency in the Inquisition records. Sometimes they are marginal players in trials of more zealous crypto-Judaizers. Frequently they are wealthy new-Christians whose minor lapses subjected their estates to the risk of confiscation. During the periods when the more rigorous crypto-Judaism was all but extirpated, these marginal crypto-Jews form the bulk of the record. The conclusion is that, although Inquisition records are not exhaustive, nor even extant for all the Tribunals in all phases of their history, in the aggregate they present detailed information for a very wide swath of the Iberian and American new-Christian communities, and in that sense can be considered representative.[15]

Another crucial point to be borne in mind is that each new-Christian community was in many respects idiosyncratic. As Roth reminds us, one cannot expect unity of practice across the new-Christian world, for over time and across space religious traditions will vary in consistency and intensity (1931–2, 2). Toledo, Ciudad Real, Segovia, Seville, Jaen, Valencia, and the like were cities with strong crypto-Jewish communities in the sixteenth century. For a host of reasons having to do with patterns of settlement, persecution, and conversion, Barcelona and Madrid were not. In the seventeenth century Portuguese Judaizers flocked to Madrid but not to Valencia. In the New World, a century after the conquest Judaizers tended to congregate in Mexico City and a few of the other major cities, while their presence in the Yucatan, northwest Mexico, or Central America was minimal. Novinsky (1972b) has shown that in the seventeenth century the new-Christian communities of Brazil's northeast were substantially different from the communities of the south. While one can hazard some generalizations about the nature of crypto-Judaism in the aggregate, one must be very cautious about applying them to any specific community at any specific time.

It is tempting to give special importance among Inquisition documents to the Edicts of Grace, which apparently list the religious customs of the Judaizers with great thoroughness. Yet they must be used with some caution as guides to contemporary Judaizing practices. By 1500 they were in common use in assisting informers to determine whether their neighbors were crypto-Jews. They were reissued for centuries without substantial change (Lea 1906, 2:92), and rarely kept up with the evolutionary trends of crypto-Judaism. Their standard form was an admonition for anyone knowledgeable of heresy to come forward and confess, to which was appended a long, detailed, fairly comprehensive guide to Jewish practices as well as a sample of typically Jewish statements of belief. These compilations represented an abstract total set of Jewish practices, and not a description drawn from observation of the customs of any particular community of Judaizers. Moreover, as Roth and others remind us, the Inquisition's views about Judaism were founded "largely upon Biblical teachings and historic reminiscence" and not on the post-Talmudic rabbinical traditions (1931–2, 2). Nevertheless the Edicts of Grace are largely accurate (although not comprehensive) in their depiction of normative Judaism, even though the religious repertoire of most Iberian crypto-Jews was much less broad and tended to include some practices not routinely listed in the Edicts. Ironically, the Edicts became more accurate over time as Judaizing *conversos* who had lost first-hand knowledge of normative Judaism came to rely on the Edicts of Grace themselves as their most accessible guide to Jewish practice.

Fortunately, in addition to an enormous corpus of Inquisition documents of qualified reliability and representativeness, historians have a large number of other sources available to them. These include autobiographies, Jewish *responsa* literature, contemporary chronicles in Spanish, Portuguese, Latin, and Hebrew, and information about contemporary Jewish customs from the crypto-Jewish Diaspora in Italy, Holland, North Africa, and Turkey. None of these is without its idiosyncratic biases, but again, in the aggregate, they are reasonably consistent with the data about crypto-Judaism found in Inquisition records and help in the reconstruction of a full and reliable picture of crypto-Jewish religious and social customs.

## DID MARRANISM REALLY EXIST?

There can be no doubt that something clearly identified as crypto-Judaism, or Marranism, flourished in Iberia for at least the two and a half centuries following the Expulsion and mass conversions. The weight of the evidence offered by the vast quantities of Inquisition documents and the host of corroborative material from sources both Jewish and Christian, Iberian and non-Iberian, leads to an unassailable conclusion: crypto-Judaism and a strong Jewish identity were very real phenomena among many new-Christians.[16] In Spain the crypto-Jewish identity was formed during the hundred years when new converts and practicing Jews continued to live side by side. In Portugal it was the result of the sudden, global conversion of the Jews in 1497 and the forty-year delay before the establishment of the Portuguese Inquisition, a delay that allowed crypto-Jewish modalities to take root in an environment relatively free of interference.[17] The phenomenon lasted from at least the middle of the fifteenth century through the beginning of the eighteenth, and in a few instances even longer.

Although the nature of Iberian crypto-Judaism varied considerably from time to time and from place to place, several common threads run through it from start to finish. Crypto-Jewish practices derived from those of normative Judaism. Along the way they reduced in number, grew less complex in their details, and added a veneer of Christian practice and belief. Moreover, throughout its long history crypto-Judaism was beleaguered, forced into secrecy by repressive religious, political, and social campaigns waged against it. As a result crypto-Jews developed complex strategies of furtiveness that in significant ways shaped their social and religious practices. New-Christians, whether Judaizers or assimilationists, lived in constant fear of discovery. They incessantly monitored their own behaviors lest a tiny slip bring ruin down on themselves, their families, and their possessions. They tended to live two lives, one private and one public, and their collective schizophrenia became one of their identifying characteristics.[18]

Nevertheless some historians have continued to question the dimensions and even the very existence of the crypto-Jewish phenomenon. For radical historians crypto-Judaism was invented by the Inquisition, except for a handful of orthodox Jews whose practices carried over into their conversion.[19] Although it has been amply demonstrated that throughout the Iberian dominions the Inquisition played an important role in the transmission and codification of crypto-Judaism, it does not therefore follow that the Inquisition created Marranism.[20] As is often the case, the truth lies somewhere in the middle, in ground occupied by historians like Révah and more recently Pullan, for whom

> Crypto-Judaism did exist, but did not survive just as a consequence of the unfailing loyalty of Jews to Judaism. The Inquisition had a part in the survival of secret Judaism, but it was not merely a crude and cynical forger of evidence. By the very questions it asked, by its Edicts of Grace, and by making the public aware of the possibility of secret Judaism, it helped to keep its memory alive. . . . It may also be that a sense of Jewishness, if not a knowledge of Judaism, was kept alive not only by the Inquisition but also by other social devices, and particularly by the statutes disqualifying persons tainted with Jewish blood from municipal office [and other positions]. . . . Such measures drove the

conversos to become, in a fairly high degree, an endogamous group holding itself apart from the Old Christians, and forming its own associations and clubs. (1983, 204–5)

## THE TAXONOMY OF NEW-CHRISTIANS: JUDAIZERS VERSUS ASSIMILATORS

The most deep-seated controversy among historians is around the degree to which *conversos* tended toward crypto-Judaism or toward assimilationism. Another way of putting the question is to ask just how Jewish the *conversos* were. Over the past five centuries most answers to this question have tended to reflect the political agendas of their authors. A second controversy, related to the first but much more universal in scope, arises from the historical difficulty in agreeing on the criteria for deciding just exactly what being a Jew means. This conundrum cannot be ignored, because it shapes the terms of the Judaizing-versus-assimilating controversy.

The first definitional approach is biological and racial: a Jew is someone who has a Jewish mother.[21] This approach suggests that some important racial traits are passed genetically and also recognizes the socio-cultural principle of the power of family education in transmitting religious education. Physical stereotyping is based on this approach. And the Spanish purity-of-blood laws, while largely political and economic in nature, were grounded in this definition, as was much of the rhetoric of Iberian religious intolerance.[22]

The second approach has to do with belief: a Jew (or Judaizer) is a person who believes what a Jew believes. Leaving aside the very thorny question of what constitutes the complete corpus of Jewish belief (which, unlike Catholic dogma, does not have a living, divinely inspired, supreme papal authority to certify it as true), it is the case that during the period in question certain beliefs were widely held to be the essence of the difference between Judaism and Catholicism. These were the belief in a unitary God (contrasted with the belief in the Christian tripartite God), belief that the Messiah had not yet come but was coming, and belief that the Law of Moses had not been abrogated in any way by the Christian Law. Profession of any of these beliefs was sufficient to brand a person as a Judaizer. Even the utterance of a proverb that was thought merely to reflect one of these beliefs was enough to invite suspicion.

The third approach has to do with practice: a Jew (or Judaizer) is a person who practices what a Jew practices. Traditional Judaism, which emphasizes the expression of belief through religious practice, has evolved an extremely complex set of behaviors that governs almost every human activity from dawn to dawn and from birth to grave. Easily codifiable, as in the Edicts of Grace, and easily observable, as seen in the evidence given later in this book, these practices tended to define Judaizing for both Inquisitors and adherents. The problem is often one of degree: how much observance constitutes Judaizing?

The fourth approach is one of self-concept: Judaizers are people who think of themselves as Jews. Time and again Inquisition testimony includes statements in which self-concept took precedence over practice, statements such as "I lit the Sabbath candles only in my heart,"[23] or "it is enough to fulfill the precepts with your thoughts in your heart."[24] Particularly in the later stages of crypto-Judaism, when most practices were forgotten or when circumstances made any overt observance problematical, some portion of Iberia's new-Christians continued to think of themselves as Jews.[25] Révah considers this an expression of "potential" rather than "real" Judaism, but recognizes it nonetheless as a sincere expression of affiliation (1969, 54).

The fifth approach to the question focuses on the external anti-Semitic environment: Judaizers are people whom other people think of as Jews. This definition occasioned the tragedy of the seventeenth-century *conversos* who were barred from their chosen professions by the purity-of-blood laws even though they were incontrovertibly Christian by definitions two, three, and four. This approach, too, was the root cause of many otherwise well-assimilated *conversos* choosing to become crypto-Jews when their external milieu forced them to assume caste consciousness and when the Edicts of Grace provided a blueprint for Judaizing.[26] *In extremis*, when the Inquisitors extend their torches or the Nazis tip the canisters of Zyklon B gas, this external definition is the one that counts.[27]

On the definitional question, from the very first moments of the *converso* phenomenon, polarized positions were advanced, sometimes simultaneously.[28] Legally the new-Christians were Christians. Baptism admitted them to the saving power of Christ and made them subject to the Church's jurisdiction in matters of faith. Traditional theological arguments voided the distinction between old- and new-Christians, asserting that the date of one's conversion was irrelevant.[29] But the political and social realities of the fifteenth century argued to the contrary. One was compelled to recognize the fact that, while some converts had embraced Christianity enthusiastically out of sincere religious conviction, others had been coerced, whether physically in the urban riots or psychologically as a result of the disputations and the propaganda barrages.[30] The first group were likely to be hyper-Catholic; the second were likely to retain an affinity for their former Jewishness, an affinity that could manifest itself in a variety of ways. One also had to recognize the nearly universal fact that people tend to impart their religious convictions to their children, so that the distinction between forced and willing converts was likely to be mirrored in the second and even subsequent generations. There was also the complex socio-economic reality to be considered: both the small old-Christian middle class and the peasantry, as well some segments of the nobility, resented the fact that for reasons of education and tradition the *conversos* were attaining dominant positions in the emerging capitalistic urban centers. They saw that this was true both of the "good" *conversos* who were truly Christian and the "bad" *conversos* who continued to behave in many ways as Jews.

As we have seen, positions hardened toward the end of the fifteenth century. To isolate *conversos* from the conservative influences of practicing Jews was a major policy thrust of the 1480s, which culminated, quite explicitly, in the language of the 1492 Edict of Expulsion. Increasingly churchmen lumped all new-Christians with the Judaizers and considered even the most tenuous remnants of Jewish practice proof of Jewish identity.[31] This rationale dominated the Inquisitorial frame of mind, which found justification for its operations in proving the equation *converso* = crypto-Jew. The contemporary orthodox Jewish community, on the other hand, whether in Spain or abroad, tended to consider any deviation from strict observance to be proof of apostasy. As Netanyahu has unwaveringly asserted, for the rabbis the majority of *conversos* were fully gentile.[32] Some modern historians have also taken extreme positions on both sides of this question.[33]

One major early exception to the polarizers was the chronicler Hernando de Pulgar, who in his c. 1490 *Chronicle of the Catholic Monarchs* astutely placed the *conversos* in a shifting, ambivalent world of divided loyalties and skittish beliefs:

> Though they kept the Sabbath and some of the Jewish fasts, they did not keep every Sabbath, nor fast on all the fast days. If they performed one ceremony, they omitted another, so that they were untrue to both laws. And in some cases the husband was found to observe some Jewish ceremonies and the wife to be a good Christian; some of their children might be good Christians, while another might hold Jewish beliefs. And within a single household there could be diverse beliefs, each one hidden from the other.[34]

This view is much closer to that held by most modern historians: the *conversos* were, like most groups of human beings, both diverse and inconsistent. For that matter, a single individual might vary his or her practice over time, might begin believing one thing and end up believing quite another, or might even hold contradictory beliefs simultaneously. It is therefore not very useful to try to devise a single descriptor for the wide range of *converso* beliefs and customs. Yet neither is it profitable to talk only about individuals or about small communities at one particular point in time.

More useful is to try to visualize the *conversos* along the spectrum that runs from wholly Christian to wholly Jewish, recognizing that even the two polar designations admit a wide variety of beliefs and practices and that the points at which any spectrum is segmented into distinctly perceived colors are, in some sense, arbitrary. While there is a good deal of variance according to time and place,[35] *conversos* can generally be thought of in four broad groups according to their self-concept. Some thought of themselves as (1) Christians; some as (2) Jews; some as (3) seekers of truth caught between the two religions; and some as (4) skeptical dropouts, for whom religion was as unimportant as the times allowed it to be.[36] Within each of these broad categories of self-identity there were a variety of subgroups distinguishable by how these four basic philosophical orientations were put into practice. Within a category a particular individual might belong to more than one subgroup.

TYPE 1

*Type 1a: Conversionist zealots.* Many of the late fourteenth- and fifteenth-century converts who were intellectually convinced that Christianity had supplanted Judaism and were swept up in the fervor of their choice devoted their lives to missionary activities among their former coreligionists. Some of these people, like Pablo de Santa María, Pedro de la Caballería, and Jerónimo de Santa Fe, were the authors of most of the learned, virulent, anti-Semitic tracts of the conversionist century. Some of them, like the Dominicans Tomás de Torquemada and Diego de Deza, the first two Inquisitors General, became the early senior staff of the Inquisition. Some denounced their Judaizing friends or family members to the Holy Office.[37]

*Type 1b: Christian reformers.* Some new-Christians, persuaded to convert by an idealized vision of Catholicism, were acutely disappointed by what they found to be discriminatory practices of the Church, particularly the Inquisition and the purity-of-blood laws. From the 1480s to the 1520s some of the loudest voices raised against these two institutions came from first- and second-generation *conversos* like the chronicler Hernando de Pulgar, the archbishop Hernando de Talavera, and Erasmian scholars like the historian Juan de Vergara and the Valdés brothers.[38]

The distinguishing characteristic of this group of *conversos* is their compulsion to express their dissatisfaction with the status quo. Sometimes what they expressed was militant idealism. They brought to their chosen crusades a vision of a more perfect Catholicism, a more equitable Church, or an improved society. Very often these were second- or third-generation *conversos*, who had no personal recollections of Judaism or in some cases even of the Jewish roots of their families, but who were nurtured in an environment of intellectual curiosity and emotional commitment to idealistic goals. Some of Spain's great church reformers, like Saint Teresa de Avila, Beatus Juan de Avila, and Fray Diego de Estella, are in this tradition.[39] So too are many of the Spanish late-medieval and Golden Age writers in whose works run strong thematic currents of tolerance, equity, and profound unease with current governmental, religious and societal practices. In this group of *conversos* one might consider the playwrights Gil Vicente, Juan del Encina, Lucas Fernández, Bartolomé de Torres Naharro, Diego Sánchez de Badajoz, and Miguel de Carvajal; humanistic essayists like Fray Luis de León and Benito Arias Montano; poetic ironists from Antón Montoro, Juan de Valladolid, Rodrigo Cota, Juan Alvarez Gato,[40] and many other late fifteenth-century "songbook" (*cancionero*) poets to the baroque giant Luis de Góngora; chroniclers like Hernando de Pulgar; and so forth.

Others in this group vented their frustrations in the creation of fictional universes (Castro 1965, 185). Some wrote "escapist" literature. Diego de San Pedro and Jorge de Montemayor wrote sentimental or pastoral novels, creating worlds where love reigns supreme. Others like García Rodríguez de Montalvo composed chivalric novels, where single, extraordinary individuals had the power to put things right with the world. Some were satirists, creating worlds that exemplified both the positive and negative aspects of human relationships and institutions. Often their works were steeped in irony. Among these conflicted souls were prose fiction writers like Diego de San Pedro, Fernando de Rojas, Francisco Delicado, Mateo Alemán, probably the anonymous author of *Lazarillo de Tormes*, and possibly even Cervantes.[41] Although these authors span more than a hundred years and their works are widely different in both style and intent, their common threads are a concern for equity and toleration and a conception of a universe held together not by the tinkerings of an interceding God but rather by the complex and contradictory web of imperfect human interrelationships.

*Type 1c: Heterodox Catholics.* Very close in spirit to the Christian reformers were the *conversos* who might best be termed heterodox Catholics. In the sixteenth century the intellectuals among them were attracted by the diverse religious movements that characterized the early days of the Reformation. Many found inspiration in the writings of Erasmus. Some were Illuminists or early Protestants (Juan and Alfonso Valdés).[42] Many (like the reformer Saint Teresa de Avila and Fray Luis de León), seeking an idealized personal relationship with God, explored the paths of mysticism.

*Type 1d: Christian professionals.* Even among those Christian *conversos* not given to zeal, a considerable number became professional clergy. Many entered the priesthood or joined monastic orders for the same mix of religious, economic, and personal reasons that motivated their old-Christian colleagues. Many used a clerical career as an entry into a variety of intellectual pursuits. Some entered church politics; in the fifteenth century alone more than a half dozen rose to the rank of bishop (Roth 1992, 377). But an additional reason moved some *conversos* to become clerics: these people saw the Church as an ideal haven, with a clerical career as an overt symbol of their commitment to Christianity and their definitive rejection of their family's Jewish past.[43] During the conflictive third quarter of the fifteenth century some of these *converso* clerics, like the Dominican Lope de Barrientos, argued that persecution of *conversos* was a serious disincentive to further conversions (Roth 1992, 374).

*Type 1e: Low-profile Christians.* The preferred goal of the vast majority of Christianizing *conversos*, however, was anonymous assimilation. In a way these people are the hardest for the historian to perceive because those who succeeded in this strategy disappeared. But representatives of the myriad who fell just short of success appear frequently in the trials, or in the seventeenth century in the depositions for purity-of-blood certificates, where we see them vigorously attempting to establish a sustained family tradition of Catholic orthodoxy and minimizing the importance of their remote Jewish ancestors.

TYPE 2

While the first type of *conversos* were characterized by their primary identification with Christianity, the second type conceived of themselves primarily as Jews, differing only in the breadth and exclusiveness of their observance of Jewish customs and in the extent to which they defined pro-Jewish as anti-Christian.

*Type 2a: Observant Judaizers.* This is the group about whom we know the most, for it was the group most energetically pursued by the Inquisition and, in turn, the most visible and likely to be caught. We have already looked at the evolution of their beliefs and practices from the days of their coexistence with the Jewish community in the fifteenth century up through their almost complete eradication, or assimilation into Christianity, by the start of the eighteenth.[44] Overall, these *conversos* were characterized by their observance of as many Jewish customs as they knew and as their circumstances would allow. They celebrated the major events in their family's life cycle in the Jewish fashion, they observed a number of holidays as fully as they were able, they strove to remember or reconstruct Jewish prayers, they cherished and repeated the scraps of Hebrew passed on to them in their oral tradition, they labored to keep a kosher home, and they reassured themselves with declarations that Judaism was superior to Catholicism in every way. Although by very soon after the Expulsion their vision of Judaism was heavily influenced by their Catholic milieu, and in fact in many ways became a syncretic blend of Jewish and Catholic elements, they continued to regard their particular brand of Judaizing as very much akin to the normative Judaism practiced outside the Iberian Peninsula. Members of this group were those Judaizers most likely to accept, or even court, martyrdom, perceiving virtue in death at the hands of the Inquisition.[45]

*Type 2b: Accommodationist Judaizers.* These *conversos* were similar to the last group except in the depth and rigor of their overt expressions of their Jewish identity. They tended to practice only those aspects of Judaism they found convenient or safe. They yielded to economic pressures and the threat of discovery and kept their businesses open on the Sabbath. They observed a few holidays sporadically and paid little attention to the Jewish ceremonial aspects of life-cycle events. Occasionally, particularly in the years just prior to the Expulsion, groups of Judaizing *conversos* joined a particular religious house (such as the Jeronymite monasteries of Guadalupe[46] near Cáceres or La Sisla[47] in Segovia) so that they could maintain some measure of crypto-Jewish community life in the shelter of the monastery walls. Accommodationist Judaizers tended toward the negative in their Jewish observances: they sometimes fasted, but rarely hosted the holiday feasts; they refrained from eating pork when they could, but did not de-vein their meat or soak it to remove the blood. They still thought of themselves primarily as Jews, but when pressed frequently said that they kept most of Judaism's tenets only in their hearts. In Gebhardt's words they were Catholics without faith and Jews without knowledge, though Jews by desire (cited in Pullan 1983, 205). Their children were likely to assimilate wholly into Catholicism. Overall, among crypto-Jews this type was probably the most numerous.

*Type 2c: Anti-Catholic Judaizers.* These *conversos* tended to express their Jewish identity in negative attitudes toward Catholicism and its trappings. To an extent this group overlaps with the preceding two. Many first-generation *conversos*, whose childhood education as Jews had sharpened the differences between the two religions, found it almost impossible to accept the sacraments in good faith. The supernatural aspects of Catholic ritual were incomprehensible to them. The transubstantiation of the eucharist seemed implausible, and if it was true then consuming the eucharist would seem like cannibalism. The emphasis on concrete representations of the deity in painted or carved images seemed to them like idolatry. Inquisition testimony suggests that they often gave vent to these feelings in expressions of skepticism or outright scorn. For later generations of Judaizing *conversos*, who perforce received a Catholic education as children and who possessed a much shallower understanding of normative Judaism, the expression of negative feelings about Catholicism became a central part of their self-concept as Judaizers. They accepted the iconographic holiness of Catholic cult items and occasionally made the mistreatment of these items—wiping off the chrism, beating a crucifix, trampling a consecrated host—an integral part of their Judaizing.[48]

TYPE 3

The first two groups of *conversos* tended to be relatively sure of their religious identity. Members of the third type tended to have a much more ambiguous self-concept.

*Type 3a: Vacillators.* For some *conversos* the road to assimilation as Catholics was filled with switchbacks. This category does not refer to the willing converts of the late fourteenth and fifteenth centuries, who often came to their new religion in stages marked by a wavering between the two faiths, but rather to those who were born new-Christian and raised in an ambiance that included both Catholic and Jewish practices. Within this category there were several groups whose identifying characteristic was their vacillation, or alternation, between the two religions. As Chapter 8 of this book makes clear, most of these people were raised initially as Catholics, for it was dangerous to entrust the family's secret of Judaizing to children who had not yet reached the age of discretion. When the children were finally initiated into Judaizing, which generally occurred during their early adolescence, they might well be reluctant to change their primary self-concept from Catholic to Jew and for a time might waver, or alternate, between the two. Sometimes when one parent was an old-Catholic and one a Judaizing *converso* a child might be caught between competing religious identities, which compounded the complex choices of adolescence. Some members of this group were religious chameleons who in their travels or even at home were Jews to the Jews and Christians to the Christians.[49]

*Type 3b: Syncretists.* I am not referring here to the largely unconscious syncretism that pervaded crypto-Jewish beliefs, such as the Christian-like belief in personal salvation through belief in the Law of Moses, or the occasional syncretic practice, like refraining from eating pork for forty days before Passover. Rather, this relatively small group of *conversos* tended to believe that it was possible to practice both religions simultaneously. These were people like the Valencian *converso* Pedro Besant, who confessed in 1486 that every morning he prayed the Our Father and recited the articles of faith and then washed his hands and recited his Jewish prayers (Haliczer 1990, 214). Or like the Portuguese *cristão novo* Manuel Rodrigues, accused in 1573 of saying that "when he was in church the Christian things seemed right to him, and when he went outside he returned to blindness."[50] Or like the Ecijan lawyer Periáñez de Mesa, who said in 1591 that "some relatives of his had taught him the Law of Moses and that he had observed it together with that of Jesus Christ our Lord."[51] The line between the vacillators and the syncretists is in many instances arbitrary, for some new-Christians practiced both or either or neither of the two religions as circumstances dictated. Chaim Saruc, consul of the Levantine nation in Venice, said of Gaspar Ribeiro in 1580: "A Marrano . . . is one who steers by two rudders: that is, he is neither Christian nor Jew" (Pullan 1983, 209). In addition many of the so-called remnant Marranos of the twentieth century fit among the syncretists. They tend to be almost wholly Catholic in beliefs and practices, yet they continue to identify simultaneously as Jews or Marranos or descendants of Jews and sometimes retain some few vestigial Judaic practices which they do not see as conflicting in any way with the essence of their Catholicism.

### Type 4

The first three types of *conversos* were characterized by their commitments in varying degrees to Judaism and Catholicism. Members of the fourth type tended to reject both religions.

*Type 4: Skeptics.* Since all Iberian crypto-Jews were also required to practice Catholicism, any affirmation of Judaism was also a rejection of Catholicism, what Révah termed a "collective, clandestine repudiation of the Catholic mentality," which meant that "their entire public life, both religious and philosophic, was condemned to insincerity."[52] It follows that to some extent any manifestation of crypto-Judaism was simultaneously an expression of skepticism, one that was, moreover, cloaked in hypocrisy. But some *conversos*' antipathy to faith went far beyond this kind of inherent skepticism. A considerable number of *conversos* recoiled from the incessant religiosity of their times, and from the personal religious crises that beset them and their families, by withdrawing into skepticism. Baer finds the roots of this skepticism in the fourteenth- and fifteenth-century Jewish flirtation with Averroism (1966, 2:148, 253–9). Often this skepticism expressed itself in the Averroistic idea that the soul dies with the body and that there is no afterlife. Sometimes it was much broader and extended itself to a general disdain for religion sometimes expressed as a Sadducean-like secular attitude that saw the Law as a material alliance assuring prosperity in this world (Domínguez Ortiz 1955a, 19). While the quiet dropouts do not appear very often in Inquisition documents by virtue of the success of this strategy in avoiding attention, I suspect that this behavior was extremely widespread. It is reflected in the paltry Judaizing and the poor church attendance of many new-Christians, who participated in little more than the obligatory annual mass and confession.

All four types of *conversos* were likely to run afoul of the Inquisition. The Judaizers, vacillators, and skeptics were all outside the canons of Church orthodoxy and thus, according to the logic of the times, a threat to the coherence of the Christian state. They were considered potent heretical catalysts in urgent need of identification, rehabilitation, or elimination. And even the assimilationist new-Christians were closely scrutinized for signs that might indicate that they, too, were infected with the virus of heresy. Even vestigial customs that had nothing to do with belief—such as an aversion to pork or an affinity for personal hygiene—might call down the apparatus of investigation. The customs of this vast and varied group of people, customs that ranged from the most trivial echoes of medieval Jewish habit to the most profound commitments to observance of the Law of Moses, are detailed in the remainder of this book.

## Notes

1. In each of the following sections the first numbers given are the most widely accepted estimates.
2. In 1991 Suárez Fernández estimated the Jewish population of Castile in the fifteenth century as substantially under 100,000 (1991, 232).
3. Baer's estimates are substantially below these numbers. The best discussions of these numbers remain Caro Baroja 1961, 1:182–9 and Netanyahu 1966, 238–48. Unless otherwise indicated, this section follows Caro Baroja.
4. At that time the only *aljamas* with more than 300 families each were Segovia, Toledo, Trujillo, Guadalajara, Ocaña, Almazán, Soria, Avila, Valladolid, and Murcia. Most had only 40–50 families. There were no *aljamas* in Asturias, only one (Vitoria) in the Basque country, and only two (Orense and La Coruña) in Galicia (Suárez Fernández 1991, 338).
5. A reasonable review of the data and the arguments is found in López Martínez 1954, 91–8.

6. García Cárcel 1985, 250. Of the cases heard by the Toledo tribunal in 1485–1500, 99 percent were for Judaizing; in Barcelona in 1488–1501, 99.3 percent; in Valencia in 1484–1530, 91 percent. By the 1530s the early purges were essentially over: from 1540 to 1549 in Castile only 5.9 percent of the Inquisition investigations were for alleged Judaizing (Haliczer 1987, 10–11).

7. Most studies of local tribunals in the last decade include a statistical summary by category of the cases tried and their disposition. Good examples are Bel Bravo 1988 [Granada]; Blázquez Miguel 1986b [Murcia]; 1990 [Madrid]; Pérez 1986 [Majorca]; Dedieu 1978 [Toledo].

8. The largest number of cases, 11,247 (26.6%), were for heretical utterances; the second largest, 10,444 (24.7%) were for people accused of Islamicizing.

9. This is the conclusion of Caro Baroja 1961, 1:188 and Márquez Villanueva 1980, 63, among others.

10. As best we can tell, only occasionally did Inquisitors blatantly fabricate evidence. The best-known example is the Córdoban Inquisitor Diego Rodríguez Lucero in the early sixteenth century (Lea 1906–7, 1:194–5).

11. One might argue that in the Inquisitorial environment of omnipresent threat to one's life, property, and soul, as well as those of one's family and friends, all testimony was in effect coerced. In my view this does not automatically render all Inquisition testimony invalid.

12. The magnitude and variety of eyewitness testimonies refute Novinsky's argument that trial proceedings are unreliable because "confessions recur with identical bureaucratic formularies, monotonously, throughout the centuries" (1982, 6). I do not accept Saraiva's conclusion with regard to Portugal that Inquisition archives are not credible because their main purpose was to justify the Inquisition and so the testimony they recorded is not reliable. Nor, given the enormous similarity with regard to the customs of the crypto-Jews that one finds in the bulk of the documents, do I accept Saraiva's admonition to Révah that one may not generalize from a large sample of the documents but is rather obliged to read them all (1985, 17). For a review of this controversy see Nahon 1973 and Rivkin 1980, 106–7. For recent historiography of the Spanish and Mexican Inquisitions see Bujanda 1991 and Greenleaf 1991. See also Van der Vekene 1982–3.

13. In making this point Novinsky overstates her case when she says that "every imprisonment, unconditionally resulted in confessing Judaism" (1982, 6). For a review of the debate about the validity of confessions see Lorence 1982, 39–47.

14. I am not in agreement with statements such as Liebman's that "the number of Jews unearthed by the Holy Office constituted only an insignificant percentage of the total number present in New Spain" (1970, 288–9).

15. There are historiographic biases as well. One must never forget that until very recently most studies of the Inquisition and of crypto-Judaism were written by British Protestant, Spanish Catholic, or Jewish historians, many of whom had ideological or emotional axes to grind. As M. Cohen and others have pointed out, historians whose principal interest is documenting the persistence of crypto-Judaism have undoubtedly given a disproportionate weight to the portion of the record that emphasizes the persistence of crypto-Judaism (1972, 278). The data presented in this book, which attempts to document examples of the widest possible range of crypto-Jewish customs, should not be presumed to give substance to this bias. For a brief review of this controversy see Contreras 1991, 129–30.

16. In his defense of this conclusion, M. Cohen stresses the webs of detailed Judaizing activities confirmed and reiterated by witnesses unaware of each other's testimony (1972, 281).

17. Pullan considers these the two basic conditions under which clandestine religious groups are likely to become established, arguing that in other circumstances the old religion is unlikely to persist beyond the "first generation of defiant or bewildered converts" (1983, 201–2).

18. A. García calls this a "double life, a split personality, a terrible personal duality in religion and language" (1987, 54).

19. This is the view of Saraiva, who uses Portuguese Inquisition sources, and of Netanyahu, who, relying primarily on Jewish sources, concludes: "It was not a powerful Marrano movement that provoked the establishment of the Inquisition, but it was the establishment of the Inquisition that caused the temporary resurgence of the Spanish Marrano movement" (1966, 3). For Novinsky this thesis holds for Portugal and her colonies in the seventeenth and eighteenth centuries (1982, 4). Pullan summarizes this set of views: for these historians "Marranism existed largely in the heads of the authorities and of those who became their accomplices and collaborators. It was the creation of all-powerful inquisitions and their dangerously elastic procedures" (1983, 203). For a review of this controversy see Yerushalmi 1971, 21–42.

20. For Brazil Novinsky concludes that when Inquisition activity suddenly intensified it was to a large extent responsible for "bringing back to the old faith many people who at that point had only vague memories of it" (1972b, 37). Well into the seventeenth century there are instances of the Inquisition's creating crypto-Jews in ways that were even perceived by their contemporaries. For example, in 1648 in Brazil the vicar of Salvador was denounced for having affirmed that "the Inquisitors must want for there to be Jews because in their writings they taught them how to be one, and what they were to do, and how they were to sin" (*os senhores Inquisidores deviam querer que houvesse judeus pois nos ditos papéis lhe ensinavão como havião de ser e o que havião de fazer, y como havião de pecar*) (1972b, 142).

21. Although some aspects of Judaism are passed patrilineally—such as membership in the priestly caste of *cohanim*—in this basic definition the mother takes prominence over the father for two reasons: motherhood is incontrovertible, while paternity is sometimes in question, and mothers were traditionally viewed as assuming prime responsibility for transmitting the religious ethos of the household.

22. Typical language was that of a 1525 decree that barred from the Franciscan order "descendants of Jews up through the fourth generation" (*descendientes de judíos usque al quartam generationem*) (Sicroff 1960, 152). The statutes of the cathedral of Córdoba in 1577 denied benefices to people "descended from *conversos* and Jews" (*que descendían de generación de conversos y judíos*) because people of this lineage are "sowers of discord, fond of innovation of and argument, ambitious, presumptuous and malcontented, and wherever they are found there is little peace" (*es generación cizañadora, amiga de novedades y discusiones, ambiciosa, presuntuosa e inquieta, y donde quiera que está esta generación ay poca paz*) (Domínguez Ortiz 1992, 142). The Inquisitor Juan Escobar de Corro (Llerena c. 1628) wrote that "from the moment of its conception . . . every fetus permanently carries with it the moral attributes—in the case of the Marranos, the moral depravity—of its parents" (cited in translation by Patai 1988, 76). Francisco de Torrejoncillo wrote in his 1691 *Centinela contra judíos*: "To be enemies of Christians . . . it is not necessary to be of a Jewish father and mother. One alone suffices. . . . The Holy Inquisition has discovered in our times that up to a dis-

tance of twenty-one degrees [of consanguinity] they have been known to Judaize.... Wet-nurses who are chosen to suckle their sons [of princes] must be Old Christians, for it is not proper that the sons of princes should be suckled by Jewish vileness, because that milk, being of infected persons can only engender perverse inclinations" (cited in translation by Yerushalmi 1982, 16).
23. Catarina Fernandes in Coimbra, 1573 (Azevedo Mea 1982, 344).
24. So said "rabbi" Alonso de Córdoba Membreque to his congregation in Córdoba in 1511 (Gracia Boix 1983, 57).
25. Typical is the attitude of Francisco Mendes de Castro, who in 1707 in Brazil said that his brother "believed in the Law of Moses, but didn't practice any customs, because he was a soldier" (Bromberg 1984, 93).
26. McGaha 1991 considers that "deprived of any real knowledge of Judaism, and hence any meaningful Jewish identity, they were at the same time not accepted as true Christian Spaniards, though many of them were just as fanatical in their Christian beliefs and just as ardent in their patriotism as their fellow citizens. They were not proud, defiant Jews, but people whose involuntary 'Jewishness' was a cruel trick of fate, a meaningless burden that they could not escape."
27. Some approaches consciously mingle these definitions. For example, Novinsky considers the new-Christians to be Jews for three reasons: "They were considered Jews by the society in which they lived, and were never allowed to assimilate completely; ... they constituted an ethnic group which identified itself with the Jews, not through their orthodox Jewish religion, but through their exclusion from global society; and thirdly, because their suffering derived from their 'Jewish condition' " (1982, 5).
28. Thus Fray Prudencio de Sandoval in his 1604 biography of Charles V both acknowledges that Christianity embraces all believers equally and damns the descendants of Jews as being racially blemished: "I know that in the divine presence there is no distinction between Gentile and Jew, because One alone is the Lord of all. Yet who can deny that in the descendants of the Jews there persists and endures the evil inclination of their ancient ingratitude and lack of understanding, just as in the Negroes the inseparable quality of their blackness" (cited in translation by Yerushalmi 1982, 16).
29. These arguments were frequently based on the parable of the two sons laboring in the vineyard (Matthew 21:28–32).
30. From the very first, Hebrew writers made the distinction between forced (*anusim*) and willing (*meshumadim*) converts. Christian polemicists too, whether arguing for tolerance for all Christians or for the harsh treatment of false converts, tended to make the distinction. A good example of this awareness and of its political consequences is found in the *Libro llamado del Alborayque* (1488). See Gitlitz 1992, 3–4.
31. For Baron "the majority of the Spanish clergy and laity viewed any deviation from Christian orthodoxy, however minor, as a manifestation of subversive feelings liable to undermine the ethno-religious unity of the Spanish people" (1969, 13:350).
32. "The overwhelming majority of the Marranos at the time of the establishment of the Inquisition were not Jews but ... Christians.... The minority that still adhered to Judaism in the three decades preceding the establishment of the Inquisition was, save for temporary and inconsequential reactions, constantly diminishing in size and influence; that it would have, in all likelihood, soon faded into nothingness, had not the process of assimilation been violently interfered with by the repellent and bewildering actions of the Inquisition.... Jews generally regarded the Marranos not only as apostates, but also as gentiles,

and ... saw in their continued stay in Spain definite proof of their willingness to practice Christianity" (1966, 3, 60). As M. Cohen points out, even those rabbis who considered the new-Christians to be Jews "felt compelled to marshal the most exquisite arguments to prove this point, and thereby obliquely attested to the serious interruption in their Jewish identity" (1972, 280). I believe that on these points the main lines of Netanyahu's analysis are accurate, despite some weaknesses of context and logic pointed out by G. Cohen 1967 and others.

33. For Kamen, the late fifteenth-century *conversos* were all Judaizers: "Of the thousands of Jews who in the course of the preceding century had been forced by execution and massacre to accept baptism, very few embraced Catholicism sincerely. Many, if not most, of them continued to practice the Jewish rites in secret" (1965, 30). Similarly, Blázquez Miguel considers that *conversos* were never able to put aside their essential Jewishness (*Estos conversos, en su gran mayoría, continuaban siendo judíos en el fondo de sus corazón*) (1989, 145). Baer too, although he documents the wide range of attitudes current among late fifteenth-century *conversos*, basically holds to the view that "Conversos and Jews were one people, united by bonds of religion, destiny and messianic hope" (1966, 2:424). For Baer the story of these *conversos* "is not one of racial 'remnants' which had lost their Jewish characteristics, but of a large population-group, the majority of whose members adhered, consciously and by conviction, to the living Jewish tradition" (1966, 2:278). Haim Beinart too has concluded that "the conversos were, and remained, Jews at heart, and their Judaism was expressed in their way of life and their outlook" (1981a, 23), though in my view his superb documentation of the Extremadura *converso* community suggests greater diversity of commitment than that. Many historians (Liebman, Greenleaf, Böhm, etc.) go so far as to equate crypto-Judaism with normative Judaism, or in extreme cases even to equate *converso* with Jew, using the term "Jew" to refer to them both (see M. Cohen, 1972, 281–3, who even shows how other heterodox Catholics were sometimes labeled Jews). Most modern scholars, on the other hand, recognize that many *conversos* ended up in an ambiguous middle world. This is Blázquez Miguel's eventual conclusion (1989, 145), and is shared by Domínguez Ortiz 1971, 18, Caro Baroja, Haliczer, and many others. Precisely the opposite view was advanced by Netanyahu, based on his readings of Jewish sources: "the new-Christians at the beginning of the [14]80s were not Jews, in practice or in spirit, but assimilated to the core, Christianized, and anti-Jewish," "detached from Judaism, or rather, to put it more clearly, Christians" (1966, 205, 3).

34. *E aunque guardavan el sabado y ayunaban algunos ayunos de los judios, pero no guardaban todos los sabados, ni ayunaban todos los ayunos, e sy façian un rito no façian otro, de manera que en la una y en la otra ley prevaricavan. E fallose en algunas casas el marido guardar algunas çeremonias judaycas, e la mujer ser buena christiana; e el un hijo e hija ser buen christiano, e otro tener opinion judayca. E dentro de una casa aver diversidad de creençias, y encubrirse unos de otros* (1943, 2:210). Pulgar's obsession with the theme of lineage and his mordant commentary on relations of his time between old-Christians and *conversos* have been admirably analyzed by Cantera Burgos (1944).

35. The evolutionary nature of crypto-Judaism is unfairly minimized by historians such as Roth, for whom there was very little change after the passing of the generation that converted: "Henceforth, we can trace a continuous and homogeneous tradition, still carried on by that heroic residue of the New Christians so dramatically rediscovered in Portugal in our own day" (1931–2, 4).

36. Taxonomies for the *conversos* run the gamut from erroneous simplicity (all Judaizers or all assimilated Christians) to systems that give explicit recognition to their diversity.

Among the more useful are those of Haliczer, who sees in the 1480s in Valencia (1) crypto-Jews struggling to preserve tradition, (2) fervent Catholics, (3) and *conversos* who practice both religions (1990, 211). Pullan finds a wide range of attitudes within three basic types of *conversos* in mid-sixteenth-century Venice: (1) people cut off from Judaism but who identify with it; (2) people happy to assimilate to Catholicism had they been allowed; and (3) opportunists attached to neither faith (1983, 206–8). For Pullan the Venetian *conversos* are "studies in ambiguity and vacillation." Caro Baroja's taxonomy (1961, 1:275) is widely used. His six basic types are (1) good Catholics; (2) heterodox Christians; (3) Talmudists [by which he means orthodox, normative Jews]; (4) heterodox Jews; (5) skeptics; (6) vacillators. Faur's recent classification of *conversos* into four groups (those who wanted to be Jews, Christians, both, or neither) (1990, 113–24; 1992, 41) is very similar to mine.

37. Among Jews the informer, whom they labeled with the derogatory Hebrew term *malsin*, was particularly despised. For vivid examples see Caro Baroja 1961, 1:277–84.

38. Many of these intellectuals and those of the following group are treated in Baron 1969, 13:75–84, 342–52, which has excellent bibliographic information. See also Kamen 1965, 58–73. For Talavera see also Beinart 1971, 443–4; Hernando de Talavera 1961. Domínguez Ortiz 1965 reviews arguments for and against a *converso* literary mentality; Asensio 1967 summarizes the risks of ascribing a *converso* zeitgeist to these writings.

39. For Márquez Villanueva these three verged on religious anarchism in their common detestation of ecclesiastical organization, imperial policy, the purity-of-blood mania, the Inquisition, and violence employed in the name of religion (1965, 328–9).

40. The profound sense of alienation which pervades the works of these poets of the courts of Enrique IV and the Catholic Monarchs is displayed in a variety of contradictory attitudes toward the *conversos*. See Caro Baroja 1961, 1:284–91; Rodríguez Puértolas 1968, 51; Scholberg 1971, 303–60; Márquez Villanueva 1960; Arbós 1981; Gitlitz 1972.

41. While there is no strong biographical evidence that Cervantes was from a family of *conversos*, his *Don Quijote* and many of his shorter novels and theatrical pieces are perhaps the Golden Age's best expression of the traditional *converso* themes of equity and multicultural toleration. Works such as Rojas's *Celestina* and the *Lazarillo de Tormes* remain popular perhaps because, as McGaha speculates (1991), "as in the case of many Holocaust survivors, their experience convinced them above all of the essential absurdity of the human condition, and that is why many readers today find their writings so relevant to our own times."

42. See Bataillon 1937; Selke de Sánchez 1980.

43. Some historians assert—with slim evidence, I believe—that crypto-Jewish families often sent a son into the priesthood so that he might funnel Biblical knowledge to them and, by keeping their church contacts within the family, protect them from dangerous scrutiny (for example M. Cohen 1968, 40).

44. Historians commonly overlook the well-documented tendency of the offspring of observant Judaizers to join the assimilationists. For example, Faur asserts that the "faithfully Jewish ... *conversos* at all times ... felt a part and parcel of the Jewish Diaspora, hoping for ... their own eventual reintegration into Jewish society" (1992, 46).

45. *Conversos* might understand this virtue within the Jewish tradition of sanctifying the Holy Name of God (*kiddush ha-shem*) through martyrdom, or within the Christian tradition of achieving personal salvation through extreme sacrifice, or in terms of the honor of being an example to other Judaizers to remain steadfast in their faith.

46. Sicroff 1965; Rábade Obradó 1990a, 162–83.

47. Fray Juan de Madrid said quite explicitly that "he had only become a monk so as to better observe the Jewish Law, because in the monastery no one saw him" (*Non se avia metido*

*frayle salvo por guardar mejor la ley de los judios, por que en el monasterio non era asy visto*) (Baer 1936, 477). Cf. Beinart 1961, 182; Blázquez Miguel 1986a, 62; León Tello 1972, 80; Rábade Obradó 1990a, 345. Of the 17 *converso* monks studied by Rábade Obradó in the Toledo Inquisition Archives, 15 were Jeronymites (1990, 471).

48. These aspects of Judaizing are discussed in Chapter 5. For Révah, the rejection of Catholicism as idolatry is one of the defining characteristics of crypto-Judaism.

49. The *Libro llamado el Alboraique*, an anti-*converso* pamphlet c. 1488, skewers this group with a string of negative metaphors: "When they find themselves with Jews they say: 'we are Jews'; and when they find themselves with Christians they say: 'we are Christians.' . . . There are animals called bats which fly at night and have teeth; they say to these animals: 'we are like you, for we have teeth'; that is what the Jews say. They say to the birds: 'we are like you and we have wings to fly to the sky.' And they are not wholly animals nor wholly birds" (*Quando se hallan con los judíos, dizen: somos judíos, quando con los christianos: somos christianos. . . . Hay animales, que llaman murciélagos, que andan de noche y tienen dientes; dizen a los animales: como vos somos, ca dientes tenemos; así lo dizen los judíos; dizen a las aves: como vos somos y alas tenemos para volar a el cielo. Y ni son aves del todo ni animales del todo*) (1954, 400). Some of these people were frank opportunists. In Paraíba, Brazil, in the 1640s the Portuguese *cristão novo* Manoel da Costa, in an eerie echo of the *alboraique*, was said to be a Jew among Jews, a Catholic among Catholics, and a Dutch Protestant among the Dutch, praying as easily with one as with the other (*quando falava com judeus dizia que era judeu, quando falava com cristãos dizia que era cristão e quando falava com holandeses dizia que era de sua religião, e lia pelos seus livros e ia a sua Igreja*) (Novinsky 1972b, 160–1).

50. *Dise que naquele tempo nem cria nem deixava de crer nelles porque quando estava na igreja lhe pareciam bem as cousas dos christãos e como se sahia logo lhe tornava a cegeira* (Azevedo Mea 1982, 312).

51. *Unas parientas suyas le habían enseñado la ley de Moisés y que la había guardado juntamente con la de Jesucristo Nuestro Señor* (Gracia Boix 1983, 332).

52. *Le marranisme est un refus collectif clandestin de la mentalité catholique. . . . Toute leur activité publique, religieuse ou philosophique, était donc condamnée à l'insincérité* (Révah 1968, 328).

# Part II

## The Religious Customs of the Crypto-Jews

## CHAPTER IV

# The Crypto-Jewish Belief System

When the *converso* descendants of Iberian Judaism found themselves isolated from traditional Judaism and immersed in a world of Christian belief, the central tenets of their beliefs underwent profound changes. It is clear that within a generation after the Expulsion most *conversos* had become more Christian than Jewish. Even those among them who elected to Judaize and clung to whatever remnants of practice and belief they could muster were at the same time practicing (if not always believing) Catholics. The crypto-Jews had no Jewish books, no one to instruct their children in Hebrew, no Talmudic scholars to refine the understanding of the adults, and no Sabbath afternoon study sessions in which to debate the finer points of the Law. Although even after the Expulsion generation died away some clusters of crypto-Jews continued to practice their old religion communally, the data we have about their religious conversations suggest that the Judaism these people discussed with their friends was neither very deep nor very orthodox. It was likely to be an oral transmission of knowledge from the most learned Judaizer to the others or else gossip about the fate of various members of the community. And the discussion was just as likely as not to follow the members' morning attendance at mass. These people rapidly lost familiarity with the subtleties of Jewish theology and the complexities of Jewish observance.

For these people, who undoubtedly constituted the majority of the crypto-Jews, Judaism ceased to be an autonomous, self-referential system. Instead, Christianity became their common reference point, the template against which their crypto-Jewish beliefs and practices were measured. Increasingly they were not Judaizers who were therefore different from the Christians, rather they were Judaizers insofar as they differed from Christians. While it is foolhardy to over-schematize human beliefs, which always vary to some extent with the individual, among Iberian crypto-Jews three sorts of patterns of belief emerged with respect to Christianity.

Some crypto-Jewish beliefs were in explicit contrast with Christian beliefs; to a large extent their validity lay precisely in their being different. Thus crypto-Jews would say, "the Christian God is plural, while ours is singular." Or, "the alleged Christian Messiah has come, while ours is yet to come." Or, "Christian prayer requires the intercession of a saint, while our prayer goes directly to God."

Other crypto-Jewish beliefs gradually assimilated Christian theological concepts, becoming similar in essence while retaining only the thin veneer of a Jewish label as their difference. For example, Christian belief in the necessity of advocacy with the deity by Christian saints was adopted by some crypto-Jews with a shift to belief in the advocacy of Jewish saints. For a few, lighting candles to Christian images evolved into lighting candles to Jewish holy figures like Moses or Tobit.[1] The most important and widespread example of assimilation of Christian belief among the crypto-Jews was the erosion of the Jewish concept of communal salvation: most crypto-Jews came to accept the Christian concept of personal salvation of the soul through belief in Jesus, merely changing belief in Jesus to belief in Moses or in the Law of Moses.

Still other crypto-Jewish beliefs were based on an aggressive rejection of Christian beliefs and practices. The majority of crypto-Jews did not accept the divinity of Jesus, the virginity of Mary, the Trinity, Christian saints, the sacraments, or the sanctity of religious images and icons. A number of crypto-Jews went beyond passive non-acceptance to define their Judaism by aggressively ridiculing the hated symbols of Christian dominance. This aspect of crypto-Jewish beliefs will be treated in Chapter 5.

While the gradually assimilating crypto-Jews appear to have constituted the vast majority, it is also true that a few crypto-Jews contrived to remain linked over time to the wellsprings of Jewish tradition. A minute number of them preserved Jewish books. Another small minority traveled abroad and renewed their Judaism among the open practitioners of the religion in cities like Amsterdam, Leghorn, or Salonica. Visitors from abroad were pumped by the stay-at-homes for details of Jewish observance. Thus as late as the middle of the seventeenth century we find individual crypto-Jews, and even scattered groups, whose practice of Judaism and knowledge of Jewish belief was relatively sophisticated.

Nevertheless there was a common core of what can be considered crypto-Jewish dogma. No matter how sophisticated crypto-Jewish practice remained or how attenuated it became, almost all of those in Spain, Portugal, and the colonies who continued to think of themselves primarily as Jews clung to five basic principles that constituted the essence of their Jewishness: (1) God is one; (2) the Messiah has not come, but is coming; (3) belief in the Law of Moses is a prerequisite for individual salvation; (4) observance is required in addition to belief;[2] and (5) Judaism is the preferred religion. These five principles defined crypto-Judaism for the two hundred fifty years from the Expulsion to the eventual assimilation of the vast majority of the descendants of the *conversos*.

Today in the twentieth century the few scattered remnant crypto-Jewish communities are for almost all intents and purposes practicing Catholics. Their Jewishness is reduced to tenuous vestiges of former beliefs and practices among which even these five points are only sporadically represented. These modern "Judaizers" are really not Judaizers at all. They attend mass, embrace the sacraments, and fill their homes with Christian iconography. Yet they sometimes abstain from taking communion or from adding the *Gloria Patri* to their prayers. Others affirm their belief in a unitary God and see no conflict between that and their Catholicism. For some their Jewish identity is merely that: thinking of themselves as Jews while in all outward appearance and inward belief they are as Catholic as their neighbors.

This chapter examines the principal beliefs of crypto-Judaism, including their views with respect to fortune and to Jewish "saints" in addition to the five core concepts listed above.

## 4.1. ONE GOD

The central and most common precept for the Iberian crypto-Jews was the belief in a unitary God in contrast to what they considered to be the tripartite or plural God of the Christians. Jews are uncompromising monotheists for whom belief in a single God is the most important article of faith. The affirmation of monotheism is the first two of the Ten Commandments (Exodus 20:2–3) and the substance of Judaism's most often repeated prayer, the *Shema*: "Hear, O Israel, the Lord our God, the Lord is one."[3] Over the centuries testimony before the Inquisition was very consistent on this point. The *conversa* Donosa Ruiz, who was tried in Teruel in 1484, was reputed to have prayed every day to God "to protect her from her enemies, by whom she meant the Christians, idolaters who worship three Gods instead of one."[4] A memorandum about the customs of Judaizers prepared for the Granada Inquisition in 1593 listed as their very first characteristic that they believe that "there is one omnipotent God, and they deny the plurality of the ... Holy Trinity."[5] María de San Juan [Baeza 1573] testified that "her mother had told her that she must believe in the one single God who created the heaven and the earth, and not in any other."[6] Her sister Juana de San Juan, ironically reflecting the Christian view of the afterlife, was certain that "Christians were blind and would go to Hell because they did not believe in a unitary God."[7] Alonso Fernández de Aguilar, of Ecija, was punished in Córdoba in 1597 because he testified that "he had never believed in more than one God and had not held Our Lord Jesus Christ to be God."⁸ Antonio Bocarro Francês [Goa 1624] was accused of saying when the host was elevated in mass: "Only the most high Lord, God of Israel, is owed honor and glory for He is the God above all Gods, the God above all Lords. Blessed and praised and magnified is His single holy name as He was and will be forever and ever."⁹ In 1626 the Bachelor Francisco Maldonado de Silva testified to the Inquisition in Santiago de Chile that he believed that "there was only one God, to whom they owed their being, and whom they should worship."¹⁰ Raphael Cortés de Alonso [Majorca 1687] reported that the *chueta* Pedro Onofre Cortés had said: "You can only adore a single God. That is very clear, because it says in Deuteronomy that one must adore a single God and not adore images. God cannot be many because He is an infinite being and no one can have seen His face."¹¹ The crypto-Jews believed that their unitary God heard their prayers directly, without the need to employ intercessors such as Mary or the saints. In 1589 in Mexico Doña Guiomar, wife of Luis de Carvajal, expressed this idea clearly when she preached that "there was no more than one true God, . . . and that prayers should be directed only to God, and not to Jesus Christ, nor his mother."¹² Even though some later crypto-Jews were unsure about the precise nature of their unitary God,¹³ this belief that the deity is unique and immutable was characteristic of crypto-Jewish beliefs throughout the Iberian possessions and has survived well into the twentieth century among remnant crypto-Jewish communities in Portugal, where many of the crypto-Jewish prayers that have been collected assert belief in a unitary God.¹⁴

Some Spanish Jews and a few members of the first generation of *conversos* tended to emphasize this belief in God's unitary nature by using the term *El Dió* for God instead of *Dios*. Although *Dios* is derived from the Latin nominative singular *Deus*, Spanish Jews and Judaizers considered the "s" indicative of the tripartite, plural Christian God.¹⁵ In fifteenth- and sixteenth-century literature use of the term *El Dió* was a shorthand way of indicating Judaizing tendencies or Jewish descent (Shepard 1982, 40–2). A number of mid- to late fifteenth-century satirical poems attacking the *conversos* characterize them as worshipping *El Dió* rather than *Dios*. For example, the Conde de Paredes says of the notorious *converso* Juan Poeta, "Look what *El Dió* has done for your cursed race."¹⁶ In the burlesque poem on the "Wedding of Rodrigo Cota" several characters swear their oaths by *El Dió* (Gómez-Menor 1970, 102–4). In 1505 Lope de Arriaga was reported to have said, "By *El Dió* this cannot be!"¹⁷ In Portuguese the same phenomenon occurred. For example, in Gil Vicente's 1525 *Farce of Inés Pereira* the Jew Vidal announces his entry and signals his Jewishness with the words, "In the name of God, here we are," using *Deo* for God instead of the more normal Portuguese term *Deus*.¹⁸ Among some *conversos* this pseudo-singular name for God was so ingrained that they carried it over into their new religion, and were observed referring to a crucifix as *Dió* (Carrete/Fraile 1987, 71). But the difference between *Dió* and *Dios* was far from trivial, as perceptive analysts of *converso* condition on occasion pointed out. In his early sixteenth-century play about Joseph's sojourn in Egypt, for example, Miguel de Carvajal went so far as to have Joseph's proto-Christian good brothers call God *Dios*, while the evil proto-Marrano brothers refer to God as *El Dió* (Gitlitz 1972, 262–3).

## 4.2. THE MESSIAH

A second set of crypto-Jewish beliefs dealt with the concept of the Messiah. Medieval Jews rejected the idea that Jesus was the Messiah or indeed that the Messiah had come. Many Judaizers, like Juan González Daza [Ciudad Real 1484], who was accused of "not believing that the Messiah had come,"[19] and Gonçalo Vaez, a Portuguese student in Granada, who told Inquisitors in 1571 that he did not believe that Jesus was the true Messiah,[20] were convicted for expressing this disbelief. Other Judaizers were accused merely of waiting, of expressing simple faith that their Messiah would come.[21] Beyond this central tenet, medieval Jewish messianism was a complex blend of two differing traditions, which Scholem calls the popular-mythological tradition and the philosophical-rationalist tradition. Popular mythology held that there would be no continuity between the present and the messianic age but that the new order would rise on the ashes of history. Esoteric exegeses of certain Biblical and Talmudic texts sketched out a scenario of the pre-messianic chaos and apocalyptic imagination supplied the rest.

Most testimonies in this vein incorporate a mishmash of ideas. The *converso* Fernando de Madrid told the Inquisition around 1491 that some years earlier he had preached a sermon about the calendar of impending cataclysmic change: that "in 1487 there would be no justice in the world; that in '88 the cattle would be rounded up; and that in '89 all would be reduced to a single Law." The Messiah would appear in Palos de Moguer [Cádiz]. "He would bring with him the philosopher's stone, which would turn a bar of iron into silver, and a bar of steel into gold. And he would reveal the treasures of the sea. And that when he came his property would be worth 100.000 marevidis. . . . People would leave their wives and children to go where he was."[22] According to Diego de Simancas, a Jew in Seville said that the Messiah would avoid the Inquisition by arriving as a fish in the river Guadalquivir (Caro Baroja 1961, 1:407). The wonders to be worked by this apocalyptic Messiah defied logic but often gladdened the heart by offering hope of raising the dead and rejuvenating the living. This was the message of Diego Díaz Nieto, who testified in Mexico in 1601 that "the Messiah was to be a son of King David and not a son of God, and that the Messiah would redeem the entire world, that He would cause deceased Jews to arise from their graves, and that some Christians would incur eternal punishment" (Liebman 1970, 194). In 1543 an old woman named Margarida Gomes told the Lisbon Inquisition that she had heard Beatriz Mendez say that "the Messiah was still to come and would make her young again; and she began to dance and sing a song in which the word 'Adonai' was heard."[23]

Many *conversos* believed that the apocalyptic messianic age would not begin until the Jews had sufficiently atoned for their sins. This belief underlay the 1570 testimony of Isabel Alvares, of Torre de Moncorvo, who told her Inquisitors in Coimbra that "the persecution that the *cristãos novos* were now suffering was because the Jews had not waited for Moses for the forty days it took him to bring them the Law, and after twenty days they sinned . . . and God was angered by this and made them wander in captivity for this sin until the promised Messiah would come."[24] A hundred years later in Majorca Ana Cortés reported to the Inquisition that her father Joseph Cortés had told her that "they were awaiting the Messiah who was to come, and that He would not come until the Hebrew people had finished doing penance for their sins."[25] Of course many *conversos* thought that their most egregious sin was to have converted in the first place. As Fernando de Madrid put it in 1491, before the Messiah could appear the *conversos* must first suffer for having become Christians.[26]

The catastrophic tradition was very widespread and its fantastic mythology was firmly rooted in popular belief. Linked to it was a utopian belief in a complete and radical change in the natural order of things. Typical was the testimony of Pedro Serrano of the Puebla de Montalbán [Toledo], who saw the persecutions of the 1480s as the precursors of a new age in which "those who were now suffering would become prosperous—by which he meant the heretics,—and that those who were now enjoying life were like serpents—by which he meant the good Catholic Christians,—. . . and that the first would soon triumph over the others."[27] Other *conversos* focused on the reestablishment of Jerusalem and the triumph of the ideal of a peaceful, contemplative Jewish nation. While the new world order was delightful to contemplate in the ideal, at the same time the radical transformation it implied was threatening to established rabbinical authority. Rationalist approaches to messianism, perhaps most influentially exemplified in Maimonides, downplayed the idea of disruptive last days and speculation about the nature of the new order or the process of achieving it, arguing that one could only know the details of the redemptive process after it had been completed. The rationalist approach was never as popular as the apocalyptic-utopian approach (Scholem 1973, 8–15).

This was particularly true in Spain, where the tumultuous events of the fifteenth century indicated to many Jews and *conversos* that the coming of the Messiah was imminent.[28] The prevalent vision of the Messiah was that of a divinely inspired, righteous human being who would lead the scattered diaspora of Judaism back to the promised land of Palestine, where they would thrive as a perfectly harmonious religious state.[29] Medieval Jewish apocalyptic literature was rich, if inconsistent, in its discussion of the attributes of the Messiah, the characteristics of the chaotic "last days" that would prefigure His coming, the nature of the prophet who would announce Him, and calculations of the date of His coming. When one highly touted date elapsed without the Messiah's having come, rabbis lamented that the

Jewish people were not yet sufficiently righteous to accept Him, and they set another date (*Enc. Jud.* 11:1411–3). Periods of violent social unrest were often interpreted as the beginning of the "last days" and as such triggered frenetic messianic speculation. For Jews and crypto-Jews the whole series of chaotic events in Iberia from the late fourteenth to the late seventeenth centuries (the 1391 massacres, the 1413–4 Disputation of Tortosa, the fall of Constantinople in 1453, the 1480 founding of the Inquisition, the 1492 Expulsion, the visit of David Reubeni to Portugal in 1524, the loss of the charismatic Portuguese King Sebastian in Africa in 1578) set off this messianic fervor, and the historical record abounds with speculations and calculations, and with false messiahs and prophets.[30]

The predominant note in the messianic yearnings of Iberian crypto-Jews is for freedom from Inquisition persecution, a freedom which would be attained when a messianic leader would transport them to a promised land. This was a double dream, incorporating both an exodus from the lands of persecution and an in-gathering of the diaspora in a Jewish homeland, generally with Jerusalem as its center. This was the vision of Juan de Moya [Cuenca 1490], who was accused of having dreamed of emigrating to Jerusalem, which he called the promised land (*Canpo de Promisión*). He reputedly said that God would do well by the *conversos* because they were descended from Jews, who "do not believe that the Messiah has come, but rather that He is still to come."[31] It was also that of Joan Livinyana of Orihuela [Valencia 1500], who believed firmly that the Messiah was to come soon to rescue the *conversos* from their troubles.[32] And of the *converso* shoemaker Juan de Segovia, who reportedly said around 1500 that the Messiah "was to take them to the promised land, where they would eat from golden plates, and that after the *conversos* had left for the promised land it would not rain for seven years."[33] And of María Alvarez, of Herrera, who said around 1500 that now "the great fish Leviathan was dead, and which meant that soon the *conversos* would be brought out of captivity."[34] And of the *converso* who around 1501 narrated his vision of the Messiah on a golden throne, surrounded by martyrs of the Inquisition, promising to come soon to take *conversos* to the Promised Land (Caro Baroja 1961, 1:406).

Common to most of these speculations was the sense of immediacy: not only would the Messiah come, his arrival was imminent. This idea fired up the *cristão novo* community of Coimbra in the early 1580s, for in 1583 the Coimbra Inquisition heard a number of *cristã nova* women tell how they thought the coming of the Messiah to be at hand. Filipa Fernandes, of Seia, affirmed that the Messiah was sure to come within the year.[35] Beatriz Gonçalves told them that when He came she was anxious to go with the Jews to the Promised Land.[36] And Isabel Lopes, of Vila Flor, added that the old-Christians would become mules to carry the new-Christians there.[37] Francisco Maldonado de Silva told his Inquisitors in Lima in 1627 that he had fasted forty days for the Messiah who was promised in the Law.[38] As we will see in a moment, there was similar Messianic fervor among Mexican Judaizers in the 1640s, and the examples could be multiplied almost at will.

Although this double yearning to leave Iberia and to be in-gathered in the Promised Land was particularly strong among the Expulsion generation, it persisted throughout the crypto-Jewish experience. Thus Isabel Alvares, of Torre de Moncorvo, told her Inquisitors in Coimbra in 1570 that "God reserved for the Jews the good that He had prepared for them, and that when the Messiah came he would transport them to another better land, and he would give them good food without their having to work, as God had done before the coming of Christ."[39] Gonçalo Vaez told the Granada Inquisitors in 1571 that when the Messiah came he would free the Jews.[40]

Later Judaizing new-Christians sometimes incorporated beliefs about the ten Lost Tribes of Israel into their messianic speculations. Izabel Luiz [Lisbon 1572] reported that she had heard the *cristãa nova* Filipa Marques say that "the Messiah was still to come and would bring the twelve tribes of Israel."[41] Francisco Maldonado de Silva [Lima 1627] reportedly asserted that "he was of the two tribes of Israel that were preserved in the earthly paradise awaiting the end of the world, which was imminent, for God to assemble them."[42] Ana Cortés [Majorca 1678] reported that her father Joseph Cortés had told her that "there was a tribe and a half which was dispersed and lost out in the world, and that Moses and Aaron would come and take them out of captivity."[43]

Despite the cultural pressures exerted by the Christian environment, most of these statements of messianic dreaming are much more Jewish than they are Christian. As Scholem has stated, Judaism saw redemption "as an event which takes place publicly, on the stage of history and within the community. It is an occurrence which takes place in the visible world and which cannot be conceived apart from such a visible appearance." Christianity, on the other hand, saw redemption as "an event in the spiritual and unseen realm, an event which is reflected in the soul, in the private world of each individual, and which effects an inner transformation which need not correspond to anything outside" (1971, 1). For Jews, salvation, whether individual or communal, was a product of righteous fulfillment of the precepts of the Law, irrespective of any Messiah; for Christians, salvation was individual and required mediation by the Messiah.

After the Expulsion the Christian concept of the Messiah gradually replaced the Jewish concept for many crypto-Jews. Crypto-Jews continued to reject Jesus as the Messiah, but some of them now waited not for a human, politically oriented Messiah, but for a divine, miraculous Messiah whose mission included not only the establishment of a Jewish state but also the salvation of Jewish souls. Some crypto-Jews confused this Messiah with Moses (Roth 1931–2, 8); a few, adapting the Christian concept of a satanic "anti-Jesus" and hoping that the coming Jewish Messiah would destroy the Church, confused the coming Messiah with the Antichrist. Fernando de Madrid, a Castilian *converso* some of whose 1491 testimony has already been cited, referred to the Messiah as the Antichrist and said that "whoever did not want to believe in the Antichrist, each day would have a limb amputated until they believed in him and stopped believing in Jesus Christ."[44] Catalina Gutiérrez [Baeza 1573] confessed that "she had heard talk of some letters which said that a child had been born who was not of the Holy Mother Church, but rather of the Law of Moses, and she hoped that the time of the coming of that child would arrive soon.... And she understood that the child who was to come was the Antichrist."[45] A curious version of this Christianized crypto-Jewish Messiah may even have survived into the twentieth-century American Southwest. Clemente Carmona told David Nidel in New Mexico in 1980 of his family's syncretic messianic beliefs: "The Christ doll tradition in our family is meant to represent the messiah as a child [who] we always expect to come sometime. A Christ doll was passed down from one generation to the next, from one family to another" (Nidel 1984, 254).

In this environment it was only natural that a gifted speaker with an enthusiastic message about an imminent Messiah could have a profound effect on his immediate listeners and on the *converso* community in which they found themselves. This was the case of Bachelor Alonso de Córdoba Membreque, who was accused by several witnesses in Córdoba in 1504 of having preached around 1500 in a clandestine synagogue that "Elijah would come soon to take them out of these lands of captivity and take them to the Promised Land."[46] The sermon is noteworthy for its rich detail and for featuring a number of *converso* preoccupations: the preeminence of Jewish Law and the desire to prove it to the old-Christians; the wavering *converso* fidelity to Jewish Law; the desire that old-Christians not benefit by the misfortunes of the *conversos*; and even the desire to find eligible Judaizing mates for their children. One witness provided a summary of Córdoba Membreque's sermon:

> On the road to the Promised Land they would find a river of milk and another river of water. And in one of them all the old and young *confesos* would bathe, and everyone who bathed in that river, the old and the young both, would become twenty-five years old. And when Elijah came to take them from these lands and take them to the Promised Lands, the earth would shake, and the sun and the moon would die, and the sky would open, and the sea would turn to blood, and the trees would dry up, and a great hail storm would come and punch holes in the houses and flatten everything. And a great river would come and sweep away all the goods, estates and wealth that the *conversos* left behind here, so that the old-Christians would not be able to make use of them. And Elijah would cause all the earthquakes and storms so that all the *conversos* would believe in him and would see the wonders that he worked so that they would repent of the beliefs which they had had or which they had shown to the Christians. And after the earthquakes had passed, Elijah would come as an angel and would ask all the *conversos* what it was they believed, and if they truly believed in the Law of the Jews, and if they had held the Christian Law to be true and had believed in it. And he would absolve them so that they might return to the Law of the Jews, for if they did not believe in it they could not enter the Promised Lands. And that he would ask them what prayers of

the Jewish Law they knew, and in what fashion they prayed them in order to know whether they were truly of the law of the Jews. And then later, those who truly believed in the Jewish law and were firm in it he would have to get undressed, and he would dress them in [?] white shirts, without a trace of any other color but white, and he would dress them in white shoes. And they would have many lighted candles in their hands. And he would take them through the cities and towns and places where the *conversos* were, all in a procession in plain sight of everybody. And in the middle of the cities and towns and places he would preach in such a fashion that he would convert all the old-Christians into believing and following the law of the Jews. Later Elijah would take all the *conversos* with him to the Promised Lands. And halfway along the road was a cave from which would emerge all the young *converso* men who were in the Promised Lands, and these *converso* youths who came out of the cave would marry the *converso* girls from here who were of marriageable age. And on the road to the Promised Lands they would not eat anything but unleavened bread and another kind of bread made without leaven, but rather out of flour they call couscous.[47]

Other witnesses supplied additional and sometimes contradictory details of the sermon. When Elijah came "a man would appear in the moon, and then the sun and moon would die and there would be great darkness for three days and nights." There were not two miraculous rivers but three: "one of milk, one of honey, and one of blood, and the miraculous rejuvenation would come from bathing in the river of milk. The Judaizing *conversos* would leave all their troubles behind in those rivers, but those who did not believe in the Law of Moses would not be able to go any further." "In the promised land cousins would marry cousins, and that in those lands . . . many goods and riches were reserved for them." Córdoba Membreque also said that "in order to hasten what they desired, they should keep all the Jewish fasts."[48]

This sermon evidently impressed the local crypto-Jewish population deeply, for evidence of several subsequent conversations is given in the trial. For example, when Martín Alonso went to moneychanger Hernando de Barrionuevo to ask for a loan, Barrionuevo replied that "what did he want money for, because Elijah was about to come to take the *conversos* to the promised land." On one occasion Alonso met Juan Castil the silk maker in the street, and Castil told him the same thing (124). Another day he met the doctor Master Pedro in the street, and Master Pedro said to him: "Have you heard what they are saying all over town? . . . The Messiah has not yet come, and that they expect that Elijah will come soon."[49]

Among the Iberian overseas possessions, Mexico seems to have been the place where the strongest messianic sentiments were recorded. In 1589 Luis de Carvajal told Inquisitors there that "God was going to send the Messiah to help the people of Israel." He also said that "his father had told him that before the arrival of the Messiah they were waiting for every day, first Elijah would come, to prepare the way for the Messiah."[50] In 1591 Francisco Ríos Matos was accused of "hoping for the coming of the Messiah which would give [the Jews] wealth and raise them to glory" (Liebman 1964, 98). Diego Díaz Nieto testified in Mexico in 1601 that the coming "Messiah was to be a son of King David and not a son of God" (Liebman 1970, 194). In the great *auto de fe* in Mexico in 1649 several Judaizers were reported to have made predictions regarding the Messiah. Doña Blanca Enríquez, burned in effigy in the *auto*, was accused of saying that the Messiah would come in 1642 or 1643.[51] Gaspar de Fonseca, also burned in effigy, had said He would come in 1631 or 1632. Inés Pereira, reconciled in the *auto,* was reputed to be destined to give birth to the Messiah. Her family "would place her in the middle of the drawing-room and surround her with burning candles. They worshipped her and adored her as a person from whom would be born their redeemer and chief." When Inés was pregnant Justa Méndez, who was later burned in effigy in the *auto*, used to stand her on a table and dress her in a "tunic of voile" so that the Jews could worship her.[52] Sebastián Román, who died prior to the *auto* and was burned in effigy, was accused of marrying Doña Geronyma Esperanza, who was burned in effigy in Puebla, whom he knew to be "of the Hebrew nation . . . in order that the Messiah might be born from the marriage" (Liebman 1974, 231). Ana Núñez, reconciled in an *auto* the year before, conflated these ideas with the Christian concept of the Messiah, saying that her father had taught her that the coming Messiah was to die for them.[53]

With all this attention placed on the coming Messiah, and with the natural human proclivity to both charlatanism and credulity, it is not surprising that the fifteenth, sixteenth, and seventeenth centuries saw the emergence of a number of self-styled messiahs. Among the more noteworthy were the mystic teenager Inés Esteban in the village of Herrera del Duque, shortly before 1500, who said that she had talked with the Messiah, and that He had raised her to Heaven where she could see the souls of the martyrs of the Inquisition seated on golden thrones. Her followers in the region believed she was the prophet of the Messiah who would appear some night soon to take them to the Promised Land. Seventy-seven of them were burned in an *auto de fe* in Toledo in 1501.[54] In the 1530s Luis Dias, a Portuguese tailor from Setúbal, persuaded many people that he was the Messiah. He had many followers who circumcised themselves, were mystics, and lived together in a community. He was burned in Lisbon in 1541.[55] Another Portuguese false Messiah, known as *o judeu do zapato* (the shoemaker Jew) was burned in Evora in 1542 (Caro Baroja 1961, 1:409). Mexican Judaizers of the 1640s hoped that Gaspar Váez Sevilla, who was reconciled in an *auto de fe* in Mexico in 1646, would be the Messiah the Kabbalists were predicting.[56]

Among European Jews the period of intense messianic speculation culminated, and largely ended, with their religious leaders' embarrassment at having been taken in by the false Messiah Shebtai Zvi, who, after enlisting the enthusiasm of much of European Jewry in the 1660s, apostatized in Turkey and converted to Islam.[57] In Spain messianic speculation died down at roughly the same time, due less to the Sabbatean debacle than to the fact that by then most crypto-Jews were largely assimilated into mainstream Catholicism.

## 4.3. The Afterlife

Judaism and Christianity differ markedly in their concept of the afterlife. Traditional Judaism emphasizes fulfillment of the precepts of the Law of Moses as a method of achieving righteousness for its own sake, not to ensure the soul's salvation. While traditional Judaism does number among its tenets belief in the resurrection of the dead, with divine reward for the righteous and punishment of the wicked, these concepts are not the keystones of its theology. While many medieval Jews believed in some manner of resurrection of the righteous in the Promised Land after the coming of the Messiah, the concept of personal salvation of the soul in a Christian sense is foreign to traditional orthodox Judaism. Unlike Christianity, Jewish philosophy and rituals give little attention to the idea of individual salvation or to the concept of a physical heaven, somehow a replica of earth, in which human souls will be joined with loved ones for blissful eternity.

Nonetheless the majority of crypto-Jews swiftly adopted the Christian idea of salvation.[58] In fact, almost from the first days of conversion the centerpiece of the crypto-Jewish religious creed was the belief that salvation of each individual soul was only possible through the Law of Moses and not the Law of Christ. This affirmation seems to have varied little over time. Juan Ramírez [Ciudad Real early 1480s] said that he prayed with his sister and friends "with the intent of saving themselves in the Law of Moses, considering that Law to be the best one and thinking to save themselves in it."[59] Similarly, fourteen-year-old Rafael de Granada testified in Mexico in 1642 that his mother had taught him that "the Law of Moses was the good and true law, necessary for his salvation, and not the Law of Jesus."[60] In the same spirit in 1656 in Mexico Fernando de Medina insisted that salvation could only be achieved through the Law of Moses, for which he would gladly die.[61]

First generation converts who accepted the Christian idea of personal salvation were faced with an important theological dilemma: was salvation possible for the souls of their parents who had died as Jews? Although the Church answered firmly in the negative, some of these newly minted Christians continued to pray for the Jewish souls of their departed. Many of them wished their dead parents well with phrases which appear over and over in Inquisition testimony around the time of the Expulsion, and which undoubtedly echoed the Hebrew expression *alav ha-shalom* (may he rest in peace). Pedro de Guadalajara [Almazán 1503] was heard to wish his parents a good eternity. María Varca wished hers a good eternity in the Law in which they had died. Graciana Laínez hoped that God would give her parents good "breath" because they were such good people and had died as Jews.[62]

Frequently specific Jewish practices were seen as a prerequisite for the soul's salvation, as in the statements of Gracia de Teba and María González in Ciudad Real in 1513 "that keeping the Sabbath was good for the salvation of their souls."[63] Only occasionally was this basic belief in salvation augmented with any hints about the nature of the life beyond, as in the additional statement of María González that when she died "her soul would find rest with that of Moses our Rabbi."[64] Rarer still among the crypto-Jews are references to eschatological folklore, such as the legend told by the *converso* weaver Gabriel de Aranda, who was denounced in 1501:

> There was a Jew, the son of a wealthy Jewess, who went and returned from paradise, and an angel showed him heaven and hell. He wanted to stay in paradise, but God had him taken out of there and said to him: "Come out of there, friend of God." But he did not want to. And God ordered him to come out. And he said that he did not want to, because God had said that whoever saw his house could not be lost. And thus he remained in paradise. And that Jew came to summon those who were about to die. And thus he came and went.[65]

Overall, this conflation of the Jewish idea of righteousness through obedience to the Law and the Christian idea of salvation through belief is the single most powerful example of syncretism in the crypto-Jewish religion.

As with other aspects of crypto-Jewish religion, whose point of reference was almost always Christianity, for some crypto-Jews Jewishness was asserted less by affirming Jewish belief than by rejecting Christian eschatology. They were particularly skeptical about the Christian cosmography. Statements of disbelief in Heaven, and particularly doubts about the reality of Hell and Purgatory, were commonplace. Many *conversos* agreed with Juan de Buendía, who was heard to say in Calatayud sometime prior to 1488 that Hell did not exist.[66] Frequently this skepticism was translated into an affirmation that this world alone was the sum total of human existence. This belief was current among many new-Christians even before the Expulsion. The Jew Acach Xuet [Calatayud 1489] testified how the *converso* Juan de Sayas had remarked that "in this world everything is air except birth and death and that the soul of a dog comes into the body of a man and that of a man into the body of a dog."[67] About the same time the *converso* Jaime Martínez de Santángel, of Teruel, was heard to say that "in this world is where glory and honor are, for in the other there is no hell nor heaven. God is nothing more than a tree, the leaves come out in summer and winter cuts them and they fall. That how God makes and unmakes people."[68] The *converso* Diego López allegedly remarked "that the soul of a man is no different from that of a little goat or a hen when they cut its throat, and that after death, where are the souls to be found? And that there was nothing besides eating and drinking and the pleasure that a man takes, nothing but living and dying."[69] The *converso* Francisco Hernández de Diego Sánchez

[Soria 1489] allegedly said that "there was nothing but birth and death, that the day he was born the world began, and the day he died it ended."[70] Baer identifies this current of belief among fifteenth-century *conversos* as a prolongation of Averroistic tendencies that had led many Jewish intellectuals two centuries earlier to philosophical positions which denied or were at best indifferent to the concept of an afterlife (1966, 2:148, 253–9). To this philosophical current must be added the influences of what Márquez Villanueva terms the Epicurianism, atheism, and Sadduceanism that formed part of the intellectual milieu of the late fifteenth century (1961, 49).

Implicit in this attitude was a skepticism about the existence of the soul as something separate from the body or transcendent to human life. Guiomar Fernandes [Lisbon 1543] was heard to say that "she didn't know what the soul was because she could not see it."[71] In 1582 in Granada the Antequeran *converso* Joan Sánchez [Granada 1582] said "that the soul was nothing but a breath."[72] Sarcastic skepticism creeps through the words of a *conversa* named Aldonça Laínez of Almazán [Soria], who was heard to say with regard to the Expulsion: "This misfortune came at an unfortunate time . . . except for these souls that people say we are saving."[73] The natural corollary of these beliefs was that Catholic rituals whose purpose was to speed the passage of souls into Heaven were hollow. The *converso* priest Fernand Sánchez [Soria 1502] allegedly told a parishioner not to worry about contributing money for masses, saying "I never saw anything more excessive than spending money for these masses, because the dead have no need of it, for even if they are suffering in Purgatory this won't make them get out any faster; because when a man dies God already knows the mercy He is going to show him."[74]

A few *conversos* seem to have carried their skepticism over the border into atheism. The *converso* thief Alfonso Texedor [Osma 1491], for example, when threatened with excommunication reputedly denied the whole Christian concept of God, the soul, and the afterlife: "Hey, take care of your own soul; for there is no God, nor Holy Mary, nor Christ; it's all bunk." Alonso the butcher [Soria c. 1491] framed his denial in more strictly Jewish terms, focusing on God the creator: "The heaven and the earth were already made; they were not created by the hand of God; they were already set in their courses."[75] Juan de Aranda was reported to the Inquisition of Soria in 1491 to have said that "he disbelieved in God and the seven pairs of angels closest to Him."[76]

This attitude of scornful disbelief was even more common in the years following the Expulsion and was identified as a major characteristic of Judaizers in Edicts of Grace such as that published in Evora in 1536 (Furtado 1925, xxxiii). This skepticism was so common that it expressed itself proverbially in an expression which appears in scores of trials: "Let me do well in this world and you won't see me do poorly in the other."[77]

Even at a distance of five hundred years often we can capture the poignancy and immediacy of individual experience in these skeptical statements. In 1487 in

Calatayud a successful *converso* merchant expressed his contentment when he remarked that "there is no other heaven than the market of Calatayud."[78] But more commonly suffering is the dominant mode in these statements, sometimes coupled with the belief—similar to that of some mid-twentieth-century existentialists—that Hell or Purgatory is nothing more than a metaphor for the suffering imposed on people in this world. Poverty is one cause of this hell on earth. The *converso* Gonzalvo Ruiz (d. 1478) was accused in Teruel of having said "that he did not believe that there was any other paradise than being rich, nor any other hell than being poor and having to beg from another."[79] Isabel de Santángel, a *conversa* of Tarazona, was heard to remark in the 1480s that she could not believe "that there was a purgatory nor a hell nor devils nor suffering in the other world, as they say, but only suffering in this world."[80]

This idea frequently verged on incorporating a hedonistic view that the purpose of existence is to enjoy pleasure, and there is no use worrying about the next world. In Ciudad Real, Juan de Torres said that around 1469 he had been asked by Juan Falcón:

> What were the things he most desired in this world. And [Torres] replied: "Salvation for my soul." Juan Falcón said: "What is this salvation?" This witness replied: "I would like to do the sorts of things that would make me go to Paradise, and not to Purgatory or to Hell." Falcón said: "Don't give me that Paradise and Purgatory and Hell stuff!" This witness said: "Who can doubt it?" And Falcón answered: "I will tell you what Paradise and Purgatory and Hell are all about. Paradise is having sufficient wealth to be able to give charity and never lack anything; and sometimes having and sometimes not is Purgatory; to know poverty, that is Hell. And don't let them make you believe that there is any other Paradise or Purgatory or Hell."[81]

Juan de Salcedo reported in Aranda in 1502 that Ferrand de Guernica, a pot maker from Soria, gave as a reason not to convert and remain in Spain:

> the belief, as I believe, that you are only born to die, and there is nothing else in this world but birth and death. And after God created the world He left everyone with their own fortune, good or bad. Whoever has enough to eat and drink and meet his other needs in this world, that man is in paradise; and the poor man is in hell. What they say is true, by God's body, that see me comfortable in this world and you won't see me suffer in the other. For a man would give eighty turns in hell to have honor and possessions in this world.[82]

Similar sentiments were expressed by Diego Mexías, a *converso* priest of Soria, who was reported in 1502 to have told a parishioner "not to let anyone tell her there was a heaven and a hell; for there is nothing else but birth and death, and to have a pretty girl and enough to eat, there is nothing but birth and death."[83] The roots of these attitudes can be found as early as the fourteenth century, by which time many Iberian Jewish intellectuals had adopted a hedonistic, world-centered philosophy of life Baer associates with the Aristotelians and particularly with the philosopher Averroes. Central to Averroistic thought is the idea that the soul disappears when the body dies. The Spanish Averroists were, in Baer's view, particularly susceptible to conversion:

> [These Jews] sought to enjoy all the cultural values and treasures of enlightenment, while their ties with the traditions of their own people slackened more and more. Eventually they turned to the Catholic Church which, though its principles, too, were irreconcilable with their religion of the intellect, nevertheless offered them a reasonably coherent system of dogmatics as well as a rich tradition of humanism and secular culture. (1966, 2:148; cf. 2:253–9)

While some of these people accepted Christian dogma in its entirety and even became Christian apologists, many others carried their skepticism into the new religion, not only rejecting the Christian cosmography but expressing a more profound disbelief in any afterlife at all.

Most *conversos* made no effort to define a competing Jewish concept of the afterlife: rejection of Christian concepts was sufficient for defining Jewishness. But from time to time we can hear *conversos* attempting to reconcile the conflicting views of their two religions with regard to life after death. Pedro Mendes believed in a kind of reincarnation whose roots can probably be traced to the Kabbala, saying in 1505 that "when people died their souls entered the bodies of the newborn."[84] Gonçalo Vaez told the Granada Inquisitors in 1571 that "there was no Purgatory nor Hell but rather a sepulcher which the Jews call Hell; and that he would prove it to them with authoritative scriptural citations."[85] In the 1640s Margarita de Rivera confessed to the Mexican Inquisition a peculiar mix of beliefs about the afterlife. She was accused of saying that there was no Hell, but also of affirming that Judaizers who have sexual relations with Christians go there. She also believed in a "temporary punishment for people who were not very good Jews in this life, where they would suffer as oxen, or snakes, or other animals, or as door hinges."[86] Tomás Treviño de Sobremonte, who was accused in Mexico in the 1650s, held a more conventional view of Heaven. He reputedly said that "there was no Purgatory, because everyone who dies goes to one place, which he understood was called the Elysian Fields, and that they remained there until the Messiah came to take them to heaven." He also believed that they stayed in the "bosom of Abraham" until the Messiah came for them.[87]

The little information we have suggests that the eschatological beliefs of modern Portuguese Judaizers are much closer to those of orthodox Christianity in their acceptance of a three-tiered afterlife consisting of Hell, Purgatory, and Heaven. Amílcar Paulo reports that in this century in Pinhel, Portugal, when a crypto-Jew dies the family distributes hot bread, saying "May the soul of our deceased come out of Purgatory as the steam comes out of this bread."[88] Vasconcelos reports that some modern Portuguese new-Christians believe "the souls of those who have done good deeds will go to God, and that those of sinners will go to the dark regions until they expiate their sins, at which point they will rise to God. At the same time they deny belief in Hell, Purgatory, or the Devil" (1958, 173).

## 4.4. FORTUNE

Belief in an omniscient, omnipotent, benevolent God fosters the conviction that what happens to the individual or to the collective is the result of divine intervention in response to behavior (righteousness or wickedness) or petition (prayer). Christianity and Judaism differ in the relative weight given to the behavior of the individual and of the community in influencing the deity's response. Medieval Jews believed that a record of collective righteousness was a prerequisite condition for the coming of the Messiah. Moreover, they believed that Jewish history was a product of God's response to their collective behavior. As we have seen, this is one reason why the centuries of Jewish persecution, debasement, and misfortune took such heavy philosophical toll and why the discouragement of the fourteenth- and fifteenth-century Iberian Jewish communities made them particularly susceptible to conversion.

Some crypto-Jews assigned ancient causes to their current misfortunes. In 1570 the new-Christian Isabel Alvares, of Torre de Moncorvo, was charged by the Coimbra Inquisition with having affirmed that "the persecution that they were now suffering was because the Jews would not wait forty days for Moses to give them the Law, but rather they sinned after twenty days by counting the nights as days; and God was angry with them and made them wander in captivity for this sin until the coming of the Messiah who was promised to them."[89] But most crypto-Jews tended to believe that their current dire straits were a result of Iberian *conversos*' communal tendency toward assimilation.[90] Jewish and *converso* philosophers used this principle in explaining the reasons for the 1391 riots, the disputations, the forced conversions, the establishment of the Inquisition, and the Expulsion. This explanation was particularly prevalent among people who had suffered through the events leading up to the Expulsion, or who had experienced the upheavals of the Expulsion first-hand. The *converso* Gonçalo de Barbas, of Sigüenza, testified in 1501 that he believed that "if misfortune has come to us we deserve it, because we do not observe the ceremonies nor the other things that we are supposed to, and that is why we were sent into exile."[91] In 1589 in Mexico Luis de Carvajal was accused of telling his friends that "because they did not keep the Law of Moses nothing good happened to them; in this world they did not have riches nor temporal goods, nor in the next world would they have glory."[92]

Crypto-Jewish beliefs with regard to fortune were of two sorts. On the one hand, as we have seen, crypto-Jews perceived their communal status as the result of God's acting justly with respect to their communal behavior. Most crypto-Jews also tended to adopt a more personal view of fortune, which is to say, their relationship with an interventionist deity. For these people strict adherence to Jewish practice was a means of ensuring their individual good fortune. In a variant of the traditional anti-Semitic stereotype of Jewish prosperity many *conversos* believed that their personal wealth sprang from divine favor secured by their mode of worship. Leonor Alvarez's defense in 1512 for refusing to sell a fish on the Sabbath was that "by behaving in that fashion God had brought them and was bringing them much fortune, and they had gained much wealth and they had married off two daughters and given each one a hundred thousand *marevidis*; and if they behaved any other way they believed that God would not show them favor."[93] Antonia Cardosa said in Lisbon in 1538 that she heard Isabel Nunes, a *cristãa nova*, say that "people who lived in the Law of Moses would never lack for anything."[94] This belief that their religion would act as a kind of talisman persisted among latter generations of *conversos* as well. In 1582 in Granada Joan Sánchez, from Antequera, told Inquisitors "that he was proud of being a descendant of Jews because he saw that they were rich and he wanted to be rich too, and for this reason he was proud of being a *confeso*."[95] Similarly, Elvira de Santo Fimia told Inquisitors in Granada in 1592 that she observed Jewish fasts only because Marina de Mercado had told her that doing so would make her rich.[96] In 1647 fifteen-year-old Simón de Valencia reported to the Mexican Inquisition that his father had told him that the Law of Moses was good and that "God had given them money for following it."[97]

## 4.5. JEWISH SAINTS[98]

A further example of syncretism was the late adoption by crypto-Jewish communities of a set of "Jewish saints" similar to Christian saints in their ability to work miracles and intercede with the deity. Moses figured large in this slate, as did Esther: their popularity derived from the fact that they each were seen as the savior of the Jewish people from alien religious oppression. Looking at the examples chronologically we can easily perceive the increasing Christianization of the concept. For most early *conversos* Moses, for example, was the traditional Jewish Biblical hero. Alvaro Gonçalez of the Canary Islands was accused in 1525 of saying that "Moses was buried on Mount Sinai, but that no one has ever approached his tomb, as whenever anyone attempts to do so it is removed to another spot" (Wolf 1926, 43). By 1571 the new-Christian João Mendes, of Trancoso, was charged by the Coimbra Inquisition of attributing Christ's miracle of the loaves and fishes to Moses.[99] In 1593 Marina de Mercado, of Granada, reputedly declared that Moses was a kind of semi-deity who had the power to intercede with God, for she had said that "God through Moses had opened up twelve paths through the Red Sea and that Moses could help her [Catalina de Rojas] a great deal ... and that Moses would save her and she should believe in him."[100] A generation later in Mexico Ana Núñez said she had been taught that Moses was the only God (García 1910,

199), and María de Zárate was accused of having lit candles before a painted image of Moses and some other images which are described in her trial in great detail.[101] By that time the syncretism of the Jewish Moses with a Catholic-like saint was complete: Gaspar Váez Sevilla told the Mexican Inquisition around 1646 that "when his mother [Juana Enríquez] was pregnant with him she hoped that she would give birth to the Messiah, and she prayed the nine stations to a Saint Moses which a certain Catholic woman had painted on leather."[102] Yet even this total equation of Moses with Jesus is occasionally seen among fifteenth-century *conversos*, such as the unnamed woman who in 1487 in Aranda de Duero was accused because "when the host was elevated she said: 'Lord Moses, it is You I worship!' "[103]

As the previous examples indicate, sometimes Judaizers kept statues or pictures of these saints in their homes. Branca Dias was accused in Bahia in the 1590s of "having some little saints which she worshipped; they had horns like cows and were not like the saints in church."[104] An indictment of *chueta* customs [Majorca 1674] notes how the crypto-Jews avoided Catholic images and instead kept in their homes pictures of Old Testament saints such as Moses, Joshua, Aaron, Abraham, Elijah, Joseph, and others.[105] As time went on the variety and number of crypto-Jewish "saints" increased. Fray Gaspar de Carvajal testified in Mexico in 1589 that the *converso* Baltazar Rodríguez had spoken to him "of various saints of the Old Testament, such as Tobit and many other prophets, Isaiah, Job, and others." He added that "his sister, Doña Mariana, had told him the story of one of the Old Testament saints, but he did not remember whether it was Tobit or Judith."[106] Luis de Carvajal, Gaspar's brother, in his trials spoke of Saints Moses, Susanna, Abraham, Job, and Jeremiah.[107] Among many modern Portuguese crypto-Jews, Saints Raphael, Tobit, and the Guardian Angel are also popular.[108] According to Paulo, Portuguese new-Christians in Belmonte venerate *Santo Moisésinho* and *Santa Rainha Ester*. They often keep pictures of the two in their homes. Sometimes they also have a picture of the Christian Holy Guardian Angel, *o Anjo da Guarda* (1970, 80–1).

## 4.6. THE RELIGIONS COMPARED

The conversionist atmosphere that pervaded Spain prior to the Expulsion invited Jews and *conversos* to compare every aspect of Judaism and Catholicism.[109] Whether in formal disputations such as those in Tortosa in 1413–14, or in the anti-Jewish sermons preached on street corners from the end of the fourteenth century, or in the interfamilial debates that must have surrounded each individual's decision to convert, the question of which religion was better, or true, was of constant concern. After the Expulsion the question remained with perhaps even greater intensity in the context of the temptations of assimilation. The debate over the relative merits and even the compatibility of the two traditions was an inescapable part of daily life, as Judaizing new-Christians attended church and kept the Sabbath, and baptized their children and fasted on Yom Kippur, and struggled on a daily basis with contrasting faiths and practices. That any new-Christians at all committed themselves to fulfill the obligations imposed by their crypto-Judaism is remarkable. To do so, and to keep their sanity, the Iberian *conversos* who continued to Judaize generally adopted one of three attitudes with regard to the relationship between the two religions: (1) that their strong belief in the superiority of Judaism somehow mitigated their continuing Christian practices; (2) that, while God prefers Judaism, He does not care all that much exactly how He is worshipped; (3) or that, since both Judaism and Christianity are valid approaches to God, a mixture of the two is entirely acceptable. These approaches contrasted with the majority of society's exclusivist views. *Conversos* who believed with most Jews that Judaism alone was valid and required exclusive commitment tended either to emigrate or to accept martyrdom. And *conversos* who believed with most Christians in the exclusive truth of Christianity assimilated as fast as they were able.

It is not surprising, then, that those *conversos* who persevered in their adherence to Judaism considered Judaism to be the better of the two religions, and that affirmation of this belief became an important part of their religious identity. In its most basic form, this was a simple assertion, such as that of Alfonso de Toledo, a Jeronymite monk from Sisla, who in 1487 was accused of affirming that Judaism and the Law of Moses was superior to Christianity,[110] or that of Simão Fernandes [Lisbon 1583], who allegedly claimed that the new-Christian Law was better than the old-Christian Law,[111] thus implying that new-Christians were synonymous with Jews. But *converso* belief in the innate superiority of Judaism manifested itself in a variety of other ways. First generation converts, particularly those of the Expulsion generation, tried to find psychologically acceptable ways of justifying their actions to themselves. One was to affirm that God would soon cause Christianity to pass and thus it was licit to wait out the impending restoration of Judaism. These were the views of Juan de la Sierra [Ciudad Real 1484], who was accused of saying "that the Law of Moses was good and true, and that the Law of the Christians was a joke and could not last long, and he proved it with many Scriptures from the Prophets and many books which he had and with the Bible."[112] Even after hundreds of years of evidence to the contrary, some crypto-Jews continued to believe in the imminent collapse of Christianity. Juan Méndez de Villaviciosa reputedly told the Mexican Inquisition around 1647 that once he had told his Judaizing friends that "soon everyone would keep the Law of Moses, and all who did would dress in red clothes. This made everyone very happy, and they celebrated with a banquet."[113]

Prior to the Expulsion, Judaizing new-Christians frequently expressed their true feelings by showing a deep respect for those who had remained Jews. In 1490 Juan Ramírez, a *converso* of Soria, was accused of saying to a Jew who was walking by, "You go first, for you are worth more than I, for you are going to say *Kaddish* in the synagogue."[114] In 1494 the wife of Juan García expressed the same sentiment when she reported that "her father had said that the Jews would witness many persecutions, but that whoever remained a Jew would be blessed; and he himself died a Jew. And she believed it too."[115] Others gave voice, often bitterly, to the folly of their decision to convert. In 1501 in Aranda Juan Martínez del Abad reported that one day when he and Alonso Lopes were stitching shoes Martínez said that because Lopes "did not bring his wife back they are not Christians, because they were converted by force." Lopes replied: "I swear to God that you speak true, for we used to have a good Law."[116] Even some crypto-Jews who had been born as *conversos* continued to recall the time when their families—and themselves by extension—had been Jews. In 1573 testimony was given in Granada how the *conversa* Catalina of Santacruz, when she was being verbally mistreated and punched by her old-Christian neighbors when they were together at the village oven, "ran crying down the street; and when someone asked her why she was crying she replied: 'I would be better off if I had remained in the Jewish Law rather than turn Christian.' "[117] Other *conversos* disparaged the motives of Jews who followed them on the path to conversion. Once around 1491, for example, the *converso* Fernando de Madrid was talking with friends when they heard the news that a particular Jewish woman had become Christian. Madrid reputedly cried, "That slutty whore, how could she become Christian in times like these. I wish to God I could change my [current] Law for hers."[118]

Many later Judaizers took advantage of every opportunity to compare Judaism favorably with Christianity. Alvaro González [Canary Islands 1520s] said that "God had made more miracles for Moses and for the Jews than he had made for the Christians."[119] In 1527 Antonio Ferrandes, of Maqueda, was said to have shown similar disrespect for Catholicism in a conversation with Santos García when he claimed that he had Santos's debt written in his account book. "Your book is the Evangels," Santos answered. Antonio replied: "My book is truer than the Gospels."[120] In 1572 Antónia Vaz, of Matosinhos, told the Coimbra Inquisition that "new-Christians lived under a better Law than old-Christians."[121] When their passions were excited some *conversos* seem to have thrown caution to the wind in comparing the two religions. It is difficult to imagine what might have moved Gracia de Gabiría [Logroño 1570] to

> publicly brag that she came from the caste of Jews; to praise the Jews and their Law; to say that *judío* meant "just"; and that Jews were better than Christians; and that they would come into power and would be greatly feared; and that the greatest honor one could bestow on her was to call her and her children Jews; and that her Law was better than that of the Christians; and that because she was a Jew God gave her greater wealth than the Christians; and that buying from Christians at three and selling at seven was no sin.[122]

Occasionally the comparison was on racial grounds that with undoubtedly unintentional irony mirrored the old-Christians' purity-of-blood statutes. For example, according to a 1492 trial Diego de Madrid, of Garcimuñoz, was alleged to have said in 1485 "that the blood of the Jews was clean and good, and that the Jews had royal blood . . . and because the Jews had such pure blood God had chosen Our Lady for the Incarnation."[123] Often an arrogance derived from certainty of belief comes through in these statements. In Mexico in 1624 Tomás Treviño de Sobremonte declared to the Inquisition that "the true Law was that which God had given Moses in the desert, and that God was not playing a child's game in which he would first give one Law and then another."[124] In 1656 in Mexico Fernando de Medina explained to his jailers that he wore a white shirt over his prison clothes to show that Judaism was the better and cleaner law (Wiznitzer 1962a, 259). Even among the later *conversos* who had all but given up their Jewish practices one can often perceive an emotional attachment to the superiority of Judaism. For example the Portuguese-Peruvian *converso* Garci Méndez de Dueñas [Lima 1623] was accused of Judaizing, but of Judaizing badly because he didn't keep either religion very well. "The truth is that although in his heart he considered the law of Moses to be good, and that of the Christians to be bad, he had not scrupulously observed the ceremonies of the Law of Moses, nor had he done the things [required by] the evangelical law, because he had considered it wrong."[125] Even today this attitude can be found among some of the remnant crypto-Jews. With an irony that she surely did not intend or even perceive, in 1980 Beatriz da Purificação Prada, of Carção, Portugal, gave Manuel da Costa Fontes some *presunto* (cured ham) and "gleefully declared that anything made by the hands of a Jewess was better and cleaner than something prepared by a Christian" (Fontes 1993, 75).

Other Judaizers seem to have taken a perverse kind of pleasure and pride in the solidarity of the persecuted. Around 1570 a *cristãa nova* beggar in Lisbon said that "her Law of Moses was better than that of the old-Christians . . . because those raised in it do not have to go begging from door to door like other poor unfortunates; rather they gave her food to eat and no one of her generation [meaning new-Christian] would ever die of hunger."[126] Gaspar Dias [Bahia 1590s] evidently responded to a taunt that he was a *cristão novo* by saying that "he considered it the greatest honor to be a new-Christian and he was publicly proud of being a new-Christian."[127] Similarly, Manuel de Sosa y Prado [Mexico 1964] allegedly claimed that "the most honored people and the best people in the world were the Jews." Another time when someone said they would rather be a thief than a Jew, Sosa allegedly replied that "he would rather be a Jew than a thief."[128]

Another sector of the crypto-Jewish community reacted to their unmerciful buffeting in the fifteenth-century war of creeds by asserting that religious truth transcended the form that any particular religion might give it. That is to say, God is God, and it does not matter overmuch how He is worshipped. Thus it is not uncommon to find crypto-Jews around the time of the Expulsion claiming that salvation was possible under any law provided one behaved righteously. Or that there were no significant differences among Judaism, Christianity, and Islam. In the

Jeronymite monastery of Guadalupe in 1485 the *converso* Friar Fernando de Briuiesca was accused of saying that "a man could be saved in all three Laws."[129] Similarly, the *converso* Juan de Sayas [Calatayud 1489] allegedly remarked that "I am going to commend my soul to all three Laws, and whichever has the best claim to it can have it."[130] His neighbor Simón de Santa Clara was denounced for having said that "neither the Law of the Christians, nor that of the Jews, nor that of the Moors can know the truth; for my part I say that I believe that there is nothing except birth and death." He also allegedly remarked that "I have a God made of wood; I have kept the holy Law of Moses, I have kept the Law of Jesus Christ, and if right now Saint Mohammed should come out, by God!, I would keep all three; and if it were all to end tomorrow I would not fear God because I had walked in all three Laws."[131] Gregorio Laínez [Almazán 1500] confessed that "sometimes he thought and said to himself . . . who really knows which was the best Law, this Law of ours or that of the Jews or the Moors?"[132] The *converso* cloth shearer Gonzalo de Torrijos [Toledo 1538] once casually remarked that "God did exist and the Moors were right when they said they could be saved within their law as well as the Christians in theirs."[133]

Some *conversos* held that, although Christianity was perfectly fine, to take it up they had abandoned a Law that was equally good or perhaps even better. Juan de Garças was heard to have remarked in 1496 or 1497 that God favored those who turned Christian, and Lope García replied, "I don't know; we used to have a good Law and I believe we have as good a one now. Up until now we have worn three capes and now we wear four."[134] In similar fashion a woman named Graçia [Sigüenza 1501] allegedly remarked that "the Law we have now is good, but the Law we used to have was also good and we were perfectly fine then."[135]

Some *conversos* even believed it was possible to practice both religions simultaneously. For some *conversos* of the Expulsion generation, if one was good, two was better. Thus when Mencía Rodríguez de Medina's [Guadalajara 1492–3] "son was sick she visited all the churches in town barefoot and said lots of masses and donated some oil for the synagogue lamps." She also used to go to the synagogue where she "knelt before the Torahs and worshipped them and said prayers to them, believing that they would ensure her salvation."[136] Although this type of syncretism was soundly condemned by Catholic theologians,[137] it was increasingly common among the later generations of crypto-Jews, whose Jewish identity was likely to be little more than a vague self-concept, a reminiscence of Jewish background, an emotional tie to "Jewishness," and a mild antipathy to many Christian beliefs and practices. Under those conditions, a person born and bred a Catholic saw no contradiction in continuing to self-identify in some way as a Jew. Among *conversos* of the Expulsion generation this feeling often expressed itself as an ambivalence or vacillation, rather than as true religious syncretism. Joan Livinyana, of Orihuela [Valencia 1500], said that "he was not firm in one faith or the other."[138] Pedro de Ripoll, of Albarracín, wavered in his belief and practice. For a while in the 1470s he observed the Sabbath and festivals and kept the dietary laws, but he also attended mass, confessed to a priest, and worked on Saturday. He dealt socially with Jews yet criticized his wife for the same thing. When the Inquisition came in the 1480s he began to eat pork for the first time and began to quarrel with his wife about her continued adherence to the old customs. He would not eat the *matza* she bought from the Jewish baker. After a life of continuous stress between the two religions and a sporadic adherence to crypto-Judaism, Ripoll was burned in 1522 (Haliczer 1990, 215). In later generations it was likely to be the children— exposed to crypto-Judaism only after their childhood Catholicism had already taken root—who vacillated. In the accusations by the Coimbra Inquisition in 1568 against Branca de Azevedo, whose age is not given, we can sense genuine confusion about whether she was Jewish, or Christian, or both.

> She believed in the Law of Moses, hoping to be saved in it, and waiting for the Messiah, believing that he was still to come, and that the only ceremony she observed was to fast. . . . She talked about this belief in the Law of Moses with some other people and they all told her that Law was good, and she could be saved in it; but she, Branca d'Azevedo, didn't know what the Law was . . . nor what the Jews believed in. And when she was asked if at that time she ceased believing in Our Lord Jesus Christ, she said that she always believed him to be God and that she never separated herself from His Holy Faith.[139]

Branca de Azevedo is a good example of the hybrid *converso* who—in Gilman's words—"tended to waver between the two laws, keeping portions of each, and ending by losing the comfort that unthinking conformity to either might have given them" (1972, 190).

But there are also many examples of new-Christians who seem to have believed that some fusion of the two religions was viable. The *converso* Pedro Besant [Valencia 1486], unlike his sister Brianda Besant, who considered herself wholly Jewish and acted as a leader of the crypto-Jewish community in Teruel, professed to believe in both religions. He told Inquisitors that he had learned Christian prayers but continued to discuss Judaism with his friends. He said that every morning he prayed the Our Father and recited the articles of faith and then washed his hands and recited his Jewish prayers (Haliczer 1990, 214). Similarly, thirty-four-year-old Manuel Rodrigues, of Linhares [Coimbra 1573], allegedly claimed to believe in the two religions simultaneously: "He said that during that time he neither believed those things nor ceased to believe them, because when he was in church the Christian things seemed right to him, and when he went outside he returned to blindness."[140]

By the third and fourth generation of converts this view became well entrenched. Catalina de Rojas and her sisters were accused in Granada in the 1590s of saying that she practiced both religions: "that Moses could help her a lot, and that because of the reckoning she had to give to God she never drew away from

Jesus Christ nor from His mother nor did she cease hearing mass on festival days." Leonor de Rojas added "that even though she did those things [Judaized], she understood that it was not contrary to the Holy Catholic Faith, and that you could observe both of them." Juana de Rojas said that she observed Jewish customs in order to be saved, but that "when they taught them to her she did not believe that they were incompatible with the Law and faith of Jesus Christ."[141] In the same way Dr. Periáñez de Mesa, a seventy-year-old lawyer from Ecija, confessed in Córdoba in 1591 that "some female relatives of his had taught him the Law of Moses and that he had observed it together with that of Jesus Christ Our Lord."[142] Doña María Alvarez [Granada 1595] gave Inquisitors good theological reasons why she abstained from eating certain foods. She said that "they had been prohibited by the Law that God gave to the saints of the Old Testament and to the chosen people of Israel before Our Lord Christ was born. And that her mistake was to have observed the customs of that Law, thinking that even though Our Lord Jesus Christ had come, that it had not ceased to be valid, but could still be observed. And that is why she had not confessed it." She swore that "she had always been wholly adherent to the faith of Jesus Christ even though she did the things she said under the misunderstanding which she had had."[143] And in Mexico in the 1650s María de Zárate was accused of having said that "God the Father did not get angry at people who served God the Son, nor did God the Son get angry at people who served God the Father; and that therefore in cases of doubt the safest thing was to serve the Father, without ever mentioning the Holy Spirit."[144]

For many *conversos*, coupled with the abiding faith in the superiority of Judaism was the conviction that no matter how terrible the forces arrayed against it, Judaism would survive. The *cristão novo* Manoel Peixoto [Lisbon 1556] expressed this clearly when he said that "no matter what evil they work on us we will always go forward and multiply; and although they tried many times to destroy us, and even though now they are together and even more numerous than they were, the more they burn them the more they [i.e., the new-Christians] will have the superior hand at the end because their Law is better, and blessed are those who can suffer and not turn back and die in [that Law] because then they will go directly to Moses who is in heaven and because Moses sees that their faith is firm they multiply more every day."[145]

We must never forget that syntheses of beliefs or practices, like the ones summarized in this chapter, only give us a sense of the breadth and depth of new-Christian practices in the aggregate. Each individual crypto-Jew was idiosyncratic in his or her belief. Each individual's set of beliefs was perforce a product of his or her family background and childhood training, the prevailing ethos of the community, and the other individual crypto-Jews who may have served as models. Only the study of an individual case can provide a compilation of what a given individual believed and did. Frequently the prosecutor's summary indictment of an accused individual gives such a list. In rare cases the Judaizing *conversos* themselves provided the summary information. A good example is Juan de Buitrago, a Spanish

Jew who in 1492 went to Portugal before he converted and returned in 1495 to Valladolid, moving later to Segovia and eventually to Ayllón. At age eighty he presented a list of his beliefs to the Inquisition:

- Don't work on Saturday, because the Old Law so commands.
- God did not order vigils. He commanded three things: clothe the naked, feed the hungry, give water to the thirsty.
- God did not order the mass nor anything like it.
- Circumcision is not a sin: Christ himself was circumcised.
- Saint Jerome had translated those passages of the old Testament that favored Christians, leaving out those which were prejudicial. (Blázquez Miguel 1986a, 152)

## Notes

1. Tobit, a brave Jew exiled to Assyria by King Shalmaneser, and the angel Raphael figure prominently in the Book of Tobit, one of the apocryphal books included in the Vulgate. Even though Tobit is not included in the Jewish versions of the Bible, the story was popular among medieval Jews.

2. The Portuguese Judaizer Diego Juárez de Figueroa reputedly said to Mexican Inquisitors in the 1640s that "Jews keep six hundred and seventy two laws" (*Que los preceptos que guardan los judíos son seiscientos y sesenta y dos*) (García 1910, 101). Some seventeenth-century crypto-Jewish thinkers tried to reconcile the importance of observance with the fact that most of their contemporaries had largely abandoned Jewish practice. Antonio Homem, the *converso* Professor of Canon Law at the University of Coimbra, was said to have preached in a Yom Kippur sermon in 1615 that "while living in persecution it was sufficient to have in mind the intention of performing the precepts of the Law" (Roth 1931–2, 5).

3. Deut. 6:4. The persistence of the *Shema* is discussed in Chapter 15 along with other crypto-Jewish prayers.

4. *Siempre ruega al Dios que la guarde de sus enemigos reputando a los xristianos por enemigos y ydólatras, creyentes en tres dioses y no en uno solo* (Llorca 1942, 134).

5. *Que hay un Dios Todopoderoso y niegan la pluralidad . . . de la Santisima Trinidad* (García Fuentes 1981, 434).

6. *Su madre le había dicho que había de creer en un solo Dios que hizo el cielo y la tierra y en otro no* (Gracia Boix 1983, 137). See also Monsalvo Antón 1989, 121 [Osma 1491]; Baião 1921, 105 [Portugal 1537].

7. *Los cristianos eran ciegos y se habían de ir al infierno porque no creían en un solo Dios* (Gracia Boix 1983, 139).

8. *No había creído más que en un solo Dios y que no había tenido por Dios a Jesucristo Nuestro Señor* (Gracia Boix 1983, 330). For a similar statement from Brazil see Furtado 1929, 370 [1594].

9. *Solo altissimo domino Deo Israel debetur omnis honor et gloria quia ipse est Deus super omnes Deos, et dominus super omnes dominos, benedictum, laudatum et super exaltatum sit solum nomen Sanctu eius ex hoc nunc et usque in Saeculum et in Saeculum Saeculi* (Caro Baroja 1961, 1:405–6). See also Yerushalmi 1971, 36.

10. Böhm 1963, 40. Maldonado's case is also discussed in Medina 1890, 174.

11. *No se puede adorar sino a un solo Dios, que es cosa tan clara, como dijo el Deuteronomio, que a un solo Dios se deve adoración y a sus imágenes no se la dé, y es tan claro que de Dios no puede haver copia porque es un ser inifinito y no ay quien le pueda haver visto su cara* (Selke de Sánchez 1972, 247).

12. *No había más que un Dios verdadero, . . . y que las oraciones que rezase las enderezase a sólo Dios y no a Jesucristo, ni a su madre* (Toro 1932, 216).

13. Ana Núñez, reconciled in a Mexican *auto* in 1648, said that her father had taught her that "there was no God but Moses" (*No había más Dios que Moisén*) (García 1910, 199).

14. (1970, 55–6). See Chapter 15, which deals with prayer.

15. This need to differentiate Jewish and Christian concepts of God is reflected by the seventeenth-century renowned Latinist etymologist Sebastián de Covarrubias, who says with regard to the term *Dios* that Christians "to show the power of a thing and to magnify it, even though it is singular we put it in the plural" (*Para mostrar la fuerça de una cosa y para engrandecerla, siendo una, la ponemos en número plural*) (Covarrubias 1611, 474).

16. *Mirad quanto hizo el Dio / por vuestra gente maldita* (Castillo 1982, 2:236).

17. *Para el Dió no será* (Carrete/Fraile 1987, 34; see also 98, 112; Carrete Parrondo 1985, 63, 86, 153).

18. Vicente (1984, 2:439); studied by Teyssier 1959, 217–9.

19. *Non creya que era venido el Mexías* (Llorca 1939, 141).

20. García Fuentes 1981, 98. For a few of the hundreds of similar examples see Carrete Parrondo 1980, 253 [Cuenca 1493]; Azevedo Mea 1982, 1, etc. [Coimbra 1570s]; Böhm 1984, 219 [Chile 1584]; Furtado 1929, 77 [Bahia 1593]; Medina 1890, 179 [Chile 1627].

21. For some of the numerous examples see Carrete Parrondo 1980, 253 [Cuenca 1474]; Caro Baroja 1961, 1:406–12; Blázquez Miguel 1986a, 165–74; Wolf 1926, 23 [Canary Islands 1520]; Böhm 1963, 20–1 [Chile 1550s]; Azevedo Mea 1981, 176–7 [Portugal 1584]; Furtado 1929, 143, 417 [Brazil 1593–5]; Liebman 1970, 61 [colonial Mexico]; García 1910, 199 [Mexico 1648].

22. *Que el anno de ochenta e siete no avie de aver justicia en el mundo y el anno de ocho avie de ser corral de vacas y el anno de nueve avie de ser toda una ley. . . . Ha de traer una piedra filosofal, e que sy en una barra de fierro con ella tocare, se tornaria plata, e sy en una de acero, se tornara oro, e en la mar se le mostrarian los tesoros, y que luego que venga, que su fasienda valia cient mill mrs. . . . E los otros dexaria a su muger e a sus fijos e se yria con el donde estubiere* (Cantera Montenegro 1982a, 35). See also Baer 1936, 513–5.

23. *Que o Messias havia ainda de vir e de a tornar moça e começou bailando e dizendo uma cantiga em que se ouvia a palavra "Adonay"* (Baião 1921, 137).

24. *A perseguição que agora tinham era por os judeus nam esperarem por Moises quarenta dias, dentro nos quaes lhes avia de dar a lei e aos vinte peccarem . . . e Deus enojado disso os fazia andar em cativeiro por este pecado até vir o Messias que estava prometido* (Azevedo Mea 1981, 157; see also 1982, 223).

25. *Que ellos esperaban el Messías que había de venir, y que no avía venido hasta tanto que el Pueblo Hebreo ubiesse acavado de hacer penitencia de sus pecados* (Selke de Sánchez 1972, 278).

26. *No podia venir el mexias, fasta que los conversos pagasen, por que se avian tornado christianos* (Cantera Montenegro 1982a, 35).

27. *Los que agora padecian avian de tornar a estar prosperos, lo qual desya por los hereges, e los que agora se gozavan heran como syrpientes, lo qual dezia por los buenos e catolicos christianos . . . que avyan de tornar a prevallescer sobre los otros que ansy se gozavan* (Baer 1936, 476).

28. Earlier disturbances also led to outbreaks of messianism as was the case, for example, in Avila in 1295 (Suárez Fernández 1991, 127), or in Cisneros in 1393 (Silver 1927, 108). For a review of Spanish messianic literature see Carrete Parrondo 1980, 251–3. Even the 1480s anti-*converso* pamphlet *Libro del Alboraique* hypothesizes that the Messiah is coming soon, and that after centuries of ignorance the Jews will convert to *Adonai*, their true God, and to their King the Son of David (López Martínez 1954, 398–400).

29. The traditional medieval rabbinical view was that the Messiah would "defeat the enemies of Israel, restore the people to the land, reconcile them with God, and introduce a period of spiritual and physical bliss. He was to be prophet, warrior, judge, king, and teacher of Torah" (*Enc. Jud.* 11:1411). For a detailed analysis of the debates over the nature of the Messiah at the Disputation of Tortosa, and the speculations about the coming of the Messiah around the time of the Expulsion see Baer 1966, 2:174–210, 424–31.

30. The bibliography on false Messiahs in Spain and Portugal and among the Jewish communities of the Sephardic diaspora is copious. Among the more important works are Azevedo 1955; Klausner 1955; Silver 1927; Edwards 1984b. See also Baer 1966, 2:352–8; Baron 1969, 13:328–9.

31. *Venir de linaje de judíos, donde no cree el adveniminento pasado del Mexía, antes cree questá por venir* (Carrete Parrondo 1980, 255–6).

32. *Mostra a certes persones hun salm comprenien totes les tribulacions dels conversos en que estaven dientli com Deu hauria a venir sobre ells y trametre lo seu mesies* (García Cárcel 1985, 205).

33. *Los avia de llevar a la tierra de promysyon, donde avian de comer en platos de oro, e que despues de ydos los conversos a la tierra de promysyon, non avia de llover syete annos* (Baer 1936, 528).

34. *Hera muerto el pez leviatan e que en seyendo muerto aquel pez avian de salir los conversos del cativerio* (Baer 1936, 530).

35. *Não tardaria hum anno que não viesse* (Azevedo Mea 1982, 434).

36. *Avia de vir tempo em que os judeus avião de ir a terra da promissão, ella, Re, creo e teve pera si e desejou chegar a este tempo pera ir la com elles* (Azevedo Mea 1982, 439).

37. *Avia de vir hum dia bendicho, em que os christãos velhos avião de ser mulas dos christãos novos, pera se irem pera huma certa terra, esperando pollo Mesyas* (Azevedo Mea 1982, 451). A poetic expression of these sentiments, recited to the Lisbon Inquisition in 1582, has been translated into English by Lazar 1991, 187–8.

38. *Era de aquellos dos tribus de Hisrrael que estaban guardados en el paraiso terrenal aguardando la fin del mundo, que vendria presto para que Dios los juntase y los hiciese mayor cantidad que a sus pasados* (Böhm 1984, 284). See also García de Proodian 1966, 345.

39. *Deus tinha guardado aos judeus o bem que lhes avia de dar e que vindo o Messias os avia de transplantar em outra terra milhor, lhes avia de dar mui bem de comer sem trabalharem, que asi o soya Deus de fazer antes da vinda de Christo* (Azevedo Mea 1981, 157; see also 1982, 223).

40. *Quando viniese avia de libertar los judios* (García Fuentes 1981, 98).

41. *O Messias ainda havia de vir e havia de trazer as doze tribus de Israel* (Baião 1921, 195).

42. See N38, García de Proodian 1966, 345.

43. Que avía tribú y medio que andaban esparçidos y perdidos por el mundo, y que avían de venir Moysén y Arón a sacarlos de captiverio (Selke de Sánchez 1972, 278).

44. E dixo mas que el que non quisiere creer en el dicho ante cristo que cada dia le cortarian un mienbro, fasta que le creyesen e dexasen de creer a jesu Christo (Cantera Montenegro 1982a, 35). See also Baer 1936, 513–5.

45. Había oído decir de unas cartas que decían que había nacido un niño y entendía que no era de la Santa Madre Iglesia, sino de la ley de Moisés y deseaba que llegase el tiempo de la venida del niño. . . . Y que el niño que había de venir, entendía que era el anticristo (Gracia Boix 1983, 141–2). See also Cantera Montenegro 1982a, 35.

46. Helias avia de venir a sacarlos del captiuerio en que estauan et lleuarlos a las tierras de promisión (Gracia Boix 1982, 48).

47. En el dicho camino de las tierra de promisión, avian de hallar vn Rio de leche y otro rio de agua, e que en el vno dellos, se avian de bañar todos los confesos viejos e moços, e que todos los que asy en el dicho Río se bañasen, asy los viejos como los moços, se avian de tornar cada vno de edad de veynte et çinco años, e que al tienpo quel dicho Elias viniese a los sacar destas tierras para los leuar a las dichas tierras de promisyon, que avia de tenblar la tierra, et que el sol e la Luna, se avian de morir, et que los çielos se avian de abrir, et que la Mar, se avia de tornar sangre, e que los arboles se avian se secar, et que avia de venir muy grande tenpestad de piedra, et que se avian de caler las casas e haserse todo llano, et que auia de venir un Rio muy grande y avia de leuar todos los bienes, haziendas y riquezas que acá dexasen los conversos, por que no gozasen dellos los Xriptianos viejos, e que todos los dichos terremotos et tenpestades, auia de haser Elias, por que creyesen en el todos los conversos, e viesen las marauillas que hazia et por que se arrepentiesen de la creençia que auian tenido o mostrado a los xriptianos, et que pasados los dichos terremotos, auia de venir el dicho elias en figura de Angel, et que les avia de preguntar a todos los conversos que es lo que creyan, e que sy creyan bien en la ley de los Judios, e que sy la ley de los Xriptianos avian tenido et creydo, que el les absolueria por que tornasen a creer la ley de los Judios, e que sy en aquella non creyesen, non podian pasar a las tierras de promisión, e que les auia de preguntar que orazionas sabian de la ley de los Judios e de que manera las dezian, para saber dellos, sy estauan bien en la dicha creençia de la dicha ley de los Judios, et que luego, a los que creyesen bien en la dicha ley de los Judios, et estouiesen firmes en ella los auia de haser desnudar a todos, las ropas que tenian, e les avia de haser vestir camisas blancas amogiladas, syn tener en ellas otro color, saluo todo blanco, e vnos calçones blancos calçados, e sendas candelas en las manos, ençendidas, et que los avia de sacar por las çibdades e villas et logares donde estouiesen los conversos, todos en proçesión a vista de todo el mundo, et que en mitad de las çibdades, villas et logares, auia de predicar de tal manera, que convirtiese a todos los Xriptianos viejos, que toviesen e creyesen la ley de los Judios, et que luego, el dicho Elias, auia de leuar consigo a todos los conversos a las tierras de promision, et que en medio del camino, estaua vna cueva de donde avian de salir todos los moços conversos que estauan en las dichas tierras de promision, et que estos moços confesos, que de la dicha cueva saliesen, se avian de casar con las moças confesas que de acá fuesen por casar, e que en el camino, quando fuesen a las dichas tierras de promision, que non auian de comer otra cosa syno pan çençeño et otro pan que no auia de tener levadura, syno, fecho de vna harina que llaman coscoja (Gracia Boix 1982, 48–9).

48. Avia de paresçer vn onbre en la luna, e despues se avia de morir el sol e la luna, e que avia de durar tres dias con sus noches grande escuridad. . . . Tres Rios, vno de leche y otro de miel, e otro de sangre. . . . En aquellos Rios avian de quedar todos sus males, et que el que no creyese la dicha ley de Moysen, que avia de quedar alli. . . . Allá en las dichas tierras de promisión, avian de casar primos con primos, et que . . . les estauan aparejados muchos bienes et requezas. . . . Por que

*mas presto se cunpliese lo que deseauan, que ayunasen todos ayunos de Judios* (Gracia Boix 1982, 56, 58, 47–48).

49. *Para que queria dineros, que aora avia de venir Helias e avia de lleuar los conversos a las tierras de promision. . . . Aveys oydo eso que dizen por la çibdad? . . . Que no es venido el Mexias, y que esperan a Elias* (Gracia Boix 1982, 123, 129).

50. *Dios enviaría al Mesias para ayudar al pueblo de Israel. . . . Su padre también le decía que antes de que viniese el Mesías a quien aguardaban cada día, había de venir Elías, a aparejar los caminos del Mesías* (Toro 1932, 239, 260).

51. Liebman 1974, 193. For additional information see Roth 1931–2, 8; Lewin 1987, 240–6.

52. Liebman 1974, 101, 206, 218. See also García 1910, 214.

53. *No había venido el Mesías que había de morir por ellos* (García 1910, 199). Wiznitzer attributes this flurry of messianic speculation to Mexican crypto-Jews' terror of the Inquisition. Yet such intense speculation did not routinely occur in the other places where the Inquisition was severe (1962a, 267).

54. Caro Baroja 1961, 1:407–8; Beinart 1981a, 459–61; Carrete Parrondo 1980; Rábade Obradó 1990a, 210–24.

55. Coelho 1987, 199; Caro Baroja 1961, 1:409.

56. Liebman 1975, 152.

57. For a comprehensive overview of the Sabbatean movement see Scholem 1973.

58. As I was revising these lines the morning newspaper brought a striking example of how thoroughly the pervasive dominant culture can shape the beliefs of the religious minorities who are submerged in it. Elaine Goldbaum wrote to the doctor who helped her commit suicide: "I am Jewish and have been raised to believe that suicide is a *mortal sin*. Dr. Jack Kevorkian, your assistance in medicide *will get me into heaven*" (*Providence Journal-Bulletin*, Feb. 9, 1993, p. B1; emphasis added).

59. *Fue preguntado: que con que yntençion se juntauan a rezar e resauan este confesante e la dicha su hermana las dichas orazioneS. Dixo que con yntençion de saluarse en la Ley de Moysen, teniendo aquella ley por la mejor e pensandose de saluarse en ella* (Beinart 1981b, 42; see also 3:102, 565).

60. *La ley de Muissen era la buena, verdadera, necesaria para su salbacion y no la de Jesus* (AGN Vol 402 doc 2, 500a).

61. *Persistía con toda expresión y claridad en que se podía salvar y se salvaba en la ley de Moisés, y que era buena y que moriría por ella si fuese menester* (Wiznitzer 1962a, 260). For some of the innumerable additional examples of this belief see Roth 1946, 133; Llorca 1935, 16 [1484]; Fita y Colomé 1893, 291 [1485]; Carrete Parrondo 1985, 37, 54 [1490]; Llorca 1942 [1494]; Beinart 1981b, 42, 347, 364 [Ciudad Real 1511]; Cantera Montenegro 1982b, 57 [Laguardia 1515]; Caro Baroja 1961, 1:442 [1527]; Azevedo Mea 1982, 267 [Coimbra 1571]; Bel Bravo 1988, 124 [Granada 1593]; Lewin 1954, 182 [Peru 1611]; 122 [Mexico 1624]; Adler 1899, 12, 70 [Mexico 1645]; Wolf 1926, 245 [Canary Islands 1660]; Selke de Sánchez 1972, 107 [Majorca 1678]; Silva 1896, 9 [Brazil 1726]; Schwarz 1925, 108 [twentieth-century Portugal].

62. *Que dios le diese buen siglo; . . . Que Dios les diese buen siglo a su ley; . . . Que Dios les diese fuelgo, tan buenos heran, los quales murieron judíos* (Carrete/Fraile 1987, 59, 60, 70; cf. 65, 79, 81, 102). *Fuelgo* may be a translation of the Hebrew *ruakh*, which has several related meanings: wind, breath, spirit, soul, ghost.

63. *Dezian que guardar el sabado hera bueno para saluar las animas . . . por guardar los sabados se abian de saluar* (Beinart 1977a, 294, 296).

64. *Como que su alma con la de Mose Rabenu* (Beinart 1975, 656).

65. *Vn judío, fijo de vna judía rica, yva e venía a paraíso, e que vn ángel le mostró el paraíso e el ynfierno; e que se quería quedar en paraíso, e Dios le mandaua sacar de allí, e que le desya: "Sal de aquí, amigo de Dios," y él no quería. E que Dios le mandó que saliese; e quél dixo que no quería, que El avía dicho que el que su casa viese no podía ser perdido. E que así se quedó en el paraíso. E que aquel judío venía a llamar a los que se avían de morir. E que así yba y venía* (Carrete Parrondo 1985, 129). Carrete Parrondo has not located the story in the rabbinical literature.

66. Marín Padilla 1983b, 338. See also Furtado 1929, 352 [Brazil 1594]; Liebman 1975, 101 [Mexico 1602]. It follows that new-Christians were equally skeptical about Limbo (Furtado 1929, 93 [Bahia 1593]).

67. *¿No sabes que este mundo todo es ayre sino nacer y morir y que el anima de hun perro entra en el cuerpo de hun hombre y la del hombre en el cuerpo de hun perro?* (Marín Padilla 1983b, 306; cf. 341).

68. *En este mundo es la gloria y la honrra, que en el otro no hay infierno ni paraíso. Que Dios no es más que un árbol, que el verano face las hojas, el invierno las lanza y se caen. Así es Dios facer y desfacer gentes* (Marín Padilla 1983b, 338–9).

69. *Le oyo desir que la anima del onbre no era sino como la de vn cabrito e de vna gallina quando la degollauan e, despues de muerta, ¿a dónde fallarán las animas?, que no avia otra cosa sino comer e beber e el plaser que ombre tomara, e no avia otra cosa sino naçer e morir* (Moreno Koch 1977, 356).

70. *No avía otra cosa sino morir e naçer, que el día que nacía era mundo para él, e que el día que moría era fin* (Carrete Parrondo 1985, 137; cf. 46, 51, 123).

71. *Não sabia o que era a alma porque a não via* (Baião 1921, 142).

72. *Que el anima no hera mas que un huelgo* (García Fuentes 1981, 274). See the reference to Graciana Laínez earlier in this chapter.

73. *En ora mala vino el negro mal . . . syno por estas ánimas que disen que saluamos* (Carrete/Fraile 1987, 24).

74. *Nunca vi cosa más demasiada que gastar dineros en estas misas, porque los fynados no tienen neçesidad dello, que avnque estén en penas de purgatorio por eso no salen más presto que han de salir, porque quando el onbre muere ya sabe Dios los benefiçios que han de salir* (Carrete Parrondo 1985, 67).

75. *Anda, cura de vuestra ánima, que no ay Dios ny Santa María ny Christo ninguno, que todo es burla. . . . Que los çielos e la tierra fechos se estavan; e que non avían seydo fechos por mano de dios, que se andavan por su curso* (Monsalvo Antón 1984, 120).

76. *Descreo de Dios e de siete pares de ángeles, los más cercanos dél* (Carrete Parrondo 1985, 52). The angels may be a reference to Revelation 8:2.

77. *En este mundo non me veáys malpasar, que en el otro no me verás malpasar o malandar, lo vno désto* (Carrete/Fraile 1987, 69 [Almazan 1501]; cf. 23, 33, 207, 123). For other examples see Carrete/Fraile 1987, 107, 123; Marín Padilla 1983b, 337 [1481, 1491]; Carrete Parrondo 1985, 40, 94 [1490]; Baião 1921, 121 [1541]; Furtado 1929, 440 [1595]. This saying was current among some old-Christians as well, as in the case of Juan de Morales Abarve, laborer of Jaen, punished in Córdoba in 1571 for using the saying. Roth interprets the proverb as indicative of Averroism. For additional discussion of this commonplace see Baer

1966, 2:286, 369; Caro Baroja 1961, 1:371; Gilman 1972, 91–2; Shepard 1982, 91–7; and a forthcoming book by Francisco Márquez Villanueva.

78. *No hay más paraíso que el mercado de Calatayud* (Cabezudo Astráin 1950, 282). See Gilman's discussion of the irony in this statement (1972, 85).

79. *Que no creia que habia otro paraiso si non ser rico, nin otro infierno si non ser pobre e haber de demandar a otro* (Sánchez Moya/Monasterio Aspiri 1973, 140). For another example see Carrete Parrondo 1985, 127 [1501].

80. *Hoviese purgatorio ni infierno ni diablos ni penas en el otro mundo, asi como dizen, sino las penas deste mundo* (Marín Padilla 1983b, 336). For other examples see Carrete Parrondo 1985, 140 [1502]; Lewin 1971, 481 [Mexico 1665].

81. *Pregunto el dicho Juan Falcon a este testigo y dixole que que deseos eran los que en este mundo mas deseaba; e respondio este testigo e dixo: Saluaçion para mi anima. El dicho Juan Falcon dixo: Esta saluaçion ¿como es? Dixo este testigo: Querria hazer tales obras que fuese a parayso, y no al purgatorio ni al infierno. Dixo el dicho Falcon: ¡Asy que me des parayso y purgatorio e infierno! Dixo el testigo: ¿Quien dubda en ello? E dixo el dicho Falcon: Yo hos dire que duelo es parayso y purgatorio e infierno: tener mucha riqueza sobrada para dar y que non le falte nada [es paraiso]; y horas tener y horas no tener es purgatorio; pobreza conosçida, este es infierno, y non vos hagan creer que ay otro parayso ni otro purgatorio ni otro infierno* (Beinart 1974, 556; cf. 1977a, 245).

82. *Quánto más que creo, como yo creo, que nace para morir, que no ay otro en este mundo syno nasçer e morir, que después que Dios crió el mundo e cada vno dexó con su dicha, buena o mala, quel que bien tyene de comer e de beuer e lo que ha menester en este mundo, aquél está en el paraiso y el pobre está en el ynfierno; que bien dizen la verdad para el Cuerpo de Dios, que en este mundo no me veas malpasar que en el otro no me verás penar; que ochenta buelcos da onbre en el ynfierno por tener en este mundo lo que ha menester e honra* (Carrete Parrondo 1985, 155).

83. *No os hagan, señora, entender que ay parayso ni ynfierno, que no ay otra cosa syno naser e morir, y tener gentil amiga y bien de comer, que no ay syno naçer e morir* (Carrete Parrondo 1985, 78; cf. 52). See also Ollero Pina 1988, 91 [Seville 1481]; Monsalvo Antón 1984, 122–4 [Osma 1490s].

84. *Morían aquellas ánimas de los muertos entrauan en los cuerpos de los que naçían* (Carrete/Fraile 1987, 97).

85. *No avia purgatorio ni ynfierno sino una sepultura la qual los judios llaman ynfierno y se lo enseñaria provandolo con auctoridades de la escriptura* (García Fuentes 1981, 98).

86. *Alguna pena temporal para los que no fueron tan buenos judíos en esta vida, padeciendo penas, ya en bueyes, ya en culebras, ya en otros animales, ya en quicios de puertas* (García 1910, 69).

87. *No había purgatorio, porque los que morían iban a un campo, que entiende, se llamaba el Campo Elíseo, y que allí estaban hasta que viniese el Mesías para ir al cielo. . . . Iban al seno de Abraham o al Campo Elíseo* (Lewin 1971, 28, 34).

88. *Que a alma deste nosso finado saia do purgatório como o bafo sai deste pão* (1985, 28).

89. See note 24.

90. Christian historians of the time also tended to ascribe the Jews' current debased state to a different set of sins both ancient (killing Christ) and modern (refusing to convert to Christianity).

91. *Sy mal nos a venido nosotros somos meresçedores dello, que no fasyemos las çeremonias nin las cosas que avíamos de faser, que por eso nos vino el destierro* (Carrete/Fraile 1987, 113).

92. *Por no guardarla, no le sucedía cosa bien, ni tenían en este mundo riquezas ni bienes temporales, ni después la gloria* (Toro 1932, 221; cf. 214).
93. *Dixeron que haziendolo de aquella manera les avia hecho Dios mucha merçed y les hazia, y avia[n] ganado mucha hazienda y avian casado dos hijas y dado a cada vna çient mil maravedis, y que sy otra cosa hiziesen, que creherian que Dios non les haria merçed* (Beinart 1977a, 335).
94. *Toda a pessoa que vivese na ley de Mousem que nunca lhe falleçeria nada* (Baião 1921, 106; cf. 109).
95. *Se holgava de ser descendiente de judios porque los veya ricos y el deseava serlo y por esto se preciava de confeso* (García Fuentes 1981, 276).
96. *Ayuno de la manera q. esta dicho porq. la dha Marina de Mercado le dezia que haziendo aquellos ayunos seria rica y la rea lo hazia por ser rica y no por ser de la ley de Moysen* (Bel Bravo 1988, 168). For a similar claim see Coelho 1987, 223 [Portugal 1637].
97. *Dios les dava dineros por ella* (Nunemaker 1946, 21).
98. For prayers featuring Jewish saints see Chapter 15.5.
99. *Moises fora ho que fartara cinco mil homens com cinco pães e dous pexes e não Noso Senhor Jesu Christo* (Azevedo Mea 1982, 245).
100. *Dios hauia avierto por Moysen doze carreras por el mar bermejo y q. Moysen la podia ayudar muncho . . . que Moysen la hauia de saluar y q. creyesse en el* (Bel Bravo 1988, 132–3).
101. Lewin 1971, 26, 36–8, 148, 289, etc.
102. *Estando la dicha su madre preñada de él, aguardaron pariese al Mesías, y ella hizo nueve estaciones a un Santo Moisén que tenía pintado cierta católica en un guadamaci* (García 1910, 53).
103. *Al tienpo que alçavan la hostia desía: "Señor Moysén, en ty adoro"* (Carrete Parrondo 1985). See also Baião 1921, 181 [1559].
104. *Tinha huns santinhos que adorava que tinhão corninhos como vaquinhas e não eram como os da igreja* (Furtado 1925, 443; cf. 1929, 38, 56). Another Bahian new-Christian kept images that were like *pacas*, rabbit-sized Brazilian rodents (*tinha huns santinhos como pacas*) (Furtado 1929, 33, 47).
105. *No tienen en sus casas pinturas de Nuestro Señor Jesu Christo ni de su Bendita Madre la Virgen Maria Nuestra Señora ni otras de Santos del Testamento nuevo y tienen muchas del viejo como son: de Moysen, Josue, Aron, Abraham, Elias, Joseph, y de otros muchos Patriarcas y profetas* (Braunstein 1936, 184).
106. *De algunos santos del Testamento viejo, como Tobías y otros muchos profetas, Isaías, Job y otros . . . doña Mariana su hermana doncella le refirió a éste en romance la historia de uno de los santos del Testamento viejo, que no se acuerda si fue de Tobías o Judit* (Toro 1932, 226).
107. Cohen (1973, 100). According to Roth, by the seventeenth century crypto-Jewish religion commonly included references to Saints Raphael, Tobit and Esther (1931–2, 6). See also Lipiner 1969, 170 [Brazil 1590s]; Furtado 1929, 95 [Bahia 1593]; Braunstein 1936, 111 [Majorca 1670s]; Selke de Sánchez 1972, 268 [Majorca 1686].
108. Reverence for certain holy figures, or saints, is also common today among Moroccan Jewery.
109. See Baer's classic analysis of this period (1966, 2:139–243).
110. Beinart 1961, 177. For other examples see Fita y Colomé 1884, 402) [1484]; Carrete Parrondo 1985, 33 [1490], 104, 113 [1501]; Baião 1921, 142- 3 [1543]; Reguera 1984, 182 [Calahorra 1546]; Furtado 1929, 353–4, 469–70 [1594]; Liebman 1975, 168 [Peru 1711]; Liebman 1970, 297 [Mexico, 1795].

111. A lei dos cristãos novos era melhor que a dos christãos velhos (Baião 1921, 211).

112. Dezia que la Ley de Moysen hera buena e verdadera, e que la Ley de los christianos hera burla, e no podia mucho durar, e probaualo con muchas escrituras de profetas y con muchos libros que tenia e con la Bliuia (Beinart 1981b, 565).

113. La ley de Moisén presto se había de guardar por todo el mundo y vestirse de colorado los que la guardaban, de que hubo en todos grande alegría, rematándola con una grande cena (García 1910, 118).

114. Pasa tú, que más vales que yo, que vas a decir cabdís a la sinoga (Carrete Parrondo 1985, 22).

115. Avía dicho que los judíos se avían de aver en muchas persecuçiones, pero que bienaventurado sería el que después se hallase judío; el qual morió judío. E que ella asy lo creya (Carrete Parrondo 1985, 142).

116. Porque no traya su muger a esta tierra por çierto tenemos que no soys christianos, pues que fuystes christianos por fuerça. . . . Juro a Dios que desís la verdad, que buena ley teníamos (Carrete Parrondo 1985, 109).

117. Yendo llorando por la calle le pregunto otra persona porque lloras y ella havia dicho "mas valiera que me estubiera en la ley de judia que no bolverme cristiana" (García Fuentes 1981, 164).

118. O puta vellaca, agora se yva a tornar christiana en tal tienpo. Plugyera a dios que yo pudiera trocar mi ley por la suya (Baer 1936, 514- 5).

119. Mayores milagros avia hecho Dios por Moyses y por los judios que aquello [que hizo por los christianos] (Beinart 1977b, 53).

120. Vuestro libro—contesta Santos—es evangelio, e respondio el dho. Antonio, herrador: mio libro dize mejor verdad quel evangelio (Carrete Parrondo 1972,145).

121. Os christãos novos vivião em milhor ley que os christãos velhos (Azevedo Mea 1982, 336; cf. 427).

122. Por jactarse publicamente que uenía de casta de judios, alabando los judios y su ley, y que judio quería dezir justo y que los judios son mejores que los christianos y que han de venir a mandar y ser muy temidos y q. la mayor honrra q. la podían dar a ella y a sus hijos era llamarlos judios y q. era mejor ley que los christianos y q. por ser judia le daba Dios mas bienes y rriquezas q. a los christianos y que comprar por tres y vender por siete no era nada (Simón Díaz 1946, 98).

123. Que la sangre de los judios hera buena y linpia, y que eran los judios de sangre real . . . aun por ser tan linpia sangre la de los judios avia Dios escogido a Nuestra Señora para su encarnaçion (Moreno Koch 1977, 370).

124. La verdadera Ley era la que Dios había dado a Moisés en el desierto, y que no era negocio de niños que Dios se había de mudar dando una vez una Ley y después otra (Lewin 1954, 122).

125. La verdad havia sido, que, aunque havia tenido en su coraçon la ley de Moyses por buena y la de los cristianos por mala, no havia hecho cumplidamente las ceremonias de la ley de Moyses, ni hecho cosa de la ley evangelica por haverla tenido por mala (García de Proodian 1966, 282).

126. Milhor era a sua lei de Moisés que a dos christãos-velhos . . . e os que nella criam não andavão a pidir pelas portas como os outros mal aventurados, antes davão de comer a outrem e que nenhum da sua geração morrera de fame nem avia de morrer (Azevedo Mea 1981, 157).

127. Respondeo que essa era a milhor posta e a maior honra que elle tinha que era ser cristão novo e pubricamente se prezava de cristão novo (Furtado 1925, 443).

128. Que la gente mas honrrada, y mejor que hauia en el mundo eran los judios. . . . Antes quería ser Judío que ladrón (AGN Vol 529 doc 11, 270a). For a similar Brazilian example [Bahia 1593] see Furtado 1929, 116.

129. *Se podía saluar hombre en todas tres leyes* (Sicroff 1965, 110). For similar examples see Carrete Parrondo 1985, 55, 72–3, 107, 123. See also Monsalvo Antón 1984, 125–6 [Osma 1490s]; Baião 1921, 162 [1552].
130. *Entiendo de encomendar mi anima a todas las tres leyes y la que mejor derecho tenga, que se la lieve* (Marín Padilla 1983b, 306).
131. *Ni de la ley de los christianos ni de la de los judios ni de la de los moros no sende puede saber la verdat; de mi os digo que creo que no ay sino nacer y morir. . . Yo al Dio en un tallador lo tengo; yo he tenido la ley sancta de Moysen, yo he tenido la ley de Ihesu Christo y aun si agora salliesse o viniesse un sant Mahoma, ¡por el Dio! de tres la faria, y si esto acabase no avria miedo al Dio pues todas las leyes avia andado* (Marín Padilla 1983b, 306–7).
132. *Algunas vezes pensó e desía entre sy . . . que quién sabía quál hera mejor ley: ésta nuestra o la de los moros o judíos* (Carrete/Fraile 1987, 70).
133. *Dios era verdad e los moros dezian verdad que se salvaban tambien los moros en su ley como los cristianos en la suya* (Gilman 1972, 84; translation Gilman's).
134. *No sé; que buena ley teníamos y creo que la tenemos tan buena. Fasta agora trayamos tres capillas y agora trahemos quatro* (Carrete/Fraile 1987, 48). The number four in this reference remains a mystery.
135. *Buena ley es la que tenemos, mas buena ley hera la nuestra e vien nos estávamos* (Carrete/Fraile 1987, 57).
136. *Teniendo un fijo mal, anduuo todas las yglesias descalça e hizo dezir muchas misas y enbio a las lamparas de la xinoga vna ves vna escudilla de azeyte. . . . Muchas vezes yva a la xinoga e se hincaua de rodillas delante de las atoras e las [a]doraua e fasya oraçion dellas, creyendo que por aquellos avia de ser salua* (Cantera/Carrete 1975, 195–6). For a similar case see Rábade Obradó 1990a, 439 [Toledo 1487–8].
137. Fray Hernando de Talavera, for example, wrote around 1487 that to think that one could live by both Laws simultaneously was rank heresy (*Si el tal cristiano guarda y piensa que se pueden guardar ambas leyes juntamente de Moisén y de Cristo, testamento nuevo y viejo, es hereje muy errado*) (Hernando de Talavera 1961, 171).
138. *No estava ferme en la una fe ni en la altra* (García Cárcel 1985, 205).
139. *Cria na ley de Moises, esperando salvar se nela e asi esperava polo Mesias, crendo que avia ainda de vir e porem que não fizera mais cerimonias que jejuar. . . . Outras pesoas com quem comunicara a dita ley de Moises e que todas dezião que esa ley era bôa e nela se podião salvar, mas que ela, Branca d'Azevedo, não sabia que ley era . . . e que não sabia em quem os judeus crião e perguntada se no dito tempo leixara de crer em Noso Senhor Jesu Christo, dise que sempre O tivera por Deus e que nunqua se apartara de sua Santa Fé* (Azevedo Mea 1982, 41, 98).
140. *Dise que naquele tempo nem cria nem deixava de crer nelles porque quando estava na igreja lhe pareciam bem as cousas dos christãos e como se sahia logo lhe tornava a cegueira* (Azevedo Mea 1982, 312; cf. 362, 375).
141. *Y que Moysen la podría ayudar mucho, y que por la quenta que a de dar a dios nunca se apartó de Jesuchristo ni de su madre ni dexava oir missa las fiestas. . . . Entendió que aunque hiziesse aquello no era contra la sancta fee catholica, y que lo uno y lo otro se podia hazer. . . . Al tiempo que se lo enseño no creyo ser contrario a la ley y fee de Jesuchristo* (Bel Bravo 1988, 32, 137).
142. *Unas parientas suyas le habían enseñado la ley de Moisés y que la había guardado juntamente con la de Jesucristo Nuestro Señor* (Gracia Boix 1983, 332).
143. *Prohibidos en la ley que dio Dios antes que naciese Christo Nuestro Señor a los santos del testamento viejo a el pueblo escojido de Hisrael, y que lo que esta rea a herrado es en aver guardado*

*estas cosas de aquella ley, pensando que aunque fuese venido Nuestro Señor Jesuchristo, no avia cesado, sino que todavia se podia guardar y que esto no lo a confesado. . . . Siempre a estado entera en la fee de Jesuchristo aunque hacia las cosas dichas con la duda que tiene dicho* (García Fuentes 1981, 457–8).

144. *Que no se enojaba Dios Padre que sirviesen los hombres a Dios Hijo, ni tampoco se enojaba Dios Hijo de que sirviesen al Padre, y que así en caso de duda lo más seguro es servir al Padre, sin hacer nunca mención del Espíritu Santo* (Lewin 1971, 212).

145. *Por mal que nos façao sempre avemos de hir adiante e ser multiplycados e por synal que os estroyrã muitas vezes e que agora estavã juntos e tam populosos e mais do que erã e que por mais que hos queymasen avyam de ter mão ate o cabo porque era mylhor a sua ley e que bem aventurados erã os que podía sofrir e nã tornar atraz e morrer nella e que logo daque hiam direytos a Moyses que estava nos ceos e que por elle Moyses ver que tinhã firme fee nelle os multiplycava cada dia mays* (Baião 1921, 174).

CHAPTER V 🌿

# Attitudes toward Christian Beliefs

Particularly during the period preceding the Expulsion, when Christian proselytizing and coercion resulted in the conversion of tens of thousands of Jews who were then left to assimilate into Christianity on their own without any systematic education in Christian beliefs or practices, the position of many *conversos* with regard to their new religion was one of profound ignorance. They did not understand the Trinity or the transcendental aspects of the sacraments, nor did they know the prayers and ceremonies of Catholicism. They were like Juan del Hoyo [Ciudad Real 1493–4], who, when Inquisitors asked if he were a Christian, disconcerted them by saying that "he wasn't sure" (*no lo sabe cierto*). He believed in Christ but thought that the Passion was still a future event and certainly did not believe that Christ was literally present in the eucharist. The Inquisitors ordered him to be educated. Or they were like young Catalina Alvarez de Alarcón, who, when she realized the danger her family were in because they did not know which of their family practices were indicative of Judaizing or precisely what they were supposed to do as Catholics, begged her confessor to teach her mother the basic principles of Catholicism (Rábade Obradó 1990a, 358). These people tended to be unassimilated new-Christians, not crypto-Jews.

One of the characteristics of many Iberian crypto-Jews, on the other hand, was their tendency to define their Jewish identity negatively by repudiating all things Christian. Expressions of this negativism range from skepticism, disbelief, and scornful mockery to blasphemous speech and behavior. The first set of behaviors rest on the crypto-Jews' inability to accept the basic tenets of the Christian faith;

the second, paradoxically, imply some measure of belief against which to vent feelings of frustration and fear, anger and rebellion.

Early medieval attitudes about Jews, which were brought into the realm of Church policy at the Fourth Lateran Council in 1215, characterized Jews negatively in two related though slightly contradictory ways.[1] On the one hand, Jews were seen as stubborn unbelievers, unwilling to accept the self-evident truths of Christianity or to admit that the New Law had abrogated the Old. According to this vision the Jews, who were blinded by their stubbornness, were evil because they foolishly would not accept the God-man Jesus as their Messiah. They were lost, and therefore damned, because they had not the wisdom to acknowledge the Christian truth, although a simple commitment of belief would redeem them. In the second vision Jews were seen as agents of the Devil, compelled by their Satanic master to attack, pervert, or undermine Christianity through blasphemy and sacrilege. The contradiction, unperceived or at least unspoken by most Christian polemicists, is that it makes no sense to desecrate the host unless one believes that it is truly imbued with magic power, either as the literal body of Christ or in some other transcendental way as the essence of the hated Christian religion.

These beliefs abetted the late fifteenth-century campaigns to brand the Jews as diabolical anti-Christian activists.[2] These campaigns fed on an intensifying stream of accusations of host desecration and ritual murder culminating in the 1491 La Guardia case, already discussed in the Introduction to this book, in which flimsy circumstantial evidence was used to convict several Toledan Jews of a pastiche of ritual crimes, including the murder of a child whose body was never found and who in all likelihood never even existed. La Guardia was an egregious example of a political trial, a case trumped up to hammer home a political point at a time when the Inquisition's lobbying of the Catholic Monarchs to expel the Jews was at its peak. Despite the many propagandists who have asserted the truth of the La Guardia events,[3] the allegations are by any standard incredible. The accusations were non-specific; no material evidence was brought forth; the testimony included serious contradictions; and the convictions were based almost exclusively on testimony coerced by torture.

If ritual murder accusations such as those of La Guardia were untrue, as is almost certainly the case, are we similarly to believe, as do most modern Christian and Jewish historians, that all the accusations that Jews and *conversos* profaned Christian religious symbols are equally untrue? The question itself is for many historians unthinkable[4] but it cannot be avoided, for Inquisition literature abounds with accusations and confessions that new-Christians ridiculed the Holy Family, mistreated crucifixes, desecrated hosts, and parodied the sacraments.

*Converso* attitudes toward Christian beliefs and ritual were of course diverse. As we have seen in Chapter 4, very rapidly after the Expulsion generation had passed away, and inexorably in succeeding generations, most Jewish customs and beliefs were forgotten, ultimately pared down to little more than the basic belief in a unitary God and a coming Messiah. The practice of Judaism, which stresses active observance of customs dictated by the Mosaic Law, became so dangerous in the face of the vigilance of the Inquisition that observing by doing gradually gave way to observing by not-doing: Jewishness determined by the traditional practice of the Mosaic Law evolved into a Jewishness defined negatively. In subsequent chapters of this book we will see that many of the positive aspects of Jewish festival observance tended to be replaced in crypto-Judaism by avoidance: the Purim carnival gave way to the Fast of Esther; the feasts of Rosh Hashanah and Hanukah dropped from the liturgical calendar and the Yom Kippur fast assumed extraordinary importance. The myriad activities crucial to maintaining a kosher home disappeared, while avoidance of pork was retained. Whether moved by fear or ignorance, confusion or apathy, some new-Christians gradually pared their Judaizing down to a small nub of self-concept: I am still a Jew because I think of myself as a Jew.

The staunchest Judaizers, such as the forced converts who never relinquished their commitment to Judaism, from the earliest days of conversion rejected every tenet of Christian belief. Although they were required to adhere outwardly to the practice of their new religion—attending mass, baptizing their children, observing the principal Christian festivals—they did so with an absence of belief and a skepticism that often expressed itself as scorn. At the other end of the spectrum were those converts who wholeheartedly embraced the theology and practice of Catholicism and, insofar as they were consciously able, eschewed every vestige of their former practices and beliefs. Between these two extremes lay a wide range of attitudes toward things Christian.[5] Some *conversos* chose to believe and practice elements of both religions, achieving a measure of religious syncretism. Others rejected belief altogether, drifting toward skepticism or even agnosticism.

For many *conversos* who struggled to remain Judaizers in the face of rapidly eroding Jewish knowledge, the essence of their Jewish identity was a strong affirmation of not being Catholic. While they could not fulfill the *halakhah*, they could derive some comfort and some measure of Jewishness by giving vent to their negative attitudes toward Catholicism, including the theology, practices, and the ritual realia of their new religion. Crypto-Jews often expressed their negativism vocally in words that Christian jurists defined as blasphemy (evil speaking or impious irreverence) and physically in deeds that were labeled sacrilege (outrage committed on consecrated persons or things; profanation of the sacred).

These attitudes and acts ranged along an escalating scale of overt negative actions: (1) denial, or expressions of disbelief, often coupled with philosophical refutation or assertion of Jewish counter-beliefs; (2) verbal disparagement, ridicule, or scorn, often heavily tinged with irony; (3) parody; and (4) physically aggressive actions. Many crypto-Jews denied the divinity of Jesus or the holy nature of Mary, the saints, and the Trinity. Some crypto-Jews mistreated Christian images, overlooking the fact that this mistreatment amounted to a tacit acceptance of the Christian assertion that the statues were privileged or holy. With the same theological inconsistency, some crypto-Jews parodied the Catholic sacraments, religious ceremonies, or dietary practices. As we will see in this chapter, a few of the vestigial crypto-Jewish practices that have survived into this century faintly echo this theme of anti-Catholicism. The copious Inquisition material suggests that some of the acts and expressions shown in the table were common among crypto-Jews, while others were relatively rare.

|  | Jesus | Mary | Saints | Sacraments | Holidays |
|---|---|---|---|---|---|
| Blasphemy |  |  |  |  |  |
| (1) Disbelief | common | common | common | common | occasional |
| (2) Ridicule | common | common | common | common | occasional |
| Sacrilege |  |  |  |  |  |
| (3) Parody | — | — | — | occasional | — |
| (4) Abuse | common | occasional | occasional | occasional | — |

## 5.1. Blasphemy: Disbelief and Ridicule

### 5.1.1. Jesus

The most common way to affirm Jewish identity by venting negative feelings about Christianity was with simple expressions of disbelief, sometimes coupled with the affirmation of a corresponding Jewish belief. Belief in Jesus as the Christ is the linchpin of Catholic theology and was therefore the aspect of the new religion most vigorously rejected by Judaizing *conversos*, who routinely denied that He was divine, that He was a member of a three-part Godhead, or that He was the Messiah. The concept of the Trinity was particularly difficult for *conversos* to understand. Typical was the confusion of Hernando de Avila, of Ecija, who was punished in 1598 in Córdoba for having said, among other things, that "the Holy Trinity has only two persons." The witness did not remember "which of the persons was placed in doubt."[6] Francisco Valero [Toledo 1489–9] affirmed that God had three natures: one for Christians, one for Jews, and one for Moslems (Rábade Obradó 1990a, 381). The Brazilian school teacher Bento Teixeira [Bahia 1593] after singing a trinitarian ditty with his pupils—"Three in one, one in three, that's God in His divinity"—told them the proposition was false.[7]

Even before the Expulsion, assertive crypto-Jews routinely denied the divinity of Jesus or disbelieved in His miraculous birth.[8] In the following generation this disparagement intensified. Simão Vaz, of Lisbon, said in 1541 that God "had no need of putting himself into the womb of a woman and that the Messiah was not God."[9] Joana Vaz, of Aveiro, told the Coimbra Inquisition in 1567 that Jesus was not the son of God but merely a prophet.[10] The Mexican crypto-Jew Diego Díaz Nieto said in 1596 that "Jesus was a learned man but not a son of God."[11] Sometimes *conversos* affirmed that Jesus himself had been a circumcised Jew. In 1492 Martín de Inburgo reported hearing Lorenzo Casal's wife say that "because the Law of Moses was good Our Lord Jesus Christ had chosen to be a Jew for thirty-three years, and had had himself circumcised."[12] In 1511 in Ciudad Real Cristobal de Avila reported that Rodrigo de Villarubia had said that "Jesus Christ had been clipped, as clipped as all those clipped Jews."[13] *Conversos* occasionally took delight in making these points. In 1686 in Majorca a man named Billa reputedly had this conversation with his Inquisitors. "They asked me why I did not want to worship Jesus Christ, and I answered that I would be very happy to worship and follow the Law of Christ and that they should teach it to me. They showed me the Credo, and I responded that the Law that they were teaching me was not the Law of Christ but rather that of the twelve Apostles, because the Law that Christ and Mary kept was that of Moses. And that made them lose the thread of their argument."[14]

Sometimes crypto-Jews employed the logic of scholastic debate in their rejection of Christian dogma. Manuel Gómez Navarro testified around 1590 in Mexico that "he didn't believe that Jesus was the Messiah since the prophecies of the Old Law had not been fulfilled with the coming of Jesus and that Jesus had been hanged because he was a false prophet."[15] In 1615 in Mexico the Judaizer Cristobal de Herrera was said to have remarked that, since the Jews had prophesied that the Messiah must be a king, and Jesus was not, he could not have been the Messiah (AGN Vol 309 doc 4, 185b). In 1626 the Bachelor Francisco Maldonado de Silva was tried in Chile for, among other things, saying that "Christ could not have been the Messiah because his mother was not of the house of David."[16] Pedro Onofre Cortés confessed in Majorca in 1686 to having said that, "although the Christians say that Christ is God, it cannot be, because he was born and died, and God is infinite, and is not born and cannot die, because He is the creator, and His greatness does not fit in a man. In order to forgive sins He did not need to become a man, because His mercy is so great that it has no limit."[17] But he also reportedly said that Christians "adore a man, Christ, who cast spells."[18]

Sometimes *conversos*' denials of Jesus' divinity were emotional, venting feelings in scornful, disrespectful ways. Such were the words of Gonçalo López de Arnedo, who was accused in 1490 of having cursed Jesus by spitting and saying "I deny that whipped sodomite Jesus Christ, and if I had him I'd crucify him again."[19] The eighty-year-old *converso* Juan Beltrán, of Brihuega, around 1515 was said to disparage his Christian obligations with these words: "I worship you, carpenter; I worship you, carpenter."[20] Early crypto-Jews devised scornful nicknames for Jesus so as to avoid speaking His name. A favorite nickname, allegedly used by Abraham Seneor in 1490, was "that other man" (*otohays*–Heb.).[21] Brazilian new-Christians [Bahia 1593] referred to Jesus as "the unfortunate one" (*o malaventurado*) (Furtado 1929, 97–8). In 1501 in Coruña del Conde [Soria] Pedro Núñez was denounced for having said: "I am amazed the way these people continually talk about the Passion; because here when they kill a brother or a relative, particularly if they execute him legally, they don't want anyone to talk about him, and these people talk about Him all the time."[22] Juan López [Aranda 1502] allegedly quipped that "this God they have is born every year and every year they kill him."[23] Frequently in the Inquisition testimony we find denigrating expressions such as that of Francisco Maldonado de Silva, who was accused in Chile in 1626 of saying that "Christ was a drunkard and a glutton who liked to go to weddings,"[24] and that He "had preached the magic arts, with which He had deceived the ignorant people."[25] It was common for *conversos* to disparage Christ's miracles as tricks of a cheap magician.[26] In 1642 a witness told the Mexican Inquisition about a conversation involving Juan de León in which someone said that

> Our Lord Jesus Christ was a fraud, and when He died the princes said He was a fraud, and so that the people would recognize it as well they tied to His leg a sign with certain words written on it, and that then He rose up and said He was not the son of God, and that everything He did was a trick, and then He died again, and He went flying about in the air with all the souls of the Apostles and Catholics behind Him saying: "Because of You! Because of You we fly about this way."[27]

It was particularly difficult for the new-Christians to believe that Jesus had succeeded in bringing back people from death. Pedro Rodríguez [Ciudad Real 1483] reputedly said that "Jesus Christ had not brought Lazarus back from the dead but rather the Church had invented this and it was all a joke."[28] In 1615 in Mexico the Judaizer Cristobal de Herrera disparaged Jesus' miracles, saying that "in those days there were lots of spell casters who brought back the dead."[29]

While most crypto-Jews professed not to believe in Jesus' divinity or saving power, others seem to have acquired heterodox opinions about the biography and nature of the Christian savior. Alvaro Gonçalez was said to have told Juan Fernandez around 1517 that Portugal was "a land of dogs who said that the Crucified was their God ... and further said that the Crucified, playing ball one day in the Synagogue, read a writing which he saw there, and which taught him all those things which he professed to know, and that because of what he had said their God had commanded them to hang Him on a tree" (Wolf 1926, 33). Pero Gonçalez of Las Palmas was reported to have said that "in Jerusalem there is a pool, and an angel descends daily, and moves the waters thereof, and he who enters the pool first is cured, and Jesus Christ passing this place told a sick man who was there to take up his bed and walk, and in so doing He had broken the Sabbath, and that as breaker of the law He was justly condemned" (Wolf 1926, 32; cf. 63). Around 1505 the *converso* Pedro López [Almazán] was denounced for reputedly having said that "the Law of Jesus Christ that we have now is a good Law, for when our Lord went up to heaven on a long ladder the angels said that a great man was ascending dressed in red."[30]

Still other *conversos* saw Jesus and Christianity as an ancient and possibly divine plot against the Jews. Juan Salcedo told the Inquisition in Aranda in 1502 that around 1494 he witnessed a commemoration of the Passion in the Plaza of Santa

Clara in Soria with a *converso* named Santacruz, and that at the point where they were dragging the one they were commemorating Santacruz said,

> "What do you think of what they are doing here? It is such a joke that these people make fun of themselves when they hurl such insults as they are doing. What man alive can believe this stuff; if they just preached it and said 'this is what happened,' a man could believe it, but not by making such ridicule. What man alive could believe that God would put himself through this. And He was the Son of God? What Father would put his Son through this? If you don't believe me, look at those nobles who are over there, who don't pay any attention. Just the foolish people do." And then this witness and the others responded. "Leave it alone, for the love of God. Let's not talk about it. Whatever way it is we have to swallow it. . . . God be cursed if I can believe that it happened this way; rather someone must have invented it to cause trouble for the Jews."[31]

Gonçalo Váez, a Portuguese student living in Granada, told Inquisitors there in 1571 that "Jesus had been a scourge sent by God to punish humankind."[32] Doña Blanca Enríquez, who was burned in effigy in Mexico in 1649, was accused of saying that "when God gave the law to Moses on Mount Sinai, He showed him a crucified Christ, predicting that from this sign and because of Him the people would suffer many persecutions and hardships, particularly through the Inquisitions, as experience had taught them" (Liebman 1974, 193).

From the earliest manifestations of crypto-Judaism right up through the last remnants, many crypto-Jews expressed their negativism by avoiding—insofar as was possible—any mention of Jesus at all. The habit was well enough known to have formed part of the anti-*converso* jibes of late fifteenth-century satirical poetry such as the burlesque "Wedding of Rodrigo Cota," in which a character reports that whoever says "Jesus" at the *converso* wedding feast will get no meat balls.[33] Examples from trial testimony are legion. According to a 1485 trial in Ciudad Real, *conversos* "forbade their relatives and Christian children to name . . . the name of Our Savior Jesus Christ or to perform any Christian rite or ceremony."[34] Ruy Díaz Nieto [Mexico 1603] "would not name Jesus Christ Our Lord, but rather only the Lord, which is Jewish talk."[35] Similarly, the denouncing witness added, "when some Christian greets [Díaz Nieto or his friends] by saying 'Praised be Jesus Christ,' instead of replying 'Forever,' they reply 'God be praised.' "[36] Isabel Núñez told Inquisitors in Ciudad Rodrigo in 1623 that her family avoided saying the name Jesus by substituting "Cristóbal Sánchez."[37] María Ruiz testified in Ciudad Real in 1511 how some fifteen years earlier she had seen "how every time they said 'Jesus' during the Passion, Juan de Teva . . . spit. This witness was alert to look to see if his spitting came from some other reason or whether he did it to insult the Passion. And he was very attentive in watching and he saw that every time they said 'Jesus,' Juan de Teva spit without coughing and without other reason. And sometimes it happened that they said 'Jesus' two or three times all at once and every time he spit;

and if they delayed saying 'Jesus' he never saw him spit until they said it."[38] As we will see in the discussion of prayers in Chapter 15, it was particularly common for *conversos* to delete references to Jesus from their recitations of Christian prayers. Typical were Lucía Ruiz's accusations against Inés López in 1511 that "when she crossed herself she would say 'in the name of the Father' and would never say 'in the name of the Son,' except beginning eight days ago when the Inquisition came to this city; then this witness saw her cross herself once and say 'in the Name of the Father and the Son.' "[39]

### 5.1.2. Mary

Crypto-Jews expressed a very similar set of attitudes with regard to the Virgin Mary. Orthodox Catholics believe Mary to be a descendant of the house of David who was impregnated by the Holy Spirit and who retained her virginity through Jesus' conception and birth. From late medieval times Mary had gained a prominence in popular worship second only to that of Jesus. She took on the attributes of the mother and protector of humankind and the principal intercessor with God on behalf of a sinful humanity. Some *conversos* tried to assert the positive aspect of their Jewish roots by appropriating Mary as a Jewish figure. Juan de Madrid, a Jeronymite monk from Sisla [Segovia], around 1487 said that Mary had been a Jewess for twenty years.[40] According to a 1492 trial, Diego de Madrid was heard to say in 1485 "that the blood of the Jews was clean and good, and that the Jews had royal blood . . . and because the Jews had such pure blood God had chosen Our Lady for the Incarnation."[41] Nicolau Sastre [Majorca 1672] reported that he had heard *chuetas* say that "they came from a better lineage than old-Christians because the Mother of God was a Jew, and that they descended from her line."[42]

But most Judaizing *conversos* tended to be skeptical about all these matters. Frequently their disrespect slipped out in the common expressions of everyday life. Diogo Thomaz, for example, was denounced in Lisbon in 1551 for once having referred to Our Lady as "our stork."[43] In 1490 the *converso* Gonçalo López de Arnedo was accused of having cursed Mary by saying " 'I deny God and Holy Mary,' by throwing figs at them and saying 'this is for God, this is for Holy Mary.' "[44] In 1665 a witness reported to the Mexican Inquisition that "when a friend asked María de Zárate for a dress for an image of Our Lady that the friend had, Doña María replied that there was no need; and at that moment she broke wind and said 'That's for you and the Virgin.' "[45] In Bahia [Brazil] in the 1590s the new-Christian Bento Teixeira was even accused of swearing oaths "by the pubic hair of the Virgin Our Lady."[46]

Sometimes *converso* skepticism targeted Mary's immaculate conception. Antonio Silbeira y Cardoso told Mexican Inquisitors in 1694 that the baker Manuel de Sosa y Prado had said that "the conception of Our Lady had not been immaculate, because Saint Ann had been married three times."[47] But the most common disparagements centered on Mary's virginity, her chastity (i.e., the paternity of Jesus), her lineage as a member of the House of David, and her power as intercessor with God. Luis Sánchez, a *converso* canon of Soria, was reported in 1490 to have said: "I deny God and Holy Mary and the old whore Holy Mary and the sodomite her Son."[48] Elvira de San Juan, of Baeza, testified in 1572 that her mother had taught her that "Our Lady had not given birth as a virgin and that she had had more children than just Jesus Christ, and that she was married to Joseph."[49] A sixteenth-century Portuguese *cristã nova* named Cerveira was denounced to the Inquisition for saying that Mary was no more a virgin than was her own mother.[50] Pedro Onofre Cortés was denounced in 1687 to the Majorca Inquisition for saying, among other things, that "Mary was a woman who had two sons, one named John and the other Jesus."[51] Frequently the disparaging remarks relied on sexually oriented humor. Thus João Lopes was denounced in Lisbon in 1543 for saying, with respect to Mary's virginity, that "you can't make cheese without curds." When he was asked what he was talking about he replied, "Just so, a woman cannot conceive without the seed of a man."[52] In 1558 in Lisbon the *cristão novo* Garcia Mendes d'Abreu was denounced for denying the virginity of Mary with the phrase "how can you draw a yolk out of an egg without breaking the shell?"[53]

As they did with other supernatural aspects of Christian history, *conversos* tended to seek mundane explanations for allegedly miraculous happenings. In 1626 the Bachelor Francisco Maldonado de Silva testified to the Inquisition in Lima that he believed that "it was a lie to say that Mary was a virgin when she gave birth to Our Lord, because she was only a woman married to an old man and she went out somewhere and got pregnant and was not a virgin."[54] Others elaborated on the story. Leonor González was accused in 1484 of having taught her servants "that Holy Mary was a Jew who had married a Jewish charcoal seller who used to get up at dawn to make charcoal and a Christian [!] came to see her and lay with her and she got pregnant from him and gave birth to Jesus Christ. And that as soon as he was born they put him into the run-off pipe of a pool, and that gave him that crown he has. And in that time in that pool there was a huge drain that was like a saw and he got hung up there, which was that Passion that Jesus Christ went through."[55] In 1642 a witness told the Mexican Inquisition about a conversation involving Juan de León in which someone said:

> Our Lord Jesus Christ had not been conceived by the Holy Spirit, but rather he was the son of a carpenter, and Our Lady had been having her period as all women do, and for that reason Saint Joseph had not wanted to come to her, because it was a ceremony of the Law of Moses for men not to come to their wives under these circumstances, and that the people who guarded her left the doors of her house open, and when the carpenter who lived near Our Lady saw that she was alone and the door was open he went in to see her, and that is how our Lord Jesus Christ was engendered. And our Lady thought that the man who was with her was her husband Saint Joseph. And because he was conceived contrary to the custom of the Law our Lord Jesus Christ turned out

to be such a bad and deceiving man. And because Saint Joseph saw that his wife was pregnant, she fled so that he would not kill her.[56]

Frequently *converso* derision carried over into statements that not only was Mary not a virgin, she was a common prostitute. A witness denounced Catalina de Zamora in Ciudad Real in 1484 by saying that "she had seen her throw figs at Our Lady the Virgin Mary; and the girl asked her why she did it, and she replied that God should bring her misfortune if Our Lady were not a little Jewish whore."[57] Catalina evidently asked if Mary wasn't a "common woman who . . . bled like other women?' "[58]

The general *converso* disparagement of Christian reliance on intercessors with the deity was often focused on Mary. In Oporto in the sixteenth century the daughters of António Fernandes were denounced because someone heard them remark that the midwife who aided their mother to give birth had done well by not calling on Mary for help.[59] In 1571 Beatriz Dias, of Caminha, told the Coimbra Inquisition that she had told some women who were talking about the Virgin: "You talk about Our Lady, she's no better than the bogeyman."[60] In 1484 in Ciudad Real Alonso de Camargo reported something that Juan Falcón had told his brother around 1471:

> Juan Falcón asked this witness's brother after he had nearly drowned in the river: "When you fell in the river to whom did you pray for help?" His brother said: "To the Virgin Mary." He replied: "Weren't you being foolish in praying to the Virgin Mary, because while she put on her cloak and went to ask her Son, you would drown. If you ever fall in again, pray to the Lord." And this witness heard this. And his brother grabbed a dagger and wanted to kill him. And thereafter this witness's father ordered that in his house no one speak about the Catholic faith, and whoever mentioned it would be at fault.[61]

Tomás Treviño de Sobremonte was tried in 1647 in Mexico for Judaizing. Among the accusations was a conversation reported by his thirteen-year-old son Rafael. Evidently while on a trip to Guadalajara his son prayed to the Virgin to make it stop raining and "Treviño, with great anger and greatly disturbed because of the deep-seated hatred he has for the Queen of the Angels our Lady, said to him: 'Shut up, you horse, God has no mother; if He created us how could He be born? All that is nonsense; there is only one God who created the heaven and the earth and everything the Church believes is nonsense.' "[62] Joam de Paz, a teen-age *converso* from Bahia, was reported in 1593 to have said that "when I finish praying the Hail Mary I have a bitter taste in my mouth."[63]

### 5.1.3. SAINTS

The role of the saints as advocates with the divinity provoked similar skepticism among many *conversos*. Traditional Catholic saints are "those human members of

Christ recognized by the Church, either traditionally or by formal canonization, as being in heaven and thus worthy of honor" (*New Cath. Enc.* 12:852). Catholics believe that saints are able to work miracles and that they may intercede on behalf of sinners with the deity. Traditional Judaism, on the other hand, respects holy figures but does not officially sanction them, consider them superhuman, or rely on them for intercession with God. Although crypto-Jewish attitudes toward the saints are not reported in the Inquisition literature with the frequency of their attitudes toward Jesus or Mary, it is clear that when most *conversos* thought of the Christian saints it was with both skepticism and disrespect. Doctor Gómez de Ayllón [Huete 1489] used to become incensed if any of his patients invoked a saint. He would break off whatever he was doing and exclaim: "Let that saint come and take care of you!"[64] Nearly two hundred years later in Mexico María de Zárate was accused of having been similarly skeptical of the power or holiness of Christian saints.

> Of Saint Benedict of Palermo she said, how can there be a black saint? [She said that] Saint Ignatius had been a great glutton and had died seated on a chamber pot; keeping his feast was a bad thing because the Fathers of the Company [the Jesuit order] had paid a lot of money for it to be observed. And Saint Peter Martyr, when he was an inquisitor, had burned his own father, so how could you believe that a saint could be so cruel to his father? And of Saint Felipe de Jesús, the holy martyr of these realms, they say that to escape martyrdom he had fled prison, and afterward they caught him and martyred him against his will.[65]

As with Jesus and Mary, *converso* references to the saints were sometimes humorous and frequently pejorative or gross. As with denigration of the Holy Family, these attitudes preceded the Expulsion but intensified as time elapsed.[66] The baker Manuel de Sosa y Prado [Mexico 1694] was reported to have called the miracles of Saint Francis "nonsense" [*pataratas*] and to have referred to a portrait of the Saint with the epithet "dumb pig" [*cochino tonto*] (AGN Vol 529 doc. 11, 270b). Among the accusations brought against Nuño de Figueroa by the Mexican Inquisition in the 1640s was that of having little respect for the saints. Seeing a picture of St. Lawrence, he said "that the smoke that came off of that man on that fiery grill must have turned the beams black, it had been burning for so many years."[67] He also allegedly composed an indecent poem about the canonization of the Mexican Saint Felipe de Jesús. In 1485 it was reported of Juan Falcón that "if he said 'John,' he said 'May the evil John come for you.' "[68] Rodrigo, a rag dealer in Soria, was accused in 1490 of saying "I don't believe in God or in that fucking Saint John."[69] Juan González [Toledo c. 1500] used to joke about the whore Saint Mary Magdalen (Rábade Obradó 1990a, 382). María Marina reported in 1501 how Pedro Moreno, a *converso* priest of Valdecuendes [Soria], listening to a conversation about the saints, responded to a statement "that Saint Peter held the keys to heaven by saying derisively: 'Yes he does, in his underpants.' "[70]

### 5.1.4. Images

Jews and Judaizers took very literally the Mosaic prohibition against worshipping images, as stated in the Second Commandment and reiterated several times in the Torah. They tended to interpret as idolatry the veneration Catholics showed to statues and paintings of the Holy Family, the saints, and other figures. Repeatedly in the Inquisition testimony we find statements that denigrate the images as being merely wood or metal or that mock the Catholics for being so credulous as to worship them. Typical were the 1583 remarks of the Portuguese *cristã nova* Isabel Lopes, of Duas Igrejas, that "the painted saints were nothing more than pictures that somebody had painted,"[71] or of María de Palma, who confessed [Granada 1593] that when she was eleven a neighbor named Marina Hernández had told her that "Jesus Christ and the other saints were painted and made of wood by men."[72] Neither this attitude nor its logical corollary that images merited no special adoration was tolerated by Church authorities.[73] Alonso Fernández de Aguilar, of Ecija, was punished in Córdoba in 1597 because "he did not believe that one should venerate images."[74] Antonio Vélez [Almazán 1498] disparaged images with the Hebrew phrase "strange worship" (*avodazará*), which has the sense of "idolatry" (Carrete/Fraile 1987, 117). In 1545 Margarida d'Oliveira was denounced in Lisbon because when speaking about a crucifix she said, "what benefit can God bring to the world through this?"[75] When Francisco Maldonado de Silva was denounced for Judaizing by his sister Isabel [Lima, Peru 1626], she accused him of saying—among other things—that the adoration of wooden images was idolatry,[76] and that "looking at a crucifix that she had around her neck hanging from a rosary, he said that he did not believe in it, and that Christ was just a stick, for if he were what the Christians said he was it would be glowing."[77] In 1665 in Mexico María de Zárate was accused of having said that "all Christians were going to hell, for being idolaters and adoring images and the image of Jesus Christ and of wooden saints." She also reputedly said that "adoration of images was idolatry, and that they should not be worshipped; only the spirit should be worshipped, and none of its images."[78] Similarly, Lucina and Perpétua Rodríguez [Canary Islands 1655] were reported to have said that "the Virgin of Candlemas does not work miracles. [Can anyone] believe a piece of wood can work miracles?" When an image of the Christ Child caught fire, Lucina was heard to remark, "What did it matter if it burnt or not, since it is only a piece of wood."[79] These attitudes were so prevalent that they were included in a memorandum of Judaizing customs presented to the Inquisition in Granada in 1593, which stated that Judaizers "completely deny the worship of images, saying that they are only gold, silver or wood."[80]

Insofar as they were able, Judaizing *conversos* avoided keeping Christian images in their homes. Inquisition testimony makes clear that servants, neighbors, and other informers took special note of the lack of images in *converso* households. Typical of the thousands of such reports was the allegation in 1484 that Donosa Ruiz, of Teruel, "never kept in her house any altar to the Virgin Mary nor to Jesus

Christ or his saints, the way Christians do and before which they are accustomed to pray."[81] Likewise the slave Isabel testified against Juan Ramírez in 1511, saying that "in the large rooms where they read [the Torah] there were no statues of Our Lord or Our Lady."[82] Going a step further, some *conversos* tried to avoid any circumstance that would require them to perform acts that might be construed as the forbidden worship of images. Typical was testimony about how Clara de Rivera [Mexico 1646] "refused to enter churches so that she would not have to bow to the saints, because that was the worst sin that Judaizers could commit."[83] In a similar case in 1596 in the Philippines Ruy Pérez was accused of not taking his hat off when he passed by a cross (Uchmany 1982, 97), and in 1635 in Lima the Portuguese *converso* Rodrigo de Avila was tried because he "did not take off his hat to the Cross, nor did he bow to the images, or the saints, or the Holy Sacrament."[84] Evidence given in the trial of the *converso* Enrique Fuster [Valencia 1489] suggests that he was more devout in these matters than even his Jewish friends. One day the Jew José Alfaro visited him and said he wanted to go see a Christian procession in honor of the Virgin. Fuster was horrified, replying that "it would be a sin and that the Bible prohibited idol worship" (Haliczer 1990, 214).

5.1.5. SACRAMENT OF BAPTISM

The seven Catholic sacraments are those rituals by which supernatural grace is imparted. Two of the seven—baptism and the eucharist—are generally considered necessary to the soul's salvation.[85] New-Christians found that these two sacraments played an extremely important part in their religious lives and, in keeping with the attitudes we have been observing, the Judaizers among them tended to be skeptical about both. Unlike belief in the divine nature of the Holy Family and the saints, the application of the sacraments involved specific actions. Thus Judaizing new-Christians not only disparaged them but insofar as they were able they avoided them or took steps to counteract their effects.

Baptism is considered to be "the sacramental entrance into the people of God," supplanting Jewish practice as "the fulfillment and replacement of circumcision" (*New Cath. Enc.* 2:54, 57). The proper religious initiation of a newborn baby was as important to Judaizing *conversos* as to any parents.[86] Circumcising the infant boys, to mark them with the sign of the covenant between God and Abraham, was far too dangerous to be practiced regularly. And baptism in the church was far too public a ceremony to be neglected. Thus almost all *converso* babies were baptized. For some crypto-Jews, the birth of a baby and the attendant ceremonies were a cause for celebration in the community; these people made a special point of attending the baptisms of their coreligionists, which they turned into a kind of reaffirmation of their crypto-Jewishness. This is what Catalina Martín suggested when she said in 1511 that the González sisters in Ciudad Real "never went to mass on Sundays nor holidays nor other weekdays unless they had been invited to some baptism or the reading of the marriage bans of some *converso*."[87] However, this was not the most common attitude. Rather, as we will see in Chapter 7, when *converso* parents brought the baby home they routinely scrubbed off the holy oil as if to erase the stigma of their conversion and sometimes used the occasion to give the baby a Jewish name. In 1485 Françisca Fernández testified against Beatriz Núñez in Guadalupe, saying that when her children were born "she saw that when they brought the infant home from the baptism they had a pot of hot water; and after the godparents had gone and they had eaten fruit, her master and mistress and a serving girl named Marina, whom they greatly trusted, shut themselves up in a room with the water and locked the door. And she believes that they scrubbed the infant, because she heard it cry." Johanna Fernández said that she saw them "wash their foreheads, and scrub them with a cloth, which they said they did to take off the hair; and they really scrubbed a lot."[88] The attitude that underlay this behavior was radical disbelief; as the new-Christian Luis Mendes [Bahia 1593] put it succinctly to a friend of his, "your baptism is shit."[89]

Still, by mid-seventeenth century, at least in Mexico, some crypto-Jews had evolved their own form of baptism. Isabel Duarte's blessing was particularly prized. The summary of the 1646 *auto de fe* describes it this way: "She used to bless in the Jewish fashion all the Jewish infants there were in this city. They called on her for that reason. She anointed them superstitiously, and one suspects that she pacted with the Devil."[90]

### 5.1.6. Sacrament of the Eucharist

The most frequent sacrament is the celebration of the eucharist in the mass, a religious service which reenacts the sacrifice of the Last Supper and during which Christ is believed to become physically present in the wine and in the host, or eucharist (ceremonial bread) consumed by the parishioners. From the time of the Fourth Lateran Council Christians were required to confess and take communion at least once annually and to attend mass weekly. As Christians, *conversos* were compelled to attend mass. Many did so unwillingly, advancing any excuse not to have to attend. Antonio Platero of Roa [Soria], for example, was denounced in 1502 for going fishing during mass. Asked why he avoided mass he replied: "What nonsense, what nonsense!"[91] In 1505 it was reported that Pedro Laínez "stayed in bed until after the principal mass; and when they told him to get up and go to mass he told them to let him sleep."[92] Some crypto-Jews claimed that other commitments kept them from mass. Inez de Faria denounced Master Gil Vaz Bugalho in Portugal in 1537 for "pretending to be in charge of the house so as to avoid going to hear the sermon."[93] Many *conversos*, even those who were under overt suspicion of Judaizing, only attended mass when coerced. Manuel Gil told Mexican Inquisitors in 1603 that Ruy Díaz Nieto and his family, who were awaiting the conclusion of their case in the prison of the Holy Office in Mexico City, never went to mass "except when the warden forced them to go to the Santo Domingo church."[94] The records also suggest that Judaizing *conversos* did what they could to prevent anyone in their households from attending. Manuel de Puigmija's wife Violante prevented their Christian servants from attending mass in Valencia in the early 1480s (Haliczer 1990, 220). The Portuguese Diego Pérez, a new Christian living in Huancavelica [Peru], was accused of "never having let his wife nor her family hear mass."[95] In 1673 in Lima Rodríguez de Acevedo was accused by one of his young slaves of not teaching his slaves their prayers or allowing them to go to mass (Medina 1890, 241). Frequently attendance at mass was a matter of contention within the family, for feelings among Judaizing *conversos* ran high when they saw one of their number attempting to assimilate. Witness this scene, reported to the Evora Inquisition around 1580. The *cristão novo* Brites Alvares went to the house of the shoemaker Luis Fernandes to get a light for her fire. While she was there the bell began to ring for mass, and Luis' wife Catarina Martins asked her why she was not going to mass. Brites replied that she was going to go later. Diogo Lopes, a visitor in the house, said: "If you were my daughter, I would break your legs; first, because you eat blood sausages, and second, because you go to mass so often." João Gomes, who was also present, said: "Why do you go to mass? You're going to worship a piece of paper. Take the paper and tack it to the wall and worship it." Brites protested that she was going there to worship Jesus Christ, and when she left Catarina remarked: "You can't tell her anything; she's a saint-sucker."[96]

Even when they attended mass, most crypto-Jews seem to have done as much as they could to avoid active participation. Donosa Ruiz [Teruel 1484] was accused of "not kneeling when they ring the bell for prayer nor when they elevate the Body of Christ."[97] Typical also was the behavior of the *converso* Juan de Sevilla [Toledo 1486], who in the prison church was alleged to face the wall to pray when everyone else was reciting the *Salve* and to turn his face aside so as not to look at the altar.[98] Testimony in 1505 indicated that in the Church of Sant Salvador of Almazán the *conversa* mother of Diego de Luján "used to sit toward the outside in a place where you could not see the altar where they were saying mass."[99] In 1505 a *converso* was accused because "when they raised the host and the chalice he never looked at the altar, but rather at a wall of the church."[100] Another strategy was recorded by the Mexican Inquisition in 1648. When Blanca Enríquez would go to mass allegedly she would cover her eyes. "Taking a handkerchief out of her sleeve, she would pretend to wipe her face so as not to see the host and chalice raised. When she passed the altars with her mother they would make the sign of a fig underneath their shawls, and would spit at them and make fun of the saints who were up there."[101]

Blanca Enríquez was far from alone in expressing her disrespect for the mass and all it symbolized. In 1505 Isabel Laínez was reported to "have turned her back to the altar on leaving church and to have expressed her reverence with her butt."[102] In 1546 Jorge Alvarez, of Laguardia, was tried because he threw a fig at the holy sacrament and exposed his private parts to the cross and to an image of the Virgin.[103] Pedro Homem, a carpenter from Lisbon, was accused in Brazil in 1591 because "when he went into a church instead of taking off his hat he settled it more firmly on his head."[104] Alonso Rodrigues, of Maqueda [Toledo], was accused in 1528 of never taking off his hat in church during mass. The witness also reported that he never saw Rodrigues "beat his chest."[105] Ana d'Olivera used to sit in church gossiping with little reverence to God,[106] as did Beatriz de Acosta, who "did not pray, but rather sat near her relatives where they put their heads together and talked when they raised the host."[107] Branca Dias was accused in Brazil in the 1590s of denigrating the priests who were saying mass by referring to them as "chained dogs."[108] When the host was elevated the *cristão novo* Duarte Dias Enriquez [Pernambuco 1593] "looked down and with his mouth and nose made gestures and grimaces which did not show devotion but clearly seemed to be disrespectful to the holy sacrament."[109] The Portuguese Judaizer Francisco de Acosta [Mexico 1647] showed his disrespect for the mass by "pulling his beard, and putting his finger on his nose, actions which indicated threat, hate, and an evil heart."[110] Ana Gómez, who was burned in the great Mexican *auto de fe* of 1649, was accused along with her family because "when the Holy Host was raised, they made the *higas* under the cloak and sometimes they spit. She lowered her face in order not to look at the Host" (Liebman 1974, 126). Pedro López, a *converso* priest in Cuenca, was accused in 1489 of having so little respect for the mass that "he would get up from lying with his woman and without praying or atoning would go to say mass the way a Jew or a Moor might do." He also "took the altar sheets from the consecrating table where the Passion of Christ is re-enacted and threw them or had them thrown very obscenely on the bed where he slept with his woman."[111]

At the heart of these behaviors was a profound disbelief in the supernatural aspects of the mass. For Catholics the host, or eucharist, is "the Sacrament of the New Law in which the body and blood of Jesus Christ are really and substantially present under the consecrated Species of bread and wine as the spiritual food of Christians" (*New Cath. Enc.* 5:599). At a particular point in the mass the bread and wine are raised up by the priest and, for believers, are changed essentially in the miracle of transubstantiation. The miracle of the consecrated host was particularly hard for crypto-Jews to swallow. For them the transubstantiation of the eucharist into the literal body of Christ was implausible; contrarily, if it was true then consuming the eucharist seemed to them like cannibalism. The polemical *Libro del Alboraique* of the mid-1480s draws attention to this new-Christian aversion to the doctrine of the eucharist, alleging that, even though many Jews were converted by Christ himself, when they found that they were to be required to eat Christ's flesh they said: "This is a hard lesson; who can believe it? . . . And they did not want to follow Jesus Christ any longer, thinking that they would have to eat His flesh."[112]

For most *conversos* the eucharist was nothing more than a piece of bread. They would have agreed with Antonio Gonçalez when he said in Las Palmas in 1526 that he remembered his father saying to his mother that "God being present in the Host was nonsense."[113] Manuel Gómez Navarro testified in Mexico around 1590 that the host was only a piece of dough. In 1596 his friend Luis Carvajal told the

Inquisitors that the host was moldy (Liebman 1970, 175, 178). Gaspar Coelho [Bahia 1593] disparaged it as only so much tapioca.[114] When asked about the sacraments Fernando el Zarco [Cuenca 1491] allegedly "swore to God that it was all bunk from the Pope to his cape."[115] Particularly scornful were some of the new-Christians who had joined the clergy. In the Jeronymite monastery of Guadalupe in 1485 *converso* monks routinely expressed skepticism that the host was truly the body of Christ. When the wafer was elevated, one muttered "If You are God I worship you; if not, not." Another said that "I am worshipping You, Lord, if you are there."[116] One Guadalupe monk even appeared at the altar rail asking for a "cookie" (*torta*).[117] Pedro López, a *converso* priest in Cuenca, was accused of saying that "he thought no more of eating the host than of eating a slice of onion."[118] Pedro García [Almazán 1505] disparaged a rumor that a *converso* priest had been arrested for selling a host to another former Jew named Judah by saying: "It wasn't made of gold or silver; what could Judah have wanted with a piece of bread?"[119] In 1549 the Portuguese *cristão novo* cleric João Manuel was said to have complained, as he was preparing to say mass, that "they want me to believe that the Host that the priest is kneading at night with his mistress the next day becomes the true and complete God!"[120] These attitudes were common among the Judaizing *converso* clergy, for whom familiarity with Catholic ritual bred not respect but contempt. In 1487 Juan de Buendía accused the *converso* Jeronymite monk Friar Diego de Burgos, of San Bartolomé de la Lupiana, of elevating the host upside down during the mass and of later excusing himself by saying that "God is on every side."[121] In church Isabel Sánchez [Cuenca 1490] used to mutter the verse: "The bread and wine I see, in Moses' Law I believe."[122] Paulo and Schwarz even found twentieth-century Portuguese Judaizers in Pinhel murmuring on entering a church: "I do not worship bread or stone, but the only the great God who governs all alone."[123]

Not only were *conversos* compelled by their circumstances to attend mass, they like everyone else also had to receive the consecrated host, believe in it or not. One common *converso* avoidance strategy was described in the 1505 denunciation of Beatriz, wife of Martín de Velacha of Almazán: "When they distributed the host this woman took it and stuck it in her mouth and then turned her head and spit it out."[124] María Lopes, of Bahia, was also said to spit out the host rather than swallow it.[125] The Franciscan monk Friar Martín de Abbas reported in 1632 that he had seen an old *conversa* in San Juan de Luz who "having received the host had stuck out her tongue and removed the Body of Christ with her handkerchief."[126]

In addition to expressing their skepticism, the Judaizing *conversos* who were forced to attend mass sometimes tried to turn the experience into a positive expression of their Jewish beliefs. The most common approach, which appears in testimony in dozens of trials, was to couple a denial of the eucharistic miracle—and the plurality of the Trinity—with an affirmation of the one, invisible God. Marina de Avila said in Granada in 1592 that she was instructed by her half-sister that when the priest raised the host she should say: "I see a piece of bread; I believe in the Lord instead." And when they raised the chalice she should say: "I see wine and bread; I love you, Lord, instead."[127] The practice was so common that a memorandum of Judaizing customs presented to the Inquisition in Granada in 1593 stated that "they deny the sacrament of the altar, saying that in the bread there is only bread, and when it is elevated they say 'I see a piece of bread; I love you, Lord, instead.' And the same happens with the wine, when they say 'I see water and wine; I worship Adonai divine.' "[128] This custom seems to have been standard practice among the Portuguese. In 1543 the *cristão novo* shoemaker Gonçalo Vaz was said to have said, when the host was elevated: "old bread and wine, and I believe in the Law of Moses."[129] The *cristão novo* Fernão Soeiro [Pernambuco 1594] was denounced by someone who observed him at mass. "When the priest elevated the consecrated host he saw Fernão Soeiro on his knees beating his breast, and he heard him say the following words: 'I believe in what I believe, I believe in what I believe, I believe in what I believe.' "[130] Paulo notes the persistence of this custom even today among new-Christians in Covilhã, Portugal, who on entering a church say: "I enter this church, but I do not worship stick nor stone; nor do I worship bread or wine. I only come to worship the living God of Moses."[131]

Despite these efforts of *conversos* to salvage their forced attendance at church and to turn it to the purposes of crypto-Judaism, Inquisition testimony makes clear that the incessant pressure from neighbors and public officials drove many new-Christians half crazy. Even the omnipresent church bells ringing out the start of yet another religious service weighed heavily on their spirits. In 1489 the *converso* Diego López was reported to have said (some twenty years earlier) when he saw people going into mass: "where are these crazy lost souls going with their ding dong ding?"[132] Diego de Soria [Soria 1491] expressed similar exasperation when they rang the bells for mass in San Gil: "May God damn those bells of San Gil; they never stop saying 'Come in, come in.' "[133] The *converso* Antonio Laínez [Almazán 1505] allegedly said that they ring the bell for mass not to go to see God but rather "they ring to go to see the devil."[134] To these beleaguered *conversos* the mass was spiritually inconsequential, characterized by María de Sarauia in 1490 as a pack of nothing."[135] Similarly, when the Inquisitors came to Almazán in 1505, Catalina Laínez told a neighbor not to go to church to hear "preaching . . . because why did she want to listen to those nothings."[136] They believed that the mass served no useful purpose in this world or the next. A 1536 Portuguese Edict of Faith, for example, instructs informers to look for people who say that "the sacrifices and the Masses performed in the Holy Church provide no benefit for souls."[137] For other *conversos* it was worse than that, for they considered that belief in the miraculous power of the mass kept people from seeking effective earthly solutions to their problems. It was reported in 1489 that Doctor Gómez de Ayllón, of Huete, became incensed when the mother of one of his patients said that she was commissioning a mass for her daughter's health. Gómez shouted at her: "A mass for her health! Do you believe there is a mass that can restore health? Don't you believe it."[138]

### 5.1.7. SACRAMENT OF LAST RITES

When a Catholic is afflicted with an imminently life-threatening illness a priest administers the last rites, which is also called extreme unction (and is now generally known as the anointing of the sick). Consecrated olive oil is applied to the external sense organs and certain prayers are recited. As formulated at the Council of Trent, which drew together the scattered medieval theological pronouncements about last rites, its effect is said to be "the Grace of the Holy Spirit, whose anointing takes away sins. . . . It also comforts and strengthens the soul of the sick person by arousing in him great confidence in the divine mercy," and enables him to "more easily resist the temptations of the Devil. . . . This anointing occasionally restores health to the body if health would be of advantage to the salvation of the soul" (*New Cath. Enc.* 1:571).

For many *conversos* the act of death was their final opportunity to make a statement about their true religious beliefs. Their Catholic spiritual advisors, eager to press the battle for the soul down to the last moment, urged that they accept the last rites of the Church, which, as dying Catholics, they were compelled to do. Nonetheless some *conversos* whose Jewish identity was particularly strong refused and disparaged the sacrament of extreme unction. This rejection was far from trivial, for even aside from theological considerations the earthly punishments for Judaizing could extend beyond the grave with exhumation and burning of the dead person's bones, confiscation of family property, and stigmatization of descendants. Yet rejection of last rites appears to have been fairly common among the first generations of *conversos* and there are occasional examples even into the seventeenth century.

As with the other Christian sacraments, this rejection had two main aspects. *Conversos* frequently derided the efficacy of last rites. A witness reported to the Mexican Inquisition in 1642 that a woman had told Juan de León that, when her friend was dying and they brought her the holy sacrament, she told her that it was nothing at all.[139] A *converso* named Lloreynte, from Navapalos [Burgo de Osma, Soria 1501], used stronger terms, saying that "the chrism, what is it but shit?"[140] Others described it with a mocking tone. Gracia Ibáñez [Soria 1502] allegedly said that when she was sick "they confessed her, and communed her, and smeared mud on her."[141] And most Judaizing *conversos* tried to avoid last rites altogether. Alonso Sánchez testified against Juan Ramírez [Ciudad Real 1511] saying that "when Ramírez was ill certain people had told him . . . to confess . . . and receive the holy sacraments, but that he . . . always made excuses not to do it."[142]

### 5.1.8. SACRAMENT OF CONFESSION

For Catholics confession is "the manifestation of personal sins to the Church in the person of a duly authorized priest for the purpose of obtaining sacramental absolution by virtue of the power of the keys," which is to say, the power to absolve vested in the Church by Christ when He gave Peter the keys to heaven (*New Cath. Enc.* 4:131). *Conversos* were reticent about participating in the Catholic sacrament of confession and absolution for two reasons that are made clear by the frequent Inquisition testimony regarding this sacrament. First, *conversos* tended not to believe in the necessity of a priest to intercede with the deity in securing forgiveness or in the power of the priest to absolve one of one's sins. In addition, they were afraid that their confession of anything having to do with their Judaizing might lead to major complications with the Inquisition. Both of these reasons are explicit in the memorandum of Judaizing customs presented to the Inquisition in Granada in 1593, which stated that "they deny that confessors have power to absolve sins and for that reason they only confess trivial things in order to make fun of confession and because they are afraid of the Inquisition."[143] The power to control inherent in the requirement of sacerdotal confession was not lost on the Judaizers: in 1545 in Lisbon Fernão da Pina was said to have said that "in the Old Law there was only mental confession," and that the Pope had ordered vocal confession "so that lay people would be more subject to the Church."[144]

As with the other sacraments, the aversion of Judaizers to confession tended to manifest itself in two ways, disparagement and avoidance. For Judaizers the central point was that their religion permitted them to speak directly to God without the need for priestly mediation. Testimony returns to this point over and over again. Marina Fernández [Toledo c. 1500] felt it was "better to make a hole in the ground and tell your sins to it . . . than to tell a confessor, or any human being." [145] Elvira de San Juan said in Baeza in 1572 that "confession was to be made only to God."[146] Her sister Bernardina added that her mother had taught her "not to confess, even if the confessors asked her to, because Jews did not confess to the priest but rather to God, saying: 'Lord, in this and in this other I have offended you.' "[147] In 1589 Luis de Carvajal told his Inquisitors in Mexico that "confession to a priest was against the Law of the Jews, who confessed only to God."[148] Juan de León said in the Mexican Inquisitorial prison in 1645 that "When I truly confess I kneel in a corner and confess to that man [God], who is not deaf."[149] Testimony suggests that privacy and solitude were important to crypto-Jews who wanted to confess their transgressions. Turning to face a corner of the room, or the wall, was an accepted method of shutting out the rest of the world. Blanca Alonso, of Huete, was reported to have said around 1491 that Church confession was invalid and that it was sufficient for her to confess herself, at home, facing the wall (Blázquez Miguel 1987, 48). The recent convert Blasco Rodrigues echoed this sentiment [Soria 1491] when he allegedly stated that the only difference between his former religion of Judaism and Christianity was that "we confess to a man and they confess to the wall."[150] In the last analysis, for many *conversos*, as for Ysabel the wife of Pero Alonso of Roa [Soria 1502], "confession is gobbledygook."[151]

Not surprisingly, *conversos* considered avoidance the best strategy. Teresa Lopes testified in the 1484 Ciudad Real trial of Rodrigo Marín and Catalina López that she had heard Rodrigo ask Catalina if she had confessed, "and she responded that every time the priest asked her if she had sinned she told him: 'May God trouble him; I would as soon dig a hole in the garden and confess my sins there.'"[152] When avoidance was impossible, prevarication was the next recourse. Isabel de Rivera was accused by the Mexican Inquisition around 1646 of saying that "it was a sin to confess . . . and that they would tell the Catholic confessors four lies just to comply with Christian expectations."[153] In 1627 the Bachelor Francisco Maldonado de Silva, who was tried in Chile, said that when he confessed his sins to a priest in his mind he was confessing them to God not the priest, and that he only confessed those he had committed against the Law of Moses.[154]

At least in one instance prior to the Expulsion, *conversos* dealt with Christian confession by adapting it to their crypto-Jewish needs. In a 1484 trial it was reported that "Juan Escogido and [a man called] 'Rotten' were confessors of the converts." A certain *conversa* woman, too, "used to go to console and hear the confessions of the dying in the Jewish fashion."[155]

### 5.1.9. OTHER CHRISTIAN RELIGIOUS PRACTICES

Fifteenth-century Spanish Catholics would make the sign of the cross with their right hand over their forehead, shoulders, and breast for a variety of reasons: it was a visible sign of their Catholic faith; it represented acceptance of the mysteries of the eucharistic sacrament at mass; and it invoked the protection of the deity against evil for themselves and their loved ones. Understandably, the custom of making the sign of the cross was another practice despised by Judaizing *conversos* as emblematic of what they considered to be the superstitious nature of the new religion. In a 1484 trial in Ciudad Real a *converso* was denounced because "he forbade his family members and Christian children to cross themselves."[156] Phelipe Guillem, a new-Christian knight of the order of Jesus Christ, was accused in Brazil in 1591 because "when he crossed himself he crossed himself with a fig, and his excuse was that his thumb was doubled under."[157] Manuel de Acuña, a Portuguese resident in Jaen, was punished in 1745 in Córdoba for "being most observant in the Law of Moses, and of crossing himself with his left hand in scorn for the Cross."[158] Catalina González testified against María González [Ciudad Real 1511], saying that "every time her little eight-year-old son, Fernando, used to come from school he would kiss his mother's hand. And after he had kissed it, she would put it on his head and draw it down across his face without crossing him."[159] When they rang the bell for the *Ave Maria*, Teresa Sánchez [Garcimuñoz 1490s] allegedly did not cross herself but rather she crossed her hands over her head."[160]

Quantitative prayer, in particular praying the rosary, was another Christian practice commonly disparaged by the Judaizing *conversos*. The rosary is a string of beads whose arrangement helps Catholics order and number their recitation of certain cycles of prayers, notably the *Ave Maria*. Rosaries became popular in Europe in the fifteenth century. *Conversos* took several approaches to rosaries. Many people, like the *cristã nova* Gracea Rodrigues, accused in 1543, thought they were inconsequential. Rodrigues was accused of remarking, when she saw two black women in the street praying their rosaries: "Beads, beads; bunk, bunk."[161] To judge from both literary and trial evidence, assimilating new-Christians and hypocritical new-Christians often carried a large rosary as a visible symbol of their adherence to the new religion. This was the case with María de Zárate [Mexico 1650s], who was accused of "holding a rosary in her hands only for appearances' sake, because she always held it still and did not move the beads."[162] Judaizing *conversos* sometimes criticized such people for their outward display of Christian piety. Ana Lopes [Lisbon 1543] was denounced for saying to the wife of Manuel Soares, when she saw her praying her rosary: "Traitor! You pray the beads and you are of our caste! If you were truly of our caste you would not pray the beads."[163] Lopes seems to have been one of those *conversos* who tried to avoid contact with rosaries as they would with any other Catholic religious item. Another was Perpétua Rodríguez [Canary Islands 1655], who replied to an accusation that the reason why she did not take a rosary to church was because "she kept count on her fingers" (Wolf 1926, 145). The Portuguese Antonio Silbeira y Cardoso told Mexican Inquisitors in 1694 that the baker Manuel de Sosa y Prado did not even own a rosary (AGN Vol 529 doc 11, 269b).

Judaizing *conversos* routinely disparaged the Christian custom of making pilgrimages to distant or local shrines. Juan Lagarto was denounced in Sigüenza in 1501 for having said that "people who go on pilgrimages got no more benefit than they would from kissing the butt of the animals who carried them."[164] Similarly Isabel Lopes, of Vila Flor, was accused [Coimbra 1583] of scoffing with her new-Christian friends at a pilgrimage to a shrine of the Virgin.[165] They tended to feel the same way about religious processions. The *conversa* Violante Santángel [Teruel 1486] was accused of watching the Holy Week processions from a window of her house with her daughter Gracia and other *conversas* and of laughing and joking and making fun of the Christian rites as the procession passed (Sánchez Moya/ Monasterio Aspiri 1973, 130). In 1624 in Cartagena de Indias Domingo de Costa, who was born in the village of Picanzos in Coimbra, Portugal, was tried because on Holy Thursday he blew his trumpet and cried "look at the procession; there goes Jesus to the house of all the devils."[166] Even *conversos* who were under suspicion of Judaizing sometimes continued to scoff. In the Mexican Inquisitorial prison in 1646 Juan de León and two friends hung in the windows to watch a passing procession. León allegedly said, "Let's watch the procession of these lousy black dogs and make fun of it, and we'll have an amusing time." When the parade began he said: "Look at how ceremonk-ishly these deceivers are parading." One-eyed Medina said, "They do what they see the Spaniards doing." León went on, "Did you see the face of that one who looks like he is threatening someone with false testimony?" "And," the informant indicates, "he was talking about an image of holy Christ that was carried in the procession."[167]

The late medieval Catholic liturgical calendar's never-ending succession of Church holidays exasperated the new-Christians. García López was accused by Juan de Salcedo in Aranda de Duero in 1502 of having said that "when we were Jews we were bothered by one festival that came once a year, and now every day is a holiday or festival; too much and never ending."[168] By far the most bothersome to *conversos* were the many days—particularly Fridays and the forty days before Easter—on which it was forbidden to eat meat. A large proportion of the new-Christians who ran afoul of the Inquisition were accused of violating these prohibitions. Juan González, of Casarrubios, and his wife ate meat, milk, and cheese during Lent (Beinart 1975, 650). Hundreds of new-Christians were like Rodrigo Marín of Ciudad Real, who in 1485 violated Lent by eating eggs.[169] Donosa Ruiz [Teruel 1484] was said to "make her Moorish women Judaize by forcing them to eat meat on days when it is prohibited by the Holy Mother Church."[170] *Conversos* in Toledo in the early sixteenth century reputedly masked the cooking odors in their houses during Lent by "burning wool and sardine heads and cloves of garlic to mask the smell."[171] In fact, eating meat during Lent was one of the items included in a late fifteenth-century memorandum of *converso* customs: "They eat meat during Lent and on other days prohibited by the church without having the need, thinking that they can do so without sinning."[172] It was so prevalent that even inside the monastery of Guadalupe in 1485 *converso* monks routinely violated Christian fast days.[173] Because they did not believe in its rationale, they saw no reason why they should obey the rules. The attitude of Pedro de la Fuente, of Las Palmas, who allegedly affirmed in 1531 that "Lent was made for fools" (Wolf 1926, 92), is altogether typical. Most *conversos* paid Lent as little heed as possible, varying their normal routine not one whit. The Portuguese Antonio Silbeira y Cardoso [Mexico 1694] said that he was scandalized that after Good Friday mass the *converso* baker Manuel de Sosa y Prado had gone home to sleep with his *dama*, and she was a single woman (AGN Vol 529 doc 11, 269b). However, some *conversos* were more malicious about their rule-breaking. Simón Rodríguez Maroto, of Jumilla, was accused in 1618 of gorging himself on meat every Friday merely for the pleasure of breaking a Christian precept (Blázquez Miguel 1986b, 210–1). Andrés Medrano, of Genevilla [Alava], was accused in 1573 of throwing a party on Good Friday and of playing his guitar. At the party they allegedly played a game called "San Mazmarro" in which "a kneeling 'saint' was hit in the face with wet rags while the attacker chanted 'Saint Mazmarro, may God free me from you as from the Devil' " (Monter 1990, 157–8).

In the same fashion, while Judaizers did what they could to observe the Jewish Sabbath on Saturday, on Sunday they were very likely to work, both because labor was necessary to their ability to survive and because it was another back-handed way of expressing their commitment to Jewishness. Juan Sánchez Exarch [Teruel 1484] was accused of dealing and making contracts on Sunday and of maliciously walking about on Sundays and other Christian holy days.[174] Diego Hurtado, a *con-*

*verso* from Almazán who pastured large flocks in Extremadura around 1500, used to order his servants to do a variety of tasks on Sunday.[175] Branca Mendes, a *cristãa nova*, was accused [Portugal 1541] of "making marmalade on Sundays and not doing anything at all on Saturdays."[176] Diego Gomes was denounced [Toledo 1510] because "on the Sundays and holidays that the Holy Mother Church orders to be observed Diego Gomes combed and clipped the manes of his horses and made a blacksmith's servant work at the forge. . . . And in his household . . . they did not recognize Sundays or holidays."[177] An *auto de fe* in Madrid in 1720 noted that Luisa del Valle and her daughter Antonia de Tudela had violated Christian fast days by dancing and playing the guitar (Lera García 1987, 93).

The skeptical *converso* attitudes we have been discussing in this chapter extended to every aspect of Christian religious life. Brazilian new-Christians [Bahia 1593] disparaged the infallibility of the Pope (Furtado 1929, 30, 42). Bulls and indulgences came in for special ridicule. In 1486 Juan Peraile, of Bordonales, near Belalcázar, reputedly said that "indulgences and remissions of sins that the holy apostolic Roman fathers give out to the Christian faithful are of no use for the remission of sins."[178] Luis (formerly Abraham) García, a bookseller in Talavera, said that the bulls were jokes.[179] The Portuguese Diego Pérez, a new-Christian living in Huancavelica [Peru], was accused in 1625 of "never having taken a bull of the holy crusade, but rather making fun of it, tearing it up in front of his wife."[180] In 1647 fifteen-year-old Simón de León told the Mexican Inquisition that his father Duarte de León had never taken a Bull of the Holy Crusade but rather "had made fun of them, saying that they were of no use."[181] For the Judaizing *conversos* the New Testament was bereft of divine inspiration. Hearing a friend swear on the New Testament in 1497, Pedro Mendes remarked: "The Gospels—are they something?"[182] Gonçalo Váez, a Portuguese student living in Granada, told Inquisitors there in 1571 that "there was no reason to believe the Gospels because they had been written by fishermen."[183] The new-Christian Pero Rodrigues, of Lamego, was charged [Coimbra 1583] with having scoffed at religious confraternities.[184] The Mexican Inquisition heard testimony around 1646 how Clara de Rivera "denounced the adoration of relics."[185] In fact many *conversos* held the entire Christian religion in low regard. Typical were Isabel Alvares, of Torre de Moncorvo, who was charged by the Coimbra Inquisition in 1571 of having stated that the law of the Christians was a joke;[186] or Alvar González, who was accused in the 1520s in the Canary Islands of believing that "everything that Christians say or do is wind," that Christianity is "a joke," and that Christians are "dogs who would come to a bad end";[187] or the sexton in Uclés [Cuenca c. 1490] who advised a *converso* who was having a hard time affirming the articles of the Credo to lighten up because, after all, "believing in the Christian faith or in Don Moses was all the same thing."[188]

It is not surprising then that Judaizing *conversos* developed a set of negative labels to apply to sincere Christians or that they disparaged them in a variety of ways. Sixteenth-century Portuguese *cristãos novos* denigrated old-Christians with epithets like "enemy dogs" (*cães inimigos*), "sons of Edom," "Moabites," or even the Hebrew term *goyim* (Pimenta Ferro Tavares 1987, 96). Liebman reports that the Hebrew word *horkos* ("idolaters") was sometimes applied to Christians in the New World.[189] An indictment of *chueta* customs given to the Majorcan Inquisition in 1674 notes that the *chuetas* called the Catholics "Canaanites" (*cananeos*) and "rabble" (*canalla*) (Braunstein 1936, 185). Other comments were more pointed and more personal. When Melchor Rodríguez López, a Portuguese cacao farmer in Mexico in the 1640s, heard of a crime that had been committed against a Christian, he said that it did not bother him for the person had not been a Judaizer (García 1910, 193). Juan de Teva, arraigned in Ciudad Real in 1513, asserted "that any day that he didn't deceive some Christian before breakfast he was not in his right mind, and that he would not eat breakfast until he had deceived some Christian."[190] For out and out venom it is hard to surpass the prayer attributed to the *converso* Juan Díaz in Ciudad Real in 1484: "Blessed be *Adonai* who did not make me a pig for Christians to eat, and Blessed be *Adonai*, my God and God of my fathers: kill them and destroy them and return them to our Law and to our Commandments."[191]

## 5.2. Sacrilege: Parody and Abuse

The thousands of such comments sprinkled through Inquisition documents from the 1480s through the next three hundred years reveal unequivocally the skepticism and antipathy that many Judaizing *conversos* held for the Christian religion—Jesus, Mary and the saints, the sacraments, and the whole gamut of Christian religious observances. Avoidance of Christian practices and blasphemous speech—momentary aggressiveness, angry derision, irony, or gently mocking ridicule—appear to have been the most common expressions of this skepticism. Common to all the incidents is an aura of disrespect that often consisted of verbal abuse or offhand remarks that expressed fundamental scorn. These attitudes were in no way unique to *conversos*, of course, for mocking disrespect of authority is a constant human response to feelings of powerlessness with regard to that authority. The latter Middle Ages are pervaded with what Monsalvo Antón calls an "interclass, popular culture which is irreverent, which undermines the solemnity of religion, which is skeptical of high-sounding words, morally corrosive, and surprisingly self-satisfied and even proud of swimming in waters of marginality" (1984, 118). Still, despite the presence of these attitudes in society at large, the consistency with which they are attributed to the Judaizing *conversos* is evidence of the *conversos*' profound sense of alienation as a group.

But the documents also reveal that some *conversos* seem to have taken the further step of expressing their negative feelings in actions the Christian authorities considered sacrilegious. Gonzalo Sánchez de Guadalupe, of Talavera de la Reina, was accused in 1489 of "throwing figs at the statues" when he came out of church.[192] A *converso* student named Estíbares [Soria 1492] was denounced for having made a rude gesture to an image he saw through a church door and for saying: "Cursed be the people who adore such things and believe in them."[193] Juan de Cordova, a new-Christian from Tlemcen [Morocco] living in Guadix, was reported [Granada 1575] to have called a row of crosses "skewers" and when reproached by a friend said that "they looked like gibbets for hanged men."[194] Ines Rodrigues [Brazil 1590s] said that she saw Alvaro Lopez "looking intently at a crucifix which was on the altar, and he threatened it putting his finger on his nose two or three times, and pulling his beard, and after that he threw two or three figs at it" (Furtado 1925, 549).[195]

From the *converso* point of view, many of these acts seem to have been intended to be funny. Often they were performed in group settings, where several *conversos* had come together for religious or social reasons. Like much ethnic humor, these sacrilegious jokes served the purpose of reaffirming group identity by disparaging the hated "Other." They mocked what the crypto-Jews saw as Christian credulity, ceremoniousness, or mistaken values. Since the nature of a parody is to imitate an action, these behaviors tended to focus on the administration of the Christian sacraments. I have not found examples of humorous parody of the sacraments prior to the Expulsion, but a handful of sixteenth-century examples will give an idea of how later Judaizers sometimes poked fun at what they could not accept. The *converso conquistador* of Mexico, Hernando de Alonso, was accused in 1529 of many things, including a ceremony performed after the baptism of his *mestizo* son on the island of Cuba: "One Thursday, after covering the Holy Sacrament, they took a male child, and pouring wine over its head and all that was dripping from the child's parts, they collected and drank, and said, singing, around the child, a psalm about Dominus Deus Israel of Egypt."[196] Fernão Pires, a sixteen-year-old new-Christian, was denounced in Bahia, Brazil, in 1591 for baptizing a puppy in a lake in a mock Christian ceremony.[197] It was reported in 1505 that some *converso* friends went to visit the ailing Françisco de la Fuente in Almazán [Soria]. They said, "'Let's give him the sacraments,' and they brought him a host made of mud and a cross made of horns and they put the host and the horn cross in a tambourine and they covered the host and the cross with a hat and they prayed over it as if they were going to administer the sacraments."[198]

Of a more serious nature, and devoid of any humorous intent, are the many hundreds of reported incidents of *converso* mistreatment of Christian ritual items. Some of these alleged events occur before the Expulsion, but they are much more frequent afterwards. Typically both Jewish and Catholic historians of the crypto-Jews have tended to discount these reports as trumped-up continuations of the traditional medieval accusations of host desecration and image flogging. But it seems to me that (1) these accusations are so prevalent, both in Spain and Portugal and in the colonies, and (2) they are such an obvious logical extension of the tendencies toward overt negativism we have been discussing, and (3) so many of these accusations meet the tests of credibility that we should not reject them out of hand.

Let us take a look at one illustrative example that appears to meet the common tests of documentary veracity. The incident allegedly occurred in Aragon in 1482 or 1483. The cleric Miguel de Almazán claimed that early one Holy Week morning he and his mother witnessed a group of *conversos* scourging a crucifix at the home of Gonçalvo Garcia de Santa María. He alleged that among the more than thirty named participants were several members of the prominent Santángel and Caballería families. In a downstairs, windowless room, Almazán saw a large cypress crucifix set into the floor next to a flaming brazier. At one end of the room was an enormous Hebrew book, open on an ornate bookstand. Many of the *conversos* were wrapped in mourning shawls. They stood half bowed over, with their arms folded, facing the crucifix. Almazán claims that he was an eyewitness to the actual whipping, which was carried out by the town crier [*corredor de orellas*] Juan Belenguer and an old man named Ortigas, and that his father later repeated to him the terrible names the two men called the image and told him that the brazier was in order to burn the crucifix when they had finished. This was clearly a ritual act with assigned roles. According to Almazán, Juan de Pedro Sánchez, who held a document in his hand, played the part of Pilate; Juan de Juan Sánchez was Annas; and his brother Luys was Judas. Almazán testified that when the *conversos* saw him come into the room they were frightened and made him go out again. Testimony from a number of other witness tended to confirm these events (Baer 1936, 465–6).

Prior to the Expulsion the most prominent accusations of host desecration and mistreatment of images—such as in the La Guardia case—do not meet the tests of credibility. They appear to have been concocted as part of the virulent anti-Jewish propaganda barrage unleashed by clerical polemicists. In the fifteenth century this barrage included numerous accusations of ritual murder. As best I can tell, none of these accusations meet the tests of credibility we have discussed,[199] and there are no allegations of ritual murder occurring after 1492. But from 1492 on, as crypto-Judaism in relative isolation from normative Judaism underwent shifts from positive toward negative observance, and as Jewish identity became increasingly defined as non-Christian, or anti-Christian, the numbers and credibility of sacrilegious incidents increased. While to my knowledge there is not a single credible instance of a sacrilegious act committed by a *converso* against another human being, there are innumerable instances of both host desecration and the mistreatment of Christian images.

For Christians the consecrated host, or eucharist, was literally the body of Christ and as such was the religion's single most sacred ritual object. As mentioned previously, crypto-Jews tried to avoid mass. They frequently disparaged the miracle of the eucharist and when forced by circumstance to take the host into their mouths often tried to spit it out. A more deliberately insulting strategy was used by

Luisa del Valle and Antonia de Tudela, her daughter, who were penanced in a 1720 *auto de fe* in Madrid because they had put the sacred hosts in their shoes and thrown them out after the communion service.[200] In 1589 in Lisbon a *cristãa nova* was accused because twice she went to mass with her mother and sister and they allegedly "took the host in their respective mouths and brought it home and buried in under the floor and when it was buried they trod on the floor shouting 'Dog, dog.'"[201] These incidents suggest that at least some crypto-Jews considered the host in some way "special" enough to merit their aggressive disrespect and mistreatment. This mixture of attitudes can be seen in the 1525 indictment of the *converso* Diego Riquel of the Canary Islands that, when a priest passed carrying the host, he "turned his head away saying 'Thou comest in an evil hour'" (Wolf 1926, 39).

As we have seen, crypto-Jews were rarely able to accept the Spanish Catholic obsession with images of Jesus, Mary, and the saints, for to them the painted or carved images seemed to be concrete evidence of idolatry or even polytheism. The expression of their negative feelings ran the gamut from disbelief and scorn to the physical mistreatment of the images. The crucifix, which from the early Middle Ages has been the principal icon of Christianity, was targeted by crypto-Jews with great cynicism and hostility both as an object of Christian idolatry and as emblem of that aspect of Christianity they found hardest to accept: the divinity of Christ. The Church, of course, considered the desecration of a crucifix to be sacrilege of the most serious kind; not only did it symbolize Christ, but Jesus was in some sense present in the image, so that physical harm to the crucifix was in a way physical harm to His sacred person. Paradoxically, for crypto-Jews to vent their rage on the crucifix indicates that they too held some measure of belief in its sacred power. Allegations of mistreatment of the crucifix appear with such frequency in the literature, in so many widely-separated locales, and with such varied evidence, much of it eyewitness, that either some degree of credence must be given to its having occasionally occurred or one must believe that dozens of Inquisitorial courts, independent of each other, elicited testimony and confessions of crucifix mistreatment. I am inclined to believe that it did occur, for it is consistent with a pattern of crypto-Jewish disrespect for the material trappings of Christianity.

Frequently the disrespect manifested itself in petty mistreatment of the crucifix. In 1537 in Mexico the *conquistador* Alonso de Avila, a *converso*, was accused of "having a crucifix under his desk and of putting his feet on it" (Uchmany 1977, 97). In 1650 Jerónimo Valle, a student in Toluca [Mexico], was denounced for allegedly jumping over a crucifix that was on the floor (Liebman 1975, 153; Pimenta Ferro Tavares 1987, 93). In 1541 in Lisbon the *cristã nova* Isabel Gomes was denounced because when her friend Maria Fernandes was baking and drew a cross on top of a loaf of bread Isabel rubbed it out.[202] One overtly disrespectful practice was to make the crucifix a witness or participant in sexual acts. In 1491 in Frías [Soria] Juana Sánchez de Castro said "that she had often seen a crucifix in doña Aldonza's bed, and it was not put there for honest reasons."[203] In the 1590s Diogo Castanho of Bahia had "carnal relations with a black slave who was lying on a crucifix."[204] Another way to show disrespect was to spit, urinate, or defecate on the image. The new-Christian Joam Nunes [Bahia 1593] was said to have kept a crucifix over his chamber pot and to have mocked the cross while urinating on it.[205] One day in 1643 in a Mexican Inquisitorial prison a prisoner "kissed the feet of an image that was painted on the wall with charcoal, and Juan de León said to him . . . 'What are you kissing there? A little charcoal?' Thereby he showed his disrespect for the prisoner's worship of the image. And it happened that when he knelt to pray, as I have said, Juan de León drew near him and turned his back on him; similarly, when the person crossed himself or prayed León would spit on the floor as if he were making fun of him."[206] In 1486 Ynes Gonçalez told Inquisitors that her mother Mari Sánchez took a crucifix that was kept at the foot of her bed and threw it in the privy.[207] Similarly, in 1654 Catalina Silva, a Portuguese *conversa* in Murcia, was accused of smashing a clay image of Jesus with a hammer, gathering up the pieces, and burying all of them in the latrine except for one piece which she threw in the garbage (Blázquez Miguel 1986b, 141). In 1587 the new-Christian Filipa Fernandes, of Seia, was charged by the Coimbra Inquisition of treating a painted crucifix in her cell with unspeakable irreverence.[208]

Much more common, however, are reports of crypto-Jews deliberately inflicting injury on the crucifixes, generally by beating them. In 1499 in Las Palmas a slave of Juan Crespo reported that "his mistress was in the habit of beating holy images" (Wolf 1926, 4). Alvar González was said to have fled the Azores in 1504 after having been accused of flogging a crucifix.[209] In 1547 the new-Christian Beatriz de Olivera, of Logroño, was tried because allegedly "she whipped and stabbed a crucifix that had an image of Christ on it and threw a fig at it and tossed it in the river."[210] In 1571 the new-Christian Cristóvão Coronel, of Monção, was charged by the Coimbra Inquisition with having beaten a crucifix with some leather straps.[211] Hernando de Avila, a *converso* from Ecija, was punished in 1598 in Córdoba because "he took a crucifix and threw lots of stones at it."[212] María de Peralta was denounced in Bahia, Brazil, in 1591 for "holding an image of the child Jesus in her left hand and pummeling it with her right, saying 'Now take this, now take this.' "[213] In fact in Pernambuco in the 1590s mistreating the crucifix seems to have been a widespread aspect of crypto-Jewish behavior. According to testimony given during the Inquisition's visit to Brazil, Gregorio Nunes,[214] Pedralvares Madeira,[215] Catarina Alvares (Furtado 1929, 143), and Clara Fernandes[216] flogged a crucifix. Ana Franca spit on it (Furtado 1925, 368). Branca Dias threw one across the room, saying "I send you to the Devil."[217] João Nunes and Gregorio Gonçalves urinated on it.[218] Gracia Luis was accused of giving a crucifix to her son to play with and saying that "it was not sacred and it was all right for him to play with it."[219] Despite what seems to have been an epidemic of such accusations, the

Brazilian Inquisitors appear to have dealt with each case of crucifix mistreatment on its merits and occasionally found an accused *cristão novo* to be innocent (Furtado 1929, 241–3).

The frequency of these sorts of accusations increased in the seventeenth century. In 1630 in Madrid several Portuguese Judaizers were accused of gathering every week to ritually whip a crucifix, which reputedly bled and wept (Monter 1990, 306). In 1653 in Santa Cruz [La Palma] a slave testified that he had seen the merchant Diego Rodríguez "on the Friday and Saturday nights of the two months he was in his service take a crucifix from the box where he kept his sword and clothes and thrash it with a leather whip for about half an hour each time, or until he became fatigued" (Wolf 1926, 137). In 1674 in Lima Rodríguez de Acevedo was accused by his slave of beating a crucifix on Saturday nights (Medina 1890, 241). In 1689 the seventeen-year-old servant Ventura Binimelis testified in Majorca against her mistress Isabel Cortés, saying that she had seen her "with an image of Holy Christ in her left hand . . . and with some cords that she had in her right hand she gave the Holy Christ cruel blows for about a half hour; and she was saying angry words to the Holy Christ." The accusations were firmly denied.[220] In 1696 Pedro Carretero was sentenced to the galleys because on Fridays he and four friends used to give an ivory crucifix thirteen lashes.[221] An *auto de fe* in Madrid in 1720 identified twenty families whose Judaizing included "mistreating our Lord Jesus Christ, saying that He was a great magician, and burning the Holy Image of His crucifixion."[222] The increasing frequency of these incidents as time went on suggests that the overt expression of hostility toward Catholic religious icons became more important to crypto-Judaism as the breadth and depth of other Judaizing practices diminished.

Some *conversos* seem to have used considerable ingenuity to find ways to express their disrespect for Catholic images. In 1554 in Mexico Juan de Astorga was accused of "inserting crosses between the cork and the sole of the shoes he made."[223] Liebman reports the case of Latin-American storekeepers who "placed a cross under the threshold of their stores. Whoever deliberately stepped on the threshold when entering received a discount" (Liebman 1982, 103). In the 1649 trial of María de Zárate in Mexico the following custom was given: "Stockings were manufactured on which a representation of Christ was placed on the sole, making the normal use of the stockings a desecration of Christ" (Liebman 1970, 282).

Not surprisingly, mistreatment of images of Mary and the saints paralleled mistreatment of the crucifix, although it was much less commonly reported. In 1500 in Gumiel, Soria, Francisco Calderón was reported to have said some eight years earlier that "that image there is not Holy Mary, and if you threw it in the fire it will burn well . . . I could warm myself there all right."[224] María González was accused in 1511 because "once, when she was given a painted image of Our Lady the Virgin Mary, she took it and treated it with humor and scorn, and threw it into a stinking pool that was near the kitchen, and after she had thrown the image in she spit on it."²²⁵ Margarita Gonçalez [Las Palmas 1530] testified that one night a twelve-year-old girl ran into her house crying: "Do you know, Madam, that Hernando Xerez the deaf is beating a statue of Our Lady which he has in a little room in his house?" And that wishing to find out whether the tale was true she "went into the house and saw the statue in the room described by the girl" (Wolf 1926, 90–1). The *cristão novo* Pedro Martins Cabeças [Lisbon 1541] was denounced because "he went to the hermitage of Vallongo and through the door threw stones at a statue of Our Lady and broke a statue of Saint Lucy."²²⁶ Alvaro Sanches, a Brazilian *cristão novo*, told the Inquisition in Bahia in 1591 that his father-in-law, Gaspar de Barrios, had once taken "a *Flos Sanctorum* [*Lives of the Saints*] and with a pin had scratched out a figure . . . of Our Lady, and he scratched out the crown and part of the head."²²⁷ The *conversa* Leonor Gutiérrez, of Hita, who had fled to Portugal, was tried in absentia in 1538–9. One of her serving girls said that on Saturdays "she would find an image of Our Lady that Leonor had at the head of her bed turned face to the wall."²²⁸

Rosaries, too, came in for their share of abuse. Diego Pérez, a Portuguese new-Christian living in Huancavelica, Peru, was accused in 1635 of breaking rosaries (Medina 1887, 2:27). In 1647 thirteen-year-old Ana Núñez told the Mexican Inquisition that once Simón de León had lent a friend of hers a rosary. "And when she had finished praying the beads like a good Catholic, she had put it on her bed with a new ribbon . . . and when she came back she found the ribbon torn and the cross and beads on the floor."²²⁹ In 1586 the *cristão novo* Diogo Pereira was denounced in Lisbon "for jumping on a Book of Hours."²³⁰ Diego Pérez of Huancavelica was also accused of "stomping on bags of relics."²³¹ Francisca Texoso, age fifty-eight, an unmarried baker, was accused by the Mexican Inquisition in 1646 of having a strange recipe for bread: "So that they would sell more, and that it would come out whiter and tastier, she and her sisters kneaded it with water which they had previously used to wash certain unsavory parts; and they made certain circles and Jewish rites over the dough as if they were blessing it."²³²

Even if we should find that the facts alleged in any one of these individual incidents fail to meet our criteria for convincing evidence, in the aggregate this array of accusations, widely separated in time and place, paints a consistent picture of *conversos* expressing their disdain for their adopted religion with a coherent set of negative behaviors. And many of these incidents are narrated with substantial detail that decreases the likelihood that the incidents were Inquisition fabrications. Let two examples illustrate this point. Sebastián Pérez was accused in Ciudad Rodrigo in 1625 by an unnamed eyewitness of having gathered with some friends one Saturday night to mistreat a crucifix.

> Through a hole in the door he saw that in the doorway of the room on a little stand or bench was a statue of Christ on a cross. He saw that there were six people in the room, four women and two men, including the accused and one

of his brothers. One by one they walked on their knees over to the Christ, and when they got to the doorway where it was placed they put their hands together before their breasts, just like when young boys play *mocarro* [a hitting game?]. The first one approached the Holy Christ on his knees and with his two hands together gave him a blow in the face like a slap, and then on his knees with his hands still held together in front of his chest walked backwards and said: "He didn't laugh; we haven't lost." Then this one got up and another went forward the same way and said the same words and did the same thing. And the witness watched until all six people had done it. And then he saw that one of the women took the image of the Holy Christ and went inside with it. . . . And he said that all six people are new-Christians who were Jews.[233]

The witness went on to say that the house was empty when he went there the next Saturday to see if they did it again, but instead he found them in the house of another member of the group performing the same ceremony. This time, angered, he shouted at them, and they put out the light.

In a somewhat similar incident in 1647 in Mexico, fifteen-year-old Simón de Valencia reported how his parents had mistreated a crucifix in the privacy of their home: "His father [Duarte de León] and mother shut themselves in the storeroom with him . . . and his brother Francisco and his sisters Clara and Antonia. And when Francisco had brought from his bedroom upstairs a Holy Christ about a half yard long, his parents put it upside down on the counter and beat it, telling it that its law was not the good one. And this went on for about an hour." The details of this episode were confirmed by Antonia, who added that the children all sat on white boxes, that their father used a switch of branches, like the one he beat the children with, and that he told Christ that "He was a trickster, that He had not come to the world, and that it was His fault they were suffering." She said that once when he did this her mother fainted and they had to carry her upstairs while her father continued. An anonymous witness reportedly said that when she heard the blows she asked "who they were beating so severely? Simón told her they were beating a cat because it had eaten some fish. And she asked why it didn't yowl under so many blows? And he replied that they stuffed its mouth shut." But the witness said that the beatings went on for so many nights it could not have been a cat.[234]

As we have seen in this chapter, crypto-Jewish attitudes toward Christianity were predictably negative. Crypto-Jews tended to view Christianity as an untrue or empty religion, the scourge of the Jews. Around 1489 the Aragonese *converso* Pedro de Almazán was accused or having said, "May the first person who turned Christian lie in an unsettled grave."[235] They empathized with Pedro Laínez, also of Almazán, who was said in 1505 to have cried "Cursed be the one who prohibited the Old Testament."[236] Those who accepted the Christian view of the afterlife tended to believe—like Francisco Maldonado de Silva, who was denounced in Lima, Peru in 1626—that all Christians were going to Hell.[237] One weapon in their struggle against assimilation was the constant, overt expression of this negativism. They tried to prevent their family members or servants from going to church. A black slave in the Canary Islands testified in 1520:

> Castillo's father-in-law said to [her] when she was kneeling: "Listen, don't kneel when I ask you to bring me a jug of water, I am not your God or your Holy Mary who can save you." . . . And Castillo took away her rosary and beat her for carrying it, and because she called out "Ave Maria!" he beat her still more severely, saying "Take this for the love of Holy Mary, and for the love of God." . . . [She] says that her employers tried to terrify her into adopting their customs, but she would not. . . . And that two or three times Castillo has made her carry a bench on her shoulders, saying "Carry the cross as Christ carried it," and has beaten her while she did so. (Wolf 1926, 23)

In 1647 fifteen-year-old Simón de Valencia reported to the Mexican Inquisition that when his parents used to beat him "they would put a stick in his mouth, tied like a gag, to keep him from saying 'stop for the love of God and for the Most Holy Virgin.' "[238] It is in this context that the physical abuse of Christian religious iconography must be placed.

A number of conclusions can be drawn from all of this. The first is that very soon after the Expulsions many Iberian crypto-Jews developed a sense of Jewish identity that was defined with reference to Catholicism rather than to traditional Judaism. I am not talking here about religious syncretism, by which I mean things like the adoption of a Christian-like concept of personal redemption achieved through belief in the Law of Moses or the observance of Yom Kippur by abstaining from eating pork for the forty days previous. Crypto-Jews did those things too, but within a system—no matter how derivative of Christian practice—that they considered to be fulfillment of traditional Jewish law. Rather, I am referring here to a crypto-Jewish self-concept that was negative in essence: it defined Judaism in large measure as a rejection of all things deemed to be Catholic.

Second, this negativism expressed itself along a continuum of practices that ran from word to deed. The most universal were expressions of disbelief in the holy nature of Jesus, Mary, the saints, the sacraments, and every other clearly identifiable aspect of Christian culture. This disbelief easily slipped from irony into scorn or ridicule and the sorts of disparagement which can be heightened by rude physical gestures. These attitudes were expressed by some old-Christians and *moriscos* too, of course. But the documents suggest that for many crypto-Jews such acts transcended mere casual expressions of disrespect and were instead an important part of the individual's concept of him- or herself as a crypto-Jew. Moreover, many crypto-Jews carried these negative attitudes into the realm of their own religious practice. Within the relative security of exclusively *converso* environments they might build group esprit by engaging in humorous parody of the Christian sacraments. In groups or by themselves, they might strengthen their sense of Jewishness by physically mistreating the realia of Catholicism, particularly images of the holy family.

Third, this abuse was confined to inanimate objects. I have not found one single instance of crypto-Jewish ritual mistreatment of any living being.[239] The traditional Central European allegations of ritual murder were indeed libels, introduced into Spain in the fifteenth century as part of the orchestrated, intense anti-Semitic propaganda war that culminated in the establishment of the Inquisition and the Expulsion of the Iberian Jews. While allegations of ritual murder were a stock part of the anti-Semitic propaganda arsenal after 1500, they were not leveled with the sort of specificity that would allow the Inquisition to bring *conversos* to trial. Indeed, there is no evidence whatsoever that such acts ever formed part of Iberian crypto-Jewish ritual.

For the most part these negative attitudes toward Christianity must be inferred from the actions of individual crypto-Jews. Rarely did a crypto-Jew clearly articulate the motivation for the kind of negative observances I have been talking about and that are so prevalent in the historical record. The closest to a self-realization of what was going on may be these words of Juan de León, recorded in a Mexican Inquisitorial prison in 1645:

> In order not to do anything that these deceivers do (he was talking about Catholic Christians) I do everything upside-down, and on meat days I ate fish, and during Lent I ate meat. Because, why should I live in deceit like they do? Let them screw themselves and bring me meat, which is why they called me a Jewish dog: for if I were a Christian I would not be eating meat during Lent. I observe my Law the way it ought to be observed, and I have to be different from them in everything."[240]

# NOTES

1. When the Fourth Lateran Council instituted the Jew badge, it essentially declared the Jews, qua heretical unbelievers, to be infectious as though they carried some biological disease. Fearing "contagion," they required Jews to live apart from Christians and forbade social intercourse or business relationships in which Jews might exert sway over Christians.

2. These legends made their way into the early lists of allegedly Judaizing customs. For example, a Valencian Edict of Grace of 1484 labels as a Judaizer anyone who "mocks the Passion by beating or crucifying some chicken or man or animal or sheep" (*En vituperi de la passio de nostre Redemptor ha açotat o crucificat algun gall, home, animal o anyell*) (Llorca 1935, 16). In sixteenth-century Oporto the new-Christian Henrique Bentalhado was actually accused of crucifying a chicken in parody of Christian worship (Pimenta Ferro Tavares 1987, 94).

3. An edition of Lope de Vega's seventeenth-century play about the incident, *El Niño inocente de la Guardia*, was published in Hitler's Germany. As I revise these lines I find that Robert Morrison has again asserted that the alleged victim was a true Catholic saint (1992, 181–3).

4. It is hard to follow the logic of Baer, who admits the credibility of some of these charges but then dismisses others out of hand: "Jews and *conversos* were capable of at times

breaking crucifixes or trampling them underfoot, but scourging is unthinkable" (1966, 2:362). Caro Baroja is one of a few recent Spanish historians who admit the possibility that such things might have happened in an ambiance charged with negative feelings about Christianity (1961, 2:431). Liebman supports this view: "The practice of beating images and crosses with the figure of Christ was pursued in Spain and Peru, as well as in New Spain, by Negroes and slaves as well as Jews" (1970, 344). Gilman too recognizes *converso* "blasphemies often involving a hatred of the newly imposed ritual so intense that they became . . . a kind of worship in reverse" (1972, 197).

5. Edwards raises two cautionary notes: first, that even a small, tightly-knit community was likely to exhibit a wide variety of opinions; and second, that although diverse views like those discussed in this chapter were common among crypto-Jews they were not unique to them, and that strong currents of religious scepticism run through much of the late medieval European experience, Christians and Jews alike. Even limiting his investigation to one Spanish province, Soria, in the first decade following the Expulsion, he concludes that "virtually every theological and philosophical option which has so far become available to humankind was espoused by someone in this region of Spain in the late 15th century" (1988, 24).

6. *No son más que dos personas de la Santísima Trinidad . . . sobre cual de las personas puso duda* (Gracia Boix 1983, 347). See also Blázquez Miguel 1987, 52 [c. 1491].

7. *Cantandosse hum dia . . . a cantiga seguinte, trino sollo, e uno, uno sollo e trino, no es otro alguno, sino Dios divino, ho ditto Bento Teixeira dixera que esta proposição era falsa* (Furtado 1929, 42–3).

8. Beinart 1961, 182; 1981, 316; Carrete Parrondo 1985a, 19, 161.

9. *Deus nã tinha necesydade de se meter no ventre de huna molher e que o mesyas nã avya de ser deus* (Baião 1921, 129).

10. *Nam cria que . . . Jesu Christo era Deus nem o Messias senam hum profeta* (Azevedo Mea 1982, 21; cf. 178).

11. *Un hombre docto* (Liebman 1970, 194).

12. *Desía que la ley de Muysén era buena e por ser buena avía querido Nuestro Señor Ihesu Christo ser judío treynta e tres años, e se quiso çircunçidar* (Carrete Parrondo 1985a, 161).

13. *Ihesu Christo, que avia seydo retajado, tan retajado como los retajados e judios* (Beinart 1977a, 207). See also Beinart 1961, 182 [1487].

14. *Quando ellos me dezían por qué no quieres adorar a Jesuchrysto, les respondí que yo venía muy bien en adorar y hazer la ley de Chrysto, que me la enseñasen, que yo también la quería guardar. Y ellos me enseñavan al Credo, y yo les respondí que la ley que ellos me enseñavan no era la ley de Chrysto sino la de los doze Apóstoles, porque la que guardava Christo y María era la de Moysés, y con esso les hazía perder su cuento* (Selke de Sánchez 1972, 264).

15. Liebman 1970, 175. See also Furtado 1925, xxxiii [Evora 1536].

16. *Xristo hijo de Joseph no era el Mesias, por que su madre no era de la casa de David* (Medina 1890, 176). See also Böhm 1963, 42.

17. *Aunque digan los chrystianos que Chrysto es Dios, no puede ser, por quanto es nazido y muerto, que Dios es infinito, ni es nazido, ni puede morir, porque él es criador y su grandeza no se pondría a hombre; porque él por perdonar pecados no tenía neçessidad de hazerse hombre porque su misericordia es tan grande que no tiene limitación* (Selke de Sánchez 1972, 260).

18. *Adoran un hombre, Christo, que fue un hechisero* (Selke de Sanchéz 1972, 247–8).

19. *Reniego del puto Ihesu Christo açotado, que si le tomase yo le tornaría a cruçificar* (Carrete Parrondo 1985a, 19).

20. *Adórote carpintero; adórote carpintero* (Caro Baroja 1961, 1:433). For similar examples see Azevedo Mea 1982, 11 [1567]; Baião 1921, 186 [1571]; Gracia Boix 1983, 141 [1573]; Lewin 1954, 122 [Mexico 1624].

21. *Oto ha-Ish* (Fita y Colomé 1893, 417). For a Portuguese example (*esse homem*) see Furtado 1929, 96 [Bahia 1593].

22. *Marauíllome desta gente en mentar de contino esta Pasión, porque quando acá matan a vn hermano o pariente, en espeçial sy le matan por justiçia, non quieren que ge lo menten, y esta gente nunca hasen syno mentalla* (Carrete Parrondo 1985a, 90).

23. *Este Dios que tienen cada año les nasçe e cada año lo matan* (Carrete Parrondo 1985a, 152).

24. *Quien pensaba que era Cristo sino un hombre comedor y bebedor que se andaba en bodas* (Lewin 1954, 187). See also Böhm 1963, 40.

25. *Había predicado el arte mágica, con que había engañado algunos ignorantes* (Böhm 1963, 47).

26. Beinart 1977a, 216–7; Bohm 1984, 47; AGN Vol 309 doc 4, 186a.

27. *Nuestro Señor Jesucristo fue un embustero que cuando moría decían los príncipes que lo era, y diciendo el pueblo que cómo lo conocerían por tal, le pusieron una cédula con ciertas palabras escritas en una pierna, y que entonces se levantó y dijo que no era hijo de Dios, que todos eran embustes suyos y se volvió a morir, y que andaba volando por los aires y tras él todas las almas de los apóstoles y católicos, diciéndole: ¡por ti! por ti andamos de esta manera* (Lewin 1977, 248).

28. *Que Ihesu Christo no avia resuçitado a Lazaro, syno que la Iglesia lo avia compuesto, y que hera burla* (Beinart 1977a, 216–7).

29. *Entonses habia muchos hechizeros que resusçitaban muertos* (AGN Vol 309 doc 4, 186a).

30. *Dixo . . . Pero Lopes: "Buena ley es la de los cristianos que agora tenemos, que quando Nuestro Señor subió a los çielos por vna escalera larga dezían los ángeles que yva vn onbre largo, vestido de colorado"* (Carrete/Fraile 1987, 86).

31. *"¿Qué os paresçe desto que pasa aquí? Tan grande burlería desta generaçión que ellos mismos hazen burla de sy mismos en hazer tan grandes vituperios como hazen; que qué onbre viuo, con que tal pueda creher, que ya sy lo predicasen y dixesen 'esto pasó' más lo crehería onbre, que no haziendo estos escarnios; que quál viuo onbre ay que tal creha que Dios se ponía en tal tentaçión. ¿Y ser Hijo de Dios hera? ¿Quál padre abría que pusiese a su hijo en tal cosa como ésta? Sy no, beslo por esos cavalleros que están alrededor, que no hazen sentimiento ninguno, salvo la gente neçia." Y que entonçes este testigo e los otros sus conpañeros respondieron: "Dexadnos, por amor de dios, non hablemos en ello, que tal qual es le avemos de tragar." . . . Maldita sea yo de Dios sy lo puedo creher que ello pasó asy, synon que alguno lo levantó por hazer mal a los judíos* (Carrete Parrondo 1985a, 143).

32. *Nuestro Señor Hjesucripto avia sido un açote que Dios envio para castigar los hombres* (García Fuentes 1981, 99).

33. *Quien ¡Jesú! diga en la çena, / que no coma albondiguilla* (Gómez-Menor Fuentes 1970, 105).

34. *Proybiendo a sus familiares e fijos christianos que non . . . nonbrasen el nonbre de nuestro salvador ihesu christo nin fesiesen çerimonia nin cosas de christiano* (Santa María 1893b, 369).

35. *No nombrando a Jesu Christo nro. Sr., sino al Señor, que es lenguaje de Judios* (AGN Vol 271 doc 1, 3a). See also García 1910, 101 [1647].

36. *Quando algun christiano los saluda, diziendo Loado sea Jesu Christo, en lugar de dezir "por siempre," responden, "sea Dios loado"* (AGN Vol 276 doc 14, 428b).

37. *Por no tomar en la boca a Jesucristo le llamaban Cristóbal Sánchez* (Sierro Malmierca 1990, 178).

38. *Vio este testigo como cada vez que dezian Ihesus en la Pasyon, Juan de Teva . . . escopia, e que este testigo estava sobre auiso para mirar sy su escopir proçedia de todas otras e de alguna otra*

*cavsa, o sy lo hazia por escarnio de la Pasion, e que estuvo atenta a verlo, e vio que todas las vezes que dezian Ihesus, escopia el dicho Juan de Teyva syn toser y syn proposyçion, e que algunas vezes acaeçia que dezian Ihesus dos o tres vezes a reo, e todas vezes escopia, e que sy tardava de dezir Ihesus nunca le veya escopir, fasta que lo dezian* (Beinart 1981b, 326; cf. 332).

39. *E quando hysyan ademan de santiguarse alguna vez, desya "en Nonbre del Padre" e nunca desya "en Nonbre del Hijo" ni mas, saluo de ocho dias aca, despues que la Ynquisiçion esta en esta çibdad, que la vio este testigo santiguar vna ves, e dixo "en Nonbre del Padre e del Hijo"* (Beinart 1977a, 88).

40. Beinart 1961, 182. See also Baião 1921, 121 [1541].

41. *Que la sangre de los judios hera buena y linpia, y que eran los judios de sangre real . . . aun por ser tan linpia sangre la de los judios avia Dios escogido a Nuestra Señora para su encarnaçion* (Moreno Koch 1977, 370).

42. *Ellos vienen de mexor casta que los christianos viexos porque la Madre de Dios era Judía, y que ellos vienen de aquella casta* (Selke de Sánchez 1972, 115).

43. *Por ter chamado a Nossa Senhora nossa Cegonha* (Baião 1921, 157).

44. *"Reniego de Dios e de Santa María," dándoles pugeses: "ésta para Dios, éste para Santa María"* (Carrete Parrondo 1985a, 19). A fig is a sexually charged rude gesture made by making a fist with the thumb protruding between clenched fingers.

45. *Le pidió . . . un vestido para una imagen de Nuestra Señora que tenía; . . . respondió que no la había menester, y ventiscó por detrás en aquel instante y dijo para ella y para la Virgen* (Lewin 1971, 477). In Bahia [1593] the new-Christian Manoel Dias was said to have farted at the Virgin (*Alevantou a perna e deu hum grande traque, diante da imagem da Virgem*) (Furtado 1929, 43).

46. *Pello pentelho da Virgem Nossa Senhora* (Furtado 1925, 511). Cf. Furtado 1929, 69, 130.

47. *La concepçion de nuestra Señora, porque hauia sido casada Señora Santa Anta tres veçes* (AGN Vol 529 doc 11, 270b).

48. *Reniego de Dios e de Santa María e de la puta vieja de Santa María e del puto de su hijo* (Carrete Parrondo 1985a, 33; cf. 34, 61).

49. *Nuestra Señora no había parido virgen; y que había tenido más hijos que a Jesucristo, que había sido casada con Josep* (Gracia Boix 1983, 136). See also Furtado 1929, 191 [Brazil 1594]; Halkin 1953, 402 [1650]; Selke de Sánchez 1972, 247 [Majorca 1687].

50. *Asy he ella vyrgem como he a may que me pario* (Pimenta Ferro Tavares 1987, 94).

51. *Aquella muger Maria fue una muger que tuvo dos hijos, el uno se llamava Juan y el otro Jesus* (Selke de Sánchez 1972, 247).

52. *Nã ha hy queijo sem qualho. . . . Pois asy nã pode conceber nhuna molher sem semente de barão* (Baião 1921, 137–8).

53. *Como se pode tirar huma gema de hum ovo sem se quebrar?* (Baião 1921, 178).

54. *El decir que la Virgen había parido a Nuestro Señor era mentira, porque no era sino una mujer que estaba casada con un viejo y se fué por ahí y se empreñó y no era virgen* (Böhm 1963, 40).

55. *En su casa del dicho su amo decretauan y enseñauan a sus criados lo siguiente: Que Santa Maria era judia, que avia casado con vn carbonero judio, y que madrugo a faser carbon y que vino vn christiano a uilla y se echara con ella, y se enpreñara del y pario a ihesu Christo; y que lo tomaron como nasçio y lo metieron en vn aluañar de vna aluerca, y que alli se fisiera aquella corono que tiene; y que en aquel tienpo, en la aquella aluerca avian vnas colas grandes que paresçia en siryllas, y que alli lo colgaron, y que aquella era la Pasion que Ihesu Christo avia pasado* (Beinart 1974, 323).

56. *Nuestro Señor Jesucristo no era concebido por obra del Espíritu Santo, sino que era hijo de un carpintero y habido estando* [sic] *nuestra Señora con la costumbre ordinaria de las mujeres, y*

*por esta ocasión no había querido San José llegar a ella, por ser ceremonia de la Ley de Moisés no llegar los hombres a las mujeres en semejantes ocasiones, y que los que la guardaban dejaban las puertas de sus casas abiertas, y viendo el carpintero, que vivía cerca de la casa de nuestra Señora, que estaba sola y la puerta abierta entró a verla, y de esta suerte engendró a nuestro Señor Jesucristo, pensando nuestra Señora que el hombre que con ella estaba era su marido San José, y que por haberse concebido contra la costumbre de la Ley salió un tan mal hombre y embustero como nuestro Señor Jesucristo, y que como San José había visto preñada a su mujer, ella se había ido huyendo porque no la matara* (Lewin 1977, 248).

57. *Le vido dar higas a Nuestra Señora la Virgen Maria; e le dixo la moça por que lo haçia; e le dixo que duelos la diese Dios, que era Nuestra Señora vna puta judihuela* (Beinart 1974, 389).

58. *Que nuestra señora la Virgen Santa Maria era una muger comun. E que estonçes respondio la dicha Catalina, ¡que maravilla!, ¿nunca oyestes vos desir que era una ensangrentada?* (Beinart 1974, 388). For similar remarks see Caro Baroja 1961, 1:442; Carrete Parrondo 1985a, 61, 165 [1491]; Baião 1921, 126 [1541]; Reguera 1984, 183 [Basque Country 1554]; Azevedo Mea 1982, 205 [Coimbra 1570]; García Fuentes 1981, 99 [Granada 1571]; 213 [1586]; Furtado 1925, 254, 272 [Brazil 1591]; Liebman 1970, 178 [Mexico 1596]; Lewin 1954, 187 [Chile 1626].

59. *Boa molher esta que não chama pella Maria* (Pimenta Ferro Tavares 1987, 94).

60. *Vós outros falais em Nosa Senhora e Ella he tam boa como o cuco* (Azevedo Mea 1982, 282).

61. *Dixo el dicho Juan Falcon a su hermano deste testigo, porque se abia querido ahogar, que cayo en el rio: Cuando cayste en el rio ¿A quien te encomendaste? Dixo su hermano deste testigo: A la Virgen Maria. Dixo el: No fueste nesçio en encomendarte a la Virgen Maria, que mientras tomase su manto y lo fuese a rogar a su fijo, fuera el ahogado. Otra ves non te acaeste, syno encomiendate al Señor. Esto oyo este testigo, e su hermano echo mano [a] un puñal e lo quiso matar; e estonçes su padre deste testigo le requerio que en su casa non fablase en la Fe Catholica, sino que si lo mentase fuese a su culpa* (Beinart 1974, 561).

62. *Treviño con grande saña y alboroto por el entrañable odio que a la Reina de los Angeles Señora Nuestra tiene, le dijo: "calla, caballo, que no tiene Dios Madre, que si nos hizo a nosotros, ¿cómo pudo nacer? Que todo es patarata, que no hay más que un solo Dios que crió el cielo y la tierra, y todo lo que cree la Iglesia es patarata"* (Lewin 1954, 141–2).

63. *Quando acabo de dizir a Ave Maria amargame a bocca* (Furtado 1929, 78).

64. *Pues venga ese santo a curar de vos* (Blázquez Miguel 1987, 46).

65. *Decía de San Benito de Palermo que ¿cómo podía ser santo un negro? Y de San Ignacio que había sido gran goloso y comelitón, y que había muerto sentado en un servicio, y que era mal hecho guardar su fiesta, porque los padres de la Compañía por dinero habían alcanzado se guardase. Y que San Pedro Mártir, siendo Inquisidor, había quemado a su padre, y que así no se podía creer que fuese santo siendo tan cruel con su padre. Y de San Felipe de Jesús, santo mártir de estos reinos, decía que por huir del martirio se había huído de la prisión, y después lo habían cogido y contra su voluntad lo martirizaron* (Lewin 1971, 498).

66. For example, Beinart 1961, 182; 1974, 389, 560–1; 1977a, 248; Carrete Parrondo 1985, 33–4, 61, 88.

67. *Del humo que salía del fuego en que estaba aquel hombre en las parrillas, se habían puesto negras las vigas, según parecía haber de años que lo estaban asando* (García 1910, 78).

68. *Si desia Juan, desian: Mal Juan venga por ti* (Beinart 1974, 560).

69. *Descreo de Dios con sant Juan hodido* (Carrete Parrondo 1985a, 34).

70. *[Que] Sant Pedro tenía las llaues del çielo, respondió el dicho clérigo como por escarnio: "Sy, en la çinta"* (Carrete Parrondo 1985a, 101).

71. *Os santos pintados não erão mais que pinturas que as gentes pintavão* (Azevedo Mea 1982, 450).

72. Bel Bravo 1988, 146. For similar remarks see Wolf 1926, 43 [Las Palmas 1524]; Azevedo Mea 1982, 11 [Coimbra 1567]; Sierro Malmierca 1990, 117 [1580s]; Furtado 1925, 242 [Brazil 1591]; García Fuentes 1981, 462 [1595]; Lewin 1977, 243, 245 [Mexico 1643].

73. The *converso* polemicist Fray Hernando de Talavera, for example, whose *Católica impugnación* dates from around 1487, attempted a neoplatonic rebuttal of the *converso* arguments on this point: "The Christian Church . . . does not worship those images, be they painted or sculpted, be they of wood or stone . . . as the idolatrous pagans and foolish gentiles did. . . . We keep and honor the images because they recall to our memory and represent to us those people and things of which they are images, and they remind us of them" (*La Iglesia cristiana . . . no adora a aquellas imágenes, agora sean de pincel, agora de bulto, quier sean de palo, quier de piedra . . . como las adoraban los paganos idólatras y necios gentiles. . . . Tenemos y honramos las imágenes porque nos reducen a la memoria y nos representan a aquellas personas y cosas, cuyas imaginaciones son, y nos recuerdan de ellas*) (Hernando de Talavera 1961, 138; cf. 187).

74. *Ni creía que se debiese veneración a las imágenes* (Gracia Boix 1983, 331; cf. 136, 141).

75. *Que mercé pode fazer deus ha tera com isto?* (Baião 1921, 146).

76. *Adorar imagenes era idolatrar, y que Dios habia mandado antiguamente que no adorasen imagenes de palo, que era idolatria* (García de Proodian 1966, 341).

77. *Mirando una cruz que la testigo tenia al cuello en un rosario, dijo que no creia en ella, y que Xristo era de palo y si fuera lo que los xristianos decian resplandeciera* (Böhm 1984, 284).

78. *Todos los cristianos iban al infierno, por ser idólatras en adorar las imágenes delas imágenes de Jesucristo y de los santos hechos de palo. . . . El adorar las imágenes era idolatría, y que no se debían adorar, sino a solo el espíritu, y no a ninguna de sus imágenes* (Lewin 1971, 481, 26). See also García 1910, 69 [Mexico 1646].

79. Wolf 1926, 153–4. See also Carrete Parrondo 1985a, 101 [1501].

80. *Niegan generalmente la adoracion de las imagenes diciendo que solamente es oro, plata o palo* (García Fuentes 1981, 434).

81. *Nunca tuuo ni tiene ni costumbró tener en su casa oratorio de la Virgen María ni de Jhu. Xristo ni de sus Santos, segunt que xristianos costumbran tener e delant de los quales fazen oración* (Llorca 1942, 134).

82. *E que en los dichos palaçios donde leyan no avia ymagen ninguna de Nuestro Señor ni de Nuestra señora* (Beinart 1981b, 99). For other examples see Lewin 1954, 186 [Chile 1626]; Azevedo 1921, 450 [Portugal].

83. *Rehusaba entrar en los templos por no arrodillarse a los santos, por ser el mayor pecado que dicen los judaizantes se puede cometer* (García 1910, 91).

84. *Que no quitava el sombrero a la cruz, ni hacía reverencia a las imágenes ni a los santos ni al santísimo sacramento* (Medina 1887, 2:128). As late as 1737 in Ouro Preto (Brazil) Manoel da Costa Ribeiro, a new-Christian, was convicted of having similarly insulted a crucifix (Wiznitzer 1960, 158).

85. The other five are penance (confession), matrimony, anointing of the sick (or dying), confirmation, and holy orders.

86. For Marrano circumcision/baptism/*hadas* customs see Chapter 7.

87. *Nunca yvan domingos a Misa ni fiestas ni otros dias de entre semana sy no las conbidavan pa algund bavtismo o velaçiones de algunos conversos* (Beinart 1977a, 163). It still seems to be the case in this century in Belmonte, Portugal, where a *cristão novo* baby on the tenth day after birth is taken to the church to be baptized (Paulo 1985, 144; 1970, 87).

88. *Quando trayan de baptizar la criatura, tenían una caldera de agua caliente; e acabados de yr los conpadres e dada fruta, se metían el dicho su amo e ama e una moça marina, de quien ellos fiavan mucho, en una cámara e metían allá el agua e cerravan la puerta; e cree este testigo que lavavan la criatura, porque la oya llorar. . . . Les lavava las fruentes, e gelas fregava con un paño, e dezía a este testigo que lo fazía porque se les quitase el vello, e gelas veya mucho refregar* (Fita y Colomé 1893, 300, 302). By the late fifteenth century these practices were compiled among the customs of the Judaizers: "when their children are born they circumcise them and give them Jewish names and they scrape off the chrism and wash them after they have been baptized" (*Cuando nacen las crituras las circumcidan y ponen nombres de judios y las hacen raer la chrisma y lavar después de baptizados*) (Santa María 1893c, 182). See also Llorca 1935, 15 [Valencia 1484]; Beinart 1974, 198–9, 517–8, 524; Baer 1966, 2:337; López Martínez 1954, 177 [Castile late fifteenth century]; Marín Padilla 1981–2, 278–90 [Aragon late fifteenth century]; Wiznitzer 1960, 14 [Brazil]; Liebman 1970, 54 [Mexico 1527], 97 [Mexico 1639].

89. *Vosso baptismo he de merda* (Furtado 1929, 86).

90. *Y santiguaba a modo judaico a las criaturas de los judíos que había en esta ciudad, y para ello era llamada, ensalmándolas supersticiosamente y con sospechas de pacto con el demonio* (García 1910, 61).

91. *¡Qué bullas! ¡qué bullas!* (Carrete Parrondo 1985a, 147).

92. *Se estaua en la cama fasta que salían de misa mayor; e le desían que se leuantase para yr a misa e desía que le dexasen dormir* (Carrete/Fraile 1987, 76). For examples of similar behavior see Carrete Parrondo 1985a, 149; 1972, 143 [1528]; Wiznitzer 1960, 159 [Brazil 1726]; Paulo 1985 [Portugal twentieth century].

93. *Os sabbados atinha notado que o guardavam, vestindo se de festa, fingindo-se doente o dono da casa para não ir a Relação* (Baião 1921, 106).

94. *Sino es quando el alcayde los lleua a sancto Domingo que aquello es de fuerça* (AGN Vol 276 doc 14, 413b).

95. *Su muger, a quien no consentía oir misa, ni a su familia* (Medina 1887, 2:27).

96. *Se fôreis minha filha, houvera-vos de quebrar as pernas: à à uma porque comeis chouriços de sangue; e à outra porque andais tanto e is tantas vezes à missa. . . . A que is à missa? is adorar um pouco de papel. Tomai o papel e ponde-o na parede e adorai-o. . . . Para que dizeis nada àquela que é uma papa santos?* (Coelho 1987, 211–2).

97. *Non costumbró ni costumbra de genollarse quando tanyen las oraciones ni quando tanyen a la elevación del Corpus Xristi* (Llorca 1942, 134).

98. *Se vuelve cara tras e resa la cara hasia la pared, e quando los otros presos dysian la salve, que buelve la cara hasia atras y no mira el altar* (Baer 1936, 446).

99. *Por donde ella se posaua hera la parte de fuera y en logar donde no podía ver el altar donde se desía la misa* (Carrete/Fraile 1987, 90).

100. *Mientras alçaron el Corpus y el calis, nunca miró al altar, saluo vna pared de la yglesia* (Carrete/Fraile 1987, 52). For similar examples see Carrete Parrondo 1985a, 35, 97 [1490]; Gilman 1972, 97 [1525 Toledo]; Beinart 1977b, 54 [Ciudad Real 1520s]; Pimenta Ferro Tavares 1987, 93; Azevedo Mea 1982, 432 [Coimbra 1583]; Liebman 1982, 102 [Mexico].

101. *Sacando de la manga el pañuelo, hacía que se los limpiaba, por no ver alzar la hostia y cáliz; y al pasar por los altares con su madre, les iban dando higas debajo de los mantos, escupiéndolos y mofando de los santos que en ellos había* (García 1910, 209). See also Liebman 1974, 147 [Mexico 1649]. Some of this behavior carries over into this century among people who describe themselves as Judaizers. Anne Cardoza reports that her grandmother, Pauline, who

emigrated from Gerona to Buenos Aires to the United States, would attend mass but never take communion (Cardoza 1989, S2).

102. *Al tienpo que se salió vio que boluió las espaldas fasya el altar e fiso la reuerençia con el posadero* (Carrete/Fraile 1987, 34).
103. *Daba pugeses e higas* (Reguera 1984, 183). See also Baião 1921, 122 [1541].
104. *Em vez de tirar o chapéo da cabeça o afincara maís na cabeça* (Furtado 1925, 257).
105. *Non le vio herirse en los pechos* (Carrete Parrondo 1972, 143).
106. *Inquieta com pouco reverencia a Deos buscando sempre com quem trave practica* (Furtado 1925, 377).
107. *No rezaba y se sentaba junto a sus parientes y juntaban las cabezas y se ponían a hablar cuando alzaban el Santo Sacramento* (Contreras 1982, 603).
108. *Ah, cães encadeados* (Lipiner 1969, 168).
109. *Abaixando a cabeça fazia com ella e com a boca e com o nariz muitos momos e geitos que não erão de devoção, mas claramente lhe parecerão serem de industria feitos enjuriosos contra o santissimo sacramento* (Furtado 1929, 75).
110. *Se echaba mano a la barba y ponía el dedo sobre la nariz: acciones de amenaza, odio, y dañado corazón* (García 1910, 113).
111. *En levantándose de cabe su mançeba, syn reçar e syn reconçiliar, yba a deçir misa como sy la dixera vn judío o vn moro . . . [quitaba] las sávanas del altar sobre donde está el ara y sobre donde se haze memoria de la Pasyón de Christo, y echáualas y mandáualas echar muy desonestamente en la cama donde dormiesen él y la dicha su mançeva* (Carrete Parrondo 1979, 52).
112. *Duro es este sermón, ¿quién lo creerá? . . . y no quisieron seguir más a Jesuchristo, pensando que carnalmente lo havían de comer* (*Libro llamado el Alboraique*, 402).
113. Wolf 1926, 68. For similar expressions see Fita y Colomé 1884, 402 [Córdoba 1484]; Carrete Parrondo 1985a, 55, 71, 72, 101, 168 [Soria 1491]; Reguera 1984, 183 [Basque Country]; Furtado 1925, xxxiii [Evora 1536]; Baião 1921, 146 [Portugal 1543]; Gracia Boix 1983, 132, 135 [Córdoba 1572]; Azevedo Mea 1982, 202, 246, 261 [Coimbra 1570–1]; Liebman 1975, 101 [Mexico 1603].
114. *Vinha de comungar da igreja de Sam Pedro e que era laa muita gente e não avia particulas pera tanta então o ditto Gaspar Coelho dixe . . . não avia ay tapioca* (Furtado 1929, 80; cf. 86).
115. *Juro a Dios todo es burla desde el Papa hasta la capa* (Carrete Parrondo 1989, 65).
116. *Si eres Dios, yo te adoro; si non, non. . . . Así adorote, Señor, si ahí estás* (Sicroff 1965, 100).
117. Sicroff (1965, 100). For similar expressions see Carrete Parrondo 1985a, 124 [Soria]; Sierro Malmierca 1990, 120, 178 [Ciudad Rodrigo 1580s, 1623].
118. *Que no se daua más comer aquella hostia que vn casco de çebolla* (Carrete Parrondo 1979, 52).
119. *Pues Fudá ¿para qué quería pan?* (Carrete/Fraile 1987, 50).
120. *Querem-me a mim fazer crer que ha ostea que o clerigo esta fregindo ha noyte com sua mançeba que ao outro dia esta aly deus inteiro e verdadeiro* (Baião 1921, 151).
121. Beinart 1961, 190. Another witness accused him of "carrying the cross upside down as if he were going to throw it in some scandalous place" (*Cabeça ayuso que parescia que la leuaua a echar en algun lugar desonesto*) (Sicroff 1965, 101). See also Baer 1966, 2:337.
122. *Pan y vino veo y en la Ley de Moysén creo* (Carrete Parrondo 1985b, 101).
123. *Eu não adoroo pau nem a pedra / mas o grande Deus que tudo governa* (Paulo 1985, 103). See also Schwarz 1925, 19, 79.

124. *Al tienpo que dauan la pas vido este testigo cómo la susodicha tomó la pas e vn poco de pan benito e se lo metió en la boca, e luego boluió la cabeça e escupió* (Carrete/Fraile 1987, 34).

125. *Cada vez que tomava o Sanctissimo Sacramento o tomava da boca e ho hia lançar em hum munturo* (Furtado 1925, 345).

126. *Haviendo recibido la forma havía sacado la lengua y quitado de ella con un pañuelo el cuerpo de Xpo. Nro. Sr.* (Domínguez Ortiz 1955, 569; cf. 90). See also Wolf 1926, 6 [Canary Islands 1505]; Liebman 1982, 100 [Mexico].

127. *Adorando esta rea al sanctissimo sacramento le dixo la dha su media hermana que no lo adorase, sino quando alçase el clerigo en la missa la Ostia dixesse una torta de pan veo, en ti Señor adoro y creo diziendolo por Dios que estaua en el çielo, y quando alçase el Calix hauia de dezir pan y vino veo en ti Señor adoro y creo* (Bel Bravo 1988, 151).

128. *Niegan el sacramento del altar diciendo que en las especies del pan solo hay pan y quando hacian adoracion decian una torta de pan beo en Dios adoro y creo y lo mismo en las especies del vino diciendo agua y bino beo en Adonay adoro y creo* (García Fuentes 1981, 434).

129. *Pão e vinho vejo, e creio na lei de Moysés* (Baião 1921, 141). See also Pimenta Ferro Tavares 1987, 94.

130. *Quando o sacerdote alçava a Deos alçando a ostia cõsagrada vio ao ditto Fernão Soeiro estar de joelhos batendo nos peitos e lhe ouvio dizir as pallavras seguintes, eu creo o que creo, eu creo o que creo, eu creo o que creo* (Furtado 1929, 377). See also Baião 1921, 146 [1545].

131. *Nesta igreja entro, mas não adoro pau nem pedra; também não adoro pão nem vinho; venho unicamente adorar ao Deus de Moisés vivo* (Paulo 1985, 28).

132. *"¿A dónde van los locos, perdidos, con su delin, delin?"* (Moreno Koch 1977, 356). See also Beinart 1977a, 297, 481; Carrete Parrondo 1985a, 89.

133. *Desía quando tañían a misa en Sant Gil o a ver a Dios: "Duelo dé el Dió con aquellas canpanillas de Santa Gil, que nunca fasen syno desir: ¡Vienga, vienga!"* (Carrete Parrondo 1985a, 63).

134. *Tañen a ver al diablo* (Carrete/Fraile 1987, 67). See also Wolf 1926, 23 [1520].

135. *Hevelayud* = Hebr. *hebel hayu* (Carrete Parrondo 1985a, 46).

136. *La predicaçion . . . que para qué quería yr a oyr aquellas nadas* (Carrete/Fraile 1987, 68).

137. *Os sacrificios, e Missas, que fazem na Sancta Igreja não aproveitão para as almas* (Furtado 1925, xxxiii).

138. *¡Que misa de salud! ¿E vos creeys que ay misa de salud? ¡Non lo crays!* (Blázquez Miguel 1987, 46).

139. *Le había dicho . . . cuando traían al Santísimo Sacramento que aquello era nada* (Lewin 1977, 245). See also García 1910, 59.

140. *La crisma, ¿qué es syno merda?* (Carrete Parrondo 1985a, 113).

141. *Confesáronme e comulgáronme e enlodáronme* (Carrete Parrondo 1985a, 76).

142. *Que estando asy malo, çiertas personas le dixeron . . . que se confesase . . . y resçibiese los Santos Sacramentos; e que el . . . sienpre se escusaua e escuso de no haserlo* (Beinart 1981b, 102). For similar examples see Furtado 1929, 76, 378 [Bahia 1593–4].

143. *Niegan . . . que no ay potestad en los confesores para perdonar pecados y por esto no confesaban sino cosas lebes para hacer burla de la confesion y por miedo de la Inquisicion* (García Fuentes 1981, 434).

144. *Na lei velha só havia a confissão mental, . . . que o Papa ordena a confissão vocal . . . para os leigos estarem mais sujeitos á egreja* (Baião 1921, 145).

145. *Fazer un hoyo en el suelo e desir alli sus pecados . . . y non desirlo al confesor, nin a ningund onbre terrenal* (Rábade Obradó 1990a, 383).

146. *La confesión se había de hacer a solo Dios* (Gracia Boix 1983, 136).
147. *Su madre le había dicho que no lo confesase, aunque los confesores se lo preguntasen, que los judíos no se confesaban al sacerdote sino con Dios, diciendo: "Señor en esto y en esto te he ofendido"* (Gracia Boix 1983, 133). See also Lewin 1954, 182 [Peru 1611]; Medina 1890, 174 [Chile 1627].
148. *La confesión al sacerdote era contra la ley de los judíos, los cuales se confesaban a solo Dios* (Toro 1932, 258).
149. *¿Qué es confesarse? Que es embuste. . . . Cuando me confieso de veras, en un rincón me pongo de rodillas y allí me confieso y digo cuánto he hecho a aquel hombre, que no es sordo* (Lewin 1975, 94; cf. 63, 146, etc.). See also Lewin (1977, 315).
150. *Nosotros nos confesamos a honbre y ellos a la pared* (Carrete Parrondo 1985a, 56; cf. 72, 90).
151. *El confesar que hera chicharabachas* (Carrete Parrondo 1985a, 146). Sephardic rabbis, writing from outside Spain, recognized the skepticism with which *conversos* approached the sacrament of confession. Rabbi Sa'adía ben Danán wrote from Oran, sometime shortly after 1492: *¡Hacer con la boca o con los labios una confesión de nada, bajo la amenaza de la espada . . . ! Aun los peores entre ellos, los que se las dan de herejes o escépticos, no dan importancia alguna a esta nonada de los gentiles y en su corazón no puede creer que tenga contenido alguno* (Levi 1982, 35).
152. *Rodrigo Marin, su marido, la pregunto si abia confesado, e ella le respondio que cada ves que el clerigo la preguntava el pecado le desia: Duelos le de dios, mas que faria vn hoyo en su huerto e que alli confesaria sus pecados* (Beinart 1974, 546). See also Azevedo Mea 1982, 450 [Coimbra 1583]; Bel Bravo 1988, 149 [Granada 1592].
153. *Y que era pecado confesar, comulgar y oir misa y rezar el rosario; y que a los confesores católicos se les dijesen cuatro embustes para cumplir con el pueblo cristiano . . .* (García 1910, 59). See Rábade Obradó 1990a, 383 [Guadalupe 1485].
154. Böhm 1963, 40. See also Medina 1890, 183. Echoes of this attitude persist among Portuguese Judaizers of this century. Ninety-year-old Deolinda Mota of Rebordelo, Portugal, told Manuel da Costa Fontes in 1980 that "before going to confession she says a Crypto-Jewish prayer at home" (Fontes 1993, 78).
155. *Oyó decir que Juan Escogido e el Podrido, vesinos desta cibdad eran los confesores de los confesos. . . . Yngeriéndose a consolar e confesar a los enfermos en artículo de la muerte asy como judío* (Santa María 1893a, 195; cf. 199, 201).
156. *Proybiendo a sus familiares e fijos christianos que se non santiguasen* (Santa María 1893b, 369). The trials contain hundreds of accusations of this sort.
157. *Quando se benzia se benzia com huã figa e que dava por desculpa que tinha o dedo pollegar comprido* (Furtado 1925, 338).
158. *Ser observantísimo de la lei de Moises, signarse con la siniestra mano en desprecio de la Cruz* (Gracia Boix 1983, 615). See also Carrete Parrondo 1985a, 35 [1490]; Beinart 1961, 190; Azevedo Mea 1982, 261 [Coimbra 1571].
159. *E que todas las vezes que venia del escuela vn hijo pequeño de hedad de ocho años, quen se llamaua Fernando, e besaua la mano a la dicha su madre, e que despues que gela auia besado, gela ponia encima de la cabeça por la cara abaxo, syn lo santiguar* (Beinart 1977a, 268).
160. *Quando tañían el Ave Maria que no se santiguava, saluo que ponia las manos crusadas sobre la cabeça* (Moreno Koch 1977, 359). See also Beinart 1981b, 418. This custom too has echoes among people who think of themselves as the remnants of Iberian secret Judaizers. Anne Cardoza reports that her grandmother, Pauline, who emigrated from Gerona to

Buenos Aires to the United States, at mass "would touch her forehead or face or shoulders in various places so that it would look as if she was making the sign of the cross. What she really was doing was whispering *Adonai*" (Cardoza 1989, S2).

161. *Contas, contas, bulraria, bulraria* (Baião 1921, 143).

162. *Tomaba un rosario en ellas por apariencia, porque siempre lo tenía en un ser y nunca meneaba las cuentas* (Lewin 1971, 27).

163. *Aleivosa, vos rezaes por cōtas e fazeis-vos da nossa casta. Se vos forens de nosa casta nã rezaries por contas* (Baião 1921, 136).

164. *Los que yvan a romerías que no les aprouechaua más que besar en el salvonor a las bestias que llevauan* (Carrete Parrondo 1985a, 103).

165. *Avendo de ir em romaria a huma ermida de Nossa Senhora antes que a ella fosse, esteve em casa zombando com outras pessoas da sua nação do que havia de fazer na romaria em desprezo de Nossa Senhora* (Azevedo Mea 1982, 451). See also Coelho 1987, 204 [1570s].

166. *Ande la procesión, que va ahí Jesus en casa de todos los diablos* (Medina 1899b, 97).

167. *Estémonos aquí para ver pasar la procesión de estos perros negros y sarnos y haremos un poco de burla, y tendremos un rato de entretenimiento. . . . Juan de León dijo: "Miren estos embusteros cuales andan ceremoniáticos." Y Medina el tuerto dijo: "Hacen éstos lo que ven hacer a los españoles." Y dijo León: "viste qué cara aquélla que parecía que estaba amenazando y jurando en falso" . . . y esto lo decía por un santo Cristo que iba en la procesión* (Lewin 1975, 167–8). See also García 1910, 75.

168. *Quando héramos judíos enojáuamoslos con vna pascua que vernía de año a año, y agora cada día pascua e fiesta carga e soberual* (Carrete Parrondo 1985a, 149).

169. Beinart 1974, 544. See also Beinart 1975, 650.

170. *Fazía judaizar a sus moras induziendo e constrinyendo aquellas a comer carne en días prohibidos por la sta. madre yglesia* (Llorca 1942, 149). See also Sánchez Moya 1958, 189 [1485]; Beinart 1961, 190 [1487]; Moreno Koch 1977, 358; Carrete/Fraile 1987, 77.

171. *Que quemase lanas e cabeças de sardinas e cabeças de ajo, porque non oliese* (León Tello 1972, 73).

172. *Comen carne en quaresma y otros dias prohibidos por la yglessia sin tener necessidad, creyendo y teniendo la pueden comer sin pecado* (Santa María 1893c, 183). See also Fita y Colomé 1892, 488 [1484]; 1893, 291 [1485]; Sánchez Moya 1958, 158 [1485]; Uchmany 1982, 99; Carrete Parrondo 1985a, 24, 33, 35, etc.; Baião 1921, 104 [1540]; Azevedo Mea 1982, 241 [Coimbra 1571]; Osorio 1980, 186 [1638]; Liebman 1974, 135 [Mexico 1649].

173. Sicroff 1965, 100. See also *Libro del Alboraique* 393, 401.

174. *El domingo negociaua y fazía contratos. . . . Y en vilipendio y menosprecio del santo día del domingo, el dicho reo ha costumbrado y costumbra caminar el día del domingo e otros días de fiestas mandados guardar por la Yglesia* (Llorca 1939, 130–1).

175. *Los domings los enbiavan camino con bestyas por pan e por otras cosas al molino e a otras partes.* When they asked him why, Hurtado answered, *tanbién hera menester de comer e faser algo aquel día como los otros* (Carrete/Fraile 1987, 55).

176. *Aos Domingos fazia marmelada e aos sabbados não fazia cousa alguma* (Baião 1921, 105; see also 106, 109).

177. *Los más domingos e fiestas que la santa madre iglesia manda guardar el dicho Diego Gomes hazía las crines a sus vestias e las trasquilava e las fazía labrar de fuego a un mozo criado de un herrador. . . . E que en su casa . . . no se conocía ser domingos ni fiestas los tales días* (Gómez-Menor 1973, 98).

178. Las indulgencias y remissiones de los pecados que los santos padres apostolicos de Roma conceden y acostumbran dar a los fieles christianos, no aprovechan para remission de los pecados (Baer 1936, 473).
179. Eran burlas estas bulas (Gilman 1972, 91).
180. Nunca había tomado bula de la santa cruzada, haciendo menosprecio de ella, rompiéndola a su muger (Medina 1887, 2:27).
181. Haziendo burla y chanza de ella y diziendoles que no la hauian menester (Nunemaker 1946, 25).
182. Los Euangelios son algo? (Carrete/Fraile 1987, 97).
183. No avia para que creer la ley evangelica porque la avian escripto unos pescadores (García Fuentes 1981, 98).
184. Dava ao demo as confrarias do Santissimo Sacramento e da Misericordia, zombando dellas e dando a entender que não erão boas (Azevedo Mea 1982, 447).
185. Vituperando la veneración de las reliquias (García 1910, 91).
186. Que a lei dos cristãos era todo bulrra (Azevedo Mea 1982, 223).
187. Todo lo que los christianos dizen y hazen es viento . . . hera burla todo. . . . Canes, que an de venir estos canes a mal fin (Beinart 1977b, 53–4). Cf. Furtado 1929, 143 [Bahia 1593].
188. Dezía . . . Hernand Sanches Castro a cada artículo: "Creo en vn Dios verdadero," y que dixera el sacristán entonçes: "Vámonos e non ge lo dedes, que el creer de fe y don Mosé todo es vno." E que por esto que dixo echaron al sacristán a rehenpujones (Carrete Parrondo 1990, 172).
189. Liebman 1982, 103. See also García 1910, 243; Liebman 1974, 204–5.
190. Estaua hablando de los christianos y el dixo que el dia que antes que se desayunase no engañaua a los christianos, no estaua en su seso ni se desayunava fasta aver engañado a algund christiano (Beinart 1981b, 320; cf. 2:521).
191. Bendito Tu, Adonay, en que no me fiste puerco para que me comiese el christiano, y Bendito Adonay, Dio myo y de mis parientes, matalos y destruylos, tornalos a nuestra Ley y a nuestros Mandamientos (Beinart 1974, 572).
192. Hacer higa a las imágenes (Blázquez Miguel 1986a, 55). For other examples from around Toledo see Gilman 1972, 95.
193. Maldita sea gente que a tal adora y en tal cree (Carrete Parrondo 1985a, 162).
194. Espetos . . . parecen palos de ahorcados (García Fuentes 1981, 147).
195. Elle olhando fittamente pera hum crucifixo que estava no altar o ameaçou pondo o dedo no nariz duas ou tres vezes e pondo outras tantas a mão pelas barbas, e despois disto lhe deu duas ou tres figas.
196. Psalm 114. Uchmany 1977, 107; cf. Conway 1928, 22–3.
197. Dezia que os bautizava, perguntando-lhe coo te chamão, Limão, e elle lhe-punha o nome Limão, e a outro punha o nome Hamham e os metia na agoa, como quando bautizam huã criança (Furtado 1925, 485).
198. "Vamos a darle los sacramentos," e que llevaron vna ostia hecha de lodo e hizieron vna crus + de cuernos e posieron la dicha ostia e la crus de los cuernos hen vn pandero e covijaron la ostia e la crux con vn sonbrero, e fueron rezando como quien yva a darle los sacramentos (Carrete/Fraile 1987, 89).
199. Although Jews were accused of ritual murder in 1435 in Majorca, 1452 in Valladolid, in 1454 in Tavara (Valladolid), in 1468 in Sepúlveda, and in 1490 in La Guardia, in no case was concrete evidence found to implicate Jews. In fact, only in the Tavara case could it even be proved that a crime had been committed.

200. Lera García 1987, 93. For a similar example in 1619 see Webster 1889, 358.
201. *Tiraram a hostia da bocca respectiva e trouxeram-nas para casa e enterraram-na no chão e, depois de enterrada, pisaram o chão, chamando "Cão, perro, perro"* (Baião 1921, 230). For a similar example, see Muñoz de la Pena 1970, 374–6.
202. *Amassando d'uma vez pão lhe fizera uma cruz como é costume, o que Isabel Gomes desmanchou* (Baião 1921, 119). Echoes of this attitude are found among modern Portuguese crypto-Jews, where new-Christians in Argozelo (Bragança, Portugal) during Holy Week carry a ceramic crucifix and as they march in the processions say: "The more I drag you, the more I want to drag you" (*Quanto mais te arrastro, mais vontade tenho de te arrastar*)(Paulo 1985, 28).
203. *Vio muchas vezes vn cruçifixo en la cama de . . . doña Aldonça y echado por allí, non onestamente* (Carrete Parrondo 1985a, 166).
204. *Tinha ajuntamento carnal com huã sua negra metia debaixo della hum crucifixo* (Furtado 1929, 15). For similar cases see Furtado 1925, 357 and Carrete Parrondo 1985a, 166.
205. *Hum dia se posera a ourinar sobre o ditto crucifixo, dizendo as pallavras seguintes, lavai vos laa* (Furtado 1929, 124; cf. 29, 34, 68).
206. *Llegando . . . a besar los pies a una imagen que estaba pintada en la pared con carbón, dijo el dicho Juan de León, oyéndolo ambos dos sus compañeros, ¿qué está besando allí? ¿un poco de carbón? haciendo menosprecio de la adoración que dicho preso hacía a la imagen, y que sucedía a las veces que cuando se pondía a rezar, como dicho es, el dicho Juan de León y [sic] llegándose cerca dicho preso le volvía el dicho Juan de León las espaldas, y asimismo cuando dicho preso se santiguaba o rezaba escupía en el suelo, como haciendo hurla el dicho Juan de León* (Lewin 1977, 377; cf. 379).
207. *Un crucifixo que conpro su padre . . . el qual traya a los pies de la cama por el suelo, le avia echado la dicha Mari Sánchez en una privada* (Baer 1936, 448). Another witness said that Juan de León had taught her and her friends to "spit on their shirts" in accord with ceremonies of the Law (*Usaban escupir las camisas, porque el dicho Juan de León se lo enseño por ceremonia de la dicha Ley*)(Lewin 1977, 245). The exact meaning of this phrase is unclear.
208. *A huma imagem de hum crucifixo de Nosso Senhor Jhesu Christo que tinha pintado em huma parede do aposenteo onde ella, Re, estava presa, fez tais irreverencias que por honestidade se não referem* (Azevedo Mea 1982, 434; cf. 454).
209. Beinart (1977b, 51). Straightforward accusations like this one are the sort most frequently found in the Inquisition documents. See Blázquez Miguel 1987, 52 [c. 1491]; Rábade Obradó 1990a, 385 [Toledo 1484–99]; Liebman 1970, 53 [1536]; Blázquez Miguel 1986a, 79 [Talavera 1616]; Webster 1889, 348 [1619]; Liebman 1975, 160 [Cuba 1613]; 163 [Cartagena, Colombia 1644]; Rojas 1937, 194 [1637]; Adler 1899, 62–3, 85 [Mexico 1643].
210. *Porque azotaba y apuñalaba un crucifijo en que estaba la imagen de Cristo Nuestro Redentor y le daba higas y lo echó en un río* (Reguera 1984, 183).
211. *Açoutar per vezes hum crucifixo que tinha nas mãos com huns azorrages e lhe fazer outros desprezos* (Azevedo Mea 1982, 260).
212. *Tomó por certero una cruz y le tiró muchas pedradas* (Gracia Boix 1983, 347).
213. *Tendo o na mão esquerda lhe deu com a mão dereita bofetadas em ambas as faces, dizendo ora tomai, ora tomai* (Furtado 1925, 485).
214. Gregorio Nunes was said to have struck a crucifix four years earlier on shipboard while uttering this verse prayer expressing faith in the Messiah: "Eagles and lions / will conquer the fortress, / will gain the highest honor, / will slay the dragons; / and all embroiled in struggle, / in dire confusion, / the clear lions will ascend / with someone of the blood of

David" (*Aguilas e leones, / ganarao la fortaleza, / subiram em tanta Alteza, / que amansen los dragones, / y todos rebueltos en lid, / vernam en sus confusiones, / subiram francos leones, / con uno de sangue de David*) (Wiznitzer 1960, 20, 181). See also Lipiner (1969, 115).

215. María Alvares testified in Pernambuco in 1594 that she had seen Pedralvares Madeira, a *cristão novo*, take a large crucifix from the wall of his room "and holding it by the foot with one hand he stood in the middle of the floor and took some straps and gave it many blows on the head, arms, feet and body, and after he had beat it for a long time he threw it scornfully on the table" (*Chegou ao ditto crucifixo e com huã mão ho tomou pello pee da cruz e se veo com elle ao meo da camara e com a outra mão com huãs deceprinas que nella tinha deu muitos açoutes no ditto crucifixo dando lhe pela cabeça, braços, peis e todo o corpo e despois que por espaço de tempo ho açoutou o lançou e remesou com desprezo sobre a ditta taboa*) (Furtado 1929, 201; cf. 239).

216. It was reported that Clara Fernandes used to beat her crucifix while muttering "You brought me here, so You give me something to eat!" (*ás me de dar de comer que tu me trouxeste qua*) (Furtado 1925, 261).

217. *Dou-te ao demo* (Lipiner 1969, 168).

218. *Tinha em sua casa hum crucifixo ou imagem em hum lugar, çujo e deshonesto . . . apar de un vaso inmundo em que fazia seus feitos corporais* (Furtado 1929, 27, 34, 319); . . . *huma imagem de Christo crucificado na cual todos os da sua familia e congregação hiam mijar* (Furtado 1925, 319; cf. 448, 556). For additional biographical information about the family of João Nunes see Lipiner (1969, 194–203).

219. *Aquillo que não era sagrado que bem podia folgar com elle* (Furtado 1929, 408).

220. *Tenía un Santo Christo en la mano izquierda . . . y con unas disçiplinas que tenía en la mano derecha, le daba crueles açotes al Santo Christo por espaçio de media ora; y deçía palabras raviosas y con cólera al Santo Christo* (Selke de Sánchez 1972, 92). For a similar case see Lewin (1954, 229) [Peru 1637].

221. Liebman (1982, 102). In discussing this case Liebman reports that beating images was "the most common manner of exhibiting contempt and soul-burning hatred of Christianity . . . throughout Spain and in every part of the New World under Spanish dominion."

222. *Ultrajando a n. Sr. Jesuchristo; diciendo era el mágico grande, y quemando su Santa Efigie crucificada* (Lera García 1987, 93).

223. Liebman (1970, 123). Anne Cardoza, who identifies herself as a Marrana, reports that her grandmother, Pauline, who emigrated from Gerona to Buenos Aires to the United States, used to "sew Catholic medals and crucifixes in the hems of skirts and pillows" (Cardoza 1989, S2).

224. *Aquella que está allí figurada no es Santa María, que sy la ponen en el fuego bien arderá. . . . Avn yo bien me calentaría a ella* (Carrete Parrondo 1985a, 88).

225. *Vna vez, dandole vna tabla en que estaua pintada la ymagen de Nuestra Señora la Virgen Maria, ella la tomo, e como la ovo tornada, con burla e escarnio que della hizo, la arrojo en vn albañar muy suzio que estaua cabe la cozina, e despues de asi echada la dicha ymagen, la escopio* (Beinart 1977a, 248; cf. 268).

226. *Fora a uma ermida de Vallongo e por uma porta atirara pedras á imagem de Nossa Senhora e quebrara uma imagem de Santa Luzia* (Baião 1921, 113).

227. *Tomou hum Flox Sanctorum e com hum alfinete picou hua figura que estava debuxada . . . de Nosa Senhora e lhe picou a coroa e parte da cabeça de Nosa Senhora* (Furtado 1925, 46; cf. 374).

228. *Hallava vna ymagen de Nuestra Senora que tenia en su cabeçera de su cama la cara vuelta a la pared* (Cantera/Carrete 1971, 264).

229. *Hauiendole resado la dicha su muy conjunta catholicamente, y poniendole encima de su cama . . . en voluiendo hallaba echa pedazitos la cinta, y la cruz y las quentas por el suelo* (Nunemaker 1946, 25).
230. *Saltar en cima de um livro de Horas* (Baião 1921, 222).
231. *Pisando bolsas de reliquias* (Medina 1887, 2:27).
232. *Y para tener mejor venta el pan que amasaba y que saliese más sabroso y blanco, ella y sus hermanas le amasaban con agua que antes les había servido de lavarse ciertas partes inmundas, haciendo algunos círculos y ritos judaicos en forma de bendiciones sobre la masa* (García 1910, 51).
233. *Por la puerta de la casa vió por un agujero della que en la puerta de un aposento que avía enfrente de la puerta de la calle estaba puesta en un taxo o banquillo una imagen de un Cristo de bulto puesto en una cruz, y vió que estaban dentro de la dicha casa en el çaguan de ella seis personas, las quatro mugeres y las dos hombres, que eran el reo y un hermano suyo, y uno a uno yvan de rodillas hacia donde estaba el Cristo y llegando a la dicha puerta donde estaba llevando las manos puestas y juntas delante del pecho, de la manera que quando los muchachos juegan al mocarro; llegaba el primero que yba de rodillas al Sto. Cristo y con ambas las manos juntas como las llevavan, le dava en el rostro a modo de bofetada un golpe, y luego de rodillas se bolvia retirando hacia a atras con las manos puestas como queda dicho u deçía—no se río no emos perdido—y luego se levantava éste y yva otro por los mismos pasos diciendo las mismas palabras y hacía lo mismo, y que el testigo lo estuvo mirando hasta que las dichas seis personas hicieron uno por uno lo que ha declarado: Y luego vio que una de las dichas mugeres tomó la imagen de el Sancto Cristo y se entró con ella en el dicho aposento. . . . Y diçe el testigo que las dichas seis personas son todos cristianos nuevos de judíos* (Sierro Malmierca 1990, 188–9).
234. *Su padre y su madre, enserrandose en el almaçen juntamente con este confessante, . . . y de su hermano Françisco, y de sus hermanas Clara y Antonia, y haviendo bajado de arriba el dicho Françisco vn Santo Christo, que estaban en su aposento donde dormia, del tamaño de media bara, lo tendian boca abajo los dichos sus padres en el mostrador, le daban de porrasos, diçiendole que no era la buena su ley, y que duraba como vna ora. . . . Que era vn embustero, y que no hauia venido al mundo, y que por el padecia trabajos. . . . Que açotes eran aquellos tan recios y a quien? Y le respondia que a vn gato, porque se comia el pescado. Y que diciendole, que si no gritaria con tantos açotes? La respondia que le tapaba el la boca* (Nunemaker 1946, 21, 42–3, 51).
235. *Mal poso oviesse el primero que se tornase christiano* (Marín Padilla 1983b, 296).
236. *Maldito fuese quien avía vedado el Testamento Viejo* (Carrete/Fraile 1987, 20).
237. *Los que decian que eran cristianos se iban al infierno* (García de Proodian 1966, 341).
238. *Le ponia vn palo en la boca, amarrado como mordaza, por que no le pidiesse que lo dexasse por amor de Dios y por la Virgen Santisima* (Nunemaker 1946, 21).
239. The one possible exception, discussed above, is Fernão Pires's alleged baptism of a puppy [Brazil 1591].
240. *Yo por no hacer cosa que hacen estos embusteros (diciéndolo por los católicos cristianos) lo hago todo al revés, y en carnal comía pescado y en cuaresma carne, porque ¿para qué he de andar con embustes como ellos? Si no molerlos y que me traigan carne, por eso me dijeron que era perro judío, que si yo fuera cristiano y no comiera carne en cuaresma, yo guardo mi Ley como se debe guardar, y en todo he de ser diferente que ellos* (Lewin 1975, 97).

# CHAPTER VI

# Superstitions

At the root of all superstitious practice is a belief in powers that go beyond the physical laws of the universe and the transcendental relationships of authorized religion. Whether its application is to ensure health or physical security or to attain some heartfelt desire in matters of vengeance or love, superstition invokes irrational forces. It tends to presuppose the power of certain inanimate objects (such as stones, herbs, or a loved one's shoe); it tends to believe in the existence of personified agents of natural forces (such as fairies or elves, dibbuks or devils); and it tends to accept the idea that certain people have, or can acquire, the gift of accessing these forces and controlling them.

What separates superstition from religious belief is its degree of official sanction. Both Jews and Christians are comfortable with the concept that divine favor is predisposed through prayer and righteous behavior while divine wrath is called down by sin. Both consider to be superstition the belief that good luck is coercible through the invocation of protective spirits or the use of amulets or that bad luck stems from spilling salt or crossing the path of a black cat. Both Jews and Christians tend to believe that the directions of future history are foretold in the Bible; both classify the belief that the future can be read in the tarot deck or the entrails of a goat as superstition.

Despite the disapproval of their religious mentors, the everyday residents of Iberia, whether they were Sephardic Jews or their Christian neighbors, shared a common Mediterranean cultural predilection toward certain superstitious practices.[1] Medieval Jewish writers such as Maimonides criticized the practice of so-called magic, but with little success, for Hebrew medical and scientific treatises of the next several hundred years routinely included magic and superstitious practices in their discussions of cures, remedies, charms, amulets, destinies, fortunes, signs, omens, and so forth, frequently citing as authorities in addition to Jewish sources Christian writers or writers of pre-Christian antiquity (*Enc. Jud.* 11:708–14). Many rabbis continued to protest, but Jewish opposition to magic was never as vigorous as it was among Christians from the late fifteenth through the seventeenth centuries.

After 1480 the Inquisition took to itself the task of rooting out the most egregious magical practices among Christians, and trials that prosecute superstitious practice abound, often without identifying the family background of the accused. The record may indict Costanza Fulano for brewing love potions without specifying whether she was an old-Christian, a *conversa*, or a *morisca*, let alone whether she was sincere in her Christianity or still a practicing crypto-Jew. Nonetheless, sometimes the records do indicate that some specific practice was considered indicative of a person's Judaizing. In those instances we can be fairly certain that the practice was thought to be limited to Judaizers or to be common among them to a much greater extent than among old-Christians. However, the authorities might assume the "Jewishness" of some superstitious practices because they incorporated such artifacts as a scrap of Hebrew writing or a snippet from a *tallit* or prayer shawl, articles associated with Jewish religious practice, without taking into consideration that the custom might also be widely practiced by other religious groups who merely substituted one "magic" item for another.

This chapter discusses several superstitious practices that are in some way explicitly identified as indicative of Judaizing. Superstitions related to predicting the future are followed by superstitions related to influencing events.

## 6.1. Fortune Telling

Iberian *conversos* shared with other Mediterranean peoples an extensive repertoire of strategies for foretelling the future. Comets, shooting stars, and the alignment of the heavenly bodies were widely believed to prefigure momentous events; for that matter, in the late Middle Ages the sciences of astronomy and astrology were largely one in the same. The only way Mencía Rodríguez de Medina [Guadalajara 1492-3] differed from her Christian or Moslem neighbors when she asked a wise man to interpret the stars for her was that the astrologer she consulted was Jewish.[2] But the stars were distant and many people preferred specific, local, personalized methods for reading what lay in store for them or their loved ones. The most specifically Jewish of these practices, reported in both Spain and the New World, has to do with the New Year season. In Castile on Rosh Hashanah some *conversos* would take off their clothes and wrap themselves in blankets, then go outside in the moonlight and take off the blanket. If any part of the body had lost its shadow, imminent death was indicated (Blázquez Miguel 1986a, 180–1). In colonial Mexico, if on Yom Kippur a person saw the headless shadow of oneself or another person, it was an omen that the person would die within the year (Liebman 1982, 127).

Other fortune-telling practices attributed to *conversos* in the trial documents were almost certainly widespread among Mediterranean cultures and in fact in other Inquisition materials are ascribed to old-Christians or to *moriscos*. One of the most common methods involved the mandrake root, thought since antiquity to possess a variety of magical qualities.[3] The *conversa* Teresa Sánchez was accused in 1490 of using "mandrake to look at her fortune and what would be in store for her."[4] Her contemporary the *conversa* Violante de Calatayud owned and allegedly worshipped a mandrake. In 1486 Jaime de Santa Clara was said to have one which he kissed so as to never be poor (Marín Padilla 1983b, 265). A century later in Pernambuco, Brazil, Lianor Martins was said to have a mandrake shaped like a woman, which with a wolf's tooth and a letter from Saint Arasmo she used on Saint John's eve in a ceremony to ensure that men and women loved each other (Furtado 1929, 109). Despite the fact that the Inquisition sometimes interpreted the use of the mandrake as indicative of Judaizing, it was clearly a part of the pan-European culture of superstition.

This is likely to be the case with a variety of other fortune-telling aids commonly employed by Judaizing *conversos*. The probability of safe return from a journey, or of recovery from an illness, or of other matters of life or death were the questions most often put to these fortune-telling devices. In order to tell whether someone would recover from an illness, in the late fifteenth century one Jew dropped an egg white into a water basin and said, "See here whether your brother will recover."[5] Marina Sánchez was accused in Soria in 1502 of divining whether there would be a death in the village by seeing whether her bread came out of the oven with a crack in it; if it was a big crack an adult would die, if a small crack a child (Carrete Parrondo 1985a, 86). In 1491, in order to know whether her lover, a priest of Santo Tomé of Soria, was safe in Rome, Catalina de Violante was accused of "placing in a tin frying pan a stone or an oak image of a child with a staff in his hand and using it to see . . . if her lover was alive and on his way home."[6] Others used a mixture of commonly obtained items to peer into the future. In order to know whether a traveler would return in good health, a Castilian *converso* read his fortune in grains of wheat, coal, and salt, reciting, "Omens, omens, I conjure you by the Creator who created you, by the sun which shines on you, and by the air which blows over you that you answer truly what I am about to ask."[7] In 1520 the *conversa* Elvira, wife of Diego de Ayala, of Hita, was accused of consulting with a fortune teller (*adivina*) named Elena about the alleged death of her son. "She took some grains of wheat and barley and salt and blessed them and shook them in her hands and told her that . . . her son was alive."[8] In the Canary Islands Alvaro Gonçalez was said to have "employed a Negro to cast spells to discover whether the Inquisition would be established in the islands" (Wolf 1926, 43).

Other favorite questions had to do with matters of the heart. For example, a witness told the Mexican Inquisition in 1643 that she had heard a *conversa* friend say that

> before she got married she had fasted from Thursday to Saturday, according to the ceremony of the Law of Moses, to see whom she would marry. And that Saturday night she had put herself at the window in order to hear the first name that was spoken in the street. She heard the name Jacinto, by which she understood that she would undoubtedly marry someone of that name. Juan León said that they did the same thing in his country, Leghorn, and that he had done the same thing when Simón Váez Sevilla was a prisoner, to see whether or not he would get out.[9]

## 6.2. Attracting Fortune and Avoiding Misfortune

Belief in malefic agents, be they devils, imps, neighborhood witches carrying a grudge, or the generic "evil eye," may be universal among humankind. Believers commonly try to ward off these agents of evil by carrying some protective charm or amulet on their persons. Amulets were often medallions stamped out of some metal and containing Hebrew or Arabic words or religious symbols.[10] *Nóminas* were Hebrew or Arabic phrases, written on paper or parchment and sewn into the clothing or carried in a bag hung around the neck.[11] Both were extremely popular in antiquity and among medieval Jews who believed in the power of the divine Word to ward off a variety of evils.[12] To judge from both peninsular and colonial records,[13] they appear to have been equally popular among Judaizing new-Christians well into the seventeenth century. A late fifteenth-century compendium of new-Christian customs accuses *conversos* of "getting married in the Jewish fashion and wearing Jewish amulets."[14] In 1484 Fernando de Trujillo said in Ciudad Real "that María Díaz had taken a Hebrew amulet from him, and he doesn't remember how much she paid for it, and she told him it was for her daughter."[15] In 1490 in Soria Rabbi Ça Seteui reported that Juan Pérez's cousin had "an amulet written in Hebrew which he would not give him for any price, which had been useful to him for all sorts of things, and after he had it God had favored him." Pérez begged him for it, and finally he gave it to him, instructing him "to show it proper respect, for it would be very useful to him."[16] When Ruy García was arrested by the Inquisition in Soria in 1502 they found in his sleeve an amulet written in Hebrew (Carrete Parrondo 1985a, 76). In the early sixteenth century Diego Belmonte in Cuenca had an amulet written on rectangular paper with a red border. It had seven circles, four on the angles, in which his name was written, along with the Sun, Moon, Jupiter, and Venus. In the central circle was written, "Mercy from Adonai. In the name of Tamaniel, Osiel, and Haziel I conjure you to grant grace, charity and pity to whoever wears this amulet."[17] Isabel Núñez of Ciudad Rodrigo had an amulet which was a solid gold horseman with a white sword riding on a lamb which was half gold and half silver (Blázquez Miguel 1986a, 183). In 1572 Bernardina de San Juan, of Baeza, said that her brother Diego had brought her from Italy an "amulet, written with the names of the Messiah, Emmanuel, and other names of God in Hebrew, and when they took her prisoner she had thrown it in the river so they would not find it on her." Her sister Isabel de San Juan added that a soldier had given it to her brother, that "by carrying that paper with her she would be free from her enemies," and that the paper bore words like those in the verses of San Bernardo, of which she remembered *agios atanatos, uti misis, dominatoribus y o, adradon eloyn, o adonay alas*. She said that she was concerned that it might be a Lutheran amulet, so she asked if the words were all right. When asked further about the amulet she replied that it contained these names: *Agolite Voritan, Alapau Elepretan, Soygin Adocheo, Atiliano Diezmar o Enmanuel u Obratiel o Eterrenayn o Apipe o Avalean, o Erite, o Nas, Pintax Comonara, Cotreture o Adradon Van Gayn, Salomixios Labetan, Efete Sute a Monte, Pan Saun Agios, Tetragamaton Vatusalar, Taglas Agonto, Ebiel Ciencia o Alas, Entoria o Timisis Dominatoribus*, but that she did not know what they meant. Her sister Elvira de San Juan added that it had the names *Adonai, Saday*, and *Paletin*.[18] Matías Rodrigues de Olivera, a Portuguese Judaizer reconciled in Mexico in 1649, was accused of wearing on a chain around his neck a gold medal with a Hebrew letter on it (Wiznitzer 1962a, 248). There appear to be echoes of this practice among alleged remnant crypto-Jews today: the Arizonan Ruth Flores Reed, who was raised in Mexico, claims that her family has preserved from ancient times a silver amulet that bears the Ten Commandments in Hebrew (Snyder 1992, 19).

According to the Inquisition documents, frequently these amulets were invoked against specific ills. In the late fifteenth century Judaizers from Cuenca and Sigüenza wore amulets to protect against palsy and sore legs (Cirac Estopañán 1942, 89). In 1488 it was reported that a rabbi had given the *converso* Alonso de la Cavallería a personalized Hebrew amulet to protect him against his enemies.[19] It was reported in 1492 that when the wife of a *converso* named Esplugues, in Valencia, had stopped conceiving children he asked a Jewish physician for a Hebrew amulet.[20] When her daughter was sick sometime around 1515, Costanza Gómez, of Huete, seeing that Christian prayers were insufficient to cure her, asked a local Judaizer to sell her an amulet to hang around the child's neck (Blázquez Miguel 1987, 54). By the early seventeenth century some crypto-Jews evidently relied on protective icons that were much more similar to the crucifixes or saints' images worn by their Christian neighbors than they were to the classic Hebrew-letter amulets worn by their ancestors. According to a 1637 Argentinean letter of indictment, a boat reportedly came to Buenos Aires with a cargo of medals bearing the image of Moses (Rojas 1937, 195; Medina 1890, 152).

Casting spells was another method of influencing future events. Often the ceremony required the use of props or potions. Frequently the spells incorporated fragments of traditional prayers or formulaic utterances that resembled prayers.[21] Although Inquisition documents are frequently rich in detail about the spells cast by alleged witches, only a few of these spells are tied specifically to *conversos*,[22] and even those are not likely to be restricted in their use to the descendants of Jews. Typical of these generic practices was the one reported in the Canary Islands in 1524, where a new-Christian abbot named Diego Fernandes, of Córdoba, was said to have shown a new-Christian woman "who was anxious for the return of her husband from the Indies, how to make use of the seal of Solomon. She was to take a candle in one hand and place the other over the seal holding it between the fingers and turn about seven times" (Wolf 1926, 31; cf. 95–7). Among some later new-Christians Hebrew prayers had passed from being vehicles for an individual's communication with God to having the kind of talismanic power associated with amulets or spells. In San Cristóbal de Tenerife in 1636 Marcos Meneses consulted a "Jew" named Mardoqueo in the Inquisition prison and reportedly told Juan de Justiniano that "the Jew was a very learned man, and knew many things, and had taught him a prayer to be used in affliction, which he had taken down in writing, and that the Jew had said that in using it, having certain papers, he would obtain money and never be poor. The said Marcos Meneses having volunteered to translate the prayer into Spanish, from Hebrew, for the benefit of the deponent, the latter refused" (Wolf 1926, 127).

Iberian new-Christians shared with their neighbors a belief in malefic power of the "evil eye," a kind of generic, all-encompassing negative force threatening to turn any positive event into tragedy.[23] Spoken compliments were thought to have a magnetic effect on the evil eye and thus were to be avoided or accompanied by protective gestures. In 1492 the *conversa* Isabel Amorós, of Valencia, said that when certain Christians looked at her she made a superstitious sign to avert the evil eye.[24] The *conversa* Antona Ferrer was accused in 1490 of protecting a child against the evil eye by passing her open hand across the child's face, spitting, and saying "long live the child."[25] Ana Enríquez, who died in prison before she could be burned in the Mexican *auto de fe* of 1649, was accused of praying to free people from the powers of the evil eye (Wiznitzer 1962a, 247). Once the evil eye had affected a person it—like any other demonic force—had to be exorcised. A complex ceremony of exorcism is described in the 1494 testimony of the *conversa* Leonor of Cifuentes:

> Some eleven or twelve years ago, more or less, a neighbor of mine who was called Juan del Castillo and his wife Mari Sanchez had a son who must have been at that point a year and a half or two years old. This child was skinny and did not prosper and did not eat, but only cried, and his father and mother asked what they should do with him. And there was a Jewess in Cifuentes to whom they told this story, and she told them that they should beg in three households comprised of a father, a mother, a father-in-law, and a mother-in-law, and in which the woman of the house was named Maria; that they should

ask for flour in each house; that they should take the flour and knead it into a loaf of bread and a cake. They should give the cake in charity to the first poor man they saw. And they should take the bread and with it the child along with three people who have to be his father, who is called Juan del Castillo, his mother—and they begged me that I should be the third person, and that's what I did. And all three of us went with the child to where we could not hear a hen or a cock, and on the road there we did not talk to a single person. There in the countryside we dug a hole and we put the child in it, wrapped in his clothing. We put the bread next to the head of the child and each one of the three of us drew aside in a different direction. We returned to the hole and took the bread and since the child's hands were stuck into it, we pulled them out and we divided the bread into three pieces and each one took a piece and threw it in a different direction, and each one said three times: "Sands of the countryside take this crying and return it to me as silence." And, then we took the child from the hole and stripped him and buried his clothing in the hole and we dressed him in other clothes and we came back. We met a man and we asked him how we should call this child we have found. He said: "My name is Juan," and whatever name he might say that is the name we had to call him for seven or eight days at home. And when we got to Juan del Castillo's house, we made a bath for the child with rosemary and hyssop. All this happened about eleven years ago more or less and I think that's all there is to say and I swear by it.[26]

Conversos, like their neighbors, believed that certain acts attracted misfortune. Catalina Martínez [Almazán 1505] believed that holes in the street in front of her house would attract death.[27] According to Liebman, in the Americas *conversos* believed that "clothes worn inside-out would bring misfortune."[28] They also believed that "hands folded on the top of the head would bring misfortune" (Liebman 1970, 85). According to Liebman, bedclothes in the Americas had to be pulled tight; if not, "the souls of the dead might lie upon them and torment the sleeper" (Liebman 1982, 105; 1970, 85). Diego Juárez de Figueroa, a participant in the 1647 *auto de fe* in Mexico City, was said to believe that Judaizers did a number of things to avert bad luck:

> When they get up they try to immediately cover the bed, because they believe that some soul [of some dead person] will go into it. . . . They will not allow a lighted candle to be placed at the foot of the bed. . . . They will not talk about their good fortune, believing that talking about it will make it go away. . . . They will not sweep the house at night, nor look at themselves in the mirror; they consider it very unlucky to cross the fingers when you clasp your hands, or to put their hands over their heads. . . . And whether they are well or sick, if they are in bed and some funeral procession goes by, they have to get up out of bed.[29]

In the accusations brought against Margarita de Rivera, another Mexican *conversa* of the 1640s, it was said that "when she had a bad dream she would go and confess it so as to transfer the bad omen onto her confessor."[30] Fourteen-year-old

Rafael de Granada [Mexico 1642] reported that his aunt Isabel had said that Luis Núñez had said that "you must bury a human skull and put beans in the eyes, but that his aunt had not told him what it was for, nor did he know if they did it."[31] One explanation is found in the trial of her contemporary Margarita de Rivera, of whom Mexican Inquisitors said that "to make herself invisible she would plant beans in the eyes and nose of a skull." In Castile to protect themselves against witches some new-Christians put a variety of herbs on doors and windows of their houses.[32] According to a late fifteenth-century compendium of new-Christian customs, "Jews used to be in the habit of cutting the finger- and toenails and burying them under the ground so that people could not cast superstitious spells with them and so that on Judgment Day they would be gathered and buried; and they used to do the same thing with molars and other teeth."[33] Shortly after 1650 Domingo de Guzmán, from Salónica, was accused in Ocaña of keeping his nails "cut square like a Hebrew priest."[34] In the Americas nails were not cut the day of the new moon (Liebman 1982, 105).[35]

The range of practices for attracting or repelling fortune appears to have been as wide as the human imagination. In 1486 the *conversa* wife of Pedro de Ejea was reported to have protected him by not sweeping the house the day of his departure (Marín Padilla 1983b, 260). In Teruel in the 1480s the *conversa* Rica Martínez protected her husband by pouring a jar of water over him when he set out on a trip.[36] The *conversa* María González put drops of oil in the water she gave her children to drink so that they would have good luck (Beinart 1975, 654). To protect herself from the pernicious power of bad dreams, Mencía González [Guadalajara 1492] would mutter "Dreams of Joseph, wiles of Jacob, his father."[37] In Coimbra in 1573 Ana Fernandes told the Inquisitors that some fellow new-Christians had told her not to work on the Sabbath so that God would protect her son who was in the Indies.[38]

Sometimes specific places were thought to be imbued with bad or good luck. When Tomás Treviño de Sobremonte was denounced to the Mexican Inquisition in 1647, among the charges was that "in Guadalajara a certain observer of the Law of Moses did not want to leave the house he was living in because Treviño and his wife had lived and Judaized there and had left it filled with good fortune."[39]

In looking at these cases of allegedly superstitious practices one must discount those instances in which an old-Christian observer ascribed magical significance to what might be a very ordinary new-Christian religious custom. An example is the description of what appears to have been a Sabbath meal in Ciudad Real around 1513. Catalina de la Villa testified that Mayor González "ordered Juana González to set a table in the large room which was over the cellar and that she should set it with white table cloths over a carpet and that she should put small white folded napkins on the table. And this witness assumed that she set the table for the spirits."[40] Likewise, one must reject the occasional references to blood libels that creep into old-Christian testimony with respect to new-Christian practices.

For example, a Portuguese Edict of Grace in 1536 says that Judaizers "on Saint John's Eve or on Christmas Eve pour out the water and the wine from all their pots and pitchers and kettles and buckets, saying that on those nights the wine becomes blood."[41]

## 6.3. Love

As Fernando de Rojas's novel *La Celestina* (1499) makes clear when Calixto has recourse to the witch Celestina to help him secure the affections of Melibea, there is little people will not do for love, and in this *conversos* seem to have been no different from anyone else.[42] Costanza López, of Molina de Aragón, a seamstress, secured her lover's affection by sewing a dead man's bone into a slit in the side of his shirt and reciting: "As Christ has engendered this bone and this flesh in the womb of his mother, just so may love be engendered between this wife and the husband who owns this shirt."[43] In the 1520s the *conversa* Leonor de Barzana was convicted in Toledo of giving potions to women to help win the affection of their husbands or lovers (Blázquez Miguel 1989, 187). The sisters Catalina and Leonor de Rojas told the Granada Inquisition around 1563 that they had been told that keeping the Sabbath and the dietary prohibitions and fasting on Jewish holidays would ensure their getting married (Bel Bravo 1988, 132–3). The new-Christian Violante Carneira was denounced in Bahia, Brazil, in 1591 for reciting a spell to make a man fall in love with a woman. She twice whispered in his ear, "*Hoc est enim corpus meum*" (Furtado 1925, 488).

The *conversa* Margarita de Rivera was accused by the Mexican Inquisition in 1646. It was said that "to control men she used the ashes of swallows that had been toasted alive and buzzard brains."[44] Fourteen-year-old Rafael de Granada told Mexican Inquisitors in 1642 that in his aunt Isabel's house several *conversa* women had told him "that to win someone's affection it was good to toast some swallows, powder them, and give them to drink to the person you want to enamor. And he witnessed how they had brought swallows to his house and how Isabel roasted them and made powder of them and gave them to Luis Núñez to drink."[45] A similar potion could be made with the brains of a cow.[46] In the Americas the "hair of an unmarried woman had to be dried well after washing and put into buns or no gentleman would woo and marry her" (Liebman 1982, 105; 1970, 85).

## 6.4. Cures

In an age when medical science was at best haphazard, people tended to rely heavily on both folk medicine and what we now call superstition to cure them. Theoretical treatises about medieval medicine and our evidence of medieval medical practice suggest that no clear distinction was made between medicine and what today we would call magic. Folk medicine, which largely consisted of the application or infusion of certain herbs, did not generally concern the Inquisition. Anything that smacked of spells or potions, on the other hand, did, and therefore appears with some frequency in the documentation. There is no reason to believe that any of the practices listed below were exclusively Jewish or *converso*, with the possible exception of the so-called "ceremony of the drops," which consisted of foretelling the success of a cure by interpreting the spattering pattern of olive oil dropped into a hot frying pan. Thus when someone was sick Clara de Puxmija (d. 1455) and her husband "performed the ceremony of the drops for him."[47] It was reported in 1486 that in Zaragoza when the *conversa* Isabel de Bello's children were sick she was seen to throw some drops of oil into a pan and say certain words over them (Marín Padilla 1983b, 255). Donosa Besante, the wife of Antón Ruiz of Teruel, was accused in 1486 of making *las gotillas* while murmuring, "Saday, Adonai" (Sánchez Moya/Monasterio Aspiri 1973, 136). At her arraignment in 1521 Ynés de la Higuera too was accused of "having the droplets cast for her when she was sick, and of agreeing to it."[48] This ceremony seems to have persisted only in Spain and only into the middle of the sixteenth century.

The repertoire of strategies that were believed to effect a cure was broad. Some combined traditional herbs with special prayers or rituals. In the first third of the sixteenth century the Toledan *conversa* Leonor de Barzana for illness made a potion of various herbs and incense soaked in water; she rubbed the potion on the woman's hands ears, and breast, and then boiled the remaining potion under her so the vapors reached her legs and the rest of her body; although the cure was labeled *converso*, the prayer Leonor recited was "Saint Anne gave birth as a virgin, Saint Mary gave birth to Christ, Saint Isabel to Saint John. As this is true, may this ill be cured."[49] In the Americas *conversos* cured *jaqueca* (headache), *acaque* (migraine headache), and *tarbadella* (sunstroke) with remedies of tobacco, sweets, and hot chocolate (Liebman 1982, 104). Some *conversos* believed that a cure could be effected by reciting spells over the sick person's belt (Blázquez Miguel 1986a, 183). A 1449 anti-*converso* tract accused the converts of "taking the sashes of pregnant women to the synagogue and touching them to the door knockers, saying that that would hasten their labor."[50] Some believed that the power of the dead could be harnessed to help the living. For example, reputedly one could cure a sick eye by taking soil from the tomb of a good man, dissolving it in water, and painting the eye with it (Blázquez Miguel 1986a, 183; Carrete Parrondo 1985a, 54). In Molina late in the fifteenth century a *conversa* put a human skull under her husband's pillow in order to cure him (Cirac Estopañán 1942, 103). Some dressed out the sick room like a shrine. A 1484 case reports that the old-Christian Juan Jiménez, of Albarracín, went to visit his sick *converso* friend Gil de Gonzalvo Ruiz and found him "in an interior room in a bed under a canopy, and that at the four corners of the bed were four candelabra with many candles."[51] Others performed acts of charity on the sick person's behalf. In 1501 in Aranda the laborer Juana Peres was denounced for having asked a Jewess some thirteen years before how to cure her son. The answer was: "donate a pound of olive oil to the synagogue."[52] The same stratagem was used to recover lost property (1985, 160). Still others used amulets made of Jewish religious objects. Some American *conversos* believed that a piece of *matza*, which Manuel Carrasco called a "relic," placed on the head could cure a headache.[53] Beatriz Jurada [Toledo c. 1500] believed it would ensure a safe pregnancy and delivery (Rábade Obradó 1990a, 437). According to one report, even an infant's colic could be cured by magic: *conversos* would stuff clothing into the mouth of a water jar when a child was crying in order to stop the crying (*atapar planto*) (Cirac Estopañán 1942, 90).

Infertility was thought to be another illness curable through prayer or magic. Queen Isabel herself journeyed to the remote monastery of San Juan de Ortega, near Burgos, to invoke holy power in helping her conceive a son. Recourse to wise old women to proscribe aids to get—or keep from getting—pregnant was common. These might range from simple herbs, such as those that a Jewish women had prepared for the *conversa* María López, of Calatayud, around 1489,[54] to full-fledged magic. The Toledan *conversa* Leonor de Barzana early in the sixteenth century proscribed for impotence that the afflicted buy the Gospel of San Juan or the prayers of Our Lady, Saint Cebrian, and the Count,[55] and that they carry with them written notes that had touched certain relics. She also asked for nail clippings, hairs from various parts of the body, a piece of chewed bread, and money for wax candles.

# Notes

1. Cirac Estopañán 1942 makes this point when he puts the superstitions of Castilian Judaizers into their broader cultural context. See also Blázquez Miguel 1986a, 180–6.
2. *Fue a vn judío que sabia de estrelleria a le preguntar algunas cosas* (Cantera/Carrete 1975, 196).
3. Medieval Jewish texts recognized the special powers of the mandrake plant, which is mentioned in the Talmud; Josephus (first century CE) says that the roots adhere so strongly to the ground that one must harness a dog to them to pull them out, after which the dog dies vicariously for its master. In his *Guide for the Perplexed* (3:29) Maimonides inveighs against Jews who were deluded about the mandrake plant (*Enc. Jud.* 11:870).
4. *Mandragula para mirar sus hados y hechos venideros en ella* (Moreno Koch 1977, 358). See also Beinart 1981b, 556; Cirac Estopañán 1942, 73; Cantera Montenegro 1985, 88 [Molina de Aragón 1480s]; Carrete Parrondo 1985, 128.
5. *Ved aquí cómo no puede escapar vuestro hermano* (Cirac Estopañán 1942, 57).
6. *Para saber si era biua vn su enamorado que se llama Pero Hernández de Berlanga, cura de Santo Thomé, de Soria, el qual estaua a la sazón en Roma, que hizo vna ymagen de petre o de robre en vna sartén de alambre, a figura de vna persona de niño con vna varilla en la mano, e que en aquello vio que . . . su enamorado era viuo e venía por el camino* (Carrete Parrondo 1985, 21). See also Blázquez Miguel 1986a, 185.

7. *Suertes, suertes, conjuroos por el Criador que os crio; con el sol que alumbro o con el aire que os meneo, que digais la verdad desto que os pregunto* (Blázquez Miguel 1986a, 184).

8. *Tomo çiertos granos de trigo e çevada e sal e lo santiguo e los rebolvio con las manos e dixo a este declarante que . . . su hijo hera bivo* (Cantera/Carrete 1971, 261).

9. *Antes de casarse, había ayunado desde jueves a sábado por ceremonia de la Ley de Moisés, para saber con quién se había de casar, y que el dicho sábado en la noche se había puesto en la ventana para oír el primer nombre que se nombraba en la calle, y había oído el de Jacinto, por donde entendió que se había de casar infaliblemente con cierta persona de aquel nombre, a lo cual dijo el dicho Juan de León que lo mismo se usaba en su tierra, en Liorno, y que él había hecho lo mismo cuando estaba preso Simón Váez Sevilla, para saber si había de ser suelto o no* (Lewin 1977, 249).

10. The Sephardic museum in Toledo has at least one example of a fifteenth-century Hebrew amulet.

11. Carrete Parrondo 1987, 54. They were sometimes called *nominas de moro* or *herçes* (from Arabic *hirz* = amulet). *Conversos* frequently would protect themselves against the evil eye or other malefic forces with an amulet around the neck (Blázquez Miguel 1986a, 182).

12. For Jewish medieval use of amulets see Schrire 1966, and the *Enc. Jud.* 2:906–11.

13. Liebman concludes that among Marranos in colonial Mexico amulets were thought to ward off catastrophe (1970, 85).

14. *Cassan a modo judayco y trahen nominias de judíos* (Santa María 1893c, 182).

15. *Dixo que la dicha Maria Dias tomo a este testigo vna nomina de ebrayco, e que non se acuerda cuanto le dio por ella, e le dixo como la queria para su fija* (Beinart 1974, 58). See also Carrete/Fraile 1987, 54; Beinart 1974, 389.

16. *Vna nómina escripta en hebrayco, que non la daría por ningund preçio, que lo avía aprouechado a todas las cosas del mundo, que después que la tenía le avía hecho Dios merçed. . . . Que la tomase e touiese buena deuoçión con ella, que çierto le aprouecharía mucho* (Carrete Parrondo 1985, 25).

17. *Misericordia de Adonay. En el nombre de Tamaniel y Osiel y Haziel, yo vos conjuro que le pongais graçia, misericordia y piedad al que trae esta nómina* (Blázquez Miguel 1986a, 182).

18. *Había traido una nómina, escritos nombres de Mesías, Enmanuel y otros nombres de Dios en hebraico y cuando venía presa la había arrojado en el río porque no se la hallasen. . . . Trayendo aquel papel consigo sería liberado de sus enemigos* (Gracia Boix 1983, 132, 134, 136). See also Blázquez Miguel 1986a, 182.

19. *Vet ahi essa nomina que me dio el rav viejo ciciliano, rabi que teniades en esta aliama, fecha a mi nombre y contra enemigos* (Baer 1936, 455).

20. Baer 1966, 2:360. According to Baer, Esplugues was also found with some Hebrew books on alchemy in his possession.

21. While revising this chapter in Guatemala in December of 1992, I visited a pre-Columbian site called Bilbao on a knoll in the midst of a canefield near the town of Escuintla. A family of nine had hired a local priestess to exorcize the demons that were causing the family's daughter to receive failing grades in high school. The family lit candles, burned incense, and presented offerings of food and liquor before a large stone head protruding from the hill. Using formulae evocative of those found in *La Celestina*, the priestess conjured the protective intervention of Christ, the Virgin, a variety of saints, and Adonai [!], and then led the family in a pastiche of prayers that included fragments of the "Hail Mary" and the "Our Father."

22. Wiznitzer points out that although the Mexican Inquisition tried many people as witches, none was ever identified as a Judaizer (1962a, 268).
23. On the other hand, crypto-Jews were not routinely accused by the Inquisition of practicing black magic to cause people harm, although some popular anti-Semitic literature such as Lope de Vega's *El Niño inocente de La Guardia* did make such charges. Neither do we commonly find accusations of cursing (that is, invoking a malefic power to harm someone), which is often a part of superstitious practice. I have not found evidence of specific curses, or even of the act of cursing, ascribed to *conversos*, other than the allegedly blasphemous utterances against the Christian religion that are treated in Chapter 5.
24. *Quant alguns christians de natura la miravan, feya certa supersticio dient que cechs fossen los ulls dels goys que la havien mirada* (Baer 1936, 516).
25. *Bivas fillas* (Marín Padilla 1983b, 255).
26. *Abrá onze o doze años, poco más o menos, que un vezino mío, que se llama Juan del Castillo, e su mujer Mari Sánchez tenían un fijo que podía aver entonçes año e medio o dos años, e esta criatura era flaquito, e non medrava, e non comya, e non fazia syno llorar. E preguntaba el padre e la madre que qué le farían. E acertóse a casa en Çifuentes una judía, a quien contaron el caso, e ella les dixo que pidiesen por amor de Dios en tres casas qve toviesen padre, e madre, e suegro, e suegra, e la señora de casa se llamase María, e que pidiesen harina de cada casa, e que tomasen la harina, e amasasen un rollo e una torta; la torta diesen por Dios al primer pobre que viniese, e que tomasen el rrollo, e con él la criatura, e que fuesen tres personas, los quales fueron su padre, que llaman Juan del Castillo, e su madre, e me rogaron que yo fuese la otra persona, que yo lo fize así. E fuemos todos tres juntos con el niño fasta donde non sonase gallo ni gallina, e que en el camino fablásemos a la yda a persona ninguna. Et fezimos en el campo un hoyo, e metimos dentro el moçuelo con sus envolturas, y posymos el rollo metido por la cabeça del niño, e desviámonos todos tres de allí cada uno a su parte. E volvimos al dicho hoyo, e tomamos el rollo, e estavan las manos del niño metidas por él, e lo quitamos, e lo hezimos tres pedaços, e cada uno tomó el suyo, e los arrojamos cada uno a su parte, e cada uno dixo tres vezes: "Arenas del campo / tomad este llorado / y dáme tu callado." Et después sacamos la criatura del hoyo, e los desnudos, e enterramos sus envolturas e vestidos en el hoyo, e le vestimos otras, e nos venimos, e topamos a un onbre, e le preguntamos: ¿Cómo le llamaremos a este niño que nos avemos hallado? Dixo: Mi nombre se llama Juan. E cualquier nombre que dixera, le avremos de llamar syete o ocho días en su casa. Y en llegando a casa del dicho Juan del Castillo fezimos un vaño al dicho niño con romero e ysopo. Acaesció esto avrá onze años, poco más o menos tiempo, e yo creya esto todo, e tenía fee en ello* (Cirac Estopañán 1942, 90–1). Cf. Cantera Montenegro 1985, 87 [Molina de Aragón 1480s].
27. *Se lo tomava por agüero, desiendo que luego venía la muerte quando los mochachos fasyan semejantes joyos delante las puertas* (Carrete/Fraile 1987, 95).
28. Liebman 1982, 105. See also Liebman 1970, 85; García 1910, 101 [1647].
29. *Cuando se levantan, procuran lugo tapar la cama, porque creen que la ocupa alguna alma. . . . No consienten quede de noche, a los pies de la cama, la vela encendida. . . . Que no comunican sus buenos sucesos, temiendo se les desvanezcan publicándolas. . . . Y que no consienten barrer la casa de noche, ni mirarse al espejo, y que tienen por muy malo cruzar los dedos juntando las manos, ni poner los brazos sobre las cabezas. . . . Cuando sanos o enfermos están en la cama y pasa algún entierro, se han de levantar de ella forzosamente* (García 1910, 101–2; cf. 208).
30. *Cuando soñaba algún mal sueño, iba a confesarse por echar el mal agüero en el confesor* (García 1910, 68).

31. *Que se enterrasse una calabera de persona, y en los ojos se le pussiessen unas habas, y q no le dixo la dha su tia para q es esto, ni sabe si se hizo* (AGN Vol 394 doc 2, 519a).

32. *Bragas, trébedes, ruda, ervatum, escova y asador* (Cirac Estopañán 1942, 186; Blázquez Miguel 1986a, 181; Cantera Montenegro 1985, 86 [Molina de Aragón 1480s]).

33. *El cortar de las uñas y enterrarlas debaxo de tierra lo acostumbraban hacer los judíos, porque con ellas no se les hiciessen supersticiones y porque el día del juicio final estuviessen cogidas y enterradas, y lo mismo acostumbraban hacer de las muelas y dientes* (Santa María 1893c, 187).

34. *Cortadas en esquina, como sacerdote hebreo* (Blázquez Miguel 1986a, 79).

35. For a discussion of Judaic practice regarding the nails, and for examples of such practices, see Chapter 10.4.

36. Marín Padilla 1983b, 260. See also Sánchez Moya/Monasterio Aspiri 1972, 114, 136; Blázquez Miguel 1986a, 184.

37. *Sueños de Yuçef, solturas de Jacob, su padre* (Cantera/Carrete 1975, 179).

38. *Algumas pesoas de sua naçam he diseram que não trabalhase aos sabados pera que Deos lhe guardase hum filho que andava na India* (Azevedo Mea 1982, 337).

39. *En la dicha ciudad de Guadalajara cierto observante de la Ley de Moisés no se quería mudar de la casa en que vivía, porque en ella había vivido y judaizado este reo y su mujer, y la habían dejado llena de ventura* (Lewin 1954, 149).

40. *Mandava a Juana Gonçales que pusyese vna mesa en el palaçio que esta sobre la cueva, la qual ella ponia con vnos manteles linpios e debaxo su alhonbra, y ponia en la dicha mesa vnos pañezicos pequeñitos, repregados, blancos, y tenía de plaser, y . . . presumia este testigo que ponia en la dicha mesa para el duende* (Beinart 1981b, 386).

41. *Lanção ás noites de Sam João Bautista, e do Natal, na agoa dos cantaros e potes, ferros, ou pão, ou vinho, dizendo, que aquellas noites se torna a agoa em sangue* (Furtado 1925, xxxii). See also Saraiva 1969, 164.

42. The copious bibliography relating to Rojas's work deals frequently with the subject of witchcraft and of love potions. For a discussion of *converso* love potions see Blázquez Miguel 1986a, 185–6.

43. *Como Christo habia engendrado aquel hueso y aquella carne en el vientre de su madre, así pusiese amor entre la esposa y el marido proprietario de aquel jubon* (Blázquez Miguel 1986a, 185–6).

44. *Y procuró, para hacerse invisible, sembrar las habas en los ojos y narices de una calavera; y usó el dar los polvos de golondrinas tostadas, vivas, y los sesos de zopilotes, para amansar [a] hombres* (García 1910, 69).

45. *Para quererse bien era bueno tostar unas golondrinas y darlas hechas polbos, a beber a la persona que querian quisiesse bien. Y vio que haviendose traido las golondrinas a su cassa, la dha Isabel las tosto e hizo polbos y se las dio a beber al dho Luis Nuñez* (AGN Vol 394 doc 2, 519a).

46. Liebman 1970, 85. See also Liebman 1982, 105; García 1910, 64 [1646].

47. *Le hazian la ceremonia con gotillas* (Sánchez Moya/Monasterio Aspiri 1972, 132). See also Cirac Estopañán 1942, 92; Cantera Montenegro 1985, 85–6 [Molina de Aragón 1480s]; Carrete/Fraile 1987, 103 [Almazán 1505].

48. *Y estando mala le hecharon gotillas y lo consentio* (Beinart 1981b, 593; cf. 3:604).

49. *Alucena, romero, culantro seco e incienso. . . . Santa Ana parió virgo, / Santa María a Jesucristo, / Santa Isabel a San Juan: / así como esto es verdad, / así sane este mal* (Cirac Estopañán 1942, 96).

50. *Llevando las cintas de las mugeres preñadas a la dicha Ginoga a tañer las aldavas, diciendo que por aquello auían de parir más aína* (Benito Ruano 1957, 331).

51. *En una retreta acostado en una cama debajo de un pabellón e que a los cuatro cantones de la dicha cama estaban cuatro candeleros con sendos cirios* (Sánchez Moya/Monasterio Aspiri 1973, 1121).

52. *Le mandó lleuar vna libra de aseyte a la sinoga* (Carrete Parrondo 1985, 106).

53. *Estando enferma de dolor de cabeza una judía, la ofreció una reliquia que traía consigo para que se quitase el dolor, y sacó del pecho una bolsa y de ella un pedazo de pan cenceño o sin levadura, que por tal le conoció luego la judía, y se lo puso sobre la cabeza, diciendo que aquel pan ácimo, cenceño o sin levadura, era su reliquia* (García 1910, 73 [1646]). See also Liebman 1982, 105; 1970, 85; Wiznitzer 1962a, 240.

54. *Me fizo una jodía para empreñar, medecinas* (Cabezudo Astraín 1950, 276).

55. *Oraciones de Nuestra Señora, de San Cebrián y del Conde* (Cirac Estopañán 1942, 95–6).

## CHAPTER VII

# Birth Customs

Like all peoples, Spanish Judaizing *conversos* marked the key moments in their life cycles with ceremonies that helped them establish the individual's place in the grand order of the universe. Birth, marriage, and death were occasions for reaffirming their basic beliefs. The Catholic religion, to which they all nominally belonged and in which some of them wholeheartedly believed, considered these events to be holy, sanctifying them with the sacraments of baptism, marriage, and extreme unction. Because Judaizing *conversos* were Catholics in a society vigilant of religious practice, they had no choice but to participate in the sacraments. But choice with regard to their child's Jewish affiliation also had to be made almost immediately, so for many *conversos* birth and other life-cycle events provided an opportunity to reaffirm their Jewishness.

## 7.1. Birth

The historical record is very sketchy about ceremonies attendant on actual *converso* births. In the fifteenth and sixteenth centuries births invariably occurred at home, generally with female family members or midwives in attendance. The birth itself seems to have been devoid of religious ceremony, although presumably a woman would be comforted during a difficult labor by prayers of her family, friends, or clergy. To judge from the record, Christian clergy do not seem to have been present at *converso* births. In reading thousands of documents the single reference

I have found to any religious professional attending a *converso* birth occurred just prior to the Expulsion: María González was accused before the Inquisition around 1485 because "when she was giving birth, the rabbi who lived across the street and another Jew came to her house to pray to God to keep her safe, and they prayed over her awhile."[1]

Despite the sketchiness of the written records, *conversa* women, like their old-Christian counterparts, must have called on the deity to keep them safe in childbirth and to help them endure the pain. One such prayer is reported from Almagro: "May *Adonai* come, all-encompassing, greatly enlightened, well-provisioned. With You, worthy Lord, I take shelter, for You placed Your house on high so that neither harm, nor malice, nor hurt should come to Your tents which the Kings entrusted to You."[2] Azevedo Mea found a similar prayer in a large number of Portuguese trials from the 1580s in Coimbra (1981, 165). This prayer is a version of Psalm 20, which is a common part of Jewish folklore associated with births (*Enc. Jud.* 4:1051). Nonetheless the semi-private nature of the birth experience must have served to keep such prayers from coming to the attention of Inquisitors.

The only other example I have found of a birth-related prayer was recovered by Vasconcelos from a *cristão novo* community in the mountains of central Portugal in 1933. The ethnographer reports that the new baby was lifted up and this prayer was recited: "O great God, I offer you this little angel. Take note of him; do not forsake him; shield him with Your divine arm of blessing, filled with grace and mercy." Then the baby was held to the breast and this prayer was said: "This be the blessing of Adonai, of Abraham, of Isaac, of Jacob, of Moses and of Aaron. May the blessing of the Lord cover him!"[3]

## 7.2. NAMES

Among both primitive and modern societies nouns, people's names in particular, resonate with a kind of magic power. In many respects the name *is* the thing. To speak the name aloud conjures up the thing's presence, as Fernando de Rojas's Celestina and other witches, real and fictitious, have known throughout the ages. To speak the name of a person aloud incurs the risk of attracting the attention of the spirits and subjecting the named person to jeopardy. On the other hand, some names may be thought of as defensive, for by linking a person to a source of supernatural power, such as a saint, they invoke the power's protection. On a purely human level names also provide a kind of social shorthand, indicating to the socially sensitive listener the named person's ethnicity, religious affiliation, and even socio-economic status. All these factors came to play in *conversos*' selection and use of names.

According to normative Jewish tradition, both male and female children are named eight days after their birth, male children at the circumcision ceremony and female children in the synagogue when their father is called to the Torah. I have not found any references to these practices,[4] with the exception of a single report that in modern Portugal eight days after a child is born the new-Christians recite a prayer in which they speak the child's name for the first time (Paulo 1970, 87). On the other hand, as section 4 of this chapter makes clear, the seventh or eighth day after the birth was commemorated by many crypto-Jews in other ways.

Most Judaizing *conversos* had at least two "first" names. One, given at baptism, established the child's Christian—which is to say official—identity. Normally, but not universally, this would be the name of the Christian saint on whose day the child was born or baptized or a name of some member of the Holy Family and their close associates: María, José, Juan, and so forth. This Christian name was used invariably in all legal documents, although prior to the Expulsion some *conversos* continued to use their former Jewish names with a sense of pride. A good example from Toledo is Fernando González Husillo, who, it was reported to Inquisitors around 1489, signed papers in the Christian fashion, because it was required, but added his Jewish name.[5] Still, as the earliest observers of crypto-Jewish customs pointed out, even those *conversos* who wanted to hide their Judaizing frequently gave their children a Jewish name as well as a Christian one.[6] For example, when Luis de Heredia was circumcised by a Jewish *mohel* sometime just prior to the Expulsion, he was given the Jewish name *Jacobiquo*.[7] Even after the Expulsion some *converso* families continued to use their Jewish names in private. This name was probably used in moments of tenderness; it was undoubtedly used in occasions of religious observance. In times of stress it might also be uttered unthinkingly in public, subjecting the family to grave risk. In Calatañazor [Soria] in 1501 Pedro Grande said that he had seen the *conversa* Catalina, wife of Pedro Sánchez de Tapia, calling to her son in the street: " 'Juanico, fijo.' And since he did not answer she called to him three or four times . . . 'Araquigüelo.' "[8]

Sometimes an adult deciding to Judaize would adopt a Jewish name. For example, in 1484 Donosa Ruiz, of Teruel, was accused of "having changed the name that was given to her at her baptism, which was Catalina, calling herself by her own authority Donosa."[9] Sometimes a *converso* would imbue a normal Christian name with a special meaning relevant to his own personal circumstances. Captain Francisco Gómez Texoso, a Portuguese new-Christian who came to Mexico in the 1640s, reported to the Inquisition that "his maternal grandfather had been baptized when he was already grown and given the name Tristán Manuel, because he would live an unhappy life for having allowed himself to be baptized out of fear of being burned as a rebel; . . . from that derived the name Tristán used by all the members of his family."[10] More frequently, as was pointed out to the Majorcan Inquisition in 1674, *conversos* would choose Christian names whose source was the Old Testament (Braunstein 1936, 184).

The majority of Judaizing *conversos* had at least two family names as well. The first was their Hispanic surname, in itself likely to be complex. As they do today, but even more chaotically, late medieval Hispanic family names joined the principal surnames of both the father and the mother in some fashion (e.g., Juan Gómez Martínez might well have a father named Pedro Gómez Serrano and a mother named Mercedes Martínez Cárdenas). In the fifteenth century the rules for combining parents' names were just beginning to stabilize, with the result that a *converso*'s compound family names are often not a reliable guide to the individual's lineage. Moreover, in the fifteenth century common people were just beginning to take surnames for themselves. At first *conversos* routinely took three sorts of surnames: the name of the town where they lived, or of the saint on whose day they were baptized or the church in which they were baptized, or of the Christian godparents who stood up with them at the baptismal font (Gilman 1972, 123). In an attempt to assume status they sometimes also appropriated aristocratic names. Later, when Inquisition pressure increased, they sometimes attempted to increase their anonymity by Smith-Jonesing themselves with the most common sorts of names: Spanish names like Gómez, Núñez, or Henríquez and Portuguese names like Fernandes, Dias, Lopes, Mendes, or Ribeira. Common Portuguese *converso* names like Nogueira, Pereira, and Pinheiro, were equally frequent among the old-Christian populace (Pimenta Ferro Tavares 1987, 42). The numerous indices of people tried for Judaizing by the Inquisition make patent the unremarkable nature of *converso* surnames.[11]

In addition to their common, or Christian, surnames, many Judaizing *conversos* maintained in secret their family's traditional Jewish surname. We know of the tendency of Judaizing *conversos* to preserve their Jewish names from the testimony of people who had left Iberia either to take up Judaism openly somewhere else or to live their double lives in a more tolerant atmosphere. Salomón Machorro told Mexican Inquisitors in 1642 that when he visited Leghorn, in Italy, he found many Spanish *conversos* living as Jews and using their Jewish names.[12] The list of the eighteen Founders of the Sephardic congregation in London in 1664 include three whose names combine Iberian and Hebrew elements: David Abarbanel Dormido, Moseh Baruh Louzada, and Abraham Coen Gonsales (Hayamson 1951, 422).

## 7.3. Circumcision

Christians welcomed the newborn infants into the body of the Church through the sacrament of baptism. All *converso* children, as Christians, were baptized,[13] but, as we saw in Chapter 5 in our discussion of the sacraments, on returning from the church Judaizing parents frequently scrubbed the chrism from the infant's forehead. Although circumcision is entirely different from baptism, they were often linked in the minds of the Christian Inquisitors.[14] Circumcision is not a sacrament in the Christian sense (i.e., it is not essential to Jewishness in some transcendental way); but it is reckoned by Jewish sages as among the most important precepts Jews must observe, for it commemorates the covenant between God and Abraham as described in Genesis 17:11–14 and symbolizes the parents' dedication of the male infant to a Jewish way of life.

The ritual of circumcision involves the surgical removal of the foreskin from the penis. Although circumcision is generally performed by an observant Jewish male who has been especially trained in the art, a *mohel*, or circumciser, may be any observant Jew. Because of its ritual importance and the indelible evidence of Judaizing it presented to the scrutinizing eyes of the Inquisition, circumcision offered special challenges and special dangers to the Iberian crypto-Jews. Since circumcision was so specifically Jewish, and in addition involved a sexual organ, it was a favorite theme for anti-Jewish satirists and polemicists. A strikingly large number of satirical court poems of the mid- to late fifteenth century make comic reference to circumcision.[15]

Prior to the Expulsion, circumcision was relatively common among Iberian *conversos*. Among the Spanish Jewish communities the circumcision of a male child was an occasion for great celebration. *Conversos* routinely attended these ceremonies and the parties that accompanied them, sharing the family's joy as if the family were their own—which it very often was (Marín Padilla 1981–2, 287–8). When *converso* children were circumcised in Spain prior to the Expulsion, sometimes Jewish family members or friends would come to the *converso*'s house to join in the celebration, although after the Inquisition was generalized in 1480 this tended to happen less frequently because of the danger involved. Often the circumcision was performed right after the child returned from being baptized in the church.[16] The combination of scrubbing off the chrism and performing the circumcision symbolically negated the power of Christianity and dedicated the child to Judaism.

The preferred time for circumcision was eight days after the infant was born. But for *conversos* not circumcised in infancy there were later opportunities to affirm their Jewish identity in this way. In 1485 several *converso* monks of the Hieronymite monastery of Guadalupe were found to have been circumcised; it is unclear whether this occurred when they were infants or adults (Sicroff 1965, 97). In Huesca in the mid-1460s there was even a campaign among the Jewish community to bring adult *conversos* back into the Jewish fold and to perform the ceremony on those who had not been circumcised as infants.[17]

In mixed marriages between a *converso* and an old-Christian spouse, circumcision of their male children was often a point of contention. Shortly after 1492 Hernando de Soria, of Sigüenza, was accused of making his wife have their children circumcised (Blázquez Miguel 1986a, 73). Alonso Franco lamented in the early 1490s that "we have such trials: those of us who are married to old-Christian women, even though we would like to circumcise our children we cannot for fear of them."[18] The circumcision was so important among some *converso* families that they reckoned time by it: in 1501 Fernand Ruiz reported in Aranda that two years previous he had overheard Françisco Texedor say that so and so happened " 'at the time we circumcised my son;' and then he said, 'at the time we baptized him.' "[19]

Circumcision was such blatant evidence of Judaizing that it was not widely practiced among Judaizers. There are a few circumcisions reported for the children of the Expulsion generation,[20] but there are only sporadic examples from throughout the Iberian world for almost three hundred years after the Expulsion. The Portuguese *converso* Manuel Fonseca [Lima 1608] had been circumcised during a visit to Leghorn on his way to the New World.[21] In 1714 in Cuenca Gabriel de Córdoba was found to have been circumcised (Lera García 1987, 95). And as late as 1788 the Mexican Inquisition found that the *converso* Franciscan monk Rafael Crisanto Gil Rodríguez had circumcised two of his friends (Liebman 1975, 132; Chinchilla Aguillar 1953, 185). There are also cases of self-circumcision.[22] Although such examples are scattered and tend to be relatively rare, among some groups of crypto-Jews, and at some times, circumcision seems to have been relatively common. Because the discretion of young children could not be taken for granted, among some crypto-Jewish groups circumcision was delayed for many years. Braunstein found no examples at all of infant circumcision among even the most strictly observant *chuetas* of Majorca in the seventeenth century (1936, 104). Among other groups, for example the Mexican crypto-Jewish community of the early seventeenth century, infant circumcision was relatively common. In the approximately 120 Mexican Inquisition cases between 1620 and 1649 reviewed by Hordes, 38 people were found guilty of having practiced circumcision (1980, 214).[23] Much detail about the specifics of these circumcisions is given in trial transcripts and in the summaries of the *autos de fé* of 1646–9.[24] The most detailed of these Mexican descriptions comes from the Sobremonte case. Tomás Treviño de Sobremonte was accused by the Inquisition of having had his son Rafael circumcised in Mexico sometime prior to 1647:

> One afternoon, around five o'clock, . . . his wife and mother-in-law locking the door ordered the boy to take off his pants, and they told him to be quiet . . . and they held him tightly on their laps. He came like a rabbi with his head covered and with a little knife or another sharp little tool. He knelt down in front of the boy, and with full devotion and turning his eyes and thoughts to heaven, as one who was performing a great service for the God of Israel, he took the genital member of his son and holding it in his left hand, with the little knife or tool he cut it full across, in the part between the foreskin and the glans. He wrapped the member in some bandages, and put his son to bed for several days, giving him light food and pastries and sweets to eat. And some nights they lit a wax candle in his room from the time of evening prayer until dawn. Two days after he got up from bed his wife washed the boy with hot water, from his knees down, and dressed him in a clean shirt.[25]

Another testimony in the same case reports that the clean clothes were "a sign of their joy in seeing him circumcised."[26]

Because circumcision was such an important emblem of commitment to Judaizing, it drew a great deal of attention from Inquisitors. Consequently, we know in considerable detail how circumcisions were performed by those Judaizers in later generations who retained the custom. For knowledgeable Judaizers the ceremony was not unlike that performed even today in normative Judaism.[27] Prior to the Expulsion the *mohel* who performed the circumcision on *converso* children was often a Jewish rabbi; after the Expulsion someone in the *converso* community had to act as rabbi or the child's father had to take on the responsibility. Fifteen-year-old Simón de León confessed in Mexico in 1647 that "one Friday morning, before they arrested his mother, his father shut himself in the bedroom next to the pantry with his brother Pancho for a good time, and that Pancho had come out crying, with blood running from the head of his private part."[28] Sometimes the *converso* community was privileged to receive clandestine visits of rabbis from abroad. For example, in 1635 the conversos of Madrid contracted the *mohel* Isaac Farque, from Amsterdam, to come to Spain to circumcise their children (Caro Baroja 1961, 1:421). Gabriel de Granada, reconciled in the 1646 Mexican *auto*, said that "at his mother's insistence he had been circumcised as an infant by a certain famous rabbi who had come to Mexico and who was a relative of his father."[29] Occasionally a *converso* businessman who had the opportunity to travel outside Spain would have himself circumcised in some foreign country, as was the case of the Portuguese new-Christian Gonzalo Báez de Paiba, who in 1658 had himself circumcised in Bayonne. In his trial he left this detailed description:

> This is how the circumcision was done. On top of a table covered with the richest table covering that could be found in the place, and on a white towel, an open Bible and another little book of Hebrew prayers were placed, along with a fine china plate as white as Talavera ware, and a razor and some tweezers and two lighted candles in candle sticks. And after everybody who was there had prayed . . . the daily service which consists of Psalms and different prayers, they had the witness sit down on a stool and Antonio Rodrigues Pacheco stood close behind him as godfather. Antonio Guiote took one candle and Doctor Franco López took the tweezers and Master Moses picked up the little book and recited some short prayers in Hebrew, and so that the witness might speak some words of the prayers he had him repeat them, having Master Moses pronounce them first. But he was not familiar with them nor understood what they meant. Then Moses took hold with the tweezers of that part of the masculine member which was to be cut, giving the tweezers to the Doctor so that he might hold on to said part. Then Master Moses cut the said part of the masculine member, while repeating at the same time the Hebrew words. When all that was finished they brought a little glass of lemonade which had been made for this occasion.[30]

The physical evidence of circumcision, the lack of foreskin, was in most cases irrefutable evidence of Judaizing. Luis Núñez Pérez told Mexican Inquisitors in 1642 that Juan de León "had a sign on him that would be very dangerous if he was arrested, because he would not be able to deny being a Jew, and the sign was that he was circumcised."[31] Circumcised Judaizers had to be extremely cautious in their urinary habits, their bathing, and their sexual activity, lest they be identified and denounced. Inquisitors routinely required a medical inspection of suspected Judaizers. And the accused sometimes went to great lengths to provide other explanations for the physical evidence, saying that their lack of foreskin was the result of illness or accident. By the seventeenth century in Mexico some Judaizing *conversos* did not remove the foreskin at all, but rather scarred it with a longitudinal cut in an attempt to comply with the requirement of the law and deceive the Inquisitors. When Inquisition doctors examined Gabriel de Granada in Mexico in 1645 they "found a mark . . . running longitudinally and with a scar, made apparently with a cutting instrument" (Adler 1899, 112–3). This operation was normally done when boys were between the ages of nine and fourteen (Liebman 1970, 76–7).

Occasionally a Judaizer would scar some other part of the body in substitution for the rite of circumcision, and this could be performed on women as well as on men. In one of the most peculiar and unusual episodes to appear in the documentation, Duarte de León Jaramillo, who was burned after the 1642 Mexican *auto*, was accused of circumcising his eldest son in the normal fashion. "For the other children, he cut a good-sized piece of flesh from the left shoulder with a new knife. He took this and threw salt upon it and threw it into some live coals and then this inhuman Jew ate it roasted" (Liebman 1974, 132). In 1647 Simón de León confirmed this tale. He told the Mexican Inquisition that when he was nine he saw his father Duarte take a certain woman friend of theirs into his storehouse where he

> stripped her naked to the waist and told her that he wanted to make a mark on her left shoulder as a sign that she was a Jewess. And binding her eyes with a towel from Rouen, and tying her hands at the wrist with a handkerchief, he saw him cut with a knife from her left shoulder a piece of flesh . . . the size of a half *real* coin, which bled profusely and gave her great pain. And Duarte de León put certain powders into the wound and bandaged it, and dressed her again, and took that piece of flesh and roasted it in the coals of a little brazier and ate it.[32]

In later testimony a doctor certified that Ysabel Núñez and her daughters Ana and Antonia all had this mark on their shoulders (Nunemaker 1946, 52; cf. 32, 62; Lewin, 1971, 159, 161–3).

Lastly, for a few exalted *conversos* circumcision could serve as a defiant affirmation of Jewishness, a final rebellious overture to martyrdom, often performed in the very Inquisition prisons. In 1635 Francisco Maldonado de Silva, a surgeon from Tucumán, in Argentina, confessed in Lima that "he had circumcised himself with a knife and finished by cutting off the foreskin with some scissors."[33] He also let his beard grow, and said that he wanted to die a Jew.

But the eager martyrs were few, vastly outnumbered by the quiet, unassuming Judaizers who mainly wanted to be left alone. Because of the danger of discovery, for most of them circumcision ceased being a viable component of Judaizing. Even before the Expulsion we hear converts lamenting how they feared to circumcise their children. Some *conversos* rationalized that keeping the Jewish law in any measure counted as a kind of circumcision of the heart. Nevertheless, the staunchest Judaizers continued to circumcise their children—or themselves as adults—as a sign of the ancient covenant between God and Abraham. Parents had to take care to see that their children did not exhibit themselves to curious neighbors. At some point, as well, parents would have to explain to the child the circumstances and significance of his circumcision, and hope he had reached the age of discretion. In testimony given shortly after the Expulsion, for example, Luis de Heredia told Inquisitors that when he was eight or nine years old he asked his mother "Mother, the boys say I am clipped, that there is something wrong with my member." His mother explained: "Son, your grandfather Luis de Hereda brought to the house some Jews named master Juçe Toriel, the doctor, master Salamon Avayut . . . and in the presence of these Jews and your grandfather he circumcised you and took a little blood from your member and gave you the name Jacobiquo and gave you four *reales* and when they circumcised you you were four or five years old."[34]

Like so many other Jewish rituals, later *conversos* reinterpreted circumcision within the Christian context that was so central to their lives. As the Christian idea of personal salvation began to permeate crypto-Judaism's belief system, circumcision was by analogy held to convey the saving power of baptism. Juan Pacheco de León told Mexican Inquisitors in 1643 that "circumcision among Jews is the same as baptism among Christians."[35] *Chuetas* in Majorca in the 1670s believed that circumcision was essential to salvation (Selke 1972, 150). Even an orthodox Jew like Isaac Cardozo (1603?–83), writing outside Spain, believed that circumcision was a "mysterious sacrifice" and that "without this seal of circumcision the Jew cannot be saved."[36]

## 7.4. HADAS

Celebrations were held both before and after the circumcision ceremony. A widespread folk custom was to party all night prior to the circumcision in order to scare away evil spirits. In Yiddish-speaking Europe this custom is called a *vahknakht* (*Enc. Jud.* 5:576); in the Ladino-speaking Levant it is often called a *veula*, or vigil. The Iberian version of this custom appears to have been called *hadas*.

The origin of both the celebration and the term is obscure. Baer considers the word to be derived from the Hebrew *ḥadash*, meaning *new* or newborn (1966, 2:335). But there are stronger arguments for a derivation from the Latin *fatum*, meaning *fates*.[37] In fact the *hadas* celebration may even be a vestigial Roman custom (Levine 1982, 180). The custom was not unknown among Christians in Spain as well, for it is cited in Juan Ruiz's fourteenth-century *Libro de buen amor*.[38] Until recently Sephardic Jews of Salonica practiced the *fadamiento* for female children by inviting friends and their rabbi to dine with them and officially name the child (Molho 1950, 79–81).

The celebration was held for both male and female children. The *hadas* were thought of as corporeal supernatural beings. Sometimes an offering such as a saucer of honey might be put out to attract the *hadas*.[39] In 1511 Alvaro Huerta, of Castillo de Garcimuñoz, had a servant girl clean his house and sweep the floor so that the barefoot *hadas* would not stumble when they visited.[40]

The night of the *hadas*, seven days after the infant's birth,[41] family and friends would gather at the home of the newborn with presents for the baby and its mother. For example, the Jewess Sol Bellida reported that in 1489 when her sister-in-law had a son a *conversa* woman sent "a colored sash and a linen suit" to her house "the night of the *hadas* ceremony when they do what they are accustomed to doing at a circumcision."[42] The infant, wrapped in white clothing (Beinart 1974, 241), would be cleansed in a basin of water into which had been put a variety of objects indicative of plenty, wealth, and good fortune. The documentary record is remarkably consistent in its descriptions of this bath.[43] A description from Castile in the 1480s reports that "the seventh night after the birth they put the infant in a basin of water and throw in gold, silver, seed pearls, wheat, barley and other things, and they wash the infant there reciting certain words; and this is called the *hadas* which they do to infants."[44] An almost identical description appears in an Edict of Grace from Mexico in 1639: "On the seventh night after the birth of a child, they take a vessel with water, throwing into it gold, silver, a misshapen pearl, wheat, barley, or other things, [then] washing the child in this water reciting certain words. Or having made guardian angels or fairies [*hadas*] for their sons."[45]

After the child was bathed traditional prayers would be recited, traditional blessings would be given,[46] and traditional songs would be sung[47] invoking the protection of the good fates, or fairies for the newborn child. After the cleansing ceremony itself the family and friends would eat traditional sweet foods[48] and drink and party all night. Often there were musicians[49] and people danced. Sometimes people played cards (Marín Padilla 1981–2, 286). In 1484 it was said of Juana de Çibdad, of Ciudad Real, that "in her house, whenever a child was born they would do the *hadas* ceremony for him or her in the usual fashion, dressing the infant in clean white clothing, and many young women and others came to play and dance on the seventh night."[50]

There is abundant evidence that the *hadas* ceremony was customary in Spain around the time of the Expulsion, but it seems to have quickly dropped from the repertoire of Judaizing practices. I have not found any witnesses to the ceremony later than 1537, although the *hadas* is described in Edicts of Faith as late as 1639.[51] Similarly, I have not found any references to the custom in Portugal until this century, when in 1952 Machado reported a reminiscence of this custom among villagers in the Mogadouro region of Portugal. "When they have children, they throw into the water used for the child's first bath all the coins and gold objects they possess, or that their intimate friends possess, so that the new-born infant will never lack for wealth or abundance of material goods."[52] However, the custom was well known among Sephardic emigrant communities in the eastern Mediterranean, where it left remnants into the twentieth century.[53]

## 7.5. WET NURSE

Before the Expulsion *conversos* sometimes gave a child to a Jewish wet nurse (*nodriza*) immediately following the baptism. This probably did not have any deep religious significance, for there is evidence of *conversas* of that period hiring Moorish or Christian wet nurses as well. After the Expulsion the wet nurse was generally a Judaizer. Marín Padilla cites three examples from Teruel in the 1480s of *conversa* women engaging Jewish wet nurses for their infants and several examples of them giving their children to Moorish or Christian women to nurse.[54]

## 7.6. PURIFICATION, *TEBILAH*

According to Leviticus 12:2–8 a woman is "unclean" for seven days after the birth of a son and fourteen days after the birth of a daughter. She is "impure" for periods of forty or eighty days respectively. In traditional Judaism the rite of purification, or *tebilah*, involves a visit to the ritual bath, or *mikvah*. After giving birth *conversa* women often performed ritual ablutions before resuming normal activities.[55]

Perhaps because the numbers of "impure" days were so readily ascertainable in the Bible and the Biblical instructions were so clear, Judaizing *conversos* sustained the custom of ritual purification for a very long time in both Iberia and the Iberian possessions. While "impure," *conversa* women abstained from a number of religiously significant activities. The Jewish prohibition against entering the synagogue during the impure phase was readily extended to the church. Bernardina de San Juan, of Baeza, testified in 1572 that her mother had taught her that "anyone who attended a women giving birth should not pray for three days; and the woman who bore a son should not pray for forty days, nor for sixty if she bore a girl, because it was a requirement of the Law."[56] There are examples from the late fifteenth and early eighteenth centuries of *conversa* women refraining from entering a church for forty days after giving birth (Santa María 1893c, 182; cf. Lewin 1939, 26). They also abstained from sexual relations with their husbands. In 1490 Biuas, the wife of the Jew Salomón Leví, reported to the Inquisition of Soria a conversation she had had with the *conversa* Ana Rodríguez some ten years earlier. Biuas said that "when Jewish women gave birth to daughters they must remain seven weeks apart from their husbands, and when they gave birth to sons thirty days." And Ana

Rodríguez replied: "well I, whenever I give birth, whether it is a boy or a girl, for thirty days I won't go into a church or into my husband's bed for purity."[57]

While during late medieval times the visit to the *mikvah* had replaced the complex purification ceremonies described in Leviticus, within a hundred years after the Expulsion Judaizing *conversos*, perhaps ignorant of post-Biblical traditions, were mimicking some of the ancient procedures. In 1591 the wife of Gaspar Dias da Vidigueira, of Bahia (Brazil), was accused of "taking her newborn son after forty days to an abandoned hermitage, and there offering him up with two apples according to the Law of Moses."[58]

Remnants of after-childbirth purification ceremonies have surfaced in this century among the *cristãos novos* of the Trás-os-Montes region of Portugal. Even today some *conversas* in Beiras and Trás-os-Montes do not go to church for forty days following childbirth (Paulo 1985, 29). Paulo reports that in Belmonte, Portugal, when a woman has given birth she cannot undress or change her clothes for thirty days (Paulo 1985, 144). The modern Portuguese tradition has preserved fragments of prayers such as this one to purify women after childbirth, which is recited by modern Portuguese new-Christians in Lagoaça and Pinhel: "Blessed are You Adonai, God, King of the world, who sanctified us through Your holy and blessed commandments, and permitted us to live to this day, choosing us from the gentile peoples and drawing us away from those who are in error, and giving us these commandments for the purification of our souls. Amen."[59]

## 7.7. OTHER

Birth-connected customs of the late medieval Jews reflected the superstitious practices of their Christian neighbors. For example, when María González's children were born she anointed "their palms and underarms and the soles of their feet with myrrh."[60] In 1493 "a person came into the house of a sister of Juana, who had just given birth, for a light for her fire, and the mother said not to give her a light because the baby had not yet been baptized; and then Isabel ... said: 'Give her light, it is all right to give it to her, for my father was a rabbi.'"[61]

It is only natural that over the centuries a number of superstitions and folklore customs related to birth have been added to the *conversos*' repertoire of Judaizing practices. In the modern *cristão novo* communities of Portugal several of these birth-related customs have been recovered. Paulo reports that in this century in Belmonte, Portugal, when a woman is about to give birth they hang a cock's head over the door to her room.[62] Paulo also reports that among *cristãos novas* in modern Portugal a woman who has recently given birth must be protected from evil and therefore cannot be left alone for a single instant. While friends and relatives are with her they sing the ballad of Jonah, but if the baby is a girl the new-Christians in modern Portugal make no expression of joy (Paulo 1970, 86).

## NOTES

1. *Quando ella estaua de parto, vinieron a su casa el rabí que biuía enfrente della y otro judío a rogar al Dio que la escapase, e resaron cabe ella un rato* (León Tello 1972, 82). Cf. Beinart 1975, 654.

2. *Vinoão Adonay, mor cubritura, solombrado, abastado, a ti digno Adonay, me abrigo que alto puseste tuas moradas, asi não vira mal nem malicia nem chagas as tuas tendas que os Malachis te encomendarão* (Blázquez Miguel 1984, 76). The text of this prayer appears garbled and the translation is tentative.

3. *O meu Grande Deus, eu vos ofereço este anjinho. Tomai conta dele; não o desampareis; abençoai-o com o vosso divino braço de bênção, cheio de graça e misericórdia. . . . Seja a bênção de Adonai, de Abraão, de Isaac, de Jacob, de Moisés, e de Arão. A bênção do Senhor o cubra!* (Vasconcelos 1958, 207–8).

4. Levine notes the absence of specific references to these customs in her examination of early Inquisition trials in Toledo (1982, 178).

5. *Por manifestar su coraçon nonbrava se por nonbre de judio, en que quando dava e otorgava algunas escrituras e las fyrmava de su nombre, por conplir con los christianos, ponia un nombre en christianiego e junto con el ponia su nonbre en ebrayco* (Baer 1936, 510).

6. Santa María 1893c, 182; cf. Furtado 1925, xxxii [Evora 1536]; Medina 1899b, 26 [Colombia 1610 Edict of Faith].

7. Marín Padilla 1980, 250. Cf. Llorca 1942, 148 [Teruel 1484]; Baer 1936, 747 [Toledo 1487]. Solomón Machorro also told Inquisitors in Mexico in 1642 that "he did not know whether or not his parents had called him David, Luna, Salomón, Raquel and Israel Machorro out of hate for the Christian religion, but if they had it was not his fault, because he was a baby at the time" (*No sabe si los nombres que se pusieron sus padres y pusieron a este confesante, llamándolo David, Luna, Salomón y Raquel e Israel Machorro fue en odio a la religión cristiana, y cuando lo haya sido él no tuvo culpa de esto, por ser entonces niño*) (Lewin 1977, 191).

8. *Venía disiendo a vn su fijo: "Juanico, fijo," e como no le respondió dixo por dos o tres veses la susodicha a . . . su hijo: "Araquigüelo"* [diminutive of the Hebrew name *Arragel*] (Carrete Parrondo 1985, 113). Cf. Wolf 1926, 43 [Canary Islands 1524].

9. *Hauerse mudado el nombre impuesto en el baptismo, que era Cathalina, llamándose por su propia auctoridat Donosa* (Llorca 1942, 148).

10. *A su abuelo materno le baptizaron en pie y se hizo poner por nombre Tristaon Manuel, porque tristes días viviría por haberse dejado baptizar, de temor de que no le quemasen por rebelde, contra su voluntad, recibiendo el agua del santo bautismo, de que se ha derivado el apellido de Tristán usado por todos los del linaje de dicho Francisco Gómez Texoxo* (García 1910, 52).

11. I know of no surnames used exclusively or even preponderantly by *conversos*. The Inquisition, always vigilant to identify new-Christians so as to scrutinize them for crypto-Judaizing, never used surnames as a guide. The long lists of common so-called *converso* family names that historians like Böhm have assembled from Inquisition testimony and other sources (1984, 99–120) are strikingly similar to lists found in the telephone directory in any major Hispanic city. Still, there are a number of onomastic studies dealing with Sephardic and *converso* naming traditions. All the indices of Judaizers tried by the Inquisition are good indicators of the names prevalent among *conversos* in that particular area. Other lists of names can be found in Pérez 1986, 26–8, 196ff.; Levy 1987, 3–4; Molho 1950.

12. *Trató y comunicó con mucho y diferentes hombres y mujeres observantes de la dicha Ley de Moisés, unos nacidos allí y en Italia y otros en España, según oyó decir, y todos tenían y usaban*

*nombres de judíos* (Lewin 1977, 132). Cf. Yerushalmi 1980, 5; Roth 1931–2, 31; Levi 1982, 46–8; Israel 1990, 249.

13. Marín Padilla cites two cases prior to the Expulsion in which *converso* families managed to avoid having their children baptized (1981–2, 279).

14. According to an Inquisition manual from the time of the Expulsion, "when children are born the [Jews] circumcise them and give them Jewish names and when the [children] are baptized they scrub off the chrism and wash them" (*Cuando nacen las criaturas las circumcidan y ponen nombres de judios y las hacen raer la chrisma y lavar después de baptizados*) (Santa María 1893c, 182). Cf. the 1610 Colombian Edict of Faith cited by Medina 1899b, 26.

15. To cite one of many examples, a poet named Román replied to a poetic satire by the *converso* Cordoban tailor Antón de Montoro by telling him that "because you are a good tailor, you ought to sew a hood for your prick" (*Pues que soys buen alfayate / que hagáys a vuestra pixa / capirote*) (Castillo 1882; cf. poems nos. 969, 979, etc.).

16. This was a favored time for Judaizers after the Expulsion as well: as late as 1590 in Brazil Ana de Oliveira was accused of circumcising her sons after they had been brought back from their baptism (Lipiner 1969, 154). On the other hand, this incident must be considered atypical, for Lipiner's investigations suggest that this was the only circumcision performed in the Brazilian colonies.

17. In Huesca the rabbi Abraham Abballi circumcised several *converso* children and at least one adult, taking care that "the foreskin that they cut off be put in a basin" (*el prepucio y cuero que le cortan ponen en un bacin*) and singing the blessing, "Blessed be He who has brought us to this circumcision" (*Vendito sea el que nos ha traydo a circuncidir*) (Marín Padilla 1981–2, 62–7).

18. *Ved qué trabajo tenemos nosotros, los que somos casados con mugeres christianas viejas, que aunque querríamos circuncidar nuestros fijos, non lo osamos faser por cabsa dellas* (Fita y Colomé 1887, 45).

19. *"Dígos que quando retajamos a mi fijo," e luego tornó a desyr: "Quando lo bautysamos"* (Carrete Parrondo 1985, 134).

20. For example, Carrete/Fraile 1987, 25 [Almazán 1502]. Rábade Obradó speculates that evidence in the Toledo Inquisition files that sometimes gravely ill children were circumcised indicates that their parents were thereby invoking divine aid for their cure (1990a, 371).

21. About the same time the Peruvian *converso* priest Agustín de Hoces had let himself be circumcised by some Portuguese friends (Castañeda Delgado 1989, 436, 447).

22. For Mexican examples see Liebman 1970, 77, 1620; Lewin 1971, 39–40, 159–65.

23. Liebman goes further and claims that in the 1640s all Judaizing males examined by the Inquisition were circumcised (1970, 254).

24. See Lewin 1977, 53; Nunemaker 1946, 60; Liebman 1974, 83.

25. *Un día por la tarde, como a las cinco . . . su mujer y suegra cerrando la sala mandaron al dicho su muy conjunto [su hijo] quitar los calzones, y dijeron que callase . . . y teniéndole ambas fuertemente en las faldas, vino este rabino, cubierta la cabeza y con un cuchillito u otra cosa muy delgada a modo de puntilla, y llegándose donde estaba el dicho su muy conjunto de muy tierna edad e hincándose de rodillas, para ello con toda devoción . . . y poniendo los ojos y mente en el cielo, como quien a su parecer hacía gran servicio al Dios de Israel, cogió el miembro genital del dicho su muy conjunto y teniéndole en la mano izquierda, con el dicho cuchillito o puntilla le corto a lo largo, en la parte baja que nace desde e principio del prepucio hasta el frenillo, poniéndole en dicha parte unos pañitos, acostándole en la cama por algunos días, dándole a comer carne de pluma, bizcochuelos y dulces, encendiendo este reo una vela de cera algunas noches en el aposento donde está*

*el circuncidado, desde la oración hasta que amanecía, lavándole la dicha mujer de este reo a los dos días después de levantado de la cama, con agua caliente, desde las rodillas para abajo, poniéndole camisa limpia* (Lewin 1954, 150–1; cf. Liebman 1974, 138).

26. *Señal de fiesta y alegría de verle ya circuncidado* (García 1910, 255).

27. Even generations after the Expulsion some crypto-Jews retained (or had in some other way acquired) extraordinary knowledge of detail. Juan de León reportedly told Inquisitors in 1642 that the priest who performed the circumcision for several days previous should not have sexual relations with his wife (Lewin 1977, 158).

28. *Vn dia, le parese que viernes, vio por la mañana, antes que prendiesen a su madre, que el dicho su padre se enserro en el aposentto, junto a la despensa, con su hermano Pancho vn buen rratto, y que salio llorando el dicho Pancho, y corriendo sangre de sus berguensas en la cauesa* (Nunemaker 1946, 60).

29. *Circuncidóle, siendo muy pequeño, cierto rabino famoso que estuvo en estos Reinos, pariente de su padre, a petición e instancia de la dicha su madre* (García 1910, 54). Cf. Liebman 1970, 209; Furtado 1925, 333.

30. *La forma de dicha çircuncision fue poner encima de vna mesa cubierta con vna sobremessa la mas rica que se hallo en el lugar y sobre vna toalla blanca la Biblia abierta y otro librillo de oraçiones en Hebreo y vn Plato de loça blanca que como la de talabera y en vna navaja y vnas tenaçicas y dos velas encendidas en dos candeleros y despues de auer reçado todas las personas que se hallaron presentes . . . la reça ordinaria de todos los dias que consta de psalmos y oraçiones diferentes hiçieron sentar a este en vn taburete y el dicho Antonio Rodrigues Pacheco se arrimo a las espaldas deste como padrino. Y el dicho Antonio Guiote tubo vna Vela y el Doctor Franco Lopez las tenaças y el dicho Maestro Moyses quien tomo el libro Pequeño y dijo algunas oraçiones breues en Hebreo y para que este pronunciase algunas palabras dellas se las hiço repetir Yendo el susodicho pronunciandolas primero. Pero este no sauia ni entendia lo que querian deçir. Y luego el dicho Moyses quen coxio con las tenaças la parte del Mienbro viril que se auia de cortar dando al dicho Doctor las dichas tenaças para que tubiese asida con ellas la dicha parte. Y luego el dicho Maestro corto la dicha parte del miembro viril repitiendo a vn mismo tiempo las dichas palabras Hebreas. Y acauado lo referido trajeron vn poco de limonada, que era vn vasso que se auia hecho de proposito de dicha bevida pare este efecto* (Willemse 1974, lv-lvi).

31. *Tenía una seña contra sí muy peligrosa si lo prendiesen, porque no podría negar el ser judío, porque la dicha seña era estar circuncidado* (Lewin 1977, 53).

32. *La desnudo hasta la cintura, y la dixo que la queria hacer vna señal en el hombro izquierdo, en señal de que era judia, y vendandola los ojos con vna toalla de ruan, y atandola las manos por las muñecas con vn pañuelo de narizes, sintio el que la corto del dicho hombro izquierdo con vn cuchillo vn pedaço de carne . . . como medio real, saliendola mucha sangre y sintiendo grande dolor. Y que el dicho Duarte de Leon le echo ciertos poluos, y que hauiendola puesto vn paño, la torno a vestir, y cogio aquel pedaço de carne y lo asso en vnas ascuas, que estavan en vn braserito, y se la comio.*

33. *El mismo se circuncidó con una navaja y acabó de cortar el prepucio con unas tijeras* (Medina 1887, 2:147). Cf. Böhm 1984, 47; García de Proodian 1966, 348.

34. *Madre, los mochachos me llaman rezmellado; qué mal he huvido yo en mi miembro. . . Fijo, tu aguelo Luys de Heredia truxo a casa unos jodios llamados maestre Juçe Toriel, medico, maestre Salamon Avayut . . . y en presencia de los dichos jodios y de tu aguelo te circuncidio y te saquo una poca de sangre de tu miembro que te pusieron nombre Jacobiquo y te estrenaron quatro reales y eras de edat quando te circuncidieron de edat de quatro o cinquo años* (Marín Padilla 1980, 250). Cf. Marín Padilla (1981–2, 293–4).

35. *Lo mismo es entre los judíos la circuncisión que el bautismo entre los cristianos* (Lewin 1977, 191).
36. *Sin este firmamento de berit no se puede salvar el judío* (Yerushalmi 1980, 4).
37. For discussion of the origin of the term see Beinart 1981a, 302; Blázquez Miguel 1985b, 55; Cirac Estopañán 1942, 184; Kayserling 1898, 267.
38. *El día que vos nacisteis, blancas hadas os hadaron* (Blázquez Miguel 1985b, 54). In this sense it is also used by the *converso* poet Antón de Montoro (Montoro 1990, 36, 230).
39. Blázquez Miguel 1986a, 69. María González [Cuenca 1490] used to set the table with cakes so that the *hadas* would come to "sweat" her baby (*poniendo mesa y en ella tortas e otras cosas para que viniesen las tales hadas a sudar la criatura*) (Carrete Parrondo 1985b, 103).
40. *Dixo a vna moça suya, difunta, que se dezia Juana, que barriese la casa e tirase los trastos, . . . que para quando barriese las hadas, que no tropeçasen en alguna cosa porque venian descalças* (Moreno Koch 1977, 354). Cf. Blázquez Miguel 1986a, 69.
41. Santa María 1893c, 182; Beinart 1974, 85, 241; 1975, 654; 1977a, 10 [Ciudad Real 1480s]; Rábade Obradó 1990a, 434–5 [Toledo 1485–1500]; Blázquez Miguel 1986a, 65 [Alcázar 1519].
42. *Una faxa colorada y una terna . . . de lincuelo* to her house *una noche de las hadas amanando lo que se acostumbra amanar para la circuncision* (Marín Padilla 1981–2, 285).
43. As we will see in Chapter 11, some of these practices are mirrored in *converso* funeral rites.
44. *La septena noche de el nacimiento de la criatura ponen un vacín con agua, y echan en él oro, plata, aljófar, trigo, cebada y otras cosas, y lavan allí las criaturas diciendo ciertas palabras; y esto se llaman las hadas que hacen a las criaturas* (Santa María 1893c, 182).
45. Liebman (1970, 97). An almost identical Edict of Faith was promulgated in 1610 in the Colombian city of Cartagena de Indias (Medina 1899b, 26). Strangely, I have not found evidence of the *hadas* celebration in Inquisition records from any of the Iberian possessions.
46. In 1537 in Lisbon the *cristã nova* Branca Nunes was denounced because "when her granddaughter came out she put her hand on her face, drawing it downward from the eyes, saying, "may good fairies work their magic for you" (*Quando a neta sahia lhe punha a mão no rostro, descendo com ella, dos olhos para baixo e dizendo: "boas fadas que te fadem"*) (Baião 1921, 108).
47. Marina González testified in Ciudad Real in 1484 that in 1464 "when Rodrigo de Olivos' son was born they invited her to the *hadas* and she went to his house and sang, "Hadas, hadas, may good *hadas* come to you. And many *converso* men and women were there" (*Al nasçimiento de un fijo de Rodrigo de los Olibos conbidaron a este testigo que fuese a la hadas, y se fue a casa y cantaron aquella noche: Hadas, hadas, hadas buenas que te vengan. E que estaban alli muchos conuersos y conuersas*) (Beinart 1974, 458).
48. In the village of Bolea in 1483 or 1484 Juana, wife of the *converso* Pedro Tomás, invited the neighbors in and gave the children a slice of bread with a spoonful of honey, which her husband later reported was the custom of the Jews in his native village of Gurrea (Marín Padilla 1981–2, 289). Fruit was also common (Beinart 1974, 456).
49. Drummers (1476–8; Marín Padilla 1981–2, 290) and tambourine players (1484; Beinart 1974, 456).
50. *En su casa, quando le nasçia algund fijo, lo fadauan de la manera y forma que se acostumbra entre ellos faser, vestiendo la criatura de ropas blancas e linpias, e venian muchas donçellas e otras mugeres a tañer e baylar a las siete noches* (Beinart 1974, 241).

51. For additional Spanish references see Llorca 1939, 531; Fita y Colomé 1892, 488 [1484]; Coronas Tejada 1988, 102 [1511]; Blázquez Miguel 1986a, 65 [1519]; 1987, 54 [1519].
52. *Quando lhes nascem filhos, lançam na água destinada a lavá-los a primeira vez todas as moedas e objectos de ouro que possuem, e que possam obter nas pessoas de sua intimidade, para que ao recém-nascido jamais falte riqueza e abundância de todos os bens materiais* (Machado 1952, 22).
53. Until recently the *hadas* ceremony was still practiced by the Sephardic community that had emigrated to Rhodes. For a girl baby "the parents gave a banquet to which they invited relatives and friends, among them a rabbi. The rabbi held the infant on his lap and recited a blessing for the child's good health and happiness. He also announced the girl's name as chosen by her parents. The baby was then passed around to the guests who all wished her and her parents long life. This ceremony was known as *las fadas*" (Angel 1980, 119). Cf. Levy 1987, 12–3; Dobrinsky 1986, 20.
54. (1981–2, 280). See also Blázquez Miguel 1985b, 55; Sánchez Moya 1973, 134.
55. León Tello 1972, 82; Marín Padilla 1982, 250; Liebman 1970, 97 [1639]; Selke de Sánchez 1972, 277 [1678].
56. *En tres días no había de rezar la que sirviese a mujer parida y la que paría hijo, no había de rezar en cuarenta días, ni en sesenta pariendo hija, que era precepto de la dicha ley* (Gracia Boix 1983, 133).
57. *Dixo que mandaua la Ley de Moysén a los judíos que las judías, quando pariesen hijas, questouiesen siete semanas apartadas de sus maridos, e quando pariesen hijos treynta días; e vio este testigo que . . . Ana Rodríguez dixo: "Pues quánto yo cada vez que paro, agora sea fijo o hija, por treinta días non entraré en yglesia nin en la cama del bachiller por limpieza"* (Carrete Parrondo 1985, 17; cf. 133); Marín Padilla 1982, 250. Jiménez Lozano found that in certain villages of Castilla-León well into the 1960s women kept to the house and abstained from sex for reasons of "limpieza" for forty days following giving birth (1984, 363). He considers this an example of a "culteme," one of many that indicate a broad assimilation, popularization, and ultimately trivialization of sets of customs which in former times had been explicit indicators of crypto-Judaizing.
58. *Depois de lhe nascer um filho levou ele, quarenta dias depois, a uma ermida abandonada e ofereceu dois pombos, conforme a lei de Moisés* (Wolff 1987, 30). According to Lipiner, this custom derives from Leviticus 12:6–8 or Luke 2:24 (1969, 157). See also Wiznitzer 1960, 21.
59. *Bendito Adonai, Deus, Rei do Mundo que nos santificou com as Suas santas encomendanças, benditas e santas, e nos deste vida até este tempo escolhendo-nos do povo gentio e apartando-nos dos errantes, e encomendando-nos estes preceitos para a purificação das nossas almas, Amém* (Paulo 1985, 80; see also 1970, 86); Tradições 1932, 7.51:2.
60. *Con myrra las palmas e los sobacos e las plantas de los pies* (Blázquez Miguel 1985b, 56 cites Beinart 1977a, 2:266). Marín Padilla 1981–2, 283 considers this case unique.
61. *Entrara vna persona por lunbre a casa de vna hermana de . . . Juana, quien estaua parida, e la dicha parida dixera que no le diese lunbre por que non avia bautizado la criatura; e que entonçes dixera . . . Ysabel: "Dale lunbre, que bien le puedes dar, que rabi era mi padre"* (Moreno Koch 1977, 355).
62. (1970, 144, 86). This may be a medieval custom. Levine notes that a responsum of Rabbi Solomon ben Abraham Adret (1235–1310) criticizes the superstitious custom of hanging a cock and garlic at the door of a woman who has just given birth to ward off evil spirits (Levine 1982, 179).

## CHAPTER VIII

# Education

Crypto-Judaism, by the very nature of its secrecy, was dangerous to transmit, and its transmittal grew substantially more dangerous over time. In contrast to some other aspects of *converso* spiritual life we know a good deal about when and how new-Christians received their Jewish education, because in the hope of uncovering networks of practicing Judaizers the tribunals asked probing questions about where and how the accused person was educated. When we look at the education of crypto-Jews, two general principles stand out. The first is that the education issue had to be confronted every time a practicing crypto-Jew commenced a relationship with someone whose religious commitments were either unformed (as in the case of children) or not centered on Judaism (as could be the case with potential spouses or other adult friends or associates). The second is that in the vast majority of instances the family was the principal agent of Jewish education.

In considering the processes by which *conversos* were educated in the practices of crypto-Judaism, we must bear in mind some broad distinctions between the generations and the times in which people lived. There were substantial differences in *converso* education prior to the 1492 Expulsion, during the early years of the sixteenth century, and for the generations that followed.

The generation of people who themselves converted, which with a few exceptions was prior to July 31, 1492, the date by which all Jews in Spain had to convert or emigrate, carried with them into their new religion whatever Jewish education they might have had. Many had a profound knowledge of Jewish law and practice. Moreover, most of their communities still contained actively practicing Jews, some of them members of their very own families, who could serve the *conversos* as role models. Copies of the Torah and the Talmud were available to them, as were kosher butcher shops and Jewish ritual baths. If they liked, by incurring only minor risk they could visit the local synagogue and participate in prayers. As we will see in later chapters, many of them routinely joined their Jewish brethren in observance of the festivals and the celebrations that marked major events in the life cycle. After the Inquisition was generalized in Spain in 1480, there were risks attendant on all these activities, but the risks were tolerable. For the most part the religious life of the first generation of converts was not restricted by their ignorance; theirs was a crypto-Judaism whose orthodoxy and extent were determined by their own personal choice.

The Judaizers who grew up in the early 1500s were different, for the well-spring of openly-practiced Judaism was not available to them. They had no practicing Jews as neighbors to keep fresh in their minds the traditions of Jewish observance, and the realia of Judaism—the Bibles and prayer books and ritual objects—rapidly disappeared into the flames. Many of the best educated and most strictly observant Jews of the 1490s had chosen exile over conversion, thereby diluting the storehouse of knowledge available for oral transmission. Individual *conversos* and *converso* families or small communities were experimenting with respect to how much of their Judaism could be preserved, how much was compatible with Christian practice, and how much was too risky to maintain. The memories of the *conversos'* Jewish heritage were still reasonably fresh, but with each successive year the finer details were dropping away.

By the middle of the sixteenth century, however, normative Judaism was a much more distant memory. Much of the minutiae of orthodox Jewish observance had been forgotten; many Christian concepts had invaded the *conversos'* religious beliefs. The youngsters in need of educating were likely to be the grandchildren or great-grandchildren of the people who had converted. The so-called purity-of-blood laws, the *leyes de limpieza de sangre,* excluded *conversos* from many professions and increased the benefit of not disclosing a family's Jewish ancestry. In addition the Inquisition was increasingly vigilant in scrutinizing the practices of known *conversos*.

## 8.1. The Obligation to Educate

That Judaizing parents took very seriously their religious obligation to instruct their children in the basic beliefs and practices of their ancestral religion can be inferred from the mere fact that among some families crypto-Judaism persisted for well over two hundred years. Traditional Judaism explicitly requires the transmittal of Jewish knowledge to the children of the next generation, who are seen as the religion's insurance against extinction. The fundamental commandment of Deuteronomy 11:19—"You shall teach [these words] to your children, talking of them when you are sitting in your house, and when you are walking by the way, and when you lie down, and when you rise"—is even today recited aloud as an essential component of most religious services in the synagogue.

This prayer must have formed part of the oral tradition of many crypto-Jewish families, for it appears sporadically in Inquisition testimony until quite late. For example, several Portuguese Judaizers were accused by the Coimbra Inquisition in 1583 of reciting it.[1] In the 1650s in Mexico Doña Blanca Enríquez taught the fundamentals of crypto-Judaism to "her sons, daughters, grandsons, granddaughters, and all the rest of her kin. She asserted that it was the obligation of the Jews to teach the law to their children and to the children of their children" (Liebman 1974, 192–3). Another version of this commandment was found in an eighteenth-century handwritten manual of crypto-Jewish prayers in Portugal.[2]

Several Mexican Judaizers of the mid-seventeenth century felt deeply that this obligation to educate their children, and for that matter to engender children, was essential for the perpetuation of Judaism. Around 1648 this issue was central to the education of Ana Núñez, who at age thirteen told her Mexican Inquisitors that her father had told her "that when she got married she must teach her children what he was telling her (about Judaizing), and that if they did not want to believe it, she should whip them."[3] A friend of María de Zárate's, it was reported in Mexico in 1656, told her that "she wanted to have a son to whom to teach the Law."[4] In 1665 another reported that "it was a bad thing not to teach the Law to one's children so they would know what they were to observe, because they would be lost."[5] This logic made it particularly important for young Judaizers to choose spouses who would help them educate their children in the ways of crypto-Judaism, for if they did not, their children would be lost.[6] In families divided in their religious persuasion a battle could erupt over the education of the children. One parent might attempt to force the children's Judaizing over the wishes of the other, or the parents of one of the fiancés might require Judaizing while a prospective spouse might be violently opposed.

## 8.2. EDUCATION OF SPOUSES

Frequently a separate set of dangerous choices presented itself at the time of marriage. Was the prospective spouse of the same ethnic background? If so, was he or she of the same religious persuasion? As we will see in Chapter 9, the answers to these questions had to be delicately ascertained. And if the answer was no, then, in the unlikely event that the marriage took place anyway, some sort of accommodation had to be reached with the new spouse. In marriages between a Judaizer and a non-Judaizer, be they new- or old-Christian, the Judaizing member sometimes accepted responsibility for educating the other spouse in the practices of Judaism. Most of this education seems to have taken place at home, behind closed doors, free from the prying eyes of neighbors. The American *conversa* Catalina Enríquez in 1644 underscored this compulsion for privacy when she informed Inquisitors that her husband taught her Jewish prayers when they were in bed (Liebman 1975, 113).

The records suggest that in mixed marriages the Judaizing husbands were likely to attempt to instruct their wives, not vice versa. Sometimes the non-Judaizing spouses resented this instruction or, in an attempt to save themselves, told the Inquisitors that they resented it. María González [Ciudad Real 1483], for example, testified that she only heard Jewish prayers "during the period when . . . my husband made me hear them."[7] If one thing stands out in cases like these, it is that the education of the non-Judaizing spouse was problematical, requiring time, patience, and circumspection.

This education frequently required the help of other Judaizing family members as well. Sometimes these were Judaizing members of the wife's family, who wanted to help their sister or daughter make a smooth transition into the obligations of a Judaizing marriage. Leonor Alvarez [Ciudad Real 1512] said that when "she was recently married and came to Ciudad Real to live, her married sister came from Membrilla to live in her house, and that is when she instructed her in the things contained in the Law of Moses."[8] Sometimes these were members of the wife's family who wanted to make certain the bridegroom would accommodate the bride's Jewish practices. When Simón Juárez de Espinosa wanted to marry Catalina, the widow of Diego Tinoco, in Mexico sometime in the 1630s, Catalina's brother Manuel de Acosta required that his prospective brother-in-law learn to Judaize, and he threatened to stab him to death if he ever revealed any of the family's secrets (Lewin 1977, 6). In 1642 in Mexico it was reported that Juan Méndez underwent a similar experience.[9] Pedro Onofre Cortés described in Majorca in 1686 his family's multiple attempts to impart crypto-Judaism to his wife Juana Miró. He told how he had instructed his wife in Judaism a few days after their marriage, telling her that "whoever worshipped [the Jewish God] would be given rewards and great prizes here on earth and glory in heaven, and that they would not feel the trials and miseries of the world. . . . But Juana Miró never practiced, nor would she do what he wanted." Later, after their first child was born, Juana's mother, Gerónima Pomar, came to visit, and he enlisted her help in persuading Juana to Judaize. "When [Juana] saw what her mother said she believed it and obeyed him in everything, complaining to her mother because she had delayed so long in revealing all this to her. Her mother responded, saying: 'Don't you know that your father and all your brothers are Catholic? That's why I kept it from you too. And now give thanks to the God of Israel, for he has given you a good husband who has brought you to the light of grace for the salvation of your soul.' "[10]

Education of the non-Judaizing spouse was one strategy we can observe in families divided along religious lines. Another was stealth. The Judaizing spouses—generally the wives—might attempt to leave their husbands alone but try to educate their children clandestinely. Astoundingly, in many divided families the mania for secrecy was so great that for years the Judaizing spouses apparently succeeded in hiding their true beliefs or practices from their mates.[11] This was the case of Beatriz Núñez, tried in 1485, who had moved to Guadalupe with her second husband from Ciudad Real, leaving behind the sustaining community of her Judaizing relatives. Her loneliness and her fear of revealing herself even to her husband stand out in her testimony:

> I came to Guadalupe when I married my husband; and since I was a stranger, and did not know anyone there, I did not know to whom to reveal myself. And when I considered the trouble my husband could get into, and the loss of his property, and fearing that I might suffer trouble and losses, I did not dare to do the things that I had done in Ciudad Real and that I wanted to do in my heart, for fear that my serving girls or my husband or someone else might find me out. And keeping it all as secret as I could, I sometimes fasted from morning until night, and I kept the one they call the Great Fast when I could find out when it was, and I did this ceremonially according to the Law of Moses. I declare that I did not eat pork until recently, because my husband scolded me about it; and I told him that I didn't eat it because it caused me great harm in my chest; nor did I eat fish without scales if I could avoid it.[12]

There in Guadalupe one of her sons from her first marriage, Gonçalo de Madrid, one day approached her in confidence, saying that his friends had told him "he had erred from his path, and could not be saved except in the Law of Moses, and what should he do." Beatriz says that she told him, "Son, keep a secret for me and do not reveal it to anyone in this world, because if you do you will put me and you too in great danger. I tell you that I am of the same opinion as you are, for that is what I was taught in Ciudad Real."[13] In a similar case Gaspar Váez Sevilla [Mexico 1642] confessed that he had been educated in Judaism by his grandmother, who had taught him how to fast and observe the Law. "She ordered him never under any circumstances to reveal himself to his father or mother or any other male or female relative."[14] In fact, as late as 1726 we find this reticence to reveal oneself even to one's closest relatives in the case of the Brazilian poet Jozé da Silva. Once when he was at home with his brother Baltazar Rodriguez, the brother told him that he was living according to the Law of Moses. Jozé responded that he was too, "and in this way they revealed themselves to each other as believers and observers for the salvation of their souls."[15]

Frequently one finds testimony that some member of a family was unaware of another's crypto-Jewish practices. Without the benefit of cross examination, today it is hard to know whether they were truly kept in ignorance or only claimed ignorance as a way of protecting themselves. The latter seems likely when Mexican Inquisitors in 1589 asked Luis de Carvajal how it was possible that Doña Guiomar de Carvajal could have kept the Sabbath from sunup to sundown, dressed in her party clothes, without anyone in the house including her husband knowing what was going on. Luis replied that the fact that she was in mourning disguised it (Toro 1932, 217). Equally improbable is the testimony of García de Ocaña, around 1500 and a second time around 1510, that he knew nothing at all about his wife's recurrent Judaizing. Blázquez Miguel argues persuasively that this is not so much a case of García's ignorance as of an indifference to religious practice that allowed him to live at peace with his Judaizing wife (Blázquez Miguel 1989, 182–3).

This sort of accommodation obviously sprang from the very real concern that in matters of children's education openly recognized religious differences could tear a family apart. In a case in Teruel in 1485 the mothers of Brianda Santángel and several other young girls were accused of having indoctrinated their daughters in the ways of Judaism against the wishes of their old-Christian husbands.[16] In 1572 the sisters Leonor, Bernardina, Elvira, María, Isabel, Juana, Luisa, and Micaela de San Juan testified that their mother had instructed each of them in the Jewish tradition about the time they reached puberty. Their father, an old-Christian, for a time joined them in Judaizing and at other times was opposed, and several of the sisters vacillated between the two laws.[17] Even when the source of the conflict was external to the family it impinged upon the family's ability to survive. The young crypto-Jew Francisco Alvarez said around 1600 in Galicia that "he was very concerned because in the Society of Jesus, where he was studying, they said that the law of the Jews was evil and heretical."[18] It was this concern that led him to inform the Inquisition about his parents' activities.

## 8.3. CHILDREN'S EDUCATION

Every secretly Judaizing family from the first conversions up until modern times has been faced with the same recurring vital dilemma: whether to tell the children? And if so, when? And how? As we will see, the documentary record provides a wide variety of solutions to this problem and more than one case of what ultimately turned out to be a disastrous choice for the family.

### 8.3.1. AGE AT INITIATION

Once the family had rejected assimilation in favor of ongoing Jewish identification, the problem of transmittal became crucial. At some appropriate moment the children of Judaizing *conversos* had to be initiated into the religious practices of their parents. If the subject were broached too soon, before the child was old enough to be discreet, the family's covert Judaizing could be revealed to the neighborhood. If the subject were left until the child's Christian education had taken firm hold, then the child might well denounce the family. That *conversos* were acutely aware of these dangers can be seen in the relative frequency of remarks such as those of Juan de León, who told Mexican Inquisitors in 1642 that he had not yet instructed his son Gaspar Váez because the boy was still too young.[19] Every Judaizing family had to choose the moment right for the circumstances. Historians have tended to converge on the view that most Judaizers did not reveal "the family faith to their children until they evidenced mental maturity and could be trusted to keep the secret."[20] Roth suggests that thirteen or fourteen years old was the age at which crypto-Jewish children were introduced to Judaizing, but cites examples as early as age eleven.[21] Melammed found that most *conversa* girls in Toledo in the early 1500s were indoctrinated between the ages of nine and thirteen (1985, 96). In Majorca in the 1670s *converso* children were instructed in their faith at age twelve or thirteen if they were boys or when they first menstruated if they were girls (Cortes 1985, 290). My sense is that, although the onset of puberty was frequently chosen as the moment to begin instruction in crypto-Judaism, the range of ages for initiation was far broader than that, with a substantial number of crypto-Jewish children being initiated between the ages of five and ten[22] and others not until near adulthood.[23] There is no discernible difference among practices in Spain, Portugal, and the colonies insofar as the age of beginning religious instruction. The pattern carries over into the alleged remnant crypto-Jewish communities of the twentieth century. Clemente Carmona told David Nidel [New Mexico 1980] that he had been taught about his Jewish ancestry by his parents when he was in his teens (Nidel 1984, 252). In 1989 Anne Cardoza reported that her grandmother, Pauline, who emigrated from Gerona to Buenos Aires to the United States, advised her children to "share the family secret with adult children over age 13" (Cardoza 1989, S2).

The fact that many *converso* children received their first Jewish religious instruction about the time they reached puberty may suggest that their initiation was a variation of normative Judaism's traditional Bar Mitzvah, in which at age thirteen a boy is called to read the Torah for the first time in the synagogue. The parallel is false for several reasons. One is that by August of 1492 Torah reading, together with most other aspects of traditional synagogue worship, had disappeared in Spain. Another is that the subjects covered in a crypto-Jewish initiation varied considerably from the text-centered education of traditional Judaism. A third is that the appropriate moment for children's education was governed less by any religious calendar than it was by the necessity to deal with the natural curiosity of growing children or early adolescents about their family's religious practices.

8.3.2. EDUCATIONAL METHODS

As Levine (1982, 239; 1985, 94–6) has pointed out, *converso* teachers taught Jewish practices by three methods. They taught by example, fulfilling the commandments of ritual practice and providing a role model for children and other adults to follow. They taught by explanation, persuading, preaching, proselytizing, describing Jewish practices and explaining the reasons for the various observances. And, particularly in the case of children and sometimes of spouses, they indoctrinated by command.

Evidence in many cases suggests that the process of revealing the family's Jewishness to the children was a gradual one. No matter at what age youngsters began to question their elders about their practices, some basic explanations had to be given. As the young children grew more responsible they could be introduced to more Judaizing practices and given to understand their significance. A clear statement of this process was given to Inquisitors in Granada by Doña Leonor de Montalván in 1593. Her mother died when she was five. When she was about seven, her aunt, Beatriz Hernández, began to teach her how to fast, what foods to abstain from eating, and a few basic beliefs. When she was a little older and learning the skills basic to setting up her own household they taught her how to prepare meat in the kosher fashion. Later when she began to menstruate they instructed her in the ceremonies of ritual ablution.[24] Her sister Bernardina, who confessed to Judaizing from age nine up until her marriage at age fourteen, confirmed this educational process, saying that "they instructed her on different days, and not all at once."[25] Doña Costanza Bázquez, also given penance in the Granada *auto de fe* of 1593, said that when she was about thirteen she happened to notice that her mother and her aunts were gathering together. When she asked why, her mother began her crypto-Jewish education. First she was instructed in fasting. Some six to eight months later they began to teach her the dietary prohibitions. And then in a third phase they taught her to keep the Sabbath. A clear pattern emerges from the 1593 Granada documents. In very early adolescence the girl children became aware of their mothers' fasting or their avoidance of pork. This awareness led to questioning, which in turn led to instruction: generally first in fasting, then in dietary laws and in reciting one or two prayers, and later in other Judaizing customs (Bel Bravo 1988, 134–5).

Sometimes a chance encounter or the intervention of an outsider initiated the process of religious education. Juan de la Sierra confessed [Ciudad Real 1483] that "when I was young one day I came to this city and I asked for food in my father's house. And while I was eating Alvar López de Arroyo, who at the time lived here in Almagro, came in and found me eating and asked me why I was eating because that day was a fast day and I was committing a great sin in breaking it. And he stayed awhile and began to tell me things contrary to our Holy Catholic Faith. And what with my youth he caused me to doubt. And a few days later, coming back from Almagro together with him, on the road he told me a good deal about the Law of Moses, and he even told me that if I wanted a book to instruct myself he would give it to me. But I did not want it and he did not give it to me, although he frequently told me what to do—today is such and such festival—and I kept the very least of them."[26] An anonymous witness before the Galician Inquisition described how his aunt Violante Alvarez introduced him to Judaizing on Yom Kippur in 1599 when he was fifteen. "When it was evening she called him and took him out to a field that was next to the house and said: 'Take care to fast today so that our Lord will give you life.' And as the two of them stood there, facing east, she unwrapped his head covering and taught him prayers, one of which she called the prayer of the Star, and another of the Fast, and the witness repeated the same words and when it was done he said: 'Aunt, whom are we praying to?' And she said to him: 'Look, we worship a single God, the God of Israel, your people.' "[27] This marked the beginning of his initiation into the family's religion. Luis Núñez Pérez

[Mexico 1642] testified that he had first learned about Judaism as a child from a friend in school.[28] One fact that stands out in all these examples is the importance of a bond of intimacy and trust between the instructor and the novice Judaizer. Most commonly these bonds were between children and their parents or other older relatives.[29] But they could appear just as easily between close childhood friends. Alonso Marcos [Ciudad Real 1484] said that "he and Juan de la Sierra were good friends and ate and lived together and slept in one bed. And Juan de la Sierra asked Alonso Marcos why he did not pray, and Alonso asked him what he should pray, and he answered that he should recite the prayers that Juan recited. Alonso Marcos told him that he did not know any prayers beyond the Pater Noster, the Ave Maria, and the Creed, which the Christians pray, and Juan de la Sierra told him that he would teach him prayers by which he could be saved. He showed him certain prayers, which he wrote on five or six sheets of paper, one of which began thus: 'This is recited face to the wall and it begins: *Shema Israel, Adonai Elohenu, etc.*,' and he knows it all and he prayed it from the notebook."[30]

When the children did not broach the religious subject naturally with their questioning, parents had to devise other strategies to begin their education. For the initial contact the teacher generally tried to speak to the child in some isolated setting, for it was difficult to predict what the child's first reaction would be. One favorite technique was to get the child by him- or herself in a room at home. Gabriel de Granada [Mexico 1645] confessed that when he was "thirteen years old, Doña María de Rivera, his mother, called him and when alone with him in the house . . . she told him how the law of our Lord Jesus Christ which he followed was not good, nor true, as was that of Moses." Then, once the issue had been brought into the open, his aunt Margarita de Rivera was able to take a role in instructing him (Adler 1899, 12, 56). Francisco Alvarez [Galicia c. 1600] said that "when he was ten years old his mother told him one day when they were alone that he should fast until the stars came out at night and she said it in a moment of tenderness; and thus he did it and believed that would benefit his soul."[31]

Another technique was to isolate the child away from home.[32] In a 1647 trial Luis de Valencia reported how his father had revealed their Judaism to him while they were traveling in Mexico (Osorio Osorio 1980, 186).[33] Rafael de Sobremonte said that on a trip to Guadalajara from Mexico City in the 1640s his father Tomás "made him keep the Jewish fasts, punishing him with great anger if he broke them. On fast days he took him to the river to bathe. He taught him Jewish prayers." When they got back to the capital his mother, grandmother, and aunt, seeing that he was now a Judaizer, embraced him with great joy.[34] Fifteen-year-old Simón de Valencia [Mexico 1647] reported that when he was about eight or nine "his mother and father found him alone one day in the storehouse and both told him that he must believe in the Law of Moses that they observed, in which he would be saved, that the Law of Christ that he followed was no good, and that the good law was the one they followed."[35]

One element that stands out in almost all these narrations is the recognition that the risk to the family was very real. Thus instruction most always included the injunction never to reveal the family's secrets. Rafael de Sobremonte's father warned his son that he was "entrusting him with the family secret, and advised him of the risks they were all running."[36] The father of Simón de Valencia also cautioned his son that "he must do what they told him, and that he must take care to tell no one, because the people of the street must not find out."[37] The Mexican Gaspar Váez said he had been instructed by his grandmother, who told him never to reveal himself to his parents nor any other relatives (Lewin 1977, 65–7). Joseph Cortés warned his daughter Ana [Majorca 1670s] that she "should never reveal the Law to their children until she knew whom they were going to marry."[38]

Teachers of children used a variety of methods to ensure that children accepted the Judaizing customs. Sometimes they rewarded the child materially, as did Simón de León's father, who gave his son new stockings and shoes when he agreed to Judaize in Mexico in the 1640s (Nunemaker 1946, 21–2). Or, conversely, they punished the children who showed signs of resistance or who insisted on adhering to Christian practices. Evidence given to the Mexican Inquisition in the 1640s tells a good deal about the coercive educational practices of the Duarte family. Simón de León reported that his father Duarte had gagged and beat him and dressed him in rough clothing until he finally agreed to Judaize.[39] According to one of his daughters, Duarte routinely beat and mistreated his six children to force them to pray and fast and observe the festivals according to Jewish fashion. He forbade them to associate with Christian children and scolded them when they picked up religious tag-phrases from their Catholic playmates.[40]

Still, to judge from Inquisition testimony, the majority of educational programs combined practical instruction in the observances of crypto-Judaism with indoctrination about its theology and its differences from Catholicism. A good example is Marzal Saravia's description of how his father initiated him:

> In the year 1600, when he was studying in a room in his father's house, his father came in and said to him: "My son, do you know God?" He answered that he did, and his father went on: "You probably do not know him, because there is a different kind of knowing from that they have taught you up until now. Because you have to believe in one single true God whom you must serve." And he answered: "Yes, father, that is what I believe. There is one single God in three persons who are the Father, Son and Holy Spirit." And his father said to him: "You must not believe that, it is not proven nor certain that God has three distinct persons, and so that you will believe me, I will show you a place in the Decree that recognizes the diversity of opinions." And he showed him a passage of canon law in which various opinions about the Holy Trinity were expressed, and he remained in doubt because that doctrine was new to him. And his father said to him: "Look at this and consider it slowly and you will know that what I tell you is true." With this, and with what two other people in his household told him, he was moved to believe and since then has be-

lieved that there is only one God without any difference of persons, and he ceased believing in the Holy Trinity. And then he asked his father what he was to do. And he told him that he had to perform many ceremonies and rites but that he could not do them in this kingdom on account of the danger of being discovered. And he told him that for now it was enough to fix his heart on one single God and be aided in this by the Great Fast which falls on the tenth day of the new moon of September, and he did this along with his father and many other persons.[41]

About the same period Diego Núñez de Silva, a doctor from the region of Córdoba, Argentina, testified that he had taught his son Diego de Silva the Law of Moses and had told him stories to induce him to give up believing in the Law of Christ. One day when his father found him crying from a toothache "he told him to be a Jew (as he himself was), and not to worship the way he had been; but rather he should commend himself to God in heaven as a Jew, because everything they said about Christ was made up; and that he should keep the Sabbath if he could; and that he should keep his mouth shut and not say anything to his mother or his sisters, nor anyone else, so that he might not be found out."[42]

Frequently the Inquisition files contain specific details about what the teachers considered to be the central tenets of crypto-Judaism. The Mexican Ana Núñez said in the 1640s that her parents had taught her several Jewish prayers and that the Jewish beliefs her father taught her included that Moses was the only God, that God had not died, that the Messiah who was to die for them had not yet come and would be born of a Mexican Jewess (García 1910, 199). María Gómez, burned in the 1649 Mexican *auto de fe*, "tried to make her children perfect in that which their father and grandmother taught them and she did not care that they did not learn Catholic prayers. She taught them only Judaic prayers. She did not permit them to eat bacon or anything cooked in lard." Her husband, Tomás Treviño de Sobremonte, "taught them the law of Moses: how to fast, wash, don clean clothing at the appropriate times, and the occasions with which [they] should be familiar" (Liebman 1974, 135, 138). According to the summary of the 1648 *auto de fe* Tomás effectively catechized his children. His son Rafael reported that when he was about twelve his "father used to ask him who was God? And what was the Holy Trinity? And when he answered as the Catholic catechism had taught, [Tomás] said to him: 'What a horse you are! You must answer that there is only one God, infinite, wise and good.' "[43] Sometimes, capitalizing on the Christian rhetoric of salvation with which the child would already be familiar, they held out the promise of the soul's salvation in Judaism not in Christianity.[44] This, for example, was Francisco Alvarez's argument to his son [Galicia c. 1600] (Contreras 1982, 608). Occasionally the reasons for Judaizing seem tinged with material interests. Some Judaizers seemed to believe that adherence to Jewish custom would cause God to help them prosper. The Mexican Simón de Valencia, who has been mentioned several times already, said that "many nights in the presence of his mother his father called him and his siblings, Clara, Francisco, and Antonia, and sat them all down together on the bed and told them that their Law was good, and that God gave them money because of the Law, and that the Christian Law was not good, and that they had to fast all day without eating or drinking anything until nightfall, when they must eat fish."[45]

### 8.3.3. THE EDUCATIONAL NETWORK

Both men and women seemed to have played roles in the Jewish education of their family and friends but, according to Inquisition documents, at least, the role of women teachers stands out. Education was more frequently entrusted to family members than to outsiders. *Converso* children were generally instructed in the practices of Judaizing by one or both of their parents, most frequently by their mothers. This was almost invariably true in the case of girl children and predominated with male children as well. Sometimes a grandparent or an aunt would be the agent of religious instruction. Probably the most common pattern was for children to be educated over time by a variety of Judaizing adults in their immediate and extended families.

Occasionally, however, a friend, or the community "rabbi" or "wise woman," who was often termed a "dogmatizer" by the Inquisition, would instruct the children. Sometimes the influence of a particular proselytizer was widely felt. According to Juan de León, María Blanca acted as teacher for the Mexican *converso* community [1645]. "She was observant in the Law, and kept it as it should be kept, and could read it and teach the others. She had taught it to her children, who did it very well. . . . She was very clever and knowledgeable and well-read, and very articulate. Isabel did it as well as she, and so did Margarita, who is no fool either; the rest did not do so well. Margarita has a particular talent to teach and persuade the people she wants to. She was just about to try to persuade and teach the husband of her sister Clara, but he is a dummy and a lout."[46] In the 1720s in Cuenca it was reported that several *converso* children, whose ages ranged from 13 to 18, had been taught the basics of crypto-Judaism by distinguished senior members of the community (Lera García 1987, 111).[47]

One last point remains with regard to the education of crypto-Jewish children. *Converso* adolescents, like emerging adults in any culture, sometimes broke with family traditions as a part of their personal psychological emancipation. Martín Alonso de Menbreque told Inquisitors [Córdoba 1511] that his parents had begun his Jewish instruction when he was seven or eight and that he Judaized only as long as he lived with them, which was for seven or eight more years.[48] The Granada teenagers cited earlier in this chapter, Bernardina de Montalván and Costanza Bázquez, testified in the 1590s that they kept the Jewish customs only until their marriages at age eighteen (Bel Bravo 1988, 135).

Particularly in divided families, where one spouse Judaized and the other was an old-Christian or an assimilationist *converso*, a teenager might be pulled in multiple directions. A particularly poignant and not atypical case is that of the San Juan sisters, of Baeza. María de San Juan, after first having been educated as a Christian, learned Judaism from her mother at age thirteen. She was twenty-nine when she testified in 1573. María said that one Holy Thursday she found herself attracted by the seductive emotionalism of the Christian religious processions:

> When she saw the statue of Christ and of the Mother of God, to whom she had previously been deeply devoted, and seeing all the people crying and worshipping the Christ, she was seized with great envy and heartache, the way she used to feel but no longer did. She went home and finding her father Doctor San Juan alone she asked him what a person must do to be saved, and he replied that she must be a good Christian.[49]

Evidently María's father's curiosity was piqued, for he inquired why she was asking. When she gave the teenager's typical evasion—"No reason, just because . . ."—he told her not to embroil herself in deep things. Later, when she meditated on the fact that her father was educated and that he and everybody else knew more than her mother did all by herself, she decided to become a good Christian once again.[50]

A similar tale was told to the Inquisition in 1574 by María's sister Isabel de San Juan. She had been raised Catholic until she was fourteen or fifteen, when her mother, without her father's knowledge, introduced her to Jewish practice as she had previously done for all of Isabel's sisters. Because they had to be circumspect even within the family, the Judaism of the San Juan women was reduced to the observance of the major fasts and the recitation of certain "Jewish" spells when one of the family got sick. When Isabel's sister Bernardina was arrested by the Inquisition in 1572 the family panicked and Isabel's steadfastness to Judaism began to crumble. Her mother urged Isabel to keep silent if she should be arrested too, but in her confused state Isabel could not. She told Inquisitors that when her sister was taken by the Inquisition she began to waver in her faith, saying that

> she was still in the Law of Moses, which she had sucked in her mother's milk, when she became inspired to return to the faith of Our Lord Jesus Christ; she thought that she might lose her soul and she was greatly confused. And she had reached such a state of suffering that one night she had wanted to kill herself.

In another session she said that

> she was still in doubt and did not want to deceive anyone; that if her heart was not yet firm, she was prepared to die because of it, and that she had earlier testified that she had been converted to our Holy Faith to escape death; and she tried as hard as she could to return to the Holy Catholic Faith and be firm in it, but that the more she thought about this the more she was pulled by the things her mother had taught her, and that those things alone were sufficient to make her return to the Law of Moses, but they drove her to the edge of despair. . . .

Another day she requested an audience and said that

> she was determined to live and die in the Law of Jesus Christ in which her father had died, and that she should be condemned to the Abyss and God should take no mercy on her if she should feel otherwise or if her mind should change to some other thing; and that she knew that she would die because of her vacillation, saying sometimes yes and sometimes no, but that she wanted to die in the faith of Jesus Christ; and that what had moved her to decide this was seeing that her father had been such a good Christian. Also she had performed a great penance of fasting and praying in the Law of Moses in order to marry a cousin of hers, but it had been to no avail.[51]

Pulled three ways—by her mother's attempts to educate her in Judaism, her father's attempts to do the same in Christianity, and her infatuation with her cousin—Isabel de San Juan is a striking example of a confused teenager wracked by a crisis of identity.

## 8.4. Education of Adults

The Decree of Expulsion in part justifies that drastic act by accusing Spain's remaining Jews of making great efforts to induce their converted friends or family members to return to Judaism. This allegation was also one of the principal justifications for the laws that physically separated the two communities in the late fifteenth century. It recognizes the fact that in most Iberian cities prior to the Expulsion the entire population of Jews and *conversos* formed a single extended family, laced together through generations of marriage within their small communities. The fact that in the wake of the 1391 riots large numbers of the community suddenly found themselves Christian, or that over the next one hundred years increasing numbers of Jews chose to or were forced to convert, did not rupture the age-old patterns of communal living. No matter what the beliefs of individual family members, families continued to celebrate important occasions together, at least until the Inquisition made this dangerous. The new-Christians who had Jewish family members living nearby seldom broke contact with them and even occasionally continued living with them (Pimenta Ferro Tavares 1982, 477). Any family event, from a birth and circumcision to a wedding or even a funeral, was cause to come together and celebrate the unity of family ties grounded in religious tradition.[52] Although contemporary documents make clear that before 1492 *conversos* and their Jewish relatives mingled routinely at weddings, circumcisions, and funerals, at family holiday celebrations such as Sukkot and Passover, and even at the village *mikvah,* the mere fact that these events appear in the Inquisition documents indicates how dangerous such social interactions were. Many of the events described in the 1480s trials had occurred years previous, when the pressure to separate and become wholly Catholic was not so great and the consequences of disobeying the separatist laws were minor. The documents suggest a tapering off of such interactions from 1480 up to the 1492 Expulsion, for some, no doubt, due to their increasing assimilation into Catholicism, and for others from fear of the Inquisition.

This very process of assimilation was threatening to the remaining Jewish community and to those *conversos* whose prime self-identification continued to be as Jews. The Expulsion Decree's allegation that many Jews proselytized their *converso* neighbors seems to have been true, for records of the time testify to the missionary efforts of many members of the Jewish community.[53] For example, a 1485 document accuses Don Abraham Benveniste and his wife Oropesa of instructing *conversos*: "In times past both in this city of Córdoba and in other places in our kingdom you have preached to people who were living under the name of Christians, informing them and inducing them to observe certain Jewish ceremonies and rites, and you have attracted them to Judaizing. . . . And you have advised some people who are living under the name of Christians to go to live as Jews in the Moorish lands."[54] Around 1480 Jews Isaac Hadida and Samuel Valenci taught *converso* monks Jewish prayers in the Jeronymite monasteries of Sisla and San Bartolomé de la Lupiana in the province of Toledo (Beinart 1961, 181). Other testimony indicates that in 1488, Saloman Çaporta, a Jew from Sagunto, was fined and exiled for having invited *conversos* to his home for kosher meals, reading the Old Testament to them in Hebrew, and teaching Hebrew to *converso* children" (Haliczer 1990, 218). Testimony in Aragon in 1490 stated that a certain *converso* "was a great Talmudist and taught others to read the Talmud."[55] The examples can be multiplied ad infinitum. At the same time, of course, not all Iberian Jews or well-educated *conversos* engaged in missionary efforts. Some of them accepted the missionary's burden, but perhaps an even greater number ignored or even actively scorned the *conversos*.

After 1492 openly practicing Jews were gone from Spain, but the sense of missionary zeal was perpetuated in a segment of the crypto-Jewish community for many generations after the 1492 Expulsion. Well into the seventeenth century we find examples of crypto-Jews who had proselytized *converso* family and friends to return to active Judaizing. Dr. Periáñez de Mesa, a seventy-year-old lawyer from Ecija, confessed [Córdoba 1591] that "some relatives of his had taught him the law of Moses and that he had observed it together with that of Jesus Christ Our Lord."[56] In the early seventeenth century in Portugal the widow Catherina Henriques was led into crypto-Judaism by other *cristã nova* women of her village (Roth 1931–2, 11). A particularly vivid example of this process is the attempts of the Judaizing members of Mexico's Carvajal clan in the 1590s to proselytize their nonobservant relatives. Luis de Carvajal remembered this conversation with his uncle (also named Luis), the Governor of the Province of Nuevo León. One day when they had been out riding the Governor had sent his escort of soldiers ahead and remained alone with young Luis, saying:

"You know how your father lives in the Law of Moses."

Luis responded in tears: "It is a great evil."

And the Governor said to him: "Look, that is why I love you the best of all your brothers. But you should know that your father tried to deceive me, persuading me to go back to keeping the Law of Moses. If he should try that on you, consider that the evangelical Law that our Lord Jesus Christ gave us is the true Law."[57]

Later Luis reported how his brother, Fray Gaspar de Carvajal, had tried to dissuade him from Judaizing. "Although Fray Gaspar was always talking, giving the reasons why he favored the Evangelical Law, so that they would convert to it, Luis and his brother Baltazar Rodriguez were silent, as if they agreed with him, which was a sham, because they remained in their belief in the Law of Moses."[58] Luis also said that his father had told him that everything he was teaching him about the Law of Moses could be found in the Bible, giving as example the series of holidays described in Leviticus and Numbers (Toro 1982, 242–52).

The late sixteenth-century dispersal of knowledgeable Portuguese Judaizers throughout the Iberian world provided a number of atrophying crypto-Jewish communities with an influx of fresh information and fresh zeal. Catalina de Rojas [Granada 1591] explained how she and her sisters had been instructed in Judaizing around 1560 by a Portuguese maid who served with her family and promised her that if she followed certain practices and did not tell her parents then she would soon be married. She also reported that around 1574 a one-eyed woman named Marina de Mercado informed them which days they were to fast.[59] María Méndez de Ayala [Granada 1595] reported that she had been instructed around 1582 by a Portuguese woman (García Fuentes 1981, 469). The *conversos* Manuel Rodríguez and his wife [Murcia 1610] were surprised studying a set of Jewish laws that a Portuguese student staying in their house had written out for them (Blázquez Miguel 1986b, 140).

Teenage *converso* males were often apprenticed by their parents to masters who would foster their education as Judaizers. In Valencia some new-Christian teenagers in the 1460s and 1470s were apprenticed with Judaizing *conversos* and emulated their masters' religious customs until the day when they were able to establish their own independent shops, after which time they practiced their Catholic faith exclusively. It is difficult to tell whether the adolescents were responding to their masters' conversionist zeal or just prudently trying to fit in (Haliczer 1990, 216–7). Perhaps the most common attitude was one of laissez faire: Jews would provide services like kosher slaughtering or *matzot* to *conversos* when asked, they would accept their charity or their donations of oil for the synagogue when offered (Haliczer 1990, 218), and, if they were kin, they would celebrate together with them important family occasions like births, weddings, and funerals.

By the middle of the sixteenth century it had become extremely dangerous in the Iberian kingdoms or their overseas possessions to be found with books in Hebrew or with any sort of Jewish instructional material. Judaizing *conversos* could avail themselves of four sources of information about Jewish customs and beliefs: oral tradition;[60] the Old Testament, particularly in Latin editions that were fairly easy to obtain;[61] the Edicts of Faith themselves; and travelers returning from abroad with first-hand accounts of normative Jewish practice.

Ironically, it was the very Edicts of Grace, which were lists of Judaic customs published by the Inquisition to aid in the identification of Judaizers, that provided a consistent, detailed source of knowledge about many Jewish customs.[62] Mexican Judaizers talked quite openly about their reliance on the Edicts of Faith. When Juan de León was accused [Mexico 1643] of teaching Judaism to the Blanca de Rivera sisters he replied that "they knew more than he did about when a certain festival occurred, because in the Edicts of Faith that were publicly read you could hear all the rites and ceremonies of the Law of Moses."[63] The *autos de fe,* in which detailed lists of the offenses of convicted heretics were read aloud to the assembled throngs, were a similar source of knowledge. Thirty-year-old Belchior Fernandes was accused [Coimbra 1574] of having said with regard to the Laws of Moses that "if he knew about them it was from having heard them read in the copies of the sentences that the students from the village of Sea wrote down from the *autos de fe* and read to them."[64] In 1665 testimony in Mexico a witness described how she learned how to Judaize: "When they began to hold the *autos de fe* in this city, around the year 1646, more or less, she heard them read out the rites and ceremonies that the Jews practiced, all of which she attempted to emulate."[65]

Returning travelers were a particularly important educational resource. As Spain became a commercial and political world power beginning in the sixteenth century, Spaniards increasingly traveled outside the Iberian Peninsula. After the Expulsion from Spain and the scattering of the Sephardic Jews, networks of Jewish/*converso* families often had members in Turkey, North Africa, and various European countries. In the course of doing business many of the Iberian *converso* members of such families traveled with some frequency to countries where Judaism was practiced openly. The Judaizers among them, who had often been waiting for a chance to come out of the closet, sometimes began to practice openly as Jews, even having themselves circumcised and adopting their ancestral Jewish surnames. Not surprisingly, the émigré community actively proselytized among this group. In 1587 João de Victoria appeared before the Inquisition in Lisbon to confess how he had been instructed in Judaism. "When he was studying Latin in the school of Santo Antão, one of his sisters married one Alvaro Rodrigues, a new-Christian from Antwerp, whom João accompanied to that place. There he asked his brother-in-law and his sister where he should go to hear mass, which caused them to laugh at him. Thereafter they began to induce him to become a Jew."[66]

Others *conversos* returned to Spain with fresh tales of how Jews in other lands practiced their religion. Braunstein reports how in Majorca in the mid-seventeenth century "one Converso described to another certain Jewish practices he had seen observed among the Jews in Leghorn. The description of these ceremonies soon became the common property of all the Conversos" (1936, 96). Some *conversos* returning to Spain from such places as Amsterdam, Istanbul, or Leghorn even braved the risk of bringing back books. On rare occasions Jewish missionaries themselves journeyed to the Iberian kingdoms or their colonies in the hopes of bringing *conversos* there back into Judaism. For example, in the 1640s a so-called "French Jew" named Isaac de Castro visited the *cristão novo* community of Bahia, Brazil, for the purpose of persuading its members to return to Judaism (Novinsky 1972b, 134–5).

One of the most detailed descriptions of the relationship between travel and Jewish education is the tale told Inquisitors by the Portuguese informer Estevan de Ares de Fonseca in Madrid in 1635.[67] Like most such autobiographical confessions, it is often self-serving and—particularly with regard to motives and sincerity of conversion—must be taken with a grain of salt. Nonetheless it is a convincing description of the missionary efforts consistently waged by Jews and Judaizers, in and out of the Iberian Peninsula.

> He said that he was born and raised in the City of Coimbra, and then at the age of fourteen or fifteen he left that city to go to Lisbon, and after having studied Latin in the Jesuit school in Coimbra he later traveled to other cities and towns in Portugal. . . . And that when he reached the age of about seventeen he was imprisoned by the Inquisition in Lisbon, where after three years he was released as reconciled. And from there he went to Seville. [He describes other travels in Spain.] Afterwards he went to Bayonne in France, nine or ten years ago, where he remained about two months. And he had gone to Bayonne as a Catholic, believing what the Holy Mother Catholic Church believes and teaches, as he had always held and believed, in spite of the fact that in order to save his life he had confessed to the Inquisition in Lisbon that he was a Jew, even though the truth was that he did not even know that there were Jews, nor had what being a Jew meant ever come to his attention.
>
> A Jew who lived in Bayonne, a Portuguese who had been reconciled in the same *auto da fe* in Lisbon, who was called Don Nicolás López Villareal, a native of Oporto, in Portugal, who currently resides in Bayonne, began to try to persuade him to be a Jew, to follow the Law of Moses, and to abandon that of Our Lord Jesus Christ. To this he would not lend an ear nor give consent.
>
> Instead he returned to Spain. [He describes more travels.] From Pamplona, having had notice that a relative of his whose name was Doctor Duarte Enríquez was in Bordeaux, he returned to Bayonne and there he met Miguel Fernández de Fonseca, a Portuguese . . . who took him to the city of Bordeaux. And on the road and after they reached the city he tried to persuade him to be a Jew and abandon the law of Our Lord Jesus Christ and to pass over to the Law of Moses which was the true law in which one must be saved and not the other. With this, and also with the persuasive arguments which the now deceased Doctor Duarte Enríquez and [he lists several other names] made that he should follow the Law of Moses, this witness was ready to return again to Spain. . . . Instead they had him set sail first to Amsterdam in Holland where

he also had relatives. . . . and they tried to persuade him to be circumcised before setting sail because if he were to die at sea he could not be saved if he had not been, and it was good practice to carry the mark of the Lord.

[In Amsterdam he was welcomed by several Jews who] received him with great celebration and rejoicing, telling him that it was the Lord's miracle that someone who had been living blindly in the Christian law should by undreamed-of means become a Jew.

And then they began to try to make him a Jew. They wanted to circumcise him, saying that even if it were by force and against his will they were going to circumcise him because he was the son of a mother descended from Israel. And when they saw that this witness did not want to be circumcised nor become a Jew they placed him in the company of a rabbi of theirs called Mortera, a preacher of the said Law of Moses, so that he could persuade him to follow it. And when he had been with him for six months and they finally saw that they could not convince him, they excommunicated him in the synagogues so that no Jew would speak to or with him. And when he had been some days, fifteen or sixteen, without anyone speaking to him nor helping him, finally he consented to be circumcised. And they circumcised him and gave him the name David. . . .

And some three years after they had made him a Jew and circumcised him, he went to Leghorn and Venice and Trapana and Salonica and other parts of Italy and Turkey where he remained more than a year going in and out of the synagogues like a Jew. . . . [He describes more travels.] He resided in Amsterdam until last year, 1633, when he returned to the city of Rouen in France where in the Cathedral he was reconciled publicly and solemnly with the Holy Mother Church. . . .

And later, since he had no means to remain in Rouen, he returned [with a friend] . . . to Antwerp, where they looked for a means to sustain themselves and became delivery men in the market. When they had been there five or six months the Portuguese Jews of Antwerp, especially [he gives a long list of names] tried to persuade them to become Jews again in Amsterdam, offering them great incentives.

# Notes

1. *Ensina las as aos teus filhos, e aos filhos de teus filhos, pera que as diguão ao seu lançar, e ao seu alevantar* (Azevedo Mea 1982, 430; cf. 238).

2. *Repetilas has a teus filhos, e fallarás nellas, onde q.r q. te achares; na tua caza, no teu andar, na carreira, ao levantar, e q.do te deitares: escrevelas-has em humbraes de tua caza, e todas as vezes q. as ouvires repete-as no teu coração. e com toda a tua . . . tem ás em tuas mãos, trá-las sembre em teus olhos: communicas a teus filhos, p.a q. igualm.te fallem nellas onde quer q. estiverem, assim nas suas cazas como na tua, em seus passos, em suas carreiras, ao deitar, ao levantar; escreve-as sim em humbraes de tua caza, p.a q. tambem se multipliquem teus dias, e os filhos de teus filhos sobre a terra* (Paulo 1970, 66–7).

3. *Que cuando fuese casada, enseñase a sus hijos lo que él la decía, y que si no la quisiesen creer, los azotara muy bien* (García 1910,199).

4. *Deseaban tener un hijo a quien enseñar la Ley* (Lewin 1971, 230).

5. *Era mal hecho no enseñarla* [la ley judía] *a los hijos para que supiesen la que habían de seguir, porque se perdían* (Lewin 1971, 494).

6. *Vituperaban a los portugueses que estaban amancebados, no por el pecado que cometían en ello, sino porque lo estaban con cristianas viejas, pudiendo estarlo con judías o casarse con doncellas de su ley, y quedaban los hijos que habían en cristianas viejas, echados a perder y sin quien les enseñase su ley, que es el fin porque se casan los judaizantes unos con otros* (García 1910, 252).

7. *Yo niego aver oydo las dichas oraçiones judaycas tan continuamente como los christianos la Misa, et sy algunas, serian en el dicho tienpo que confese quel dicho mi marido me las faria oyr del* (Beinart 1974, 75; cf. 546; 1977a, 486).

8. *Fue rezien casada y vino a morar a Çibdad Real y moraron juntas . . . Vino la dicha su hermana casada de La Menbrilla a la dicha Çibdad Real y se vino a morar en la casa desta confesante, y que entonçes le amostro las dichas cosas de suso contenidas de la Ley de Moysen* (Beinart 1977a, 329).

9. *Ana Suarez . . . le dixo como el dho Juan Mendez guardaba la ley de Moysen, y que para cassarlo con ella le saco al campo Manuel Albarez de Arellano, y le dixo que para cassarlo con la dicha doña Ana aura de guardar la dha Ley de Moysen. Y que el dho Juan Mendez la empeço a guardar desde entonces porque hasta allí hauia sido fiel y Catholico Christiano* (AGN Vol 402 doc 1, 26b).

10. *A todos los que le adorarían, los daría galardones y premios grandes en la tierra y en la Gloria de los Çielos y que no sentirían los trabaxos y miserias . . . Pero . . . Juana Miró nunca hizo, ni menos quiso hazer lo que él dezía . . . Con que viendo ella lo que la dicha su Madre le dezía, la creyó y obedeçió en todo, quexándose de su Madre porque mucho tiempo antes no la havía avisado y dicho todo esto. Y a las horas respondió su Madre diziendola, ¿No sabes tú que tu Padre y todos tus hermanos son cathólicos? Y assí yo también me guardaba de ti. Y aora haz de hazer muchas graçias al Dios de Israel pues te ha dado tan buen marido que te ha sacado al lumbre de la graçia para salvaçión de tu alma* (Selke de Sánchez 1972, 259–60).

11. I have addressed this issue in 1993a. Testimony before the Mexican Inquisition in 1656 indicates that the revelation of the secret Judaizing of one spouse was considered legitimate grounds for divorce. In the charges against María de Zárate it was noted that "for old-Christians, cohabitation with Jews was an understandable cause of great horror, and that when they became aware of it it was grounds for divorce; and that several spouses who had unfortunately contracted marriage with an observer of the Law of Moses had tried this and been granted divorce" (*Y que siendo ocasión justa de gravísimo horror para los cristianos viejos la cohabitación con judíos y notados de este delito que da causa al divorcio, y lo han intentado y conseguido algunos de los cónyuges a quienes por desgracia les ha sucedido contraer matrimonio con persona observante de dicha Ley de Moisés*) (Lewin 1971, 231). See also Melammed 1985, 101; Rábade Obradó 1990a, 432 [Toledo 1485–1500].

12. *Yo vine aquí a Guadalupe casada con mi marido; e como yo era estrangera e non conoscía a ninguno desta tierra, non sabía a quien me descobrir; e mirando los trabajos de mi marido e pérdida de su fasienda e temiendo non me viniesen más trabajos y pérdidas, non osava faser las cosas asy como en villa Real segund las tenía en el coraçon e las deseava faser, por miedo que mis moças ni mi marido ni otra persona alguna non me lo entendiesen; y escondiéndome lo más secreto que pude, ayuné çiertas veces desde la mañana fasta la noche el día que disen el ayuno mayor quando lo podía saber, y esto por çerimonia de la ley de moysén. Digo que non comía toçino salvo de poco acá, porque me reñía sobre ello mi marido; y desíale que lo fasía porque me fasía mucho mal a los pechos, nin otrosy pescados syn escama quando lo podía escusar* (Fita y Colomé 1883, 291).

13. *Le avian dicho que estava errado e que non se podía salvar salvo por la ley de moysén, e que le dixese qué era lo que tenía. E yo le dixe: fijo, tenme secreto e non te descubras a persona ninguna deste mundo, porque pornás a ti e a mí en grande peligro; que yo te digo que esta mesma opinión tengo yo, que asy me lo consejaron en Villa Real* (Fita y Colomé 1883, 292).
14. *La dicha su abuela lo empezó a reducir a la observancia de la dicha Ley y le mandó que, en ninguna manera, lo revelase a su padre ni a su madre ni a ninguna otra parienta ni pariente* (Lewin 1977, 67).
15. *Seu irmão Baltazar dice a elle confitente, que vivia na lei de Moizes, e elle confitente lhe respondeo, que tambem vivia na dita lei e por este modo se comunicaram por crentes e observantes da mesma para salvação de suas almas* (Silva 1896, 13). For years the South American *converso* Francisco Maldonado de Silva successfully concealed the Judaizing he had learned from his father from everyone in his family, including his wife. But in 1626 in Chile he revealed his secret adherence to Judaism to his sister Isabel when they were alone together at a spa near the city of Santiago. She wrestled with the knowledge for eight months and then denounced him to the Inquisition (García de Proodian 1966, 341, 348).
16. *Las sobredichas Brianda, Alba, Leonor, Violante e Gracia, cada una dellas, cuando las dichas cosas cometieron, eran menores en edad de cada veinte años e fueron inducidas por sus madres, so cuyo poder e mando estaban* (Sánchez Moya 1958, 158).
17. Gracia Boix 1983, 131–42. For a similar case in Mexico see Lewin 1977, 54, 63, etc. [Mexico 1642].
18. *Tenía muchos escrúpulos porque en la Compañía de Jesús, donde estudiaba, se decía que la Ley de Judíos era mala y herética* (Contreras 1982, 607–8). For a similar case of vacillation see Rábade Obradó 1990, 350–2.
19. *Como por ser todavía muchacho Gaspar Váez, su hijo, no le enseñaban la dicha Ley* (Lewin 1977, 16).
20. Liebman 1970, 162. Additional seventeenth-century Mexican data is found in Lewin 1977, 400.
21. (1931–2, 10–11). See also Caro Baroja 1961, 3:127 [Spain 1720s].
22. Age 6: Portugal in mid-seventeenth century (Yerushalmi 1971, 64). Age 7: Córdoba in 1511 (Gracia Boix 1982, 120); Granada in 1593 (Bel Bravo 1988, 128–9). Age 9: Granada in 1593 (García Fuentes 1981, 462; Bel Bravo 1988, 121); Mexico in 1647 (Nunemaker 1946, 21). Age 10: Galicia in 1600 (Contreras 1982, 607–8); Mexico in 1649 (Liebman 1974, 149).
23. Age 18: Cuenca in 1720s (Lera García 1987, 111). Age 19–20: Majorca in 1680s (Selke de Sánchez 1972, 258). Age 28: Mexico in 1642 (Lewin 1977, 109).
24. *Le começaron a dezir que ayunase y que no hauia de ser como hasta alli hauia ayunado sino no comiendo en todo el dia hasta la noche, y que aunq. era niña que lo probase que era muy bueno, y que no comiese toçino porq. era suçio ni cosa ahogada ni conejo ni liebre, y que creyesse en vn solo dios, y no en ymagines y que esto es lo bueno, y despues de algunos dias que era mayor le dixeron q. pues era ya para gobernar casa tubiese quenta con ella y a la carne que le truxesen para comer le quitase el seuo de la rriñonada, que era malo, y los moriscos lo comian, y passando algunos dias porq. yvan a temporadas a su casa le dixeron, que quando le baxasse su rregla se labase todo el cuerpo por limpieza* (Bel Bravo 1988, 128).
25. *Lo qual le dixo en differentes dias, y no en vna vez todo* (Bel Bravo 1988, 129).
26. *Seyendo de poca hedad vine vn dia de camino a esta çibdad y demande de comer en casa de mi padre; y estando comiendo, entro vn Alvar Lopez del Arroyo, que a la sazon era vezino desta çibdad [Almagro] y fallome comiendo, y dixome que por que comia, que aquel dia era dia de ayuno,*

*que pecava mucho en lo quebrantar, y el espero ende y enpeçome a desir tantas e tales cosas en contrario de nuestra Santa Fe Catolica a que con moçedad y niñez me fizo dubdar en algo, e dende a algunos dias, viniendo de Almagro, a que ovimos de benir juntos, y en el camino el alego tanto de la Ley de Moysen, y avn dixome que si queria vn libro por onde yo me enseñase, quel me lo daria, el qual yo no quiso ni menos el me dio, salvo que muchas vezes me dezia lo que avia de fazer—agora es tal fiesta—y las menos guardava* (Beinart 1981b, 547).

27. *Siendo ya la noche lo llamó la rea* [Violante Alvarez] *y lo sacó a un ejido junto a la casa y le dixo: -Mira que ayunes este día para que Nro. Señor te dé vida; y estando en pie ambos hacia donde sale el sol, la rea le fue destocando y le fue diciendo oraciones que la una decía ser de la Estrella y otra del Ayuno y el testigo iba diciendo las mismas palabras y acabado éste le dixo: -Tía, por quién rezamos? y la dicha rea le dixo: -Mira que adoramos a un solo Dios, el de Israel, tu pueblo* (Contreras 1982, 607).

28. *Declaró que siendo muchacho le había enseñado la dicha Ley y catequizado* [!] *en ella otro su compañero con quien anduvo a la escuela* (Lewin 1977, 53).

29. This pattern is evident in the transmission of crypto-Judaism even up to our times. For example, ninety-year-old Deolinda Mota of Rebordelo, Portugal, told Manuel da Costa Fontes in 1980 that she had learned crypto-Judaism, which she called the new law (*lei nova*) from an old aunt with whom her parents had left her. Later she learned Catholicism from her parents (Fontes 1993, 77).

30. *El dicho Juan de la Sierra y este Alonso Marcos eran mucho amigos e comian e bivian en vno e dormian en vna cama. Y el dicho Juan de la Sierra dezia a este Alonso Marcos que por que no rezava, y este Alonso Marcos le preguntava que que avia de rezar, y el le dezia que rezase oraçion como el las rezava; este Alonso Marcos le dezia que no sabia otras oraçiones sino el Pater Noster e Ave Maria e Credo, como lo rezan los christanos, e el dicho Juan de la Sierra le dixo que el le demostraria oraçiones con que se salvase. . . . Le demostro çiertas oraçiones, las quales le escrivio en çinco o seys pliegos de papel, las quales o alguna dellas sabe que se dize en esta manera: Vna que se dize buelta la cara a la pared, comiença: Sema Ysrael Adonay Elohenu, etc., e la sabe toda, e la rezava por el dicho quaderno* (Beinart 1981b, 564).

31. *Dice el reo, Francisco Alvarez, que siendo de diez años su madre le dixo un día que estaban solos que hiciese un ayuno hasta la noche salida la estrella y lo dixo enterneciéndose con el reo y ansí éste lo hizo y creyó que aquello ayudaba su alma* (Contreras 1982, 607–8).

32. Isolation was important for the initial indoctrination of adults as well. The mill outside Mexico City where Sebastián Cardoso and his wife lived was one place where Mexican Judaizers tried to bring other new-Christians back to Judaizing. Testimony suggests that it was useful because it was safe, isolated, and comfortable (*Se escogió por parte segura para reducir al judaísmo a algunas personas, aprovechándose de lo apartado y cómodo del sitio*) (García 1910, 263).

33. This strategy was common in Spain as well. See Beinart 1983, 289.

34. *Le hizo apostatar de nuestra santa fe católica y hacer los ayunos de la ley de Moisén, castigándole con sumo enojo y saña si quebrantaba alguno, llevándole en tales días a bañar al río; y le enseñó oraciones judaicas* (García 1910, 257–8).

35. *Le cogieron vn dia a solas en el almaçen su padre y madre, y le dixeron ambos que creiesse en la Ley de Moyseen que ellos guardaban, y que era por donde se havia de salvar, que la Ley de Christo que seguia no era buena, que la buena era la que ellos seguian* (Nunemaker 1946, 21–2).

36. *Encargándole el secreto, por el riesgo que corría* (García 1910, 258).

37. *Que mirasse no lo dixesse a nadie, y que no lo supiessen los de la calle* (Nunemaker 1946, 22).

38. *Nunca muestran a los hixos la ley hasta que saven con quien se cassan* (Selke de Sánchez 1972, 257–80).
39. *Viéndole algo terco o que no percibía lo que en este particular le decían, lo redujo su padre a malos tratamientos, vistiéndole de paño burdo y dándole camisa de manta (género de que se da a los esclavos), y por muy leve ocasión cogiéndole y amarrándole, desnudo, en cueros, en una escalera, y otras veces a la ley de bayona, poniéndole un palo en la boca, amarrado como mordaza, porque no le pidiese que lo dejase por amor de Dios y por la Virgen Santísima; y le daba tantos azotes, que le ponía su cuerpo más morado que un tafetán. Teniéndole ya judaizante, mudó de tratamiento, vistiéndole bien y llamándole con los demas sus hermanos y hermanas para tratar de qué buena era la ley que seguían y cómo por ella le daba Dios dineros* (García 1910, 199).
40. *Porque cuando venía de la amiga decía loado sea el Santísimo Sacramento, y la mandaba que sólo dijese buenos días, buenas tardes tengan. Y si se descuidaba y hablaba con ella alguna persona católica, la miraba con notable saña y cólera, y se tiraba de las barbas en señal de su enojo, y después la llamaba y la decía que si no le había mandado que no dijese aquello, sino buenos días o buenas tardes tengan; y respondiéndole que las demás muchachas, cuando ella las acompañaba a su casa, decían loado sea el Santísimo Sacramento, le decía su padre que sus madres eran unas viejas y que por eso las dejaban decir aquello; que él la enseñaría otras oraciones* (García 1910, 197–8). Cf. Liebman 1974, 132–3.
41. *En el año de 1600 estando en casa de su padre estudiando en un aposento, entró el dicho su padre y le dixo: -Hijo mío ¿conoces a Dios?, y él respondió que sí, y su padre le replicó: -No lo debes conocer porque hay un conocimiento diferente del que te han dicho hasta ahora, porque tú solamente has de creer en un Dios verdadero al que debes servir; y él le contestó -Sí padre, así lo creo; hay un solo Dios y Tres Personas que son Padre, Hijo y Spíritu Sancto. Y su padre le dixo: -No lo debes creer así, no está asentado ni es cierto que dios tenga Tres personas distintas y para que lo creáis os mostraré un lugar en el Decreto donde se reconoce la diversidad de opiniones. Y le enseñó un canon en el que referían algunas opiniones acerca de la Santísima Trinidad y él quedó dudoso por ser nueva tal doctrina y su padre le dixo: -Miradlo y consideradlo despacio y conoceréis ser verdad lo que os digo. Con lo cual y con lo que otras dos personas de su casa le dixeron, se movió a creer y creyó desde entonces que no había más que un solo Dios verdadero sin distinción de personas dexando de creer en la Santísima Trinidad y después dixo a su padre qué debía hacer y éste le dixo que se habían de hacer muchas ceremonias y ritos pero que esto no podía hacerse en este reino por el peligro de ser descubierto y le dixo que le bastaría por agora poner su corazón en un solo Dios y ayudarle el Ayuno Grande que caya a los diez de la luna del mes de septiembre y esto lo hizo él y su padre y otras muchas personas* (Contreras 1982, 607).
42. *Le dijo con deseo que fuese judío (como él lo era), que no había de ser de esa manera, sino encomendándose a Dios del cielo como judío porque lo que se decía de Cristo era todo compuesto, y guardase el sábado si pudiese, y callase la boca sin decir cosa a su madre y hermanas, ni a persona nacida, porque no fuese descubierto*. Núñez added that "he had begun to instruct him when he was very little, because the child was incapable and not very bright" (*Había comenzado a enseñar al dicho su hijo siendo de muy poca edad, y que era un mozo algo incapaz y corto de entendimiento*) (Böhm 1984, 222–3). Cf. Medina 1890, 141.
43. *Miren este caballo; no has de decir sino un Señor infinito, bueno y sabio* (García 1910, 256).
44. Melammed found that this was the thrust of half of the explanations in Toledo from 1492 to 1520 (1985, 94).
45. *Muchas noches en presençia de su madre, llamaba el dicho su padre a este confessante y a sus hermanos: Clara, Françisco y Antonia, y sentandose en çima de la cama, todos juntos trataban de que era buena su ley, y que Dios les daba dineros por ella, y que la ley de los christianos no era*

buena, y que havian de ayunar, estandose sin comer ni beber en todo el dia hasta la noche, que havian de çenar pescado (Nunemaker 1946, 21–2).

46. María, la hija de Blanca, que era observante de su Ley y la guardaba como se debe guardar, y la podía leer y enseñar a muchos, y que ella había enseñado a sus hijos, y que lo hacían muy bien, . . . Era muy discreta, entendida y leída, y que se podía comunicar muy bien, y luego a Isabel que lo hacía también como la otra, y Margarita, que no es lerda nada en eso, que las demás no tanto; y que la Margarita tenía gracia particular para enseñar y reducir a los que ella quería, y que ya andaba en vísperas de reducir y enseñar al marido de su hermana Clara, pero que es un tonto y un salvaje (Lewin 1975, 97).

47. Remnants of this custom apparently have survived into the twentieth century. João Antonio Ferreira at age eighty in 1929 talked about the crypto-Jewish community in Bragança. He said that there were "women called priestesses who had the mission of teaching religion to the children" (*Havia tambem umas mulheres, a quem chamavamos sacerdotisas, que tinham a missão de ensinarem a religião ás creanças*) (Barros Basto 1929, 3.17:1).

48. Dixo que hera de hedad de syete o ocho años poco mas o menos quando sus padres le dezian lo susodicho e el lo començo a guardar. Preguntado que tanto tienpo lo hizo e guardo, dixo que syete o ocho años, mientras estouo en poder de los dichos sus padres (Gracia Boix 1982, 120).

49. Yendo a ver la disciplina, cuando vio la imagen de Cristo y de la Madre de Dios, de quien antes era muy devota y toda la gente llorar y adorar al Cristo, le dio grande envidia y dolor de corazón, como antes lo solía hacer y entonces no y viniendo a su casa con grande sobresalto no sabía que se hacer y halló solo al Doctor San Juan su padre y le preguntó que había de hacer una persona para que se salvase y le había respondido que ser buena cristiana (Gracia Boix 1983, 137).

50. Le preguntó que había de hacer una persona para que se salvase y le había respondido que ser buena cristiana y creer lo que la Santa Madre Iglesia de Roma; y que fuese diciendo las palabras del credo y las creyese todas y le había dicho que por qué se lo preguntaba y le había respondido que no más de para sabello y su padre le había dicho que no se metiese en honduras y considerando que su padre, que era letrado y toda la gente sabían mas que su madre sola, desde entonces se había vuelto a ser buena cristiana (Gracia Boix 1983, 137).

51. Estaba todavía en la ley de Moisés, que como la mamó en la leche, cuando le daban inspiraciones de volverse a la fe de Nuestro Señor Jesucristo, pensaba que se había de perder su ánima y estaba en gran confusión; y que había llegado a tanto el trabajo que había tenido, que una noche se había querido matar. . . . En otra audiencia dijo que todavía se estaba dudando que no quería engañar, que si no tenía su corazón firme, tenía propósito de morir por ello, y que había dicho antes que estaba convertida a Nuestra Santa Fe por liberarse de la muerte; y que se ayudaba cuanto podía para volverse a la Santa Fe Católica y estar firme en ella y cuanto más pensaba en esto tiraban tanto della las cosas que su madre le dijo y enseñó, que si eran solamente, le hacían volver a la ley de Moisés, mas la ponían a punto de desesperar. . . . Otro día pidió audiencia y dijo que estaba determinada de vivir y morir en la ley de Jesucristo como murió su padre y que fuese confundida en los abismos y no hubiese misericordia della Dios cuando otra determinación tuviese y su corazón se mudase a otra cosa; y que bien sabía que había de morir por las variaciones que había tenido en decir una vez si y otra no, mas que había de morir en la fe de Jesucristo; y que la causa que le había movido a esta determinación era ver que su padre había sido tan buen cristiano; y que ella había hecho grandísimas penitencias de ayunos y oraciones de la ley de Moisés para casarse con un primo suyo y no le habían aprovechado (Gracia Boix 1983, 135).

52. Marín Padilla lists these unifying familial-religious events: "births, circumcisions, weddings, illnesses, deaths; Jewish and Christian religious holidays; Sabbaths; fast and feast days; Lent, Corpus Christi, etc." (1981–2, 275). Baer asserts that "cultured *conversos* of the

upper class yearned for their old friends and kindred, for their people and the tradition of their ancestors" (1966, 2:272–4, 272). Cf. Caro Baroja 1961, 1:387, 468.

53. For Haliczer this was less true in the Kingdom of Valencia, where "coolness and reserve rather than zealous wooing implied by the Decree of Expulsion seems to have characterized the attitude of Valencia's remaining Jews" (1990, 218).

54. *En algunos tiempos pasados, estando en esta çibdad de Cordoua e fuera della e en otros lugares de nuestros regnos auiades indusido e informado e predicado a algunas personas, que biuian so nombre de christianos, que fisiesen algunas çerimonias e rictos judaycos e los auiades atraydo a judaysar. . . . E que auiades sydo en consejo e ayuda a algunas personas que biuan so nombre christianos se fuesen a biuir a tierra de moros como judios* (Beinart 1986, 55).

55. *Era gran talmudista y enseñaba a otros el Talmud* (Cabezudo Astraín 1950, 276).

56. *Unas parientas suyas le habían enseñado la ley de Moisés y que la había guardado juntamente con la de Jesucristo Nuestro Señor* (Gracia Boix 1983, 332).

57. *Le dijo estas palabras sabeis como vuestro padre vive en la Ley de Moisés, y éste le respondió llorando: es muy gran maldad, y el dicho Luis de Carvajal le dijo entonces: mira que por eso os quiero mas, que a todos vuestros hermanos; por que sabed que a mí me quiso engañar vuestro padre, persuadiéndome que me volviese a la guarda de la Ley de Moisés, y mira que si a vos os lo dijere, que pongais por delante que la ley evangelica que nuestro señor Jesucristo dió es la verdadera.*

58. *Aunque fray Gaspar quedaba siempre hablando, dando sus razones en favor de la ley evangelica, para que se convirtiesen a ella, y éste y Baltazar Rodriguez su hermano callaban, como a manera de sujetarse a ellas, era fingidamente, porque se quedaban en la creencia de la Ley de Moisés.*

59. Bel Bravo 1988, 132. For a similar case see García Fuentes 1981, 482.

60. For a discussion of the prayers and rituals transmitted orally by Iberian Judaizers see Chapter 16.

61. For a discussion of the books available to Judaizers see Chapter 14. Very occasionally the reading of the Old Testament might lead a *converso* to take up Judaizing on his own. For example, the Portuguese doctor Diego Núñez de Silva, a resident of Tucumán, Argentina, said that when he was a resident of the village of Juli, in the Province of Chuchuito, around 1584, "he had read in the Old Testament by himself, and concentrating only on the outer crust he had come to have many doubts about his faith, and he left the faith of Jesus Christ and passed over to that of Moses, thinking that it was good for the salvation of his soul" (*Habiendo leído el testamento viejo por la Biblia para sí a solas, leyendo solamente la corteza había venido a tener muchas dudas en la fe, y dejar la de Jesucristo y pasarse a la ley de Moisés, teniéndola por buena para la salvación de su alma*) (Böhm 1984, 220).

62. The text of an Edict of Faith is included as an appendix to this book.

63. *Lo sabían mejor que este confesante y cuando caía la dicha pascua, y que en los edictos de la Fe que se publicaban oían todos los ritos y ceremonias de la dicha Ley de Moisés* (Lewin 1977, 176–7).

64. *Disse que elle nunqua fora judeu nem fizera cousas da ley de Moyses e que se algumas sabia, era por has ouvir ler em treslados de sentenças que os estudantes da villa de Sea tomavão nos autos da Fé e has hião ler* (Azevedo Mea 1982, 378).

65. *Cuando se empezaron a hacer los autos de la fe por los años de cuarenta y seis, poco más o menos, en esta ciudad, la dicha persona oía leer los ritos y ceremonias que hacían los judíos, lo cual todo procuraba hacer* (Lewin 1971, 489).

66. *Tendo estudado latim no collegio de Santo Antão, uma sua irmã casou com um Alvaro Rodrigues, christão novo de Anvers, a quem acompanhou para essa terra. Ahi perguntou ao seu cu-*

nhado a ao irmão d'elle, Antonio Carvalho, onde se deveria ir á missa, de que elles se riram. Começaram no depois a induzir para ser judeu (Baião 1921, 225).

67. A transcription of this Spanish document was published by Caro Baroja (1961, 3: 332–6). Like many autobiographical statements, it was recorded by the Inquisition's scribe in the third person.

# CHAPTER IX ❦

# Marriage and Sex

Jewish Law, taking literally the Biblical command to be fruitful and multiply, requires men and women to marry if at all possible. The renunciation of marriage is seen as alien and celibacy impedes rather than enhances personal sanctification. This attitude explains the sentiments expressed by some *conversos* that the celibacy of the monastic cloister was unnatural. For example, several *converso* witnesses in the 1591–3 trials in Granada denigrate clerical celibacy. The case against Marina de Avila accused her of saying that "one should not be a nun because it would not lead to salvation." The case against Beatriz de Alarcón accused her of saying that "God wanted women to marry and not become nuns."[1] A witness told the Mexican Inquisition in 1643 that the *converso* Juan de León had told him that in Jewish Law "it was not good for a girl to die unmarried, because she would be condemned."[2] This view prevailed among the Mexican crypto-Jewish community of that time. Blanca Enríquez went so far as to say that the need for Judaizing children was so great that "it was licit for Judaizing men and women to live together without being married, as long as it was within their Law."[3] Isabel Duarte said that Judaizers were of the opinion that *conversa* girls should not become nuns "because they would be lost to Judaism and because that would put an end to the possibility of succession that was so important to them."[4] Thus, for a number of reasons even beyond the natural urges of the flesh and conventions of society, *conversos* were under pressure to marry.

The process of choosing a mate was more difficult for *converso* families than for the Hispanic population at large because the questions of ancestry and religion could not be avoided. Although the *converso* and Jewish communities mingled socially with considerable freedom during most of the fifteenth century they could not intermarry, for as Christians *conversos* were legally barred from wedding practicing Jews. When only one of two already married spouses chose to convert the marriage was not automatically ended, but the religious difference was sufficient grounds for either spouse to seek to have it dissolved and, in Aragon at least, this generally occurred. While spouses could remain in a mixed marriage they could not contract one.

*Conversos* could, however, marry old-Christians, and prior to the 1480s many new-Christians sought spouses among Spanish old-Christian families. Fourteenth- and early fifteenth-century converts were offered social mobility and easy assimilation as an incentive to convert, and one concrete sign of increased social acceptance was marriage into an old-Christian family. For the old-Christian partner, often a member of a semi-impoverished but important family, intermarriage was a strategy for improving financial conditions.[5] By the early sixteenth century it was well known that so many wealthy *conversos* had contracted marriage with the upper classes that there was scarcely a noble house in Spain that could not look—with extreme nervousness—at some demonstrably Jewish ancestors.[6] In some of these early mixed marriages of convenience the *converso* spouses continued to Judaize; prior to 1492 they were likely to maintain ties with their Jewish relatives. In other mixed marriages the assimilationist *converso* spouses strove to put their Jewish heritage behind them as fast as they could.

As the fifteenth century waned, the trend toward marriage between old- and new-Christians slowed. As converts grew more numerous and began to dominate the bureaucratic, intellectual, and business sectors of Spain's newly-developing urban capitalistic society, the so-called purity-of-blood laws (*leyes de limpieza de sangre*) were adopted, which prohibited them from entering certain occupations.[7] The percentage of *conversos* who continued to Judaize was sufficiently large that in the common mind the assimilation into Christianity of all *conversos* had become suspect. By 1480 the Inquisition had been established in Spain to ensure the Catholic orthodoxy of the converts. For old-Christians this combination of circumstances made marriage with a new-Christian a decidedly disadvantageous proposition; at the same time it continued to be an attractive strategy of assimilation for *conversos* who were so inclined. On the other hand, by the time of the Expulsion the external environment had become so hostile to Judaizers that *conversos* who wished to continue to identify as Jews had to rely on strategies of clandestineness to maintain their religious practices. The choice for marriageable new-Christian teenagers tended to be polarized: marry an old-Christian—if you could—and try to escape your Jewish past, or marry a Judaizing new-Christian and try to preserve Jewish customs within the shelter of a close-knit *converso* environment. This chapter looks at the complexities governing one's choice of mate and at *converso* marriage and divorce ceremonies, before concluding with a brief discussion of some other issues related to sexuality.

## 9.1. Exogamy versus Endogamy

For *conversos* whose main desire was to assimilate as fully as possible into their Spanish Catholic surroundings, marriage with old-Christians was a good tactic and a key part of their efforts to be thought of as old-Christians themselves. For such people exogamy, or marriage outside the group, rapidly became the rule.[8] Those who were successful in their attempts to assimilate generally disappeared from historical view, so we know very little about their feelings toward the issues we have been discussing. But those who were only partially successful tend to appear in the historical record at the very point in which their assimilation began to break down. We know a fair amount about why they intermarried and even more about why many of them regretted having done so.

Frequently the reason cited for marrying an old-Christian is love, and emotional commitment is just as frequently cited as a reason for a *converso*'s ceasing to Judaize. Documents from the 1480s include many statements such as that of Brianda de Santángel, who confessed in 1486 in Teruel that she had stopped Judaizing in order to marry an old-Christian (Sánchez Moya 1958, 170). Francisco de Torres, of La Almunia de Doña Godina, told a friend one day around 1488 that he had become a Christian because he was in love, but that he had come to regret it since now "because of his wife he could not eat Sabbath stews or any other Jewish food except on the sly."[9] But it is often hard to take these statements entirely at face value, for it is difficult to assess the degree to which love and other motivations mix in a young person's decision to break with his or her Judaizing family.

Love and a sense of family responsibility were undoubtedly factors in leading many Judaizing *conversos* to decide to remain in Iberia rather than take up Judaism openly in one of the freer lands of Europe or Africa. The rabbis of the Sephardic diaspora had to take these very real human emotions into consideration as they wrestled with legal issues facing the displaced families. One seventeenth-century responsum of Rabbi Yom Tob Zahalon specifically mentions the case of a Judaizing *converso* who refused to emigrate, saying that "I love my wife and children who are Christian."[10]

In both pre- and post-Expulsion Spain the most common *converso* marriage was to another *converso*.[11] But these marriages too could be "mixed" in the sense that one spouse might adhere to the old religion while the other was assimilationist. *Converso* families were large and diverse. It was not uncommon for one daughter to kindle the Sabbath candles at home while another sang in the choir at a nearby convent, or for one son to preach to his *converso* neighbors about the virtues of the

Mosaic Law while another was saying mass. Even before the Expulsion, while Jews were still in evidence, *conversos* might come from vastly different family traditions: because large numbers of conversions had begun as early as 1391, by the end of the fifteenth century it was quite common for a brand-new convert to marry a *converso* whose family had been Christian—superficially or sincerely—for several generations. Yet, even so, most *converso* families that continued to Judaize to at least some degree continued to offer a protective environment for other Judaizers who joined the family through marriage.

*Conversos* tended to prefer other *conversos* as spouses for several reasons. For some it was a matter of business: they hoped to keep family money and property within the *converso* enclave. Much more important, those families which were struggling to keep the Jewish traditions vital and who lived with the Inquisition looking over their shoulders were extremely reluctant to run the risk of having an "outsider" scrutinize their religious practices and perhaps disclose the Judaizing (or allegedly Judaizing) customs of *converso* members. Coupled with this was what Gilman described as "the desire for a domesticity in which one could be oneself, in which self-imposed masks and muzzles might at last be laid aside."[12] For these *converso* families endogamy, marriage within the group, rapidly became the rule. Because endogamous marriage seems to have been recognized as a precondition for the survival of Judaizing customs, the pro-assimilation Portuguese politicians of the late 1490s tried to prevent recent converts from marrying each other, but biases of both old- and new-Christians made this unlikely to happen (Pimenta Ferro Tavares 1987, 46, 76). It is understandable that endogamous marriage prevailed among remnant groups even into the twentieth century. It is also not surprising to see the unhappiness, interpersonal strife, and sometimes ruin that came to families that brought an "outsider" into their homes through marriage.

Among *conversos* endogamy was the overwhelming preference.[13] Quantitative surveys of individual *converso* communities tend to confirm this. For example, Hordes calculates that among colonial Mexican new-Christians 95 percent of the marriages were within the community (1980, 118). More than half of the 625 *cristãos novos* condemned in Lisbon from 1683 to 1746 were of exclusively Jewish descent.[14] The majority of the crypto-Jews tried in Murcia in the last great wave of trials (1715–25) had married endogamously, often with their distant relatives (Martínez Millán 1989, 331). One of the charges brought against the "Hebrew Nation" in Majorca in 1674 was that they married only among themselves.[15] In fact, different status groups within the Majorcan *chueta* communities did tend to limit marriage to their social equals. Raphael Cortes de Alfonso [Majorca 1685] reported that "it was common knowledge that no one who was observing . . . would marry anyone who was not also observing, and that was considered a good marriage. . . . And among them there was a difference because some families were considered better than others; there were also families of lesser status, also observers, and they also married among themselves. . . . And when one of the first families married someone of the lesser families, they said that they had married poorly."[16] Although *converso* endogamy was never universal, the presumption of universality lead some rabbis to rule that for emigrating new-Christians to claim Jewish status it was sufficient for them to demonstrate that their fathers had descended from Jews (Patai 1989, 76).

This tendency to endogamy has characterized crypto-Jewish communities right up to the meager remnants who have surfaced in the twentieth century. The crypto-Jewish communities in Portugal were particularly close-knit. Paulo reported that in this century in Belmonte, Portugal, new-Christian children are only allowed to dance with other new-Christians (Paulo 1985, 144). Vasconcelos observed that until around the First World War modern Portuguese new-Christians never married old-Christians, and that after that they began to do so, with some reluctance (Vasconcelos 1958, 205). Still, as late as 1980 Beatriz da Purificação Prada, of Carção, reported to Manuel da Costa Fontes that her Portuguese village used to be divided into Jews and Christians, each of which only married within their group (Fontes 1993, 75).[17]

These trends and the reasons for them are even more dramatic when one listens to the testimony of the *conversos* who were personally involved. Some *conversos* explicitly interpreted endogamy as a strategy for group survival. Bernardina de San Juan, of Baeza, testified in 1572 that her mother had taught her that Jews should not mix their blood with that of gentiles through intermarriage.[18] In 1573 Luisa Nunes was denounced to the Inquisition of Coimbra in part for having said that "new-Christian men only married new-Christian women, because they could not break their law which ordered them to marry their relatives."[19] The official Summary of the 1648 Mexican *auto de fe* in its condemnation of Rafaela Enríquez and her family gives a beautiful and concise rationale for crypto-Jewish endogamy: "They cursed the Portuguese men who had taken mistresses, not for the sin they were committing, but because they had chosen old-Christian women, when they could have chosen Jewesses, or even married young women of that faith. For the children whom they had with old-Christians were lost, without anyone to teach them their Law. That is why the Judaizers marry one another."[20]

In speaking of their children's marriages, *conversos* expressed a wide range of feelings. Ferrand Gomes [Soria 1491] said: "I want to marry my daughter to a man of my generation and lineage, so that if they call her Jewess then she will be able to call him Jew, and if she cooks some casserole or stew for him than the two of them can eat it together."[21] Gomes seems to have recognized the advantages of the sense of solidarity that comes from sharing one's status as a despised minority. His second point is that the day-to-day habits of crypto-Judaism, such as its traditional recipes, are best when shared.

Other testimonies exude a kind of xenophobic loathing of the hated "other." Antonio Rodríguez Arias's wife Doña Blanca Enríquez was accused of not permitting "her daughters to have amorous relations with or contract marriage with a person who was not of the same kind . . . or who did not promise to join them prior to the wedding. She said that she did not want to see her daughters and granddaughters in misery, married to foreigners with whom they would come to die accursed among enemies [Catholics]" (Liebman 1974, 193; cf. García 1910, 50, 122). Inquisition testimony from the early eighteenth century from Cuenca indicates, for example, that once "there was a great argument in the house of one Miranda, between him and his wife, for having married their daughter to a boy whose name the witness does not remember but who came from Extremadura, and was the son of an old-Christian captain. . . . Miranda was against marrying his daughter except to someone of full Jewish ancestry."[22]

Family solidarity was key. It was so important that Mexican Judaizers felt it altogether appropriate to insist that any prospective family member swear an oath of intention to Judaize within the marriage. Simón Juárez de Espinosa [Mexico 1642] testified that two years earlier he had fallen in love with Juana, the widow of Diego Tinoco, and wanted desperately to marry her. His prospective brother-in-law, Manuel de Acosta, objected on the grounds that Simón was not an observant Judaizer. The series of events and the dialogue leading up to this marriage, as recounted by Simón to his Inquisitor, are one of the most vivid testimonies to the problematic nature of *converso* relationships with regard to matters of religious observance.

> He asked Manuel de Acosta, the husband of Doña Isabel Tinoco, insistently for Doña Juana's hand in marriage, but Manuel put him off and strung him along, saying that he had a defect that meant that they did not dare offer him their daughter in marriage, but they would not tell him what the defect was. And when he persevered in asking them for her, and that they tell him what the defect was, they told him that it was being a Creole [a person born in the Americas], and that they were not sure that in the future he would be a man of substance who would be able to earn a living. He responded that if that was the only defect they had found, he considered himself a man of substance, as were all the honorable Creoles who had been born in this city [of Mexico].

Simón continued to beg, saying that the "defect" was not a defect at all, but Manuel continued stringing him out for several weeks more. Finally one day Manuel told him the truth:

> One day Simón went to the shop which Manuel de Acosta had set up in the plaza and Manuel told him that the reason they couldn't marry was not because of the defect of being a Creole, as they had told him, but for a much greater defect that he had which he could not as yet reveal to him, but which he would say in due time. Simón insisted that he tell him, which Manuel promised to do when they were alone. He was so anxious to find out and rid himself of this worry that he went to Manuel de Acosta's house one Easter Sunday—it was two years ago that this happened—and he asked him to do him the favor of telling him what was this defect that kept them from letting him marry Doña Juana. Manuel replied that he had spoken to his mother-in-

law, and they were agreed that he could marry so long as he was a God-fearing man. Simón replied that they had probably noticed that he had always been a God-fearing man, and he was a good Catholic Christian.

At that point a priest came in to look for a friend of his, . . . so they all began to talk. And while they were talking he thought about the words that Manuel de Acosta had said. And he began to suspect that they thought he was a Jew, because of the words Acosta had said. And when the priest had taken his leave, Manuel de Acosta said that they should go for a walk because he had something to say to him. And locking his house, which was in the Alcaicería, they strolled as far as the Alameda, and by the water pipes behind the park, next to the Veracruz Church, when the two of them were alone, Manuel repeated that if they were going to marry, as he wanted, he would have to be a God-fearing man. And if Simón wished, Manuel would send him to Juan de León[23] who knew lots of prayers and would teach them to him. And Simón replied that he had been a Catholic Christian since his baptism, and that he knew Christian doctrine and lots of prayers that he could teach León. And Manuel replied that the crux of the matter was that if he wanted to marry Juana de Tinoco, then he had to become a Jew. He said it clearly, in those very words. And when Simón heard him he grew pale and disturbed, so much so that he could not say a word. And when Manuel de Acosta saw him like this he grew terrified and angry, as he was of such a choleric nature, and he repeated to Simón that he should understand that he had not said anything to him, whether he should get married or not. And if he ever spoke of it he would kill him wherever he might find him.

Simón said that they would not get married. And they started to go back. And Simón was upset all the way back to his house, which was in the Calle de los Donceles, where Manuel de Acosta said good-bye to him. And he could not sleep at all that night for thinking about what had happened.[24]

Evidently at some later point Simón Juárez changed his mind, for eventually he did marry Juana Tinoco, and he did begin to Judaize along with the rest of his in-laws (Lewin 1977, 74–6).[25]

It was of paramount importance to maintain the Judaizing ethic of the family. One common strategy was to provide strong disincentives for breaking the family's religious solidarity. When any sort of mixed marriage occurred, the Judaizing members seem to have tacitly agreed—or perhaps even conspired—to make any non-Judaizer unwelcome. This was particularly true when a young *converso* married an old-Christian. When Fernando de Lucena married an old-Christian girl in the early sixteenth century, his family disparaged her as a whore (Gilman 1972, 115). In 1552 Izabel da Gama testified in Lisbon that her father-in-law Manuel Lopes, when he found that his son's wife was an old-Christian, "told his son that he was in mortal sin because a marriage with an old-Christian was not just a matter of pork."[26] In 1573 Ana Fernandes told the Coimbra Inquisition that certain relatives of hers wanted to do her harm because she had married an old-Christian without their permission.[27] Rafael Valls [Majorca 1670s] taught Judaizing *chuetas* that they would be shunned if they married old-Christians. Children of mixed marriages were sometimes called *mulattos* or mixed-bloods. The parents of children who married old-Christians sometimes went so far as to wear black and observe mourning customs for them (Cortés 1985, 289). The Jewish community outside of Spain tended to approve of these policies, for they encouraged the maintenance of Jewish tradition; a late seventeenth-century responsum by Rabbi Yom Tob Zahalon of Venice says explicitly that "if a Converso family in the Peninsula was found to intermarry with Old Christians, it was ostracized by the others" (Yerushalmi 1971, 20).

Unfortunately, in many families these policies functioned as an open invitation for adolescent rebellion. Over and over again the documents reveal the tragedies of Judaizing families in which the teenage children, whether for love or spite, sought out old-Christian spouses. Three examples will suffice:

Ana Gonçalez [Las Palmas 1526] reported

> that her father had despatched her mother and her brother Silvestre to Madeira to find a Jewish husband for her, but when they brought the Jew [i.e., Judaizing *cristão novo*] with them to La Palma she would not marry him, declaring that she would never marry a Jew; she states that in spite of their opposition she secretly married Pedro Hernandes, a Portuguese and old-Christian.

She further stated that when her parents found out about the marriage

> her father tore his beard, and her mother tore her hair, because she was marrying an old-Christian, that after her marriage her father said to her in her mother's presence: "Daughter, the Jewish creed is good and it allows relations to inter-marry, the man whom you have married is a vile dog who will never support you. If you wish I will send you to your aunt in Lisbon, she is very rich and will marry you to one of her kindred." That several times her father had attempted to persuade her to leave her husband, and on one occasion having overheard her parents and her brother Silvestre saying that there was nothing for it but to gag her and put her on board a ship, she sent for her husband, who after talking with her parents came to her and taking her by the arm asked whether she would return with him, which she was about to do, when her mother clutched her by the arm and implored her to remain, and after many angry words had passed and her parents had called down curses on her, the prisoner left the house with her husband. (Wolf 1926, 59, 57)

A similar case was reported in Bahia (Brazil) around 1590. Catherina de Almeida reported to Inquisitors that Fernão Pires had his daughter locked up and would not let her speak to anyone, but that Almeida had managed to communicate with her through a barred window. The daughter told her that her father had threatened to kill her if she told anyone about her Judaizing and protested that, although her father would not let her marry the man she wanted, she would never marry a Jew.[28]

When María Rodríguez secretly married an old-Christian in the 1560s, her father—according to a 1586 Valencian trial—beat her so severely that she still bore the scars. Even though she later married a *converso*, the Valencian new-Christian community so rejected her that in resentment she turned *malsin* against her father and many of his friends (Haliczer 1990, 231–2).

The mania for endogamy within close-knit and increasingly tiny Judaizing communities led to habits of consanguinity that bordered on incest and ran the risk of genetic inbreeding. In 1501 in Aranda it was reported that Fray Francisco de Aranda accused Pedro Núñez de Santafé of still being a Jew "because you marry with your cousins and nieces and your relatives."[29] In the seventeenth century the Mexican Portuguese Judaizer Luis Fernández Tristán married his own niece after requesting a dispensation from Rome. The scribe notes that "marrying a Judaizante within the family is a Jewish custom" (Liebman 1974, 222; cf. 231). Anne Cardoza reports that the family of her grandmother, Pauline, who emigrated from Gerona to Buenos Aires to the United States, always married endogamously. "On both my mother's and my father's side, cousin marriages had taken place for generations back, for another rule of the code was to stay genetically Jewish by marrying only relatives, such as cousins. My father's brother was my maternal grandmother's second husband. My uncle's youngest brother married my mother" (Cardoza 1989, S2). Paulo reports that twentieth-century new-Christians of Belmonte, Portugal, often marry cousins. He tells of having observed a number of people with rickets and night blindness. He reports having heard several times, "We are pure; we only marry cousins; we are Jews on all four sides."[30]

One approach to mitigating this tendency was to make a conscious effort to seek spouses from other *converso* communities. One man in the 1630s traveled regularly from Mexico to Italy to find Jewish or *converso* spouses (Liebman 1975, 108, 128). Other Mexican Judaizers sought wives in Pisa, Ferrara, Leghorn, and Amsterdam (Liebman 1970, 75).

A few points remain with regard to choice of spouse. One is that, since Catholicism prohibits multiple marriage, and since *conversos* were all nominally Catholic, polygamy was not practiced in the *converso* communities and in fact had all but died out in Jewish Spain by the time of the Expulsion. Another is that girls, and to a lesser extent boys, tended to marry young and to marry partners chosen by their parents. In sixteenth-century Albacete new-Christian women generally married at age twelve or thirteen, the documents tell us, so as to learn their husband's Judaizing ways while they were still malleable (Blázquez Miguel 1985a, 74). In colonial Mexico, too, Judaizing women were usually married around age thirteen (Liebman 1970, 75). A third point is that a variety of common superstitions influenced the choice of spouse among *conversos* just as it did with any other segment of the population.[31]

## 9.2. Divorce

Jewish law permits divorce for reasons of fraud, physical or mental mistreatment, impotence[32] or sterility, unfaithfulness, and a host of other factors. It also permits divorce in the case of prohibited marriages such as close consanguinity or marriage to a non-Jew. There is evidence that under this provision around the time of the Expulsion the conversion of one of the spouses was considered sufficient grounds by both Jews and Catholics for dissolving the marriage. When in the 1480s in Aragon María de Pisa converted to Catholicism against the wishes of her husband, she was considered to be divorced and soon after married a Christian. Similarly, when Azarías Chinillo, of Calatayud, converted he left behind his Jewish wife and soon married an old-Christian woman (Marín Padilla 1982, 261). In the charges against María de Zárate in Mexico in 1656, it was noted that "for old-Christians, cohabitation with Jews was an understandable cause of great horror, and that when they became aware of it it was grounds for divorce; and that several spouses who had unfortunately contracted marriage with an observer of the Law of Moses had tried this and been granted divorce."[33] The fact that Catholic Law prohibited divorce in all but the most extraordinary circumstances, and that Jewish Law permitted it, meant that well into the seventeenth century divorce was considered to be indicative of Judaizing. A Mexican Edict of Grace in 1639 makes this connection, citing as a Jewish custom the "parting of their ways which is when some person goes on a separate road" (Liebman 1970, 97).

Many complexities stemmed from the fact that *conversos* adhered to two separate legal systems. This was particularly evident when a marriage fell apart. Sometimes one *converso* spouse, perhaps the Judaizing member of the couple, chose to emigrate in order to practice Judaism openly in some other country and eventually decided to marry someone else who was also a Jew. What sort of divorce was required, and who should grant it?

Problems could also arise when a husband died leaving a wife childless, because the ancient Jewish custom of levirate marriage required that a childless widow marry the brother of her deceased husband so that the family bloodline would continue. This custom is derived from Deuteronomy 25:5,[34] which commands that "if brothers dwell together, and one of them dies and has no son, the wife of the dead shall not be married outside the family to a stranger; her husband's brother shall go in to her, and take her as his wife, and perform the duty of a husband's brother to her." Although this did not seem to happen with great frequency, a few examples appear in the trials. In an early eighteenth century case from Cuenca a witness's "aunt Isabel Fernández, when she was dying, said to her husband Antonio Rodríguez that when she died he was to marry Josepha Hernández, her niece, according to the ceremony that Jews observe in marrying the nearest blood relative of their [deceased] spouse."[35] The custom surfaces as late as 1745, when Manuel de Acuña, a Portuguese *converso* living in Jaen, was punished in Córdoba as a Judaizer because "he cohabited with the wife of the deceased who was also a Jew in order to comply with the Law."[36]

When a *converso* husband died the widow might emigrate, and then she would require a sort of legal quitclaim from her former brother-in-law in order to remarry a Jew. A picturesque version of the ceremony that releases a brother from this duty, called *halishah*,[37] is described in a late fifteenth-century compendium of crypto-Jewish customs:

> It was a commandment of the Jewish law that when a brother died the other living brother could marry the widow of his brother *Ad Suscitandum semen fratris* [for the continuation of his brother's seed]. And if he did not wish to marry the wife of his brother, it was necessary to put on a leather shoe which Jews used to keep hidden with their valuables. The shoe had twelve laces and twelve knots and when it was put on the right foot, his sister-in-law, the widow, would come and spit on it, signifying that just as those twelve knots were untied so would the bond and obligation of that marriage be dissolved. And from there on each one could freely marry whomever they preferred but not unless they did that ceremony of release from obligation as is written in the five books of Moses. This was to take place even though the brother of the dead man was married to another woman, because in that law a man could have two wives or more if he did not have children. If they had children they could get married only once. And, if they had children the living brother did not need to do this ceremony of the shoe, since the reason for the brother to marry the widow was to give progeny to the dead man. And that's why they had to name the first son who might be born with the name of the dead brother. That's why they said that the seed of the brother would be continued.[38]

Another version of this ceremony was reported in 1489, when the *converso* Juan Axalón was accused of giving his sister-in-law a "letter of release" because he was intending to go to Naples.[39] Later, around 1490, he went through a formal ceremony of release:

> Then a Jew came and put a [leather] shoe on one of his feet and a cloth shoe on the other and tied certain knots on it . . . and then his Jewish sister-in-law came in, . . . the one he was giving license to marry, and took his foot to untie the knots that the Jew had tied and he struggled with his Jewish sister-in-law so that she could not remove that shoe because the Jews . . . had told him that this is what he had to do to give her permission; and finally his sister-in-law untied the knots . . . and took off the shoe . . . and when it was off she spit on the ground and banged the shoe on the ground and that was the end of the ceremony . . . and they gave him fourteen ducats and away he went.[40]

## 9.3. THE MARRIAGE CEREMONY

As one of the most important life-cycle events, weddings were perceived by Judaizing *conversos* as an opportunity to reaffirm their Jewish commitments. All *conversos* were required to be married in the Church but, even so, Judaizing *conversos* prior to the Expulsion tended to celebrate their marriage with as much traditional Jewish ceremony as they could muster. From the signing of the nuptial agreements to the bedding of the new couple and the paying of the bill for the wedding party, *converso* weddings of the first post-Expulsion generation tended to be Jewish to the core. In fact, prior to the establishment of the Inquisition the marriage guests would often include both Jews and *conversos* and the festivities might take place in the *judería* as well as in the *converso*'s home. Once the generation of converts that had first-hand knowledge of Jewish life prior to the Expulsion had passed away, most of these customs fell into disuse; in fact many of them seem to have left no trace at all after 1492.

The period leading up to a *converso* wedding generally involved intense preparations. The two families would agree on the terms of the dowry.[41] The house would be cleaned and food for the wedding guests bought and prepared. Before the *conversa* Aldonza Ruiz was married in Teruel in 1478, some Jews even came to her mother's house and whitewashed it (Sánchez Moya 1973, 333). If the homes of the two families were at all distant from one another, transportation had to be arranged. Before 1480 *conversa* women might be festively escorted according to local Jewish custom. For example, around 1467 the *conversa* Angelina de Santángel went from Barbastro to Ainsa (Huesca) to marry the merchant Domingo. When they passed through the village of Naval "three Jewish women came outside singing with a Jewish child in their arms, and they went with the bride and her party to the inn of Ainsa, called Ramon's. They went inside and the Jewish women put the child on the lap of the bride and said to her: 'Within one year, daughter, may you have one like this on your skirt, may the Creator grant it.' "[42] Then immediately before the ceremony the prospective bride would bathe, at home or, if it could be arranged, at the local *mikvah*. Sometimes the bride bathed between the Catholic and the Jewish ceremonies. Catalina de Zamora testified in Ciudad Real in 1484 that she saw María Díaz "wearing a veil in the church, as the Christians do . . . and they told her that she had to be veiled again by a Jew called Trujillo, and that she had to bathe in cold water . . . and they took her and wrapped her in a sheet and bathed her in a stream or river which passed by the gate of the town."[43]

The Talmud prescribes two components to the Jewish wedding ceremony: *Kedushin*, or betrothal, and *Nissu'in*, the wedding ceremony under the canopy, or *huppah*. The traditional wedding blessing (*Birkat Erusin*) is "You are consecrated unto me with this ring according to the law of Moses and Israel" (*Enc. Jud.*, 11:1032). The weddings of Judaizing *conversos* might include these two elements, but since all *conversos* were nominally Catholics they had to receive the sacrament of marriage in the Church as well. There appears to have been no pattern as to which ceremony had to come first. *Conversas* in Ciudad Real in 1484 like Catalina de Zamora were church married and then later married a second time by a Jew (Beinart 1974, 53). Her contemporary María Alvarez, of Toledo, married her husband at home and then "the priest of Santa Justa married us" (León Tello 1972, 82). In almost all reported instances the Judaizing *conversos* considered the Jewish ceremony to be the one that truly married them and the Christian merely for the purpose of complying with the demands of society.[44] On leaving Iberia some *converso* couples who had been married only in the Church would be remarried in the Jewish tradition. Roth cites cases of Portuguese couples remarried in London as Jews up through the end of the eighteenth century (1931–2, 30). A witness told the Mexican Inquisition in 1643 that Juan de León had told him that "Catholic marriage was no good, that the marriage that observant Jews practiced in his land [Italy] was better, and for that reason that when married couples from here went there they would get married again there according to the ceremony of the Law."[45]

Before the actual marriage ceremony the two families generally negotiated and signed a *ketubbah,* or wedding contract, which identified the dowry and specified the bride's financial rights.[46] This was so important that a marriage might be considered invalid if it were not done. Jacob Abençuçan [Zaragoza 1482] confessed that he had been born Christian, that some twenty years ago he had married, had traveled to Malaga to have himself circumcised, and then had returned to Seville where he found his wife had given birth. After her purification they traveled to Guadalcanal where "we were married and made a *caçuba* in the Jewish fashion."[47] In later years the *ketubbah* had to be negotiated, signed, and archived in great secrecy. An indictment of *chueta* customs given to the Majorcan Inquisition in 1674 notes that marriage contracts were drawn up and signed by the relatives of the bride and groom, at certain specified hours, often in orchards, cloisters, or church cemeteries.[48] While the *ketubbah* does not appear to have been widely used among later crypto-Jews, there are examples of it from colonial Mexico (Liebman 1970, 75).

From the early years some full descriptions of new-Christian weddings survive. According to 1482 testimony in Zaragoza, some ten years previous the *conversos* Jaime de Montesa and Costanza López were married in Calatayud on Good Friday noon. Jaime had first gone to mass. A large number of *conversos* and one or two Jews attended. According to their maid, Inés, they closed themselves in a room with Jaime's squire, Costanza's mother, the town doctor Francisco Martín, and three Jews, where, it was reported, they settled the terms of the marriage contract and saw that the dowry was paid. Bernardo de Ribas reported that the words that were said were those of the Catholic wedding ceremony. Fernando Torrellas recalled that a Catholic chaplain married them. According to other testimony Francisco Martín took the couple by the hand, and the groom put a ring on the hand of the bride and said: "Let this be a good sign, and may God give us sons and daughters." When the bride emerged from the room where they had been betrothed her maid Inés reported that her hand was "covered with rings." She asked her if the groom had given her the rings, and she replied that "these two rings were given to me by my mother's relatives, Sento Avayut and Jehuda Avayut."[49] Jaime announced, "Now they are wed, wish them good fortune. . . . Come, everyone dance."[50] Some of the guests ate spinach and hake, but one or two took only bread and water.[51]

The sequence of events at this *converso* wedding is typical of others that dot the Inquisition records. A large crowd of the new spouses' friends and family were in attendance. The two families acknowledged the dowry and witnessed the signing of the *ketubbah*. Some respected, learned person presided. This might be a so-called rabbi (that is, a person locally reputed to be particularly knowledgeable in Jewish lore) or even, as in the case cited above, a priest. The actual wedding ceremony might take a number of different forms. The Portuguese miner Pedro López de Morales told the Mexican Inquisition in the 1640s that when he had married his Judaizing cousin in Madrid "the men and women sat on their heels with their heads down, their hands together, and their heads covered. They were like that for a long time, while another Judaizer read from a book the precepts and ceremonies of the Law of Moses. And when they had finished this ridiculous ceremony, they went off happy that they had assured a good fortune for the bride."[52] The report of the Mexican *auto de fe* of 1648 included a description of a different sort of wedding ceremony. "When they did not have a rabbi they just exchanged vows, and later, to comply with Catholic custom, took the steps that the Church requires. When there was a rabbi, they called him so that he could recite the blessings over a glass of wine, and give it to the bride and groom and family to drink; then they threw the glass in the air and broke it, after having first sprinkled the remaining wine around the room so that they would be fruitful with their children and that the wealth of the Christians would accrue to their houses."[53] Participants treated these weddings as formal religious services. Tomás Treviño de Sobremonte [Mexico 1647] was charged that at his wedding "he covered his head with a knotted pocket handkerchief, the way the Hebrews do."[54]

Whatever was said in the actual service, these ceremonies generally seem to have ended with a uniting of the bride's and groom's hands. Occasionally, as in this description of a new-Christian wedding in the Brazilian city of Bahia in 1590, it consisted of very little else. A new-Christian named Manoel da Veigua testified that "in this city a new-Christian man married a new-Christian woman who was a relative of his according to the customs and rites of the old Law. Other relatives of theirs joined their hands and performed the ceremonies and threw them into bed in the Jewish fashion. And after her pregnancy had begun to show they sought a dispensation because they were related and they got married by the Church."[55] Frequently rings were exchanged.[56] María Alvarez, of Toledo, described her marriage ceremony which took place sometime prior to the Expulsion this way:

> The day the papers were signed before Francisco Rodríguez, the scribe, the night before that day my husband came to my father's house where I was and sat next to me on a bench and took my hand and put a ring on my finger and told me that with that ring he was taking me for his wife according to the Law of Moses, and he told me that I should respond to

him saying that I accepted him as my husband. And he said that that was what a Jewish doctor named don Yuça had told him to do. And after this, when I married my husband, the priest of Santa Justa . . . married us.[57]

Sometimes the Catholic ceremony was augmented by the spouses' declaring to each other their adherence to Judaism, as Tomás Núñez de Peralta told the Mexican Inquisition in 1642, saying that "the night he married Beatriz Henríquez he and she declared to each other that they adhered to the Jewish law."[58]

Following these ceremonies a blessing for the new couple's happiness and fruitfulness was recited. Sometimes wine was drunk after an appropriate blessing.[59] According to 1484 testimony, at the wedding of María Díaz in Ciudad Real "the Jew Trujillo came with a cup of wine in his hand and said certain words and had the bride and the groom drink from it."[60] Peruvian crypto-Jews manufactured a wine for their ceremonial use. In Mexico *kiddush* was often recited over liquid chocolate, "prepared from the cocoa bean and made frothy by the use of a swizzle stick twirled between the palms of the hands" (Liebman 1975, 119).

Few of these customs have survived into modern times except in Portugal, where several two-ceremony weddings—a Catholic church wedding and a Jewish wedding replete with rings and the blessings of Abraham, Isaac, and Jacob—have been reported. Schwarz describes one of these weddings. Several days before the civil ceremony the bride and groom, each with two friends, stood among their families. A family member joined their hands, bound them with a linen cloth, and pronounced a blessing: "In the name of the God of Abraham, Isaac and Jacob, I join you into one. May you fulfill His benediction."[61] To judge from other reports, the most important aspect of this ceremony was the joining of new spouses' hands. Vasconcelos recorded a 1933 Portuguese new-Christian wedding ceremony conducted by a woman, Maria José da Cunha. After three days of fasting the bride and groom at sunset took hands and the leader said three times: "I join you together in the name of the living God, with the blessing of Isaac, of Jacob, and of Abraham. May the Lord marry you and join you for good. May it be with the blessing of Adonai, and Abraham and Isaac and Jacob, and Moses and Aaron." Da Cunha sprinkled rose petals and olive leaves over the couple, and all shouted "*Hallelujah!*"[62]

Paulo reported another Portuguese wedding in which friends and relatives gathered in the bride's home. The groom's family entered and said: "I come to ask the hand of your daughter for my son." The bride's father responded: "I give it to you with great honor." Everyone congratulated the couple with the phrase "May luck be with you!"[63] Then the women sang a ballad narrating a romance between Judah and Tamar.[64] Seven days after the ceremony the couple fasted all day with two friends of the groom and two of the bride. At the end of the fast they celebrated the actual wedding with this blessing:

Blessed be the great God Adonai, who created happiness, satisfaction, the groom, the bride, love and brotherhood, delights and pleasures, friendship and peace. O Lord, our God, may Your city of Jerusalem be built soon to the sound of happiness, to the sound of the groom and the bride emerging from their festivity. Blessed are You, God, who causes the married couple to prosper.[65]

## 9.4. THE WEDDING PARTY

Prior to the Expulsion weddings in the *judería* were usually attended by friends and relatives on both sides of the religious line. It was not unusual for the family's Christian friends or business associates to be in attendance as well, although custom or law might separate the different groups within the festivities. Judging from the fact that Gonzalo Jarada, a councilman of Trujillo, was accused in 1489 of "going to honor the weddings of some Jews, because that is the custom in the city of Trujillo,"[66] in the 1480s it was common for the entire community of old-Christians, *conversos*, and Jews to attend Jewish weddings. All groups contributed lambs to the celebration. In Aragon prior to the Expulsion *conversos* frequently attended Jewish weddings and took part in the festivities. *Conversa* girls helped adorn the bride. They witnessed the ceremony and ate and drank and danced and sang with their Jewish friends and relatives. If the party went late, occasionally they slept over in the Jewish quarter. In 1476 a *conversa* named Leonor stayed three weeks in the Jewish quarter for her friend Clara's wedding. The *conversa* girls watched the ceremony from behind a curtain (Marín Padilla 1982, 270–2). Francisco Cambila, of Ejea de los Caballeros [Aragon], confessed that from 1470 to 1490 he frequently visited his Jewish relatives, that he attended their weddings and dined with them, at a separate table, eating their food and drinking their wine (Marín Padilla 1982, 288).

Sometimes, but less frequently, Jews attended *converso* weddings. Curiously, some Jewish weddings just prior to the Expulsion were paid for by wealthier new-Christians. In some cases this was for reasons of family ties or for maintaining supportive links with the Jewish community. In Calatayud in 1488 the *converso* Alonso de Santa Cruz offered to pay for the wedding of Yucé Buena Vida's eldest daughter if the Jew would send him Sabbath stew every Friday (Marín Padilla 1982, 266). In others it may well have been a way of expiating the guilt that new-Christians felt at having converted. The *converso* Juan Pérez de Ariza was denounced in 1489 for having given charity to the Jews for the weddings of Jewish orphan girls (Marín Padilla 1982, 266).

Weddings themselves were a cause for communal celebration. Gifts of clothing, jewels, or food were exchanged among family and guests. In Aragon around the time of the Expulsion it was customary to give *converso* brides cloth, clothing, or jewels. Inquisition documents record gifts of a silver chain, silver and bronze spoons, rings, clogs, shoes and shoe liners, scarves, towels, shirts, bolts of cloth, and other items (Marín Padilla 1982, 270–1, 288–91). In Aragon it was also customary for the parents of the newlyweds (especially Jewish newlyweds) to give gifts to their guests and friends and relatives in honor of the wedding. Gifts of food were common; the documents attest to gifts of fowl, including chickens, ducks, and geese, cuts of meat, and so forth. Occasionally jewels were given.[67] Little information about *converso* wedding gifts is found in later texts.

The wedding festivities featured a banquet. The foods offered to guests frequently included honey or honey cake, which symbolized the wishes of all present for a sweet future for the new couple. In Aragon around the time of the Expulsion wedding feasts often included meat, cakes and pastries (especially round crullers or doughnuts called *rosquetas*), and fruit. Wine was generally served (Marín Padilla 1982, 270). Tomás Treviño de Sobremonte [Mexico 1647] was charged with having begun his 1629 wedding by eating "some crullers made with honey in memory of the honeycomb that the angel had brought out of the storehouse [?] for the daughter of Potiphar when she married Joseph, which ceremony Treviño explained like a rabbi to the guests."[68] After the Treviño wedding meal was over "blessings were recited and cold water was thrown on each hand prior to praying. The hands were dried 'with a towel in a peculiar way' " (Liebman 1970, 246).

While the Treviño family celebrated their wedding with a feast, other Mexican Judaizers of that time took the opposite tack. The Portuguese miner Pedro López de Morales told the Mexican Inquisition in the 1640s that when he had married his Judaizing cousin in Madrid "they celebrated the wedding with a solemn fast."[69] Micaela Rodríguez, reconciled in the 1648 Mexico City *auto de fe*, said that when a Judaizing friend got married, "she, her mother, her sisters, and nieces and nephews fasted for the success of that marriage."[70]

In twentieth-century *converso* weddings in Portugal, foods from several holiday traditions seem to have been blended. Paulo reports that in this century in Belmonte, Portugal, at a new-Christian wedding a light meal is served. On the table is a wine chalice, salt, bitter herbs, honey, an apple, and unleavened bread. The bride and groom drink from the same cup (1985, 145). He reports another wedding table set with sweets, figs, *medronhos,* and *aguardiente* (1970, 84).

Often following the wedding there was dancing to music that was sometimes provided by groups of professional *converso* musicians. There is evidence that in Aragon just prior to the Expulsion some *converso* musicians made a living by playing at Jewish and *converso* weddings. Such was the case of Juan de Zaragoza, who played flute and drums, and a man named Tribulet who played the tambourine.[71] After the ring ceremony at the Calatayud marriage of the *conversos* Jaime de Montesa and Costanza López, which was described earlier in this chapter, Jaime announced: "Now they are wed, wish them good fortune.... Come, everyone dance." When Inés objected that it was Good Friday and people were praying, Jaime insisted to such an extent that it seemed that the wedding would not be valid without dance as a public expression of joy.[72] Martín, a tambourine player in Soria, told the Inquisition in 1501 that he and his son the *dulzaina* player Juan Navarro attended the wedding of the *converso* Alonso in Almazán (Carrete Parrondo 1985a, 117). One suspects that, as is the case in many cultures, ribald jokes and pranks were a part of wedding festivities. The *converso* notary of Calatayud Juan Blasco said he used to go to Jewish weddings to eat and "to play jokes," but that that was not a sin because it was not a Jewish ritual.[73] The custom was common in Daroca as well.

Eventually the bride and groom were led off to the bridal chamber. The next morning they were separated and kept apart for a week before being allowed to resume marital relations. This tradition, derived from Leviticus 18:19 and 20:18, which prohibits sexual relations during any sort of vaginal bleeding or menstrual flow, was initially widespread. At a 1504 *converso* wedding "they gave the bride . . . to Alonso Laínez, her husband, and they shut them in. Two nights later they took her from him and did not give her to him again . . . until Sunday of the following week. And they watched over them on Thursday, and the groom went to his mother's house and the bride to her parents' house . . . and they didn't give her to him again until they took the newlyweds to the house where they were going to live."[74] At a Soria wedding in 1501 the guests "went with the bride's godmother and her sister-in-law to the bridal bedroom and dragged the bride out of bed by her feet and left the groom alone with the witness and his son to have lunch. The witness asked the groom why he let them do this to him, and he said: 'They won't give her to me for seven days.' "[75] This custom seems to have persisted sporadically for nearly two hundred years, although with interpretive embellishments. For example, in 1678 Ana Cortés reported to the Inquisition in Majorca that her father Joseph Cortés had instructed her "that when it came time to marry that she should abstain from consummating the marriage for three days, and that following those three days she should commend herself very sincerely to God, and that this was done in memory of Sarah, for the Devil had killed her seven husbands, and that with the help of the angel Saint Raphael, who burned the liver of a fish, and with the odor and the prayers, the Devil was driven off, and Sarah enjoyed her last husband."[76]

## 9.5. Sexual Customs

Sexual relationships outside of marriage go against the tenets of both Catholicism and the Jewish Law, but have always been a part of human behavior. Ample evidence from the thirteenth through the fifteenth centuries suggests that the sexual behaviors of Spain's Jews were heavily influenced by those of their Christian and Moslem neighbors, and that the sexual codes by which Spain's Jews lived were less rigid than those north of the Pyrenees (Assis 1988). These behaviors carried over into the *converso* community. While sexual behavior per se did not fall within the jurisdiction of the Inquisition, two issues were of concern to the tribunals: homosexual acts and disavowal of the fact that fornication—defined by the Church as sexual relationships not sanctified by marriage—was considered a sin.

On the latter point, documents suggest that, whether from naïveté or guile, defendants who had been charged with fornication frequently claimed ignorance of the law. In later years this was as true of Judaizers as it was of the general populace; typical was the declaration of Diogo Nunes [Brazil 1590s] "that having carnal relations with an unmarried woman was not a mortal sin so long as you paid her for her trouble."[77] Others affirmed that Judaism differed from Christianity in condoning pre-marital sex. Margarita de Rivera, a Judaizer, confessed that for a man and woman who observed the Law of Moses sex before marriage was not a sin (Liebman 1975, 108). Antonio José da Silva, who was born in Rio de Janeiro, confessed in 1726 in Lisbon that his aunt Dona Esperança had persuaded him to live by the Law of Moses so that he could have sexual relations with her maid, since that was not a sin in Judaism (Wiznitzer 1960, 154). Da Silva testified that "in the Law of Moses simple fornication was not a sin."[78]

Laws prohibiting sexual activity between Jews and Christians had been promulgated in Spain beginning with the fourth-century Council of Elvira and continuing through the Middle Ages, with a frequency and a vehemence that underscored their ineffectiveness.[79] Love—or lust—always seems to have found a way, and the Inquisition documents bring to light numerous instances of sexual relationships outside of marriage. María de Pisa confessed in the 1480s in Zaragoza that "when she was a Jew she had a Jewish lover and that even now the Jewish lover slept with her after she was a Christian."[80] The *converso* Leonardo de Santángel was denounced in 1488 for having a Jewish mistress with whom he ate and slept in her house in the Jewish quarter of Calatayud. The *conversos* Martín Salvador and Francisco Climent were similarly denounced (Marín Padilla 1982, 265).

Extra-marital relationships of any sort tended to be considered scandalous. The scandal was compounded when they crossed religious lines, for they were perceived as threatening by Judaizing *conversos* intent on preserving the exclusiveness of their endogamous society. The *conversa* widow Vellida of Trujillo was arrested for conducting several scandalous affairs between 1481 and 1490 with married Christians (Melammed 1991, 119). The old-Christian Alonso de las Torres testified in 1484 that around 1469 he used to "keep company" with a *conversa* girl and that "one day she begged him that when he was coming to be with her that he be as circumspect as possible, because she was much criticized by the *conversos*, especially by the elder Juan Falcón, who called her a bitch because she was sleeping with an old-Christian, saying that it was against the Law."[81] In the 1640s Margarita de Rivera (mentioned above) averred that for a Jewish man to have sex with a Christian woman was not a sin, but that for a Jewish woman to have sex with a Christian man condemned her to Hell (Liebman 1975, 108). Adultery could be a cause of great concern to the Judaizing community: the Portuguese Judaizer Diego Juárez de Figueroa went so far as to tell the Mexican Inquisition in the 1640s that "the souls of adulterous Judaizing women appear before God with their faces covered with a dirty rag."[82] The social pressure for endogamy led observant crypto-Jews to discourage any sexual relations with old-Christians. Isabel de Rivera said in Mexico in the late 1640s that devils would come for any Judaizer who had sex with a Christian.[83]

It should also be pointed out that some Judaizers married exogamously and then converted their spouses to Judaism. Some *converso* men formed liaisons with unmarried women or with their own servants or slaves (Melammed 1991, 119) and then attempted to induce children of these unions to Judaize. Racial mixing was more likely to occur in the American colonies than in Iberia. The family circumstances of any individual Judaizer could be quite complex. For example, the official summary of the 1646 *auto de fe* in Mexico cites in some detail the case of the mulatta Judaizer Esperanza Rodríguez, who was born in Seville around 1574 to a black Guinean slave and the new-Christian dressmaker Francisco Rodríguez. Esperanza married the German sculptor Juan Baptista del Bosque, who brought her to Guadalajara, and when he died she became a slave to Catalina Rodríguez, a principal Judaizer in that city. Esperanza's two daughters, the mulatta Juana del Bosque (who married a fugitive Portuguese Judaizer), and María del Bosque, were also sentenced as Judaizers.[84] The Portuguese Judaizer Duarte de Torres, "reconciled" in an *auto* in Mexico the following year, had married Josefa Ruiz, a mestiza of Indian mother and Spanish father, who lived in Pátzcuaro, Michoacán (García 1910, 105). Pedro López de Morales, of Portuguese descent, a miner from Ixtlán, Guadalajara, was said to have a bastard daughter of mixed blood (*mestizuela*) whom he wanted to send back to Spain to learn Judaizing from some of his relatives.[85] In colonial Brazil, too, it was common for male immigrants to marry—or at least have children with—their female black slaves. If the father was a Judaizer frequently the mulatto children were raised as Judaizers (Wolff 1987, 35–43).

Last, a percentage of *conversos*, like every other group of people, engaged in homosexual practices, and occasional references to homosexuality appear in the trials. The Brazilian Inquisition seems to have been particularly homophobic and its documents also indicate that both old- and new-Christians engaged in homosexual activity. To cite just one of many examples, the *cristão novo* Salvador Romeiro was accused in Pernambuco (Brazil) in 1595 of having ceased marital relations with his wife and having engaged in sexual activity with a number of men.[86] This is not an isolated case, for the investigations in Brazil in the 1590s alleged homosexual activity among a number of men and women, both new- and old-Christians.

## Notes

1. *Y que no fuese monja porque no era estado para su salvación. . . . Que Dios queria mas que se casasen que no que se metiesen monjas* (Bel Bravo 1988, 89).

2. *Que en ella no era bueno morir doncellas, porque se condenaban* (Lewin 1977, 242, 247). For a similar example see García 1910, 59.

3. *Tenían permiso para amancebarse judías con judíos, y no era pecado entre ellos el estarlo con las de su ley* (García 1910, 205–6).

4. *Por la imposibilidad de reducirlas al judaísmo, como por acabarse por este camino la sucesión tan deseada entre ellos* (García 1910, 61).

5. See Kamen 1965, 28–30.

6. As was pointed out in the Introduction, this was both common and scandalous. The sixteenth century saw the publication of several politically motivated genealogical essays, such as the *Libro verde de Aragon* and the *Tizón de la nobleza de España*.

7. The best study of this movement remains Sicroff 1960.

8. In Spain *converso* exogamy and the corresponding social expansion of *conversos* tapered off rapidly after the generalization of the purity-of-blood statutes in the 1540s (Contreras 1991, 131). For colonial Mexican examples of *converso* exogamy see Alberro 1988, 203. A surprising number of mixed marriages are cited in the Pernambuco investigations of the 1590s, with the children described as "half new-Christians" (*meo cristão novo*) (Furtado 1929, 145, 153, 175, 222, etc.).

9. *No podia comer hamines y viandas judaicas por causa de su muger sino a scondidas* (Marín Padilla 1982, 246). For a similar case see Pimenta Ferro Tavares 1982, 440.

10. *Ahavti et ishti v'et b'nei sh'b'goyot* (Yerushalmi 1971, 30).

11. Of the 625 people found guilty of Judaizing by the Lisbon Inquisition betwen 1683 and 1746, 58% were considered to be of exclusively Jewish descent. According to Baron 1965, 10:85, rabbis outside Iberia considered *converso* endogamy to be so much the norm that they did not require documentation of lineage to establish the Jewishness of emigrating converts. For a discussion of the psychological context of *converso* endogamy see Gilman 1972, 113–7. Official Spain, recognizing how endogamy retarded assimilation, sometimes tried to legislate against it. In Extremadura there was even an attempt to force *conversos* to choose spouses from old-Christian families, but little came of it (Sanabria Sierra 1984, 162).

12. Gilman 1972, 116.

13. This tendency to *converso* endogamy was noted by Jewish rabbis outside Spain. In the early years of the sixteenth century Rabbi Sim'ón ben Selomó Durán wrote, in confirming the validity of *converso* marriages, that *estos conversos, durante su permanencia en tierra gentil, en su mayoría contrajeron matrimonio con descendientes de conversos; sólo una minoría contrajo matrimonio con los hijos de Edom* (Levi 1982, 33).

14. Baron 1969, 13:85. Lorence's research on mid-seventeenth century rural Portuguese communities, on the other hand, attributes their "disintegrating character" to the fact that so many of the Judaizers had intermarried with old-Christians (1991, 101).

15. *Los que de ellos se mezclan con christianos en caso de matrimonio lo tienen por muy grande afrenta y los dicen los demás que son de la Nación, que son mal mezclados y los tienen a mucha baxesa* (Braunstein 1936, 184, 57).

16. *Era en común estimación de todos que ninguno que fuesse de la observancia . . . se cassase con otra que no fuesse de la mesma observancia, y no lo tenían por buen matrimonio. . . . Y entre ellos había differencçia porque había unas familias que eran tenidas en mayor estimación que otras; había también otras familias inferiores, también de la observancia, y éstas cassavan también entre sí. . . Y quando una de las familias primeras cassava con otro de las familias inferiores, dezían que había cassado mal* (Selke de Sánchez 1972, 36–7).

17. For some additional examples of endogamous *converso* marriage from the fifteenth to the twentieth century see Blázquez Miguel 1985b, 53–4; Carrete Parrondo 1985, 65 [1491]; Blázquez Miguel 1986a, 71; Lipiner 1977, 38; Schwarz 1925, 36; Vasconcelos 1958, 228 [1933]; Nidel 1984, 257.

18. *Que los judíos no se casasen ni mezclasen su sangre con la de los gentiles* (Gracia Boix 1983, 133).

19. *Os christãos novos cazavam com as christãs novas e que elles não aviam de quebrantar ha sua lei que lhes mandava que casasem con as parentas* (Azevedo Mea 1982, 300).

20. *Vituperaban a los portugueses que estaban amancebados, no por el pecado que cometían en ello, sino porque lo estaban con cristianas viejas, pudiendo estarlo con judías o casarse con doncellas de su ley, y quedaban los hijos que habían en cristianas viejas, echados a perder y sin quien les enseñase su ley, que es el fin porque se casan los judaizantes unos con otros* (García 1910, 252).

21. *Casar mi fija con honbre de mi generaçión e ralea, que si la llamaren judía que ella le pueda a él desir judío, e que si ella le enguisare a él algund enguisado o caçuela que lo coman él tanbién con ella* (Carrete Parrondo 1985, 63–4).

22. *Avia una gran pendencia en la casa de dicho Miranda, entre él y su mujer por haver casado esa a su hija con un mozo que avía estado en Extremadura cuyo nombre no save, si que era hijo de un capitan christiano viejo, y de una judía observante contra el gusto de dicho Miranda que no quería casar a su hija sino fuese con quien fuese judío por todas partes* (Lera García 1987, 111).

23. León, AKA Salomón Machorro, was the unofficial rabbi of the Mexican crypto-Jewish community at this time. All this testimony is a part of León's trial.

24. *Habiéndoselo tratado a . . . Manuel de Acosta, marido de doña Isabel Tinoco, pidiéndoles por mujer a la dicha doña Juana con mucha insistencia, y luego se excusaron y lo fueron entreteniendo diciéndole que tenía un gran defecto por el cual no se atrevían a ofrecerle a la dicha su hija por mujer, sin declararle por entonces qué defecto era, y perseverando este confesante en pedírsela y que le dijesen qué defecto era, le dijo que era el ser criollo y que no se aseguraba que en adelante sería hombre de bien y sabría ganar de comer, a lo cual les respondió que si no era otro el defecto que le ponían, que él se tenía por hombre de bien como lo eran los criollos honrados que habían nacido en esta ciudad. . . . En cierta ocasión llegó este confesante al cajón de mercaderías que tenía en la plaza el dicho Manuel de Acosta y hablándole en [cortado] del dicho negocio le dijo que el no casarse no era por el defecto que le hubieran dicho de ser criollo, sino por otro mucho mayor que tenía, pero que entonces no se lo podía decir, que a su tiempo se lo diría, y este confesante le hizo mucha insistencia en que se lo dijese y le prometió de decírselo a solas, y con deseo de saberlo y salir de cuidado, fue este confesante a casa del dicho Manuel de Acosta un día de pascua de resurrección, que hizo dos años que esto pasó, y le dijo que hiciese merced de decirle la falta que tenía porque no le daban por mujer a la dicha doña Juana, y el dicho Manuel de Acosta le respondió que ya tenía dispuesta la voluntad de la dicha su suegra, con calidad que este confesante había de ser muy temeroso de Dios, a lo cual le respondió que se reparaban en eso siempre el haber sido muy temeroso de Dios y era católico cristiano, y en este punto entró un clérigo que se iba a buscar compadre suyo que vivía en casa del almirante Juan López de Olaya, con el cual se puso a parlar, y mientras lo hacía reparó este confesante en las palabras que le había dicho el dicho Manuel de Acosta, y tuvo alguna presunción de que tuviese a este confesante por judío, pues le había dicho las dichas palabras, y despidiéndose el dicho clérigo, le dijo a este confesante el dicho manuel de Acosta que se fuesen a pasear y le diría lo que más tenía que decirle, y cerrando su casa, que era en la alcaicería, se fueron paseando hasta La Alameda y a la cañería que está detrás de ella, junto a la parroquia de la Veracruz, y estando solos volvió el dicho Manuel de Acosta a decirle que para casarse, como pretende, había de ser muy temeroso de Dios, y si quería este confesante lo enviaría*

*a casa de Juan de León . . . el cual sabía muchas oraciones y se las enseñaría, y este confesante le dijo que él era cristiano católico desde que había recibido el agua del bautismo y sabía la doctrina cristiana y muchas oraciones que le podría enseñar a él, el cual le respondió a este confesante en resolución, si quería casarse con la dicha doña Juana de Tinoco había de ser judío, diciéndoselo claramente por las dichas palabras, y oyéndolas este confesante se demudó y turbó de manera que no le acertó a hablar palabra, y viéndolo de esta manera el dicho Manuel de Acosta, aterrado y colérico por ser, como era, de terrible condición, se volvió a decir a este confesante que hiciese cuenta que no le había dicho cosa alguna, ora se casase o no se casase, porque si lo decía lo había de matar dondequiera que lo hallase, y este confesante le respondió que no se casaría y se tornaron a volver, y todavía turbado este confesante hasta que lo dejó en su casa en la calle de los Donceles, el dicho Manuel de Acosta despidióse de él, y toda aquella noche estuvo desvelado este confesante de lo que le había pasado* (Lewin 1977, 74–6).

25. For additional information about this case see Hordes 1980, 119 and Liebman 1974, 188.

26. *Que estava em peccado mortal por quanto casamento de christã velha era nó de porco* (Baião 1921, 160).

27. *Humas pesoas suas conjuntas que lhe queriam fazer mal por ela, Re, se casar com seu marido, christão velho, sem licença dellas* (Azevedo Mea 1982, 337).

28. Furtado 1925, 529. In a similar case in Guadalajara [1492–3] Juana García's father locked her up because she was involved with a certain [old-Christian] squire, and she donated oil to the synagogue so that God would soften his heart toward her (*Su padre la tovo ençerrada por çiertos amores que dixo que tenia con vn escudero . . . Dio . . . para azeyte a la sinoga, porque la engraçie Dios en ojos de su padre*) (Cantera/Carrete 1975, 160).

29. *Porque vos casáys con vuestras primas e sobrinas e con vuestras parientas* (Carrete Parrondo 1985, 107).

30. *Nós somos puros, só casamos com primos, somos judeus dos quatro costados* (Paulo 1970, 116).

31. For example, Diego Calderón was told by a master Diego in Coruña del Conde around 1491 not to marry a woman who had already buried two husbands because, he alleged, that was contrary to the Old Law (Carrete Parrondo 1985, 67).

32. For example, Liebman cites a 1642 case where a *conversa* woman was granted a divorce because of her husband's impotence (1970, 234).

33. *Y que siendo ocasión justa de gravísimo horror para los cristianos viejos la cohabitación con judíos y notados de este delito que da causa al divorcio, y lo han intentado y conseguido algunos de los cónyuges a quienes por desgracia les ha sucedido contraer matrimonio con persona observante de dicha Ley de Moisés* (Lewin 1971, 231).

34. See also Genesis 38:8.

35. *Su tía Isabel Fernández, al tiempo de morir dio al dicho Antonio Rodríguez, su marido, que en muriendo ella reciviere por mujer a dicha Josepha Hernández, su sobrina carnal, según la ceremonia que observaban los judíos al casarse con la pariente transversal más cercana de su mujer* (Lera García 1987, 112).

36. *Cohabitó despues con la muger del difunto que tambien era judia para cumplir con la escritura* (Gracia Boix 1983, 615).

37. Neuman 1942, 2:55–7. Cf. Marín Padilla 1982, 293; Yerushalmi 1971, 25–7.

38. *Hera mandamiento en la ley judayca que muerto el hermano, el otro hermano sobreviviente se podía cassar con la mujer viuda de su hermano ad suscitandum semen fratris; y en casso que no quissiesse cassarsse con la mujer de su hermano, hera necessario que se calçasse un çapato de*

*cuero que solían tener recóndito los judíos en sus archivos; el qual çapato tenía doce correas y doce lazos; y puesto aquel en el pié derecho venía la dicha viuda su cuñada y escupía en él, signifficando que como aquellas corregüelas doce se desatavan, anssí se destaban el vínculo y obligación del dicho cassamiento; y de allí adelante cada uno se podía cassar libremente con quien bien visto le fuesse; y de otra manera sin hacer la dicha ceremonia y soltura el uno y el otro, como se contiene en los cinco libros de Moyssén; y que también havía lugar esto, aunque el hermano de el muerto fuesse cassado con otra muger, porque en aquella ley bien podían tener los hombres dos mujeres, y más no teniendo hijos, porque si los tenían no se podían cassar sino una vez; y por esso el hermano que vivía, no hera necessario hacer la dicha ceremonia de el çapato, porque la intención de casarsse dos hermanos con una muger era por exercitar la progenie de el muerto, y por esso se havía de llamar el primer hijo que nasciera de el nombre de el hermano muerto, y por esso dice que havía de suscitar el simiente de su hermano* (Santa María 1893c, 188).

39. *Carta de quitación.*

40. *Empues vino hun judio y escalçole a este confesante el hun çapato y calçole otro çapato como de voldres y echole en el dicho çapato ciertos nudos . . . y vino luego la cunyada . . . judia a quien dava licencia de se casar y tomole del pie para le desfazer los nudos que el judio le havia echado y quitarle el dicho çapato y este confesante forceava con la dicha judia su cunyada que no ge lo quitase aquel capato porque le dixieron los judios . . . que assi lo havia de hazer dando la dicha licencia y assi a la postre . . . su cunyada le quito los nudos . . . y le quito el capato . . . y quitado que lo huvo . . . escupio en el suelo y batio el capato en tierra y assi se hizo toda la cerimonia que se havia de hazer . . . le daron a este confesante quatorze ducados y assi se vino* (Marín Padilla 1982, 293–5).

41. This is a presumption. Perhaps because the custom of dowry was not exclusively Jewish, dowries are not mentioned as a Judaizing custom in any of the documents I have consulted, with the exception of one report that, when modern Portuguese *cristãos novos* wed, the parents arrange their children's weddings and always negotiate a formal dowry (Vasconcelos 1958, 203). As will be seen below, *ketubbot*, or formal wedding contracts, are mentioned in the documents with some frequency.

42. *Salieron tres judias con hun jodiguello pequenyo en las manos cantando y dende fueron aconpanyando a la dicha novia y a los que hivan con ella al meson del dicho lugar de Nabal, llamado de Ramon; y dende que fueron ende, dize, las dichas judias echaron en la falda de la dicha novia el dicho jodiguello y le dixieron tales palabras a la dicha novia Angelina: -desde hun anyo, fija, ende tengas otro tal en la falda, placia el creador* (Marín Padilla 1982, 269).

43. *Viendola velado con su marido en la yglesia, como fasen los christianos . . . la dixeron que la auian de tornar a velar por mano de vn judio que se llamava Truxillo, e que la auian de bañar en agua fria; . . . la tomaran e la cobijaran vna sauana e la bañaran en vn arroyo o rio que pasaua por su puerta en la villa* (Beinart 1974, 53). According to testimony from Molina de Aragón just prior to the Expulsion, Christians bathed so infrequently that for a bride to present herself clean at the altar constituted a prima facie case for Judaizing (Carrete Montenegro 1985, 81). The prenuptial ritual bath, or *banyo di novia*, has remained an important custom among Ladino-speaking Jews in the eastern Mediterranean. Levy reports that in this century in Rhodes a wealthy groom would rent an entire bath house and send an elaborate meal for the female guests at the bath (Levy 1987, 20). The party at the *mikvah* was often called the *bogo de baño* (Dobrinsky 1986, 56).

44. Paulo reports that in this century in Belmonte, Portugal, new-Christians have a church wedding only so that they will not be outcast legally and socially for living in sin. He recounts the case of a couple married in the Jewish law for twelve years, with three children,

who finally had a church wedding so that the husband would not lose his job as a mailman (1985, 144).

45. *El matrimonio que convenían los católicos no era bueno, que mejor era el que los observantes hacían en su tierra, y tanto que cuando iban a ella algunos observantes casados de los de acá se volvían a casar allá, de acuerdo con la ceremonia de la Ley* (Lewin 1977, 242; 247).

46. Marín Padilla summarizes the bibliography through 1982 referring to Hispano-Jewish *ketubbot* (1982, 250). As late as 1514 Mencía Belázquez sued to recover her dowry from the estate of her late husband (burned for his homosexual practices), adducing her 1480 Hebrew *ketubbah*, signed by both Jewish and *converso* witnesses, as proof of her claim (García Casar 1989, 95).

47. *Fizimos nuestro matrimonio et le fix caçuba a modo de judios* (Marín Padilla 1982, 250; cf. 253–60).

48. *Para tratar y afectuar todos los contratos matrimoniales se acostumbraron juntar los parientes de ambas partes en huertos, claustros o en cementerios de la Iglesia y conventos a ciertas horas que para solo este efecto tenian señaladas* (Braunstein 1936, 185). For another example see Cortes 1985, 289.

49. *Que buen simán fuese, que el dio les dase fillos y fillas* [Siman: Hebrew = good omen]. *Estos dos anillos me han dado los parientes de mi senyora, Sento Avayut e Jehuda Avayut.*

50. *Ahora ya son desposados, dezitles que buena pro les haga . . . Sus, baylar todos.*

51. Marín Padilla 1982, 253–60. For descriptions of Mexican new-Christian weddings in the 1630s see Liebman 1970, 97.

52. *Se sentaron en cuclillas y boca abajo los hombres y mujeres, con las manos puestas y cubiertas las cabezas, y estuvieron así por largo tiempo, mientras leía en un libro otro judaizante las ceremonias y preceptos de la ley de Moisén; y acabada esta ridícula ceremonia, muy contentos aseguraron el buen suceso que había de tener la judía desposada* (García 1910, 124).

53. *Los judíos, entre sí, se habían de casar debajo de su palabra en estas partes donde no tenían sacerdote de su ley, y después, por cumplir con los católicos, hacer las diligencias que ordena la Iglesia; y cuando hubiese rabino, le habían de llamar para que sobre un vaso de vino hiciese sus bendiciones y les diese a beber a los desposados y padrinos, tirando a lo alto el vaso y quebrándole, habiendo antes derramado el vino que sobró por la sala, para que fuesen fecundos de hijos y se les viniesen a casa las riquezas de los cristianos* (García 1910, 205). See also Wiznitzer (1962a, 244). The custom of breaking the glass must have been excedingly rare, for this is the only reference to it I have found.

54. *Se ató con un pañuelo de narices la cabeza, cubriéndola toda a usanza de los hebreos* (Lewin 1954, 142). Cf. Liebman 1970, 246 [1629].

55. *Se casarão hum cristão novo com huma cristãa nóva parentes ao modo e com os ritos da lei velha e que outros seus parentes lhes derão as mãos e lhes fizerão as ceremonas e os lançarão logo na cama ao modo judaico e que depois de ella estar prenhe pubricamente então pedirão despensação do parentesco e se casarão em fórma da Igreja* (Furtado 1925, 320).

56. For the use of rings see Baer 1966, 2:355; Blázquez Miguel 1988, 54; Braunstein 1936, 185 [Majorca 1674].

57. *Quel día que se fizieron iso recabdos por ante Francisco Rodríguez, escribano, que a la noche deste día, el dicho mi marido vino a casa del dicho mi padre do yo estaua e se asentó a par de mí en un vanco e me tomó la mano e me puso en el dedo una sortija e me dixo que con aquella sortija me tomaua por muger según la ley de Moisés y me dixo que yo le respondiese que yo le resçibía por marido. Et que aquello le avía dicho que hiziese vn judío físyco que se llamaua don Yuça. Et después desto, me desposó con el dicho mi marido, el cura de Santa Justa . . . nos veló* (León Tello

1972, 82). For similar descriptions see Baer 1966, 2:497; López Martínez 1954, 185; Blázquez Miguel 1985b, 54; Liebman 1970, 75, 245.

58. *La noche que se casso con la dha Beatriz Henriquez su muger se declararon este confessante y ella por obserbantes de la ley de Moysen y como las guardaban* (AGN Vol 402 doc 1, 51b).

59. In 1706 in Lisbon an old-Christian girl named Catherina Soares Brando described to the Inquisitors a new-Christian wedding she had attended in Rio de Janeiro some eight years before. According to Wiznitzer, "men and women assembled in separate rooms for the wedding banquet. When the servants retired after the banquet, one of the women raised her glass, proposing a toast: 'Let all present drink the blood of Christ.' In response, someone was heard to say: 'All of us here belong to the Nation, except that bitch of a bird dog'" (*Todas bebessem o sangue de Christo. . . . Todos aqui somos da nacão e so aquela perra perdigueira não è*) (1960, 147).

60. *Vino el dicho judio Trujillo con vna taça de vino en la mano e dixo çiertas palabras e dioles a beuer al nouio e a la nouia* (Beinart 1974, 53).

61. *Em nome de Deus de Abrahão, Isaac e Jacob eu vos uno; cumpri vós a sua benção* (Schwarz 1925, 62–3). See also Paulo 1985, 145.

62. *Eu vos uno e vos ajunto à voz do Grande Deus vivo. A bênção de Isaac, de Jacob e de Abraão. E o Senhor vos case e vos ajunte com bens. Seja a bênçao de Adonai e de Abraão e de Isaac e de Jacob e de Moisés e de Arão* (Vasconcelos 1958, 228).

63. *Venho pedir-vos a mão de vossa filha—para meu filho—. . . . Vo-la dou com muita honra. . . . Be-siman tob!* (Paulo 1970, 84).

64. *Judah é bom trovador, / mas também sabe bailar;*
   *na guitarra é um primor / rouxinol no seu cantar.*
   *Numa festa de Purim / Judah falou a Thamar,*
   *cantou, dançou e no fim / dela foi s'enamorar.*
   *E tão grande era a paixão / desde judeu trovador,*
   *que não ganhava o seu pão, / mas cantava o seu amor.*
   *Rico o pai de Thamar / ao pobre nosso cantor*
   *sua filha não quiz dar / p'ra dar a um velho doutor.*
   *Numa noite de luar / Judah foi a casa dela,*
   *p'ra cantar e suspirar, / debaixo já da janela.*
   *Ouvindo tão grande dor, / a linda bela Thamar*
   *fugiu co'o seu trovador / p'ra com ele se casar.*
   *E foram sempre a correr, / sempre sem nunca parar,*
   *até à porta bater / do Ribi-mor Eleasar.*
   *Não temais, ficai aqui, / esperando o pai de Thamar*
   *lá lhes disse o bom Rabi, / e logo o foi procurar.*
   *Convence o pai tão rude / o nosso doutor Rabino,*
   *C'um preceito do Talmud, / e com razões de ladino.*
   *Casou Judah com Thamar / unindo o seu grande amor,*
   *muita gente foi lá bailar / nas bodas do trovador.*
Paulo 1970, 84; see also 117–80; Tradições 1928, 2.12:7–8.

65. *Bendito seja o Grande Deus de Adonai, que criou a alegria, a satisfação, o noivo, a noiva, o amor e a fraternidade, as delícias e os prazeres, a amizade e a paz. / Senhor, nosso Deus, que bem depressase ouça na cidade, de Jerusalém a voz da alegria, a voz do noivo e a voz da noiva saindo do seu festim. Bendito sejas Tu, Adonai, que fazes prosperar os casados* (Paulo 1970, 84). For additional examples of modern Portuguese crypto-Jewish weddings see Paulo 1970, 117–8; Schwarz 1925, 36; Barros Basto 1928, 3.17:1; Vasconcelos 1958, 200, 207.

66. *Fue a honrar las bodas de algunos judios porque es costunbre en la çibdad de Trujillo* (Beinart 1980, 288, 336).
67. Marín Padilla 1982, 270–80, 288–91; cf. Carrete Parrondo 1985, 44.
68. *Comieron al principio unos buñuelos con miel a la memoria de aquel pañal que el ángel mandó sacar de la botillería para la doncella hija de Putifar cuando se casó con José, explicando como rabino este reo esta ceremonia a todas las dichas personas* (Lewin 1954, 142). Cf. Liebman 1970, 76, 246. Liebman 1974, 140 relates this custom to the Promised Land flowing with milk and honey, as found in Joshua 5:6, Judges 14:19.
69. *Celebrando las bodas con un solemne ayuno* (García 1910, 124).
70. *Hizo con su madre, hermanas, sobrinos y sobrinas un ayuno por el buen suceso de aquel casamiento* (García 1910, 244).
71. These two musicians also played when a new Torah was put in the synagogue (Marín Padilla 1982, 276).
72. *Ahora ya son desposados, dezitles que buena pro les haga. . . . Sus, baylar todos* (Marín Padilla 1982, 253–60).
73. *Scarnio o trufa . . . hun majadero de tocho [u otra cosa] trufatoria* (Marín Padilla 1982, 284).
74. *Dieron la novia a . . . Alonso Laynes, su marido, y les ençerraron; y pasadas las dos noches se la quitaron y no se la dieron . . . fasta el domingo de la otra semana; y los velaron en jueves, y el novio se fué a casa de su madre y a la novia touieron en su casa . . . sus padres . . . y non se la dieron fasta que les lleuaron a los novios a la casa donde avían de morar* (Carrete/Fraile 1987, 29; cf. 107, 118). The custom is alluded to only once in the Aragonese Inquisition records studied by Marín Padilla 1982, 292. See also Blázquez Miguel 1988, 54; Represa 1987, 35 [Almazán 1500]; Lewin 1954, 143 [Mexico 1647]; Liebman 1982, 124; 1970, 245; 1974, 137 [Mexico 1649].
75. *La dicha madrina e otra su cuñada de la novia tomaron la novia por los pies de la cama e sacáronla de la cama e dexaron del novio solo con este testigo e su hijo armosando. E este testigo dixo al novio que por qué lo consentya, e le dixo el novio: "Pues no me la an de dar en estos syete días"* (Carrete Parrondo 1985, 117).
76. *Quando llegasse a desposarse, se abstubiesse de consumar el matrimonio por tres días, y después de los tres días encomendarse muy de veras a Dios, y que esto se haçía en memoria de Sara, que el Demonio la havía muerto siete maridos, y que con la assistencia del Angel San Raphael, que quemó el higado del pescado, y con el olor y las oraçiones, se apartó el Demonio, y goço Sara del último marido* (Selke de Sánchez 1972, 276). Levy reports an interesting remnant of this custom in Rhodes from early in the twentieth century: "On the seventh day of the *hupa* the groom would go to the market and buy a fish. When he came home, he would find the bride locked up in the bathroom, usually guarded by a member of the family. He then had to pay some money to that person to free her. When she left the bathroom, he would throw the fish at her feet . . . as a token of fertility" (Levy 1987, 21).
77. *Dormir carnalmente com huã molher solteira não era peccado mortal pagando lhe seu trabalho* (Furtado 1929, 189–90).
78. *Não era pecado na lei de Moizés a simples fornicação* (Silva 1896, 9).
79. For example, Canons 16 and 78 of the Council of Elvira [c. 300 CE]; Laws of Constantius [339]; Memorial of the Jews presented to King Reccesswith [654]; Title 24: Laws 8 and 9 of the *Siete Partidas* of Alfonso X [1265] (Marcus 1960, 4, 21, 38–9, 101–2). According to Assis, despite the severity of these laws, there is only one known case where the death penalty was exacted, and that involved a Jewish man and a nun (1988, 44).
80. *Quando era judia tenia hun enamorado judio et que ahun agora dormia con ella el dicho enamorado judio despues que era christiana* (Marín Padilla 1982, 261). Given the number of

references in the municipal legal charters (*fueros*) to sexual relations between Christian men and Jewish women, they must not have been particularly rare (Dillard 1984, 206–7).

81. *Le rogava que las veses que oviese de yr a estar con ella, que fuese lo mas secreta que pudiese, porque ella era mucho reprochada de los conuersos, espeçialmente de Juan Falcon el uiejo, que la llamava perra porque dormia con christiano viejo, disiendo que era contra ley* (Beinart 1974, 559).

82. *Las judías adúlteras, parecen sus almas en juicio delante de Dios, cubiertas las cabezas con un trapo sucio* (García 1910, 101).

83. *A los judíos que se mezclaban con cristianos, se los llevaban los diablos* (García 1910, 59, 205). Views of this sort did not keep some liaisons from taking place. In fact the Mexican *conversas* Rafaela and Micaela Enríquez were the reported lovers of no less than the Inquisition notary Eugenio de Saravia and the Inquisitor Francisco de Estrada y Escobedo (Alberro 1988, 205).

84. García 1910, 47, 56, 77. See also Wiznitzer 1962a, 240.

85. García 1910, 125. See also Wiznitzer 1962a, 242.

86. Furtado 1929, 393; cf. 53; 279, 395, 437–8, 443–4.

# CHAPTER X

# Ritual Purification and Hygiene

Traditional Judaism gives a good deal of attention to personal hygiene, prescribing a variety of routines of cleanliness, each with its special prayers. Both men and women are required to be clean before engaging in any religious ritual. The cleanliness is physical in the sense that it requires that any trace of dirt, offal, or blood be washed away. But it is also symbolic, requiring rituals and prayers to prepare one psychologically for religious experience. The purification of hands before praying will be discussed in Chapter 15. The purification of cooking and eating utensils will be discussed in Chapter 19. Aspects of purity/impurity or of hygiene connected with death will be found in Chapter 11. Superstitious practices involving the finger- and toenails are described in the third section of this chapter. While Judaism requires good personal hygiene of both men and women, it gives particular emphasis to the woman's reproductive system.

## 10.1. THE RITUAL BATH

The laws governing menstrual hygiene are among the most complex in Judaism. An entire section of the Mishnah, the tractate *Niddah*, deals with the menstruant, as does the *Shulḥan Arukh* (YD 183–200). The essence of the law is that for a minimum of five days during her period and for seven days after the last show of blood a woman is considered impure, or *niddah*, and may not engage in normal relations with her husband or fulfill certain religious duties until she has immersed herself in the *mikvah*.

The *mikvah* is a pool or bath of a certain prescribed size which is reserved for ritual ablutions. Jewish law dictates that it must be filled with running water (i.e., not drawn water). Again, the laws and traditions governing its size, care, and use are complex. No seriously orthodox Jewish community can be without a *mikvah*, and both documentary and archaeological evidence for the existence of Spanish *mikvaot* prior to the Expulsion are substantial.[1] In fact, the remains of the medieval *mikvah* in Besalú (Gerona) have become a tourist attraction.[2] Since Christian legislation generally prohibited Jews from washing in the same facilities as Christians, the medieval *mikvah* frequently also served Jews as community bathhouse or had a bathhouse associated with it. Prior to the Expulsion Judaizing *conversa* women might—with increasing risk as time went on—use the community *mikvah*. The charges brought against Sancho de Çibdad [Ciudad Real 1484] because the women of his family "used to go to bathe after their periods in the pool of Juan de Herrera" were typical of this period.[3] A witness in Segovia said that in the early 1480s Diego Arias's wife Elvira González, though a *conversa*, used to visit the *mikvah*. Once when a neighbor asked her where she was going she whispered "to the bath house where they perform *tebilah*" and then was there for about an hour.[4] Elvira also performed her ablutions at home. In 1487 the *conversa* Isabel Arias testified that she used to pour water over the head of Elvira González who was standing naked in a basin.[5]

After the Expulsion it was too dangerous to maintain a separate *mikvah* facility, so ritual ablutions were generally performed in a large basin in someone's house. Thus in the early 1500s in Ciudad Real María González seems to have taken over responsibility for the tradition by maintaining a makeshift ritual bath in her home.[6]

It was customary to go to the *mikvah* on the eve of the Sabbath and of major holidays. However, the main function of the ritual bath, according to the laws of *niddah*, which govern almost every aspect of feminine reproductive hygiene, was to cleanse women at the conclusion of their menses and after childbirth. As the rabbis continually asserted, the purpose of ritual immersion was spiritual, not physical cleanliness (*Enc. Jud.* 11:1534). Nonetheless the prescribed bath was such that women emerged physically cleansed. They were required to remove all articles of clothing, rings, and jewelry, so that the water would touch every part of their bodies, and they were required to scrub under their fingernails and toenails.

Ritual bathing in all three of these circumstances—after menses, after childbirth, and before the Sabbath and festivals—appears to have been the norm among the first generation of converts. Inquisition trials of the time make frequent reference to the custom, in language that suggests that everyone thoroughly understood what was involved. Statements such as the prosecutor's assertion that Isabel González "performed *tebilah* as the Jewish women do,"[7] which even incorporates the Hebrew term for the custom, are not uncommon in the period preceding the Expulsion. Moreover, since observance of the laws regarding feminine hygiene and ritual purity and impurity is an essential part of traditional Jewish observance, it is not surprising to see that in simplified form they seem to have persisted among

Judaizing *conversas* for a very long time, both in Spain and Portugal and in their overseas possessions. For example, Luisa Ramírez [Granada 1591] was accused along with several other women of "washing herself every month at the end of her period."[8] Similarly, Ynés de Torres was instructed "to wash her legs when she had her period."[9] Seventeenth-century Majorcan *chueta* women were required to "bathe in a warm solution of wild marjoram, or oregano, and salt" (Braunstein 1936, 105; Selke de Sánchez 1972, 105). Rafaela Enríquez [Mexico 1640s] was accused of bathing with her women friends on holiday eves, "bathing with hot water, and then pouring jars of cold water on each other's backs according to the ceremonies of penance of their law."[10]

## 10.2. Activities Prohibited in an Unclean State

Traditionally the woman who has undergone any sort of menstrual flow is considered impure, or *niddah*, and until she has immersed herself in the *mikvah* she is forbidden to do several things.[11] The prohibition against having carnal relations with her husband derives directly from Leviticus 18:19: "You shall not approach a woman to uncover her nakedness while she is in her menstrual uncleanness." Among knowledgeable crypto-Jews these prohibitions seem to have been practiced both before and long after the Expulsion with little change. Castellana Gencor [Teruel 1485] was accused of not sleeping with her husband during her menses, nor of eating with him at the same table, nor of taking anything from his hand. Before returning to his bed she washed herself with cold water all over.[12] Maria Alfonso de Herrera [Toledo 1501] reported that "when she had her period or had just given birth she drew her bed away from her husband's and did not draw near to him again until she was clean and had washed herself and cut her nails."[13] In 1642 Isabel de Ribera told her Mexican Inquisitors that she had been taught by Juan de León that "when women had their periods they could not go to their husbands, nor eat what they were to eat, nor touch them with their hands, because it was forbidden by the law."[14] In 1647 Simón de León told the Mexican Inquisition that "sometimes he saw that his father and mother drew their beds apart, and did not eat together at noon but rather by themselves, and that this lasted a week or two and then they became friendly again."[15]

The traditional interpretation of these laws extends the state of uncleanness to persons, utensils, clothing, and other items that have come into contact with the impure woman (Leviticus 15:19–30). In addition, both woman in their unclean state and men who have become impure through contact with them are enjoined from fulfilling certain religious duties until they have undergone the purification ritual (Leviticus 15:31). Among the prohibited activities is uttering certain prayers or entering a synagogue. Bernardina de San Juan [Baeza 1572] testified that her mother had taught her that "when her period came she should not pray for eight days nor speak the name of God, because during those days women were unclean until they had washed their entire body."[16] Similarly, Ynés de Torres [Granada 1591] said that she had been instructed that women should not pray when they had their periods.[17] A memorandum of Judaizing customs presented to the Inquisition in Granada in 1593 stated that "when women had their periods they were not to pray nor look at the sky, for it was a sin."[18] Not surprisingly, some later Judaizing new-Christians extended this prohibition to govern attendance at church. Thus Hernando Alonso reportedly told his wife in Mexico in the 1520s that during her menses she should not go to mass "because in your present condition you would profane the Church." She reportedly replied: "These are old ceremonies of the Jews which are not observed now that we have adopted the law of evangelical grace." Alonso said this was a pretext to keep his wife from going out (Liebman 1970, 114).[19] In Majorca Judaizing women in the 1670s were not permitted to eat cooked food during their periods (Selke de Sánchez 1972, 277).

## 10.3. OTHER ASPECTS OF RITUAL PURIFICATION OR PERSONAL HYGIENE

Other aspects of personal hygiene were also governed by Jewish laws and traditions. For both men and women washing the fingers and toes and cutting the nails and hair all received ritual attention. Women's monthly ablutions required that the fingernails and toenails be scrubbed clean. But when it comes to cutting the nails the rules applied to both men and women. According to the Talmud (*Niddah*, 17a; *Mo'ed Qatan*, 18a): "Three things are said with respect to the nails: he who burns them is pious; he who buries them is wise; and he who throws them away is evil." These practices were basic enough to be enumerated in the Edicts of Faith,[20] and were in fact widely observed by crypto-Jews, with very little variation by region or over time. Maria Alfonso de Herrera [Toledo c. 1501] testified that "the night before the Yom Kippur fast she bathed and cut her nails according to ceremony and threw them into the fire."[21] Maria González [Ciudad Real 1511] confessed that once when she was cutting her fingernails a woman asked her why she let her nails fall on the ground rather than gathering them together and making a hole and burying them, because that's what her mother had done."[22] Juana Martínez [Cuenca 1490] used to keep all her nail parings to be buried with her when she died.[23] Inez de Mérida [Ciudad Real 1513] declared that some thirteen years earlier she saw her mother sometimes cut her nails and gather them together and make a hole in the ground and put them there and cover them with earth. At other times she threw them in the fire.[24] The Portuguese Judaizer Diego Juárez de Figueroa [Mexico c. 1647] told Inquisitors that Judaizers "do not cut their nails in the order of their fingers, but rather they cut the first, then the third, then the fifth, and they make tiny pieces of the parings and throw them away."[25] Schwarz reports that among Portuguese Judaizers the custom of burning nail parings has persisted into the twentieth century (Schwarz 1925, 19).[26]

These customs were all practiced widely among crypto-Jews. Other customs having to do with hygiene or ritual purity surface from time to time in the Inquisition records, but their relative rarity indicates either that they were practiced only sporadically, or that they were not identified as typical of Judaizing. For example, in 1541 it was reported to the Lisbon Inquisition that Violante Fernandes "made her husband wash his hands before they enjoyed themselves in bed,"[27] but this is the only reference to the custom that I have found. A more unusual custom is alluded to in a remark recorded in 1524 in the Canary Islands, when Diego de Xerez was heard to say that the Genovese are like Jews because "women in your country do not cut their hair" (Wolf 1926, 30).

# NOTES

1. For pre-Expulsion *mikva'ot* see Millás y Vallicrosa 1965 [Besalú, Gerona]; Torres Balbas 1956 [Zaragoza]; González Simancas 1929 [Toledo].
2. In 1967 I was informed by a local guide that the pool was used by Jewish men to wash their feet before going in to hear mass[!].
3. *Se yuan a vañar en sus tienpos a vna cuenca de Juan de Herrera* (Beinart 1974, 240).
4. "*¿Dónde his a tal ora?,*" *a lo qual respondió: "Calla, no digas nada, que bamos al baño donde se faze la tibulá," y estubieron allá por espacio de una ora, poco más o menos* (Carrete Parrondo 1986, 50).
5. *Por su mandado la echó del agua encima de la cabeza, estando ella desnuda, en una bacina puesta* (Carrete Parrondo 1986, 42).
6. Beinart 1977a, 274, 385. See my Chapter 12, note 11. For additional details for Ciudad Real see Beinart 1974, 24; 1977a, 294.
7. *Fiso la tebila como fasen las judias* (Beinart 1974, 239). For other examples see Beinart 1974, 243; Fita y Colomé 1883, 299.
8. *Labarse al cavo de cada mes quando se le quitava su rregla* (Bel Bravo 1988, 114). For this epoch see also García Fuentes 1981, 435, 470.
9. *Que quando les acudiese el mes se hauian de labar las piernas* (Bel Bravo 1988, 140).
10. *Haciendo sus baños con agua caliente y echándose unas a otras, por las espaldas, algunos jarros de agua fría, por ceremonia y penitencia de su ley* (García 1910, 249).
11. The rules regarding impurity after childbirth derive from Leviticus 12:1–8 and were discussed in Chapter 7.
12. *No dormian en uno y se tevilaban . . . echandose agua fria por somo* (Sánchez Moya 1972, 136).
13. *Quando estava con my flor o estava parida apartava cama de my marido e no me llegava a el fasta que estava linpia e me banava e cortava las unas* (Levine 1982, 195). For a similar example from 1593 see García Fuentes 1981, 435.
14. *Cuando las mujeres estaban en su regla no habían de llegar a sus maridos ni comer de lo que él había de comer ni poner la mano en ellos, porque era prohibido en la ley* (Lewin 1977, 32; cf. 48).

15. *Algunas veçes veia que su padre y su madre apartaban camas, y no comian a mediodia juntos, sino de por si, y duraba esto vna semana y dos, y luego se volvia a amistar* (Nunemaker 1946, 25).

16. *Cuando le bajase su costumbre, no rezase en ocho días ni mentase a Dios, porque en aquellos días estaban sucias las mujeres hasta que se lavasen todo el cuerpo* (Gracia Boix 1983, 133).

17. *Que quando les acudiese el mes . . . no hauian de rezar* (Bel Bravo 1988, 140).

18. *La muger con su regla ni abia de reçar ni mirar al cielo porque era pecado* (García Fuentes 1981, 435).

19. For other examples see Uchmany 1977, 106; Conway 1928, 22. Edicts of Faith from Lima, Peru (and from Cartagena, Colombia in 1610; see Medina 1899b, 26) also identify as Judaizers women who refrain from entering churches for forty days after giving birth (*guardase cuarenta días después de parida, sin entrar en el templo*). For Lewin this is a classic case of religious hybridism 1946, 28.

20. An Edict of Faith from Cartagena, Colombia, in 1610 lists "cutting the nails and trimming the hair, and preserving or burning the cuttings" (*cortándose las uñas y las puntas de los cabellos, guardándolas o quemándolas*) (Medina 1899b, 26).

21. *La noche antes de ayuno mayor me bañava e cortava las uñas por cerimonya e las echava en el fuego* (Levine 1982, 195).

22. *Vio como este confesante se cortaba vn dia las vñas de las manos. E dixo a este confesante por señas la dicha Galana que para que dexaba caher las vñas en el suelo, que las allegase e cogiese e hiziese vn hoyo e las enterrase, que asi lo hasia la dicha su madre* (Beinart 1977a, 258).

23. *Las vñas que cortava guardávalas todas, disiendo que las quería para echar en su sepultura* (Carrete Parrondo 1985b, 97).

24. *Vio esta confesante algunas vezes cortarse las vñas [a] la dicha su madre, e juntarlas e hazer vn huyo en el suelo e meterla alli e cobrirlas con tierra, e otras vezes las hechaba en el fuego* (Beinart 1981b, 361).

25. *Las uñas no las cortan como se siguen los dedos, sino desde el primero al tercero, y de éste al quinto, y las hacen menudos pedazos y las arrojan* (García 1910, 102).

26. For additional sixteenth- and seventeenth-century examples see Beinart 1981a, 301; cf. Liebman 1975, 105; 1970, 73, 96; Lewin 1971, 497. For an eighteenth-century example see Lewin 1939, 25.

27. *Fazia lavar as mãos ao marido antes de se deitar na cama* (Baião 1921, 126). Washing the hands after sexual intercourse is required by traditional Judaism (*Enc. Jud.* 12:999 cites *Shulḥan Arukh* OH 4:18).

# CHAPTER XI

# Death and Funeral Customs

The mystery and inevitability of death exerted a powerful conservative influence over *conversos*. Those who were now sincere Christians prepared themselves to die according to Christian ritual. But many others, those who vacillated in belief or maintained a proclivity toward Judaism, at the time of their own death or faced with the death of a loved one sought consolation in their ancestral religion. For the Judaizer it was just as important not to die as a Christian as it was to die a Jew: thus Judaizers routinely refused Catholic last rites or washed off the chrism that the priest had applied. The many Jewish customs associated with death and mourning are visibly different from Christian practice and so drew special attention from the Inquisition. Every Edict of Faith listed these customs in detail. Here, for example, is a typical compendium of customs from the text of a Mexican *Edicto de fe* dated 1639:

> If when some person is at the point of death, he turns to the wall to await death and then [the corpse] is washed with warm water, shaving the beard and under the arms and other parts of the body, and attiring it with clean linen, under drawers, and shirt and cover, which is folded over the top, and putting a pillow with virgin soil under the head, or money in the mouth, or a misshapen pearl or some other thing. Or singing some funeral dirge or throwing out the water from the large jars and emptying all the containers with water in the house of the deceased and all other houses of the area as a Jewish custom; eating fish and olives on the floor behind the doors; not meat because of sorrow of their loss; not leaving the house for one year in accordance with the observance of the laws. Or if they are buried in virgin soil or in a Jewish cemetery. (Liebman 1970, 97)

All these death-related customs and many others appear routinely in testimony before the Inquisition.[1]

## 11.1. Dying

No matter under what religious flag *conversos* sailed during their lifetimes, when they neared the harbor of death their true, and often earliest, beliefs came to the fore. For some *conversos* the deathbed reaffirmation of Judaism assured their place in the continuum of ancestral tradition. For others, particularly those who had accepted the Christian concept of an afterlife whose entry ticket was fervent belief, it offered the hope of Jewish "salvation." Thus it was not uncommon to see a flurry of Judaizing activity around the deathbed of even the most assimilationist *conversos*, even though the practice of Jewish funeral rites exposed the surviving family members to possible detection and destruction. Moreover, along with the reaffirmation of Jewish practices at the deathbed there was likely to be a heightened rejection of anything that smacked of Christianity.

For this reason we often find that dying Judaizers rejected Christian images, clerical consolation, or the Catholic last rites. Many Judaizers from Teruel in the early sixteenth century would wash off the chrism before they died (Sánchez Moya/ Monasterio Aspiri 1972, 114; cf. 137, 139). When Manuel González died [Guadalajara 1492] he allegedly ordered that no Christian attend him and that no cross be brought anywhere near him.[2] When Ana Rodriguez was dying [Bahia c. 1590], her daughters importuned her to accept a crucifix, but she cried "Take it away, take it away." Her daughter Beatriz Antunes said to her: "Mother, don't dishonor us, for we are married to men who are noble old-Christians." But still her mother would not do it.[3] Isabel de Rivera [Mexico 1646] testified that when her father was dying "she and her mother and sisters tried to prevent his being given the holy sacraments. But when he had received the eucharist, she drew near him and said: 'Look, sir, this is nothing.' And he replied: 'Yes, daughter, I know.' "[4] The avoidance of last rites was such a diagnostic characteristic of crypto-Judaism that some churches were alerted to look for special signs. In 1672 in Majorca parishes were warned how Judaizers "let the parish churches know [only] after they have already died, pretending to be very concerned and urging the Parish priests to hurry up . . . and when they get to the house with the Holy Sacrament they tell them . . . that they did not get there in time, because just a moment earlier the person had croaked."[5] This aversion is taken to its extreme in a twentieth-century Portuguese legend which alleges that when new-Christians are certain a dying relative will not recover they asphyxiate him rather than let the priest come to administer last rites.[6]

When faced with the imminent death of a loved one, it is human nature for family and friends to want to engage in leave-taking activities. For practicing Jews, spending time with the sick or dying fulfills the traditional halakhic requirement to visit the sick (*bikur holim*). For people who believed in a benevolent, interventionist God, prayer for the recovery, comfort, or easy passage of the dying was a natural deathbed activity. Prior to the Expulsion, in religiously divided families Judaizing new-Christians would frequently attend the deathbeds of their Jewish relatives. When the Jewess Doña Sol was dying around 1453 her *conversa* daughter Clara Escobar went to her home to attend her. Clara was present at her death and participated in all the funeral ceremonies (Marín Padilla 1983b, 292). Similarly, at the point of death some new-Christians preferred to be comforted by Jews. A 1449 anti-*converso* tract even accused the converts of "reconciling themselves at the time of their death with learned rabbis and Jews who were learned in their Law."[7] In 1489 in Calatayud Rabbi Solomon Axequo testified that around 1472 the *converso* Pablo de Daroca was near death and summoned him to his bedside. Pablo asked him for "a little Jewish confessional book called the *bidduy* in which the Jews pray when they are about to die," which the rabbi explained to the Inquisitors was part of the Yom Kippur prayer book. Pablo prayed from it, did not die, and then kept the book.[8]

After the Expulsion the most common practice was for active Judaizers to try to help their coreligionists to die a Jewish death. Some new-Christians seem even to have made it their special mission to attend to the dying. Santa María mentions the case of a certain *converso* in 1484 "who insinuated himself to console and confess in the Jewish fashion the sick who are near death."[9] In later years some new-Christians made a business of providing shrouds to the crypto-Jewish community. This seems to have been the case of the Portuguese Manuel Alvarez de Arellano, reconciled in Mexico in 1647, who served the colony as the *converso* mortician. Alvarez traveled back and forth from Spain, importing, among other things, shroud linen from Rouen (Liebman 1964, 103; Liebman 1975, 41). A similar situation prevailed in the Balearic Islands, where an indictment against *converso* customs delivered to the Majorcan Inquisition in 1667 reports that the community had "a man to prepare the shrouds for the men, and a woman for the women."[10] Sometimes the Judaizing intent of these deathbed visits was evidenced by everyone's studied avoidance of Christian prayers. Leonor de San Juan [Baeza 1572] declared that "she suspected that her mother did not die a Christian because she had begun to recite the prayer of San Josep."[11] Ana Pérez [Las Palmas 1625] testified that five years previous, when Polonia Gonçalez was dying, since no priest was at hand Catalina Domínguez "came to the sick person and by way of helping her to die, exhorted her to call upon King Gideon. And the deponent seeing that no mention was made of Jesus Christ or his mother, or the Saints, as is customary at such times, was amazed" (Wolf 1926, 119). Some remnant Portuguese *cristãos novos* appear to have cast their deathbed prayers in the Christian mold. In 1952 Machado reported that when someone is dying and is in great pain new-Christian villagers in the Mogadouro region of Portugal pray novenas for them: that is, nine people pray three times a day for nine days (Machado 1952, 41).

One of the most common and most persistent death-related customs is for family or friends to turn the dying person's face toward the wall.[12] The custom appears to derive from 2 Kings 20:2, which recounts how when Hezekiah was dying he "turned his face to the wall, and prayed to the Lord," who then healed him. A 1639 Mexican Edict of Grace considers as a sign of Judaizing that "when some person is at the point of death, he turns to the wall to await death" (Liebman 1970, 97), and many Judaizers, such as Clara Rodríguez [Yepes 1643], were accused of turning their sick spouse's face toward the wall before death.[13] In some places this custom persisted even after its original intent had been transformed. Bernardina de San Juan's mother [Baeza 1572] taught her that "when someone was about to die you should turn their face toward the East so that they suffer less."[14]

According to custom, when a Jew dies the body must not be left unattended from the moment of death until the burial (*Enc. Jud.* 5:1426). When Pedro Veles, of Almazán, died in 1505, Teresa Sancho "stayed alone with him . . . and a lamp was burning at the head of the bed."[15] When her mother-in-law died in Mexico around 1630 Isabel Núñez stayed awake all night to maintain a vigil over the corpse. According to Liebman, "such a vigil is mandatory because of the possibility that actual death may not have occurred" (Liebman 1970, 245).

## 11.2. Preparation of the Corpse

Traditional Jewish law dictates the way in which a corpse must be prepared for burial, prescribing that specific attention be given to cleansing and enshrouding the body of the deceased. For example, the gloss to *Shulḥan Arukh* (YD 352:4) commands that when someone dies "they cut his nails," and this was widely practiced by Judaizers from pre-Expulsion times right up to the present. Ana Fernandes was accused by the Coimbra Inquisition in 1573 "that when someone died they enshrouded him in the Jewish fashion, and washed his body with hot water and trimmed the nails of his feet and hands and cut the hair on his head."[16] The *Mishnah Torah* (Maim., Yad. XIV,4,iv,1) and the *Shulḥan Arukh* (YD 352:4) also command that "they cut his hair." These were normative practices among medieval Iberian Jews, and an early compendium of Judaizing customs says that when a Judaizer dies "they wash him with hot water, shaving his beard and underarms and other parts of the body."[17] A century and a half later, according to a 1651 deposition before the Mexican Inquisition, when Fray Juan de Segueta was about to die he wanted to make certain that his corpse would be properly prepared: "he called an Indian barber to shave his underarms, beard, and other private places of his body, which was done. And he requested to be dressed in clean clothes to die."[18]

The ancient practice of cleansing the body of the deceased is called in Hebrew *tohorah* (*Enc. Jud.* 15:1188–9). It derives from the belief that "when the soul departs from the body, it beholds the Divine Countenance. It is therefore proper to cleanse and wash the body thoroughly before it faces its Maker."[19] It is also related to Eccl. 5:15, "as he came, so shall he go," which is interpreted to mean that since babies are washed when they are born, so too shall they be washed when they die (*Enc. Jud.* 15:1189). Catalina de Torres said in 1489 that when Juana López's father-in-law died Juana "ordered her to put some water on to heat and throw barley in it; and when the water was hot they had some boards and a kneading trough (*artesa*) brought, and they poured it in there and bathed him."[20] The need to wash the dead could be acutely felt by the dying themselves. Luis de Carvajal's father [Mexico 1589] allegedly said to Luis as he was dying, "Son, wash my body so that I won't go dirty into the grave."[21] For the survivors the injunction was even stronger. Catalina de Rivera [Mexico 1642] thought it proper to wash the Judaizer's corpse and hair (Lewin 1977, 47). The primary responsibility fell to the deceased's family.[22] María de Zúñiga [Mexico 1642] described in detail how the Portuguese new-Christian couple Gaspar Suárez and Rafaela Enríquez cleaned the corpse of their deceased two-year-old son Enriquillo: "They put him on top of a buffet and they took off his clothes. Then a Mulatta woman named María de la Concepción, who lives in the same house, brought hot water and a cloth and began to wash off the child, and cleaned him thoroughly, from top to bottom with the cloth. And I asked her why she was washing a thing which the earth was going to swallow up, and at that point she stopped washing him."[23] While the deceased was generally washed by his or her relatives at home, the washing evidently served as an occasion for the Mexican crypto-Jewish community to come together, for Margarita de Rivera [1646] was accused of being "extremely ceremonious, and always being present at the enshrouding of Jews and Jewesses, and at the washing of their bodies."[24] Moreover, the *Mishnah Torah* (Maim., *Yad.* XIV,4,iv,1) requires that a body be rubbed "with divers spices." In accordance with this precept, Brianda Lopes [Lisbon 1543] testified that when Isabel Fernandes's daughter died she washed her body with herbs (Baião 1921, 139). In the mid-seventeenth century the Portuguese Antón Rodríguez, of Tembleque, was accused of washing his deceased wife's body in wine (Blázquez Miguel 1986a, 79). In Majorca in the 1670s the bodies of deceased Judaizers were washed with water and anointed with oil (Cortes 1985, 290). Prior to the washing all the windows of the house were closed.[25] It also seems to be the case, as these examples confirm, that in the Iberian world it was normally the women's task to wash the corpse (Levine 1982, 203).[26] All these customs were common among early Judaizing *conversos* throughout Spain,[27] Portugal, and the Iberian possessions, and most of them persisted for as long as there were crypto-Jews.

The remnant crypto-Jews of Portugal have preserved many of these traditions. In Belmonte when someone dies the family fetches water in an earthenware pitcher from the nearest fountain to wash the corpse (Paulo 1970, 145). The Portuguese new-Christians wash out the mouth of the deceased so that "the devil won't come to take hold of the soul and carry it to hell."[28] Vasconcelos transcribes this modern Portuguese prayer recited while washing the body of the deceased: "Wash this soul, Lord, / with the water of salvation; / free it from sin, / give it Your divine blessing. / Humble and repentant, / he asks the Lord for forgiveness."[29]

Traditional Jewish law is also quite specific about the way in which a corpse must be clothed in preparation for burial. For example, the *Mishnah Torah* (Maim., Yad. XIV,4,iv,1) requires that "they cover the face of the dead in order not to shame the poor whose faces have turned livid as a result of undernourishment." To cite a late example, in seventeenth-century Galicia the servant Blanca Oliveira said that "when her master died, her mistress and other Portuguese new-Christian women prepared him for burial by putting rings on his fingers and a very valuable knitted linen handkerchief over his face."[30] Frequently the corpse's head was covered with some sort of cowl. Around the time of the Expulsion this was referred to ironically as a *sambenito*, from the name of the garment the Inquisition required certain penitents to wear. Juana López [Garcimuñoz 1489] was accused of "washing the dead, shrouding them and putting a *sambenitillo* over the shroud." When her father-in-law died "they laid him out on some boards and put a shroud over his long *sant benitillo*."[31] Sometimes, in fact, witnesses described without any sense of irony the crypto-Jewish burial garments in terms of the habits of Christian religious orders. A new-Christian in Bahia around 1591, for example, was said to have been buried in the Jewish fashion with a cloak of the order of Saint Francis (Lipiner 1969, 170, 176). When Mexican Judaizers died, Leonor Núñez [burned in the *auto de fe* of 1649] "enshrouded them according to the Jewish rites and ceremonies and would have them wear the habit of Carmen because it [the Order of Carmen] was of the patriarchs and prophets" (Liebman 1974, 144). Similarly, Blanca Enríquez [Mexico 1648] ordered a Judaizing seamstress to put the necessary pleats into her mother's shroud, which had been sewn from Rouen cloth to look like the albs that the Catholic priests wear.[32] It is always possible that these descriptions are merely the result of Catholic witnesses or scribes looking for an appropriate metaphor to describe crypto-Jewish mortuary dress. On the other hand, it may be that some crypto-Jews used an outer Catholic religious habit to conceal an inner shrouding in the Jewish fashion. This seems to have been the case for María de Zúñiga [Mexico 1642], whose testimony about washing her son's body was cited above. She went on to say that to enshroud him "they heated up a clean shirt and heated and perfumed it over a brazier and they dressed the child in it. And then the wife of Gaspar Suárez . . . said that they should go to her house and bring something to enshroud the child. They brought a whole piece of new linen, and another piece of new yellow baize cloth and they enshrouded him with it, wrapping his body. And over it they put a black habit of Saint Nicholas [decorated] with stars of gold and silver."[33]

It seems to have been universally customary for Judaizers to enshroud the corpse in brand-new linen. The use of pure linen derives from Lev. 19:19. Linen is holy because it was used in the coverings for the Tabernacle (Ex. 26:1, 31, 36; 27:9, 16) and for the vestments of the priests (Ex. 28:15; 39:27–9; Lev. 16:4). According to Sperling, the *Maaver Yaabok* says that linen is used because "flax, the plant from which linen is derived, grows during the season of the early rains and is symbolic of the Tree of Life" (Sperling 1968, 293). To guard against unseemly ostentation at the time of death, the *Mishnah Torah* (Maim., Yad. XIV,4,iv,1) requires that the body be dressed "in an inexpensive shroud sewed with white linen thread." An early description of crypto-Jewish customs, for example, stated that they prepared their dead by wrapping them "in shrouds of new linen, with breeches, a clean shirt, and a pleated cape."[34] The custom was widely adhered to. Isabel Rodrigues [Evora 1571] was accused in part because she allegedly wrapped a deceased relative in "a new linen shroud and shirt and other articles of new clothing that had never been washed."[35] In the same vein Catalina de Rivera [Mexico 1642] testified that when someone dies they should be wrapped in new linen with all the trimmed-off parts tucked in with him, so that nothing would be sticking out when they buried him.[36] In Spain *conversas* sometimes expressed a preference for a homespun shroud. For example Bernardina de San Juan [Baeza 1572] was of the opinion that when someone died the "shroud should be of homemade linen."[37] In the Americas commercially woven shrouds from Rouen were preferred perhaps, according to Liebman, because "there were several Jewish-owned factories in Rouen manufacturing this linen." After 1620 linen from Holland was also prized.[38] Special consideration seems to have been given to using the entire piece of linen without cutting or tailoring it. Thus Beatris Antennas [Bahia 1592] declared that when someone in her house died "she enshrouded them in a full-sized *lançol*, without removing any strip or piece of cloth from it no matter how big it was, and fastening the shroud only with ties, so as not to sew it with a needle."[39]

Generally before being shrouded the corpse was dressed in good clothes, often made of linen. The traditionally preferred color was white, which the *Shulḥan Arukh* (YD 352:2) links to Eccl. 9:8. As late as the 1720s some *conversos* were recorded as going to great lengths to ensure that their burial garments were of this color. When she was dying Isabel Fernández, of Tembleque (Toledo), even made her husband get her a Dominican monk's habit from Madridejos because it would both meet the requirement for white and ironically dissemble her commitment to crypto-Judaizing (Caro Baroja 1961, 3:126). However, on the whole the quality of the clothing seems to have been more important than its color. Thus the *conversa* Beatriz Núñez [Guadalupe 1485] was accused of dressing the corpse of Diego González with "his trousers and cape the way she knew they did in Ciudad Real."[40] According to testimony in the trial of Inés López [Ciudad Real 1511], "when they dug up certain converts from the cemetery of Saint Francis in this city to see if they had been buried as Jews . . . they found them dressed like Jews with bloomers and shirts and stockings and other Jewish items of clothing; and not one of them had a cross."[41] Catharina Sanbrana [Lisbon 1543] dressed the corpse of her daughter with "a golden hair net and a napkin with a golden fringe, and a braid with a red ribbon and a finely woven dress."[42] While dressing corpses in good clothes seems to have been nearly universally practiced among sixteenth-century Judaizing *conversos*, these customs are mentioned rarely in the later documents.[43]

The requirement to tie up the jaws of the deceased (*Shulḥan Arukh* YD 352:4) sometimes led to the use of a chin strap. For example, around 1489 in Aragon a niece of the *conversa* Violante Matheu was buried in "linen stockings which came up a little above the knee and a shroud and a chin strap."[44] When the *converso* Berenguer de Torrellas died in Aragon in the 1480s a woman "made him some linen stockings and fixed a hair net on him and covered his face with a cloth and with certain bandages bandaged his eyes and mouth the way the Jews do their deceased."[45]

Again, there are several very common Jewish traditions related to clothing the corpse which do *not* appear in the documents pertaining to *conversos*. Among these customs are pouring nine measures of water over the body; after attending the body washing the hands with salted water; and burying a deceased male in the *tallit* he used during his lifetime (*Enc. Jud.* 15:1188–9; 4:1519). Either these were not current among Jews in Iberia or they did not make the transition to the new-Christian environment.

Many religions consider death to be a literal journey from this world to an afterworld that is outside time or space but somehow still at a physical distance from the world of the living. This view is not as dominant in Judaism as it is in other eastern Mediterranean religions or in Christianity, all of which give importance to an Underworld, or Hades, or Hell to which the souls (or spirits, or bodies) of the deceased travel after death. Nonetheless Biblical Judaism speaks of a realm of the dead, or *she'ol* (Isa. 14:9–12; Ezek. 32:17–32, etc.), and Talmudic, Midrashic, and Rabbinical debates seek to understand its nature. Deut. 26:14 hints at the custom of placing food offerings in the coffin or the grave, but evidently this practice was not common in post-Biblical times (*Enc. Jud.* 4:1519), and on the whole there is little scriptural or traditional Jewish justification for putting articles into the tomb to accompany the deceased on his or her journey to the afterworld. Iberian Jews and *conversos*, however, commonly sought to ease the journey of the deceased with offerings of food and money, so that grave offerings appear with great frequency in documents that detail *converso* burial customs.

Among crypto-Jews the custom seems to have varied little over the centuries. In a 1490 trial it was reported that a witness asked the deceased's daughter "to give him a silver *quartillo* which he put in the dead man's hand, saying to him: 'take this to pay for your first lodging.' "[46] When Alfonso Díaz died in 1509, Catalina González put a coin and a candle in the sleeve of his shroud (Blázquez Miguel 1987, 55). When Francisco Rodríguez de Matos died in Mexico in the early seventeenth century his family put a gold coin under his body (Liebman 1970, 82). The testimony of Diego Juárez de Figueroa [Mexico 1647] suggests the reason for this unusual placement of the coin. He said that when a Judaizer dies "from fear of the

Inquisition they put into his rectum the gold that they would normally put in his mouth and ears."[47] In early twentieth-century Portugal *cristãos novos* sometimes put a coin in the corpse's mouth and a second coin and a piece of bread in the coffin (Paulo 1970, 145). Others passed a gold or silver coin across the mouth of the deceased and then offered it to a poor person (Schwarz 1925, 37; cf. Paulo 1970, 28, 145). Then this prayer was recited three times:

> You'll go to the valley of Jehosephat / and find a lion there;
> if he asks you for meat, give him bread;
> if he asks you for a sign, give him money;
> if he inquires which Law is yours, / tell him the Law of Moses.
> May he let you pass by / freely and untrammeled
> where God allows, / where God orders.
> If he asks you who made you, / tell him it was a Jewish woman
> who brought you into this world;
> may he do to you what he knows how,
> and not do to you what he should.[48]

Often, instead of money, seed pearls, or misshapen pearls, were placed in the coffin. The custom is mentioned in the earliest compendium of crypto-Jewish customs[49] and appears frequently thereafter on both sides of the Atlantic. Blanca de Villanueva, of Quintanar del Rey [Cuenca 1490s], used to put into the deceased's mouth a seed pearl followed by a drop of milk squeezed from her breast (Blázquez Miguel 1986a, 69). In Bahia in the 1590s it was even reported that Ana Rodriguez was saving the jewels from her wedding so that she could be buried in them when she died.[50] Gabriel Granada [Mexico 1642] said that when Diego Antunes died his grandmother "ordered him to go to her house and ask Doña Catalina de Rivera, his aunt, for some grains of seed pearls, and he went to her house to ask for them in the name of his grandmother, and the said Doña Catalina gave him wrapped up in a piece of paper, two or three small pearls, which this confessant took and gave to the said Doña Isabel Duarte, and . . . he has heard it said that when some observer of the law dies, they put gold or pearls in his mouth to be interred with him."[51] The same year Rafaela Enríquez reported a similar experience when Blanca Enríquez was dying. "When she was near death she sat up in bed and had a little Michoacán bull brought to her. Opening it with her own hand, she took out a string of pearls whose ends were finished with gold. And taking it by one of the ends she handed it to one of her daughters—the witness did not remember which one—telling her to keep it to put it into her mouth when she died. And after she died it was placed in her mouth—though she does not remember by whom."[52] Many other examples could be cited.

Since many new-Christians visualized the loved one's departure for the afterlife as a literal journey, they took care to provision the traveler. In Castile in the 1490s *conversos* put a piece of bread and a coin in the deceased's mouth "so that he would rest there in peace and not travel in poverty because of some debt."[53] When Alfonso Díaz died in 1509, Catalina González opened his mouth with her fingers and put a grain of coral and a hazelnut in it (Blázquez Miguel 1987, 55). Testimony from Ciudad Real in 1511 indicates that "when Doctor Tomás de Cuenca came to this city he had certain dead people dug up.... They say that they found jugs of water with them."[54] Catalina Muñoz added that when *converso* graves were opened "they found one of them buried with a piece of cheese as big as a fist."[55] Blázquez Miguel reports the Castilian custom of putting drops of mother's milk in the coffin, especially for a deceased infant (1985b, 58; 1986a, 69).

The documents occasionally refer to other items buried with the deceased. The most curious may be a Mexican case from the 1640s. When Blanca Enríquez died in Mexico in 1642, according to Catalina de Rivera, Pedro de Espinosa took a paper full of her teeth and threw it into her tomb, which was in the Carmen Convent.[56] Liebman thinks these may have been a set of false teeth (1974, 194; 1970, 268), but Enríquez's daughter later testified that before dying her mother had told her "to take from her little desk the teeth and molars that had fallen out, or been pulled out, while she was alive, and to put them into her grave with her."[57] One item that did *not* accompany Judaizers into the grave was the crucifix, and the Inquisition considered the absence of crucifixes a sure indication of Judaizing. Catalina Ruiz told Inquisitors in Ciudad Real in 1511 that "when they dug up certain *conversos* from the burial ground of San Francisco in Ciudad Real to see if they had been buried as Jews . . . they found them with pleated pants and shirts and shoes and many other Jewish clothes and none of them had a crucifix."[58]

## 11.3. FUNERALS

The actual funeral services in traditional Judaism are relatively simple affairs. The coffin is brought on the shoulders of the pallbearers into the cemetery prayer hall. The prayer *Zidduk ha-Din* (acknowledgment of the Divine judgment) or Psalm 16 is recited. As the body is being lowered into the grave Psalm 91 is recited while the attendees pray for peace for the deceased. The traditional prayer *Kaddish* (see Chapter 15.4) is recited. Contemporary Jewish funerals outside Iberia, such as the Italian Jewish funeral described by Juan de León in prison in Mexico in 1645, follow this same pattern. According to León, when a Jew dies "they take him to our synagogue, and there men and women sing over him."[59] León adds picturesque details about the funeral procession. "If while we are taking him to be buried we should pass one of those deceivers who is not of our Law [a priest], the body is returned home and we wait three days before taking it to the place where we have to take it, because it is an omen of fortune among us, and we consider it a bad sign."⁶⁰

The documents dealing with post-1480 *converso* customs do not describe their funeral services in any great detail. Observing Jewish custom at public funerals was suicidal, and even private funerals could be dangerous in that death attracted attention and might heighten the scrutiny of neighbors alert for Judaizing. Nonetheless one occasionally finds indications that Judaizers tried to preserve some semblance of Jewish ritual. As with other social occasions, prior to the Expulsion Jews and new-Christians often mingled at funeral services. The Jew Acat Abcacar described in 1488 in Calatayud how the *conversas* Sol and Clara Escobar attended a Jewish burial in which after the body was laid in the grave they touched the coffin and said "May God pardon him."⁶¹ And a late fifteenth-century satiric poem by Alfonso Alvarez on the death of the *converso* Alfonso Ferrandes alleges that Ferrandes wanted to be attended by a *shamas* to pray from the Torah for him and to sing him a hymn and a lament in sorrowful meter. Ferrandes also reputedly left his winding sheet to a Jew as a sign of righteous charity so that he would pray for him in his grave.⁶² Often a number of people—perhaps the ritual *minyan* of ten adult men—were in attendance. In funerals of the first post-Expulsion generation prayers might be recited in Hebrew. In 1527, when Juan de Silva died in Atienza, his old-Christian in-laws and the entire *converso* community gathered in two upstairs rooms of his house. The old-Christians went downstairs to watch the door, perhaps against thieves. Juan Rodríguez delivered a eulogy extolling Silva's Jewish life and praising the Law of Moses. He prayed in Hebrew, which the young people did not understand, while the older people chanted the responses. The men had their heads covered. They closed by singing some Spanish *guayas*.⁶³ Elena de Silva [Mexico 1642] reported attending a funeral at a person's home where she found thirteen persons "and the defunct was in the middle of the parlor covered with a new cloth and she who went to condole noticing it asked those present why they had put a covering over the defunct for she had remained beautiful and with her natural features. . . . [Someone] answered it is because we put a little gold in her mouth and that if she should empty it that they could not see it" (Adler 1899, 82).

It is likely that *conversos* on both sides of the Atlantic attempted to follow the Jewish custom of burying the deceased person as quickly as possible. When Leonor Váez Sevilla died in Mexico sometime prior to 1649, her mother pointed out that one "whom they bury on the same day may not be placed in a coffin as is done on other days." Moreover, because she died on Friday, she had to be buried before the start of the Sabbath. Her mother said that "she had become an angel by virtue of her death especially since she had died on Friday, which is a day of veneration in their law" (Liebman 1974, 221).

At Jewish funerals the Aramaic prayer *Kaddish* is recited after the grave is closed with earth (*Shulḥan Arukh* YD 376:4). By reciting this prayer of praise to God, "the mourner acknowledges submission to God's judgment and the acceptance of His justice" (Sperling 1968, 297–8). Also common were prayers that wished the departed peace, or a good fate, or a good afterlife. The documents contain numerous references to the funeral *Kaddish* and sporadic references to other prayers recited at or after crypto-Jewish funerals.[64] In Aragon in the late fifteenth century it was common for *conversos* to say over the graves of their departed Jewish or Judaizing relatives, "May God pardon him in his Law."[65] María de Villalpando [Soria 1501] accused Guiomar López of wishing her deceased father well by saying: "'May God have my father in Paradise,' or 'a good fate,' one of those. And her father died a Jew."[66] A few of these funeral prayers remain among Portuguese *cristãos novos* of this century, such as this one sung as the coffin is being carried out of the house: "May the Guardian Angel protect you! May the Guardian Angel guide you! May the Angel Saint Raphael pray to the Lord for you."[67] Some modern Portuguese *Cristãos-novos* on entering a cemetery recite: "May God save you who passes by, / you once were living, just as we; / we will become just as you. / There in heaven where you are / pray to the Lord on our behalf, / for in this vale of tears / we will pray to the Lord for you."[68]

More common in the documents are references to the surviving members of the family accepting the obligation to continue praying for the souls of their departed long after the actual funeral. Prior to the Expulsion crypto-Jews might even contract with openly practicing Jews to recite the *Kaddish* in their stead for their departed relatives or even for themselves. For example, Blanca Fernández [Garcimuñoz], shortly before she died in 1475, "sent two bushels of wheat to the Jewish rabbi (çofar) of Huete to say some prayers for her soul."[69] Similarly the *converso* Joan López Coscolla [Calatayud 1489] gave the Jew Asser Advendavit money to go to his mother's grave to "say a prayer in Hebrew."[70] It is often difficult to tell whether these *conversos* were electing a way to fulfill their obligation with minimal risk, or whether they had decided that it was more proper for a Jew than for a convert to say *Kaddish* for relatives who had died as Jews. But occasionally the issue was broached directly. The *converso* Pedro de Guadalajara accepted the obligation to recite *Kaddish* and continue to pray for his parents who had died as Jews, and in 1505 he answered Inquisitors' objections to this practice by saying, "What is done well is never lost and may do some good."[71] But even well after the Expulsion many *conversos* continued to recite the *Kaddish* for relatives who had also been *conversos* at the time of their death. Emigrated Jews still said *Kaddish* for *converso* relatives who had died and were buried in Spain. The legitimacy of this custom was debated with some heat, but most rabbis, such as Rabbi David HaKohen of Patras, Greece, who wrote early in the sixteenth century, said that it was proper for Jews who had escaped from Spain to recite *Kaddish* for their parents who had died as *converso* apostates.[72] As with many *converso* rituals, this one evolved over the centuries as the traditional prayers were forgotten and *conversos* composed others to take their place. One of the most complete prayers was preserved in the Mexican archives when in 1642 Rafael de Granada recalled for Inquisitors—in somewhat garbled fashion—a mourning prayer his mother María de Rivera had taught him, which was to be recited during the Wednesday fasts for the souls of the departed:

> Serene abode of pleasure,
> high abode,
> underneath the wing of the divinity
> as one of the saints
> Like a light of the heavens
> You shine and clarify
> the flight of bones.
> Pardon for sins,
> accommodation of the rebellious,
> Mercy, Clemency,
> Good reward
> For the world to come
> has departed the soul
> of So and So,
> who departed this world
> having lived very few years.
> By the will of He who dwells in the heavens,
> King of kings,
> shelter his soul
> and honor him
> beyond his delight
> as in a high orchard
> as in a spring of water
> for Your waters are never lacking.
> May the soul of So and So
> come within your grasp,
> accompanying
> those who sleep in Hebron
> with David, with Solomon
> and with all the prophets of the Lord,
> and may the soul of So and So
> be tied to you with a ring,

> with the dead of the dead
> of Our Dead. Amen.⁷³

More traditional prayers for the dead have been preserved among Portuguese *cristãos novos* of this century, such as these from the region of Belmonte:

> God of Abraham, take this soul into you holy hands. Amen.
>
> Oh the most exalted God of Jacob, which is the name of the Lord, this is said and done for the soul of ——, who departed this world on the holy night of [*capaz*] so that his sins be reckoned, and before God they all be forgiven. Amen.⁷⁴

This modern Portuguese prayer blesses the meal that the family and friends take eight days after the funeral:

> May the Lord of heaven be eternally blessed, for He gives us so many gifts, and in our time we have so many troubles; we accept with good grace the sustenance which we eat, the grace with which we are served after this death, amen. Let us sing in great victory: "O, Lord, take this soul to Your divine glory."⁷⁵

One of the principal differences between Jewish and Christian burial customs in the Middle Ages was that Christians practiced double inhumation: that is, they generally buried a body a first time until it had completely decomposed and then dug it up to bury the bones a second time in a permanent resting place. Often a body would initially be placed in a communal pit and the bones later removed to a final resting place that might also be communal. Acceptable Christian burial sites included the churchyard, the church floor, or stone crypts within the church or church grounds. To Jews all these practices, particularly the practice of secondary burial, were abhorrent. Reburial received special condemnation in the codified laws of the *Shulḥan Arukh*. YD 362:4 commands that Jews "not place two coffins one above the other," and 363:1 states that "one should not remove a corpse and bones from a dignified grave to [another] dignified grave." The *conversa* Graçia [Sigüenza 1501] gave voice to this repugnance when she said that "it seems to me that one of the worst things in this Law we have now is to bury people one on top of another, and to take out the bones and reinter them. In the Law we used to have we did not bury people one on top of the other but rather in virgin soil."⁷⁶

Jewish tradition dictated that the deceased be buried in virgin soil that had never been used for any other purpose. Jews maintained their own cemeteries in part to ensure that the ground remained untouched.⁷⁷ For purposes of burial Orthodox Jewish tradition accounts for converts, permitting those who expressed their Jewishness in their final hours to be buried within the Jewish cemetery in a special corner reserved for converts, suicides, and people of poor reputation (*Enc. Jud.* 5:275). Thus during the years before the Expulsion, when converts and Jews were still living side by side in Spain, it is likely that some *conversos* were given Jewish burial.

After the establishment of the Inquisition, when Jewish-style burial became dangerous, *conversos* adapted traditional Jewish practice to their own needs. Sometimes a *converso* burial ground would be established next to a Jewish cemetery, or a particular sector of a Christian burial ground or a particular parish church would become known as being "reserved" in some way for *conversos*. In 1483 or 1484 the Jew Mayr Abenpesat observed several *conversos* in Calatayud burying a deceased *converso* right next to the Jewish cemetery. He reported that one of them, named García, said to his friend Jaime, "As for me, I want to be buried in the *converso* cemetery over there, right next to the Jewish cemetery with only an adobe wall in between."[78] Alvaro de la Higuera [Ciudad Real 1521] testified that the *conversa* "María de la Higuera was buried in Alcázar de Consuegra in Saint Sebastián, outside the town, where all the converts are buried in the field outside that church."[79] *Conversos* in Toledo wanted to be buried in the meadow of San Bartolomé so as "to be buried alone in virgin soil, as the Jews do, and not be buried in the church."[80] In Mexico Judaizers were often buried at the Convento del Carmen in San Angel. Women were dressed in the habit of the order (Liebman 1975, 124; cf. 1970, 97) [1639]. In Pernambuco Judaizers in the 1590s were buried in the hermitage of Nossa Senhora da Concepção because it contained virgin soil.[81]

The concern to bury in previously untouched ground is expressed over and over again in Inquisition testimony. The *cristã nova* Isabel Fernandes [Lisbon 1541] gave a picturesque explanation to Inquisitors for why Jews seek virgin soil and disapprove of the Christian custom of reutilizing graves: "When they are put into holes where other dead people have lain all their sins stick to the one who is lying there."[82] Around 1598 in La Roda (Albacete) Simón Rodríguez Feijoso stated that he wanted to be buried in a grave where no one had been buried before, because the Bible says that cleanliness of the body is like cleanliness of the soul.[83] Inquisitors were well aware that burial in virgin soil was one of the tell-tale signs of crypto-Judaism. A Portuguese Edict of Faith of 1536 instructs informers to be alert for burials "in virgin soil and in very deep graves."[84] The word went out in Majorca in the seventeenth century that *chuetas* buried their dead "in virgin soil outside the churches near a stream of fresh water."[85]

Some *conversos* sought burial in brand-new churches where presumably the soil had not previously been broken. In 1501 in Burgo de Osma [Soria] Diego Pérez de Gijón reported a conversation about a new-Christian funeral in 1497. He said it was foolish to bury the woman in a half-built church that might never be finished, and Alonso de Mena replied: "Sir, she didn't make a mistake; rather she very cleverly chose a pretty burial, to be laid in virgin soil."[86] Diogo Dias [Bahia c. 1591] reported that Heitor Antunes was buried in a newly built hermitage because "he was a Jew, and that is why he asked to be buried in that place which was virgin soil, which Jewish custom requires for burials."[87] Later when his son wanted to move the bones his mother would not let him. Even in the mid-seventeenth century the Portuguese Antón Rodríguez, of Tembleque, was accused of burying his wife in a hermitage where no one had been buried before.[88] Other *conversos* would scoop up a handful of virgin soil and sew it into a pillow that would be placed under the head of the deceased in the coffin, thus symbolically fulfilling the requirement that the deceased lie on virgin soil. The practice was already current among crypto-Jews prior to the Expulsion, with many examples like Juan González and his wife, who around 1472 put a pillow of dirt under the head of a *converso* friend at his funeral.[89] In fact the early compendia of crypto-Jewish customs also refer to the pillow of dirt,[90] as do many subsequent Edicts of Grace.

The pillow of virgin soil is both a symbolic act and a dissemblance strategy. Using newly built churches for burial was another dissemblance technique. In extreme cases—probably more rumored than fact—Judaizing *conversos* would have a sham coffin buried according to Christian ceremony and then later, secretly, bury their loved one according to Jewish practice.[91] In Castile around the time of the Expulsion there were many rumors of burying coffins filled with logs or stones to fool Christians. Although Blázquez Miguel claims there are no substantiated cases (1985, 57), at least one case, that of Tolosana Puxmija, of Teruel, who died around 1470, is described in considerable detail in Inquisition testimony. Witnesses state that Pedro and Antonio Nadal buried her secretly and then put a heavy log in the coffin, which they buried in the Monasterio de la Merced.[92] Similar is the case of Martín Fernández Cachito [Herrera, Toledo] who seems to have been buried in his garden under a pomegranate tree that his daughter Inés was supposed to take care of. Local rumor had it that a greyhound had been buried in his coffin in the church of Santa María (Rábade Obradó 1990a, 440).

When, in the nineteenth century, civil cemeteries were established in many Latin countries, *conversos* would bury their dead there rather than in the Catholic graveyards. In Portugal Schwarz found twentieth-century Judaizers burying their dead in civil cemeteries (1925). In 1929 Arturo Carlos de Barros Basto pointed out to the French journalist Lily Jean Jarval the crypto-Jewish cemetery in Bragança where there were more plain stones than crosses (Jarval 1929, 2).

## 11.4. THE FUNERAL MEAL

On returning from burying the deceased the first item of business was to feed the mourners. Because tradition says that at the first meal after the funeral (*se'udat havra'ah*) you cannot eat food you yourself have prepared, the meal was usually prepared by neighbors or friends.[93] The post-funeral meal around the time of the Expulsion in Castile was called a *cohuerço*.[94] Levine traces this word to the Latin *confortiare* and cites several Iberian variants: *cogüerzo, confuerzo, cohuerzo* (1982, 210), all of which are common in the documents.

Jewish tradition dictated that after funerals certain foods should be served and eaten in a certain way. Eggs were the most common mourning food, followed by lentils. The *Kol Bo* (first known edition 1490) says that the initial meal after the burial should be eggs and lentils, which are "symbolic of the roundness of the world and the mourning which comes to all."[95] *Shulḥan Arukh* (YD 378:9) commands that "at first they provide the mourner's meal with eggs or a dish of lentils as a symbol of mourning." But among Iberian Jews and *conversos* lentils were rare, while most documented funeral meals include eggs. Sometimes these were cooked in ways that de-emphasized their symbolic roundness. For example, in Toledo in the late fifteenth century relatives sent a mourning family "an omelet and two pears and two loaves of bread and grapes and a pitcher of water . . . in a basket covered with some white cloths."[96] But most eggs were probably hard boiled. Among the alleged Judaizing customs of Marina González [Ciudad Real 1484] was that she ate eggs at her mother-in-law's *coguerço* (Beinart 1974, 312). In Yepes in 1643 mourners ate eggs and salad (Blázquez Miguel 1986a, 80). Elena de Silva [Mexico 1642] reported that

> when a friend died she went to see the corpse and found Gabriel de Granada and twelve other persons there. And after they took away the said defunct to be buried the said Gabriel or another person . . . brought some eggs boiled hard and . . . a person . . . taking them from the said Gabriel . . . got up from where she was sitting and she went around giving to each one of the persons . . . his egg and at the same time expressing her condolences standing up on foot, and then she did the same with the persons related to the deceased, and having finished giving the said eggs the said person . . . took her own turning up her eyes towards heaven and giving her own self the condolence saying, it is certain that her soul is enjoying God, for the number of eggs came so exact to the persons who are connected by blood with the defunct. (Adler 1899, 82)

Rafaela Enríquez testified that these eggs were called *aveluz*.[97] Likewise Blanca Enríquez [Mexico 1648] said that after the funeral "blood relations of the deceased had to eat a cold hard-boiled egg, without salt (called the *aveluz*), as a sign of the pain they were feeling, and whoever brought it to the house was esteemed by the God of Israel."[98] When her father died, after she had eaten one *aveluz* she and his sister and another Judaizing woman "went into an empty room, and rushed around it several times, leaving the *aveluz* there for the first Catholic man or woman who should come in, so that the misfortune and bad luck should fall on them, for by that ceremony they believed that they themselves were free of it."[99] Micaela Enríquez testified that you "took away the bad luck of the *aveluz* by eating fish at noon."[100]

At post-funeral meals chicken was rarely served and beef almost never.[101] Early compilations of crypto-Jewish customs mention this prohibition,[102] as do many later trials.[103] In 1688 Ana Cortés reported to the Inquisition in Majorca that her father Joseph Cortés had instructed her "that when anyone on Sayell Street died she was not to eat meat for twenty-four hours until the corpse was buried, unless it was a child."[104] In a 1505 case mourners were said to eat "nothing but a casserole of Swiss chard with cheese and grated bread."[105] In Majorca in the 1670s Judaizing mourners ate only rice fried in olive oil, which they called "funeral food."[106] Even when old-Christians attending a *converso* funeral ate meat, the crypto-Jews were likely to abstain. Juan de Chinchilla testified in Ciudad Real in 1484 that when someone died in Almodóvar he would go to funeral banquets and "at their table they ate chicken and the converts on the floor ate chickpeas and eggs."[107]

For the post-funeral communal meal fish was a popular substitute for meat. Juana García [Ciudad Real 1484] said that when Bachelor Abudarme died in 1472 "they prepared the funeral banquet for him there and for nine days ate fish and eggs."[108] When Juana de Valdeolivas's mother [Garcimuñoz c. 1489] died, "for a whole week they ate no meat, but only fish."[109] When one of Catalina Ruiz's relatives died in Huete the family returned from the cemetery and dined on eggs and fish (Blázquez Miguel 1987, 47). Inquisitors in Ciudad Rodrigo in the 1580s reported that the new-Christian Gómez sisters, Ana and Catalina, never again ate meat after their mother died, but only fish (Sierro Malmierca 1990, 112). Isabel de Rivera [Mexico 1640s] confessed that, when her father died, for seven days a long list of Mexican Judaizers sent food to their house, especially fish.[110] The same custom was observed in Majorca in the 1670s (Cortes 1985, 290)[111] and appeared as a diagnostic for Judaizing in most Edicts of Faith in both Spain and Portugal.[112]

Tradition also prescribed that mourners show their grief by symbolically upsetting the comfort of their homes. The most common way was by eating while sitting on the ground or at low tables, a custom derived from the *Jerusalem Talmud*'s interpretation of Job 2:13 (Sperling 1968, 301). The *Mishnah Torah* (Maim., *Yad.* XIV,4,v, 17–8; xiii,3) and *Shulḥan Arukh* (YD 387:1) require the mourner to "overturn the couch": "When the time for sleeping or eating [arrives] he may sit [or sleep] on an overturned couch, but during the entire day he may not sit even on an overturned couch save on the ground." This custom was universal among Spanish Jews. It is frequently mentioned in pre-Expulsion Inquisition documents that refer to *converso* attendance at Jewish funerals. For example, Juan de Chinchilla, of Ciudad Real, said that he "attended funeral banquets at the home of [the Jew] Çuçen, on the floor, in the Jewish fashion."[113] Some crypto-Jews ate on the ground, but many also sat at low tables, which are often called in the documents *almadraques*.[114] Casarrubios's García family mourned at low tables in the 1470s (Beinart 1975, 651). When Luis Vélez died (Almazán 1505) his family set their tablecloth on a small basket they had overturned on the floor.[115] When Fernando Husillo [Toledo 1485] responded to an accusation by denying that this was a specifically Jewish custom, he was not believed (Baer 1966, 2:351).

In addition to eating at low tables, it was reported that when one of Catalina Ruiz's relatives died [Huete 1519], the family sat on a rug which they had turned upside down to eat their eggs and fish (Blázquez Miguel 1987, 47). Most of these customs appear to have persisted, and are common among Ladino-speaking Jews even today (Dobrinsky 1986, 91).

## 11.5. Mourning

Immediately following the burial the surviving family began a formal period of intense mourning. While a *converso* burial was a public event, generally under the auspices of the Church and always to be carried out with some circumspection, the mourning at home was a private, family affair and therefore a suitable vehicle for the reaffirmation of Jewish identity. Although the documents are relatively silent about *converso* funeral customs, they are rich in details about mourning customs.

Traditional Jewish mourning is divided into four periods, each dated from the time of burial: 3 days, 7 days, 30 days, and 1 year. The first three days after the funeral are naturally the most intense. During that period mourners are not considered receptive to words of comfort, so that friends and relatives are required to refrain from offering consolation.[116] When Juan González Daza's father died [Ciudad Real 1484], "the first day he ate fish and eggs at a low table while sitting on the floor, and that ceremony lasted three days."[117] Beatriz Gonçalves [Evora 1583] said that when her son died she abstained from eating meat for three days, and would have fasted for seven had her health been better (Azevedo Mea 1982, 439, 450).

The first full week of mourning, called *shivah* [Heb. = seven], is derived from Gen. 50:10, which states that Joseph mourned his father for seven days, or from Amos 8:10, which states that "I shall turn your feasts into mourning." According to the *Mo'ed Katan* (20a), "the feast of Succoth is celebrated for seven days; accordingly, mourning should last seven days also" (Sperling 1968, 299). It may also be related to the seven days of mourning Joseph observed on the death of Jacob (Gen. 50:10). The *Mishnah Torah* (Maim., Yad. XIV,4,xiii,10) requires that "one should not weep for the dead more than three days nor lament for him more than seven days." *Conversos* in Casarrubios del Monte in the 1470s observed seven days of mourning (Beinart 1975, 652). When Gabriel de Granada [Mexico 1643] learned of the death of his father Manuel, he and seven friends

> did on the seventh day after receiving the news fast for the soul of said Manuel de Granada.... The six preceding days the said Gabriel with a person very nearly related to him stayed in the house retired without going out as a ceremony of the law of Moses... and that on the eve of the second day a certain person whom he named sent the supper in order that the said Gabriel and the aforesaid persons should keep the fast. And that the said six days preceding the seventh of the said fast five persons whom he named sent things to eat....
> And the said dinners were of fish because on such days the Jews eat fish for the sake of their dead.[118]

The seven days of *shivah* are followed by twenty-three days of less intensive mourning, totaling thirty. This period of a full month of moderate mourning may derive from Deut. 34:8, which was the period that the people of Israel mourned Moses (*Mo'ed Katan* 83c). The *Mishnah Torah* (Maim., *Yad.* XIV,4,vi,1–2) requires that for thirty days mourners refrain from "cutting the hair, putting on pressed clothes, taking a wife, attending social festivities, traveling on business" (*Mo'ed Katan* 22b–23a; 27b). Many new-Christians did as Juan de Loperuelo [Aragon 1483], who when his father died kept his children in the house for thirty days.[119]

This thirty-day period is followed by another, of eleven months, to make an entire year of progressively less intense mourning. The full year is most generally observed after the death of a parent (*Mo'ed Katan* 22a). A document from the late fifteenth century mentions *conversos* "sitting on the floor behind closed doors where they eat fish, olives, but not meat, and out of grief for the deceased they do not leave the house for a year."[120] Similarly, a Mexican Edict of Grace of 1639 refers to the custom of "not leaving the house for one year in accordance with the observance of the laws" (Liebman 1970, 97).

Over time most crypto-Jews seem to have kept this mourning calendar, although there were variations in it even before the 1492 Expulsion. Juana García testified in Ciudad Real in 1484 that her family ate the *cohuerço* of fish and eggs for nine days.[121] In Aragon in the late fifteenth century mourners sometimes kept to their houses for eight days, as did Gracia de Esplugas [Zaragoza 1487] who mourned for eight days behind closed doors (Marín Padilla 1983b, 286; cf. 322). Antón Ruiz [Teruel 1484] mourned the death of his nephew Mose Alazar by going to his brother-in-law's house for fifteen days (Sánchez Moya 1973, 133). Seventeenth-century Mexican crypto-Jews, who tended to be preoccupied with issues of calendar, varied in their mourning schedules. Antonio Méndez was reported in 1603 to have said that "in the other times the Jews used to fast eight days for their parents in sign of mourning, but nowadays one has to do what the world requires."[122] Some forty years later Isabel de Rivera said that for one's parents it was customary to fast on the seventh day. Rafael Enríquez said that it was customary to eat fish for nine days.[123] The three-day, month, and year-long periods were also observed sporadically well up into modern times. Modern remnant crypto-Jews conform to this pattern. Early twentieth-century Portuguese Judaizers left a lamp burning for the eight days that the family sat at home, on low benches, receiving relatives and friends who came by three times daily to pray. The family would abstain from meat, and fast entirely on the eighth day, the thirtieth day, and the end of the third month after the death (Schwarz 1925, 37). Paulo finds that during the first eight days of mourning twentieth-century Portuguese new-Christians eat no meat; on the ninth and thirtieth days they fast, and again at the end of the third, sixth, and ninth months (1970, 95).

Traditionally Jewish mourners were required to demonstrate their grief by abstaining from certain happy, fulfilling, or ostentatious activities. Mourners were "not to leave the house, perform manual labor, conduct business transactions, bathe, anoint the body, cut the hair, cohabit, wear leather shoes, wash clothes, greet acquaintances, and study the Torah" except for the sorrowful portions (*Mo'ed Katan* 15a–b, 23a) (*Enc. Jud.* 12:489). The *Mishnah Torah* (Maim., *Yad.* XIV,4,v,1; 15–16) and the *Shulḥan Arukh* (YD 384:1) forbid the mourner for seven days from reading "the Pentateuch, Prophets or Hagiographa, Mishnah, *Gemara, Halakot* or *Aggadot.*"

As a symbol of their unhappiness mourners would accept certain discomforts of the flesh, or mortify their flesh, or destroy certain items that were valuable to them, such as clothing. Many of these practices have traditional sources. For example, the rending of clothes, or *K'riah*, is attested to several times in the Bible: Gen. 37:29, 37:34; Josh. 7:6; Job 1:20; and so on. The most popular of these activities was rending clothing, for which there are elaborate rules in the *Mishnah Torah* (Maim., *Yad.* XIV,4,viii,1–10;ix,1–15), the *Shulḥan Arukh* (YD 340:1) and *Mo'ed Katan* (20b). When Alonso González Aserrafe died around 1472, Juan González and his wife María tore their clothes (Beinart 1975, 652). Rodrigo de Rojas said that he saw Juan González mourning his daughter by "tearing his hood, from grief, which he heard said was a Jewish ceremony."[124] In Mexico the surviving spouse tore his shirt (male) or cut the waistband of her skirt (female).[125]

Refraining from bathing is found in 2 Sam. 12:20. The *Mishnah Torah* (Maim., *Yad.* XIV,4,v,1;vi,2) and the *Shulḥan Arukh* (YD 380:1;381:1) also forbid the mourner to bathe.[126] A prohibition against washing clothes is derived from 2 Sam. 14:2 (*Mo'ed Katan* 15a-b; *Shulḥan Arukh* (YD 389:1) (Sperling 1968, 297). Antón Ruiz [Teruel 1484], for example, mourned the death of his nephew in his brother-in-law's house for fifteen days and did not change his clothes in all that time. When Violante Moniz's husband died in Bahia in the 1590s, Violante "never again until the day she died washed her dress nor slept in a bed."[127] Consonant with the idea of mourning by mortifying the flesh, when *conversa* women in Brazil in the late sixteenth century were left widowed, as a symbol of mourning when they sat down they would lift their skirts and sit with their bare skin against the ground.[128] In Majorca in the 1670s close relatives of the deceased would not bathe or leave the house for a month (Cortes 1985, 290).[129] Although the *Mishnah Torah* (Maim., *Yad.* XIV,4,v,1) and *Shulḥan Arukh* (YD 380:1) also prohibit mourners from wearing shoes, this custom surfaces in the record only rarely, such as when the wife of the *converso* Pedro Cruillas, of la Cedacería, Aragon, was said to have mourned him around 1466 in bare feet (Marín Padilla 1983b, 321).

Crypto-Jewish mourners also strove to exhibit overt symbols of their grief in their homes. Jewish tradition, for example dictates that after a death all the mirrors in the house be turned toward the wall (*Enc. Jud.* 5:1426). Liebman reports that many colonial Mexican Judaizers followed this custom (Liebman 1975, 124). Some *conversos* went further in decorating their houses for mourning. Juan de Salcedo [Aranda de Duero 1502] reported how shortly after Diego Delgado's wife died, "he found him removed to a small room, hung with black drapery, the doors and windows closed. He was barefoot and had his cape pulled over his head, the fringe up to his mouth. He was exactly like the Jews are during the seven days, when some close relative has died."[130] A new-Christian in Bahia in the 1590s was accused of decorating his house with branches as a sign of mourning.[131] A memorandum of Judaizing customs presented to the Inquisition in Granada in 1593 stated that "when someone died you must unfasten the hangings in the death room."[132]

Traditionally Judaism views death as contaminating with some kind of impurity anyone or anything which has come in contact with it. Anybody who has touched a dead person is thereby unclean and must be purified (Num. 19:14). By extension the house where someone has died has become ritually unclean and must be purified ceremonially before normal business can be conducted in it (*Shulan Arukh* YD 371:1). Among Iberian crypto-Jews a number of mourning rituals had to do with cleaning and purifying the place where the death occurred and the people who had come in contact with the corpse. Micaela Enríquez [Mexico 1648] reported that when her grandmother died the women all went and bathed in her house.[133] Brazilian new-Christians in Bahia, for example, swept their houses clean when the deceased was removed from the house and then brought in new brooms.[134] Ynés Alvarez de Herrera [Granada 1593] was accused "of having washed her body and her head because she had been present at the death of the deceased."[135] In an example that suggests that the impurities resulting from death were associated with menstrual impurity, the Mexican Judaizer Antonio Vaez Tirado, burned in 1649, ordered the women in his family "not to wear the undergarments that they had worn at the time of their mothers' deaths" (Liebman 1974, 129). Modern Portuguese new-Christians exhibit the same concerns. When one of them dies the house becomes *trefle* and has to be purified by sprinkling salt water with an olive branch into the corners of the house while praying: "Just as the sea is salty / the God of Israel is savior. / May God 'disimpure' [*desintrefle*] this house, / and everything that is in it."[136] Vasconcelos reports additionally that, as soon as they remove a newly deceased Portuguese new-Christian from his bed, they remake the bed with brand-new bed clothes and maintain it for seven days (1985, 200).

Mourners were expected to refrain from certain "happy" activities. For example, fasting is sometimes associated with traditional Jewish mourning practices.[137] Among the *conversos* it seems to have been practiced mainly by colonial Judaizers; in the seventeenth century some Mexican *conversos* fasted on Wednesdays in honor of their departed loved ones. When Gabriel de Granada [Mexico 1643] learned of the death of his father Manuel, he and seven friends fasted during daylight hours for a full week of mourning (Adler 1899, 69). The Brazilian new-Christian Violante Antunes did not fast, but she said [Bahia c. 1590] that when her husband died she stopped eating "anything that tasted good."[138] During the period of intense mourning it was also common to abstain from sex. For example the Mexican Judaizer Antonio Vaez Tirado, burned in 1649, "ordered all married daughters of deceased Jewesses not to sleep with their husbands" (Liebman 1974, 129).

This sense of impurity carries over to one's religious life. Some crypto-Jews even believed that they were to refrain from prayer until the period of mourning had passed. Many Judaizers in Castile thought that people sitting *shivah* could not pray to God (Blázquez Miguel 1986a, 57), and a memorandum of Judaizing customs presented to the Inquisition in Granada in 1593 stated that "people who are in mourning should not eat meat for seven days nor pray to God."[139] When the Brazilian new-Christian Ana Rodríguez's husband died she would never again go into the church where he was buried (Furtado 1925, 392).

One of the most overt signs of grief was the intonation of funeral laments or dirges. Traditionally Jewish mourners would wail and lament and beat their breasts as one expression of their grief. The composition and recitation of funeral laments are attested to many times in the Bible (2 Sam. 1:17; 2 Chron. 35:25; etc.). According to the *Mo'ed Katan* (23a) the custom of chanting funeral laments (*endechas*) may derive from Jer. 9:17–18: "Consider, and call for the mourning women to come; send for the skillful women to come; let them make haste and raise a wailing over us." The *Shulḥan Arukh* 344:1–3 gives rules relating to lamentation. Breast-beating is related to Isaiah 32:12. All of these customs were common among Judaizing *conversos*. Prior to the Expulsion some Jews, and some new-Christians as well, seem to have made a living as professional mourners. According to a 1484 trial in Ciudad Real a *conversa* named "Catalina de Zamora had as a profession writing and reciting funeral poems for the dead."[140] Professional mourners seem to have disappeared about the time of the Expulsion, although as late as the mid-seventeenth century a certain Mexican woman was known to lead the lamenting at *converso* funerals. And the custom seems to have been preserved—or revived—by twentieth-century Portuguese crypto-Jews. Machado reported in 1952 that when some new-Christian dies in the Mogadouro region of Portugal professional women mourners come and cry and wail and give the deceased instructions and messages for people who have died previously (1952, 43). Vasconcelos also reports that when a Portuguese new-Christian dies professional mourners[141] pray three times daily for seven days by the bed where the person died.

Loud lamentation was a distinctive feature of late medieval Judaism and by extension crypto-Judaism, and as such attracted the attention of the Inquisition. As late as 1639 a Mexican Edict of Grace considers as a sign of Judaizing "singing some funeral dirge" (Liebman 1970, 97), and a few years later in 1645 the Mexican *converso* Juan de León described new-Christian burial customs to a friend by saying that "when someone dies people show great emotion and observe many fasts for him and pray for him."[142] The data from around the time of the Expulsion are explicit about loud mourning at funerals. When Lope Sánchez [Garcimuñoz 1490] died, his daughter and another *conversa* "recited funeral poems and sang, beating their breasts the way the Jews do."[143] One such song in Molina de Aragón in the

1480s began: "Bring the beautiful woman out; may good fortune be hers . . . alas, alas."[144] Some dirges were sung in unison, some responsively, as in the case of Isabel García [Hita 1520–3] in which a servant described how the women would sing and weep and "a certain person called out the songs and Isabel and the other women sang responses, weeping and swaying."[145] In Aragon in the late fifteenth century mourners were given scraps of cloth, which were kept in boxes especially for that purpose, with which to dry their tears (Marín Padilla 1983b, 286–7, 290). Inquisition witnesses frequently remark on what to them appeared to be the intensity of this lamentation. Isabel García, cited above, was accused "of singing funeral laments while walking around the bed of the deceased, and sometimes getting up on the bed, . . . sometimes climbing down." Among the songs she reputedly sang was "I, the unhappy wife, went to the fields to pick herbs."[146] When Ana Rodriguez's husband Heitor Antunes died in Bahia (Brazil) in the 1590s, Ana "sat half-naked on the floor and sang laments for him, bobbing her head." Her priest reported that she did the same when her daughter Violante died.[147] When Nicolás de la Guerra [Canary Islands 1631] visited the home of Fernan Pinto, a Portuguese, "he found him with his two sons, and another person unknown to him, lying on the floor with bent heads, covered all with a black cape, and making gestures and noises as though they were all weeping" (Wolf 1926, 122). Francisca Núñez, burned in effigy in Mexico in 1649, was accused of leading laments at funerals of Judaizers. "She went out with the women to another room. The women removed the silken veils that they were wearing and launched into the ridiculous ceremony, *Avelus*,[148] or the feeling of violent grief for the deceased, and reciting a very long Jewish prayer to send [the soul] to heaven" (Liebman 1974, 204; cf. 221). Likewise Juan Méndez de Villaviciosa, a Portuguese merchant who appeared as a Judaizer in the 1647 *auto de fe* in Mexico, was described as a habitual lamenter at Jewish funerals,[149] as was Rafaela Enríquez.[150]

Another common crypto-Jewish sign of mourning was for survivors to light a memorial lamp in honor of the deceased. Traditionally during the seven days of *shivah* a candle is left burning because "it is said that the soul of the departed derives some joy and comfort from this glowing light 'as the soul of man is the lamp of the Lord' " (Prov. 20:27) (Sperling 1968, 295). Before the Expulsion crypto-Jews might commission a memorial lamp to be lit in their local synagogue. For example, in 1488 it was reported in Calatayud that the *conversa* Clara had given the Jew Acat Abcatar money to buy oil to light a lamp for the soul of her mother Sol (Marín Padilla 1983b, 332). More common was to kindle the lamp at home. In 1484 Juana Garçia accused Ysabel, the wife of Alonso Falcón, of mourning her father-in-law in 1472 by putting in "the kitchen where the man had died a basin of water and a lighted lamp for nine days."[151] Among Judaizing *conversos* this custom seems to have persisted only sporadically, although there are examples as late as mid-seventeenth century such as Ana Núñez [Murcia 1654], who kept a candle lit for three days after her husband's death (Blázquez Miguel 1986b, 142). And the custom survives among the modern Portuguese *cristãos novos*, many of whom keep a lamp lighted for eight days in the room where someone died.[152]

Another whole set of mourning customs has to do with water. According to the *Shulḥan Arukh* (YD 339:5), "it is a custom to pour out all drawn water in the neighborhood of the corpse." The *Kol Bo* is of the opinion that this is "in order to announce the death to the neighborhood without having to spread the bad tidings by word of mouth."[153] Levine (1982, 199) says that it is to warn the Jewish priests, or *Cohanim*, that the house is ritually impure. She cites two other traditional reasons as well: that pouring out the water is symbolic of the extinction of life, or the pouring out of the soul. There was also a superstitious fear that the Angel of Death would stir up the water and drip blood in it. Blázquez Miguel relates it to the belief that it is so that the Angel of Death can wipe his sword, and also so that the soul might not be able to bathe for seven days.[154] Bernardina de San Juan's mother [Baeza 1572] taught her that "when someone died you should pour out all the water that was in the house, because the soul would bathe in any water that it found; and on the eighth day in the very place the deceased had expired, and at the very hour, you should put a porcelain bowl for the spirit of the deceased to bathe."[155]

Whatever the explanation, the custom was common enough throughout the *converso* world to be seized upon by Inquisitors as one of the principal indicators of Judaizing.[156] Early compilations of crypto-Jewish customs list this practice[157] as do many later Edicts of Faith.[158] A memorandum of Judaizing customs presented to the Inquisition in Granada in 1593 stated that when someone died you must "pour out all the water in the house and for seven houses around."[159] It appears regularly in Inquisition testimony. For example, sometime prior to 1484 in Teruel, when a Jew died Francés de Puxmija filled a jug with hot water and sent it to the *judería*, where it was taken into the house and poured out the window (Sánchez Moya/Monasterio Aspiri 1972, 113). In another trial a witness stated that "when the mother of Diego Laynes, a new-Christian, died [in 1505], they ordered the maid to pour out the water, and they said that the deceased's soul was there."[160] This custom survives in Portugal (Schwarz 1925, 37) and is likewise found among many Ladino-speaking Turkish Jews.[161]

Among some crypto Jews the death-contaminated water was not to be replaced during the period of most intense mourning. Marina de Coca testified in Ciudad Real in 1484 that when the *converso* Juan Gonçales de Santistevan died, for nine days "they drew no water from the well."[162] Alfonso de Chinchilla's wife [Almagro 1503–4] "when someone died covered up the well according to Jewish custom so that the souls of the dead would not come there to bathe."[163] This custom may be derived from the fact that when Miriam died the well dried up (Num. 20:2).

The taboo nature of water that had been in the presence of death can be perceived clearly in the crypto-Jews' reluctance to drink it. In 1489 the *conversa* Juana de Valdeolivas, of Garcimuñoz, was charged that when her mother died, "they did not drink the water that was in the house the day she died."[164] Guiomar Roiz

[Evora 1573] said that some thirty years earlier when someone died her stepmother said that "even though they had water in the house you could not drink it, but only the fresh water that she sent for."[165] Fernão Lopes of the Azores [Lisbon 1573] was denounced because, among other reasons, "when someone died at his house . . . he did not want to drink the water that was in the pitchers because his mother had told him not to."[166]

The funeral customs relating to water are among the most persistent and contradictory of the crypto-Jewish tradition. On the one hand, as we have seen, it was deemed necessary to pour out all the water that had been witness to the act of death. On the other hand, many *conversos* would set out a basin of water after a death had occurred, presumably so that the soul of the departed could come to drink or wash. This was common practice in Ciudad Real in the years preceding the Expulsion. Juana Garçia testified there in 1484 that when the Bachelor Abudarme died in 1472 "on his wife's command this witness put in the kitchen where the young man had died a basin of water . . . for nine days, so that the soul could come and bathe."[167] When Diego Lopes died in 1481 "in a large room where [he] died they put a basin of water and some white towels and some needles [?] and nine little lamps for the soul of said Diego Lopes."[168] When the Mexican Francisco Rodríguez de Matos died, "a jar of water and a washcloth were left in the room so that the soul of the departed would be able to wash and dry. There was also deposited nearby some simple food and an egg without salt."[169] Diego Juárez de Figueroa [Mexico 1647] affirmed that "because they believe that the souls of the dead, transformed into birds, come to drink or to bathe, they put a pitcher of water and a hand towel next to the bodies of the deceased."[170] Similarly, Blanca Enríquez [Mexico 1648] said that it was because the souls of the dead "came to bathe and wash away their sins."[171] Similarly, in Aragon it was the custom to put a glass of water on the window sill for nine Sabbaths and mourning days so that the soul could come to refresh itself.[172] As with other mourning customs, the length of the mourning period tended to vary. Elvira Gutiérrez of Baeza testified in 1573 that when someone died "on the eighth day she would put out a pitcher of water so that the soul could come and wash."[173] This custom, too, persists among some Turkish Sephardic communities.[174]

It was particularly important that this water be fresh. In Castile around the time of the Expulsion tradition held that fresh water must be brought from at least seven houses distant from the house where someone died (Blázquez Miguel 1986a, 57). A memorandum of Judaizing customs presented to the Inquisition in Granada in 1593 stated that when someone died "for seven days you must drink water freshly brought from the fountain."[175] It was reported in Pernambuco in 1594 that when a slave died in her household Maria Alvares "had all the water poured out of the pitchers that were in the pitcher rack in the room where they drank and had them filled with fresh water from the fountain." She explained that she did it "because the slave's dying in that room left an unclean odor."[176] The custom survives among some modern Portuguese new-Christians, who bring water from a fountain in a new pitcher, which they then break and scatter the pieces in the river (Vasconcelos 1985, 228).

## 11.6. CHARITY

Although making charitable contributions at the time of death is not a common Jewish practice, with the exception of paying the funeral expenses for indigent Jews,[177] it appears to have been introduced into the *converso* repertoire of customs in the mid-seventeenth century and to be widespread in the twentieth-century Portuguese *cristão novo* community. The most common manifestation was bringing food to the mourning family during the period of *shivah* (*Shulḥan Arukh* YD 378:1). Juana Rodríguez testified in Mexico in 1642 that when a Judaizer dies "it is a ceremony of the law of Moses . . . to send something to eat to the widower or widow or to his greatest friend or nearest relation and . . . Gabriel [de Granada] sent to her the hard boiled eggs and chocolate which was eaten by the said widow and her children" (Adler 1899, 93). But other charitable acts were recorded as well. When Gabriel de Granada's own father died in Mexico around 1643, for example, he left about "three hundred dollars" (*pesos?*) so that "every Wednesday seven fasts of the said law of Moses had to be made, and that an alms of one dollar should be given to the person who kept the fast, and that if there should be more than three hundred dollars they should be distributed amongst some of the poor observers of the law of Moses after they had kept the said fasts for his soul for the supper of that day" (Adler 1899, 74; cf. Liebman 1970, 83). At the trial of the Seville liquor dealer Gabriel Gomes Navarro [Lisbon 1673] a special supper for the dead was described. For seven nights after the funeral they set a table with a loaf of bread and a glass of water, adding a new loaf each night. When the seven days were up they gave the seven loaves to someone outside the family (da Cunha e Freitas 1952, 21).

Modern Portuguese new-Christians preserved this last custom and invested it with a variety of what appear to be local traditions. In Vilarinho dos Galegos, Portugal, when someone dies the family makes his bed and sets a place for him at the table as if he were alive.[178] Moreover, they sometimes dress a poor man in his clothes, sit him in his place at the table, and put all the bread in the house on the dead relative's bed, saying: "Take this, lion, leave the soul of this dead man when he crosses the Jordan river."[179] This meal may be repeated several times. When a Judaizer dies in Covilhã the family twice weekly invites a poor person to the table in the deceased's place and serves him the deceased's favorite foods (Paulo 1970, 55). Other new-Christians host a sumptuous but meatless lunch for the poor on the eighth day after someone dies and again at the end of the first, sixth, eleventh and twelfth months. The lunch is called "for the good of the soul" [*bem de alma*] (Paulo 1970, 95–6).

Portuguese remnant Judaizers also practice other forms of charity. Some give seven coins to new-Christian beggars when they are washing the body, when they take the body from the house, and again when they lower it into the grave (Vasconcelos 1985, 209; cf. Dobrinsky 1986, 103). Schwarz reported that they would distribute alms at every corner the funeral cortege passed on the way to the cemetery, and then for a year they would invite a poor person to every Sabbath meal (Schwarz 1925, 37; cf. Vasconcelos 1985, 209). Vasconcelos also reports that when a Portuguese new-Christian dies they donate the bed clothes to the poor (1985, 200). These customs are practiced by Portuguese Judaizers, but it is unclear whether the customs are Jewish in their essence. Some are clearly not. For example, in Pinhel, Portugal, when some Judaizer dies the family distributes hot bread, saying "May the soul of our deceased one come out of Purgatory the way the steam comes out of this bread."[180]

## Notes

1. On the other hand, there is no mention in the documents of several other common Jewish traditions related to preparing the corpse: leaving the body untouched for several minutes after death and placing a feather on its lips to make certain that no flicker of life is left; the eldest son or nearest relative gently closing the eyes and mouth; placing the body on the floor with the feet toward the door "to indicate the escape of the impurity"; and covering the body with a sheet (*Enc. Jud.* 5:1425–6; 15:1188).

2. *Non llegase a él christiano, nin le cosiese la mortaja, nin le metiese christiano en el ataud, nin le vañase, e mandó que non le pusiesen crus despues de muerto, teniendola por cosa reprovada* (Cantera/Carrete 1975, 177).

3. *Ella o não queria ver, dizendo, tiraio láa, tiraio láa, e que Breatiz Antunes . . . lhe dixera, mãi, não nos deshonreis, que somos casadas com homens cristãos velhos, e nobres, e contudo que a dita velha Anna Roiz tornara a dizier, tiraio láa, tiraio láa, e não o quizera veer ao dito crucifixo* (Furtado 1925, 479). See also 330; Sierro Malmierca 1990, 194 [1620s].

4. *Procuró estorbar, con su madre y hermanas, que no recibiese los santos sacramentos, y habiendo recibido el de la Eucaristía, se llegó a él y le dijo: señor, mire que esto no es nada, y respondió: ya lo sé, hija* (García 1910, 59).

5. *Acostumbran avisar en las Parroquias después que ya son muertos, fingiendo mucho cuydado y dando mucha prissa a los Párrochos; . . . y aviendo llegado a sus casas . . . con el Santísimo Sacramento, les dizen que . . . no an sido a tiempo, que en aquel punto an acabado de espirar como unos pollitos* (Selke de Sánchez 1972, 120).

6. Some also speculate that it is so that the dying person will not give himself away to the Inquisition. The alleged stranglers are called *abafadores* or *afogadores*. There are no proven cases of which I am aware. See Paulo 1970, 29; Schwarz 1925, 38–41; Machado 1952, 43 [1952]; Vasconcelos 1985, 174–8; Barros Basto 1928, 2.13:2; Lipiner 1977, 11–12.

7. *Reconçiliarse al tiempo de la muerte con rabíes doctores e judíos maestros en su ley* (Benito Ruano 1957, 331). See also Carrete Parrondo 1986, 141.

8. *Hun librico di conffesion que los judios tienen y lo claman el budduy, que lo fazen los judios quando se quieren morir* (Marín Padilla 1983b, 299). See also Carrete Parrondo 1986, 141.

9. *Yngeriéndose a consolar e confesar a los enfermos en artículo de la muerte asy como judío* (Santa María 1893a, 195).

10. *Tienen dos personas que son de la misma Nación: un hombre para coser y amortajar a los hombres y una muger para las mugeres* (Braunstein 1936, 188).

11. *Tenía sospecha que no murió cristiana por haber comenzado avezar* [sic] *la oración de San Josep* (Gracia Boix 1983, 137). The identification of this prayer, which obviously was thought to be indicative of Judaizing, is unclear.

12. According to Marín Padilla the custom was relatively rare in Aragon (1983b, 315), although it appears frequently in documents from Castile, Portugal, and the Americas.

13. Blázquez Miguel 1986a, 80. For additional examples of this custom see Blázquez Miguel 1986a, 56, 140 [1610; 1639]; Liebman 1974, 218 [Mexico 1649]; 1975, 100; Cortes 1985, 290; Braunstein 1936; Selke de Sánchez 1972, 121 [Majorca 1670s]; Lewin 1939, 26 [Americas eighteenth century].

14. *Le volviesen hacia Oriente cuando se quisiesen morir, porque no penasen tanto* (Gracia Boix 1983, 133; cf. Santa María 1893c, 182).

15. *Este testigo quedose sola con él . . . e vn candil ençendido . . . questaua a la cabeçera* (Carrete/Fraile 1987, 116).

16. *Amortalhar hum defunto ao modo judaico, lavando o todo com agoa quente e cortando lhe has unhas dos pés e das mãos e os cabellos da cabeça* (Azevedo Mea 1982, 337). For other examples of this custom see Furtado 1935, xxxii [Evora 1536]; Saraiva 1969, 164 [Portugal 1536]; Cohen 1973, 101 [Mexico 1589]; Furtado 1929, 100 and Wiznitzer 1960, 14 [Brazil 1593]; da Cunha e Freitas 1952, 20 [Lisbon 1673]; Paulo 1970, 28 and Machado 1952, 43 [twentieth-century Portugal].

17. *Muerto, le laban con agua caliente rapándole la barba y debaxo de los brazos y otras partes del cuerpo* (Santa María 1893c, 182). For other examples of this custom see Blázquez Miguel 1985b, 56; Azevedo Mea 1982, 337 [Coimbra 1573]; Medina 1887, 1:128 [Peru 1578]; Cohen 1973, 101 [Mexico 1589]; Liebman 1970, 97 [Mexico 1639]; Lewin 1939, 26 [eighteenth century]; Liebman 1970, 82 [Mexico 1785]; Machado 1952, 43 [twentieth-century Portugal].

18. *Mando llamar a vn yndia barbero a quien mando dho Pe Fray Juan de Segueta que le rrapase axilas, barbas como las demas partes secretas de todo su cuerpo como lo hizo, y que se mando uestir de limpio para morir* (AGN Vol 506 doc 11, 526a).

19. Rabbi Simeon ben Zemach Duran (1361–1444), cited by Sperling 1968, 292.

20. *Le mandaron poner vna poca de agua a calentar e echar çeuada dentro e, despues de caliente el agua, mandara traer vnas tablas e vna artesa e lo sacaron alli e lo vañaran la dicha Juana Lopes* (Moreno Koch 1977, 366).

21. *Hijo lávame este cuerpo no vaya asi sucio a la tierra* (Toro 1982, 227).

22. Beinart 1981a, 281; Melammed 1991b, 158–9.

23. *Le echaron encima de un bufetillo, y le desnudaron, y luego una mulata llamada María de la Concepción que vive en la misma cassa, traxo agua caliente y un paño y començo a labar al dho nino y le labo todo, volviendole de arriba abajo, con el dho panio, y diciendo esta declarante, que cossa que hauia de comer la tierra, que para que hera labarle con lo qual se dexaron de labar* (AGN Vol 402 doc 1, 7a).

24. *Era sumamente ceremoniática y se hallaba a los amortajamientos de los judíos y judías, y a los lavatorios de sus cuerpos y a las demás ceremonias ridículas que en semejantes ocasiones hacen los judaizantes* (García 1910, 68).

25. Braunstein 1936, 107. Modern Ladino-speaking Jews in the Levant wash the body three times with soap and warm water, twice with plain warm water, and then the head a last time with cold water. Then water is poured over the entire body (Dobrinsky 1986, 88).

26. For additional examples of cleansing the corpse see Beinart 1974, 1:292, 309; 3:685; Furtado 1935, xxxii [Evora 1536]; Azevedo Mea 1982, 249, 337 [Coimbra 1571–3]; Cohen 1973, 101 [Mexico 1589]; Furtado 1929, 100 [Brazil 1593]; Chinchilla 1953, 184 [Guatemala 1609–26]; Liebman 1964, 102; 1970, 97; 1975, 117, 151 [Mexico 1623–49]; da Cunha e Freitas 1952, 20 [Lisbon 1673]; 82 [1785].

27. Marín Padilla's research suggests that around the time of the Expulsion the custom of shaving and washing the body was more commonly practiced in Castile than in Aragon (1983b, 316).

28. *Vem o demónio, tenta aquela alma e leva-a para o inferno* (Paulo 1985, 64) See also Vasconcelos 1985, 228 [1933].

29. *Lavai, Senhor, esta alma / com água de salvação, / Limpai-o de pecados, / Deitai-le a vossa divina benção. / Humilde e arrependido, / ao Senhor pede perdão* (Vasconcelos 1985, 209). See also Paulo 1985, 64 and Vasconcelos 1985, 173 [Portugal twentieth century].

30. *Cuando murió su señor, su señora y otras portuguesas cristianas nuevas pusiéronle al enterrar anillos en las manos y un lenzuelo de puntas de mucho valor por el rostro* (Contreras 1982, 601).

31. *Vañava los difuntos, amortajandolos y poniendolos vn sanbenitillo sobre la mortaja . . . Le vistieron vna mortaja sobre vn sant benitillo largo* (Moreno Koch 1977, 366).

32. *Sacase de un cofre la mortaja de ruan nuevo, que había años tenía cortada al modo de las albas de que usan los sacerdotes de la Iglesia Católica, para que se la cosiese cierta judía con los pliegues necesarios* (García 1910, 207). Her sister Rafaela Enríquez reputedly added that Mexican Judaizing women routinely prepared their own shroud when they were married (*tratando de la obligación que las judías tenían, cuando se casaban, de hacer sus mortajas de lienzo nuevo, y guardarlas y preparar lo demás necesario . . . para su muerte*) (García 1910, 250).

33. *Calentaron una camissa limpia y la calentaron y saumaron, en un brasero y se la vistieron al dicho niño, y luego la muger de Gaspar Suarez . . . dixo que fuessen a su cassa y trajessen con que amortajar aquel niño, y traxeron lienço nuebo en un pedaço y otro pedaço de bayeta amarillo nuebo, con ello le amortaxaron, rebolbiendoselo al cuerpo, y sobre el le pusieron un abito de san nicolas negro con estrellas de oro, y plata* (AGN Vol 402 doc 1, 7a-b).

34. *Los amortajan con lienço nuebo, calçones, y camisa limpia, y capa plegada* (Santa María 1893c, 182).

35. *Embrulhando a com camisa e lançol novo e outras peças de pano cru que nunca fora lavado* (Azevedo Mea 1982, 292).

36. *Los amortajan con lienzo nuevo, y las cortaduras de las mortajas las ponen con ellos porque no queda nada fuera* (Lewin 1977, 47).

37. *La mortaja fuese de lienzo casero* (Gracia Boix 1983, 133).

38. Liebman 1970, 81; 1974, 155, 157; 1975, 124 [1649]. For additional examples of shrouding see Santa María 1893c, 182; Fita y Colomé y Colomé 1883, 293 [1485]; Furtado 1935, xxxii [Evora 1536]; Azevedo Mea 1982, 249, 279 [Coimbra 1571]; Medina 1887, 1:128 [Peru 1578]; Sierro Malmierca 1990, 96, 188, 191 [Ciudad Rodrigo 1580s, 1625]; Wiznitzer 1960, 14 and Furtado 1929, 100 [Brazil 1593]; Blázquez Miguel 1986a, 140 [Castile 1610]; Liebman 1970, 97 [1639]; Lewin 1977, 47 [Mexico 1642]; 82 [1785]; da Cunha e Freitas 1952, 20 [Lisbon 1673]; Schwarz 1925, 36 [twentieth-century Portugal].

39. *Os manda amortalhar em lançol inteiro sem lhe tirar ramo näe pedaço algum por grande que o lançol seja e atalos amortalhados somente com ataduras, mandando que os não cosam com algulha* (Furtado 1935, 133). For additional biographical information about the Antunes family, see Lipiner 1969, 122–43.

40. *Que lo amortajasen con sus calçones e capa como sabía que se fazzía en çibdad Real* (Fita y Colomé 1883, 299).

41. *Quando auian desenterrado a çiertos conuersos del honsario de Sant Françisco desta çivdad para ver sy estauan enterrados como judios . . . avian hallado enterrados como judios con çaraguelles e camisas e calçones e con otras muchas vestiduras como judios e syn thener cruz ninguno dellos* (Beinart 1977a, 2:90).

42. *Lhe poserão huma coyfa douro e hum paninho de franja douro e hum trançado que levava huma fita encarnada e asy huma camisa de desfiado* (Baião 1921, 141). This custom, like so many others, was reinforced by travelers' tales of Jewish practices in other lands. In the Mexican Inquisitorial prison in 1645 the *converso* Juan de León said that back in Italy when a Jew dies they "dress him in the best clothes he has and take him to our synagogue" (*Le ponen el mejor vestido que tiene y lo llevan a nuestra sinagoga*). He also said that in Italy "they put certain things in the deceased's mouth, according to ceremony, and on other parts of his body, mixed with perfumes, in the manner of the Jews" (*Los metían en muriendo en la boca algunas cosas, que son ceremonias, y en otras partes de su cuerpo, mezcladas con olores, a la usanza de los judíos*) (Lewin 1975, 148–9).

43. Modern customs are sometimes contradictory. In this century in Belmonte, Portugal, when someone dies they dress the corpse in brand-new white clothing, taking care to use nothing of color (Paulo 1970, 145). Vasconcelos reports, on the other hand, that modern Portuguese new-Christian dead are generally clothed in black, with a white shirt, in the Catholic manner (Vasconcelos 1985, 173).

44. *Calcones de lienço que le subian un poco encima de la rodilla e con una mortalla e una barbillera* (Marín Padilla 1983b, 316).

45. *Fizo hunos calçones de lienço y pusole huna cofia y hun trapo por la cara y con ciertas vendas envendolo por los ojos y por la boca de la manera que los judios fazen a sus muertos* (Marín Padilla 1983b, 316). See also Saraiva 1969, 164 [1536]; Sierro Malmierca 1990, 96 [1580s].

46. *Le diese vn quartillo de plata, el qual le puso en la mano, disiendole: "Tomad, que lleues para la primera posada"* (Moreno Koch 1977, 356). See also 355; Furtado 1935, xxxii [Evora 1536]; Paulo 1985, 64 [Portugal twentieth century].

47. *Y que por miedo del Santo Oficio, les ponen en la vía ordinaria el oro que les habían de poner a los difuntos en la boca y oídos* (García 1910, 101).

48. *Ao Vale de Josafat irás / um leão encontrarás;*
    *Se te pedir carne, dá-lhe páo; / Se te pedir senha, dá-lhe dinheiro;*
    *Se te procurar de que lei és, / Diz-lhe que és de Moisés.*
    *Que te deixe passar / livre e desembaraçado*
    *para onde Deus te deixar, / para onde Deus te mandar.*
    *Se perguntar quem te compôs / diz-lhe que foi uma hebreia*
    *que neste mundo ficou, / que te fez o que sabia,*
    *não te fez o que devia*

(Paulo 1985, 145; Machado 1952, 43). For additional examples of the practice of putting coins in the deceased's mouth see Blázquez Miguel 1987, 45 [1489]; 1986a, 254 [early eighteenth century]; Saraiva 1969, 164 [1536]; Baião 1921, 119 [1541]; Wiznitzer 1960, 39 [Brazil late eighteenth century]; Liebman 1970, 97 [Mexico 1639]; Lewin 1977, 47 [Mexico 1642]; Roth 1931–2, 28.

49. *Les ponen . . . en la boca moneda de plata, aljófar o otras cosas* (Santa María 1893c, 182).

50. *Tem guardado as joias de quasou pera se enterrar com ellas quando morrer* (Furtado 1925, 338).

51. Adler (1899, 37, 42). For other examples see Saraiva 1969, 164 [1536]; da Cunha e Freitas 1952, 20 [Lisbon, 1673]; Liebman 1970, 83, 97; 1975, 100 [Mexico]; Lewin 1977, 47 [Mexico 1642]; Wiznitzer 1960, 14 [Brazil]. This practice occurs so frequently, in both Spain and the colonies, that Liebman's assertion that "the custom may have been adopted from some of the Indians" is not credible (Liebman 1970, 83).

52. *Estando la dha doña Blanca Enrriquez cercana a la muerte, hauiendose sentado en la cama hiço traer en eso un torillo de Michoacan y abriendolo ella mesma por su mano saco un aspador de perlas con estremos de oro y sacando uno de los dhos extremos y se lo dio a una de sus hijas q no se acuerda esta confesante qual fuese diciéndole q la guardare para metérselo en la boca en espirando lo qual despues de auer espirado se lo metio en la voca, no saue quien* (AGN Vol 402 doc 1, 34b–35a). Michoacán, a region two hundred miles west of Mexico city, was known and is still known for its lacquerwork chests and figures.

53. *Para que holgase alla en pas e que no viniese tan ayna por otro debdo suyo* (Blázquez Miguel 1985b, 58). *Ayna*: from the Hebrew 'Ani = poor. See also Blázquez Miguel 1986a, 69; Liebman 1970, 83; Machado 1952, 43 [1952].

54. *Quando vino el doctor Thomas [de Cuenca] a esta çibdad e hizo desenterrar çiertos muertos . . . dizen los allauan vnas botijas de agua* (Beinart 1977a, 90).

55. *Hallaron a vno enterrado con vn pedaço de queso tan grueso como el puño* (Beinart 1977a, 93).

56. *Oyó decir entonces, aunque no se acuerda a cual de sus hermanas, que un papel de dientes de la dicha doña Blanca Enríquez lo llevó Pedro de Espinosa, y lo echó en la sepultura en que la enterraron en el convento del Carmen* (Lewin 1977, 47).

57. *Que de un escritorillo sacasen los dientes y muelas que se le habían caído y sacado mientras vivió, para que se los echasen en la sepultura, cuando la metiesen en ella* (García 1910, 207).

58. *Quando auian desenterrado a çiertos conuersos del honsario de Sant Françisco desta çiudad para ver sy estauan enterrados como judios . . . avian hallado enterrados como judios con çaragelles e camisas e calçones e con otras muchas vestiduras como judios e syn thener cruz ninguno dellos* (Beinart 1977a, 90). See also Moreno Koch 1977, 364.

59. *Lo llevan a nuestra sinagoga, y allá le cantan los hombres y mujeres* (Lewin 1975, 148).

60. *Si acaso cuando lo llevamos a enterrar pasa alguno de estos embusteros que no son de nuestra Ley se vuelve el cuerpo a su casa y hasta que pase el tercer día no lo llevamos a donde lo hemos de llevar, porque es azar y agüero entre nosotros, y lo tenemos por mala señal* (Lewin 1975, 148).

61. *Son celemonias que los jodios fazen quando algun pariente lievan a enterrar, que acompanyan el cuerpo y algunos lloran; y quando ya le dexan enterrado cada huno toca en la sepultura y dize: Dios te perdone* (Marín Padilla 1983b, 292).

62. *Algunt ssamas* [Heb. = sexton], */ porquel reze en el Homas* [Heb. = Five (books of Moses)] */ e le canten con buen son / vna huynna* [Heb. = lament], *vn pysmon* [Heb. = hymn], */ bien planidos por compas. . . . / Al qual manda ssu sudario / en senal de çedaqua* [Heb. = Righteous charity] */ porque rreze tefyla* [Heb. = prayer]/ *desque ffuere en su fonsario* (Baena 1966, #142).

63. Caro Baroja 1961, 1:439–40. See Melammed 1991b, 162–5. See Chapter 15.7 for use of the term *guayas*.

64. For additional funeral prayers see Azevedo Mea 1981, 165 [1580s]; for twentieth-century Portuguese prayers see Machado 1952, 43–7; Paulo 1970, 64–6; 1985, 64–6; Schwarz 1925, 76–8, 86–7, 103–4; Vasconcelos 1985, 208–9.

65. *Dios te perdone. . . Dios le perdone en su ley. . . Buen poso aya en su ley* (Marín Padilla 1983b, 292–5).

66. *"Dios le dé parayso a mi padre"* o *"buen siglo,"* lo vno desto. El qual dicho su padre murió judío (Carrete Parrondo 1985a, 126; cf. 123). To judge from Inquisition trials the phrase was common among Christians and Moslems as well.

67. *O Anjo da Guarda te guarde! / O Anjo da Guarda te guie! / O Anjo Santo Rafael / Peça ao Senhor por ti* (Paulo 1970, 96).

68. *Deus vos salve lá passados, / fostes vivos como nós, / nós seremos coo vós, / lá nesse ceu onde estais / pedi ao Senhor por nós, / que, neste vale de lágrimas, / pediremos ao Senhor por vós* (Schwarz 1925, 76–7). Versions of this poem in Spanish are current among Spanish Christians—I recall seeing it engraved over the gate of the municipal cemetery in Logroño—; eighteenth-century English-language versions are found in every New England graveyard.

69. *Mandó que diesen por su anima dos fanegas de trigo para el çofar de los judios de Huete por que dixese algunas oraçiones por su anima* (Moreno Koch 1977, 364). Çofar is a Hebrew word that means schoolmaster or teacher and by implication rabbi.

70. *Decir un responso en hebraico* (Cabezudo 1950, 282).

71. *Lo bien fecho nunca se perdía e aprouechaua* (Carrete/Fraile 1987, 59).

72. Freehof 1973, 147. See also Levi 1982, 47–8.

73. *Folgansia Compuesta / estancia alta / debajo del ala de la divinidad / en grado de sanctos - / Como Lustro de los Cielos / ylustra y esclarece, / escapamiento de guessos. / Perdon de culpas / allegamiento de rebeldes, / Piedad, Clemencia, Partebuena = / Para el mundo venidero / allí se aparto el alma / de fulano o fulana / q se aparto de este mundo / en brevedad de años. / Per boluntad del morador de los cielos / Rey de los Reies / ampare su alma / y le de onrra / sobre su folgança / como huerto alto / como manadero de agua / que nunca faltaron sus aguas / y sobre su asida / sea el alma de fulano o fulana / acompañada / con durmientes en Hebron / con David, con Salomon, y / con todos los prophetas del Señor. / Y sea el alma de fulano o fulana / atada contigo de aro / con los muertos de los muertos / de Nros Muertos. Amen* (AGN 402, doc 2, 517G-18a).

74. *Deus de Abraão, ponde esta alma na Vossa santa mão. Amém. . . . Ao alto Deus de Jacob, que é o nome do Senhor, esta vai dita e feita por alma de _____, que deste mundo partiu na noite santa de capaz* [sic] *ao outro dia de capuz, para que os seus pecados lhe sejam procurados e, diante daquele Deus, lhe sejam todos perdoados. Amém* (Paulo 1970, 146; 1985, 89–92).

75. *Bemdito sempre louvado seja o Senhor dos altos Ceus, que nos da tantos bens seus, e em nós tem tantos cuidados: aceitemos de bom grado o mantimento que comemos, graça com que o servimos depois da morte, amen! Cantemos com grã victoria: -O Senhor leve esta alma á sua divina Glória!* (Schwarz 1925, 86).

76. *De las cosas que peor me paresçe en esta ley que agora thenemos es enterrarse vnos sobre otros e sacar los huesos e tornarlos otra ves dentro; que en la ley que soliamos tener non nos enterramos vnos sobre otros, syno en tierra virgen* (Carrete/Fraile 1987, 58; see also 122); Beinart 1974, 309, 312.

77. A 1410 last will and testament from Alba de Tormes refers to Jewish burial in a "legal plot" (*campo dinado* [din: Hebr. "judgment/court"] . . . *en tierra tuesta, nin tañida nin tocada*), that is, one maintained according to Jewish law with undisturbed soil (Amador de los Ríos 1875, 964).

78. *Quanto yo, no me quiero enterrar sino en el fosar de los convesos . . . estava ay, quasi junto con el dicho fosar de los judios que no ay sino huna tapia en medio* (Marín Padilla 1983b, 327). In many cities in Aragon *conversos* founded brotherhoods [*cofradías*] in the name of some saint for the purpose of burying their members appropriately (Hinojosa Montalvo 1993, 40).

79. *La dicha Maria de la Higuera se enterro en Alcaçar de Consuegra en San Sebastian, fuera de la villa, donde todos los conversos se enterravan en el canpo fuera de la dicha yglesia* (Beinart 1981b, 601; cf. 641).

80. *Por estar solo y en tierra virgen, commo hazen los judíos, por no se enterrar en la yglesia* (León Tello 1972, 85).

81. *Jorge Dias mercador e Gracia da Villa outrossi mercador cristãos novos já defuntos que estão enterrados na ermida de Nossa Senhora da Concepção desta villa se mãodarão enterrar nella por ser terra virgem* (Furtado 1929, 54).

82. *E porque lançauão em couas onde já jouveraã outros defunctos que todos os pecados daqueles que aly jaziam se lhe apegauã* (Baião 1921, 129).

83. Blázquez Miguel 1985a, 65. For other examples see Blázquez Miguel 1985b, 57; Liebman 1975, 100; Blázquez Miguel 1985b, 76 [1593]; etc.

84. *Em terra virgem, e em covas muyto fundas* (Furtado 1935, xxxii) [Evora 1536].

85. Braunstein 1936, 107, 188. For additional examples of burial in virgin soil see Marín Padilla 1983b, 328–30; Furtado 1935, xxxii [Evora 1536]; Azevedo Mea 1982, 299 [Coimbra 1573]; Furtado 1929, 378 [1594]; Liebman 1970, 97 [1639]; Lewin 1977, 47 [Mexico 1642]; Liebman 1974, 157 [Mexico 1649]; Lewin 1939, 26 [twentieth century]; Lipiner 1977, 52.

86. *Señor, no lo erró, mas antes hiso como discreta e escoj[i]ó gentyl enterramiento enterrarse en tierra virgen* (Carrete Parrondo 1985a, 112).

87. *Era Judeu, e que por isso se mandara enterrar naquelle lugar que era em terra virgem na qual se costumão enterrar os judeus* (Furtado 1925, 478; cf. 255, 340).

88. Blázquez Miguel 1986a, 79, 56. For an eighteenth-century example see Blázquez Miguel 1985a, 69.

89. Beinart 1975, 651; see also 1974, 309, 312.

90. "They put under their head a pillow of virgin soil" (*Les ponen a la cabecera una almohada con tierra virgen*) (Santa María 1893c, 182).

91. For modern burial customs of Ladino-speaking Jews see Dobrinsky 1986, 87–95.

92. Sánchez Moya/Monasterio Aspiri 1972, 122, 13. The rumor is also discussed in Marín Padilla 1983b, 325; Floriano Cumbreño 1924, 579–81.

93. Mo'ed Katan 27b; Shulḥan Arukh YD 378:1. See also Levine 1982, 210.

94. In 1489 Elvira Sánchez "made a funeral banquet for the deceased" (*Hasia cohuerço a defuntos*) (Moreno Koch 1977, 357). See also Carrete/Fraile 1987, 77; Coronas Tejana 1988, 201.

95. Sperling 1968, 294. Melammed recalls the tradition (Genesis Rabbah 63:14) that "eggs are sealed and lentils have no mouth; the mourner is symbolically lacking a mouth because he cannot greet others" (1991b, 161).

96. *Una tortilla de huevos e dos peras e dos panes y uvas e agua en vn cántaro . . . en una çestilla, cobierta con vnos manteles blancos* (León Tello 1972, 85).

97. AGN Vol 402 doc 1, 34a; cf. Vol 402 doc 2, 518b. This is probably the Hebrew word for mourning: *Avelut* (Wiznitzer 1960, 244).

98. *Se había de comer por las personas que le tocaban en sangre o parentezco un huevo duro y frío, sin sal [llamado el aveluz], en señal del dolor que tenían, y quien los traía a la casa del difunto, tenía gran mérito para con el Dios de Israel* (García 1910, 205). See also Liebman 1975, 124.

99. *Habiendo comido el aveluz del huevo sin sal por el dolor de la muerte de su padre, se entró, en compañía de su hermana, de Micaela Enríquez, y de otra judía famosa, en un aposento que es-*

*taba vacío, y se pasearon a toda priesa muchas veces por él, para dejar allí el aveluz para el primer católico o católica que entrase en él y le cayese encima la desdicha y mala ventura, que por aquella ceremonia creían estar libres* (García 1910, 209).

100. *Habiendo comido al media día cosas de pescado para limpiarse de la desdicha e infortunio de su aveluz* (García 1910, 245). The Granada trial provides the peculiar detail that the person who distributed the funeral eggs stood on one foot (Liebman 1970, 83). For additional examples of funeral meals see Roth 1931–2, 29; Wiznitzer 1960, 14; Fita y Colomé 1883, 293 [1485]; Blázquez Miguel 1986a, 72 [Sigüenza 1492]; Coronas Tejada 1988, 201 [Jaen 1511]; Furtado 1935, xxxii [Evora 1536]; Saraiva 1969, 164 [1536]; Adler 1899, 16; [Mexico 1645]; Liebman 1964, 103; 1970, 83; 1974, 221, 233 [Mexico 1645–9]; Levy 1987, 24 [twentieth century]; Dobrinsky 1986, 91, 104 [twentieth century].

101. This may be in accord with Deut. 26:14 or Dan. 10:3; the *Shulḥan Arukh*, YD 341:1 states that "one who suffered a bereavement . . . eats not meat nor drinks wine."

102. "Sitting on the floor behind closed doors they eat fish, olives, but not meat" (*Comen en el suelo tras las puertas pescado, aceytunas, y no carne, por duelo del diffuncto*) (Santa María 1893c, 182).

103. See, for example, Beinart 1974, 1:545; Marín Padilla 1983b, 322 [1483]; Furtado 1925, 275 [1591]; 1935, 132, 139 [1592]; Blázquez Miguel 1986a, 140 [1610]; Liebman 1970, 97 [1639]; Selke de Sánchez 1972, 100 [1677]; Machado 1952, 47 [1952].

104. *Quando moría alguno de la Calle de Sayell, no se avía de comer carne en 24 horas hasta que fuesse enterrado el cadaver, si no es que fuesse niño* (Selke de Sánchez 1972, 274).

105. *Una olla de açelgas con queso e pan rallado . . . e no comieron otra cosa* (Carrete/Fraile 1987, 116–7).

106. Cortes 1985, 290; cf. Selke de Sánchez 1972, 100.

107. *Comian gallinas a su mesa y los conuersos en el suelo garuanços e huevos* (Beinart 1974, 176). Liebman reports that Justa Méndez, burned in effigy in the Mexican *auto de fe* of 1649, said that when someone died in her family they "threw freshly slaughtered meat and fish under the bed in which she had died" (1974, 219), but he ventures no explanation for the custom.

108. *Le fisieron ally el cohuerço e comieron en el suelo nueve dias pescado y huevos* (Beinart 1974, 309).

109. *Cuando murió su madre en toda la semana no comieron carne, sino pescado* (Moreno Koch 1977, 353).

110. *Todos los siete dias despues de aver muerto el dho su padre, les embiaron de comer. . . . Guardaron la costumbre ordinaria de embiar de comer cossas de pescado quando muere algun observante de la dha ley* (AGN Vol 402 doc 1, 27b). See also Liebman 1970, 97.

111. For other examples see Beinart 1974, 292, 312; Fita y Colomé 1883, 293 [1485]; León Tello 1972, 84–5; Coronas Tejada 1988, 201 [1511]; Furtado 1929, 101 [1593].

112. Evora in 1536 (Furtado 1935, xxxii); Mexico in 1639 (Liebman 1970, 97).

113. *Comio a los cohuerços en casa de Çuçen, en el suelo, en modo judayco* (Beinart 1981a, 305). As Beinart notes, this description was so common as to be almost formulary. For similar examples over a wide time span see Fita y Colomé 1883, 293 [1485]; Beinart 1974, 309; Llorca 1939, 141 [1484]; Santa María 1893c, 182; Coronas Tejada 1988, 201 [Jaen 1511]; Melammed 1991b, 160–2 [Spain early 1500s]; Saraiva 1969, 164 [1536]; Blázquez Miguel 1986a, 59; Adler 1899, 69 [Mexico 1645]; Liebman 1970, 80; Lewin 1939, 26 [eighteenth century]; Paulo 1970, 92 [twentieth-century Portugal]; Levy 1987, 24 [twentieth-century].

114. Probably from the Arabic *almatrah* = cushion or large pillow.

115. *Pusieron media fanega en el suelo o otra cosa baxa donde pusieron los manteles . . . tenían mesa alta en que solían comer antes que muriese* (Carrete/Fraile 1987, 116–7). See also Beinart 1981b, 3:641. A *converso* from Barbastro in 1491 added the detail that when some relative died "he would eat at a low table and . . . from new bowls and plates as per Jewish ceremony" (*Comia aquel dia encima del almadraque zollado e comia en scudillas e vaxilla nueva por cerimonia judayca*) (Cabezudo 1963, 284). See also Wiznitzer 1960, 14.

116. Sperling 1968, 301 cites *Midrash Rabba Vayikra*, Ch. 18.

117. *Quando murió su padre, que comió el primero día en suelo encima de vna almadra, quería pescado e huevos e que duró tercero día en aquella cerimonia* (Llorca 1939, 141). See also Furtado 1929, 101 [Brazil 1593].

118. Adler 1899, 69, 80–2. For additional examples of a crypto-Jewish seven day mourning period see Liebman 1970, 83; 1974, 214; 1975, 124; and García 1910, 124 [Mexico]; Moreno Koch 1977, 366 [Garcimuñoz]; García Fuentes 1981, 435 [Granada 1593]; Adler 1899, 69 [Mexico 1645]; Haliczer 1990, 234 [Madrid 1710s]; Paulo 1970, 28, 146; 1985, 89 [twentieth-century Portugal].

119. Marín Padilla 1983b, 323; for other examples see Cortes 1985, 290; and Selke de Sánchez 1972, 276 [Majorca 1670s].

120. *Comen en el suelo tras las puertas pescado, aceytunas, y no carne, por duelo del diffuncto no saliendo de cassa por un año* (Santa María 1893c, 182). For a later example [Hita 1520] see Melammed 1991b, 164. Jiménez Lozano found that in certain villages of Castilla-León well into the 1960s Christian mourners ate fish, hard-boiled eggs and olives at funerals (1984, 362–3); he considers this an example of a "culteme"; see my Chapter 7 note 57.

121. *Le fisieron ally el cohuerço e comieron en el suelo nueve dias pescado y huevos* (Beinart 1974, 309). See also León Tello 1972, 84.

122. *En otro tiempo usauan los judios por luto ayunar ocho dias por sus padres, pero agora se asse cumplir con el mundo* (AGN Vol 276 doc 14, 419a).

123. AGN Vol 402 doc 1, 27b, 34a.

124. *Rasgando el capus, de la pena, e avía oydo desir que era çerimonia judayca* (León Tello 1972, 83).

125. Liebman 1975, 127. For additional examples see Beinart 1975, 545; Moreno Koch 1977, 366 [Garcimuñoz]; García 1910, 245; and Liebman 1975, 124 [Mexico]; Paulo 1970, 28, 146. Modern Ladino-Speaking Jews gather at the house of the deceased after the funeral to symbolically cut two pieces of clothing, an outer garment and an undergarment, which is called *cortar keria* (Dobrinsky 1986, 91).

126. Some new-Christian mourners in Portugal in this century do not shave for thirty days after a loved one's death (Paulo 1985, 89; 1970, 93).

127. *Nunca mais vestio camisa lavada nem dormia em cama senão no chão* (Furtado 1925, 379; cf. 258, 538).

128. *Fez o pranto diferente do que usam os cristãos levantando as fraldas e asentando se com as carnes no chão* (Furtado 1925, 275; cf. 392, 401).

129. Sánchez Moya 1973, 133. For other examples see Liebman 1974, 129 [Mexico 1649]; Braunstein 1936, 107 [Majorca 1670s]. Paulo reports that new-Christians in Portugal in this century do not change for eight days the bedclothes in the bed where someone has died. Each day they go into the room and pray: "May God grant you a good night. You used to be like us, and we will be like you" (*Boa noite te dé Deus, / Tu já foste coo nós / E nós seremos coo vós*) (Paulo 1985, 65).

130. *Estaua retraydo en vna cámara pequeña, enparamentada de paramentos negros, çerradas las puertas e ventanas, e descalço e el capirote metido en la cabeça, e la veca reboçada a la voca. E estaua así como los judíos suelen estar en los syete días, quando se les muría pariente çercano* (Carrete Parrondo 1985a, 152).
131. *Emramarão a casa* (Furtado 1925, 315).
132. *Se abian de descolgar las zalas donde estaban despues de muertos* (García Fuentes 1981, 435).
133. *Bañándose en la mesma casa de estos endiablados difuntos* (García 1910, 245).
134. *Quando levavão o defunto pera fóra mandava varrer as casas e despois de varridas botar as vassouras fóra e mandava trazer outras vassouras novas pera casa* (Furtado 1925, 315).
135. *Se labo el cuerpo y cabeza por haverse allado presente a la muerte de dho diffunto* (Bel Bravo 1988, 114).
136. *Assim com o mar é salgado / Deus de Israel o salvou, / Deus desintrefle esta casa / e tudo o que nela ficou* (Paulo 1970, 146). See also Machado 1952, 44.
137. Its origins are traced to 2 Sam. 3:35; Esth. 4:3; Ezra 10:6 (*Enc. Jud.* 12:485).
138. *Não comendo cousa que lhe soubese bem* (Furtado 1925, 258).
139. *Las personas que se hallaban presente no abian de comer en siete dias carne ni hacer oracion a Dios* (García Fuentes 1981, 435).
140. *Esta misma Catalina de Çamora tenia por ofiçio de endechar los muertos e desir las endechas* (Beinart 1974, 388). See also Beinart 1981b, 685; Blázquez Miguel 1986a, 72; Sánchez Moya 1973, 117.
141. *Oficiantes contratadas ou rezadeiras* (Vasconcelos 1985, 200).
142. *En muriendo uno todos hacen muy gran sentimiento y le hacen muchos súchiles y oraciones* (Lewin 1975, 148).
143. *Endecharon y cantaron, dandose palmadas como fasen los judíos* (Moreno Koch 1977, 356). See also Llorca 1942, 149 [1484]; Cantera/Carrete 1971, 270 [1522]; Furtado 1935, xxxii [Evora 1536].
144. *Sacalda a fuera a la fermosura, buena sea su ventura . . . guayas, guayas* (Cantera Montenegro 1985, 84).
145. *Çierta persona nombra las cantares, e luego la dicha Ysabel e las otras personas continuavan el cantar e lloravan y sabadeavan* (Melammed 1991b, 164).
146. *Endechauan . . . andando al derredor de la cama del difunto, subiendo vnas vezes ençima de la cama . . . e otras vaxandose. . . . Fuy al canpo, la mal casada, e cogi las yervas* (Cantera/Carrete 1971, 262).
147. *Asentando se com as carnes no chão guajando com a cabeça. . . . A vio dentro em huã casa pequena assentada no chão sobre a terra . . . e estaua pranteando a ditta morta toda cuberta com o manto guajando se toda como se diz em vulgar abaixando muito a cabeça e tornando a a levantar baqueando se desta maneira muitas vezes* (Furtado 1925, 275, 364).
148. Liebman surmises that this derives from the Hebrew *Avelei* which means mourners. According to Roth, in Mexico the traditional funeral banquet was called *aveluz* (= Hebrew: aleph beth lamed vav tav) (Roth 1931–2, 30). We have seen earlier in this chapter that the word may also have referred to hard-boiled eggs.
149. *Era el plañidero de sus mortuorios.*
150. *No hubo mortuorio de judío o judía que acabase sus desdichados días, en que no se hallase haciendo el oficio de plañidera y cuidando se hiciesen en sus cadáveres y entierros todas las invenciones y supersticiones de que se vale esta pérfida gente* (García 1910, 117, 250).
151. *Este testigo puso en la cozina donde el dicho bachiller murio, por mandado de su muger, vna escudilla con agua y vn candil ençendido que estuuo ally nueue dias, para en que se vañase el alma*

(Beinart 1974, 309). For other examples see Beinart 1974, 312; 590; Marín Padilla 1983b, 316 [1488]; López Martínez 1954, 1860; Rodrigues 1937, 11.80:4.

152. Paulo (1970, 92); cf. Vasconcelos 1985, 174. It is still common today among many Ladino-speaking Jews (Dobrinsky 1986, 91, 106).

153. Sperling 1968, 290.

154. For these and other explanations see Blázquez Miguel 1985b, 56; Furtado 1935, xxxii; Gracia Boix 1983, 133; Azevedo Mea 1982, 362. It may also be related to Psalm 20:15 (Liebman 1970, 82).

155. *Cuando alguno se muriese derramasen toda el agua que hubiese en casa, porque se iba a bañar el alma en cualquiera agua que hallaba; y al octavo día en el mismo lugar y hora que espiró pusiese una porcelana en que se había de bañar el ánima del difunto* (Gracia Boix 1983, 133). For a similar example see Carrete Parrondo 1985a, 30 [1490].

156. See Melammed 1991b, 157–8. Marín Padilla considers the custom common in Castile but rare in Aragon 1983b, 319.

157. *Derraman por las cassas de los diffunctos el agua que tienen los cántaros y tinajas quando mueren* (Santa María 1893c, 182).

158. For example, that of Evora in 1536 (Furtado 1935, xxxii) and Mexico in 1639 (Liebman 1970, 97).

159. *Derramar todas el agua de casa y de siete casas a la redonda* (García Fuentes 1981, 435). Melammed finds that Spanish Judaizers seem to have defined the immediate neighborhood as two house on each side of where the death occurred (1991b, 158).

160. *Le mandó a la moça derramar el agua quando murió su madre de Diego Laynes, christiano nueuo, e desían que estaua alli el ánima del defunto* (Carrete/Fraile 1987, 68). For some other examples see Moreno Koch 1977, 366 [Garcimuñoz 1480s]; Blázquez Miguel 1986a, 56 [Castile]; Carrete Parrondo 1985a, 29, 30, 63, 64, 162 [1490–1502]; Saraiva 1969, 164 [1536]; Blázquez Miguel 1985b, 56; Baião 1921, 114 [1541]; Azevedo Mea 1982, 6, 362 [Coimbra 1567–73]; Gracia Boix 1983, 133 [Cordoba 1572]; Wiznitzer 1960, 14; Furtado 1925, 243, 315, 379, 552; 1929, 100, 364, etc.; 1935, 23–4 [Brazil 1591–4]; Liebman 1975, 124 [Mexico]; Sierro Malmierca 1990, 191 [Ciudad Rodrigo 1620s]; Adler 1899, 93 [Mexico 1642]; Lipiner 1977, 59–60; Paulo 1970, 146 [twentieth-century Portugal]. Jiménez Lozano found it in Grajal de Campos (León) in the 1960s 1984, 365. See note 120 of this chapter.

161. In Salonica up until modern times water was poured out at both the house of the deceased and the houses next door (Molho 1950, 174).

162. *No sacaron en aquellos dias agua del poço* (Beinart 1974, 175).

163. *Quando alguno murio tapava el pozo disiendo que no se vinyesen alli a bañar las almas de los muertos por guardar e cunplir la çerimonia que los judios guardavan en sus mortuorios* (Melammed 1991b, 162).

164. *No vevieron del agua que estava en casa el dia en que ella murió* (Moreno Koch 1977, 353).

165. *Ainda que tivesse muita água em sua casa nem dela havia de comer nem beber senão de água nova que mandava buscar* (Coelho 1987, 210).

166. *Quando morresse alguma pessoa em casa que não haviam de beber aquela água que estivesse em casa* (Pereira 1979, 190). The family of this Brazilian Judaizer was studied by Lipiner 1969, 144–64. For similar examples of this custom see Azevedo Mea 1982, 157 [Coimbra 1569]; Blázquez Miguel 1986a, 141 [Castile 1654]; Selke de Sánchez 1972, 276–7 [Majorca 1678].

167. *Este testigo puso en la cozina donde el dicho bachiller murio, por mandado de su muger, vna escudilla con agua . . . que estuuo ally nueue dias, para en que se vañase el alma* (Beinart 1974, 309, 312). See also Sierro Malmierca 1990, 95 [Ciudad Rodrigo 1580s].

168. *Pusieron en vn palaçio donde el dicho Diego Lopes fallesçio vna escudilla llena de agua e vnas tovajas blancas e vnas agujas salmar e nueve candilejas ençendidas por el alma del dicho Diego Lopes* (Beinart 1974, 598). See also López Martínez 1954, 186.

169. Liebman 1970, 82, citing Jiménez Rueda, *Herejías y supersticiones en la Nueva España*, 93.

170. *Creen que las almas de los difuntos, transformadas en pájaros, van a beber o bañarse, y para eso, junto a los cuerpos difuntos, ponen un jarro de agua con un paño de manos* (García 1910, 101).

171. *Porque su alma se iba a bañar y lavar de los pecados en ella* (García 1910, 205; cf. 209, 210).

172. Blázquez Miguel 1986a, 57; Marín Padilla 1983b, 324; Melammed 1991b, 162.

173. *Poner al octavo día una jarra de agua para que se viniese a lavar el ánima* (Gracia Boix 1983, 140).

174. Levy reports a remnant of this custom from the Ladino-speaking community of Rhodes in this century. When someone died "a pitcher of water was placed outside the front door. This pitcher was known as a 'librik' and was made of earthenware. . . . Immediate family, relatives and neighbors came to visit; and as they went out the front door, they would wash their hands with the water from the 'librik.' The 'librik' remained there and was used until after the funeral procession returned to the home" (1987, 23).

175. *Beber siete dias agua recien trayda de la fuente* (García Fuentes 1981, 435).

176. *Mãodava lançar fóra a agoa dos potes que estavão na cantareira da salla donde ella bebia e tornar a enchellos dagoa fresca da fonte. . . . Ho fizera por lhe morrer na ditta sala a ditta escrava e deixar fedor* (Furtado 1929, 273–4; see also 364, 385; 1935, 32 [1591]); Lipiner 1977, 60.

177. For example, the *conversa* Violante de Castro was accused in 1489 in Aragon of donating a shroud around 1478 for the funeral of the child of the Jew Clara de Bonafos (Marín Padilla 1983b, 296).

178. Paulo 1970, 27, 50, 55. See also Machado 1952, 47 [1952]; Vasconcelos 1985, 174.

179. *Pega, leão; deixa a alma deste defunto enquanto passa o rio Jordão* (Paulo 1970, 28). See also Machado 1952, 44, 47 [1952]; Paulo 1985, 65.

180. *Que a alma deste nosso finado saia do purgatório como o bafo sai deste pão* (Paulo 1970, 28). See also Machado 1952, 47 [1952].

# CHAPTER XII

# Sabbath Customs

Observance of the Sabbath is the single most persistent crypto-Jewish custom. From the earliest days of Judaism the Sabbath was regarded as the most holy of Jewish festivals. Observance of the Sabbath is not dependent upon either synagogue or community, although it is greatly enriched by communal prayer and fellowship. Sabbath observance includes both positive precepts (lighting Sabbath candles, blessing the wine, studying the Torah) and negative precepts (abstaining from work).[1] The holiday was particularly well suited to clandestine crypto-Jewish observance because so many of its practices are home-centered, and this is one reason why its observance was a mainstay of crypto-Jewish adherence to ancestral practice. In fact, over time and throughout Iberia and her possessions it is the most frequent and persistent Judaizing practice.[2] This chapter examines preparations for the Sabbath, Sabbath religious observances, and Sabbath social customs and concludes with a look at traditional crypto-Jewish Sabbath recipes.

As the holiest of all Jewish holidays, the Sabbath receives the most attention in the Bible, the Talmud, the Mishnah, and rabbinical literature. The first activity mentioned in the Ten Commandments is to "remember the Sabbath day, to keep it holy" (Ex. 20:8). Legend has it that if only one Sabbath were properly observed by all Jews the Messiah would appear (Talmud Shab. 118b). Reverence for the uniquely holy nature of the Sabbath was one of the central tenets of crypto-Judaism for as long as the crypto-Jews held on to Jewish customs. Remarks like those of the Sorian new-Christian Graciana Santa Cruz—who, hearing her granddaughter say in 1502 that today was Saturday, replied: "How right you are, daughter; today is the Sabbath, and the Sabbath is a special day"[3]—are extremely common and persist almost without change well into the seventeenth century. Francisco Maldonado de Silva said in his trial in Chile in 1626 that he always "observed the Sabbath, as the law of Moses commands, because that precept seemed inviolable."[4] Ana Cortés [Majorca 1688] reported that her father, Joseph Cortés, had instructed her "that the principal festival of the law of Moses was to observe the Sabbath, and that she should keep it so strictly that she should not even pluck a leaf from a tree, nor eat anything cooked on the Sabbath."[5] Even though these sentiments were occasionally expressed in Christian terms, such as when Antonia de Oliveira [Bahia 1591] testified that her grandmother, Branca Roiz, had told her "to observe the Sabbath, because Saturdays were the true Sundays,"[6] the basic reverence for the Sabbath remained the same. The Sabbath was holy, a time for rest and reflection, for putting aside weekday quarrels. Lucía Fernández [Ciudad Real 1513] testified against Juan de Teva and Juana Núñez, saying that "he and his wife on Friday nights did nothing at all, and that on other weekday nights they would scrap and fight, both Juana Núñez and her husband, and he would scream at her. But on those Friday nights they didn't do any of this."[7]

The Sabbath was celebrated for twenty-four hours, from sundown on Friday until sundown on Saturday. The traditional Sabbath calendar begins on Thursday afternoon or Friday morning with cleaning and cooking for the holiday. On Friday evening candles were lit, the wine was blessed, and a festive family meal was served. The children received their parental blessing and the family went to bed early. Saturday's activities centered on worship, study of the Law, rest, and communal socializing. Saturday at sundown ceremonially marked the passing of the Sabbath. The documentary evidence shows that the traditional Sabbath calendar was largely maintained by the crypto-Jews in their observance of the holiday, and the wealth of detail in the documentation attests to a rich, complex, and sustained repertoire of Sabbath customs. The rhythm of Sabbath observance among crypto-Jews does not appear to have varied much from place to place or across the centuries. Even when Judaizing *conversos* could not keep every Sabbath precept they could refrain from work and, in a phrase that appears in countless sixteenth- and seventeenth-century Inquisition cases, "keep the Sabbath in their hearts."[8] People who still thought of themselves as Jews despite practicing no overt observances of any kind retained this sense of the holiness of the Sabbath. Typical was José da Silva, a Judaizing Brazilian poet [Lisbon 1726], who reported that "he kept the Sabbath only in his spirit, because since he was a student on those days he did not abstain from studying."[9]

## 12.1. Preparations for the Sabbath

Observant Jews are said to receive the Sabbath as if she were a bride coming for the first time into the home of her betrothed. It is not surprising, then, that preparations for the Sabbath include a strong emphasis on cleanliness.[10] Iberian crypto-

Jews, particularly women, would bathe themselves on Friday afternoon. Especially in the years immediately following the Expulsion, Judaizing women would gather at one of their houses to turn the Sabbath bath into a light-hearted, communal celebratory experience. At María González's house [Ciudad Real 1512] "on Friday nights the witness and all the women she had named bathed themselves according to Jewish ceremony in a large basin of water that had been heated with chamomile and other herbs, which María González warmed and set out. . . . And when she had the water ready she sent for this witness and all the other women on Friday night to come and bathe. The youngest bathed before the older women, and the older women washed the younger women all over their bodies."[11] Another witness said that "the water was heated with rosemary and orange peels," or "with herbs and chamomile."[12] María González herself confessed that "other people bathed with her at that time, and that they shut themselves in an interior patio so that the serving women would not see them."[13] This Sabbath bath does not differ significantly from one described by the Mexican crypto-Jew Simón de León in 1647. He reported that his father Duarte de León "bathed his body in hot water which one of Simón's two sisters heated for him, sometimes on Friday, other times on Saturday night, in a tub in his room . . . taking turns, one daughter on Friday and the other on Saturday."[14] In later testimony we learn that it was a wooden tub that his father bought one Friday in the market, and that the daughters heated the water with rose petals. Simón confessed that he himself did not bathe at home, but rather "he took his bath in the pool in Chapultepec on Sunday with the other Catholic children."[15]

When a full ablution was not possible, crypto-Jews washed what they could, with particular attention to their feet, nails, hair, and sexual organs. Diego de Zamora and his colleagues who were *converso* Jeronymite monks in San Bartolomé de la Lupiana used to wash their feet on Sabbath eve.[16] Catalina Enríquez [Mexico c. 1593] was also denounced for washing her feet and cutting her nails on Friday afternoons before the Sabbath (Liebman 1970, 169; cf. 96). According to the testimony of Manuel Gil [Mexico 1603], Ruy Díaz Nieto always "trimmed his hair on Fridays because it is a special ceremony of the Jews, and because it is a sin for them to trim their hair, beard or nails on the Sabbath."[17] Gil also said that one Friday evening about nine o'clock he had caught Ruy Díaz Nieto's friend Antonio Méndez at his bath. "He saw him standing naked on top of a large hearth on which they cooked for him. When the [water and] herbs were hot, and in the presence of Gil and a black servant he had named Juan Angola, he washed his groin and legs, and with a knife scraped the bottoms of his feet, and cut his nails. And on a stand next to the window he saw a razor and on the floor the signs of his having cut the hair from under his arms and from his private places, because he saw the hairs there. And what surprised him was to see that he would not let the Negro wash him, as he usually did."[18] It was reported to the Lisbon Inquisition in 1726 that José da Silva, the Judaizing Brazilian poet, honored the Sabbath by "washing himself on Friday evening from the waist down."[19]

After the bath, but for that matter even if they had not bathed, Judaizers traditionally put on clean clothes to welcome the Sabbath. This custom was so widespread and well known that it was listed in every compilation of crypto-Jewish customs, from the late fifteenth century[20] through the innumerable Edicts of Faith of the sixteenth and seventeenth centuries. To *conversos*' old-Christian neighbors this custom was objectionable both for religious reasons and because it seemed ostentatious. According to 1484 testimony in Ciudad Real, María Díaz and her daughters "dressed up on Saturdays and primped like great ladies."[21] Occasionally witnesses described the Sabbath clothes with details that confirm the elegance of this display. María González confessed in 1512 that some ten years earlier she and a friend "used to go visiting on Saturdays all dressed up; the wife of Rodrigo de Chillón wore a dress of thin black velvet and purple damask, and this witness wore a white *fustan* in summer, and a clean shirt."[22] Beatriz Gomes [Evora 1570] reported that on Friday nights she put on a clean shirt and a clean kerchief on her head.[23] Of Caterina de Figueredo, a Brazilian *christaā nova* [Pernambuco 1594], it was reported that on Saturdays "she wore the best clothes she owned, the overdress of silk, a new blue sash overlaid with another good green sash, and a clean blouse and a clean jacket of white Dutch linen, and a clean cowl in her hair."[24] During the reign of Felipe III, when the starched, ruffled collar was the principal male item of adornment, according to Duarte Rodríguez [Mexico 1603] "one Saturday morning, between six and seven, he saw [the *conversa*] Isabel Rodríguez with a large clean collar in her hands for her husband Sebastián de la Pena, and two small clean collars for her two sons."[25]

Some crypto-Jewish women tended to their appearance in other ways as well. María Díaz and her daughters [Ciudad Real 1484] "kept the Sabbath and dressed up and put on makeup."[26] If fine clothes were not available, then at least the clothing had to be clean. Rodrigo de la Sierra [1513] said that "his mother used to tell him many Saturdays: 'Put on a clean shirt, damn it!, and take off your sash if it is dirty, Devil take you!' "[27] And if poverty limited a crypto-Jew's ability to celebrate the Sabbath in proper style, then Judaizers did what they could. Another witness in a 1513 trial said that "she also sometimes put on a clean shirt on Saturday, but she did not put on a clean hair cowl, inside or outside, because she only owned the one she had on."[28] Fifteen-year-old Simón de León [Mexico 1647] confessed that "his father . . . put on clean clothing and bedclothes Friday nights, but that he did not, because he only had two shirts and those had to do for both him and his brother Jorge. And they each had to go around undressed when they washed their shirts."[29]

As important as cleansing the body in preparation for the Sabbath was cleaning the house. In fact, bathing and house cleaning prior to the Sabbath were such widespread practices among Judaizing *conversos* that they were invariably mentioned in the Edicts of Grace as one of the identifying characteristics of crypto-Judaism.[30] On Friday afternoon the house would be swept and the dirt or wooden floor would be sprinkled with water to keep the dust down. This too was an activity easily observed by one's neighbors, so it often appears in trial testimony. In 1484, for example, Catalyna Martínez said that she went to Juan Dávila's house one Friday evening "at dusk and found him and his wife [at home], the house swept and watered down and the table set with white tablecloths, and the two of them sitting at it."[31] Similarly, in 1510 Diego Gómez [Toledo 1510] was denounced because "on the Sabbath his house was swept and watered down and washed out and decorated and scented with perfume and incense,"[32] these last being practices that probably derived from those of Spanish Moslems. Wealthy crypto-Jews enlisted the help of their servants or slaves in these preparations. Branca Dias [Pernambuco 1595] was accused of having her black slaves wash the floor of her house in preparation for the Sabbath.[33] But this was always dangerous, for non-Judaizing servants could easily reveal the family's secrets to Inquisitors.

Evidently some new-Christians swept their house in an idiosyncratic fashion related to their respect for the holy word, although this seems to have been noticed only rarely by Inquisitors. Isabel Núñez [Ciudad Rodrigo 1623] was reported to sweep her house on Fridays from the outside in,[34] and Yerushalmi cites another instance of a *converso* " 'sweeping the house the wrong way' [*varrer a casa as avessas*]; i.e., sweeping the dirt from the entrance toward the inside of the room, rather than out through the door." He finds the reason in an essay by Moses Hagiz (1671–1750), who says that "it was a custom of the Spanish Jews not to sweep through the doorway out of reverence for the *mezuzzah* on the door post" (Yerushalmi 1971, 37).

An important part of cleaning the house for the Sabbath was changing the bed and table linen. The very first compilations of crypto-Jewish customs referred to washing the family linen prior to the Sabbath (Santa María 1893c, 182), and the custom was practiced virtually without change for as long as crypto-Jews continued to observe the Sabbath. Thus Violante Vaz [Evora 1571] was accused of putting freshly washed sheets and blankets on her bed to honor the Sabbath.[35] Isabel Lopes [Evora 1583] reportedly told the Inquisition that "to honor the Sabbath on Friday afternoon she cleaned the house and the shop and put washed linens on the bed, and if some of the linens were new she said that first she had to moisten one corner before putting them on the bed."[36] Pedro Abella, of Barbastro, was accused in 1491 of putting out clean towels on Friday night.[37] A late fifteenth-century satiric poem from a court poet named Román against the *converso* poet Antón de Montoro lists among his Judaizing customs that on Friday he set the table for two days.[38] Over the centuries hundreds of Judaizers were similarly accused of putting "clean cloths on their tables . . . to honor the Sabbath."[39]

Because no work could be done on the Sabbath the business of preparing for the holiday had to be completed by sundown on Friday night. This included both shopping[40] and the preparation of the Sabbath meals, which will be considered later in this chapter. Although fasting in preparation for the Sabbath is not widespread in Judaism (*Orekh Ḥayyim* 249), it was frequently practiced by the crypto-

Jews. In fact, according to Blázquez Miguel most Castilian crypto-Jews in the sixteenth century observed the Sabbath fast (1986, 62). Luis de Valencia [Mexico 1638] was also accused of fasting on Friday to prepare for the Sabbath (Osorio 1980, 185–6). In fact, this custom was particularly popular among New World Judaizers; in Brazil it persisted until at least the eighteenth century (Wiznitzer 1960, 159).

Lastly, some Judaizers in the years immediately after the Expulsion finished their preparations for the Sabbath by going to bed earlier than on other nights. Beatriz López, of Hita [Toledo c. 1520] reported that "she used to go to bed earlier on Friday nights than on other days in order to honor the Law of Moses."[41] But as marital intimacy was an expected part of Sabbath observance,[42] perhaps that too influenced the decision to cut the evening short. The González sisters in Ciudad Real scented their Friday bath water with sweet herbs (Beinart 1977a, 274) perhaps because they were washing not only to honor the Sabbath, but also because they expected to have sexual relations with their husbands that evening. Lucía Fernández in 1511 testified against her mistress María González, saying that "on those Friday nights when her mistress bathed she did not do any work; and when she came in off the patio from bathing she would go to bed with her husband. And the two of them didn't do anything else on Friday night."[43] A Mexican trial in the 1630s revealed that Luis Pérez Roldan required his wife to have relations with him on Friday evening (Liebman 1970, 245). Among the accusations brought against Isabel Núñez, burned in effigy in the great Mexican *auto de fe* of 1649, was that "every Friday night she went to sleep with her husband, leaving his dying mother unattended because it was an inviolable precept which they affected. . . . Married couples had to sleep together on Friday nights even though they had had quarrels and without even considering a sudden fit of illness" (Liebman 1974, 168). Perhaps this explains the statement of Juana Núñez [Ciudad Real 1512] that "she used to go to bed earlier Friday nights than other nights of the week for the pleasure of it."[44]

## 12.2. Friday Evening Religious Observances

Home ritual plays an important part in the observance of the Sabbath. But communal Sabbath prayer too has always exerted a strong attraction to the observant Jew or Judaizer. In normative orthodox Judaism there are three communal Sabbath services: the Friday afternoon prayers that begin just before sunset and conclude with the regular evening prayers during which the Sabbath is formally welcomed (*Kabbalat Shabbat*); the Saturday morning service during which a portion of the Torah and of the Prophets (haftarah) are read; and Saturday afternoon's additional prayers (*musaf*). The *havdalah* ritual, which traditionally marks the "going out" of the Sabbath (*motz'et shabbat*), is usually performed at home. In the decades immediately following the Expulsion crypto-Jewish observance tended to follow this pattern, although, since Jewish books had all but disappeared in 1492, crypto-Jews celebrated without reading the Torah or reciting prayers too lengthy to have lodged in the oral tradition. In normative Judaism all these activities are important, but among most groups of crypto-Jews Sabbath observance seems to have been largely on Friday evening. These observances were largely home-centered and reserved for the family and their closest friends.

Frequently the service would begin with special prayers or hymns to welcome the Sabbath. This was a solemn moment requiring the full attention of family members in attendance. Juan Sánchez Exarch [Teruel 1484] first went "to an antechamber and washed his hands, saying a prayer during which he would not allow anyone to speak, except through signs."[45] The opening Sabbath ceremony could take many forms. The new-Christian might go outside to search the heavens for the first stars that indicated that the Sabbath had come, in accordance with the tradition that the Sabbath begins "when three stars of medium size become visible" (Maim., *Yad*. III,1,v,4). Pedro de Higueras testified against Leonor de la Oliva [1521], saying that some years before on "Friday nights she went outside to pray to heaven when the stars had come out, and he saw her do this many Friday nights."[46] Sometimes the ceremony took place later in the evening. In 1512 Alonso Sánchez said that he and Isabel de los Olivos "got together to pray . . . on Friday nights, an hour or two after dusk . . . and after they had prayed each one went home."[47]

Even up into the seventeenth century the Friday evening observance sometimes included blessing one's children. Blanca Enríquez [Mexico 1642] "blessed her grandson, Gaspar, on Fridays before dusk by placing her hands on his head, bowing her head, and saying, 'May the Lord bestow upon you and your children the blessings of Jacob and Israel' " (Liebman 1970, 270). Other times, particularly in the years around the Expulsion, the Friday evening gathering might involve more people than just family, and might include a communal reading, as when Alonso Rodríguez [Ciudad Real 1483] testified that one Friday night he saw a *converso* named Alvaro "in his large room, up some stairs, sitting with a hood over his shoulders and head, reading to many *conversos*."[48]

Perhaps the most important part of the crypto-Jews' home Sabbath ritual was the kindling of the special Sabbath light. This is wholly in accord with normative Judaism. Traditionally on the Sabbath at least two lamps are lit in recognition that the injunction to keep the Sabbath appears twice in the Pentateuch (Ex. 20:3; Deut. 5:12–15). The laws governing the lighting of Sabbath lamps are given in the Talmud (Shab. 25b, 31a) and in the *Mishnah Torah* (Maim., *Yad*. III,1,v). Lighting Sabbath candles or lamps is one of the most persistent crypto-Jewish customs. Not only does it receive mention in every Edict of Grace, it appears in almost every Inquisition record from the earliest days until the middle of the seventeenth century. Levine (1982, 29) argues that oil lamps were much more common than tallow candles until the seventeenth century; but Inquisition records suggest that among some groups oil lamps lasted even longer than that. In fact the custom of lighting an oil lamp rather than candles persists among some Turkish Ladino-speaking Jews, as does the custom of lighting multiple lamps, sometimes as many as seven in honor of the seven days of the week.[49]

Mexican Crypto-Jews tended to use candles instead of oil lamps, and they treated them differently from everyday illumination. In Mexico in the 1580s the circle of the Carvajal family kept the candles they used for religious purposes separate from those they burned for illumination (Liebman 1970, 173). According to Duarte Rodríguez [Mexico 1603] only whole candles were lit on Friday nights at the home of Ruy Díaz Nieto, even though most other nights they only burned candle ends.[50] Even after his first imprisonment and reconciliation Díaz Nieto persisted in lighting a whole tallow candle on the Sabbath and leaving it lit until it burned out.[51]

In Judaizing *converso* homes the routine associated with lighting Sabbath lights was complex and dangerously visible. First the lamps had to be carefully cleaned. Alvaro González de la Higuera testified against Inés de la Higuera [Ciudad Real 1521] saying that "he saw her kindle her lights on Friday nights and observe the Sabbath, and that he also saw her light them other nights. And that Friday nights he saw them scald them in a flame and clean them earlier than on the other nights, and they set them burning behind a closed door in a large room, below the room where they slept."[52] In 1484 the wife of Juan González Escogido cleaned her lamps by boiling them, according to a witness, in "a pot of melted syrup [wax?]."[53] Often, particularly in the early years, these lamps were part of elaborate candelabra. Alfonso Iniesta of Alfaro [Aragon 1490] said that "one Friday afternoon he saw the maid, Marica, cleaning some iron lamps that were set on an iron stand, on which stand there may have been seven or eight little lamps, in the same form he had seen in the house of Don Bueno, a Jew of this town, . . . and they lit these lamps on Friday nights behind the doors of their room."[54] Diego Gómez of Toledo [Toledo 1510] was denounced because an informer saw on Friday nights "in a large room which is by the front gate of his house certain lamps set on a chandelier suspended from a hemp rope."[55]

For oil lamps new wicks had to be prepared. Tradition holds that the wick must be made of "a substance to which the flame adheres firmly, such as hatcheled flax, linen cloth, cotton cloth, and the like" (Maim., *Yad.* III,1,v,5), that the lamp must burn oil (v,8), and that the light is to be kindled by a woman (v,3).[56] In 1504 in Córdoba in a clandestine synagogue the rabbi Alonso de Córdoba Membreque instructed the congregation "to use new cotton wicks in honor of the Sabbath." Then everyone who was present "before they left the synagogue made wicks of new cotton for their lamps and after they had made them they washed them in the water in which the rabbi and all the others had washed their hands."[57] The González sisters Beatriz, Leonor, and Isabel [Ciudad Real 1511] on "Friday nights ordered their black slave Françisca to clean three lamps which they had, and when they were clean and the sun had set Juan de la Sierra's wife said to the slave: 'Look if the sun has set and light these lamps.' The slave cleaned the lamps and put in new wicks and lit them."[58] Inquisition depositions frequently refer to the fact that in well-to-do homes a servant was asked to prepare the Sabbath lamps, for if the mistress of the house had a servant to do the rest of the cleaning, it would draw suspicion for her to clean the Sabbath lamps herself. Yet, as Inquisition testimony makes all too clear, servants quickly perceived the pattern of lamp cleaning on Fridays and with the help of the publicly read Edicts of Faith were not slow to identify it as a sign of Judaizing. Lucía de Lillo [Ciudad Real 1511] said that some four years previous María González "every Friday night ordered her to light two clean lamps with clean wicks earlier than on weekday nights, and that one of them she put in the bedroom where her master and mistress slept."[59] On Friday nights in Coimbra in 1569 Graça de Leão also used to light a lamp with two new wicks (Azevedo Mea 1982, 156). Lighting Sabbath lamps with new wicks persists even among remnant crypto-Jews in Portugal. In 1952 Machado reported that new-Christian villagers in the Mogadouro region of Portugal on Friday light "the Lord's lamp" (*a candeia do Senhor*), which is filled with olive oil, and uses a new linen wick made by twisting an odd number of strands (Machado 1952, 37–8).

Most denunciations to the Inquisition for Judaizing routinely merely list candle lighting among their accusations, suggesting that the custom was well enough understood to require little in the way of corroborative description. Mari Aluares was accused in 1491 in Soria of "lighting lamps on Friday night and praying over them like a Jew as she lit them."[60] The Iniesta family [Alfaro, Aragon 1490] "lit lamps on Friday nights behind the doors of their room."[61] In the Jeronymite monastery of Guadalupe in 1485 several *converso* monks were accused of lighting candles on Friday nights so openly that the prior had to warn them to stop (Sicroff 1965, 99). Occasionally additional details are given. André Monteiro told Inquisitors in Bahia around 1590 that, when he had seen Manuel Lopes keep the Sabbath back in Lisbon, Lopes "and his sisters would gather in a circle and light the candles and perform certain ceremonies."[62] In Mexico in the 1580s the Carvajal family and their friends dedicated the Sabbath lamps to the souls of the dead, "so that through them the deceased of Israel might attain glory and rest." The wicks would contain one strand for each of the deceased. When lighting them they would say, "I see this one for So-and-so; . . . [may God] give him eternal bliss" (Cohen 1973, 133). As innumerable testimonies make clear, Judaizing women in their homes, Judaizing monks in their monasteries, and, when they were able, Judaizing prisoners in their Inquisition jails all lit the Sabbath lamps. The custom was neglected only by those crypto-Jews who were for some reason unable to kindle the Sabbath lights—such as Catarina Fernandes [Coimbra 1573] who declared that "because she was blind and did not control the use of her hands she only lit the Sabbath candles in heart."[63] Roth is correct in observing that this is without doubt the most persistent of *converso* customs (Roth 1931–2, 20).[64]

The blessings traditionally recited over the candles are short and easily committed to memory; thus they persisted in the oral tradition with very little change down through the centuries. Many of these traditional blessings were recorded by Inquisition scribes. Catharina Alvares Dalegre [Lisbon 1543] allegedly recited this prayer over the Sabbath candles: "These are the holy and blessed prayers that our God commands us to say when we kindle the Sabbath lamps with clean olive oil."[65] Filipa Fernandes [Coimbra 1583] told Inquisitors that she recited over the Sabbath candles a prayer that began: "May our candle burn clear and white now and forever."[66] In the seventeenth century Majorcan *chuetas* would bless their candles by saying "Praised be the name of God."[67] In Cataluña Judaizers might chant "Blessed are You, my true Lord, Adonai."[68] Portuguese Judaizers in Castile used this prayer when lighting candles: "Clear and white may this candle be for us, now and always."[69]

Once the lamps were lit, tradition dictated that they be allowed to burn until they extinguished themselves of their own accord. The often cited González sisters [Ciudad Real 1511] were accused of kindling Sabbath lamps which "burned all night and they did not put them out. And when they went to bed they filled them with oil."[70] Some *conversos* even took steps to make the Sabbath lamps burn longer. One of the González sisters said that María González "made her put in the lamp that she set in her bedroom a grain of salt, saying that it would make the light last longer."[71] Because leaving the Sabbath lamps lighted violated the usual imperative to conserve expensive oil, crypto-Jews had to be careful to have explanations ready to parry awkward questions. Juana Sánchez [Garcimuñoz 1490] was accused of lighting a Sabbath lamp with two wicks. A witness reported that she "asked if she should put out the lamp, and her mistress told her: 'Leave it, child, because I want it to burn.' And this witness asked her why, and her mistress replied that it was because of the devotion she had for the Trinity that she wanted it to burn."[72] Doña Joanna [Lisbon 1543] was said to have a lamp "that came from the holy temple in Jerusalem and for this reason it never went out."[73]

It was crucial to the survival of the Judaizing family to hide Sabbath lamps from the prying eyes of servants and neighbors. The strategies of dissemblance were as varied as their imaginations. Cantera reports that in Hita Judaizing *conversos* "on Fridays would bring more oil into their homes than they usually did and would order their servants to go to bed before they did."[74] The Carvajal sisters [Mexico 1580s] used to place the Sabbath lamps in a special room where they could burn unobserved until they went out (Cohen 1973, 132). Micaela Enríquez [Mexico 1648] reported that in her mother's house "on Friday nights they would light in the name of the Lord a lamp made of a wick floating in a little bowl of olive oil, putting it inside an empty box so that their slaves would not see it, and it would burn there all night."[75] Other New World *conversos* placed their candles under a table or covered the windows with a black cloth (Liebman 1982, 102). Tomás Treviño de Sobremonte, burned in Mexico in 1649, hid his Sabbath like a tree in a forest: he told the Inquisitors that "in order not to violate the Sabbath by extinguishing the candles lit for religious reasons and in order not to arouse the suspicions of his servants, he did not blow out the candles on week nights in the upstairs room that he used for his midnight prayers" (Liebman 1970, 147).

Kindling a special lamp for the Sabbath is a key component of the crypto-Jewish rituals discovered in Trás-os-Montes early in this century. In 1929 Arturo Carlos de Barros Basto took the French journalist Lily Jean Jarval to a poor crypto-Jew's home in Bragança, where he asked an old woman to recite some prayers. "The woman covered her head with a white cloth . . . She went off mysteriously for the Sabbath lamp . . . which she put in our hands. Then she faced east. Her face, deep-lined from poverty, was illuminated; tears rolled from her eyes, and with a trembling voice she chanted: 'The blessing that the Lord gave the sun, the moon, to Jacob and Abraham and Isaac and holy Sarah and holy Raquel extend to this poor pilgrim' "[76] New-Christian villagers in the Mogadouro region of Portugal light Sabbath candles with this prayer: "Blessed is my God, my Lord, my Adonai, who orders us to keep His holy commandments, blessed and holy, and to light this twisted wick to brighten and gladden this holy night of the Lord, so that the Lord will bring light to our souls and will free us from error and sin. Amen, Lord. May this rise to heaven."[77] While preparing their lamps they also recite this blessing: "Praised be the Lord, who has ordered me to keep His holy commandments. The Lord has said that I shall wash my hands with clean water before twisting this linen, and that I burn olive oil in His holy lamp, in the holy name of the Lord, amen."[78]

Today the secret kindling of the Sabbath lamp has become a principal motif in the folklore surrounding the crypto-Jews. Most people who consider themselves to have descended from remnant crypto-Jews report some version of the custom of hiding candles. Liebman claims that in 1964 and 1965 he interviewed nuns in Mexico and Lima who "light candles on Friday nights and place them under a table covered by a long cloth, so that the flame is not visible." They reported that their mothers had taught them to do this, and that it was the obligation of the eldest daughter (Liebman 1982, 112). Fierman recounts a recent anecdote from Ciudad Juárez, Chihuahua, in which a man named José Nevárez told a man named Prieto that his mother and grandmother, in Zacatecas, had lit candles on Friday night. He claims to have met other Mexicans as well in the El Paso area who remember lighting candles on Friday night (Fierman 1987, xii, 15). Twentieth-century Judaizers around Bragança in Portugal were observed lighting a *candeia do Senhor* inside a clay pitcher on Friday afternoons to welcome the Sabbath.[79] A man in 1989 recalled that in his Catholic Cuban grandfather's house "we would light candles on Friday evenings, always in a concealed place" (Anon. 1989, S5). Anne Cardoza reports that her grandmother, Pauline, who emigrated from Gerona to Buenos Aires to the United States, would light votive candles on the Sabbath. They used "little red or blue glass Catholic votive candles" and would light them "in the bedroom, sometimes even in the bathroom, but never on the dining room table, lest someone say you were a Jew" (Cardoza 1989, S2). In fact, every Jewish community, and every Hispanic country, has its version of the tale of the crypto-Jews who each Friday night light a candle inside a pitcher, or down in their basement, so that no one will see them. While there are scattered references to lighting candles inside a box, there are no reliably documented instances of lighting the candle inside a pitcher. Nonetheless, the persistence of the legend is testimony to the need of modern society to believe in the continuity of faith and the ingenuity of the human spirit.

## 12.3. SATURDAY RELIGIOUS SERVICES

Among observant crypto-Jews Saturday morning was almost always given over to prayer. Some *conversos* prayed alone. Prior to the Expulsion, Judaizing converts could at some risk attend the synagogue with their former coreligionists. After 1492 specially designated areas in the *converso* home substituted for the prohibited synagogues,[80] and family members and sometimes guests would gather there for the Sabbath prayer. Generally they came together only once each Sabbath. In some towns it would be on Friday evening; in others on Saturday morning. Sometimes the Sabbath observers would stay over, praying through the night.

In the rare instances in which the clandestine synagogue was open to a broader spectrum of the Judaizing public, the records show that some coded indication might be devised to call the faithful to prayer.[81] Thomas Lopes [Pernambuco c. 1579] allegedly signaled Judaizers to come to the synagogue by walking in the street with one shoe on and a cloth tied around one toe of the other.[82] Margarita de Rivera [born in Mexico City 1610] reported that Judaizers were called to prayer by "a Negro [who] was dressed in a red suit and went through the streets playing a tambourine" (Liebman 1982, 122). But given the relative rarity of such descriptions in the records it is reasonable to assume that most crypto-Jews came together on Saturday morning by prior arrangement, without the need for any sort of encoded signal. In the early years arrangements tended to be casual: Ysabel de los Olivos testified [Ciudad Real 1512] that a woman named Florencia called them to prayer, and "sometimes she sent her black slave Isabel, and that other times she doesn't remember who called them or whether they went by themselves."

Prior to the Expulsion observant crypto-Jews often attended synagogue services with their former co-religionists. Buena Pero González de Pozuelo [Atienza 1491] used to go to the synagogue on Saturday to "see the Torah."[83] Sancho de Contreras reported in 1484 that he had seen the *converso* Diego Arias wearing his tallit and praying on the Sabbath in the synagogue with the Jews.[84] Those who did not held Sabbath services in their homes or sometimes even in remote locations in the countryside.[85] Once inside whatever space had been designated as the synagogue, the Judaizers would pray according to their means and knowledge.[86] In the years prior to the Expulsion and for the first half century after, it was not unusual for them to have some knowledge of Hebrew and to use some carefully hoarded Jewish prayer book. There was generally a reader, who took the role of rabbi, covering his head with a white cloth, sometimes a table cloth, as if it were the ritual tallit. Diego Arias, a rich *converso* spice merchant who became tax collector for Enrique IV, frequently celebrated the Sabbath for his *converso* friends in his home or, if they were traveling, in the inn at which they were lodging. Jacob Castellano, an official of the Jewish community of Medina del Campo, in 1486 described one of these Sabbaths to the Inquisition:

> And there in his lodgings Diego Arias put out of the room to which he and the Jews had withdrawn all of the Christians who were there.... And there was a table set for dinner with a cloth, and two benches. He took a cloth that was on the table and climbed up on a bench which was in front of a bed that was there, and put the cloth over his head the way the Jewish chaplain puts on the large *taler* to pray, and he began to sing a responsive prayer that the Jews say on the Sabbath or any of their festivals when they go up to the pulpit or *tebá*. He recited this with a melody, the way Jews do and with as much grace and more."[87]

Prior to the Expulsion it was not unusual for crypto-Jews to continue to possess Jewish books. For example, Juan Díaz [Ciudad Real 1484] allegedly read from Hebrew books on Friday nights and Saturdays, "sitting in a doorway of his house, and many *converso* men and women came to hear him read, and they filled the doorway and sat around him and responded aloud as he read, bobbing their heads."[88] More often the prayer service was held indoors. On the Sabbath in the 1480s the Díaz family of Ciudad Real "closed themselves up in a large room and read in a book with their heads covered."[89] Other witnesses said that Juan Díaz used to read to his wife from "a book that said: God of Abraham, God of Isaac, God of Jacob."[90] Other witnesses said that the women of the family used to read together, "saying, among other words: 'If you knew or understood which are the three books of the Holy Law, *Rebeca la chirimia, barach Adonai barach.*'"[91] Alfonso Sánchez testified in 1511 that "some thirty years ago, more or less, he and his sister Florencia... were locked in a large room of the house of Florencia and her husband Juan Ramírez, and that Ramírez read to his sister from a small book of Jewish prayers; and... it was on Saturday mornings and sometimes in the afternoons, and occasionally on Friday nights.... And after Juan Ramírez and the others had recited the Jewish prayers, they talked with one another about things which go against our faith and against Christians, and they made fun of the law of the Christians, and how they were deceived and blind, and how the Law of Moses was good and true and through it they would be saved, and how all the rest was nonsense."[92] On the whole these descriptions of new-Christian Sabbaths prior to the Expulsion are very similar throughout Spain, and resemble this 1489 Calatayud Sabbath: "On a candelabra which was in the center of the room there were many small oil lamps, which were lit; and that man who had come was entirely covered with a white cloth, his head and his whole body, and he set on a table a book from which he read while the others, who were behind him, gestured with their heads and with their bodies, and they were there more or less three hours."[93]

For many years after the Expulsion Sabbath observance appears not to have changed very much. Elvira González [Ciudad Real 1511] confessed how "she and the wife of Juan de la Sierra, and Leonor, her daughter, and Isabel González . . . observed the Sabbath all together, and did not perform any work. They went up into a little room which is over the gate to the street, and they took there a little book of Jewish prayers and they prayed from it, sometimes one of them, and sometimes another. And sometimes what they read from the book was: 'Creator, Creator.' And that is how they passed the time."[94] In 1543 Catharina Annes told the Lisbon Inquisition that Manuel Soares and his wife "kept the Sabbath and Friday nights they lit a candelabra with many wicks, gathering their whole family into a room far removed from the rest of the house where they read from some large books saying: "I see, I don't see; I see, I don't see."[95]

Sabbath observance among later generations was so routine that investigators rarely pumped for details. Common are bare-bones descriptions such as this one, from Bahia in 1591, of "a house where certain people gathered on Friday nights until Saturday after dinner."[96] But from time to time an individual trial included a wealth of detail. Sometimes snippets of Sabbath prayers are transcribed. For example, Mexican Inquisition documents contain considerable information about the practices of the Carvajal family in the 1580s. The family routinely gathered on the Sabbath. Luis or Baltasar, or, if they were not present, one of the women, would conduct the service. Readings were in Latin, with just the *Shema* and its response in Hebrew. The service began with recitation of Psalm 51:17, followed by this prayer: "Comprehend me, O Lord, in Thy help, and forget not to help me. . . . Lord of the world, I come before Thee to pour forth my soul with a sacrifice of prayers, entreaties, cries and petitions. I come before Thee for tokens of mercy and to ask Thy compassion." The main part of the service was verses from the Psalms, including 92, 103, 121, and 148, together with original poems and prayers composed by family members and friends and paraphrases of the Bible in Latin or Spanish (Cohen 1973, 135; cf. 207–8). Liebman found that other seventeenth-century colonial Mexican Judaizers used to recite this Sabbath prayer in Portuguese: "He who sings will drive away his sorrows; / he who cries will make them worse: / I sing in order to dissipate / the suffering that torments me."[97] In 1657 Gaspar Enríquez, resident in Toledo, was arrested for keeping the Sabbath and for reciting this Spanish prayer: "Oh living eternal God, who created the heaven and the earth and gave life and being and courage to all beings, free us, great Lord of the heaven and the earth."[98] Judaizers in Majorca in the 1670s prayed on Friday night through the intercession of San Tobit. They welcomed the Sabbath with a version of the *Kabalat Shabbat* which they learned from the book *Ramillete de Flores*.[99] Specifically Jewish books were by then exceedingly rare, but as late as the eighteenth century a Sabbath prayer book was circulating among Portuguese new-Christians.[100]

In the Trás-os-Montes region the pattern of Sabbath observances among twentieth-century Portuguese new-Christians is closer to the calendar of normative Judaism than are most of the sixteenth- and seventeenth-century examples. This suggests that a re-education in Jewish custom may have occurred somewhere along the way with sources extraneous to the crypto-Jewish tradition.[101] Schwarz in 1925 found Portuguese Judaizers still gathering three times on the Sabbath to pray (Schwarz 1925, 30). Paulo collected several twentieth-century Sabbath prayers in Portugal. He reports that on Friday nights some crypto-Jewish women put a linen towel over their heads and recite this prayer three times: "I offer my prayers, my praises, in praise of You, Lord. May all that I ask of You be granted. In the name of the Lord, Adonai, amen." The rest of the family respond: "Blessed and praised, magnified, raised, manifested, revealed, honored, celebrated and exalted be the seventy names of God. Adonai, amen."[102] Another Sabbath prayer was collected in Bragança in 1926: "Today is the holy Sabbath, the holy Sabbath of the Lord, which the Lord made for His rest, so that we might praise, exalt and glorify His holy and blessed names."[103] On Saturday morning in Belmonte *criptojudeus* gather in someone's home, where a woman (*rezadeira*) leads them in prayer: "On a Holy day like today / God took pleasure and rested, / His holy flags set out, / and his pennants raised on high, / and the names of the Lord / were pronounced and declared / by the mouths of all the winds / augmented by the animals. / Sabbath, Sabbath, Moses, Moses, / on the Sabbath you shall not work. / You must occupy yourself with serving and worshipping / the great God Adonai. / There has never been another nor will there be. / Praised be the Lord who gives us life, / Amen. Lord, [may these prayers] rise to heaven, and reach heaven."[104]

## 12.4. OTHER SABBATH ACTIVITIES

On Saturday, most observant crypto-Jews seem to have spent their Sabbath activities between communal prayer and visiting with their friends and relatives. The most important component of this activity, of course, was observance of the strict requirement not to work on the Sabbath. The Fourth Commandment (Ex. 20:10) states that "the seventh day is a Sabbath to the Lord your God; in it you shall not do any work, you or your son, or your daughter, your manservant, or your maidservant, or your cattle, or the sojourner who is within your gates."[105] Based on this, the Mishnah (*Shab* 73a) lists 39 prohibited activities. Abstention from work was a cardinal precept almost universally observed by Judaizers from the earliest days up until modern times. As a negative action (like fasting or abstaining from eating pork) it was somewhat easier to conceal than positive actions (like circumcision or conducting a Passover *seder*). Edicts of Faith, such as that of Valencia in 1484, call attention to people "who celebrate the Sabbath by not doing any work or permitting that anyone in their household work."[106] Judaizers from Spain in the 1480s[107] to Mexico in the 1640s[108] to twentieth-century Portuguese new-Christians have all abstained from labor on the Sabbath.[109]

Many crypto-Jews interpreted the injunction against working on the Sabbath with extraordinary strictness. Diego Juárez de Figueroa [Mexico c. 1647] explained that "on the Sabbath you may not even lift a straw from the ground."[110] *Conversos* routinely considered the injunction against labor to include physical labor, commerce, household tasks, lighting the fire, and traveling. Testimony in Ciudad Real in 1484 accused some *conversos* because "on Saturdays, to honor and observe the Law of Moses, they did not do business, nor would they handle money, just like the Jews do."[111] Gomes de Chinchilla [Ciudad Real 1484] declared that he saw Maria Dias and her daughters "praying, and he asked them for money to buy food and they did not want to give it to him because it would interrupt their prayer."[112] María de San Juan [Baeza 1573] reported that her mother said that God had commanded "that Friday nights they should not leave the pot on the fire nor the kitchen rags hang outside to dry."[113] In Brazil the school teacher Bento Teixeira was denounced [1593] because "on Saturdays he did not hold class and he ordered his students not to come to class saying that he did not want to have class on Saturdays."[114] Similarly, in 1594 in Pernambuco João Picardo denounced the new-Christian goldsmith Ruy Gomes because "when the witness asked the goldsmith to sell him some gold earrings for his wife the goldsmith responded that he did not have them; but then the following day that was Sunday in the morning before mass the witness saw the goldsmith in his shop with a hammer in his hand making the things of his profession and he asked him to sell him the earrings and the goldsmith sold them to him."[115] Mexican crypto-Jews felt the same way. Captain Esteban de Lemos testified in 1604 that the *converso* merchant Ruy Díaz Nieto refused to sell anything on Saturday. He reported that one Friday night a woman asked Díaz Nieto to send her a new cowl the next day and he replied: "Daughter, don't you see that tomorrow is Saturday?"[116] Juan de León [Mexico 1642] explained that "the Sabbath was a festival, and that on it you cannot work from four in the afternoon on Friday." León also said that it was forbidden to bear arms on the Sabbath.[117] Juana Enriquez went so far as to "slice the bread and cut the meat into bite-size pieces prior to the Sabbath so that the use of a knife would not be necessary on the Sabbath" (Liebman 1982, 119). In 1636 Antonio Cordero was denounced in Chile for not selling on the Sabbath. He stated that "I will not sell today, because it is Saturday, nor tomorrow, which is Sunday."[118] Some Mexican Judaizers carried these abstentions even further. In the great *auto de fe* of Mexico in 1649 Pedro Mercado was burned in effigy for, among other things, taking "his merchandise out of his house on Saturday so as to sell it in the streets but, in fact, he did not sell. Instead he returned to Jews that which he had repaired. He sent this little youth to do this latter form of work but he himself had no intention of vending his wares on such days so that he would not lose the merit of observing his holidays" (Liebman 1974, 180).

The prohibition against travel was also widely observed. Juan de Fes [Ciudad Real 1484] testified that "on Friday afternoon [he and Sancho de Çibdad] came to Linares, and the next day Saturday he did not want to leave there, because the witness knows that he kept the Sabbath."[119] The *converso* Jeronymite monk Diego de Burgos, of San Bartolomé de la Lupiana, around 1487 reported a certain "Dominican brother who would avoid walking in the street on the Jewish Sabbath" (Beinart 1961, 190). In 1501 it was reported in Soria that some five years earlier the *converso* Martín de Gonán had said that he would not travel on Saturday because "he would not break the Sabbath because of his devotion to Our Lady."[120] The Portuguese-Peruvian *converso* Garci Méndez de Dueñas [Lima 1623] was accused of Judaizing, but of Judaizing badly, because sometimes he walked on the Sabbath.[121] In 1657 Antón de Almeida was arrested by the Inquisition. Although he knew very little about Judaism, he considered the Sabbath its central tenet and told the Inquisitors that "even if by doing so he would gain the entire world he would not walk on Saturday, because it is the day God rested."[122]

The Edicts of Faith all enjoined people to look for patterns of abstention from labor, and the Inquisition trials give a good deal of attention to strategies the *conversos* used to dissemble their not working. In the 1480s in Segovia Diego Arias used to pretend to be sick on Saturday and then would recover and eat meat on Saturday evening.[123] Luzia Fernández said that her mistress Juana Núñez [Ciudad Real 1513] "some Friday nights . . . pretended to be sick and said that her head ached and she threw herself down on two pillows. And other Saturdays, when she also pretended to be sick, she threw herself down on a couple of pillows and then later, in the afternoon, she recovered."[124] Inés de Mérida [Ciudad Real 1513] said that "when Pedro de Villarreal's wife came to her mother's house on Saturdays to enjoy herself, she brought her distaff and skeins of flax and sometimes wool to be worked, and she put them on a bench or on the floor and she did not spin or do any work, and when she departed in the evening to her house she took it all with her still unspun."[125] One approach was to complete necessary tasks prior to the Sabbath. A *converso* in Evora in the 1570s ordered everything that was usually done in the Catholic houses on Saturday done in his house on Friday, including such things as kneading, washing the pots and dishes and tableware, changing the bed linen, etc."[126] Ruy Díaz Nieto [Mexico 1603] allegedly prepared his Sabbath meal on Friday afternoon and then, when it was time for prayer, put out the fire of his stove.[127] That these strategies too could be dangerous can be seen in testimony such as Tomás Treviño de Sobremonte's confession [Mexico 1624] that when he saw his mother and cousin kneading bread on Saturday, when they used to bake on

Friday, he asked why, and she replied that "Luis Martínez, her brother, had come to her on bent knee to beg her with his hands clasped together that she pay attention to what people were noticing, and for this reason she kneaded on Saturday. But God knew how it pained her in her heart not to observe the Sabbath, and God only ate [was concerned with] hearts."[128] The hiring of gentiles to perform necessary tasks was not common among Judaizing *conversos*, although it was common among Jews prior to the Expulsion.[129]

Many crypto-Jews extended the prohibition against labor on the Sabbath to their old-Christian servants, even at the cost of incurring great risk of being denounced by those very servants. Inés García testified against her mistress Beatriz Núñez [Guadalupe 1485], saying that "her mistress would not let her sift on Saturday, but made her sift on Sunday when people were at mass." Johanna Fernández added that "on Saturday they would not let her knead or wash or soap the clothes or sift, except on Saturday nights after it had gotten dark; . . . and they made her spin on Sundays."[130] Catalina Martín testified against the González sisters [Ciudad Real 1511], alleging that on the Sabbath "they would not even let her or a black woman named Francisca who was in the house light a fire. And if they did, it was only to make a small fire to heat up a little water for washing."[131] In 1501 Enrique Hurtado was said to have ordered the shepherds who worked for him in Extremadura "to rest on Saturdays and to work on Sundays."[132]

Semi-observant Judaizers were often berated by their family members for not adhering to the Sabbath restrictions more rigorously. Brianda de Santángel [Teruel 1485] admitted that she had observed "her mother refrain from sewing on Saturdays and that she had ordered her and her sister Alba not to sew; even so it was true that on those days she saw her give and take money and poke at the fire."[133] Gracia Ruiz [Teruel 1486] confessed that "on Saturdays she did not spin, at her mother's orders, but that she did wash and sew and card and do other light tasks."[134] Inés de Mérida [Ciudad Real 1511] admitted that "sometimes on Saturday she would begin to work, and her mother would say to her: 'Stop that, Devil take you, don't do that.' And if she kept on doing it her mother scolded her and beat her with whatever she had in her hand."[135] António Gomes [Coimbra 1573] reported that he used to scold his relatives when he saw them working on the Sabbath.[136]

Other new-Christians who found themselves unable to observe the Sabbath strictly expressed their emotional dismay clearly to the Inquisitors. For many new-Christians the requirement to keep the Sabbath, like other aspects of crypto-Judaism, shifted from active observance toward intent. In 1504 in Córdoba in a clandestine synagogue rabbi Alonso de Córdoba Membreque was said to advise his congregation to abstain from work on the Sabbath, "but if they could not do it, to fulfill the precepts with their thoughts in their heart." His brother Martín Alonso Membreque confessed in 1511 that "he had kept many Sabbaths as best he could, although he had bought and sold on Saturday."[137] In 1595 in Granada Ysabel de Montilla, who identified herself as a former Judaizer who had been misled by her mother, said that her mother told her to keep the Sabbath, but "although she wanted to keep them she did not think she kept them because she had work to do on that day and because of her love for the people in her house."[138] Theologians concerned with justifying crypto-Jewish practices took special note of the merit of intention. Antonio Homem, the *converso* Professor of Canon Law at the University of Coimbra, was said to have preached in a Yom Kippur sermon in 1615 that "while living in persecution it was sufficient to have in mind the intention of performing the precepts of the Law" (Roth 1931–2, 5). Immanuel Aboab, a crypto-Jew who returned to Judaism in Amsterdam, in his *Nomologia* (1629) gives the justification for the interior practice of Judaism. Aboab cites the Epistle of Jeremy from the last chapter of the apocryphal Book of Baruch as justification for worshipping openly as a Catholic and secretly as a Jew: "When ye see a multitude before you and behind bowing down ye shall say in your hearts: Thou alone art to be praised, O Lord" (Roth 1931–2, 5). This principle gave comfort to half-assimilated Judaizers over a wide span of time throughout the Iberian territories. Several trials from the region of Coimbra, Portugal, in the 1570s make it particularly clear how this principle played out in practice. In Coimbra at this time it was common for new-Christians to lessen the amount they worked on the Sabbath or to say that they observed the Sabbath only in their hearts. In other words, although they continued to work on Saturday, when questioned they felt compelled to reaffirm their intention to observe the Sabbath. Two possible reasons for these affirmations suggest themselves. The first is that the *cristãos novos*, consumed with guilt for having abandoned their Judaizing practices, expiated their laxity through confession. The second is that by confessing to this relatively minor transgression they might secure a lighter sentence for themselves. In either case, the Coimbra trials indicate six distinct patterns of observance:

(a) Not abstaining from work for general fear of being discovered.[139]

(b) Not abstaining from work for fear of being discovered because they lived in a tiny village.[140]

(c) Not abstaining from work because they had old-Christian servants who might denounce them.[141]

(d) Not abstaining from work because they were married to an old-Christian.[142]

(e) Not abstaining from work because they needed the money.[143]

(f) Working only intermittently.[144]

The obverse of abstaining from work on the Sabbath was to engage in positive leisure activities. While not nearly as frequent in the documentary record as data about refraining from labor, from time to time we catch glimpses of the Judaizing *conversos*' leisure activities. Primary among them was visiting with other *conversos* to discuss Jewish law or merely to share their Jewishness through fellowship and affirm their steadfastness to the ancestral religion by communally accepting the risk that gathering on the Sabbath entailed.

In a 1484 trial a *conversa* woman was accused of "keeping the Sabbath with her sons and daughters, putting on clean holiday clothes, and going to visit with her relatives."[145] María González [Ciudad Real 1511] alleged that "Juana Núñez and Inés López told her how they used to observe the Sabbath, and on how many other Saturdays Juana would have a good time . . . without her; because they used to tell her everything, and she would tell them everything, and they would reveal to each other the things they did against our Holy Catholic Faith."[146] She also said that "in the summer her women friends and she gathered in her house some Saturdays after eating, while people were napping; but that in the winter they did not get together so often."[147] Branca Dias [Pernambuco 1593] was denounced because "on Saturdays she invited her grown-up daughters to come to her house along with some other younger daughters that she had, and all of them ate with her even though none of them came to eat with her on other days of the week."[148] Diego Gómez [Toledo 1510] was denounced because on the Sabbath "his son Iñigo played his guitar and rested as on a holiday."[149] Lucia Fernández [Ciudad Real 1513] testified against Juan de Teva's family, saying that "on Saturdays they got up late, at the time they ring the bell for the Principal Mass, while other days they got up at dawn."[150] In 1593 Inés Fernandes was denounced for spending her Saturdays "sitting in a hammock reading books without doing any other work."[151] Antonio Méndez, a prisoner of the Holy Office in Mexico in 1603, "after dinner on Friday night as the prisoners strolled about used to play a guitar and sing the 'Rivers of Babylon.' "[152] It was reported [Canary Islands 1655] that in the Rodríguez family "the women do no work on Saturday but sit talking together alone, and afterwards drop their hands and point to the ground. . . . This deponent hears them talking in their own tongue on the Saturday and pointing to the ground" (Wolf 1926, 145, 148).

The traditional ceremony of separation from the Sabbath, or *havdala*, does not seem to have been practiced by the crypto-Jews. Still, at least in the first years after the Expulsion, crypto-Jews continued to observe the Sabbath strictly until the first stars had appeared on Saturday night. The most detailed description I have found of the end of a Sabbath was reported to have occurred near Viana (Logroño) around 1505. Pascual García said that

> some four or five years ago, when he was going from Viana to Almarihil for a wine barrel, around dusk, along the road . . . by an arroyo near Almarihil, he saw Pedro López de Hituero and Sancho de Velasco, new-Christians, residents of this town, who were strolling along the banks of the arroyo, up and down. And they asked him "Where are you going, Pascual?" He told them he was going to Almarihil for a barrel . . . and Pedro López and Sancho de Velasco told him: "Go get it and come back; you will find us here when you come back and we will all go together." And the witness was gone for a half hour, and when he returned he found them there, and when he got near them he said: "Help me here, for the barrel is slipping on me." And they told him that they couldn't, that he should wait a moment. And even though they were not doing any-

thing they did not want to help him. And he adjusted his barrel, and when he had adjusted it they said to him "Wait for us." And he stopped and waited for them. And after a little while, waiting there, he heard . . . how Pedro López . . . said to Sancho: "Let's go, there is no sunshine left." And it was true that there was no sun, because it had gone behind the hill and it looked like it had set. And Sancho . . . answered him: "There is plenty of time, let's go." And they still stayed there, and the witness could not get them to move. And he said to them: "Let's go from here, it is nearly night and we won't be able to see where to go." And then a bunch of donkeys, which this witness was bringing back unloaded, began to bray, and he couldn't get them to move, as hard as he tried. And a little after this he heard Pedro López say to . . . Sancho de Velasco: "Look at the star." And the other turned to look at it and then he said to . . . Sancho: "Let's get going, let's hurry up."[153]

## 12.5. SABBATH MEALS

Since the Mosaic Law prohibits doing any sort of work on the Sabbath, meals had to be prepared in advance and left to warm overnight. The *Mishnah Torah* explains the conditions under which meals prepared on Friday may be left on the fire so as to be eaten warm on Saturday (Maim., *Yad.* III,1,iii,3–16). Because the Sabbath prohibitions against labor include making a fire, Sabbath meals were generally kept warm by holding them in an iron pot on a banked fire. Thus one-dish meals such as stews or casseroles were the norm. A late fifteenth-century memorandum about crypto-Jewish customs describes one Sabbath stew and gives its historical rationale. "*Ani*, which means hot food, was usually made with fat meat, chickpeas, lima beans, green beans, hard-boiled eggs and any other vegetable. It was cooked all night on Friday, because on Saturday the Jews could not cook food. And that dish was kept hot on its warming oven until mealtime on Saturday. And thus preparing this *ani* was a principal way of keeping the Sabbath. And its meaning is that the Jews kept *mannah* from one day to the next, and all that *mannah* turned to worms except that which they cooked on Friday for Saturday, and that did not turn to worms. Because of that Jews make *ani* on Friday for the Sabbath."[154]

The Sabbath dish was called by different names in the different regions of Iberia. The *converso* Juan Sánchez Exarch [Teruel 1484] was accused of "ceremonially eating a Sabbath dish called *Hamyn*." This was sometimes made of chickpeas and spinach or chard[155] and was also called *trasnochado*.[156] In Segovia in the 1480s the dish was called a *caliente*.[157] Bernáldez says that the *conversos* "ate and drank a great deal, and never lost the Jewish custom of snacks and pots of *adefina*, snacks of onion and garlic, refried with olive oil; and they fried their meat in olive oil."[158] The family of Diego Enríquez [Toledo 1580] was denounced for making an *adafina* on Fridays that consisted of meat with parsley, onion, chard, and mint.[159] Joan Sánchez [Granada 1582] described how in his master's house they used to make a "Jewish" dish called *boronia* (García Fuentes 1981, 275). In each region the most common and economical foods, such as chickpeas, rice, or other grains, formed the basis for the Sabbath stew. Rita Besante [Teruel 1485] reported that her mother had her maids cook a Sabbath stew of meat, chickpeas, and cabbage.[160] María González [Ciudad Real 1511] used to make "casseroles of eggs and cheese and parsley and coriander and spices, and sometimes she made them with eggplant and sometimes with carrots, according to what was in season, and they used to eat those casseroles cold."[161] In a 1520–3 trial a *conversa* from Hita was accused of making a one-pot Sabbath dish of chickpeas, onions, spices, and honey (Cantera/Carrete 1971, 262). The Fernandes family [Bahia 1591] on the Sabbath ate a "special yellow-colored dish ... made from grains, meat, oil, onions and spices."[162]

The majority of these Sabbath dishes also included meat. Often they resembled modern-day stews. Clara de Puxmija (d. 1455) of Teruel used to make a Sabbath dish as follows: "She broke some eggs into a copper [?] skillet and after they were cooked she sprinkled on them chopped meat that had been braised with onion. And simultaneously she beat other eggs and poured them on top. And she took another pan with broth and put it on top, and you could smell all the odors mixed together."[163] Beatriz Núñez and her husband [Guadalupe 1485] allegedly used to prepare a stew of lamb stomach and feet with chickpeas for the Sabbath.[164] The *converso* Master Bernal and his wife [Almazán (Soria) 1505] prepared "a dish of cow head and internal organs with garlic and spices which they ate on Saturdays."[165] Blanca Ramírez's [Toledo 1523] Sabbath meal was "chickpeas and beans, the fattest available meat or udder, put in a pot with eggplant, if they were in season, with dried coriander and caraway and cumin and pepper and onion. And they called those spices and onion *guesmo*, and the aforesaid stew began to cook at sundown until the next day at noon. And when they wanted to cover it up the night before they would put in Swiss chard that had been sliced and chopped and pounded; and if there were no Swiss chard they put in radish leaves." The testimony gives a second recipe as well: "Friday night they cooked meat balls and another stew pot of Swiss chard with its spices and chickpeas, and when they were going to bed they covered them with an iron pot with burning coals in it, and the next day they uncovered the stew pot and ate from it."[166] In Barcelona in the sixteenth century the Sabbath stew tended to be spinach, chickpeas, lamb, salt meat, and eggs. In Toledo it was chickpeas, white beans with meat, and sometimes coriander and cumin and pepper. In Murcia it was mainly chickpeas. In the Canary Islands it was goat meat stewed with lots of onion and olive oil, accompanied by unsalted barley cakes (Blázquez Miguel 1986a, 59–60).[167] Sometimes the Sabbath stew was eaten with hard-boiled eggs, which could also be easily prepared the day before. The Aragonese *converso* Pedro de la Cavallería was said in 1492 to eat Sabbath stew and hard-boiled eggs on the Sabbath.[168] Poor Judaizers might eat meat or fish only on the Sabbath, and this too is noted in an occasional trial, such as that of Francisco Fernandes in Coimbra in 1568 (Azevedo Mea 1982, 51).

On the other hand, some crypto-Jews conscientiously avoided meat on the Sabbath. Manuel Gil told Mexican Inquisitors in 1603 that Jewish law prohibits fasting on the Sabbath and "therefore Ruy Díaz Nieto around noon on Saturdays would eat Lenten foods, but nothing containing meat."[169] Occasionally fish took the place of meat. Isabel González [Ciudad Real 1511] allegedly "used to cook on Friday for the Sabbath casseroles of fish and sardines, sometimes with eggplant and onions and coriander and spices."[170] The Mexican Ruy Díaz Nieto used to prepare on Friday afternoon a Sabbath meal of "chickpeas, eggs, salt fish, fresh fish, and tuna, all stewed together," portions of which he sent to his friends.[171] In Ciudad Real and Andalucia the Sabbath meal commonly included fish and eggplant, or sometimes carrots and white beans (Blázquez Miguel 1986a, 59).

Other favorite Sabbath dishes around the time of the Expulsion were sausages made of meat, eggs, vegetables, and spices stuffed into an intestine. Beatriz Núñez and her husband made a Sabbath dish by stuffing a sheep's intestine with ground liver and egg yolks and spices.[172] In 1501 a witness said that Diego and Catalina, *conversos* of Soria, had meat brought on Thursday night for cooking that night or Friday morning. Catalina "chopped the meat . . . with spices and took the intestines of a lamb which they brought to her . . . on Thursday and filled them with that chopped meat and tied them with string when they were plump and fried them in beef fat."[173]

Another favorite was the *empanada*, a pie or pastry filled with meat or sometimes fish. In 1488 Diego García Costello's wife was accused in Aranda of making "fish pies on Friday for the Sabbath."[174] Shortly after 1492 Hernando de Soria of Sigüenza was accused of cooking sheep heads for several hours, chopping them finely, sprinkling them with cheese and spices, and making *empanadillas* [meat pies] to fry in olive oil and soak in honey (Blázquez Miguel 1986a, 72). In the 1590s the Fernandes family of Bahia made for the Sabbath a kind of meat pie, "putting ground meat into the bread dough with olive oil and onions and grain and spices and other things, sealing it tight with dough around it and putting it into the oven until it was cooked."[175]

In the summer, or when circumstances made it difficult to hold over hot food, another Sabbath option was a cold meat or salad plate. For example, María Sánchez testified in 1485–6 that on Saturday in Guadalupe she had seen lots of *conversa* women sitting by the doors of their houses eating salad with vinegar.[176] Lucía Fernández alleged that Juana Núñez [Ciudad Real 1513] for lunch used to give them "lettuce and radishes and cheese and cress and other things that she does not remember."[177] *Conversos* also had recourse to these cold foods when circumstances denied them access to a hot meal prepared prior to the Sabbath and carried over. Judaizers in Majorca in the 1670s who were unable to make a Sabbath stew, for example, ate only bread and olives (Cortes 1985, 286).

The written record only infrequently mentions special desserts for the Sabbath. Liebman reports that Friday night meals in colonial Mexico frequently ended with halvah, which is a kind of ground nut pastry, or quince paste [*membrilla*] (Liebman 1970, 79).

For twentieth-century remnant crypto-Jewish groups, grain stews or fish dishes tend to be the Sabbath choice. In 1925 Schwarz found Portuguese Judaizing women preparing on Fridays a dish usually made of fish and vegetables, never of meat (Schwarz 1925, 30). Anne Cardoza reports that her grandmother, Pauline, who emigrated from Gerona to Buenos Aires to the United States and who identified herself as a descendant of crypto-Jews, on the Sabbath would prepare a meal of "a porridge of cooked whole rye, wheat, brown rice, millet, lentils, and chickpeas, with celery, carrots and parsley" (Cardoza 1989, S2). As with other crypto-Jewish customs, Sabbath meals are often shaped by the Catholic context of crypto-Judaism. For example, Vasconcelos reports that some modern Portuguese new-Christians abstain from eating pork on Fridays and Saturdays (Vasconcelos 1958, 173).

One custom that is common in normative Judaism does not appear to be found among the Iberian crypto-Jews. In a tradition derived from Exodus 16:22, 29, two special loaves of bread (*ḥallah*, pl. *ḥallot*) are placed on the Sabbath table, blessed by the man of the house, and eaten. The closest hints to such practice are a few references around the time of the Expulsion such as in the testimony of Alonso Rodríguez [Ciudad Real 1483] who one Friday evening around 1467 went into the house of a *converso* named Alvaro and "saw a table set with white cloths and some loaves of bread set out on it."[178] But, given the absence of post-Expulsion references to the Sabbath *ḥallah*, this custom seems to have been rarely practiced by crypto-Jews.

Finally, the Sabbath lore of the crypto-Jews was, like so many other aspects of their culture, very eclectic. For example, Ana Fernandes [Coimbra 1573] allegedly did not work on the Sabbath because "some people of her Nation had told her not to work on the Sabbath so that God would keep watch over her son who was in the Indies."[179] Esperança Gómez [Canary Islands 1570] testified that her niece told her that "she never baked bread on Saturday, and that if bread were baked on that day and given to the poor, the charity was not acceptable to God" (Wolf 1926, 99–100). Occasional folk tales from ancient Jewish tradition surfaced in the memory of crypto-Jews even as late as the mid-seventeenth century. For example, María de Zárate [Mexico 1656] allegedly said that "in a certain very remote part of China, there was a river whose stones were continually knocking against each other on weekdays. And when the Sabbath came they grew calm."[180] This reference is to the legend of the Sambatyon River, across which the ten lost tribes were exiled by the Assyrian king Shalmaneser. The river ran rapidly for six days and grew quiet on the seventh, thus preventing the escape of the tribes, who would not travel on the Sabbath. The legend appears in antiquity in sources as diverse as the *Targum* and Pliny the Elder, was popularized in 1489 by Obadiah of Bertinoro, the great commentator on the Mishnah, and appears as late as the seventeenth-century work

*Mikveh Yisrael* of Menasseh ben Israel (*Enc. Jud.* 11:1425–6; 14:762–5). How it got to colonial Mexico remains to be seen.

## NOTES

1. According to Levine's discussion of the Sabbath customs of the first post-Expulsion generation of *conversa* women in Toledo, "technically, the *Torah* requires the Jew to observe (*lishmor*) and to remember (*lizkor*); according to rabbinic interpretation the former requirement entails thirty-nine activities that are forbidden on the Sabbath, while the latter actually refers to *quiddush* (blessing of the wine). Other observances such as lighting candles, providing two breads (*ḥallot*) for the meals, and eating three meals (*se'udot*), are, according to majority opinion, based on later rabbinic ordinances. According to *halakhah* [Jewish Law], a Jew who has not engaged in the proscribed activities and who has made *quiddush* has observed the Sabbath" (1982, 52).

2. To cite just one example, of the roughly 120 Mexican Inquisition cases between 1620 and 1649 reviewed by Stanley Hordes, 39 people were found guilty of observing the Sabbath. Most were sentenced to exile and confiscation of property (1970, 213).

3. *Bien dizes, fija, ques sábado, quel sábado se fiso saluado* (Carrete/Fraile 1987, 109).

4. *Había guardado los sábados, conforme lo manda la ley de Moisés, por parecerle inviolable* (Lewin 1954, 191). See also Medina 1899a, 184.

5. *La fiesta principal de la ley de Moysén era guardar el Sábado, y que éste le avían de guardar con tanta observancia que ni aún oja de un árbol se avía de arrancar, ni comer cosa guisada de Sábado* (Selke de Sánchez 1972, 274).

6. *Que guardasse os sabbados porque os sabbados erão os verdadeiros domingos* (Furtado 1925, 76). See also Lipiner 1969, 155.

7. *Amos y dos non hazian nada en los viernes en las noches, e que las otras noches de entre semana, que desmontavan e devanavan, asy la dicha Juana Nuñes como el dicho su marido, e el hazia pleyto, e que aquellos viernes en las noches no hazian cosas ninguna de las susodichas* (Beinart 1981b, 324).

8. Azevedo Mea 1982, 35, 62, etc.

9. *Aguarda dos sabados só no animo, porque como era estudante não deixava nos ditos dias de continuar o seu estudo* (Silva 1896, 10; cf. 34).

10. The Talmud is explicit with regard to personal cleanliness on the Sabbath: Shab. 25b, 31a; Sanh. 95a; etc.

11. *E aquellas noches de viernes todas las susodichas y este confesante se vañavan aquellas noches de viernes por çerimonia judayca en vna tinaja grande con agua cozida con yervas, manzanilla e otras yerbas, la qual agua hazia e tenia aparejada la dicha Maria Gonçales . . . e enbiaua a llamar a este confesante e a todas las susodichas las dichas noches de viernes quanto tenia aparejada el agua para que se viniesen a vañar; e que las mas moças se vañavan primero que las viejas, e las viejas les vañavan a las moças todo el cuerpo* (Beinart 1977a, 274).

12. *Hazia calentar agua con romero e cascaras de naranjas . . . con yervas, mançanilla e otras yervas* (Beinart 1977a, 385, 388).

13. *Que se vañavan otras personas entonçes con ellas, e que ençerravan en aquel xarayz porque non las biesen las moças de sus casas* (Beinart 1977a, 256). See also Beinart 1974, 24, 545; 1977a, 151, 214, 294; 1981b, 324, 473, 489; Liebman 1974, 106, 187 [Mexico 1649].

14. *Se bañaba el cuerpo con agua caliente, que le calentaba vna de dichos dos hermanos del dicho Simon de Leon, los viernes vnas vezes, y otras los sabados en la noche, en vna batea y en su aposento, . . . trocando los dias, si el vno el viernes, el otro el sabado.*

15. *Adonde se iba a bañar era a la aluerca de Chapultepeque los domingos con los otros muchachos catholicos* (Nunemaker 1946, 39–40).

16. Beinart 1961, 187 [1487]. Cf. Azevedo Mea 1982, 211 [Coimbra 1570].

17. *Si se a de hazer la barba siempre es en viernes, lo qual es ceremonia precissa de los judios y precepto de pecado el cortarse el cauello, barba, o las uñas en sabado* (AGN Vol 276 doc 14, 414a).

18. *A las nueve de la noche suuio este to. al apossento del dho. Antonio Mendez y le hallo desnudo encima de un tebrillo grande donde tenia a que le cozinaran. Hechas las dhas hieruas caliente, y se estaua lauando, y en presencia de este to. y del un negro bocal que tiene llamado Juan Angola se lavo los muslos y piernas, y se rajo con un cuchillo las plantas de los pies y se corto las uñas, y vio que tenia junto assi sobre el poyo de la ventana una nauaja y en el suelo seniales de auerse quitado los pelos de debaxo de los braços y de las partes secretas porque vio los mismo pelos, y lo que la marauillo mas fue no consentir que el dho negro le lauasse, como otras vezes lo solia hazer* (AGN Vol 276 doc 14, 427b). See also Liebman 1970, 201.

19. *Lavando-se na vespera da cintura para baixo* (Silva 1896, 10).

20. "They keep the Sabbath to honor the light of Moses, and they wear clean shirts and their good holiday clothes" (*Guardan por fiesta los sabbados a honrra de la luz de Moyssen, y se visten camissas limpias y otras ropas mejores de fiesta*) (Santa María 1893c, 182).

21. *Se vestian los sabados e se atauiauan como vnas grandes señoras* (Beinart 1974, 57). For an example from 1726 in Brazil see Wiznitzer 1960, 159.

22. *Las susodichas yvan alli los dichos sabados bien atabiadas, que la de Rodrigo de Chillon llevaba vn sayco de terçiopelo negro, angosto, de damasco morado, e este testigo llevaba vn fustan blanco quando hera en berano, e camisa linpia vestida* (Beinart 1977a, 294).

23. *Vestindo nelles camissas lavadas e pondo toucados lavados* (Azevedo Mea 1982, 201).

24. *Se vestio nelles do milhor vestido que tinha afóra os vestidos de seda vestindo se de huã saia de pano bom azul nova chaã e de outra saia vermelha boa tambem chaã e de camisa lavada e de jubão lavado de Olanda ou de linho muito alvo com su coifa lavada na cabeça* (Furtado 1929, 361; see also 31, 45, 51, etc.).

25. *El dicho sabado por la mañana entre las seis y las siete vio este to. a la dicha Isabel Rodriguez en las manos un cuello grande limpio para el dho Sebastian de la Pena su marido, y dos pequeños tambien limpios para dos hijos* (AGN Vol 271 doc 1, 9a).

26. *Guardauan el sabado madre e hijas e se vestian de fiesta aquel dia e se afeitauan* (Beinart 1974, 55).

27. *E que la dicha su madre dezia a este testigo confesante algunos sabados: ¡Vistete, diablo, vna camisa linpia, e quitate el sayo quanto es suzya, dete al diablo!* (Beinart 1981b, 359–60).

28. *E que esta confesante se vestio algunas vezes los sabados camisas linpias, e que no se tocaba tocas linpias ni por fuera, porque no tenia esta confesante mas de lo que traya sobre sy* (Beinart 1981b, 360).

29. *Su padre . . . se ponia ropa limpia, camisas y sauanas en la cama los viernes en la noche y que este confesante no se la ponia, por no tener mas que dos camisas y seruir ambas a el y a hermano Jorje. Y aun se quedaua en cueros, quando le cauia la uez que le lauarian la suya* (Nunemaker 1946, 45). For additional examples of dressing up for the Sabbath see Moreno Koch 1977, 358 [Garcimuñoz 1490]; cf. Llorca 1939, 130 [1484]; Fita y Colomé 1892, 488, 499, 501, 516 [Ciudad Real 1484]; Sánchez Moya 1958, 167, 196 [Teruel 1485]; Carrete/Fraile

1987, 81 [Almazán 1505]; Beinart 1977a, 165; 1981b, 396 [Ciudad Real 1511]; Furtado 1925, xxx [Evora 1536]; Baião 1921, 178 [1558]; Azevedo Mea 1982, 450 [Coimbra 1583]; Medina 1887, 192 [Peru 1578]; Lipiner 1969, 167 [Brazil 1591]; Adler 1895, 56 [Mexico 1607]; Blázquez Miguel 1987, 60 [Huete 1623]; Lewin 1954, 127 [Mexico 1624]; García de Proodian 1966, 342, 418 [America 1626, 1636]; Osorio 1980, 185 [Panama 1638]; Liebman 1974, 187 [Mexico 1649]; Wolf 1926, 242 [Canary Islands 1665]; Lipiner 1977, 34–5; and Wiznitzer 1960, 159 [Brazil eighteenth century]; etc.

30. For additional examples of cleaning house for the Sabbath see Beinart 1981b, 395–6; Furtado 1925, xxxi [Evora 1536]; Azevedo Mea 1982, 102ff. [Coimbra 1569]; Medina 1887, 1:192 [Peru 1578]; Lipiner 1969, 167 [Brazil 1591]; Liebman 1974, 187 [Mexico 1649]; Selke de Sánchez 1972, 118, 274 [Majorca 1670s]; Wiznitzer 1960, 159 [Brazil 1737].

31. *Vn biernes en la noche . . . entro en su casa en anochesçiendo e que los fallo a el e a su muger, la casa barrida e regada e su mesa puesta con manteles blancos, y ellos asentados a ella* (Beinart 1974, 301–2).

32. *Tiene los días de los sábados su casa varrida e regada e lavada e ataviada e olorosa e sahumada* (Gómez-Menor Fuentes 1973, 97).

33. *Nas mesmas sestas feiras á tarde mandava a ditta Branca Dias lavar a louça de casa pellas suas negras* (Furtado 1929, 31).

34. *Vió a la rea barrer la casa desde fuera para dentro* (Sierro Malmierca 1990, 177).

35. *Traveseiro e lançoes lavados por honra dos sabados* (Azevedo Mea 1982, 241).

36. *Por honra dos ditos sabbados a sesta feira a tarde, alimpando e mandando alimpar a casa e o estanho e lançando lançoes lavados na cama e se alguns dos lançoes era cru, dizia que se avia de molhar primeiro huma ponta, que o lançassem na cama* (Azevedo Mea 1982, 452). For additional examples see J. Azevedo 1921, 448; Pereira 1979, 189 [Azores 1573]; Liebman 1970, 169 [Mexico 1590s]; Uchmany 1982, 99 [Philippines 1597]; Liebman 1975, 163 [Cartagena, Colombia 1636]; Liebman 1974, 187 [Mexico 1649]; Wiznitzer 1960, 159 [Brazil 1726].

37. *Mudando toballas limpias en aquel dia* (Cabezudo Astraín 1963, 282).

38. *Poner la mesa / que s'este para dos días* (Castillo 1882, #994).

39. *En la messa manteles limpios . . . por honrra del sábado* (López Martínez 1954, 179). For additional examples see Baer 1966, 2:366; Beinart 1974, 150 and Llorca 1939, 130 [Ciudad Real 1480s]; Wolf 1926, 22 [Canary Islands 1520]; Pereira 1979, 189 [Azores 1573]; Liebman 1975, 163 [Cartagena, Colombia 1636].

40. To cite a modern allegedly crypto-Jewish example, Clemente Carmona told David Nidel in New Mexico in 1980 that in his family the women "shop on Fridays and try to get home as soon as possible" (Nidel 1984, 253).

41. *Acostandose mas temprano en las dichas noches los dichos viernes que en los otros dias de entre semana por honrra de la Ley de Moysen* (Levine 1982, 53).

42. The Mishnah explains that marital relations are a Sabbath delight and that therefore "scholars in good health should fulfill their conjugal duty every Friday night" (Maim., *Yad.* III,1,xxx,14).

43. *Aquellas dichas noches de viernes que se vañava la dicha su ama no hazia hazienda ninguna, que luego, en saliendo del xarayz de vañarse, se yva [a] acostar con el dicho su marido. E que sus amos y dos no hazian nada aquellos viernes en las noches* (Beinart 1977a, 385; see also 1981b, 324).

44. *Se yva acostar mas tenprano las dichas noches de viernes que holgava que las otras noches de entre semana* (Beinart 1977a, 496).

45. *Retraerse ante cámara o así mesmo quando se laua las manos, e que durante la dicha oración no permite que ninguno le fable, sino por senyales* (Llorca 1939, 134).

46. *El biernes en la noche se salia a hazer oraçion al çielo hazia las estrellas asentada, lo qual le vido hazer muchos biernes en las noches* (Beinart 1981b, 690).

47. *Fue preguntado que que dias se juntavan a rezar las dichas oraçiones; dixo que los viernes en las noches a vna ora o dos de la noche . . . y de que avian rezado, se yvan cada vno a su casa* (Beinart 1977a, 559). See also J. Azevedo 1921, 448.

48. *Viernes en la noche . . . vio al dicho Aluaro . . . en aquel palaçio puesto encima de vnas gradas, asentado con vn capirote pusto [sic] en el ombro e en la cabeça, e que ally estaua leyendo a muchos conversos* (Beinart 1974, 150).

49. Dobrinsky 1986, 240. Schwarz found twentieth-century Portuguese Judaizing women lighting on Friday afternoons a *candeia do Senhor* made of pure olive oil with a seven-strand wick of pure linen, and reciting this prayer: "Blessed be my God, my Lord, my Adonai, who has commanded us through His blessed holy commandments to light this twisted wick to illuminate and celebrate this holy night of the Lord, so that the Lord will illumine our souls and grant us lives free from trials, hardships and sins. Amen, Lord, etc." (*Bemdito meu Deus, meu senhor, meu Adonai, que nos mandou e nos encomendou com as suas encomendanças bemditas e bem-santas que acendessemos esta santa torcida para alumiar e festejar a noite santa do Senhor, para que o Senhor nos alumie a nossa alma e nos livre de culpas penas e pecados. Amen, Senhor, etc.*) (Schwarz 1925, 30, 62–3).

50. *Vela entera de medio real* (AGN Vol 271 doc 1, 1b).

51. *Le ha visto ençender quasi todos los viernes con particular cuydado una uela entera de sebo antes de la oración y ponerla en un candelero limpio sobre una mesa . . . y aunque se acostauan quedaua encendida* (AGN Vol 276 doc 14, 14a).

52. *Vio a las dichas . . . ençender los candiles los biernes en las noches e guardar los sabados, e que tanbien que los vio ençender las otras noches; e que los biernes en las noches gelos veya quemar en el fuego e limpiarlos e ençenderlos mas tenprano que las otras noches, y los ponian ençendidos detras de vna puerta de un palaçio, vaxo donde dormian* (Beinart 1981b, 601). For similar examples see Beinart 1981b, 640; Furtado 1925, xxxi [Evora 1536]; Pereira 1979, 189 [Azores 1573].

53. *Vido cozer en su casa una caldera de arrope de los candiles* (Santa María 1893a, 199).

54. *Que un viernes a la tarde vido que la otra criada, Marica, estaba limpiando unas crisoletas de fierro, que staban fincadas en una varilla también de fierro, en la qual varilla podía haber fasta siete o ocho crisolillas, de la misma forma que había visto poner en casa de don Bueno, jodío desta villa . . . que dichas crisoletas eran para enzenderlas por la noche los amos, en viernes, detrás del paramento de sus cambras* (Cabezudo Astraín 1950, 277).

55. *Vio las dichas noches en un palaçio que está frontero de la puerta de la dicha casa, ençendidas çiertas candelas puestas en una almenara e colgada de un cordel de cáñamo* (Gómez-Menor Fuentes 1973, 98).

56. In the Americas single men lit the candles if they had no women in the household (Liebman 1982, 119).

57. *Que les pusiesen mechas de algodon nuevas por honrra y guarda del sábado . . . Antes que se fuesen de la dicha sinoga, hizieron mechas de algodon nuevas para los candiles e que despues de fechas, las lavaron en el agua con que el dicho Rabi e todos se avian lavado las manos* (Gracia Boix 1982, 51).

58. *Los viernes en las noches mandavan las susodichas a Françisca, la negra, que alinpiase tres candiles que tenian e despues de linpios, quando se ponia el sol, dezia la dicha muger de Juan de la*

*Sierra a la dicha esclava: Mira sy es puesto el sol, ençiende esos candiles. E que la dicha esclava alinpiava los dichos candiles e los ponia sus mechas nuevas e los ençendia* (Beinart 1977a, 164).

59. *Todas aquellas noches de viernes por mandado de la dicha su ama, encendia este testigo dos candiles limpios con mechas nuevas mas tenprano que las otras noches de entre semana, e que el vno ponia en la camara donde dormian los dichos sus amos* (Beinart 1977a, 266).

60. *Açendía candiles los viernes tarde e fazía su oraçión como judía quando los açendía* (Carrete Parrondo 1985a, 59).

61. *Dichas crisoletas eran para enzenderlas por la noche los amos, en viernes, detrás del paramento de sus cambras* (Cabezudo Astraín 1950, 277).

62. *Com suas irmãas se ajuntava em róda e acendiam candeas e faziam certas ceremonias* (Furtado 1925, 414).

63. *Não ascendia o candieiro a sesta feira a noute por ser cega e não poder com as mãos, contudo em seu coração ho acendia* (Azevedo Mea 1982, 344).

64. For a variety of examples of Sabbath candle lighting see Fita y Colomé 1893, 291 [Guadalupe 1485]; Sánchez Moya 1958, 166 [Teruel 1485]; Carrete Parrondo 1985a, 21 [Soria 1490]; Moreno Koch 1977, 358 [Garcimuñoz 1490]; Carrete/Fraile 1987, 62, 68 [Almazán 1605]; Fita y Colomé 1892, 499, 501 [Ciudad Real 1484]; Beinart 1974, 54; 1981b, 387 [Ciudad Real 1480–1520]; Gracia Boix 1983, 3 [Córdoba 1570s]; Baião 1921, 104, 119 [1537]; Azevedo Mea 1982, 103, etc. [Coimbra 1569]; García Fuentes 1981, 99 [Granada 1571]; Pereira 1979, 189 [Azores 1573]; Furtado 1929, 247 [Brazil 1594]; Sierro Malmierca 1990, 169 [Ciudad Rodrigo 1608]; Liebman 1982, 102, 119 [Mexico]; Wolf 1926, 242 [Canary Islands 1655]; Nidel 1984, 250 [New Mexico 1980].

65. *Estas sã as encoméndanças benditas e santas que nos enconmendou o nosso deus que açendesemos candea em noyte de sabbado com azeite d'oliva limpa* (Baião 1921, 134). For additional modern blessings see Machado 1952, 38–9; Schwarz 1925, 62–3, 82.

66. *Clara e alva sse acenda nossa candea agora e sempre* (Azevedo Mea 1982, 434).

67. *Quando enciendan el candil, dixese "Alabado sea el nombre de Dio"* (Braunstein 1936, 99).

68. *Beneyt tu, lo meu senyor verdader, Adonay* (Blázquez Miguel 1988, 75).

69. *Clara e alva se acenda nossa candea, agora e sempre* (Blázquez Miguel 1986a, 75). For additional prayers see Azevedo Mea 1981, 164 [1580s].

70. *Que ardian toda la noche, e que no los matavan; e que quando se querian acostar los hinchian de azeyte* (Beinart 1977a, 164).

71. *En aquel candil que ponia en la dicha camara le hechase vn grano de sal, diziendo que por que durase mas ençendido* (Beinart 1977a, 266). According to Levine, this custom can be traced back to rabbinic times (1982, 48). For a probable source see *Tosefta Shabbat* (ed. Zuckermandel) II, Jerusalem, 1953, 112.

72. *Preguntó este testigo si mataria el candil, e que la dicha su ama le dixo: "Dexalo, hija, que quiero que arda"; y que este testigo le preguntó que por qué, e la dicha su ama le respondio que por deuoçion que tenia de la Trinidad queria que ardiese el dicho candil* (Moreno Koch 1977, 360). For a similar example from Evora in 1536 see Furtado 1925, xxxi.

73. *Vinda da casa sancta de Jerusalem e que, por causa d'isso, nunca se apagava* (Baião 1921, 139).

74. *Los viernes traian a su casa mas aceite que los demas dias y ordenaban que la servidumbre se retirara antes que ellos* (Levine 1982, 48).

75. *Encendían, los viernes en la noche, en el nombre del Señor, una candileja hecha de hilas en una escudilla con aceite, poniéndola dentro de una caja vacía para el intento, porque no la viesen las esclavas, y allí ardía toda la noche* (García 1910, 244).

76. A mulher cobre a cabbeça com um pano branco. . . . Vai misteriosamente buscar a lampada sabática. . . . E deu-a para as nossas mãos. Depois, ela olha para o oriente. O seu rostro sulcado pela miseria ilumina-se, os seus olhos rolam lágrimas, e, com uma voz tremula, psalmodia: "a benção que o Senhor votou ao sol, á lua e a Jacob e a Abraão e a Isac e a Santa Sárah e Santa Raquel e a este povo peregrino" (Jarval 1929, 3).

77. Bendito meu Deus, meu Senhor, meu Adonai, que nos mandou e nos encomendou com as suas santas encomendanças, benditas e santas, que acendêssemos esta torcida, para alumiar e festejar a noite santa do Senhor, para que o Senhor nos alumie a nossa alma e nos livre de culpas e pecados. Amen, Senhor. Ao Céu vá (Machado 1952, 37). See also Schwarz 1925, 62–3.

78. Louvado seja o Senhor, que me fez e me encomendou nas suas santas encomendanças. Deixou o Senhor dito que lavasse as minhas mãos com água esclarecida para fazer esta torcida de linho, de linhal, para queimar e arder com azeite de oliva santa em candeleta, pelo nome santo do Senhor. Amen (Machado 1952, 37–8). See also Paulo 1981, 143.

79. Schwarz 1925, 16; cf. Paulo 1981, 143; 1985, 50.

80. See the description of synagogues in Chapter 17.

81. Vnas veses llamaua a esta confesante la dicha Florençia e otras veses la enbiaua a llamar con su negra Ysabel, esclaua de la dicha Florençia, e que en los otros no sabe quien los llamaua o sy se venian de suyo (Beinart 1981b, 39).

82. Costuma em certos dias e tempos atar hum pano no dedo do pé e andar assim por esta villa, servindo isto de signal para outros cristãos novos irem ajuntar se a Camaragibi a fazerem a esnoga (Furtado 1929, 54). See also Furtado 1929, 85, 480; Lipiner 1969, 90.

83. Ver çéfer Torá (Carrete Parrondo 1985a, 52).

84. Le abía bisto en la sinoga con su sanbenito de estameña como judío y cantando y que mejor voz tenía (Carrete Parrondo 1986, 22).

85. In the 1480s Diego Arias sometimes celebrated the Sabbath with friends in a cave, or wine cellar, near the city of Segovia (Carrete Parrondo 1986, 44).

86. Specific Sabbath prayers are treated in Chapter 15.

87. Tomó el dicho Diego Arias y echó de la cámara e retraymiento en que estaba con los dichos judíos a todos los christianos que allí estaban fuera. . . . Y so una messa que estaba allí puesta para comer con una alcatifa encima, la qual estaba sobre dos bancos, e tomó unos manteles que estaban encima de ella e subióse sobre una banca primero que estaba delante una cama que allí estaba, e púsose los dichos manteles sobre la cabeza de la forma e manera que se pone el capellán judío el taler mayor para facer oración, y enpezó de cantar a so boz vn responso que diçen los judíos en sábado o en otra qualquier su fiesta, luego en subiendo a la cátedra o tebá, el qual deçía mucho a son, según y en la forma que los judíos le dicen y con tan buena gracia y mejor (Carrete Parrondo 1986, 106).

88. Juan Dias leya en libros ebraycos desde el uiernes en la tarde y el sabado en vn portal, y que venian alli muchos conbersos y conuersas a le oyr leer, el portal lleno y sentados todos all derredor, e davan bozes todos a tienpo de leer, sabadeando con las cabezas (Beinart 1974, 559). The custom of swaying to and fro while praying, which the Spaniards called sabadear, is discussed in Chapter 15.

89. Aquel dia sabado y desde el viernes a mediodia se ençerrauan en vn palaçio e alli leyan todas en vn libro, las cabeças cubiertas, sabadeando (Beinart 1974, 55).

90. El dicho Juan Dias leya el viernes en la noche y el sabado, estando su muger oyendole sabadeando, desian en el libro: Dios de Abraan, Dios de Ysaque, Dios de Jacob (Beinart 1974, 289). These words are the start of the traditional Benedictions that are at the heart of the Sabbath service.

91. *Desian entre otras palabras: Si supieses o entendieses quales son los tres libros de la Ley Sacra, Rebeca la chirimia, barach Adonay barach* (Beinart 1974, 55).

92. *Podra aver treynta años, poco mas o menos, que este confesante e su hermana Florençia . . . se ençerrava en vn palaçio de la casa de la dicha Florençia e del dicho Juan Ramires, su marido, e que este confesante leya a la dicha su hermana vn libro pequeño de oraçiones judaycas; e que . . . eran en dias de sabado a la mañana e a las veses en la tarde, e algunos viernes en las noches. . . . E que despues que el dicho Juan Ramires e los susodichos auian rezado las dichas oraçiones judaycas, platicavan vnos con otros en cosas que son contra la fe e contra los christianos, que hazian burla de la ley de los christianos, como estavan engañados e çiegos, e que la Ley de Moysen hera la buena e verdadera e que por ella se avian de salvar, e que todo lo otro hera burla* (Beinart 1981b, 41, 92).

93. *Dentro de la sala susodicha y en un candelero que había enmedio había muchas crisoletas con azeite, enzendidas, y aquel hombre que había venido estaba todo cubierto con una tela blanca, la cabeça y todo el cuerpo y tenía sobre una mesa un libro en el que leía y los otros estaban detrás del, faziendo gestos con las cabeças y con las personas y estuvieron allí tres oras poco más o menos* (Cabezudo Astraín 1950, 280).

94. *Esta confesante y la muger del dicho Juan de la Syerra, e Leonor, su hija, e Ysabel Gonsales . . . guardavan algunos sabados todas juntas, no hasiendo cosa ninguna en ellos. E que se subian en vna saleta que esta ençima de la puerta de la calle, e que alli lleuavan vn librico de oraçiones de judios y resavan en el, vnas veses la vna, otras veses la otra. E algunas veses desia en el dicho libro: Criador, Criador. E que estauan asy holgando* (Beinart 1977a, 171).

95. *Guardavam os sabbados e nas sextas feiras á noite accendiam um candeeiro com muitas "matullas," junctando-se em casa d'elle a familia toda, n'um quarto muito reservado onde liam por uns libros grandes, dizendo: "Veo, nã veo, veo, nã veo"* (Baião 1921, 136).

96. *Havia uma casa onde desde as sextas-feiras à noite até o sábado depois do jantar se recolham certas pessoas* (Lipiner 1969, 92).

97. *Quem canta, seu mal espanta; / quen chora seu mal aumenta: / Eu canto para espalbar / a paixao que me altormenta* (Liebman 1970, 64).

98. *O vibo eterno Señor que çielo y tierra criaste y a toda criatura diste vida y ser y valor, libranos, gran Señor del çielo y tierra* (Blázquez Miguel 1989, 212).

99. Cortes (1985, 286, 293). See also Roth 1931–2, 6; Braunstein 1936, 99.

100. Tradições 1928, 2.11:7.

101. For collections of modern Portuguese Sabbath prayers see Vasconcelos 1958, 225–6; Tradições 1932, 7.51:2–3; Paulo 1947, 21:137, 8.

102. *Ofereço estas minhas orações, estes meus louvores, em louvor de Vós, Senhor, tudo o que vos peço seja atendido em todo. Em nomne do Senhor, Adonai, amém. . . . Benditos e louvados, engrandecidos, realçados, manifestados, descobertos, honrados, festejados, exaltados sejam os setenta nomes do Senhor. Adonai, amém* (Paulo 1981, 143). Canelo speculates on the Kabalistic origin of the seventy (more usually seventy-three) names of God (Canelo 1987, 108–9). For other examples see Paulo 1985, 79–80, 89–91.

103. *Hoje é dia do santo sábado, santo sábado do Senhor, que fez o Senhor para seu descanso, para sabermos louvar, exaltar e glorificar os seus santos e benditos nomes* (Tradições 1928, 3.15:8).

104. *Tal dia Santo, como o de hoje, / folgou o Senhor e descansou, / suas santas bandeiras compostas, / como os pendões levantados, / e os nomes do Senhor / foram ditos e declarados, / por boca de todos os ventos / e criaturas aumentados. / —Sábado, Sábado, Moisés, Moisés, / au Sábado nada farás. Ocupar-te-has em servir e adorar / o Grande Deus de Adonai. / —Não há outro nem*

haverá, / louvado seja o Senhor que a vida nos dá, / amém, Senhor, ao Céu vá, ao Céu chegue (Paulo 1981, 145).

105. See also Gen. 2:1–3; Ex. 16:22–30; 21:13; 31:14–5; 34:21; Num. 15:32–6; Isa. 58:13; etc.

106. *Si ha celebrat los dissaptes no fent faena ni permetre que se'n fes en sa casa ab intencio de seruar la ley mosayca* (Llorca 1935, 15). See also Fita y Colomé 1892, 485–6 [1484].

107. Alfonso Sánchez said in 1511 that some thirty years earlier he had observed a *conversa* named Florencia "keep some Sabbaths by not doing a lick of work on them" (*Vio a la dicha Florençia . . . guardar algunos sabados no hasiendo hasienda alguna en ellos*) (Beinart 1981b, 43).

108. Juan de León told Mexican Inquisitors in 1642 that the prohibition against work on the Sabbath was so strong that "although his father was a very rich man, if they brought him any kind of business letters, even if they were very important, he would not open them on Friday afternoon nor all day on Saturday" (*Siendo hombre muy rico, que si le traían algunas cartas de cualquier negocio que fuese, aunque importase mucho, no las abriría el viernes en la tarde ni el sábado en todo el día*) (Lewin 1977, 68).

109. Modern Portuguese *criptojudeus* around Belmonte only refrain from work on the Sabbaths that fall in the months before Passover and Yom Kippur (Canelo 1987, 95).

110. *Que en los sábados no han de . . . alzar una pajuela del suelo* (García 1910, 101).

111. *Los dichos sabados, por honra e guarda de la dicha Ley de Muysen, non tratauan ny avn tomaron ni dauan dineros, segund que lo fasen los judios* (Beinart 1974, 11). A late fifteenth-century satiric poem from Román against the *converso* poet Antón de Montoro lists among his Judaizing customs that on the Sabbath he would not touch money (Castillo 1882, #994).

112. *Vio . . . estar ellas resando e demandarles este testigo dineros para conprar de comer e que no gelos quisieron dar por no quebrar su oraçion* (Beinart 1974, 56). For other examples see Beinart 1981b, 324; Llorca 1939, 130 [1484]; Sánchez Moya 1958, 158 [Teruel 1485]; Carrete Parrondo 1985a, 107 [Soria 1501]; Wolf 1926, 22, 224 [Canary Islands 1520, 1660]; Liebman 1970, 170 [Mexico 1590s]; 145 [1655].

113. *Que el viernes en la noche no dejasen la artesa tendida ni los trapos al sereno* (Gracia Boix 1983, 137; cf. 141).

114. *Em todos os sabbados o ditto mestre náo fazia escolla e mandava que nelles não fosse ninguem á escolla dizendo que não era sua vontade ter escola aos sabbados* (Furtado 1929, 40). For additional biographical information about Bento Teixeira and his family see Lipiner 1969, 204–12.

115. *Lhe dixe elle denunciante que lhe vendiesse huns pensamentos de ouro de orelhas pera sua molher e o ditto ourives lhe respondeo que não nos tinha, então no dia seguinte que era domingo pella menhaã ante missa . . . vio estar o ditto ourives na tenda aberta com hum martelinho na mão fazendo cousa de seu officio e se chegou então elle denunciante a elle e lhe pedio que lhe vendesse os ditos pensamentos e ho ditto ourives lhe vendeo então os dittos pensamentos* (Furtado 1929, 316; cf. 466–7).

116. *Hija, no veis que mañana es sabado* (AGN Vol 271 doc 14, 437b).

117. *Los sábados son de guarda por días festivos, sin trabajar en ellos desde el viernes a las cuatro de la tarde* (Lewin 1977, 48).

118. *Digo que no he de vender hoy, que es sábado, ni mañana que es domingo* (Medina 1890, 2:101).

119. *Llegaron vn viernes en la tarde a Linares, e que otro dia sabado non quiso partir de alli, porque sabe que guardaua el sabado* (Beinart 1974, 17). For similar examples see Llorca 1939, 131 [1484]; Liebman 1970, 119 [1536]; Liebman 1975, 193 [Peru 1595].

120. *Por deuoçión de Nuestra Señora non quebrantaua los sábados* (Carrete Parrondo 1985a, 116).

121. *No los havia guardado tan puntualmente, por haver caminado en ellos* (García de Proodian 1966, 282).

122. *Si yo supiera ganar un mundo no caminava en dia de sabado, porque es dia del descanso de Dios* (Blázquez Miguel 1989, 213).

123. *Finxe estar malo los sábados e comía carne a la noche y lo facía por olgar el sábado* (Carrete Parrondo 1986, 29).

124. *Algunas noches de viernes . . . se hazia mala la dicha su ama e dezia que le dolia la cabeça, e se hechava sobre dos almohadas. E que otros dias de sabados, que tanbien dezia que estaua mala, e se estaua hechada sobre vn par de almohadas, e que luego, a la tarde, la veya buena* (Beinart 1981b, 324). For similar examples see Beinart 1981a, 265; J. Azevedo 1921, 448; Wiznitzer 1960, 159 [Brazil 1737].

125. *E quando la dicha muger de Pedro de Villarreal venia alli los sabados a holgarse en casa de la dicha su madre, traya su rueca e çerros de lino e algunas vezes lana para tramar, e lo ponia en vn poyo o en el suelo e no hilaba ni hazia cosa ninguna, e quando se yva a la noche a su casa se lo llevaba por hilar* (Beinart 1981b, 360).

126. *Mandava em sua casa que o serviço que em as casas dos católicos se soiam aos sábados fazer se fizesse às sexta-feiras assim como amassar, lavar estanho, arame e prata, mudar leçóis nas camas, etc.* (Coelho 1987, 207).

127. *A la oracion auia apagado el brassero de lumbre en que las guiso* (AGN Vol 276 doc 14, 422b).

128. *Que Luis Martínez, su hermano, había ido de rodillas a pedirle con las manos puestas, que mirase lo que se notaba, y que por esta causa amasaba los sábados; que Dios sabía lo que sentía en su corazón no poder guardar aquella fiesta, y que Dios no comía sino corazones* (Lewin 1954, 127).

129. For example, Juan Ferrer confessed in 1488 that around 1475 the Jews of Zaragoza used to call him to light their fires on the Sabbath, and that once he did that at a wedding and was paid two *sueldos* and invited to the party (Marín Padilla 1982, 276). Testimony in Aragon in 1490 mentions "on the Sabbath sending a messenger to kindle the fires of the Jews" (*Los sábados enviaba un mensajero a fazer fuego a los judíos*) (Cabezudo Astraín 1950, 276). For similar examples see Marín Padilla 1983a, 224; Carrete Parrondo 1985a, 40, 61 [1490]; Melammed 1985, 104; Cantera/Carrete 1975, 182.

130. *No le quería dexar çerner el sábado, e fazíala çerner el domingo mientras en misa. . . . Ningund sábado la consyntían amasar él ni su muger, ni lavar, nin enxabonar, ni haser colada, salvo los sábados en la noche después de anochecido . . . e le mandavan filar los domingos* (Fita y Colomé 1893, 300–1). See also Haliczer 1990, 220 [Valencia 1480s].

131. *Ni avn dexavan haser fuego a este testigo ni a vna negra que estava en la dicha casa, que se llama Françisca. E que quando mucho, que les dexavan hazer vn poco de fuego pa calentar el agua para fregar* (Beinart 1977a, 163). Exodus 35:3 explicitly prohibits the kindling of a fire on the Sabbath. For similar examples see Beinart 1981b, 448; Wolf 1926, 89 [Canary Islands 1530].

132. *Folgar los sábados e trabajar los domingos* (Carrete/Fraile 1987, 61; cf. 55). See also Blázquez Miguel 1987, 52 [c. 1491].

133. *Vio que su madre se abstenía de filar en los días de sábados y mandaba a ella y a su hermana Alba que no filaban, verdad es que en aquellos días le vió dar y tomar dineros y tocar el fuego* (Sánchez Moya 1958, 170–1). See also Azevedo Mea 1982, 8 [Coimbra 1567].

134. *Los sábados no filaba por mandado de su madre, pero que zabonaba e cosía e aspaba e facía otras faciendas livianas* (Sánchez Moya 1958, 197). For similar cases see Gracia Boix 1983, 137 [Córdoba 1573]; Furtado 1929, 32 [Brazil 1593].

135. *E algunas vezes esta confesante começaba a hazer labor, que los dichos sabados la dicha su madre desia a este confesante: Dexa eso, dete el diablo, non fagas nada. Y sy porfiaba este confesante a hazerlo, la dicha su madre reñia a esta confesante e la daba con lo que esta confesante tenia en la mano* (Beinart 1981b, 360; cf. 396–7).

136. *Pelejando com huma dellas per a ver trabalhar naquelle dia* (Azevedo Mea 1982, 334).

137. *Et que los que lo que asy non lo pudiesen haser, conplir e manterner, que lo hiziesen y cunpliesen con los pensamientos de coraçon. . . . Guardo muchos Sabados lo mejor que podia, conmo quera que en ellos conpraua e vendia* (Gracia Boix 1982, 57, 117).

138. *Aunque deseava guardarlos no se acuerda averlos guardado por tener que hacer aquellos dias y por amor de la gente de su casa* (García Fuentes 1981, 465).

139. *Aver medo de ho entenderem* (Azevedo Mea 1982, 301). *Gardava os sabbados de trabalho na vontade e os não gardava por obra por estar em logea onde vendia mercadoria e aver medo de ser sentido* (Azevedo Mea 1982, 448, etc.).

140. *Nem osava por viver em aldea.*

141. *Guardando os sabados de trabalho na vontade e nam nos guardava na obra por nam ousar por ter moças cristãs velhas em casa* (Azevedo Mea 1982, 35; cf. 62, 95, 151, etc.).

142. *Não podia guarda los por obra, por ser molher de christão velho* (Azevedo Mea 1982, 327; cf. 295, etc.).

143. *Não deixava de trabalhar neles por ser molher pobre* (Azevedo Mea 1982, 113). *Porque era pobre e lhe era necessario trabalhar nelles* (Azevedo Mea 1982, 298; cf. 40, 129, 150, etc.).

144. *Guardava os sabados de trabalho a pedaços, deixando de trabalhar nelles algumas horas* (Azevedo Mea 1982, 114). *Guardava os sabados de trabalho a pedaços, travalhando nelles menos que nos outros dias* (Azevedo Mea 1982, 128).

145. *Su muger e hijos e hijas guardaban el sábado vestiéndose Ropas linpias y de fiesta, y se ivan a ber parientes* (Santa María 1893a, 199). See also Llorca 1939, 131 [1484].

146. *Las dichas Juana Nuñez e Ynes Lopez le desian a este confesante como guardavan aquellos dias de sabados e que otros muchos sabados holgavan las dichas Juana . . . syn este confesante, porque ellas se los dezian a este convesante y este convesante a ellas, y se descubrian vnas a otras de las cosas que hazian contra nuestra Santa Fe Catolica* (Beinart 1981b, 346).

147. *Se juntauan todas las susodichas y este confesante en la dicha casa algunos sabados despues de comer, mientras dormia la gente, en verano que en los ynviernos no se juntauan tantas vezes* (Beinart 1977a, 485).

148. *Nos sabados chamava acima do sobrado as dittas suas filhas e as outras filhas mais moças que então tinha, e todos hiam então acima jantar com ella sendo costumadas a nunca irem jantar com ella nos outros dias da semana* (Furtado 1929, 31).

149. *Tañía una vihuela e holgava como día de fiesta* (Gómez-Menor Fuentes 1973, 49). According to Gómez-Menor Fuentes this Iñigo López is a good candidate for authorship of the anonymous proto-picaresque novel *Lazarillo de Tormes* (69).

150. *E que otro dia sabado, que se levantavan tarde, quando querian tañer a Misa Mayor, y que los otros dias se lavantavan en amanesçiendo* (Beinart 1981b, 324). See also Beinart 1977a, 385, 508; Furtado 1929, 31 [Brazil 1593].

151. *Estando sembre nelles deitada em huã rede lendo por livros sem fazer outro nenhu serviço nem trabalho* (Furtado 1929, 65).

152. *Los dichos viernes despues de cenar ha oydo este al dho Anto Mendez cantar estando taniendo una guitarra, cuuando presos passauan los Rios de Babilonia* (AGN Vol 271 doc 1, 5a).

153. *Pascual Garçía, labrador, veçino de Viana . . . , dixo . . . que avrá quatro o çinco años que vn sábado, yendo este testigo desde Viana a Almarihil por vna cuba, serya a ora de bísperas, pasando por el . . . camino, vido cabe vn arroyo que está cabe el dicho Armahil, a Pero Lopes de Hituero e a Sancho de Velasco, christianos nuevos, veçinos desta . . . uilla, que se andavan paseando por ribera del arroyo, el arroyo arryba e el arroyo abaxo, e dixeron a este testigo: "¿A dónde ys, Pascual?" e este testigo les respondió e dixo que a Almarahil por vna cuba, e . . . Pero Lopes e Sancho de Velasco le dixeron: "Pues yd y veníos, que aquí nos hallarés quando vengáys y yrnos hemos todos." Y tardó este testigo allá más de media ora, e quando voluió se los halló allí; e de que llegó junto con ellos les dixo: "Ayudadme aquí, que se me cae esta cuba," y ellos dixeron que no podían, que esperase vn poco, y avnque no hasían cosa ninguna no le quisieron ayudar, y este testigo adobó su cuba, y de que la ovo adobado le dixeron los susodichos: "Esperadnos," y este testigo se detovo e los esperó; e dende a poco rato, estando allí, oyó . . . cómo dixo . . . Pero Lopes a . . . Sancho: "Vamos, que ya no ay sol," e no paresçía sol ninguno, porque estaua cubierto con la cuesta e paresçía que hera puesto; e respondiole . . . Sancho: "Tienpo ay harto, vyajemos," e ansy estouieron vn poco deteniéndose, que no los podía este testigo sacar de allí; y este testigo le dixo: "Vamos de aquí, que es noche y no veremos por dónde yr." Y entonçes començaron fablar sendos asnos que tenían vasíos, y trayanlos delante sy, y venían a çaga deste testigo, que casi no andavan nada por much priesa que él les dava. E de a poco oyo este testigo cómo dixo Pero Lopes a . . . Sancho de Velasco: "Cata el estrella" y boluió el otro a verla; y estonçes dixo . . . Sancho: "Vamos, aguijemos"* (Carrete/Fraile 1987, 87–8; cf. 115).

154. *El ani, que quiere decir cossa caliente, que se acostumbraba a hacer con carne gorda, garbanços, fabas, judías, huebos duros, y de otro cualquier legumbre; lo qual todo cocía toda la noche de el viernes, porque los judíos el sábado no podían guisar de comer; y aquel guisado estava caliente en su fogaril fasta la hora de comer el sábado; y anssí el guisar de este ani hera principio de la guarda de el sábado en signifficación que los judíos guardaban manna de un día para otro, y todo el dicho manna se les tornava gusanos, salvo lo que cozían el viernes para el sábado, porque aquello no se bolvía gussanos, y por aquel ressppeto los judíos hacían el ani el viernes para el sábbado* (Santa María 1893c, 187).

155. *Come por cerimonia judayca del sábado vn comer vulgarmente llamado Hamyn . . . garuanços e espinazas o uerças* (Llorca 1939, 130–1). See also Sánchez Moya 1958, 158 [Teruel 1485]; García Casar 1990, 178 [Cuenca 1480s]; Cabezudo Astraín 1963, 283 [Barbastro 1491]; Baer 1936, 462 [1492]; Carrete Parrondo 1985a, 152 [Soria 1502]. Liebman defines *amin* as a broth that was "used for the sick and faint and by women during pregnancy" (1970, 80).

156. A late fifteenth-century satiric poem from Román against the *converso* poet Antón de Montoro lists among his Judaizing customs that he would not eat anything the Rabbi prohibited, but only *trasnochado* (Castillo 1882, #994).

157. *Diego Arias rogó a su padre de este testigo que le ficiesse facer un caliente para el sábado* (Carrete Parrondo 1986, 98).

158. *Ansé eran tragones y comilones, que nunca perdieron el comer a costumbre judaica de manjarejos, e olletas de adefina, manjarejos de cebollas e ajos, refritos con aceite, y la carne guisaban con aceite* (Bernáldez; cited by López Martínez 1954, 183). See also Carrete Parrondo 1986, 51, 60, etc. [Segovia 1487]; Cantera/Carrete 1971, 262 [Hita 1520].

159. Blázquez Miguel 1989, 195. Jiménez Lozano found that in certain villages of Castilla-León well into the 1960s, the expression *ir de adafina* was used for a cold meal prepared to be taken on a journey (1984, 362). He considers this an example of a "culteme" (see Chapter 7 note 57).

160. *Facía guisar a sus mozas carne con garbanzos e berzas para el sábado* (Sánchez Moya 1958, 172). For a similar example see Carrete Parrondo 1985a, 155 [Soria 1502]; Cantera/Carrete 1975, 156 [Guadalajara 1520–3].

161. *Caçuelas . . . hechas de huevos e queso e perexil e calantares e espeçias, e que algunas vezes las hazian de verenjenas e otras vezes de çanahorias, como hera el tiempo, y que comian frias las dichas caçuelas* (Beinart 1977a, 251). See also Beinart 1977a, 479; 1981b, 390, 394, 418, 482.

162. *Era amarella . . . que se fazia com grãos pisados, e a carne picada e adubos* (Furtado 1929, 31; cf. 57). Cf. Wiznitzer 1960, 25 [Brazil].

163. *Estrellaban los huevos en una sarten de ambre* [sic] *y apres que eran fechos echaban encima carne picada sofreida con cebolla, y pares batian otros huevos y los echaban encima, y tomaban otra sarten con rescaldo y ponianla encima, y asi se oleaba todo* (Sánchez Moya/Monasterio Aspiri 1972–3, 131).

164. *Vientres e pies de carnero . . . e que lo cozían con garvanços* (Fita y Colomé 1893, 299, 301).

165. *Cabaheas de lyvyanos de vaca e de cabeça de vaca y de las entrañas, y con sus ajos y espeçias, y las hazían y las comían los sábados* (Carrete/Fraile 1987, 37–8; cf. 78).

166. *En la qual echauan garvanços e avas; y carne de lo más gordo que se podía aver o ubre, echávase en la dicha olla, e si era tiempo de verengenas echáuanlas, y echauan más culantrillo seco e alcaravea e cominos e pimienta e çebolla; e aquestas espeçias e çebolla, llamávanlo guesmo, e la dicha olla se començava a guisar desde ora de bísperas fasta otro día a la ora de comer; quando la querían cubijar antenoche, echauan azelgas cochas e picadas e machacadas, y si no avía acelgas, echauan hojas de rávanos. . . . El viernes en la noche, echava vnas pelotas cozidas e sancochadas e otra olla de açelgas con sus espeçias e garvanços, e quando se yvan acostar dexavan vna caldera sobre la dicha olla con lunbre, e otro día, sábado, hallavan descocha la dicha olla e comían della* (León Tello 1972, 70–1).

167. For additional recipes for crypto-Jewish Sabbath dishes see Arbós Ayusa 1981, 78–9 [mid-fifteenth century]; Fita y Colomé 1892, 485, 487, 499 [Ciudad Real 1484]; Blázquez Miguel 1986a, 55, 59; 1987, 52 [c. 1491]; Kayserling 1898, 267; Azevedo Mea 1982, 111, etc. [Coimbra 1569]; Liebman 1974, 106 [Mexico 1649].

168. *Hamin y huebos hammados* (Baer 1936, 463). *Ham* = Hebr. warm. This was also a favorite of *conversos* of that time in Huete (Guadalajara), who prepared them by boiling eggs with onion skins, olive oil, and ashes (Blázquez Miguel 1986a, 57). *Huevos haminados* are still a favorite dish of Sephardic Jews of Turkey, who boil the eggs in water to which onion skins have been added to dye the eggs a maroon color.

169. *Ruy Diaz en los dhos sabados come a medio dia cossas quaresmales; y no cossa de carne* (AGN Vol 276 doc 14, 415b).

170. *Sienpre acostunbrava . . . la dicha Ysabel Gonsales guisar los dichos viernes para loss sabados caçuelas de pescado y sardinas, e las vezes con verengenas e con çebollas y culantron y espeçias* (Beinart 1977a, 163).

171. *Adreçar despues de medio dia mucha comida de garbanços, hueuos, pescado salado y pescado frescho, y atún* (AGN Vol 276 doc 14, 422b).

172. *En una tripa de carnero o macho echar hígado machado e yemas de huevos e espeçias* (Fita y Colomé 1893, 299, 301).

173. *Su ama picaua la . . . carne con espeçias e tomaua de las tripas del carnero que trayan en los . . . jueues, e rellenáualas con aquella carne e atáualas con hilos e quedauan como redondas, e las freya con manteca de vacas* (Carrete Parrondo 1985a, 115–6).

174. *Hasía empanadas de pescado el vyernes para el sábado* (Carrete Parrondo 1985a, 173).

175. *Lançavão a carne picada na panella com azeite e cebolla e grãos e adubos e outras cousas, e barravão lhe o testo com massa ao redor e metiamna dentro em hum forno onde estava até se cozer* (Furtado 1929, 57). See also Lipiner 1969, 167 [Brazil 1591].

176. *Estavan muchas conversas comiendo verdura con vinagre a las puertas* (Baer 1936, 447).

177. *Que les daua la dicha su ama a merendar lechugas e ravanos e questo e mastuerço e otras cosas que este testigo no se acuerda* (Beinart 1981b, 324).

178. *Viernes en la noche . . . vio vna mesa puesta con vnos manteles blancos en ella tendidos e vnas tortas de pan en ella puesta* (Beinart 1974, 150).

179. *Algumas pesoas de sua naçam he diseram que não trabalhase aos sabados, pera que Deos lhe guardase hum filho que andava na India* (Azevedo Mea 1982, 337).

180. *En cierta parte de la gran China, había un río cuyas piedras continuamente se estaban dando golpes una con otras todos los días de la semana, y llegado el sábado se sosegaban* (Lewin 1971, 218).

# CHAPTER XIII

# Holidays

Inquisition documents are rich in descriptions of the Jewish festivals. In part this is because the holidays, or at least certain holidays, were central to the crypto-Jews' religious observance and to their self-identification as Judaizers. In part it is because the observance of Jewish holidays was one of the most incontrovertible indications of Judaizing practices among *conversos*, so the protocols of examination used by the Inquisition put a good deal of emphasis on the holidays. In these descriptions a number of trends in the crypto-Jewish observance of traditional Jewish festivals can be observed.

The first trend is that the most holy of Jewish holy days, Yom Kippur, the Fast of Atonement, was pre-eminent in the Jewish liturgical year. The next most frequently observed holiday was Passover, followed by Purim and Sukkot. The many other holy days in the traditional Jewish liturgical calendar appear but rarely. The second is that, from the very earliest days of persecution, fasts played a more important role in crypto-Jewish customs than did feasts. Several reasons converged to make this so. Many Jewish theologians in the fifteenth century believed that Judaism was in such a sorry state because Jews collectively and individually were in a state of sin. Fasting was the principal self-mortification that demonstrated a Jew's remorse and determination to atone. It also expressed grief at the succession of calamities that had historically befallen Judaism. There was also the practical matter that it was more difficult to perceive abstinence than it was to observe the overt celebration of festivals. Yom Kippur was the most important crypto-Jewish fast day, but Purim, renamed the Fast of Queen Esther, was a close second. In addition, some colonial Mexican Judaizers fasted during daylight hours during the week of

Passover and some modern Portuguese new-Christians fast the first, fourth, and seventh days of Passover.

The third trend is that crypto-Jews consistently blended traditional Jewish observance with local customs. This was particularly true with regard to foods, where local delicacies or the availability of certain foods determined what was incorporated into traditional meals. The fourth is that with time the historical bases of the holidays became garbled, even to the extent of the traditional villain of the Purim story, Haman, being referred to as a saint. Moreover, traditional holiday observances became encrusted with superstitions that in their way also become traditional.

This chapter treats the major Jewish holidays in the order in which they occur during the liturgical year: Rosh Hashanah, Yom Kippur, Sukkot, Simhat Torah, Hanukkah, Purim, Passover, and Shavuot. The chapter concludes with a discussion of several other minor holidays that were observed sporadically by the crypto-Jews.

## 13.1. ROSH HASHANAH

Although Rosh Hashanah, the beginning of the Jewish liturgical year and the start of the so-called ten Days of Awe that culminate in Yom Kippur, is in normative Judaism one of the most important holidays, it seems to have been observed by crypto-Jews with great rarity.[1] The traditional date of Rosh Hashanah is the first day of the Hebrew month Tishri, which generally occurs in September. While crypto-Jews occasionally went to great lengths to calculate the dates of other Jewish holidays, a concern with the precise date of Rosh Hashanah does not figure in documents relating to the Iberian crypto-Jews. The infrequent references to the holiday usually allude to it as the Festival of the Horn (*La pascua del cuerno*). Sometimes a Hebrew version of the name was recorded, such as in an early sixteenth-century Portuguese Edict of Grace where it is called *Rofagana* (Coelho 1987, 209) and a 1623 trial where it is called *roçana* (Sierro Malmierca 1990, 178). There are occasional references to blowing the *shofar*, or ram's horn, on Rosh Hashanah, but there is very little else.

The description of the holiday in a memorandum of crypto-Jewish customs during the reign of Fernando and Isabel undoubtedly described the traditional holiday as it was understood by Spanish Jews just prior to the Expulsion:

> The Festival of the Horn signifies that on that day God created the world and freed Isaac from being sacrificed by Abraham, his father, and because instead of having to sacrifice his son, Abraham found the ram to sacrifice, its horns tangled in some brambles. And because of this the Jews on that festival blow the horn in memory of Isaac's not having had to be sacrificed. It is a day of remembrance which falls on the first day of the moon of September."[2]

Most descriptions of the crypto-Jewish celebration of Rosh Hashanah are from the Expulsion generation. For example, in 1484 the Jew Esdra Çaçon accused the *converso* Pero González de Madrid of reading "from a book and they were prayers which the Jews say on the Festival of the Horn."[3] Similarly, Juan de Santa Clara was accused in Toledo of having asked the Jew David Aben Pando for a prayer book [*çidur*] to celebrate the Feast of the Horn (León Tello 1972, 81). After the Expulsion generation was gone the holiday surfaces only rarely. In the 1623 case from Ciudad Rodrigo referred to above Inquisitors accused Isabel Núñez of a large array of Judaizing practices, including "keeping the festival of eight and fifteen days which is called *Roçana*."[4] On September 10, 1603, the Mexican *converso* Ruy Díaz Nieto and his friends celebrated a holiday by dining on "pastries, *turcos*, cakes, filled breads and blancmange."[5] "While this feast is not identified as Rosh Hashanah in the document, it seems likely, for on the same page the testimony describes a Sukkot celebration on September 21.

Inquisitors occasionally took note of what they considered superstitious practices associated with the crypto-Jewish festivals. Thus crypto-Jews in Fregenal (Extremadura) were accused in the late sixteenth century of hanging a bag around their neck on Rosh Hashanah so as never to lack money during the rest of the year (Blázquez Miguel 1986, 154).

## 13.2. YOM KIPPUR

Crypto-Jews generally considered Yom Kippur to be the most solemn and important festival in their liturgical year. Trials prior to the Expulsion describe observances in great detail, and trials through the end of the seventeenth century in the Iberian Peninsula and its overseas dominions routinely supply evidence of Yom Kippur observance. The holiday even figures in the religious life of the remnant communities of the twentieth century. Observance of Yom Kippur was for the Iberian crypto-Jews an essential component of self-affirmation that annually solidified their Jewish commitment.

Yom Kippur is the holiday known among crypto-Jews by the widest range of names. In some parts of the Iberian world a form of the Hebrew name survived in terms such as *equipuz, antepur, cinquepur,* or most commonly just *Quipur*.[6] Other names recognize the pre-eminence of the holiday in the liturgical year, calling it the Great Day (*El día Grande*)[7] or the Fast of the Greatest Day (*El ayuno del Día Mayor*).[8] Still other names, such as the Fast of Expiation (*El ayuno de la Expiación*)[9] or the Fast of Pardoning (*jejum das perdoanças* or *ayuno del perdón*),[10] point to the holiday's nature as a day for seeking and granting pardon for transgressions. Most commonly, however, it is called simply the Great Fast (*jejum mayor* or *ayuno mayor*).[11]

The proper date for the Yom Kippur fast was of great concern to crypto-Jews, who endeavored both to remember the date and to promulgate it among their coreligionists. In fact, some Judaizers even accepted the risk of writing down the exact date of this and other holidays. The *conversa* Gómez sisters [Ciudad Rodrigo

1588] maintained a written calendar of the Jewish festivals,[12] as did the Portuguese-Argentinean Diego Núñez de Silva [Chile 1602], who said "he had written down the cycles of the moon in order to know [the dates of] the fasts of the Jews."[13] When the Bachelor Francisco Maldonado de Silva [Chile 1627] was found with a "small, parchment-bound notebook containing some Jewish prayers and the calendar of the festivals of the Law of Moses," he told the Inquisitors that "he had copied it from the Calendar of Psalms of Genebrando."[14] Simón de Osorio of San Combadan, Portugal, who later lived in Quito, Ecuador, was accused [Lima 1635] of "carrying with him the calendar of Jewish holidays in code, which was found among his papers while he was in prison."[15]

This concern for the precise dates of the Jewish holidays lasted for a long time among Portuguese Judaizers. Schechter recounts that in 1819 two country gentlemen appeared at a Jewish service in Lisbon, where Jews had been permitted to hold services openly since 1800. The two "threw themselves down before the ark.... They had come to Lisbon from the Trás-os-Montes, and there in Lisbon wished to know when the Kippur was held, and returned to the country, bearers of the date for the year 1819" (Schechter 1917, 73).

Some Judaizers found an easy solution in equating the Hebrew date for the holiday, the tenth of Tishri (Lev. 23:27), with the tenth of the Christian month of September. This was such common practice among New World Judaizers that a person who suggested a more accurate date, as did Manuel Mello in Guadalajara [Mexico] in the mid-seventeenth century, was bitterly resisted.[16] On the other hand, most crypto-Jews recalled that the traditional Jewish calendar was reckoned by the moon, which led them to equate the tenth of Tishri with the tenth day after the new moon of September. This was the case with Juana de San Juan [Baeza 1573], who said that "one had to fast on the tenth day of the September moon, which they call the Great Day," and with countless other crypto-Jews.[17] Some remembered the new moon but forgot about the tenth day: in 1593 it was reported in Pernambuco that *cristãos novos* used to gather at the new moon in August in a synagogue in the village of Camaragibi (now Santiago) to pray on Yom Kippur (Furtado 1929, 75). As is the case with other crypto-Jewish holidays, some new-Christians remembered the date of Yom Kippur by associating it with the Catholic liturgical cycle, in this case the Feast of Saint Matthew.[18] Other Judaizers associated it with the agricultural cycle. Francisca Vaz [Lisbon 1543] reported that Yom Kippur comes at the grape harvest.[19] Judging from these examples, some crypto-Jews attempted to be as precise as possible in the dates of their holiday observances, while for others an approximate date was sufficient.[20]

Moreover, as time went on many crypto-Jews seemed to lose sight of the fact that Yom Kippur is celebrated traditionally for a single day. In some parts of Aragon even around the time of the Expulsion Yom Kippur was "kept continuously for four or five days before the Feast of Booths [Sukkot]."[21] Bachelor Francisco Maldonado de Silva [Lima 1627] said that he observed Yom Kippur for four days, even though only one was required, because he wanted God to forgive him his sins.[22]

Several very detailed general descriptions of Yom Kippur observances have come down to us from the first two hundred years following the Expulsion. Common threads in these descriptions are concern about the proper date; preparations for the holiday; descriptions of and explanations for the fast; petitions to God for forgiveness for sin; worshippers requesting and granting pardon to each other for any harm they might have done during the preceding year; blowing the ram's horn, or *shofar*;[23] and the meal that breaks the fast. A late fifteenth-century memorandum of Judaizing customs lays out the basic practices and their justification:

> The Fast of Kippur, which means pardon, signifies the forty days in which Moses was up on Mount Sinai without eating or drinking, waiting the light and forgiveness which God was to give the people of Israel for their sin of idolatry.[24] Because of his prayers God forgave them and gave them light. And thus Jews in thanks for that gift are accustomed to keeping that fast, and are accustomed to asking forgiveness one of the other, and the younger ones kiss the hands of their elders. And that Fast of Pardoning falls on the tenth day of the moon of the month of September.[25]

An Aragonese Rabbi named Simuel, testifying in Teruel in a *converso* trial in 1485, elaborated on this basic pattern:

> It is true that according to the Law of Moses Jews are only obligated to fast for the forgiveness of their sins. But the wise men [rabbinical tradition], in order to assist the fasting, commanded that the following ceremonies be observed: Not to wear shoes, but rather reed or cloth slippers. Not to wash your hands or face with water merely to take pleasure in it; but it is permitted to wipe your face in the afternoon with damp cloths. The law says not to eat anything until nightfall. It is untrue that they have to wear a hood on their heads. As for being in the synagogue, it is not required if there isn't one, because you can fast out in the countryside. Blowing the horn (and if they blow it it is after the fast, in the evening) is a separate ceremony not related to the fast. And that day it is also the custom to forgive each other and encourage peace and good feelings among each other. But if all this is missing, they must still fast.[26]

Felipe de Adahuesca described in the 1489 Aragonese trial of Violante Santángel what seems to have been an outdoor celebration of Yom Kippur. He reported that around 1469:

> At the time of the grapes and the figs, all the *confesos* of Barbastro went out to the orchards two by two, four by four, six by six, eight by eight, and ten by ten. They strolled up and down in the orchards and did not work that day, which is when the Jews are accustomed to fast. . . . You could see in their faces they were nearly fainting, or dead. They did not go back to their houses until nightfall, nor did they eat all day long until the evening. At night they ate meat and hens and made a great party. . . . And when he was asked if they were formally

or informally dressed or were barefoot, he said that they were formally dressed, but that some of them were without shoes in just their stockings. He saw that before they ate they said Jewish prayers which he did not understand, and they all hit themselves.[27]

Later descriptions of Yom Kippur observances tend to echo the early reports. Although there was some variation from place to place, sophisticated Judaizers on the whole related the seriousness of the holiday to the fact that it marks the moment annually when God judges souls.[28] Even well into the seventeenth century the fuller descriptions of Yom Kippur practices tend to mirror one another. For example, Gabriel de Granada [Mexico 1645] confessed how his mother had instructed him to observe Yom Kippur:

> Every year he kept the fast of the Great Day. The previous evening one must bathe and put on clean clothing, and dine on fish and vegetables. Then wax candles must be lighted and set on a clean cloth. And one must pray at midnight the prayers of the said law, and ask each other for forgiveness and embrace one another and make peace among those who had quarreled. And at midnight they had to go to sleep, leaving the candles lighted until they burned out of themselves. The next day they had to fast without eating or drinking until evening when the star had come out, when they would again eat fish and vegetables and other things, but not meat. . . . They lit four or five wax candles and set them on a clean cloth on the floor of the room in which they slept, and they sat there until midnight. [Gabriel] and his brother had their hats off because they had been told that they should not cover their heads. And each of them was praying by himself all the prayers they knew of the said law of Moses.[29]

The next morning his mother told him "to go out and walk around for the whole day wherever he liked, but not to eat or drink anything because that would violate the fast."[30]

The preparations for Yom Kippur, as for other Jewish holidays of great solemnity, were similar to the preparations for the Sabbath. At the heart of all of them was a concern for personal and environmental cleanliness. In the pre-Expulsion days when it still was possible, *conversa* women would perform their purifying ablutions prior to Yom Kippur in the communal *mikvah*. Typical was the case of Blanca Martínez, who three decades after the fact was accused in Toledo of "one day before the great fast going to the bathhouse of the Jews."[31] After the Expulsion both men and women tended to bathe at home. Tomás Treviño de Sobremonte [Mexico 1624] described how on Yom Kippur eve around four in the afternoon his mother went into a bath room "and washed and bathed her entire body in a large tub, and he thinks it was with warm water; and having dried herself off and put on a new dress, she called him into the room to wash his whole body the way she did, according to the ceremony of preparation for the Great Fast which was the following day."[32] In Mexico in the 1640s the Machorro women used to bathe together in one of their houses (Lewin 1977, 41). On the other hand Salomón Machorro and his male Judaizing friends used to bathe the morning before Yom Kippur in the community bathhouse called "japones," and afterward they put on clean clothes and snacked on roast egg, wine, and pastries. What is most amazing is that they were accused of taking this semi-public bath according to Jewish ritual.[33] Other times the ablutionary bathing would take place in a nearby river;[34] in fact this is still the case among remnant Portuguese Judaizers of the twentieth century, where villagers make an evening procession (*romagem*) to the bank of a river on Yom Kippur eve to purify themselves with a ritual ablution.[35]

As with the Sabbath, new-Christians wore clean and if possible new clothes on Yom Kippur. This seems to have been particularly important to Mexican Judaizers. Tomás Treviño de Sobremonte [1624] testified that on Yom Kippur both he and his mother put on new clothes (Lewin 1954, 126). Ruy Díaz Nieto [1603] was denounced for, among other things, buying new clothes in September, including "a suit of brown cloth, high-topped shoes and regular shoes and a pleated collar and a new hat."[36] Mathias Rodríguez de Olivera [1649] reported that Mexican Judaizers "would wear some new article of clothing on that day regardless of how poor they were."[37] Likewise their houses had to be clean and pure for Yom Kippur, as seventeen-year-old Filipa Cardosa stipulated [Coimbra 1583] when she said that for the Great Fast of September she bought new dishes and scrubbed all her wooden dishes, cupboards, benches, and chests.[38] Preparation for the holiday was generally women's work. Among assiduous Judaizers it represented a major investment of time, effort, and, of course, risk. Ana Cortés [Majorca 1688] followed her father's instructions about how "on the eve of this fast they cleaned the whole house, and their clothing, and they washed their whole body and put on their best clothing to honor the fast. Similarly, the night of the feast they put clean linen on the table, and on the bed, and they asked pardon of one another." She added that her father also told her that "that day one ate fowl and other good things, and made a great feast, ostentatiously; but they did not eat lamb, because during the month of September they did not eat lamb that was slaughtered by someone else's hand. And . . . that day they should put on a great show, and if they could make *cocas bambas* [a kind of pastry] they should, and sweets as well, unless they were prepared by those dogs who keep the Law of Grace, and then they should not buy them."[39] One additional preparation for Yom Kippur is found among modern Portuguese *cristãos novos* of Belmonte, who prior to the holiday visit the graves of their departed.[40]

Since Yom Kippur is considered to be a Great Sabbath, a *shabbaton*, lamps were traditionally lit for Yom Kippur as for the Sabbath. As with the Sabbath, attention was given to cleaning the lamps and preparing new wicks. As with the Sabbath, the lamps were allowed to burn out of their own accord. And, as with the Sabbath, candles and oil lamps seem to have been used indiscriminately. Simão Alvares, of Oporto, told the Coimbra Inquisition in 1573 that on Yom Kippur eve "he lit a porcelain lamp of olive oil with three new twisted wicks and left it lighted until it burned itself out."[41] In Mexico Salomón Machorro and his circle of friends [c. 1640] began Yom Kippur with one of the men or women lighting three or four wax candles on a clean white linen cloth placed on the floor.[42] Gabriel de Granada and his family around 1645 "lighted four or five wax candles and put them on the floor of a bedroom, on a clean towel; and afterwards his mother, grandmother, and aunts recited some prayers of the Law." Each person separately lighted candles, and they let the candles burn themselves out.[43] One seventeenth-century Mexican case associates a seven-branched candelabra with the Yom Kippur holiday. And, as with the Sabbath, dissemblance strategies were required. Some Mexican women lit candles for "several nights prior to Yom Kippur so that when the Great Day arrived the candles were accepted without curiosity by servants and Christian neighbors" (Liebman 1970, 65). Ancient Jewish custom has made Yom Kippur a time as well for the lighting of the traditional memorial candle in honor of a deceased loved one [*Kol Bo* 68]. One Mexican case from 1648 alleges that on Yom Kippur Rafaela Enríquez lit so many candles for both the living and the dead that "it looked like some glowing Catholic shrine, for there were more than eighty of them."[44] In our times Portuguese *cristãos-novos* on Yom Kippur eve also illuminate their houses with lights in memory of their deceased relatives (Schwarz 1925, 31).

Because Yom Kippur was a Great Sabbath, the Sabbath rules against performing any sort of labor were in effect (*Mishnah Torah* [Maim., *Yad* III,3,i,2]). These rules seem to have held without change from before the Expulsion right up to modern times. In a 1490 trial in Cerezo de Río Tirón (Burgos) Fernando de Peñafiel was accused of avoiding work on Yom Kippur by going out to the villages, allegedly to see about debts people owed him. His wife wrapped her hand in a bandage so she would not have to spin (Carrete Parrondo 1985a, 167). The *converso* Juan Pacheco [Mexico 1642] testified that "he once went to Pedro Tinoco to ask him to desist from studying and attending classes at the university on Yom Kippur. The inquisitors thought this request was contrary to Jewish law since Jews were accustomed to studying on holy days. Juan explained to them that on those days study was restricted to holy texts" (Liebman 1970, 270; cf. Lewin 1977, 92–3). And Paulo reports that in this century in Belmonte, Portugal, even the new-Christians who have married old-Christians and are thus alienated from the community close their stores on Yom Kippur (1985, 149).

For crypto-Jews by far the most important part of the Yom Kippur observance was the fast. From ancient times the fast has been the traditional heart of the Yom Kippur observance. Lev. 16:29–31, 23:28–32, and Num. 29:7 require that Jews "afflict themselves" on the Day of Atonement, and the rabbis identified five principal classes of afflictions: abstaining from food and drink; from washing oneself for pleasure; from anointing the body; from wearing leather shoes; and from engaging in sexual intercourse. From the earliest days of crypto-Judaism through the present, the fast of Yom Kippur has been observed with great rigor, while the other prohibited activities have been observed sporadically. Unlike most other fasts, which require one to abstain from eating only during daylight hours, the Yom Kippur fast was total, and was observed for a full twenty-four hours except in the case of children, pregnant women, and the infirm. Prior to the fast *conversos* ate hearty food to carry them through the following day.

On the theory that if one fast is good two are better, many Portuguese Judaizers in the 1570s used to fast during the daylight hours for the five or even ten days prior to Yom Kippur.[45] In the 1620s the South American Judaizer Francisco Maldonado de Silva kept the Yom Kippur fast for four days.[46] Twentieth-century Portuguese Judaizers retain a curiously syncretic version of this custom. João Antonio Ferreira at age 80 in 1929 reported that in the crypto-Jewish community in Bragança "from the time of the new moon of September no pork could enter the house."[47] Vasconcelos adds that many modern Portuguese new-Christians would abstain from eating pork for the forty days prior to Yom Kippur, and from any kind of meat for the eleven preceding days (1958, 210) before fasting on Yom Kippur itself (Schwarz 1925, 30).

Much more common than pre-Yom Kippur fasting, however, was the need to fortify oneself with food prior to undertaking the twenty-four-hour fast. This crypto-Jewish custom too had its origin in pre-Expulsion times. Rabbi Simuel of Teruel testified in 1485 that "the night before the fast it is the ceremony of the Jews to eat chicken and other solid food."[48] Several detailed descriptions of preparations for the feast before the Yom Kippur fast exist; this one was recited by Mariana, a maid in the *chueta* family of Margarita Martí [Majorca 1678]:

> They cooked all night many different dishes . . . and they ate in their main room, where they did not eat other days, on their biggest table set more sumptuously than on other days. And they made new clothes and put them on . . . and Margarita Martí also dressed her children up. And that same afternoon, because she [Mariana] perceived so much commotion, curious to know if they were doing the same thing all over the neighborhood, she went into the house of the brothers Miguel and Antonio Cortés, and of Balthazar Martí . . . and Isabel Forteza. . . . And she saw that they were all dressed up as on a festival, and that there was a great stirring in their kitchens, just as in her masters' house.[49]

Braunstein adds that Majorcan *chuetas* broke out newly purchased salt for this occasion (Braunstein 1936, 101). Mexican crypto-Jews were also accustomed to feasting prior to the Yom Kippur fast. Around 1645 Gabriel de Granada and his family dined before the fast on fish, eggs, and vegetables, which they washed down with chocolate (Adler 1899, 13, 81). Mathias Rodríguez de Olivera [Mexico 1649] said that he used to send "fish, candy and other things to other persons of the same false belief [Judaism] so that they could eat on those fast days" (Liebman 1974, 87). In the 1640s Salomon Machorro and his friends preceded one Yom Kippur fast with eggs, salad, and meat pies (*empanadas*) and another with fish and vegetables (Lewin 1977, 25, 43).

The fast itself was undertaken with great solemnity,[50] for most Judaizers believed along with Juan de Madrid, a *converso* Jeronymite monk from the monastery of Sisla (Segovia) who testified in 1487, that "whoever fasted on the Day of Atonement would be rewarded by God."[51] In Teruel [1485] a *conversa* was accused of believing "that in order to be saved she had to fast the Fast of Kippur, because that was necessary for the salvation of her soul."[52] Francisco Luis [Mexico 1649] said with regard to Yom Kippur that "whoever did not fast would have his soul cut" (Liebman 1974, 84).

For crypto-Jews the fast began and ended at dusk according to ancient Jewish custom. A Valencian Edict of Grace of 1484 calls attention to people "who observe the Fast of Pardon and other Jewish fasts and do not eat until nightfall when you can see the stars."[53] Testimony in Ciudad Real in 1484 stated that "on the Great Fast, as the Jews call it, they are barefoot all day and they neither eat nor drink and pray until nightfall."[54] Some *conversos* fasted with their friends: María González [Ciudad Real 1511] said that she "fasted twice with Juana Núñez . . . not eating the whole day, and in the evening eating eggs and other things she had in her house."[55] Pedro Núñez Franco [Ciudad Real 1513] confessed that he and his friends "did not eat all day until nightfall, and at night they ate meat and embraced one another."[56]

As with other crypto-Jewish observances, dissemblance was in order. Diego Díaz Nieto [Mexico 1601] stated that he celebrated Yom Kippur in the Indian village of San Pedro (near Pachuca) because, Liebman says, "his failure to eat on a fast day in an Indian village would occasion no disclosure of his religion" (Liebman 1970, 194). Judaizers in Majorca in the 1670s followed Yom Kippur by observing seven days of holiday during which they abstained from work by pretending to be sick (Cortes 1985, 287). Curiously, in the seventeenth century some rich Judaizers paid others to fast for them, as did Isabel de Miranda, of Madrid, who gave someone 300 *reales* to fast for the soul of one of her relatives (Blázquez Miguel 1986, 62).

The end of Yom Kippur might be marked with a final prayer and a bit of food to end the fast symbolically. The Galician maid Blanca Oliveira was puzzled when she saw "many people coming into her masters' house, and she saw that when the first star had come out one of them, a Portuguese man, had given to each one of the people who were there a slice of bread, and then all of them began to pray, while facing one wall of the bedroom."[57] But after that feasting was in order. Although in Castile Judaizers might "break their fast with fowl and other meat,"[58] in Aragon, Portugal, and the colonies fowl or fish seem to have been the preferred foods. In the late fifteenth century Rabbi Simuel of Teruel testified that "after the fast, in the evening, they ate chicken."[59] The Family of Aldonza Deli of Teruel broke their fast with doves.[60] Inquisitors accused Isabel Núñez [Ciudad Rodrigo 1623] of a large array of Judaizing practices, including the fact that her family broke the Yom Kippur fast "with *matza* and a salad dressed with oil and vinegar and ground dirt [sic]."[61] Isabel Rodríguez, an eighty-year-old illiterate *conversa* [Toledo 1677], allegedly broke her Yom Kippur fast with trout, fruit, chickpea stew, olives, fritters with honey, and chocolate with biscuits (Blázquez Miguel 1989, 215). Gabriel Gomes Navarro [Lisbon 1673] reported that his family would break the Yom Kippur fast with anything except meat: grapes, fruit, fish, bread, or wine (da Cunha e Freitas 1952, 19). Tomás Treviño de Sobremonte [Mexico 1624] declared to the Inquisition that on Yom Kippur night he and his mother and her friends ate "some fish dish, which was required because it was a ceremony of said Law."[62]

Ethnographers have collected substantial information about the ways in which twentieth-century Portuguese new-Christians break their fast. First they wash their mouths three times (Vasconcelos 1958, 222);[63] then before eating they recite this blessing: "Just as the Lord gave His holy blessing to the line of Abraham, Isaac and his son Jacob, may the Lord extend to us and all our family His holy blessing." To which all reply: "May this rise to heaven, may this reach there, for the honor and glory of the holy name of the Lord. Amen."[64] Vasconcelos reports that after the Yom Kippur fast new-Christians can eat no kind of meat until they have eaten fowl (Vasconcelos 1958, 210). Paulo found that some groups break fast with a fish dinner and that before eating they take three grains of salt in their hand and say:

> I beg Your permission, Lord, / to break my fast.
>
> Make me happy and constant / to serve and love You.
>
> Just as this salt / comes out of the sacred sea,
>
> Lord, draw my soul / away from sins and sorrows.
>
> Praised be the Lord, / as now I break my fast:
>
> God give me life and health / to obey His holy Law.[65]

While a restrained, somber mood dominated the twenty-four-hour period of Yom Kippur prayer, the feast that broke the fast was clearly a happy occasion, for after breaking their fast twentieth-century Portuguese new-Christians sing and dance for the honor and glory of God (Vasconcelos 1958, 172).

As mentioned previously, fasting was only one of the principal classes of "afflictions" Jews were required to undertake for Yom Kippur. Another was abstaining from wearing leather shoes. Almost as frequently as they fasted, observant crypto-Jews went barefoot on Yom Kippur, in accord with the *Mishnah Torah*'s prohibition against wearing shoes (Maim., *Yad.* III,3,i,5; iii,7). Roth explains that the custom has its origin in the behavior of Moses before the burning bush (1931–2, 24). The custom was recorded in the fifteenth-century memorandum describing crypto-Jewish customs (Santa María 1893c, 183) and was part of the standard *converso* observance of Yom Kippur right up to modern times.[66] Colonial Mexican Judaizers not only went barefoot, but during Yom Kippur prayers they went to surprising lengths to remain perfectly still during the long prayers. The *converso* Jorge Rodríguez Tabara stood on bricks, fulfilling the Orthodox rule that the leader in prayer should not move his feet (Liebman 1982, 107), and Pedro Arias de Maldonado, too, was accused in 1649 of praying barefoot and standing on bricks on Yom Kippur (Liebman 1974, 228). Inquisitors in Ciudad Rodrigo in 1623 accused Isabel Núñez of a large array of Judaizing practices, including the fact that in her home "they observed a great fast for three days and threw ashes on their heads, and one of them on foot with his feet together prayed their prayers."[67] Some later Judaizers added sleeping on the floor to the requirements of Yom Kippur. Francisco Maldonado de Silva was accused in Chile in 1626 of saying that one of the "corporeal afflictions" required during Yom Kippur was to sleep on the floor (Böhm 1963, 47), and as late as 1952 Machado reported that on Yom Kippur new-Christian villagers in the Mogadouro region of Portugal sleep on the stone floor (Machado 1952, 40).

With regard to the prayers commonly recited by crypto-Jews during the Yom Kippur observances, the documentary record provides substantial evidence both of general prayer practices and of specific texts of prayers. In normative Judaism, on Yom Kippur itself prayer begins at sundown on Yom Kippur eve and continues almost without break until sundown the following day. Some crypto-Jews held as many as five separate services during the twenty-four-hour period.[68] Other Judaizing new-Christians on both sides of the Atlantic were accustomed to praying straight through the night on Yom Kippur. For example, in Mexico in 1624 Tomás Treviño de Sobremonte declared to the Inquisition how on Yom Kippur eve

> after everyone else in the house had gone to bed, between ten and eleven at night, he went over to Diego de Almanza's house with Leonor Martínez, his mother, and Ana Sánchez, and together they went up to a bedroom where Ana de Almanza, Diego's daughter, and Luisa Martínez were sleeping. And leaving her husband Diego de Almanza still asleep, Luisa Martínez went up to Ana Almanza's room, where they were all gathered praying, and speaking about the Law. And they said how everyone had to fast the next day, that was the day of the Great Fast. And that during the most of that night, or all of it, each as best she could should remain standing or walking back and forth according to the ceremony required by the Law of Moses. And they were there until two in the morning, talking about the Law and praying.[69]

This same custom was reported in the trial of the Spanish liquor dealer Gabriel Gomes Navarro [Lisbon 1673]. After the meal on Yom Kippur eve everyone would walk around the table all night, barefoot, praying for the dead and reciting this prayer: "May the Lord be magnified and glorified for ever. You raised me up so that my enemies could not conquer me. Raise me up, heal me with Your divine medicine. You pulled my soul out of a cave, You made my body from the dust, You kept watch over my soul. Hear, hear, Lord, as I sing praises to the Lord. Salvation, salvation, salvation, salvation be with our souls forever."[70]

The solemnity of the beginning of the Yom Kippur celebration helped to impress young crypto-Jewish initiates of the importance of the tradition that was being passed to them. A niece of the Galician *conversa* Violante Alvarez described the start of Yom Kippur in these words:

> The first fast she kept when she was fifteen years old was the Great Fast of 1599. When it was night the prisoner [Violante Alvarez] took her out to a field next to the house and said to her: "Take care to fast today so that Our Lord will grant you life." And the two of them on foot facing the setting sun the prisoner uncovered her hair and recited prayers, one which she said was the prayer of the Star and another of the Fast and the witness said the same words. And when they had finished she said to her: "Aunt, why are we praying?" And the prisoner replied: "You know that we worship one God alone, the God of Israel your people."[71]

Frequently crypto-Jews would begin these marathon prayer sessions with a request for the Deity to favor their worship. A late example comes from an eighteenth-century new-Christian prayer book discovered in Portugal: "I come before you, Lord, in fasting; not for lack of bread, nor of anything. I mortify my flesh, my blood is written in heaven, I hope for Your divine blessing, Lord God of Adonai. Amen."[72] New Christians in Portugal in this century begin Yom Kippur by lighting the olive-oil-burning "lamp of the Lord" and reciting: "Blessed is my God, my Lord, my Adonai who commanded us to keep His holy and blessed commandments, to light this lamp to illumine and gladden the holy night of the Lord, so that the Lord will illumine our souls and free us from error and sin. Amen, Lord. May this rise to Heaven, may this reach Heaven."[73]

The traditional Yom Kippur liturgy stresses the themes of confession, repentance, atonement, and forgiveness.[74] Confession of sin tends to be public, generic, and communal. These themes also appear frequently in the crypto-Jewish prayers that have made their way into the public record. On the whole a very somber mood prevailed. A late fifteenth-century satiric poem from Román against the *converso* poet Antón de Montoro lists among his Judaizing customs that on the day of the Great Fast he was shut up inside all day moaning and weeping.[75] Certain psalms and lamentations were particularly popular; Luis García, of Talavera (formerly Rabbi Abraham), was accused of having "chanted the prophecies of Jeremiah and Isaiah and other prophecies, chanting them in low voice in the manner and tone in which the rabbis used to chant them in the synagogue to honor their law."[76] In Mexico on Yom Kippur in 1590 the incarcerated Luis Carvajal prayed on his knees, saying: "O Almighty, for the sake of Thy Holy name and for Thy Great Day which You have made so that we might fast and repent our sins, pardon us and have mercy on us."[77] Gabriel de Granada recited this prayer to the Mexican Inquisition in 1642:

> Lord, my soul called upon Thee to deliver me from the fire and flame that I may not be burned or scorched. Here am I in this desert, turned into a plant [*servato*] where great trouble shall overtake me. Into thick darkness shall they cast me where neither brother nor cousin can aught avail me. One thing, my God, shall I ask of Thee, that Thou remember my soul and deliver it at the mouth of a cave and going out at a door, and that I may not amuse myself except in counting the Stars of Heaven or throwing water in the Sea.[78]

Similarly, on Yom Kippur eve [Mexico 1642] Doña Catalina de Rivera was reported to have sat in her room next to the Yom Kippur candles and recited with her sisters prayer that began "I have sinned, I have sinned, Lord."[79] As is common in Jewish prayer services, these sorts of lamentations and petitions generally begin by praising the Deity in His many attributes. This is the theme of this verse prayer that in 1644 the American *conversa* Micaela Enríquez said was recited on Yom Kippur: "Now we are going to bed / and we pray to God, / to God, my Lord, / than whom there is no equal, / nor has there been nor will there be, / blessed be He who gives us life."[80]

As with other crypto-Jewish festivals, the most learned Judaizer in the group would take on the role of leader. For example, Francisco López Díaz was accused in Mexico of attending a Yom Kippur service sometime in the 1630s where one man acted as rabbi to a group of Judaizers, "reading from a book to them in Hebrew the rules of the fast; making them sit down, stand up, and deeply bow their heads. The men's heads were covered with hats and the women wore long head clothes. A large number of candles were lit."[81]

The last major component of crypto-Jewish Yom Kippur observance, in accord with Yom Kippur's emphasis on atonement and forgiveness, is formal pardoning of family, friends, and associates within the *converso* community. Either during the days immediately preceding Yom Kippur or on the holiday itself, crypto-Jews attempted to settle any outstanding moral debts or obligations they might have. This was a common practice among Jews prior to the Expulsion and was featured strongly in the Yom Kippur celebrations of the early *conversos*. In 1485 in Ciudad Real the prosecutor's summation accused Juan Martínez de los Olivos and his friends of "on the day of the Great Fast they ask each other for forgiveness, ceremonially, as the Jews do, saying that all their sins are forgiven on that day."[82] Similarly, Juan Sánchez Exarch [Teruel c. 1485] went barefoot and hooded to the house of a man named Puxmija "to ask forgiveness of Puxmija, because it had been about five years since he had spoken to him."[83] In the 1460s the *conversos* Diego Arias and his wife Elvira González on Yom Kippur would embrace their Jewish relatives and ask their pardon.[84] Asking formally for forgiveness appears to have been a feature of Iberian crypto-Jewish observance right up to modern times.[85] In 1543 in Lisbon Francisca Vaz said that on Yom Kippur all transgressions must be forgiven.[86] In colonial Mexico around 1645 observant Judaizers "embraced each other and prayed for forgiveness from each other, and they kissed the hand of the oldest of their . . . relations who gave her blessing to all of them saying: 'May God make ye good' " (Adler 1899, 117). Gaspar Váez recalled for Mexican Inquisitors in 1642 how one Yom Kippur his friend Juan de León "persuaded him to go to the house of Doña Leonor de Rojas, his aunt, to speak to her, because for a long time he had been angry at her, and he recalled that he persuaded him to go also to talk to Doña Elena de Silva, his aunt, with whom he had also not been communicating, telling him that he was obliged to do it because it was a ceremony of the Law."[87]

Some crypto-Jews also expressed their atonement through acts of charity, although references to the custom are quite rare. Leonor Rodrigues was convicted by the Coimbra Inquisition in 1567 because, among other things, she said that on "the Fast of Kippur she gave greater charity than at other times."[88] Twentieth-century Portuguese new-Christians, too, on Yom Kippur eve distribute charity to the poor.[89]

In accord with general Sabbath and holiday practice, from Expulsion times granting forgiveness on Yom Kippur was linked to the blessing of one's children in affirmation of their continued commitment to crypto-Judaism. A memorandum prepared for Inquisitors in the late fifteenth century says that "the [conversos] pray Jewish prayers and at night ask forgiveness one of the other, the fathers putting their hands on their children's heads saying: may you be blessed by God and by me for keeping the Law of Moses and its ceremonies."[90] Sometimes, as in Mexico in the 1640s, this appears to have been little more than the standard parental blessing. Juana Enríquez was accused in 1642 in Mexico of going to her mother's house on Yom Kippur eve, where she "found seven or eight wax candles lit on a buffet.... She asked her mother for a blessing. She stood and bowed her head. Her mother put her hand on her head and blessed her: 'May the blessing that God gave Jacob and Isaac descend to her and to all her children.' "[91] But often it was tied explicitly to the act of Yom Kippur forgiveness. According to a Ciudad Real trial in 1484 "the day of the Great Fast the wife of Juan Daça, the scribe, and their children came to ask forgiveness of Hernando de Theba's mother and they kissed her hand, because they were her relatives, and she put her hand on their heads."[92] Heitor Lobo, of Lamego [Coimbra 1569], testified that "before breaking the fast certain people who had been fasting with him knelt before him and asked his forgiveness, and he passed his open hand across their face and gave them God's blessing and his own."[93]

As with the other Judaizing customs sketched in this study, individual *conversos* tended to select from the crypto-Jewish tradition those practices which they knew of, or which they felt comfortable observing. Public observance of Yom Kippur was, of course, all but impossible, which renders suspect a 1593 allegation that in Brazil *cristãos novos* used to go in procession to their synagogue to pray on Yom Kippur. A Florentine visitor to the region, Felipe Cavalcanti, reported that it was an annual custom on the new moon of August to go in carts decorated with branches to Camarigibe to celebrate the fast of Kippur. Lipiner believes that this is probably a reference to Sukkot, not Yom Kippur, and to September not August (1969, 93), and it may be an example of the use of a pilgrimage to a local Catholic shrine as cover for a crypto-Jewish practice. Contrary to this example, almost always when groups of crypto-Jews came together they took care to avoid prying eyes. The most typical Yom Kippur observance must have been a clandestine fast and a furtive coming together in someone's house to recite whatever fragments of prayer remained in the family's oral tradition.[94] From time to time, however, the documents provide a glimpse of the elaborate way a Jewishly sophisticated *converso* celebrated Yom Kippur. One of the most detailed descriptions of a Yom Kippur celebration comes to us from the Portuguese trial of Antônio Homem, who was burned by the Inquisition in 1624.

> The house in which the fast was to be celebrated was prepared by whitewashing the floor; in one part was placed a table covered with a silk cloth, set with candlesticks with lighted candles; from the center of the room hung a great tin candelabra with many candles. And at the appointed hour all the people who were going to attend the solemn festivity came into the house dressed in their best clothes, their beards trimmed, their feet bare, without capes, their hats on their heads, and they sat along the wall. On some of those fasts they wore white vestments that came down to their waist, and they put some straps with amulets attached on their heads, and they had their arms crossed. And during many of these solemnities, in which the prisoner Antônio Homem often took the part of priest, he was seated on a backed chair preaching to some people, exhorting them to live in the law of Moses, referring to certain authorities of the Old Testament; and at certain passages the people performed *guayas*, raising their eyes to the sky, clapping their hands together and lowering their heads to their chests, bowing this way and that. And the prisoner repeated some Psalms of David without the *gloria patri*, and among them was the *In exitu Israel de Egipto* [Ps. 114] and the *Super flumina Babilonia* [Ps. 137] and the *De profundis clamavi* [Ps. 130]. And when they got to the verse that says *Et propter legem tuam sustinui te Domine* he explained that this meant that they were to suffer trials and persecutions for the sake of the Lord's law, and that they should forever hope in the Lord, and that is also what was meant by the verse of the same Psalm which said *A custodia matutina usque ad noctem speret Israel in Domino*, and that by that verse David meant that the fast was to be . . . from morning until night, and that is how they would gain from God what David had promised in the next verse, which is: that the loving-kindness of God and the redemption of the people of Israel would be of great dimension, and that He would forgive them all their sins. And after spending some time in this preaching and in similar ceremonies which he performed for the people in attendance in order to strengthen their belief in the law of Moses, some other priests dressed him—sometimes in this house and sometimes outside—in a long, well-fitting garment, setting on his head a sort of miter that was closed on top and decorated with a golden plaque. And those priests of the law of Moses who attended him were dressed in silk vestments. They handed him a censor [?] with which the prisoner perfumed a few steps around that altar, where sometimes there was a little altar-stand with a painting of Moses and another of someone who had been handed over to the secular authorities and burned as a Jew. Then they perfumed the prisoner, who blew into a horn and made a low sound several times during that day. And on that altar was a Bible from which the prisoner read several chapters of the Old Testament, and recited Psalms of David, in which the entire day was spent. At the end of the day the prisoner preached another sermon in which he exhorted them to practice the law of Moses. . . . And at the end of the sermon that the prisoner preached at the

gathering of the Great Fast everyone who attended kissed his foot, and he blessed them in the Jewish manner, putting his hand on their head and running it down over their face. And he did this so that the people who attended those acts would consider him to be the Great Priest of the law of Moses.[95]

The records of the trial of André de Avelar in 1623 include additional information about the Yom Kippur services at which Antônio Homem officiated: After reading certain passages the congregation

> performed *guayas*, raising their eyes to heaven, holding the palms of their hands together, lowering their heads to their chests and bowing at the waist. And after they prayed like this for an hour in preparation for the great fast, the main priest got up and went into a more hidden place where he stayed for a quarter of an hour, after which he blew three quiet notes on a horn, at which the people who were waiting outside performed three *guayas* in the aforesaid manner. Then the prisoner, and a certain number of the other people to attend him, went back into the secret place, and after they were with him another quarter of an hour the horn sounded another three times and the people waiting outside performed another three *guayas*.[96]

The priest's robe was an "alb, decorated at the corners with fringes of the same silk which dragged on the ground, decorated all around with little silk bells which were not silver so that they would not make a sound, and tied with a belt."[97] The priest's miter bore "two golden plaques, one with the figure of Moses and the other with a serpent."[98] The incense ritual was even more elaborately described:

> The prisoner and the rest of the congregation stood on both sides of the altar, wearing vestments of a certain color. When they were all standing they began the ceremony, which they termed a "sacrifice." The prisoner, kneeling, took the censor containing incense and embers from some special charcoal which was easily lit and burned during the entire day. He gave it to the main priest, who from time to time shook incense at the altar in a certain way, then giving the censor back to the prisoner and bowing with a great *guaya* and bowing his head slightly. Then the prisoner shook incense at the other attendees, and they all performed *guayas* among each other all during the incense ceremony.[99]

The priest "recited by heart certain Psalms and then explained them in Latin, saying that the law of Moses was still good today."[100] They terminated the ceremony by "making a vow on a certain book that they would hold the fast day sacred, and that they would never reveal it, because it could cost them their lives because of the great harm that could fall on People of the Nation."[101]

## 13.3. SUKKOT

Lev. 23:39–43 and Num. 29:12–39, which describe the customs of the festival of Sukkot in some detail, provide a basis for the observance of the *conversos*. The basic elements of the holiday are that it commemorates the harvest; that it lasts for eight days (nine in the Diaspora), the first and last of which are to be considered Sabbaths; and that during the holiday observers dwell in huts, or "booths," made of "the fruit of goodly trees, branches of palm trees, and boughs of leafy trees, and willows of the brook" (Lev. 23:40). Special tractates of both the Mishnah and the Talmud provide additional instructions with regard to Sukkot, but these were largely inaccessible to *conversos*.

Among crypto-Jews Sukkot was known by a variety of names, including its traditional Hebrew name. By far the most common names had to do with the custom of building booths; thus it was known as *La pascua de las cavañuelas* (Santa María 1893c, 186) or *La fiesta de las Cabañuelas* (Beinart 1974, 242). A twentieth-century New Mexican festival that may have a remote connection to Sukkot is called by a Mexican word that means "hut," according to Clemente Carmona, who told David Nidel in 1980 that his New Mexican family used to celebrate "an autumn festival called *jacales* at which booths were built. Meals were taken in the huts, and it was believed that seven 'saints' paid a visit to them." He added that around 1960 Bishop Davis began actively to discourage such practices.[102]

Leviticus 23:39 gives the date of Sukkot as the fifteenth day of the seventh month of Tishri, or five days after Yom Kippur, and this date was generally known to the observant *conversos*. The Mexican *converso* Juan de León [1643], for example, said that "*Succoth* was celebrated five days after the fast of Kippur in the month of September."[103] As with the dates of other holidays, *conversos* often related Sukkot to the lunar calendar. Diego Mora, of Quintanar de la Orden, was accused in 1589 of celebrating fifteen days after the new moon of September in thanks for the harvest (Blázquez Miguel 1986a, 67). A late fifteenth-century compilation of Jewish customs describes the holiday this way:

> Sukkot is the Feast of the Booths, which falls on the fourteenth or fifteenth day after the new moon of September and lasts for nine days. The first two are days of special observance and the last is called Simhat Torah which means joy, for it was on that day they finished reading the five books of the Law and began again right after this holiday, and because they lived in booths in the desert, and praised God because usually it rained on that holiday. And they keep the last two days of these nine and the day before which is called *araba* and is one of the last three days.[104]

Perhaps because it was so readily accessible in the Bible, this calendar was recalled by *conversos* for many hundreds of years. In 1688 Ana Cortés reported to the Inquisition in Majorca that her father Joseph Cortés had instructed her "that two or three days after the Fast of Pardon came seven consecutive festival days in which she was not to work.... And that after the seven days she was to eat stewed [?] beans and roast chicken."[105]

In normative Judaism four particular species of fruits, the so-called *arba'ah minim* (palm-*lulav*; myrtle-*hadassim*; willow-*aravot*; citron-*etrog*), are brought into the booth (*sukkah*). A memorandum given to the Inquisition in the late fifteenth century states that "the Festival of Booths, which falls on the fifteenth of September, recalls when the children of Israel went forth from Egypt, and went into the desert and for forty years lived in booths and huts. And in remembrance and memory of this Jews make these huts, constructing them of cane, willow, fennel, and other vegetables and fruits, according to the season. And these huts have to be made outside, in a place from which you can see the sky, which were like the ones the Jews had in the desert. The huts last for nine days, during which they give thanks to God for the harvest of the fruits of the land, and for seven of the nine days Jews were obligated to eat inside the hut."[106] A Valencian Edict of Grace of 1484 labels as Judaizers people "who make in their houses booths of fennel or other branches in memory of the Booths of the Jews."[107] In a 1492–3 trial in Toledo Ruy García Serrano was accused of celebrating Sukkot in the traditional fashion. "On the Festival of Booths he took the grapefruit [the traditional *etrog*] and the palm branch [the traditional *lulav*] in his hand and recited the prayers that the Jews recite, saying *Anna adonay osiana*, as the Jews do."[108] However, the *arba'ah minim* seem to have been dropped early from Sukkot observance, for they are rarely mentioned in documents dealing with *converso* customs beyond the first generation or two.

The festival of Sukkot was widely practiced among Judaizing *conversos* from the earliest days up through the end of the sixteenth century in Spain and the Spanish possessions. This is surprising because the booths traditionally constructed for Sukkot are easily observable and run counter to the trend of clandestineness. Nonetheless in Spain Sukkot lasted for a century after the Expulsion. References to it after that time are sporadic. In the New World the holiday had disappeared by mid-seventeenth century (Liebman 1982, 123). In northern Portugal by the late sixteenth century Sukkot was apparently rarely celebrated, or at least rarely noticed by the Inquisitors. In the 634 cases of Judaizers reported from the Coimbra Inquisition between 1567 and 1583 there is only one reference to the Feast of Booths (Azevedo Mea 1982, 114). As with most observances, however, it was strongest in the years close to the Expulsion date.

The most common feature of new-Christian Sukkot observance was the construction of huts, or booths, near the Judaizer's principal residence. Numerous descriptions from around the time of the Expulsion detail the normative Jewish practice of that time.[109] *Conversos* or their servants would scour the countryside for the appropriate branches and fruits. In 1490 Fray Juan de Victoria reported to the Inquisition that one day before Sukkot he had been walking out near San Lázaro and had seen the *converso* Gonçalo Sanches Cauallero "riding on a mule; and it was the eve of the Festival of Booths, one hour before sundown, and in his hand he had a branch of green willow, and he rode along praying and bobbing his head; and he saw that Gonçalo Sanches Cauallero was so deeply involved in his prayers that although he passed right by him Sánchez never saw him or spoke to him. He just rode along praying and swaying with his branch in his hand."[110] Another witness said that when Sánchez saw him coming he hid the branch under his cape.

The booths were constructed adjacent to the house or, if possible, in the central courtyard. It was important that the branches be woven loosely enough to permit glimpses of the sky. A witness in Ciudad Real said how *conversos* he knew "make booths at the entrances to their gates and break open a piece of the roof."[111] In those early days of *converso* culture observance of Sukkot was so central to Judaizing that even *converso* priests who retained an identification with Judaism continued to build their huts in the traditional ways. Salamón Leuí testified in Soria in 1490 that ten years earlier he had gone into the house of Pero López, the priest of Cornago [Logroño] whose father had been a Jew, and had seen "how he had the willow branches stretched over some poles, from wall to wall, . . . the way Jews make booths at their festival."[112] Around 1488 the monk García Zapata of Nuestra Señora de Sisla in Toledo was said to have woven certain branches over the ceiling of his cell, which he told his colleagues was to cheer him up. He pretended to be sick, which provided an excuse for him to be visited there by some other Judaizing monks (Blázquez Miguel 1986a, 62). It is clear that prior to 1492 *conversos* nostalgic for traditional Judaism were accustomed to visiting with their Jewish friends in their booths during the Sukkot holiday. A striking example of this yearning for Jewish experience was the case of Juan de Cuéllar, a Segovian who converted sometime prior to 1486 and who not only "continued to frequent the house of Abraham Seneor for six months, every morning and evening, and sometimes in the afternoon, to hear him pray . . . under guise of doing business with Don Abraham; [but] sometimes he comes up to our booths at Sukkot to do business with Don Abraham at his table."[113]

During Sukkot these booths served as a focal point for communal activity. They were commonly the site of the family meal, which was often shared with friends. In 1484 in Ciudad Real Rodrigo Marín and his wife Catalina López were accused of having "kept the Holiday of Booths, fasting until the first star came out at night, and afterwards in the evening they ate chicken and other meat all nine days of the feast of Booths."[114] The custom was so prominent among Judaizing *conversos* that a late fifteenth-century satiric poem from Román against the *converso* poet Antón de Montoro lists among his Judaizing customs that he was accustomed to eating *matza* on the Festival of Booths.[115] The holiday was particularly attractive to young people, and most booths seem to have kept a supply of sweets on hand. Violante Santángel was said in 1485 to have gone with the wife of Martín Ruiz to the *judería* to see the booths, and that there they looked at them and went into them and the wife of Martín Ruiz went into the booths and brought them out drinks and candy.[116] When she was a little girl she and her sister accompanied their mother to the *judería* to visit the booths. The two girls shopped in the market and were courted by the Jewish boys. Later they were offered *confites* by a woman named Bonjorna (Sánchez Moya/Monasterio Aspiri 1972–3, 118). Her sister Leonor Santángel was said to have gone to the *judería* to watch the bulls run and to see the booths and eat *priscos* [?].[117] Juan Sánchez Exarch, a *converso* from Teruel, was accused in 1484 of making a booth in his house or, if he could not, in someone else's house, of meeting with other Jews there, of conducting ceremonies and of eating nougat candy.[118] Recalling the days before the Expulsion, María de la Higuera recalled in 1521 that she used to go into the booths just to look at them.[119]

*Shemini Atzeret* [= Solemn Assembly; see Num. 29:35] in normative Judaism is celebrated on the eighth day of Sukkot with a memorial service and with prayers for rain. One possible description of a *Shemini atzeret* observance and of *converso* nostalgia for the old ways of Judaism comes from Calatayud from 1489. A witness there reported that "when the Jews of Calatayud took out the Torahs in the street to pray for rain . . . she saw [the *converso*] Simon de Santaclara, the father, in a window of Pazagon's house. And when the Jews were doing that ceremony blowing their horns and singing and wailing so that it would rain, she saw how Santaclara wept and rubbed his lips like any Jew who was praying and weeping (not the ones who were singing out loud). And, she saw Simon nestled in that window where he could look at the Torahs and the whole ceremony."[120]

The last day of Sukkot, called Simḥat Torah (The Rejoicing of the Law), is treated in the next section of this chapter as a separate holiday.

The most outrageously daring crypto-Jewish Sukkot I have heard of was in 1603 in the Mexico City Inquisition prison, where the *converso* Sebastián Rodríguez, his family, and friends found themselves awaiting disposition of their cases by the Holy Office. Admittedly the prison was loosely run and permitted some comings and goings from the family members who were required to provide basic maintenance for the prisoners. Despite their incarceration, on September 21, 1603, they contrived to celebrate Sukkot right inside the prison. In the report of the informer Captain Lemos: "On the Saturday evening before that Sunday, Sebastián Rodríguez sent him to get lots of branches, which he did, bringing in four Indians loaded up with willow branches with which they decorated the corridors and the patio. They set out tables in the corridor which leads to the patio, and from which you can see the sky. And the food was brought to the table [in front of] the room of Sebastián Rodríguez, at which were seated Costanza Rodríguez, Isabel Rodríguez." There follows a long list of names of people in attendance. Among the dishes served was some sort of "Mexican fowl stuffed with eggs and salt pork." Even the prison warden, Diego del Spinossa, participated, along with his wife, who were told that the party was to celebrate the wedding of Sebastián Rodríguez.

The document says that "Juan López and the son of Isabel Rodríguez, whose name was Simon, served at the table. And after eating there was music and dancing. Antonio López, his sister Leonor Díaz, and a musician from Puebla, whose name he does not know, all sang." The songs they sang were "cathedral songs." Three members of the group, "Ruy Díaz Nieto, Hector de Fonseca and Antonio Díaz Márquez, would not eat at that table . . . because there was salt pork on the table and things cooked with lard," but they took branches to decorate their own rooms, in which they sat praying while the party went on.[121]

## 13.4. SIMHAT TORAH

In normative Judaism Simḥat Torah, which occurs on the twenty-third of Tishri, the last day of Sukkot, has special significance because it marks the end and the beginning of the annual cycle of reading portions of the Torah in the synagogue. On Simḥat Torah both the last portion of the current cycle and the first portion of the next cycle are read, signifying that the study of the Torah can never be completed. Traditionally the congregation parades the decorated Torah scrolls around the synagogue with great rejoicing and singing.

It is understandable that Simḥat Torah is so rarely mentioned in documents dealing with crypto-Jewish religions customs, for in post-Expulsion Iberia for the most part there were no formal synagogues, no Torah scrolls, and no regular cycle of reading from the Torah. One of the two references I have found appears in the late-fifteenth century description of Sukkot cited earlier in this chapter.[122] The second is a description of a *converso*'s visit to a synagogue outside of Spain in the early seventeenth century:

> Hector Méndez Bravo, a Portuguese informer, said in 1617 that he had seen Portuguese Jews in Venice observing a holiday "when a parchment roll written in Hebrew, called the Law, is produced and carried in festivity round the Synagogue by all the men in [new] clothes. (Roth 1943–4, 232)

## 13.5. HANUKKAH

Hanukkah, a relatively minor holiday in the Jewish liturgical year, celebrates the Maccabean Jews' victory over the Syrian Greeks in the year 165 BCE and the restoration of worship in the Temple in Jerusalem following that victory. Tradition says that when the restorers entered the defiled Temple they found only enough oil for the altar lamp to last one day, but that miraculously it lasted for eight days until new oil could be produced. Therefore the holiday, also known as the Festival of Lights, is celebrated by lighting candles or lamps at home and by eating foods fried in oil. Hanukkah is observed for eight days beginning on the twenty-fifth of the Hebrew month Kislev (which generally falls in December).

Although the festival of Hanukkah has assumed major importance in twentieth-century Western culture, probably because of its close proximity to Christmas, it appears to have been of minor significance in pre- or post-Expulsion Iberia. There are a few references from around the time of the Expulsion to Spanish Jews celebrating the holiday. Only two pre-Expulsion Spanish Hanukkah lamps are known to survive.[123] A memorandum prepared for Inquisitors in the late fifteenth century says that Judaizers "celebrate the Feast of Candles and they light them one at a time up to ten, and then they blow them out; and they pray Jewish prayers."[124]

In the 1470s the recently converted Fernando de Trujillo continued to celebrate Hanukkah in the fashion of the Jews (Beinart 1983, 83). And in 1484 his friend María Díaz was accused in Ciudad Real of keeping "the Feast of the Little Candles ... by lighting nine lamps."[125] References to Hanukkah after the Expulsion period are rare. Testimony before the Evora Inquisition in 1536 states that Doctor António Valença, of Mogadouro, taught people the date that *hanuca* was celebrated (Coelho 1987, 209). And a probably anachronistic Mexican Edict of Faith (1639) talks of burning ten candles (Liebman 1970, 97). Around 1615 the António Homem circle in Coimbra was observing a *paschoa das candelilhas* (Lorence 1991, 97). But for the most part the holiday dropped off the crypto-Jewish calendar. In the 634 cases tried by the Coimbra Inquisition between 1567 and 1583 there is only one possible oblique reference to Hanukkah. Seventy-four-year-old Isabel Lopes, of Vila Flor, in the section of her conviction that deals with the Sabbath, was accused of lighting a lamp "with clean oil and six or seven wicks."[126] The handful of twentieth-century references to crypto-Jewish celebration of Hanukkah—such as the report that it is sometimes celebrated in Portugal as the Feast of the Little Candles or even "Little Christmas"[127]—probably derive from the modern Jewish observance of Hanukkah or the calendar association of Hanukkah with Christmas. This is almost certainly the situation in New Mexico, where Clemente Carmona told David Nidel in 1980 that in December "we have a festival that sort of coincides with Hanukkah. We call it *las fiestas de los Reis,* and you light candles. You keep lighting candles until you have eight or nine candles at the family altar." He added that they call it the Festival of the Kings so that any Christian who discovers it will think it is an early celebration of the Christian holiday of Epiphany on January 6.[128]

## 13.6. Purim

Purim commemorates the deliverance of the Jews of Persia from the genocide which King Ahasueros' minister Haman plotted against them, as narrated in the Book of Esther. Traditional Jewish synagogues preserve this book in the form of a scroll, known as the Scroll of Esther (*Megillat Esther*) or merely the *Megillah.* On Purim eve in the synagogue the *Megillah* is read aloud while the congregation—notably the children—cheer every mention of the story's hero, Mordechai, and drown out the name of its villain, Haman. Except for the noise-making of children, these basic outlines of the Purim festival were well known to Iberian Jews prior to the Expulsion, as a memorandum of Judaizing customs prepared for Inquisitors in the late fifteenth century makes clear. It calls Purim "the day of the stars, on which Jews used to donate to the poor in commemoration of King Ahasueros' saving the people of Israel at the behest of Mordechai and Queen Esther;

for he was going to kill them on the advice of Haman, as it is written in the book of Queen Esther."[129] The *converso* Antonio de Avila's testimony in Segovia in 1488 is typical: he said that some twenty years earlier he had visited the *conversa* Isabel Arias to read her "the story of King Ahasueros in the form of a *megillah* that was written like a Torah."[130] There may have been other special prayers associated with the holiday as well, as an Inquisitor's reference in 1524 in the Canary Islands to the Prayer of Saint Esther may indicate. Pero Gonçales [Las Palmas 1524] was asked "how many times he had said the prayer of Queen Esther, but he would not answer. This question deponent put to him because he is known to have said that Queen Esther was born for the salvation of many."[131] Among Iberian Jews and *conversos* the holiday was generally known by its Hebrew name of Purim, although astonishingly it was also known in some quarters as Saint Haman's Day![132] While in the Ashkenazi tradition Purim has taken on carnival-like aspects of humorous disguises, play acting, and general revelry, these characteristics are not mentioned in documents having to do with Iberian Jews or *conversos*.[133]

Among *conversos* much more popular than Purim itself was the Fast of Esther (*Ta'anit Esther*), which occurs on the thirteenth of Adar, the day before Purim, and commemorates the fact that Esther fasted before she approached King Ahasueros to plead for the Jews (Esther 4:15–16). Because fasts were much easier and safer for the crypto-Jews to keep than feasts, the Fast of Esther grew to rival the feast on the following day and eventually came to be the equal of the fast of Yom Kippur. Probably because of its theme of deliverance and the fact that the crypto-Jews could identify with the oppressed captives living in the threatening environment of ancient Persia, Purim appears to have been enormously popular among the Jews of Iberia and its overseas possessions. It is clear that among Iberian *conversos* Esther was esteemed as a historical deliverer of her people. Later generations of new-Christians frequently referred to her as Saint Esther, a name by which she is recalled by remnant new-Christian communities in the twentieth century, among whom she is venerated almost like a Christian Saint.[134] Until recently *cristãos novos* from Belmonte hung pictures of Holy Queen Esther in their homes (Fontes 1989a). Clemente Carmona told David Nidel in New Mexico in 1980 that his family used to celebrate "Saint Esther's holiday." It was mainly a holiday for women, "dedicated to mothers teaching their daughters the ways of the home and such." They held a big party and served the meat turnovers called *empanadas*. They drank wine which was blessed by the oldest person present. The women "lit candles to Saint Esther and other saints." Around 1960 Bishop Davis began actively to discourage such practices (Nidel 1984, 253–4).

Although in normative Judaism the Fast of Esther is kept for a single day, many crypto-Jews observed it for a longer period, often for three days.[135] Rita Besante confessed in Teruel in 1485 that she "kept the three Fasts of Queen Esther,"[136] while Isabel Gomes was accused in Portugal in 1541 of keeping the Fast of Esther for four or five days (Baião 1921, 119).[137] As with other traditional Jewish holidays, once the Expulsion generation had died away Judaizing *conversos* had difficulty in fixing the precise date of Purim. The *Mishnah Torah* says that the *Megillah*, or scroll of Esther, must be read on the fourteenth of Adar (Maim., *Yad.* III,10,i,4), which tends to occur in March. Gonçalo Váez [Granada 1573] said that "the fast of queen Ester is for three days, and it falls in the month of September,"[138] while a memorandum about Judaizing customs prepared for the Granada Inquisition in 1593 placed it in the month of June (García Fuentes 1981, 434). Iberian new-Christians tended to relate Purim's date to the lunar calendar. In Majorca in the 1670s Judaizers kept the fast of Esther two days after the new moon in March (Cortes 1985, 287). Seventeenth-century Portuguese *conversos* observed it on the full moon of February (Roth 1931–2, 27), while Majorcan *chuetas* of the same period observed it on the eleventh day after the new moon of March (Braunstein 1936, 101). Paulo reports that in this century new-Christians in Belmonte, Portugal, celebrate the feast of Esther during September (1985, 57).

The fast of Esther was observed by Judaizing new-Christians much as was the fast of Yom Kippur, except that people fasted during daylight hours only. The late fifteenth-century memorandum of Jewish customs reports that "they fast the fast of Esther which they call the Destruction of the Holy Temple, . . . not eating on those days until the first star is out at night, and those nights they do not eat meat. And the day before the fast they wash themselves and cut their nails and trim their hair."[139] In 1688 Ana Cortés reported to the Inquisition in Majorca that her father Joseph Cortés had instructed her to keep the three fasts of Esther "on three consecutive days, abstaining from eating or drinking until nightfall, but that since she was a little girl she should not keep more than two, the first and the last. At night they should eat fish, except the last night when she, without her mother finding out, should prepare chickpeas with spinach in a pot with *broçats* and *garvellones*."[140] Some new-Christians believed that observance of the Purim fast would bring them good luck. A *converso* from Garcimuñoz in a 1491 trial reported that "my grandmother Maria Sánchez is a Jew, and tonight she told me that she was celebrating because it was a fast that they call the day of Saint Haman, and that whoever fasts today will not die during the coming year, because on a day like that God is sitting at your right hand."[141]

As with Yom Kippur, Judaizers tended to break the Fast of Esther with fish, chicken, or vegetable dishes while avoiding meat. Rita Besante confessed in Teruel in 1485 that "after [the Fast of Esther] she ate good chickens or hard-boiled eggs with parsley, and that she didn't keep any other ceremonies, except to fast and not eat until evening."[142] In Mexico in the 1640s Judaizers broke their fast with fish and vegetables (Adler 1899, 16). In Majorca in the 1670s they used fish, peas, and spinach (Cortes 1985, 287).[143] Seventeenth-century Majorcan *chuetas* concluded the fast of Esther, as they did the fast of Yom Kippur, by asking "one another's pardon by kissing hands and saying: 'God will pardon us as He has pardoned the Patriarchs'" (Braunstein 1936, 102).

## 13.7. Passover

The festival of Passover commemorates the departure of the enslaved Jews from Egypt, as is described in Exodus and elsewhere in the Bible. In the words of Abraham Millgram, for Jews Passover became "the annual occasion for dramatizing the ideal of freedom as a religious objective in the life of the Jew and in the collective life of the Jewish people," a time for reaffirming confidence that "God would again redeem the Jewish people from exile and degradation" (1971, 200). From the years of the earliest conversions in Iberia, Passover played an important part in crypto-Jewish religious life. After the Sabbath and Yom Kippur it was the most important crypto-Jewish holiday.

The Passover festival was of such importance that it was recognized both by crypto-Jews and their persecutors as THE Jewish festival. It was often referred to without any descriptive modifiers as the *Pascua de los judíos*[144] or, in a name preserved among modern Portuguese *cristãos novos*, the *Santa festa* (Paulo 1970, 99). In many texts, even late ones, some form of the Hebrew name *Pesah* is preserved.[145] Some names for the festival, like *La pascua del cordero* (lamb), focused on the paschal lamb.[146] The most common terms drew attention to the Passover custom of eating unleavened bread. Among Spanish speakers it was known as *Pascua del pan cenceño*[147] or the *Fiesta del pan centenyo*.[148] In Portuguese it was called the *Pascua do pão asmo*[149] or the *Jejum das filhós*.[150] Among Catalán speakers on the east coast of the Peninsula it was called *Pasqua del pa alís*.[151]

Traditionally the Passover is celebrated for eight days beginning on the fourteenth of the Jewish month of Nissan, which usually occurs in April. As with other Jewish festivals, crypto-Jews had difficulty precisely identifying the date of Passover. Without access to the Hebrew calendar *conversas* like the Mexican María de Zárate tended to fix the date by the Julian calendar, as can be noted by her testimony in 1656 that the "festival of the lamb was on the first day of April."[152] Gonçalo Váez, a Portuguese student, told the Granada Inquisition in 1573 that Passover was celebrated in the month of March (García Fuentes 1981, 98, 434), as did Luis de Carvajal [Mexico 1589] (Toro 1932, 243). Some reckoned by the moon, a practice carried over into the twentieth century in which Portuguese new-Christians celebrate the *Santa Festa* on the fourteenth day of the new moon of March (Paulo 1970, 99). The most convenient benchmark for *conversos* was the Christian Holy Week and, more broadly, the forty-day calendar from Ash Wednesday through Lent to Easter. Bernardina de San Juan [Baeza 1572] testified that her mother told her that "from Holy Thursday until the next Thursday was the Jewish Passover."[153] Guiomar Dias, of Santa Marinha, Portugal, told the Coimbra Inquisition in 1573 that she celebrated Passover on a Wednesday during Lent with a *seder* that followed a day-long fast.[154] Trials in Granada in the early 1590s also link Passover to Holy Week (Bel Bravo 1988, 91), as did the testimony of Catalina de Rivera, who told Mexican Inquisitors in 1642 that the Festival of the Lamb falls just before the Christian Holy Week.[155] Some *conversos*—or some scribes—just got it wrong: Antonio Cardoso, of Barajas (Madrid), who testified in 1652, told Inquisitors that he used to celebrate the seventeenth day after the new moon of September, from which date he ate the bread of affliction for nine days (Caro Baroja 1961, 1: 469).

Under normal circumstances Passover is celebrated for eight days, with the celebratory communal meal, or *seder*, held on the first evening. Prior to the Expulsion Judaizing *conversos* were able to celebrate Passover with their Jewish friends or relatives. Typical was the experience of a *converso* named Papudo, from Burgos, who spent the holiday with the father of the Jew Yudá Rabinuça, "eating with him the celery and bitter herbs that they eat on the first evening of that festival, and of the unleavened bread and [special] foods, along with everyone else who was at the Jew's house; and he recited the Jewish prayers with him."[156] In like fashion Pedro García de Alonso Arias said that he used to spend Passover with a Jew named Peñafiel (Carrete Parrondo 1986, 83). In March of 1500 in Valencia a clandestine synagogue was discovered in the home of the merchant Miquel Vives and a group of Judaizers was found to be observing the Passover *seder*: "there were many unleavened breads, and many lights, candles, and lamps, and there were a lot of people present."[157] Roth notes that some crypto-Jews held their *seder* after the first two days of the festival had ended as a way of throwing off Inquisitorial attention (1931-2, 22-3). But by the time the generation of the Expulsion had faded away there was very little consistency in the number of days during which the Passover was celebrated. Even within a single new-Christian community the length of Passover might vary. While in Mexico in the 1590s Catalina and Manuel Enríquez observed the Passover for eight days, Diego Díaz Nieto celebrated it for seven days.[158] Around Coimbra in the late sixteenth century Passover was celebrated for four days (Azevedo Mea 1982, 434), five or six days (163), six or seven days (196), seven or eight days (280), or ten days (430).

In the main, Passover observances among crypto-Jews were fairly standard. A memorandum prepared for Inquisitors in the late fifteenth century says:

> the feast of unleavened bread is in memory of those flat cakes that the children of Israel carried on their shoulders when they crossed the Red Sea. Because the crossing took seven days they had only the flat cakes to eat, and thus Jews on the seven days of Passover eat only unleavened bread in memory of the above, as it says in [left blank]. . . . Seven days you shall eat unleavened bread. It is also called the holiday of *Phase*, which means Passover, as it is written at the beginning of Joshua.[159]

This is an accurate outline of the traditional basic tenets of Passover as it was consistently observed by crypto-Jews over the next several centuries. In the seventeenth century some Majorcan *chuetas* also recalled the connection between Passover and the giving of the Law at Mount Sinai. In 1678 Ana Cortés reported:

In the spring, on a certain day she does not remember, but last year it was Holy Thursday, she was to observe a fast called the Feast of the Lamb, not eating or drinking the entire day. And after this fast she was to celebrate the Passover that lasted for seven days. And then she should slaughter a lamb which was to be roasted whole, and to invite all her relatives to a feast. And the bones were to be burned, which commemorated the sacrifice of the law of Moses. And on those seven days she had to eat unleavened bread, nor could she have any leaven in the house. And that she was to prepare little flat cakes on new brick, and to cook them on the fire, and these were to be distributed among her relatives.[160]

The two most important components of Passover observance are a meal at which the story of the Exodus from Egypt is recited and special dietary regulations featuring the exclusive consumption of unleavened bread, generally called *matza*. The *seder* ceremony itself has a fairly consistent tradition. The family gathers; the table is set with the Passover dishware and the traditional foods, whose symbolic items are often set on a specially marked *seder* plate which is one of the family's few private ritual items; wine is set out; and the *Haggadah*, or book of the Passover service which has been part of Jewish tradition from the Middle Ages and which narrates the events of Exodus, is placed on the table or, if there are several, distributed to the participants. Candles are lit as for the Sabbath, the *kiddush* over the wine is chanted, and the participants retell the story of the deliverance from Egypt as related in the *Haggadah*.

In normative Judaism the custom on Passover is to eat while in a half-reclining position, but this must not have been widespread among the crypto-Jews, for the only reference I have found appears in the recollections of Pedro de Tinoco, who was reconciled in the great Mexican *auto de fe* of 1649. He said that he had learned Passover customs from his grandmother, whom "he helped knead the unleavened bread. . . . She told him to remain reclining and keep his head covered and not to eat any other bread during those days. He said that on the evening of those days [text reads "Holy Thursdays"], as a sort of communion, he put a small piece of that bread with some herbs and parsley in his mouth" (Liebman 1974, 111).

In part because the Passover liturgy is conducted at home, not in the synagogue, the *seder* was well suited to crypto-Jewish worship, and it is mentioned frequently in documents dealing with the crypto-Jews. Many descriptions of the Passover *seder* center on Passover ritual foods; in fact reports of new-Christian *seders* from the time of the Expulsion are especially detailed in this respect. In 1484 it was said of María Díaz that "she celebrated the Feast of Unleavened Bread which they begin by eating lettuce, celery and other green vegetables . . . sow thistles [?] and vinegar, and another ceremony which they make with *maror*, which means bitter, and certain little cakes of unleavened bread."[161] Leonor González was seen [Ciudad Real 1484] "at the head of the table [where] she blessed the unleavened bread and the wine, and that everyone who was at the table ate and drank of it."[162] Later descriptions tend to minimize these factors, merely recording the fact that the *seder* was held and that *matza* and wine were consumed. Around Coimbra in 1573 Judaizers celebrated Passover by "fasting all day and then eating at night in company of other persons, reciting to each other how they did this in the observance of the law, and that at night they came together and ate flat cakes and drank wine."[163] In Mexico Luis de Carvajal the Younger enacted the Exodus story at his *seder*. "The reader wore a white garment over his clothes with a belt tightened over his waist. He paced back and forth as he read aloud, with a staff in his left hand and the Bible in the other" (Liebman 1982, 121; 1970, 68–9). They all sat together at a large table in the home of Luis's brother-in-law and read psalms of praise, particularly the song of Moses, *Cantemus Domino glorioso* [Ex. 15:1–18].[164] Colonial Mexican *conversos* had no *Haggadah*, but read the Exodus story directly from the Vulgate (Liebman 1982, 121; 1970, 67). Reciting the Passover story while standing up or walking around in symbolic reenactment of the Exodus from Egypt was a common feature of new-Christian *seders*. Diego Mora, of Quintanar de la Orden, was accused in 1589 of eating on Passover while standing (Blázquez Miguel 1986, 67). And Juan de León told Mexican Inquisitors in 1642 that on Passover you have to eat the Paschal lamb while standing.[165] Roth, too, reports that *converso seder* participants "stood, booted, their sticks in their hands, in literal fulfillment of the Biblical precept" (1931–2, 22). There is evidence that at least in Mexico in literal accord with the instructions in Exodus 12 some *conversos* smeared the blood of the sacrifice on the inside of their door posts at Passover.[166]

The consumption of *matza* was for Iberian crypto-Jews even more important than the *seder* itself, essential not for the furtherance of Jewish tradition but, as Isabel Gomes, of Trancoso, put it to the Coimbra Inquisition in 1574 when she was accused of making and eating five unleavened breads for Passover, for the salvation of her soul.[167] Normative Judaism is scrupulous about the Passover dietary restriction against eating any sort of leavened bread or having any sort of leaven in the house on Passover. Inquisitors noted of María Díaz [Ciudad Real 1484] that "during that whole festival she did not eat any other sort of bread, performing ceremonies with it as the Jews are accustomed to do."[168] Testimony before the Evora Inquisition in 1536 states that "whoever was required to eat unleavened bread during the Passover could not have in his house any leavened bread, and if he had it he was not observing the festival."[169]

The search for leaven (*bedikat hametz*) on the evening prior to Passover was and is a standard event marking the beginning of the Passover holiday. From the silence of the documentation, it does not appear, however, to have been an important part of crypto-Jewish observance. Pre-Expulsion Jews kept separate sets of dishes for Passover, so that Passover food would not come into contact with anything that might have been "contaminated" by touching leaven, a custom that seems to have persisted through the end of the sixteenth century. In 1484 [Ciudad Real 1484] it was said of Beatriz, the wife of Rodrigo the Alcaide, that "they bought new crockery for that festival";[170] it was said that María Díaz's family "the whole holiday ate only on dishes and plates and pots and pitchers that were brand new, as is the custom of the Jews; ... they ate from new dishes which had never touched leavened bread, and if they ate [on any old plates] these were made of copper or some other metal or wood, and they had first been scalded with boiling water and then washed with cold water."[171] Testimony before the Evora Inquisition in 1536 suggests that there were so many Judaizers in the region that even old-Christians had adopted the custom of changing their dishes during the holiday season for the Festival of Resurrection.[172] Filipa Fernandes, of Seia, was accused in Coimbra in 1583 of eating "unleavened breads that she kneaded in a new bowl [?] and shaped [?] on a new board that had not touched any other flour, and wrapped in a new towel."[173]

The elimination of leaven was not the only preparation for Passover. As they did for other Jewish festivals, for Passover some crypto-Jews readied themselves with purification rites that included both cleansing and fasting. In the most orthodox Jewish communities, firstborn males traditionally fast on the eve of Passover because the Jewish firstborn were saved during the tenth plague (Ex. 13; *Enc. Jud.* 6:1196). Among crypto-Jews this custom appears to have been practiced only sporadically. Judaizers around Coimbra in the 1570s celebrated a Passover that they called the *jejum das filhós* (the fast of the flat cakes) (Azevedo Mea 1982, 359, etc.). A witness told Inquisitors in Mexico in 1665 that María de Zárate fasted "on April first which they said was the Festival of the Lamb which God had commanded them to keep."[174] In fact, according to Liebman some colonial Mexicans fasted during the day for the whole week of Passover. He explains that fasting "had become so ingrained that many thought that every holiday had to be accompanied by a fast" (Liebman 1970, 69). Judaizers in Majorca in the 1670s observed the day before Passover as a fast which they called the Fast of the Newborn (*Ayuno del Natalicio*). It was preceded by a banquet during which the family's firstborn was presented to the assemblage in his father's arms.[175] For them this banquet seems to have replaced the traditional Passover *seder* (Cortes 1985, 288).

All other things aside, the preparation and ritual consumption of *matza* dominated the crypto-Jews' observance of Passover. *Matza* is the name given to the flat cakes of unleavened bread eaten by Jews on Passover in fulfillment of the Biblical commandment [Ex. 12:17–20] and to recall the hurried departure from Egypt that prohibited waiting for the bread to rise [Ex. 12:39]. *Matza* is made from flour and water, without any leavening, and is mixed and baked quickly so as to avoid any natural fermentation. In Spain *matza* was called *pan centenyo, pan cenceño, pan ácimo,* or *pan cotazo.* In Valencia it was called *pa alís* (García 1987, 85). In Portugal it was called *pão ázimo, pão asmo, pão santo,* or *filhós.*[176] Around Coimbra in the late sixteenth century it was called *bolos asmos* (Azevedo Mea 1982, 17, etc.). Antonio Cardoso, of Barajas (Madrid), testified in 1652 that on Passover he used to eat "the bread of affliction" (*pan de la aflicción*) (Caro Baroja 1961, 1:469). Many documents do not name the *matza* but refer to it in terms that are unmistakable.

María González said in 1513 that on Passover she ate "cakes as white as snow, tasteless, with a slight flavor of olive."[177]

Sometimes *matza* was prepared at home but, since not everyone had an oven at home, baking was often done in a communal oven. Prior to the Expulsion Iberian *conversos* could usually obtain *matza* from their Jewish neighbors, although there is evidence in some cases that a *matza* baker continued to supply the community after his conversion. Violante Sánchez Exarch and Francisco Belluga sent wheat to the Teruel *judería* and got back *matza*.[178] The Augustinian friar Licentiate García de Vera [Garcimuñoz 1490] wrote to his friends outside the monastery and received from them in return packages of *matza*, which he ate himself and distributed in slices to other monks in his monastery just as if it were the host.[179] After the Expulsion the preparation and distribution of *matza*, like other Jewish cult items, became extremely problematical. It attracted the attention of Inquisitors, who saw in the distribution network a map of the Judaizing community. Even so, in some communities a particular crypto-Jewish baker would supply the rest of his Judaizing friends with *matza*. Rodrigo de Castro, of Huete, confessed to the Inquisition in 1615 that he and relatives in the region used to exchange *pan centeno* during Passover (Blázquez Miguel 1987, 60). In the mid-seventeenth century *matza* was supplied in Mexico City by the Montoya family and distributed by Rodrigo Tinoco, who also served as sexton of the synagogue.[180]

It was common in Iberian villages and cities for each family to grow (or purchase) its own wheat, to have it ground, and—sometimes—even to prepare the loaves at home. But since most Spaniards and Portuguese households did not maintain an oven, it was more common to have the bread baked by a professional baker or at the home of someone, often a wealthy member of an extended family group, who did have the proper facilities. The fee for this service could be cash money but was more frequently a portion of the ground flour. This pattern can be seen in the preparation of *matza* as well. In a 1484 trial in Ciudad Real this method of making *matza* was described: "During Lent, around Holy Week, in her home she [María González] prepared the unleavened bread which the witness took to be baked in Diego González' oven."[181] According to testimony in 1487, even after her conversion Diego Arias's wife Elvira González continued to prepare *matza* for the Jewish and *converso* communities of Segovia and to conduct the Passover *seder* in her home. The González/Arias oven was a community gathering place. Maestre Gerónimo (formerly Rabbi Moshe) testified that "on many Passovers, when the Jewish women went to bake their unleavened bread at the oven of Diego Arias, which is inside the walls of his house, when they came out from baking it I saw how they went to eat lunch with the wife of Diego Arias; the Jewish women brought it to be baked and each one of them left her two or three cakes of that unleavened bread; . . . the women were her sisters and nieces."[182]

When Passover concluded it was permitted to eat leavened bread once again. Until 1492 the Jewish community relied on their Christian or even *converso* neighbors to supply them with a leavening "starter" to get their bread making going again. One deposition from about the time of the Expulsion recalled how around 1450 a witness from Soria had seen the *conversa* wife of Ruy Sánchez the day after Passover send some Jews "leavened bread and a kid and vegetables ... so they could come out of the Festival of Unleavened Bread, and also some yeast."[183] In like fashion, when Passover was over Diego Arias's *conversa* wife Elvira González used to have a slave take leavened bread and lettuce and greens to the Jew Jacob Melamed's father's house and bring back some cakes of unleavened bread for her.[184] Although I have not found this custom mentioned in later Inquisition material, it seems reasonable to suppose that Judaizers either did not wholly purge their houses of leaven, or obtained a starter from their non-Judaizing friends.

The documents provide us with a number of recipes for *matza*. Most *matza*, such as the *pan de la aflicción* (bread of affliction) prepared by Antonio Cardoso, of Barajas (Madrid) in the 1650s, was simply a plain dough of flour and water, mixed without salt or yeast.[185] Micaela Enríquez [Mexico City 1648] used her mother's recipe for "little wheat cake, kneaded in a new tub, and baked before the embers." She added that her mother "would not let her touch it with her hand, but that her mother would place a piece of it in her mouth, saying certain words which seemed like the communion that the priests give."[186] Some *matza* was enriched with eggs, such as that from Francisco Suárez's wife's recipe [Soria 1505]; her friends "prepared flat bread, i.e., unleavened bread, and they kneaded it with an egg, and put olive oil in the dough."[187] But Iberian crypto-Jews often used spices to introduce flavors into their *matza*. Angelina, the wife of Christóual de León, of Almazán (Soria), "made the dough of flour and eggs, and formed some round, flat cakes with pepper and honey and oil. She cooked them in an oven and she did this around Holy Week."[188] Juana de Fuente, also of Almazán, said in 1505 that she and the wife of Ruy Días "made some cakes separately of another dough that had no leavening and they kneaded it with white wine and honey and clove and pepper, and they made about twenty of those and they kept them with the scrolls in his storage chest."[189] When materials for traditional *matza* could not be obtained, crypto-Jews substituted local foods that did not contain leaven. Judaizers around Coimbra in the late sixteenth century sometimes substituted cooked chestnuts for *matza*.[190] Luis de Carvajal told the Mexican Inquisition in 1589 that on Passover "because he did not have unleavened bread he ate corn *tortillas*, since they had no yeast."[191] Sixty years later Juan de León [Mexico 1642] reported that one Passover he ate "corn tortillas, fish and vegetables" (Lewin 1977, 46).

As with any other Jewish ritual item, *matza* had to be prepared clandestinely and then carefully concealed. In 1484 Rodrigo de Torres reported how in Leonor González's house "he found under a bed seven or eight cakes of unleavened bread wrapped in a towel inside a basket. It was during Lent."[192] In the late fifteenth century a Valencian *converso* stated that the *matza* had to be hidden from the servants in their house.[193] Sancho de Mora testified in Ciudad Real in 1511 that the year before, "when Juan Ramírez was unwrapping certain papers and writings on the table where he had his desk, this witness saw how a host which was among those papers fell to the floor. The host was not quite so large as those which the priest consecrates nor so small as those that they give for communion; rather, it was a medium-sized round host. And when the host fell, it seemed to this witness that Juan Ramírez was upset. And Juan Ramírez said to those who were present 'Watch out, don't step on it. I have it to take with some pills.' "[194] The Gómez sisters [Ciudad Rodrigo 1580s] had another strategy: "They baked some flat cakes of bread, white and without color, which were unleavened, baking them in the coals of the fireplace. And all throughout Holy Week, when they were eating they handed pieces to one another under the table . . . trying to make certain that no one saw them. And all throughout the Feast of the Resurrection the witness saw them eating it in that way, even though they had put ordinary bread on the table."[195]

The traditional Passover *seder* includes a number of foods with ceremonial significance. Exodus 12, Num. 9–11, and Deut. 16:2–4 require the Passover consumption of the Paschal lamb, unleavened bread, and bitter herbs. The lamb signifies the lamb whose blood was used to mark the gates of the Jews over which the Angel of Death passed on the night of the tenth plague. While modern observance substitutes a roasted lamb shank for the Paschal lamb, in Iberia the Biblical precept was taken literally and the Passover consumption of a whole roast lamb persisted for two and a half centuries after the Expulsion. Cristovão Lopes, a physician from Evora, was burned in 1570 in part because each year he would eat "at the feast of the unleavened bread a one-year-old unblemished white lamb."[196] In Mexico, too, crypto-Jews tended to choose a white lamb (Liebman 1970, 68). Diego Mora, of Quintanar de la Orden, was accused in 1589 of keeping the Passover, eating lamb while standing up on the eve of the holiday (Blázquez Miguel 1986, 67). Juan de León told Mexican Inquisitors in 1642 that on the Passover "the lamb has to be cooked whole and you have to eat it standing up, without damaging a single bone of the lamb."[197] The complexity of customs with regard to the Paschal lamb can be seen in the testimony of the Mexican Judaizer Luis de Carvajal in 1589. He said that his father had taught him that Passover

> was observed in that Law of Moses in memory of when God brought the children of Israel out of Egypt, and passed through the desert to the Promised Land; that the Passover lasted seven days during which one had to eat unleavened bread; and also on that festival you take a small white lamb and you cut its throat, and with the blood you anoint the lintels of your doorways, because that is what God commanded the children of Israel to do when He took them out of Egypt. And when it was dead it had to be roasted whole, without breaking a single bone, and eaten while standing as if you were ready to march. And you consume it entirely, so that nothing is left over. And you should have your staves in your hands and your belts pulled tight. And you eat it so that nothing is left over; if perchance something is left over you give it to a neighbor. And

on the same festival one was to eat the lamb with bitter lettuce, and with unleavened bread. And the festival was called *Phase*, which means pass-over, and it lasted seven days; and the first and last days of it were to be kept as a festival [Sabbath]. And the lamb has to be killed and eaten on the evening before the first day, at night.[198]

The bitter herbs (*maror*) of Passover recall the bitterness of the Jews' enslavement in Egypt. Over the centuries, tradition has added several other foods to the *seder*: a mixture of apples, nuts, and wine, called *ḥaroset*, symbolizes the mortar employed by the Jews to build the Pharaoh's cities; salt water recalls the parting of the Red Sea, and also the tears of bitterness wept by the Jews in Egypt; a roast egg symbolizes the free-will offering at the Passover feast that celebrated the Jews' deliverance. Four cups of wine are traditionally consumed at the *seder*. The wine, *matza*, and bitter herbs are all mentioned frequently in Inquisition documents. Other Passover foods are cited in the documents as well. Juan de Lucena's *conversa* mother was accused in 1471 of on Passover eating only *hormiguillos*, which were stews made of bread (or *matza?*) crumbs, ground almonds, and honey (Carrete Parrondo 1985a, 54). Marcos Alonso testified in Ciudad Real in 1484 that they ate their *matza* at Elvira González's house together with "vegetables the first night, with celery and parsley and with other vegetables that he cannot remember."[199] Isabel Gomes was accused in 1541 in Lisbon because "on the Passover she did not eat meat during the eight days and she made unleavened bread."[200] Judaizers around Coimbra in the 1560s on Passover often ate eggs, rice, chestnuts, and dried fish.[201]

Modern Portuguese Judaizers too on Passover tend not to eat meat but rather cod or other fish fried in olive oil (Paulo 1985, 151; 1970, 100), or *bacalhau* balls, rice, and grain. Additionally, the first day's meal is always eaten cold (Vasconcelos 1958, 214). Other Portuguese new-Christians eat white beans and chestnuts.[202] In 1952 Machado reported that on the three days following Passover new-Christian villagers in the Mogadouro region of Portugal do not eat meat, and before they are permitted to eat pork again they have to eat some sort of fowl (Machado 1952, 40). Because these foods are not mentioned in fifteenth- and sixteenth-century documents, I suspect that the extensive range of Passover foods given in accounts of modern Portuguese *cristãos novos* reflects a post-Expulsion insertion of Judaizing customs or borrowing from regional Portuguese cuisine rather than a continuum of tradition from the fifteenth century.

The celebration of Passover is one of the Judaizing customs most fully documented among twentieth-century Portuguese *cristãos novos*. On the whole their observance seems to be a mixture of holdover crypto-Jewish customs combined with Portuguese regional customs, Christian practices, and genuine innovations, some of which may have derived from their contacts with Ashkenazi Jews during the last few decades. For these Judaizers the preparations for Passover begin long before the holiday itself. Passover's dietary requirements seem to have induced a concern for diet in the preparatory period as well. Some of them fast. Others, in an improbable if logical extension of traditional dietary concerns, prepare for Passover beginning on Purim by abstaining from eating pork (Paulo 1970, 99) for a period that roughly coincides with Lent. Canelo reports that on Passover modern Portuguese *criptojudeus* from around Belmonte go out in the fields and cut hawthorn branches to decorate their houses (1987, 105). Many clean their houses. Vasconcelos reports that on Passover in twentieth-century Portugal new-Christians wear linen underwear and put linen sheets on the bed (Vasconcelos 1958, 222). For some people the concern for cleanliness, in its sense of ritual purity, carries over into the holiday itself, during which some new-Christian couples do not sleep together.[203] On Passover eve new-Christian women light the "Lord's lamp" (*candeia do Senhor*), an oil lamp with a new wick made of seven strands, which they have twisted together while reciting certain prayers (Paulo 1970, 99–100). During the eight days of Passover new-Christians in Belmonte keep five oil lamps lighted on a table decorated with flowers (Paulo 1985, 56; Vasconcelos 1958, 221). During the Passover holiday itself, modern Portuguese new-Christians tend to treat the eight days somewhat differently. Paulo reports that some of them fast the first, fourth, and seventh days of Passover, which they consider days of complete rest. Three times a day they pray. The morning of the fourth day they wrap a piece of *matza* in a lettuce leaf and swallow it without chewing (1985, 150; 1970, 100; Machado 1952, 39).

Understandably, many of their customs have to do with the preparation and use of the Passover *matza*. In 1952 Machado reported that new-Christian villagers in the Mogadouro region of Portugal make *matza* as follows. They select the wheat grain by grain, grind it, mix it, knead it, and cook it. The dough is covered with a new cloth, and after it is cooked it is wrapped in a clean towel (Machado 1952, 39). Schwarz in 1925 described Judaizers celebrating Passover in groups in private homes. Everyone dressed in white. On one side of the room braziers and bowls of white flour and water were ready to prepare the *matza*. The women who made the *matza* prayed continuously. Before baking it they threw a pinch of dough into the fire; according to Canelo this was in hope that it would burst open and bring good luck (1987, 106). When the *matza* was baked the congregants embraced each other, gave thanks for the *pão santo*, and wrapped it in white towels to take it home. Wine for the holiday was prepared separately from other wine. During the whole holiday the Judaizers abstained from work and gathered three times daily for prayer (Schwarz 1925, 33–5).

Several ethnographers have recorded prayers that the Portuguese women sing while preparing the *matza*. Paulo found that as the dough is mixed a prayer-woman (*rezadeira*) prays to the Lord. "Blessed are You, Lord, our King, God of all things and all the world, who sanctified us with Your holy and blessed commandments; blessed are You for giving us life to reach this time and to keep Your divine, holy precepts, preparing this bread as a precept. Lord, make us reach Zion with peace and happiness. Amen."[204] As in Machado's report, the dough is covered with a new cloth, and after it is cooked it is wrapped in a clean towel while reciting this prayer: "In honor and praise of the holy names of the Lord! In remembrance of our brothers, when they left Egypt and entered the Promised Land. Amen."[205] Vasconcelos transcribed another *matza*-making song: "The fourteenth day of the new moon / of the first month of the year, / Israel and her brothers / depart from Egypt. / They sing songs / of praise to the Lord. / Where are you taking us, Moses? / Here in his desert place / where there is no bread (?) nor firewood / nor pasturage nor cattle? / Etc."[206] As with most Judaizing groups it is important to abstain from eating leaven as well as to eat *matza*. Twentieth-century crypto-Jews in Covilhã and Belmonte in Portugal abstain from eating any bread at all on the first two days of Passover and eat *matza* only on the third (Schwarz 1925, 16). For some of these crypto-Jews the *matza* takes on an almost talismanic importance. Around Belmonte modern *criptojudeus* set aside one piece of *matza* each year and save it with those of past years in a special place to be brought out next Passover (Canelo 1987, 106).

Paulo reports that in this century new-Christians in Belmonte, Portugal, place on their *seder* table three trays: one with *matza*, one with a roasted lamb bone and a roasted egg, and one with herbs and sauce. On one side of the trays they place a cup with vinegar or salt water and a sweet made of almonds and apples (1985, 57). The *seders* around Belmonte feature communal singing of a Passover song inspired by Moses' hymn in Ex. 15: "Today we sing to the Lord / the singular God of glory, / who threw the horses and riders / into the deepest sea. Etc."[207]

The ethnographers have also observed how modern Portuguese crypto-Jews take part of their Passover celebration out into the countryside. In Belmonte new-Christians often go on picnics during Passover. They pray and dance and sing songs like this one: "Magnified and exalted / is the high God of Abraham. / May He free us from the deep sea / and bring us to the Promised Land."[208] Machado found that new-Christian villagers in the Mogadouro region of Portugal go in procession to the river on the last day of Passover. As they march they pray: "Let us praise and magnify the great God of Abraham, / may He free us from the great sea / and take us to the Promised Land." When they reach the bank they cross the stream twelve times; one of them keeps track with twelve leaves which he shifts from one hand to the other as they cross. As they cross they say: "The sea opened, the people crossed, the God of Israel has commanded it." Then they return home singing: "Let us praise and magnify the great God of Israel / who freed us from the great sea and this cruel river."[209] Schwarz cites a slightly different version of this custom. The *cristãos novos* go to a stream and pluck branches and beat the water chanting "See Moses with his staff raised to part the water of the salty sea, etc.," and then keep the branches for a year and use them to light the braziers on which the *matza* is made the following year.[210] Canelo calls the custom "cutting the waters" (*cortar as águas*); he adds that if they can't go to the river each family dams up a little water in their yard and observes the ceremony there (1987, 107–8).

## 13.8. Shavuot

Shavuot, or the Feast of Weeks, celebrates the harvest in accord with the directions in Exodus 23:16: "You shall keep the feast of harvest, of the first fruits of your labor, of what you sow in the field." Tradition has it that Shavuot is also the anniversary of the giving of the Ten Commandments on Mount Sinai. The holiday occurs on the sixth and seventh days of the Hebrew month of Sivan, seven weeks (actually fifty days) after Passover. Since Biblical times, when Shavuot was the occasion for a pilgrimage in which Jewish males brought the first harvested fruits in offering to the Temple in Jerusalem, there has been very little observance associated with this holiday, other than stressing in the synagogue ritual the themes of harvest and of the giving of the Law. The references to Shavuot in documents relating to the crypto-Jews are both rare and generic.

Testimony in 1484 in a Ciudad Real trial refers to *conversos* keeping "the Fifty Days Feast, which they call the Giving of the Law."[211] Inquisitors in Ciudad Rodrigo in 1588 took note of the fact that the Gómez sisters possessed a written calendar of the Jewish festivals that included "the fast of the breaking of the tablets of the law,"[212] but they alleged no actual observance of the festival. There is some evidence that Shavuot was observed sporadically in colonial Mexico. At his trial in Mexico Luis de Carvajal referred to a holiday which he called Festival of First Fruits.[213] And in Mexico in the first decade of the seventeenth century both Jorge de Almeida (Adler 1895, 46) and Mariana de Carvajal (Liebman 1970, 67) were accused of celebrating Shavuot 40 days [sic] after Passover. Taken as a whole, this evidence suggests that the holiday was not of great importance to Jews in pre-Expulsion Spain and that, with the exception of a few Judaizers in colonial Mexico who took their inspiration directly from the Bible, it died out among the *conversos* shortly thereafter.

## 13.9. Other Fasts

As we have seen, fasting was one of the most important aspects of crypto-Jewish religious observance. The first part of this section introduces a number of additional fasts observed by Iberian Judaizers; the last part deals with general customs related to fasting.

In addition to the fasts of Yom Kippur and of Esther, the post-exile period of Jewish religious history has recognized four fasts in commemoration of Biblical events. One of these, the fast on the ninth of the Hebrew month of Tevet that marks the beginning of the siege of Jerusalem, does not appear to have been observed at all among crypto-Jews. The other three were observed sporadically.

A. The seventeenth of Tammuz, which commemorated the breaching of the walls of Jerusalem (Jer. 39:2) and other calamities on that date (*Shulḥan Arukh* OH

549:2) was generally celebrated by fasting (*Enc. Jud.* 6:1195). The only reference to this fast that I have found among *conversos* precedes the Expulsion. Juan Sánchez Exarch, a *converso* from Teruel, was accused in 1484 of keeping the fast of Tammuz (Llorca 1939, 133).

B. The Fast of Gedaliah, on the third of Tishri, commemorates the assassination of Gedaliah, a benevolent administrator appointed by the Babylonian conquerors to rule Jerusalem. The Mishnah says that the third of Tishri is a fast day "because Gedaliah, the son of Ahikam, was slain on that day, thus extinguishing the last remaining ember of Israel's independence and making her exile complete" (Maim., *Yad.* III,9,v,2). Although I have found no records of this holiday's having been observed in Spain, it does appear in the Gómez sisters' written calendar of the Jewish festivals unearthed by Inquisitors in Ciudad Rodrigo in 1588, where it is referred to as the fast of "Degedelias and the siege of Jerusalem."[214] There are references to this fast having been kept sporadically in Portugal, where it was observed on the day after the New Year (Roth 1931-2, 28). And in the 1670s Majorcan *chuetas* were said to keep the fast of Gedaliah (Cortes 1985, 287), which was preceded by a meal of fish (Braunstein, 1936, 101). The absence of other data about crypto-Jewish observances suggests that the Fast of Gedalia was not part of the native Iberian Jewish ritual, but rather may from time to time have been introduced into the Iberian territories by returning travelers who had observed the custom in other lands.

C. Tisha b'Av, the ninth day of the Hebrew month of Av, which generally falls in mid-summer, commemorates the anniversary of the destruction of the First and Second Temples (Jer. 52:12–13) and, according to the Mishnah (*Ta'an.* 4:6), recalls as well several other calamities that had befallen the Jews. With the exception of Yom Kippur it was traditionally the most solemn Jewish fast day and the only other fast observed for a full twenty-four hours. In normative Judaism the three weeks prior to Tisha b'Av, beginning with the fast of the seventeenth of Tammuz, are considered a period of official mourning in which no weddings or other enjoyable activities are permitted. On Tisha b'Av itself a gloomy atmosphere prevails; even the study of the Torah, except for the books of Job and Lamentations, is prohibited. The central theme of the holiday is calamity as the result of laxity of Jewish observance; for this reason it was of particular importance to crypto-Jews, who saw in their own circumstances a reflection of the events of Tisha b'Av.

Judaizers accurately recalled Tisha b'Av's historical commemoration of the destruction of the Temple in Jerusalem, and the holiday was observed by crypto-Jews with little variation throughout the Iberian world at least until the end of the seventeenth century. The *converso* monk Alfonso de Toledo in the Monastery of Sisla [Toledo c. 1480] reportedly asked the Jewess Vellida, "When is the fast that the Jews call *tisabaf* which is when the holy temple was lost?"[215] Inquisitors in Ciudad Rodrigo in 1588 took note of the Gómez sisters' written calendar of the Jewish festivals, which included "the fast of the destruction of the temple two times."[216] In a 1610 Edict of Grace from Cartagena de Indias the holiday is called "the fast of *Re*-

*beaso*, commemorating the loss of the holy temple" (Medina 1899b, 26). That the holiday's dominant mood was black and its central feature was the fast were evident in testimony of the late fifteenth-century *conversa* María Alvarez, of Guadalajara, who reported that she fasted on the Jewish "Bitter Day."[217] Alfonso Vaz Cordilha told the Portuguese Inquisition in 1540 that "he used to eat on the floor the eve of the day that they lost Jerusalem."[218] Juan Molina [Huete 1491] was said to go once a year to the synagogue, on Saint Ann's day, and to weep all the time he was there (Blázquez Miguel 1987, 47); the Jewish fast nearest to Saint Ann's day (July 26) is Tisha b'Av, to which this probably refers. In the New World Judaizers abstained from eating meat for three weeks prior to Tisha b'Av and they fasted on the day (Liebman 1982, 123; 1970, 62, 270). This is probably the sense of Pedro Tinoco's statement [Mexico 1649] that he fasted "on those unfortunate weeks around the month of July which commemorate the destruction of the Temple in Jerusalem" (Liebman 1974, 111). In Majorca in the 1670s Judaizers ate lentils and hard-boiled eggs in July in commemoration of the destruction of the Temple (Cortes 1985, 287). In northern Portugal by the late sixteenth century, however, Tisha b'Av seems to have been less popular, for it was rarely noticed by the Inquisitors. In the 634 cases reported from the Coimbra Inquisition between 1567 and 1583 there is only one reference to the holiday of *tesabeat* (Azevedo Mea 1982, 6). As is the case of many crypto-Jewish customs, native knowledge of Judaizing was from time to time enriched by returning travelers. The Portuguese informer Hector Méndez Bravo quoted above said in 1617 that he had seen Portuguese Jews in Venice keeping the fast of "Thesabão, when Jerusalem was destroyed by Titus and Vespasian; he thinks it falls in June or July. No food was consumed until night and on the following day. Lamentations like those of Jeremiah were recited and signs of mourning shown" (Roth 1943–4, 231).

Beyond these generally recognized fasts, some Iberian crypto-Jews kept a variety of other specific fasts that tend to be much less commonly observed in normative Judaism.

D. Yom Kippur Katan (Minor Yom Kippur). Some Jews observe the fast called the Minor Yom Kippur on the last day of each month (*Enc. Jud.* 6:1195–6). While I have not found records of this fast being observed in the Iberian territories, the Portuguese informer Hector Méndez Bravo said in 1617 that he had seen Portuguese Jews in Venice observing what appears to be a different fast, which he termed the "Small Kippur," some seven days before Yom Kippur (Roth 1943–4, 231).

E. *Rosh Hodesh* (New moon). Traditional Judaism considers each month's new moon a joyous occasion to be celebrated with special prayers. The celebration does not appear to have been common among crypto-Jews, although there are very sporadic references such as those of Elvira de Mora [Alcázar, Castile 1590], who recalled observing the first day of the month as a holiday (Melammed 1992, 162). In most cases *Rosh Hodesh* takes precedence over other requirements to fast, but by the seventeenth century a few Judaizers in widely separated areas were observing the new moon as a fast day. Isabel Núñez [Ciudad Rodrigo 1623] allegedly "showed respect for the moon by dedicating three fasts to it, especially when it was the new moon."[219] Some seventeenth-century Majorcan *chuetas* fasted on the day following the appearance of the new moon (Braunstein 1936, 102). On the other hand, the appearance of the new moon was observed festively in seventeenth-century Mexico. Francisco López de Fonseca confessed to the Mexican Inquisition that he kept the festivals of the New Moon,[220] and Clara Núñez said her parents had taught her to "worship the new moon, standing at the window, bowing to it the way her uncle did."[221] In Mexico only Simón Montero confessed to actually fasting on the New Moon.[222]

A number of the fasts observed by Iberian crypto-Jews seem to be innovative additions to normative Jewish practice.

F. *Bordón del alma*. Blanca Juárez was accused by the Mexican Inquisition in 1648 of keeping a number of Jewish fasts, among them one called "the staff of the soul" (*bordón del alma*) (García 1910, 213).

G. *Bredos*. Some Judaizers in northern Portugal in the 1570s celebrated the fast of *bredos*.[223] I have been unable to relate this citation to traditional Jewish observance. The Portuguese word *bredos* indicates the amaranth, a kind of plant with purple flowers.

H. Elijah. Guiomar de Cáceres told the Coimbra Inquisition in 1573 that she fasted one day a week for forty weeks to honor the fast of Elias, who fasted for forty days.[224] 1 Kings 19:8 tells how the food Elijah was given by the angels lasted him for forty days on Mount Horeb, but there is no traditional Jewish fast day in honor of Elijah.

I. Judith. In colonial Mexico Judaizers sometimes observed a Fast of Judith. Isabel Carvajal, for example, told Inquisitors in the 1590s that as Esther and Judith fasted "so that God might free Israel from the indignation of King Ahasueros and Haman and King Nebuchadnezzar and Holofernes," she fasted "so that God might free her and some other people from persecutions, difficulties, and afflictions."[225] Although Judith is widely venerated as one of the strong women of Judaism, there is no traditional fast in her honor.

J. Moses. José Sánchez was accused in Mexico in 1659 of "fasting on the fourth of September, because they said that was the day Moses had died."[226]

K. The Fast of Lentils. In 1688 Ana Cortés reported to the Inquisition in Majorca that her father Joseph Cortés had instructed her "that in the month of July she had to observe a fast called the fast of lentils which she thought was in commemoration of Saul [Esau] who sold his birthright to Jacob for a plate of lentils, and that that night they must prepare lentils for dinner and boil eggs in them until they were hard, and eat them with fish and whatever else they had."[227] Braunstein is of the opinion that this must have been the fast of Tisha b'Av (see above) (1936, 102).

L. *Natalinho.* Among some twentieth-century Portuguese new-Christians *Natalinho* (the birth) is a twenty-four-hour fast observed on the eleventh day of the November moon (Schwarz 1925, 35). Vasconcelos thinks this may be in imitation of Christmas (1958, 214). Canelo observes that it is not a full fast, for the Portuguese Judaizers only abstain from eating meat (1987, 117).

A large number of prayers associated with fasting have been preserved in the documentary records, particularly in Portuguese trials in the latter half of the sixteenth century. Nearly all of them incorporate the same themes: contrition for sin, symbolized in self-mortification and willingness to sacrifice; the merit of asceticism; and requests for divine favor. Violante Gomes, of Seia, recited this prayer for fasting to the Coimbra Inquisition in 1573: "You, Lord, who created the heavens and the earth and separated day from night, remember me and receive this fast made in holy service to You."[228] The Coimbra tribunal also recorded this prayer: "Lord, I come before You in fasting and not in sin; on the day of my fast I call on You, that You receive my great affliction and console my heart with the coming of David and with coming of the Messiah David."[229] Bernardo Rodrigues [Bragança 1593] recited a simpler version for the eve of a fast when the first stars come out: "Blessed be the name of the Lord who created you, may He help me bear this fast in contrition for my sins."[230] In other areas self-inflicted suffering seems to have been associated with fasting. The Judaizing Carvajal family in Mexico in the 1580s used to wear hair shirts to mortify their flesh on fast days and on some other occasions (Cohen 1973, 209). A prayer recorded in Castile about the same time alludes with traditional symbolism to a sacrifice of flesh: "When my household was in celebration and I sinned, I fasted and drew out its blood and its fat with great diligence, and I forgave them their sins. Just so, Lord, may this my fast, and my fat be little, and my blood be little. Receive it, Lord, in Your attention and forgive me my sins."[231]

The same themes weave through eighteenth-century examples of fasting-prayers from both Spain and Portugal. These examples come from Castile:

> God who gave me my soul, pure and clean as the sun which You created and formed to give You honor. Remember me for the sake of Abraham, his obedience and fear of God which led him to sacrifice his son for You, Lord. Then, with fury and grandeur the hand of God unleashes that which is tied: receive our prayer.[232]

> Blessed is the light of the day and the Lord who sends us daylight, peace and joy, salvation for our souls and succor for our lives.[233]

> In this fast which today You have commanded, great God of Israel, I offer You my life, so that You may free me from jails, prisons, and the other evils of this world. Amen. Blessed be the Lord of Israel. Amen.[234]

This prayer for before fasting was recorded in an eighteenth-century manuscript from Rebordelo, Portugal:

> I come before You in this fast, Lord, not from lack of bread, or of anything else; my flesh is weak and my blood is written in Heaven, in hope of Your divine blessing, Adonai, Amen. My God, help me to pray this day in the name of the Lord, Adonai. Amen.[235]

There are many other examples from this century, such as this fasting prayer from the Portuguese villages of Carção and Pinhel:

> Blessed and praised be my God Adonai who commanded us to exorcise the devil to the infernal regions. Lord, God of Israel, I ask You for permission to offer You all that I do this day. I hope that my offer may serve to reach Your divine presence, and that it may be for the good of my soul so that I may live and die in Your holy service. Amen.[236]

As has been mentioned several times previously, fasting received extraordinary emphasis in the Iberian crypto-Jewish tradition, in part because fasts were relatively easy to dissemble and in part for psychological reasons having to do with the attractiveness of physical penance in atonement for the transgression of conversion and assimilation. While fasting is at heart a solitary act, several of the sentences from the Coimbra Inquisition in the 1570s make reference to the habit of fasting in community,[237] either for a sense of communal solidarity or to strengthen each other's resolve to withstand the hunger. Besides the annual fasts we have already discussed, many crypto-Jews were faithful to a minor Jewish tradition of fasting on Mondays and Thursdays in accord with certain prescriptions in the *Mishnah Torah* (Maim., *Yad.* III,9,i,5). Although the specific days of the week sometimes varied,[238] these weekday fasts were widely observed by crypto-Jews. María González [Ciudad Real 1513] testified that they "kept the Jewish fasts two days a week, which she believes were Monday and Friday or Thursday, and each one fasted all day in her house until dinner. And after they had eaten they gathered in the house of Diego de Teva's wife, and there, together, they chatted and told each other how they had fasted and what they had eaten."[239]

These weekday fasts were especially strong in the Portuguese tradition in the sixteenth century. Among Judaizers in northern Portugal in the 1570s the Monday and Thursday fasts were known as *tannis* or *thanys* [= Hebrew *ta'anit*-fast].[240] According to one witness the *thanys* could be observed on any weekday. The Monday/Thursday fast is mentioned in a large portion of the 634 sentences handed down in Coimbra between 1567 and 1583 (Azevedo Mea 1982, 355, etc.). Of the roughly 120 Mexican Inquisition cases between 1620 and 1649 reviewed by Stanley Hordes, 60 people were found guilty of observing Jewish fasts (Hordes 1980, 213). In the seventeenth century these weekday fasts were practiced in the Azores according to the trial of Fernão Lopes [Lisbon 1573], who was accused of following his mother's instructions to fast during the day on Mondays and Thursdays.[241] A 1591 Edict of Grace from Brazil refers to the *converso* custom of fasting all day Monday and Thursday.[242]

The trial of Ruy Díaz Nieto [Mexico 1603] provides a particularly vivid example of the importance of the weekday fasts to some Judaizers. According to the informer Manuel Gil, even after Ruy Díaz Nieto was reconciled by the Inquisition and set free he continued to keep the Jewish weekday fasts, not eating "until one hour beyond nightfall. Then he ate things cooked by his own hand like fish, chickpeas, eggs, and other vegetables, all cooked with olive oil because he never cooks with lard. [Gil] says that he knows that he doesn't eat all day because he goes out selling early in the morning with his pack, and at noon he comes to the street of Santo Domingo and he comes into [Gil's] store and asks for something to eat for the Indian who carries his pack. And when [Gil] invites Ruy Díaz to eat he refuses, saying that he had eaten his lunch early in the morning, and that he would not eat again until evening."[243]

Most crypto-Jews seem to have adhered to the tradition that only the fasts of Yom Kippur and Tisha b'Av are full fasts in the sense that they last twenty-four hours. A typically large portion of the Coimbra Inquisition sentences, for example, refer to Judaizers fasting during the daylight hours.[244] A minority of Judaizers, widely scattered in time and place, held for a more rigorous fasting. María de San Juan testified in Baeza in 1573 that her mother had told her that "fasts were to be a full twenty-four hours."[245] An *auto de fe* in Madrid in 1720 identified twenty families whose Judaizing included observing Jewish fast days and fasting for twenty-four hours (Lera García 1987, 93).

Crypto-Jews also recognized that under certain conditions people were exempt from the requirement to fast. The *Mishnah Torah* permits women not to fast when pregnant (Maim., *Yad.* III,9,i,8), and traditionally the sages exempted from fasting both pregnant and nursing women (Tosef. to Ta'an. 2:12; 3:2; cited in *Enc. Jud.* 6:1193). María González [Ciudad Real 1513] testified that among her friends "some kept more fasts than others, and that because she was always either pregnant or had just given birth, she rarely fasted."[246] Similarly, Mencia Muñiz [Granada 1595] reported that her sister-in-law told her to fast on a Jewish fast day but that she excused herself because she was pregnant.[247] Sick people were exempted for much the same reason. Several of the trials of Judaizers in Coimbra in the 1570s refer to exemptions from fasting for being ill or weak.[248] Leonor Lopes [Coimbra 1568] did not consider herself excused from fasting because she was in poor health, but she did consider that reason to space her fasts out rather than fasting on consecutive days.[249] Juan Pacheco de León told Mexican Inquisitors in 1643 that Pedro de Espinosa was a Judaizer, "although he did not fast because he was sickly."[250] Then as now, children bore long fasts with difficulty. Fifteen-year-old Simón de León confessed in Mexico in 1647 that "he ran away because he broke a fast that his father had ordered him to keep because he could not bear the hunger. And the person he asked for chocolate was his sister Antonia."[251]

To judge from the case of the Mexican Judaizer Tomás Treviño, crypto-Jews prepared for these minor fasts with their usual attention to personal and environmental cleanliness. Treviño's son Rafael charged in 1647 that his father made him fast several times, telling him at the river in Guadalajara "that first he had to bathe at night, and when they got home they would put clean clothes on themselves and the table; and then they ate hard-boiled eggs and fish with oil and vinegar."[252] Care was taken not to defile the fasts with Christian practices. Alvaro Pacheco [Pernambuco 1591] taught his cousin how to fast in the Jewish way on Mondays and Thursdays, taking care not to recite one Our Father or Hail Mary during the whole day (Lipiner 1969, 155). Sometimes other signs of asceticism were linked to the fasts. Francisco Maldonado de Silva [Chile 1627] allegedly said that "fasts had to be with bodily affliction, such as God commands in Deuteronomy, and the afflictions were wearing hair shirts, sleeping on the ground, not eating meat, nor eating all day until nightfall when the stars had come out."[253]

These minor fasts were broken with meals very similar to those which followed the Yom Kippur and Esther fasts. Francisco de Vergara [Lima 1636] broke his fasts with fruit and fish and eggs and other "Friday foods."[254] María de Castro, born in Madrid, was accused [Lima 1736] of breaking her fasts with a meal of fish and salad (Lewin 1954, 269). Juan de León and his Mexican *converso* friends used to precede their fasts with sweets, fruit, and chocolate, and break the fasts with salad, eggs, sweets, and chocolate, or with fish marinade (*escabeche*), olives, cheese, bread, fruit and wine. They never ate meat before or after a fast and as good colonial Mexicans they invariably finished up their meals with a cup of the native festive drink: chocolate (Lewin 1977, 67, 81).

Crypto-Jews used a variety of strategies to conceal their fasting from the eyes of non-Judaizing neighbors and servants. According to Braunstein, seventeenth-century Majorcan *chuetas* used to dissemble their fasts by "sitting themselves at the table but not eating a morsel" or taking food "to the top floor of their houses upon one pretext or another, but it was later found untouched" (1936 103). In 1589 Fray Gaspar de Carvajal testified that he had seen his sister Isabel "pretend that she was eating, and then take out whatever she had in her mouth and throw it under the table, where he later saw it."[255] The servant of a Galician *converso* said that "his master had fasted during Lent in order not to be discovered."[256] In Majorca in the 1670s Judaizers concealed their fasting by sitting at the table without eating, carrying the food into a room where they left it untouched, or leaving their houses on fast days (Cortes 1985, 288). Some new-Christians tried to conceal their fasting even inside the Inquisition prisons. Filipa Cardosa [Coimbra 1583], for example, "on [Jewish] fast days had meat in her cell and did not eat. Rather, in order not to be discovered in her Judaizing she used some exquisite inventions and dissemblings, hiding the meat and placing it in a place where it could not be found, such as in her dirty water and in other places."[257] Doña Ana de León Carvajal [Mexico 1640s] reported that "at lunch time she would ask for something to eat and, instead of eating, she hid the food and kept it and chewed on a piece of paper to make believe that she was eating" (Liebman 1974, 123).

The Mexican Inquisition files from the mid-seventeenth century are particularly rich in details about how fasts were hidden. For example, in 1642 Pedro

Tinoco declared that he would disguise his fasts by walking around the city all day.[258] Blanca Rodríguez and her mother and her friends "accompanied each other to the fields in order to conceal the fact that they were not eating at midday" (Liebman 1974, 192). When Juana Rodríguez lived in Granada, in Spain, she and her husband "and their children went out to Triana [the gypsy quarter] and into the caves when they made the fasts of their law. They would not return until the supper hour, according to the Jewish rites" (Liebman 1974, 215). Juan de León said that he sent his servant on errands to the country on fast days so that the boy would not see him (Lewin 1977, 44, 175). In order not to drink hot chocolate in the morning on fast days, the *converso* slave merchant Fernando Rodríguez talked about how great his expenses were and that it was making him poor."[259] Catalina de Rivera testified that on Yom Kippur "Simón Váez and his wife pretended to have a fight that day so that they would not have to eat and so that their servants and slaves would not know that they were fasting but would think that they were not eating because they were angry."[260] The León Jaramillo family adopted the same strategy: "to disguise their fasts the father and son pretended to fight, and the son, pretending to be afraid, would leave the house, and the father, pretending to look for him on horseback, would go outside the city to search in the orchards."[261] Similarly Amaro Díaz Martaraña and her husband "would have a falling out with each other in the middle of the day in order not to eat [on fast days].... When chocolate was brought to them they would pretend to be offended and spill it on the servants. In the evening they would become reconciled with each other" (Liebman 1974, 184; cf. 190–1, 196). Manuel Núñez said that he would disguise his fasts by pretending to have a headache and staying home the whole day. He put aside the eggs they gave him to eat them at night.[262] Sebastián Vaz de Azevedo "pretended to be sick and would remain in bed" (Liebman 1974, 89; cf. 190, 196). María de Rivera fasted on Wednesday so that neighbors would think she was honoring the Virgin of Carmen.[263] And Isabel Enríquez would take her friends to spend the day in the patio of the Convent of Santiago.[264]

Another popular technique for dissembling was to contract with someone else to fast for you and discharge you of your obligation. This custom seems to have been widely practiced in Portugal, where several of the trials of Judaizers in Coimbra in the 1570s refer to paying a third party to fulfill one's obligation to fast.[265] It was also common in Mexico. Roth reports the custom of "paying a third person, or leaving a legacy, for vicarious afflictions" and even cites the case of a Mexican professional faster (Roth 1931–2, 7). As late as 1714 in Madrid it was reported that "Francisco de Miranda had said that he did not keep the fasts himself but that he paid others to fast for him and for his family."[266]

Iberian Judaizers fasted for a whole host of reasons, the most common of which was to ensure—in the Catholic sense—the salvation of their soul (Melammed 1985, 103–8). Other reasons seem to have their roots in ancient Jewish tradition which derives from the Bible's suggestion that fasts are for the purpose of averting or ending catastrophe (1 Kings 21:27–9; 2 Sam. 12:22–3), for improving communication with God (Ex. 34:28), or for forgiveness (Is. 58). Some Judaizers saw their fasting, and other ascetic acts as well, as a kind of penance that earned them merit with God in proportion to their suffering. This seems to have been the motivation of Beatriz Hernandes and Beatriz Henriques, of Oliveira do Conde, who in Coimbra in 1571–3 were accused of fasting for the purpose of mortifying the flesh in order to please God,[267] and of Leonor Lopes, of Pinhanços, who was tried in Coimbra in 1571 for, among other things, fasting to support her prayers to God.[268] Others considered their suffering to atone for ancient sins. In Brazil in the 1590s, for example, Antonia d'Oliveira said that "Jewish fast days were observed to atone for the worship of the Golden Calf" (Wiznitzer 1960, 17).

Other Judaizers felt that fasting would impress the Deity with the sincerity of their prayer and improve the chances of some particular request being granted. Some of the petitions were of a communal, historical nature, such as that of the mother of Bernardina de San Juan, of Baeza, who fasted to influence the outcome of the deliberations at the Council of Trent. Bernardina testified in 1572 that "when the Council of Trent was coming to an end, her mother had fasted forty days without eating until nightfall, and had kept silent, and prayed repeatedly that it should determine that all Christians should keep the Law of Moses and praise God instead of Jesus Christ, because they were living in deception. And her mother had made her fast for the same reason."[269]

The majority of petitions were of course much more personal in nature. By far the most frequent have to do with curing illness. Pedro Fernández de Alcaudete, treasurer of the cathedral of Córdoba, was sentenced in 1484 because "when he was in pain and in great discomfort he fasted for himself or had someone else fast for him the fasts of the Old law, so that he might be freed from suffering."[270] In 1485 Brianda Besante confessed in Teruel that "once when her little daughters were on the point of dying, a Jewess named Zahara told her that if they kept the fasts of the Jews God would grant health to her daughters. And for four years she fasted on the fast the Jews keep in the month of September."[271] Juan de León was accused in Mexico in 1643 of having gone to visit a woman who was sick in her throat and having told her that he and a friend would fast for her health. The woman was worried that this would tip the friend to the fact that she was a Judaizer.[272]

If volunteers could not be found to pray for one's health, rich Judaizers sometimes would pay to have a third party fast to cure someone of an illness (Blázquez Miguel 1986, 62). The *cristão novo* Manoel Marques said in prison in Lisbon in 1556 that Christovão Dias told him to observe the Jewish fasts in order to be set free.[273] In 1587 in Lisbon Margarida Rodrigues was said to have been advised "to keep the Fast of Queen Esther so that God would free her sister, Beatriz Aires, from the Inquisitorial talons."[274] Similarly, María de Zárate was accused in Mexico in the 1650s of fasting so that her husband, Francisco Botello, would be freed from the Inquisitorial prison.[275] Roth Reports that it was common to fast for the living or the dead, "for the good of a departed kinsman or on behalf of some person in the clutches of the Inquisition" (Roth 1931–2, 28). Fasting for protection or for freedom from prison was also common. Isabel Rodríguez, an eighty-year-old illiterate *conversa* in Toledo, was accused in 1677 of fasting whenever loved ones went on a journey so that God would protect them (Blázquez Miguel 1989, 215).

Unlike that of Catholicism, the Jewish concept of afterlife does not include a Purgatory in which sinful souls serve out a sentence that can be reduced for them through penance, prayer, and charitable acts. Nevertheless this concept seems to underlie the strong crypto-Jewish concern for fasting for the benefit of the souls of one's departed loved ones. Fasting for the souls of dead Judaizers was particularly widespread in seventeenth-century Mexico, where Doña Ana de León Carvajal was so venerated by her fellow Mexican Judaizers that "they used to ask her to fast for their deceased, feeling that her fasts would be more acceptable to the God of Israel than those of other Judaizers" (Liebman 1974, 123). Isabel Duarte, too, who appeared in the 1646 *auto*, was described as "a great faster, who received charity for fasting, charging Jews a *real* for each fast."[276] Margarita de Rivera told Mexican Inquisitors in 1642 that Beatriz Enríquez had given her grandmother some ten *pesos* "so that she and her daughters would keep that number of Jewish fasts for the soul of Doña Blanca Enríquez, who [before dying] had given some five hundred *pesos* to Doña Beatriz to distribute among people who observed the Law so that they would fast for Doña Blanca." They kept the fasts "on various Wednesdays, because those are the days you fast for the deceased."[277] She was also to "distribute her dresses and underclothes to Judaizing women to pray for her soul."[278] About the same time in Mexico Juan de León allegedly met with nine other Judaizers to fast for the soul of a certain dead person. Catalina de Rivera said that "the first thing you eat after you have fasted for someone's soul is a soup made of bread soaked in salt water."[279] This custom was practiced elsewhere as well. Fernão Lopes, of the Azores, was accused in 1573 in Lisbon of saying that "the fasts of Pardon and of Queen Esther were better than the fasts of the Christians, and that they ensured the salvation of your soul."[280] In the seventeenth century Isabel de Miranda, of Madrid, reputedly paid 300 *reales* for someone to fast for the soul of one of her relatives (Blázquez Miguel 1986, 62).

For some *conversos* fasting for the souls of the departed assumed an almost mystic intensity. Leonor Núñez, named in the great Mexican *auto de fe* of 1649, seems to have fasted to induce visions:

> She influenced people to fast three days for the souls of the deceased. Then she would feign revelations and relate that the soul for whom they had been fasting was in a good place. On one occasion in which she had celebrated a fast for her family, she imagined that a miracle, made by the God of Israel, had occurred, as it does to the fine Jews because they serve Him carefully. The ceiling in the house where she lived fell but it had not caught them in it, and this caused her to break out in paeans of praise of the virtues of herself and her family. She pointed out to Thomas Treviño de Sobremonte [her son-in-law]

that whenever she fasted a beautiful and clear image would appear to her and she said, "Son, when I make these fasts, it seems that I am in the glory [of God] and if I were to die in such a moment, I would go straight to Heaven and see the God of Israel." (Liebman 1974, 144)

The range of motives for fasting and their importance in the lives of Iberian Judaizers can be seen in the behavior of Juan de León and Francesco Botello, who were observed at length in the Mexican Inquisitorial prisons in 1645. A substantial part of the Judaizing of these two men centered on fasts, which they called *súchiles*. They fasted on weekdays and on the Sabbath. They fasted in support of specific supplications: for freedom, that their leg irons be removed, that the prison window be opened, etc. León recounted how before his imprisonment he had fasted in the home of Simón Váez because it was comfortable to fast there. "Everyone got together, mother and daughters and sons-in-law and grandchildren, everyone of the lineage of Simón Váez and his wife, and we did it with the greatest care and secrecy in the world. We all joined in the living room as if at a light meal, with great dissembling, so that even if someone came in from outside they would not know, because we all communicated by signs."[281] According to Botello there were strict rules that governed fasting: "Let it be as it ought to be, bathing ourselves, dressing ourselves well with clean clothes, leaving a light burning all night, praying while we are on our knees, just as you have told me, everything that we can and should do." León told him "that's how we'll do it; and remember that it must be with the knees crossed."[282]

# Notes

1. The evidence of observance of Rosh Hashanah is sporadic and reinforces Roth's opinion that this holiday was almost completely neglected by the *conversos* (1931–2, 21). For examples of its celebration, see also Selke de Sánchez 1972, 97; Liebman 1982, 123; Lorence 1991, 100 [Portugal 1600s]. A 1403 document orders Valencian Jews to leave the city on *capdany* ["head of the year"] so that new-Christians would not be tempted to celebrate the holiday with them (Hinojosa Montalvo 1993, 115).

2. *La pascua de el cuerno signiffica que en tal día crió Dios al mundo y libró a Issac del sacrifficio que Abrahaam, su padre, querría hacer de él; y porque Abrahaam halló el carnero de que hiço el sacrifficio en lugar de su hijo envuelto, y travando los cuernos entre unas çarças; y a signifficación desto los judios en tal pascua acostumbravan tocar el cuerno en memoria de la dicha liberación de el sacrifficio de Isaac, que era día de remembración y caya el primero día de la luna del mes de septiembre* (Santa María 1893c, 185).

3. *Este testigo leyó en el dicho libro, y heran unas oraciones que los judios dizen en la pascua del cuerno* (López Martínez 1954, 136). See also Gracia Boix 1983, 3 [1484]; Fita y Colomé 1884, 402 [1484].

4. *Tenían sus pasquas que celebraban ocho y quinçe días, que las llamaban Roçana* (Sierro Malmierca 1990, 178).

5. *Pasteles, turcos, tortas, empanadas y manjar blanco* (AGN Vol 271 doc 1, 10a).
6. *Equipuz* (Tejado 1950, 64 [Colombia early seventeenth century]). *Çinquipul* (Ollero Pina 1988, 98 [Andalucia 1482]). *Cinquepur* (García 1910, 102 [Mexico 1648]). *Antepur* (Azevedo Mea 1982, 31 [Coimbra 1567]; García 1910, 102 [Mexico 1648]). *Quipur* (Santa María 1893c, 185 [Spain late fifteenth century]).
7. Osorio 1980, 173 [1609]; Liebman 1974, 84 [Mexico 1649]; Lewin 1977, 20 [Mexico 1642].
8. Bel Bravo 1988, 101 [Granada 1590s].
9. García de Proodian 1966, 351. Prior to the Expulsion it was sometimes called the day of *axora* [*a çara*], or Day of Woe (Cantera Montenegro 1985, 69).
10. Azevedo Mea 1982, 158 [Lamego 1569].
11. Braunstein 1936, 100. Sixteenth-century Portuguese new-Christians called it the *Jejum mayor* (Furtado 1925, xxxi [Evora 1536]), and also the *jejum do Quipur* (Azevedo Mea 1982, 31 [Coimbra 1567]). Seventeenth-century Majorcan *chuetas* also called it *El ayuno Mayor* (the Great Fast) (Braunstein 1936, 100). Modern Portuguese new-Christians call it the *Grande Jejum* (Vasconcelos 1958, 222).
12. *Al tiempo que la dicha Catalina Gómez fue presa le hallaron en las manos los ministros que la prendieron dos librillos escriptos de mano con repertorio de los ayunos de la ley de Moysen y oraçiones della, desde el año de ochenta y çinco, y razón de quando se an de ayunar los ayunos del día grande* (Sierro Malmierca 1990, 131). Prior to the Expulsion, of course, *conversos* consulted their Jewish neighbors with regard to the dates of the festivals; for some examples see Cantera Montenegro 1985, 62 [Molina de Aragón 1497].
13. *Tenía escritas las lunas para saber los ayunos de los judíos* (Böhm 1984, 221).
14. *Allose al reo entre sus papeles un quadernito de ochavo afforado en pergamino con algunas oraciones judaicas, y con el calendario de las fiestas de la ley de Moyses y Pascuas della. . . . Que habia sacado el calendario de Genebrando [?] sobre los salmos* (Böhm 1984, 284, 288). See also Medina 1899a, 186.
15. *Traía el calendario de sus fiestas en cifra, que se le halló entre sus papeles, quando en prisión* (Medina 1887, 2:127).
16. Liebman 1982, 107. For the tenth of September see also García de Proodian 1966, 350 [Peru]; García Fuentes 1981, 98 [1573]; Toro 1932, 244 [Mexico 1589]; Bel Bravo 1988, 165 [Granada 1592]; Lewin 1977, 69 [Mexico 1642].
17. *Le mandaba ayunar . . . en septiembre a diez de luna, que llamaban el día grande* (Gracia Boix 1983, 139). See also Contreras 1982, 607; Liebman 1970, 65; 1982, 121; Adler 1895, 46 [1607]; Böhm 1963, 47 [1627]; Selke de Sánchez 1972, 97 [1677]; Roth 1931–2, 22; Paulo 1970, 97 [twentieth-century Portugal]. An interesting dissemblance strategy is also recorded among modern Portuguese Judaizers who sometimes celebrate Yom Kippur on the eleventh day of the September new moon so as—Vasconcelo speculates—to avoid Inquisition scrutiny (1958, 210). See also Canelo 1987, 99.
18. *El dayuno de quipur, que cae por el mes de septiembre, hacia San Mateo* (Sánchez Moya 1966, 276). Among ignorant Judaizers sometimes the association with Christianity was closer still. A witness in 1665 in Mexico may have alluded to Yom Kippur when she told Inquisitors that María de Zárate used to fast "on the fourth of the month of September because they said that was the day when the Messiah had died" (*A los cuatro del mes de setiembre, porque decían que era el día en que había muerto Mesías*) (Lewin 1971, 488).
19. *O dia do Quipur, que vem no tempo das uvas* (Baião 1921, 136). See also Bel Bravo 1988, 101 [Granada, 1590s].

20. *Los judíos estaban encerrados e dayunaban, que era el fin de agosto o en principio de septiembre* (Sánchez Moya 1966, 279).

21. *El dayuno de Quippur es continuamente cuatro o cinco días antes de la Pascua de las Cabanillas* (Sánchez Moya 1966, 279).

22. *Abia hecho el ayuno de la expiaçion que es a los 10 de setiembre por 4 dias, sin comer ni beber en todos ellos; y que aunque el precepto de su lei no era mas que de un dia, el reo por devoçion y para que Dios le perdonase sus pecados le habia hecho de quatro* (Böhm 1984, 288). See also Medina 1899a, 184.

23. References to the *shofar* are quite rare. See, for example, Cantera Montenegro 1985, 67 [Molina de Aragón c. 1460].

24. In 1556 in Lisbon the wife of the *christão novo* doctor Pedro da Motta explained the origin of Yom Kippur this way: fasting is "in memory of the fast which the Jews kept in remembrance of the redemption God granted them when he took them out of captivity" (*Por memorya do jejum que os judeus fizeram por aquela memorya e redencão que Deus por elles fizera em os tirar do Captiveiro*) (Baião 1921, 176).

25. *El ayunar el ayuno del quipur, que quiere decir perdón, signiffica los quarenta días que Moyssén estuvo sin comer ni bever en el monte Synay, esperando la luz y perdón que Dios havía de dar al pueblo de Isrrael por el pecado de la ydolatría; el qual Dios por sus ruegos perdonó y les dió la luz; y anssí los judíos por aquella merced que les hiço acostumbravan de hacer el dicho ayuno, acostumbravan demandarse perdón los unos a los otros, y los menores besavan las manos a los mayores; y el dicho ayuno de el perdón solía caer a diez días de la luna del mes de septiembre* (Santa María 1893c, 185).

26. *Dixo que es verdat que por la Ley de Moisen, los judíos son obligados a dayunar solamente dayuno para perdonación de sus pecados; pero los doctores para ayudar al dicho dayuno, mandaron facer las cirimonias siguientes: no calzar zapato, pero esparteña, sí, o zapato de paño; non lavar las manos nin la cara con agua simple por razón de tomar deleite; pero con manteles remojados de parte de la tarde, sí. Es de ley no comer ninguna cosa fasta la noche. Es falso que hayan de tener capucho en la cabeza. A lo de estar en la Sinoga, no es obligado si no la tiene, que en el campo puede facer el dayuno. De tocar el cuerno, y si lo tocan después de pasado el dayuno a la noche, es por cirimonia y no es cirimonia del dayuno. E símesmo aquel día se acostumbraban a perdonar y facer mucha paz y concordia entre ellos. Pero si algo desto fallare, el dayuno queda en su firmeza* (Sánchez Moya 1966, 294).

27. *En el tiempo de las ubas y también de los figos, todos los confesos de Barbastro iban llegados a los güertos de dos en dos, de cuatro en quatro, de seys en seys, de ocho en ocho, de diez en diez, paseando en los güertos y no fazian fazienda aquel día, en que acostumbraban a dayunar los judios, . . . porque les veia las caras esmayadas, de muertos y no venian fasta la noche a sus casas, ni comian en todo el dia fasta la noche, e en la noche comian carne e gallinas e fazian gran fiesta. . . . Ynterrogado si estaban vestidos o spoxados o scalços dize que bestidos estaban, empero algunos descalços en peales e alli vió antes de comer, que dezian oraciones judaicas e no las entendia e que facíanse todos un golpe* (Cabezudo Astraín 1963, 271–2).

28. For example, Luis de Carvajal told the Mexican Inquisition in 1589 that "on the Great Day of Pardoning . . . God judged the souls" (*El día grande del perdón . . . en aquel día particularmente juzgaba Dios las ánimas*) (Toro 1932, 244). Substantial information about the Yom Kippur observances of the Carvajal family is found in Cohen 1973, indexed under "Great Day."

29. *Cada año hacia el ayuno q llamauan el dia Grande, y q la vispera del se avian de bañar y de llevar limpio senando a la noche pescado y legumbre, y despues se auian de ensender candelas de*

*cera, poniendolas sobre un lienzo limpio y hauian de resar a la media noche las orasiones de la dha ley y que se auian de pedir perdon y abrasarse los unos a los otros y amistarse los que hubiesen reñido. Y que a la media noche se auian de ir a dormir, dexando las dichas belas ensendidas hasta que se acabasen. Y que el dia siguiente se auian de estar sin comer ni beuer hasta la noche salida la estrella y auian de volver a senar pescado legumbres y de otras cosas y no carne. . . . Ensendieron quattro o sinco candelas de cera y en el suelo de la rrecamara en que dormian las pusieron sobre un lienso limpio y estubieron hasta serear a media noche estarse siempre todos senttados y este confessante y su hermano con los sombreros sueltos porque le adbirttieron todas q no se havian de tocar las cabessas, y estubieron rresando cada una para si las oraciones que saven de la dha ley de Moysen. . . .*

30. *Que fuese a pasear todo el día adonde quisiesse. Y no comiesse ni bebiesse cossa alguna porque quebrantara el dho ayuno* (AGN Vol 402 doc 2, 504a-b). See also Adler 1899, 13.

31. *Vn día antes del ayuno mayor, yr al vanno de las judías* (León Tello 1972, 75).

32. *Habiéndose entrado en ella se lavó y bañó todo el cuerpo la susodicha, en una batea grande, y le parece que fué con agua tibia; y habiéndose enjugado y vestido camisa nueva, le dijo a éste que entrase en la dicha despensa y se lavase todo el cuerpo, como ella lo había hecho, por ceremonia necesaria para prevención del dicho ayuno del Día Grande, que era el siguiente* (Lewin 1954, 126).

33. *La víspera de este ayuno se fueron a bañar al baño de los japones . . . y allí, se acuerda se vistieron ropa limpia y comieron unos huevos asados, vino y marquesotes, y, le parece, que fue por la mañana* (Lewin 1977, 69; cf. 80, 20, 30).

34. "Sometimes when the Great Fast of the Jews was approaching the day before I went to the river to bathe myself according to the ceremony" (*Algunas veses quando venía el ayuno mayor de los judíos el día antes yva al río a bañarme por çelimonia*) (López Martínez 1954, 181).

35. Paulo 1985, 93. For other examples of pre-Yom Kippur bathing see Adler 1899, 13 [Mexico 1645]; Liebman 1970, 65, Paulo (1970, 97), and Vasconcelos 1958, 171 [twentieth-century Portugal]. The concern is clearly with both physical and spiritual cleanliness. Carrying this practice to an extreme, modern Portuguese new-Christians are said not to let strangers or menstruating women into the room where people are fasting because they would render the fast impure (*trêfo*) (Vasconcelos 1958, 211). For these *cristãos novos* Yom Kippur's sanctity is fragile and great care must be taken that it not be defiled. If while walking on the street on Yom Kippur they meet a funeral cortege, it is considered bad luck. It is also bad luck to encounter a priest, an image of Christ, or a church. Thus they do whatever they can to stay home (Vasconcelos 1958, 171).

36. *Un vestido de paño pardo y vorzeguies y çapatos nuevos y cuello deramissa y cree que tanbien sombrero nuevo* (AGN Vol 276 doc 14, 433a).

37. Liebman (1974, 87). This custom persists even today among remnant Portuguese Judaizers, who wear their best clothing on Yom Kippur (Schwarz 1925, 31). See also Paulo 1970, 97; Vasconcelos 1958, 171, 210.

38. *Comer pera o tal dia em louça nova e lavando e esfregando toda a louça de pao, arcas, bancos, escabellos, como pera festa do tal dia* (Azevedo Mea 1982, 430).

39. *En el qual día se cenava aves, y cosas buenas, y hacían gran cena, con ostentazión; pero no comían carnero, porque en el mes de Septiembre no comen carnero por ser muerto por mano agena. Y la víspera de este ayuno se limpiaba toda la cassa, y toda la ropa, y se labraban todo el cuerpo y ponían la mexor ropa en sus personas, por honra de la festividad del ayuno; y por lo mesmo la noche de la cena se ponía en la mesa ropa limpia, y en la cama, y se pedían perdón los unos a los otros. . . . Para aquel día se avía de hacer gran ostentazión, y si podían hacer cocas*

*bambas las hiciessen, y aun confitura también, si no que la hacen manos de la canalla que guardan la ley de graçia, y por esso no la compraban* (Selke de Sánchez 1972, 272–3).

40. Paulo 1985, 56. This custom persists among Ladino-speaking Sephardis in the Levant (Dobrinsky 1986, 345).

41. *Na noite antes do tal dia enchia huma porçolana de azeite e lhe punha tres torcidas novas e as deixava ficar acesas atè se apagarem por si* (Azevedo Mea 1982, 299; cf. 76).

42. *Y habiéndosele dado las candelas de cera, que entiende fueron tres o cuatro, las encendió y sobre un paño de lienzo limpio las puso en el suelo, en un aposento pequeño donde todas vivían* (Lewin 1977, 41; cf. 46, 64).

43. Adler 1899 13–4; cf. 68, 73–4.

44. *Encendiendo, tal vez la víspera de un ayuno del día grande, tanto número de velas de cera por vivos y muertos, que parecía un lucido monumento de los católicos, y pasaban de ochenta* (García 1910, 249).

45. *Jejuando pelo mes de Setembro dez dias arreo e apos delles o jejum do Quypur* (Azevedo Mea 1982, 101; cf. 102, 121, 147, etc.).

46. See note 22.

47. *Durante a lua de setembro, desde o seu começo, não entrava carne de porco em casa nenhuma* (Barros Basto 1929, 3.17:1).

48. *La noche antes de dayuno es cirimonia de judíos comer gallinas e substancias* (Sánchez Moya 1966, 283).

49. *Guisavan de noche differentes guissados buenos . . . y çenavan en la sala prinçipal, donde otras vezes no çenan, en mesa grande más bien adereçada que otros dias; y se compusieron y mudaron vestidos, y dicha Margarita Martí también compuso los hixos. Y que aquella misma tarde, como sentía ésta tanto ruydo, por curiosidad de saver si hazían lo mesmo en la veçindad de la Calle, entró en casa de Miguel Cortés y Antonio Cortés, hermanos; y Balthazar Martí . . . y vio que estavan vestidos todos como de fiesta, y que también andavan con gran tráfago en la coçina, al modo y de la mesma manera que en cassa de dichos sus amos* (Selke de Sánchez 1972, 98–9).

50. Modern *criptojudeus* in the area of Belmonte purify their mouths by washing them out three times with water before beginning the Yom Kippur fast (Canelo 1987, 95).

51. Beinart 1961, 182. For a similar opinion from Brazil in 1726 see Wiznitzer 1960, 154.

52. *Haberse de salvar ayundando el Ayuno de Quipur, y aquel ser necesario a la salvación de su ánima* (Sánchez Moya 1966, 299).

53. *Si ha dejunat del perdo o altres dejunis dels Juheus no menjant fins a la nit vistes les estreles* (Llorca 1935, 16).

54. *El Ayuno Mayor que disen los judios, e estan descalços en todo el dia, e non comer ni beuer e resar hasta la noche* (Beinart 1974, 58). For other examples see López Martínez 1954, 180 [Spain 1490s]; Fita y Colomé 1892, 515 [1484]; Llorca 1939, 133 [1484]; Adler 1899, 15 [Mexico 1645]; Lewin 1954, 146 [Mexico 1647]; Cortes 1985, 286 [Mexico 1679]; Haliczer 1990, 234 [Madrid 1710s]; Wiznitzer 1960, 154–8 [1726–32].

55. *Ayuno este confesante dos ayunos con Juana Nuñez . . . non comiendo en todo el dia hasta la noche, e que a la noche comian huevos e otras cosas de su casa* (Beinart 1977a, 254).

56. *Que no comian en los dichos dias en todo el dia hasta la noche, e que a la noche çenavan carne y se abraçaban vnos a otros* (Beinart 1981b, 425).

57. *Que viniese mucha gente a la casa de sus amos y que ella vio por la noche, salida la estrella, que un hombre portugués le daba a cada uno de los presentes, una rebanada de pan, y luego se pusieron todos a rezar mirando a una pared de la alcoba* (Contreras 1982, 601).

58. *A la noche desayunandose con aves e otras carnes* (Beinart 1974, 58).

59. *El dia de dayuno a la noche, comen gallinas* (Sánchez Moya 1966, 283).

60. *No comieron fasta a la noche, que comieron palomas* (Sánchez Moya 1966, 285).

61. *Questa mesa la tenían puesta por la pasqua del día grande y le echaban tierra muy cernida y comían de aquel pan [que masaban sin levadura ni sal] la noche siguiente del ayuno con una ensalada con açeite y vinagre y la dicha tierra molida* (Sierro Malmierca 1990, 178).

62. *Algunas cosas de pescado que así habían de hacer por ser también ceremonia de la dicha Ley* (Lewin 1954, 126). For other examples see Willemse 1974, 29; Roth 1943–4, 230 [Venice 1617]; Adler 1899, 13 [Mexico 1645].

63. For examples from the Eastern Mediterranean during this century see Dobrinsky 1986, 345.

64. *Assim como o Senhor botou a sua santa bênção á lā e ao lino, a Abraão, a Isaac, ao seu filho Jacob, bote o Senhor sobre nós e toda a nossa familia a sua santa bênção. . . . Ao céu vá, lá chegue, para honra e glória do nome santo do Senhor. Amen* (Vasconcelos 1958, 172).

65. *Licença te peço Senhor / para me vir desenjuar, / que me faças feliz e constante / para te servir e amar. / Assim como este sal / saiu do mar sagrado, / me tire o Senhor minha alma / de penas e pecado. / Louvado seja o Senhor, / que já me desenjuei: / Deus me dê saúde e vida / P'ra cumprir sua santa Lei* (1970, 98).

66. See Beinart 1974, 24, 58; Baer 1966, 2:351 [1471]; Llorca 1939, 133 [1484]; Beinart 1975, 653; Carrete Parrondo 1985a, 560 [1491]; Blázquez Miguel 1986, 62; Sánchez Moya 1966, 288; Carrete Parrondo 1980, 255; Baião 1921, 136 [1543]; Azevedo Mea 1982, 422, 430 [Coimbra 1583]; Lorence 1991, 96 [Coimbra 1615]; Roth 1943–4, 230 [Venice 1617]; Liebman 1970, 96 [1639]; García 1910, 206 [1648]; Liebman 1974, 111, 228 [Mexico 1649]; Lewin 1939, 25 [eighteenth century]; Wiznitzer 1960, 13 and Dobrinsky 1986, 343 [twentieth century in the Levant].

67. *Que ayunaban un ayuno grande de tres días y echaban çeniça sobre sus cabeças y uno dellos con los pies juntos en pie reçando sus oraçiones* (Sierro Malmierca 1990, 178).

68. Roth 1931–2, 24.

69. *Después de haberse recogido toda la gente de su casa de éste, como entre diez y once de la noche, pasaron por la dicha puerta a casa de dicho Diego de Almanza, las dichas Leonor Martínez, su madre, y Ana Sánchez y este confesante, y juntos subieron a un aposento donde dormía Ana de Almanza, doncella, hija del dicho Diego de Almanza y de Luisa Martínez; y dejando dormir al dicho Diego de Almanza, su marido, subió la dicha Luisa Martínez al aposento de la dicha Ana de Almanza, su hija, donde los referidos estaban juntos, rezando y hablando de la dicha Ley, y comunicaron cómo todos habían de ayunar al día siguiente, que era el ayuno del Día Grande; y que lo más de aquella noche o toda ella, cada cual como mejor se hallase, habían de estar en pie o paseándose por ceremonia necesaria de la dicha Ley de Moisén, y estuvieron en esta forma hasta las dos de la mañana, hablando de materias de la dicha Ley y rezando oraciones de ella* (Lewin 1954, 126–7).

70. *Exaltado e glorificado sejais, Senhor, para sempre. Vós exalçareis a mim para que meus inimigos se não vinguem de mim. Exalçar-vis-ei, amèzinhar-me-eis com a vossa divina mèzinha. Da cova tirastes a minha alma, o corpo ficou na terra, a alma a guardastes. Ouvi, ouvi, Senhor, cantar louvores ao Senhor. Salvação, salvação, salvação, salvaçvão seja com as nossas almas para sempre* (da Cunha e Freitas 1952, 20). For other examples see Liebman 1970, 65; Azevedo Mea 1982, 452 [Coimbra 1583]; Adler 1899, 41, 68 [Mexico 1645].

71. *El primer ayuno que hizo cuando tenía quince años fue en el día Grande de 1599. Siendo ya la noche lo llamó la rea y lo sacó a un ejido junto a la casa y le dixo: -Mira que ayunes este día para que Nro. Señor te dé vida; y estando en pie ambos hacia donde sale el sol, la rea le fue destocando*

y le fue diciendo oraciones que la una decía ser de la Estrella y otra del Ayuno y el testigo iba diciendo las mismas palabras y acabado éste le dixo: -Tía, por quién rezamos? y la dicha rea le dixo: -Mira que adoramos a un solo Dios, el de Israel, tu pueblo (Contreras 1982, 607).

72. *Deante de vós, Senhor, venho em jejum, nanja por falta de pão, nem de nada; minhas carnes a enfraquecer, meu sangue escrito no ceu, eu esperando pela vossa divina benção, Senhor Deus de Adonai. Amen* (Tradições 1928, 2.11:8).

73. *Bendito meu Deus, meu Senhor, meu Adonai, que nos mandou e nos encomendou as suas santas encomendanças, benditas e santas, que acendessemos esta torcida para alumiar e festejar a noite santa do Senhor, para que o Senhor nos alumie a nossa alma e nos livre de culpas e pecados. Amém, Senhor. Ao Céu vá, ao Céu chegue* (Paulo 1970, 97–8).

74. For a description and analysis of the traditional Yom Kippur liturgy see Millgram 1971, 224–61. Schwarz found twentieth-century Portuguese Judaizers on Yom Kippur breaking their prayer into five sessions 1925, 31; 63–5.

75. *Estar encerrado / el buen ayuno mayor / con lágrimas y dolor* (Castillo 1882, #994).

76. *En especial cantaua profecías de Jeremías e Ysaías e otras profecías, cantándolos baxos en la manera e tono que las cantauan los tiempos pasados los rabíes en la sinoga, por honra de su ley* (León Tello 1972, 77).

77. Liebman 1970, 177. Other Yom Kippur prayers of the Carvajal family are given in Cohen 1973, 136.

78. Liebman 1970, 66 gives David Fergusson's translation of this prayer. Cf. Adler 1899, 17.

79. *Esta confesante y las dichas sus hermanas . . . estuvieron un rato en el dicho aposento sentadas juntas a las candelas, y esta confesante rezó la oración que empieza Pequé, pequé Señor* (Lewin 1977, 41).

80. *Agora nos acostamos / y a Dios nos encomendamos / a Dios, mi Señor / que no hay otro mejor / ni le hubo ni le habra / bendito aquel que vida nos da* (Liebman 1982, 117).

81. *Leyéndoles en un libro en lengua hebrea la institución de aquel ayuno; haciéndoles sentar, levantar e inclinar profundamente las cabezas; teniendo los hombres las cabezas cubiertas con sombreros y las mujeres con tocas largas; encendiendo mucho número de candiles* (García 1910, 223). Judaizers in Majorca in the 1670s on Yom Kippur were also observed to have covered their heads with handkerchiefs (Cortes 1985, 287).

82. *En el dio del Ayno Mayor, demandando aquel dia perdon a otros, e otros a ellos, çerimonyalmente, como fasen los judios, disiendo serles perdonados todos sus pecados aquel dia* (Beinart 1974, 524; see also 1981b, 566; 1975, 653).

83. *Vido uno, que se llama el Royo vino el día del Dayuno de la Perdonanza de los judíos a casa del dicho Puxmija, e traía una capilla puesta en la cabeza, e apiés descalzos entró por un portiyo. E vinía a demandar perdón al dicho Puxmija, que había cinquo años, poco más o menos, que no se fablaban* (Sánchez Moya 1966, 298).

84. *Se abracaron con el dicho maestre Samaya y se demandaron los unos a los otros perdon* (Carrete Parrondo 1986, 121).

85. Roth 1931–2, 24. For other examples see Liebman 1982, 109; 1970, 66 [1642]; Lewin 1977, 46 [Mexico 1642].

86. *No dia do jejum de Quipur se deveriam perdoar todas as culpas* (Baião 1921, 138).

87. *Persuadió a este confesante a que fuese a casa de doña Leonor de Rojas, su tía, a hablarle, porque este confesante había mucho tiempo que estaba disgustado con ella, y también le parece que le persuadió a que se fuese hablar también a doña Elena de Silva, su tía, con quien asimismo no se comunicaba, diciéndole que era ceremonia de la Ley y tenía obligación de hacerlo* (Lewin 1977, 68).

88. *No dia do jejum do Quipur dava maiores esmolas que nos outros tempos* (Azevedo Mea 1982, 1).

89. Paulo 1970, 97. See also Vasconcelos 1958, 210. The custom persists among Eastern Mediterranean Sephardis (Dobrinsky 1986, 342–3).

90. *Reçan oraciones de judios y las noches se piden perdón unos a otros poniendo los padres a los hijos las manos sobre las cabeças diciendo: de Dios y de mí seays bendecidos por lo que dispone la ley de Moyssén y sus ceremonias* (Santa María 1893c, 183).

91. *Hallo encendidas unas siete u ocho candelas de cera sobre un bufete . . . y pidio la bendicion a la dha su madre, puesta en pie, y baxa la cabeça, a donde se puso la mano y le dixo que la bendicion que Dios auia echado a Jacob, y a Ysac cayese sobre esta confeste, y sobre todos los sus hijos* (AGN Vol 402 doc 1, 20b). For other Mexican examples see Lewin 1977, 46; García 1910, 213 [1648].

92. *El dia del Ayuno Mayor venian a pedir perdon a la madre del dicho Hernando de Theba la muger de Juan Daça, escriuano, e sus hijos, e le besauan la mano, porque eran parientes, e ella les ponia la mano sobre la cabeça* (Beinart 1974, 147).

93. *Antes que cease certas persoas, que com ele o jejuvão, se asentavão de giolhos diante delle e lhe pedião perdão a elle lhes corria a mão aberta pela cabeça e lhes dizia que a benção de Deus e a sua as cobrise* (Azevedo Mea 1982, 158).

94. Vasconcelos reports that sometimes modern Portuguese new-Christians would celebrate Yom Kippur out in their vineyards so as to avoid suspicion. There the women and men would separate into two groups and each would spend the day praying under direction of a leader of the same sex. But even in modern times most Portuguese new-Christians would celebrate at home, where, unobserved, they could pray from the Bible, especially the Psalms (1958, 200, 211).

95. *Preparava-se a casa em que se havia de fazer o dito jejum alcatifando-se o pavimento dela, e a uma parte se punha um bufete coberto com um pano de seda, e nele castiçais com velas acesas, e no meio dela se dependurava um candieiro de latão com muitos lumes; e à hora assinada entravam todas as pessoas que se achavam na dita solenidade para a dita casa com melhores vestidos, barbas feitas, descalços, sem capas, nem chapéus na cabeça, e se encostavam às paredes, e em alguns ditos jejuns se lhes vestiam umas vestes brancas, que chegavam até à cinta, e se lhes punham umas correas com nôminas atadas pela testa, e estavam com os braços cruzados, e em muitas das ditas solenidades, em que o réu Antônio Homem fez por muitas vezes o ofício de sacerdote, estava assentado em uma cadeira despaldas, e dela fazia prática às ditas pessoas, exortanto-as a que vivessem na lei de Moisés, refirindo-lhe algumas autoridades do testamento velho, e as ditas pessoas em certos passos da prática faziam guayas, levantavam os olhos ao céu, punham as palmas das mãos viradas uma para a outra baixando as cabeças até os peitos, e inclinando-as a uma e a outra parte, e o réu repetia alguns salmos de David, sem gloria patri, e entre elas era o In exitu Israel de Egypto e o Super flumina Babilonia e o De profundis clamavi e chegando ao verso que diz Et propte legem tuam / Sustinuit te Domine dizia entender-se que por amor da lei de Deus haviam de sofrer trabalhos e perseguições, e que haviam de esperar em Deus em todo o tempo e que esto significava o verso do mesmo salmo que seguia, que diz A custodia matutina usque ad noctem speret Israel in Domino e que também David quisera dizer no mesmo verso que o jejum havia de ser . . . desde a manhã até noite, e que se assim o fizessem alcançariam de Deus o que David prometia nos versos seguintes a saber: que seria a misericórdia de Deus e sua redenção para o povo de Israel mui copiosa, e que lhes perdoaria todas as suas culpas; e depois de gastar um espaço nesta prática e em outras semelhantes, que fazia aos circunstantes, a fim de os confirmar na crença da lei de Moisés fazendo-se esta preparação algumas vezes na mesma casa, e outras na de*

*fora, revestiam ao réu outros sacerdotes, em uma veste larga e comprida, pondo-le um modo de mitra na cabeça, a qual era cerrada por cima e no meio tinha uma lâmina de ouro, e os ditos sacerdotes da lei de Moisés, que lhe assistiam estavam revestidos em umas vestes de certa seda os quais lhe administravam um turíbulo com o qual o réu incensava em certos passos o dito altar, em que algumas vezes estava um retábulo coma figura de Moisés e outro com a de certa pessoa que foi relaxada à justiça secular, e quimada por judeu, e depois incensavam ao réu, o qual tocava uma busina em tom baixo por algumas vezes no decurso do dito dia, e no sobredito altar estava uma bíblia pela qual o réu lia alguns capítulos do testamento velho, e recitava salmos de David noque se gastava todo o dia e no fim dele fazia o réu outra prática em que encomendava observáncia da lei de Moisés. . . . E no fim das práticas que o réu fazia, nos ajuntamentos no jejum do dia grande lhe iam todos os circunstantes beijar o pé, e ele lhes lançava a bênção ao modo judaico, pondolhes a mão pela cabeça e correndo lha pelo rosto; o que se lhe fazia por ser tido das pessoas que se achavam naquels atos por Sumo Sacerdote da lei de Moisés* (Lipiner 1977, 87–9).

96. *Todos em certos pasos faziam guaias, levantando os olhos ao céu e as palmas das mãos em compostura, abaixando a cabeça até os peitos e inclinando-a para as ilhargas. E feita esta prática por espaço de uma hora que nela gastavam por modo de preparação para o dito jejum grande, se levantava o dito sacerdote principal e entrava em outro lugar mais secreto onde se detinha por um quarto de hora e depois tocava uma buzina três vezes, mansamente e ao som dela os ditos circunstantes no lado de fora, onde ficavam entretanto, faziam-se tres guaias na forma sobredita e logo o Réu, com alguns deles em certo número, entravam no dito lugar mais secreto para serem assistentes do dito sacerdote principal e depois de estarem com ele mais de um quarto de hora tornava a soar a dita buzina três vezes e os circunstantes no dito lugar de fora tornavam a fazer as ditas guaias.*

97. *Certa alva guarnecida nas pontas ao redor com uma tira da mesma seda que arrastava pelo chão, rodeadas de campainhas de certa seda e não de prata por não serem sentidos e cingido com um cordão.*

98. *Duas lâminas de ouro de certa feição em uma das quais estava a figura de Moisés e na outra a da serpente.*

99. *O Réu, com os mais assistentes, estavam repartidos nos lados do altar, revestido com outro gênero de vestes de certa cor. E estando assim todos e os mais circunstantes em pé para começarem o dito ato, a que chamavam sacrificio, o Réu de joelhos, tomava o turíbulo com incenso e brasas de certo carvão artificioso que se acendia facilmente e durava todo o dia e dava ao dito sacerdote principal, o qual por algumas vezes incensava o altar de certo modo e tornando o turíbulo ao réu e sendo incensado por ele e reverenciado com uma guaia grande lhe fazia uma pequena inclinação com a cabeça e logo o Réu incensava os mais assistentes somente, fazendo-se guaias entre si de parte a parte e as mesmas faziam os mais circunstantes enquanto durava esta cerimônia de incensar.*

100. *Rezava de cor alguns salmos e os interpretava em latim, dizendo que aum hoje a lei de Moisés era boa.*

101. *Faziam juramento sobre certo livro prometendo ter segredo nos ditos atos de jejum, sem nunca os descobrirem, ainda que lhes custasse a vida pelo grande prejuízo que se poderia seguir à gente da nação* (Lipiner 1977, 89–91).

102. Nidel 1984, 253–4. See also Snyder 1992, 19.

103. *Sucod se celebra cinco días después de pasado el ayuno de Quipur del mes de setiembre* (Lewin 1977, 274 [Mexico 1643]). See also Santa María 1893c, 186 and Blázquez Miguel 1986a, 67 [Toledo 1589].

104. *Çuco es pascua de las cabanuelas, cae a quatorze ala XV de la luna de septiembre y dura nueve días los primeros dos de guardar de premia y el çaguero destos dos llaman çinhatora que*

*quiere dezir alegria, porque en aquel día se acabaron los cinco libros de la lei y tornóse a encomendar después esta pascua porque anduuieron en el disierto en cabañas xlanos y por dar loor a dios que sienpre solía caer agua en tal pascua y guardan los dos çagueros destos nueve e antes se llamaua día de araba y es el uno de los tres dias çagueros* (López Martínez 1954, 179).

105. *Dos o tres días después de dicho ayuno de perdón venían siete fiestas contínuas en que no se avía de trabaxar . . . y que passados los siete días de fiesta, el día siguiente havían de comer fava parada y pollo asado* (Selke de Sánchez 1972, 273).

106. *La pascua de las cavañuelas, que cae a quince días del mes de septiembre, significa quando los hijos de Isrrael salieron de Egipto, y fueron por el dessierto quarenta años apossentados por cavañas y borrascas [barracas? = huts], y a esta signifficación y en memoria de esto hacían los judíos las dichas cavañuelas poniendo en ellas cañas, salces, ynojos y otras verduras y fructos, según la concurrencia del tiempo; y las dichas cavañuelas se havían de hacer a la serena y en lugar que se viesse el cielo, como heran las que los judíos tenían en el desierto; las cuales cavañuelas duraban nuebe días, haciendo gracias a Dios porque eran acogidos todos los frutos de la tierra, y los siete días de los nuebe heran obligados los judíos de comer debaxo de la dicha cavañuela* (Santa María 1893c, 186).

107. *Si ha fetes fer en casa seua barraques de fenoll o altres rames en memoria de les cabanyelles dels Juheus* (Llorca 1935, 16).

108. *En las pascuas de las cabanuelas se yva a casa de judios e entrava en sus cabanuelas e tomava la toronja e la palma en la mano e desya e resava las oraciones que los judyos resan dysyendo, "anna adonay osiana" como los judios fasen* (Levine 1982, 136). Levine identifies the prayer as part of the *Hallel*, derived from Psalms 113–8, which is recited on Passover, Shavuoth, and Sukkot. For a pre-Expulsion example from Molina de Aragón see Cantera Montenegro 1985, 69.

109. Some later *conversos* seemed to have abandoned this custom and treated Sukkot as if it were merely a special Sabbath. Around 1593 Catalina and Manuel Enríquez were accused in Mexico of celebrating Sukkot by praying and refraining from work. There is no reference in her trial to constructing booths (Liebman 1970, 170).

110. *Yua caualgando en vna mula; y que era la vigilia de la . . . Pascua de las Cavañuelas, vna ora antes que anocheçiese, e que lleuaua en la mano vn ramo de salze verde, e que yua rezando e sabadeando; e que tanto vio este testigo que . . . yua enbebeçido en lo que rezaua que este testigo pasó en par dél e que . . . non le vio nin habló. E que así se fue rezando e sabadeando con su ramo en la mano* (Carrete Parrondo 1985a, 36, 48).

111. *Ellos fasen las cabañuelas en las entradas de sus puertas y ronpen un pedaço de tejado* (Beinart 1981a, 295). See also Baer 1966, 2:366.

112. *Tenía los sazes tendidos sobre varas, de pared a pared . . . segund que los judíos suelen hazer las cabañuelas en la dicha su pascua* (Carrete Parrondo 1985a, 50).

113. *Las noches no biene a otra cosa salbo a oyr la oración so color de negociar con don Habrahén, e se nos sube a las cabañuelas a negocar con don Habrahén e a su mesa* (Carrete Parrondo 1986, 36).

114. *Guardaban las Cabañuelas, e ayunavan fasta la noche la estrella salida, e que despues los vio çenar a las noches gallinas e otra carne todos nueve dias de la fiesta de las Cabañuelas* (Beinart 1974, 545; see also 1975, 653).

115. *Comer cenceño / la fiesta de Cabañuelas* (Castillo 1882, #994). This is probably a conflation with Passover.

116. *Algunas vegadas fueron . . . a mirar las cabanillas e allí estaban mirándolas y entraban dentro y la testigo les sacaba colaciones de confites e que esto es verdad.*

117. *Alguna vegada fue a la judería y a ver correr bueyes y mirar las cabanillas y allí alguna vez fizo colación de priscos* (Sánchez Moya 1958, 177, 180). For a similar example see Carrete Parrondo 1985a, 66 [1502].

118. *Fazia cabanillas de ramos y las fazia fazer en su casa, y en caso que en su casa no podiesse, se yua a vna casa de sus parientes y amigos malos xristiano o judíos y allí fazía cabanillas e con otros se congregaua, donde fazía todas las cerimonias que judíos costumbran en tales días fazer, comiendo en aquellas y faziendo collaciones con turado y con otras cosas* (Llorca 1939, 131). See also Fita y Colomé 1884, 402 [1484].

119. *Entraron en cabañuelas de judios solo para verlas* (Beinart 1981b, 606).

120. *Cuando los jodios de Calatayud sacaron por rogarias las Thoras a la calle, pa que lloviese . . . vio estar en una ventana de casa de Pazagon a Simón de Santaclara padre y que cuando los jodios fizieron aquella . . . ceremonia tocando los cuernos, cantando y faziendo plantos, porque lloviese, vio cómo el dicho Santa Clara ploraba mucho y mecía mucho los labios como quien reza tanto como qualquier jodío que rezase e plorase, de los que no cantaban a altas vozes y que dicho Simón, estando amagado dentro de dicha ventana podía mirar las Thoras y toda la ceremonia* (Cabezudo Astraín 1950, 282). In traditional Judaism on the seventh day of Sukkot, *Hoshanna Rabba*, seven circuits of the synagogue are made and willow branches are struck against the reader's lectern as a sign of the renewing powers of nature. In 1484 some Ciudad Real *conversos* were accused of observing Sukkot by "reading night and day in a book, all night, and they did not take their clothes off all that night until the next day" (*Vido como en vna Fiesta de las Cabañuelas de los judios, que el dicho Alonso Gonsales de Teba leya de noche y de dia en vn libro toda la noche, e que nunca se desnudaron aquella noche fasta otro dia*). Beinart considers that this may be a reference to the day of *Hoshanna Rabba* [= Great Rejoicing] (1974, 242).

121. *El sabado vispera del dho domingo mando a este el dho Sebastian Rgz fuesse a traer muchos ramos, y este lo hizo assi, y traxo quatro indios cargados de sahuzes con que enrramaron los corredores y el patio poniendo las messas debaxo del corredor que sale al patio donde se via el çielo y la comida se lleuaua a la messa del aposento del dho Sebastian Rodriguez en el cual estauan las dhas Costança Rgz, Isabel Rodriguez. . . . Ave de la tierra rellena con huevos y tocino. . . . Un Juan Lopez y un hijo de la dha Isabel Rz que se llama Simon sirvieron a la messa y despues de comer huuo musica y vailes y cantaron el dho Anto Lopez y su hermana Leonor Diaz, y un mancebo musico de la Puebla que comio alli que no le sabe el nombre. . . . Despues de auer comido cantaron los cantares de la Yglesia Mayor. . . . Rui Diaz, Hector de Fonseca, y Antonio Diaz Marquez no quisieron comer en la dha messa . . . por auer tocino en la messa y cossas quissadas con manteca* (AGN Vol 271 doc 1, 10a-12a; Vol 276 doc 14, 446a-7a).

122. *Çuco es pascua de las cabanuelas, cae a quatorze alsa XV de la luna de septiembre y dura nueve dias los primeros dos de guardar de premia y el çaguero destos dos llaman çinhatora que quiere dezir alegria, porque en aquel día se acabaron los cinco libros de la lei* (*Ceremonie judeorum*, quoted by López Martínez 1954, 179).

123. Both are of stone and date from the twelfth or thirteenth century, after which date bronze lamps came into use. A lamp made of Pyrenean marble, found in Avignon, is now in the Klagsbald family collection in Jerusalem; another, found in Gerona in 1982, is in private hands (Narkiss 1988).

124. *Celebran la fiesta de las candelillas, y las encienden de una en una hasta diez, y despues las tornan a matar; y reçan oraciones judaycas* (Santa María 1893c, 184). Precisely this text appears in a 1610 Edict of Faith in Cartagena de Indias (Medina 1899b, 26).

125. *Le vido guardar la Pascua . . . de las Candeillas . . . las pascuas ençendian nueue candiles* (Beinart 1974, 58, 54).

126. *Accendendo o candieiro com azeite limpo com seis ou sete torcidas* (Azevedo Mea 1982, 452).
127. *Paschoa das candelilhas . . . Natalhino* (Roth 1931–2, 26).
128. Nidel 1984, 261. Ramon Salas, from Albuquerque, also remembers his family lighting eight *lumenarias* on the days preceding Christmas (Snyder 1992, 19).
129. *El Purín hera día de estrellas, que acostumbraban dar los judíos a los pobres en signifficación de la liberación que el rey Assuero hiço al pueblo de Isrrael que no muriesse a instancia del Mardocheo Nodriço de la reyna Esther; lo qual hiço por conssejo de Amán, como paresce en el libro de la reyna Esther* (Santa María 1893c, 185–6). The reference to stars probably has to do with the lots traditionally cast at Purim.
130. *Puede aber beinte y tres años poco mas o menos que este testigo por medio de su padre fue a leer a ysabel arias . . . la ystoria del rey asuero en forma de megilla que esta escrito como tora* (Carrete Parrondo 1986, 58). See also Gutwirth 1981, 100.
131. Wolf 1926, 63 notes that this prayer is probably from the Apocrypha: The Rest of Esther, xiv, 3–19.
132. *Día de sant Hanan* (Moreno Koch 1977, 365 [1491]). See also Llorca 1942, 133 [1484]. A fourteenth-century stone Purim cup with a Spanish language inscription [*Rei Ahashwerosh i la reina Ester*] in Hebrew letters is in the Cluny Museum in Paris (Narkiss 1988, 13).
133. In the trial of Juan Pacheco in Mexico in 1642 there is a reference to games being played at the end of Purim, but it is unclear whether these were observed in Spain, Mexico, or Italy (Liebman 1970, 269). A trial in Cuenca in the 1480s reports a *converso* who distributed wine to his Jewish relatives on Purim (García Casar 1990, 178).
134. Cohen speculates that crypto-Jews may have transferred to Esther some aspects of the Catholic apotheosis of Mary (1973, 97).
135. The *Shulḥan Arukh* prescribes a one-day fast on the thirteenth of Adar. Flavius Josephus, on the other hand, who was much read by crypto-Jews (see Chapter 15.2), talks of a three-day fast (Lewin 1987, 232–3). Today the Fast of Esther is observed in limited numbers of Jewish communities, among them the Sephardic communities of Morocco and the Levant (Millgram 1971, 285; Dobrinsky 1986, 383, 387).
136. *Facía los tres ayunos de la Reina Ester . . .* (Sánchez Moya 1958, 173).
137. For other examples of the Fast of Esther see Roth 1931–2, 26; Llorca 1939, 133 [1484]; Schwarz 1925, 108; Furtado 1925, xxxii [Evora 1536]; Azevedo Mea 1982, 4 [Portugal 1567–83]; García Fuentes 1981, 98, 434, 469 [1573–95]; Toro 1932, 214 [Mexico 1589]; Liebman 1964, 98 [Mexico 1596]; Lorence 1991, 97 [Coimbra 1615]; Lewin 1977, 23, 41 [Mexico 1642]; Caro Baroja 1961, 1:469 [Madrid 1652]; Selke 1972, 97, 104 [Majorca 1677]; Wiznitzer 1960, 158 [1732]; Lewin 1939, 25 [eighteenth century]; Vasconcelos 1958, 214 and Lipiner 1977, 84–5 [twentieth-century Portugal].
138. *El ayuno de la reina Hester que son tres dias y cae por el mes de septiembre* (García Fuentes 1981, 98).
139. *Ayunan el ayuno de la reyna Ester que llaman el Perdimiento de la cassa sancta, . . . no comiendo en dichos días hasta la noche salida la estrella, y en aquellas noches no comen carne; y un día antes se lavan por los ayunos cortándosse las uñas y puntas de cabellos* (Santa María 1893c, 183). The description seems to confuse the Fast of Esther with the Fast of the ninth of Av, discussed later in this chapter. For a similar description from Mexico see Liebman 1970, 96 [1639].
140. *Y la dixo que los tres ayunos se hacían en tres días contínuos, no comiendo ni bebiendo en todo el día hasta la noche, y porque ésta era muchacha, no ayundaría más de dos, que era el primero y el último. Y a la noche se avía de cenar pescado, si no es la última noche, que la mandó*

*que, sin que su Madre lo supiesse, guissase garbanços con espinacas, cazuela de broçats y garvellones* (Selke de Sánchez 1972, 272).

141. *Mi avuela Maria Sanchez es judia, que esta noche me dixo que holgaua por que era dia de ayuno e le llamaua dia de sant Hanan, e queste dia el que ayunaua non moria aquel año, por que tal dia como aquel se sentaua Dios a la diestra* (Moreno Koch 1977, 365).

142. *Facía los tres ayunos de la Reina Ester y enllas comía buenas gallinas o huevos duros con perexil y que no facían otras cirimonias, salvo ayunar absteniéndose de comer fasta la noche* (Sánchez Moya 1958, 173).

143. For other examples of breaking the Purim fast see Pereira 1979, 189 [1573]; Caro Baroja 1961, 1:469 [1652]; Willemse 29, 101; Adler 1895, 46 [Mexico 1607]; Adler 1899, 16 [Mexico 1645].

144. Beinart 1974, 49. See also Gracia Boix 1983, 132.

145. *Phase:* Santa María 1893c, 186; Toro 1932, 214 [Mexico 1589]. *Pessa:* Lewin 1977, 274 [Mexico 1642].

146. *La pascua del cordero:* Lewin 1977, 22 [Mexico 1642]; Selke de Sánchez 1972, 274 [Majorca, seventeenth century].

147. Festival of the unleavened bread: Santa María 1893c, 186; cf. Beinart 1974, 58; Lewin 1977, 274 [Mexico 1642].

148. Llorca 1939, 121 [1484].

149. Festival of the unleavened bread: Azevedo Mea 1982, 7 [Coimbra 1567].

150. Fast of the fritters: Azevedo Mea 1982, 298, 315, etc. [Coimbra 1573].

151. Festival of the unleavened bread: García 1987, 61 [Valencia, late fifteenth century].

152. *Se debía de guardar la pascua del cordero, que era el primer día de abril* (Lewin 1971, 27, 218).

153. *Desde el Jueves Santo hasta otro jueves siguiente era Pascua de los judíos* (Gracia Boix 1983, 132).

154. *Hum jejum de judeus em huma quarta feira de quaresma, sem comer em todo o dia señao a noute, em companhia de outras muitas pesoas de sua naçam . . . e todas cearam a noute juntas grãos, pescada seca e filhós e se declararão como faziam aquelle jejum daquella maneira por ser da ley dos judeus* (Azevedo Mea 1982, 333). Edwin Berry, who lives near Albuquerque, "recalls his mother making what he says resembled unleavened bread once a year around Lent. It was like a long biscuit, and it was eaten only a few days of the year" (Shapiro 1989, S4).

155. *Hay una pascua que cae antes de la semana santa de los cristianos que llaman del cordero* (Lewin 1977, 46).

156. *Comió del apio e cosas amargas que comen la víspera de la dicha pascua, e del pan çençeño e viandas, que todos [estaban] en casa del dicho judío, e rezó oraçiones judiegas, que sabía rezar* (Carrete Parrondo 1985a, 160).

157. *Se hacía la pascua judía, con panes aliis, muchas luces, candiles, lámparas y había mucha gente* (García 1987, 83–5).

158. Liebman 1970, 170, 195; see also 1975, 190 [Peru 1641].

159. *La pascua de el pan cenceño signiffica y es en memoria de aquellas tortas cotacas que los hijos de Isrrael llevaron encima de los hombros quando passaron el mar bermejo; porque siete días les duró el passar no comieron sino las dichas tortas cotacas; y anssí los dichos judíos no comían en los siete días de las pascuas sino pan cenceño en memoria de los susso dicho, como lo dice el texto de . . . [dejado en blanco]: septem diebus azyma commedetis; que también se llama pascua de el Phase; que Phase quiere decir pascua, como está escripto en Iesué, in principio* (Santa María 1893c, 186). The word *Phase* was used by Judaizers in sixteenth-century Mexico as well. It

appears to be a traditional name for the Passover and not, as Liebman speculates, a word invented to throw Christians off the track (1970, 72).

160. *Por el tinpo de la primavera, en çierto día que señaló y no se acuerda . . . sólo que este año pasado fue el Jueves Santo, se avía de hacer un ayuno que llaman de la Pasqua del Cordero, no comiendo ni bebiendo en todo el día. Y que después de este ayuno se avía de celebrar la pasqua y duraba siete días; y que entonces se mataba un cordero y se asaba entero, con el qual se haçía un combite a todos los Parientes; y los huesos se avían de quemar, lo qual significava sacrifiçio de la ley de Moysén. Y que en estos siete días se havía de comer pan sin lebadura, ni se podía tener lebadura en casa; y que se avían de hacer unas cocas sobre un ladrillo nuevo, y cocerlas al fuego, y éstas se avían de repartir entre los Parientes* (Selke de Sánchez 1972, 274).

161. *Celebran la pascua del pan cenceño, y comiençan a comer en lechugas, appio, o otras verduras. . . . La Pascua del Pan Çençeño . . . las dos primeras noches, en que comen lechugas e apio e çerrajas e vinagre, e otra çerimonia que fasen de maror, que quiere desir amargo, e con çiertas tortillas de pan çençeño pequeñas* (Beinart 1974, 58). See also Santa María 1893c, 183; Sánchez Moya 1958, 170 [1485]; Liebman 1970, 96 [1639]; Llorca 1939, 131 [1484].

162. *Avian vido a la çerera [Leonor González] en casa del dicho su amo, que la ponian a la cabeçera de la mesa e que aquella bendesia el pan çençeño y el vino, e que de aquello comian e beuian todos los que a la mesa estauan* (Beinart 1974, 322).

163. *Fez hum jejum a que os judeus chamão das filhós, sem comer em todo o dia senão a noute em companhia de outras pesoas, declarando se todas como o faziam por ser da dita ley e a noute se ajuntarão a comerão as filhós e beberão vinho* (Azevedo Mea 1982, 359).

164. Toro 1932, 247. For examples of modern Portuguese Judaizing prayers related to Passover see Vasconcelos 1958, 225, 233–4.

165. Lewin 1977, 32. See also Toro 1932, 243 [Mexico 1589].

166. Roth 1931–2, 25. See also Liebman 1970, 68; Nidel 1984, 261 [New Mexico, early twentieth century].

167. *Celebrou huma pascoa de pão asmo na somana de Ramos, fazendo cinco bolos sem formento e hos comera por lhe parecer que era bom pera salvar a alma* (Azevedo Mea 1982, 375; see also 422, etc.). The Christian-like concept of the personal salvation of one's soul is discussed in Chapter 4.

168. *En la Pascua de los judios comio pan çençeño, segund que los judios lo suelen comer, y en toda la dicha Pascua non comia otro pan, e fasiendo con ello otras çerimonias que en la tal Pascua acostunbran faser los judios* (Beinart 1974, 49).

169. *Quem havia de comer pão asmo não podia ter em sua casa, no tempo da páscoa, nenhum pão levedado e tendo-o não guardava a páscoa* (Coelho 1987, 209). See also Baião 1921, 119 [Portugal 1541].

170. *En toda la dicha Pascua non comio saluo en escodillas e platos e ollas e jarros e otras vasijas todo nueuo, segund forma e costunbre de judios. . . . Mercavan barro nuevo para aquella fiesta* (Selke de Sánchez 1972, 274). For the custom of putting out new dishes for Passover see also Llorca 1939, 132 [1484]; Baer 1966, 2:366; Sánchez Moya 1958, 170 [1485]; Rábade Obradó 1990a, 437 [Toledo 1485–1500]; Furtado 1925, xxxii [Evora 1536]; Azevedo Mea 1982, 196, etc. [Coimbra 1567–83]; Liebman 1982, 118 [Mexico].

171. *En vasijas nueuas que non vuiese llegado a elas pan libdo, e si en algunas comya eran de cobre o de palo o de otros metales, y esto seyendo muy bien escaldadas con agua herviendo e despues con fria* (Beinart 1974, 49, 58, 456, etc.). The *Mishnah Torah* prescribes this method of purifying dishes so that they may be used on Passover (Maim., *Yad.* III,5,v,23–6).

172. *E costume em páscoa de ressurreição todos os cristãos-velhos comprarem louça nova, scilicet, panelas e tigelas de fogo e fogareiros para guisarem seus manjares, que na dita páscoa da ressurreição mais que em outra se costumam fazer, porque a louça velha serviu na quaresma em peixe e não serve em carne. E por isso compram a louça nova na dita páscoa comummente todos os cristãos-velhos sem haver nenhum que a deixe de comprar. E por isso se vende somente na somana maior mais louça de barro e de malega juntamente que em seis meses do ano* (Coelho 1987, 209).

173. *Comendo nelles bolos asmos que amaçava numa gamelinha nova e pineirava por pineira nova que não tivesse pineirado outra farinha e punha o ditto pão asmo em toalhas novas, cruas, e no ditto tempo o não comia pão levado* (Azevedo Mea 1982, 434).

174. *En especial a primero de abril, porque decían que era la pascua del cordero que Dios mandaba guardar* (Lewin 1971, 488).

175. Braunstein 1936, 102 relates this to Exodus 13:2, 11.

176. *A costumbrado de guardar e solempnizar la pascua vulgarmente llamada del pan centenyo, comiendo en aquella pan cotazo* (Llorca 1939, 131 [1484]). See also Paulo 1970, 100; Vasconcelos 1958, 212; Llorca 1939, 131 [1484]; Paulo 1970, 100; Vasconcelos 1958, 212; Azevedo Mea 1982, 359.

177. *Comia de vnas tortas blancas como la nieve, desabridas, como olivadas* (Beinart 1977a, 2: 390).

178. Sánchez Moya/Monasterio Astraín 1972–3, [72] 123. For other examples see Llorca 1942, 131 [1484]; Sánchez Moya 1958, 172 [1485]; Carrete Parrondo 1986, 30 [1486].

179. *Escriuya e enbiaua cartas secretamente a sus amigos e onbres sospechosos a nuestra religion christiana e con el mensajero desas tales cartes le enbiauan los tales sospechosos a este religioso pan çençeño, y no sola mente lo comia é, mas avn por faser judaysar e apostatar a otros religiosos les daua sendas reuanadas dello como quien de pan bendito entre christianos* (Moreno Koch 1977, 361).

180. Liebman 1970, 80; see also 148 [Mexico 1646]; García 1910, 76 [1646].

181. *Ella masaba en su casa el pan çençeño en la Quaresma, por la Semana Santa, lo qual yva este testigo a cozer al horno de poya de Diego Gonsales* (Beinart 1974, 483). For similar examples see Beinart 1981b, 565; Fita y Colomé 1892, 486, 513 [1484]; Azevedo Mea 1982, 45, 128, etc. [Coimbra 1568–9]; Sierro Malmierca 1990, 132, 178 [1588, 1623]; Liebman 1975, 88 [Mexico 1642].

182. *El día que las susodichas cocían el pan cenceño que las conbidaba en su casa la dicha muger de Diego Arias e les facía fiesta e comía del pan cenceño. . . . Que muchas pascuas del pan cenceño, quando las judía yban a cocerlo al orno del dicho Diego Arias, que es pared en medio de la dicha su cassa, e quando salían de lo cocer bía este testigo cómo se entraba a merendar con la dicha muger de Diego Arias, las judías lo trahían a cocer y cada una de ellas le dexaba dos o tres tortas de aquellas del pan cenceño; . . . las quales eran sus hermanas y sobrinas* (Carrete Parrondo 1986, 41, 51, 81). For a full treatment of the half-assimilated Arias family, see my *Los Arias Dávila de Segouia, entre la iglsia y la sinagoga* (Bethesda, Md.: International Scholars Press, forthcoming).

183. *Enbió . . . al salyr de la dicha pascua con pan lyudo e vn cabrito e yeruas . . . para con que salyesen de la . . . pascua del Pan Çençeño, e leuadura* (Carrete Parrondo 1985a, 27; cf. 38, 44).

184. *Inbiaba pan leudo y lechugas y berdura a cassa de su padre de este testigo, salida la pasqua del pan cenceño, con una esclaba, la qual esclaba traya una torta de pan cenceño que le daban en cassa de su padre de este testigo* (Carrete Parrondo 1986, 103).

185. Caro Baroja 1961, 1:469. See also Sierro Malmierca 1990, 178 [1623].

186. *Que eran unas torticas de harina, amasadas en un lebrillo nuevo y después tostadas al rescoldo. . . . La daba un pedacito de una de ellas, no consintiendo la tomase en la mano, sino que su mesma madre se la daba en la boca, diciéndole ciertas palabras en remedio de la comunión que dan los sacerdotes* (García 1910, 243–4).
187. *Masar pan çençeño, conviene a saber syn leuadura; y que la masó con vn huevo e le echó aseyte a la . . . masa* (Carrete/Fraile 1987, 109).
188. *Su ama fasía con masa [y] huevos vnas tortillas redondas, con pimienta e miel e aseyte, e las cozía en el forno; e quésto fasía la Semana santa* (Carrete/Fraile 1987, 32).
189. *Masaron otras tortas aparte, de otra masa syn leuadura e amasada con vino blanco e miel e clauos e pimienta, e que fasían e masauan dellas fasta veynte . . . y que las guardauan con los rollilos en su arca* (Carrete/Fraile 1987, 35).
190. *Comendo nelle castanhas cozidas em lugaur do pão asmo* (Azevedo Mea 1982, 26; 186 etc.).
191. *Por no haber pan cenceño comía tortillas de maiz, por no tener levadura* (Toro 1932, 243). See also Cohen 1973, 134; Liebman 1970, 73.
192. *Fallo debaxo de vna cama vna çesta enbueltas en vnas tobajas syete o ocho tartas de pan çençeño; era Quaresma* (Beinart 1974, 325).
193. *El pa alís . . . calia amagar-lo i guardar-lo de les criades de ma casa* (García 1987, 61).
194. *Que desenboluiendo çiertas escripturas e papeles de la mesa donde tiene su escriptorio el dicho Juan Ramires, vio este testigo como se le cayo en el suelo vna ostia que estaua entre los dichos papeles; la qual dicha ostia ni era tan grande como las que consgra el saçerdote ni tan pequeña como las que dan quando comulgan, syno que era vna ostia mediana redonda. E que quando cayo la dicha ostia le paresçio a este testigo que se turbo algo el dicho Juan Ramires; e dixo el dicho Juan Ramires a los que pesentes stauan: Mirad, no la pises, que la tenia para tomar vnas pildoras* (Beinart 1981b, 67; 105).
195. *Asaron unas tortas de pan, estendidas y muy blancas y descoloridas, que entiende no tenían lebadura, asándolas en las brasas de la chimenea, y que en todo los días de la Semana Santa, quando comían, se daban unas a otras por debajo de las mesas pedaços del, recatándose de la que testifica, y a lo que paresçía procurando comerlo sin que se hechase de ver, que en todos los días de Pascua de Resurrecçión, lo vio comer a las dichas, de la mesma manera, aunque ponían en la mesa del pan ordinario* (Sierro Malmierca 1990, 113–4).
196. *Um cordeiro de um ano, branco, sem malha, por páscoa de pão asmo* (Coelho 1987, 208).
197. *Lo han de asar entero y lo han de comer en pie, sin lastimar ningún hueso al cordero* (Lewin 1977, 32). See also Roth 1931–2, 24; Braunstein 1936, 103 [Majorca seventeenth century]; Liebman 1970, 69.
198. *La Pascua, que se guardaba en aquella Ley de Moisés, en memoria de cuando Dios sacó de Egipto a los hijos de Israel, y los pasó por el desierto a la tierra de promisión, la cual Pascua duraba siete días, en los cuales se había de comer pan cenceño sin levadura, y también en la dicha pascua tomar un cordero pequeño y blanco y degollarlo, y con la sangre untar los umbrales de las puertas: porque así Dios lo había mandado hacer a los hijos de Israel cuando los sacó de Egipto, y así muerto lo habían de asar entero, sin quebarle ningun hueso, y comerlo en pie como quien está para caminar, sin que quedase nada, teniendo báculos en las manos y ceñidos por las cinturas, que se habia de comer de manera que no sobrase nada, y si acaso sobrase darlo a un vecino, y ansí mesmo se habia de comer el dicho cordero con lechugas amargas, y con el pan cenceño, en la cual pascua que llamaban del Phase, que quiere decir la pasada, y duraba siete dias, se habian de guardar como fiesta, el primero y ultimo día de ella, y el cordero se había de matar y comer la víspera del primero día de ella en la noche* (Toro 1932, 243).

199. *El qual dicho pan hazia en su casa la dicha Eluira Gonçales . . . e lo cozio en vn horno de la puerta dentro en su casa y lo comian todos los dias de pascua, que diz que son siete o ocho dias, y lo comian con verdura la primera noche, con apio o peregil e con otras verduras que no se acuerda bien* (Beinart 1981b, 565).

200. *Numa Paschoa não comeu carne nem nas oitavas e fizera pão asmo* (Baião 1921, 119).

201. Azevedo Mea 1982, 11, 248, 333, etc. Anne Cardoza reports that her Catalonian grandmother, Pauline, who has been cited previously in this study, on the Passover would eat "lentils, honey cakes, and greens, no meat, sometimes fish, vegetables and grains." She said her grandmother would make *matza* "by mixing water and rye flour or chickpea flour, kneading it, and throwing it into the fire or oven" (Cardoza 1989, S2).

202. *Feijão branco e castanha* (Vasconcelos 1958, 222).

203. Vasconcelos 1958, 222. See also Canelo 1987, 106.

204. *Bendito Tu, Adonai, nosso Rei, Deus de todas as coisas e de todo o mundo, que nos santificaste nas santas encomendanças, benditas e santas, e bendito que nos deste vida para chegarmos a este tempo e para observarmos os Teus divinos e santos preceitos, tomando o pão por preceito. Fazei-nos Senhor, chegar a Sion com paz e alegria. Amém.*

205. *A honra e louvor dos nomes santos do Senhor! Em lembrança dos nossos irmãos, quando sairam do Egipto e entraram na terra de Santa Promissão. Amém* (Paulo 1970, 101). See also Tradições 1932, 7.51:3.

206. *Catorze da lua / primeiro mês do ano, / parte o povo do Egipto / com Israel seu irmano. / Cantigas que vão cantando / ao Senhor vão louvando. / Adonde nos trazes, Moisés? / Aqui neste povoado, / adonde não há pau nem lenha / nem menos pastos nem gado? / Etc.* (Vasconcelos 1958, 212–3; Paulo 1985, 94–6).

207. *Cantemos hoje ao Senhor, / Deus de glória e singular, / que o cavalo e o cavaleiro / lançou no profundo mar. / Etc.* (Vasconcelos 1958, 185–8). For other versions see 211; Paulo 1981, 146; 1970, 100; Schwarz 1925, 72–5.

208. *Louvemos e engrandeçamos / ao alto Deus de Abraão, / que nos livre do mar largo, / nos leve à Terra da Promissão* (Paulo 1985, 150). For additional Passover picnic songs see Paulo 1970, 102; Machado 1952, 39–40; Vasconcelos 1958, 214; Nidel 1984, 251. Anne Cardoza reports that her grandmother also celebrated the Passover with outdoor picnics (Cardoza 1989, S2).

209. *Louvemos e engrandeçamos ao Alto Deus de Abraão, / que nos livre do mar largo, / nos leve á terra da Promissão. . . . O mar se abriu, o povo passou. / Deus de Israel o mandou. . . . Louvemos e engrandeçamos ao Alto Deus de Israel, / que nos livrou do mar largo e daquele rio tão cruel* (Machado 1952, 40).

210. *La vem Moisés com a sua vara alçada a bater no mar selado* (Schwarz 1925, 33–5). The full text of this prayer and the song are given in the appendix to Schwarz 1925, 72–5. See also Paulo 1985, 150. Some Moroccan Sephardis go out into their fields on the seventh day of Passover to bless the fruit trees (*birkat ha'ilanot*) (Dobrinsky, *Treasury*, 263–4).

211. *La Pascua de Çinquesma, que llaman ellos de Dada de la Ley* (Beinart 1974, 58). A 1403 Valencian document calls it *Pasua de Cinquagesima* (Hinojosa Montalvo 1993, 115).

212. *Del quebramiento de las tablas de la ley* (Sierro Malmierca 1990, 131).

213. *Pascua de las primicias* (Liebman 1970, 67). See also Cohen 1973, 20.

214. *Degedelias y por el cerco de Jerusalén* (Sierro Malmierca 1990, 131).

215. *Quándo era el ayuno que los judíos llaman tisabaf, que es quando se perdió la casa santa?* (León Tello 1972, 80). In Molina de Aragón c. 1471 the holiday was called the Fast of the Holy Temple (*el ayuno de la Casa Santa*) (Cantera Montenegro 1985, 68). See also Beinart 1961, 179; Liebman 1970, 96 [1639].

216. *De la destruición del templo dos vezes* (Sierro Malmierca 1990, 131). María Alvarez, of Guadalajara, in the 1490s called it the "bitter fast" (*el ayuno amargo*) (Cantera/Carrete 1975, 148).
217. *Ayunava el dia del ayuno amargo de los judios* (Levine 1982, 103).
218. *Comyaã no chão na uespera do dia em que elles perderão Jerusalem* (Baião 1921, 110).
219. *A la luna la respetaban haciéndole tres ayunos, especialmente quando era nueva* (Sierro Malmierca 1990, 178).
220. Liebman calls it *Conjunctions de Lunas* (1974, 100). See also García 1910, 101.
221. *Adorase la luna nueva, parada a la ventana, haciéndola reverencias, como lo hacía su tío* (García 1910, 219).
222. Liebman feels that the Inquisition transcriber, Bacanegra, raises this idea out of proportion, observing that the New Moon festival is only observed by the very most orthodox Jews and that its observance does not traditionally include fasting (1974, 158). This prayer for the new moon was found in the Mogadouro region of Portugal in this century: "May the Lord bless the moon and me, who are his creations. As the moon is yours in the heavens, may I be yours on earth. As I can see you and not touch you [gesture with the hands toward the moon], may my enemies not be able to do me ill" (*Benza Deus a lua e a mim, que sou criatura. Assim como tu és lua no Céu e eu criatura na terra, assim como te vejo e não te posso alcançar (gesto com a mão para alcançar a lua), os meus inimigos me não possam fazer mal*) (Machado 1952, 37). See also Paulo 1985, 78, 102; Vasconcelos 1958, 185. Rabbi Jacob Hurwitz has suggested to me that this prayer is reminiscent of the traditional *Birkat Ha-levana*. Another curious new moon custom was recorded in New Mexico in 1980, when Clemente Carmona, who considers himself a descendant of crypto-Jews, said that his sister-in-law "at the beginning of each month puts grass and new coins on the [family] altar" (Nidel 1984, 259).
223. *O jejum que os judeus chamão dos bredos* (Azevedo Mea 1982, 204, 355).
224. *Huma pesoa de sua naçam lhe ensinar que fizese hum jejum de quarenta, que he em quarenta somanas hum jejum em cada huma dellas a honra do profeta Helias que jejuara quarenta dias* (Azevedo Mea 1982, 361).
225. Cohen 1973, 134. See also Liebman 1970, 72; Toro 1932, 214, 226 [Mexico 1589].
226. *Ayunaba . . . a cuatro de septiembre, porque decían que era el día en que había muerto Moises* (Lewin 1971, 33).
227. *Por el mes de Julio también se avía de hacer un ayuno, que se llama de las lantejas, que le parece era en memoria de Saul que vendió su Mayorazgo a Jacob por una escudilla de lentejas, y también a la noche se avían de guisar lantejas para cenar, y en ellas se coçian huevos con cáscara hasta que estuviessen duros, y los cenaban demás de pescado, y lo demás que tenían* (Selke de Sánchez 1972, 273).
228. *Vos, Senhor, que criastes os ceos e a terra e apartastes o dia da noute lembrai vos de mym e recebey este jejum em Voso santo serviço* (Azevedo Mea 1982, 298).
229. *Senhor, diante de Vos vengo em ajuno e não de pecado em dia de mio juno vos llamo, que recebais minha grande affeição e consoleis meu coração com a vinda de David e com a vinda de Mecea David* (Azevedo Mea 1981, 164).
230. *Bendito seja o nome do Senhor que te criou, e me queira levar este jejum en conta dos meus pecados* (da Cunha e Freitas 1952, 18). A longer version of this prayer appears in the trial as well.
231. *Quando la casa estava en fiesta la vez que pecava ayunava y sacava su sangre y su sebo delante de su acatamiento y perdonavales su pecado. Asi, señor, este mi ayuno, mi sebo sea poco mi sangre sea mengue rreçibillo, señor, delante vuestra acatamiento y perdoname mi pecado* (Bláz-

quez Miguel 1988, 76). Millgram points out that the affliction of one's soul through fasting was "regarded by the rabbis as a personal sacrifice, an offering of one's 'blood and fat' upon the altar [Ber. 17a]" (1971, 361).

232. *Dios que el alma me disteis, pura y limpia como el sol tu la criasteis y formasteis, para que te de honor. Miembrame por Abraham, su obediencia y temor sacrifico a su hijo por obedecerte, señor. Luego, con furia y grandeza el brazo de tu temor desata la que esta atada, recibe nuestra oración* (Blázquez Miguel 1988, 77). Rabbi Jacob Hurwitz has suggested to me that this prayer is reminiscent of the priliminary prayer of the morning service.

233. *Bendita la luz del dia y el señor que nos la embia nos de paz y alegria y salvaçion para el alma y remedios para la vida* (Blázquez Miguel 1988, 76). This prayer was recited after fasting, and before eating, as the family looked at the sky through a window.

234. *Este ayuno que oi hes hecho gran Dios de Isrrael a mi vida os ofrezco, Señor, porque me libreis de carzeles, prisiones y cosas malas deste mundo. Amen. Vendito seais Señor de Isrrael. Amen* (Blázquez Miguel 1988, 254).

235. *Deante de vós, Senhor, venho em jejum nanja por falta de pão, nem de nada, minhas carnes enfrequeci e meu sangue escrito no Ceu, eu esperando pela vossa divina benção, Adonai, Amen. Meu Deus, me dai auxilio para vos fazer este dia de preces em nome do Senhor, Adonai. Amen* (*Tradições* 1928, 2.10:5; cf. 1928, 2.11:8).

236. *Bendito e louvado seja o meu Deus de Adonai que nos encomendou e recomendou que desconjurássemos o demónio e toda a parte infernal. Licença, Senhor, Deus de Israel, Te peço para o fazer este dia de hoje que Te ofereço tudo quanto nele obrar; espero que seja oferta capaz de apresentar na Vossa divina presença e seja para bem da minha alma para que viva e morro no Vosso santo serviço. Amém* (Paulo 1985, 80). For additional prayers relating to fasting, see Azevedo Mea 1981, 164 (1580s); Schwarz 1925, 71–2.

237. *Os quaes fez em companhia de outras pesoas, declarando se todas que os faziam por serem da lei dos judeus* (Azevedo Mea 1982, 326; cf. 309, 312, etc.).

238. Mondays and Thursdays (Ollero Pina 1988, 102 [Andalucia 1482]); Mondays, Thursdays, and Saturdays (Carrete Parrondo 1985a, 52 [Atienza 1491]); Tuesdays and Fridays (García de Proodian 1966, 418 [Lima 1636]). A witness told Inquisitors in Mexico in 1665 that María de Zárate fasted on Sundays and Wednesdays, and sometimes on Mondays as well (Lewin 1971, 469, 488).

239. *Todas las susodichas ayunavan algunos ayunos de judios dos dias en la semana, que cree que heran el lunes y el viernes o el jueves, e que cada vna ayunava en su casa e çenava. E que despues que avian çenado, se venian a juntar a la dicha casa de la dicha muger de Diego de Teva, e alli, estando juntas, platicavan y se dezian vnas a otras como avian ayunado e lo que avian çenado* (Beinart 1977a, 390).

240. *Jejuns de segundas e quintas feiras a que os judeus chamam Tannis, sem comer em todo o dia senam a noite* (Azevedo Mea 1982, 78; 205, 254, etc.).

241. *Eram jejuns das segundas e quintas-feiras que se haviam de jejuar sem comer senão à noite* (Pereira 1979, 189).

242. Wiznitzer 1960, 13; cf. 17, 161. For other examples of weekday fasting see Lipiner 1977, 92 [Brazil]; Melammed 1992, 165 [Castile 1590]; García Fuentes 1981, 434 [1593]; Willemse 1974, lviii; Adler 1895, 46 [Mexico 1607] and 1899, 15 [Mexico 1645]; Cortes 1985, 287 [1670s]; Selke de Sánchez 1972, 103 [Majorca 1677]; Roth 1931–2, 27.

243. *Hasta la noche con mas de una hora despues de auer anochecido, que come cossas guisadas por su mano como son pescado, garuanços, huebos y otras legumbres todo guissado con azeyte porque jamas guissa con manteca, y el desir que no come en todo el dia lo colige por ser que se sale temprano de cassa con su petaca a vender, y se viene a medio dia a la calle de*

*Sto Domingo a donde ha entrado algunas vezes a la tienda deste testigo y pedido de comer por un indio que trae, con la petaca, y convidandole a comer al dho Ruy Diaz no lo quiso aceptar, diziendo, que el almorzaua por la mañana y que no voluia a comer hasta la noche* (AGN Vol 276 doc 14, 415a).

244. For example, *fazia jejuns sem comer em todo o dia senam a noite* (Azevedo Mea 1982, 1, 2, 3, etc.).

245. *Que el ayuno había de ser de veinte y cuatro en veinte y cuatro horas* (Gracia Boix 1983, 138).

246. *Vnas hazian mas ayunos que no otras, e que este confesante, porque estava sienpre preñada o parida, ayunava pocas vezes* (Beinart 1977a, 390). See also Liebman 1982, 100 [Mexico].

247. *Le dixeron a esta rea que ayunase sin comer en todo el dia, pero que ella se escuso porque estava preñada* (García Fuentes 1981, 454).

248. *Com sua doença nam podia jejuar. . . . Jejou alguns annos os tres dias de jejum da Rainha Esther, sem comer em todo o dia senam a noite e por ser fraca num jejuava mais que o primeiro dia* (Azevedo Mea 1982, 34, 35; cf. 62, 224, etc.).

249. *Jejou os tres dias do jejum da Rainha Esther e por ser fraqua e os nam poder jejuar areyo os jejuou interpolados* (Azevedo Mea 1982, 92).

250. *Era observante de la Ley de Moisés, aunque no ayunaba porque era achacoso* (Lewin 1977, 201).

251. *Es verdad que se huio por hauer quebrantado vn ayuno que le mando hazer su padre, no pudiendo çufrir la hambre. Y que a quien pidio chocolate fue a su hermana Antonia* (Nunemaker 1946, 45).

252. *Se había de bañar por la noche, y venidos a casa se pusieron ropa limpia en personas y mesa, y cenaron juevos en agua y pescado con aceite y vinagre* (Lewin 1954, 142).

253. *Que los ayunos habian de ser con aflixiones corporales, como lo manda Dios en el Deuteronomio, y las aflixiones eran cilicios, dormir en el suelo, no comer carne, ni comer en todo el dia hasta la noche, salida la estrella* (Medina 1899a, 185).

254. *Entonces cenaba fruta y pescado y güevos y otras comidas de viernes* (García de Proodian 1966, 418).

255. *Le vió algunas veces en la mesa que hacía que comía, y luego sacaba el bocado que tenía en la boca y lo echaba todo bajo la mesa, a donde después veía la comida* (Toro 1932, 225–6).

256. *Que por la Cuaresma su amo había hecho el ayuno por no ser descubierto* (Contreras 1982, 601).

257. *Os tais dias de carne a Re tinha em seu aposento e a não comia, antes por aõ ser sintida nem descuberta em seu judaismo, uzava de invenções e dissimulações exquisitas, escondendo a dita carne e deitando a em parte onde não podesse ser achada como era nas agoas sujas e em outras partes* (Azevedo Mea 1982, 430).

258. *Se paseó aquel día por esta ciudad, para disimular el hambre* (Lewin 1977, 91).

259. *Por no beber chocolate por la mañana, encarecía mucho el gasto que tenía y que los empobrecía* (García 1910, 107).

260. *Su mujer doña Juana Enríquez, ella y su marido Simón Váez, fingían una riña cuidadosa para no comer aquel día y que los criados y esclavos no conociesen que ayunaban, sino que no comían por estar enojados* (Lewin 1977, 45). See also García 1910, 197.

261. *Por disimular los ayunos, fingían padre e hijo riñas, y el hijo, fingiendo temor, se salía de su casa, y el padre, haciendo del que le iba a buscar a caballo, se iba a los alrededores desta ciudad hacia las huertas* (García 1910, 110)).

262. *Estándose sin comer todo el día con achaque de que tenía jaqueca, y que para esto guardaba los huevos que le daban, para cenar de noche* (Lewin 1977, 118).

263. *Ayunando los miércoles con ocasión del escapulario del Carmen, para más disimularse* (García 1910, 69).
264. *En los días de ayuno, por disimularse, se iba . . . a la plaza y patio del convento de Santiago con otros judaizantes* (García 1910, 115).
265. *Mandou jejuar outros jejuns de judeus da somana e dava esmola a que lhos jejuava* (Azevedo Mea 1982, 185; cf. 252, 292, etc.).
266. *Le havia dicho que él tampoco hacia los ayunos sino que dava limosnas a otras personas para que los hiziesen por él y su familia* (Lera García 1987, 94).
267. *Não comese senão a noute porque quanto mais quebrantase a carne, mais merito avia diante de Deos* (Azevedo Mea 1982, 295, 326).
268. *Jejuava pella semana quando queria fazer algua rogativa a Deos* (Azevedo Mea 1982, 294).
269. *Cuando el Concilio de Trento estaba para acabarse, había ayunado su madre cuarenta días sin comer hasta la noche y traía silencio y rezaba muchas devociones porque se determinase en él, que todos los cristianos guardasen la ley de Moisés y alabasen a Dios y no a Jesucristo porque vivían engañados y para el mismo efecto le había hecho ayunar a ella* (Gracia Boix 1983, 133).
270. *Cuando se vió en agonías y trabanos, ayunó por sí e hizo ayunar a otras personas los ayunos de la Ley Vieja, por los cuales fuere librado de penar* (Gracia Boix 1983, 3).
271. *Teniendo algunas criaturas para se morir, le dixo una judía que se llamaba Zahara que si dayunaba los dayunos que los judíos tienen, luego Dios les daría salud a las dichas sus criaturas, y que dayunó cuatro años, un día que los judíos dayunan en el mes de septiembre* (Sánchez Moya 1966, 276).
272. *Se llegó a su cama el dicho Juan de León un día por la mañana y le dijo que aquel día ayunaba por su salud, y que en nombre de ella había dicho a cierta persona que ayunase por el mismo fin, lo cual sintió la dicha persona, porque no quería que supiese la tal persona que ella guardaba la Ley de Moisés* (Lewin 1977, 236). For other examples of fasting to effect a cure see Roth 1931–2, 7; Llorca 1942, 149 [1484]; Carrete Parrondo 1985a, 158 [1489]; Blázquez Miguel 1987, 45 [1489]; Baião 1921, 182 [1559]; Azevedo Mea 1982, 254, 303 [Coimbra 1571–3]; Wiznitzer 1960, 18 [Brazil].
273. *Lhe aconselhara a que praticasse o jejum dos judeus para ser solto* (Baião 1921, 174). See also Ollero Pina 1988, 104 [Andalucia 1482]; Fita y Colomé 1892, 513 [1483]; Azevedo Mea 1982, 296, 327 [Coimbra 1571–3].
274. *Que practiasse o jejum da rainha Esther para Deus livrar sua irmã, Beatriz Aires, das garras Inquisitoriaes* (Baião 1921, 224).
275. Lewin 1971, 27. Echoing the well-known traditional Spanish ballad of "Princess Jimena's complaint," Zárate also swore not to sleep between sheets until her husband was freed.
276. *Era sumamente ayunadora y para ellos recebía limosnas, tasándose entre los judíos la de cada ayuno en un real de a ocho* (García 1910, 61).
277. *Le dio a su abuela de este confessante d. Blanca Mendez de Reuiera algunos pesos q. le parece serian dies para q hiciesse ella y sus hijas otros tantos auinos de la dha ley por el alma de la dha d. Blanca Enriquez la qual dexo como quinientos pos a la dha d. Beatriz porq. se repartiessen entre obserbantes de la dha Ley para que ayunassen por la dha d. Blanca. . . . Los hizo entre diferentes miercoles porq en tales dias se hazen por los difuntos* (AGN Vol 402 doc 2, 517a).
278. *El repartirlos con sus vestidos y ropa blanca entre judaizantes, para que ayunasen por su alma* (García 1910, 207). See also Adler 1899, 15 [Mexico 1645]; Liebman 1974, 144 [Mexico 1649].
279. *Cuando se ayuna por algún difunto de la dicha Ley se come lo primero cuando se cena a la noche una sopa de pan mojado en agua y sal* (Lewin 1977, 21, 46, 237).

280. *Jejuns judaicos . . . como no das perdoanças e da Rainha Ester, como eram melhores que os jejuns dos cristãos e que os faziam por salvaçao da alma* (Pereira 1979, 193). See also Azevedo Mea 1982, 295, etc. [Coimbra 1567–83; Furtado 1925, 75 [1591].

281. *En casa de Simón Váez había la mejor orden para hacer los súchiles, . . . se juntaban todos, y la madre e hijas y yernos y nietos, y todos los de su linaje de Simón Váez y de la mujer, y que lo hacíamos con el mayor secreto y recato del mundo, nos juntábamos todos allí en la sala y en una merienda, con mucho disimulo, que aunque entrara alguna persona de fuera no lo podía echar de ver, porque nos entendíamos todos por señas* (Lewin 1975, 84, 70, 76, 89, 166).

282. *Sea como se debe, bañándonos, poniéndonos muy bien con él, con ropa limpia y luz encendida la noche, haciéndole alguna oración y estando de rodillas, como tú me has dicho, todo lo que se pueda y como se debe hacer. Y León le dijo: así se hará, y advierte que de rodillas cruzadas, es como se hace* (Lewin 1975, 143).

# CHAPTER XIV 🌱

# Books

Most educated male Jews in fourteenth- and fifteenth-century Iberia knew Hebrew sufficiently well to be able to pray the liturgy and to read the Torah. Extensive private libraries of religious, philosophical, and medical books in Hebrew were common and large numbers of Iberian Jews were able to speak and write the language with ease.[1] On the whole, pre-Expulsion *conversos* had access to these intellectual resources. First generation converts, of course, brought into their new lives whatever Jewish education they had had prior to their conversion. Moreover, up until the establishment of the Inquisition some *converso* children continued to receive a Hebrew education in the schools maintained by the Jewish community. At first many new-Christians continued to keep Hebrew Bibles or prayer books in their homes. A typical example was the *converso* Juan Díaz, who in the 1460s in Ciudad Real allegedly read "every Saturday in a Bible and other books as large as the Bible."[2]

Traditionally, by far the most important Jewish religious books were the Torah (the first five books of the Bible, often called the Five Books of Moses, the Pentateuch, or simply the Five [Ḥumash]), and the entire Old Testament, followed closely by the Talmud (ancient compilation of Jewish oral law) and then the Hebrew prayer book, or *siddur*. Before the Expulsion each Jewish community in Iberia possessed a number of Torahs, which might be brought out in procession and paid homage on public ceremonial occasions just as the Christian community would parade the crucifix.[3] The Talmud was a particular target of medieval churchmen for its alleged blasphemous references to Mary and Jesus.

The Talmud and other Jewish books were burned publicly on several occasions in France in the thirteenth century.[4] While public book burnings were not common in medieval Spain, in 1263 Jaime I of Aragon did order the Jews of his kingdom to delete references to Mary and Jesus from their copies of the Talmud or else have them burned (*Enc. Jud.* 15:769). And in the cataclysmic events of the Expulsion itself many Jewish books were burned. For example, in 1501 Antonio Triguero reported to the Soria Inquisition that at the time when the Jews were returning from Portugal they burned Torahs in the plaza of Coruña del Conde, and Martín García was heard to say: "Oh, how much good Law is burning today!"[5]

Within a very few years after the Expulsion Hebrew books had all but disappeared and knowledge of Hebrew among the Judaizing converts had dwindled to almost nothing. I have found no references after 1480 to *conversos* possessing a copy of the Talmud, although in 1490 the *converso* Luis Sánchez, the master of the household of the King of Aragon, was accused of "being a great Talmudist and of teaching the Talmud to other people."[6] In sixteenth-century Spain, struggling internally to control its *converso* heretics and its mystics and at war externally with the schismatic Protestant movement, not only Hebrew books were considered dangerous; the sixteenth century's religious conflicts and exploding access to information meant that all books touching on religion were potentially subversive. In this atmosphere the relative paucity of Jewish religious books in the hands of *conversos* is not surprising.[7]

Nonetheless, as we will see in this chapter, some Jewish books were retained—at great risk—and treasured by the crypto-Jewish communities. When they could not find key traditional Jewish books, crypto-Jews reconstructed them as best they could from the segments of traditional Hebrew literature which had been translated into Latin to serve as Christian holy books. And when these too proved difficult to obtain crypto-Jews were innovative in finding material from other sources to serve their religious needs.

## 14.1. The Bible

Spanish *conversos* before 1492 were able to read—or listen to—the Torah in the synagogues of their Jewish friends, although once the Inquisition began its work they incurred substantial risks in doing so. In 1488 the Jew Michel de Bonaboya, of Zaragoza, used to read the Bible in Hebrew to *conversos* of that city, including the vice chancellor Alonso de la Cavallería, and he bragged that "they enjoy listening to me and learning about many things from me, because they know that I do it very well."[8] Fernando de Madrid was accused in 1491 of "going to the homes of the Jews and begging them to read him from the Prophets, which they did."[9] The people who denounced these *conversos* often took note of the special reverence they showed to the Jewish written word. In 1492 it was reported that the distinguished Aragonese *converso* Jaime de la Cavallería used to kiss the Torah with his lips and touch it with his eyes when he went into the synagogue to pray with the Jews.[10] Antonia Astoriano [Aranda de Duero 1502] testified that, when the Duke and Duchess of Albuquerque were married around 1490 and the Jews took out the Torah to welcome the duchess, the *converso* Diego de Palencia behaved like a Jew when he "bowed to the Torah and told everyone to bow to it, because it was our Law."[11] María Alonso of Huete [Cuenca 1491] used to "cause cloth to be spread out at the door of her house, when the Torahs were to pass by."[12] In the decades before the Expulsion wealthy *conversos* such as Segovia's Arias Dávila family might purchase a Torah for their local synagogue or donate a cloth cover or metal adornment for the Torah scrolls.[13] In private, and sometimes in public, crypto-Jewish *conversos* lamented having been deprived of the consolation offered by their familiar religious texts. Marina Martín [Almazán 1505] told how when she went to Aldonza Laínez's house to spin she frequently heard Aldonza curse the people who had banned the Torah, as she sighed and lamented "Ah, Old Testament, ah, Old Testament."[14]

For a short while after the establishment of the Inquisition, some members of the Judaizing *converso* community continued to keep a Hebrew-language Old Testament, or some portion of it, in their homes. For that matter, even for a decade or two after the Expulsion some crypto-Jews secreted their Hebrew books in their homes. Juan Ramírez [Ciudad Real 1512] allegedly retained "a big book, which he first said was covered with parchment and later said with colored paper, in which they read Jewish prayers, and the book was the size of a full parchment page. . . . It was a big book, the size of a Bible."[15] During those years many of Ciudad Real's *conversos* continued to keep Jewish books in their homes, until finally the books were rounded up and brought to the home of Juan de Arévalo, a member of the Town Council (Beinart 1977b, 87, 90). Some Torahs bedecked with silver bells were observed in the home of Francisco Laínez [Almazán 1505],[16] and another witness reported that when the Inquisitors came to Almazán, Rodrigo Díaz Laínez threw his Torah into the well in the patio of his house.[17] From time to time caches of these books turned up unexpectedly. For example, a man named Suero reported [Soria 1501] that when he was repairing the house of Juan de Salcedo he broke through a wall and discovered

> some documents written on parchment in Jewish letters, wrapped in another clean parchment. . . . He asked Salcedo what he would give him to return to him the Jewish documents he had found in his house . . . and Salcedo begged him to show them to him. The witness showed him, but did not let him take them in his hands, but rather kept them in his own hands. Salcedo . . . read a little and said that they were of Moses [e.g., a Torah], and that he wanted to take them to burn them in an oven that he had in his house. The witness did not let him, but instead took them to his own house and burned them.[18]

Since Hebrew books were difficult to buy on the open market, some bilingual *conversos* dedicated themselves to copying and translating books. Shortly prior to the Expulsion the *converso* Francisco Castellano confessed in Toledo that "I copied a book of prayers of the Law of Moses into Spanish, and another book of Sancho de la Caua, in which book I read sometimes . . . and I gave these books and some others to a Jew some days ago, and later I told him to burn them." Diego López was another new-Christian copyist, testifying that once "I copied a book of some twenty pages of the Law of Moses for a lady."[19]

After the Expulsions, unauthorized possession of a Hebrew book was considered prima facie evidence of serious Judaizing. For some careers with a rich professional literature exclusively in Hebrew this caused problems. In 1497 in Portugal an exemption to the ban on Hebrew books was granted to *converso* physicians who were as yet unable to read medical texts in Latin (Pimenta 1987, 36). But the ordinary Judaizing *converso*'s concern was not with science but with religion. Because the possession of books in Hebrew was exceedingly dangerous, Judaizing *conversos* turned increasingly to Christian books from which they could glean a real or surmised Jewish content. The most important of these Christian books, of course, was the Latin Vulgate version of the Bible. *Conversos* derived the bulk of their knowledge about Jewish practices from their reading of the Latin Old Testament and, as we will see in Chapter 15, they adopted portions of it, most notably the Psalms, for their liturgical uses. The polylingual spiritual leaders of the Expulsion generation were easily able to make these Latin materials accessible to their *converso* colleagues. For example, the same Luis Sánchez of the Aragonese king's household who was accused of being a Talmudist was also accused of reading "in Latin the Jewish Bible, and then speaking it aloud in Spanish."[20] Even a century later in Pernambuco the *cristão novo* school teacher Bento Teixeira used to gather women together on Saturdays to read to them from the Bible in Latin and in translation.[21] His contemporary Francisco Lopes also used to read to his friends from the Old Testament in Portuguese passages dealing with Moses' prayers and the ten plagues.[22]

"In translation" meant in the vulgar language, in this case Portuguese. As the religious conflicts of the sixteenth century intensified, the Church was increasingly reticent to make the Bible in the vulgar languages accessible to common people, who might interpret it in heretical ways. From 1502 on a license was required to publish any book in Spain. Beginning in 1547, the Inquisition in Spain periodically published lists of prohibited books.[23] From the very first these lists included translations of the Bible into the vernacular languages, as well as the works of Erasmus, foreign philosophers, and in fact an astoundingly wide range of materials.[24] Publication, sale, or even possession of forbidden volumes could result in imprisonment and death. Despite this pressure, *conversos* at least until the mid-1500s often possessed Old Testaments in translation. It is fairly common to find data about people like Alfonso de Toledo, a Jeronymite monk of Sisla, who was tried in 1487 for striving "to read the Bible as much as possible in the Spanish translation" (Beinart 1961, 176; also Baer 1966, 2:349), or the *converso* Master Gil Vaz Bugalho, who was denounced in Lisbon in 1538 for possessing a translated Bible.[25]

## 14.2. BIBLE SUBSTITUTES

When even these books were denied to them, Judaizing new-Christians relied on other methods for communing with the Old Testament wellsprings of their religious beliefs. Detractors noted their enthusiasm for Old Testament stories in church sermons. Antonio Méndez [Mexico 1603] was alleged "to be especially fond of those sermons which quoted liberally from the Old Testament, and to have praised the preacher who quoted them. He did not admire them as prefigurations of other passages of the Gospels, as was the intent of the preachers, but for themselves alone, as stories."[26] Or they talked among themselves about the Old Testament whenever they had the chance. Izabel da Gama, of Elvas, denounced her husband Henrique Lopes in 1552 for "preaching to her at night about the Bible and about Jewish things."[27] In Pernambuco Antonio Mendes used to enjoy telling Old Testament stories to his family on Saturday and his wife Violante read the Old Testament even more than he.[28] Manuel de Sosa y Prado, a baker, was denounced [Mexico 1694] as a Judaizer because Sosa and his brother used to talk about the story of Esther, which left them saddened and contrite; and they were very fond of the Old Testament.[29]

*Conversos* used a wide range of other religious and literary materials as a source of inspiration and information about the Old Testament. The favorites were books that dealt in any way with Old Testament subjects, whether or not they were overtly Christian in their orientation. Among the books most commonly mentioned in trial testimony (listed alphabetically) were

> *David perseguido* (Lozano?). This book was most likely the long, moralizing work by the Doctor of Theology Cristobal Lozano, published serially between 1652 and 1663. In recounting the Old Testament story of David, the book engages in a variety of novelesque, historical, and philosophical digressions. The book was extremely popular in the late seventeenth century and went through several editions. When threatened by the Inquisition in Majorca, Raphael Valls burned his copy of this book in 1677. (Braunstein 1936, 97)

> *De bello judayco* (Josephus). Several witnesses in the 1691 posthumous trial of Diego Forteza in Majorca claimed that Josephus's account of the first-century Roman wars against Jerusalem was much read among Judaizers (Selke de Sánchez 1972, 42). The *Jewish Wars* was translated into Spanish in Seville in 1492, in Antwerp in 1555, in Madrid 1557, and in many subsequent editions. Despite the fact that the Spanish translation appeared on the first Spanish Index of prohibited books in 1559 (Sierra Corella 1947, 228), the book was frequently found in *converso* libraries.[30]

> *Espejo de consolación* (Ribadaneyra?). The book referred to is probably by Fray Pedro Ribadeneyra. Around 1605 in Lima Duarte Enríquez was accused of say-

ing that "there was no book like the *Mirror of Consolation*, which contained the whole of the Holy Scripture, and Abraham, Isaac and Jacob, and many other favors that God had done for the Jews," and that he would pay anything for a copy of that book.³¹ In 1603 Antonio Méndez was accused in Mexico by Manuel Gil of "having brought into the room where he lived [with Gil] a copy of the *Espejo de consolación* which contains many Old Testament stories. One night he read in it with great feeling. He wanted to keep it in [Gil's] bookcase, but [Gil] would not let him because he thought it was one of the prohibited books. Méndez replied that that one book was worth more than all the others that [Gil] had."³² This was another of the books Raphael Valls burned in Majorca in 1677 to keep them from the Inquisition (Braunstein 1936, 97).

*Flos sanctorum* (Villegas).³³ This enormously popular five-volume compendium of saints' lives, the *Flowering of the Saints*, was published by Alonso de Villegas Selvago between 1580 and 1603. Among other things, it provided biographical material on a number of Old Testament figures. An amplified book with the same title was published by the Jesuit historian Fray Pedro de Ribadeneyra in 1599–1604. The Portuguese *converso* Duarte Rodriguez [Veracruz, Mexico 1646] "used to read *Flos Sanctorum* of Villegas and the lives of the Patriarchs and prophets, Judith and Esther."³⁴ Gonzalo Váez, burned in the Mexican *auto* of 1649, also prayed from the *Flos Sanctorum*, which he called "the missals in the vernacular" (Liebman 1974, 152). Pedro Onofre confessed in Majorca in 1678 that the *Flos Sanctorum* was popular among Judaizers because it contained "chapters which dealt with the favors God had done for the people of Israel and the Patriarchs of the old Law."³⁵

*Monarchía Ecclesiástica* (Ramón y Zamora? Pineda?). Selke de Sánchez finds that this was the book most commonly mentioned in Majorcan Inquisition proceedings of the 1670s and 1680s. She suggests that the work's alternate title was the *República Christiana* and that it was most likely the work of Fr. Jerónimo Ramón [Román?] y Zamora titled *Repúblicas del mundo divididas en tres partes* (Salamanca, 1595).³⁶ On the other hand, the title might refer to the Franciscan Juan de Pineda's *Monarchía eclesiástica o Historia universal del mundo desde su creación*, published in Zaragoza in 1576, which was a best seller of its time. Both of these books contain ample Old Testament material. Pineda's *Monarchía* is considered one of the most learned books of the Spanish Renaissance, citing almost every author of note from classical antiquity up to Pineda's time.

Sem Tob's *Coplas*. This long series of four-line stanzas on moral, religious, philosophical, political, and folk wisdom, composed in Castilian in the fourteenth century by Rabbi Sem Tob ibn Ardutiel of Carrión, was incorporated into the liturgy of *conversos* of Molina de Aragón in the years just prior to the Expulsion.³⁷

*Símbolo de la fe* (Granada). Liebman asserts that Fray Luis de Granada's *Introducción al símbolo de la fe* (*Symbol of Faith*, first published in Salamanca in 1583) was widely read in Mexico at the end of the sixteenth century because of its excerpts from the Prophets, especially Zechariah and Ezekiel.[38] Some of Granada's other works appeared on the Spanish Index of prohibited books in 1559 (Sierra Corella 1947, 227; Kamen 1965, 99). Ironically, in the 1640s Sebastián Cardoso argued in his defense to the Mexican Inquisition that while he had observed some Jewish practices in his heart he was a true Christian; that he prayed catholic prayers and read religious books like those of Fray Luis de Granada (García 1910, 262). Galanes (1988, 168) argues that the *Symbol of Faith* was a source of spiritual nourishment for all sorts of groups: orthodox Christians read it as a source of piety; *conversos* appreciated its de-emphasis of lineage; the religiously ambivalent found consolation in Fray Luis's acceptance of various paths to truth; crypto-Jews used it as a source of enlightenment about the Jewish symbols of faith and for information about the Old Testament. But Pero Anriques [Bahia 1594] was certain that it was a source of inspiration mainly for "the blind, stubborn Talmudists . . . who found in it things from their Talmud."[39]

Evidently several other books recounting Old Testament history were circulating among Mexican Judaizers in the 1640s. The summary of the *auto de fe* of 1646 says, for example, that seventy-year-old Isabel Texoso "was very fond of reading about the lives of the Patriarchs and prophets of the Old Law."[40] Two books of the Apocrypha were popular among the *conversos* for similar reasons. According to Liebman, the book of Judith was widely read in Mexico at the end of the sixteenth century because of the book's "strong religious orientation, [which] serves as an inspiration for patriotism and piety" (1970, 153). The book of Tobit was also widely read in Mexico at the end of the sixteenth century because "the principal character is consumed by his Judaism and the sadness of being in exile" (Liebman 1970, 153). In 1593 it was reported in Pernambuco, Brazil, that the *cristão novo* Jorge Diaz de Paz used to read to his friends from the history of Tobit in Spanish (Furtado 1929, 95, 452).

*Conversos* avidly sought and preserved vulgar language versions of the Psalms, for these Biblical hymns tended to play an important part in crypto-Jewish liturgy.[41] Some *conversos* treasured handwritten versions of the Psalms, which were circulated among the community or handed down from generation to generation. Tomás Treviño de Sobremonte [Mexico 1649] admitted that his mother owned a notebook with the seven penitential Psalms, which included some in her own handwriting (Wiznitzer 1962a, 233). But these were not the only sources of the Psalms in the vulgar languages. Almost any book—no matter how Catholic—that contained a Psalm was co-opted by the crypto-Jews. The two most commonly used seem to have been

Book of Hours. This most common of Catholic prayer books together with the Dominican *Day-book* were read in colonial Mexico because they included the seven penitential Psalms and other material taken from the Old Testament (Liebman 1970, 153; Cohen 1973, 208). Many *conversos* such as Alfonso Vaz [Lisbon 1545] possessed a "Book of Hours of Our Lady which contained the Psalms of David."[42] In 1665 testimony in Mexico a witness told how she had asked the *conversa* María de Zárate "to give her in Spanish the Psalms that they prayed, but they told her that it was not possible to give them to her in Spanish, because they were not allowed to have them written, but that she should buy a Book of Hours to learn them from."[43]

*Ramillete de flores* (Aboab?). The book referred to may be the *Perach Schouschan, Ramillete de Flores* (*Bouquet of Flowers*), published in Amsterdam in 1687 by Isaac de Matitya Aboab.[44] Braunstein identifies this book as the "treasure-trove of prayers" of Majorcan *chuetas* in the seventeenth century (1936, 99). In 1694 the Portuguese native Antonio Silveira y Cardoso reported to the Mexican Inquisition that the Judaizer Manuel de Sosa y Prado "did not own religious books, but only a *Ramillete de divinas flores* from which he constantly read the Psalms of David."[45]

## 14.3. Prayer Books

After versions of the Old Testament, prayer books were the crypto-Jews' most important religious possessions. To an extent these books continued the traditions of late medieval Jewish prayer books. Attempts had been made to standardize the Jewish prayer book, or *siddur*, as early as the tenth century, but each local Jewish community's customary order of service continued to have great standing throughout the Middle Ages (Millgram 1971, 367–73). After the introduction of the printing press into the Iberian Peninsula late in the fifteenth century a number of Hebrew *siddurim* were published. The first was the *Seder Tefillot* in 1490 (*Enc. Jud.* 13:987). In fact, despite the restrictive atmosphere of the times the corpus of printed *siddurim* in pre-Expulsion Iberia was extraordinarily rich. Of the 175 known Hebrew *incunabulae*, 62 (35%) were published in the Iberian Peninsula: in the Spanish cities of Montalbán, Guadalajara, Hijar, and Zamora, and in the Portuguese cities of Lisbon, Leiria, and Faro (*Enc. Jud.* 8: 1326).

References to Hebrew language *siddurim* in use by *conversos* are fairly common among the generations preceding the Expulsion. Many of these references come from the 1480s from the region around Ciudad Real, whose community has been particularly well documented. Juan Grande reported that in 1459 "he had found in the house of Juan Díaz, the rag merchant . . . a small book which told the ceremonies for Hanukah and Rosh Hashanah and Selichot and the Feast of Unleavened Bread and many other Jewish prayers."[46] María Díaz and her family too were seen "praying from a Jewish book called a *siddur*."[47] Alonso Sánchez testified that in the early 1480s he used to read to the Ramírez family "from a small book of Jewish prayers; and . . . this happened Saturday mornings and sometimes in the afternoon, and sometimes Friday nights."[48] Francisco Martínez [Soria 1501] was said to have "a book written in Hebrew called a *çidur*, which contained all the prayers that the Jews pray during the whole year, each in its own season."[49] Occasionally in modern times prayer books from the period of the Expulsion have been discovered hidden in Spain. One extensive late fifteenth-century *siddur* in Catalán was found in 1848 in Barcelona.[50]

More common are reports of the persistence of booklets of crypto-Jewish prayers in Spanish, Portuguese, or Catalán. Documents from the early 1480s suggest that prayer books in Castilian and Valencian were in common use among *conversos* and Jews too in the kingdoms of Castile and Aragon prior to the Expulsion (Baer 1966, 2:346, 355, 359, 361). Johanna Desfar [Valencia 1487] was accused of "having a book of hours of Jewish prayers in Valencian and in Hebrew from which she often read."[51] The *conversa* Aldonza González reported in 1468 that "a Jew named Rabbi David, who lives in Segovia, used to come to my father's house sometimes [in the 1460s]. And when he saw that they were teaching me to read he said: 'Would you like to buy a little Spanish book of good prayers for you to read?' And he insisted so much that I bought it. He told me that reading in it and keeping the great fast would cause God to show me great mercy. . . . And when I showed the book to an uncle of mine who was an abbot, and asked him what it was, he told me that it was against our holy Catholic faith and I should destroy it."[52] Alonso Sánchez [Ciudad Real 1512] accused Isabel de los Olivos of having a book "in which they prayed that began *Adonai* and was written in Spanish and was the size of a quarter of a parchment sheet."[53] The market for these bilingual prayer books was due in part to the fact that many new-Christian families rapidly had lost their fluency in the Hebrew language. But another reason had to do with crypto-Jews' clandestine lifestyle. Francés de Puxmija [Teruel c. 1484] had a book of Jewish prayers rendered in Christian writing so as not to call attention to them (Sánchez Moya/Monasterio Aspiri 1972, 113).

But, as is the case with Hebrew Bibles, Hebrew *siddurim* disappeared from most *converso* households very quickly after the establishment of the Inquisition. For prayer most Judaizing *conversos* had to rely on their knowledge of the oral tradition; a few possessed handwritten collections of prayers, occasionally in Hebrew, but more often in the vulgar tongues. By the end of the first decade of the sixteenth century *siddurim* were for all intents and purposes gone, since references to them after that date are exceedingly rare. For example, of the 634 cases of Judaizers tried by the Coimbra Inquisition between 1567 and 1583, Hebrew books are only mentioned once: Manuel Lopes, of Viseu, was accused in 1573 of praying on Yom

Kippur at home with some friends from Hebrew books that they held in their hands.[54] Still, from time to time even into the early eighteenth century there are reports of Iberian Judaizers praying from Hebrew-language *siddurim*. In 1626 in Zacatecas (Mexico), Tomás Gómez, a native of Castello Branco, Portugal, accidentally dropped a small, handwritten book of prayers in a local store. The storekeeper gave it to the Inquisition. Sixteen years later Gómez was tried in Mexico and fined, whipped, and banished from the Indies. The book contained a version of Psalm 97, a pastiche of several other Psalms, the *Shema*, the *Amidah*, and the *Kedushah*, all common components of the standard Jewish prayer book.[55] Among Francisco Maldonado de Silva's possessions [Lima 1627] was found a "small, parchment-bound notebook containing some Jewish prayers and the calendar of the festivals of the Law of Moses."[56] Nearly a hundred years later Jorge de Almeida, tried in absentia in Mexico in 1707, was accused of possessing a liturgy and some other Hebrew volumes (Roth 1931–2, 12).

The communities of the Sephardic Diaspora, particularly in the publishing centers of central Europe, Italy, and the Low Countries, worked hard to prepare religious material—particularly *siddurim*—that could be smuggled back into the Iberian Peninsula for use by the crypto-Jews who remained there.[57] Kayserling's pioneering bibliography (1890) of Dutch Sephardic publications details a large number of these. In addition, foreign-published titles appear with frequency in Inquisition testimony. João Baptista told the Lisbon Inquisition in 1577 that in Flanders he had been given a book of Jewish prayers with the title *Livros ladinos em linguoa espanhola* (Baião 1921, 205). The leather-covered booklets of Jewish prayers described by Francisco Botello to the Mexican Inquisition in 1649 were almost certainly of foreign provenance (Wiznitzer 1962a, 253), since we have no evidence of a local crypto-Jewish book industry. Raphael Valls, tried by the Inquisition in Majorca in the 1670s, used to read from a book called *Almenara de la luz* that contained "examples and spiritual exercises for the observer of the law of Moses" (Braunstein 1936, 97). The book is probably Isaac Aboab's *Menorat ha-Maor* (*Candelabra of lights*), translated as *Almenara de la luz* by Jacob Hages, the head of the Leghorn rabbinical school, and published in that city in 1656 (Kayserling 1890, 73). Travelers' reports, too, attest to the common use of Spanish or Portuguese language or even bilingual *siddurim* among Jews of the Sephardic Diaspora. For example, Fernando de Medina told Mexican Inquisitors in 1656 that he had visited synagogues in France where the rabbi prayed in Hebrew and everyone followed the service in a book of his own language, in his case Spanish (Wiznitzer 1962a, 258).

The only crypto-Jewish community to have preserved a significant number of *siddurim* into modern times is that of the Beira Alta region of Portugal. As late as 1929 Antónia Candida da Costa Martins, of Oporto, had two manuscript collections of prayers that had been handed down in her family (Paulo 1981, 141).[58] In

1981 Moisés Abraão Gaspar of Rebordelo (Bragança) produced a manuscript in eighteenth-century handwriting entitled "Book of Prayers to the Almighty God Most High" (*Livro de Orações ao Altissímo Deus todopoderoso*).

## 14.4. OTHER RELIGIOUS BOOKS

Of course the books cited so far in this chapter were not the only Jewish religious books that circulated among some of the new-Christian communities. Trial testimony and inventories of prisoners' possessions provide many other hints, although frequently the citations do not provide enough data for us to positively identify the books in question. What is clear is that new-Christians found religious inspiration in the widest possible range of written materials. Some seem to have been of overtly Jewish content. For example, in Toledo at the end of the fifteenth century Juan de Toledo confessed that "sometimes he read in a book called the '613 commandments of the law of Moses.' "[59] Something called the *Consejos de Salomon* was used for consolation and prayer at Yom Kippur in colonial Mexico (Liebman 1970, 66, 154). Also current in New Spain was the Spanish translation of Shlomo Ibn Verga's *Shevet Yehudah* (*Staff of Judah*), which recounts persecutions of the Jews across history, philosophizes about the reasons for popular hatred of the Jews, and criticizes the moral and social lapses of modern Jews.[60] Others were secular works that touched on religious matters, such as printed editions of plays on Old Testament themes. The Portuguese Judaizer Manuel de Sosa y Prado [Mexico 1694] was found to own, in addition to the *Remillete de divinas flores* and the *Cronicon*, the book of *Macabeos* and some collections of plays (AGN Vol 529 doc 11, 271a). Sometimes the most unlikely source, such as the *converso* Antonio de Nebrija's 1492 dictionary, might inspire a new-Christian to intensify his or her Jewish identity. Bachelor Rodrigo Fernández Correa, of Veracruz, told Inquisitors in Mexico City around 1647 that he had begun Judaizing when he was twelve because, "while he was studying the introductory curriculum, once he was looking up a word in Antonio Nebrija's *Vocabulario*, he had found an explanation of Jewish fasts, which gave him a great blow because then he understood how he had sinned."[61] Much work remains to be done in this area, beginning with a comprehensive, detailed index of titles cited in Inquisition trials.[62]

Occasionally we have detailed information about the books utilized for the religious preparation of a Judaizing *converso*. Luis de Carvajal's confessions in Mexico in the 1590s, for example, document his study at the Franciscan Colegio de Santiago Tlatelolco with Fray Pedro de Oroz. There young Carvajal studied the Bible, including the Apocrypha, Ribadaneyra's *Mirror of Consolation*, Hebreo's *Dialogues of the Love of God*, the *Guide of Sinners*, and Granada's *Introduction to the Symbol of*

*Faith*. He read the Dominican Jerome Oleaster's 1569 commentary on the Pentateuch, which introduced him to Maimonides's thirteen tenets of faith (although not formally identified as such) and to Nicolas of Lyra's *Glosses*. Based on these books Carvajal composed a number of short religious tracts and poems, which he circulated among his crypto-Jewish friends (Cohen 1973, 201–3). Inquisition inventories of *converso* libraries also give us a more rounded picture of a particular Judaizer's intellectual formation. In the 1602 inventory of the library of the Portuguese-Argentinean Judaizer Diego Núñez de Silva, among the several dozen medical books were Fray Luis de León's *Nombres de Cristo* (*Names of Christ*) in three volumes, Juan de Orozco's *Emblemas morales* (*Moral emblems*), and an early book of plays of Lope de Vega (Böhm 1984, 232). León's *Nombres*, first published in 1583, is one of the most elegantly written books of the Spanish Renaissance. Its principal theme is the presence of God in all aspects of creation and the resultant beauty of the created world. It may have been attractive to Judaizers because of its abundant citation of Old Testament material. The Augustinian Fray Luis de León was himself a descendant of *conversos*. Bishop Juan de Orozco's *Emblemas* (Segovia, 1589), which draws moral consequences from a series of allegorical pictures, was one of the most popular emblem books of its day. Sometimes these library inventories provide graphic evidence of the success of efforts by Jews of the Sephardic Diaspora to smuggle books into the Iberian Peninsula or the colonies. One of the most extensive libraries was that of Luis Méndez Chaves, who was accused in the middle of the seventeenth century, somewhere in the Americas, of possessing a large number of Jewish books, including a number in Hebrew (García de Proodian 1966, 478–9):

> Two copies of the "Order of the five annual *tahaniot*": which are the fasts of *tebet*, Esther, the 17th of Thamuz, the 5th of Av, and Gedaliah. Printed in Amsterdam, 5390–1630, by Efraín Bueno and Jonah Abrabanel in the print shop of Menasseh ben Israel.[63]
>
> Book of festival prayers, Printed in Amsterdam, 5401–1641, by Efraín Bueno and Jonah Abrabanel in the print shop of Nicolas Rabestein.[64]
>
> Treasury of *dinim* (laws) of Menasseh Ben Israel. Printed by Viahu Aboab, 1445 [sic].[65]
>
> Prayers for Rosh Hashanah and Yom Kippur, with the addition of the prayers of forgiveness (*selihot*), translated into Spanish. Printed in Amsterdam by David Avenatar Mello in 5377–1617.[66]
>
> Monthly prayers and holiday prayer book printed by Menasseh Ben Israel in Amsterdam in 5397–1637.[67]
>
> A "Confessional of prayers of forgiveness."[68]

## NOTES

1. Baer 1966, 2:72. For a short while even after the Expulsion some *conversos* such as Almazán's Mestre Bernal [1505] were able to hang on to their Hebrew and Arabic medical books (Carrete/Fraile 1987, 28).

2. *Vido que todos los sabados leya el dicho Juan Dias en vna Bribia e en otros libros grandes como la Bribia* (Beinart 1974, 576). For a similar example see Böhm 1984, 219 [Chile 1584]. Another witness said that Díaz was in the habit of "reading in the Lamentations of Jeremiah, and the book had pictures and was bound with a decoration of flames like in a brazier. This witness asked him what it was, and he said that it was the Holy Fire of the Holy of Holies which Jeremiah was going to hide so that it would not be taken by the enemies who were going to destroy Jerusalem" (*Le fallo leyendo en los plautos de Jeremias; estaba el libro estorado, y tenia vnos fuegos como brasero. Preguntole este testigo que que cosa era aquello, e el dixo que era el Fuego Santo del Santo Santorum, que Jeremias lo tenia para lo esconder por que non fuese tomado de la mano de los enemigos que abian de destruyr a Gerusalem*) (Beinart 1974, 576).

3. Evidence of this public, ceremonial use of the Torah abounds in medieval Iberia. For example, Rodrigo Yáñez's fourteenth-century poem describes the entry of Alfonso IX into Sevilla this way: *Cavalleros bofordando / todos con gran alegrança; e a la gineta jugando / tomando escudo e lança. / E los moros e las moras / muy grandes fiestas fazían, / los judíos con sus Toras / estos reyes reçebían* (Amador de los Ríos 1875, 341).

4. For example, Maimonides's works were burned in Montpelier in 1233 and some twelve thousand manuscripts of the Talmud burned in Paris in 1242 (Milgram 1971, 624).

5. *O, quánta buena ley se quema oy* (Carrete Parrondo 1985a, 96). Some books were lost as well in the anti-*converso* disturbances of the middle of the fifteenth century, such as the 1449 riots in Ciudad Real (Roth 1992, 382).

6. *Era gran talmudista y enseñaba a otros el Talmud* (Cabezudo Astraín 1950, 276). Luis Sánchez, the son of Eleasar Usuf of Zaragoza, was one of five *converso* brothers who held high offices in Fernando's court (Madariaga 1940, 194; Kayserling 1894, 24).

7. For a general discussion of *conversos*' access to religious books see Kamen 1965, 94–6; Roth 1931–2, 12; Gutwirth 1981, 90–1.

8. *Lio adalgunos la biblia que toman plazer descuchar me e de saber de mi algunas cosas, por que saben que lo se yo bien fazer* (Baer 1936, 454).

9. *E asymesmo se iva a casa de judios e les rogava que le leyesen las profeçias e se las leyan* (Cantera Montenegro 1982a, 35).

10. *Vio asimesmo, como los dichos Juhan quondam y Jayme la Cavalleria vesavan la dicha tora, y el dicho Jayme no solamente la vesava con la voca, pero ahun con los ojos tocava en ella* (Baer 1936, 460).

11. *Fizo reverençia a la Torá, e les dixo que omiliasen todas a ella, que aquella era nuestra ley* (Carrete Parrondo 1985a, 141).

12. *Fizo tender ropa a su puerta por donde pasasen las dichas Atorás* (Carrete Parrondo 1978, 18).

13. Arias's wife Elvira González donated an "amulet" with the Hebrew inscription "Adonay" (*vna nómina que traya y tenía en que tenía e traya escritas çiertas letras ebraycas e nombres de Adonay, la dió a un judío para que ge la llebase e pusiese a la sinoga por reliquias*). Around 1462 Diego Arias purchased at the Medina fair a Torah for Avila's Andrin synagogue, and a few years later he had red velvet cloth cut for a Torah cover (*napa* = Heb. *mapah*) for a synagogue in Madrid (Carrete Parrondo 1986, 141, 120, 61).

14. *Maldito fuese quien avía vedado el Testamento Viejo. . . . ¡Testamento Viejo! ¡Ay, Testamento Viejo!* (Carrete/Fraile 1987, 20).
15. *Otro libro tenia el dicho Juan Ramirez, grande, vna vez dixo de cubiertas de pergamino e otro de cubiertas coloradas, en que tanbien leyan las dichas oraçiones judaycas, e que hera el dicho libro de pliego entero. . . . El libro grande, que era de la Bribia* (Beinart 1977a, 558–9).
16. *Avía hallado vna Torá con vnos cascaueles e canpanillas de plata, arrymada a vn paramento* (Carrete/Fraile 1987, 70).
17. *Aquella noche que posando en casa de Ruy Dias Laynes vn padre inquisidor, avían echado a vn pozo, questá en el patín de la casa, vna Torá* (Carrete/Fraile 1987, 84).
18. *Vnas escripturas de pergamino escriptas de letra judiega enbueltas en otro pergamino linpio. E como este testigo las halló dixo a . . . Salcedo qué le daría por le tornar vnas escripturas que avía hallado en su casa, judiegas. . . . Sazedo rogó a este testigo que ge las mostrase; e este testigo le mostró dellas e non ge las quiso dexar en sus manos, saluo teniéndolas este testigo en su mano. Leyó . . . Sazedo vn poco e dixo cómo heran de Moysén, e que las lleuase al horno que tenía en su casa a quemar. E este testigo no lo quiso faser, saluo lleuólas a su posada e que allí las quemó* (Carrete Parrondo 1985a, 119). According to Carrete, Salcedo was the former Rabbi Yantó, who emigrated as a Jew to Portugal but in 1499 converted and shortly thereafter returned to Spain. Fragments of a Hebrew Bible turned up inside a wall in Molina de Aragón in 1649 (Cantera Montenegro 1985, 72).
19. *Yo trasladé un libro de oraçiones de la ley de Moysen en romance, de otro del dicho Sancho de la Caua, en el qual dicho libro yo leya algunas vezes . . . el qual con otros libros yo di a un judío días ha, al qual después dixe que los quemase . . . . Yo escreví un libro de hasta veynte hojas de la ley de Moysen para una dueña* (León Tello 1972, 78).
20. *Leía en latín la Biblia de los judíos y luego la decía en romance* (Cabezudo Astraín 1950, 276).
21. *O mãodava chamar, certos dias da semana pera lhe declarar a biblia de latim em linguagem* (Furtado 1929, 56).
22. *Lhe declarasse em lingoagem hunos certos capitolos . . . que se continha as bençãis que Mojsés dizia aos filhos de Israel guardando a ley de Deos e as pragas e maldiçãis que lhes dezia que teriam se não guardassem a ley de Deos* (Furtado 1929, 95, 452). See also Furtado 1925, 305; Lipiner 1969, 170.
23. The earliest Indices were derived from lists of books prohibited by the University of Louvain, or by Rome. The first autonomous Spanish Index appeared in 1559 (Kamen 1965, 98). The Index of 1559 specifically prohibited the Bible in translation (*en nuestro vulgar, o en otro qualquier, traducida en todo o en parte*), as well as any book dealing with Jewish ceremony (*todos los libros hebraycos, o en cualquier lengua escriptos que contengan ceremonias iudaicas. . . . Todos cualesquier libros scriptos en hebraico, o en otra vulgar lengua que sean de la ley vieja*) (Sierra Corella 1947, 224, 232).
24. Kamen categorizes these as follows: "all books by heresiarchs; all religious books written by those condemned by the Inquisition; all books on Jews and Moors with an anti-Catholic bias; . . . all vernacular translations of the Bible, even by Catholics; all devotional works in the vulgar tongue; all controversial books between Catholics and heretics; all books on magic; . . . all pictures and figures disrespectful to religion" (1965, 96).
25. *Uma Biblia em lingoagem* (Baião 1921, 106). For more on this subject see Llamas 1944, 1951; Morreale 1960; Sephiha 1970.
26. *No alaua sino los passos del Testamento Viejo y se enternesçe con ellos, alaua mucho al predicador que trae muchos. No los celebra por figurar de otros passos de los sagrados evangelios con-*

*forme al intento de los predicadores, sino solamte tratandolos como la letra fuera como aficionado a tales historias* (AGN Vol 276 doc 14, 420b).

27. *Veio denunciar o seu marido Henrique Lopes, que ás noites lhe prégava coisas da Bibla e dos judeus* (Baião 1921, 160).

28. *Muito mais que o dito seu marido lida e vista na biblia e sempre contar e declarar as istorias da lei velha da biblia* (Furtado 1925, 443).

29. *La Historia de Esther, y los dos se lastimauan de ella, mostrandose mui contritos, y aficionados al testamiento Viejo* (AGN Vol 529 doc 11, 269a).

30. Kamen 1965, 99. For some of the numerous Mexican examples see Lewin 1971, 27, 66 [Mexico 1650s]; Lewin 1987, 192; AGN Vol 529 doc 11, 271a [Mexico 1694].

31. *No había libro como el Espejo de Consolación, en el cual estaba toda la Sagrada Escritura, y Abraham, Isaac y Jacob, y otras muchas mercedes que Dios había hecho a los judíos* (Lewin 1987, 201). For other examples see García 1910, 104 [colonial Mexico]; Liebman 1964, 104; 1970, 154, 165, 201; 1975, 70, 172 [colonial Mexico]; Gracia Boix 1983, 139 [Andalucia 1573]; Baião 1921, 232 [Portugal 1587].

32. *Traxo un dia al dho apossento donde los dos vivian un libro de los de espejo de consolaon donde se tratan muchas historias del testamo biejo. Hauiendo leydo en el una noche con mucha ternura lo quiso guardar en un escritorio de libros de este to, y no queriendo se lo consentir diziale paresciasen de los prohibidos. Respondio el do Antonio Mendez que ualia mas aquel solo libro que quantos este to tenia* (AGN Vol 276 doc 14, 420b).

33. This title was used for several books. The Index of 1559 prohibits a *Flos sanctorum*, printed in Zaragoza in 1558, but does not list the author's name (Sierra Corella 1947, 227).

34. Liebman 1964, 103. See also García 1910, 104; Liebman 1970, 153, 243; 1987, 201 [colonial Mexico]; Baião 1921, 250 [Portugal 1597]; Caro Baroja 1961, 3:129 [Spain 1730s].

35. *Contenían differentes capítulos que tratan de algunos beneficios que Dios hizo al pueblo de Israel y a los Padres de la ley antigua* (Selke de Sánchez 1972, 41). See also Braunstein 1936, 97.

36. Selke de Sánchez 1972, 41. See also Braunstein 1936, 97.

37. Pedro Bernal testified that he had not prayed from Genesis, but he had frequently read or heard the *Coplas of Rabbi Santo* and likewise had read the seven penitential Psalms and other prayers in the vulgar language (*Dixo que en el Genesi nunca leyo, e que ha leydo e oydo algunas vezes las coplas de Rabi Santo. E ansymismo ha leydo los syete Salmos penitençiales, e otras oraçiones en romance*) (Cantera Montenegro 1985, 75).

38. Liebman 1970, 153. See also Cohen 1973, 68, 131, 193. Lewin cites a number of passages from Granada's book of presumed interest to crypto-Jews (1987, 187–200). Granada's other principal work, the *Libro de Oración* (*Book of Prayer*), published in 1554, was so popular that it went through twenty-three editions by 1559, when it appeared on the Index of banned books. Fray Luis fought the ban and eventually had the book approved at the Council of Trent (Kamen 1985, 82).

39. *Os tais judeus, talmodistas . . . erão cegos e pertinaces e que leesse o livro do simbollo que fez frei Luis de Granada e que nelle acharia cousas de seu talmud* (Furtado 1929, 161).

40. *Era muy amiga de leer las vidas de los patriarcas y profetas de la ley antigua* (García 1910, 63; cf. 68, 108).

41. When Maria de Peralta asked her new-Christian friend Bento Teixeira [Bahia 1594], the school teacher, to translate the Psalms for her, he presumed that she too was a crypto-Jew (*Lhe disse se lhe queria elle tornar em linguagem huns psalmos, e logo elle denunciante presumiendo que ella lhe dezia aquillo com tenção judaica*) (Furtado 1929, 164). For crypto-Jewish use of the Psalms as prayers, see Chapter 15.

42. *Um libro de Horas de Nossa Senhora, em que vinham os psalmos de David* (Baião 1921, 144).
43. *Aunque pidió y solicitó que le diesen los psalmos en romance que ellos rezaban, dijeron que no era posible dárselos en romance, porque no se podían tener escritos y que comprase unas horas en que aprenderlos* (Lewin 1971, 487).
44. Kayserling 1890, 103. The book's full title is *Perach Schouschan, Ramillete de Flores, colhido no jardin das artes, que levaã o estudiozo ao saber: breve compendio do que em sustancia contem cada sciencia, e sua definição, contem 50 discursos, tratados de grande noticia.*
45. *Solo tenia el Ramillete de divinas flores donde leyia de continuo los Salmos de David* (AGN Vol 529 doc 11, 271a).
46. *Fallo en casa de Juan Dias, trapero . . . vn libro pequeño en que estaban las reglas de las Pascuas de Hanuca e Roxaxania y del Zelahod y del Pan Çençeño y otras muchas oraçiones judaycas* (Beinart 1974, 575).
47. *Resando en vn libro judayco que se dise çidur* (Beinart 1974, 55).
48. *Podra aver treynta años, poco mas o menos, que este confesante e su hermana Florençia . . . se ençerrava en vn palaçio de la casa de la dicha Florençia e del dicho Juan Ramires, su marido, e que este confesante leya a la dicha su hermana vn libro pequeño de oraçiones judaycas; e que . . . eran en dias de sabado a la mañana e a las veses en la tarde, e algunos viernes en las noches* (Beinart 1981b, 41). See also Fita y Colomé 1892, 501, 516 [1483].
49. *Vn libro escripto en abrayco que se llamaua çidur, donde tenía todas las oraçiones que los judíos desían e resauan en todo el año, en cada tienpo lo suyo* (Carrete Parrondo 1985a, 122).
50. It has been edited by Riera i Sans (1971–5), who in his footnotes cites several other examples. See also Caro Baroja 1916, 1:119, 388.
51. *La dita Johanna per obseruacio de la ley de Moyses ha tengut e tenia vnes hores de oracions judayques en pla y en hebraye, en les quals legia moltes vegades* (Llorca 1935, 23).
52. *Vino a mi un judio que entrava e salia en casa de mi padre algunas veses, el qual se desia rabi David, el qual mora en Segovia, e vido que me mostrava a leer, e dixo: Queres conprar un libro pequeno en romance de buenas oraciones en que leaes, e el me siguio tanto que gelo conprase, e yo le conpre, e el me dixo que leyendo en el e ayunando el ayuno mayor que me avia de fase dios mucha merced. . . . e mostrando el libro a un mi tio abad ove de saber, que era, e dixo me que era contra nuestra santa fe catolica que le ronpiese* (Baer 1936, 478).
53. *Fue preguntado que que tal hera el libro que rezavan y como escomençava. Dixo que Adonay, y que estava escrito en romançe e que seria del tamaño de menos de medio quarto de pliego* (Beinart 1977a, 558).
54. *Paseando pella casa, rezando por livros em hebraico que traziam na mão* (Azevedo Mea 1982, 368).
55. Lewin 1987, 214–23. According to Lewin, Angel Rosenblat considers it a copy of a sixteenth-century text, handwritten in Spanish by someone whose native language was Portuguese.
56. *Allose al reo entre sus papeles un quadernito de ochavo afforrado en pergamino con algunas oraciones judaicas, y con el calendario de las fiestas de la ley de Moyses y Pascuas della* (Böhm 1984, 284).
57. There is evidence of widespread book smuggling. For example, from a ship crewed by Muslims and Jews that ran aground in Gibraltar in 1629 officials confiscated six prayer books in Hebrew and Spanish which had been printed in Venice for smuggling into Spain (Domínguez Ortiz 1981, 611). Liebman documents a flourishing trade in religious books between Manila and Mexico (1970, 290).

58. Portions of other twentieth-century Portuguese *siddurim* have been published by Schwarz 1925; Barros Basto 1928b; Paulo 1970, 67–77, 113–4; 1985, 117; and Fontes 1989a, 1989b.

59. *Algunas bezes en vn libro que se llama seysçientos e treze mandamientos de la ley de Moyse* (León Tello 1972, 77).

60. Liebman 1970, 153. The first edition in Hebrew in 1553 or 1554 was in Adrianople. It was translated into Spanish and published in Amsterdam in 1640 by Meir de León (Kayserling 1890, 80).

61. *Estudiando menores, buscando un vocablo en el Vocabulario de Antonio de Nebrija, había hallado uno particular para explicar el ayuno de los judíos, de que había recibido en sí un golpe muy grande* (García 1910, 129).

62. The Archivo General de la Nación in Mexico City is currently engaged in producing such an index for the more than 1500 volumes of Inquisition documents housed there.

63. *Orden de los cinco Tahaniot.* Listed in Kayserling 1890, 53. The *tahaniot* are the fasts of forgiveness.

64. Precise identification of this book is difficult. Kayserling 1890, 53 lists two *Orden de oraciones de mes* by Bueno (1648, 1649), and an *Orden de Ros Asanah* (1652).

65. *Thesouro dos Dinim que o povo de Israel he obrigado saber e observar* (Amsterdam: Eliau Aboab, 5405–1645). Listed in Kayserling 1890, 91.

66. Kayserling says that Melo, a new-Christian who emigrated to Amsterdam and died in 1646, published only a 1626 translation of the Psalms (1890, 89–90).

67. *Orden de las Oraciones del mes con los mas necessario, y obligatorio de las tres fiestas del año como tambien lo que toca a los ayunos, Hanucah y Purim* (Amsterdam: Menasseh ben Israel, 5397–1636) (Kayserling 1890, 82).

68. *Orden del selioth, de harbith, y confesion de el malcut.* I have been unable to identify this book.

## CHAPTER XV

# Crypto-Jewish Ritual and Prayer

For the observant Spanish male Jew prior to the Expulsion, almost every routine daily activity was sanctified by prayer. Jews prayed when they first arose in the morning, at mid-day, and when they went to bed. For their morning prayers they wrapped tefillin around their arm (see Chapter 18). They prayed when washing their hands and both before and after partaking of food. They blessed their children. They prayed when they left their houses and murmured another prayer when they entered again. They repeated hymns of praise whenever they perceived God's blessings, and they asked God for help whenever they were in need. They also prayed communally in the local synagogue on the Sabbath and festivals. Some visited the synagogue every morning and evening as well.

Pre-Expulsion Jews in Iberia varied in their knowledge of the Hebrew language and Jewish ritual,[1] but a substantial number of them had broad knowledge of Judaism and adhered to traditional orthodox practices. Synagogues functioned wherever there was a sizable community and Jewish homes pulsed to the rhythms of Sabbath and festival worship. Before the establishment of the Inquisition many converts continued to pray openly with their former coreligionists at home or in the synagogues. As we saw in Chapter 14 it was fairly common for *conversos* to possess Hebrew prayer books. Even after 1480, and up until the Expulsion in 1492, some new-Christians continued to keep books, although circumspectly, and *conversos* who wished to pray as Jews were able to do so. Some common prayers were memorized, but pre-Expulsion Jews continued to be able to rely on manuscript or printed material.

After the Expulsion, possession of any Judaic documents invited disaster. Some few crypto-Jews relied on carefully hidden written religious material, but in the main the liturgy had to be transmitted orally. A few prayers, such as the *Shema*, remained in the oral tradition for a surprisingly long time. But with each passing year the liturgical scope narrowed. Increasingly prayers were passed along in the vernacular languages with only snippets of Hebrew to give a flavor of the original. Latin Bibles were accessible, and among crypto-Jews certain portions of the Bible, such as the Psalms and the canticle of Moses, were considered "Jewish" and became central to their liturgy. The more talented crypto-Jews composed their own prayers, often in verse, and many of these were handed about and memorized by their contemporaries. As Braunstein points out, it came to be believed that "it made little difference what one said in prayer, so long as the intention of the prayer was to communicate with the God of Israel."[2]

Fragments of prayers are scattered throughout Inquisition documents in both Spain and Portugal. They were recorded in large numbers in Portugal from the 1570s onward, largely because at that time the Portuguese Inquisition introduced questions about prayers into their protocol of interrogation. However, by the beginning of the seventeenth century the liturgy had largely been reduced to the *Shema*, the Psalms, a handful of blessings, and various hymns of praise and supplication. A hundred years later only the *Shema*, a few Psalms and bits of blessings were left. There are two exceptions to the above generalizations. One is that the occasional crypto-Jew who was particularly learned, or had a superbly retentive memory, or who was of a poetic bent, might command a repertoire of prayers that substantially exceeded the few scraps of liturgy commonly retained by crypto-Jews. Examples from Mexico are Luis de Carvajal "the younger" [1590s] and Tomás Treviño de Sobremonte [1630–40s]; examples from South America are Francisco Maldonado de Silva [1620s] and José de Silva [1720s]. Sometimes the repertoires of crypto-Jewish communities, such as that in Mexico in the 1640s, were enriched by the fact that some of their members had previously resided in orthodox Jewish communities in Europe (Israel 1970, 129). There are also sporadic reports of Jews from other lands visiting Iberia. In 1570, for example, the Coimbra Inquisition said that Leonor Coutinha, of Vila Flor, gave alms to "a certain person who came from the land of the Jews to collect charity for oil for the synagogues and to tell them on what day the Jewish fasts fell."[3] The second exception is in the Trás-os-Montes region of Portugal, where an extensive assemblage of crypto-Jewish prayers was collected in the early years of this century. These prayers, which are almost wholly in the Portuguese language, constitute a fairly complete liturgy, with prayers for the major life events such as birth, marriage, and death, prayers for the Sabbath, and prayers for the daily and annual calendars of worship. Because these prayers were passed along in the oral tradition they are often incomplete or garbled, and thus are sometimes difficult to translate coherently.[4]

This chapter focuses on crypto-Jewish prayers that were part of the daily liturgy in the home (15.1), including prayers related to food and to hand-washing (15.2) and for special occasions (15.3). It looks at the communal liturgy (15.4), including those prayers that were defined with respect to Christian ritual (15.5). It closes with some observations about the physical demeanors associated with crypto-Jewish prayer (15.6) and with the persistence of Hebrew (15.7). Prayers related to specific life-cycle events, special rituals, or festivals have been dealt with in their respective chapters: birth (Chapter 7), marriage (9), death (11), the Sabbath (12) and the festivals (13), feminine hygiene (10), and kashrut (19).

## 15.1. THE DAILY CYCLE OF PRAYER

Tradition dictates that Jews pray a minimum of three times daily: in the morning on arising (*shaḥarit*), in the afternoon (*minḥah*), and in the evening (*arvit*). For each of these occasions a cycle of prayers is prescribed that includes, among other things, a series of benedictions, the *Shema*, a silent prayer recited while standing (*Amidah*), and a selection of Psalms. There is substantial evidence that Judaizing *conversos* through at least the seventeenth century understood and followed this cycle of prayers.[5] Maria Rodrigues, of Lamego [Coimbra 1569] allegedly prayed "certain Psalms three times each day: that is, in the morning, at noon, and at dusk."[6] Seventeenth-century Mexican Judaizers were particularly attuned to this daily calendar. In his prison cell in Mexico in 1642 Juan Pacheco reputedly had a Hebrew prayer book and prayed each day at 5:00 and 10:00 in the morning and at 3:00 and 6:00 in the afternoon (Liebman 1970, 270). Tomás Treviño de Sobremonte, burned in Mexico in 1649, told the Inquisitors that "he prayed four times every day: about one hour upon arising, a half hour in the afternoon, a similar time shortly after Angelus, and for about an hour at midnight." Isabel Núñez, burned in effigy in the same *auto*, prayed three times daily.[7] Both Antonio Méndez and Ruy Díaz Nieto [Mexico early 1600s] were allegedly very regular in their twice daily prayers. In the morning Méndez

> in his undershirt would go to the window of his room and thrust his head outside and face east, moving his lips as if he were praying some secret thing, and rolling his eyes upward until the whites showed. After he was dressed he would pace up and down in his room, his arms folded on his breast the way Ruy Díaz does, with his hat on. And at night it was the same thing. He would not eat until he had prayed for everyone. Sometimes when the witness pressed him to eat, he responded that he could not eat until he had finished praying his rosary, but he did not have a rosary.[8]

María de Zárate [Mexico 1665] allegedly had taught one witness to recite the seven penitential Psalms "in the morning after washing the hands and before eating anything, going outside to pray where you can see the sky, looking toward where the sun sets; and at night in the same fashion, after you see the first star which appears, which is called the star of Venus."[9] Among some *conversos* this cycle of repeated prayer came to verge on the Christian practice of quantitative prayer. Catalina de Laguna [Granada 1590s], for example, claimed to pray a certain crypto-Jewish prayer twelve times a day so that she would become wealthy.[10] María de Matthos [Avila 1740s] kept track of the number of fasts she observed and the prayers which accompanied them (Caro Baroja 1961, 3:134).

*Shaḥarit*, the dawn prayer, with its eight components is the most elaborate of the obligatory three daily prayers. Traditionally Jews wear their prayer shawls (tallit) and put on their phylacteries (tefillin) during the recitation of *shaḥarit* on weekdays.[11] Evidence suggests an uninterrupted commitment of serious Judaizers to reciting *shaḥarit*, and a clear knowledge of its importance in the liturgy.[12] In 1491 Juan de Lucena was accused before the Inquisition of Soria of reciting the morning prayer "in Hebrew, standing up, his face turned toward the wall, bobbing his head" (Carrete Parrondo 1985a, 57). Pero Fernandes da Rosa [Coimbra 1583] used to recite this prayer upon waking: "I give myself over to the Lord of the World who created the heavens and the earth," while Simão Lopes da Guarda reported that in the morning he recited Psalms 6, 32, 51, and 130 that are the traditional preliminary prayers of *shaḥarit*.[13] In 1665 testimony in Mexico described the morning prayers of María de Zárate:

> When she rose from her bed she washed her hands and picked up a rosary, without crossing herself, only for appearances' sake . . . and she drew near to a pillar of the house that was reserved for this purpose and she crossed her hands and prayed the Psalm *Miserere Mei* in Spanish. At the end she bowed her head and said "praised be the most holy Lord, God of Abraham, Isaac and Jacob." And at the very end of the Psalm she used to say: "heifers will be placed on your altars. . . ." She recited the Psalms sometimes three times and sometimes six; and in between times she demanded a deep silence. And if one of the children made noise Doña María would slap him until he was quiet.[14]

Literally dozens of *shaḥarit* prayers have been recorded among Portuguese *cristãos novos* in this century.

Three themes are woven into traditional *shaḥarit* prayers: praise for the Deity in His role as creator, particularly for the creation of the morning light; thanks for having brought the worshipper safely through the night; and request for further assistance and protection. The joy of the miracle of creation and of waking to a new day predominate. An early Catalán *shaḥarit* prayer expressed this idea in simple verse: "Blessed is the day / and blessed He who sends it."[15] In the late seventeenth century Majorcan *chuetas* prayed upon rising: "Thank you my God for the light of the new day by which you call us to your service."[16] In 1674 Brites Henriques [Lisbon 1674] recited a more complex formulation of these motifs: "Blessed is the light of day, / and the Lord who sends it. / May He give us grace and happiness, / and knowledge to do His bidding, / so that when we die we will appear in the kingdom of light."[17] António de Sá Carrança [Coimbra 1701] recited this verse: "I get up in the morning, / in the morning, at dawn. / I go to pray my psalms / to the Lord. / Whoever trusts in God / will not lack favor. / Blessed and glorified / be the name of the Lord."[18] A lengthy verse prayer recorded in Mogadouro de Vilarinho in 1934 begins: "Now the black roosters sing, / as do the angels at every hour, / so that we will remember / to magnify, serve and praise / the holy name of the Lord / when the beautiful dawn breaks."[19]

Other versions stress the joy at having survived the night, as in this prayer from Castile: "Blessed and praised are You, Lord, who wakens me live and well with my soul in my body. I slept like a dead man. You gave me linen and cloth to cover myself, ears to hear with, hands and feet to walk with, and thus I, a sinner, am unworthy of praising Your holy virtues. May angels give You thanks in the heavens and humankind on earth. For all of the good things You have done for me and do each day and night; blessed is the day, blessed is the power of the Lord who sends light and clarity with the keys of understanding."[20] Or this one from Juan López de Armenia [Toledo 1590]: "Praised be the Lord who had awakened me alive and healthy, in peace and safe from the mists of night. May He give me His light and life and grace in order to serve Him."[21] Tomás Treviño de Sobremonte [Mexico 1644] said that his father had taught him this semi-rhyming prayer on waking up: "Blessed be the light of the day and the Lord who sends it out. All peoples praise the Lord, all nations praise the Lord, because He has supported us. And the truth of the Lord remains forever."[22] The several wake-up prayers that were recorded in Portugal in the 1930s include this one: "O Guardian Angel, / Angel who is my guide, / now that you have freed me from the trials of the night, / free me from the dangers of the day";[23] and this one from Bragança: "I give you thanks, divine King, / blessed is Your power, / for You permitted me, Lord, / to reach this morning hour. / I give You my soul and my life, / blessed King of truth, / for, Lord, I am not worthy, / still, show me Your mercy."[24]

Very often these themes of praise and thankfulness are combined with a request for further favors. Brites Henriques [Lisbon 1674] prayed: "Praised is the Lord, who created the light. May You keep me constant in Your service, my Lord, to be worthy of receiving Your gifts."[25] A Majorcan maid to the *chueta* Pedro Onofre Cortés observed in 1677 how each morning her master "went up on the terrace roof, and having washed his hands and face, knelt down and looking at the heavens, with great devotion prayed." The text that Onofre gave to the Inquisition was

> You, great God who created the Heaven and the Earth, and me and all creatures, be glorified and your holy name be praised. You have preserved me this night and brought me to see the light of day. May you give me good days and good years for the sake of your divine benevolence, and may you be my shield and my aid. Care for my needs with your holy help, and have mercy on me and forgive me my sins, according to your divine benevolence and for your glory's

sake. Grant me the grace of your holy glory to the end of my days, when you will be praised and glorified forever. Amen.[26]

These themes remain in modern Portuguese *shaḥarit* prayers, such as this one, recorded in Belmonte:

> Come now beautiful dawn; / come now bright day; / come O God most high / with Your holy, blessed joy! / May God free me / and all the people of Israel / from dead men—from evil encounters; / from living men—who are evil enemies; / from the harm of biting dogs; / from rushing water and burning fire / and people's tongues. / All we can not free ourselves from / You free us, o great God Adonai, / and all your people. / Amen, Lord. May this prayer rise to heaven, may it reach heaven![27]

The *minḥah* ritual of afternoon prayer, given the relative infrequency with which it appears in testimony, seems to have been less commonly observed by Judaizers. There are only occasional references to prayers at noon, such as this one reported from Castile in the sixteenth century: "Blessed are You, O Lord, who allowed me to see this mid day without losing hope and without experiencing the dangers and trials of this world; may it please You, Lord, to let me see this mid day and many other full days with fewer sins and greater dedication to Your holy service."[28] On the other hand, prayers at noon or early afternoon are common among modern Portuguese *cristãos novos*. An example is this afternoon prayer from Rebordelo: "I come to begin my prayers before You, Lord; my God, help me to praise You, to magnify You. In the name of the Lord, Adonai, amen."[29]

Traditionally the *ma'ariv* prayers are recited at sundown and the *niylit* prayers upon going to bed. Both were common among crypto-Jews. Because the *Shema* requires Jews to speak of the teachings of the Torah upon going to bed, the evening service opens with the common benedictions, focusing on praise of God the creator of the night. A standard version was recited by Luísa Antónia [Coimbra 1583]: "Blessed art Thou, Adonai, our God. By Your command the nights fall. Your knowledge opens doors. With Your wisdom You change the hours, command the stars in the sky according to Your will, create day and night and envelop the light in the darkness. . . . You gave Your people the law and commandments; Lord gladden us with the words of Your law."[30] Crypto-Jews used the emergence of the first star from the twilight sky as a signal for when to say these prayers. Beatriz Pérez [Granada 1575] and her mother "would go to the window at night to say the prayer of the star."[31] Rafael de Sobremonte said that when he and his father were coming back to Mexico City from Zacatecas in 1643, "he saw that his father would stop in some gully they found and would wash his hands, and take the handkerchief that he had knotted around his waist and cover his head with it, and wrapped in his cape he would stand there reciting the prayers of the law of Moses."[32] Leonor Martínez [Mexico 1648] reported that "her grandmother had taught her Jewish prayers, taking her out twice to pray every evening, sitting down and looking at a certain star which she indicated. Often before praying she would have [Leonor] sing certain glosses which were for the purpose of attracting her to Judaism. Then she would take her to look at the stars, and when the one they were looking for had set, they would both pray those prayers."[33] Francisco Botello [Mexico 1659] used to "go outside to pray in the garden of the house they lived in in Tacubaya, an action which was undoubtedly Judaizing in nature, because they look for a place and time to see the evening star and watch it come up which is wholly alien from the customs of Catholic Christians, who for this purpose go into the most hidden parts of their houses to pray before some image."[34]

Sometimes these prayers were combined with those traditionally recited just before going to sleep. As with the other prayers of the daily cycle, they frequently began with an expression of praise ("Blessed and praised are You, Lord, who gave the staff of Aaron to sainted Moses, and who ordered him to cleave the rock so that we would have clean hands to praise you with"[35]) and a request for forgiveness ("Extend Your grace over me; relieve my inadequacies; wash my misfortunes with Your hands and fill them with glory and contentment; may my humble thoughts praise You, Lord"[36]). Clara Henríquez [Granada 1593] used to pray from her bed: "I lie down in the power of Adonai for many are His mercies and He will have mercy on me"; to which she would add: "Lord God, reveal your truths so that we will not walk in error."[37] Even more common were requests to be kept safe through the night. In 1484 Alonso Marcos said that he had heard Juan de la Sierra pray before going to sleep: "Lord, I am Yours and my dreams are Yours."[38] Also common throughout Iberia was the prayer "May the Lord grant us a good night, and the great God of Israel wake us to good"[39] or more simply, "Let us lie down, Father, in peace," which is a part of the traditional *ma'ariv* prayer.[40] Frequently, particularly among Portuguese crypto-Jews, a Guardian Angel or some other protective spirit might be invoked. For example, in 1573 Maria Lopes, of the Azores, recited these prayers to the Lisbon Inquisition: "Protect me, Angel Raphael, from all suffering." "Protect me, Adonai, Angel Gabriel, Angel Uriel [?] free me from all suffering."[41] Modern Portuguese evening prayers, of which there are a profusion, reflect these traditional themes of praise, supplication, and yearning for protection.

> May I lie sleeping in my bed; / may my doors be closed / with the keys of Abraham; / may good things enter, / may bad things be kept away, / and the angels of the Lord, / be with me.[42]
>
> May I lie sleeping in my bed; / may five angels be found there, / two at my feet, three at my head / and the Lord most high in front of me.[43]
>
> May the Lord give me a good night to my body and soul, salvation for souls, peace for the world, glory for the dead, peace to the living. O Lord, free us from our enemies, who speak of us well and do us ill, from bad men and bad women and tongues that say whatever they like.[44]

> May God bless me from feet to head as He blessed Isaac and Jacob. O blessed Lord, let me sleep. Lord keep me this night and all through tomorrow. O omnipotent Lord, keep me in Your company.[45]
>
> May God cover me from my feet to my head with the blessing of Isaac and Jacob. May the blessed Lord grant me sleep. May the Lord keep me this night and tomorrow morning and the whole day.[46]

Some crypto-Jews completed their daily cycle of prayer at midnight. Elvira Alvarez [Ciudad Real 1484] said that ten years earlier she had heard "Sancho de Ciudad get up at midnight to pray saying: '*Abraham, Adonai*,' and other things she does not remember." María Díaz added that she heard him "get up at midnight and read like a Rabbi making a *berakhah*, which lasted some two hours."[47] A century and a half later Tomás Treviño de Sobremonte [Mexico 1647] was charged with "getting up in his undergarments, wrapping in a cape, and buckling on his shoes, to pray at midnight, with his head covered and his glasses on. First he washed his hands, for which he had a jar of water sitting on a chest. And drawing near the light he prayed from a little Book of Hours, spending about three quarters of an hour at it, and then going back to bed when he had finished praying."[48]

What is clear in all these testimonies is the centrality of prayer in the lives of the Iberian crypto-Jews. This point could not be expressed more clearly than in the words of Ferrand Alvarez [Aranda de Duero 1502], who reputedly told Juan de Salcedo "that he just wasn't himself the day that he did not pray, nor did he think that God blessed him that day. And the day he had to travel he was content, because then he could pray as he pleased." He then added, contrasting his prayer with Christian observance: "We go to church, they say the mass, we don't know what they are saying or not saying. They elevate when they say they are elevating and we look at them and I don't know what else. Know that I am never entirely myself the day that I don't recite a prayer."[49]

## 15.2. Prayers Related to Food and Hand Washing

Prayers related to hand washing and to eating, while not figuring per se in the daily calendar of prayer, were part of almost every crypto-Jew's routine. These prayers tended to be recited in the home, not the synagogue, and to form part of private, not communal, worship. While there was always the danger of being observed by one's servants, or of being denounced by some non-practicing member of the family, these home prayers were safer than those which required communal participation. Moreover, they tended to be brief and their daily repetition facilitated their retention in an individual's memory. As a result, at least in their simpler forms, they tended to persist until quite late among crypto-Jews.

The ceremony of washing the hands (*netilat yadayim*) appears to be of rabbinical rather than Biblical origin. The hands must be clean prior to the ritual washing, which is not for hygienic purposes but rather for religious purification. In fact, when water was unavailable dirt could be used. A fifteenth-century compendium of Judaizing customs recognizes that "before they pray they wash their hands with water or earth,"[50] and a new-Christian named Graçia [Burgos 1492], mother of the rabbi of Los Arcos who had not yet converted, "used to wash her hands with dirt before reciting the *Kaddish* with her son."[51] However, hands were most generally cleansed with water. Traditionally the hand is immersed up to the wrist, or water is poured over both hands, wetting them up to the wrist. Rings and other impedimenta are removed so that the water may come in contact with the entire hand. Hands are washed three times upon arising as part of the *shaḥarit* liturgy, and once before eating bread, each time reciting the blessing ". . . and commanded us concerning the washing of the hands."[52] Sometimes hands were dipped into a basin, as in the clandestine Cordoban synagogue where around 1504 Alonso de Córdoba Membreque recited "the prayer for clean hands while first washing his hands; and that in the same water where the rabbi washed . . . the other people who were there washed their hands; each one said the prayer for cleaning the hands."[53] But more frequently water from a pitcher was poured over the hands, a custom that was interpreted as peculiarly Jewish, or at least that seems to be the sense of a late fifteenth-century satiric poem against the *converso* poet Antón de Montoro, which lists among his Judaizing customs that he washed his hands at the spout of a pitcher.[54] The reason for the pitcher was ably explained by the *converso* Diego Díaz Nieto [Mexico 1601] when he testified that "the hands were not to be put into the jar, but rather water was to be thrown directly from the jar over the hands and face since immersion of the hands would have dirtied the water. Washing was necessary because night dreams were under the aegis of demons" (Liebman 1970, 195).

This ritual ablution was considered an essential precursor to prayer. Lope García [Soria 1502] testified that in the 1470s he had observed a *converso* named De la Moneda pray at night when they were lodging together in a room near the synagogue: "And when De la Moneda heard the Jews praying, he asked this witness to get up and bring him the wash pitcher, and this witness got up and gave it to him. And after he had washed his hands De la Moneda prayed things in Hebrew while he was still lying in bed. And when he was asked why he washed his hands and was lying in bed, he said that it was because the Jews were accustomed to washing their hands before praying."[55] In the sentences of Portuguese Judaizers in Coimbra in the 1570s there are frequent reports of washing hands before praying. Typical is the case of Branca Dias, accused of "praying three or four prayers with Jewish intent, and washing her hands in the Jewish fashion before she began and again when she finished."[56] Similarly, one of the accusations against Tomás Treviño de Sobremonte [burned in Mexico 1649] was that "after eating, this perfidious Jew washed his hands with cold water because he did not want to remain *trefa,* which means contaminated."[57]

The prayer most commonly recited during this ablution by sixteenth-century Portuguese Judaizers was some variant of "Lord, You who commanded us on Zion to wash our eyes, and our head and our hands . . ."[58] Tomás Treviño de Sobremonte declared that his mother always washed her hands, mouth, and eyes after eating, and that he did as well, reciting the prayer she had taught him: "Blessed be mighty *Adonai,* who in Your teachings taught me to wash my hands, mouth and eyes in order to praise and serve You, and praise and honor of the Lord and the Law of Moses."[59] Occasionally a crypto-Jew would even add to the *netilat yadayim* a phrase specific to the Iberian experience. In the Membreque synagogue in Córdoba around 1504, for example, the congregants allegedly said that "just as they were washing their hands in that water, just so they would wash their hearts clean of any belief in the Law of the Christians."[60]

A number of prayers for the washing of hands have survived among modern Portuguese *cristãos novos*. Two of the most common are

> Lord, wash me with the water of salvation, / forgive me my sins, / for You know well what they are. / Give me peace in this world, and salvation and pardon / and help in the other, / for all is in Your divine hands, / Lord Adonai, Amen.[61]

> Praised be the Lord, who gives me water to wash and a cloth to dry myself; in this way may the Lord give me grace to serve Him and knowledge to praise him, *Adonai*. Amen.[62]

Jews traditionally recite benedictions both before and after eating. The blessing preceding the meal is brief, thanking God for creating bread[63] (and on special occasions, wine), foods that symbolize the full bounty of creation. Variants of these simple prayers are found throughout the crypto-Jewish experience. In a 1484 trial in Ciudad Real it was reported that *conversos* "blessed the bread in the Jewish fashion, and then blessed a glass of wine."[64] The Mexican *conversa* Leonor de Cáceres, tried in 1601 (at age 14) and again in 1652, used to recite before meals: "Lord God, true creator, may Your favor never fail even in the uninhabited deserts."[65] In the trial of the Seville liquor dealer Gabriel Gomes Navarro [Lisbon 1673] this prayer over wine, fruit, or bread was recorded: "Blessed be He who created you from the dust of the earth to be food and sustenance for sinners; may He renew our souls to serve God in the high heavens."[66] Another blessing was recited over fish: "Blessed be the Lord who raised you in the waters of the sea as sustenance for sinners."[67]

The much more elaborate traditional prayers following the meal thank God in turn for the food which has just been consumed, the gift of the land of Israel, the rebuilding of Jerusalem (no matter that it still lay in ruins), and for preserving Judaism from destruction.[68] The grace after meals is alluded to frequently in Inquisition testimony; however, the bulk of these allusions give few specifics, instead merely mentioning that a grace was said. In the early days even relatively uneducated Judaizers were likely to know some version of this prayer. Juana Fernández la Brisela, of Molina de Aragón, just prior to the Expulsion testified that when her family finished eating her mother would say "Blessed be He whose food we eat. Blessed be He. Blessed is His memory for ever and ever," while her father would make them recite the Pater Noster![69] María Alvarez [Toledo c. 1500] told Inquisitors that this was the only Jewish prayer that she knew (Rábade Obradó 1990a, 438). Miguel Pelligero [Soria 1491] said that he was eating with Pedro Núñez when Núñez's grandson put his hands together and began to pray. Núñez slapped him and said: "What's with this *Adonai*? This is not a good time to be praying!"[70] Luis Fernández Tristán, who was burned in effigy in the great Mexican *auto de fe* of 1649, was charged with the fact that "after the supper he would go to a window and give thanks to the God of Israel" (Liebman 1974, 223).

The preserved texts of such prayers suggest that they were much simplified from the pre-Expulsion models. Typical was the prayer of the *converso* Juan Díaz [Ciudad Real 1484], who "when he ate blessed the table, saying: 'Let us praise God who has given us what we eat and drink, blessed be He and his Holy Name.'"[71] In some graces Moses came to take on the advocacy role Jesus plays in the Christian counterparts of these prayers. The Portuguese goldsmith Diogo Alvares [Evora 1619] reported that he used to say this grace after meals: "Moses, we worship you. We give you thanks for the favors you do for us every day, in every hour."[72] Gabriel Gomes Navarro [Lisbon 1673] recited this prayer after eating: "Blessed be the Lord who gives us so many of His gifts; blessed be the prophet Moses for his assistance to the Jews."[73]

The modern crypto-Jewish graces recorded in Portugal echo these trends but omit the references to Moses. In Felgueiras and Belmonte this grace is recited: "May what we eat be sufficient, may what we drink serve us as medicine, and may what is left over be a blessing. Let us praise the Lord because His goodness is eternal. Amen."[74] Another grace from Belmonte is "Just as You, Lord, created bread to signify Your bounty, Lord may you give me the bounty of Heaven and earth to celebrate Your festivals, and may You be pleased to use me in Your holy service. Amen."[75] Machado records another variant: "Blessed thanks be given to the Lord for the gifts which He has given us and will give us. O Lord who now gives us what we need, sustain us in every hour. For Your holy and divine good, free us from suffering and from all evil. Amen, Lord. May this rise to heaven."[76]

While the benedictions over food are recited at every meal, the blessings over wine (*Kiddush*) are reserved for the Sabbath and festivals. They focus on the wine, but their true import is to thank God for His gift of the holy days. Evidence of the *Kiddush* is most prevalent in trials just prior to the Expulsion and varies little from testimony to testimony: "They bless the table according to the custom of the Jews, and they drink Kosher wine, and they take a glass of wine and say certain words over it, and then each drink a sip."[77] The Ciudad Real crypto-Jewish community was completely traditional in reciting the *Kiddush*. In Juan Falcón's house "when they set the table for Saturday and on other days, they put on it a large glass of wine; and after they were seated to eat Juan Falcón read from a book, and afterwards he whispered certain words over that wine glass and blew on it and then gave everyone a drink of that wine."[78] Another report concerned the González family:

> That day was Saturday, and he saw how Alonso González, after he had eaten, took a glass of wine in both hands and began to pray and bob his head over it, and he began to raise it above his head like the chalice when they elevate it [in mass], and then he lowered it, and then he and his wife and children who were all present around the table began to pray and bob their heads. He drank a little and gave it to his wife and his children, and after this his children kissed his hand, and their mother's hand, and he put his hand on their heads. The witness saw this from behind some large earthenware vats where they did not see him.[79]

In Soria around 1496 [testimony 1505] a curious addition to the traditional *Kiddush* is noted: "they took a little wine and blessed it and then threw a little of it into the lamp."[80] These customs persisted with little variance over the next two hundred years. In Toledo in the sixteenth century the head of the *converso* family "took a glass of wine in his hand and prayed over it and everyone took sips of that wine." Other cases refer specifically to "blessed wine."[81] *Chuetas* in Majorca in the seventeenth century recited an *Idus* [*Kiddush*] that they learned from the book *Remillete de Flores*. They said the *Idus* "with a cup in hand, and after drinking a little [wine] out of it, the master of the house gave it to his wife to drink. All this was done in accordance with the instructions of the book, in remembrance of the practice of the Jews who, upon leaving the synagogue on Friday evening, went to their homes, and recited this prayer with a wine-cup in hand, allowing all the circumcised to drink of it."[82]

## 15.3. Prayers for Specific Purposes

In traditional Judaism significant events and routine daily activities were both likely to be sanctified by prayer. Some prayers were tailor-made for specific situations, while others, of a more general nature, might be applied to a number of circumstances. The prayers most likely to persist were relatively brief and thus easily committed to memory. Many were designed for intimate domestic occasions in which they might be uttered relatively freely. Not surprisingly, these circumstances allowed crypto-Jewish families to pass these prayers along in the oral tradition for many generations.

Among the most long-lived were the blessings (*Birkat ha-bonim*) that parents uttered over their children. An early compilation of Judaizing customs described this blessing in its most basic form: "They put their hand on top of the head, drawing it down over the face without making the sign of the cross, which they say recalls the blessing that Jacob gave to Menasseh and Ephraim, his grandchildren, sons of Joseph born in Egypt, when he put his hands on their heads and blessed him as is written at the end of Genesis in the testament of Jacob."[83] Testimony in hundreds of cases suggests that this was a very accurate description. *Converso* fathers in the Castilian village of Casarrubios used to bless their children with their hands on the children's heads, saying "May God grant you fortune," to which the children replied "May God bless you."[84] María González [Ciudad Real 1511] confessed that "she often blessed certain people in the Jewish fashion, when they kissed her hands, by placing her hands on top of their heads and drawing them down over their face, as the Jews are accustomed to do."[85] In Juana González's house too the young people kissed the older people's hands and the older people put their hands on the heads of the younger, without making the sign of the Cross.[86] In later years the procedure did not vary much. Branca Campos, a *cristãa nova* abbess tried by the Inquisition in Coimbra in 1623, said that the blessing was given "by placing an open hand on top of the head and passing it over the face while saying: 'God of Abraham, God of Isaac, and God of Jacob.' "[87] A modern version of the traditional mode of blessing, described as a prayer for washing the face, comes from Bragança from the 1930s: [The hand is placed on the head]: "*Adonai*, Lord, turn Your holy and divine face to mine; You before, I behind You, I will have not fear, or terror, nor will any evil thing befall me. I will be guided and governed by the great God *Adonai*." [The hand is drawn down across the face to the chest.] "God bring His holy and divine blessing on me, on my husband and on my children."[88]

Kissing the hand plays a prominent part in the twentieth-century Portuguese holdovers of this custom. Vasconcelos, for example, records these four new-Christian ways of blessing: (1) With the palm of the hand turned toward the light, touching the head with the back of the fingers, drawing the hand down across the mouth, and kissing it. (2) Drawing the hand from the head to the mouth, and kissing the hand, then bringing it to the chest and beating the chest several times. (3) Drawing the hand from the belt across the shoulders and to the top of the head, and repeating this circle three times. (4) Touching the mouth, then the chest, then the forehead, and then pointing to heaven and saying: "May the words of my heart rise from my mind to God."[89] Similarly, Clemente Carmona told David Nidel in New Mexico in 1980 that in his family, which considers itself to be crypto-Jewish, the women give the more powerful blessings, and that he always kissed the hand of the person who was blessing him (Nidel 1984, 254). Paulo found this absolutely normative rendition of the traditional priestly benediction (*Birkat cohanim*, found in Num. 6:24–6) in Vimioso and in Pinhel: "May the Lord bless you and keep you. May the Lord make his countenance shine on you and have mercy on you. May the Lord turn His divine face to you and grant you peace. Amen."[90]

The persecuted and clandestine nature of the crypto-Jewish religious existence heightened the importance of prayers for deliverance from all sorts of ills, and these prayers are common in the record until quite late. Some are merely generic cries for help.[91] Some request freedom from one's enemies. For example, Filipa Mendes, of Vinhais, recited this prayer in Coimbra in 1586: "I commend myself to God so that no additional evil may befall me; You go up to the heavens and count the stars and descend to earth and measure the waters and weigh the branches and measure the blasts of the wind. The mercies of God are stronger to save me than are the evil deeds of my enemies to afflict me or to do me ill."[92] Other prayers seek deliverance from the Inquisition prisons. Beatriz Henriquez, of Oliveira do Conde, recited this prayer in prison in 1574: "Lord, as You freed those who were in Egypt, opening the sea for them in twelve paths, just so free me from this prison in which I find myself" (Azevedo Mea 1981, 168). Nine years later Isabel Lopes, of Miranda do Douro, was overheard reciting this prayer in prison: "Lord, as You took out Your servants and brought them to the Promised Land, just so, Lord, may You take me out of all my troubles."[93] María de Rivera [Mexico 1642] recited this prayer for deliverance from illness: "O Great God of Israel, / who gives health to Your people, / grant health to me / and to my husband and children."[94] This much more complex example comes from Argozelo, Portugal, in the twentieth century: "Lord, God of Abraham, God of Isaac, God of Jacob, God of our forefathers, for who You are, Lord, I beg You for the sake of Your great name; I am not worthy of Your mercy; Give me health, Lord, as a merciful Father who remembers me, Lord, and has pity on my state. Do not let Your creations lack Your sustaining help, Lord; so that the peoples will ask where is our God now, who does not remember us, since it is certain that He is distant from us. Do not abandon me, Lord, nor my possessions. Blessed are those who rely on You, O powerful God of Israel, to fulfill the promise made to Abraham, our Father. Amen."[95] Sometimes distressed *conversos* learned by heart poetic pleas of supplication, or even composed their own. These three were recorded in the trial of María de Rivera in prison in Mexico in 1642:

> 1. My soul cries out to You
> to free me from fire and flame
> so that I will not burn nor be consumed.
> My God, I want to ask You for one thing,
> that You give me one thing in charity:
> remember my soul
> which is waiting [unclear text]
> may it be saved.
> I see myself in great trouble;
> they will throw me in great darkness;

neither cousin nor brother will be able to help me;
but only the things that I will do with my hand
and that You will do, Lord of truth.
Free me
from rabid dogs,
from hurtful swords,
from going indoors,
from going out of caves.
Let me be delighted by no other thing
than by witnessing the stars in the sky,
than by witnessing the water in the sea.[96]

2. O evening of the Lord,
may you be well received.
I commend myself to You, King of Adonai.
May You save me and protect me
from anger, from ire, from sudden death,
from rushing rivers,
from burning fires,
from the waters of the sea,
from the waters of the earth,
from living men,
from dire danger, from dead men,
from evil encounters
and from other dire dangers.
May my soul be free and unbound. Amen.[97]

3. Assist us, great Lord
for we wander in great affliction
from land to land
on account of our sins.
Do not forget us
Alleluia, alleluia, Adonai, Sabaot [Lord of Hosts].[98]

A number of crypto-Jewish prayers seem to sublimate this desire for freedom into a desire for peace. Clara Nunes, of Trancoso, [Coimbra 1584] used to pray: "Grant me peace to my right, peace to my left, peace in front of me, peace with my husband, peace with my children and peace with whoever wishes me well."[99] And this prayer for peace was recorded in an eighteenth-century manuscript from Rebordelo, Portugal: "Lord, You who are seated on the throne of mercy, give me peace. By Your will favor my soul as a leaf in the morning [dew]. Give me understanding, Lord, like the whitest snow, and grace with which to serve You. In the name of the Lord, Adonai. Amen."[100]

A variety of other crypto-Jewish prayers have found their way into the record. These might be for occasions as ordinary as setting out on a journey. Gonzalvo Ruiz [Teruel 1480] in the 1450s used to stop in the doorway when he left the house, bow three times to the door post, put his hands over his face, and raise them to his forehead.[101] Rabbi Mose Mohejo told the Toledo Inquisition in 1488 that F. de Jahen's wife begged him one night to take her to the synagogue. "When they got there she begged him to take out the Torah. She fell to her knees before it and wept and cried out certain prayers that her husband might have a safe journey, and she donated some money for oil for the synagogue."[102] Castilian crypto-Jews might pray: "Walking we give thanks to the Lord, whosoever confides in the Lord shall not lack favor."[103] The wife of Juan García [Aranda 1502] told him that "whenever she left the house to go to mass, as soon as she put her foot outside the door she would say: 'I commend myself to you, God of my father, God of Abraham, God of Isaac, God of Jacob, and in You I believe and trust, and everything else is nothing but vanity.' "[104] Bernardo Rodrigues [Bragança 1593] would recite this prayer when setting out on a journey: "Blessed be the name of the great Lord who created you, may He direct my steps, as He directed the chosen people of Israel."[105] Garci Sánchez de las Cosillas [Cifuentes 1490s] never set out on a journey without reciting the *levaya* [?] which the Inquisition identified as the Jewish blessing for travel (Blázquez Miguel 1986a, 55), and in fact a 1610 Edict of Faith from Cartagena [Colombia] still identified a prayer called "the ruayá, which is when a person sets out on a journey."[106] As with the other areas we have looked at, many travel prayers seem to have survived into the twentieth century. Paulo recorded this one in Felgueiras [Portugal]: "Lord, my spirit is governed by Your hand. Adonai, God of truth, make me walk straight among my enemies. O Lord of all things, be served, and open a straight path for me, as You, Lord, opened a path for Israel in the Exodus from Egypt. Amen."[107] *Cristãos novos* in Pinhel might say: "Accompany us on the Holy path of the Lord as You accompanied the son of Tobias. You chose to accompany him as a just man; may You protect me as the sinner I confess that I am. No one is equal in soul or life to the Lord; I shall praise Him so that at the end of my life He will give me glory."[108] Vasconcelos recorded in the 1930s in Portugal this prayer for traveling.

Adonai, guide me on a straight path because of my enemies; level the roads for me. May I be armed with the arms of Adonai. May I be covered with the cloak of the Lord. May we have the [?] of Saint Tobias on our bodies, so that we will not be imprisoned, nor wounded, nor killed, nor put in the hands of our enemies, nor tied with bonds. May we all be guided and accompanied by the power of the Lord. May the good things we see and hear be for us. May blessed Adonai be our salvation, and our guide, and our company with peace and calm, during night and day, and at the noon hour.[109]

Prayers for a number of other occasions have survived among modern Portuguese *cristãos novos*. Some are for occasions as trivial as winding one's watch. "May the Lord give the hours, / our troubles be over, / our goods be increased, / our sins be forgiven; / may we lie down in the lap of the Lord; / may the Lord's law be published here / and in the holy temple in Jerusalem. Amen."[110] Prayers for good harvest, such as these from Lagoaça and Pinhel, are common: "Blessed are You, our God, King of the World, who sanctified us through Your commandments, blessed and holy, holy and blessed, who gave us this life so that we would come to this time to give You infinite praise. O great God of Israel, You created the fruit for our sustenance; at all times may You, Lord, give us the sustenance to continue to serve You."[111] "As You created this flowering and beautiful tree, the most pleasant of all trees, just so may the Lord be pleased to bring us pleasant holidays, dedicating our fruit to His holy service. Amen."[112] "As You, Lord, created these flowers as a symbol of happiness, so, Lord, grant me peace and happiness to make a pleasant holiday for You, dedicated to Your holy service."[113] Finally, the documents record a number of prayers to be recited while giving charity, such as this one, from an eighteenth-century Portuguese prayer book: "In holy honor and praise of the Lord, I offer this meager charity in the holy name of the Lord. Accept it and use it for His holy glory. Accept this little gift as if it were great; may it help me serve the Lord and do His work and to free us from sin and from trouble, from poverty, and so that the Lord will free us from the hands of others, from the power of enemies, and from offending God. Adonai, amen."[114] Another is this one: "I offer this charity in honor and praise of the sacrifice of the Lord. May the blessing that the Lord extends to His beloved chosen saints be extended to this charity offering."[115]

## 15.4. Prayers from the Communal Liturgy

The structure of the daily synagogue rituals, despite its apparent complexity, is relatively straightforward and has not changed much in its overall outlines in the last five hundred years. As with private devotions in the home, prayers are conducted three times daily: *shaharit* in the morning, *minhah* in the early afternoon, and *ma'ariv* in the evening. Of the three the morning service is the longest and most complex, consisting of an opening series of benedictions (pl. *berakhot*; sng. *berakhah*); a selection of verses praising God in His various attributes (*zemirot*), to which are often added prayers seeking forgiveness (*taḥanun*) and asking for divine aid; a declaration of the unity of God (*Shema*); a formulary series of prayers which is recited while standing (*Amidah*); a prayer of consolation (*Kaddish*) which is recited at least once by the reader and again by congregants who are in mourning; and a closing priestly benediction. In addition to the above prayers it may include the public reading of a portion of the Torah and a supplementary selection from the Prophets (*haftarah*), each preceded and followed by formulary benedictions. The afternoon and evening services follow the same general pattern but are less extensive and omit the Torah reading. Within this general structure there is some freedom with regard to which Biblical verses are chosen for praising, for seeking forgiveness, or for supplication. On the other hand, a number of specific prayers and hymns within these general categories are commonly repeated; these are often referred to by the Hebrew word with which they open (*Alenu, Adon olam, Ein kelohenu, Yigdal*, etc.).

Certain parts of the crypto-Jewish liturgical tradition were remarkably resilient, while other parts eroded rapidly as isolation from mainstream Judaism and assimilation took their toll. As we have seen in earlier chapters, soon after the Expulsion Jewish literature all but disappeared, so that the transmission of liturgy relied almost exclusively on the oral tradition. Over time this shift from written to oral tradition inevitably triggered a number of significant changes and innovations in the traditional Jewish modes of worship:

- The range of the liturgy narrowed.
- Prayers tended to be shortened and simplified.
- Vernacular versions of traditional prayers replaced Hebrew.
- But a few Hebrew prayers, or isolated Hebrew expressions, survived for a long time.
- Newly composed vernacular prayers were added to the crypto-Jewish liturgy.
- Bits of Christian liturgy were adapted for crypto-Jewish use.
- Quantitative prayer entered the liturgy.

Trials in the decade prior to the Expulsion provide evidence to the fact that crypto-Jews, many of whom continued to associate religiously with their Jewish neighbors and family, were conversant with the full scope of Jewish liturgy. For new-Christians like the influential Diego Arias in Segovia, attendance at the local synagogue was part of their daily routine. Once the synagogues and books disappeared the liturgical repertoire of most crypto-Jews was strikingly reduced. Nevertheless, in sixteenth-century trials and occasionally even later we find traces of the principal prayers of the Jewish liturgy.

Without question the prayer that most commonly turns up in the public record is the *Shema*, Judaism's principal affirmation of monotheism.[116] In normative Judaism the *Shema* is recited as part of every daily prayer service and at several points in holiday liturgies. The full prayer is formed of Deut. 6:4–9, 11:13–21, and Num. 15:37–41. The *Shema*'s opening mandate—"Hear, O Israel, the Lord our God is one" (Deut. 6:4–9)—which proclaims the unity of God, is probably the best known and most often repeated prayer in Judaism. To this proclamation is added the doxology *Barukh Shem*—"Blessed be the name of His glorious kingdom for ever and ever." In many Inquisition documents this prayer is alluded to by its Hebrew name[117] or by reference, in translation, to its initial verse, such as in the 1484 accusation that María González recited in Spanish "a well-known Jewish prayer that the Jews consider their principal prayer that begins: 'Hear, O Israel.' "[118]

The *Shema* in translation was likely to be recited in any of the Peninsula's vernacular Romance tongues. For example, Joan Celma [Valencia 1491] confessed that he frequently recited the *Shema* in a mixture of Catalán and Hebrew.[119] María Lopes [Azores 1573] recited this Portuguese version: *Ouve Israel: Adonai é o nosso Deus. Adonai é uno. Bendito é o nome para a eternidade e perfeição* (Pereira 1979, 187). The Coimbra Inquisition in the 1570s recorded another fragment in Portuguese: *Ensina las as aos teus filhos, e aos filhos de teus filhos, pera que as diguão ao seu lançar, e ao seu alevantar* (Azevedo Mea 1982, 430). Frequently testimony indicates that often the *Shema* was the only Hebrew prayer a crypto-Jew was able to recite. Typical was Juan Ramírez [Ciudad Real 1513], who was denounced among other reasons because he said that "the prayers he prayed were Jewish and he prayed them from a Jewish book he had, for he did not know them by heart, except for the *Shema Israel*, a few words of which he recited by heart, along with some prayers in Spanish."[120] Despite the unfamiliarity with the Hebrew language of most Inquisition scribes, they wrote down many versions of the *Shema* that are recognizable today.[121]

If crypto-Jews possessed any written prayers at all, they were likely to include the *Shema*. Alonso Marcos testified in 1484 that Juan de la Sierra [Ciudad Real 1484] possessed "certain prayers, which were written on four or five sheets of paper, one of which read as follows: 'One which is to be said facing the wall, which begins: *Shema Israel, Adonai Elohenu*, etc.,' which he knows in its entirety."[122] In 1574 when a wall of a Portuguese new-Christian's house in Cabeço de Vide fell down, a paper with Hebrew writing tumbled out. A local canon translated it as the complete text of the *Shema* (Coelho 1987, 205). These written texts help explain the persistence of the fuller versions of the *Shema* that appear from time to time in the Inquisition documents. One of the most complete, found in an eighteenth-century Portuguese manuscript, is also one of the last to be recorded. It begins in Hebrew—"*Y eh. o. v. a. Schem. Y. A. Ela. hèno. A. Eha. Baruque Yova Bouquetu. Zim. Olan. Bahe*"—and then continues extensively in Portuguese.[123]

The *Amidah*, which is recited silently while standing and is an important part of the three daily services, is referenced in several trials from the time of the Expulsion. Typical is that of Alonso Marcos [Ciudad Real 1484], who testified that he used to pray "the *Amidah*, which begins: '*Adonai*, open my lips and my mouth to pronounce Your praises, etc.' "[124] In 1472 Jamila la Bancalera overheard Gonzalvo Ruiz, of Teruel, say "*Cadoz, cadoz, Adonai Cebahot*," a prayer taken from Isaiah 6:3, which is part of the *Kedushah*, the reader's repetition of the *Amidah* (Sánchez Moya 1973, 141). Tomás Treviño de Sobremonte [Mexico 1625] recited to his Inquisitors the prayer "Holy, Holy, Holy is the Lord of Hosts, the whole earth is full of His glory" (Liebman 1970, 241). The *Amidah* is also called the *Shemoneh Esreh* (Eighteen Benedictions) and contains these opening words which Diego Nieto [Mexico 1601] recited to Inquisitors: "O Lord, open my lips that my mouth may declare Thy praise."[125] Liebman in fact reports that some New World *conversos* knew the entire *Shemoneh Esreh* (Liebman 1982, 111).

The *Alenu*, the traditional closing prayer of each daily service, was reported with far less frequency, and in fact seems to have existed largely in the vernacular, such as the Catalán version reported by the Valencian new-Christian Joan Celma in 1491.[126] We also find traces of the *Takhnun*, the penitential prayer recited every day as part of the morning *shaḥarit* service (Millgram 1971, 461–3), as reported, for example, by Juan Ramírez [Ciudad Real 1513]: "Take pity, take pity, Lord, on us and on our affairs; O Creator, O Creator, take pity on us."[127] The *Modim*, a common prayer of thanksgiving, was reportedly recited by Isabel de Aguila, of Atienza, who was burned in 1541 (Caro Baroja 1961, 1:442). Surprisingly the *Kaddish*, an Aramaic doxology which is repeated in nearly every Jewish service and in addition forms a central part of the ritual of mourning, is seldom mentioned in the records. The few references to the *Kaddish* come from around Soria in the 1490s, where people like the *converso* Hernando de Alcalá [Calatañazor 1490] were accused of visiting the synagogue specifically in order to say "*cadís*" (Carrete Parrondo 1985a, 46; cf. 160, 174).

After the *Shema* the second most central prayers in crypto-Jewish ritual were the Psalms. The portions of the Psalms that express contrition and that praise and petition God are incorporated into nearly every Jewish religious service. In fact more than half of the Psalms find their way into some part of the standard liturgy.[128] Since many of the Psalms are supplications to a just God who rewards steadfast commitment to Judaism with rescue from adversity, crypto-Jews found their themes comforting.[129] Psalms were relatively available to the *conversos* in Latin Bibles, Books of Hours, and a variety of other Catholic devotional writings. Early crypto-Jews such as Luis Fernández [Ciudad Real 1503] were still able to pray the Psalms in Hebrew.[130] Even before the Expulsion, however, crypto-Jews were just as likely to recite the Psalms in one of the Peninsula's Romance languages. Psalms 46, 84, and 91 were sung in Catalán in the 1480s and 1490s.[131] The *converso* Esperandeu Salvador [Zaragoza 1485] allegedly owned a Book of Hours in Spanish that contained several Psalms and the prayers of San Cebrián and San Agustín, and he used to pray from it in church (Marín Padilla 1983b, 300). Judaizers in Bahia in the 1590s were accused of praying the Davidic Psalms in Portuguese (Lipiner 1969, 92). Perhaps even more common than vernacular versions of the Psalms were Latin texts, which circulated fairly freely. The psaltery that Rodrigo Alfonso confessed to having read in his cousin's house [Guadalupe 1484] was probably in Latin.[132] During his second trial in Mexico in 1595 Luis de Carvajal was found to have in his possession a small book entitled *Salmorum* (Lewin 1987, 213). When in 1627 the Bachelor Francisco Maldonado de Silva was tried in Chile, he transcribed for his Inquisitors by memory the Latin text of Psalm 10 (Lewin 1987, 213).

Perhaps the most popular Psalms among the crypto-Jews were the so-called seven Psalms of David, or seven Penitential Psalms. Medieval Jews were accustomed to sing a different Psalm each day of the week as part of the morning *shaḥarit* service. In the Catholic liturgy the seven Penitential Psalms were sung during the forty days of Lent. In the Vulgate these are Psalms 6, 31, 37, 50, 101, 129, 142; in the Jewish numeration they are Psalms 6, 32, 38, 51, 102, 130, 143. Possibly because of the easy accessibility of these Psalms, which tended to be packaged in a group in Catholic devotional works, they remained central in crypto-Jewish liturgy for a very long time. Juan de León was accused [Mexico 1643] of "reading from a paper the penitential Psalms in Spanish . . . in eight-line stanzas."[133] María de Zárate [Mexico 1655] was particularly fond of these Psalms: "Desiring to be saved, she prayed from her Book of Hours the Psalm *Miserere Mei* and immediately afterwards the rest of the seven penitential Psalms."[134]

Other groupings of Psalms were popular among crypto-Jews as well. Sometimes the groups were merely referred to as Davidic. Thus it is hard to know exactly which Psalms Manuel de Fonseca [Cartagena, Colombia 1610] had memorized in Spanish (Liebman 1975, 176), or which Psalms Graça Lopes [Coimbra 1567] recited "each morning and night [when she] prayed the twelve psalms of David in honor of the twelve paths that God opened in the Red Sea for the children of Israel."[135] At other times we know what the grouping was. For example, in Portugal in the 1570s crypto-Jewish liturgy incorporated Psalms 18, 25, 27, 32, 37, 51, 97, 121, 130 (Azevedo Mea 1981, 159–61). Simão Lopes da Guarda [Coimbra 1583] in the morning recited Psalms 6, 32, 51, and 130 (Azevedo Mea 1981, 162).

A favorite among crypto-Jews was Psalm 121, traditionally recited in time of crisis, danger, or illness. Francés de Puxmija [Teruel 1484] was observed praying it in Spanish on Passover.[136] Blázquez Miguel records a late fifteenth-century Castilian version of this Psalm.[137] Catalina Alfonso [Huete 1493] knew it in another Spanish version.[138] Other crypto-Jews constructed prayers from a pastiche of verses from the Psalms. For example, in 1596 Diego Díaz Nieto reported to the Inquisition in Mexico (as did his wife Catalina Henríquez, in a slightly different version, in 1643) this prayer, which combines original verses in Spanish and Portuguese with verses taken from several of the Psalms:

> High God of Abraham / Powerful King of Israel / Thou who hast listened to
> Ismael / a man of great piety ; Thou who dwellest as Lord / in the heights, /
> Listen to this sinner / who calls Thee from the depths. / Since Thou openest
> roads and fountains / to all creatures, raise my eyes to the mountains / from
> whence shall come my help. / My help shall come from the Lord. / He who
> made heaven and earth. / Free us from so much war, / though we are those who
> worshipped / alien gods, in which I, too, have erred / and I confess to that
> great sin within me. / Help shall come from Adonai, / Thou who made the
> heaven and earth. Have pity on me, Lord, / without my deserving it. / Transform my weeping / into song for Thee. / Open my heart; / so that I may always
> praise Thee, / let my soul not be silent.[139]

Psalms were, of course, central to Catholic liturgy as well. Most crypto-Jews seem to have de-Christianized the Catholic versions of the Psalms by omitting the "Glory to the Father, the Son, and the Holy Ghost," the doxology traditionally appended to the Psalms since the time of Augustine (Salomon 1982, 65). This omission was an especially telling sign to Inquisitors of a *converso*'s commitment to Judaizing and thus is frequently noted in trial testimony. The Portuguese student Gonçalo Váez [Granada 1571] reported that "he had persuaded a person in Salamanca to buy one of those Psalteries that do not have the *Gloria Patri* at the end of the Psalms, because it seemed to him a sin to say *Gloria Patri* because he believed that there was no more than one God and therefore there was no need to give glory to the Father and the Son and the Holy Spirit."[140] Ysabel de Montilla's mother [Granada 1595] taught her a Psalm, telling her that "when she said it in front of other people she should add '*gloria patri et filio et espiritu sancto*,' and when she said it alone it was only 'glory be to God.' "[141] Prisoners of the Mexican Inquisition, according to an informer in 1603, sometimes "after dinner on Friday night . . . stroll about . . . reciting the Psalms in Spanish without the *Gloria Patri*" (AGN Vol 276 doc 14, 418b). For that matter, the Trinitarian doxology was routinely omitted by the crypto-Jews wherever it appeared in the Catholic liturgy. Felipe Nunes, of Trancoso, [Coimbra 1571] allegedly closed her prayers by saying "instead of the *Gloria Patri*, 'May we be glorified before God when we render him holy service.' "[142] Jerónimo Rodrigues [Coimbra 1598] was accused of closing his prayers not with the *Gloria Patri* but with *Laus Tibi Domine Rex Eterne Glorie* (Azevedo Mea 1982, 85). The candy maker Antonio Leal [Lima 1618] finished his prayers with "Praised be God," instead of "Praised be Jesus Christ."[143] María de Zárate [Mexico 1650s] closed her prayers with the words "Praise be to the most holy Lord, God of Abraham, Isaac, and Jacob."[144]

Since every traditional Jewish daily prayer service includes prayers of praise, contrition, and supplication, it is not surprising that these themes pervaded the crypto-Jewish liturgy as well. Hymns of praise seem to have been particularly common in the latter stages of crypto-Judaism and range from simple to extensive and complex. Francisco Botello recited to Mexican Inquisitors in 1649 this brief prayer of praise: "Praised be the most Holy God of Israel, or the most Holy God of the

Hosts."[145] In 1625 in Lima the Portuguese Juan Acuña de Noronha, resident of Santiago de Estero [Argentina], was accused of praying: "Praised be God; blessed be the Lord of heaven; great is the God of Israel, Abraham, Isaac and Jacob."[146] The hymns of praise recorded in the 1701 Coimbra trial of Antônio de Sá Carrança and the 1713 trial of Salvador Pimentel, both from Bragança, stitched together a variety of Biblical verses (da Cunha e Freitas 1952, 21–2). Justa Méndez allegedly recited this one in 1596: "Let us joyfully sing praises of the Lord. No one who relies on Him goes unrewarded by His favor."[147] A much more extensive prayer was reported in the sixteenth century from Quintanar de la Orden:

> We are obliged to praise the Lord in all things because He did not make us like the gentiles of the world, nor did he set our fate like that of those communities; because they bow in vain and in emptiness pray to a god who does not speak. We bow to the King of kings, Lord of lords, holy and blessed, who stretched out the heavens and knew how to make of the foundations of the earth our home and our fortress. Turn your heart to Adonai, for my Lord is powerful in the heavens above, and on the earth below all are cast aside except Him; and there is no other except Him, as is written in His true and holy law. I shall hope in the Lord; I shall ask of Him mercy and grace with my tongue together with the people. I will speak to That Man with a clean heart and the odor of the holy house, amen. In our days, amen, in our nights, amen, in our lifetime may the city of Zion be built, may Your sacrifice be in Jerusalem, amen and amen. With permission of those present I ask You, Lord, to magnify the law and honor it for the love of . . . those here on earth. Keep me, Lord, on Your holy paths.[148]

In the mid-seventeenth century Manuel López, of Burgos, startled the tribunal by sinking to his knees and reciting: "*Adonai*, blessed is the powerful king who created the heaven and the earth; all powerful and eternal forever in the law which He gave on Mount Sinai; the true and holy *Adonai*, the blessed, who reigns in Jerusalem with Israel forever; the miracles of *Adonai* will be seen on your people, and the anger of *Adonai* on the gentiles."[149] Francisco Maldonado de Silva in his 1627 trial in Chile recited from memory the whole of Moses' thanksgiving prayer from Deuteronomy 30 (Böhm 1963, 46; Medina 1899a, 184). Hymns of praise are also copious among new-Christians in Portugal in this century.[150]

In the minds of some *conversos*, accustomed to the Catholic emphasis on serial repetition of brief prayers, quantitative praise took on great importance. The instructions for this prayer of praise from an eighteenth-century Portuguese new-Christian prayer book say that it is to be recited seventy-three times: "Blessed and praised, magnified, lifted up, manifest, revealed, honored, feted, and exalted by the seventy-three names of the Lord, Adonai. Amen." Another, "May the Lord be blessed and praised and magnified," was to be recited one hundred times.[151]

Prayers of supplication are common in Inquisition records, particularly up to the middle of the seventeenth century. Liebman found several versions of two prayers of supplication in Mexican records between 1596 and 1644: "O Lord our God, do not keep me in perpetual scorn for the sake of your name and your people,"[152] and "O Great God of Israel, You who heard Daniel, hear my prayer. You who reign on high, Lord, have mercy on me; without Your help I will be turned to lamentation. Open my heart to sing to You and to praise You forever, and preserve my soul."[153] The Mexican *conversa* Leonor de Cáceres recited this prayer at her first trial in 1601 (at age 14) and repeated it again in 1652: "Look at me, Lord, and hear me for I am poor and in need."[154] In 1678 Ana Cortés recited to the Inquisition in Majorca a prayer that her father Joseph Cortés had taught her that began: "Our mighty Father / who every day performs wonders," and ended "Great God of Israel, / You who have opened a road / in the sea and on dry land / have mercy and pity on us / for the sake of who You are."[155] An eighteenth-century Castilian example was "On the dry tree the Lord created those green leaves; thus may God keep us in peace and health and free us from our enemies."[156] Paulo recorded this supplication in Belmonte, Portugal, in this century: "God give us the faith of Abraham, the contrition of David, the wisdom of Salomon, the victory of Gideon, the warning that was given to Lot, the happiness of Jacob, the spirit of Elijah, the charity of Tobias, the patience of Job. Lord, God of Adonai, amen."[157]

These prayers of supplication are related to the traditional prayers asking for forgiveness (*selihot*), series of which form a special order of service recited on fast days and during the High Holidays. A large number of prayers, many of which were composed during the Middle Ages, are considered *selihot*, and they were particularly popular among *conversos* of the Expulsion generation. In 1484 Juan Díaz was accused in Ciudad Real of owning a book that gave the laws of Hanukkah, Rosh Hashanah, *selihot* and the Passover.[158] In 1503 Luis Fernández confessed in Ciudad Real that he frequently prayed çeliah [sng. of *selihot*] early in the morning.[159] In Aranda [Soria 1502] Jorge Martines reported that once when he was staying with Juan de Salcedo he reproached him for praying in the middle of the night and Salcedo replied: "Shut up, I am saying *selihot*, I am saying *selihot*, so that God will take me out of this çara, which means 'trouble.' "[160]

Christian authorities often identified prayers as "Jewish" by their opening invocations of the Patriarchs or reference to the Deity by one of His traditional Jewish attributes. The most common opening formula, at least at first, was the one reputedly recited in a clandestine synagogue in 1504 in Córdoba: "O great, high King, redeemer, Abraham, Isaac, and Jacob."[161] In Castile *conversos* were likely to recite "My Lord Adonai, grant me good fortune, my Lord Adonai, and free me from the power of my enemies so that I can magnify You."[162] Majorcan Inquisition documents toward the end of the seventeenth-century record several prayers for arising in the morning (and also for washing hands and for slaughtering foul) that all begin with the formula: "Into your hands, Lord, I commend my soul."[163] The sentences handed down by the Coimbra Inquisition in the 1570s contain references to a variety of common opening formulas for Judaizing prayers: "God who created the heaven and the earth . . ." "God of Abraham . . ." "Adonai, Adonai, remember me . . ." "Praised be the name of the Lord . . ."[164] The Coimbra trials also provide a wide range of formulaic invocations and supplications:

- Our Lord, grant us peace, and preserve our King for the sake of a good life and peace, and extend the tent of your kindness over us . . .

- Save me, Lord of the highest heavens . . .

- Lord, save me and remember me in my trials and have mercy on me. . .

- God spoke to Abraham and said to him: Abraham, take your son Isaac who you love and go up to Mount Moriah . . .

- O great God of Abraham, o great God of Israel, You who heard Daniel, hear my prayer . . .

- Most worthy Adonai, my God, my shelter, my strong and firm castle, my great Lord in whom I trust . . .

- I get up now and place myself in Your power, Lord, who are filled with so many holy kindnesses . . .

- Just as You, Lord, took your servants out [of Egypt] and brought them to the Promised Land, just so, Lord, take me out of all my misfortunes . . .[165]

From time to time versions of traditional Jewish hymns also surface in the Inquisition records. Catalina Alfonso [Huete 1493] was accused of reciting what appears to be part of the popular hymn *Adon Olam*, said to have been composed in Spain by Solomon ibn Gabirol in the eleventh century: "There is no one but you, God, alone, who is glorified in the council of angels; blessed be our God, blessed be our God, blessed is our creator; in you there is no beginning nor end; you live and are not mortal and never died nor were buried."[166] One of the most popular hymns was the *Eḥad, mi-yodea*, a counting song based upon the traditional list of the attributes of God.[167] This version was recited in Cataluña in 1512:

Who knows and understands what is one?
One is God in Heaven, *barukh hu, barukh shemo.*
    Who knows and understands what is two?
Two are Moses and Aaron,
One is God in Heaven, *barukh hu, barukh shemo.*
    Who knows and understands what is three?
Three are our forefathers, Abraham, Isaac and Jacob, . . . etc.
Four are the mothers of Israel, Sarah, Rebecca, Leah and Rachel, . . . etc.

Five are the books of the Law, . . . etc.
Six are the days of the week,[168] . . . etc.
Seven are the days with the Sabbath, . . . etc.
Eight are the days to circumcision, . . . etc.
Nine are the months of pregnancy, . . . etc.
Ten are the commandments of the Law, . . . etc.
Eleven are the brothers of Joseph, . . . etc.
Twelve are the tribes of Israel, . . . etc.[169]

## 15.5. Christian Influences

As Catholics living in a pervasively Catholic world, crypto-Jews in both Spain and Portugal were immersed in Christian liturgy and symbolism. It is only natural that they adapted Christian ritual to their own purposes. In addition to de-Christianizing Catholic prayers by dropping references to the Trinity, as we have seen above, many crypto-Jews modified specific Christian prayers. Often the Inquisition testimony suggests a kind of generic adaptation. Isabel Texoso [Mexico 1646], for example, was accused of having modified a number of Catholic prayers for use by Jews.[170] Roth cites the cases of Pedro Alvares, who stated in his 1594 trial that "he used to commend himself to God with Christian prayers."[171]

The most common crypto-Jewish adaptations were of the ubiquitous *Pater Noster* (Matt. 6:9–13; Luke 11:2–4). These were facilitated by the fact that the *Our Father* itself is an amalgam of several common Jewish prayers: "Our Father who is in heaven" (*Avinu sh'bashamayim*) is a phrase found in many Hebrew prayers; "May it be Your will" (*Yehi ratzon*) are the opening words of the prayer recited after the Torah reading on Mondays and Thursdays; "May Your name be hallowed and may Your kingdom come" (*V'yitkadesh shemai rabba . . . v'yamlikh malkhutai*) is part of the *Kaddish* (Brookes 1959, 138). *Conversos* of the Expulsion generation, of course, were familiar with many traditional Jewish prayers and had little need to adapt the prayers of their Christian coreligionists. The only evidence of *Pater Noster* adaptations I have found from that time is Pedro Rodríguez's assertion [Guadalupe 1485] that the innkeeper Manuel González had prayed for him "a Jewish *Pater Noster*, which goes *Pater noster, de tuhel de tuhel amaharón*, etc."[172] But by the end of the sixteenth century crypto-Jews throughout the Iberian world were praying the *Pater Noster*. In 1589 in Mexico Doña Guiomar, wife of Luis de Carvajal, allegedly counseled crypto-Jews that "one should only pray the *Pater Noster*, and no other prayers, except the penitential Psalms."[173] The Evora Inquisition heard in 1637 how Manuel Gonçalves taught the local new-Christian women "to pray Our Fathers and Ave Marias and to offer them to Moses." A similar practice is reported from 1657.[174] Isabel Martí y Cortès [Majorca 1678] recited this idiosyncratic version of the *Our Father*: "Our powerful father, / who every day works miracles, / have pity, great God, on us / and on your simple sheep / who are stung by bees / with such great affliction. / You who are powerful, eternal God / have pity on them. / May Your name be sanctified / now and forever. / Lord, show us your light, / do not keep it hidden. / If in times past our people / have strayed from You / Lord, may they be forgiven, / as is written in Your sacred law. / You, great God, who art in heaven, / seated on Your holy throne, / have pity, great God, on us, / and Your people who yearn for You."[175] On the other hand Duarte Lopes [Evora 1591] prayed the "Our Father" by default: he said that "he believed in the God of Heaven who gave the Law to Moses and that he prayed to him the Our Father" because he did not know any Jewish prayers.[176]

The Judaized "Our Father" remained popular even into modern times. José da Silva, a Judaizing Brazilian poet, testified to the Lisbon Inquisition in 1726 that "he recited the Our Father without saying Jesus at the end."[177] And a long gloss on the *Pater Noster* was recorded in Portugal in 1936: "Holy God, merciful God, / omnipotent God, / Continue, my God, being / *Our Father*. // Lord, treat as Your own, / such a troubled people, / who lives with the single hope / *that you are in heaven.* / Etc."[178]

Other Christian prayer-related customs were adapted as well. Some crypto-Jews even accepted the Apostles' Creed, although with the crucial modifications indicated by Bachelor Bartolomé Ruiz, a surgeon, who was denounced [Soria 1502] for having said that the "Credo was made by the Apostles, and it only goes as far as *iudicare viuos et mortuos.*"[179] Gaspar Gomes [Bahia 1644] evidently claimed that he "prayed the rosary to keep the Law of Moses" and that he prayed "two hail Marys and two Our Fathers for the Law of Moses."[180] The further from the date of conversion, the more likely the crypto-Jewish communities were to adopt Christian models. The crypto-Jewish communities of Portugal in this century produce several examples, such as this crypto-Jewish credo recorded in 1927 in Bragança:

> I believe in omnipotent God, creator of the heavens and the earth and all that is contained therein.
> I believe in You, Lord, and in Your holy and blessed law.
> I believe in You, Lord, the only true God.
> I believe that You saved Your people from the Red Sea and drowned their enemies.
> I believe in You, Lord, the only true God, who is the divine King and the King of glory, for only You are the King of kings, God of gods, Lord of lords, Father of fathers.
> Therefore, Lord, I trust in Your divine mercy which, Lord, will save me and free me from all danger and troubles and evil encounters.
> I trust, Lord, that You will free me from the bonds of the king, from the power of unjust justice, from evil neighbors, from evil tongues, from envious

eyes; and from that which we cannot free ourselves, nor overcome, may the great God of Israel free us and keep us.

The prayer concludes with a long list of evils from which freedom is sought.[181]

Traditional Jewish prayers commonly invoked God as the God of Abraham, Isaac, and Jacob or the God of Moses. These phrases did not entirely drop from crypto-Jewish ritual, but they are not cited in the documents with great frequency. Traditional prayers commonly also make reference to the assistance God granted Biblical figures such as Moses, Daniel, Jonah, and Esther, suggesting that similar favors are merited in the supplicant's particular case. Prayers of this sort often appear in the written records. Isabel Amorós [Valencia 1492] allegedly prayed that God "deliver us here as You delivered the people of Israel," and as He delivered Judith.[182] Isabel Lopes recited this prayer for freedom while in prison in Coimbra in 1583: "I call on You, Lord, from the deeps. Jonah called You and You took him from the belly of the whale. Just so, Lord, take me from these chains in order to serve You."[183] Brites Henriques [Lisbon 1674] requested that God "give me the help and favors / that You promised to Daniel. / May the coming of the Messiah / be in our days. / Send us as messenger / the prophet Moses to take us from captivity."[184]

The Catholic prayers with which new-Christians were familiar often invoked the Virgin, or some saint, to act as intercessor with God. While the need for a supernatural advocate is a concept foreign to traditional Judaism, crypto-Jews readily adapted the theology of the majority religion to their own needs. There is evidence of this process occurring even prior to the Expulsion. Juana Lopes [Garcimuñoz 1492] allegedly greeted her friends with the phrases "May Abraham protect you," and "May Abraham be your home."[185] This may also be the sense of the references to Mencia Suárez's [Ocaña 1488–90] prayers to Joseph (or Joshua). Catalina Gómez said that before the Inquisition took Mencia Suárez to be tortured, Mencia "gave her a prayer of Joseph to keep for her, which she has done. And that today, when they released her from prison, she threw it behind her bed." Aldonza Gómez reported that "in the Inquisition jail she had seen one of Suárez's books that contained a prayer to Joshua, in which the name *Adonai* appeared several times."[186] The instances of Jewish "saints" multiplied rapidly in the years following the Expulsion.[187] Esther was popular among crypto-Jews because, as Yerushalmi observes, the story of a Jewish queen who hid her true faith in order to save her people was a kind of "archetypal Marrano" (Yerushalmi 1971, 38). The new-Christian Paulo Rodrigues [Coimbra 1573] was charged with having said that "just as the old-Christians are devoted to Saint Catherine of Sienna and other saints, the new-Christians are devoted to Queen Esther."[188] Doña Juana Enríquez, reconciled in the Mexican *auto de fe* of 1649, was accused of venerating Saint Moses (Liebman 1974, 107), while Ana Núñez told Mexican Inquisitors in the 1640s that her parents had taught her to worship Moses and to pray to him: "Our Father, Our Father,

God save you, God save you, amen, amen."[189] Isabel Martí y Cortès [Majorca 1678] recited her crypto-Jewish version of a prayer to *San Raphael*.[190]

One characteristic of twentieth-century Portuguese crypto-Judaism is its veneration of Jewish saints, angels, and holy figures of all sorts. *Cristãos novos* from Belmonte until very recently used to hang pictures of St. Moses in their homes.[191] This hymn to Moses was recorded among crypto-Jews in Bragança, Portugal in 1937: "When we came to the sea / we cried out to Moses; / Moses answered us / with a voice full of pain / calling out to the great God of Israel / to assist us. / Let us praise the east, / let us praise the west / let us praise the great God of Israel / for ever and ever. / O great God of Israel, / holy and just and blessed / be Your Holy Name / written on Mount Sinai."[192] The Guardian Angel is another popular protector. This rhymed prayer was recorded in an eighteenth-century manuscript from Rebordelo with the instruction to repeat it thirteen times: "Guardian Angel, Bird of the Lord, the most divine, divining Lord! I beseech the unending Lord; go speak to God for me."[193] This prayer to the *Anjo da Guarda* was recorded in this century: "Guardian angel, accompany me and keep me on the path to truth. Do not let me do things that will offend the Lord. Observe my suffering and report it to the Lord. If I die, watch over me; if I live, accompany me."[194] Modern Portuguese crypto-Jewish prayers also make frequent references to the miraculous events of the Old Testament. The sacrifice of Isaac is a popular motif,[195] as is the story of Jonah.[196] A text of a prayer directed to the three youths of Babylon was recorded in Bragança in 1927.[197] A long prayer invoking Habacuc was recorded among crypto-Jews in Portugal in 1932: "When the Prophet Habacuc was out in the fields with his shepherds, giving thanks to the Lord . . ."[198]

## 15.6. THE PRACTICES OF PRAYER

Medieval Iberian Jews prayed with a motion that was described by observers as a swaying back and forth and a bobbing of the head. The origins of this custom are mysterious. It appears to have no Biblical source. In the twelfth century the Spanish philosopher Judah Halevi thought it derived from several people trying to read from a single book: "Each of them was obliged to bend down in turn in order to read a passage and to turn back again. This resulted in a continual bending and sitting up, the book lying on the ground. . . . Then it became a habit through constant seeing, observing, and imitating, which is human nature" (Millgram 1971, 360). The *Zohar* (3:218b-19a) explained it mystically by saying that "the soul of a Jew is attached to the Torah as a candle is attached to a great flame" (*Enc. Jud.* 13:983). Whatever its origin, from the very first Inquisition cases in the 1480s this swaying motion was considered a prominent characteristic of Judaizers. Spaniards labeled this motion *sabadear*, thus linking it with Sabbath worship. But abundant documents make clear that crypto-Jews swayed at prayer both alone at home and in communal worship, both while standing and while sitting. Typical is 1501 testimony from Almazán, which reported that when the *conversa* Elvira de Alves prayed she "turned toward the wall and for a while was seated *sabadeando*, raising and lowering her head."[199] In 1573 Inofre de Figueiredo said that he had spied Helena Soares, of Bragança, praying. "She was sitting on her bed between the linens, her head and shoulders covered by a shawl, and she was swaying her body forward and backward, lowering and raising her head, and then she bent forward and touched the wall with her head, even though she was sitting down."[200] A Brazilian Judaizer [1591] "joined the palms of his hands together and clapped his hands and separated them and clasped them again and lowered his head and raised it again, and bowed his body down and straightened up again."[201] It is unclear in these testimonies whether the *conversos* consciously retained the swaying motion as a sign of their commitment to crypto-Judaism, or whether the old habit prevailed even well into the processes of assimilation.

The documents also make frequent reference to Judaizers taking three steps forward and backward as they prayed, a custom Millgram ascribes to a symbolic drawing near to God, as in Genesis 18:23, and taking leave of God at the end of prayer (1971, 358). This stepping forward and backward commonly framed the recitation of the *Amidah*, but Iberian Judaizers seem to have extended it generally to their prayer. The *converso* Alonso Lopes [Burgo de Osma 1501] was observed out in the countryside to "go down into a gully, near a thorn tree, and stand in front of the thorn tree. And there he lowered and raised his head and took some steps forward and others backward; and sometimes he bowed his head so low that it seemed he touched the ground."[202] Similarly, a 1527 trial refers to *conversos* who "made certain bowing motions with their bodies and with their heads every three moments and took three steps backwards and forwards and what they were praying was in Hebrew."[203]

Iberian Judaizers as they prayed also bowed low to the ground, stretched out their arms, or opened and closed their fingers in accord with Biblical descriptions such as the 1 Kings 8:54 picture of King Solomon at prayer. The sentences handed down by the Coimbra Inquisition are remarkably rich in descriptions of these prayer practices. Typical is the description of Maria de Fonseca, of Aveiro, who "frequently prayed in the Jewish fashion, standing, sitting, or kneeling with her hands raised—first having washed them—closing and opening them from time to time, and lowering and raising her head." Beatriz Dias, of Caminha, folded her hands on her breast as well. Graça Rodrigues, of Oporto, was described as praying with her open eyes raised to the light. Guiomar Cardosa, of Fonte Arcada, from time to time raised herself on tiptoe in her prayers. Helena Soares prayed while seated in her bed. "She opened her hands some ten times and closed them again, clapping them together. And she did this for about a quarter of an hour." She also "turned her head from side to side," and "turned her fingers as if she were praying her beads."[204] Brazilian Judaizers in the 1590s seemed to have prayed in much the same fashion. Anrique Vaz [Bahia 1591] allegedly worshipped while "sitting on a stone, with a hat on his head, praying the Psalms of David in Portuguese. While he prayed he brought his hands together and clapped his palms and drew them apart, and brought them together again, and lowered his head and raised it again, and swayed his body downward and upward. He often did this at nightfall, next to a large window where he could see the stars."[205] In the Americas some *conversos* prayed "with outstretched arms or with arms crossed over the chest or, when seated, with hands overlapping on the lap. During a recital of the *Shema* the left hand was used to cover the eyes and the right was placed over the heart" (Liebman 1982, 107).

It is traditional in synagogue services for Jews to rise at certain times and face Jerusalem. Judging from testimony, some Iberian Judaizers may have continued to do this. Marina González and her *converso* friends [Ciudad Real 1484] prayed in the patio of their house "turned toward where the sun rises and praying while bobbing their heads like Jews."[206] This custom was particularly common in Mexico, where new-Christians like the Carvajals [1580s] used to turn toward the east while they prayed (Cohen 1973, 208). A 1603 deposition describes the Mexican *converso* Ruy Díaz Nieto at prayer this way: "After he washes his hands, he sits upon a chest that he has in his room and crosses his arms over his breast. On his head he wears a large piece of cloth wound the way the Moors wear it. Facing east, and raising his eyes to heaven, for more than an hour . . . he prays in a language that you cannot understand."[207] Likewise Isabel Núñez, burned in effigy in 1649, was accused of praying "three times daily, covering her head with a hood, a handkerchief over her hands, turning her face to the East" (Liebman 1974, 167).

In most synagogues the reader's platform and the ark where the Torahs are kept are situated in the east to facilitate reverence for the holy city. But in most of the Iberian world crypto-Jews merely turned their faces toward the wall to pray, without apparent regard for which wall it was. Again, testimony is abundant. Alonso Marcos testified in 1484 in Ciudad Real that Juan de la Sierra "showed him certain prayers, which he wrote down on five or six sheets of paper, which said—or at least one of them said—as follows: 'One which is said facing the wall begins: *Shema Israel, Adonai Elohenu*, etc.,' and he knows it all the way through."[208] María Díaz and her daughters [Ciudad Real 1484] used to "pray facing the wall with their feet together."[209] Elvira de Alves [Sigüenza 1501] prayed "turned toward the wall and was there for a while sitting down, swaying back and forth, raising and lowering her head."[210] The *conversa* wife of Ferrand Alvarez had once said to Juan de Salcedo [Aranda 1502]: "Come here, Juan de Salcedo; you, who were the rabbi, do it just like my husband, who walks around the house praying in the morning and the afternoon and the evening, turning his face toward the wall. I would rather have a punch in the eyes than see him do it. And I don't know what he is praying, because I don't understand it."[211] This was also the custom in the Canary Islands where it was said of Gaspar de Paiva [Las Palmas 1581] that "being at a certain house when the Angelus rang, although all present knelt down, went apart into a corner close to the wall and stood with head humbly bent down and his hat in his hand. That on another occasion he was lying down at the ringing of the Angelus, and though called upon to kneel down, only smiled and turned his face to the wall, remaining so until the prayer was concluded" (Wolf 1926, 110). And Antonia Núñez described her father's and uncle's prayers to the Mexican Inquisition around 1648 this way: "Each of them stands behind the two doors of the room, facing the wall, my uncle's head covered with a white cloth like a monk's cowl, and my father's too."[212]

The Old Testament records several scenes of Jews praying while kneeling or lying prostrate in sign of their humility before the deity. However, since for medieval European Jews these attitudes were associated with Christian ritual, the practices were largely abandoned (Millgram 1971, 356–7). Iberian crypto-Jews, who tended to be ignorant of the rabbinical tradition and to base their practices directly on Old Testament models, frequently knelt to pray, but their kneeling for prayer may just as easily have been an imitation of Christian models of reverence. There are occasional references prior to the Expulsion to *conversos* like Sancho de Çibdad [Ciudad Real 1484] "praying kneeling on the floor" and "throwing himself bellydown on the floor."[213] But few went to the extremes of the *converso* Pedro el Romo [Soria 1490], who allegedly "had fallen on his knees in . . . the synagogue and had crossed himself, and that Diego had done the same and prayed an Our Father and a Hail Mary."[214] By the early seventeenth century such practices had become common among Iberian Judaizers.

In the colonies they seem to have been the norm. In Mexico [1580s] the Carvajal family used to kneel to pray on fast days (Cohen 1973, 208). In a letter Francisco Maldonado de Silva wrote from his cell in Lima to the "Synagogue of Rome" before he was burned in 1638, he said that every Sabbath he prayed on his knees (García de Proodian 1966, 385). In 1645 while in prison in Mexico Juan de León described to his friend Francisco Botello how one properly prays: "I get on my knees, resting my weight on my legs and bending my body very low, looking at the ground, with my hands together and my head very low, looking at the ground, my hands held together with the finger tips pointing up. And you must do this in the corner of the room, which is how they do it in my region, with the lamp lit."[215] Similarly, Tomás Treviño de Sobremonte [Mexico 1647] "used to pray in his storeroom, from a little Book of Hours, sometimes on his knees and other times standing."[216] As late as 1819 two country gentlemen appeared at a Jewish service in Lisbon, where Jews had been permitted to hold services openly since 1800, and "threw themselves down before the ark . . . on their knees fervently praying. They had come to Lisbon from the Trás-os-Montes" (Schechter 1917, 72).

Testimony tells us a good deal about the vocal style in which crypto-Jews prayed. In traditional Judaism most prayers were not recited but rather chanted in a manner that Inquisition informers easily recognized as Jewish. The guttural nature of the Hebrew language also drew their attention. The laborer Miguel [Ciudad

Real 1511], for example, reported that he often heard his master singing his prayers, and although "he did not understand what they were singing . . . he knew it was not Christian praying, because they chanted back in their throats as if they were strangling."[217] A *converso* witness in a 1527 trial said that "when he recited the prayer . . . he spoke deep in his throat and his voice was harsh as when the Jews pray, and the witness says that back when there were still Jews he saw them swaying back and forth and praying in their throats."[218]

In crypto-Jewish communal prayer frequently one member of the group read the prayers or recited them from memory and the rest of the congregation added certain refrains in unison. The practice carried over from that of the Iberian synagogues, for we know that *conversos* like Hernando de Alcalá [Calatañazor 1490] used to attend the local synagogue and chant the responses with the Jews (Carrete Parrondo 1985a, 46). In the clandestine synagogue frequented by Juan de Córdoba Membreque [Córdoba in 1504], "everyone responded together in unison to what the Bachelor Membreque preached to them. . . . At the end of the prayer . . . they all responded in unison 'Amen.' "[219]

## 15.7. THE PERSISTENCE OF HEBREW

First generation adult converts carried their knowledge of Hebrew with them into their new-Christian existence,[220] and even after 1492 there is evidence to the fact that some of them taught the rudiments of Hebrew to their children as well. It was extremely dangerous to possess any material written in Hebrew, of course, so that perforce the continuance of the language depended on oral transmission. Pious Judaizers learned what they could of the Hebrew liturgy by rote. Often *conversos* did not understand the meaning of Hebrew words but continued to recite them, or an approximation of them, believing the traditional sounds to be the most efficacious means of communicating with the deity. It seems likely that for other *conversos* repetition of a scrap or two of Hebrew prayer was a way of asserting their Jewish identity.[221]

The *converso* generation preceding the Expulsion, of course, lived in a milieu in which knowledge of Hebrew was extremely common. Many *conversos*, like Brianda Besant [Teruel 1486], were said to pray in Hebrew every day (Haliczer 1990, 213). The *converso* Pedro Alfonso was so well known as a Jewish scholar in Valencia in the 1480s that "when a Jew who was carrying a Hebrew book was asked who in Valencia could read it, he answered, Pedro Alfonso." Alfonso was even reputed to speak Hebrew at home with his wife (Haliczer 1990, 212). The *converso* priest Fernando de la Barrera was accused in Cuenca in 1491 of writing in Hebrew when he wanted to keep something secret (Carrete Parrondo 1979, 57). Another *converso* priest, Juan Rodríguez, from Tajaguerçe [Soria], in 1487 still kept a box with a Hebrew inscription that read: *Vahí Adonai et Yosúa vahié somó becholaraz*.[222]

Testimony from the years following the Expulsion is equally explicit about the ability of many *conversos*, men and occasionally women as well, to read or even speak the Hebrew that they had learned in their childhood. This is probably what is meant by the accusation that Fernand Laço's wife [Miranda de Ebro 1501] was heard "talking like a Jew."[223] In 1505 Juan Fernandes testified that "wishing to write to Gramel Ferran, and not knowing how, he begged a certain Ximenez to write for him, that he signed the letter in Hebrew characters, as he used to do before his conversion to Christianity, not having learned any other kind, but that he had no wish to offend against the Catholic Faith, or observe any Jewish custom, but merely because he knows no other writing" (Wolf 1926, 8). As late as 1543 Diogo Fernandes da Cruz named to the Lisbon Inquisition five *cristãos novos* whom he had heard speaking Hebrew.[224] However, for most children of the Expulsion generation true knowledge of Hebrew had all but disappeared, except for a few oaths or scattered words or phrases in oral tradition.[225] And even among the Expulsion generation there is evidence that knowledge of Hebrew was slipping away from many *conversos*. At a crypto-Jewish prayer service in Córdoba in 1504, for example, "the rabbi said the prayers in Hebrew and then repeated them in Spanish."[226]

As might be expected, the largest number of Hebrew expressions in *converso* speech focus on religious concerns.[227] Most common of all are the fragments of Jewish prayers that have been discussed earlier in this chapter, particularly those that invoked God with His Hebrew name *Adonai*.[228] These were not specific prayers per se. Rather the single word *Adonai* was a talisman that made almost any prayer Jewish in essence. Sometimes, in fact, crypto-Jews merely substituted the word Adonai where a Christian prayer might invoke Jesus or Mary. This is the sense of the accusation leveled against *conversos* in Ciudad Real in 1484–5 that "sometimes when they should have named our Lord Jesus Christ and Our Lady they called on and named *Adonai* and *Amaysgrael*."[229] But most often these invocations of *Adonai* were truncated versions of traditional Jewish blessings. For example, Marina González's family [Ciudad Real 1484] often was heard to say "May *Adonai* be praised."[230] Alonso Sánchez, of Badajoz, said in 1511 that before the Expulsion he used to pray "*Adonai, Adonai*, have mercy on us, O Creator of heaven and earth and the sea and the sand."[231] The sentences handed down by the Coimbra Inquisition in the 1570s make occasional references to prayers to *Adonai*, such as eighteen-year-old Felipa de Mesquita, of Vila Real, who was accused in 1571 of "talking about *Adonai*," and Guiomar Lopes, of Grajal, who recited a prayer that began "Blessed are You, *Adonai*."[232] The American *conversa* Catalina Enriquez in 1644, at age 60, reported that she believed only in *Adonai* (Liebman 1982, 113). The term occasionally survives in twentieth-century Portuguese *cristão novo* liturgy, as in this verse prayer: "*Adonai, Adonai*, in whom I place my trust . . . I live in delight and hope, for God promised our father Abraham to enable all the 'people of the Nation' to take joy in His manifestations! We, for our sins, walk in error, in a foreign land, without a shepherd! Have pity on us and show us Your mercy, Lord."233 In addition, twentieth-century Portuguese crypto-Jews tend to replace the Christological closing formula of Christian prayers ("In the name of the Father, the Son, and the Holy Ghost") with their own formula: "In the name of the Lord, *Adonai*, Amen" or "Amen, Lord; may my prayers rise, may they reach Heaven."234

Frequently a *converso* was reputed to have recited a *berakhah*, retaining the Hebrew word for a blessing. For example, Sancho de Çibdad [Ciudad Real 1484] was reputedly heard "around midnight reading like a rabbi making a *berakhah*."235 A late fifteenth-century satiric poem lists among Antón de Montoro's Judaizing customs that he was accustomed to saying a *berakhah* over the wine.236 In 1610 an Edict of Faith from Cartagena [Colombia] speaks of saying the *berakhah* over a glass of Kosher wine (*vino casero*) (Medina 1899b, 26). As with other Hebrew expressions the word was sometimes garbled by Inquisition scribes: Inés González de la Rueda denounced Fernand Alvarez in 1501 in Soria for praying like a Jew and saying *Bahá* and other words she did not understand.237

A number of Hebrew interjections also remained current among new-Christians. Many were casual invocations of the deity. The Hebrew word *ḥai* (life; live!) survived in Almazán, where in 1505 Pedro de Guadalajara was reported to have asked: "Don't you believe, *ḥai Adonai* [may God live on], by the Law of Moses that I speak the truth?" And then, after an embarrassed silence, he continued: "O, God, what people have become accustomed to, they cannot leave behind."238 Clara de Puxmija [Teruel late fifteenth century] would cry out *Saday* or *Alhar* when someone sneezed.239

*Guayas*, the Hebrew term equivalent to "alas!" was extremely common among *conversos* of the Expulsion generation. Leonor González [Ciudad Real 1484] reputedly lamented the baptism of a *converso* child by exclaiming "*Guay* the baptism!"240 Juana Lopes la Rabeuera [Garcimuñoz 1488] "was heard to say to her children: 'Ay, *guayas*, *guayas*,' like the Jews say, lowering her head as she said it."241 When María Alvarez [Almazán 1505] was in pain she cried out in Hebrew "Ay, *guayas*, two or three times, and [her husband] told her to be quiet, because the house was full of people."242 In the trial of Leonor Gutiérrez of Hita, who had fled to Portugal and was tried in absentia in 1538–9, it was reported that one Holy Friday she had seen some peasant women crying in the church of Caspueñas in Hita. She allegedly said: "Why all these *guayes*? May an evil *guay* befall you! Aren't you sick of *guay*-ing for Him all the time?"243 By long tradition *guay* was also used to refer to a dirge, a formal expression of grief sung or recited at funerals.244 At the funeral of Juan de Silva [Atienza 1527], for example, these *guayas* were sung: "Ay, ay! / What a good Jew he has been. / And he was always faithful / in the Law of Moses. / He died like a good Jew. / May God pardon him."245 Isabel de Hita [1520–3] "went to console certain people who were shut in behind closed doors on account of a certain death and there with the other women she sang *guayas* in the Jewish fashion."²⁴⁶ In fact these showy laments were so characteristic of Jews of this time that a number of mid- to late fifteenth-century satirical poems, such as the burlesque "Wedding of Rodrigo Cota," characterize the *conversos* as people who use the term *guayas*.²⁴⁷ There are occasional instances of this term being used even into the seventeenth century in Portugal, where it referred specifically to ritualized lamentations. For example, Don Antônio Homem, condemned in 1624, was accused of "sitting on a chair preaching to some people, exhorting them to live in the law of Moses, referring to certain authorities of the Old Testament, and at certain passages the people performed *guayas*, raising their eyes to the sky, clapping their hands together and lowering their heads to their chests, bowing this way and that."²⁴⁸

Among the Expulsion generation the word *meldar* was retained to indicate the reading of Jewish religious books. The *Libro del Alboraique*, for example, characterizes *conversos* as continuing to "*meldar* from religious books in the Jewish fashion,"²⁴⁹ and in a late fifteenth-century satiric poem the *converso* poet Antón de Montoro is chided because he was still accustomed to *meldar* and study the law.²⁵⁰ The term shows up in Inquisition testimony as well. Alonso de la Fuente's son [Calatañazor 1501] rushed in one day and, addressing his father by his old Hebrew name, said "Mayr, give me some bread, because I have to go to *meldar*." His father reputedly responded by slapping him and sending him out of the room.²⁵¹ When Juan Ramírez [Ciudad Real 1511] and his friends prayed "they did it like when the Jews *meldavan*, raising and lowering the head."²⁵² Although a few of these terms like *guay* and *meldar* persisted, most tended to drop out of usage in a generation or two. For example, an act of charity was sometimes referred to by its Hebrew name *tzedakah*, as when the *converso* Pedro Abella [Barbastro 1491] was accused of "having given money to the communal *tzedakah* fund, and other donations to poor Jews."²⁵³

Many Hebrew pejorative expressions were retained as well. Gentiles (in this context non-Jews, non-Judaizers, or old-Christians) were often labeled with the term *goy*. Francisco de Aguila reported to the Inquisition in Aranda de Duero in 1502 that Juan de León had said to him: "You know what the Jews say: 'So many *goyim*; so many dogs!'"²⁵⁴ The ubiquitous Inquisition spies, and for that matter anyone who denounced a crypto-Jew to the Inquisition, were likely to be called by the Hebrew term *malsín*, which means an informer or slanderer.²⁵⁵ For example, Bacharel Simão Nunes told the Lisbon Inquisition in 1541 that her new-Christian friends called Fernão Nunes "a *malsín* because he had told about the money they were channeling to Rome."²⁵⁶ The term was also used as a verb: around 1486 the Segovian jeweler Abrahán Memé promised Mosé Zaragoza and his son Isaac to keep his mouth shut from fear that that they might *malsinar* to the bishop about them.²⁵⁷ The Hebrew term for bastard (*mamzer*) was also fairly common. In 1491 Fernando de Aylón [San Martín de Trevejo, Cáceres 1491] allegedly called Alonso de León a *mançer* and a *roeca*.²⁵⁸

Among the Expulsion generation other pejorative terms also remained current. María López [Almazán 1505] was reported to have asked about her husband's hurt toe: " 'What's this *guezarah* about this foot, because it never gets better?' The witness [the doctor Maestre Pedro] states that he does not know what it means, but that he believes it means 'what bad luck,' because at an earlier time, when there were still Jews, he often heard this word."[259] Vernaldino de Gumiel de Mercado [Soria 1489] reputedly cursed in Hebrew while he was weaving, saying: "'May it be *Orsemor!*' and he cursed and said that he loved his mother, who was a Jew and died at sea, more than Our Lady the Virgin Mary."[260] In 1490 María de Sarauia was reported to have said that mass was *hevelayud*, which the witness defined as a pack of nothing.[261]

In the conflictive, polylingual society of fifteenth-century Spain, Hebrew was used in environments other than prayer, of course. Much as secularized modern American Jews may use a word or two of Yiddish or Hebrew in their speech, *conversos* through the end of the seventeenth century would occasionally slip into their speech expressions their watchful neighbors would identify as Hebrew. The tendency of newly converted Jews to use Hebrew expressions was widely satirized in the burlesque poetry of the courtly songbooks (*cancioneros*) of the late fifteenth century. Many of the poets collected in the *Cancionero de Baena* [1445] or the *Cancionero general de Hernando de Castillo* [1511] were themselves recent converts, and they wrote for an educated audience that was comprised in part of *conversos* and in part of old-Christians perfectly familiar with the *converso* ambiance. Just as the Jewish comedians of the Catskill Mountains "Borscht Belt" resorts in the middle of the twentieth century peppered their speech with Yiddish expressions for a knowing audience of both Jews and gentiles, so did the Castilian *cancionero* poets use ethnic linguistic humor to show off their wit or their pain and to get laughs.[262] And just as a large number of Yiddish expressions have become part of the modern American lexicon, so too did a number of Hebrew phrases or expressions become a part of common Spanish speech.[263]

# NOTES

1. Frehoff argues that a portion of Spanish medieval Jewry was not adept at ritual, which led the rabbis to bring into the synagogue much of what in other countries remained as home ritual (1964).

2. (1936, 111). This attitude may well derive from the Averroist philosophy popular among Spanish Jews of the fifteenth century (Baer 1966, 2:255–6).

3. *Huma certa pesoa que veo da terra dos judeus a tirar esmola pera o azeite das sinagogas e de lhe dizer a dita pesoa os dias em que caião os jejuns dos judeus* (Azevedo Mea 1982, 219).

4. Several collections of crypto-Jewish prayers are available in print, often as parts of larger works dealing with some aspect of crypto-Judaism. These include Spain (Spanish language): Caro Baroja 1961, 1:422–5; Blázquez Miguel 1988, 66–83; Cortes 1985, 292–4;

Selke de Sanchez 1972, 279–86; 1986, 236–42; Braunstein 1936, 194–202. Spain (Catalán language): Riera i Sans 1975, 349–64; 1971–5, 70–90. The American colonies (Spanish language): Böhm 1963, 90–6; Liebman 1970, 154–7, 261–3; Lewin 1975, 116, 144, 167. Portugal pre-twentieth century: J. Azevedo 1921, 484–6; Azevedo Mea 1981, 156–78; Paulo 1970, 65–7; Schwarz 1925, 95–105; Tradições 1929, 3.18:4–6; 3.21:6–8; 3.22:6–8. Portugal twentieth century: Canelo 1987, 95- 211; Machado 1952, 22–49; Orações 1938, 3; Paulo 1970, 84–123; 1981, 142–7; 1985, 60–109; Schwarz 1925, 48–97; Vasconcelos 1958, 172–235. In addition, nearly every issue of *Ha-Lapid* includes twentieth-century Portuguese prayers. See also Lazar 1991, 184–99.

5. For echoes of this calendar of prayers among twentieth-century Portuguese *cristãos novos* see Machado 1952, 24–6; Schwarz 1925, 49–51; 96- 7; Vasconcelos 1958, 183–4.

6. *Rezava e lya os ditos psalmos tres vezes em cada hum dos ditos dyas, a saber, pela menhã, ao meo dya e a vesporas* (Azevedo Mea 1982, 128; cf. 451).

7. Liebman 1970, 247. See also 1974, 139, 167.

8. *Se va . . . en camissa a la ventana de su apossento y hecha la cabeça fuera mirando hojo al oriente meneando los lauios, que paresçe reza alguna cossa secreta voluiendo los ojos en blanco. Y despues de vestido ya passeandose por el apossento los braços sobre el pecho de la manera que los pone el dho Ruy Diaz en cuerpo y el sombrero puesto, y a la noche ni mas ni menos, y no cenara hasta auer rezado por todo el mundo, y apretandole este algunas vezes a que çene ansy, le ha respondido que no a de çenar hasta acauar de rezar su rossario, no trayendo rossario* (AGN Vol 276 doc 14, 418b–9a).

9. *Por la mañana lavándose luego las manos y antes de comer, y antes de comer cosa alguna, yéndose a rezar aparte donde viese el cielo, hacia donde el sol se pone, a la noche de la misma manera y se viese la primer estrella que aparece, que llaman la estrella de Venus* (Lewin 1971, 487).

10. Bel Bravo surmises that the prayer was the *Shema* (Bel Bravo 1988, 97).

11. Although these prayers are the obligation of the individual, and are therefore to be said at home, today these three services are also commonly held in the synagogue (*Enc. Jud.* 14:1257).

12. Blanca Enríquez told Mexican Inquisitors around 1648 that her family prayed every morning, "and would not even drink their chocolate until they had finished praying" (*Ni almorzando chocolate hasta haber acabado de rezar*) (García 1910, 208).

13. *Encomendo me ao Senhor do mundo que fez o ceo e a terra* (Azevedo Mea 1981, 162).

14. *Cuando la dicha doña María se levantaba de la cama se lavaba las manos, tomaba un rosario, sin santiguarse, sólo por apariencia, . . . y se arrimaba siempre a un poste de la casa que tenía señalado o destinado para esto y cruzaba las manos y rezaba el psalmo de Miserere Mei en romance, y al final humillada la cabeza decía alabado sea el Santísimo Señor, Dios de Abraham, Isaac y Jacob, y a la postre del psalmo solía decir: se pondrán sobre tu altar becerros, . . . y la oía rezar dicho psalmo unas veces tres veces y otras seis, teniendo en el entretanto gran silencio en jurar. Y si alguna vez los muchachos hacían ruido, daba la dicha doña María una palmada para que callasen* (Lewin 1971, 471).

15. *Beneyt lo dia i beneyt lo que l'envia* (Blázquez Miguel 1986a, 74).

16. *Gracias Dios mío por la luz del nuevo día por la cual nos llamas a tu servicio* (Cortes 1985, 293).

17. *Bendita la luz del dia, / el Señor que la envia. / Ella nos dé graça e alegria, / e saber para fazer a sua vontade, / para que quando morrer possamos apparecer no reino da claridade.* Symbolically light has come to mean the Torah. For modern versions of this prayer see J. Azevedo 1921, 485; Paulo 1985, 61.

18. *Levantei-me de manhana, / de manhana, ao alvor. / Fui rezar os meus salmos / ao Senhor. / Quem en esse Deus confia, / não lhe faltará favor. / Bendito e glorificado / seja o nome do Senhor* (da Cunha e Freitas 1952, 21).

19. *Já os galos pretos, cantam, / os anjos a toda o hora, / para que acordemos / engrandecer servir e louvar / o nome Santo do Senhor / ao romper da bela aurora* (Tradições 1934, 9.67:3). For other modern versions see Vasconcelos 1958, 181–2; Tradições 1928, 2.10: 7.

20. *Bendito y alabado seais vos, señor, que me levantastes vivo y sano con el anima en las carnes dormia como un muerto, diste me lienço y paño con que me cubriese, oydos con que oyese, pies y manos con que andubiese, por eso yo pecador yndigno de alabar vuestros santisimos alabamientos los angeles os den graçias en el çielo y las gentes en la tierra. Por tantos bienes como me aveys hecho y me hazeys de cada dia y days en la noche benido es el dia, bendito el poder del señor que la luz y claridad enbia con llaves de entendimiento.* (Blázquez Miguel 1986a, 74). For a similar example from Majorca in the 1660s see Braunstein 1936, 194–5; analyzed by Lazar 1991, 192. For modern Portuguese examples see Machado 1952, 22–4; Schwarz 1925, 47–8; 95–6; Vasconcelos 1958, 181–2, 215, 224, 231–2; Fontes 1992, 460 [1980]; Tradições 1934, 9.67: 3–4.

21. *Alabado sea el Señor que me a amanecido bivo y sano y seguro y en paz de la tiniebla de la noche; me de su luz y vida y gracia para que le sirva* (Yerushalmi 1971, 36).

22. *Bendita sea la luz del día, y el señor que nos lo envía. Alabad al Señor todas las gentes; Alabad al Señor todos los pueblos. Porque ha confirmado sobre nosotros, y la verdad del Señor permanecerá para siempre* (Wiznitzer 1962a, 235). The translation is Wiznitzer's.

23. *O anjo da minha guarda, / anjo da minha guia, / já que me livraste das trevas da noite, / livrai-me dos perigos do dia* (Vasconcelos 1958, 232), See also Tradições 1928, 3.15:8.

24. *Graças te dou, rei divino, / bendito o vosso poder, / que me deisastes, Senhor, / chegar a hora d'amanhecer. / Alma e vida te entrego, / bendito rei da verdade, / que eu, Senhor, não vo-lo mereço, / tende de mim piedade* (Vasconcelos 1958, 181).

25. *Louvado seja o Senhor / que assim é esclarecido; / sê tu, meu Senhor, servido / de constante me fazer, / para eu o teu bem possa merecer* (J. Azevedo 1921, 485). The first phrase is part of the Sabbath *shaḥarit* prayer.

26. *Los más días del año por la mañana subía al terrado, y haviéndose lavado las manos y la cara, hincado de rodillas y mirando al Çielo con mucha devoción reçava. . . . Tu grande Dios que has criado al Çielo y la tierra, y a mí y a toda criatura, seas glorificado y alabado tu santo nombre; que me has guardado en esta noche y me has dejado ver la luz del día, me dés vuenos días y buenos años por tu Divina Bondad y seas mi guarda y mi ayuda; y socorra mis neçessidades con tu santo remedio, y tengas misericordia de mí, perdón de mis peccados, y assí lo espero de tu Divina Bondad por gloria tuya. Y me harás graçia para alcançar al fin de mis días tu santa Gloria, en que serás alabado y glorificado para siempre, Amén* (Selke de Sánchez 1972, 100; cf. 186–7).

27. *Já lá vem a bela aurora / já lá vem o claro dia, / já vem o altíssimo Deus / coa Sua santa, bendita alegria! / Senhor me libre a mim / e a todo o Povo de israel / de homem morto—mau encontro, / de homem vivo—mau inimigo, / Cão danado, para danar, / de águas correntes, fogos ardentes / e de lingua de más gentes. / Tudo de que não nos pudermos livrar / livrai-nos, ó grande Deus de Adonai, / a todo o Seu povo que for e vier / Amém, Senhor, au Céu vá, au Céu chegue!* (Paulo 1985, 61). For a variant designed for fast days see Paulo 1985, 62.

28. *Bendito seais vos, señor, que me dejastes ver este medio dia sin salimiento de anima sin otros peligros y tribulaçiones desde mundo, plega vos, señor, que me dejeis ver este medio dia y otros muchos enteros con menos pecados y mas a vuestro santisimo serviçio* (Blázquez Miguel 1986a, 74).

29. *Diante de Vós, Senhor, venho empeçar a rezar; meu Deus, dai-me auxilio para Vos louvar, engrandecer; en nome do Senhor, Adonai, Amém* (Paulo 1985, 68). This closely parallels the language of Psalm 145, which begins the traditional minḥah service. For other examples see Paulo 1985, 67–70; Tradições 1928, 2.10:5.

30. *Bento tu, Adonay, nosso Deos, que com teu mandamento anoitecem as noites e com sabedoria abre as portas e com entendimento mudas as horas e ordenas as estrellas no ceo como he tua vontade e crias dia e crias noite e envolves a luz entre as escuridades . . . a teu povo deste lei e encomendanças, far nos has Senhor alegrar com verbos de tua lei* (Azevedo Mea 1981, 162). This is a close rendering of the first paragraph of the traditional ma'ariv service and may also be similar to the traditional prayer *Asher bi-dvoro*. I am grateful to Rabbi Jacob Hurwitz for noting this similarity and for pointing out several other connections between these crypto-Jewish prayers and the modern liturgy.

31. *Se ponian a una ventana de noche a hazer oracion a la estrella* (García Fuentes 1981, 149).

32. *Veía a su padre irse a cualquier arroyo que hallaban y se lavaba las manos, quitaba el paño de manos que traía ceñido a la cintura y cubría con él la cabeza, y arrebozado con la capa, se estaba en pie rezando oraciones de la ley de Moisén* (García 1910, 257).

33. *La enseñó su abuela oraciones judaicas, llevándola dos veces, todas las noches, a que las rezase sentada y mirando a una estrella que la señalaba, haçiéndola muchas veces que, antes que rezase, cantase ciertas glosas, enderezadas a inclinarla al judaísmo, y luego la llevaba a mirar las estrellas y, en cayendo la que buscaban, ambas rezaban aquellas oraciones* (García 1910, 233).

34. *Entrarse a orar al jardín y huerta de la casa en que vivían en Tacubaya, acción sin duda ninguna de judíos judaizantes que buscan sitio y lugar para ver la estrella y observan el tiempo de su nación y totalmente ajena de las costumbres de los cristianos católicos, que se retiran en lo más escondido de sus habitaçiones a este efecto, delante de alguna imagen* (Lewin 1971, 442). See also Cortes 1985, 293 [Majorca seventeenth century].

35. *Vendito y alabado seays vos, señor, que diste la verga de Aron al santo Moysen mandastes hender la pena para que fuesemos limpios de manos para que os alabasemos* (Blázquez Miguel 1986a, 75). For some twentieth-century counterparts see Schwarz 1925, 51–2, 104; Vasconcelos 1958, 216, 232; Tradições 1932, 7.51:3; 1934, 9.67:4.

36. *Esparciras señor sobre mi tu graçia, sobre mis torpeças que reliebe, labaras con tus manos mis desgraçias hinchendolas de gloria y contento, alabete señor mi humilde pensamiento* (Blázquez Miguel 1986a, 75).

37. *Acuestome en poder de Adonay que muchas son las suas piadades y apiadarme a . . . Señor dios descubre tu las verdades porq. no andemos engañados* (Bel Bravo 1988, 180).

38. *Señor, yo soy tuyo e mis sueños tuyos seran* (Beinart 1981b, 564). Rabbi Jacob Hurwitz notes that this prayer is traditional after a bad dream and is also recited by the congregation during the priestly benediction.

39. *Buenas noches nos de el Señor y el gran Dios de Ysrrael nos levante con bien* (Blázquez Miguel 1986a, 74).

40. *Echanos, nuestro Padre, en pas* (Riera i Sans 1975, 352 [Valencia 1512]). See also Blázquez Miguel 1986a, 74.

41. *Guarde-me o Anjo Rafael de toda a angústia. . . . Adonai me guarde, o Anjo Gabriel, o Anjo Sorosel me livre da angústia* (Pereira 1979, 187). This is the beginning of the traditional prayer *Hashkibenu abinu le-shalom*.

42. *Na minha cama me deitei, / as minhas portas fechei / com as chaves de Abrahão; / os bons entrarão, / os maus sahirão, / os anjos do Senhor / comingo estão* (Schwarz 1925, 51).

43. *Na minha cama me deitei, / cinco anjos nela achei, / dois aos pés, três a cabeceira, / o Altíssimo Senhor ande na minha dianteira* (Schwarz 1925, 51). Rabbi Jacob Hurwitz suspects that

this prayer, with four angels—often mentioned by name—and not five, derives from traditional bedtime prayers.

44. *O Senhor nos dê boas noites á alma e ao corpo, salvação para as almas, paz como todo o mundo, glória aos mortos, paz aos vivos. O Senhor nos livre dos nossos inimigos, de quem bem nos fala e mal nos quer, do mau homem e da má mulher e da boca que diz o que quer* (Vasconcelos 1958, 216 [Bragança 1930s]).

45. *Deus me benza dos pés até a cabeça com a benção de Isac e Jacob. O Senhor bemdito me adormeça, o Senhor me guarde esta noite e amanhã todo o dia, o Senhor todo poderoso me guarde na sua companhia* (Tradições 1927, 2.8:8). This prayer was recited before going to bed.

46. *Deus me benza dos pés à cabeça com a bênção de Isaac e Jacob. O Senhor bendito me adormeça. O Senhor me guarde esta noite e amanhã todo o dia* (Paulo 1985, 62). In this book Paulo gives examples of eleven other bedtime prayers (62–4).

47. *A la media noche se leuanto el dicho Sancho de Çibdad de la cama en pie, y que oyo como resaua disiendo: Abraham, Adonay, e otras cosas que no se acuerda. . . . A ora de la media noche leer como rabi hasiendo la baraha, que duro fasta dos oras* (Beinart 1974, 20). See also Carrete/Fraile 1987, 50. This may be a reference to *selihot*.

48. *Se levantaba este reo en calzón blanco y con una capa, enchancletados los zapatos, a media noche, a rezar, cubierta la cabeza y con los anteojos, y se lavaba antes las manos, que para ello tenía un jarro lleno de agua, encima de la caja; y llegándose cerca de la luz rezaba en unas horitas, en que gataba como tres cuartos de hora, volviéndose a acostar en acabando de rezar* (Lewin 1954, 147–8).

49. *No estaua en sy el día que no desya oraçión, ni entendía que le fasya Dios bien; e que el día que yba camino que se olgaua, que la desya a su plazer. . . . Vamos a la yglesia, dizen la misa, no sabemos lo que dize ni qué no. Alçan quando dizen que alzan e vemos no sabemos qué más. Sabed enteramente que no estó en mí el día que no digo oraçión* (Carrete Parrondo 1985a, 145).

50. *Antes que recen, se lavan las manos con agua o tierra* (Santa María 1893c, 183).

51. *A la dicha Graçia avía visto responder al cadix, lauándose primero las manos con tierra* (Carrete Parrondo 1985a, 160). For other examples see Azevedo Mea 1981, 164; Baião 1921, 174 [Portugal 1556]; Liebman 1970, 96 [Mexico 1639]; Lewin 1977, 46, 145, etc. [Mexico 1642]; Machado 1952, 24; Paulo 1985, 66–7; Schwarz 1925, 49; Vasconcelos 1958, 182–3 [Bragança 1932- 6].

52. The *Shulḥan Arukh* devotes several sections (OH 92, 158–62) to hand washing (*Enc. Jud.* 2:84; 12:998–9). Traditionally the hands also must be washed ritually after cutting the nails, combing the hair, touching the genitals, engaging in sexual intercourse, excreting wastes, removing the shoes, or leaving a cemetery. Hands are washed before prayer, eating bread, reciting grace, eating parsley at Passover, or giving the priestly blessing.

53. *Antes que el dicho Rabi començase a rezar esta oraçion de linpias manos, se lavava las manos, et que en aquella misma agua, quel dicho Rabi se lavava, vió conmo se lavaron del dicho Juan de Córdoba Menbreque y las otras personas que allí estauan . . . vió e oyó conmo . . . todas las otras personas que allí estauan, quando asy se lavavan las manos, en la dicha agua, rezavan todos e cada vno por sy la dicha orazion de linpias manos* (Gracia Boix 1982, 50).

54. *Lauar las manos / por pico de aguamanil* (Castillo 1882, poem #994).

55. *Quando oyó resar a los judíos, hizo levantar a este testigo que le diese aguamanos, y este testigo se leuantó y se la dio; y después que se ovo lavado las manos el dicho de la Moneda resava cosas de abrayco estándo echado en la cama. Preguntado que por qué se lavava las manos y se estuvo echado en la cama, dixo que porque los judíos acostunbravan lauarse las manos antes que resasen* (Carrete Parrondo 1985a, 177).

56. *Com a mesma tenção de judia rezou por tres ou quatro vezes orações, lavando primeyro que começasse as mãos e quando acabava de rezar has tornava a lavar por cerimonia judaica* (Azevedo Mea 1982, 297; cf. 52, 221, etc.).

57. Liebman 1974, 137. For other examples see Carrete/Fraile 1987, 50, 85 [Almazán 1505]; Baião 1921, 126 [Lisbon 1541]; Liebman 1975, 186 [Peru 1609].

58. *Senhor, Vós nos encomendastes em terras de Syon que lavasemos os olhos, e a cabeça e as mãos* (Azevedo Mea 1982, 445).

59. *Bendito sea el Poderoso Adonai que en las enseñanzas me enseñaste a lavar las manos, boca y ojos para te alabar y servir, en loor y honra del Señor y en la Ley de Moisén* (Lewin 1954, 128).

60. *Quando se lavauan las manos dezian que asy como ellos se lavauan las manos en aquella agua, que asy se lauasen sus coraçones de tener en ellos ninguna creençia de la ley de los Xriptianos* (Gracia Boix 1982, 50).

61. *Senhor, lavai-me como a água da salvação, / perdoai-me os meus pecados, / que bem sabeis os que são. / Dai-me neste mundo paz / e no outro salvação / perdão e remédio, / que tudo está no Vossa divina máo. / Senhor de Adonai, Amém* (Paulo 1985, 67). Since water is used post mortem for the final cleansing of sins, this may be a death-related prayer.

62. *Louvado seja o Senhor, que me deu água para me lavar e pano para me limpar, assim o Senhor me dê luz e graça para O servirmos e entendimento para O louvarmos, Adonai. Amém* (Paulo 1985, 66). A variant of this prayer has been reported from Belmonte: "Lord, just as You give me this water to wash with, this towel to dry myself, eyes to see, ears to hear and mouth to speak, Lord give me grace to know how to serve and love You. Amen" (*Senhor, assim como me deste água para me lavar, toalha para me limpar, olhos para ver, ouvidos para ouvir e boca para falar, assim Senhor me dê graças para O saber servir e amar. Amém*) (Paulo 1985, 66).

63. Mishnah, Berakoth 6:1. The source of the blessing is Psalm 104:14.

64. *Bendesían la masa judaycamente bendisiendo a la postre un vaso de vino* (Santa María 1893b, 369). Traditionally these blessings are recited in the opposite order.

65. *Señor Dios verdadero hacedor que en los desiertos nunca habitados no falta Tu favor* (Liebman 1982, 115).

66. *Bendito seja Aquele que te criou do pó da terra para sustento e alimento dos pecadores, nos renove as nossas almas para fazermos serviços com elas ao Deus dos altos ceus.*

67. *Bendito seja o Senhor que te criou nas águas de mar para sustento dos pecadores* (da Cunha e Freitas 1952, 19). Modern Portuguese new-Christians recite this prayer over salt before they eat their first meal of the day: "I ask Your permission, Lord, / to break the night's fast. / Make me happy and constant / in order to serve and love You. God of Adonai, Amen, Lord! / Just as this salt / comes from the holy sea, / may the Lord draw from my soul / sins and misfortunes. / Praised be the Lord, / for now I have broken fast. God grant me health and life / to fulfill His holy law." (*Licença te peço, Senhor, / Para me vir desenjuar, / que me faças feliz e constante / para te servir e amar. / Deus de Adonai, ámen, Senhor! / Assim como este sal / saiu do mar sagrado, / me tire o Senhor minha alma / de penas e pecado. / Louvado seja o Senhor, / que já me desenjuei: / Deus me dê saúde e vida / p'ra cumprir sua santa lei*) (Vasconcelos 1958, 184 [Bragança 1932- 6]). Rabbi Jacob Hurwitz finds this prayer reminiscent of a traditional short prayer recited after eating fruit.

68. Millgram 1971, 293–5. The Hebrew term for these prayers is *Birkat Hamazon*. They derive from Deut. 8:10 and its elaboration in Mishnah, Berakhoth 6:8 (Gaon 1990, 210). For additional prayers after meals see Schwarz 1925, 51.

69. *Bendito Aquel que comemos que lo suyo. Bendito El. Bendita su memoraçion, a por con syglo y syenpre* (Cantera Montenegro 1985, 79).

70. ¿Qué Adonay? ¡Que agora no aprouecha resar! (Carrete Parrondo 1985a, 60).

71. Quando comia bendesian la mesa, desiendo: Bendigamos a Dios que de lo Suyo comemos e de lo Suyo beuemos, Bendito sea El y el Su Santo Nonbre (Beinart 1974, 576; cf. 1:241). See also Blázquez Miguel 1986a, 75. According to Rabbi Jacob Hurwitz, this may be the prayer *Mezuman*, which comes before *Birkat Hamazon*.

72. A ti, Moisés, adoramos! A ti, graças damos pelas mercês que cada dia nos fazes, cada hora! (Coelho 1987, 216).

73. Bendito seja o Senhor que nos dá tantos bens seus, bendito o profeta Moisés para amparo dos judeus (da Cunha e Freitas 1952, 20).

74. O que comemos seja para fartura, o que bememos nos sirva de medicina e o que nos sobra seja de bendição. Louvemos ao Senhor porque Ele é bom para sempre. Amém (Paulo 1985, 78).

75. Assim como Vós, Senhor, criaste o pão significando os bens, assim vós, Senhor me darás os bens dos Céus e da terra para vos fazer Páscoas que vos sejam agradáveis empregando-me no Vosso santo serviço. Amém (Paulo 1981, 144). See also Tradições 1932, 7.51:3.

76. Benditas graças dadas au Senhor pelos bens, esmolas ue nos fez a está para fazer. O Senhor que nos deu para agora, que nos abasteça para cada hora. Pelo santo e divino bem, nos livre da miséria e de tudo quanto mau for. Amen, Senhor. Ao Céu vá (Machado 1952, 26). Clemente Carmona told David Nidel in New Mexico in 1980 that he recalled "being taught to knock a piece of bread from the table at the outset of a meal. He explained that one silently could say the blessing over the bread while bending down to retrieve it if a priest happened to be at their table" (Nidel 1984, 251).

77. Bendicen la messa a usso y según costumbre de judíos, y beben vino cassero [kosher], y toman un vasso con el vino, y dicen ciertas palabras sobre él, y dan a beber a cada uno un trago (Santa María 1893c, 184). See also Fita y Colomé 1893, 322 [1485]; Liebman 1970, 97 [1639].

78. Quando ponian la mesa el sabado e en otros dias para comer, que ponian en ella vn vaso grande de vino, e que desque se asentavan a comer, que el dicho Juan Falcon leya en vn libro, e despues desia çiertas palabras callando sobre aquel vaso de vino e aspiraba sobre el con resollo, y despues, que daba a beuer a todos de aquel vino (Beinart 1974, 559; cf. 1:290, 524).

79. Aquel dia era sabado, sabe y vido como el dicho Alonso Gonçales, despues que obo comido, tomo vn vaso con vino con amas manos y començo de resar y sabadear sobre el, y començolo de leuantar sobre la cabeça como caliz quando alzaua, y tornolo luego a abaxar, y torno a rezar y sabadear sobre el su muger e sus hijos estauan todos presentes en derredor de la mesa, beuio el vn poco e dio a su muger e a sus hijos, e despues desto besaronle la mano sus fijos, e asimismo a su madre, y el pusoles la mano sobre la cabeça. Este testigo vido todo esto estando tras vnas tinajas donde no le veyan (Beinart 1981b, 568–9). Traditionally the blessing of family members precedes the *Kiddush*. See also Carrete Parrondo 1985a, 160 [Burgos 1502].

80. En su casa tomava vn poco de vino y lo bendesía, y luego echaua vn poco dello en la lunbre (Carrete/Fraile 1987, 30; cf. 121). See also Beinart 1974, 23.

81. Un vaso de vino en la mano e resaron sobre él e beuieron a soruillos de aquel vino. . . . Vino de la berahá (León Tello 1972, 74).

82. Tambien leia otra que se intitula Idus de recibimiento de sabat, lo qual decia con una taza en la mano, y haviendola dicho bevia un poco, y dava de bever a la . . . su muger, y esto lo hazia porque el libro lo decia, y que los hebreos quando salian de la Sinagoga de viernes por tarde por celebrar el Sabado devian en su casa esta oración con una taza de vino en la mano y davan de bever á los sircunstantes (Braunstein 1936, 99–100).

83. El poner de la mano encima de la cabeça bajándola por la cara abaxo sin santiguar, dice que significa la bendición que Jacob dió a Manassés y a Effrayn, nietos suyos, hijos de Joseph, nacidos

*en Egypto, quando les pusso las manos encima de la cabeça y les bendixo como está escripto al fin del Génesi en el testamento de Jacob* (Santa María 1893c, 184). The reference is to Gen. 48:14.

84. *Dios os haga bienaventurados . . . Dios os bendiga* (Beinart 1975, 653). See also León Tello 1972, 75.

85. *La dicha Mari Gonsales daua e dio muchas vezes la bendiçion a la manera judayca a çiertas personas, al tienpo que le besauan las manos, poniendoles la mano estendida sobre la cabeça e baxandosela por la cara abaxo, como le tenian por costunbre de hazer los judios* (Beinart 1977a, 248; cf. 2:256, 438, 441).

86. Blázquez Miguel 1986a, 69; cf. 64. For many similar examples see Beinart 1981b, 569 [1483]; Fita y Colomé 1893, 293 [1485]; Sicroff 1965, 99 [Guadalupe 1485]; Beinart 1961, 182 [1487]; Carrete Parrondo 1985b, 99 [Cuenca 1490]; Furtado 1925, xxxii [Evora 1536]; Coelho 1987, 1:210 [Evora 1549]; Furtado 1925, 136 [Brazil 1592]; Liebman 1970, 96 [1639]; Lewin 1977, 250 [Mexico 1643]; Lipiner 1977, 33.

87. *Deus de Abraão, Deus de Isaac, e Deus de Jacob* (da Cunha e Freitas 148; cited by Fontes 1993, 83). A good example of this blessing occurs in Gil Vicente's 1525 Portuguese *Farsa de Inês Pereira* (Vicente 1984, 2:448). Gil Vicente's Hebraisms are studied by Teyssier 1959, 199–226. For modern versions see Schwarz 1925, 82 [1925]; Vasconcelos 1958, 172, 208 [1958]; Paulo 1985, 80 [1985].

88. *Adonai, Senhor, volvei a vossa santa e divina face á minha; vós diante, eu detrás de vós, não terei medo, nem pavor, nem causa má me empecerá. Serei guiado e governado pelo grande Deus de Adonai. . . . Deus me deite a sua santa e divina bênção sobre mim, sobre o meu homem, sobre os meus filhos* (Vasconcelos 1958, 182).

89. *Pelas palavras que saem do coração suba a minha mene até Deus* (Vasconcelos 1958, 223).

90. *O Senhor te abençoe e te guarde. O Senhor mostre a Sua face e se compadeça de ti. O Senhor volva o Seu divino rosto para ti e te dê paz. Amém* (Paulo 1985, 80). For other examples see Tradições 1932, 7.51:2; 1934, 9.67:3.

91. Typical are these two allegedly recited by Catalina López [Cuenca 1490]: *que le valiese Adonay, Dios biuo . . . Adonay, Adonay, adoléscete de mí* (Carrete Parrondo 1985b, 100).

92. *Deus que me encomendo que me não posa ninguém mais mal fazer nem empecer, que ao ceo subir e strelas contar e a terra decer e agoas medir e framas pesar e vento medir as braçadas, maiores são as piedades de Deus para me salvar que as maldades de meus inimigos que para me empecer nem me fazer mal* (Azevedo Mea 1981, 168). See also Schwarz 1925, 53.

93. *Assi como Vos, Senhor, sacastes aquelles vossos servos e os levastes a terra da promissão, assi Vos, Senhor, me saqueis a mim de todos os trabalhos* (Azevedo Mea 1981, 168).

94. *Oh, alto Dios de Israel / que das salud a los tuyos, / me darás salud a mí / a mi marido e hijos* (Lewin 1977, 112).

95. *Senhor, Deus de Abraão, Deus de Isaac, Deus de Jacob, Deus dos nossos pais, por quem és, Senhor, Te peço pelo teu nome grande, não mereço que tenhas piedade de mim, dande-me Senhor saúde como Pai clementíssimo que te lembres Senhor e compadeças do meu estado, não consentindo, Senhor, que as tuas criaturas fiquem desamparadas faltando-lhes o teu amparo e então às gentes onde está agora o nosso Deus, que nos não acode; é certo que dos seus está apartado, não Te afastes, Senhor, de mim nem de todas as minhas coisas. Benditas sejam as criaturas que confiam em Ti, poderoso Deus de Israel, para que nos seja cumprida a promessa que foi dita a Abraão, ao nosso Pai, Amém* (Paulo 1985, 78–9). Also given in Tradições 1932, 7.51:2. See also Machado 1952, 29–30.

96. *Y mi alma por ti clama / que me la libres de fuego y de llama / q no se me queme ni se me arda. / Una cosa mi Dios te quiero pedir. / Por limosna mi Dios me la quieras dar / q de mi alma te*

*quieras acordar / aguiando entre* ——— [unclear text] / *esta salbatta / en grande aprietto me e de ver / en grande escuridad me an de meter / que no me a de valer primo ni hermano / sino las obras q yo hijiere por mi mano / y tu señor de la verdad / me quieras librar / de perro rabioso / de espada dañossa / entrada de puerta / salida de cueba / q no me entretenga en otra cossa / sino enconttrar estrellas del sielo / sino enconttrar agua en el mar* (AGN Vol 402 doc 2, 506b).

97. *O noche del Señor, / por bien seas venida / encomiendome a ti, rey de adonai. / Q me libres y ampares / de ira, de saña, de muerte supitaña / de rios corrientes / de fuegos ardientes / de aguas de la mar / de aguas de la tierra / de ombre bivo / de mal peligro, / de ombre muerto / del mal encuentro / y de otro mal peligro. / Sea mi alma libre y solta. Amen* (AGN Vol 402 doc 2, 506b-7a, 567a).

98. *Que no se acuerda bien de los* ——— [unclear text] / *sino de lo q se sigue / socorrenos Gran Señor / q andamos atribulados / de tierra en tierra / por mal de nosos Pecados / no lo seamos de vos / aleluya aleluya adonay sabaot* (AGN 402, doc 2, 507a).

99. *Paz a minha direita, paz a minha esquerda, paz a minha dianteira, fez comiguo, paz com meu marido, paz com meus filhos e paz com quem me quer bem* (Azevedo Mea 1981, 168).

100. *O Senhor, que estaes assentado em cadeira de piedade, dae-me paz; como vontade favoreci a minha alma como a folha da manhã; como a neve esclarecida, dai-me, Senhor entendimento e graça como que vos sirva. Em nome do Senhor, Adonai. Amen* (Tradições 1928, 2.10:7).

101. Sánchez Moya 1973, 112. The doorpost is where the mezzuzah would traditionally be placed.

102. *Y ydos a la xinoga le rogo que sacase el atora y hincose de rodillas delante della e lloro e hizo alli llorando ciertas rogarias por su marido que viniese con bien, e dio dinero para azeyte a la xinoga* (Baer 1936, 479).

103. *Caminando vamos dando graçias al señor, a quien en el señor confia no le faltara favor* (Blázquez Miguel 1988, 76).

104. *Quando salía de casa e yva a misa, que en sacando el pie de la puerta dezía: "A ti, Dió de mi padre, me ecomiendo, Dió de Abraham, Dió de Ysaque, Dió de Jacó, y en tí creho y en tí fío, que todo lo otro es nada y vanidad"* (Carrete Parrondo 1985a, 142).

105. *Bendito seja o nome daquele grande Senhor que te criou, e me queira encaminhar, assim como encaminhou o povo de Israel escolhido* (da Cunha e Freitas 1952, 18).

106. *Hiciesen el ruayá*, que es cuando alguna persona parte camino (Medina 1899b, 26). Cf. Cantera Montenegro 1985, 75 [Molina de Aragón 1480s], where it is termed *benaya*. Prior to the Expulsion, of course, *conversos* consulted their Jewish neighbors with regard to the dates of the festivals.

107. *Senhor, com a Tua mão era convertido o meu espírito. Adonai, Deus da verdade, endireitai-me entre os meus inimigos. Seja servido o Senhor de todas as coisas, mas abrindo-me a carreira direita, assim como Tu, Senhor, a abriste a israel quando saiu do Egipto. Amém* (Paulo 1985, 78).

108. *Acompanha-nos ao Santo caminho do Senhor assim como acompanhas-te o filho de Tobias: a êle como justo o quizeste acompanhar e a mim como pecador tu me quererás amparar e eu confesso que o sou, não há outro igual com alma e vida ao Senhor hei-de louvar para que no fim da minha vida a gloria me queiras dar* (Tradições 1932, 7.51:2).

109. *Adonai, guiai-me na rectidão por causa dos meus inimigos, aplana os caminhos perante mim. Co'as armas de Adonai estou eu armado; co'o manto do Senhor acobertado; o fel de S. Tobias no corpo, para que não sejamos presos, nem feridos, nem mortos, nem nas mãos dos nossos inimigos postos, nem em laços embaraçados. Por o poder do Senhor sejamos todos acompanhados e guiados. Os bons que nos virem e que nos ouvirem por nós serão. Adonia bendito seja a nossa salvação, a nossa guia, a nossa companhia, com paz e sossego, de noite e de dia, a horas do meio-dia* (Vasconcelos 1958, 215–6).

110. *As horas do Senhor sejam dadas, / nossos trabalhos acabados / nossos bens aumentados, / nossos pecados perdoados, / no regaço do Senhor deitados, / a Lei do Senhor seja publicada / aqui e além / na casa santa de Jerusalém* (Schwarz 1925, 78).

111. *Bendito tu, nosso Deus, Rei do Mundo, que nos santificaste nas Tuas santas encomendanças, benditas e santas e santas e benditas, e nos deste vida para chegamos a este tempo e para Te darmos os infinitos louvores. O grande Deus de Israel, criaste o fruto para o nosso sustento, em todo o tempo Tu, Senhor, sejas servido a dar-nos o sustento necessário para continuarmos no Teu santo serviço. Amém* (1985, 81); also in Tradições 1932, 7.51:3.

112. *Assim como Vós criastes esta frontosa árvore e formosa, a mais agradável de todas as árvores, assim o Senhor seja servido dela para fazermos Páscoas agradáveis empregando o seu fruto no Vosso santo serviço. Amém* (1985, 81); also in Tradições 1932, 7.51:3.

113. *Assim como Vós, Senhor, criastes as flores para símbolo de alegria, assim Vós, Senhor, dai-me paz e alegria para Vos fazer Páscoas agradáveis empregando-as no Vosso santo serviço. Amém* (1985, 81) also in Tradições 1932, 7.51:3.

114. *Em santa honra e santo louvor do Senhor, ofereço esta limitada esmola aos santos nomes do Senhor. Aceite e se sirva dela para santa honra e glória Sua. Aceite o pouquinho por muito, sirva para o Senhor me fazer servo Seu e para nos livrar do pecado e da miséria, da pobreza, e para o Senhor nos livrar de maõs alheias, e do poder de inimigos, e o Senhor nos livrar de ofendermos a Deus. Adonai, Amém* (Tradições 1928, 2.10:7). Paulo also claims to have recorded this prayer in Carção [Portugal] in this century (1985, 102).

115. *Ofereço esta esmola em honra e louvor e sacrificio do Senhor. A bênção que o Senhor botar sobre os seus santos queridos e escolhidos, bote o Senhor sobre esta esmola* (Vasconcelos 1958, 185).

116. A curious exception to this rule seems to have been the *cristão novo* community around Coimbra in the second half of the sixteenth century, for of the more than 600 cases of Judaizers tried there between 1567 and 1583, the *Shema* is only mentioned once (Azevedo Mea 1982, 21).

117. See for example Caro Baroja 1961, 1:442; Beinart 1961, 177; Gracia Boix 1982, 117.

118. *Vna oraçion judayca publicamente escripta, las quales tienen los judios por mas prinçipal, que comiença: Oye Ysrael* (Beinart 1974, 478).

119. *Ojes, Ysrael, Adonay nostreo Déu, Adonay hu* (Riera i Sans 1975, 349).

120. *Las oraçiones que rezaua eran de judios e las resaua por vn libro judayco que tenia, porque de coro no las sabia, salua el Xema Ysrael, que dixo de coro algunas palabras y lo otro en romançe* (Beinart 1974, 3, 12; cf. 27, 97).

121. *Samma Israel, Adonai, eloheno, Adonai hanat. Baro sem queovot malfotot leolam vahet, Adonai* [Valencia 1492] (Riera i Sans 1975, 350). *Samay saraell Adonai ala eno Adonat asat tora; samay saraell Adonai ala eno asat sama sat; samay saraell Adonai ala eno Adonai asat samay sat; sem cabotum machotum e olam vaet tara sit va llano* [Cataluña sixteenth century] (Blázquez Miguel 1988, 69). *Senis Israel, adonai alueno aga / Barosein quebo malento leo lambuiel / Oye Isrrael adoiai Judio* [Mexico 1589] (Liebman 1970, 163–4; cf. 178, 241). *Sema Adonai Histrael, baruc sem, malhuto.* Also: *Semac, baruc, quebot, . . . malhuth, leolam baet, deaftahet, Adonai, selo ehat, behot lefath ut sol naftehar, uhol mobeavu a debarim, aele hacer hanuhim besabetha hayom hal lebaneha de dibertaum bam besiteha, de beteha, beteha badereh, usumeha o cumeha usatem leoda ayadeha beayn letotafot beneja usatam almijus beteha o bisereha* [Mexico 1645] (Lewin 1977, 70; cf. 169, 286). About the same time Tomás Treviño de Sobremonte recited this version to Inquisitors: *Sema, Adonai, Beruto, Ceolan, Banel* (Wiznitzer 1962a, 230). Many other examples are found in the compilations of prayers listed in note 4 to this chapter.

122. Le demostro çiertas oraçiones, las quales le escrivio en çinco o seys pliegos de papel, las quales o alguna dellas sabe que se dize en esta manera: Vna que se dize buelta la cara a la pared, comiença: Sema Ysrael Adonay Elohenu, etc., e la sabe toda (Beinart 1981b, 564).

123. Bemdito A. nosso R. e R. de todo o m. q. governa a luz, cria a escurid. e faz paz e produz tudo: Bem dito tu A. n. D. q. formaste as luminarias, e com hum. m.ioso amor nos amaste sempre: Bem dito tu A. q. com g.de e avantajada piad.e nos socorreste. / Bemdito tu A. n. R. e R. de todo o m. q. ama o seu povo com g.de amor. / Amarás ao teu Deus como todo o teu coraçao, com toda a tua alma, com todo o teu ser: Estarão estas m.as palavras q. hoje te recom do sobre teu coraçao; repetilas has a teus filhos, e fallarás nellas, onde q.r q. te achares; na tua caza, no teu andar, na carreira, ao levantar, e q.do te deitares: escrevelas-has em humbraes de tua caza, e todas as vezes q. as ouvires repete-as no teu coraçao. e com toda a tua . . . tem ás em tuas mãos, trá-las sembre em teus olhos: communicas s teus filhos, p.a q. igualm.te fallem nellas onde quer q. estiverem, assim nas suas cazas como na tua, em seus passos, em suas carreiras, ao deitar, ao levantar; escreve-as sim em humbraes de tua caza, p.a q, tambem se multipliquem teus dias, e os filhos de teus filhos sobre a terra. Dice A. a M.es falla a filhos de I. e dize-lhes q. fação zizi ourelas de seus vestidos, e q. o m.mo recommendem ás suas gerações em ourelas de fio cardado; e q. p.lo Zizi olharão, ese lembrarão das m.mas recommendaçoes. Adverteos, dice o S.r das minhas advertencias p.ara q. não vão após seus olhos, nem após, seus corações que após elles andarão errados e presta-lhes m.as admoestações p.ra que sejão santos e fieis aoseu Deos. A. Sr. nosso, não ha outro Deus mais do q. Elle, nós somos. seu povo, e Elle hé nosso R. q. nos remio de todos os fortes (Paulo 1970, 66–7).

124. E otra que se llama el Amida, que comiença: Adonay, abre los mis labios e mi boca te anunçiara tu alabamiento, etc. (Beinart 1981b, 564). These words are from Psalm 51:17, which begins the Amidah. For similar instances see Riera i Sans 1975, 352 [Valencia 1512]; Adler 1895, 56 [Mexico 1607].

125. Adonay, Adonay, shawfavsi tiftaw ufi yagid t'chelawsechaw (Liebman 1970, 193). For other pre-Expulsion examples from Molina de Aragón see Cantera Montenegro 1985, 74.

126. Sobre nós per a loar al Senyor de tot per a donar grandea al creant principat (Riera i Sans 1975, 349).

127. Diziendo entre otras oraçiones de judios que rezaua: Apiadate, apiadate Señor sobre nosotros e sobre nuestras cosas, o Criador, o Criador, apiadate sobre nos (Beinart 1981b, 12). See also Beinart 1981a, 281; 1977a, 282, 552; Liebman 1982, 114.

128. In the Yom Kippur shaharit service alone portions of more than twenty Psalms are chanted (Millgram 1971, 62–3). The incorporation of Psalms into the crypto-Jewish liturgy has been sketched by Lazar (1991, 191–9).

129. What Lewin calls the trascendencia de los salmos en la emocionalidad criptojudía can be seen in the fact that when David Abenatar Melo arrived in Holland, after having survived torture at the hands of the Portuguese Inquisition, he prepared a translation of the Psalms into Spanish "so that in our being and our wandering we sing them, and others can help us weep in the time of our affliction and others may console us and help us praise the Lord" (Para que en nuestro estar y en nuestro andar los cantemos, y los que sirven para llorar en el tiempo de nuestra aflicción y los que para consolación y alabanza del Señor) (1987, 203).

130. E ansymesmo rezava los syete salmos penitençiales en ebrayco (Beinart 1977a, 137). Cf. 282; Azevedo Mea 1982, 42 [Coimbra 1568].

131. Riera i Sans 1975, 349–51. Versions of Psalm 91 are found in several collections of prayers of the Judaizers (Lazar 1991, 193).

132. *Me acuso, señores, que algunas vezes leya en aquel salterio que dixe en casa de unas primas mías* (López Martínez 1954, 136).
133. *Leyó un papel . . . en que estaban escritos los psalmos penitenciales en romance, sin gloria patri y en octavas* (Lewin 1977, 230).
134. *Deseando salvarse consecutivamente rezaba . . . el psalmo del Miserere Mei y todos los demás siete psalmos, que son penitenciales, quitando lo que está añadido del Gloria Patri, etc. en cada psalmo y las oraciones que están al fin de ellos en las horas* (Lewin 1971, 487; cf. 27).
135. *Rezava cada dia polla menha e a noite doze salmos de David a honra das doze carreiras que Deus abrira no mar Roxo aos filhos de Israel* (Azevedo Mea 1982, 26).
136. *Alcé mis ojos a los montes atalayando dónde verná la mi ayuda de aquel fazedor del cielo y de la tierra.* He also prayed Psalms 67 and 130 (Sánchez Moya 1966, 112–3). See also Azevedo Mea 1982, 38 [Coimbra 1568].
137. *Canto grados alcaie* [sic] *al señor mis ojos, a los montes, a los montes del señor, venga del señor mi ayuda, mi defensa, mi abrigo, mi vandeo, mi consejo, Adonay, façedor y criador de los çielos y de la tierra no dara tropieço el señor en los mis pies; no mires, señor, mis guardas que son guardas de Ysrael, que el señor me guardara sobre mi mano derecha el sol del dia, no se me fiera la luna de la noche, no se me escurezca, guarde el señor mi vida, mi alma, mi salida, mi venida de peligros y contrarios, amén* (Blázquez Miguel 1988, 70).
138. *A ti alço los mys ojos a los montes que moras en los çielos e en todo lugar senoreas, fesiste çielos e tierra, sacaste los hijos de la ley cativa, no te aduermas ny te adormyras guardador de Ysrael tu guardas my entrada e my salida toda ora de noche e de dia, tu nombre altisimo sea castillo e fortaleza y ençima de mi cabeça panes y escudo y estandarte que me libre* (Blázquez Miguel 1986a, 55).
139. *Alto Dio de Abrahan / Rey forte de Isrrael / tu que ouuiste a ismael / ouue a minha orazón / tu que en las grandes alturas / te aposentas Señor / ouue a esta pecadora / que te chama das bas juras / pois tu que a todas criaturas / abres caminos e fontes / alzo meus ellos aos montes / donde vira minha ajuda / minha ajuda de con Adonay / a que fes o ceu a ha terra / líbranos de tanta guerra / pues que somos os teuos seyes / de adorar ed Dioses alleihos / coissa en que tanto ho me encerra / eu confesso que en mi se encerra / gran pecado que en mi ay / minha a juda do con Adonay / ee que fez eo ceu y aterra* (Liebman 1970, 155–7; cf. AGN Vol 402 doc 2, 506a–b, 564a). For other Psalms found among crypto-Jews see the compilations of prayers cited at the beginning of this chapter, also Azevedo Mea 1982, 38, 284, 430 [Coimbra 1568]; Lewin 1954, 123–4 [Mexico 1624].
140. *Persuadió a otra persona en la ciudad de Salamanca y a que conprase un salpterio de los que no tienen gloria patris al fin del salpmo porque le parescia que era pecado dezir gloria patris porque el dicho Gonçalo Vaez tenia y creya que no avia mas de un solo Dios y ansi no tenia para que dar gloria al padre y al hijo y al espiritu santo* (García Fuentes 1981, 98).
141. *Quando lo dijese delante de otras personas lo dijese con "gloria patri et filio et espiritu sancto," y quando lo dijese a solas solamente gloria sea a Dios* (García Fuentes 1981, 465). For other accusations of omitting the *Gloria Patri* see Santa María 1893c, 181; Wiznitzer 1960, 14 [Brazil]; Furtado 1925, xxxii [Evora, 1536]; Gracia Boix 1983, 133 [Córdoba 1572]; Azevedo Mea 1981, 159 [Portugal c. 1570]; Pereira 1979, 193 [Azores 1573]; Bel Bravo 1988, 99 [Granada 1590s]; Kohut 1904, 151 [Manila 1601]; Adler 1895, 45 [Mexico 1607]; Medina 1887, 2:145 [Lima 1635]; Lewin 1987, 214 [Lima 1581–1641]; Liebman 1970, 97 [Mexico 1639]; Lewin 1977, 230 [Mexico 1643]; Lewin 1954, 148 [Mexico 1647]; Lewin 1939, 25 [Argentina eighteenth century]; Lipiner 1977, 78 [Brazil]; Paulo 1981, 142 [Portugal twentieth century].

142. *Em lugar de Gloria Patri, dezia* "Gloria sejamos ante Deos quando foi seu sancto serviço" (Azevedo Mea 1982, 268; cf. 278). See also Blázquez Miguel 1989, 216 [Toledo 1677].
143. *Loado sea Dios.* / *Loado sea Jesucristo* (Liebman 1975, 197).
144. *Alabado sea el santísimo señor Dios de Abraham, Isaac y Jacob* (Lewin 1971, 27).
145. *Loado sea el Santísimo Dios de Israel, o el Santísimo Dios de los Exercitos* (Wiznitzer 1962a, 253). The translation is Wiznitzer's.
146. *Loado Dios; el Señor del cielo sea bendito; ¡qué grande es el Dios de Israel, Abraham, Isaac y Jacob!* (Medina 1899a, 149).
147. *Cantemos con alegria* / *alabanzas al Senor* / *que nadie que en el confia no le falta* / *Su favor* (Liebman 1982, 115). This is from the beginning of Psalm 95 and the end of Psalm 34.
148. *Somos obligados a alabar al señor en todo y por todo porque no nos hizo como los gentios de la tierra, ni puso nuestra suerte como la de ellos comunidades, porque ellos se humillan a vano y a baçio hazen oraçion al dios que no habla, nosotros nos humillamos ante el rey de los reyes, señor de los señores, santo y bendito, que estendio los çielos y ençimiento la tierra morada y fortaleza sabia y tornarasen tu coraçon que Adonay y poderosso es mi señor en los çielos de arriba y en la tierra de abaxo todos son desechados a fueras de el y no ay otro sino el, como esta escrito en su santa y verdadera ley, esperare en el señor, demandalle he merçed y graçia de lengua con ayuntamiento de gentes, hablare con contar al baron ques la limpieça de mi coraçon con la fragaçion de la casa santa, amen. En nuestros dias, amen, en nuestras noches, amen, en nuestra vida sea fragada la ciudad de Sion sea tu sacrificio en Jerusalen, amen con amen, con liçençia de los presentes plega ti, señor, de engrandeçer la ley y de honralla por amor de los . . . de la tierra, administrame, señor en tus santas carreras* (Blázquez Miguel 1986a, 68–9; cf. 69–70). The first part of this prayer resembles the traditional *Alenu* and the last part is a pastiche of various traditional prayers.
149. *Adonay, bendito es el rey poderoso que creó el çielo y la tiera sumo y eterno para siempre la ley que dio en el monte Sinay, la verdadera y santa, Adonay, bendito, reinará en Jerusalen con Ysrael para siempre, maravillas de Adonay se berán sobre su pueblo, yras de Adonay sobre los gentiles* (Blázquez Miguel 1986a, 214).
150. Paulo 1985, 70–8. Deolinda Mota and Francisco dos Santos Gaspar each recited a version of this prayer to Manuel da Costa Fontes in Rebordelo in 1980: "Adonai, Lord, I submit; / Adonai, Lord, be with me. / In the mouths of all humankind / may the Lord be praised and magnified" (*Adonai, Senhor, me benzo,* / *Adonai, Senhor, comigo.* / *Na boca de todo o nascido,* / *o Senhor sempre louvado e engrandecido*) (Fontes 1993, 82). For additional prayers see Azevedo Mea 1981, 166–7 [1580s]; Schwarz 1925, 58–9 [Portugal twentieth century]; Tradições 1928, 2.10:5–8; 1934, 9.68:6; 1935, 10.72:2–3; Fontes 1992 [Portugal 1980].
151. *Benditos e louvados, engrandecidos, realçados, manifestos, descobertos, honrados, festejados, exaltados sejam os setenta e tres nomes do Senhor, Adonai. Amen. . . . Bendito e louvado e engrandecido seja o Senhor* (Tradições 1928, 2.11:8).
152. *Senor Dios nuestro* / *no traigais en escarnio perpetuo* / *por birtud de buestro nombre* / *a buestro pueblo* (Liebman 1982, 113).
153. *O alto Dios de Abraham* / *Dios fuerte, Dios de Israel* / *Tu que oiste a Daniel* / *oye me oracione* / *Tu que las grandes alturas. Apiadate Senor* / *sin ayuda de me* / *trastorno no mi lloro. Por cantar a Ti,* / *abre mi corazon para que siempre te loe* / *mi alma no caye* (Liebman 1982, 113–4). See *Mishna Tannit* 2.4. Manuel da Costa Fontes has informed me in a letter [1991] that this prayer persists in the oral tradition in Portugal.
154. *Inclina Señor Tus ojos y oyeme porque pobre y necesitada, etc.* (Psalm 86:1) (Liebman 1982, 114–5).

155. *Padre Nuestro Poderoso / que cada día haceis maravillas / . . . Gran Dios de Israel / Vos que avés hecho camino / en la mar y en la tierra / Ayais merced y piedad / por ser vos quien sois* (Selke de Sánchez 1972, 279–80). For another version see note 175.
156. *En aquel arbol seco crio el señor aquellas hojas verdes, asi dios nos crie con paz y salud y nos libre de nuestros enemigos* (Blázquez Miguel 1988, 78).
157. *Deus nos dê a fé de Abraão, a contrição de David, a ciência de Salomão, Vitória de Gedeão, aviso que teve Loth, a felicidade de Jacob, espírito de Elias, a caridade de Tobias, a paciência de Job. Senhor, Deus de Adonai, amém* (Paulo 1981, 147). See also Tradições 1928, 2.10:7.
158. *Vn libro pequeño en que estaban las reglas de las Pascuas de Hanuca e Roxiaxania y del Zelahod y del Pan Çençeño* (Beinart 1974, 575). Modern Sephardis recite the *selihot* for 40 days from the beginning of the month of Elul until Yom Kippur. The first day they generally recite the *selihot* at midnight, after that generally prior to morning prayers (see the *Shulḥan Arukh, Orekh Ḥayyim* 581:1). Also see Levine 1982, 84.
159. *Reze los maytines del çeliah* (Beinart 1977a, 137).
160. *Calla, que digo çilhod, que digo çilhod, por que Dios me escabe de esta çara, que quiere desir peligro* (Carrete Parrondo 1985a, 72).
161. *Nuestro alto Rey Redentor Abrahan, Ysac e Jacob* (Gracia Boix 1982, 50).
162. *Mi señor Adonay, dadme ventura, mi señor Adonay, y libradme de poder de enemigos donde yo pueda engrandeçeros* (Blázquez Miguel 1986a, 75).
163. *En vuestras manos, Señor, encomiendo el alma mía* (Psalm 31:6). This prayer appears in the evening service just before the *Shema*; it is also recited before sleep and at the end of *Adon olam*.
164. *Se encomendava a Deos que fez os ceos e a terra, o mar e as areas, rezando orações de judeus* (Azevedo Mea 1982, 26; cf. 55, 79, 102, 151, 197, 258, 295–7, 327, 450).
165. *Deite nos, Noso Senhor, em paz e alevante Noso Rey pera vidas boas e paz e espanda sobre nos a cabaria de piedade* (Azevedo Mea 1982, 258) . . . *Valei me Senhor dos altos ceos* (274) . . . *Senhor valley me e acorey me a este trabalho e avey misericordia* (339) . . . *Falou Adonay Abrahão e dise lhe: Abrahão, toma teu filho Isaac que amaste e vai te ao Monte Morial* (422; cf. 430) . . . *O grande d'Abrahão, o grande d'Israel, Tu que ouviste a Daniel, ouve minha oraçvão* (422; cf. 430) . . . *Digno Adonay, meu Deu, meu abrigo, meu castello forte e firme, meu grande Senhor, em que me eu fio* (422) . . . *Alevantar me ei agora em poder de Vos, Senhor, cheo de muitas sanctas piedades* (445) . . . *Assi como Vos, Senhor, sacastes aqueles vossos servos e os levastes a terra da promissão, assi, Vos, Senhor, me saqueis a mim de todos os trabalhos* (450).
166. *No nynguno sino tu solo dios que glorifica en el consejo de los angeles bendito nuestro dios, bendito nuestro dios, bendito nuestro criador en ti que no ovo comienso ny fyn ny acabamyento byvo y no mortal que no fuiste muerto ny sepultado* (Blázquez Miguel 1986a, 55).
167. Espinosa (1930, 391–8) traces the origin of this song back to India and cites 83 versions in diverse European languages. For other *converso* versions see Blázquez Miguel 1988, 78–9; Riera i Sans 1975, 363–4; Lazar 1991, 197; Léon 1907, 279–80 [France twentieth century]: his version adds that 13 are the attributes of God.
168. Some versions of the hymn cite instead "the six books of the Mishnah" (León 1907, 279).
169. *Quien supiesse y entendiese qual era el uno.*
    *Uno Dió en el cielo, barahu barahu simo.*
    *Quien supiesse y entendiese quales eran los dos.*
    *Dos son Moysé y Arón.*
    *Uno es Diós en el cielo, barahu barahu simo.*

*Quien supiesse y entendiese quales eran los tres.*
*Tres son nuestros parientes, Abraham, Isach y Jacob...*
*Quatro madres de Israel, Sarra, Rica, Lia y Ragel.*
*Sinco libros de la Ley.*
*Los seys dias de la sempmana.*
*Siete dias con el sabbat.*
*Los ocho dias de la circumsissión.*
*Los nueve messes de la prenyada.*
*Diez mandamientos de la Ley.*
*Los honze jermans de Josep.*
*Los dotze tribus de israel.*
*Uno es Dió en el cielo, barahu barahu simo* (Riera i Sans 1975, 351–2).

170. Liebman 1975, 146. See also García 1910, 62; Fontes 1992 [Portugal 1980].

171. *Se encomendava a Deus com as orações dos christãos* (Roth 1931–2, 16–7).

172. *Resava... un pater noster judiego, que disen pater noster de tuhel de tuheel amaharón, etc.* (Fita y Colomé 1893, 322). Another example may be the prayer that Juan Martínez Pelligero [Soria 1501] was overheard saying in mass that began: "My father Moses..." (*Padre mío Moysén*) (Carrete Parrondo 1985a, 96).

173. *Que el Pater Noster le dijo que rezase solamente, y no otra oración ninguna, excepto los salmos de la penitencia* (Toro 1932, 216).

174. *Que rezassem dois Padres-Nossos e duas Ave-Marias e as ofrecessem a Moisés* (Coelho 1987, 223–4).

175. *Padre nuestro poderós, / que tot jorn feu maravellas, / ayau pietat, gran Déu, de nós / y de las vostres simples ovelles, / que són fiblades de abelles / en tran gran afligiment. / Tu qui és poderós, Déu aternal, / vulles-te apiedar de elles. / Santificat sia el teu sant nom, / ara y tota vegada. / Monstras, Senyor, lo teu llum, / no l'em tengas amagada. / Si la nostra gent passada / per algun tems a errat, / de tu, Senyor, és perdonat, / así lo diu la Ley segrada. / Tu, gran Déu, qui en lo cel, / estàs en la tua santa cadira, / pietat, gran Déu, de nós / y el teu poble qui suspira* (Riera i Sans 1975, 362–3). For a discussion of other *Pater Noster* adaptations in Catalán see Aramón 1961, 100ff.; Selke de Sánchez 1986, 238–9.

176. *Cria no Deus dos Céus que deu a dita Lei a Moisés e a ele se encomendava com a oração do Padre-Nosso* (Coelho 1987, 211).

177. *Rezavam a oração do Padre nosso sem dizir Jesus no fim* (Silva 1896, 31). See also Roth 1931–2, 16–7; Caro Baroja 1961, 3:129, 134 [Spain 1740s].

178. *Deus santo, Deus misericordioso, / Senhor de todo o poder, / continuai, meu Deus, em ser / Padre nosso. // Trata, Senhor, como vosso, / um povo tão consternado, / que vive só esperançado, / que estais no céo. //* etc. (Vasconcelos 1958, 188–90; 226–9). For additional Portuguese versions of this prayer see Schwarz 1925, 79–82; Paulo 1985, 98–102.

179. *El Credos los apóstoles lo hezieron y no es más de fasta: Iudicare bivos ed mortuos;* that is, it omits the *Gloria Patri* (Carrete Parrondo 1985a, 68).

180. *Rezara um rozario por guarda da lei de Moisés... rezassem duas Ave Marias pela lei de Moisés e dois Padre Nossos* (Novinsky 1972b, 158).

181. *Creio em um Deus Omnipotente, criador dos céus e da terra e de tudo quanto numa e noutra parte se encerra. / Creio em Vós, Senhor, na Vossa Santa e bendita Lei, / Creio em Vós, Senhor, único Deus verdadeiro. / Creio que o Vosso povo do Mar Vermelho o salvaste e os inimogos afogaste; / Creio em Vós, Senhor, único Deus Verdadeiro, que sois o Rei Divino e o Rei da Glória, porque só Vos sois o Rei dos reis, Deus dos deuses, Senhor dos senhores, Pai dos pais. / Portanto*

*eu, Senhor, espero na Vossa divina misericórdia que me haveis, Senhor, de salvar e livrar de todos os perigos, trabalhos e maus encontros. / Espero, Senhor, que me haveis de livrar dos ferros de el-rei, do poder da justiça de portas alheias, do mau vizinho à porta, de más-linguas, dos olhos da inveja; e do de que não nos pudermos livrar, nem soubermos, nos livre e guarde o grande Deus de Israel. / Livra- nos, Senhor, de prisães, como livraste o Vosso santo profeta Daniel da cova dos leães. / Livra-nos, Senhor, de ódios e invejas como a David, quando o libraste das mvãos de Saul. / Livra-nos, Senhor, do fogo como livraste os três mancebos Ananias, Azarias e Missael. / Livranos, Senhor, de falsos testemunhos como livraste a casta Susana do falso crime de adultério. / Salva e livra todo o povo de Israel. / Livra-nos, Senhor, do poder de todos os nossos inimigos, que nos desejam fazer mal. / Perdoa-nos, Senhor, os nossos erros, as nossas maldades, as nossas culpas, o nosso pecado, as nossas iniquidades e todos os nossos maus pensamentos. / Livra-nos, Senhor do inimigo tentador. Tu és Deus imenso, imutável, sempre eterno e és Pai de misericórdia para como o Teu povo de Israel, Deus Adonai. Amém, Senhor, Amém* (Paulo 1985, 96–7). The reference to the three youths is from Daniel 1:6 and also forms part of the *selihot* prayer. See also Paulo 1970, 55–5; 1981, 145; Schwarz 1925, 61–2; Tradições 1935, 10.72: 4.

182. *O Déu, deliure'ns axí com deliurares lo poble de Israel* (Riera i Sans 1975, 350). For a twentieth-century parallel see Azevedo Mea 1981, 169–75. Not surprisingly, the apocryphal book of Judith was widely read in Mexico at the end of the sixteenth century (Liebman 1970, 153).

183. *De profundis cramarei, Senhor, de las profundezas Vos llamou Joanas y lo sacastes de lo ventre de la balena, asi me sacai, Senhor, desta cadena para vos servir* (Azevedo Mea 1981, 168). A similar plea appears in the sentence of Maria Lopes, of Lamego, in Coimbra in 1570 (*Que a livrase de peryguos e asym como livrara a Jonas e outros profetas* (Azevedo Mea 1982, 204).

184. *Dá-me ajuda e favores / que prometeste a Daniel, / esta vinda do Messias / seja, Senhor, em nossos dias. / Mandenos por mensageiro / o Profecta Moyses que nos tire / do captiveiro. Amen* (Schwarz 1925, 95; cf. 48, 55–7). There is a modern Portuguese version of this prayer: "Great God of Israel, / great strength of Abraham, / since You heard Daniel / hear my prayer" (*Grande Deus de Israel, / grande forte de Abraão, / já que ouviste a Daniel, / ouve a minha oração*) (Paulo 1985, 105). See also Tradições 1928, 2.11:7; de Cunha e Freitas, 21–2 [1701].

185. *¡Abraham te guarde! . . . ¡Abraham sea tu morada!* (Moreno Koch 1977, 366–7).

186. *Dio a este testigo una oracion de Josep, para que ge la guardase, e que este testigo la ha tenido, e que oy quando la sacaron de la carcel, la echo tras de una cama. . . . En la cárcel desta iquisyción vido un libro de la beata Suares que tenía una oración de Josué, en que desía muchas veses el nombre de adonay* (López Martínez 1954, 136). Baer considers the reference to be to Joseph (1936, 480).

187. For a general discussion of Jewish "saints" see Chapter 4.

188. *Asi como os christãos velhos tinham devaçam em Santa Caterina de Sena e outros santos asy os christãos novos tinham devaçam a rayna Hester* (Azevedo Mea 1982, 308). Vasconcelos reports that modern Portuguese new-Christians frequently pray to Saint Esther (1958, 223). See also Nidel 1984, 254.

189. *Padre nuestro, padre nuestro, Dios te salve, Dios te salve, amén, amén* (García 1910, 197–8).

190. Riera i Sans 1975, 363. See also Braunstein 1936, 196 [1660s Majorca]. For modern versions see Schwarz 1925, 59–60; Tradições 1927, 2.8:8; 1928, 2.11:7. For a modern crypto-Jewish funeral prayer to Saint Raphael see Paulo 1970, 96; 1985, 98.

191. Fontes 1993, 74. Clemente Carmona told David Nidel in New Mexico in 1980 that his family honors Moses as a saint and lights candles to him. He also said that among his

"Jewish" friends the women "light candles supposedly to the saints, but they will never tell you which saints." He added that some women "will light a wick in a bowl of olive oil" (Nidel 1984, 254).

192. *Quando nós ao mar chegamos / logo por Moisés chamamos / Moisés nos respondeu / com uma voz muito dolorida / chamai pelo grande Deus de Israel / que vós sereis socorridos / Louvamos ao nascente / louvamos ao poente / louvamos o grande Deus de Israel / para todo o sempre. / Oh! grande Deus de Israel / Santo e justo e bemdito / o Nosso Santo Nome / no monte Sinai éste escrito* (Tradições 1937, 11.80:8).

193. *Anjo Custodio, Ave do Senhor, ao Divino Divinal Senhor sem fin, pedi, clamae a Deus por mim* (Tradições 1928, 2.10:5).

194. *Anjo da Guarda, acompanhai-me e guardai-me no caminho da verdade. Não permitais que eu faça coisas com que ofenda o Senhor. Apresentai minhas misérias, dizei-as ao Senhor. Se eu morrer, velai-me, se viver, acompanhai-me* (Machado 1952, 41; cf. 42). For other examples see Tradições 1928, 2.12:5; Schwarz 1925, 52; Paulo 1970, 80–1, 91; 1981, 147; 1985, 63; Vasconcelos 1958, 173, 232 [1933]. For a funeral prayer to the Guardian Angel see Paulo 1970, 96.

195. Schwarz 1925, 57–7; Paulo 1985, 82–3. Azevedo Mea 1981, 163 provides a sixteenth-century antecedent.

196. Paulo reports that in modern Portugal when a child is born new-Christian friends and family stay with the mother during the first night and sing the ballad of Jonah (1970, 87; 118–20). See also Paulo 1985, 87- 8; Tradições 1934, 9.67:4–5.

197. Tradições 1935, 10.72:3. For other examples see Paulo 1985, 85; P. Azevedo 1910, 189.

198. *Estando Abbacuc Profeta no campo com seus pastores, dando graças ao Senhor* (Tradições 1932, 7.51:3). See also Schwarz 1925, 48, 55–7; Paulo 1985, 83–4.

199. *Se voluía a la pared y estava vn rato asentada sabadeando, alçando e abaxando la cabeça* (Carrete/Fraile 1987, 30; cf. 72, 105). See also Carrete Parrondo 1985a, 29 [1490]; Caro Baroja 1961, 1:434; Beinart 1974, 24, 164, 242, 564; 1981b, 38, 42, 99; Furtado 1925, xxxii [Evora 1536]; Lipiner 1977, 123–4 [colonial Brazil]; Liebman 1970, 96 [Mexico 1639]; Willemse 1974, 29 [Spain 1650s].

200. *Vio que ella estava asentada na sua cama antre os lançois cuberta com uma mantilha po-los hombros, estava meneando o corpo pera baixo e para cima, digo, pera diante e per detras, abayxando e alevantando a cabeça e despois encostou a parede a cabeça, asi como estava asentada* (Azevedo Mea 1982, 338–9).

201. *Rezando ajuntava as palmas das mãos e batia as palmas e tornava a afastar as palmas, e tornava a ajuntá-las e abaixava a cabeça e tornava a levantá-la, e baqueava o corpo para baixo e para cima* (Lipiner 1977, 124). See also 1969, 92.

202. *Se entró en vn rehoyo, junto con vn espino, e púosose en pie delante el espino; e estando allí abaxaua a alçaua la caveça e andaua çiertos passos adelante e otros atrás; e algunas abaxaua tanto la cabeça que paresçía que llegaua junto con el suelo* (Carrete Parrondo 1985a, 111).

203. *Hazian çiertas humiliaçiones con los cuerpos y con las cabeças cada tres beçes y daban tres pasos hazia atras y hazia adelante y lo que ansi rezaban hera en ebrayco* (Caro Baroja 1961, 1:442).

204. *Rezar ao modo judaico per muitas vezes, estando em pé e assentada e de joelhos com as mãos alevantadas, lavando as primeiro, cerrando as e abrindo as de quando em quando, movendo a cabeça para baixo e para cima. . . . Tendo as mãos abertas e apartadas huma da outra e de quando em quando as ajuntava e depois punha nos peitos huma sobre a outra, judaizando desta maneira como os judeus custumam en seu rezar. . . . Estando em pé com os olhos na lux e as*

mãos abertas alevantadas. . . . Pondo se algumas vezes nas pontas dos pés. . . . Abrio as mãos obra de dez vezes e as tornava a cerar, afastando as huma da outra e que ela estaria nisto obra dum coarto d'ora. . . . Bolia com a cabeça de quando em quando, dum ombro pero ho outro. . . . Bolia com os beiços como que rezava com as contas penduradas na mão (Azevedo Mea 1982, 34, 282–3, 322, 338–9; cf. 11, 26, 48, 259, etc.).

205. Vio muitas vezes . . . por-se num canto como o capello da capa na cabeça e rezar os psalmos de David em lingoagem e rezando ajuntava as palmas das mãos e batia as palmas e tornava afastar as palmas e tornava ajuntalas e abaixava a cabeça e tornava a levantalla e baqueava o corpo pera baixo e pera cima e ás vezes fazia esto a boca da noite junto de huã grade olhando pera as as estrellas (Furtado 1925, 336; cf. 393). These customs were common in colonial Mexico as well (Liebman 1970, 72, 345).

206. Estauan todos bueltos hazia donde sale el sol e rezauan sabadeando con las cabeças a manera de judios (Beinart 1974, 310; cf. 312).

207. Se sienta sobre una arca que tiene en su apossento despues de auerse lavado, y cruza los braços sobre el pecho, y tiene puesto en la cabeça un gran paño de tocar a manera de los que traen los moros, y esta puesto al Oriente, y levantados los ojos al çielo rezando sin entendersele lo que reza . . . mas de una hora (AGN Vol 271 doc 1, 4b). See also AGN Vol 276 doc 14, 413a.

208. Le demostro çiertas oraçiones, las quales le escrivio en çinco o seys pliegos de papel, las quales o alguna dellas sabe que se dize en esta manera: Vna que comiença: Sema Ysrael Adonay Elohenu, etc., e la sabe toda (Beinart 1981b, 564).

209. Resauan a la pared los pies juntos (Beinart 1974, 59). Rabbinic tradition ascribes praying with the feet together to Ezekiel 1:7 (Millgram 1971, 355).

210. Se voluía a la pared y estava vn rato asentada sabadeando, alçando e abaxando la cabeça (Carrete/Fraile 1987, 30).

211. Vení acá, Juan de Salzedo; vos, que fuistes rabí, hazes asy como fase mi marido, que siempre anda faziendo oraçion por casa en la mañana e a la tarde e a la noche, e pónese de cara a la pared muchas vezes. Más querría que me diesen puñadas en los ojos que no vérgelo; e no sé lo que reza, que no ge lo entiendo (Carrete Parrondo 1985a, 145).

212. Poniéndose cada uno detrás de dos puertas de una sala, la cara a la pared, su tío cubierta la cabeza con un paño blanco, a modo de capirote (García 1910, 202). See also Carrete Parrondo 1985a, 29, 36 [Soria 1490]; Moreno Koch 1977, 367 [Garcimuñoz 1491]; Furtado 1929, 192 [Brazil 1594]; Liebman 1970, 96 [Mexico 1639]; Wiznitzer 1960, 14 [colonial Brazil].

213. Este testigo las vido resar de rodillas. . . . Lo vido estar resando en vn libro a grandes boses. Y que le vio como se echo de barriga en el suelo (Beinart 1974, 26). Traditionally the only time one prays prostrate is on *Yom Kippur*. For other pre-Expulsion examples from Molina de Aragón see Cantera Montenegro 1985, 72–3.

214. Pedro el Romo que se omilló de rodillas en la . . . synoga e se santiguó, e queste testigo hizo otro tanto, e que rezó este testigo un Pater Noster e Ave María (Carrete Parrondo 1985a, 36).

215. Me pongo de rodillas, cargado el cuerpo sobre las piernas e inclinado todo el cuerpo muy bajo, mirando el suelo, con las manos puestas y la cabeza muy baja, que esté mirando el suelo, y las manos hacia bajo las puntas de los dedos, y esto has de hacer puesto en un rincón, que es como se hace allá en mi tierra, y encendida la candileja mientras estás de esta suerte (Lewin 1975, 84; cf. 70, 76, 89, 166). Botello was also accused in Mexico of "praying prostrate on the ground, on his knees, his body leaning on his head which was on the ground, and praying the Psalms that way" (*Él se echaba de bruces en tierra, que es hincado de rodillas, y tendido el cuerpo de hacia la cabeza en tierra, y rezaba los salmos*) (Lewin 1971, 30).

216. *Rezando en el aposento que le servía de almacen, en dichas horitas, unas veces hincado de rodillas y otras de pie* (Lewin 1954, 149). See also Liebman 1974, 142.
217. *No entendia bien lo que cantaban, . . . pero que sabe que no hera cantar de christianos, porque cantaban de garguero como que se ahogaban* (Beinart 181b, 387).
218. *Quando dezia la dha oron . . . hablaua de garguero y la boz ronca como lo hazian los judios y q este t: quando auia judios los vio fabordear e rezar de garguero* (Caro Baroja 1961, 1:434).
219. *Todos juntamente a vna boz respondieron et dixeron a lo quel dicho Bachiller Menbreque les predicaua. . . . E al fin della . . . desyan e respondian todos a vna box, amen* (Gracia Boix 1982, 41, 50). Freehof shows that prayer in unison characterized Sephardic observance, in contrast to the Ashkenazi rite, from at least the thirteenth century (1964, 221–2).
220. Hiuce Galhon testified [Segovia 1486] that the *converso* "Alonso Días had told him that he had learned Hebrew as a child" (*Alonso Diaz, esmelador difunto, le obo dicho que siendo niño aprendia hebrayco*) (Gutwirth 1981, 90). See also Carrete Parrondo 1985a, 20, 21, 29, 32, etc.; Lazar 1991, 184.
221. For example, Don Francisco Rodríguez de Matos, one of the most learned crypto-Jews in late sixteenth-century Mexico and the father of Luis de Carvajal, knew only the *Shema*, by rote, and even there probably did not know the meaning of the individual words (Cohen 1973, 96).
222. Carrete Parrondo 1985a, 47. Joshua 6:27: "And it came to pass that God was with Joshua, whose fame extended throughout all the world."
223. *Yba pocas vezes a misa y tenía mucho la habla de judía* (Carrete Parrondo 1985a, 168).
224. Baião 1921, 143. For additional biographical information about the Diogo Fernandes family, see Lipiner 1969, 165–78. For a similar example from the Canary Islands [1526] see Wolf 1926, 56. The city of Toledo was known to have a Hebrew-speaking *converso* community even at the end of the sixteenth century if Cervantes's testimony in *Don Quijote* 1:9 is to be believed.
225. Exceptions are those *conversos* like Fray Luis de León or Martín Martínez de Cantalapiedra who entered the priesthood and became absorbed in Renaissance humanist scholarship that emphasized the study of the Bible in its original languages.
226. *Todo lo que desya en hebraico lo tornava a desir et declarar en romançe* (Gracia Boix 1982, 41–50).
227. Beinart has compiled a list of Hebrew religious terms that appear in the Ciudad Real trials in the late fifteenth and early sixteenth centuries (1981a, 341–3).
228. Hebrew = "My Lord." Covarrubias (1611, 474), ignoring its Hebrew origin, defines Adonai as *otro nombre de Dios, vale Dominus meus*. For a set of Brazilian prayers praising Adonai see Lipiner 1977, 20–1.
229. *Quando algunas veces acaso avían de nonbrar a nuestro señor ihesu christo e a nuestra señora llamauan e nombrauan adonay e amaysgrael* [the Shema?] (Santa María 1893b, 369).
230. *Les oyo dezir muchas veçes: Alabado sea Adonay* (Beinart 1974, 310). Garçia de Quintanar [Soria 1491] allegedly prayed with the words *Varahá leymán Adonay* (Carrete Parrondo 1985a, 60). Carrete Parrondo speculates that this may be *Berakah le-ne'eman Adonay* [benediction of the faithful to God]. See also Carrete/Fraile 59; Caro Baroja 1961, 1:422; Beinart 1977a, 558; Beinart 1981b, 42, 47, 55; Baião 1921, 175 [1556]; Schwarz 1925, 108 [Portugal twentieth century].
231. *Adonay, Adonay, apiadate de nos e Criador del çielo e de la tierra e de la mar e de las arenas* (Beinart 1981b, 41; cf. 102).
232. *Rezar orações que falavão em Adonay. . . . Bento Tu, Adonay* (Azevedo Mea 1982, 260, 355).

233. *Adonay, Adonay, em quem tenho confiança. . . . Vivo a meu folgo, minha esperança—a que já Deus prometeu a nosso Padre Abrãao, de gozar as tuas senhas toda a gente da nação! Nós, pelos nossos pecados, todos andamos errados, em terra alheia, sem pastor! . . . Tende de nós piedade, e misericórdia, Senhor* (Lipiner 1977, 20–1).
234. *En nome do Senhor, Adonai, Amen. . . . Amen, Senhor, ao ceu vá, ao ceu chegue* (Roth 1931–2, 16).
235. *Leer como rabi hasiendo la baraha* (Beinart 1974, 20).
236. *Desir sobre 'l vino / vuestra santa barahá / como aquel que la sabrá* (Castillo 1882, poem #994). See also Beinart 1974, 295 [1484].
237. Carrete Parrondo 1985a, 114. On the other hand, this may be an allusion to a Hebrew word meaning "cry" or "lament."
238. *¿Non cres, señor, hay Adonay, por la ley de Moysén, que dygo verdad a vuestra merçed? . . . ¡O, senor, lo que mucho an los honbres acostunbrado non lo pueden asy desar!* (Carrete/Fraile 1987, 59). An anonymous contributor to *Avotaynu* in 1989 (S5) recalled that in his Cuban grandfather's house he would hear his father and his grandfather say "Hay Adonai."
239. Sánchez Moya 1972, 133; cf. 73, 136. *Saday* = Almighty! *Alhar* [*El khai* ?] = God lives!
240. *Preguntado lo de vn bateo que avian echo de vn pariente suyo, que avia avido segund fama vn yjo suyo en vna criada suya, entre otras palabras que dixo a las quales preguntaua, dixo el dia de guay batheo, de otras palabras non se acuerda* (Beinart 1974, 324).
241. *Le oyera desir este testigo algunas veses de que mentaua a sus hijos: "¡Ay, guayas, guayas!" como dizen las judias, e baxando la caveça disiendolo* (Moreno Koch 1977, 366).
242. *Dixo . . . Mari Aluares "¡Ay, guayas!" dos o tres veses, y quel . . . liçençiado le dixo que callese, que la casa estaua llena de gente* (Carrete/Fraile 1987, 28). See also Carrete Parrondo 1985a, 87; Cantera/Carrete 1971, 262; Gil Vicente's 1532 Portuguese *Auto da Lusitânia* (Vicente 1984, 2:555) and Teyssier 1959, 219–24.
243. *¿Qué guayais? Mal guayo os cayga. ¿No estays hartas de guayarle cada día?* (Cantera/Carrete 1971, 264).
244. In a 1410 last will and testament from Alba de Tormes the Jew don Judáh requested that when he died his family and friends were to chant "Guay, guay, the righteous man is dead" (*¡Guay, guay! que ya murió el que bien façía*) (Amador de los Ríos 1875, 964).
245. *¡Guayas, guayas! / ¡Que buen judio ha sido! / Y siempre estuvo bien / en la ley de Moisén. / Murió como buen judío / Perdónele el Dío* (Caro Baroja 1961, 1:440).
246. *Yba a consolar e consolava a çiertas personas que estavan tras puerta por muerte de çierto defunto e alli juntamente con ellas estava tras puerta e hazia guayas como de judayco*. Another person described her as *guayando e cantando e llorando e haziendo palmas con las manos como lo hazian los judios* (Melammed 1991b, 163).
247. Gómez-Menor Fuentes 1970, 103. See also Gil Vicente's *Barca do Inferno* (1517). In his *Juiz da Beira* (1525?) a new-Christian laments his current religious state: *Agora que soy guayado / y negro christianejo, / ándome a calçado viejo* (Cancioneiro Geral 5:202–3).
248. *Estava assentado em uma cadeira despaldas, e dela fazia prática às ditas pessoas, exortantoas a que vivessem na lei de Moisés, refirindo-lhe algumas autoridades do testamento velho, e as ditas pessoas em certos passos da prática faziam guayas, levantavam os olhos ao céu, punham as palmas das mãos viradas uma para a outra baixando as cabeças até os peitos, e inclinando-as a uma e a outra parte* (Lipiner 1977, 79).
249. *Meldar como judíos* (López Martínez 1954, 393).
250. *Trobar en yr meldar, / trobar en saber la ley* (Castillo 1882, poem #994).
251. *Mayr, dan pan, yrme e a meldar* (Carrete Parrondo 1985a, 120).

252. *Quando . . . resauan las dichas oraçiones, que lo hasian como quando los judios meldavan, alçando e abaxando la cabeça* (Beinart 1981b, 42). The word is retained with the same meaning among modern-day Ladino-speakers.
253. *Dava dineros a la bolsa de dicha cedaqua y otras almosnas a judios pobres* (Cabezudo Astraín 1963, 283).
254. *¡Haba, goym; haba, quelabim!* (Carrete Parrondo 1985a, 153).
255. Covarrubias defines *malsín* without reference to its Hebrew etymology: *El que de secreto avisa a la justicia de algunos delitos con mala intención y por su propio interés, y hazer este oficio se llama malsinar* (1611, 781). Medieval Iberian Jewish communities went to great lengths to protect themselves against informers. For example, at the end of the fourteenth century the *aljamas* of Aragon were given the power to prosecute and inflict corporal penalty on informers (Baer 1966, 2:67–9), although a later papal bull of Spanish anti-pope Benedict XIII (1415) barred Jewish courts' jurisdiction against *quos ipsi malsines appelant* (Shepard 1982, 72). The abuses of *malsines* and attempts to curb them have given rise to a number of controversies, which are reviewed by Baer (1966, 2:444–56).
256. *Lhe chamarem malsim por elle ter descoberto o dinheiro que elles tiraram para Roma* (Baião 1921, 129).
257. *Por temor que tenía a que ge lo malsinarían con el dicho obispo* (Carrete Parrondo 1986, 56).
258. Carrete Parrondo 1985a, 171. I do not know the meaning of *roeka*, unless it is related to the Hebrew *ro'e*, which signifies someone who reads a text.
259. "*¿Qué guezará es ésta deste pie, que nunca sana?*" *y que no sabe este testigo qué quiere desir, saluo que cree que quiere desir "qué mala ventura," porque antes, quando heran judíos, les oyo desir muchas veces este vocablo* (Carrete/Fraile 1987, 83). See also Gil Vicente's *Barca do Inferno* [1507] (Vicente 1984, 2:202–3) and Teyssier 1959, 216.
260. "*Orsemor sea ello,*" *e maldezía e dezía que quería más a su madre, que fue judía e morió en la mar, que a Nuestra Señora la Virgen María* (Carrete Parrondo 1985a, 137).
261. *Venía . . . de misa, e que todo era hevelayud, que quiere dezir "todo es nada"* (Carrete Parrondo 1985a, 46). Carrete Parrondo considers the expression derived from the Hebrew *hebel hayu*.
262. Perhaps the most complex of these bilingual poems is Fray Diego's fifteenth-century poem against a *converso* from León called Juan de España (Baena 1966, 985–7). Solá-Solé and Rose have analyzed and reviewed scholarship about the poem (1976, 373–84). The genre was popular among Sephardic Jews in Amsterdam as well (Salomon 1970). Gutwirth gives several examples of *converso* humor based on slipping Hebrew allusions into everyday speech (1981, 90).
263. One example is the word *desmazalado* ("unfortunate"), comprised of a Latinate prefix and suffix and the Hebrew word *mazal* (= "fortune"), which is found in Cervantes's *La Señora Cornelia* and *El coloquio de los perros* (Shepard 1982, 39) and in Gil Vicente's 1525 Portuguese *Farsa de Inês Pereira* (Vicente 1984, 2:446). Covarrubias ignored the Hebrew derivation of the term when he defined it in 1611 as "disorderly and poorly assembled; it is a metaphor taken from merchandise which comes bundled in *maços* and tied together. Thus *amazaladas*. And unbundled means that each piece goes its own way, which is called *desmaçolar*. And from that are derived *desmaçolado* and *desmaçalado*) (*Desaliñado y mal compuesto; tomada la metáfora de las mercadurías que vienen atadas y hechas maços, y assí amazoladas, que desatadas va cada pieça por su parte, y esto se puede dezir desmaçolar. Y de allí desmaçolado y desmaçalado*) (1977, 460).

# CHAPTER XVI 🌱

# Oaths

In an age in which most people believed that the deity was omniscient and omnipotent, and in which most people hoped for some sort of salvation for their eternal souls, oaths were mortally serious. In their essence oaths tend to differ very little from culture to culture. The majority of oaths have three parts: (1) an invocation of the deity; (2) a promise, generally to perform a certain act, or that what the swearer says is true; and (3) a commitment to some penalty—often only implied—if the promise is not kept. That is, an oath is a promise that puts one's life or soul in bond.

In the Middle Ages both Jewish and Christian oaths met these conditions, but they invoked the deity and offered up the body or soul according to each religion's theological tenets. The most striking differences had to do with the invocation of the deity. The most common Christian oaths invoked Christ or the Virgin Mary. The most common Jewish oaths invoked God through one or another of His attributes deemed central to the Jewish faith. The *converso* Fernando de Madrid was said in 1491 to make oaths with the Jewish phrase: "By God, by the living God."[1] The Nunes family of Pernambuco was accused in 1595 of swearing simply "by God in heaven and by the Lord of the world."[2] Sometimes these oaths reflected the new-Christian antipathy to the multiple components of the Christian Trinity and Holy Family. For example, Rodrigo de Tardajos [Soria 1501] testified that "when he swore, he always said 'I swear by God,' and nothing else."[3]

But Judaizers were much more likely to swear by God in His role as creator of the universe. Even before the founding of the Inquisition, in 1459 a *converso* barber in Frómista was punished for swearing not by Christ but by "the God who created the heavens, the stars, the earth, the sea, and the dust" (Baer 1966, 2:285). There are written versions of oaths of this nature from the early thirteenth century in such documents as the 1232 Fuero de Aragón, which gives precise instructions about how Jews were to swear: "Swear by the miraculous name of Ananie of the strong words that Moses spoke over the sea so that it divided into twelve paths over which the children of Israel could pass on dry land, after which Pharaoh and all his host died in the Red Sea."[4] Juan de Fez [Ciudad Real 1484] was said to have sworn as follows: "As the Creator of the world is in heaven and created the heavens and the earth and divided the sea in twelve paths and saved the people of Israel from the power of Pharaoh, in this way may You, o Lord, have mercy on me and save me."[5] This oath was extremely popular in Castile. The many recorded examples include this one, which was allegedly spoken by the *converso* Jeronymite monk Alfonso de Toledo around 1487: "I swear to the Creator who created the heaven and the earth and divided the sea into twelve paths and gave the Law to Moses that this is true."[6] Bartolomé González [Guadalajara 1492] added a reference to the Tetragrammaton: "By the Law of Moses such-and-such a thing is true, and by the Creator who put His name in four letters and divided the sea in twelve paths. . . ."[7] In 1607 the Mexican Inquisition made Diego Díaz Nieto swear by the following oath, which seems to echo the concatenation of events of the Exodus story found in the Passover song *Dayenu*: "Do you swear by the Creator, who made heaven and earth and the sea, and the sands, and wrote His name in four letters, *Job, He, Vav, He*, and took the children of Israel out from the land of Egypt, and parted the sea, and gave them the manna, and gave the Law to Moses on Mount Sinai, and brought the Children of Israel through the desert and afterwards took them to the Promised Land, to tell the truth in answer to the questions?" (Liebman 1970, 196). In their oaths some new-Christians such as Fernando de Madrid [Toledo 1491] projected the idea of a liberating God into their own circumstances: "May it be the will of the God who created the heavens and the earth to take us out from the midst of this people [the Christians] who watch our every movement and among whom we live cheated of what is ours!" (Baer 1966, 2:351).

Crypto-Jewish oaths also frequently made reference to the afterlife, either invoking God as savior of souls or naming some deceased loved one whose eternal happiness presumably was also in bond to the sworn oath. In Brazil these oaths continued to incorporate the Hebrew word *olam*, which in this context means "world" in the sense of the afterworld. The *cristãa nova* Dona Lianor [Bahia 1591] confessed that "she used to swear by the world to keep the soul of her father."[8] A year later Dona Ana Alcoforada confessed that she used to swear by the "*orlon* of her father, which was the same as swearing by the world."[9] The new-Christian Antunes family as well used to swear oaths "by the World which holds the soul of my father."[10]

Since oaths are legal formulas, it was only natural that people swore by the written laws that they believed bound them. Thus Christians sometimes swore by the Gospels as Jews swore by the Pentateuch. And since certain physical religious objects were seen to be imbued with the sacred character of the deity or to focus the deity's power, Christians often swore by placing their hands on the New Testament or a crucifix while Jews in similar fashion touched the Torah scrolls. Judaizing *conversos* of the Expulsion generation continued to invoke the Torah and the Creator of the world with formulas that went back at least to the thirteenth century. Mari Lopes [Ciudad Real 1484] said that Rodrigo Marín used to call "not on Holy Mary but on Moses, and when he had to swear he would swear by the Law of Moses and the Ten Commandments."[11] The *converso* Manuel de Puxmija was said in 1486 to swear his business oaths on his friend's Hebrew prayer book and to kiss the book.[12] Segovian *conversos* like Pedro García de Alonso Arias in 1490 accepted oaths like "by the Torah of Moses" in their business dealings.[13] 1505 Testimony described how Luis Mendes, playing cards with friends around 1496, got into an argument and said: "By the Law of Moses, that's how it is!"[14] And in like vein Juan de Salcedo [Aranda de Duero 1502] alleged that more than a decade earlier Yñigo de Soria refused to go to the church of the Virgin Mary to swear, saying: "Kill that idea. I will swear the same thing here as in the church of Our Lady. Holy Mary won't bite me, because she is nothing but a stone. Why not go to the synagogue to take the Torah in our arms?"[15]

Judaizing new-Christians were extremely sensitive to the theological underpinnings implied in the different ways Christians and Jews swore their oaths; they seem to have been as eager to eschew the Christian formulas as they were to invoke the Jewish oaths. Even the hint of a Christian oath—such as swearing by the "living God" who might be construed to be Christ—could set someone off. In a 1484 trial a man reported that some twenty years earlier "Alvar Díaz, a linen dealer, and Juan Martínez del Oliva . . . were having an argument and a fight in the alley and in the street, the subject of which he does not remember. To stress the truth about what he was saying, Alvar Díaz swore by the living God; but Juan Martínez did not believe him, and said that he swore by the true law of Moses. Then, they reached an agreement and they did not fight anymore and became friends."[16] Rodrigo de Tardajos [Soria 1501] was asked whether it was true that

> he did not believe in the oaths that Christians make and did not swear them, but rather swore by the true and living Creator who created the heaven and the earth, and that he did not swear by the Gospels. He replied that he never said nor swore that, but [rather] because he saw that many Christians swore lightly and some of them said that they did not believe in the oath they took because they were not telling the truth.[17]

Francisco Maldonado de Silva [Chile 1626] refused to swear by Jesus Christ because "the law of Moses commands that oaths not be made to any gods at all."[18] Some new-Christians reputedly went so far as to use their oaths to mock what they saw as Christian credulity. Juan de Salcedo [Aranda de Duero 1502] allegedly used to swear "by the one I see who does not see me . . . by which he meant the host, which he could see, meaning that he could see God but God could not see him."[19]

# Notes

1. *Para el doy [sic; Dio?]; para el hay adonay* (Baer 1936, 513).
2. *Jurar por Deos dos ceos e pello Senhor do mundo* (Furtado 1929, 410).
3. *Quando jurava, sienpre dezía: "Juro a Dio" e no de otra manera* (Carrete Parrondo 1985a, 74).
4. *Juras por el nomne maravelloso Ananie del fuert que dixo Moysés sobre la mar, e partióse la mar en xii carreras e pasaron todos los fillos de Ysrael por seco, et murio Pharao e toda so uuest en la mar roya.* Beinart gives the sources of the Jewish tradition that holds that Moses split the Red Sea into twelve paths and that the twelve tribes crossed separately (1961, 177–8). For additional discussion of Jewish oaths in Spain from the 1320s see Bujanda/Cantera Burgos (1947); Fuentes Estañol 1978.
5. *Que el Creador esta en el çielo e crio el çielo e la tierra e partio el mar por doze carreras e saco el pueblo de Ysrael de poderio del Rey Faraon, asi, Señor, Tu me apiada e me libra* (Beinart 1974, 202).
6. *Juro al criador que crio el çielo e la tierra e partyo la mar por doze carreras e dio la ley de Moysen, esto que es mas verdad* (Beinart 1961, 177). See also Beinart 1981a, 306; Baer 1936, 475 [1487]; Medina 1899a, 181, 186 [Chile 1627].
7. *Para la ley de Muysen tal cosa es verdad, e por el criador que puso su nonbre en quatro letras e partio la mar por doze carreras* (Cantera/Carrete 1975, 176).
8. *Tinha por costume ordinario jurar pello mundo que tem a alma de seu pai.*
9. *Jurar pello Orlon de mi padre que quer dizer o mesmo que pello mundo* (Furtado 1925, 139, 174). See also Wiznitzer 1960, 16, 19. In the mid-fifteenth-century burlesque poem on the "Wedding of Rodrigo Cota" a character says of his father, "May you have a good eternity" (*Buen Olán ayas*) (Gómez-Menor Fuentes 1970, 104).
10. *Pelo mundo que tem a alma de meu pai* (Furtado 1925, 258; cf. 401).
11. *En lugar de Santa Maria llamavan a Moysen, y quando avian de jurar juravan por la Ley de Moysen y por los dies mandamientos* (Beinart 1974, 545). See also 518–9; Carrete Parrondo 1985a, 82, 153.
12. *Tractando con ellos en algunas mercaderias que le fiavan, el testis levava y unas oretas judienyas para jurar de complir en la paga el tienpo que prometia, y que vio el testis que quando el abria las dichas oras y jurava, el dicho Manuel las besava* (Baer 1936, 467).
13. *Dixo este testigo que algunas veces jurando algunos judios a este testigo para torad mosse sobre cosa de diferencia de quentas y pagas decian los judios a este testigo para torad mosse* (Gutwirth 1981, 90).
14. *Por la ley de Moysén asy es* (Carrete/Fraile 1987, 97). See also Beinart 1974, 546.
15. *Ponte duelo, que lo que jurare aquí juraré en Nuestra Sennora, que no me a de morder Santa María, que no es syno vna piedra; que no vamos agora a la sinoga a tomar céfer en braços, que quiere dezir la Torá* (Carrete Parrondo 1985a, 141).
16. *Vido a alvar dias, lençero, e a juan martines del oliva . . . que tenían una contienda e questión en la correría en la calle, no sabe sobre qué cosas; el alvar dias por faser verdad lo que desía juraba por dios bibo, el dicho juan martines non lo creya; alvar días como veya que non lo creya dixo, por la ley de moysén que es verdad; entonces se conçertaron y no ovieron más questión y luego fueron amigos* (Santa María 1983b, 363). See also Caro Baroja 1961, 1:435.
17. *Fuele dicho cómo se deponía contra él que él non creya en el juramento que hasen los christianos e quél non juraua, saluo juró por aquel Criador biuo e verdadero que crió los çielos e la tierra, e que no jurava por los Evangelios; dixo que él tales cosas dixo nin juró, saluo porque veya*

*que muchos christianos juravan liuianamente e veya que no hasían lo que juravan e que por algunos dellos dezían que non creyan en el juramento que fazían porque sabían que no juravan verdad* (Carrete Parrondo 1985a, 74).

18. *La ley de Moisés manda no juren por dioses algunos* (Lewin 1954, 190). See also Böhm 1963, 44.

19. *Jurava para aquel que veo y non me vehe* (Carrete Parrondo 1985a, 71; cf. 142).

CHAPTER XVII 🌺

# Communal Organizations, Synagogues, Rabbis

Jewish life in pre-Expulsion Iberia was highly structured, with community organizations, functionaries, and property supported through self-imposed communal taxes. Formally constituted societies took responsibility for visiting the sick, burying the dead, caring for the poor and for travelers, providing dowries for poor women, and educating children. Synagogues and *mikvahs* were built and maintained, and rooms were set aside to serve as schools. Rabbis, cantors, and kosher butchers served the community. Such documents as the 1432 *Takkanot* (Regulations) of the Valladolid community detail the structure and financing mechanisms for these institutions.[1]

As might be expected, prior to the establishment of the Inquisition and even up until the Expulsion, Judaizing new-Christians continued to rely to some extent on these Jewish institutions. As we have seen in previous chapters, many *conversos* used the communal *mikvah*, celebrated the Sabbath and the festivals alongside the Jews, and availed themselves of Jewish organizations when they marked their major life-cycle events. New-Christians frequently contributed financially to the maintenance of Jewish institutions. The synagogue and the community of which it was the most important tangible symbol continued to be a significant magnet for Judaizing new-Christians prior to the Expulsion. It was not unusual to find *conversos* like Gonzalvo Ruiz [Teruel 1487], who "had a bench in the synagogue and he defends it and allows his friends and relatives to sit on it and nobody else." He even had his illness announced in the synagogue and the congregation fasted for his restoration to health.[2] Many new-Christians continued to attend Jewish services. Martín Sánchez de Salarena [Covarrubias, Burgos 1491] was accused of frequenting the synagogue and of "going up to the synagogue lamps . . . and lighting a candle there."[3] Ruy García, an old *converso* of Soria who walked with a cane, was accused in 1490 of "going to the synagogue and going inside, and not coming out until two hours after nightfall, . . . and of going to the synagogue winter and summer, even when there was a frost or a great storm."[4] Diego Arias Dávila, the father of the bishop of Segovia Juan Arias, was denounced by numerous witnesses for visiting the synagogue to pray with the Jews (Carrete Parrondo 1986, 22). Of course this continued intermingling of Jews and new-Christians at worship was dangerous for both sides even before the establishment of the Inquisition, as the anti-Jewish and anti-*converso* riots of the 1440s and 1460s made clear. Old-Christians considered it an outrage and it made the Jews justifiably nervous.

By the 1480s Judaizing *conversos* were forced to begin to create their own social and religious institutions. As this chapter will make clear, for new-Christians of the Expulsion generation, who personally recalled the comprehensive Jewish institutions of their youth, these new structures were likely to be quite complex. In the 1480s crypto-Jews in Valencia, among them the ancestors of the Renaissance humanist Luis Vives, maintained a full set of social, professional, and charitable organizations (García 1987, 55). Even generations later some new-Christian communities, such as that of northeast Brazil in the 1590s, managed to sustain a well-organized communal life. There is evidence, for example, that they regularly collected money (*bôlsa dos Judeus*) for their communal needs. Thomaz Lopes was accused of collecting money for a Jewish lamp (*alampada dos Judeus*). There seems to have been a special religious society, called the *mordomos e confrades da Toura*; Pedro Fernandes Raphael and Luis Lopes Paredes were accused of spending half the night writing in a large book of the confraternity (*o livro da confraria dos judeus*). Judaizers who revealed the group's secrets were punished by the group: one man was thrown into a sugar vat and another chained in his house (Lipiner 1969, 90–1). But these sorts of organized activities were rare, for after the passing of the Expulsion generation most crypto-Jewish communities seem to have focused merely on maintaining some form of communal worship.

## 17.1. Synagogues

Throughout the Iberian world the simple Spanish or Portuguese terms for synagogue were used. In Inquisition documents the terms usually refer to the place where Judaizers gathered to pray, which may or may not be a location dedicated to that purpose. The most common terms were the Spanish *sinoga*[5] and the Portuguese *esnoga*.[6] Frequently the linguistic contexts make clear that what is referred to is a physical space,[7] but just as commonly the terms refer to a congregation or to a quorum (Heb. *minyan*) of Judaizers assembled to pray.[8]

Presumably every community with a Judaizing *converso* contingent of any size had established places where the crypto-Jews could gather to pray. In the early days before habits of scrutiny and circumspection had taken firm root, this might be the church, hermitage, or chapel that had been the site of the former synagogue. The most extraordinary example of this practice comes from the Aragonese town of Barbastro, where in 1415 the village synagogue was consecrated as the Hermitage Church of San Salvador. From that date until the Inquisition's investigation in 1485 it continued to serve Barbastro's *converso* community as a synagogue. The *conversos* formed a religious society (*cofradía*) of San Salvador to justify their continued attendance. No one but *conversos* could join. Behind the altar was a niche (*cadiera*) where the Torah had been kept, and near it Hebrew inscriptions were written on the wall. Several witnesses report that for a time a parchment (*cartapaz*) of some sort was kept there. A witness in the trial of Speraindeo de Santángel [1489] told how the *conversos* of Barbastro would go to the hermitage of San Salvador of Barbastro and "touch a bench near the holy water font, and they would kiss it and walk to the side of the altar, and bow in that place next to the altar which they called the 'old place.' The *conversos* would say to each other: 'Let's go to the old place,' which the witness understood, because the bench had been there from the time the hermitage had been the synagogue." Another witness told how the bench was made of brushwood (*fusta*), and how "it was the place where the Rabbi used to circumcise the baby boys. There were inscriptions and Hebrew letters painted on the wall. . . . Once he saw them worshipping and kissing the bench. . . . Before they did that they would greet each other, and pay honor to the older men. Then they would stand and turn their face toward the wall. And there were no altar statues nor figure of Jesus Christ there."[9] When the priest assigned to the hermitage realized what was happening he burned the niche and scratched out the painting (Marín Padilla 1977, 223–5).

Barbastro was a striking but not a unique case, for up to the middle of the sixteenth century there are instances of new-Christians returning to pray to what had once been the Jewish synagogue. In 1540 Francisco de Murcia, his son Melchor, and others were denounced for visiting the ruined walls of the old synagogue to, as Blázquez Miguel terms it, "meditate and lament their misfortune."[10]

Nevertheless, use of the former synagogue was the exception rather than the rule. More frequently the "synagogue" would be a meeting place in the home or place of business of a principal member of the community, for after the Expulsion the clandestine communal religious life of Iberia's crypto-Jews necessarily had to take place behind closed doors. The most common approach seems to have been to dedicate a particular room in someone's home for this purpose. From the 1480s right up to modern times reports of every new-Christian community indicated this to have been the pattern. In Teruel in 1486 the *conversa* Brianda Besant was said to be a leader of the crypto-Jewish community and to hold services in her own home (Haliczer 1990, 213). Beinart finds that in the last half of the fifteenth century in Ciudad Real some eighteen different homes served *conversos* as synagogues, although not necessarily all simultaneously (*Conversos* 273–5). In a notorious case in 1500 that scandalized the entire city of Valencia, a clandestine synagogue was discovered in the home of the merchant Miquel Vives. A Torah was discovered along with a group of Judaizers observing the Passover *seder*. The room that served as the synagogue was well decorated. "In the middle of the room was a hanging candelabra, or tin lamp, on which eight oil lamps were burning. In another part of the room . . . there was a table covered with a very rich cloth, and at the four corners of the table, and in the middle on one side and the other, six lamps of wax candles." Inside the table Bibles and other books were found. The synagogue also contained "a basin made of wire."[11] A room in Alvar González's house [Canary Islands 1524] was also kept as a synagogue, and Juan Delgado testified how "after dark when the bell for prayer had rung, he saw many of the new-Christians and *conversos* going in there to join others who had already come from that town. They would sneak into said house two by two with their faces covered like people who did not want to be seen, glancing from side to side, with their heads down, wrapped up in capes like women. Some went in and then others, and they stayed in that house a long time."[12] Pedro Anes [Lisbon 1537] reported a synagogue at the home of Beatriz de Cáceres and Branca Lopes. On Saturdays, "in the house where they lived, many new-Christian women and one dark-haired new-Christian man gathered and remained inside with the door closed and clean cloths over the windows. In the winter they would go there before dawn."[13] In Pernambuco, Brazil in the 1590s a synagogue was reported in the village of Camaragibi.[14] In the 1590s other Brazilian *Cristão novo* synagogues were reported in Perabusú, Salvador, Matoim, and Pernambuco (Lipiner 1969, 91–3). Liebman concludes that in Mexico in the midseventeenth century there were "about fifteen congregations in Mexico City and environs, at least three in Puebla, at least two each in Guadalajara and Veracruz, and one each in Zacatecas and Campeche. It is probable that there was at least one each in Mérida, Monterey, Guatemala, Nicaragua and Honduras" (1970, 57; cf. 145, 184, 255). These included synagogues in Mexico City at the homes of Simón Váez Sevilla and Tomás Treviño de Sobremonte, at the home of Duarte Rodríguez Tejoso in Veracruz, and in Guadalajara at the home of Manuel de Mello.[15] In 1622 a synagogue was reported on the Calle de Santo Domingo, in Mexico City, but the Inquisition did not follow up (Liebman 1970, 216). As the processes of assimilation eroded the Iberian crypto-Jews' commitment to communal worship, the number of clandestine synagogues seems to have declined, only to rise again for a time with the influx of Portuguese new-Christians at the start of the seventeenth century.

The so-called remnant new-Christian communities of the twentieth century follow the same pattern. In 1929 an old crypto-Jewish woman in Bragança told the French journalist Lily Jean Jarval that when she and her friends prayed "they used to sit on the floor so that the neighbors would not see them."[16] Clemente Carmona told David Nidel in New Mexico in 1980 that he knew about thirty five "Jewish" families around Albuquerque who "carry on traditional Marrano ways." "There are secret prayer rooms and meetings at different homes. We didn't have rabbis, but a person who knew most of the prayers in Ladino or Spanish, and these were called *resardores* [sic]. . . . And we had people called *levantadores* who lifted the Torah, or our form of Torah, and we kissed it before and after, and the chanting of prayers was done very quietly so as not to attract unwelcome attention" (Nidel 1984, 256).

Characteristically the room that served sixteenth- and seventeenth-century Judaizers as their synagogue had to be large enough to hold the community and private enough so that what took place there could not heard or seen by the casual observer. Generally interior or second story rooms were used. A dedicated room was required both in order to maintain its sanctity and to be able to declare it off-limits to servants. In Diego Arias's house an interior room that faced onto the walled garden served as synagogue (Carrete Parrondo 1986, 50). In the early 1500s the *converso* Rui Dias Laínez, of Almazán (Soria), "had a synagogue in his house in the basement," as did Ramiro López.[17] In Teruel in 1485 Jaime de Santángel's house was said to contain some very secret rooms, where "the servant girl, at the behest of his wife, had brought them a book from the *judería* and all of them were glued to it, along with a Jew who had come there with the servant girl."[18] Catalina Fernández said in 1484 that "many *converso* men and women of this city were upstairs in a tower of Sancho de Cibdad's house."[19] Lope de Villa Real said that when he went to Sancho's house to do business he went up to the tower, where they made him sit down and wait until "Sancho and his wife had finished their praying, turned face toward the wall like Jews; that they both went up to the tower, and that they prayed there every day."[20] Testimony indicates that Sancho's neighbor Juan Falcón also "used to go upstairs into a room to pray."[21] Marina de Horosco testified that around 1495 she had heard Francisco Laínez of Almazán say that "he had gone into a room at the end of the house, upstairs, and had found a Torah and some little silver bells in a closet."[22] The larger rooms were sometimes described in the documents as "palaces." It was said of María Díaz and her daughters [Ciudad Real 1484] "that Saturday and from Friday at noon they shut themselves in a palace and read together from a book."[23] María la Manzana [Almazán 1505] said that she had seen a synagogue in the home of Pedro and Aldonza Laínez: "it was a palace to the left of the door as you go in, which in the time of the Jews was a synagogue."[24]

While private homes were the most common meeting places for the *sinoga*, other presumably inconspicuous sites were also utilized. Manoel Bras [Bahia 1591] said that Jews (i.e., *conversos*) met at the home of Diego Lopes Ilhoa to make *esnoga*.[25] At the same time the women of the Monis family used to hold their Saturday gatherings in a building that served as a warehouse.[26] Liebman notes that in Mexico City at the beginning of the seventeenth century there was a synagogue on the corner of Calle de Reloj and Puente de Acapulco in a building that was not a private home (1970, 184).[27]

Other crypto-Jewish groups met outdoors. Yuçá Françés [Soria 1491] reported how he used to go with the *converso* Diego Fernandes "to an orchard of his, near

San Gil, and that he carried with him . . . his prayer book [çidur] and Bible [humás], which are books of the Jewish Law, and that he saw him pray . . . as a Jew in Hebrew."[28] Juan Campuzam [Canary Islands 1519] alleged that Gonçalo de Cordova "rented a garden and orchard outside the town, and many Saturday mornings passing this place, he saw sometimes as many as thirty or forty men entering there two by two, wearing long cloaks, similar to mourning cloaks, and, being thus covered, he could not recognize them. That hearing the rumor that there is a Synagogue and Rabbi on the island, he entered the orchard one day under pretext of seeing the fruit, and saw there a thatched house which was well swept and had seats" (Wolf 1926, 20). Local legend around Braganza in the early twentieth century held that the synagogue used to be on a mountain top in Bragança "called Shoe Peak where the Marranos used to gather in caves like the Huguenots."[29]

Crypto-Jewish synagogues did not reflect the glorious decoration that we see in the remnants of ancient synagogues in Toledo or Córdoba. Rooms that served as synagogues tended to be bare of decoration, for any visible Jewish cult item invited detection and prosecution and Christian iconography would have profaned the religious nature of the site. Typical was the testimony of the Brazilian *cristãa nova* Lianor Carvalha [Bahia 1591] that some fifty-five years earlier in Arzilla she had gone into the "synagogue of the Jews [i.e., new-Christians] in which there was no cross nor statue of God or the saints."[30] This absence of Christian iconography is a frequent part of old-Christian denunciations of so-called crypto-Jewish synagogues.

Nonetheless, the records suggest a common interior architecture for crypto-Jewish synagogues. At one end might be a raised bench or table, from which the leader could read the Bible or preach to the assembled group. This might be covered with a tablecloth or some other cloth specially reserved for the purpose. Whatever ordinary candles or lamps lighted the room served as cult items as well. Sometimes a niche, wardrobe, or cupboard would serve to store the holy books or to indicate where they had been stored. Testimony in 1505 described a *converso* home in Almazán with "a niche carved out of plaster, with painted doors, like where the Jews used to keep the Torah."[31] This niche was fitted with doors which when the witness went back to investigate she found locked. Lianor Carvalha, cited above, also said that the Arzilla synagogue contained "a cupboard with a painted cloth frontal from India; and inside the cupboard were the scrolls which they said were parchment, encased in linen cloth covers. And in front of this were hung oil lamps with many wicks of twisted thread."[32] In these synagogues the congregation sat on benches or sometimes stood or kneeled on the floor. If some piece of furniture were left from the days when true synagogues existed in Spain, it would receive special veneration from the community. No matter what space was chosen to serve as the *sinoga*, it was likely to be considered a privileged place, to be cleaned and lit with special care, as in this description of a colonial Brazilian synagogue: "The house in which the fast was to be celebrated was prepared by laying a carpet on the floor; in one part was placed a table covered with a silk cloth, set with candlesticks with lighted candles; from the center of the room hung a great tin candelabra with many candles."[33]

The most peculiar crypto-Jewish cult item I have seen in the Inquisition records was in fairly common use in northeast Brazil at the end of the sixteenth century. Both so-called synagogues and private homes of the 1590s were frequently said to contain a *Toura*. Several descriptions of the object exist. The one observed in a home in Tujucupapo in the district of Itmaracá was "a black wax figure of a man with two horns on his head, carrying in one hand a candle or a staff."[34] Another witness saw one about a palm in height which was "a ceramic *toura* with horns, all painted gold," kept in a niche in a private home. In a hollow in its back was a slip of paper with a prayer on it. A black slave of the family said she had been told it was a "*toura* that the Jews worship."[35]

In traditional Jewish synagogues men and women worship separately and synagogue architecture facilitated that separation. For example, the Cordovan synagogue, the Tránsito Synagogue in Toledo, and the synagogue which is now the Corpus Christi convent in Segovia have a screened upstairs gallery for women. Presumably single-story synagogues, such as Santa María la Blanca in Toledo, would have divided the congregation in some fashion. In the early days following the Expulsion crypto-Jews tended to maintain some sort of physical separation. This is the sense of María González's description [Ciudad Real 1512] of a synagogue in a private house. She says that when the men were reading a book "she does not know what book it was nor did she hear what they were reading, because she and the women she had previously mentioned were together in another room of the house."[36] However, even before the Expulsion the record suggests that in some cases men and women worshipped together in a single, undivided location, as in Sancho de Cibdad's house in Ciudad Real in the 1480s, where Sancho and his wife prayed together in an upstairs room.[37] After the passing of the Expulsion generation this was certainly the general rule.[38]

## 17.2. THE SYNAGOGUE WORSHIP SERVICE

When worship was to begin the crypto-Jews gathered, sometimes with other pretexts, at the location that served as a synagogue. In large or dispersed communities they were called to prayer with some type of secret signal. Jorge Dias de Caja, of Olinda [Brazil], was said in 1591 to have summoned the Judaizers of the city to the synagogue by walking through the streets "with a piece of white linen on his foot and a sword in his belt as a signal."[39] Margarita de Morera, reconciled in Mexico in 1646, testified that there "a Negro dressed in a red suit went through the streets playing a tambourine which was the signal for all Jews to assemble."[40] In the majority of instances, however, each small crypto-Jewish community was cohesive enough to know when to gather without requiring some special call. At the appointed time crypto-Jews would assemble under the pretext of work or socializing. Sometimes old-Christian neighbors who reported these gatherings described the congregations' demeanor as furtive. The witness who denounced the house of Alvaro Gonçalez [Las Palmas 1524] as a synagogue said that he "saw numbers of people entering there two and two at night, with bent heads and draped in their cloaks like women, looking from one side to the other before entering, as though not anxious to be seen" (Wolf 1926, 55). Not infrequently some member of the crypto-Jewish community would stand at the door to guard against unwelcome intrusions. According to Manoel Bras in Bahia in the 1590s, when the new-Christian merchant Diogo Lopes Ilhoa gathered with his friends in a synagogue some of them would patrol outside keeping watch.[41] When in the 1450s Diego Arias's watchman mistakenly let an old-Christian into a room where Arias and his *converso* friends were praying, Arias fired the man (Carrete Parrondo 1986, 51).

Either in continuance of the ancient Jewish custom of washing the hands before praying, or in imitation of the Christian dipping of the hands in holy water on entering a church, crypto-Jewish synagogues often featured a place to wash the hands. María Núñez testified in 1484 that she had seen Sancho de Çibdad and his friends "when they went into the house ask for water for their hands, and after they had washed [she] heard how they read in some book."[42] Ana Díaz accused her mistress Blanca Ramírez [Toledo 1523], saying that "at the entrance of the synagogue she saw that they washed their hands in a wash basin."[43] Bernardina de San Juan [Baeza 1572] testified that her mother had taught her that "before praying you should wash your hands and mouth first and then not speak with anyone."[44]

The worship service in a crypto-Jewish synagogue could be extremely simple and informal, consisting merely of communal recitation of prayers. Or it could approach an orthodox Jewish service both in its order of prayer and in its reliance on a rabbi to preach, read, and explain the prayers; a chanter (*hazzan*) to sing the appropriate portions of the service; and communal participation in the reading, the silent prayer, and the choral responses. The Inquisition records provide us a number of good descriptions of religious services in crypto-Jewish synagogues.

One of the most detailed is given in the trial of Juan de Córdoba Membreque in Córdoba in 1504. The fact that the rabbi, his brother the Bachelor Alonso de Córdoba Membreque, was barefoot suggests that it was a Yom Kippur service:

> Juan de Córdoba marched in procession behind the rabbi-preacher with all the others who had come together in the synagogue. . . .[45]
>
> The Bachelor Membreque wore [over his jerkin] a white linen shirt that came down to his feet. [In fact, everyone present wore a long white shirt.] And he had a white cloth over his head from [the corners of] which hung [four] ribbons which he tied under his arms. He wore white linen breeches, and he took off his high, hard-soled shoes. . . .[46]
>
> When the Bachelor Membreque was preaching . . . he got up on a bench or high chest, and from there [he read] from a book he had in his hands. . . . The

> bench was covered with a [white] altar cloth and had some cushions on it. He held two books in his hand, one green and the other red. . . .[47]
>
> While he was preaching . . . everyone was kneeling. . . .[48]
>
> Everyone responded together in unison to what the Bachelor Membreque preached to them. . . . From the book he prayed twelve prayers which had a lot of Hebrew words in them, . . . one which began "Verná Israel Adonai" [the *Shema*?]; and when he began to say it he put his hand over his eyes, and when he had finished saying it he lowered his head to the floor, as did Juan de Córdoba Membreque and the other people who were there with him. They did that at the beginning and the end of the prayer, as the rabbi did, and they all responded in unison "Amen." . . . The rabbi said the prayers in Hebrew and then repeated them in Spanish. . . .[49]
>
> Everyone raised and lowered their heads and bobbed up and down and at the end of each prayer they kissed the ground and wept, and the Rabbi kissed the book which he had in his hands when the listeners kissed the ground. . . .[50]
>
> Juan de Córdoba Membreque and the other people who were there each had in their hand a lighted white candle. And after the Bachelor Membreque had finished preaching, . . . he came down from the pulpit where he had gone up, and when he was down . . . everyone kissed his hand and he put his hand on each one of their heads, as if he were absolving them, in the Jewish fashion, without making the sign of the cross. . . .[51]

The Cordovan Inquisitors interpreted this Jewish service as a kind of anti-mass: a "ceremony which the rabbi performed in contrary to the mass, elevated on an altar, dressed in white, . . . and in place of the host, the rabbi-preacher raised an open Jewish book, and in place of the chalice, another smaller Jewish book; and Juan de Córdoba and the others who were there beat their chests, as the Christians do when they raise the Body of Christ. And when the mass was over, the Rabbi blessed them without making the sign of the cross."[52]

It was fairly common to pray facing east, as in the 1484 testimony of María Sánchez that she had seen the Bachelor Abudarme and his friends "all turned toward where the sun rises and they were praying, bobbing their heads in the fashion of Jews; this was in March."[53] It was common to pray responsively. In Cartagena de Indias in the 1620s the mulatto Diego López described prayer in the synagogue that functioned in the house of Blas de Paz Pinto: "He drew near a window and heard a person speaking in a low voice, with pauses, and he could never understand a word of it, except that sometimes he stopped and let the other people answer. . . . He was beating the side of his chair loudly with his hand as if he were lamenting what he was saying."[54] It was common to spend the day talking of the Jewish law, perhaps in ways that pointed out its differences with Christianity. For example, in Mexico in the 1640s Duarte de León Jaramillo's house served the Judaizing community as a synagogue. One of his daughters reported that they all went there "to confer and to talk about the Law of Moses, its precepts, fasts, rites and ceremonies. Each one told what they did to observe it, each one encouraging the others in the scrupulousness of their fasts. All of them together, as in a church council, affirmed the eternal damnation of Catholics, and said unseemly things against the ceremonies, processions, and other practices of Our Mother the Church."[55] Either because practices were indeed heterodox, or because old-Christian observers did not understand what they were witnessing, often the reported crypto-Jewish services were idiosyncratic in one way or another.

## 17.3. CONVERSO RABBIS

Before the Expulsion *conversos* were often led by the rabbis who served the extant Jewish community. Occasionally rabbis who themselves converted continued to serve the crypto-Jewish population. For example, after the 1474 riots in Ciudad Real many members of the *converso* community fled to Palma, near Córdoba, where Fernando de Trujillo, a Jew who later converted, served as their rabbi (Beinart 1981a, 83). But in most communities whoever was considered most knowledgeable, or most strictly observant of Jewish custom, or most saintly, was thought of as leader.

From its earliest moments, the Inquisition used the term "rabbi" frequently, and loosely, to refer to any *converso* allegedly learned in Judaism or who allegedly took a leadership role in any Jewish communal activities, from public prayer to kosher butchering or performing marriages or circumcisions. Up to 1473 the *converso* Juan González Panpán served the Ciudad Real crypto-Jewish community as rabbi. That is to say, he took charge of kosher butchering, and *conversos* gathered in his house routinely to pray. In the 1460s Juan González Daza also served that community as a sort of rabbi. Juan González Escogido used to hear the confessions of dying *conversos*, and various witnesses call him rabbi, or sometimes "confessor of *conversos*" (Beinart 1981a, 236–8, 243).

With the rare exception cited above, these people were not or had not been rabbis in any formal sense. In some instances they were not even particularly learned but were merely men who came to take a leadership role in the crypto-Jewish community. Whenever the Inquisition uncovered a nucleus of crypto-Jews of any size, the Inquisition took special care to determine who were its leaders, and these people—men, and with less frequency women[56]—were labeled "rabbis" or "dogmatizers" or even "*converso* priests." Their numbers are legion. Andrés de Medrano allegedly served as the rabbi of the Genevilla [Alava 1573] community (Monter 1990, 157). Francisco López Díaz reported to the Inquisition in Mexico in 1648 that he had attended a synagogue in Seville where "one man served as rabbi, and a prayer book in Hebrew was used" (Liebman 1975, 95). In the 1660s Raphael Valls and Pedro Onofre Cortés served the Majorcan *chueta* community as rabbis (Braunstein 1936, 105–6, 109–11). In 1720 an *auto de fe* in Madrid reported a synagogue that had been operating since at least 1707 and had elected a rabbi in 1714. The community of twenty families there decided to hire a rabbi and sent to Italy to

Leghorn for him. He arrived two months later and swore to them, his hands placed on the Torah, to observe their Law.[57]

In colonial Mexico the most famous so-called rabbi was undoubtedly Luis de Carvajal the younger (*el Mozo*), whose biography has been written by Liebman (1967). Of similar stature during the second quarter of the seventeenth century were Tomás Treviño de Sobremonte and Simón Váez de Sevilla (1970, 218, 237–51). Liebman reports the names of several other men who acted as rabbis in Mexico and other locations in the Americas in the sixteenth and seventeenth centuries (1970, 58; 234; 1974, 171). Antonio Váez Tirado prayed over the sick and officiated at his niece's wedding (Liebman 1974, 128). Váez Tirado was termed by Inquisitors the "priest of the Jews" (Wiznitzer 1962a, 229). Simón Montero, who had studied Judaism formally in France and Italy, worked hard to convert Portuguese immigrants to Judaizing.[58] Beatriz Enríquez, reconciled in 1648, testified that sometimes a rabbi was present to perform weddings for Mexico's crypto-Jews (Wiznitzer 1962a, 244). From 1638–42 Juan de León (alias Salomón Machorro), who had been educated in Leghorn and Smyrna and who had spent several years as a captive of the Muslims in Algeria, was a major dogmatizer of *conversos* in Mexico, taking on many attributes of rabbi (Lewin 1977).

In Portugal several men of substantial learning served as crypto-Jewish rabbis. Fernando Gómez, of Salonica, functioned as a rabbi in Portugal at the start of the seventeenth century. He was burned in Evora in 1608 (Roth 1931–2, 4). Diogo Alvares, a goldsmith from Beja, who was burned in 1619, served as rabbi to that city's community, reading to them from Hebrew books which he possessed (Coelho 1987, 216). A synagogue under the spiritual leadership of the professor of canon law Antônio Homem was discovered in Coimbra in 1619 (Yerushalmi 1971, 38).

In Brazil, particularly in the northeast, the situation was similar to that in Portugal. However, during the Dutch occupation, during which many crypto-Jews were able to come out of their closets and practice Judaism openly, real rabbis came from Europe to serve the community. In 1642 Aboab de Fonseca went from Amsterdam to Pernambuco to serve as rabbi of the Jewish community there during the Dutch occupation. There are rumors of another rabbi from Salonica serving the Pernambuco community. Jacobo Lagarto served as rabbi of the Tamarica community (Lewin 1939, 48–9). Paraiba was served by Captain Moses Peixotto (Roth 1932, 287). Later, in the *Grande Inquiração* conducted in 1646 in Bahia in which much hearsay evidence was gathered about 118 new-Christian residents, several people were termed *rabino* or *cádi* or even *pontífice dos judeus* (Novinsky 1972b, 133).

Nonetheless the number of crypto-Jewish communities anywhere in the Iberian world served by real, formally trained rabbis was always very small. In their absence the most learned, or diligent crypto-Jews in the community served as spiritual leaders, sustaining a crypto-Judaism of diminishing depth and complexity for as long as they were able. Martin Cohen is correct when he concludes that "the Inquisition's ordination . . . certifies [the community leaders'] zeal rather than their knowledge" (1973, 95).

One of the keys to the survival of vestigial crypto-Jewish communities today is the persistence of strong leadership that finds a way of transferring itself from generation to generation. This was clearly the case in Bragança, where in 1929 eighty-year-old João Antonio Ferreira reported that "there was an old man named Luiz Carneiro whom they called the Jewish priest, and three or four others, among whom was Manuel de Barros, the grandfather of the pharmacist of Oporto."[59] Clemente Carmona told David Nidel in New Mexico in 1980 that the local community that thinks of itself as Marrano has "had our own minor rabbis, self-ordained rabbis, who would go from village to village, especially in northern New Mexico which has whole colonies of Marrano families. These *resardores* [sic], prayer leaders, would come and visit and lead the chants. The office is usually passed from father to son. And one who shows great promise is given the handwritten prayer books." He claimed still to know one old man near Chama, but he would not reveal the name (Nidel 1984, 254).

## Notes

1. Moreno Koch 1987; see also Neuman 1942.
2. *Tiene lugar en la sinoga e lo defendia e fazia que sus amigos y parientes se asentan a ella y no otros* (Edwards 1984a, 336).
3. *Yba a las lánparas de la . . . synoga e ençendía en ellas vna candela* (Carrete Parrondo 1985a, 170).
4. *Entraua en la sinoga e estaua dentro, que non salya hasta dos oras de la noche . . . e que hizo esta continuaçión de yr a la sinoga en ynvierno y en verano, avnque elase o hiziese grand fortuna, e que era viejo, que andaua con vn palo* (Carrete Parrondo 1985a, 37). A large number of Sorian *conversos* were accused of similar behaviors in the years preceding the Expulsion. See Carrete Parrondo 1985a, 19, 60, 74, 151, 170.
5. Edwards 1984a, 336; Carrete Parrondo 1985a, 37; etc.
6. Furtado 1925, 56; etc.
7. "He went into the *sinoga* and remained inside" (*Entraua en la sinoga e estaua dentro*) (Carrete Parrondo 1985a, 37).
8. "The Jews coming together made an *esnoga*" (*Se fazia esnoga com ajuntamento de Judeus*) (Furtado 1925, 420).
9. *Algunas vezes, puyando a la hermita de San Salvador de Barbastro, tocaba en una cadiera que estaba cerca de la pileta del agua bendita y besaba aquella y andaba al costado del Altar y fazia reverencia en aquel lugar zaguero al altar que le dezian la Antigüedad, porque dezian los confesos entre ellos: "vamos a la Antigüedad," lo cual el presente deposante entendía porque era la dicha cadiera del tiempo de los judios quando dicha hermita era Sinoga. . . . Era la cadiera donde el Rabí circunzidaba a los judigüelos y habia ciertas scripturas y letras ebraicas en una paret pintadas. . . . Vió que adoraban y besaban la dicha cadiera. . . . E antes de que tocasen aquella, se convidaban los unos a los otros dando la honra a los mas viexos y mayores, aprés figuraban y se*

*volvian de cara enta la paret.... e alli no habia ningun Retaulo ni fegura de Jhesu Xpo* (Cabezudo Astraín 1963, 272–3).
10. *Meditar y llorar su miseria* (Blázquez Miguel 1986a, 70). *Conversos* in many cities in Aragon founded brotherhoods, frequently in the name of the saint in whose name the former synagogue had been consecrated; some of these *cofradías* served as burial societies (Hinojosa Montalvo 1993, 40).
11. *Enmedio de la cámara, colgado un candelero o candil de latón, en que ardían ocho mechas con aceite. Item, a una parte . . . estaba una mesa cubierta con una alcatifa muy rica, y a los cuatro cantones de la mesa, y en medio de una parte y otra, seis candelas de cera a forma de velas. . . . Una bacina de arambre* (Garcia 1987, 83–7).
12. *Vio como alli entraua despues de anochecido y tañida la oracion muchos de los dichos christianos nuevos e conuersos que alli heran venidos y otros que antes binian en la dicha villa, y que entrauan en la dicha casa de dos en dos resguardandose al tiempo que entravan como personas que no querian ser vistas, mirando a una parte e a otra, las cabeças baxas, cubiertos las capas como mugeres, y que entrauan agora vnos y de ay a vn poco otros, y que estauan dicha casa gran rato* (Beinart 1977b, 52).
13. *Na casa onde moravam, se junctavam muitas christãs novas e um christão novo, velho crespo, e depois ficavam com a porta fechada e com pannos lavados nas janellas. De inverno entravam antes de nascer o sol* (Baião 1921, 105; cf. 134).
14. Furtado 1929, 75; cf. 467, 537; 1925, 522.
15. Liebman 1964, 104–5; 1975, 127–8; Wiznitzer 1962a, 246, 266.
16. *Nós assentavamo-nos no chão para que os visinhos não nos vissem* (Jarval 1929, 2).
17. *Tenía en su casa vna synoga debaxo de tierra. . . . Estaua vna synoga so tierra en casa de Ramiro Lopes, christiano nuevo* (Carrete/Fraile 1987, 42, 84).
18. *En unas cámaras muy secretas . . . y que la dicha moza, por mandado de su señora, les había traído un libro de la judería, y que allí estaban todas plegadas y que con la dicha moza había [venido] un judío* (Sánchez Moya 1958, 186).
19. *Estauan muchos conversos e conversas desta çibdad ençima de la torre de Sancho de Çibdad.*
20. *Le fasia estar alli asentado fasta que el dicho Sancho acabaua de resar e su muger, bueltos a la pared como judios, estando anbos en la dicha torre, adonde continuauan resar cada dia* (Beinart 1974, 16, 18).
21. *Se subian a vna camara a rezar* (Beinart 1974, 560).
22. *Avya entrado en vna cámara en cabo de toda la casa, en lo alto, e avía hallado vna Tora, con vnos cascaueles e canpanillas de plata, arrymada a vn paramento* (Carrete/Fraile 1987, 70).
23. *Aquel dia sabado y desde el viernes a mediodia se ençerrauan en vn palaçio e alli leyan todas en vn libro* (Beinart 1974, 55). See also Beinart 1981b, 41, 567; Gracia Boix 1982, 42 [Córdoba 1504].
24. *En el mismo portal, a la mano ysquierda como entran, está vn palaçio, el qual quando judíos hera sinagoga* (Carrete/Fraile 1987, 72).
25. Wiznitzer 1960, 19. See also Wolff 1987, 29.
26. *Huã casa que era huã despensa* (Furtado 1925, 561).
27. Barry Schwartz, a rabbi on the United States military base in the Azores, reported in 1966 the existence on the island of Terceira of a sixteenth-century synagogue that contained at least two Torah scrolls. It was tended by two of the four remaining Jews on the island, women in their nineties. An old Jewish cemetery, with some gravestones as old as the fifteenth century, was adjacent to the building behind a brick wall (Schwartz 1966, 66–8).

28. *Se fue este testigo con . . . Diego Ferrandes a vna huerta suya, çerca de Sant Gil, e que lleuava allá . . . Diego Ferrandes su çidur e el humás, que son libros de la ley judayca, e que le veya este testigo rezar en ellos . . . como judío en abrayco* (Carrete Parrondo 1985a, 58, 59).
29. *O Alto do Sapato onde se juntavam os maranos, como os huguenotes nas cavênas* (Jarval 1929, 2).
30. *Entrou em hua esnoga de judeus na qual não hauja cruz nem imagem de Deos nê de Sanctos* (Furtado 1925, 56). See also Lipiner 1977, 67–9.
31. *Vnas como halhazenas labradas de yeso, e pintadas las portezuelas donde quando judíos tenían la Torá* (Carrete/Fraile 1987, 72).
32. *Huã cantareira cã hu frontal de pano da India pintado na qual cantareyra estauão huns rolos que deziam serem de pregaminhos em fronhados em huns sacos de pano de linho e defronte estaua dependurado hum alampadayro de muytas trocidas dazeite* (Furtado 1925, 56). See also Lipiner 1977, 67–9.
33. *Preparava-se a casa em que se havia de fazer o dito jejum alcatifando-se o pavimento dela, e a uma parte se punha um bufete coberto com um pano de seda, e nele castiçais com velas acesas, e no meio dela se dependurava um candieiro de latão com muitos lumes* (Lipiner 1977, 87–9).
34. *Huã figura feita de çera preta . . . era de homem num e na cabeça na testa tinha dous cornos feitos da mesma cera e em huã mão . . . tinha feito da mesma çera como vella, ou vara* (Furtado 1929, 13).
35. *Uma toura de barro com cornos tôda dourada. . . . Aquilo era a toura em que os judeus adoravam* (Lipiner 1969, 86–9, 168). Lipiner surmises that the rolled up Torah scrolls, covered with a cloth through which the two handles of the scrolls protruded, may have seemed to the ignorant a horned figure, which they sometimes described as a bull's head, confusing the Hebrew term *Torah* with the Portuguese term for bull's head: *toura*. Wiznitzer feels that it may have been some sort of mezuzzah (Wiznitzer 1960, 25, 31). See Chapter 18.
36. *No sabe esta confesante que libro hera ni oya lo que leyan, porque esta confesante y las susodichas mugeres estaban en otro palaçio de la dicha casa, juntas* (Beinart 1977a, 281–2).
37. Beinart 1974, 16. Nevertheless, on the whole, Beinart is of the opinion that the first generation of *converso* men and women tended to pray separately (1981a, 272).
38. Paulo reports that in this century the church in Argozelo [Bragança] is divided in half by a rope, one side for new-Christians, one side for old-Christians. The former are insulted by use of the term *judeu da corda* (1985, 28).
39. Wiznitzer 1960, 20; cf. Furtado 1925, 522. Thomaz Lopes [Brazil 1593] used to walk the streets with one shoe off and one shoe on, with a cloth wrapped around the bare foot (*quando queria dar signal pera os cristãos novos se ajuntarem en certa parte a fazer sua esnoga corria esta villa com hum pé calçado e outro descalço e com hu pano atado no descalço*) (Furtado 1929, 85). Similarly, Belchior Mendes [Bahia 1593] allegedly used to signal crypto-Jews that he was collecting contributions for the synagogue lamps by wearing a bandage on his foot (*trazia huã rodilla no pé por sinal pera os judeus lhe darem a esmola pera a alampada dos judeus*) (Furtado 1929, 61).
40. Liebman 1964, 98. See also García 1910, 71.
41. *Se fazia esnoga com ajuntamento de Judeus e que quando hums estavão dentro fazendo a esnoga, outros andavão e fóra vigiando* (Furtado 1925, 420).
42. *Quando entrauan demandauan agua a manos, e despues que eran lauados oya este testigo como, a su paresçer, leyan en algund libro* (Beinart 1974, 24).
43. *A la entrada de la synoga, vido que se lavavan las manos en un aguamanil* (León Tello 1972, 68).

44. *Cuando hubiese de rezar se lavase las manos y la boca primero y no hablase con persona alguna* (Gracia Boix 1983, 133). See also Carrete Parrondo 1980, 255.
45. *Johan de córdoba andubo en proçisyon con todos los otros que estauan en la dicha synoga e ayuntamiento, tras el dicho Raby predicador* (37). All the Membreque references are from Gracia Boix 1982, 37–58.
46. *El dicho Bachiller Menbreque estaua vestido de vna camisa blanca de lienço hasta en pies. . . . Vistió de vna camisa blanca ençima del jubon* (40). *. . . E vn paño blanco sobre la cabeça con vnas çintas colgadas del dicho paño, con que se le atava por debaxo de los sobacos. . . . Tenia quatro çintas blancas en cada esquina* (42, 48, 51). *. . . Calço vnos calçones de lienço blancos, et se descalçaua los borzeguies et çapatos* (48).
47. *El dicho Bachiller Menbreque se subia e subió . . . ençima de vn vanco o arca alta, et que dende alli por vn libro que en las manos tenia* (40). *. . . Vn bancar que estava cubierto con vna alcatyfa et vnos coxines ençima* (42, 48). *. . . Tenia en las manos dos libros, vno verde e otro colorado* (109).
48. *Entre tanto que el . . . dezia et predicaua . . . todos estauan hincados de rodillas* (43).
49. *Todos juntamente a vna boz respondieron et dixeron a lo quel dicho Bachiller Menbreque les predicaua* (41). *. . . Por el dicho libro . . . el dicho Rabi dezia, leya et rezava, doze orazíones judaicas, en las quales nonbrava muchos nonbres hebraycos. . . . Vna oraçion que comiença verná Yrrael [sic] adonay, et que al tiempo que la començaba a desir, vió conmo el dicho Rabi se ponia la mano sobre los ojos, et quando la acabava de desir, abaxava la cabeça fasta el suelo, et vió conmo asymismo el dicho Juan de Córdoba Menbreque y las otras personas que allí estauan, hazian otro tanto al prinçipio de la dicha orazion e al fin della, segun lo fasya el dicho Raby et desyan e respondian todos a vna box, amen* (50). *. . . Todo lo que desya en hebraico lo tornava a desir et declarar en romançe* (50).
50. *Alçauan e abaxauan las cabeças sabadeando et besauan todos en la tierra et llorauan fasta en fin de cada oraçion, e que el dicho Rabi besaua el dicho libro que tenia en las manos quando todos los oyentes besauan la tierra* (50).
51. *Juan de Cordoua Menbreque y las otras personas que alli estauan tenian cada vna en su mano vna candela de çera blanca ençendidas et que después quel dicho Bachiller Menbreque auia acabado de predicar, vió como se baxava del predicatorio do estaua subido et asy baxando vió como el dicho Juan de Cordoua Menbreque y las otras personas que allí estauan, besaron la mano al dicho Bachiller Menbreque y él gelas ponia e puso a cada vno ençima de la cabeça, conmo que los absoluia, a modo judaico, syn los santiguar* (41). A late fifteenth-century satiric poem from Román against the *converso* poet Antón de Montoro lists among his Judaizing customs that people would kiss his hand when he blessed them (*c'os besen la mano / y que echeys la bendicion*) (Castillo 1882, poem #994).
52. *Cierto abto quel dicho Raby fazia en contra fazen la misa, puesto en vn altar, bestido de blanco, . . . y en lugar de la ostia, alçaba el dicho Raby predicador, vn libro judayco abierto, y en lugar del caliz, otro libro judayco menor et se herian, el dicho Johan de Cordoua y los otros que allí estauan, en los pechos, segund que los Xriptianos lo fazen al tiempo que alçan el Corpus Xripto. Et despues de acabada la misa, el dicho Raby les echaua la vendiçion syn los santiguar* (37). See also 78.
53. *Vido que estauan todos bueltos hazia donde sale el sol e resauan sabadeando con las cabeças a manera de judios; esto era por março* (Beinart 1974, 310). See also 312; Baer 1966, 2:366; Adler 1875, 48 [Mexico 1607].
54. *Se arrimo a una ventana todo lo que pudo y oyo a una persona que hablaba haciendo pausas en baxa vox y nunca pudo entender ni perçebir raçon alguna, mas de que algunas vezes paraba y*

*dexaba de hablar la dicha persona y replicaban los demas.* . . . *Daba palmadas sobre el brazo de la silla reciamente y como lamentandose de lo que decia* (Tejado 1950, 70–1).

55. *A conferir y tratar de la ley de Moisén, de sus preceptos, ayunos, ritos y ceremonias, diciendo cada cual lo que en su observancia hacía, animándose unos a otros en la puntualidad de sus ayunos; y todos juntos, como en conciliábulo, difinían la condenación eterna de los católicos, diciendo gravísimos desacatos contra las devociones, procesiones y cosas de que usa nuestra Madre la Iglesia* (García 1910, 195).

56. Even before the Expulsion women took a leadership role in some *converso* communities. Brianda Besant was accused in 1486, for example, of holding religious services in her home in Teruel (Haliczer 1990, 213).

57. *Por Noviembre de 1714 nombraron los de dicha junta un ravino, para que les enseñare y embiaron dicho nombramiento a Livorna, y vino aprobado dentro de dos meses firmado de tres ravinos, y este ravino juro puestas las manos en el libro de su lei de observarle* (Lera García 1987, 93). See also Yerushalmi 1971, 11.

58. Liebman 1974, 151; 1970, 58, 218. In addition to Montero, Liebman mentions Francisco Rodrígues de Matos [1598], an unlearned man who was termed a rabbi by the Inquisition; Manuel de Morales; Isaac de Aboab [Brazil 1642–54]; Manuel Bautista Pérez [Lima, burned in 1639]; the Mexican *conversos* Antonio Rodríguez Arias and Ruy Díaz Nieto [1601]; Juan Pacheco [Querétaro 1641] (1970, 58, 80, 193–200, 268).

59. *Havia um velho, chamado Luiz Carneiro, a quem chamavam Sacerdote judaico e havia mais uns 3 ou 4 entre os quais estava Manuel de Barros, avô do farmaceutico residente no Porto* (Barros Basto 1929, 3.17:1).

# CHAPTER XVIII

# Clothing and Ceremonial Items

Exodus 13, Deuteronomy 6, 11, 22, and Numbers 15 provide the textual inspiration for a number of ritual objects which tradition has come to associate with certain aspects of daily worship. Concern with religious clothing was restricted to men. The skull cap and *tzitzit* (pl. *tzitziyot*; fringed shirt) are worn constantly by orthodox Jewish men even today as a sign of their devotion to the Law. The *tallit* (pl. *tallitot*; prayer shawl) is used to cover a man's head and shoulders during certain prayers, and the *tefillin* (phylacteries) are worn by Jewish men during certain morning prayers. The door posts of Jewish houses are marked with a kind of amulet called a *mezuzzah*; on the house's eastern walls may be hung a calligraphic decoration called a *mizrah*. Traditionally each of these items is decorated or inscribed with Hebrew letters in a way that indicates its dedication to liturgical use.

All of these items were commonly employed in the Iberian Peninsula prior to the Expulsion. From the moment the Inquisition began to cast its vigilant eye, however, prudence dictated that *conversos* rid themselves of the physical realia connected with Jewish ceremony.[1] Thus, as we will see in this chapter, with very rare exceptions these specifically dedicated items are not mentioned among the Iberian crypto-Jews after the first generation of converts. On the other hand, two of these items, the prayer shawls and hats, could easily be approximated by using articles in common usage, and references abound to crypto-Jews praying with a shawl-like mantle across their shoulders and with their heads covered.

## 18.1. TALLIT

The tallit, or ceremonial prayer shawl, is worn by orthodox Jewish men in prayer as a reminder of the obligation to comply with God's commandments in fulfillment of the prescription in Numbers 15:38–39, which states: "bid them make tassels on the corners of their garments throughout their generations, and to put upon the tassel of each corner a cord of blue; and it shall be to you a tassel to look upon and remember all the commandments of the Lord." Very often the shawls were woven with stripes of blue—or sometimes black—thread in compliance with the biblical requirement. The practice was common enough to be listed in the Inquisition's compilations of customs, such as a Valencian Edict of Grace of 1484, which labels as Judaizers people "who instruct any Jew to wear the shawl, to venerate it and to kiss it in sign of devotion."[2] And it was a common touchstone of satirists and polemicists who made frequent pejorative mention of Jewish dress, including the tallit. For example, the late fifteenth-century satiric poem from the Count of Paredes against the *converso* poet Juan de Valladolid says that the *converso* had only to look at the Christian altar cloth and it would become a fringed linen tallit of the sort Jews wear when they take out the Torah to celebrate a visit by the king.[3]

Frequently the tallit is described by old-Christian writers in terms derived from their more familiar Christian tradition. In 1483 Hernando de Teba was denounced for twenty years earlier having been seen "wearing a white alb like an abbot would wear."[4] Paintings of religious subjects involving Old Testament Jews or Jews of the time of Jesus, provided visual models of *tallitot* for the *conversos* and led to statements like the 1571 accusation that Cristóvão Coronel, of Monção, "dressed himself like a priest of the old Law when he prayed."[5] But despite their Christian context these descriptions leave no doubt as to what was being described.

While specifically dedicated, decorated *tallitot* are not often referred to in documents dealing with the post-conversion period, references to the use of shawl-like mantles is extremely common. Frequently a towel, tablecloth, or napkin was pressed into use. The prominent *converso* Diego Arias Dávila [Segovia 1460s] was variously described as "praying with a sheet wrapped around his neck in the Jewish manner"; and "with a linen *taler* on his head like a rabbi"; "with a large shawl over his head and shoulders"; and "wrapped in a tablecloth."[6] At one memorable dinner Arias "took the tablecloth off the table and put it on his head and around his body the way the Jewish rabbis put on their *taler* when they want to pray, and he climbed up on a bench and began to sing a responsum."[7]

Some sort of prayer shawl was in use among crypto-Jews until quite late in some areas, while in others it seems to have all but disappeared. For example, there is only one reference to Jewish ceremonial clothing in the more than 600 sentences of the Coimbra Inquisition in the 1570s (Azevedo Mea 1982, 260). In Mexico, on the other hand, the tradition remained strong. In the trial of Tomás Treviño de Sobremonte [1647] there are numerous references to a prayer shawl (Liebman 1970,

247; cf. Roth 1931–2, 17). Simón Montero, executed in the Mexican *auto de fe* of 1649, "was found with a wool cloak woven with his own hands in the form which is seen painted in certain pictures of [John] the Baptist preaching to the Jewish people and which he used when he recited the prayers of the law" (Liebman 1974, 159). About the same time the Núñez sisters told Mexican inquisitors how their father León Jaramillo had prayed wearing a colored silk prayer shawl.[8] As with other crypto-Jewish practices, the wearing of the tallit was from time to time reinforced by the tales of travelers returning from places where Judaism was practiced openly. Juan Cardoso, who had lived in Amsterdam, was accused in Mexico in 1647 of praying with a tallit (Liebman 1975, 52). Hector Méndez Bravo, a Portuguese informer, said in 1617 that he had seen Portuguese Jews in Venice praying while "wrapped in white mantles" (Roth 1943–4, 230). The custom remains vital among some remnant crypto-Jews of this century. João Antonio Ferreira, at age 80 in 1929, talked about the crypto-Jewish community in Bragança. He said that "on Sabbaths and fast days they put white linen towels on their heads when they said their prayers."[9] Around Belmonte on Yom Kippur modern *criptojudeus* put a cloak over their heads and recite this prayer: "Blessed be You, Adonai, our God and King of all the world who charges us with Your holy commands that would be given to us with the cloak. Amen."[10] And Clemente Carmona told David Nidel in New Mexico in 1980 that his "Jewish" friends wash their hands before eating and put the folded napkin or towel over their left shoulder to recall the traditional Jewish prayer shawl (Nidel 1984, 255).

## 18.2. Tzitzit

Numbers 15:37–9 and Deuteronomy 22:12 require men to wear a garment with tassels on the corners, blue-threaded to recall the sky and God's throne of glory. The tassels, like the mezuzzah and the tefillin, are specifically intended as reminders to observe the commandments. In Spain and Portugal they were known variously as *dit cit, cedid, çeçi*, and so forth. While the tallit and tzitzit are derived from similar injunctions in the Bible, in medieval practice they became two quite different objects. The tallit, or prayer shawl, was a long, rectangular, fringed shawl worn over the head and shoulders while praying. The tzitzit was also rectangular and fringed, but tended to have a hole in the center and to be worn as a poncho-like inner shirt. A document from the time of the Expulsion states that "before [Jews] pray they wash their hands with water or dirt, and they wear serge or tammy cloth or linen shirts with certain strings hanging down."[11]

There are frequent references to *tzitziyot* among Iberian *conversos* for the first few years after the Expulsion. Jaime Ferrer [Valencia 1485] was accused of "wearing under his shirt a *tzitzit*, which is a fringed Jewish garment like a scapular, which was folded against his abdomen, and from the four corners of which hung four knotted woolen cords."[12] The cloth cutter Diego Beltrán was accused in Almazán (Soria) in 1505 because, among other things, "above his sash he wore a little habit, open at the sides with cords hanging down at the sides; . . . it was as delicate as wool serge and yellow in color."[13] Similarly Pedro Laínez was said in 1505 to have worn "a little blue serge habit, like the honored Jews wear, similar to *tzitzit* . . . with some white cords that were hanging down off the corners of the habit."[14] After that time they appear to have rapidly dropped out of use. The early seventeenth-century reference to tzitzit in a Cartagena de Indias (Colombia) Edict of Faith[15] is probably anachronistic, for contemporary trial testimony does not refer to the fringed garments.

## 18.3. Tefillin

The custom of wearing tefillin is derived from Exodus 13:16 and Deuteronomy 6:8; 11:18. This last verse commands that "you shall therefore lay up these words of mine in your heart and in your soul; and you shall bind them as a sign upon your hand, and they shall be as frontlets between your eyes." Tefillin are small boxes containing certain key prayers, which orthodox Jewish men bind on their forehead and weak hand (i.e., the left hand in right-handed men) with leather straps, and which they wind seven times around their arm between their elbow and their wrist. The New Testament (Matthew 23:5) calls them with the Greek term for amulet: phylacteries. In Spain and Portugal they were known variously as *ataphalis, ataphalijs, estefalim, tafelines, tefelim, tefelin,* and *tephiliñs*. Praying in the morning with tefillin was routine among pre-Expulsion Jews, as many Inquisition documents of the 1480s make clear. Inés Alvarez testified in Toledo, for example, that "one of the Jews of this city who was named Garu became a Christian and was then called Pero López. . . . He kept two small Jewish books in a box in which there were little parchment scrolls with writing and some long black strips of leather."[16] Commonly crypto-Jews of the Expulsion generation continued to wear tefillin during their morning prayers. Juan Fernández de Luz, councilman of Castillo de Garcimuñoz, was accused in 1491 of "putting on tefillin . . . ; before eating he took a leather strap and bound it around his neck and tied it to his fingers . . . ; and taking out something like an amulet he read from it, his face turned toward the wall, gesturing like a Jew."[17] The practice was common enough during those years that a Portuguese Edict of Faith of 1536 instructed informers to look for "*ataphalijs*, which are leather straps tied to the arms and placed on the head."[18]

Tefillin appear to have been used commonly before the Expulsion, frequently during the first few years following the Expulsion, and only sporadically after that. But scattered examples from as late as the middle of the seventeenth century very likely mean that the custom was occasionally reintroduced by travelers who had observed practicing Jews in Europe. Hector Méndez Bravo, a Portuguese informer, said in 1617 that he had seen Portuguese Jews in Venice praying "with some leather strips on their heads, and other strips on their arms inscribed with letters in Hebrew characters, which they call *tafellim*" (Roth 1943–4, 230). In 1636 in the Canary Islands Beatriz Hernández reported that she had seen Marcos Meneses "hide in his cell when Mass was being said in the prison, and that when preparing for bed he would tie a leather strap round his head" (Wolf 1926, 128). The Núñez sisters [Mexico 1649] reported how their father León Jaramillo used to pray wearing phylacteries (*cucurucho*).[19]

## 18.4. KIPAH

The male custom of praying only when one's head is covered is not prescribed in the Bible, and in fact even into medieval times was an optional custom. But by the fifteenth century it had became a fairly widespread way of showing modesty before God. In addition, because Christians prayed bareheaded, covering the head during prayer was considered to fulfill the Talmudic injunction not to imitate the heathen (ḥukkat ha-goi). The Expulsion generation were acutely conscious of how their former Jewish customs differed from the Christian customs that they were required to adopt. Antón Tapiazo reportedly told Juan de Salcedo in Soria around 1498 what he thought of the new religion: "In the synagogue we used to sit on benches and had our heads covered, and in the church they kneel and get up so many times you would think they are playing 'Up and Down.' "[20] In addition, probably reflecting medieval Jewish practice in Iberia, the rule was considered applicable to both men and women. Thus women like María Díaz and her daughters [Ciudad Real 1484] commonly "read together from a book, their heads covered, bobbing their heads."[21]

Although Roth asserts that the custom of praying with covered head disappeared among crypto-Jews very quickly (1931–2, 17), there is ample evidence that at least in the New World it persisted at least through the seventeenth century. Brazilian Judaizers of the 1590s were accused of praying "with the hood of their capes up over their heads."[22] Rafael de Granada said in 1641 that his relative Gabriel de Granada prayed with his hat on "because they were warned by the said persons that they must not uncover their heads."[23] On Yom Kippur during those years Pedro Arias de Maldonado "did not wear his shoes and stood on bricks, and his head was covered while they recited the prayers of his decadent law until dawn" (Liebman 1974, 228). Catalina de Rivera [1642] said that when they pray "the men have to wear a hat or a cloth cap and the women have to put cowls or handkerchiefs on their heads."[24] Diego Juárez de Figueroa [1647] explained that "on the Sabbath you may not uncover your head, even though they break it because you are discourteous, nor even lift a straw from the ground."[25] Francisco López Díaz [1648] confessed that he had attended a synagogue in Seville where "the men prayed wearing hats and the women wore large headdresses" (Liebman 1975, 95). As late as 1736 María de Castro, a Madrileña living in Lima, Peru, was accused of attending services in which the men prayed with their heads covered (Lewin 1954, 269).[26]

## 18.5. MEZUZZAH

A mezuzzah (pl. *mezuzzot*) is an amulet which is placed on the doorpost of one's house in fulfillment of the commandment in Deuteronomy 6:4–9 and 11:13–21. It generally contained a small scroll of parchment with the words to those verses inscribed in Hebrew, while on the back was inscribed the Hebrew term *Shaddai* ("Almighty God," but also the Hebrew acronym for "Guardian of the Gates of Israel," *Shomer delatot Israel*). While presumably *mezuzzot* were common among the pre-Expulsion Jewish community, after conversion, and after Expulsion, nailing a mezuzzah to one's door would have been an unmistakable invitation to martyrdom. The very occasional references to *mezuzzot* in the documentation are extremely problematical.[27] For example, in Bahia in 1591 a cult item was reported in the likeness of the head of an ox, made of wood and about a span and a half (13.5 inches) long. It was called a *toura*, a name that led the inquisitors to confuse it with Torah, but which may have referred to an ox-shaped mezuzzah.[28]

The extreme rarity of Inquisition references to the use of the mezuzzah among crypto-Jews suggests that the custom did not outlive the Expulsion generation. Yet it seems to be a common part of the folklore that surrounds the alleged discovery of modern crypto-Jews. Jacob Beller claims to have seen one among descendants of crypto-Jews in Santa Maria, Brazil, in the 1960s (Beller 1969, 273). An anonymous contributor to *Avotaynu* in 1989 recalled that his elderly Portuguese Catholic aunts "whenever they leave or return to their home . . . use their right hand to tap the doorway's stone arch two or three times. . . . I had a stone mason remove the right side stone of my aunt's door which was at eye level. Behind the stone, I found a parchment scroll written in Hebrew" (Anonymous, *Avotaynu*, Crypto-Jews S5). Tony Sanchez reported in 1992 that "my great grandparents had a statue of Michael the archangel in front of their door and in the tip of his boot was a mezuzzah. Everyone going in would kiss the tip of his boot and everyone else would see what great Catholics they were" (Kaufman 1992). Thomas Benrosh, an Azorian living in southeastern Massachusetts, told me before he died in 1992 that the family of Irmelina Gonsalves, who emigrated to Norton, Massachusetts, from the Beira Alta region of Portugal, used to tap a certain place on the door frame when entering or leaving their house.

## 18.6. Mizraḥ

A *mizraḥ* is a calligraphic amulet generally placed on an interior wall of the house. They are extremely common among Moroccan Jews and may have been in use in pre-Expulsion Iberia. I have found only one reference to something that might conceivably have been a *mizraḥ*. In 1505 testimony a witness identified some religiously significant writing in the home of Pedro Laínez in Almazán: "We saw him . . . open the cupboard where there were some large letters and he spoke and prayed in a way that the witness did not understand except that when he did it he swayed back and forth raising and lowering his head and body."[29]

## Notes

1. When Rabbi Abraham Saba arrived in Portugal in 1497 and learned that the King had ordered that "every Jew who might be found with a book or with philacteries in his possession would be put to death, . . . straightaway, before I entered the quarter outside the city, I took these books . . . and dug a grave among the roots of a blossoming olive tree; there we buried them" (Lazar 1991, 181).

2. *Se es feta instruir a ningun Juheu fentse mostrar la toca, venerant aquella e besantla en senyal de deuocio* (Beinart 1974, 152).

3. *Los Corporales tornastes, / sólo por vuestro mirado, / en un lençuelo delgado, / con orillas orillado, / con que la faz cobijastes. / Ya sabeys cómo lo vsays, / segun manda vuestra ley, / cuando la Tora sacays / y cantando la lleuays / para recebir al Rey* (Castillo 1882, poem #969).

4. *Vestido vna como alua de abad* (Llorca 1935, 16).

5. *Se vestir como sacerdote da lei velha e rezar orações ao modo judaico* (Azevedo Mea 1982, 260).

6. *Una sábana echada al pesquezo a manera de judío* (Carrete Parrondo 1986, 5); . . . *un taler puesto sobre la cabeza de lienco, puesto como rabí* (28); . . . *toma una gran toca y pónesela sobre los hombros e cabeza a forma de taler* (66); . . . *se abía cobijado vnos manteles por taler, que es cobijadura de judíos* (99); see also 49.

7. *Arias tomó los manteles que estaban en la messa e púsolos por la cabeza e cuerpo como se ponen los rabíes de los judíos el taler quando quieren deçir oración, y subióse en vn banco e començó a cantar vn responso* (Carrete Parrondo 1986, 102; cf. 106).

8. *Una vestidura colorada de bombazi* (Wiznitzer 1962a, 246).

9. *Aos sabados e dias de jejuns colocavam umas toalhas brancas de linho pela cabeça emquanto diziam as orações* (Barros Basto 1928b, 3:17, 1).

10. *Bendito sejas tu Adonai, nosso Deus e rei de todo o mundo, que nos encomendou com as suas santas encomendanças para que nos houvéssemos com o manto* (Canelo 1987, 101).

11. *Antes que recen, se lavan las manos con agua o tierra, y se visten bestiduras de sarga, estameña o lienço con ciertas cuerdas colgadas* (Santa María 1893c, 183). See also López Martínez 1954, 180.

12. *Portaua damunt la camisa un dit cit, ques diu fimbria de Moysés a manera de vn escapulari, que pleguaua fins a mig ventre, e dels quatre cantóns de la dita fimbria penjant quatre cordetes de lana ab certs nucs* (Llorca 1939, 120). See also Lipiner 1977, 39.

13. *Ençima del sayo tenía vestido vn abitilo abierto por los lados con vnas cuerdas colgadas a los lados; . . . que hera delgado, como d'estameña y como vn poco amarillo* (Carrete/Fraile 1987, 36). See also Baer 1966, 2:361.

14. *Un sanbenetillo asul de estameña, como los judíos honrados lo solían traer a manera de çeçi; . . . vnas cuerdas blancas que colgauan de los cabos del santbenito* (Carrete/Fraile 1987, 74; 76). See also Carrete Parrondo 1985a, 122 [1501].

15. *Vistiéndose vestiduras de sarga, estameña o lienzo, con ciertas cuerdas o orregüelas colgadas de los cabos con ciertos nudos* (Medina 1899b, 26).

16. *Uno de los judíos que hera natural desta cibdad que se llamava Garu y se tornó cristiano e se llamava agora Pero López . . . tenía dos libros judiegos pequennos e altos en una caxuela en que tenía unos rollitos de pergamino escritos e vnas correhuelas de cuero negras e largas* (León Tello 1972, 78).

17. *Ataviavase con los tafelines. . . . Antes que comiese tomaua una correa e se la echaua al pescueço e se la ataua a los dedos; . . . sacando de alli vna como nomina y leyala hasia la pared, haziendo sus autos e gestos como judio* (Moreno Koch 1977, 367). For other examples see Wiznitzer 1960, 14; Carrete Parrondo 1985a, 43 [1490]; 122 [1501]; Saraiva 1969, 164 [1536].

18. *Os ataphalijs, que são huas correas atadas nos braços, ou postas sobre a cabeça* (Furtado 1925, xxxii).

19. Wiznitzer 1962a, 246. See also Liebman 1970, 96 [1639], 247; Lipiner 1977, 28–9.

20. *En la synoga se sentauan en sus vancos e llebauan sus capirotes, e de cómo en la yglesia se hincaban de rodillas e se leuantauan muchas veces, e paresçia que jugauan al "susete posete"* (Carrete Parrondo 1985a, 145).

21. *Leyan todas en vn libro, las cabeças cubiertas, sabadeando* (Beinart 1974, 55).

22. *Com o capelo da capa na cabeça* (Lipiner 1969, 92).

23. Adler 1899, 68. See also Liebman 1970, 198, 247; 1974, 139, 213; Lewin 1954, 148.

24. *Para rezar las oraciones de la dicha Ley . . . los hombres ponerse sombrero o montera y las mujeres tocas o paños en las cabezas* (Lewin 1977, 46). See also 27, 68, 145, etc.

25. *Que en los sábados no han de descubrir la cabeza, aunque se las quiebren por descorteses, ni aun alzar una pajuela del suelo* (García 1910, 101).

26. Fierman recounts a recent anecdote from Ciudad Juárez, Chihuahua, in which a man named José Nevárez told a man named Prieto that their father, in Zacatecas, had covered his head with a little hat (*Mi papá* [covered his] *cabeza con sombrero chiquito* [sic]) (Fierman 1987, xii).

27. A witness in Almazán in 1505 identified a scrap of parchment as one of those the Jews used to put on their doors (*era los papeles y palabras que los judíos solían tener a sus puertas*) (Carrete/Fraile 1987, 54; cf. 98).

28. Wiznitzer 1960, 25, 31. See also Furtado 1925, 395, 475. This may be the object observed in Fernão Soares's house in 1593 and described in Furtado 1929, 48. There is reason to believe that the Brazilian *touras* were some sort of ritualistic Torah icon and as such figured on the "altars" of *Cristão novo* synagogues; see discussion above. Cf. Lipiner 1969, 86–9.

29. *Le viera abrir el . . . almario adonde tenía vnas letras grandes, y que hablaua e rezava, que no lo entendía este testigo, saluo que quando lo tal fasya sabadeava baxando e alçando la cabeça y el cuerpo* (Carrete/Fraile 1987, 72).

# CHAPTER XIX

# Food and Dietary Laws

The kosher rules, the complex of prescriptions that govern what a Jew eats, derive from regulations laid down in Leviticus 3, 7, 11, and 17 and Deuteronomy 14 and enlarged and refined in later Talmudic and rabbinical tradition. Jewish dietary laws concern themselves with almost every aspect of food preparation and consumption. They govern the slaughter of animals, the preparation of meat, baking, the care of utensils, and the methods of cooking. They mandate which foods cannot be eaten in combination with one another, and which foods cannot be eaten at all. They dictate which blessings must be said over which foods. And they require that certain foods be eaten, or not be eaten, on certain holidays.[1]

Two consequences derive from the complexities of Jewish dietary regulations. The first is that, because food preparation and eating occur several times each day, observant Jews are constantly reminded of their Jewish identity. Keeping kosher becomes a kind of mantra, a series of infinitely repeated minute acts that focus the attention of men and women on their Jewishness. Keeping kosher is hard work, inconvenient, and time consuming. It is expensive. Where a Jewish community is surrounded by a gentile culture, and where assimilation is possible or even encouraged by the majority society, it is always easier for Jews not to keep the dietary laws than to keep them. Remaining observant to the kosher restrictions is an on-going affirmative act, an assertion of commitment to traditional Judaism.

The second consequence is that the dietary restrictions ensure that Jews and gentiles do not commingle because the laws effectively bar Jews from taking part in gentile social occasions. Thus Jews considered them to be a bulwark against the eroding influences of assimilation. Christian leaders felt similarly. Social intercourse around the dinner table was from the earliest days of Christian missionary efforts seen as a dangerous prelude to cultural and sexual intercourse. The episcopal Council of Elvira, held near Granada around the year 306 CE even before Roman legalization of the Christian religion, forbade Christians from taking food together with Jews (Marcus 1960, 101). Alfonso X's 1265 code of laws (*Siete Partidas*, Title 24, Law 8), which forbade "any Christian man or woman to invite a Jew or a Jewess, or to accept an invitation from them, to eat or drink together, or to drink any wine made by their hands" (Marcus 1960, 38), was a typical result of medieval Christian attitudes on this question.

Even beyond the religious importance of the formal mandates of the dietary regulations, Jewish cooking was a central part of Jewish ethnic identity. In this respect the Iberian Jews were no different from any other encapsulated ethnic group, and they closely resembled the immigrant enclaves of our century which cluster around their ethnic restaurants and grocery stores in every big city in the Americas. For immigrant communities of today, as well as for the Iberian crypto-Jews of four hundred years ago, memories of the smells emanating from childhood kitchens go a long way toward defining ethnic identity. Thus Iberian Jewish popular culture was in no small part characterized by its recipes: its use of olive oil rather than lard, its predilection for eggplant and chickpeas, its repertoire of Sabbath stews. These foods were easily recognized by Jew and gentile alike as "Jewish" foods and were often mentioned as such in Inquisition testimony.

Unlike many other Jewish religious customs, Iberian Jewish dietary practices survived among crypto-Jews for a long time. Judaizing new-Christians tended to continue to slaughter animals and fowl in the kosher fashion and to prepare them for cooking according to Jewish rite. They tended to avoid the most prominent of the prohibited foods and to continue to prepare their most cherished Sabbath recipes. Even *conversos* who tried their best to assimilate into the mainstream Catholic culture retained an aversion to some of the traditionally prohibited foods, notably pork products. Sometimes the evidence for Judaizing inveighed against a *converso* was merely that he refused to eat pork.

In the Iberian world from the 1480s until the abolishment of the Inquisition in the nineteenth century, the adherence to Jewish dietary customs had other consequences as well. One was the need to educate each successive generation of Judaizers secretly about the intricacies of the kosher regulations. Although the Talmudic and rabbinical traditions in this area were soon lost, as they were in other areas of Jewish observance, Judaizers could find detailed instruction about dietary laws both in the Old Testament and in the Inquisition's own Edicts of Faith, which tended to be quite specific about Jewish slaughtering, cooking, and eating practices. On the other hand, because Christians were well informed about Jewish dietary habits, Inquisitors and their networks of neighborhood spies tended to pay special attention to the culinary customs of their *converso* neighbors. As a consequence, readers of the trial testimony know a great deal about how *conversos* interpreted the Jewish dietary laws.

## 19.1. Forbidden Foods (*Terefah*)

Traditional Judaism prohibits the consumption of two sorts of foods that it labels unclean: those which are in any way diseased or blemished and those which are specifically forbidden by the Scriptures. According to the rules of ritual slaughter (*shehitah*), meat must be carefully inspected (*bedikah*) for any of eight types of defects that might indicate that the animal was ill or had not been slaughtered strictly according to custom. If it showed any evidence of these defects it was declared *terefah,* or unclean (*Enc. Jud.*, 6:28). *Bedikah* was included in many of the official lists of Judaizing customs, such as this one from the late fifteenth century: "*Terefah* meat is when the animal has a spot on its side, which comes from the commandment in Jewish law not to eat carrion; and thus they did not eat it, nor any animal which still had blood in its body; because a sick animal always had blood in its body."[2] *Bedikah* was the norm for the Expulsion generation. Pascual the shoemaker [Ciudad Real 1484] said that when Juan Díaz Doncel slaughtered, "if he found some ewe to be *terefah* they would not eat that meat."[3] Testimony in Almazán in 1505 told how when someone "brought a hen to sell and it was a little bit damaged, the *conversa* women told their servant boy not to buy it."[4] And there are instances of crypto-Jews performing *bedikah* for the next hundred and fifty years. Fernão Lopes, of the Azores, was accused in Lisbon in 1573 of "not eating meat from animals that died of natural causes because it still had blood in it."[5] Maria Lopez [Bahia 1591] said that she had "an aversion and disgust for chickens or any other fowl that died of illness."[6] In 1647 fifteen-year-old Simón de León told the Mexican Inquisition that when his brother chose a chicken for dinner it was "an entirely black chicken, without a single white feather."[7]

Lists of clean (*tahor*) and unclean (*tameh*) animals are given in Deut. 14:3–20 and Lev. 11:3–23. Generally in order to qualify to be eaten mammals must have cloven hoofs and be ruminants. Fish must have both gills and scales. Fowl must not be flesh-eating. These requirements excluded a large number of foods that were a routine part of the Christian Spanish diet: pork and rabbit, squid, octopus, eel, and shellfish. Lists of forbidden foods appear frequently in the trials and vary little in their content. Mayor González [Ciudad Real 1511] allegedly "never ate eel nor octopus nor hare nor rabbit nor conger . . . until the Inquisitors came to town."[8] Juana Sánchez said in 1490 in Garcimuñoz that her mistress Teresa Sánchez "never ate pork, nor hare, nor conger, nor eel, nor strangled partridges."[9] These lists were so commonplace that they became a staple of the satirical Spanish poems of the mid- to late fifteenth century that made fun of the *conversos'* adherence to Jewish dietary customs. Typical is the burlesque "Marriage of Rodrigo Cota," which says that at his *aljama* wedding party they did not serve the meat of furry animals nor fish without scales.[10] Even later generations of crypto-Jews seem to have retained knowledge of the basic prohibited foods. Isabel do Casal said in Pernambuco [Brazil 1594], that she did not eat rabbit or eel because they made her ill.[11] Schwarz found twentieth-century Portuguese Judaizers abstaining from eating pork, rabbit, hare, and fish without scales. They did, however, eat pork sausages (1925, 17).

Shellfish and scaleless fish were generally avoided by crypto-Jews. Catalina Martín said in 1511 that "she had never seen the *conversa* González sisters eat octopus or eel or any other fish without scales."[12] In Brazil in the 1590s Guiomar Fernandes used to berate fishermen for bringing her such fish. Maria de Paiva said that such fish upset her stomach. She couldn't eat eel because it looked too much like snake (Lipiner 1969, 170–1). Rafael de Granada [Mexico 1642] related how "his mother had told him that the Law of Moses prohibited eating fish with [sic] scales, but that when they gave one to him he never noticed whether it had scales or not."[13] In some environments Judaizers could even joke about such things. In 1596 the Evora Inquisition took note of a conversation between Heitor Tomas and the theologian Pêro Vaz about a dogfish. Tomas saw a man carrying a dogfish (*cação*) down the street and remarked that it was a good fish, to which Vaz agreed. Then Tomas said, "I was just kidding. You can't eat that fish." "Why?" "Because it is forbidden." "By what Law?" "By the Law of Moses. Aren't you a Jew?" "Yes," replied the theologian; "I hope to be saved in the Law of Moses."[14]

The food most assiduously avoided by crypto-Jews was pork, which in addition to not meeting the general requirements for cleanliness was specifically prohibited in Deuteronomy 14:8. *Conversos* avoided pork both because they considered it to be unclean and because it was emblematically Christian. Sometime in the 1570s Grácia Dias Correia, of Castela [Evora], told the Inquisitors that "I have never eaten [pork] and I will never eat it. I am not a pig to eat pig meat as the old-Christians do."[15] Luis de Carvajal [Mexico 1589] informed Inquisitors that Jews "did not eat bacon or any other pork; because they were only supposed to eat ruminants, and not animals that were not ruminants, such as pigs."[16] Later crypto-Jews justified their aversion to pork in a variety of folkloristic ways, even believing that it had the power to work magic transformations. João Carvalho [Goa 1627] said that he had been told that people who ate pork turned into pigs (Roth 1931–2, 19). Isabel de Rivera reputedly told the Mexican Inquisition around 1646 that Judaizers "could not eat salt pork, because pigs were men who had been cursed by God, and until they rejoined the blessed one could not eat them."[17] As with other areas of crypto-Jewish practice that were defined more by not-doing than by doing, for many *conversos*, particularly in later years, avoidance of pork became a touchstone of their Jewish identity.

Most crypto-Jews went to great lengths to avoid eating pork products. In the Jeronymite monastery of Guadalupe in 1485 the *converso* Friar Diego de Segovia did not come to the refectory if it was being served. Friar Francisco de Burgos said he gave someone else his pork ration because it made him ill. Friar Francisco de Toledo gave away his bacon and his sausage.[18] The strategies were legion. Victoria Fernandes told the Portuguese Inquisition in 1541 that "her father had a shop where he sold pork, beef and lamb, but that Catharina Fernandes only bought beef and lamb."[19] *Converso* families commonly ordered their kitchen maids not to serve them pork. In 1653 an English servant reported in Orotava (Tenerife) that he left the service of Lucina Rodriguez "because she called him an English dog for bringing a roasted rabbit to the table, and that she abused him for putting pork in the stew" (Wolf 1926, 139). In fact as late as 1720 an *auto de fe* in Madrid identified twenty families whose Judaizing included abstaining from eating pork (Lera García 1987, 93). *Conversos* tried to avoid any dish that might have even a trace of pork in it. Several Judaizers sentenced by the Coimbra Inquisition between 1567 and 1583 were accused of cooking pork only for their servants, and always in pots that were reserved for that purpose and washed separately from their other dishes.[20] Blanca Duarte [Ciudad Rodrigo c. 1584] was denounced because "once the witness cooked some pork in a pot, and when Blanca Duarte saw her take it out to eat it she ordered her to take it out of her sight, and then she took the spoon with which she had removed the pork and burned it and broke the pot in which it had been cooked."[21] In 1576 in Las Palmas Maria de Palençuela reported that one day when she was eating with Catalina Núñez, Núñez "made a sign to her son, by which they understood that he was not to eat a certain dish that contained pork. She has heard it reported that [Núñez] would refuse to eat dishes prepared for her son and his wife when they contained pork."[22] Manuel Gil [Mexico 1603] said that even when he was sick and needed to eat meat the *converso* Ruy Díaz Nieto would only eat "raisins and almonds and some conserves of fruit" until one day the *conversa* Isabel Rodríguez made him a stew.[23]

But of course any avoidance of pork was noticed and talked about by the old-Christian community that enveloped the crypto-Jews. Late in the 1480s it was reported to the Zaragoza Inquisition that, when the old-Christian Gaspar Roiz saw his *conversa* daughter-in-law pick bacon out of her food and throw it under the table, with great "displeasure and malice" he would say, "We have Jews in my house, we have Jews in my house."[24] Testimony in Majorca in 1673 described a picnic in Pedro Onofre's orchard four years earlier. "One of the things that the guests took out to eat was a stew cooked with pork sausage; one of them . . . wanted to eat it but the other . . . said, 'It has pork sausage.' And they did not eat it, but instead ate some fish and fruit which they had. And Antonio de Puigdorfila asked them why they did not eat it, that they were behaving like Jews. And they said it would do them harm; and the others who were there laughed and said to each other, 'Look at the Jews who don't want to eat the stew!' "[25] Juan del Canto [Soria 1501] said that Antón Tapiaço had told him that "he did not eat pork but he did eat food cooked with pork; and if they put a plate of pork before him and there was a bonfire there he would rather throw money in the fire than eat the pork; and if it weren't for the way people talk he wouldn't eat food cooked with pork either."[26]

It goes without saying that most Judaizing *conversos* preferred to fry their food in olive oil rather than in lard. Even the royal chronicler Andrés Bernáldez, describing Jewish and *converso* customs just prior to the Expulsion, remarked that "they cooked their meat with olive oil, which they threw in instead of salt pork or lard so as to avoid pork; and olive oil with meat is something which smells very bad when it is cooked; and thus their house and gates smell very bad because of their cooking."[27] The distinction between Jewish and Christian cooking was clearly marked by the slave Fátima, who reported in 1528 in Las Palmas that her "master told me to fry a little onion in oil in the pot, and then throw in the chickpeas, and then add a little water, after which I wash the meat and throw it in. . . . Before this I had another master, but he only ate stews such as the Christians eat, putting in the meat and bacon and then the turnips, chickpeas and cabbages."[28] Diego de Torres [Las Palmas 1527] reported that a man named Mayrena invited him to eat "meat boiled with onions and a quantity of oil, and as it seemed to deponent that this was a Jewish dish he refused to eat of it" (Wolf 1926, 82, 99). Rui Pérez [Manila 1597] was accused of only eating food prepared with sesame oil (Uchmany 1982, 99). Duarte Rodríguez [Mexico 1603] said that Ruy Díaz Nieto "did not eat salt pork, lard, or any pork product, and instead of salt pork he cooked his stews with olive oil."[29] Another witness, Manuel Gil, said that one Friday which was a meat day he caught Díaz Nieto "frying six eggs and a fish in olive oil and vinegar, and that he fried other Lenten dishes in olive oil."[30]

The preference for oil remained strong all through the seventeenth century. In 1622 Diego Enríquez Villanueva was charged with having eaten partridge cooked in oil on business trips through Andalucia (Rose 1987, 60). In the Inquisition dungeons in Mexico in the 1640s González Flores was accused of requesting "that he be given Jewish rations because he wanted to cook his own food in his manner in new pots with oil, not lard, because Jews do not eat lard" (Liebman 1974, 149). In the 1670s in Majorca a group of Judaizers was accused of cooking exclusively with olive oil.[31]

Pork was not only forbidden to Jews and Judaizing *conversos*, it was often physically repugnant to them. Because for so long it had been the principal symbol of everything that was alleged to be unclean about Christian culinary habits, they could not overcome their ingrained aversion to it. Even those early *conversos* who had assimilated religiously to Catholicism often found that they could not eat pork. Many said that it made them ill: it harmed their stomachs, throats, or eyes.[32] In the Jeronymite monastery of Guadalupe in 1485 an anonymous monk said that he vomited after eating pork (Sicroff 1965, 98). Beatriz Núñez, tried in Guadalupe in 1485, declared "that I did not eat pork until recently, because my husband scolded me about it; and I told him that I didn't eat it because it caused me great harm in my chest."[33] In a 1551 trial in Evora, Gil Vaz Bugalho was said to have said that "he didn't eat pork because it harmed his eyes."[34] Luisa Ramírez and Leonor de Silva [Granada 1590s] each reported that they abstained from eating pork because it gave them asthma.[35] Mencia de Avila refused to eat it because it gave her paralysis![36]

Even the faintest odor of pork was repugnant to many. A maid reported to the Inquisition in 1505 that nine years previous when "she was cooking some pork and her mistress [Ana Laínez] drew near the fire ... she saw how she put a cloth up to her nose because of the odor of the pork; and her mistress ... told her: 'The odor of this pork is bothering my throat.'" Her neighbor Ana del Aguila said that pork stunk (*hedia*).[37] Mayor Meléndez [Guadalajara 1520–1] used to flee the kitchen and stop up the holes in the door to escape the odor of cooking pork.[38] In Majorca in the 1670s in *chueta* houses when the maids wanted to cook pork their masters made them cook it up on the roof because the smoke bothered them (Selke de Sánchez 1972, 86).

As Inquisition trial testimony makes abundantly clear, Judaizing new-Christians found it extremely difficult to cope unobtrusively with the pork-saturated world in which they found themselves. But they continued to try. Some feigned sickness when a plate containing non-kosher food was set on the table before them. Leonor Martí, an old Majorcan woman, testified in the 1670s that "because of the bouts she had of hypochondria and her eye problems ... the doctor had told her not to eat pork or any strong food ... like rabbits, thrushes, or fish without scales."[39] Some claimed to have eaten already. Some purchased *terefah* food and then threw it out or gave it away. Some surreptitiously picked out the morsels of pork and hid them under the table or under their beds. Beatriz Pérez [Granada 1575] said, before she hanged herself in her cell, that in her house "they did not eat pork and when they were eating in front of other people, in order not to give the appearance that they were not eating it they pretended to eat it and secretly threw it underneath the table."[40] Diego Rodríguez Arias sailed from the Canary Islands to London in 1654. During the journey he asked all the passengers to share with him pieces of the pork they were eating. Several people later testified that when they got to London the meat was found hidden underneath the straw on which he slept (Beinart 1977b, 58).

Even if Judaizing new-Christians were unable to keep pork products entirely out of their houses, they often attempted to keep pork—and anything that had come into contact with pork—away from their own food. Of course each *conversa* housewife had to cope with the kosher regulations in a way in which she and her family were comfortable. One woman might consider the kitchen her private preserve and prepare all the foods herself. Another might relegate food preparation to the servants, who were in all likelihood not *conversas*, while at the same time supervising them closely. One might not allow any of the forbidden foods into the house while another might only ban pork products. Or one might allow the servants to prepare pork for themselves and non-*converso* guests, while preparing something else for the family (Levine 1982, 175). In this last case she was likely to keep the pork utensils rigorously separate from those which touched her family's food. Clara de Puxmija's maid testified in the 1480s that "they offered her five or six rashers of bacon and this witness touched them, for they were in a bag." Clara would not touch them and "for more than the next eight days she would not eat anything that this witness touched, and she would not let anyone serve her but insisted on serving herself."[41] Around 1490 Teresa Sánchez, of Garcimuñoz, was accused of "refraining from eating pork even though her children ate it; and that she would not set her bread where they had eaten it, nor put it on the table, nor cut it with the knife they used to cut it" (Moreno Koch 1977, 358). In 1505 it was said of Aldonza Laínez of Almazán that "when some servant cut bacon she had the pan cleaned and washed and even scalded."[42] In 1505 Catalina Laínez was accused of "ordering a witness to set out one pot for her and for . . . Alvaro de Luna and another pot for the witness and the serving boys; and that she should not put bacon in the stew pot that she was fixing for her and her husband, but rather beef and sometimes chickpeas and other times greens; and she ordered that that pot be stirred with a wooden spoon and the other with an iron spoon, and she did not allow the spoon from one pot to be used in the other."[43] Fernand Alvarez [Soria 1497] allegedly refused to eat a certain meal because it had pork in it, saying " 'God keep me from having to eat it. When I go to the villages I take my own prepared meat and my knife so that I won't have to have anything to do with 'them.' He meant by this the old-Christians. And he also said that . . . if he did not have prepared meat he did not take uncooked meat so that he wouldn't have to cook it on the grill with the Christians.' And he said he bought eggs and ate them roasted so as not to have to use their frying pans. And that the working people begged him to eat from their pot and he said that he was sick and could not eat it."[44] An indictment of Judaizing customs, given to the Inquisition of Majorca in 1674, describes how *chuetas* even refused to eat meat that had been slaughtered on a day in which pigs had been killed, for fear of contamination in the slaughter house.[45]

The other side of the fact that in the popular mind Judaizing was synonymous with avoidance of pork was that it put great pressure on *conversos* to prove their Christian orthodoxy by consuming pork where their neighbors could see them. In fact, this was so common that it became emblematic of the hypocritical new-Christian, as can be seen in this late fifteenth-century satiric poem directed to Queen Isabel herself by the *converso* Antón de Montoro, known by his nickname *Ropero* (old-clothes dealer):

> Oh, Ropero, sad and bitter,
> would your pain would go away!
> I am seventy today,
> and I never ceased to say
> "Virgin was our Sancta Mater."
> I swore not to the Creator;
> I communed and said the Creed.
> On fat bacon I did feed,
> and I gobbled salt-pork stew.
> I heard mass and prayed my beads,
> crossed myself and scuffed my knees,
> and yet still I was not freed
> from the stainful name of "Jew."[46]

The strategies for projecting porkophilia were varied. Some *conversos* lied about their eating habits: the Galician Ana de Medina reported in the seventeenth century that "when she talked with old-Christians she said that she ate pork and she gave them to understand that she really enjoyed fried pork."[47] Alonso Marcos [Ciudad Real 1484] stipulated that "he did not eat Christian meat, but only kosher, and he bought meat at the Christian butcher shops to put on a show for people, and later he threw it to the pigs."[48] In 1502 Juan de Salcedo said that the *converso* Diego García el Rico, of Soria, "never ate pork, nor anything cooked with pork, even though he slaughtered pigs in his household; and he had his meat cooked separately."[49] Leonor Teixeira was accused by the Coimbra Inquisition in 1573 of sometimes accepting gifts of pork, or asking for pork so that people would think she ate it, but of then giving it away to other people outside her household.[50] Rui Pérez [Manila 1597] allegedly ate pork only when he had guests.[51] Luis de Carvajal [Mexico 1589] said that his family would eat kosher food at home, but sometimes did not when they were eating away from home, so that they would not be found out.[52] The Portuguese Tomás Núñez de Peralta [Mexico c. 1646] stated that "one day, when eating at the home of a rich Jew in Mexico City, he saw that he put roast ham on the table, which scandalized him until he realized that it was only there on the chance that some Catholic might enter and see it."[53] Manuel Gil [Mexico 1603] alleged that "everyone in the Holy Office prison, except Ruy Díaz, eats salt pork. . . . They all make a great show of salt pork, and they call it their Patent of Nobility, and when they want to eat it they call for it saying: 'Let me have that Patent of Nobility.' Even if they did not normally eat salt pork, that day they would have had to because of the invited guests, particularly Pedro de Fonseca, a Minister of the Holy Office."[54]

A particularly ingenious family which was committed to avoiding pork might employ all these strategies. In 1655 in Orotava (Tenerife) the black slave Catalina testified against her master Diego Rodriguez:

> They do not eat pork, and if at any time any is sent to them they gave it away; and that . . . an acquaintance of his sent them a pig from Canary, and they killed it in the courtyard of the house, but they ate none of it, but sold it all; and that the said Gonçalo Rodriguez asked for a little of it to be roasted for breakfast, whereupon Maria, a black, taking it into the room remained there to see whether her master would eat any, but he did not, and gave it to the black boys. . . . And that the said Lucina [Diego's sister] says that neither her father nor mother ate pork, nor has she ever done so since she was born, and she breaks a china plate which has held pork, and a tin one she melts in the fire. And that one day this deponent and her companion put a piece of pork in the stew, and their mistress discovering this, seized the pan with the meat in it, and threw it into the courtyard, saying she would not have her people eat pork as it causes sore throat; and she would never allow the bucket, used to catch the blood of the pig which was killed in the courtyard, to be again brought indoors, or used for anything but the food for the fowls; and if a guest dines at the house, they put pork in the stew, but the said Gonçalo Rodriguez, Lucina and Perpetua do not take any of it, but eat eggs. (Wolf 1926, 145–6)

Although traditional Judaism is vague about whether it is licit to eat meat from the hindquarters of an animal, in Iberia the issue was of concern to some groups of crypto-Jews. A few people like Alonso Núñez [Soria 1501] who preferred the forequarter,[55] or Beatriz Ribeira [Coimbra, 1569] who was accused of "not eating the hindquarters of lamb according to Jewish practice,"[56] considered the hindquarters to be forbidden. More common is evidence suggesting a preference for hindquarter meat. Catalina de la Villa [Ciudad Real 1511] said that she only saw meat from the hindquarters brought to the house of the *converso* Mayor González.[57] Fifteen-year-old Simón de León [Mexico 1647] confessed that "his father sent their black slave Luis to the slaughter house to bring home hindquarters of lamb to eat."[58]

An additional dietary law, which prohibits combining dairy products with meat (*basar be-ḥalav*) and requires keeping separate dishes for meat and dairy products, is derived from the injunction in Ex. 23:19, 34:26, and Deut. 14:21 not to boil a kid in its mother's milk. I have only found two widely separated references to this custom. Beatriz Gonçalves, of Chacim [Coimbra 1583] considered it a sin to eat cheese with meat.[59] Leonor Martínez [Mexico 1647] indicated at her trial that she did not eat dairy products with meat (Liebman 1970, 248). Judging from the extreme rarity of such evidence, and from the absence of references to *basar be-ḥalav* in the Edicts of Faith, it appears that separating milk and meat dishes was not a standard part of the crypto-Jewish repertoire of dietary practices.

Judaizing new-Christians who felt strongly about preserving Jewish dietary regulations worked hard to ensure that anything that came into contact with their food should be ritually pure. In some new-Christian communities in the late 1480s "no one but a Judaizing *converso* was permitted to wait on the table" (Baer 1966, 2:269). This requirement also dictated that anything that touched *conversos*' food must not be contaminated by contact with non-kosher foods. For many Judaizers this meant that their pots and pans, plates, utensils, and table linens had to be stored and washed separately from any used by their old-Christian servants. Juana González denounced the de la Sierra family [Ciudad Real 1511], for example, because they "did not let her or Francisca wash the family's plates and pans with the scrub rag they used to wash the servants' dishes."[60] The servant Catalina Martín [Ciudad Real 1511] testified that Beatriz, Leonor, and Isabel González "kept their pots and spoons and pans separate, and they did not share their water jug with anyone but each other. And if anyone else happened to drink water from the jug they had set aside, they ordered that a brand new jug be brought from the plaza for them to drink."[61] Duarte Rodríguez [Mexico 1603] said that the crypto-Jew Ruy Díaz Nieto "would not take a drink unless it was in his own house from his own pitcher" and that he kept a separate pitcher to offer other people. Another witness, Manuel Gil, added that one day Díaz Nieto "came into his store dying of thirst, because he had not taken a drop of water all day although he was in great need of it. Gil said to him: 'Is water lacking in the city or in the houses you have gone into?' Ruy Díaz replied in Portuguese: 'Blessed be the greatness of the Lord for I have not drunk from anyone else's pitcher in the time I have been in this land.' "[62]

Sometimes these rules extended to table linens as well. Catalina Martín also said of the González sisters "that they would not allow their shirts or table cloths to be washed with those of the serving men nor with the witness's clothes, but rather separately."[63] To judge from Inquisition testimony, the old-Christian servants of these families were alert to their masters' kitchen habits and routinely denounced any suspicious behavior to the authorities.

Kitchenware was expensive, so Judaizers were reluctant to destroy items that were impure because of having come in contact with non-kosher food. This problem is taken into account by Jewish tradition, which provides that hard-surfaced utensils such as silverware or ceramic plates that have come into contact with a contaminating substance can be re-purified by searing them in fire or by burying them for a time in clean soil. There are a handful of references from the time of the Expulsion to *converso* families purifying their tableware by these methods. In Toledo in the late fifteenth century the *converso* Rodrigo Rofos purified his dishes by "burning the stew pots and roasting pans and knives which he was using for cooking and eating."[64] Some crypto-Jews considered boiling the tableware to be sufficient. Fernand Alvarez [Soria 1502] was accused because when his knife was used to cut some sausages he "didn't want to use it until it had been washed with boiling water."[65] In addition, Jewish tradition considers that cracked or broken dishes are not ritually pure, and we find occasional evidence from the Expulsion period that *conversos* observed this prohibition.[66] But on the whole these practices ancillary to the principal Jewish dietary laws seem to have dropped out of crypto-Jewish practice within a few years after the Expulsion.

## 19.2. Kosher Butchering (Shehitah)

In the orthodox Jewish communities of pre-Expulsion Iberia most mammals were slaughtered by professional kosher butchers; fowl were slaughtered either by the kosher butcher (*shohet*) or at home. Before the Expulsion Judaizing *conversos* were able to buy kosher meat in the butcher shops of the Jewish community, and there is ample evidence of their having done so. In 1484 Marina Rodríguez told the Ciudad Real Inquisition that "she had often seen Beatriz González . . . carrying a hen or chicken in her skirt, and when she asked why . . . she replied: 'I am going to find someone to slaughter it for me.' 'Can't you kill it yourself?' She answered: 'May God keep me from doing something like that!'"[67] Another Ciudad Real witness claimed to know of a man "not from this city who was slaughtering beef in his home, and he thinks he was a Jew, and he saw Juan Escogido go there for meat."[68] Brianda Santángel [Teruel 1485] purchased food in the *judería* and had it brought to her house.[69]

Some men seem to have specialized in providing kosher meat for the new-Christian community. Antón López told the Ciudad Real Inquisition in 1484 that Garçia Barbas "was like a rabbi because he slaughtered meat for the *conversos*."[70] The Sorian new-Christian Juan de Salcedo reported to the Inquisition a conversation that had taken place some years before when he was still the community's kosher butcher. The *converso* Fernand Gomes had come to him saying, "My good friend Yontó, you have to do me a favor which I need very much. Some relatives of mine have come from Burgos, and you have to help me out with a couple of chickens. And you have to slaughter them with the same ceremony that the Jews use to slaughter chickens for themselves."[71]

Evidently many newly converted Jews would not even consider eating meat that had not been appropriately slaughtered by a Jewish butcher. The *converso* priest Fernando de la Barrera [Cuenca 1491] was accused of having his fowl slaughtered in the kosher fashion and of saying that "he wished God had favored him with allowing him to slaughter his food himself without having to find a Jew to do it for him."[72] Fernando de Trujillo said of María Díaz [Toledo 1484] that she "never ate meat unless its throat had been cut by the witness [who had not yet converted] or some other Jew who knew how to slaughter, and she would rather go without eating than to eat meat slaughtered by a Christian."[73]

The quality of kosher meat was such that some of these men had old-Christians as well as new-Christians as clients. The *converso* Gil de Gil Ruiz (called El Dentudo), a merchant, was denounced in 1486 in Teruel. Wherever he traveled in the region even his old-Christian customers knew that if they were going to pay him in meat or fowl they had to give the animals to him alive so that he could slaughter them according to the kosher practice.[74] In the 1480s in Segovia the powerful *converso* Diego Arias made fun of a Jew who did not know how to slaughter properly, and derisively showed him how to do it.[75] After the Expulsion many Judaizers butchered at home; sometimes one or two families in a community would act as butchers for the others.[76] Even two hundred years after the Expulsion some new-Christian communities were provisioned by men who functioned as professional kosher butchers. In Majorca in the 1670s specially trained ritual slaughterers would visit the houses of *chuetas* to slaughter their animals for them with the appropriate blessings (Braunstein 1936, 98).

According to the laws of *sheḥitah* the animal to be slaughtered must be free of any defect. The butcher examines the animal closely in a process called *bedikah* to make certain that it has no physical blemish or illness that would render it impure, or *terefah*. This practice was routine among newly converted Jews in the late fifteenth century. In a 1484 trial a witness stated how "through a hole the witness saw how in a corral of Juan Escogido's house they were slaughtering a cow and had it hanging open from a pole, and he saw how Juan Escogido and two other *conversos* were peering at it closely and then looking at each other."[77] Juan de Salcedo [Aranda de Duero 1502] reported that when he was young his uncle, Lezar Caballero, "used to slaughter goats and sheep and geese, and sometime Salcedo helped him, and that he checked them over to see that they were not impure."[78] After the passing of the Expulsion generation *bedikah* appears to have been rare, but occasionally, in a particularly well-informed crypto-Jewish community such as one that maintained contact with foreign Jews, the practice was continued. Juan Pacheco reported in Mexico [c. 1650] that Jews in Italy considered that any spots on the lungs rendered an animal *terefah* but that in Mexico minor spots were overlooked. Unclean meat was given to the Christians (Liebman 1982, 126). Salomón Machorro told the Mexican Inquisition in 1643 that he remembered how beef was slaughtered by the Jews he had known in Italy: "When they have cut the throat of a sheep or cow or other animal they open its chest cavity and look at its liver, lungs and heart, and if it is *caser* (which means clean) they eat it, and if it is *trefen* (which means dirty), the Catholics eat it."[79]

Kosher slaughtering strives to minimize the animal's suffering by killing it quickly and cleanly. Thus the knife used for slaughtering must be spotlessly clean and smooth, with no nicks on the blade. Traditionally before it is used it is tested by drawing it across the thumbnail. Many conversos were like Pedro Laínez [Almazán 1505], who "tested his knife on his nail before he slaughtered a kid."[80] In Toledo early in the sixteenth century it was said of Rodrigo Rofos that "when he slaughtered some steer or fowl he tested the knife by drawing it across his thumbnail and saying: 'Blessed be our Lord the Creator who raised you for the sustenance of mankind.' "[81] Many people kept special knives reserved for kosher slaughtering and passed them along in their families for generations. At Thomas Treviño de

Sobremonte's house [Mexico 1640s] "the chickens were decapitated with a knife that had been used at the table of his mother-in-law, Isabel Núñez" (Liebman 1974, 137). In the Rodríguez home [Canary Islands 1655] "all the birds eaten in the house have their heads cut off, either by Gonçalo Rodríguez or the slaves, and that before cutting off the heads they first try the knife on their nail" (Wolf 1926, 148). Rodrigo Henríquez de Fonseca, of Málaga, was accused [Chile 1655] of having advised a witness that "any foul that he ate he should see butchered so that they would not be *terefah*, and that he should take good care of the butchering knives and not entrust them to anyone."[82] A maid of Pedro Onofre Cortés [Majorca 1673] reported that he secretly kept a special knife, "like a folding razor," for slaughtering fowl. Sometimes a neighbor would come asking for "that thing," which the maid correctly—but to the family's alarm—interpreted as the butchering knife.[83] Unlike *bedikah*, which disappeared rather quickly, Judaizers kept special knives for kosher slaughtering until quite late in the assimilation process.

In kosher butchering the bird or animal is slaughtered by bending its neck backwards and then cutting its throat with one clean motion. This was so important to Judaizing *conversos* that in 1603 in Mexico Manuel Gil said that even in jail the *converso* Ruy Díaz Nieto would only eat fowl if [the *converso*] Hector de Fonseca had slaughtered it, and that he did so by slitting their throats (AGN Vol 276 doc 14, 412b). A generation later a witness told the Mexican Inquisition that Juan de León had instructed him how to slaughter fowl properly: "A chicken was to be slaughtered by taking its head in your hand and using a knife that was very well sharpened (so that the chicken would not feel pain); and sticking it three times in the dirt and repeating three times 'Blessed be He who raised you for my sustenance and who raised me for the earth,' looking toward where the sun rises."[84] Later León himself explained that "back in his land a priest cut the hen's throat; holding its head in his hand he cut its throat with a knife that had no point nor any nicks in its blade, its sharpness tested against the fingernail, by one cut down and back, and that the blood of the hen had to be covered up."[85]

After the throat was cut the blood was then drained out on the ground, not saved for puddings or sausages as the Christian butchers were accustomed to do. The spilled blood was generally covered with dirt until no sign of it remained. This method of slaughter was so common that it became a stock element in the anti-*converso* satiric literature of the late fifteenth century, such as the poem that twits the *converso* Antón de Montoro for Judaizing by eating only lamb that had been slaughtered by lifting its head up and cutting its throat.[86] The descriptions vary little over the years. Alonso de las Torres [Ciudad Real 1484] told how some fifteen years earlier he had seen Rodrigo Berengena "slaughtering some black rams and he saw that he cut their throats . . . and he dressed them like a butcher, wearing his linen apron. And when it was time to quarter them the elder Juan Falcón and some other *conversos* came into the courtyard and Rodrigo quartered the beast and gave each one a portion and they took their quarters and hid them under their capes and one by one set off to their houses."⁸⁷ Juana García [Ciudad Real 1511] reported how she saw "Pero Franco kill a goose in the middle of his corral with a drawn sword, and that he killed it by cutting its throat."⁸⁸ Diego Mora, of Quintanar de la Orden, was accused in 1589 of slaughtering cattle with a sharp knife and reciting "Blessed be he who created you for the sustenance of mankind."⁸⁹ In 1622 Diego Enríquez Villanueva was charged with having slaughtered a ram in the Judaic fashion: "Holding the ram from behind, he cut its throat, beginning at the level of its ears, the blood falling from one side toward the front" (Rose 1987, 60). Jews and most Judaizing *conversos* shunned animals that had been killed by strangling, which was the normal practice among Christians. In fact, as late as 1720 an *auto de fe* in Madrid identified twenty families whose Judaizing included abstaining from eating foul that had been slaughtered by strangling.⁹⁰

Kosher butchers routinely covered the spilled blood with dirt or with ashes. This custom was noted both in the early compilations of Judaizing practices⁹¹ and late fifteenth-century satiric poetry⁹² and persisted until quite late. Dona Lianor, a Brazilian *cristãa nova*, testified in Bahia in 1592 that once "a slave slit the throat of a hen in front of her door and that she ordered the blood to be covered with a little sawdust from the wood she had had sawed, but she did it because there was a pig rooting there and she did not want it to eat the blood."⁹³ Duarte Rodríguez said that he had seen Ruy Díaz Nieto [Mexico 1603] slaughter fowl by cutting their throats, and that he then covered up the spilled blood with earth.⁹⁴ A maid testified in Majorca in 1678 that when her master slaughtered fowl he took it up on the terrace roof or to an upstairs room and "put ashes in a plate or basin and there they drained the blood, and then they threw it out or left it there." In 1688 someone called "la Moyaneta" explained the custom this way: "blood was the animals' soul, and therefore God ordered it to be covered."⁹⁵

The last component of kosher slaughtering⁹⁶ was the special prayers kosher butchers recited during the act. These remained remarkably consistent over time. The most common were "Blessed be he who created you for the sustenance of humankind"⁹⁷ and "Blessed be the Lord who has created the slaughterhouse."⁹⁸ Variants of the first of these appear in the case of Bernardo Rodrigues [Bragança 1593]: "Blessed be the name of the Lord who created you to be born and to die; may He put me on the proper path, rescue and save me from the power of my enemies, as He freed the people of Israel from Egypt"; and "Blessed be the Lord who created you to die."⁹⁹ In Mexico in the 1640s Thomas Treviño de Sobremonte's mother-in-law Isabel Núñez reputedly "said three times, in accordance with similar ceremonies observed by her son-in-law and at his request, a certain ridiculous prayer over the chickens" (Liebman 1974, 137). In Majorca in the 1670s when covering the blood with ashes or sand this blessing was recited: "Blessed is Adonai, our God, King of the world, who sanctified us in His commandments and required the covering of the blood."¹⁰⁰

In fact, among Judaizing *conversos* all these customs remained in use through the seventeenth century, and there are similar instances from later times. Even families that had abandoned most other Judaizing practices sometimes continued to slaughter fowl in the Jewish fashion and to avoid eating fowl that had been strangled.

## 19.3. HOME KOSHERING OF MEAT

As we have seen, in order to fulfill the requirements of the dietary laws meat must have been slaughtered in the prescribed fashion. Such meat was referred to generically as kosher meat. Meat purchased from a Jewish butcher shop was assumed to be kosher. Early Inquisition trial testimony in Soria abounds with references to kosher meat. Gonzalo the butcher of Soria used to eat "kosher meat and food" with his Jewish friends Ysaque and Mazaltó Serrano. Ruy García bought "kosher meat" from the Jew Abraén Aluo. The *converso* Diego Hernández de los Palaçios was accused of eating "kosher food" with his friend the physician Yuçé.[101]

But the matter did not rest with mere purchase. Kosher rules required that meat be specially treated before it was cooked. Because Leviticus 17:11 states that "the life of the flesh is in the blood," kosher rules prohibit the consumption of blood.[102] It was for that reason that the Coimbra Inquisition highlighted the aversion of many Judaizers to eating meat that was undercooked, or *verde*,[103] and that Luis de Carvajal told the Mexican Inquisition in 1589 that his father would not let him eat blood sausage.[104] Abhorrence of bloody meat was constant, although crypto-Jews rationalized it in a variety of ways. Beatriz Gonçalves [Coimbra 1583] reportedly "washed and salted and rinsed her meat to draw out all the blood, because she considered it a sin to eat blood."[105] Several Judaizers sentenced by the Coimbra Inquisition between 1567 and 1583, such as Felipa de Mesquita, of Vila Real, in 1571, were accused of not eating animal blood because, they said, "when anyone appeared before God with blood on his hands He would know who had been eating blood."[106]

Blood was most commonly removed by soaking the meat in several baths of water and then salting it. María Alvarez was accused in 1505 of "having her meat soaked five or six times until it became lean, and white, and dead looking."[107] Blanca Ramírez [Toledo 1523] was denounced for washing her meat three times.[108] In 1501 testimony María Alvarez said that "so that meat would not be spoiled she washed it and salted it, sometimes hanging in the air, and sometimes in a basket, although she did not do it for ceremonial reasons."[109] A *conversa* named Beatriz [Cuenca 1622] was accused of eating only the breast meat of fowl and of soaking it in water to cleanse it of blood (Blázquez Miguel 1985a, 68). Filipa Fernandes, of Seia [Coimbra 1583], allegedly "washed in the Jewish fashion the meat that came from the butcher shop in order to remove all the blood because eating it was a sin."[110] An *auto de fe* in Madrid in 1720 identified twenty families whose Judaizing included abstaining from eating meat that still had blood in it.[111] In the early years of this century Schwarz reported that Portuguese Judaizers salted and drained the blood out of the meat they prepared (1925, 17). In 1952 Machado reported a reminiscence of this custom among reputedly new-Christian villagers in the Mogadouro region who "do not eat meat the day the animal is killed, but first they cleanse it of all blood with repeated washings." Unlike other villagers, "when they kill a pig [!] they do not make use of the blood" (Machado 1952, 22). An anonymous self-proclaimed Marrano contributor to *Avotaynu* in 1989 recalled that in his Cuban grandfather's house "we washed and salted meat" (Anonymous, *Avotaynu* 1989, S5).

In addition to being free of blood, for meat to be kosher all excess fat (*chelev*) had to be trimmed away (Lev. 3:17, 7:23–5). A late fifteenth-century text describes how "removing the fat from meat and abstaining from eating it recalls how the people of Israel used to make a sacrifice to God of the fat, throwing a piece of fat the size of a walnut into the fire; and these pieces of fat were commonly taken from the loin and haunch of the beef before putting it in the cooking pot, as is written in the passages about sacrifice."[112] María Alvarez [Almazán 1505] stood over her kitchen maids until they had removed every trace of fat from the meat they were going to cook.[113] In Mexico City in 1603 Captain Lemos described how one day he had visited a new-Christian neighbor. "He went to light the brazier and warm the room in Violante Rodríguez's house, and he found a pile of pieces of fat she had removed from the meat, and he went back to Miguel Gil's room crossing himself and saying: 'This Duarte Rodríguez is a real devil.' "[114]

A third process, called porging, was required to render certain cuts of meat perfectly kosher. As explained in the late fifteenth century, "removing the sciatic vein from the legs of cattle, before they are cooked, is in remembrance of when the Angel fought with Jacob and he was left lame; and because of this the children of Israel do not eat the nerve in the leg nor the fat which is connected to it, which is the sciatic vein, as is written at the end of Genesis."[115] In Teruel in 1485 the *converso* cleric Mosén Juan Ram was accused of ordering the sciatic vein removed with the explanation that "whoever eats it goes crazy."[116] Frequently Inquisition testimony describes porging in some detail. Aldonza Laínez [Almazán 1505] was accused of de-veining a leg of lamb. "Seated at the entrance to her . . . kitchen, she had on her knees, over her skirt, a white linen cloth, and on it was a round leg of mutton or goat, and she had a knife next to her with which she had cut it through the middle, and with her fingernails or fingers she was taking off the fat and the large vein."[117] A butcher in Galicia testified that the *converso* Diego de Chaves "bought a steer from him to make beef jerky and when he had taken it home to cut it up his wife Felipa Ruiz asked him to open the leg up and take out the vein." Her husband reacted with fright and "drew her aside and told her that she should not say that in front of the butcher, although the witness heard it, and they told him not to take out the vein at which the witness stopped, although he had begun to remove it and it seemed to him a bad thing. . . . Since then he has considered it a Jewish custom."[118]

Several Brazilian witnesses told the Inquisition in Bahia in 1591–2 that they porged their meat but did not know it was a Jewish custom; rather, they thought it made the meat taste better. The *cristãa nova* Maria Lopez said that she even porged pork! "When she roasted the hind quarter of a lamb or a pig she ordered the vein removed so that it would roast better and be more tender and would not be contaminated by the congealed blood in the vein."[119] Given how often this custom is described in the documents, it may have been the most commonly followed of the kosher practices, or at least the one most observed by vigilant old-Christians.[120] But, for that matter, most of the koshering procedures remained in at least sporadic use among crypto-Jews well into the seventeenth century.[121]

## 19.4. Baking

Traditional Jewish bakers remove a pinch of dough and cast it with an appropriate blessing into the fire. The separation of this piece of dough the size of an olive, called the *ḥallah*, is prescribed in the Talmud (Shab. 2:6) and the *Shulḥan Arukh* (OH 457). As a late fifteenth-century compilation of Judaizing customs described it, "when they knead dough, they take off a piece of the dough and throw it into the fire to burn as a sacrifice. . . . The rabbi says that throwing a piece of dough in the fire is in memory of the bread that the people of Israel were obliged to give to the High Priest in sacrifice. It was one piece of bread every time that they baked in memory of the priesthood that the people of Israel lost. They used to take two handfuls of the dough and offer it to the High Priest; and when the priesthood was lost, they did it in commemoration."[122]

This custom appears to have been universal among Iberian Jews at the time of the Expulsion and was common for the next half-century or so. In a 1489 trial it was said that Elvira Sánchez "threw bits of dough into the fire when she made bread, saying as a good Jewess says: 'Blessed are You, Adonai, who commanded us according to your commandments and ordered us to make the sacrifice of the dough.'"[123] In a 1490 trial Violante González was accused of throwing "bits of the first kneaded dough into the fire in memory of the first things that the Old Testament ordered given to the priests."[124]

The separation of the *ḥallah* seems to have been practiced sporadically for the next hundred and fifty years. Several Judaizers sentenced by the Coimbra Inquisition between 1567 and 1583, such as Beatriz Rodrigues, of Lamego, in 1569, were accused of throwing exactly three bits of dough into the fire.[125] *Chuetas* in Majorca in the 1670s would throw a bit of bread dough into the fire with a prayer to God to make the bread rise.[126] There are even echoes of the custom among modern crypto-Jews. Schwarz found twentieth-century Portuguese Judaizers throwing a bit of their *matza* dough into the fire. He reported that they bless their ordinary bread dough with these words: "Blessed is my Lord, my God, my Adonai, who commands us with His blessed and holy commandments to knead this bread, for the mouth of the lion, as our brothers did in the Holy Promised Land."[127]

Normative Judaism requires the baking of a special bread for the Sabbath and the placing of two loaves on the Sabbath table. Surprisingly, neither of these customs finds its way into the documentary record. There are two possible explanations. One is that they were not widely practiced in pre-Expulsion Iberia, or at least not practiced among crypto-Jews, even those of the first generation. The other is that the practice was so ordinary as not to be considered specifically Jewish or to attract the attention of the Inquisition.

## 19.5. WINE

Although Jewish tradition prescribes no particular method for koshering wine, generally accepted practice is that in order to be considered kosher every step of the wine making process must be in the hands of Jews. References to Jewish wine abound in trials of the first generation of converts but rarely provide the sort of detail that would lead to insights about *converso* wine making. One report states that in Toledo prior to the Expulsion *conversos* would sometimes "have some Jewish man or woman come to the house to press the grapes in the vat so that the wine would be kosher."[128] But in most early Inquisition trial testimony in cities such as Soria, the abundant references to kosher wine do not go beyond mere mention of it. Antón de Ríos, the abbot of San Gil, played cards with his friends one afternoon and "drank kosher wine." One Sabbath Diego Garçia was reported to have "drunk wine that had been blessed."[129] In a 1520s trial a *conversa* from Hita was accused of "drinking home-made wine according to Jewish rite."[130] Edicts of Faith, such as the one published in Mexico in 1639, frequently cite among the Judaizers' customs "drinking *caser* wine" (Liebman 1970, 97), but specific references to kosher wine in trial testimony after the passing of the Expulsion generation are uncommon.

## 19.6. OTHER CRYPTO-JEWISH DISHES

In addition to the special Sabbath and holiday dishes, which have been described in their respective chapters, the crypto-Jews of the Iberian world cherished a number of other traditional recipes. References to these dishes are scattered throughout Inquisition documents. Some appear to have been quite common; others are mentioned only once or twice. On the whole these dishes share two characteristics. At some point in time some individual identified them as indicative of Judaizing tendencies. And today the majority of them are common in the repertoire of Hispanic or Portuguese cuisine. The inference is that none of these dishes was exclusive to Iberia's Jewish population, though at the time of the Expulsion they may have played a particularly large role in the diets of Jewish and *converso* families.

*Alfajor* (almond cookie), a cookie made of compressed almonds, walnuts and honey. According to Liebman it was popular among new-Christians in Mexico in the early seventeenth century (1970, 81). These cookies, common throughout Spain, were defined by Covarrubias in 1611 as "a certain paste made by the Moors of bread crumbs, honey, and spices."[131]

*Array hoja.* When the *converso* Sancho Cavallero remarked in 1527 in Las Palmas that he had never eaten a better tasting dish than *array hoja*, Ruy Gonçales told Inquisitors that "the dish in question is a Jewish dish of which deponent has heard the Jews in Saffi speak; especially as the said Cavallero is a convert, and the grandson, so deponent has heard, of a person condemned by the Inquisition" (Wolf 1926, 80). I do not know to what this name refers.

*Azucaque* (sugar cake). In 1491 Pedro Abella, of Barbastro, was accused of having sugar cakes and nougat candy brought from the Jewish quarter; he would eat them only if Jewish women had prepared them.[132]

Eggplant. *Conversos* were frequently accused of eating "casseroles of eggplant with eggs."[133] Eggplant as a Jewish dish appears frequently in the satirical *cancioneros* of the late fifteenth century, such as in the mid-fifteenth-century burlesque poem on the "Wedding of Rodrigo Cota," where the guests are served "lots of eggplant and Swiss chard seasoned with saffron."[134] In a satiric poem the Count of Paredes said that when the *converso* poet Juan de Valladolid kissed the paten (the silver tray used at mass to carry the consecrated host) it miraculously became an eggplant stew.[135]

Eggs cooked with onions. In Soria around the time of the Expulsion *conversos* prepared eggs by boiling them in wooden pots with onion skins.[136]

Fried bread crumbs. Master Bernal and his wife [Almazán 1505] allegedly made "*cuez* bread in this fashion: they put coriander in a frying pan with garlic and ground spices and water and oil and threw in bread crumbs and green coriander, and stirred it up and from that made *cuez* bread for Saturdays and Fridays."[137]

Meatballs. The *conversa* Beatriz Laínez [Almazán 1505] reputedly "chopped up raw meat and threw it in a mortar with spices and some eggs and blended it, and when it was blended they formed it into round balls and they fried them in a pan with oil or in a pot and they called them *albondequexos*.[138]

Meat pies. Beatriz Laínez [Almazán 1503] also "would take lamb tripe and chopped snout, throw in hard-boiled eggs with the whites chopped and the yolks whole, and with them make some pies which they put on to cook, and they ate them on Saturdays and other days when meat was permitted."[139] In Soria *conversos* made special *empanadas* called *haravehuelas* from the cow's spleen (*baxo*) and spices.[140]

Onions. Onions with a spicy sauce were a favorite dish among *conversos* in Castile in the 1480s.[141]

Radishes. A late fifteenth-century satiric poem from Román against the *converso* poet Antón de Montoro lists among the foods considered indicative of his Judaizing radishes and stuffed peppers.[142]

Sausage. According to her maid, who testified in 1505, Angelina de León, a *conversa* of Almazán, used to make a sausage called *cabaheas* (or sometimes *longanizas*) in this way: "On Sunday nights she set the heads of steers and goats to stew; and after they were cooked . . . [she] chopped them finely and stuffed them into goat tripe and smoked them; and later she ate them."[143] Twentieth-century Portuguese new-Christians make a sausage called *tabafeiras* or *alheiras*,[144] stuffing ground beef into cow tripe. No pork is used at all (Paulo 1970, 88).

Swiss chard. María Alvarez [Almazán 1505] allegedly prepared "Swiss chard, parboiling it in water and then frying it with onions in oil, and then boiling it again in the oil. And then she threw in water and grated bread crumbs and spices and egg yolks; and she cooked it until it got very thick."[145]

# NOTES

1. A useful introduction to Jewish dietary practices can be found in the *Enc. Jud.*

2. *La carne trefa, que es quando la res tiene una bela appegada del liviano en el costado de la res, significa que hera mandamiento en la ley judayca, que no comiessen carne muerta; y ansí no la comían, ni res que tuviesse sangre en el cuerpo; porque la res mortecina siempre acostumbra a tener sangre en el cuerpo* (Santa María 1893c, 184).

3. *Que si alguna carnera fallaua trefe, que non comian de aquella carne* (Beinart 1974, 292).

4. *Trayan a vender vna gallina e estava vn poco lysiada, e dixeron a su moço . . . que non la conprase* (Carrete/Fraile 1987, 91; cf. 323). See also Beinart 1977a, 152 [Ciudad Real 1483]; Carrete Parrondo 1979, 52 [Cuenca 1489]; 1985, 141 [Soria 1501]; Liebman 1975, 178 [Lima 1656].

5. *Não se havia de comer a carne da rez que morresse porque tinha o sangue dentro de si* (Pereira 1979, 190).

6. *Tinha nojo e asco as galinhas e a qualquer outra ave que moria de doença* (Furtado 1925, 32).

7. *Cogia vna gallina toda prieta, que ni vna plumita tenia blanca* (Nunemaker 1946, 25). See also Liebman 1982, 105; García 1910, 110.

8. *Su ama no come anguila ni pulpo ni liebre ni conejo ni congrio . . . salvo desde la Quaresma aca . . . porque estaba su reuerençia . . . por esta tierra* (Beinart 1981a, 398).

9. *No comia toçino, ni liebre, ni congrio, ni angila, ni perdises ahogadas* (Moreno Koch 1977, 359). See also Llorca 1935, 23 [Valencia 1487]; Beinart 1975, 650; 1981b, 398 [Ciudad Real]; Uchmany 1982, 89 [Philippines]; Saraiva 1969, 164 [Portugal 1536]; García de Proodian 1966, 432 [Lima 1636]; Selke de Sánchez 1972, 174 [Majorca 1688]; Silva 1896, 31 [Lisbon 1726].

10. *En la boda desta aljama / no se comió peliagudo / ni pescado sin escama* (Gómez-Menor Fuentes 1970, 105).

11. *Não comia coelho nem enguia por que lhe tinha nojo* (Furtado 1929, 153). See also 176, 456; Fita y Colomé 1892, 501 [Ciudad Real 1484]; Azevedo Mea 1982, 39, 46, etc. [Coimbra 1570s].

12. *En el dicho tienpo nunca les vio comer pulpo, ni anguila, ni otro ninguno pescado syn escamas* (Beinart 1977a, 164). See also López Martínez 1954, 184 [Castile 1490s]; Carrete/Fraile 1987, 86 [Almazán 1500s]; Azevedo Mea 1982, 178, 186, 286 [Coimbra 1570s]; Liebman 1975, 163 [Cartagena, Colombia 1636]; 179 [Lima 1655].

13. *Su madre le dixo como por observansia de la dicha ley de Moysen no se hauia de comer pescado con escamas pero que este confessante nunca reparo cuando se lo dauan a comer si tenia escamas o no* (AGN Vol 402 doc 2, 506a).

14. *Estava zombando. Aquele peixe não se pode comer. —Porquê? —Porque é defeso. —Em que Lei? —Na de Moisés. Não sois vós judeu? —Sim,—teria respondido o teólogo. —E na Lei de Moisés espero de me salvar* (Coelho 1987, 211).

15. *Que nunca a comera nem havia de comer. E que não era porco para comer carne de porco como os cristãos-velhos* (Coelho 1987, 207). See also García 1910, 217 [Mexico 1648].

16. *Ni comer tocino, ni otras cosas de puerco; porque el animal que rumiaba la comida se habia de comer, y no el que no la rumiaba, como el puerco* (Toro 1932, 243).

17. *Lo que habían de escrupulear, sólo era el comer tocino, poque los puercos eran hombres malditos de Dios y que hasta que los volviesen a bendecir, no se podían comer* (García 1910, 59).

18. Sicroff 1965, 98. See also Carrete Parrondo 1985a, 116 [Soria c. 1500]; Liebman 1974, 93 [Mexico 1649].

19. *O pae da testemunha vendia carne de porco, vacca e carneiro e Catharina Fernandes nunca lhe comprava senão de vacca e carneiro.* She added that Catharina claimed that pork upset her stomach: *e que quando, d'uma vez entrou em casa da testemunha e vio toucinho disse que se lhe embrulhava o estomago* (Baião 1921, 116).

20. *Não comendo carne de porco nem outra cousa com que ella se cozesse, antes a cozia apartada em huma panella pera a gente de casa e tinha panella apartada em que fazia o seu comer sem ella e tigellas apartadas em que comia, as quais se não lavavão com a outra louça, a dizia que a não comia porque a defendia a sua lei* (Azevedo Mea 1982, 452; cf. 307, etc.).

21. *Aviendo la que testifica hechado una vez un torrezno en la olla, y sacándole para comer, viéndolo la dicha Blanca Duarte mandó a la que testifica que se apartase de donde ella estaba para comerlo, y luego la dicha testificada tomó la cuchara con que se sacó el torrezno y la quemó, y quebró la olla en que se coció* (Sierro Malmierca 1990, 93).

22. Wolf 1926, 105. See also Liebman 1970, 176 [Mexico]; 1975, 163 [Cartagena, Colombia 1636].

23. *Solo comia pasas y almendras y algunas cosas de conserua* (AGN Vol 276 doc 14, 413b).

24. *Con desplazer y malenconya . . . Judios tenemos en casa mia, judios tenemos en casa mia* (Marín Padilla 1982, 247). See also Furtado 1925, 414 [Brazil 1590s].

25. *Y entre otras cosas que sacaron para comer fue un guisado con morçilla de puerco, y uno dellos . . . quería comer del dicho guisado, y el otro . . . le dixo: Aquí ay morçilla de puerco. Y no comieron del dicho guisado sino pescado y fruta que tenían. Y el dicho Antonio de Puigdorfila les dezía que ¿por qué no comeis desto?, y que comiessen los tales por quales Judíos. Y ellos dezían que les haría mal; y los demás que estavan presentes se reyan y dezían unos a otros: ¡Miren los Judíos que no an querido comer del guisado!* (Selke de Sánchez 1972, 84).

26. *No comía toçino, pero comía de lo que se guisaua con ello, e desya que sy le ponían vn plato de toçino e allí vna hoguera que ante se dexaría echar dinero a la hoguera que comer del toçino, e que sy no fuese por el desir de las gentes que no comería de lo que se guisase con ello* (Carrete Parrondo 1985a, 119).

27. *La carne guisaban con aceite, ca lo echaban en lugar de tocino e de grosura por escusar el tocino; y el aceite con la carne es cosa que hace muy mal oler el resuello; y ansí sus casas e puertas hedían muy mal a aquellos manjarejos* (López Martínez 1954, 183). For other evidence of the preference for oil see Contreras 1982, 601 [Galicia 1600s]; Blázquez Miguel 1989, 195 [Toledo 1580]; Furtado 1925, 261, 360, 493; 1929, 352 [Brazil 1590s]; Liebman 1970, 78, 200 [Mexico].

28. Wolf 1926, 86. The difference was so striking that *conversos* sometimes used it to discern whether a new acquaintance was a Judaizer. A realistic though fictional example occurs in Francisco Delicado's novel *La Lozana andaluza*, discussed in Chapter 21.

29. *No comer tocino manteca ni cossa de puerco, y en lugar de tocino hecha en la olla azeite* (AGN Vol 271 doc 1, 1b).

30. *Freir seys huebos y pescados cozido con azeyte y vinagre, y otros guissados quaresmales, con azeite* (AGN Vol 276, doc 14, 425b-6a).

31. Cortés 1985, 285. See also Selke de Sánchez 1972, 96; Lewin 1954, 152 [Mexico 1647].

32. The phenomenon was noted even among converts to Christianity in Visigothic times. In 654 CE converted Jews in Spain presented a memorial to the Christian King Recceswinth of Toledo, stating that "with regard to the flesh of animals which we consider unclean, if we should be unable to eat the same on account of our ancient prejudices, nevertheless, when it is cooked along with other food, we hereby promise to partake of the latter with no manifestation of disgust or horror" (Marcus 1960, 21). This phenomenon was recognized by the sixteenth-century Jewish historian Solomon ibn Verga when he wrote in the *Staff of Judah* that "all food to which man is not accustomed is rejected when it is presented to him, and his natural inclination is to detest it. If one were to tell a Christian to eat dog or cat meat, he would vomit and flee from it the way a Jew flees from pork" (cited by Gilman 1972, 75).

33. *Digo que non comía toçino salvo de poco acá, porque me reñía sobre ello mi marido; y desíale que lo fasía porque me fasía mucho mal a los pechos* (Fita y Colomé 1893, 291).

34. *Nam comia toucinho por lhe ser danoso aos olhos* (J. Azevedo 1921, 450). See also Coelho 1987, 208.

35. *Tenia escrupulo de comer de la olla donde se echava toçino con achaque de dezir que tenia un rrama de asma. . . . Alguna vez avia dexado de comer toçino por ser tocada de asma.*

36. *La rea comia pocas vezes toçino y las vezes que se echava en la olla no comia el caldo porque deçia que tenia perlesia* (Bel Bravo 1988, 107). See also García Fuentes 1981, 474.

37. *Asando este testigo . . . vn poco de toçino . . . estaua allí al fuego . . . su ama, e vido este testigo cómo se puso la toca delante de las narises por el olor del toçino, por que . . . su ama dixo: "Ese güesmo dese toçino se me entra en la garganta adelante"* (Carrete/Fraile 1987, 66, 30; cf. 20). See also Sierro Malmierca 1990, 130 [Ciudad Rodrigo 1588].

38. *Sy veya asar toçino se apartaba de alli e se metia en vna camara, en donde se ençerraua e atapaua todos los agujeros porque non hentrase el olor del toçino* (Cantera/Carrete 1975, 188).

39. *Por los achaques que padecía de hipocondría y mal de ojos . . . que el médico le había dicho que no comiesse toçino ni cossas fuertes . . . como conexo, tordos, ni pescado sin escama* (Selke de Sánchez 1972, 119).

40. *No comian tocino y quando comian delante de algunas personas por no dar nota de comerlo hazian que lo comian y disimuladamente lo echavan debaxo de la mesa* (García Fuentes 1981, 149).

41. *Le empresentaron cinco o siete perniles de tocino y esta deposante los toco, que estaban dentro en una talega . . . mas de ocho dias que no quiso comer nada que esta deposante tocase, y no*

*queria que nadie la sirviese sino ella misma* (Sánchez Moya 1972, 132). For similar cases see Azevedo Mea 1982, 26, 39, etc. [Coimbra 1570s]; Blázquez Miguel 1986a, 79 [Castile 1649]. Although abstention from eating pork was the norm among Judaizing *conversos*, Blázquez Miguel cites the case of Beatriz González, of Almagro, burned in 1497, who was fond of eating bacon, which she said she did for health reasons (1984, 12).

42. *Que quando algund moço partía algún toçino mandaua linpiar e lauar y avn escaldar el tal cañiuete* (Carrete/Fraile 1987, 21; cf. 43, 64, 66, 74). See also Fita y Colomé 1893, 299 [1485].

43. *Catalina Laynes mandaua a este testigo que pusiese vna olla para ella e para . . . Aluaro de Luna e otra para este testigo e para los moços de casa, e que no echase toçino en la olla que se guisaua para ella e su marido, saluo carne e algunas veses garuanços e verdura otras veses; e que le mandaua pusiese en aquella olla vna cuchara de palo e en la otra vna cuchara de fierro, e que no llegase la cuchara de la vna olla en la otra* (Carrete/Fraile 1987, 91; cf. 27). See also Beinart 1981b, 555.

44. "*Guárdeme Dios, e yo lo avía de comer; e quando voy a las aldeas liebo mi carne cozida e mi cuchillo por no tener que hazer con ellos." E esto desya por los christianos viejos. . . . Desya . . . que sy no tenía carne cozida que no la lleuaba cruda por no asarla en los asadores de los christianos. E desya que conpraua huevos e los comía asados por no haserlos en su sartén. E que los labradores le rogauan que comiese de su olla e quél les desya questaua doliente por no comer dello* (Carrete Parrondo 1985a, 176).

45. *Dexan de comer carnero en los dias que se matan los tocinos porque se matan en la misma carniceria y se cortan en las mismas tablas* (Braunstein 1936, 186). In the minds of many Christians, avoidance of pork became emblematic of the crypto-Jews, as abundant references in sixteenth- and seventeenth-century literature attest.

46. *¡Oh, Ropero, amargo, triste, / que non sientes tu dolor! . . . / Setenta años que naciste / y en todos ellos disixte: / inviolata permansiste . . . / Nunca juré al Criador. / Fize el Credo, e adorar, / Ollas de tocino grueso / torreznos a medio asar, / oír misas e rezar, / sanctiguar e persinar, / e nunca pude matar / este rastro de confeso* (Rodríguez Puértolas 1968, 316).

47. *La dicha Ana de Medina, cuando hablaba con los cristianos viejos decía que comía tocino y daba a entender lo bien que le sabía un torrezno* (Contreras 1982, 601).

48. *Este testigo no comia carne de los christianos, saluo caxer, e traya carne de las carneçerias de los christianos por haser muestra a las gentes, e despues lo hechauan a los puercos* (Beinart 1981b, 566).

49. *No come toçino ni de la vianda que con ello se guisa, avnque mata puercos en su casa, e fase guisar su olla aparte* (Carrete Parrondo 1985a, 149).

50. *Não comer carne de porco nem se cozer em sua casa, e se alguma pesoa lha dava ou ella a pedia era pera dar a entender que a comia e depois a tornava a dar a pesoas de fora* (Azevedo Mea 1982, 363).

51. Uchmany 1982, 99. See also Lewin 1954, 128 [Mexico 1624].

52. *No comían tocino ni aves ahogadas; aunque cuando estaban en México en casa del dicho Jorge de Almeida, lo echaban en la olla y lo comían, por estar en casa agena y no ser sentidos* (Toro 1932, 256).

53. *Comiendo en casa de cierto judío rico, en esta ciudad, veía que ponían en la mesa jamón asado; tuvo sumo pesar y le causaba horror, hasta que supo que era judío y que por sólo cumplimiento y por si entrase algún católico y lo viese, se ponía en la mesa* (García 1910, 85).

54. *Todos los de la carcel perpetua, ecepto el dicho Rui Diaz comen tocino. . . . Los demas judios hazen mucha ostentacion del tocino y le llaman executoria, y quando lo quieren comer lo pi-*

*den, diziendo: Daca essa executoria, y aunque no comieran el dicho tocino era fuerça comerle aquel dia por cumplir con los conuidados y en particular con el dho Pedro de Fonseca ministro de este Santo Oficio* (AGN Vol 276 doc 14, 432a).

55. *No quiso tomar el quarto trasero, syno el delantero . . . no lo haze por otro synon porquel quarto delantero non lo purgan ellos como el trasero* (Carrete Parrondo 1985a, 141).

56. *Não comya . . . o quarto trazeiro do carneiro por ceremonia judaica* (Azevedo Mea 1982, 113).

57. *Vio que todas las vezes que trayan carne del quarto traso a casa de los dichos sus amos* (Beinart 1981b, 384; cf. 398).

58. *Su padre mandaua al negrito Luis que fuese al rastro y traxese para comer en casa quartos traceros de carnero* (Nunemaker 1946, 45). See also Azevedo Mea 1982, 4, 6, etc. [Coimbra 1570s].

59. *Nem menos comia queijo quando comia carne, por ter para si que era peccado come lo* (Azevedo Mea 1982, 439).

60. *Los platos y escudillas en que los dichos sus amos comian no querian que este testigo ni la dicha Françisca los fregase con el estropajo con que este testigo y la dicha esclaua fregauan los platos e escudillas en que ellos comian* (Beinart 1981b, 556).

61. *E que tenian su olla e cocharas y escudillas aparte, e su jarro que non llegava nadie a ello syno las susodichas; e que sy alguno veuia agua con el dicho jarro que tenian apartado, que luego las susodichas mandavan traer otro jarron nuevo de la plaça para beuer* (Beinart 1977a, 163). See also Beinart 1981b, 555; Fita y Colomé 1892, 516 [Ciudad Real 1484]; Carrete Parrondo 1985a, 36 [Soria 1490]; López Martínez 1954, 184; Liebman 1975, 75 [Mexico 1649].

62. *No beber sino fuere en su cassa con su jarro. . . . Dixo . . . que venia muerto de sed por que en todo el dia no auia veuido gota de agua aunque auia tenido gran necesidad della, y diziendole este, pues falta la agua en la ciudad y en las casas donde ha entrado, respondio el dho Ruy Diaz en lengua Portuguessa, Vendicta sexa ha grandeza de Ho señor que ate agora no he veuido por jarro de otra persoha despues que estoy en esta terra* (AGN Vol 271 doc 1, 2b; Vol 276 doc 14, 418a, 415a).

63. *E que no consintian que sus camisas ni manteles se lavasen con las de los moços y este avia ni con la ropa deste testigo, syno aparte* (Beinart 1977a, 163).

64. *Quemar las ollas e tanbién los asadores e cochillos en que auía de guisar e de comer* (León Tello 1972, 72). Cf. Rábade Obradó 1990a, 47 [Toledo 1485–1500].

65. *No le avía querido tomar ni le tomó fasta que ge lo escaldaron* (Carrete Parrondo 1985a, 176).

66. For example, a late fifteenth-century satiric poem from Román against the *converso* poet Antón de Montoro lists among his Judaizing customs that he only used unbroken pots (*Olla que no quiebre*) (Castillo 1882, poem #994).

67. *Vido a la dicha Beatris Gonsales . . . muchas veses llevar en la falda vna gallina o pollo, y preguntabale este testigo que para que traya en la falda aquel pollo o gallina, desia ella: Vo a buscar quien me la mate. Desia este testigo: ¿Vos non la podeys matar? Desia ella: ¡Guardame el Señor que tal fiçiese!* (Beinart 1974, 469).

68. *Sabe que mataba en su casa carne un honbre que no era desta çibdad, y que cree que era judío, e que vido yr allí por carne a Juan Escogido* (Santa María 1893a, 200–1).

69. *Comiendo carne y hamín o otros comeres judaicos ansí guisados en las casas de sus padres y madres, . . . como enviados de la judería. . . . Algunas veces enviaban seis dineros o medio real a la judería para que les guisasen manjares e ge los truxesen los judíos a sus casas para el sábado. E que ansí mismo compraban carne de la judería* (Sánchez Moya 1972–3, 158, 166).

70. Era como Rabi, porque mataba carne para los confesos (Beinart 1974, 574).

71. Muy buen amigo Yontó, vna merçed me avéys de faser, que estó en grande neçesidad, que me an venido vnos parientes míos de Burgos, que me avéys de socorrer con vn par de gallinas en todo caso; e más avéys de faser, que las avéys de degollar con la misma cerimonia que los judíos acostunbrauan degollarlas para sy mismos (Carrete Parrondo 1985a, 122).

72. Plugiera a Dios que me hiziera tan dichoso que pudiera yo degollar la vianda que tengo de comer syn buscar judío para me la degollar (Carrete Parrondo 1979, 56).

73. Non comia carne, saluo degollada de mano de este testigo o de otro judio que supiese degollar, e antes estaua sin la comer que non averla de comer de mano de christiano (Beinart 1974, 58). See also Coelho 1987, 208 [1570s].

74. Sánchez Moya/Monasterio Aspiri 1973, 127. See also Monter 1990, 156 [Alava 1573].

75. Ben aca necio que en esto mas se yo que no tu y que tomara el dicho diego arias el pollo en su mano y ge lo mostrara de la manera que los judios lo deguellan (Gutwirth 1981, 97).

76. For a discussion of kosher butchering in Ciudad Real around the time of the Expulsion see Beinart 1981a, 281–7.

77. Vido este testigo por un agujero como en las casas de Juan Escogido en el corral estava una Res degollada e abierta colgada de un palo, que vido cómo el dicho Juan Escogido e otros dos conversos la estaban mirando e atentando e mirándose el uno al otro (Santa María 1893a, 200).

78. En casa de Lezar Cavallero, tyo deste testigo, que matauan los cabritos e a las vezes carneros e ansarones, e a las veses los mataba este testigo, e que los cataba por trefés (Carrete Parrondo 1985a, 151).

79. Degollado el carnero o vaca u otro animal, le abren el pecho y lo ven el hígado, bofes y corazón, y si está caser (que es limpio) lo comen, y si está trefen (que es sucio), lo comen los del pueblo católico (Lewin 1977, 277).

80. Vido a Pero Laynes catar el cochillo en la vña antes que matase vn cabrito (Carrete/Fraile 1987, 71).

81. Quando alguna res e ave degollaua, tentaua el cuchillo en la vña e las atrauesaua e desya: bendito Nuestro Sennor el Criador que te crió para mantenimiento del mundo (León Tello 1972, 72). See also Blázquez Miguel 1985a, 599 [1491]; Liebman 1970, 77, 96, 245 [Mexico 1629].

82. Que le había dicho que las aves que comiese las hiciese matar delante de sí y que no estuviesen trefes, y guarde los cuchillos con que se degollasen, que no los fiase de nadie (Medina 1890, 252).

83. A modo de una navaja que se doblaba . . . lo guardava con mucho cuydado, recatándose de ella. . . . "Dexadme aquello." . . . "¡El cuchillo pide!' . . . "¡Que te metes en cuchillo! ¿Qué saves tú desto?" (Selke de Sánchez 1972, 87).

84. Las gallinas se habían de degollar teniéndoles la cabeza en la mano e hincando el cuchillo muy bien afilado (porque no pene la gallina) tres veces en la tierra y diciendo tres veces Bendito sea Aquel que te crió para sustento mío y a mí para la tierra, mirando hacia la parte donde nace el sol (Lewin 1977, 250). Cf. Liebman 1970, 245.

85. En su tierra los degollaba [el] sacerdote, teniéndole[s] la cabeza en la mano los degüellan con cuchillo, sin mella y sin punta, probado en la uña con un ido y venido, cubriendo con tierra la sangre de la gallina (Lewin 1977, 277).

86. Trobar en ser carnicero / como la ley ordenó; / trobar en comer carnero, / degollado car' al Dió / qual vuestro padre comió (Castillo 1882, poem #994).

87. Estaba degollando dos carneros prietos, y que vio que los degollo . . . e adobo como carniçero, con su abantal de lienço puesto delante; e que a tiempo de quartear los carneros, que entro el dicho Juan Falcon el uiejo e otros conuersos con el, y los quarteo el dicho Rodrigo e dio a cada

vno su quarto en la mano; y ellos tomaron sus quartos e metieronlos baxo de las capas y fueronse vno a vno, cada vno camino de su casa (Beinart 1974, 558).

88. *Vio este testigo como el dicho Pero Franco mato vn ansaron en medio del corral con vna espada sacada, que le dio vna cochillada en el pescueço* (Beinart 1981b, 390). See also 1981b, 567; Fita y Colomé 1892, 486, 513, 516 [1484]; Liebman 1982, 126 [Mexico].

89. *Bendito sea aquel que te crió para el mantenimiento de la gente* (Blázquez Miguel 1986a, 67).

90. Lera García 1987, 93. See also Azevedo Mea 1982, 430 [Coimbra 1583]. Judaizers did not always follow prescribed procedures. In 1647 fifteen-year-old Simón de León told the Mexican Inquisition that his brother slaughtered a chicken as follows: "he did not wring its neck, nor cut its throat; rather while it was still alive, its feet and wings tied, he immersed it in hot water until it drowned" (*No la torcia el pescueço, ni degollaba, sino que viua, amarrados los pies y alas, la metia para que se ahogassen en agua caliente*) (Nunemaker 1946, 39).

91. "Jews bury the blood of the fowl they slaughter because it is a commandment of their law, and because the blood of fowl was not customarily used for sacrifice to God, as was the blood of other animals, as is written in the third of the five books of Moses" (*El enterrar de la sangre debaxo de tierra los judíos lo hacían de las aves que degollavan, porque hera mandamiento de la ley, y porque de la sangre de las aves no acostumbraba hacer sacriffiçio, como se hacía de la sangre de los otros animales, a Dios, como está escrito en el libro tercero de los cinco libros de Moyssén*) (Santa María 1893c, 187).

92. This is another of Montoro's Judaizing customs listed in Román's poem (*trobar en sangre coger / de lo que aueys degollado*) (Castillo 1882, poem #994).

93. *Huã sua escrava degolou sua galinha de fronte da sua porta e que ella mandou lançar em cima do sangue que estava derramado no chão hum pouco de poo de saradura de madeira que se avia serrado, porque andava ai perto hum porco e aremetia a elle pera o comer e isto fez, porque o porco não ficasse inclinado a lhe comer* (Furtado 1925, 139).

94. *Le ha visto degollar las aues que a de comer y cubrir la sangre con tierra* (AGN Vol 271 doc 1, 1a).

95. *Ponían ceniça en un plato o varreñón y allí hechaban la sangre, y la arrojaban o la dexaban allí. . . . La sangre era la alma de los animales, por esso mandava dios que se cubriesse* (Selke de Sánchez 1972, 97). For similar examples see León Tello 1972, 73 [Toledo 1490s]; Blázquez Miguel 1986a, 61 [Murcia]; Wiznitzer 1960, 13 [Brazil]; Liebman 1970, 78 [Mexico]; Wolf 1926, 148 [Canary Islands 1655]; Braunstein 1936, 98 [Majorca 1670s]. Some twentieth-century Portuguese new-Christians abstain from eating blood sausage (*morcela*) (Paulo 1970, 88). Jiménez Lozano, who found that this whole gamut of customs related to kosher slaughtering persisted in certain villages of Castilla-León well into the 1960s, considers them "cultemes" (see Chapter 7 note 57 (1984, 363–5).

96. I have found one reference to an allegedly Jewish method of skinning the animal. Miguel Hidalgo denounced Fernando Atrachon in Toledo in 1484 because some ten years earlier he had gone into his house one Sunday morning "and had found two rams that had been slaughtered that day that had their hides dressed out in the Jewish fashion" (*Tenia en su casa dos carneros muertos de aquel dia e tenian los pellejos catrinisados a manera de judio*) (Beinart 1974, 292).

97. *Bendito sea aquel que te crio para el mantenimiento de la gente* (Blázquez Miguel 1986a, 77). See also Gracia Boix 1983, 139; Sánchez Moya 1973, 340; Liebman 1970, 270 [1642].

98. *Alabado sea el señor que ha creado el degolladero* (Blázquez Miguel 1986a, 77). See also Braunstein 1936, 98 [Majorca 1670s].

99. *Bendito seja o nome do Senhor que te criou para nascer e morrer, me queira encaminhar, livrar e salvar do poder dos meus inimigos, assim como livrou o povo de Israel do Egipto.* . . . *Bendito o Senhor que te criou para morrer* (da Cunha e Freitas 1952, 18). In Toledo in 1523 Blanca Ramírez was denounced for reciting when she put meat into the stew pot, "Blessed be God who brought you forth from the interior of the earth for the sustenance of mankind" (*Bendito sea Dios que te tiró del monllento de la tierra para el mantenimiento de la gente*) (León Tello 1972, 72).

100. *Bendito tu Adonay, nuestro Dios, Rey del mundo, que nos santificó en sus mandamientos y nos encomendó la cobertura de la sangre* (Braunstein 1936, 98).

101. *Viandas e manjares caseres;* . . . *carne caser;* . . . *viandas caseres* (Carrete Parrondo 1985a, 18, 20, 35). See also Fita y Colomé 1892, 488 [1484].

102. Injunctions concerning blood are found in Lev. 7:26–7, 17:10–14, 19:26; Deut. 12:16, 23.

103. *Não comia carne de porco verde nem sange, parecendo lhe que niso pecava* (Azevedo Mea 1982, 267; cf. 65, 272, etc.).

104. *Que no la comiese; porque decía Dios, que en la sangre estaba el alma* (Toro 1932, 246).

105. *E quando [a carne] vinha do acougue, a lavava muito bem e salgava e punha a escorrer, para que lhe tirasse todo o sangue, tendo para si que comendo a carne sem fazer a ditta ceremonia peccava porque poderia comer algum sangue della* (Azevedo Mea 1982, 439).

106. *Se não avia de comer sangue de nenhuma cousa por ser defeza na ley dos judeus, e a razão porque se defendia era porque depois diante de Deos apareceria o sangue nas mãos e se conheceria quem ho comera* (Azevedo Mea 1982, 260, etc.). See also Sierro Malmierca 1990, 165 [1605].

107. *Se lo fasía lauar con çinco o seys aguas fasta que todo quedaua magro, como carne blancusca, mortezina* (Carrete/Fraile 1987, 27; cf. 32, 74). Testimony in 1623 in Ciudad Rodrigo said that meat treated this way was as white as paper (*blanca como un papel*) (Sierro Malmierca 1990, 177).

108. León Tello 1972, 71. See also Llorca 1942, 148 [1484]; Carrete Parrondo 1985a, 163 [Burgos 1502]; Sierro Malmierca 1990, 95, 130, 164, 191 [Ciudad Rodrigo 1584–1625]; Bel Bravo 1988, 106 [Granada 1590s]; Blázquez Miguel 1989, 202 [Toledo 1602]; Blázquez Miguel 1986b, 140 [Murcia 1610]; Liebman 1970, 78 [Mexico]; Braunstein 1936, 98 [Majorca 1670s].

109. *Porque no se perdiese la lauaua y la echaua sal algunas vezes en el ayre e otras vezes en vna çesta; y que no lo fazia por çeremonia* (Carrete/Fraile 1987, 26, 74). See also Llorca 1942, 148 [1484]; Sánchez Moya 1958, 166 [1485]; Blázquez Miguel 1986b, 140 [1610]; Sierro Malmierca 1990, 177 [1623]; Braunstein 1936, 98 [Majorca 1670s]; Schwarz 1925, 17. Liebman (1970, 78) reports no records of salting meat in colonial Mexico prior to 1640.

110. *Por cerimonia da ditta lei lavava a carne quando vinha do açougue pera lhe tirar todo o sangue por ter por peccado come lo* (Azevedo Mea 1982, 434).

111. Lera García 1987, 93. See also Pereira 1979, 190 [1573]; Liebman 1970, 96 [1639]; Selke de Sánchez 1972, 274 [1688].

112. *El sacar y quitar las grassas de la carne y no comer dellas signiffica cómo el pueblo de Isrrael acostumbraba a hacer sacrifficio a Dios de las grassas, hechando por sacrifficio un poco del dicho sebo tanto como una nuez en el fuego; y estas grassas communmente las solían quitar del lomo y riñonada de las resses antes de hecharla en la olla, como está escripto, en los números de los sacrificios* (Santa María 1893c, 184).

113. *Su ama mandó* . . . *que non dexaua ninguna gordura, y fasta que lo quitaua este testigo non se quitaua de allí* . . . *su ama* (Carrete/Fraile 1987, 271 cf. 20, 23, 30, etc.). For some of the

hundreds of examples of this custom see Wolf 1926, 85 [Canary Islands 1527]; Furtado 1929, 119, 387 [Brazil 1593]; Lewin 1971, 63 [Mexico 1656].

114. *Fue con occassion de calentar al brasero un parche al aposento de la dicha Violante Rgz, y hallo un bulto o pella de pedaços de sebo de la carne que deseuaba y se voluio santiguando al apossento del dho Ml. Gil, diziendo, el diablo es este Duarte Rgz* (AGN Vol 271 doc 1, 9b; see also Vol 276 doc 14, 448a).

115. *El quitar la landrecilla de las piernas de las resses, estando cruda, signiffica y es en memoria de quando el Angel luchó con Jacob y quedó coxo desta lucha; y por esso los hios de Isrrael no comían el niervo de la pierna ni la grassa que se pegaba con él, que es la dicha landrecilla, como está escripto en el fin del Génesis* (Santa María 1893c, 184). The reference is to Gen. 32:32.

116. *Quien lo comía se facía loco* (Sánchez Moya 1973, 326).

117. *Asentada a la entrada de la . . . cozina, y tenía ençima de las rodillas, sobre las faldas, vn paño blanco, de lienço, ençima dél vna pierna de carnero o macho, redonda, y la tenía hendida por medio y vn cuchillo junto con ella; y con la vñas o dedos de la vna mano estaua quitando toda la gordura e vna vena larga* (Carrete/Fraile 1987, 20). For similar examples see 73, 80; Beinart 1981b, 384, 398, 417 [1513]; López Martínez 184; Chinchilla 1953, 183 [Guatemala 1609].

118. *Le compró un castrón para cecina y cuando estaba en su casa para descuartizarlo su mujer Felipa Ruiz mandó al testigo que abriese un poco la pierna y sacase la landrecilla. . . . La llamó aparte y le dijo quedo que no dixexe aquello delante del testigo aunque éste lo oyó y le dixeron que no sacase las landrecillas con que el testigo paró aunque ya había comenzado a sacarla una y le paresció muy mal . . . y desde entonces lo tuvo por cosa de judíos* (Contreras 1982, 602). For many conversos—and occasional old-Christians—porging was merely a family custom transmitted from earlier generations and now devoid of religious significance (Rábade Obradó 1990a, 349–50).

119. *Se asa quarto trazeiro de carneiro ou porco lhe manda tirar a landoa por que se asa milhor e fica mais tenro e não se lhe ajunta na landoa o sangue emcruado* (Furtado 1925, 31).

120. For some of the hundreds of examples of porging see Llorca 1935, 16 [1484]; Fita y Colomé 1892, 501 [Ciudad Real 1484]; Sierro Malmierca 1990, 94–6 [Ciudad Rodrigo 1584–97]; Azevedo Mea 1982, 26, 28, 43, 342, etc. [Coimbra 1570s]; Lewin 1987, 226–31 [Mexico 1575–1626; Peru 1577]; Furtado 1925, 41, 133, 139, 522; 1929, 352 [Brazil 1590s]; Liebman 1975, 175 [Lima 1595]; Chinchilla 1953, 183 [Guatemala 1609]; Lewin 1954, 227 [Argentina 1622]; 42 [Mexico 1642]; Liebman 1970, 78 [Mexico].

121. For example, of the roughly 120 Mexican Inquisition cases between 1620 and 1649 reviewed by Stanley Hordes, 32 people were found guilty of observing the Jewish dietary laws. Twenty-two of them were sentenced to exile and confiscation of property (1970, 214).

122. *Quando massan, sacan una ala de la massa y la hechan en la lumbre a quemar por sacrificio. . . . El hechar un pellizco de massa en el fuego, dice el Rabbi que signiffica y es en memoria de aquel pan del pueblo de Isrrael, que hera obligado de dar al Summo Sacerdote en sacrifficio de cada una massa que los judios massaban, por razón y memoria del sacerdocio que el pueblo de Isrrael perdió, y hera que tomaban dos puñados de la dicha massa y aquello se ofrecía al Summo Sacerdote; y perdido el dicho sacerdocio, en memoria* (Santa María 1893c, 182, 184).

123. *Echava pelillas en el fuego quando masava, disiendo como buena judia "Bendito seays, Adonay, que nos encomendastes en vuestras encomendaçiones y que nos mandastes haser sacrifiçio de la masa"* (Moreno Koch 1977, 357).

124. *De primera masa pellicas en el fuego en remembranza de las primiçias que en el Testamento Viejo se mandaua dar a los saçerdotes* (Moreno Koch 1977, 357). For other contemporary examples see Carrete/Fraile 1987, 106 [Almazán]; Beinart 1975, 654; 1977a, 151, 337; 1981b,

361 [Ciudad Real]; Llorca 1935, 16 [Valencia 1484]; Blázquez Miguel 1987, 45 [Huete 1489]; Carrete Parrondo 1985a, 80 [Soria 1490s]; Moreno Koch 1977, 366 [Garcimuñoz 1490s]; Blázquez Miguel 1986a, 69 [Cuenca 1511]; Baião 1921, 138 [Portugal 1543].

125. *Quando amasava, lançava tres pelourinhos de masa no fogo por sacreficyo e ceremonya judaica* (Azevedo Mea 1982, 113; cf. 4, 6, 230, 297, etc.). See also Liebman 1970, 97 [Mexico 1639].

126. *Dios la haga crecer a la masa* (Braunstein 1936, 98). See also Cortés 1985, 285 [Majorca 1670s]. A peculiarly perverted variant of this custom was reported in New Veracruz in Mexico, where Francisca Texoso was reconciled in 1646. She confessed that "in order to have the bread which she and her brother kneaded come out white and tasty, they kneaded it first with water which they used to wash certain obscene parts and then made some circles and Jewish rites in the form of prayers over the dough" (Liebman 1964, 102). Jiménez Lozano also found this custom practiced in the 1960s in a village of the Bierzo region of León and in the Pinares of Valladolid (1984, 364–5).

127. *Bemdito meu Senhor, Meu Deus, meu Adonai, que nos encomendou com as suas encomendas bemditas e bem-santas que dizi massemos este pão, para a boca do levão, como fizeram os nossos irmãos na Santa Terra da Promissão* (Schwarz 1925, 17, 79).

128. *Venir algún judío o judía a pisar la uva en mi casa en el lagar porque fuese vino caser* (León Tello 1972, 74).

129. *Beuieron allí del vino caser. . . . Beuió vino de la barahá en sabado* (Carrete Parrondo 1985a, 18, 28, 47).

130. *Bebia el vino de la bodega según el rito judaico* (Cantera/Carrete 1971, 262).

131. *Cierta pasta que hacen los moros, hecha de pan rallado, miel, alegría y especias* (1611, 83).

132. *Se fazía traher azuquaques e turrado de la Juderia e lo fazía aparellar de judias* (Cabezudo Astraín 1963, 283).

133. *Cazuelas de verenjenas con huevos* (Moreno Koch 1977, 355 [1489]). See also Beinart 1977a, 163, 259, 295.

134. *Mucha verengena y açafrán con açelguilla* (Gómez-Menor 1970, 105). See also Arbós Ayuso 1981, 78–9.

135. *No dexemos la patena / a que la boca llegastes, / que luego que la besastes, / se dice que la tornastes / caçuela con verengena* (Castillo 1882, poem #969). In the eastern Mediterranean, eggplant stew, both with and without meat, remains a staple of traditional Sephardic cooking, where it is called *berengena guisada* (Sephardic Sisterhood 1971, 62), *yuvech* (Stavroulakis 1986, 181), or *almodrote* (Marks 1992, 18).

136. Blázquez Miguel 1986a, 59. In modern Sephardic cooking of the eastern Mediterranean these are called *huevos jaminados* (Sephardic Sisterhood 1971, 31; Stavroulakis 1986, 23; Marks 1992, 37–8).

137. *Hasya pan cuez en esta manera: que tomavan culantro en vna sartén y ajos e espeçias molidas y agua y azeyte y echavan pan desmenuzado y el culantro verde, y lo boluían todo, y hazían aquel pan cuez para los sábados y los viernes* (Carrete/Fraile 1987, 38). This seems similar to a modern Spanish dish usually called *migas*.

138. *Picauan vna poca de carne cruda e la echauan en vn mortero, e allí echauan espeçias e algunos hueuos, e majauan aquello e, después de majado fasían vnos como bodoques redondos, e los freyan en vna sartén con azeyte o en vna olla, e los llamauan albondequexos* (Carrete/Fraile 1987, 43). For an exiled Jew's nostalgia for his Spanish *albóndigas* see *adafina* in Chapter 12.5. This dish is a staple of Sephardic cooking throughout the Levant (Sephardic Sisterhood 1971, 46; Stavroulakis 1986, 186; Marks 1992, 14).

139. *Trayan algunos alvillos de carnero y del baço picado e huevos cozidos e las alburas picadas, e las yemas enteras echauan en los aluillos e fasían vnos torterillos, y echáuanlos a cozer, e después comían de aquéllos los sábados e otros días de carne* (Carrete/Fraile 1987, 43–4).

140. Blázquez Miguel 1986a, 59. Stuffed meat pies, called *empanadas* in Spain and *borekas* (from the Turkish *böreklar*) in the Levant, are common elements of both Sephardic and Spanish cooking (Sephardic Sisterhood 1971, 2–3; Stavroulakis 1986, 103). A version of this lamb-innard dish, called *pastele* or *komotin*, is common among modern Greek Sephardis (Stavroulakis 1986, 69–70).

141. *Cenaron çebollas con almodrote* (Moreno Koch 1977, 353). See also Beinart 1977a, 163. Variants of this dish are found throughout the Levantine Sephardic world (Sephardic Sisterhood 1971, 67; Marks 1992, 50).

142. *Ráuanos buenos . . . papillos rellenos / en los viernes en la noche* (Castillo 1882, poem #994).

143. *Las cabeças del buey e cabrones las echase a cozer el domingo en la noche, e después de cozidas las picaua . . . su ama y las echaua en los aluillos de los cabrones e las ponía a sahumar, e después comía dellas* (Carrete/Fraile 1987, 32; cf. 23, 56, 85, 91, 121, 122).

144. María Régulo Rodríguez documents the use of the word *alaheas* in Inquisition documents of the Canary Islands, tracing it to the Arabic term *hasawa* [to stuff] (Carrete/Fraile 1987, 24).

145. *Los viernes fasía . . . su ama açelgas sancochadas en agua e después ahogadas en aseyte e con çebollas, e allí, en el azeyte, reheruir; e después echaua allí su agua e pan rallado e espeçias y yemas de hueuos; e cozía fasta que se para muy espeso* (Carrete/Fraile 1987, 27; cf. 63). See also Arbós Ayuso 1981, 78.

# CHAPTER XX 🌿

# Conversion

In speaking of conversion[1] we must distinguish two types: change of legal status and change of heart. The first is characterized by some specific act that formally changes one's religious affiliation.[2] The second involves motive and belief, both of which are notoriously difficult to discern. Officially, between 1391 and 1492 many tens of thousands of Iberian Jews became Christian, some willingly, some under coercion. Either way, as soon as the waters of baptism touched their foreheads they were no longer Jews, at least as far as Christians were concerned. Conversion instantly changed their legal status: henceforth they were subject to the laws, obligations, and penalties imposed by the Church. Whether a given *converso* really believed in the tenets of the new religion or practiced it exclusively was, in the years before 1480, largely a matter of individual conscience. As we have seen in earlier chapters, the religious identity of the *conversos* was complex. Many newly baptized Christians continued to Judaize and to self-identify as Jews. Some practiced both religions in an unstable mix. Some believed in neither. Some tried as hard as they could to assimilate to Christian ways. Many *conversos* did not revert to Judaism even after they emigrated to lands where it was legally possible for them to do so.

We can observe the behaviors of people in these and other categories, but their beliefs are much harder to perceive—or document—than their acts. We can infer true religious conversion in the majority of those who became militant in the Catholic Church, or who became Protestant, or who returned to an active Jewish religious life. We can see it written from time to time in the spiritual autobiography left by a Pablo de Santa María, Hernando de Talavera, or Uriel da Costa.[3] And occasionally we can reconstruct the circumstances of conversion from testimony recorded in Inquisition hearings.

While a family's legal status usually changed at the instant of baptism, their true and total conversion to Christianity could take generations. In the majority of cases of true conversion what we find is not a public, well-reasoned, exemplary change of faith but rather a gradual, often subtle process of shifting one's beliefs and practices from one religion to another. This conversion often came about on intimate family battlefields, when a Judaizing spouse had to accommodate to old-Christian in-laws, or when Judaizing parents tried to impart their traditions to their Catholic-educated children. The most common pattern was the protracted atrophying of Jewish practice and Catholicizing of Jewish beliefs in an environment dominated by Christian ceremony, symbols, and rhetoric, where the very rhythms of the clock and calendar were determined by the Church. This type of progressive conversion often took place over generations: one might look at the Christian great-grandchildren of rabbis and find not a single trace of Judaism left. Another name for this sort of conversion, which is accumulated from thousands of in themselves inconsequential decisions, is assimilation.

No matter which sort we are speaking of, conversion was a deadly serious business, the key to the well-being of one's immortal soul and of one's all-too-mortal body. The reasons for conversion, as contemporary documents make clear, ran the gamut from sincere religious conviction to coercive threats to life or property, desire for social mobility, love, family pressure, opportunism, or adolescent rebellion. No matter why or when conversion occurred, it frequently occasioned the sort of identity crisis and angst that we normally associate with adolescence. The effect on the converting individual was very likely to be traumatic. We can catch glimpses of that trauma in the voices left to us by the historical record. This chapter examines the motives people ascribed to their conversion to Christianity, their emotional stress in trying to balance, or vacillate between, the two religions, the regrets they felt at having converted, and the processes by which most of them eventually assimilated.

## 20.1. Conversion to Christianity

At first those most willing to convert of their own volition tended to be people who thought deeply about their religion. Baer analyses four principal reasons why many Jewish intellectuals converted to Catholicism in the early fifteenth century, as listed in a letter from Paul of Burgos (formerly Solomon Halevi) to his former coreligionist Joseph Orabuena: material gain (*lust after riches and honor*), Averroist skepticism (*satisfy the intellect without fear and anxiety*), the national disaster Baer calls the "thunder of history" (*behold the doom of our homeland*), and the persuasive power of Christian truth revealed (*the secrets of prophecy*) (1966, 2:143–5).

A far different picture of conversion is painted by Inquisition trials from around the time of the Expulsion. Personal, social, and economic motives predominate, particularly feelings associated with the well-being of one's spouse, lover, or children. The relative paucity of claims to have converted because of some transforming religious experience, or because of recognizing the superiority of Christianity, or that its law had replaced that of the Jews, is surprising, especially given the Inquisition audience presumably receptive to such testimony.[4] For the generation that converted in the spring and summer of 1492, consideration of the horrors of the impending Expulsion, not the attractiveness of Christianity, was what moved them to convert, and the compulsions of the moment inevitably produced more de jure conversions than true changes of heart. Pedro Soler [Almazán 1501] informed inquisitors how "Pedro de Salzedo, the Count of Monteagudo's tailor, ... had remained a Jew for three days after the Expulsion edict was up ... and after three days he became a Christian; and he acted like he had left a piece of cloth at a pawn shop for three days, thinking that he would find a solution. But when he saw there was no solution, he was baptized."[5] Francisco de Cáceres [Toledo 1500] perceived this coercive atmosphere very clearly when he reportedly turned the situation on its head in a discussion with a new-Christian friend:

> If the King, our lord, commanded the Christians to become Jews or leave his dominions, some would become Jews and others would go. Some, seeing themselves lost, would become Jews in order to return to their true nature. They would be Christians, and pray like Christians, and they would deceive everyone. All would think that they were Jews, and within their hearts and by their will they would be Christians.[6]

While Spanish authorities insisted that Jews were free to choose between conversion and exile, and new-Christian clerics like Fray Hernando de Talavera argued that forced conversions were invalid,[7] evidence suggests that physical coercion and psychological pressure were sometimes employed. A striking and probably not atypical example can be seen in the testimony of the *converso* Ferrant Núñez, majordomo of the Duchess of Alburquerque, who bragged to Inquisitors in 1498 how he had once hidden Antonio Martínez in his house "so that his wife would not know about her husband's conversion and baptism; and when he was baptized I myself went to his house and had his son taken from the arms of his mother, who was crying and screaming, and I took him to San Francisco church and there he was baptized like his father."[8]

It is also clear from the testimony that coercion was sometimes used on the other side as well. Mosse Aninay Adret, a Jewish merchant of Aranda, told Inquisitors in 1489 that when he was fourteen he had wanted to become Christian, but that his family beat him and imprisoned him and eventually took him to the *converso* Alonso de la Cavallería, the Aragonese vice chancellor, who talked him out of it for several reasons: it would trouble his aged Jewish father; he would lose his rights of inheritance and have to go begging at the Christian charity houses;

and if he did not convert Cavallería would see that he was set up in business. He said that when these threats did not take away his desire to become Christian they locked him up again, and then as a last resort married him to an attractive young Jewess.[9] In another example, Rabbi Yuda of Cuéllar reported in 1491 how a Jew named Rodrigo and the Jewish niece of don Isaac Corral with whom Rodrigo was having an affair became Christian when the Jewish community ran them out, but how don Isaac managed to bribe an official and keep their baby from being baptized.[10]

To judge from Inquisition testimony, the two most prevalent reasons for conversion had to do with property and with matters of the heart. For some Jews the Christian world offered seductive opportunities for advancement. Pedro de la Caballería, who held important political offices for Juan II of Aragón, allegedly explained this to one of his Jewish friends, who had asked him why he had converted if he was continuing to observe all the Jewish customs. Pedro reputedly replied: "Silence, fool! Could I, as a Jew, ever have risen higher than a rabbinical post? But now, see, I am one of the chief councilors of the city. For the sake of the little man who was hanged [Jesus], I am accorded every honor.... Who hinders me—if I choose—from fasting on Yom Kippur and keeping your festivals and all the rest? When I was a Jew I dared not walk as far as this [i.e., beyond the prescribed limits of a Sabbath day's walk]; but now I do as I please."[11] The same sentiments were more abstractly stated by the Aragonese *converso* Pedro de Sant Joan, who allegedly said around 1492 that, although he still practiced Judaism he had turned Christian formally "because of his property and prosperity in this world."[12] Phrases such as this are echoed in many trials of the 1490s.[13]

Other *conversos* were much more specific about their financial concerns. In 1501 in Aranda Pedro Núñez de Santafé, who with his wife came back from Portugal without their children, was reported to have said that "if it were not for the debts that were owed him he would never have turned Christian or come back from Portugal."[14]

Still others converted for reasons of employment. A case [Soria 1491] particularly revealing of the family tensions and conflicts of interest that surround a decision to convert is that of García Fernández de la Isla, an accountant for the Duke of Medinaceli. A Jewish doctor named Xeteui stated that Fernández continued to talk religion with him after his conversion and that "he knew that he still had as little faith in the Law of the Christians as when he was a Jew." Fernández regretted having converted and blamed his brother for having made him do it. Diego de Burgos said that Fernández sometimes remarked that if it weren't for his wife and children he would emigrate and become a Jew again. Xeteui also reported that after Fernández converted he continued to live with his Jewish wife and had some number of children with her. His children continued as practicing Jews, and Xeteui observed them all praying together, even hearing Fernández one day call to his son: " 'Alonsito, go get the Targum—which is a Jewish book—, because I want to read.'

To which the young man replied, pointing out the irony of his father's using his Christian name, 'You call me Alonsito and you send me for the Targum?'" Eventually the pressure on the family became unbearable. Diego de Burgos reported that "the duke was badgered by some monks and other people who told him that it was a bad example to have in his house a Christian married to an infidel, and that he ought to fire him.... The duke sent him a message saying that he should convert her or the duke would take away his job. And thus he made her turn Christian," and from then on they baptized the children as they were born. Xeteui reported that once he asked Fernández if it was true that he had a new Law and a new wife, and Fernández replied: "Woe be to God, the Law is so old that it isn't worth anything, and my wife is as much a Jewess as she was before, and she was as Christian then as she is now." Fernández's wife, too, regretted that she had converted to accommodate her husband. When he was mortally wounded and they brought his body home, she was reported to have lamented: "And for this little thing I became a Christian!"[15]

For many other *conversos*, their emotional relationships with their old-Christian or wholly Christianized *converso* spouses won out over their commitment to Judaism. Francisco de Torres [La Almunia de Doña Godina c. 1488] told a friend one day around 1488 that he became Christian because he was in love, but that he had come to regret it: "It would have been better to remain a Jew and keep my law than to be a Christian; but the Devil tempted me, because for the love of a woman I turned Christian, yet I swear to God that I am as much a Jew today as the day I was born."[16] Some, like María de Castro [Soria 1490], said that they had converted "for the children's sake."[17] Some Judaizing *conversos* began their true religious conversion to Christianity when they married. As Brianda de Santángel explained it [Teruel 1485], she ceased Judaizing both because "she knew it was a bad road, and because she was about to marry an old-Christian.... Four years ago she gave up some of these customs and two years ago she gave them all up."[18] Others, wavering in their affiliation, were brought into church by the attraction of love or sex. The former Jew Jaco Abençuçan explained [Zaragoza 1482] the circumstances of his conversion this way:

> I was born Christian; ... when I was nineteen or twenty years old I married this [Christian] virgin named Johana, daughter of Johan Gonçalez the merchant.... And from the time I was very young I thought that the Law of the Christians was not good and that the Law that God gave to Moses was better. And when I was twenty years old and firm in my convictions I went to Malaga in the Kingdom of Granada and I went to the house of a Jew named Yeuda Cofer, who runs the mint for the King of Granada and there I was circumcised. And after I was circumcised I wandered through the Kingdom of Granada, but since it seemed to me that in the entire Kingdom of Granada there was no woman like mine, I risked coming back to Seville and I found my wife delivered of a daughter who was eight days old.[19]

A related example in the testimony of Charles de Goserán, who returned to Aragon in the mid-1490s, seems suspiciously self-serving, but it suggests circumstances and motives that cannot have been all that uncommon. Goserán told officials that he had only left Aragon so as to be able to convert his already emigrated family, and that "he prayed to God and He converted her and their nine children and another five members of their households and they were all baptized in Navarre." Another Aragonese convert said that "his wife and children were hardened [against Christianity] and they wanted to cross the sea. And because he thought that with time he could bring them to have faith, he arranged for them all to go to Navarre."[20] Nonetheless, evidence from Jewish sources confirms that love of family could even be a reason not to emigrate for the purpose of taking up a Jewish life elsewhere. A seventeenth-century responsum of Rabbi Yom Tob Zahalon, for example, cites the case of a *converso* who was invited three times by his family in other lands to emigrate from Spain but elected to stay, saying "I love my wife and children who are Christian."[21] Similar cases appear in Inquisition testimony. For example, a Judaizing Mexican friend of the *converso* Luis Franco said in 1626 that he could not emigrate with Franco to Flanders because he was married to an old-Christian (García de Proodian 1966, 294).

Whereas in both Spain and Portugal most conversions had occurred by the mid-1490s, there are numerous later instances of sudden breaks, not with Judaism but with crypto-Judaism. It only took one member to break the chain of transmission of Judaizing customs and to convert—de facto—all subsequent members of the family. Testimony suggests that this member was very likely to be a young woman, who in the shelter of her home had been habituated to the family's idiosyncratic ways of doing things, but then who one day discovered that the family's customs were Jewish in origin. The precipitating event could be almost anything, even the public reading of an Edict of Grace. Thirty-year-old Bernardina de Montalván [Granada 1591] said that when she was eleven an aunt had introduced her to Judaizing and that for many years she had fasted and observed the dietary laws. But some three years after her marriage to Luis Alvarez she noticed that her husband did not practice the same customs. She said that when she heard an Edict of Faith read at her parish church she realized that the customs were indicative of Judaizing, so she stopped (Bel Bravo 1988, 130). Similarly, María de Palma [Granada 1593] confessed that when she was eleven a neighbor named Marina Hernández had instructed her in Judaizing, and that she had practiced all she had been told until "when she heard the Edict of Faith read she said to herself: 'God save me; what I have been doing is from the Law of Moses!' "[22]

Discovery that a particular custom was Jewish, or discovery by the Inquisition, were not the only circumstances that broke the chain of transmission. An illuminating experience—positive with regard to Christianity, or negative with regard to Judaism—could reshape a life. In 1647 fifteen-year-old Simón de Valencia professed to the Mexican Inquisition that he stopped Judaizing when "he saw how downtrodden [the Jews] were, and he was, without anyone being willing to give him a piece of bread, calling him Jew and son of Jews."[23] María de San Juan, of Baeza, who learned Judaism from her mother at age thirteen (and who was twenty-nine when she testified in 1573), said that it was the seductive emotionalism of Christian observance that drew her back into the fold. One Holy Thursday

> going to watch the scourging [of Christ], when she saw the statue of Christ and of the Mother of God, to whom she had previously been deeply devoted, and seeing all the people crying and worshipping the Christ, she was seized with great envy and heartache, the way she used to feel but no longer did. She went home and finding her father Doctor San Juan alone she asked him what a person must do to be saved, and he replied that she must be a good Christian and believe what the Holy Mother Roman Church [taught], and recite the words of the Credo and believe all of them.

Evidently her father's curiosity was piqued, for he inquired why she was asking. When she gave the teenager's typical evasion—"No reason, just because . . ."—he told her not to embroil herself in deep things. Later, when she realized that her father was well educated and that he and everybody else knew more than her mother did all by herself, she decided to become a good Christian again.[24]

## 20.2. Assimilation

Presumably every successfully assimilated new-Christian family went through a gradual process of replacing Jewish beliefs and customs with those of their adopted religion. Some few may have quit "cold turkey," at the moment of baptism. But much more likely was a protracted process in which modes of prayer, choices of food, and the weekly rhythms of personal and home cleanliness gradually became exclusively Christian. Since the successfully assimilated do not appear in the documentary record, our knowledge of them has to be surmise.

However, the number of partially assimilated new-Christians who came before the tribunals amounted to many thousands, and they were arrested at nearly every point on the spectrum of assimilation, from near-total Judaizing to only the vaguest alleged remnants of Jewish practice. From the 1450s through the next two and a half centuries it was common to find half-assimilated *conversos* who practiced elements of both religions. A typical example was Pedro de Ripoll, of Albarracín. The Inquisition noted that in the 1470s Ripoll used to go to mass, participate in the sacraments of confession and communion, and work on Saturday, while at the same time he kept the Jewish dietary laws and observed some Sabbath customs. His circle of friends included Jews and both old- and new-Christians. He berated his wife for buying *matza* from the Jewish baker but at the same time joined her in celebrating the Passover (Haliczer 1990, 215). Ripoll's two religions coexisted in him in a state of constant tension. But there were other *conversos* who thought it philosophically licit to adhere to both religions simultaneously. Branca de Azevedo [Coimbra 1568] saw no contradiction in believing simultaneously in the Law of Moses, in which she hoped to be saved, and that Jesus Christ was God, and that she had never separated herself from His Holy Faith (Azevedo Mea 1982, 41, 98). Leonor de Rojas [Granada 1590s] asserted "that even though she [Judaized], she understood that it was not contrary to the Holy Catholic Faith, and that you could observe both of them." Her sister Juana too said that she observed Jewish customs in order to be saved, but that "when they taught them to her she did not believe that they were incompatible with the Law and faith of Jesus Christ."[25] Another example was that of Dr. Periáñez de Mesa, a seventy-year-old lawyer from Ecija, who confessed [Córdoba 1591] that "some relatives of his had taught him the law of Moses and that he had observed it together with that of Jesus Christ Our Lord."[26] As we have seen, among later generations of *conversos* even those people who thought of themselves primarily as crypto-Jews were likely to be almost wholly Catholic in their practices.

While for many *conversos* the road to assimilation was paved with mixed intentions, others at some point in their lives made a conscious decision to abandon their Jewish practices, and a few of them articulated in their testimony the reasons why they stopped Judaizing. As with the reported reasons for conversion, social pressures, particularly from their family, were prominent. In Garcimuñoz around 1500 Lope de Peñafiel's wife "stopped observing the Sabbath because her son, Alonso de Peñafiel, provisioner of this holy church, had scolded her for it."[27] Manuel González, an innkeeper in Guadalupe, testified in 1485 that when he scolded his wife for keeping the Jewish fasts she stopped.[28] Catalina de la Torre [Granada 1591] said that she stopped Judaizing after she was married "out of fear of her husband and her sisters-in-law, because they all lived together."[29]

Some steadfast Judaizers like the Mexican *cristiana nueva* Isabel de Carvajal were able to resist family pressure. Her family was split down the middle with each side trying to convert the other. Among the most telling incidents reported about this extended family is Fray Gaspar de Carvajal's report that one day around 1589 when he was praying his niece Isabel told him that she had learned from her husband that Christ did not exist. Fray Gaspar said that in a rage he knocked her down and began to beat her to try to kill her, screaming that she was an enemy of God and the saints.[30] But many others gave in and abandoned their Judaizing customs.

One must of course take with a grain of salt the information accused Judaizers provided about their families. Fear—for oneself or one's loved ones—could shape testimony, as could rancor, envy, or any number of muddying emotions. A common defense seems to have been "My spouse (parents, guardian) made me Judaize; but as soon as I was free of their influence I stopped." This defense was less nasty than it seems in those cases where at the time of testimony the allegedly coercing family member was safely in Holland, Turkey, or the grave, or had been already convicted by the Inquisition courts. The silk merchant Francisco de Ecija Zayas, of Baeza, who was arrested in 1573 at age 29, is a case in point. His father was an old-Christian and his mother a *conversa*, as was his wife Elvira de San Juan. Only after the *converso* side of the family had all been imprisoned did Francisco confess to his own Judaizing, in a way that tried to make it seem like they, not he, were to blame:

> His wife had persuaded him to believe in the Law of Moses and she had told him that his mother and sisters held to that Law; and they had taught him many details and ceremonies related to it.... And that although at the beginning he had been angry at his wife and had gone several days without speaking to her, later he told her that he believed it. And that he fasted certain days that she told him, abstaining from eating until evening, but at noon he went outside his house to eat; and he did this in order to placate his wife and not because he had left the Holy Catholic Faith. Rather he intended to go to Rome to ask the Pope for a writ to absolve him and give him secret penance because it affected his honor.... He held those beliefs for six months and later vacillated about which was the better [Law]; and after his wife was imprisoned he had been in this period of doubt for twelve months.[31]

For most crypto-Jewish families the process by which they eventually became fully orthodox Catholics was more one of evolution than of conversion. For some families the point at which they ceased being crypto-Jewish at all is imperceptible to us. In other cases the documents permit us a glimpse at the crisis points. Often these involved a teenager wrestling with choice between two faiths and with divided family loyalties as we saw in the case of the unfortunate teenager Isabel de San Juan, whose agonized alternation between the religious worlds of her father and mother contributed to the family's destruction.

The most successful assimilation strategy, followed by the innumerable *converso* families that eventually dropped entirely from sight, was to move year by year farther from orthodox Jewish practice and nearer to Catholic custom until at some point along the way the decision was made—perhaps consciously, perhaps only through procrastination—not to inform the next generation of children about the family's crypto-Jewish heritage. In those cases, barring an unfortunate challenge some day to an assertion of *limpieza de sangre*, the family's assimilation was complete.

## 20.3. REGRETS

First generation converts frequently gave voice to their regret at having chosen conversion. For some people, both crypto-Jews struggling to retain their Jewish customs and half-assimilated semi-Christians struggling to meld into a lifestyle they still found inimical, the reasons for their malaise were not always clearly articulated, or perhaps even articulable. The *conversos* who were overheard venting their dissatisfaction with their current Christian life tended to express a kind of vague but intense nostalgia for things past and a nagging regret for their former way of life, an anger at themselves for having left it behind, and a disappointment with the problematical Christian world they had joined. Some, like Ferrand Alvarez or the rag dealer Herrand Martines [Soria 1490], said no more than that they "repented of having turned Christian."[33] Others highlighted the emptiness that was left in the center of their soul by conversion. Alonso García el Blanco, a Guadalajara returnee from Portugal who was tried in the 1540s, responded to a friend's query about how he liked Christianity by saying that now he was "neither Christian, Moor, nor Jew: I don't know how I am; I am nothing, and I wish to God I had suffered a bad death there [in Portugal] and not come back here to be a Christian, for after I came back here I am blind to everything."[34] A Sorian *converso* named Iñigo [Aranda de Duero 1502] recalled fondly his life spent as a Jew, and his regrets at having converted: " 'They can't take away my seventy years. The only thing that bothers me is that our lives hang on a spoken oath,' which he said referring to the oath that the Christians make, putting one stick across another to make a +."[35] Lope Garçia [Sigüenza 1501] called his accepting baptism a bad mistake (*modorrada*) (Carrete/Fraile 1987, 47). Agustín Pérez, who converted in Valladolid around 1472, many years later reacted with these words to his Jewish son Francisco's desire to become a Christian: "How's that, my son? For I am lost, and it would be better had I not become a Christian. You have a good Law; stick with your mother."[36]

The disappointment and malaise that sprang from conversion was expressed by other *conversos* in a variety of ways. There are several eloquent examples from the *converso* community of Almazán, recorded in trials between 1501 and 1505:

- Catalina, the mother of Doctor Antonio de Alves, recalled with nostalgia the days in which she had been a good Jew living in the market district.

- Pedro López de Hituero observed that there was no way he could forget his mother's milk, which provoked a friend to say that he was as good a Jew now as he had ever been.

- Magdalena la Jaena, the wife of Luis del Peso, remarked that "back when God wished it she was like the Twelve Peers of France, but now she was like mud, nothing at all."

- Diego Méndez agreed with a friend that he could no longer follow his old customs, but then added: "even though it displeases God."

- Catalina Martínez told a friend that they had been just fine as Jews, and that the King had done wrong by them in making them convert.

- Antón del Valle asserted to some friends that if he had only gone to Portugal there was no way he would ever have become Christian.

- Diego Luján expressed his regrets with an eloquent silence that preceded his second thoughts. In a conversation about the events of Exodus a witness noted that Luján remarked that " 'the God who did those things back then was good.' And then, after a short time, he said: 'And the current God is good too,' without anyone there having to prompt him."[37]

The *conversos* of Almazán were not unique in voicing these sentiments, for during the first forty years of the Inquisition trial after trial contains clear statements of regret, nostalgia, exasperation and bitterness. And many *conversos* focused their remarks in ways that let us better understand the root causes of their frustrations. As we saw in Chapters 4 and 5, religious motives predominated. Particularly in the late fifteenth century when Jewish models were still tantalizingly accessible, or idealized in recent memory, *conversos* yearned for the fellowship and spiritual consolation of communal worship. The Aragonese *converso* Jaime de la Cavallería, for example, found it particularly difficult to abandon his former religious habits. Several witnesses in 1492 describe his coming in disguise to the Zaragoza synagogue on Rosh Hashanah around 1480. He was accompanying his Jewish friend Gento Siltón to visit Siltón's lover across the city. Rather than go directly, Jaime said: "Let's go this way, through the *judería*, to look at the festival that the Jews are celebrating tonight." When they went by the synagogue door and heard singing Jaime said: "Come on, let's go look inside this synagogue." Siltón did not want to go in because he did not have a shawl, but Jaime did have a shawl over his head, and he went and stood inside the doorway and said: "By God, look, this is how my grandfather did it when he was a Jew in this synagogue." And he began to bow and sway, and he stood there for more than fifteen minutes watching the Jews pray. Then they went to the widow's house.[38]

The Jews down the block were an irresistible magnet for many *conversos* who in the years before the Inquisition bitterly regretted their decision to turn Christian. Often their actions spoke louder than any possible words. A witness in Cuenca in the 1490s, for example, recalled how Hernand Sánchez Castro had behaved in Uclés some twenty years earlier when all the religious communities turned out to pray for relief from drought. "He saw how Sánchez went out of the church of San Andrés with the other Christians in their procession, and when they passed by the plaza where the Jews stood with their Torah, waiting for the Christian procession to pass, Sánchez stayed there with the Jews and marched with the Torah, abandoning the procession of the Christians."[39]

Another striking example is that of Juan de Cuéllar, a Segovian who converted some time prior to 1486, who continued to frequent the house of the still-Jewish Abraham Seneor for six months, every morning and evening and sometimes in the afternoon, to hear him pray. When Seneor had not yet come back from the next-door synagogue, according to one witness, Cuéllar would lie down on the floor of a nearby hallway to listen to the prayers. The witness alleges that he complained about this to people in the household: "What the Hell is Juan de Cuéllar doing here every time they are at prayer? If he has business with Don Abraham he should leave and come back." To which he got the answer: "Leave him alone. I wish you and all of us were half as devout as he is! In the evenings he only comes to hear the prayers under guise of doing business with Don Abraham; and sometimes he comes up to our booths at Sukkot to do business with Don Abraham at his table."[40] The image of Cuéllar stretched on the floor, all by himself, straining to catch the distant rhythms of Jews at prayer, is an eloquent emblem of the feelings that drove many *conversos* to continue struggling to live their lives as crypto-Jews.

But pious yearning was just a part of the attitudinal mix. Some *conversos* seasoned their continued adherence to Judaism and their disbelief in Christianity with an exasperation at the incessant ceremonies and physical icons and restrictive obligations of their new religion. This sense of exasperation lies behind the outburst of Françisca d'Aça [Almazán 1505], who when she could not get permission to eat meat during Lent, in spite of her illness, lamented: "That's what I get for having turned Christian, because before I could eat anything I wanted to."[41] Garçía López, a *converso* tailor from Soria, put the matter this way to a close friend around 1498: "When we were Jews we were bothered by one festival that came once a year, and now every day is a holiday or festival; too much and never ending. The mass we hear is worthless, and we don't understand more than donkeys, and this abbot who says it I swear to God doesn't understand any more than that dog. This is a real captivity."[42]

*Conversos* seem to have missed the social and cultural aspects of their former lifestyle almost as much as they doubted the wisdom of the religious choice they had made. In addition to continued adherence to the Law of Moses, their strong sense of nostalgia for Jewish prayer and for the comradeship of discussion of the Torah is evident. A substantial number of *conversos* of the Expulsion generation continued to meet on the Sabbath with their lifelong friends—Jews before 1492, *conversos* afterward—to discuss the Mosaic Law.[43] Similarly, as we saw in Chapter 19, in these *conversos* we perceive an intense nostalgia for the Jewish foods of their pre-conversion homes. Typical were the feelings of Francisco de Torres [La Almunia 1488], who had married an old-Christian, when he told a friend that "I was undergoing the world's worst suffering because on account of my wife I could not eat *hamines* or other Jewish dishes except in secret."[44]

Coupled with all of this was a sense many *conversos* had of having let their ancestors down by breaking with the religion of their birth, almost a sense of personal dishonor as a consequence of their choices. In 1491 the Jew Yuçá Francés told the Soria Inquisition of how his friend the *converso* Francisco Martines Serrano had "told him in tears how he was repentant and dishonored for having become a Christian."[45] In 1492 María Alvarez put it even more strongly. After a fight with her husband Fernando de Cuéllar she lamented the love that had caused her to convert and abandon her Jewish children:

> Look for what an awful man I have left my children and my husband. . . .
> It must be some ten years since I turned Christian. . . . I have Jewish children whom I hide from my husband. I have sent them money and other things, and I brought one small daughter into my house for a few days. . . . I had doubts in my heart, and one day my husband wounded me. . . . Look who I turned Christian for! I left my home and my children and my honor for the honor I have acquired with this evil man and for those wooden saints in that church.[46]

While Jews in Iberia always were in a somewhat precarious position of dependence on the benevolence, or at least grudging tolerance of the Christian power structures, after the establishment of the Inquisition Judaizing *conversos* in mixed marriages found themselves in an even more precarious environment. In a mixed marriage the non-Judaizing spouse held a potent weapon that gave him or her a decisive advantage on the quotidian battlefields of conjugal life. This, too, was a cross to bear and led to bitter expressions of regret such as that of Garçía Lopes [Aranda de Duero 1502], who reportedly complained, in continuation of testimony we heard earlier in this chapter: "This is a true captivity. Even in his own house a man doesn't dare to speak, I swear to God, or even move, because of his wife. Sometimes on the minor festivals I will do something behind closed doors in my house, maybe only some prayers. I don't dare do more. Before the women were subject to us, and now we are subject to them."[47] The *converso* Alonso Franco, married to an old-Christian, lamented in 1491: "See what trials those of us who are married to old-Christians have to suffer? For even though we would like to circumcise our sons, we do not dare to because of them."[48] What is worse is that sometimes the old-Christian partner made good on these threats, either out of spite or because of fear for the spouse's soul. One of these reasons may have motivated the wife of Francisco Botello. An informer in a Mexican Inquisitorial prison in 1646 overheard Botello talking about his wife with Juan de León, saying that if his wife were of:

> our law it might well be that I would not be here. If she kept our Law the way she keeps hers she would be canonized as a saint. I used to tell her that she was a deceiver, and what did she want with those ceremonies? And she would say to me: "someday you will see who is the deceiver, you or I"; which causes me to suspect that she might have found out something and denounced me. But woe be to her if she did it, for when I get out, if I get out, she won't be alive any more. I will deceive her and take from her everything I can and hide it away safely, and then I will give her something that will send her off to dine with the devils, may they take her soul, and I will have everything.[49]

One of the most detailed portraits to emerge from the period immediately prior to the Expulsion is that of Diego Arias Dávila, Chancellor of the Exchequer (*con-

*tador mayor*) of Enrique IV. According to the scores of witnesses who testified about the family from 1486–90, Arias and his wife Elvira González kept the Sabbath, observed the major festivals, set a kosher table, supported the synagogue, knew a good deal of Hebrew, kept Jewish ritual objects in their home, worked on Sunday, avoided going to church, and observed nearly every crypto-Jewish custom detailed in this book. Arias was bitter about his *converso* status, and blamed St. Vincent Ferrer, who had preached in Segovia in 1411, for his family's misfortune.[50] Two witnesses recalled that when Arias had heard in the mid-1450s that the family of the *converso* Maestre Francisco, the mayor of Medina de Campo, was preparing to leave Spain to take up Judaism in the Holy Land, he lamented: "Would be to God that I could do as you are doing."[51] As we have seen elsewhere in this book, Arias frequently disparaged the trappings of Christianity, particularly the saints, and sought out any occasion to share religious and social experiences with his Jewish friends. If anything, his wife Elvira was even more staunchly crypto-Jewish than was he.

The case built against them features a number of anecdotes in which Diego Arias's nostalgia for Jewish practices came to the fore. Many of these center on Jewish religious music. Diego Arias evidently had a sweet and powerful voice in which he took pride and his friends took pleasure. One witness reports how one evening at Diego Arias's house he saw him put a shawl over his head like a tallit and heard him sing evening prayers in a voice so sad and sweet that he seemed like an angel.[52] In the relative safety of Arias's home such an act was possible, if not advisable. Another relatively safe environment was out in the countryside in a group, alone or with a single friend—in this case a friend to whose son's testimony to the Inquisition in 1488 we owe the following anecdote: Rabbi Simoél heard his father, Master Josep, say that "one day out walking with Diego Arias, . . . they drew apart from the people who were with them, and Diego Arias asked master Josep if he knew how to sing anything in Hebrew. He answered that he did, and Diego Arias asked him if he knew the melody of a hymn that the Jews sing—called *Col Meuaçer*. He answered that he did, and began to sing it. Diego Arias joined in and told him he did not have the melody right, that it was more like he had started to sing, and they sang it together."[53]

Here too Diego Arias initiated the conversation, whose goals included the companionship of song, the reaffirmation of his religious roots in a shared quasi-religious act, and a desire to refresh his memory about a half-forgotten childhood melody. A familiar setting provided a sense of security: Diego Arias's defenses came down and he broke into song.

Strong drink could open the door to indiscretion too, as was reported in 1488 (Carrete Parrondo 1986, 66), and in this episode reported in 1489: One day, visiting his country house in Valdeprades with a friend named Zaragoza, he got up early in the morning, breakfasted heavily on sausage and wine, and then began to sing loudly the morning prayer. Zaragoza asked him what he was doing, to which Arias replied: "Go on, there is no Law but this one!" Zaragoza was reputed to have answered, "I don't know if he did it because of the wine or because he was out of his head."⁵⁴

For Diego Arias music was the key that opened the door to the world of his childhood memories. Judá Zaragoza recalled that one day while traveling on the road to Chinchón Arias had said to him: " 'You know, Don Judá? When I was a Jew I used to go to the synagogue on the Sabbath to say the *hararu* when they took out the Torah. . . . And I am going to say it now for you.' And he began to sing it out loud, and very nicely, like a Jew, and he took great pleasure from singing it."⁵⁵

Perhaps the most poignant of all these episodes is the following, in which we can see the pleasure that the *converso* Diego Arias still took in communal worship, the important role of music, and the clear sense of risk with which Diego Arias approached such events:

> Jacob Castellano, Jew, resident of Medina del Campo, official of the *aljamas*, sworn witness, says that it might be 26 years ago, more or less, when he was 12 years old, or slightly older, when Diego Arias de Avila . . . came to the town, where he stayed in the house of Francisco Ruiz. . . . And being there with him in his lodgings, as that was a Sabbath or a festival day that the Jews celebrate, Diego Arias expelled all the Christians from the room he was in with the Jews. Diego Arias looked around to see if some Christian remained to be thrown out and he saw this witness who was there, having gone with Don Mayr, his master, and he came up to him, and since Diego Arias realized he was a Jew he asked if he was a discreet boy, and they told him he was, and he responded: "Then he can stay. . ." And he had the door of the room barred.
> 
> And [he went over to] a table that was set there across two benches, laid with a carpet, and he took a tablecloth that was on it and climbed up on a bench which was in front of a bed in the room, and he put the cloths over his head in the way the Jewish chaplain puts on the large tallit when he prays. And he began to sing in a low voice a responsa which the Jews say on the Sabbath or the other festivals when they go up on the pulpit or *tebah*. He sang this to a melody the way the Jews say it and with as much grace or even more. He sang in Hebrew the responsa which begins: *Misurad colahy fasta cadís*, and he was singing it in Hebrew as I have said for a quarter of an hour. When he finished he got down off the bench, sighing and saying: "Oh, Jews, Jews. When you are celebrating the Sabbath, on Friday night, and you are singing *Vay hod lo asamay*, etc., you have no thought for the world, and you will never see anything as fine as that."⁵⁶

Another witness, Rabbi David Gome, who was in attendance, recalled Diego Arias's final words this way: "Oh, oh, Jews: you don't know the value of what you have!"⁵⁷

In Diego Arias Dávila we get a good sense of the worm of regret that gnawed many *conversos* from within. Arias and his friends had been forcibly expelled from a world of *convivencia*, of familiar cultural practices, of trust and comparative physical security. Rejecting the easy path to assimilation, nostalgic *conversos* like Arias, unable or unwilling to break cleanly with their Jewish past, looked over their shoulders at the culture of their youth vanishing in violence behind them. Their backward glances were captured by a historical record where some five centuries later we can still observe, in heart-rending detail, the precise moments when these *conversos*, like Lot's wife, turned to salt.

There were also moments in every *converso*'s life when nostalgia for the world left behind gave way to despair. From time to time we can catch glimpses of this, too, in the documentary record. It could be the expression of a wish to flee Spain to a place where one could again practice Judaism openly, as Diego Arias was reputed to have said around 1458, or a desire to go to Jerusalem. Or it could be an expression of the "if only . . ." variety, as when Diego Arias reputedly lamented that he would speak Hebrew better if only Vicente Ferrer had not come along to stir up the world. Or that he would not have converted if he were in Portugal and not Spain (Carrete/Fraile 1986, 63–4, 107).

## 20.4. REVERSION TO JUDAISM

One must distinguish between reconversion to Judaism, which was feasible only in certain tolerant havens outside the Iberian Peninsula and its possessions, and reversion to Judaizing, which occurred from time to time among the new-Christians.[58] Of the first, which has been discussed in recent years by a number of historians, much still remains to be said.[59] The lives of the Jewish and crypto-Jewish communities outside Iberia, however, are beyond the scope of this book.

No matter how thoroughly *converso* families considered themselves to have Christianized, as long as they themselves were aware of their Jewish past it was difficult for them to be entirely free of it. The rituals of the Inquisition, with its public readings of Edicts of Faith and its high visibility *autos de fe*, not to mention its networks of professional spies and enthusiastic busybodies, and the Iberian mania for genealogical investigation kept alive by the purity-of-blood laws ensured that even the most assimilationist *conversos* had questions of religious identity thrown up constantly in their faces. But the religious sensibilities of the *conversos* were heightened in other ways as well.

For one thing, the general intensity of religious concerns in the Europe of the Reformation and Counter-Reformation kept the possibilities of religious options solidly in the public consciousness. Moreover, Jewish practices and beliefs, even if all but dead in a particular *converso*'s immediate circle of family and friends, were kept alive by the Church in sermons and in the texts of the Edicts of Faith as a living model of behavior that said to every new-Christian, "This is what Jews believe and do; what do *you* believe?" And despite the generally feeble restrictions placed on *converso* emigration there was always the option to go to a land where one could follow a religion different from orthodox Iberian Catholicism. Thus until such time as assimilation was complete and Jewish family origins were totally forgotten, for individual *conversos* religion was never a given. They were always haunted by the specter of choice.

As we have seen throughout this book, for most *conversos* gradual assimilation into a Christian identity was the norm. That relatively few *conversos* from assimilated Christian families resumed their Judaizing is easy to understand, given the magnitude of risk of such an action. When a *converso* did resume Judaizing, it appears to have been for one of two reasons. The first, as with all of the other changes we have discussed, was family pressure. As we saw in Chapter 8 in the case of Simón Juárez de Espinosa [Mexico 1630], some families pressured prospective spouses into Judaizing as a condition of marriage (Lewin 1977, 6). In dozens of families a distant relative—an aunt, a grandmother, a cousin—might initiate a practicing Catholic young *converso* into Judaizing, using almost any crisis as an entry. Ana de Aguilar told the Granada Inquisition in 1595 that when she was twenty she became very sick and an aunt told her that "if she wanted to get well, and for God to do many things for her, she must believe only in the one true God and not believe in Jesus Christ or Our Lady."[60] In other communities the role of initiator was filled by what the Inquisition called a professional "dogmatizer" or, as was the case in Cuenca in the 1720s, by some senior member of the community (Lera García 1987, 111). Even a crypto-Jewish servant might serve as catalyst for someone's reversion to Judaism, as in Granada in 1560 (Bel Bravo 1988, 132). Some crypto-Jewish communities went so far as to use monetary incentives to induce assimilated *conversos* to join them: Gonzalo de Córdoba [Seville 1482] said that every time he came to the town where his father and brother lived they badgered him to Judaize, saying that "God gave riches to those who served Him, and that the *conversos* kept a fund to which every *converso* in town tithed, and the fund was for the needs of the *conversos*."[61]

Outside catalysts were the rule, but sometimes a reversion to Judaism might occur almost spontaneously in a *converso* whose combination of dissatisfaction with some aspects of Catholicism coupled with the kind of inquiring spirit that leads to curiosity about Judaism provoked the change of heart. Juan Méndez was one of the people whose awareness of their family circumstances drew them to reexamine their own religious convictions. Méndez [Mexico 1647] confessed that "his blood on his mother's side had inclined him to entertain doubts in matters of faith; and, if anyone had informed him that there was a Law of Moses, doubtless he would have followed it" (Roth 1931–2, 9). Another was Francisco Maldonado de Silva, who testified to Inquisitors in Lima in 1626 about his spiritual pilgrimage. Maldonado de Silva said that his father's family were all of the "caste and generation" of Jews; his mother's family were all old-Christians. As a child he lived with his mother in Tucumán, but when he was eighteen he journeyed to Callao, the port of Lima, to find his father, who had just been "reconciled" by the Inquisition. He and his father lived together as Christians for a year and a half. But one day he asked his father why Christians worshipped images if the First Commandment prohibited the worship of anyone but God. His father then confessed that he had been a Jew all along and had feigned re-conversion to Christianity only to save his life and property. With this Francisco too adopted the Mosaic law (García de Proodian 1966, 346–8). For Pedro Onofre Cortés [Majorca 1685] the catalyst was a personal crisis that led him to reassess his standing vis-à-vis the deity:

> It came to my mind that it could be that God was punishing me for having ceased worshipping Him and having turned to follow and keep the law of the Christians. . . . Whoever abandons Him to worship other gods He will punish with tribulations and great poverty, punishing them also by the hands of their enemies, and they shall go through the world mistreated and persecuted. While those who worship Him and keep His law, that He gave to His people through the hands of the Prophet Moses, He will give them happiness and wealth and victories over their enemies, and after this life He will give them Glory.[62]

# NOTES

1. For other matters relating to conversion see Chapters 1, 2, 3 and Chapter 8.

2. This first type of conversion also includes Christians, most frequently new-Christians, who became Jews. From the fifteenth through the seventeenth centuries and occasionally thereafter, some modest number of new-Christians left Iberia or the colonies and converted to Judaism in lands such as Holland or Turkey, where that was possible. In the case of males, often their conversion was marked symbolically by circumcision.

3. For Pablo de Santa María (formerly Solomon Halevi) see Baer 1966, 2:141–50. For Talavera see Hernando de Talavera (= Márquez Villaneuva) 1961. For da Costa see Acosta 1901.

4. Relatively rare are claims such as Pedro González's [Almazán 1502] that it was God's will that he convert (*Porque Dios quiso que se tornase christiano y que no fuese más judío*) (Carrete/Fraile 1987, 53).

5. *Pero de Salzedo, sastre del conde de Monteagudo, christiano nuevo, cómo avía estado judío en esta . . . villa tres días después de conplido el . . . término; e que después de tres días se tornó christiano; e que lo avía fecho compprenda que se remata en el almonedo a terçero día, pensando de aver remedio. E como vido que no ovo remedio, que se bautisó* (Carrete/Fraile 1987, 105).

6. *Si el rey, nuestro sennor, mandase a los christianos que se tornasen judios o se fuesen de sus reynos, algunos se tornarian judios e otros se yrian, e los que se fuesen, des que se viesen perdidos, tornarse y an judios por volverse a su naturaleza y que serian christianos e rezarian como christianos e engannarian al mundo, pensarian que heran judios e de dentro en el coraçon e voluntad serian christianos* (Baer 1936, 545).

7. *Traerlos a la santa fe por fuerza . . . no se debe hacer en ninguna manera especialmente en los adultos, quia caetera potest homo nolens, credere autem non nisi volens* (Hernando de Talavera 1961, 171).

8. [*Le tuvo en su casa] para que su muger no sopiese de la conversyon e bautysmo de su marido, e acabandole de bautyzar yo mismo fuy a su casa e hize tomar el hijo de los braços de su madre*

dando grandes gritos y haziendo grandes llantos y le lleve a San Francisco e ally fue bautyzado como el padre (Baer 1936, 525).

9. *Porque quieres dar mala vexedat a tu padre en hazerte christiano? No te vale mas que hare yo con tu padre que te ponga en la botiga y que tengas cargo della . . . ? No te pienses que tengas derecho en los bienes de tu padre; . . . andar en el ayre y yr pobre por los espitales; . . . Su fantasia de fazerse christiano* (Baer 1936, 456–8).

10. *Rodrigo el que se torno christiano con una sobrina de . . . don Ça que tenia por amyga, y como el aljama los corria, por aquello tornaron se christianos y quedo un ninno judio de la dicha amiga del dicho Rodrigo, e queriendo levar para lo tornar christiano, se fue el dicho don Ça al dicho alcalde Diego de Alva . . . y le pidio por merced, que aquel ninno que le tomavan, para que fuese christiano, quel lo remediase, y que el dicho licenciado le respondiera que no oviese recelo que judio se quedaria, y que le diera el dicho don Ça 500 mrs. e se quedo judio* (Baer 1936, 522).

11. *Calla, loco, y que pudia subir estando judio de rabi en suso? Agora so jurado en cap, y por un enforcadillo ahora me fazen tanta honra, y mando y viedo toda la ciudat de Çaragoça. . . . Quien me quita a mi que si yo quiero ayunar el quipur y tener vuestras pascuas y todo, quien me lo veda a mi que no lo faga, que quando era judio, en el sabado no osava yr fasta ahi, y agora fago lo que me quiero* (Baer 1966, 2:227; 1936, 463–4).

12. *En el camino fablando de las leyes al dicho mosen Pedro Sant Joan vino a dezir que el por pasar esta vida fazia las cosas como christiano que en la voluntat eran tan buen judio como este deposant, que no lo fazisa sino por los bienes y prosperidat deste mundo* (Motis Dolader 1987, 248).

13. *Por manera que el y la dicha su mujer e fijos tengan con que se alimentar. . . . Agora se falla en muy gran inopia y necesidad; . . . bienes para en que pudiesse passar esta miserable vida; . . . enpero haviendo respeto a su grande pobreza* (Motis Dolader 1987, 248).

14. *Pues nunca medre yo porque me torné christiano e avn quien me lo rogó. . . . Sy no fuera por las debdas que le deuían que no se tornara christiano ni viniera de Portugal* (Carrete Parrondo 1985a, 107; cf. 130–1). Many new-Christians from the region of Almazán testified in the early 1500s that they had emigrated to Portugal as Jews before accepting baptism and returning Spain (Carrete/Fraile 1987, 47, 69, etc.).

15. *Conosçía dél que tenía tan poca fe en la ley de los christianos como quando hera judío. . . . "Alonsyto, ve por el Targún āques vn libro de la ley de los judíos* [the Aramaic translation of the Hebrew Bible], *que quiero meldar." E quel moço le respondió: "¿Llamáysme Alonsyto y enviáysme por el Targún?" . . . Fue el dicho duque afrontado por religiosos e otras personas, deziéndole que era cosa de mal enxenplo tener onbre en su casa christiano que tenía muger ynfiel, que lo deuía echar de su conpañía, el . . . duque le enbió desir que la tornara christiana o que le quitaría el ofiçio de contador que tenía; y la tornó asy christiana. . . . Veys que pese al Dió, ya es tan vieja ley que no vale nada, que tan judía es mi muger como antes e tan christiana estaua antes como agora. . . . ¡Y por tan por* [sic] *tanto poco me torné christiana!* (Carrete Parrondo 1985a, 61–2, 161–2, 166).

16. *Mas me valiera estarme judio y guardar mi ley que no seyer christiano, que juro a dios que tan judio me estoy como el primer dia* (Marín Padilla 1982, 246).

17. *Fija, por los fijos* (Carrete Parrondo 1985a, 33).

18. *Se apartó dello porque conoció ser mal camino; y porque había de casar con cristiano de natura y por cuanto le trataban casamiento, de cuatro años a esta parte se apartó de algo de las dichas cosas y de dos años acá se apartó de todo* (Sánchez Moya 1958, 169).

19. *Yo naci cristiano . . . et siendo yo de edat dizinuebe o vinte anyos casé con aquesta muxer moça virgen que se clamaba Johana, fixa de Johan Gonçales, mercader. . . . Et por quanto de pequinito se me parecia que no era buena la ley de los cristianos et que era mexor la ley que dios dio a*

*Moyses. Et como yo fue en edat de bente anyos e fue en mi seso firme, me fue a la ciudat de Mallega del Regno de Granada; e fueme a casa de hun judio que se clama yeuda Cofer, que tiene la casa de la moneda del Rey de Granada et ali me fiz circumdir. Et enpues que fue circundido, andube por todo el Regno de Granada et por quanto me parecio no haver en todo el Regno de Granada tal muxer como la mia, arisqueme a tornar en Sebilla et trobe a mi muxer parida de huna fixa de ocho dias* (Marín Padilla 1982, 149).

20. *Como quier que el tenia ya intencion de ser christiano salvo porque queria trabajar en convertir a su mujer y fijos se hovo de yr del reyno . . . despues trabajo tanto con la dicha su mujer que plugo a nuestro sennor que la convirtio con nueve fijos e fijas e otras cinco personas de su casas y recibieron todos agua de babtismo en el reyno de Navarra. . . . Dizque la dicha su mujer e fijos que estavan algun tanto enduriados querianse passar la mar. E porque el creya que andando el tiempo los podria conduzir a la fe trabajo con ellos que fuessen a Navarra* (Motis Dolader 1987, 250).

21. *Ahavti et ishti v'et b'nei sh'b'goyot* (Yerushalmi 1980, 30).

22. *Oyendo los edictos de la fee dezia entre si hauiendolos oydo, valame dios, si esto que yo hago si es de la ley de Moysen* (Bel Bravo 1988, 146).

23. *Lo que le ha movido a dexarla es ver que andan arrastrados, como lo ha andado este confessante, sin haver quien le diesse vn pedazo de pan, llamandole de judio y hijo de judio* (Nunemaker 1946, 21).

24. *Yendo a ver la disciplina, cuando vio la imagen de Cristo y de la Madre de Dios, de quien antes era muy devota y toda la gente llorar y adorar al Cristo, le dio grande envidia y dolor de corazón, como antes lo solía hacer y entonces no y viniendo a su casa con grande sobresalto no sabía que se hacer y halló solo al Doctor San Juan su padre y le preguntó que había de hacer una persona para que se salvase y le había respondido que ser buena cristiana y creer lo que la Santa Madre Iglesia de Roma; y que fuese diciendo las palabras del credo y las creyese todas y le había dicho que por qué se lo preguntaba y le había respondido que no más de para sabello y su padre le había dicho que no se metiese en honduras y considerando que su padre, que era letrado y toda la gente sabían mas que su madre sola, desde entonces se había vuelto a ser buena cristiana* (Gracia Boix 1983, 137).

25. *Entendió que aunque hiziesse aquello no era contra la sancta fee catholica, y que lo uno y lo otro se podia hazer. . . . Al tiempo que se lo senseño no creyo ser contrario a la ley y fee de Jesuchristo* (Bel Bravo 1988, 32, 137).

26. *Unas parientas suyas le habían enseñado la ley de Moisés y que la había guardado juntamente con la de Jesucristo Nuestro Señor* (Gracia Boix 1983, 332).

27. *Avia dexado de guardar los dichos sabados por que su hijo, Alonso de Peñafiel, raçionero desta santa yglesia, se lo avia reñido* (Moreno Koch 1977, 353).

28. *Pequé que consenty a mi muger que desde que soy casado le vy ayunar un día, e porque le reñí, nunca más lo vy* (Fita y Colomé 1893, 314).

29. *No lo hizo despues de casada por el themor de su marido y cuñadas, que estauan todas juntas* (Bel Bravo 1988, 139).

30. *Estando en la villa de Pánuco a donde vino a ver a la dicha su hermana, que vivio allí doña Francisca Núñez de Carvajal, con su marido, hijos y casa, estando un día éste rezando en sus horas el Santo Oficio de Nuestra Señora, le dijo doña Isabel, hija de la dicha su hermana viuda, entre otras palabras, que no había Cristo y éste le dió un gran bofetón que dió con ella en el suelo, y arremetio para darle de coces o matarla, y le dijo con furia, enemiga de Dios y de sus Santos, y eso haz de decir, y reprendiéndola de que en su linaje hubiere persona que dijese contra Cristo Nuestro Señor, ella respondió que se lo habia enseñado su marido, cuyo nombre no sabe, mas de que era de Astorga, y luego éste le enseñó los artículos de la fe* (Toro 1932, 252).

31. *Su mujer le había persuadido a la creencia de la ley de Moisés y le había dicho que su madre y hermanas la guardaban; y le había dicho muchas particularidades y ceremonias della. . . . Y que aunque a los principios se había enojado con la dicha su mujer y había estado algunos días sin hablarla, después le había dicho que lo creâ; y que ayunaba ciertos días como ella le decía, sin comer hasta la noche y se iba a comer fuera de su casa a medio día; y esto lo hacía por asegurar a la dicha su mujer y no porque se hubiese apartado de la Santa Fe Católica, antes con intento de ir a Roma y pedir al Papa un Breve para que le absolviesen y diesen penitencia secreta por lo que tocaba a su honra. . . . Estado en la creencia seis meses y después dudaba en cual era mejor y andaba vacilando; y que después de presa su mujer, había estado en la dicha duda doce meses* (Gracia Boix 1983, 140). He was sentenced to wear the *sambenito*, to have all his goods confiscated, and to row for three years in the galleys.
32. Gracia Boix 1983, 135. See discussion in my Chapter 8, pp. 229–30.
33. *Se arrepentía porque se avía tornado christiano* (Carrete Parrondo 1985a, 22, 177). Shortly before the Expulsion Yuça Francés was heard weeping with regret and shame at having converted (*llorando como él estaua arrepentido e amansillado por se aver tornado christiano*) (García Casar 1990, 179).
34. *Que ny era christyano, ny moro, ny judio; no sé cómo me va, que no soy nada, y que plugyera a Dios que muryera mala muerte alla y no vynyera aca a ser christyano, que despues que aca vino avía çegado del todo* (Cantera/Carrete 1975, 171).
35. "*De sesenta años no me pueden quitar, e no me pesa syno que esta nuestra vida de colgada a juramento de palabras*," *lo qual desya por el juramento que fazen los christianos, que ponen vn palo sobre otro para faser la +* (Carrete Parrondo 1985a, 142).
36. "*Padre, tórname christiano*," *e que . . . su padre le dixo*: "*Anda, hijo, questoy perdido, que valiera más que no me tornara christiano, que buena ley te tyenes; vete con tu madre*" (Carrete Parrondo 1985a, 181).
37. *Quando yo moraua en barrio Mercado buena judía era. . . . Nunca oluidaré la leche que mamé. . . . Pues luego tan judío os estáys agora como estonçes. . . . Quando Dios quería hera de los dose pares; ahora es lodo y es nada. . . . Avnque pese a Dios por ello. . . . Buena ley tenían, que bien estauan quando eran judíos, y quel rey avía fecho mal en faserlos tornar . . . Por mi vida, sy yo estouiera agora en aquella tierra no me tornara christiano. . . . Buen Dios hera aquél que executaua luego; e luego, dende a poco rato, dixo*: "*E bueno el de agora*," *syn le fablar persona alguna dello de los que allí estauan* (Carrete/Fraile 1987, 30, 87, 90, 93, 95, 96, 111).
38. *Andat aca, vamos nos por la juderia y miraremos la fiesta que hazen esta noche los judios. Y asi fueron y pasaron por la juderia, y quando pasavan por la puerta de la sinoga de los torneros de la dicha aljama, sintieron, como cantaban los judios en la sinoga, y la hora el dicho Jayme de la Cavalleria dixo a este testimonio: Vat aca, entremos a mirar a esta sinoga. Y este testimonio dixo: Comno quereis que dentremos, que yo no lievo clocha, sino este tabardo? Y la hora vio este testimonio, como el dicho Jayme de la Cavalleria, asi como estava vestido con la clocha y capirot en la cabeça, que dentro en la dicha sinoga, y asi como dentrava por la puerta, dixo estas o senblantes palabras: Por el dio, veis aqui, como entrava mi aguelo, quando era judio en la sinoga, faziendo el dicho Jayme unos gestos del cuerpo, haziendo se muy drecho y alçando la cabeça, y asi dentro en la sinoga dentro de la puerta principal y estubo alli a la otra puerta que esta en un paset, y estubo alli un quarto de hora escuchando lo que estavan alli rezando los judios, y visto que estava tanto, dentro este testimonio y fizo lo sallir dalli, y assi se fueron a casa de la dicha viuda* (Baer 1936, 461).
39. *Vió como Hernand Sanches Castro . . . salió de la yglesia de Sant Andrés juntamente con otros christianos en su proçesión e pasaron por la plaçuela donde estauan los judíos con su Torá, esperando a que pasase la proçesión de los christianos, y estonçes se quedó . . . Hernand Sanches*

Castro con la Torá e proçesión de los judíos y dexó la proçesión de los christianos (Carrete Parrondo 1990, 172–3).

40. Se echaba de pechos sobre un coredor, donde se oía toda la oración, solo. . . . Este testigo dixo: . . . "¿Qué diablos haze aquí Juan de Cuéllar todos los tiempos que están en oración? Si ha de negociar con don Hebraén debe debía de hir e bolber." E respondió Alonso de Carmona: "Dexaldes vos. Ojalá la mitad de la deboción que él tiene tubiésedes vos e nosotros, que las noches no biene a otra cosa salbo a oyr la oración so color de negociar con don Hebrahén, e se nos sube a las cabañuelas a negociar con don Hebrahén e a su mesa" (Carrete Parrondo 1986, 36).

41. Tal meresco yo porque me torné christiana, que podía comer antes de todas las cosas que quería (Carrete/Fraile 1987, 45).

42. Quando héramos judíos enojáuamonos con vna pascua que vernía de año a año, y agora cada día pascua e fiesta carga e soberual, pues la misa que oymos se lo vale, que no entendemos más que asnos, e este abad que la dise que juro a Dios que creo que no sabe más que aquel perro; y agora es el catyverio verdadero (Carrete Parrondo 1985a, 149).

43. There are myriad examples of people like Francisco Martines Serrano [Soria 1491], who used to meet with friends to talk about the Torah (*Muchas veses platicava . . . con este testigo en las cosas de la ley de Moysén*) (Carrete Parrondo 1985a, 58).

44. *Estava con el mayor trabaio del mundo porque no podia comer hamines y viandas judaicas por causa de su muger sino a scondidas* (Marín Padilla 1982, 246).

45. *Le desía llorando cómo él estaua arrepentido e amansillado por se aver tornado christiano* (Carrete Parrondo 1985a, 58).

46. *Mira por que mal onbre me tornado christiana e he dexado mis fijos e mi marido. . . . Puede aver 10 annos p.m.o.m. que yo me torne chrystiana, y luego . . . tenia dubdas en mi coraçon, y un dia hyryome my marydo. . . . Mirad, sennores, por quien me torne yo chrystyana y dexi mi casa y mys hyjos y my onra por esta onra que he ganado con este mal onbre y por aquellos santos de palo que estan en aquella yglesya. . . . Yo tengo hyjos judios y ascondidas de mi marydo. Yo les he dado y enbiado dineros y otras cosas, y a una hyja mia pequenna hyse traer a mi casa y la tuvi ciertos dias en ella* (Baer 1936, 519). Many marriages were dissolved when one of the spouses converted and the other did not. Fairly common are complaints like that of an old-Christian woman named Catalina [Almazán 1505], who protested that her new-Christian husband Pablo used to berate her "because she was an old-Christian, and he used to say that God had punished him enough by depriving him of his children and his former wife, who was Jewish, and giving him her, who was an old-Christian, and if God would only cause her to die, he would never get married again except to a new-Christian like himself" (*Reñía con ella porque era christiana vieja, e le desía que farto mal le avía fecho Dios en quitarle su sangre y su conpañera, que era judía, y darle a ella, que era christiana vieja, y que sy Dios quisiese se moriese, que nunca casaría syno con christiana nueua como él*) (Carrete/Fraile 1987, 101).

47. *Agora es el catyverio verdadero, que avn en su casa el onbre no osa hablar, vos juro a Dios, para su muger, ni menearse, que algunos días de las fiestas menores haré alguna cosa ençerrado en mi casa, syno pedimientos; que no oso que antes heran ellas subjetas de nosotros; agora somos nosotros dellas* (Carrete Parrondo 1985a, 149).

48. *Ved qué trabajo tenemos nosotros, los que somos casados con mugeres christianas viejas, que aunque querriamos circuncidar nuestros fijos, non lo osamos faser por cabsa dellas* (Fita y Colomé 1887, 45).

49. *Si fuera de la nuestra pudiera ser que yo no estuviera aquí, y si lo que ella hace de su Ley lo hiciera de la nuestra fuera una santa y estuviera canonizada, y yo le decía que era una embustera*

y que ¿qué andaba con ceremonias?, y ella me decía: algún día verás quién es el embustero, si tú o yo, de que tengo algunas sospechas si a ella se le traslució algo que me acusó con los demás, pero pobre de ella si lo ha hecho en saliendo yo, que salga no ha de tener más vida, yo la engañaré y le quitaré lo que pudiere y lo pondré en buen recaudo, y le daré cosa con que la envie a cenar con todos los diablos que le lleven su alma, y me quedaré con todo (Lewin 174–5).

50. Que buen principio llegaba si no viniera esta rebuelta de lo de fray Vicente (Carrete Parrondo 1986, 94).

51. Plugera a Dios que lo pudiera yo así facer como vos (Carrete Parrondo 1986, 63, 64)

52. Con un taler puesto sobre la cabeza de lienço, puesto como rabí e cantando un salmo . . . que parecía un ángel en su boz (Carrete Parrondo 1986, 28).

53. Le dixera el dicho Diego Arias . . . que si sabía cantar alguna cosa de su hebrayco, el qual le dixera que sí, e que le dixera Diego Arias que si sabía el son de un pismoní que dicen los judíos "Col meuaçer" e que él le dixo que sí, e lo escompeçó a cantar; e que el dicho Diego Arais le ajudó e dixo que no acertaba en el son, mas que era como él lo començó a cantar, y lo cantaron entranbos (Carrete Parrondo 1986, 62).

54. Aquel día viernes comió allí morcillas casi saliendo el sol y comenzó a cantar la barahá el dicho Diego Arias, y el dicho Çaragoza dixo que le dijera: "Señor ¿y ésto?" y él respondiera: "Andad, que no ay otra ley sino ésta" (Carrete Parrondo 1986, 71).

55. "¿No sabes, don Judá? Quando yo era judío yba a la sinoga el día del sábado a deçir la hararu estando la Torá fuera. . . . Y quiéroos las agora decir," las quales comenzó a decir cantadas a voçes, con muy buena graçia, como judío, e se olgaba mucho en lo deçir (Carrete Parrondo 1986, 115). For other examples of how music tied the conversos to their past see Marín Padilla 1981–2, 275.

56. Jacob Castellano, judío, veçino de Medina del Campo, oficial de las aljamas, testigo jurado, dixo que puede aber beinte y seis años, poco más o menos, siendo este testigo de hedad de doçe años, antes de más que de menos, y viniendo a la dicha villa de Medina Diego Arias . . . posó en cassa de Francisco Ruiz. . . . Y estando allí con él en la dicha su posada, seyendo aquel día de folgar de los judíos o sábado o pasqua, tomó el dicho Diego de Arias y echó de la cámara e retraymiento en que estaba con los dichos judíos a todos los christianos que allí estaban fuera, e mirando el dicho Diego Arias si quedaba algún christiano para lo echar fuera, vió a este testigo que estaba allí presente, que abía ydo con don Mayd, su amo, que se llegaba a él, reconociendo el dicho Diego Arias que era judío preguntó a los dichos judíos que allí estaban si era mozo de seso, e dixéronle que sí, y él repondió: "Pues estese." . . . Y fiço cerrer la puerta de la cámara. Y so una messa que estaba allí puesta para comer con una alcatifa encima, la qual estaba sobre dos bancos, e tomó unos manteles que estaban encima de ella e subiose sobre una banca primero que estaba delante una cama que allí estaba, e púsose los dichos manteles sobre la cabeza de la forma e manera que se pone el capellán judío el taler mayor para facer oración, y enpezó de cantar a so boz vn responso que diçen los judíos en sábado o en otra qualquier su fiesta, luego en subiendo a la cátedra o tebá, el qual deçia mucho a son, según y en la forma que los judíos le dicen y con tan buena gracia y mejor, y el responso deçía en hebrayco, el qual enpieza: "Misurad colahy fasta cadís," y estaría en decirlo de la manera susodicha en ebrayco de la manera susodicha por espacio de quarto de ora; y acabado de deçir descindiese de la dicha banca, sospirando e diciendo: "¡Ay, judíos, judíos! quando vosotros estáis en vn Sabad, el del viernes en la noche, y estás diciendo 'Vay hod lo asamay, etc.' ¿no tenéis en nada todo el mundo y no miráis tamaño vien?" (Carrete Parrondo 1986, 106).

57. E que así acabados de deçir los dichos responso, que dixo: "¡O! ¡o! judíos, no sabéis el bien qué tenéis" (Carrete Parrondo 1986, 102).

58. People not descended from Jews rarely became active crypto-Jews, although there are occasional instances. For example, when a Mexican crypto-Jew named del Valle found his wife in the arms of an old-Christian in Pachuca in 1630, he apparently required the man to convert to crypto-Judaism as a condition for sparing his life (Alberro 1988, 211).

59. Nicolau Eimeric's 1376/1578 *El manual de los inquisidores* contains an interesting description of the ceremony former-Jews and Christians were made to go through in order to be considered Jews (Eimeric 1973, 85–6). See also Netanyahu 1966, especially 218–20; Yerushalmi 1980. Some members of Europe's practicing Jewish communities accepted responsibility for the reconversion of their *converso* brethren, both those who remained in the Iberian Peninsula and those who were still living as Christians in other European cities. Printing presses in places like Amsterdam produced Spanish- and Portuguese-language conversionist tracts for smuggling into the Peninsula (Kayserling 1890). Both apologetic and polemical literature was produced in substantial quantity (Halkin 1953, 399–400). In Contreras's view, every new-Christian was a potential emigrant once his or her commitment to Judaizing had been kindled in an evolutionary process that "begins with the New Christian and concludes with the Jew; the marrano is the intermediary stage" (1991, 130).

60. *Si queria sanar y que Dios le hiziese muchas mercedes, que no avia de creer sino en un solo dios verdadero y que no creyese que avia Jesuchristo, ni Nuestra Señora* (García Fuentes 1981, 463).

61. *Dios le dava bienes y riquezas que serviese al señor con ellas, y que le dizian que ellos tenían bolsa entre los conversos a la qual davan todos los confessos de esta çibdad de todo lo que ganavan de diez maravedis uno. Y este dicho baçin o bolsa era por las neçesidades de los dichos conversos, y que todos los sobredichos le hizieron tantas moniçiones y requerimientos que le trastornaron su huizio y le hizieron errar contra la fe* (Ollero Pina 1988, 93).

62. *Podría ser que Dios me castigasse por haverle yo dejado de adorar y haver buelto a seguir y guardar la ley de los Chrystianos. . . . Que quien por adorar otros dioses dexaría de adorarle, los castigaría con trabajos y mucha pobreza, castigándoles también por manos de sus enemigos, y que por el mundo maltratados y perseguidos yrían perdidos. Y por el contrario, aquéllos que le adorarían y guardarían su ley, la que dio a su pueblo por manos de su Profeta Moysés, que los daría feliçidades, riquezas y victorias de sus enemigos, y después de esta vida los daría la Gloria* (Selke de Sánchez 1972, 258).

# CHAPTER XXI

# The Social Contexts of Crypto-Judaism

## 21.1. Socializing with Jews

From the earliest wave of forced conversions in 1391 until the Expulsion in 1492 Iberian *conversos* continued to live in close proximity to their Jewish neighbors despite sporadic attempts to formally segregate the city neighborhoods according to religion.[1] The cities in which they lived tended to be small—rarely more than a few thousand souls, often only a few hundred—so that routine business or social activities inevitably brought Jews and *conversos* together. In their professional lives, whether buying or selling, signing contracts or borrowing money, engaging in manufacture or collecting taxes, the two groups mingled. *Conversos* met Jews on their travels to the regional commercial fairs and they often used the same network of host homes or inns. The *converso* Manuel Rodrigues [1490] used to "sleep some nights in the hospice of the Jews in the castle in Soria."[2] When the *converso* priest Fernando de la Barrera [Cuenca 1491] traveled he sometimes slept at a Jew's house (Carrete Parrondo 1979, 54–5), as did a certain Aragonese *converso* [1490] who when he "traveled stayed in Jewish homes and ate their food and drank the wine which had been blessed."[3] That other *conversos* when they traveled mixed freely with old-Christians, new-Christians, and Jews, as circumstances dictated, is confirmed by testimony such as that of Diego Sánchez de San Pedro [Ocaña 1509], who said that before the Expulsion "it was the custom for Jews to spend the night in Christian homes, and Christians in Jewish homes, particularly in places where there were fairs."⁴ When the Jew Mose Aben Xuxen found himself in Molina de Aragón on Sukkot, he built a *sukkah* at the home of the *converso* Juan Gallego and blew his silver-decorated *shofar* to invite the *converso* community to the *sukkah* (Cantera Montenegro 1985, 68).

In some parts of the Peninsula even up to the summer of the Expulsion a spirit of *convivencia* seems to have continued to prevail.⁵ Despite the laws that prohibited social intercourse between the religions, it was not unusual to find Jews and Christians attending each other's major life-cycle events, and in some communities among high-placed families this seems to have been the rule rather than the exception. In 1489 in Trujillo an old-Christian town councilman named Gonzalo Pérez Jarada was criticized because "he used to honor Jewish weddings with his presence, because that was the custom in Trujillo."⁶

The exchange of gifts on each other's major holidays was also common. Manuel Rodríguez reported that "it was customary in Huete [Cuenca 1491] at Christmas time for Jews to send to old- and new-Christians and at Passover for Christians to send to Jews fruit, eggs, and other things."⁷ The *conversa* María López [Almazán 1492] testified that "I sent some Jews leavened bread, grapes and a present of cheese, because these same Jews used to send to my husband and to me on feast days and for Christmas . . . capons and partridges and other things and fruits, and for this reason I sent them what I have said."⁸

People on both sides of the religious line were likely to be sensitive to the dietary concerns of the others. The *converso* priest Fernando de la Barrera [Cuenca 1491], for example, was accused of frequently eating with Jews at his house or at theirs, and even of allowing kosher slaughtering of fowl in his own house so as to "do them the honor of serving them meat."⁹

Even in the tense atmosphere preceding the Expulsion there is evidence that some Christians and Jews continued to support each other's charitable institutions. In the 1492 trial of Blanca Rodríguez [Huete] it was reported that "when the Jews make processions . . . they give charity to all the poor who wish to receive it, to both Jews and Christians." Moreover, "when the city rejoices either at the birth of a prince or for a victory that God might have given the monarchs, . . . the Jews take out the Torah and that day the Jews give alms to the Christians, and they receive them from them; and likewise, when the Christians go soliciting on Sundays and feast days with bowls, they receive alms from Jews."¹⁰ Especially the new-Christians continued to contribute to Jewish charities. María Alonso [Huete 1489] used to give alms to Jews who would come to her house at certain times to bless her table (Blázquez Miguel 1987, 45). *Conversos* seemed to have felt a special commitment to helping maintain the community synagogue. In fact a Valencian Edict of Grace of 1484 specifically labels as Judaizers any *converso* who "gives money or any other thing to build, repair, or decorate a synagogue."¹¹ The *converso* Juan Molina [Huete 1491] was said to go around to all the *conversos* in town to collect money for the synagogue, but since the Inquisition considered him a half-crazy old drunkard he was let off (Blázquez Miguel 1987, 47). Contributions of oil for the synagogue lamps—perhaps in symbolic commitment to keep the light of Judaism burning—seem to have been a common feature of pre-Expulsion *converso* life. This was true even among the *converso* Catholic clergy, as can be seen by the trial of the *converso* priest Fernando de la Barrera [Cuenca 1491] (Carrete Parrondo 1979, 57) and the Jeronymite monk Juan de Madrid [Segovia 1487], who was said to have given some of the monastery's oil for use in the synagogue, passing it out through the gate or through a chink in the monastery wall (Beinart 1961, 182). This sort of donation is noted as early as a 1449 anti-*converso* tract that accuses "each of the adult converts of maintaining a lamp in the synagogue, and each day giving alms for oil for those lamps";[12] it is recorded as late as 1570, when the Coimbra Inquisition said that Leonor Coutinha, of Vila Flor, gave alms to "a certain person who came from the land of the Jews to collect charity for oil for the synagogues and to tell them on what day the Jewish fasts fell."[13]

Prior to the Expulsion many *conversos* who were comparatively well off thought it their duty to help their financially disadvantaged Jewish friends and relatives, and the Hebrew word for charity, *tzedakah*, frequently appears in trials covering events of this period. The *converso* Pedro Abella [Barbastro 1491] allegedly "out of his devotion to the Jewish Law gave money to the communal charity fund, and other donations to poor Jews."[14] Rita Santángel and her daughters [Teruel 1485] were accused of "giving alms to buy oil for the synagogue, . . . and of giving alms to poor Jews"[15] and of making gifts of bread to the Jews.[16] In Segovia "the wife of Alonço Gonçalez de la Oz . . . had a Jewish brother named Don Baro for whom she secretly did much good."[17] Gonçalo López Cocodrillo [Segovia 1487] donated a shroud for a poor Jew (Gutwirth 1981, 97). Fernando Ram, of Teruel, gave alms for righteousness' sake every Friday,[18] as did Blanca Ramírez in Toledo.[19] For that matter, in some places the Jewish community seems to have actively solicited these donations. Juan García [Soria 1490] reported how a Jew had come to the *converso* Gonzalo Sánchez's house to "ask for alms with an open purse in his hand."[20]

In all but the largest Spanish cities in the years prior to the Expulsion, the entire population of Jews and *conversos* formed a single extended family, welded together through generations of marriage within the community. The fact that in the wake of the 1391 riots large numbers of the community suddenly found themselves Christian, or that over the next hundred years increasing numbers of Jews converted, did not rupture the age-old patterns of communal living. No matter what the beliefs of individual family members, on the whole families continued to celebrate important occasions together, at least until the generalization of the Holy Office in 1480. What emerges from Inquisition testimony is proof of the unwavering strength of family ties and the power of family events to draw *conversos* back into Jewish familial groups.

Family events—births, circumcisions (or baptisms), weddings, illnesses, funerals—brought the groups together. The *conversa* Violante de Santángel [Teruel 1485] confessed that "when the Jews were celebrating a wedding, the Sunday before, when other people and old-Christians went to the *judería*, her mother sent her daughters there to see the wedding ceremonies."[21] In Lérida in the late 1470s Aldonza Garreta was said to have attended the circumcisions of her friends' children and to have taken pleasure listening to music, eating traditional foods, and enjoying herself at the festivities (Marín Padilla 1981–2, 290). The Aragonese *converso* Juan Serrano confessed that around 1482, "shortly after his conversion, he went to a naming ceremony in the home of a Zaragozan Jew named Parello. When sweetmeats were served he asked if a Christian could eat Jewish foods. The *converso* Diego Maldonado replied that he could, because Christians have a "law of grace which says that anything that has been blessed can be eaten.""[22] Juan ate and drank, but later had second thoughts and related the incident to his confessor, who imposed as a penance that he wear a hair shirt for three days.[23] Similarly, the *converso* Pedro Abella [Barbastro 1491] was accused of "going to Jewish weddings and circumcisions and festivals in the Jewish quarter and of having eaten with them, wearing new clothes and honoring the Jews and consoling himself with them." The *converso* Manuel Rodríguez in Huete [Cuenca 1491] "used to go to the burials of the Jews to pray to God for them."[24]

Major Jewish festivals sparked family gatherings; in fact prior to the coming of the Inquisition it was commonplace for new-Christians to celebrate the festivals with their Jewish friends, especially the holidays whose observance involved family feasting (such as Passover and Sukkot) or communal home ritual (such as Purim). Among other reasons, traditional ethnic foods were a powerful magnet. *Conversos* could not help but notice how the *aljamas* prepared for these holidays, as the sounds of cleaning and the smells of traditional cooking filled the air. Among Jews, these holidays were occasions for gathering together the extended family, which frequently included members who had converted. In Teruel in 1485, for example, several young *conversa* girls were accused because "on Jewish festivals ... they went from their houses to the *judería* and entered into the houses of the Jews and drank and ate fruit and candy with them."[25] A 1484–5 trial in Ciudad Real (1484–5) alleged that it was common for *conversos* to "welcome Jews who wore the badge into their houses and to eat and drink with them."[26] Judging from the emphasis placed on food in the trials, it seems that for Inquisitors the consumption of food was what separated a casual visit from one with ritual significance.

The most common festival, of course, was the Sabbath, and the documentary record overflows with evidence of *conversos* who continued to celebrate it with their Jewish friends and family, often sharing their Sabbath meals. Absolutely typical was the case of Buena de Pero Gonçales, of Agreda [Soria 1491], who was accused of "continually dining with her brothers who were Jews, of eating their Kosher food and their Sabbath stews and of keeping the Sabbath with them."[27] Jaime de la Caballería, the *converso* brother of the Aragonese Chancellor, frequently took his Sabbath meal with the family of the Jewish weaver Abraham Leredi in Villanueva [Huesca 1490s], joining in on the responses to the prayers (Baer 1936, 461–2).

As we have seen in Chapter 15, communal prayer was as much a social experience as it was a religious one, and as such functioned as a magnet to draw Jews and *conversos* together. Special events, like the appearance in town of a famous preacher, might draw an audience from a broad spectrum of the community. Testimony in 1486 in Aragon indicates that when well-known Jewish "sermonizers" were speaking in the synagogues they drew crowds that included Jews, *conversos*, and even old-Christians. *Conversos* sometimes went to listen to sermons in Hebrew.[28] But *conversos* in those years did not need special events or special invitations to draw them back to the synagogues. An anti-*converso* tract dated 1449 accused the converts of "going to the synagogue every day to hear the Mosaic services and to pray against the Christians."[29] The evidence that many *conversos* continued to frequent the synagogues right up to 1492 is overwhelming. Donosa Ruiz [Teruel 1484] "would go to the synagogue of the Jews or Jewesses to pray, as the Jews do, and when she cannot go to the synagogue, she prays in her home. . . . She went to the home of her relatives and friends to pray with the other heretical, apostate, bad Christians."[30] The *conversa* Brianda Besant [Teruel 1486] even paid for a reserved seat in the synagogue so that she could attend services. On the High Holidays, or other occasions when this was too dangerous, she would go with other crypto-Jews to a house near the synagogue from which they could hear the prayers (Haliczer 1990, 213). Gonzalo Pérez Jarada [Trujillo 1489] used to pray regularly with Jews, especially on Friday afternoon. He also admitted that on Sukkot he may have walked through their huts but only because that was the only way into their houses.[31] Pedro Abella [Barbastro 1491] was accused of visiting the Jewish synagogue and of praying to [sic] the Torah, and of honoring it.[32] It is also clear from much testimony that the Jewish community was deeply concerned by the risks it incurred by permitting new-Christians to continue to worship with them, and that it sometimes took steps to put an end to it. A typical example comes from Soria [1490], where Ruy Martínez was accused of "going into the synagogues of this city and praying the prayers of the Jews, reciting prayers in the Jewish fashion; and the Jews threw him out of the synagogues and . . . Ruy Martínez shouted why were they throwing him out of the synagogue, since he wanted to pray like the Jews were praying."[33]

The picture that emerges from testimony in the late fifteenth century is one of daily interactions between Jews and *conversos*, centered on family and religious events. An exemplary case is provided by the family of the *conversa* Elvira González and her husband, Diego Arias Dávila, Chancellor of the Exchequer (*contador real*) of Enrique IV. Elvira and much of her family had been converted at the time of Vicente Ferrer's preaching in Segovia in 1411. For nearly a half century they continued to interact with their Jewish relatives, helping decorate their houses for weddings and laying out their dead for burial.[34] Elvira's Jewish cousin Jacob Melamed told how she and Diego Arias "after they had become Christians, both before they were married and afterwards, lived in his house for a long time, and they ate and drank together" (Carrete Parrondo 1986, 48). Elvira González continued going to the communal *mikvah* in secret with her sister, Leticia.[35] Until the very day she died, around 1460, Elvira González maintained an intimate friendship with her Jewish niece, Luna. Similarly, her husband, Diego Arias, never stopped giving gifts to his Jewish sister, who lived next door to him in Avila and with whom he communicated through a secret gate (Carrete Parrondo 1986, 93, 117–9). Diego Arias Dávila and his wife, Elvira González, both deceased prior to the Expulsion, were *conversos* working hard to remain Jews, not *conversos* struggling to assimilate into the Christian mainstream. Nonetheless, in the portrait of these two that emerges from Inquisition archives can be seen the conservative social dynamic that characterized the *converso* community around the time of the Expulsion.

Matters of belief aside (without belittling its strength as a contributing factor), it was the pull of family and friends, of holiday meals and other community activities, that drew the pre-Expulsion *conversos* back into the Jewish world. The prosecuting attorney's summation of the case against Elvira González is eloquent testimony of the web of habit that tied her to the Jews. He accused her of:

- on Saturdays eating *adefinas* cooked by Jews, drawing aside secretly on Saturday to eat them without being seen or noticed;
- when the Jews finished their Passover sending them leavened bread, eggs and lettuce;
- when her [Jewish] daughter was married having two Jews prepare kosher meat for her;
- sending apples to Jewish weddings;
- going to the Jewish quarter to celebrate the seven days of mourning for her [Jewish] sister who had died; . . .
- going to Jewish weddings to the Jewish quarter and remaining there;
- going to the Jewish quarter at night to the ritual bath with Jewish women;
- taking pleasure on the Sabbath with Jewish men and women and on the other festivals and feasts of the Jews; and going to the Jewish quarter to celebrate them; and later, when she was prosperous, having the Jewish women come to celebrate them with her;
- going to the Jewish quarter to visit her relatives when they had given birth, remaining there until they circumcised the infant;
- even after she had converted to our holy Catholic faith she resided in the Jewish quarter in the house of her aunt for a long time, where she conducted herself as she had before when she was a Jew;

- in her last illness, by her will and command, having two Jewish women at the head of her sickbed;
- and when she died, "they wrapped her in the Jewish fashion, with breeches and a long cape, with a hood, which Elvira had put aside in a chest; and they put a pillow of virgin dirt in the coffin, under her head." (Carrete/Fraile 1987, 123–5)

These patterns of behavior appear to have held both for the sincere converts to Christianity who despite their assimilationist goals chose not to turn their backs on their families and for the Judaizing converts who maintained family networks for the purpose of helping keep their Jewish customs alive. During those tense years just prior to the Expulsion the two groups were frequently difficult to tell apart.

After 1492 some of the same patterns continued to be observed within the different sectors of the *converso* community. In most circumstances Judaizers and assimilators continued to commingle harmoniously as business associates or as family members. For one thing, as has been often demonstrated in the course of this book, *conversos* were arrayed along a continuum that ran from tenacious Jews to fervent Christians with every intermediate gradation. Only at the extremes did people adopt exclusivist behaviors. Some *conversos* did all they could to purge their family history of traces of their true ancestry, moving to a new town, changing their names, and falsifying their genealogy. Such people did not welcome continuing contact. At the other extreme, some—perhaps most—practicing Judaizers were extremely circumspect about who was admitted to observe or participate in their Judaizing activities. They might well dine, visit, or lodge with anyone along the continuum—and in some cases even marry someone whose religious convictions and practices were widely different from their own—but they would pray, fast, or eat *matza* only with Judaizing friends in whom they had confidence.[36]

## 21.2. THE INQUISITION

From its founding in Andalucia in 1478 to its abolishment in the fragmenting, post-Enlightenment Iberian world of the early nineteenth century, the Inquisition was an inescapable presence for Iberian Christians, often shaping the course of their lives. This is not the place for a detailed discussion of Inquisition politics, procedures, or economic policies, nor is it the place to survey the evolution of contemporary attitudes about the Inquisition. Bibliography about these subjects is copious, and the principal works are listed at the end of this volume. Nonetheless, for the purposes of this book it will be useful to consider two sets of issues: the most common emotional reactions that the Inquisition elicited in new-Christians, and the coping strategies that it forced them to adopt.

Although *conversos'* reactions to the Inquisition were complex and as varied as the individuals who experienced them, four emotional patterns seem to have been dominant. (1) Fear, sometimes magnified to panic at the mortal threat which the Inquisition always represented. (2) Indignation at the way in which the Inquisition and purity-of-blood laws made mockery of the Christian concepts of equality before God. (3) Scorn, disgust, or outright loathing of the venal aspects of the Inquisition, which sometimes put greed or personal vengeance ahead of Christian piety or justice. (4) Veneration of the victims of the Inquisition as martyrs to their crypto-Jewish faith.

In turn, new-Christian strategies to cope with Inquisition pressure tended to be of three sorts: (1) Sporadic, largely unsuccessful attempts to abolish, change, weaken, or otherwise mitigate the pernicious effects of the Inquisition.[37] This included developing strategies to evade discovery and to fortify prisoners who were to suffer interrogation, often under torture. (2) Flight, either spiritual flight into clandestine crypto-Judaism, as we have seen throughout this book, escape into the attractive alternative worlds of artistic creation, or actual physical flight through emigration. (3) Assimilation. The adoption of unassailably Christian lifestyles and beliefs remains the most successful coping strategy of all. Some assimilationist new-Christians took the vanguard of militancy as the aggressive anti-*converso* propagandists of the fifteenth century.[38] Some joined the legions of new-Christian clergy.[39] Others, such as Tomás de Torquemada and Diego de Deza, the first two Inquisitors General, became functionaries of the Inquisition itself. Some falsified documents, lied in their testimony under oath, and somehow thwarted the nearly ubiquitous purity-of-blood laws.[40] The most successful of all were the quietly conforming Christians who melted away into anonymity.

The word *cataclysm* is overworked, but it accurately describes the effect on every Iberian new-Christian community when the Inquisition first came to town and the first Edict of Faith was read aloud to the assembled totality of the town's inhabitants, who, willing or not, were socially compelled to attend its proclamation. Suddenly crypto-Jewish behaviors that had once been routine became mortally risky and had to go instantly underground. Worse, prior behaviors were also actionable and any record of Judaizing, no matter how slight, put a person at risk. Moreover, anyone with even the slightest hearsay knowledge about prohibited activities was required to come forward and testify. Every citizen, whether new- or old-Christian, instantly faced the moral—and it soon became clear—mortal dilemma of whether to come forward and speak.

Echoes of the panic felt by the generation of the 1480s bubble up in testimony of the period. A colleague said that Fray Alfonso de Toledo, a Jeronymite monk of the monastery of Sisla in Toledo who was sentenced to be burned in 1485, had turned as pale as death when he heard the Inquisition was coming (Baer 1936, 475; 1966, 2:353–4). Many *conversos* were agitated into flight. Fernando de Ayllón fled from Soria to Extremadura because of the Inquisition. There in 1491 he explained his reasons to a *converso* named Josepe Pinto, who, after first ascertaining whether Ayllón was a *converso*, asked him:

> "Why are you here so far from your home region?" And [Ayllón] said to him: "Since for our sins everybody harries us, the Inquisition came to Aranda. I was a councilman at the time and didn't know what to do—unless it was to act with my staff of justice as if I were on official business and to leave. And that's why I am here. One day I went to see a prisoner, a friend of mine—he didn't give the name—and he told me to get out, because from greed for my possessions they were going to kill me. And then I wrapped these clothes in a bundle and grabbed what I could and I left and fled here."[41]

In 1502 Leonor Ramírez told Inquisitors in Soria that Dr. Diego, a *converso*, had come to her and told her that his brother had sent him an urgent letter which he read to her, which said that "he ought to take precautions, because Juan de Salcedo had condemned and burned many people in the city. And that as soon as he had read the letter he should burn it."[42] Particularly in the 1480s and 1490s, when the Inquisition's activity was at its peak and horrific tales of public burnings and of mass arrests and torture were sweeping through the new-Christian communities on what seemed like a weekly basis, panic was a reasonable response.[43]

This reaction was not limited to the first generation of Judaizers but continued for as long as the Inquisition actively campaigned against crypto-Jews. In 1516, when Violante Fernández was fleeing from Guadalajara to Portugal with her children, "in each town [she] would say they were going only as far as the next town, so that they would not be arrested as fugitives."[44] Simão Gonçalves [Coimbra 1571] helped targeted Judaizers to escape: "When certain people of his Nation were fleeing because they were afraid that the Holy Office would arrest them, and when Gonçalves heard about them and why they were fleeing, he sheltered them in his house and he gave them favor and help so that they could get away."[45] The new-Christian Lionel Mendes was reported to have fled from Oporto to Pernambuco in the 1590s because he dreaded the Inquisition, which had already arrested his sister (Furtado 1925, 318). Francisco López Díaz [Mexico 1640s] told Inquisitors how, when he was young and the Inquisition in Lisbon was intensifying, he and his siblings fled to Seville, where "some of the fugitive women changed their names and moved into a house on the outskirts of town, where they hid for a year, earning a living by washing the clothes of the men who had also fled at that time . . . and who continued to visit them, despite the risks."[46] Juan Méndez de Villaviciosa used to keep watch on the Mexican prison, so that he could advise people whose relatives had been arrested to hide their possessions and burn their papers.[47] And in fact when the Portuguese Judaizer Francisco de León Jaramillo thought that he would be taken by the Mexican Inquisition in the 1640s, he helped his father bury the family silver (García 1910, 109). About the same time Jorge Ramírez de Montilla told the Mexican Inquisition that "because he had suffered the fears and worries with which Judaizers commonly live, he had hidden some of his wealth, and sold the rest for far less than it was worth."[48]

The panic *conversos* felt for the Inquisition became a literary stereotype as well. Mateo Alemán, himself a new-Christian, recounts this story in the 1604 continuation of his picaresque novel *Guzmán de Alfarache*:

> There was a new-Christian, ripe for cooking, rich and powerful, who was living happy, fat, gay and contented in some houses that he owned, when an Inquisitor moved in next door. And with only having him nearby he grew so thin that in a few days he was reduced to skin and bones.[49]

Active Judaizers had good reason to fear the Inquisition. So did anyone who was even distantly related to someone convicted by the Holy Office. Martín Alonso Menbreque [Córdoba 1511] told Inquisitors that the reason he confessed was "from fear that they would burn him, because they had burned all his relatives and many others too."[50] One did not have to be a staunch Judaizer to experience this dread. It was enough for a person to suspect that they might not pass the litmus test of Catholicity. This is the sense of the remarks of María Maestre, of Quintana del Pidio [Burgos 1501], when she told the Sigüenza Inquisition that several of her women friends had told her that they feared the coming of the Inquisition "because they say that they require the Our Father and the Ave Maria and the Credo and the Salve Regina and other things that make people afraid."[51] *Conversos* knew that even the slightest recurrence to an allegedly Judaizing custom might spell their doom. As a formerly Jewish character recently returned to Spain put it in Miguel de Carvajal's early sixteenth-century play *The Courts of Death*, "If the little Christian—although it troubles him, and weighs on him—should Judaize even a little bit, then the knife is at his throat."[52]

Perhaps the most pernicious side effect of the Inquisition was the way in which it destroyed the foundations of trust on which harmonious human relationships depend. With the coming of the Inquisition, new-Christians were justifiably fearful of their servants, neighbors, and even family members. Whatever enemies they might have were now able to avenge themselves through denunciation. The anonymous accuser, soon universally referred to with the Hebrew term *malsín*, became the most feared and loathed of creatures. Inés García's daughter-in-law [Guadalajara pre-1492] told their Jewish friends that "she was a Christianized viper and they should beware of her."[53] Since any slip of the tongue might lead to their condemnation, new-Christians tended to be acutely self-monitoring. If someone indiscreetly veered into a sensitive subject, friends were quick to cut him or her off. Thus, when Alvaro de Prado began to complain about the Inquisition [Soria 1501], a *converso* named Gaona instantly cut him off with a hand signal.[54] When someone ventured too far in a conversation he would likely stop suddenly and attempt to swear his listeners to secrecy, but—to judge from the frequency with which denunciations of trivial conversations appear in the trial records—with little effect.⁵⁵ The Mexican *converso* Luis de Valencia described the environment this way in 1638:

> In a certain Indian village in the province of Nicaragua in the town church Luis de Valencia said to a certain person who shared his Law and beliefs: "See how these Indians even though they are barbarians have a church where they can worship and venerate God and we do not have a temple, or priest or sacrifices where we can please, respect, venerate and magnify the God of Israel. And we are forced to wander in persecution by the Inquisition, and wherever we go we do not have one safe hour. And our temple must be our hearts where we praise the Lord secretly so that the Inquisition will not seize us. For as soon as we communicate [aloud] sooner or later they arrest us."⁵⁶

Judaizers guarded themselves and scrutinized the movements of their potential enemies.⁵⁷ The poisonous nature of this endemic suspicion can be seen in a 1603 case from Mexico City. Sebastián Rodríguez, a new-Christian merchant there, had set up Duarte Rodríguez in business and invited him to board in his house. One day, while they were in the storeroom behind his shop, Sebastián said that "he had heard that [Duarte] was communicating with the Holy Office, and that he begged him by the one God to note that he had children who should not be made orphans. And his wife Costanza Rodríguez pleaded the same way."⁵⁸ That this fear was justified can be seen in the many recorded instances of people who did use the threat of denunciation to give them a powerful advantage over another person. Tomé Gómez [Michoacán, Mexico 1640] threatened a fellow *converso* with denunciation if he pressed Gómez to repay a loan he had made to him.⁵⁹ Francisco de León Jaramillo told Inquisitors [Mexico 1640] that once his father had introduced him to Judaizing he abused his knowledge about his father's Jewish practices to steal money from him for his gambling debts, realizing that his father was no longer in a position to punish him.⁶⁰

The greatest danger was not from neighbors on the street but from friends and relatives who had been arrested by the Inquisition and might under coercion implicate Judaizing *conversos* still on the outside. From bits and pieces of information that appear in the testimony, it is clear that some *converso* communities worked hard to fortify each others' resolve to remain silent. When the arrests started in Mexico in 1642, Rafaela Enríquez called her group of Judaizers together and told them that if they were arrested they should "shower threats on their fellow prisoners," warning them not to give information about them.⁶¹ Her colleague Francisco López Díaz advised his fellow Judaizers that if they were arrested they should only talk about themselves and not implicate anyone else, and that way when they got out the rest of the community would help them.⁶² Once they had been arrested, these Mexican Judaizers tried a number of strategies to try to protect their communities. While in prison they communicated with each other via a system of taps on the wall, and they used aliases so that the Inquisition's agents would not know who was speaking (García 1910, 227, etc.). They talked up their courage to fortify their resolve. Doña Ana Juárez joked with the other Judaizing women about the penance they were likely to receive, saying that "she did not want her *sambenito* to be decorated with diamonds, but rather with a yellow satin ribbon, which because of her fair skin would look good on her."[63] According to the summaries of the 1646–8 *autos de fe*, several of the Mexican Judaizers initially feigned madness so as to deflect questions and avoid having to denounce their colleagues and families.[64] Francisco Botello invented wild stories so that Inquisitors would think him mad (Wiznitzer 1962a, 252), and the Portuguese merchant Francisco Núñez de Navarro affected shaking fits. Esperanza Rodríguez, a Judaizing *mulata*, tore her clothing, pretended that a roll of rags was her infant daughter, and let herself be eaten by fleas.[65] Leonor Váez ranted and raved (Liebman 1970, 227).

In this atmosphere a kind of paranoia, both communal and individual, took hold of the new-Christian psyche. Generations grew up under the stringencies of the Inquisition. Whether they were Judaizers or assimilators, the twin pressures of the Inquisition and the purity-of-blood laws forced them, if they were to survive, to become adept at donning publicly acceptable masks. In other words, to the paranoid fear of the Inquisition was joined a pervasive schizophrenia, as each newChristian consciously had to don a public persona behind which to safeguard private spiritual or social practices. Each *converso* perched on his own shoulder and watched himself act. Each became at once the protagonist and author of his own fictionalized autobiography.

The second set of attitudes new-Christians expressed with regard to the Inquisition—and for that matter, with Spanish Catholicism in general—may be loosely categorized as indignation. New-Christians, wherever they placed themselves in the spectrum that ran from Judaizers to assimilating Christians, tended to be acutely sensitive to the contradictions between the Christian ideal of the universality of Christ's saving grace and the sharp distinctions their society drew between new- and old-Christians. In the sixteenth century many new-Christian literati stressed this theme in their works, insisting that lineage was in no way as important as true faith and good works,[66] that human beings are all descended from Adam and Eve (or from Noah),[67] that they are all on equal footing at the hour of their death,[68] and that the eucharist brings Christ's body equally to all Christians, no matter when they converted.[69] These themes occasionally surface in the trials as well, such as when Leonor Núñez [Mexico 1646] responded to an Inquisitor's question about her lineage by asserting "that she descended from Adam and Eve."[70] But the indignant protests seem to have fallen universally on deaf ears.

The third attitude commonly expressed by *conversos* was disgust. New-Christians were not shy—at least in environments they thought were private—about expressing their disdain for the venal nature of the Inquisition. The Holy Office financed its own activities with what it seized from convicted heretics.[71] Thus from the very first moments heavy fines and confiscation of property were an important component of the sentences meted out. It is not at all surprising, then, that the profit motive was widely attributed to the Inquisition by new-Christians, nor that their strident resentment frequently made its way into the Inquisition record itself. Mencia de la Peña [Escalona 1487] was allegedly of the opinion that "the *conversos* who were burned were only burned so they could seize and steal their property, and that whoever had property should realize that they also had the flames."[72] Similarly Diego de Roa [Soria 1501] insisted that "many of the Padres who seized and burned people did it only because of their property."[73] In 1484 Catalina de Zamora was heard to remark bitterly that "the Inquisition these Padres are carrying out is as much about taking *converso* property as it is about glorifying the faith. . . . Here is the heresy they found in Juan Pintado: 17 sheets and the furniture in his house. He died for this, not because he was a heretic."[74]

These attitudes persisted for as long as the Inquisition was active. In 1587 the *christão novo* Francisco Alvares was denounced to the Lisbon Inquisition for having asserted that the Inquisition palace was "a house of vice," because in it "men were stripped of their property and dishonored."[75] Seventeenth-century Brazilian *cristãos novos* generally believed, with good cause, that the Inquisition pursued them for economic reasons. In the 1640s Antam de Castro called the Inquisitors thieves (*ladrões*). Cristóvão Cerveyra, who was reconciled in a 1642 *auto da fe*, said that the Inquisitors only wanted the Jews' money (Novinsky 1972b, 142). Augustín Cortés de Alfonso [Majorca 1686] reputedly said that the Inquisitors "were dogs who had . . . taken our property as if we had worshipped the Devil!"[76] The trials of many Mexican Judaizers of the 1640s make it clear that they thought the Inquisition was mainly motivated by greed. Pedro de Espinosa put it bluntly: "The Inquisition does not want poor Jews; only rich ones." Equally blunt was Francisco López Díaz: "The Inquisition only arrests in order to expropriate property; they don't want to convert prisoners." Pedro López de Morales, a miner, said he had "dreamed that the Holy Office had taken them prisoner, and in the room in which they found themselves the Inquisitors were counting money they had taken from another Jew."[77] Manuel de Sosa y Prado [Mexico 1694] said that "the rulers of Castile and Portugal did ill in depriving Jews of their property and oppressing them so strongly it took their lives."[78]

For *conversos* like these the Inquisitors themselves were rotten to the core. Duarte Nunes [Lisbon 1553] was of the opinion that "many of the prisoners of the Inquisition were there unjustly, and the judges were more deserving of being burned than were the judged."[79] The new-Christian merchant Joam Bautista [Bahia 1590s] called the Inquisitors devils.[80] Antonio Costa Lobo [Evora 1618] said, among other things, that Inquisitors "instead of saving souls sent them to Hell. And that the Devil would take them all." And that the Inquisitors were "dogs, Cananites, Samaritans and Philistines." And that the only reason people confessed to Judaizing was because of the torture. "And that lightning should strike the Inquisitors and whole kingdom because of the vexations they had caused the people of the Nation; and the King too, because he consented to it."[81] Conversations between Juan de León (alias Salomón Machorro) and Francisco Botello in the Mexican Inquisitorial prisons in 1642 obsessed on these themes. León said that if he ever escaped he would want to live where "there are no jails like these or the sort of men who treat honored men worse than they treat Negroes." Botello replied that the Inquisitors are "cruel executioners, tormentors who will pay for it all in Hell while we are at rest." Later León unleashed a tirade against them: "What do you think of these deceivers who hang their portraits in the hall so people will think they are saints? Do they think that because they are Inquisitors they are saints, and there is no one else in the world like they are?" Botello replied: "They are haystack saints, may they be burned instead of the straw. Demons, they are demons from Hell, condemned to Hell. . . . Do you see what good works and saints they have created and are creating, taking away lives, honor, and property, and taking pleasure from doing harm; those are all reasons why the demons must consider them saints."[82]

A natural outcome of these views, even among practicing Judaizers, was the conviction that many *conversos* convicted by the Inquisition had got a raw deal. The blame fell on the venal, unjust Inquisitors, and also on the allegedly false witnesses who denounced their colleagues for reasons of fear, animosity, or profit. In trials around 1501 many members of the Soria *converso* community voiced their conviction that they were being treated unfairly. Fernán Zapatero felt that eight out of ten victims were denounced falsely. Gonzalo de Alconada's wife echoed this sentiment: "Oh, Holy Mary, husband, how many are burned because of false witnesses!" In 1501 Alvaro de Prado voiced the opinion that the Castilian Inquisition alone had burned 1500 people on the basis of false testimony.[83]

The reverse side of this coin was the belief that sincere Judaizers went to their deaths as martyrs for the true religion. This view—not unnaturally—seems to have prevailed among Judaizing new-Christians. Many thought that the Inquisition victims were martyrs because they had been persecuted unjustly. In this view false witnesses and the venal nature of the Institution as an institution, or of the Inquisitors as corrupt individuals, had prevailed. Typical was the opinion of the new-Christian silk merchant Fernão da Rocha [Lisbon 1597], who said after an *auto da fe* that "those poor little sinners died as martyrs."[84] This view was even held by an occasional old-Christian like Catalina Crespa of Ubeda [Córdoba 1569], who was accused "because when other people were speaking ill of the converts, she said that they should not speak ill of them; that many were persecuted and died even though they were blameless; and that some day all this would be perceived clearly. And it was reported that she was a great friend of the converts and of listening to the converts when they preached. She proved that she was an old-Christian and that the witnesses were her enemies. Absolved."[85]

Other new-Christians believed that the victims' martyrdom lay not in the fact that they had been persecuted inappropriately but that they had had the conviction and the intestinal fortitude to affirm their Jewish allegiance to the end.[86]

They were, in the words of a *converso* monk from the Jeronymite monastery of La Sisla in Toledo in 1495, "martyrs who had died for the Law of Moses like the Maccabees."[87] Particularly prized was these victims' steadfastness even in the face of the horrible consequences of their stubborn faith. Manoel Dias Espinosa [Brazil 1622] held that "many of those who were burned died as martyrs because they were honorable men and sustained their honor by not giving in and confessing."[88] In 1686 Pedro Onofre Cortés reported that he had asked a man named Billa about a Judaizer who had been burned: "Do you think that Jew whom they burned, the one named Alonso, did right in letting himself be burned? Because he could easily have asked for pardon and mercy and saved his life and later emigrated to his own land if that was his wish and not commit suicide, for that is a great sin. . . . Billa replied that Alonso had done well because whoever dies for his God is crowned in Heaven."[89] In a show of faith, or bravado, New World Judaizers often marked their imminent martyrdom by giving their co-religionists a so-called Judaic kiss of peace (*osculum pacis judayco*). In the Mexican *auto* of 1649 María Gómez attempted to "give the kiss of peace in the Jewish fashion" to her mother when the sentences were read.[90] Manuel Bautista Pérez, from Anzan, in Coimbra, was executed in 1635 in Lima, Peru, where among other proofs of his Judaism it was observed that "on the gallows he gave the kiss of peace to his brother-in-law Sebastián Duarte."[91]

People seem to have understood full well how martyrs were created and their usefulness in sustaining commitment to crypto-Judaism. Juan de León [Mexico 1642] said that because he and his friends observed the Jewish customs "they oppress us, and lock us in jails and dungeons, in fog and in darkness, with a thousand kinds of martyrdom in a thousand different ways, so that we become martyrs and saints."[92] María González acknowledged this process at her arraignment in Ciudad Real in 1511, allowing that "often when speaking of her husband after they burned him as a heretic, they said that of a sinner they had made a martyr." She also made clear how heroic martyrdom could be a source of consolation to the living. As a martyr her husband "had ascended to heaven; that one night he had appeared to her as an angel, as a beautiful two-year-old child, and that immediately he had disappeared."[93] The new-Christian Duarte Mendes [Bahia 1590s] was reported to have told Diogo Fernandes not to weep when his father was burned by the Inquisition because he had died for the sake of his honor.[94] In an extreme case, such as the one narrated to the Mexican Inquisition by Simón Juárez de Espinosa around 1646, his friends induced him to Judaize by taking him to the cathedral and showing him his grandfather's *sambenito*.[95] A clandestine religious confraternity was even founded in Portugal in honor of Fra Diogo da Assunção, who was burned in 1603, and another, disguised as a Society of Saint Anthony, was founded in honor of the martyr Antônio Homem (Roth 1931–2, 6). Victims of the Iberian persecution were also eulogized by Europe's openly practicing Jewish communities abroad, in literary martyrologies in a number of languages.[96]

Although most crypto-Jews, understanding full well the fate that might await them should they fall into the hands of the Inquisition, took to flight or sought the protective cover of anonymity, a few—for religious or psychological reasons that we can only guess—actively courted martyrdom. One of the most striking examples is the South American Judaizer Francisco Maldonado de Silva, who confessed his Judaizing with pride, telling the Inquisitors that "there was only one God, a forgiving God, who had given His law to Moses on Mount Sinai, which he observed in his heart and for which he was going to die." He challenged the Inquisitors "to burn him, for those who died by fire did not die, but rather God kept them forever alive." He said that "if he had a thousand lives he would give them all for the sake of observing the Law of Moses." In a letter he wrote from his cell to the "Synagogue of Rome" he "promised to die fighting with all of his strength and power against the enemies of the truth of God's law, and to observe it up to the altar of fire that I believe they are preparing for me soon so that from it God will receive me in holocaust for the sake of our sins and that He will cease His anger against me that has burned so during these times." After twelve years in prison he was granted his wish on January 23, 1639.[97]

Somewhat more common were last-minute expressions of bravado in the face of the inevitable, such as Juan de Madrid's 1486 confession from the gibbet that "as long as I have to die, better that I should die now than later. I say that the Law of Moses is the good Law, the one in which people will be saved." When the crowd heard this they stoned him.[98] One also occasionally finds the desire for martyrdom cast into the subjunctive mood by people who, with admiration for their brave colleagues or bitter regret at the living hell in which they found themselves, wished that they had had the strength to accept martyrdom themselves. This, for example, is the sense of Alvar González's [Canary Islands 1520s] lament that he had not died a martyr at the time of the great persecution.[99]

## 21.3. Dreams of Emigration

For new-Christians the possibility of emigration was always an alternative to remaining in the Iberian kingdoms. Although the movements of *conversos* were restricted by law, and obtaining an exit visa could be problematical, the evidence is overwhelming that *conversos* who were determined to leave could almost always find a way. Rare is the *converso* such as the Jeronymite monk Alfonso de Toledo (burned as a Judaizer in Toledo in 1485) who said that he had tried twice to emigrate but had twice been brought back by force, and that he would have tried again if he could (Baer 1936, 475; 1966, 2:353–4). What held most *conversos* back was a combination of personal motives that outweighed the desire to live in a land where they could practice Judaism openly. One of the most commonly expressed motives was the fear of being caught and of having the Inquisition interpret the attempt to emigrate as a prima facie case for Judaizing. Juan de Sevilla [1485] confessed that he had aborted his plans to emigrate because, when people had told him that the Jew he planned to go with was going to sell him out, he did not dare to go (Baer 1936, 445). Lope del Castillo [Aranda de Duero 1492] evidently planned to wait the Inquisition out, for he allegedly "swore to God that when the Inquisition let up a little bit he would go to a seaport and there he would become a Moor or an Arab or whatever you like, and there his children would associate with people of his choice."[100] For some other *conversos* like Ruy Díaz [Soria 1491], who said "that if it were not for his children he would go to the land of Judea,"[101] family ties were a deterrent to emigration. While this was undoubtedly true for many *conversos*, it was just as true that those who did emigrate routinely broke up their families in order to do so. Testimony in Soria in 1490 reported that for years Francisco Martínez had been saying that his intention was to give everything he had to his wife and he would send her to her father's house so that he could go to Jerusalem.[102] Leonor de Castro [Cuenca 1490] declared that her father and some other men had already left Cuenca "to go to Judea where they would all be reunited on Yom Kippur."[103] Nonetheless, for most Iberian new-Christians the dream of emigration remained a dream; whether for reasons of family, financial concerns, fear of being caught, or sheer inertia, most Judaizing *conversos* stayed put. The historical record suggests the majority of Judaizing new-Christians did not—as Maimonides' principles required—invalidate the religious significance of their conversion by seizing the first opportunity to emigrate. As we have seen in the Introduction to this book, this situation caused enormous problems for the Jewish religious authorities living abroad who were forced to decide in cases of marriage, divorce, or inheritance, whether or not an Iberian new-Christian was still to be considered a Jew.

But these dreams continued to buoy up despairing Judaizing *conversos* with hope of the possibility of a better life. If they could just hold on to their Jewishness a little longer they, or their children, could one day go to a place where the Iberian Inquisitions and purity-of-blood laws would be only a cruel memory. The simple motive for these dreams of emigration was the desire for religious freedom. Juan de Sierra [Ciudad Real c. 1503] expressed this idea clearly to his friend Antón Sánchez one day when they were out walking, saying "that in other realms, such as in the land of the Turk and other places, they let everyone follow the Law they want; because there were Moors and Jews and Christians there and they let each one live in his Law. And the way he said that it was clear that they ought to do the same in these kingdoms of Castile, and that they ought to let everyone live in the Law they preferred."[104] Most of the statements recorded in the trials are less complex, but the yearnings they reveal are just as strong. María de Zárate and a friend [Mexico 1656] hoped "that before they died they could go to a place where they could reveal publicly the Law in which they lived."[105] Catalina de Santacruz merely wanted escape the hell of her current life; according to 1573 testimony in Granada, once when she was being verbally mistreated and punched by her old-

Christian neighbors at the village oven, she ran crying down the street: "May God take me to a land where I can die in the Law of the Jews."[106]

The *conversos* of the Expulsion generation had a predilection for Turkey. Some, like María Díaz [Ciudad Real 1484], who said that she wanted to go to Constantinople to become a Jew,[107] saw Turkey as a land that encouraged the open practice of Judaism. Others appreciated that Turkey controlled access to the Holy Land. The *converso* Juan de Robles [Cuenca 1535] wrote letters to his mother expressing his desire to go to the Holy House and to Jerusalem.[108] And some looked to Turkish Palestine as the site of the long-awaited Messianic redemption. Juan de Moya [Cuenca 1490] promised a friend that he would take him to the Promised Land (*Canpo de Promisión*), Jerusalem, and that that promise would be fulfilled by the coming Messiah (Carrete Parrondo 1980, 255). Evidently some *conversos* avidly followed news reports from the East in hopes that the proper moment would arise for them to start their journey. In the trial of Gracia Lopes [Lisbon 1543] Gonçalo Dias said that "when the Emperor took Tunis from the Turks she was sad; when the Cape of Gué was taken she was happy. He heard her say . . . that she was resolved to flee to the Gulf of Salonica."[109]

*Conversos* of later generations yearned for any safe haven. The Coimbra Inquisition's sentences from the 1570s record several of these dreams. Heitor Vaz, in 1567, was accused of "telling people that he was a Jew at heart and that he wanted to go somewhere where he could live freely." Antónia Vaz, of Matosinhos, was accused in 1573 of praying that "God take her to die to Moorish lands, where she could see her mother's grave, and that if she remained in Portugal that dogs and crows should eat her and disturb her bones." Graça Garcia [Vila Real 1571] allegedly said that "she would be a good Christian only when the old-Christians were good Jews or Moors, and that she would give a great sum of money and would let them live in freedom if they would let her live in freedom in the Jewish law, without being imprisoned or punished for it."[110] Sebastião Pereira told the Lisbon Inquisitors in 1584 that a Jew named Antão de Barcellos, who lived with the ambassador Francisco da Costa, had tried to persuade him to go to the Barbary Kingdoms where he could practice Judaism openly.[111] In 1578 Juana de Mellia, who had already lived for a time in Tlemcen [Morocco], was tried in Granada for having expressed a desire to go back to the Barbary States, saying that "he wanted to go with some Moors back to his land, and that once he was there he would do like the others and observe the Jewish Law which he considered better than that of the Christians."[112]

Mexican *conversos* of around 1600 had a strong Italian connection in the person of Ruy Díaz Nieto, who had traveled there extensively. Testimony in 1604 indicates that "he was fond of talking about Florence, Ferrara, and other places," often describing Jewish practices he had seen there, and sometimes talking nostalgically "as if he were still among the Ferraran Jews."[113] A generation later the focus was on the Low Countries. Luis Franco [Cartagena, Colombia 1626] "planned to gather up all that was owed to him and to go to live in some land where there was freedom of conscience." He expressed a preference for Flanders.[114] Tomás Treviño de Sobremonte [Mexico 1647] had a similar dream. His son Rafael reported that his father had said that just as soon as some poor friends of their were released by the Inquisition, they would go to a place where they could live as they pleased, by which he meant the Low Countries.[115]

Testimony sometimes allows us to glimpse both *conversos*' hunger for particulars about Jewish life outside the Iberian territories and the elaborate fantasy worlds *conversos* dreaming of emigration must have created for themselves. A good example are the conversations recorded in the Inquisition prison in Mexico in 1643 between Juan de León (AKA Salomón de Machorro) and another prisoner. The two men's dreams of emigration to a land where Judaism could be practiced openly were mixed with naïve hopes with regard to some other features of this redemptive land. León was asked by a fellow prisoner whether it was true that in Amsterdam:

> there was a church where those of the Nation could go to participate in services? León replied that there was, and that the church was very big and well appointed. That on Jewish festival days the men and women enter separately, and the boys and girls the same; because from a very young age they teach them and read to them the Law and what they are to observe, and they teach them the prayers and they indoctrinate them with great care. And the prisoner said: "I have a great desire to see all that." And León told him: "You will see it; if That Man [meaning God] grants us life we will both see it." He then went on to explain to his friend that when they got to that land "they would give him whatever woman he might fancy, whether she was married or not; and that That Man had endowed almost all the women of that land with beauty, and it would be like picking pears. And the prisoner said to him: "I wish we were there to see it." Another time León filled his friend's head with dreams of the Italian city of Leghorn: "It is a very generous land and very inexpensive, and when they find out that you are a member of the Nation everyone favors you and helps you, so that in four days you will become rich." And the prisoner said to him: "Then it's agreed, there is no reason to stay here, nor to tarry in this evil land. Let's go where we can live without unpleasant shocks, without always dragging our noose around."[116]

## 21.4. IDENTIFYING OTHER JUDAIZERS

Secret Jews, like any other clandestine persecuted group, required methods of identifying one another without disclosing their identity to the hostile larger community that engulfed them. Crypto-Jews also required ways of speaking with each other about their group so that uninitiated outsiders would not catch on to the true meaning of what was being said. These strategies were necessary to bridge two very contradictory requirements of crypto-Judaism: the need for secrecy and the need for communal religious activity. The solution was to create a code.[117]

The written record suggests that codes were more commonly used in the seventeenth century than in the sixteenth, and in the distant American corners of the empire than in the Iberian Peninsula itself. Undoubtedly for the first generation or two after conversion, and within the relatively narrow confines of their home districts, new-Christians and those among them who Judaized were likely to know one another. But as memories faded, and the Iberian empire widened to include the Americas, the East Indies, and portions of southwestern Europe, it became increasingly important to have a method of innocently asking whether a person was a Judaizer, so that if the person was not, the true meaning of the question could pass as inadvertent. The most straightforward method—asking whether a colleague identified him or herself as a Jew—was also the most dangerous, for it could easily lead to a string of incriminating revelations, particularly if the colleague turned out to be an Inquisition spy. Juan de Heredia [Canary Islands 1632] said that "one day when he was at the house of Fernán Pinto at Laguna, . . . Pinto (who deponent understands is of the Hebrew race) said to him: 'You are one of us,' and to discover his motive in asking the question the deponent answered: 'Yes' " (Wolf 1926, 124). These issues were better approached obliquely. Crypto-Jews in seventeenth-century Galicia alluded to each others' "knowledge" in order to indicate their religious identity. "When they spoke among themselves they would say 'So and So knows the Lord, So and So is the Lord's.' " Another phrase they used was "when you get there with So and So you can go ahead, because he knows his stuff very well."[118]

In colonial Mexico in the mid-seventeenth century there were several expressions that served as a code to identify someone as a practicing Judaizer. One was a response to a question about someone's identity with the phrase "he is a very good man and comes from these parts," which indicated that the man was a Judaizer and came from a place where Jews could practice openly.[119] Another way was to say that "so and so was a son of the man."[120] Juana Enríquez gave Inquisitors another set of phrases: "Does he know something?" "Is he afraid of God?" "Does he have a good heart?" "Is he observant?" "Does he observe the Law?" (Liebman 1982, 127). Garci Méndez de Dueñas [Mexico 1623] allegedly revealed himself to a friend as a Judaizer "by greeting him and exchanging words with him and winking at him and making a sign with his face."[121] For seventeenth-century Majorcan *chuetas* the phrase "a very good man" meant an observant Judaizer; a "good person" was one who observed at least one voluntary fast each week; and "servants of God" were Jews (Braunstein 1936, 113). *Conversos* in Cuenca in the early eighteenth century reported several other code phrases. The Inquisition itself was called *pincha*; the penitential garment, or *sambenito*, was called the "saddle blanket" (*albarda*), and being crypto-Jewish was referred to as "being a member of the carder guild" or being "Basque."[122] *Conversos* also devised a set of coded greetings they could use with each other in public and other phrases for the privacy of their homes. Juan de León and Francisco Botello, prisoners of the Mexican Inquisition in 1645, greeted each other as follows: "May the Almighty give you a good day," to which the reply was "May He do as He will, and this I ask of Him" or "May He give you the same."[123] Izabel da Gama [Lisbon 1552] reported that while Henrique Lopes and his wife were relaxing he called her "Sister Jew," and he wanted her to call him "Brother Jew."[124]

But surely the most common strategy to ascertain whether an acquaintance was a crypto-Jew, or at least sympathetic to crypto-Judaism, was to dance verbally around the subject, drawing closer to the key questions with ambiguous phrases that if understood correctly would elicit revelatory, although equally ambiguous, responses, until one of the parties finally dared to become explicit. This is the essence of how Pedro Onofre Cortés [Majorca 1686] said he came to know Rafael Cortés de Alonso, who sponsored him in the silk business:

> One day when he gave me silk, he told me that he enjoyed doing favors for those poor people who knew the omnipotent God. I responded that if that were the case then God would reward him. And he replied that he knew very well what God commanded in His holy law, and therefore, just between you and me, I won't let you down. I responded that God would reward him. And he told me that he would like to go outside the city one day with me in a leisurely walk. So a few days after that the two of us went outside the walls of the city, and there, strolling up and down, we declared ourselves to each other as observers.[125]

A similar anecdote was reported in Peru in 1635, when a witness narrated to the Inquisition a discussion between two anonymous merchants about the Judaizer Francisco de Vergara's marriage to a Portuguese girl. " 'How could this Portuguese new-Christian marry his daughter to a Navarro? She must not understand what's what' (which is like saying that she must not be a Judaizer). And the merchants replied to him: 'She's no dummy; she understands very well, and has read a lot of stories, and knows by heart more than seven.' With that the person was left with the impression that the Portuguese man professed his religion, and that they dealt with each other in the same Law."[126] Sometimes crypto-Jewish practices could be encoded in similarly eloquent ways. For example, in Francisco Delicado's satirical novel *Retrato de la Lozana andaluza*, published in Rome in 1528, there is a scene in which Lozana, a *conversa* recently come to Rome from Spain, endeavors to find out whether her companions are *conversas* as well. When she tells them that she likes to cook fritters in olive oil, not in lard, they recognize her openly as one of them.[127] Though this code, based on widespread Jewish custom, would have worked anywhere, most examples involve signals that seem to have been deliberately concocted and must have had a restricted, local significance. The Panamanian Sebastián Rodríguez, for example, was accused in 1641 of signaling to his friends that he was a Judaizer by taking hold of the friend's hand and raising it to his chest (Osorio 1980, 193).

The difficulty of determining whether someone Judaized is patent in the case of the house guest who stayed with Violante Juárez in Guadalajara, Mexico, for three months in the mid-1640s. Violante and her husband, who were at the heart of the Judaizing community in western Mexico, and whose house often served as an informal synagogue, were looking at the guest as a prospective husband for their daughter. For three months they tempted him to reveal himself: "In order to arrange the marriage they scrutinized his words and actions with great care, to see if they could catch a hint of whether he Judaized. And when they saw that they could not find a clue that would serve this purpose, they treated him very badly, so that he left their house."[128] The Brazilian poet José da Silva told the Inquisition in Lisbon in 1726 how he had revealed himself to a close student friend, Luiz Terra. "When the two of them were alone Luiz Terra embraced him and said that he lived in the Law of Moses, and that João Thomaz had also told him and Luiz Terra that he lived in that Law; and he didn't know more details about how he was observant, and he did not want to reveal more to him either; to which his friend responded that in effect he lived in the Law of Moses, and this was the way they declared themselves, and it did not go any further, nor did they say who had instructed them, nor who else they had told; and they trusted each other because they were friends of the same Nation."[129] But, as testimony before the Inquisition repeatedly makes clear, even in cases of the strongest presumption of trust it was always dangerous to reveal oneself. For years the South American *converso* Francisco Maldonado de Silva successfully concealed the Judaizing he had learned from his father from everyone else in his family, including his wife. But in 1626 in Chile he revealed his secret adherence to Judaism to his sister Isabel when they were alone together at a spa near the city of Santiago. Isabel wrestled with the knowledge for eight months and then finally denounced him to the Inquisition (García de Proodian 1966, 341, 348).

Some of these problems could be solved if the crypto-Jewish community was sufficiently networked that members could recognize each other without having to resort to these risky strategies. Of course networking provided its own risks, as is indicated by the frequency with which such groups of relationships are described in the Inquisition documents. Seventeenth-century Mexican crypto-Jews cultivated these networks both in order to promote community solidarity and to locate prospective brides or grooms. Margarita de Rivera, a notable Mexican Judaizer of the 1640s, made it her business to "go out among the Jews to discover which were the most Jewish and perfectly observant in the Law of Moses."[130] When the Portuguese *converso* Francisco López Díaz arrived in Mexico in 1638, he immediately set about "declaring himself a Judaizer to many members of that community, particularly to the women."[131] López Díaz was part of the glue that held the Mexican crypto-Jewish community together in those years. Wherever he traveled he fasted with the Judaizing community. Among his activities were visiting sick Judaizers in the hospitals and bringing in charitable contributions from outlying areas for the poor Judaizers in Mexico City. He carried the news, informing various groups how well other groups were doing in adhering to the Law and who had been taken by the Inquisition. He also acted as a matchmaker, ensuring that "Judaizing women marry men of the Hebrew nation."[132]

Crypto-Jewish travelers, particularly if they intended to adhere to the dietary laws, or observe the Sabbath or festivals, needed a safe place to lodge when away from home. Many crypto-Jewish communities seem to have maintained such public houses and to have spread the word about the services they provided. The *converso* Manuel González, for example, ran the Mesón Blanco in Guadalupe in the 1480s. It was known as a haven for Judaizers traveling in Extremadura, a place where they could have a meal that conformed to the dietary laws and where *kiddush* was recited over the wine (Fita y Colomé 1893, 323). Judaizers coming to Mexico in the 1630s knew that in Veracruz they were to stay with Fernando Rodríguez. In Mexico City Simón Váez would receive them (Liebman 1982, 121). It was probably at Váez's house that Tomás López de Montforte lodged in 1637, for he described it as "the house of a rich Jew where all the Jews who come here from Spain or Portugal stay, and where people gather as in a synagogue."[133]

These networks were particularly useful in helping crypto-Jews who were newly moving into an area to acclimatize themselves. In Bahia in the 1590s Domingos Nunes da Roza, a shoemaker, denounced Gomes Fernandes, the "noseless one," for running a kind of Welcome Wagon for newly arrived Judaizers. "He said that when any new-Christian comes to this city, that he went to talk to him and help him; and that he assisted the poor new-Christians who came to this land, the foreigners who except for him found no one to assist them."[134]

## 21.5. SECRECY AND DECEIT

Judaizing *conversos* used three general strategies to deceive the watchful eyes of old-Christians with regard to their true religious practices: concealing, dissembling, and misdirecting. As we have seen frequently throughout this book, the Judaizers were adept at finding ways to conceal the practices of their religion. They tended to be deathly afraid of being observed and sought out places where their worship presumably could not be seen. One of the most unlikely hiding places was the church itself. Fray Juan de Madrid joined the monastery of Sisla in Segovia, he said in 1487, "so as to better observe the Jewish Law, because in the monastery no one saw him."[135] For *conversos* without a Catholic vocation, favorite hiding places were out in the countryside away from the eyes of neighbors and servants, or at home behind closed doors. The actions of the *converso* Ruy Díaz Nieto and his friends [Mexico 1603], who on Friday nights "ate behind closed doors, which they did not do other nights,"[136] were typical. Frequently Judaizing *conversos* prepared two dishes, a kosher meal for themselves, and a meal which overtly violated the kosher or Sabbath laws which they could exhibit to their suspicious non-Judaizing neighbors. Urraca Núñez testified in 1484 that some nine years earlier she had seen how her masters "cooked two stews on Friday for the Sabbath: they made one of fish in case someone came in and one of meat for themselves to eat."[137] Fernando Falcón [Toledo 1484] testified that once "when they were eating stew Fernando de Torres . . . knocked at the door and Catalina de Zamora and her daughter hid the stew pot under a chest and then went to see who it was, and when they recognized him they opened and closed the door and went into the house. And Catalina de Zamora said: 'when we thought it was someone else we hid the stew pot we were eating from. You gave us a fright.' "[138] Antonio Meléndez solved the servant problem by employing a girl who was deaf and blind, telling a friend that "she was the best sort of servant for them, because she neither heard nor saw."[139]

Judaizers were just as assiduous in hiding the realia associated with their worship as they were in concealing their actions. Small items like books could be stashed in a number of places. The slave Isabel [Ciudad Real 1511] said that Juan Ramírez and his family "took the book from which they used to read and they carried it to hide it in a hay loft in their house and to hide it they stuck it under the straw. Later they were not certain the book would be safe there and they took it out and put it in a storage cellar of the house and wrapped it in a burlap cloth and dug a hole and put it in there and covered the hole with earth and put a wine barrel on top of it so that it would not seem that they had placed anything there."[140] Their neighbors the Olivo family also "kept their prayer book when they were not reading from it . . . in a hole in the ground."[141] More than a century later in Mexico María de Zárate and her friends hid their Jewish books the same way: "They hid them in a hay mow in the house where they were living; but later when they took them out they were wet so they put them in the sun to dry and then hid them again together with some money and silverware in an upstairs room, making a cavity in the wall."[142]

The second strategy was to dissemble: to disguise a Judaizing practice as a Christian observance or to ascribe a Judaizing custom to some purpose other than religious observance. The preferred cover stories involved Christian practices. Hieronymus Münzer, a German traveler in Valencia around 1495, observed how *conversos* spoke loudly about going to church when their intentions were quite the opposite: "when one *converso* would say to another, 'Today we shall go to the Parish of Santa Cruz,' everyone knew that it meant they were gathering in the synagogue" (Gilman 1972, 117). Maria González [Ciudad Real 1513] protested that she was not celebrating the Sabbath by visiting with friends; rather she went to Molina's house "because Fernando de Molina's wife was baptizing a son, and they went there to honor him and not to keep the Sabbath, nor did they observe it."[143] Similarly new-Christians in Coimbra in the 1580s used the pretext of some saint's day in order to celebrate the Sabbath.[144]

Jewish prayers were sometimes given a Christian veneer for the purpose of dissembling them. Colonial Mexican Judaizers sometimes paraphrased Christian prayers and adopted Christian melodies so that "a person passing the synagogue and hearing the hymnal music might be deceived into thinking that a group of Christians were engaged in a religious observance or a rehearsal for the coming Sunday. To aid in the deception, the names of Jesus and Mary were retained in one or two places" (Liebman 1970, 70). Ruy Díaz Nieto [Mexico 1603] "used to pray with a rosary in his hands, his face turned toward the east, covered with his cape, his hat on his head . . . very clearly in the Jewish fashion" (AGN Vol 276 doc 14, 425a). The Portuguese Judaizer Diego Juárez de Figueroa [Mexico 1640s] told Inquisitors that "Jews are not permitted to name Our Lord Jesus Christ nor his Most Holy Mother, and that when they refer to the Virgin of Carmen, which they do so that Catholics will think they are invoking Our Lady, they are not speaking of her, but of Elijah."[145]

The rare Jewish book could be dissembled between Christian covers. Francisco de Ecija Zayas [Baeza 1573] owned a book called *Josefina* that dealt with the marriage of Joseph; it was "bound into a book that was four fingers thick which at the beginning had things about knights and at the end had things about our Holy Catholic Faith and in the middle the *Josefina*, and that it was bound this way in order to disguise it."[146]

Other cover stories were less overtly religious. Jewish fast days could be dissembled by pretending to have eaten. Thus Judaizers in Mexico City on Yom Kippur would walk in the Alameda park "with toothpicks in their mouths to give the impression that they had eaten."[147] A festival custom like preparing *matza*, which could stand out in the social landscape like a stately tree, could be dissembled by planting a forest around it. Thus a *converso* doctor in Lima was reported to have "prescribed unleavened bread for patients with stomach disorders throughout the year so that he could eat *matzoth* on Passover without arousing suspicion of more than a stomach complaint" (Liebman 1982, 120).

The third strategy was misdirection by engaging in ostentatious Christian practice, so that informers would not suspect an underlying adherence to Judaism. Juan González Daza [Ciudad Real 1484] allegedly went to mass only to be thought a Christian.[148] García Franco [Toledo 1491] allegedly said that he and his friends never ceased doing Christian things "because of what people say; and that is why we join certain brotherhoods and societies, or buy bulls, only so that we will show people the proper coloring."[149] Jorge Núñez [Lima 1595] only confessed and took communion so as to deceive his acquaintances (Castañeda Delgado 1989, 433). Francisco Maldonado de Silva [Chile 1626] allegedly said that "although he had heard mass, and confessed and taken communion, he did it to cover himself, and not because he understood that it was necessary for the salvation of his soul."[150] The majority of the more than 600 sentences against Judaizers handed down by the

Coimbra Inquisition between 1567 and 1583 carry the accusation that the person engaged in Christian practices only to deceive their Christian neighbors.[151]

The whole point of these strategies was to make sure that neighbors noticed them. Leonor Martínez [Mexico 1647] reported at her trial that "on festivals her grandmother used to shout in a loud voice for the benefit of their Catholic neighbors, 'Get ready, Leonorilla, we must go to mass.' However, they would only walk by the church, without going in, and would end up at her aunt's house."[152] Among other things it was said of Doña Beatriz Texoso, burned in effigy in the great Mexican *auto de fe* of 1649, that "when she prayed she held a rosary in her hand so that there would be greater dissimulation, and she did this maliciously so that people would not recognize her intentions and they would think that she was praying to Our Lady, the holy Virgin Mary" (Liebman 1974, 191). A *conversa* in Galicia "each year bought the Bull of the Crusade so that everyone would think she was an old-Christian and she told everyone she was going to buy it in order to redeem the souls in purgatory."[153] A wealthy converso might even endow a church so as to deflect the suspicion of his neighbors. This was the case in Calatayud [1487], where a *converso* named de la Cabra made a church out of an old synagogue not for "devotion to Christianity, but so that people would consider them good Christians."[154] Remnants of these attitudes and strategies are found in this century among people who consider themselves the descendants of these crypto-Jews. Anne Cardoza reports that her grandmother, Pauline, who emigrated from Gerona to Buenos Aires to the United States, advised her children to "wear big crosses, sometimes five inches in diameter" (Cardoza 1989, S2). In 1929 an old crypto-Jewish woman in Bragança told the French journalist Lily Jean Jarval that, although she had lots of Catholic religious imagery in her home, "it is to preserve appearances.... We never look at them, they are not ours."[155]

The dissembling ways of Judaizing new-Christians were so well known, or at least so widely alleged, that they became commonplaces in the political invective and the satirical literature of Spain's Golden Age. It is in this context that the father of Mateo Alemán's proto-*pícaro* Guzmán carries a rosary with beads the size of hazel nuts (*Guzmán de Alfarache* [1599], 1:1). This is why Lazarillo de Tormes's sixth master, a businessman who allows Lázaro to keep his Saturday earnings for himself, has cloaked his true beliefs by becoming a chaplain (*Lazarillo de Tormes* [1554], *Tratado* 6). This is why the young Pablos' parents, in the first version of Quevedo's picaresque novel *El Buscón* (1604), have adopted the surnames San Pedro, San Juan, and San Cristóbal (1:1).[156] And it is why a late fifteenth-century polemicist chose as an emblem for the hypocritical *conversos* the hybrid beast *Alborayque*, which, among its other attributes, has the "mouth of a wolf because these *Alboraycos* are hypocrites and false prophets, calling themselves Christians although they are not ... saying that they are Jews when they are with the Jews, and Christians when they are with the Christians."[157] These figures and hundreds like them served as emblems of hypocrisy, corrosive symbols of the interplay of reality and appearances that emerged as dominant themes in Spanish literature from the middle of the fifteenth century to the end of the seventeenth.

## Notes

1. These attempts were both legal—for example municipal ordinances requiring separation of the *aljamas*—and hortatory. In Segovia in 1485 Fray Francisco de la Peña preached against Christians associating with Jews, citing the egregious number who frequented Abraham Seneor's house (Asenjo González 1986, 327).

2. *Dormió algunas veces en el ospital de los judíos desta fortaleza* (Carrete Parrondo 1985a, 27).

3. *Cuando viajaba, moraba en casa de judíos y comía sus comeres y vino bendecido* (Cabezudo Astraín 1950, 276). Cf. Baer 1966, 2:337, 351.

4. *En aquel tienpo estava de costunbre posar los judios en las casas de los christianos y los christianos en las casas de los judios, especialmente en los lugares donde avia ferias* (Baer 1936, 542).

5. Entrepreneurial opportunities often created unusual alliances. For example, in Castellón in 1473 Fray Juan, the hermit of Santa Magdalena, Ramón Canet, a resident of Lucena, and Abraham Vires, the rabbi of Castellón, drew up a formal partnership to prospect for metal and treasure (Hinojosa Montalvo 1993, 119). Business relationships, of course, continued right up through the summer of 1492.

6. *Fue a honrar las bodas de algunos judios, por que es costunbre en la cibdad de Trujillo* (Baer 1936, 509).

7. *Era costumbre en Huete, por las pascuas de Nauidad, enbiar los judíos a los christianos viejos e nueuos, e los christianos a los judíos enbiarles por las pascuas del pan çençeño frutas e hueuos e otras cosas* (Carrete Parrondo 1978, 15–6). For similar examples see Carrete Parrondo 1977b, 30; García Casar 1990, 178 [Cuenca 1480s; both Passover and Purim gifts].

8. *Enbie algunos judios pan lebdo e huuas e queso presentado, por que los tales judios enbiauan las fiestas e pascuas de Nauidad a . . . mi marido y a mí capones e perdises e otras cosas e frutas, y a esta cabsa les enbie yo a ellos esto que dicho tengo* (Carrete Parrondo 1978, 16). For similar examples see Marín Padilla 1981–2, 275–84.

9. *Y si allí a él o a otro judío, por hazerle honra que comiese carne, si no la traía, le dexé degollar alguna carne, no me acuerdo* (Carrete Parrondo 1979, 54–5).

10. *Quando los judios hasen proçesiones . . . dan por Dios e limosnas a todos los pobres que la quieren reçebir, asy a judios como a christianos. . . . Quando la çibdad hase algunas alegrias o a naçimiento de prinçipe o por vitoria que Dios aya dado a los reyes . . . sacar los judios la Tora e aquel dia dar limosna los dichos judios a los christianos, y ellos la reçebian dellos; e asy mismo, quando los christianos andan demandando los domingos e fiestas con los baçines, reçebir limosnas de judios* (Carrete Parrondo 1978, 17–8).

11. *Si ha donats dines o algun altra cosa per edificacio, reparacio o ornament de la sinoga* (Llorca 1935, 16).

12. *Teniendo cada uno de los judíos maiores baptiçados una lámpara en la Ginoga y dando cada día dineros para aceite a las dichas lámparas* (Benito Ruano 1957, 331).

13. *Huma certa pesoa que veo da terra dos judeus a tirar esmola pera o azeite das sinagogas e de lhe dizer a dita pesoa os dias em que caião os jejuns dos judeus* (Azevedo Mea 1982, 219).

14. *Ha dado . . . dineros pa olio a la dicha Sinoga de los judios . . . e dava dineros a la bolsa de dicha cedaqua y otras almosnas a judios pobres por debocion a la ley judayca* (Cabezudo Astraín 1963, 283).

15. *Enviaban limosnas para comprar olio para la Sinagoga, e que daban limosnas a judíos pobres* (Sánchez Moya 1958, 167). See also Llorca 1936, 6; 1939, 136; and 1942, 148 [Teruel 1484]; Blázquez Miguel 1987, 45 [1489]; Carrete Parrondo 1977a, 74 [1491]; Gutwirth 1981, 96–7 [Segovia 1490s]; Beinart 1981b, 593 [Ciudad Real 1521].

16. *Algunas vegadas, por mandado de su madre, dio algún trozo de pan a dalguna judía* (Sánchez Moya 1958, 179; cf. 181, 189).

17. *La mujer de Alonço Gonçalez de la Oz a la puerta de San Martin tenía un hermano judío que se decía don Varo al cual secretamente hacía mucho bien* (Gutwirth 1981, 97).

18. *Almas a la cedaca* (Sánchez Moya 1973, 328).

19. León Tello 1972, 68. The sense of communal responsibility survived well after the Expulsion. Francisco López Díaz, a Portuguese merchant living in Mexico in the 1640s, took it on himself to gather alms from the Judaizers living outside Mexico City for distribution to the poor Judaizers of the capital (*Los judíos que vivían fuera desta ciudad le encomendaban repartiese las limosnas que inviaban a los judíos pobres que en ella estaban*) (García 1910, 224).

20. *Demandó la çedacá con vna bolsa abierta en las manos* (Carrete Parrondo 1985a, 48).

21. *Cuando los judíos facían bodas el domingo adelante cuando otras gentes e cristianos de natura iban a la judería, ella mandaba ir a las dichas sus fijas allá a ver las dichas bodas* (Sánchez Moya 1958, 182).

22. *Ley de gracia que qualquiere cosa que la vendiga la puede comer* (Marín Padilla 1981–2, 285).

23. *Ha ido e iba a bodas y circuncisiones e fiestas de judios en la juderia e ha fecho colacion en aquellas estrenando y honrando los judios y consolandose con ellos* (Cabezudo Astraín 1963, 283).

24. *Yva a los enterramientos de los judios para rogar a Dios por ellos* (Carrete Parrondo 1978, 16). See also Carrete Parrondo 1977b, 31; Caro Baroja 1961, 1:387, 468.

25. *Las dichas pascuas e fiestas de los judíos . . . se iban de sus casas a la judería e entraban en las casas de los judíos e recebían dellos frutas e colaciones de confites e otras cosas* (Sánchez Moya 1958, 167).

26. *Resçibian judíos de señal en sus casas e comían e bevían con ellos* (Santa María 1893b, 369). For similar examples see Gracia Boix 1983, 3; Fita y Colomé 1884, 402 [1484]; Carrete Parrondo 1985a, 61.

27. *Que continuamente comía con sus hermanos judíos de sus manjares e viandas caseras, e que comía adafinas los sábados e guardava los sábados* (Carrete Parrondo 1985a, 52).

28. *Rabi Simuel . . . agora bive en Medina del Canpo y es christiano y llamase maestre Fabricio, fisico, y seyendo grande filosofo, echaron fama que queria leer o predicar filosofia en la synoga. . . . Fue fama publica que fueron muchos christianos de la villa a la synoga a le oyr. . . . Yva a oyr sus sermones christianos viejos y conversos. . . . Aquel dia havia sermonado maestre Martin de Viana . . . en ebrayco a todos aquellos conversos* (Baer 1936, 466, 523).

29. *Iendo a la Ginoga cada día a oír los officios mosaicos e façer oración contra los christianos* (Benito Ruano 1957, 331).

30. *Fue a la sinoga de los jodíos o jodías a fazer oracion, como jodíos costumbran fazer, e quando no puede yr a la sinoga, faze oración en su casa. . . . Fué a una cassa de sus parientes y amigos a fazer oración con otros malos xristianos heréticos y apóstatas* (Llorca 1942, 133–4); cf. Cantera Montenegro 1985, 62 [Molina de Aragón 1497].

31. *Los viernes en las tardes rezava el dicho Gonçalo Peres meldando como judio. . . . Ellos fasen las cabannuelas en las entradas de sus puertas y ronpen un pedaço del tejado, y podria ser yo entrar e salir, por no aver otra entrada* (Baer 1936, 509).

32. *Ha ido a visitar la sinoga de los judios e ha fecho orazion a la Thora y reverencia* (Cabezudo Astraín 1963, 283).

33. *Se entraua por las sinogas desta . . . çibdad e rezaua oraçiones de los judíos en las mismas synogas, meldando como los otros judíos; e que los judíos que le echauan fuera de las sinogas, e que . . . Ruy Martines que daua bozes diziendo que por qué le echauan de la synoga, que quería haser oración como ellos, los judíos* (Carrete Parrondo 1985a, 24; cf. 60).

34. Carrete Parrondo 1986, 35, 53, 115. Further references to Elvira González are to this volume. The social relationships of the Arias clan in Segovia have been analyzed by Gutwirth 1981.

35. Carrete Parrondo 1986, 51. For other examples see Chapter 10.

36. A particularly dramatic and unusual example of both fraternization and exclusivity is the Sukkot celebration in the *Cárcel perpétua* in Mexico City in 1603 that was described in Chapter 13.

37. Kamen 1965, chapters 3 and 4.

38. Examples are Solomon Halevi, who as Pablo de Santa María became bishop of Burgos in the 1390s; Joshua Halorki, who as Jerónimo de Santa Fé led the Christian forces at the Disputation at Tortosa; and Pedro de la Cavallería, converted at Tortosa, who in 1450 wrote an apologia for Christianity called *Zelus Christi contra judaeos, saracenos et infideles* (Baer 1961, 2:139–50, 175–229, 276).

39. Cardinal Juan de Torquemada (Tomás's uncle) and a number of bishops, including Hernando de Talavera, Archbishop of Granada, and Juan Arias Dávila, Bishop of Segovia; the great Augustinian poet and essayist Fray Luis de León; and Saint Teresa of Avila, the reformer of the Carmelite Order, are but a few of many, many examples.

40. The best overview of these laws remains Sicroff 1960.

41. "*Non, mas soy converso de parte de mi madre e de parte de mi padre hidalgo.*" *Y este testigo le tornó a preguntar: "¿Pues cómo tal ome como vos andáys fuera de vuestra tierra?" Y él le dixo: "Como por nuestros pecados todos nos corren, vino la Ynquisyçión a Aranda, e yo era alcalde e la sazón no supe qué haser, synon con la vara como que yba a hacer otra cosa, salirme; e por eso ando acá. Que vn día fuí a ver a un preso, amigo mío—el nonbre del qual non le dixo—y él me dixo que me fuese, que por amor de mi fazienda me auían de matar, y luego enfardeme estos paños y apañí lo que pude; y asy me salí e ando acá fuydo*" (Carrete Parrondo 1985a, 171).

42. *Le avía enbiado vna carta con mucha priesa, la qual ante este testigo se leyó, en que desía que mirase bien por sy, que Juan de Salzedo avía condenado y abrasado a muchos en esta çibdad. E que luego, como leyese la carta, la quemase por que no se descubriese* (Carrete Parrondo 1985a, 67; cf. 34).

43. For discussion of this atmosphere of horror see Gilman 1972, especially 166–9.

44. Cantera/Carrete 1975, 157.

45. *Indo fugindo certas pesoas de sua naçam com medo de as prenderem pelo Santo Officio, o Reo, sabendo dellas, ho porque fogiam, as recolheo em sua casa e lhe deu favor e ajuda com que se ausentaram e fugiram* (Azevedo Mea 1982, 238; cf. 307, 308, 363, etc.).

46. *Algunas de las mujeres fugitivas, mudándose los apellidos, tomaron una casa retirada del comercio, donde estuvieron un año escondidas, ocupándose en lavar ropa de los hombres que en aquella ocasión habían también venido huyendo . . . que acudían a visitarlas, sin serles bastante freno el riesgo en que se hallaban* (García 1910, 254).

47. *Espiaba cuando se hacían las prisiones en las calles desta Inquisición, a pie y a caballo, para avisarles qué personas se prendían; ayudando en este tiempo a esconder bienes y a quemar papeles* (García 1910, 118).

48. *Por vivir con los recelos y temores con que viven los judaizantes, de ordinario, de ser presos por la Inquisición, ocultó y escondió y, en parte, malbarató su caudal* (García 1910, 190–1).

49. *Un cristiano nuevo y algo perdigado, rico y poderoso, que viviendo alegre, gordo, lozano y muy contento en unas casas proprias, aconteció venírsele por vecino un inquisidor y con solo el tenerlo cerca vino a enflaquecer de manera, que lo puso en breves días en los mismos huesos* (II:3:8; Valbuena y Prat 1962, 563b). A similar anecdote, which appears in the play *En los indicios la culpa*, attributed to Lope de Vega, has been analyzed by Silverman (1991, 163–4).

50. *Fue por temor que no le quemasen por que le quemaron a todo su linaje et a otros muchos* (Gracia Boix 1982, 109).

51. *Disen que demandan el Pater Noster e el Ave Maria y el Credo y la Salue Regina e otras cosas avrá onbre miedo* (Carrete Parrondo 1985a, 126). When threatened by the Inquisition in Mexico in the 1640s, Rafaela Enríquez advised her group of Judaizers "to buy little chapbooks of Christian doctrine to memorize, because they were not familiar with it" (*Para dar cuenta de la doctrina cristiana, se previnieron de cartillas, comprándolas para aprenderla, porque no la sabían*) (García 1910, 254).

52. *Y si acaso el cristianillo, / según lo siente, y le pesa, / judaizar viese un poquillo, / luego al pescuezo el cuchillo* (Carvajal 1872, 34b).

53. *Decía a los judíos que hera este testigo vna biuora achristianada, que se guardasen della* (Cantera/Carrete 1975, 158).

54. *Gaona le fizo de sennas que callase, que otramente cree que dixiera mas* (Carrete Parrondo 1985, 129).

55. One day in a fit of anger Pero Lopes Camello [Bahia 1594] began to rant about his lack of faith in Jesus and then, realizing what he had done, "clapped his hand over his mouth and said he was not feeling well and that God should pardon him; but his friends were scandalized," and one of them reported the episode to the Inquisition (*Logo acabando de dizir as dittas pallavras antes de ninguem o reprehender bateo com a mão na boca, dizendo que não fallara bem e que Deos lhe perdoasse, e todos os circunstantes se escandalizarão*) (Furtado 1929, 163). Juan de León [San Esteban de Gormaz, Soria 1502] made his friends swear by "God and the ten commandments" that they would not report his injudicious remarks, but Francisco de Aguila did anyway (*¿Juráis al Dió e a estos diez mandamientos que no me descubriréis? e este testigo le dixo que sy*) (Carrete Parrondo 1985a, 153).

56. *Y en cierto pueblo de indios de la provincia de Nicaragua en la iglesia del dixo el dho Luis de Valencia a cierta persona de su lei y profession ve aqui un señor fulano que estos indios con ser barbaros tienen iglessia donde adoran y veneran a Dios y nosotros ni tenemos templo ni sacerdote ni sacrificios donde agradar respetar venerar y ensalçar al dios de Israel y emos de andar perseguidos dela Inqqon en qualquiera parte que estemos sin que tengamos hora segura y el templo ha de ser nro. pecho donde alabemos al Señor si queremos escusar quela Inqqon nos prenda que en haviendo comunicacion o mas tarde o mas temprano nos prenden* (Osorio 1980, 233).

57. Inquisition procedure permitted the accused to adduce a list of people whose testimony should be disallowed because of reasons of personal enmity, which raised the value of keeping track of such things. For an example of such a list translated into English see Gilman 1972, 245–51.

58. *Le auian dicho que este entraua en el So Ofco, y que assi le pedia por un solo Dios, que mirasse que tenia hijos y no los hiziesse huerfanos, y lo mesmo le rogo la dicha Costanza Rodriguez* (AGN Vol 271 doc 1, 12b).

59. *Diciéndole que si más le pedía las puntas o su valor, diría lo que con él le había pasado en el judaísmo* (García 1910, 88).

60. *Desde que le redujo al judaísmo, le sufría su padre le hurtase para jugar, lo cual no hacía antes, porque con un freno le quitaba el pellejo a azotes* (García 1910, 111).

61. *Si las prendiesen, negasen sus delitos y procurasen derramar amenazas contra los que, presos, los descubriesen* (García 1910, 254).

62. *Ninguno estaba obligado a más que a confesar sus culpas y que a todos los que les sucediese semejante prisión, lo hiciesen así, para que todos los de afuera, en saliendo, los amparasen* (García 1910, 226–7).

63. *No le quería con punta de diamante sino con ribete de raso amarillo, que, como era blanca, le estaría bien* (García 1910, 196).

64. A similar strategy was followed by several Judaizers arrested by the Lima Inquisition around 1600 (Castañeda Delgado 1989, 433–4).

65. *Haciéndose simple y zonzo, y con notable diminución, variedad y revocaciones; fingiendo turbación y temores. . . . Se fingió loca, dejándose comer de piojos; diciendo y haciendo acciones y palabras con que pretendía ser tenida por tal, como eran el coger sus camisas y rasgarlas, haciendo un muñecón grande, con su mantilla, faja, brazos metidos y capillo en la cabeza; y besándole, hacía que le daba de mamar* (García 1910, 47, 49).

66. Cervantes builds on a century-long tradition when he chooses this as one of the shaping themes that runs consistently through both books of his *Don Quijote de la Mancha* (Gitlitz 1969).

67. In the 1499 *Celestina*, by the *converso* Fernando de Rojas, a young prostitute says that "deeds create lineage, and anyway we are all children of Adam and Eve" (*Las obras hazen linaje, que al fin todos somos hijos de Adán y Eva*) (F. Rojas 1968, 2:34). In Miguel de Carvajal's play *The Courts of Death* (*Las cortes de la muerte*) (c. 1540) an absurdly pompous nun boasts of a lineage that extends from Creation to Spain's currently most noble families: "I am the daughter of Adam and Eve, and as for present times, I am called Doña Casilda de Guzmán, and I have some Manrique blood too" (*Soy hija de Eva y Adán; / y si en lo del siglo toco, / llámome, según verán, / Doña Casilda de Guzmán; / de Manrique tengo un poco*) (Carvajal 1872, 16b). Cervantes makes this same point in his *Retablo de las maravillas* (c. 1614), which pokes serious fun at old-Christian pretensions of lineage by presenting a non-existent puppet show that allegedly only those of pure blood can see, and then frightening the women in the stage audience with a horde of (invisible) multicolored mice all descended from those which sailed in Noah's ark (1962, 583a).

68. See my analysis of Miguel de Carvajal's *Cortes de la muerte* (1974).

69. This is a major theme of the 1480s polemical pamphlet *Libro del Alboraique* (Gitlitz 1992, 2–3). Américo Castro first called critical attention to these ideas (1963, 207).

70. *Respondió que no sabía dar otra razón más que descender de Adán y Eva* (García 1910, 67).

71. The Inquisition required prisoners or their families to assume the costs of their confinement as well, but as this was a normal judicial procedure it seems to have evoked no protest.

72. *Los conversos que quemavan non los quemavan salvo por les tomar e robar sus faziendas, e que el que tenia fazienda feziese cuenta que tenia el fuego consigo* (Baer 1936, 473).

73. *Los padres que prendían e quemavan que muy muchos dellos no prendían e quemavan syno por caso de fasiendas* (Carrete Parrondo 1985a, 98, cf. 126).

74. *Esta Ynquisyçion que se fase por estos padres tanto se fase por tomar las fasiendas a los conversos como por ensalçar la fe. . . . Esta es la heregia que fallaron a Juan Pintado: dies e seys sa-*

*vanas y las prestas de su casa, que por esto murio que non porque era ereje* (Beinart 1974, 391). See also Beinart 1961, 179 [1487]; 1981b, 104, 372; Carrete Parrondo 1989, 64.

75. *Casa de vicio . . . tomavam a fazenda aos homens e os deshonravam* (Baião 1921, 235).

76. *Esta Canalla por adorar al Dios omnipotente nos hayan castigado y, lo que más es, tomado nuestras haziendas, ¡como si hubiéramos adorado el Demonio!* (Selke de Sánchez 1972, 266).

77. *No quería judíos pobres, sino ricos. . . . Prendía por sólo quitar las haciendas y no porque se convirtiese los reos. . . . Había soñado que los llevaban presos por el Santo Oficio, y que veía que en el mesmo aposento en que estaban, contaban los ministros el dinero que tenía el otro judío* (García 1910, 80, 225, 125). See also Lewin 1971, 466, 480 [Mexico 1665].

78. *Hacian mal los Reyes de Castilla, y Portugal, en quitarles la hazienda y oprimirlos con tanto vigor hasta quitarles la vida* (AGN Vol 529 doc 11, 270b).

79. *Muitos que estavam presos pela Inquisição eram mal presos e que mais mereciam ser queimados os julgadores que os julgados* (Baião 1921, 171).

80. *Lá vem os diablos da Inquisição* (Furtado 1925, 267, cf. 412).

81. *E que em vez de as salvarem as metiam no Inferno. E que o diablo os havia de levar a todos. E que o tribunal do Santo Oficio era tribunal do diabo e que o diabo o fizera e mandara fazer. . . . Cães, cananeus, samaritanos e filisteus. . . . [Havia de] cair um raio dos céus que havia de abrasar os inquisidores e o reino pelas vexações que faziam à gente de nação, e ao mesmo rei porque o consentia* (Coelho 1987, 217–8). María de Zárate [Mexico 1656] held the Monarch to blame for having instituted the Inquisition in the first place: "the Tribunal of the Holy Office had been badly founded, because it had been founded as a result of the jealousy that a Queen of Spain named Isabel had of a very beautiful Jewess with whom the King was having an affair" *(Había sido mal fundado el tribunal del Santo Oficio, porque se había fundado por los celos que tuvo una reina de España llamada doña Isabel de una judía muy hermosa a quien comunicaba el rey)*. This version confuses Isabel's husband Fernando with the thirteenth-century King Alfonso VII who, legend has it, had an affair with a Jewess named Raquel (Lewin 1971, 301).

82. *No vivir adonde hay estas casas y género de hombres que tratan a hombres honrados peor que a negros. . . . Son crueles verdugos, sayones, ellos lo pagarán en el infierno y nosotros tendremos descanso. . . . ¿Qué te parece de estos embusteros que porque los tengan por santos se han hecho retratos y tienen aderezada la sala con colgaduras y sus retratos? ¿Que les parece que por ser inquisidores son santos y no hay otros en el mundo como ellos? Y Botello le respondió: santos de pajares que se queman ellos y la paja no; demonios, sí lo son del infierno, que están condenados a él. . . . Has visto qué obras buenas y santos han hecho y están haciendo, quitando vidas, honras, haciendas y holgándose de hacer mal, todas éstas deven de ser entre ellos causas para ser santos de los demonios* (Lewin 1975, 78–9, 145). See also García 1910, 45, 60 [Mexico 1646].

83. *Sy quemaron dies, que los ocho quemaron por testigos falsos. . . . ¡O, Santa María!, marido, quántos se queman por testigos falsos. . . . En Castilla más son quemados de mill e quinientas personas con testigos falsos* (Carrete Parrondo 1985a, 151, 180, 129). Cf. 102, 130; Baião 1921, 146 [Portugal 1545].

84. *Aquelles pecadorsinhos morrem martyres* (Baião 1921, 249). See also Beinart 1961, 179 [1487]; Sicroff 1965, 119 [1485]; Carrete Parrondo 1985a, 132 [1501]; Wolf 1926, 10 [1505]; Baer 1936, 542 [1511]; Baião 1921, 244–55 [1583]; Roth 1931–2, 6.

85. *Porque estando otras personas diciendo mal de confesos, dijo que no dijesen mal dellos; que muchos castigaban y morían sin culpa; y que algún día claro, vendría en que se viese todo. Y fue testificada que era muy amiga de conversos, y de oir los confesos cuando predicaban, probó ser cristiana vieja y los testigos sus enemigos. Absuelta de la instancia* (Gracia Boix 1983, 43).

86. The ability to tough it out was widely admired. A *converso* tailor [Aranda de Duero 1502] allegedly told Juan de Salcedo not to worry about the Inquisition, for "I swear to you by the true God that it will not last long, for I always heard the sages say that whoever found himself still a Jew after these persecutions were over would be blessed" (*No os desmayés por esta Ynquisiçión, que esto e más hemos de pasar; mas yo's juro a Dios verdadero que no ha de durar mucho, que siempre oy desir a sabios que sería bienaventurado el que se fallase judío después destas fortunas pasadas*) (Carrete Parrondo 1985a, 149).

87. *Los que avian quemado eran martires e que yvan salvos. . . . Le alabo mucho los macabeos martires, disiendo que eran muy gloriosos e excelentes, por que murieron por la ley de Moysen* (Baer 1936, 475; see also 1966, 2:353).

88. *Muitos queimados morriam mártires por serem homens honrados e sustentar sua honra, não querendo por essa razão confessar* (Novinsky 1972b, 149).

89. *¿Juzgays que haya hecho bien aquel Judío que quemaron, dicho Alonso, con dejarse quemar? Pues bien podía pedir perdón y misericordia y salvar su vida y después yrse a sus tierras si fuesse agrado y de su pareçer y no ser homicida de si mesmo, que esso es muy grande peccado. Respondió . . . Billa que . . . Alonso havía hecho muy bien porque quien muere por su Dios, en los Çielos es coronado* (Selke de Sánchez 1972, 264).

90. *A dar el osculo de paz al modo judaico* (Liebman 1982, 125–6). See also Liebman 1975, 79, 172. Liebman believes this may be derived from the kiss of peace which according to tradition is given by God to a departing soul: Talmud *Baba Batra* 7a.

91. *Dio muestras de su depravado ánimo y de disimulado judío en el ósculo de paz que dio a su cuñado Sebastian Duarte, relaxado en el cadahalso* (Medina 1887, 2:151).

92. *Por eso nos tienen oprimidos, encerrados en cárceles y calabozos, en tinieblas y oscuridades, con mil géneros de martirios por mil modos y caminos que nos están haciendo, que venimos a ser mártires y santos* (Lewin 1975, 145). See also García 1910, 104 [1647].

93. *Hablando muchas veses del dicho su marido despues que lo quemaron por herege, dixo la susodicha que de vn pecador avian hecho vn martir, e que avia muerto martir e como martir se avia subido al çielo; e que vna noche se le avia apareçido como vn angel, como vn niño de dos años hermoso, e que asy se le avia desapareçido* (Beinart 1977a, 197). See also Baião 1921, 193 [1572].

94. *Não choreis primo que morreo pella honra* (Furtado 1925, 524). This sense of pride may also underlie the ironic code phrase that María de Zárate [Mexico 1660s] used to refer to someone who had been penanced by the Inquisition. "She said that the penitents had been knights, making the sign of the cross on her chest" (*Decía que dichos penitenciados que habían sido caballeros, haciendo con la mano una cruz en el pecho*) (Lewin 1971, 496). The reference was to the cross of Saint Andrew that was painted on the penitential *sambenitos* and the crosses the knights of the Spanish military orders wore on their breasts.

95. *Para facilitarle más su apostasía, le llevaron a la iglesia mayor y le mostraron el sambenito de su abuelo* (García 1910, 82; cf. 196, 224).

96. Popular examples from Amsterdam were Antonio Enríquez Gómez's "Ballad in honor of the divine martyr, Judah the Believer, martyred at Valladolid at the hands of the Inquisition," and Miguel de Barrios's "In lighthearted praise of the holy Law in the foundation of the Synagogue," which have been edited and translated by Oelman (1982, 176–203, 212–8, 230–43).

97. *Le prometí morir luchando con mis fuerzas y poder con argumentos contra los enemigos de su Ley y de su verdad, y observarla hasta el altar del fuego que creo que se me prepara para pronto, con el fin de que desde él Dios me reciba en holocausto por nuestros pecados y cese en mí la ira de su cólera que tanto se inflama en estos tiempos. . . . Avia un solo Dios, y que era misericordioso,*

*el cual abia dado su ley a Moyses en el Monte Sinay, la cual guardava el reo en su alma y abia de morir por ella. . . . Que le quemasen, que los que morian quemados no morian, sino que su Dios los tenia siempre vivos. . . . Si mil vidas tuviera todas las perdiera por la observancia de la ley de Moises* (García de Proodián 1966, 344–5, 350). See also Böhm 1984, 284.

98. *Ago, agora una muerte tengo de moryr, mas vale moryr agora que otra ves. Yo dygo que la ley de Moysen es la buena y en la que los onbres se an de salvar, e que entonces toda la gente apedrearon al dicho Juan de Madrid* (Baer 1936, 472).

99. *Que quando hablauan de la Ley de Moyses dezia que quien se muryera en aquel tiempo, porque hablauan de quando era judio* (Beinart 1977b, 53).

100. *Juraba a Dios que çesando vn poco las ynquisyçiones que yría a vn puerto de mar, e allí que sería moro o algrabe, o lo quél quisyese, e allí estarían sus hijos con quien él quisiese* (Carrete Parrondo 1985a, 158).

101. *Que sy no fuera por los fijos que tenia que se fuera a tierra de Judea* (Carrete Parrondo 1985a, 62). Fernando de Uclés [Cuenca 1490] confessed a similar sentiment (Carrete Parrondo 1980, 255).

102. *Daría a su muger toda la hazienda que amos tenían e que se fuese a casa de su padre, porquél se quería yr a Iherusalem* (Carrete Parrondo 1985a, 22).

103. *Se yuan a Iudea a estar todos juntos el Día Mayor* (Carrete Parrondo 1980, 255). Some twentieth-century Spaniards have kept alive (or recreated) the memory of the intensity of this dream within their families. Elie Wiesel beautifully recounts having met a Spaniard in Zaragoza who showed him a parchment preserved in his family for generations that read: "I, Moses son of Abraham, forced to break all ties with my people and faith, leave these lines to the children of my children and to theirs in order that on the day when Israel will be able to walk again, its head high under the sun, without fear and without remorse, they will know where their roots lie. Written at Saragossa, this ninth day of the month of Av, in the year of punishment and exile." Several years later Wiesel says that he met the man as an émigré in Jerusalem (Kurzweil 1980, 311–7).

104. *Hablando en cosas por el camino le dixo el dicho Juan de la Sierra a este testigo que en otros señorios, ansi como en tierra del turco como en otras partes, dexauan a cada vno estar en la ley que queria, porque alla avia moros e judios e christianos, et que a cada vno dexauan biuir en su ley. Et que de la manera de su dezir dio a entender manifiestamente que se deuia hazer aquello mismo en estos reynos de Castilla, que deuian dexar biuir cada vno en la ley que quisiese* (Beinart 1981b, 557). See also Beinart 1961, 178.

105. *Entre sí decían que tenían esperanza que antes de morir habían de pasar a parte pudiesen publicar la Ley en que vivían* (Lewin 1971, 230).

106. *Plega a Dios . . . que me lleva a tierra donde yo muera en la ley de los judios* (García Fuentes 1981, 164). Juan de León [Aranda de Duero 1502] at the time of the Expulsion expressed a similar sentiment to a departing friend: "Don't be sad about going. I wish to God that I were you and you were me. You are crazy to be sad about leaving, for you drink your death in one swallow while we stay here among this evil people, and every day we receive death at their hands" *(No estés triste por esta yda vuestra, y plugiese al Dió que yo fuese vos y vos fuésedes yo, que sois neçio en estar triste por la partyda, que vosotros tragáys la muerte en vn trago e nosotros quedamos acá entre esta mala gente, que cada día reçiuimos la muerte con ellos)* (Carrete Parrondo 1985a, 153).

107. Carrete Parrondo 1980, 254. See also Baer 1966, 2:338, 362.

108. Carrete Parrondo 1980, 253. For a similar example see Carrete/Fraile 1987, 69.

109. *Quando o emperador tomou Tunis aos turcos ella se entristeceu, quando se tomou o cabo de Gué mostrou contentamento. Ouvio dizir . . . que estava resolvida a fogir para Gulfo ou Celoniqua* (Baião 1921, 138).

110. *Dizendo a certas pessoas de sua nação que elle era judeu de coração e que desejava de se hir a parte onde o pudesse ser livremente. . . . Que Deos ha levasse a morrer a terra de mouros a ver os ossos de sua may e se morresse nesta terra que os caens e corvos ha comessem e fossem lá lançar. . . . Quando os christãos velhos fosem bons judeus ou mouros que então seria ella e os outros christãos novos bons christãos, dizendo mais que darião huma grande soma de dinheiro e que os deyxasem viver em sua liberdade para livremente poder viver na ley dos judeus, sem por isso ser presa nem castigada* (Azevedo Mea 1982, 10, 336, 289).

111. *O tem instigado a voltar para a Berberia para livremente praticarem o judaismo* (Baião 1921, 243).

112. *Queria pasar en Berberia . . . ubo determinacion de yrse con unos moros a su tierra y que puesto alla hiziera como los otros y guardara la ley de los judios y que la tubo por mexor que la de los christianos* (García Fuentes 1981, 180).

113. *Es muy afficionado a hablar de Florencia, Ferrara y otras partes; . . . hablando de si, y de los demas judios de Ferrara, como si actualmte estuviera con los judios de Ferrara* (AGN Vol 276 doc 14, 415b–6a).

114. *Pretendia recoger toda su hacienda que le debian e irse con ella a bivir a tierra donde uviesse libertad de conciencia* (García de Proodian 1966, 293).

115. *Le dijo que lo había de llevar y a su mujer y parentela a parte donde cada uno vivía como quería, y qué sólo aguardaba a que saliesen algunos pobres de los que estaban presos en la Inquisición, para socorrerlos* (García 1910, 257). See also Lewin 1954, 146; Lewin 1971, 30.

116. *¿Si en la ciudad de Amsterdam no había una iglesia adonde iban los de la nación a sus ceremonias? Y el dicho Juan de León le respondió que sí, y que era muy linda la iglesia y muy grande y muy bien aderezada, y que en la fiestas de los judíos entran los hombres aparte y las mujeres aparte, y las niñas y niños también de por sí, porque desde chiquitos los van enseñando y les leen la Ley y lo que han de guardar, y les enseñan las oraciones y los van adoctrinando con mucho cuidado, y el dicho preso dijo: gran deseo tengo de ver todo eso, y el dicho León le dijo: lo verás, dándonos aquel hombre vida lo veremos. . . . En yéndose a las dichas tierras, luego le darán mujer que escoja a su gusto, y aunque sea casada no importa, y que por la mayor parte ha dotado aquel hombre a todas aquellas mujeres de hermosura y que escogiera como en peras, y el dicho preso le dijo: en eso nos viéramos. . . . Es tierra de mucho regalo y muy barata, y que en sabiendo que era de la nación todos lo favorecerán y le ayudarán, y que en cuatro días se hará rico, y que el dicho preso le dijo: esto queda concertado de esta suerte, no hay que quedarse aquí ni qué parar en esta mala tierra, sino irnos adonde podamos vivir sin zozobras, ni tener siempre la soga arrastrando* (Lewin 1977, 323–4, 310).

117. Such strategies are, of course, not unique to the crypto-Jews, and in many ways the crypto-Jewish secret language was a phenomenon not unlike the esoteric terminology developed by the criminal underworld (in Spain in the sixteenth century called "germania") or the tough-punk world of the self-styled socially alienated (in Spain in the seventeenth century called "jaquesca").

118. *Cuando hablaban entre ellos decían fulano conoce al Señor, fulano es del Señor. . . . Cuando llegue con fulano bien podéis pasar adelante porque sabe muy bien la cartilla* (Contreras 1982, 605).

119. Liebman 1982, 127. See also Lewin 1977, 51, 78, 226 [Mexico 1642]; Cortes 1985, 293 [Majorca late 1600s].

120. *Cuando quería declarar que una persona era observante de la Ley de Moisés usaba un refrán, diciendo fulano es hijo del hombre, con que lo entendían los observantes de ella* (Lewin 1977, 70, cf. 240).

121. *Savia hera judio, despues de haverle saludado y tenido palabras de cumplimiento y guiñado y señalado con el rostro a otra cierta persona y dicho que hera judio* (García de Proodian 1966, 282).

122. *Ser de la carda y su querido . . . vizcaíno* (Lera García 1987, 112).

123. *El Todopoderoso te dé muy buenos días . . . El lo haga como puede y se lo pido. . . . A ti también* (Lewin 1975, 86, 93, cf. 138).

124. *En sus pasatempos nã lhe chamava senão Mana Judia e queria que ella lhe chamasse Mano Judeu* (Baião 1921, 160).

125. *Çierto día que me dio seda, me dijo que se agradaba de hazer bien a personas pobres de las que conoçían al Dios omnipotente; y yo le respondí que si él lo hazía assí que dios le daría bienes. Y él respondió que sabía muy bien lo que Dios mandava en su santa ley, y assí que yo a vos, no vos dejaré patir [sic]. Y yo le respondí que Dios le ayudaría. Y él me dijo que quería yr fuera de la Çiudad conmigo un día muy espaçio. Con que al cabo de días fuimos los dos fuera de los muros de la Çiudad, y assí passeándonos uno con otro nos declaramos por observantes* (Selke de Sánchez 1972, 260).

126. *¿Pues cómo el dicho portugues siendo xristiano nuebo caso la dicha su muy conjunta con un navarro? No debe de entenderse (que es lo mismo que preguntar, "no debe de judaizar"). Y los dichos mercaderes le respondieron: "No es lerdo; muy bien se entiende, y es muy leydo en historias, y sabe mas que siete." Con que la dicha persona quedo creyendo que el dicho portugues es de su profesion, y que se conocen por de una misma ley* (García de Proodian 1966, 416).

127. *Lozana: Señoras, ¿en qué habláis, por mi vida? / Teresa: En que, para mañana, querríamos hacer unos hormigos torcidos. / Lozana: ¿Y tenéis culantro verde? Pues dejá hacer a quien, de un puño de buena harina y tanto aceite, si lo tenéis bueno, os hará una almofia llena . . . / Beatriz: . . . (¡Por tu vida, que es de nostris!)* (Delicado 1528, 200; cf. 57, 178).

128. *Para efectuar el casamiento marido y mujer le atendieron con sumo cuidado a las acciones y palabras, para ver si podían rastrear que fuese judaizante; y viendo que no podían descubrir cosa que hiciese a su propósito, le dieron una muy buena pesadumbre, con que salió de su casa* (García 1910, 267).

129. *Estando ambos sós o mesmo dando a elle confitente um abraço lhe dice, que vivia na lei de Moizes, e que João Thomaz havia dito tambem a elle e Luiz Terra, que elle confitente tambem vivia na dita lei, e que por o não saber mas cedo que ella confitente a observava, é que se não quizera com elle declarar mais cedo; ao que elle confitente lhe resondeo, que com efeito vivia na lei de Moizés, e este foi o modo porque se declararam, e não passaram mais, nem diceram quem nos haviam ensinado, nem com quem mais se comunicavam, e se fiaram uns dos outros por serem amigos da mesma nação* (Silva 1896, 28).

130. *Hacía grandes pesquisas entre los judíos para saber quiénes eran más judíos y perfectos en la observancia de la ley de Moisén* (García, 1910, 68). As late as the early eighteenth century, networking also facilitated fundraising for the community. In the 1740s the Judaizers around Villanueva de la Serena waited for someone whom they thought was traveling around Spain collecting the tribute of the Law of Moses from the Judaizers, whose names he carried in a notebook (Blázquez Miguel 1986a, 255).

131. *Se comenzó a declarar con muchísimas personas por judaizante, visitando principalmente a las mujeres* (García 1910, 225). He was also accused of abusing his saintly reputation to have sexual relations (*tratos ilícitos*) with crypto-Jewish women.

132. *Los visitaba y consolaba aún en los mesmos hospitales a donde eran llevados a curar. . . . Los judíos que vivían fuera desta ciudad le encomendaban repartiese las limosnas que inviaban a los judíos pobres que en ella estaban. . . . Cuando venía de fuera, traía nuevas a los judíos desta ciudad de los que vivían en las partes y lugares en que había estado y de los progresos que hacían en la guarda de la ley. . . . Servía de espía para avisar a los demás de los que se iban trayendo a estas cárceles secretas. . . . Procuraba que los casamientos de las judías se hiciesen con hombres de la nación hebrea* (García 1910, 223–27).

133. *En casa de cierto judío rico, adonde venían a parar todos los judíos que pasaban de España y Portugal, y adonde se hacían las juntas de ellos como en la sinagoga* (García 1910, 87; cf. 223).

134. *Quando a esta cidade vinha algum cristão novo, que a elle achava pera falar por elle e o favorecer e que elle favorecia aos pobres cristãos novos que a esta terra vinhão, estrangeiros que não achavão senão a elle pera os ajudar* (Furtado 1925, 390).

135. *Non se avia metido frayle salvo por guardar mejor la ley de los judios, por que en el monasterio non era asy visto* (Baer 1936, 477). Cf. Rábade Obradó 1990b, 309. There were many such examples, the most notorious being that of the Jeronymite monastery of Guadalupe (Sicroff 1965).

136. *Cenaron a puerta cerrada no lo haciendo otras noches* (AGN Vol 271 doc 1, 8a).

137. *Guisauan caçuelas el viernes para el sabado, vna de pescado e otra de carne: la del pescado fasian para si algunos entrasen y la de carne para comer* (Beinart 1974, 322–3). See also Liebman 1982, 120.

138. *Çenando una caçuela e que Fernando de Torres . . . dio a la puerta, y que la Catalina de Çamora e su fija escondieron la caçuela debaxo de un arca, e que fueron a ver quien era e que le conosçieron e le abrieron e çerraron la puerta e se entraron en casa. E que dixo la dicha Catalina de Çamora: pensando que era otro escondimos esta caçuela que çenamos, e nos aveys dado turbaçion* (Beinart 1974, 389).

139. *Aquella hera propia para ellos, porque no veya ni oya* (Cantera/Carrete 1975, 186).

140. *Tomaron el dicho libro en que leyan las veses que tiene dicho e lo lleuaron a esconder a vn pajar de la dicha casa y lo metieron debaxo de la paja; e que despues no se aseguraron en tener alli el dicho libro e lo sacaron de alli e lo lleuaron a vna bodega de la dicha casa e lo enboluieron en vn paño de stopa e hisieron vn hoyo e le metieron alli e encubrieron el dicho hoyo con tierra e pusieron encima vna cuba para que no paresçiese que avian puesto alli cosa ninguna* (Beinart 1981b, 34). See also Beinart 1975, 655.

141. *Fue preguntado que quando no leyan en el dicho libro, que adonde le tenia. Dixo que en oyo debaxo de tierra* (Beinart 1977a, 558).

142. *Los encerraron en un pajar de la casa donde vivían, de donde después los sacaron humedecidos y los pusieron a secar al sol y los volvieron a esconder con algún dinero y plata labrada en un aposento alto, haciendo un socavón en la pared* (Lewin 1971, 230; cf. 298). Even in modern times an occasional Jewish book is discovered in its ancient hiding place. A late fifteenth-century prayer book in Catalán was found in 1848 (Riera i Sans 1971–5).

143. *La verdad es que las susodichas fueron alli el dicho primero sabado que tiene dicho porque la dicha muger de Fernando de Molina vavtizava vn fijo suyo, e que fueron alli para honrarle e non por guardar el dicho sabado, ni lo guardaron* (Beinart 1977a, 308; cf. 344).

144. *Quando algum sancto de guarda caia em dia de sabbado, ella, Re, vestia camisa lavada por honra do mesmo sabbado* (Azevedo Mea 1982, 439; cf. 450).

145. *Que a los judíos no les era permitido nombrar a Nuestro Señor Jesucristo ni a su Santísima Madre, y que cuando dicen la Virgen del Carmen, porque piensen los católicos que los oyen que invocan a Nuestra Señora, no la invocan, sino a Elías* (García 1910, 101).

146. *Dicen que estaba encuadernada en un libro de volumen de cuatro dedos y al principio había cosas de caballerías y en medio la josefina y al fin cosas de Nuestra Santa Fe Católica, que entendió estaba encuadernada así por disimular* (Gracia Boix 1983, 139).

147. Liebman 1982, 121; 1970, 66. This classic symbol of hypocrisy first appeared in the prototypical Spanish picaresque novel *Lazarillo de Tormes* (1554). *Conversos* in Andalucia [1482] also disguised their fasts by strolling in the countryside (Ollero Pina 1988, 98).

148. *Yva a misa por tener nombre de xristiano* (Llorca 1939, 141). Similarly a Galician new-Christian *confesó y comulgó sacramentalmente por Pascua porque no le testificasen, pero no porque tuviera verdadera intención* (Contreras 1982, 601).

149. *Destas cosas semejantes nunca nos apartamos, por el desir de las gentes; e por tanto non dexemos de entrar y estar en algunas confradías e cabildos, o tomar algunas veces bullas, solamente por dar color a la gente* (Fita y Colomé 1887, 45).

150. *Aunque había oído misa, confesado y comulgado, lo hacía por encubrirse y no por entender que fuese necesario para la salvación de su alma* (Garcia de Proodian 1966, 347).

151. For example, *Todos os autos que fazia de christão erão por contemplação do mundo sem crer nellas. . . . Fazia todos os autos de cristã por comprimento do mundo somente* (Azevedo Mea 1982, 116, 2).

152. *Los días de fiesta le decía su abuela a gritos (por los vecinos católicos): vamos a misa Leonorilla, e iba con ella, pasaban por las iglesias y nunca entraban en alguna, antes la llevaba a la casa de otra tía suya* (García 1910, 234–5). See also Liebman 1970, 248–9.

153. *La rea tomaba todos los años la Bula de la Cruzada porque entendiesen todos que era cristiana vieja y que decía que todos habían de comprarla para redimir las ánimas del purgatorio* (Contreras 1982, 601).

154. *Devoción de la christiandat, sino porque los creyesen que eran buenos christianos* (Marín Padilla 1980, 261).

155. *E' para salvaguardar as aparencias . . . mas nós não olhamos para elas, eles não são dos nossos* (Jarval 1929, 2).

156. Converts from Islam to Christianity were thought to behave in much the same way. This is why in *Don Quijote* (1605) the *morisco* Ricote, apparently a sincere Christian but expelled from Spain nonetheless, returns to seek out his family wearing the disguise of a German pilgrim and munching on a ham bone (2:54).

157. *El Alborayque tenía boca de lobo, esto es, que estos alboraycos son ypróquitas y falsos profetas, llamándose xrianos y no lo son . . . quando se hallan con los judíos, dizen: somos judíos, quando con los christianos: somos christianos* (*Libro llamado el Alboraique* 1954, 392, 400). As the late Sanford Shepard pointed out, this seems to be a model for a similar passage about *converso* hypocrisy in Francisco Delicado's early sixteenth-century novel *Retrato de la Lozana andaluza* (1982, 27).

# Appendix

### EDICT OF FAITH (CUENCA 1624)[1]

We the Inquisitors against heretical wickedness and apostasy by virtue of apostolic authority, etc. To all residents and inhabitants of the cities, towns and villages of this district, of every rank, condition and title . . . good health in our Lord Jesus Christ, which is true health, and may you steadfastly observe, keep and comply with our commands, which are truly apostolic utterances. Be advised that the Prosecutor of the Holy Office appeared before us to point out that we knew that for a long time in many cities, towns and villages of this district no Inquisition or general investigation had been made, so that we had no information about the many crimes that had been committed and perpetrated against our holy Catholic Faith which were still to be punished, and that this did a great disservice to our Lord and great damage and harm to the Christian religion; therefore he asked us to initiate such an Inquisition and general investigation, having edicts publicly read, and punishing those who might be found guilty, so that our Holy Catholic Faith would be extended and exalted. And we, seeing the appropriateness of his request, and wishing to provide the remedies necessary for service to our Lord, for this reason ordered the following [document] to be issued for each and every one of you. By this [document] we exhort you and require that if any of you knows, or has seen or heard say that any person, living or absent or dead, has done or has said or has held any of the heretical ideas against what our Holy Mother Roman Church teaches, or has said or affirmed any vile sounding heretical words, or scandalous or blasphemous words, against God our Lord and his Holy Catholic Faith.

## Law of Moses

to wit: if any of you has seen or heard say that any person or persons have kept any Sabbaths in honor or observance of the Law of Moses, putting on clean personal linen and their best or festival clothing, placing clean linen on their tables and throwing clean sheets on their beds in honor of the Sabbath, not kindling a fire or doing any other work on those days, beginning on Friday afternoon. Or who have porged or deveined the meat they are preparing to eat, soaking it in water to remove the blood, or who have removed the sciatic vein from a leg of mutton or from any other animal. Or who have cut the throat from one side to the other of any animals or birds which they are going to eat, saying "Blessed be the Lord who has commanded us to slaughter [in this fashion]," first testing the knife on a finger nail to see if it has a sharp edge, and then covering the blood with earth. Or who have eaten meat during Lent or on other days forbidden by the Holy Mother Church, without needing to do so, believing that they could eat it without sin. Or who have fasted on the Great Fast which is called the Fast of Pardon, going barefoot on that day. Or who have prayed Jewish prayers, and in the evening have asked forgiveness of each other, the parents putting their hands on their children's heads without crossing them or saying anything, or saying "May you be blessed by God and by me," according to the Law of Moses and its ceremonies, or who fast the fast of Queen Esther, or the fast of *Rebeaso*, which they call the Loss of the Holy Temple, or other Jewish fasts during the week, such as on Mondays or Thursdays, not eating on those days until evening when the stars have come out, and those nights not eating meat, and washing themselves the day before in prepraration for those fasts, cutting their nails and trimming their hair, and keeping or burning the cuttings, praying Jewish prayers while raising and lowering their heads which are turned face toward the wall, and before they pray washing their hands with water or with dirt, wearing garments of serge, terry cloth or linen with certain cords or little strings hanging down from the corners tied into certain knots. Or who celebrate the Festival of unleavened bread, beginning by eating lettuce, celery or other bitter herbs on those days. Or who observe the Festival of Booths, putting up huts of green branches, eating there and hosting their friends and exchanging food. Or the Festival of the Little Lights, lighting them one by one until there are ten, and then putting them out again, praying Jewish prayers on those occasions. Or if they bless the table according to Jewish custom, or drink *Caser* wine, or make the *Barahá*, taking the glass of wine in their hands and saying certain words over it, then giving each person a sip. Or if they eat meat that has been slaughtered by Jews, or eat their food with them at their tables.[2] Or who pray the Psalms of David without the *Gloria Patri*. Who wait for the Messiah or say that the Messiah promised by the Law has not come but is coming and who wait for him to remove them from the captivity in which they say they find themselves and who will take them to the promised land. Or if any woman waits forty days after childbirth to go into the temple according to ceremonies of the Law of Moses. Or if when children are born they circumcise them and give them Jewish names, or call them by them, or who after they are baptized wash off the Oil and Chrism. Or who on the seventh night after the birth of the child put it in a basin of water into which they place gold, silver, pearls, wheat, barley and other things, washing the child in that water, saying, "May you be as well supplied with the goods of this world as is this basin." Or who have made the ceremony of the *hadas* for their children. Or if anyone is married in the Jewish fashion, or performs the *Ruaya,* which is when someone sets out on a journey. Or if they wear Jewish amulets. Or if when they are kneading they take a piece of *ala* from the dough and throw it into the fire as a sacrifice. Or if when some person is at the point of death they turn him toward the wall to die, and when he is dead, they wash him with hot water, shaving his beard and underarms and other parts of his body, enshrouding him with new linen, breeches, shirt, with his cape folded on his breast, placing under his head a pillow of virgin soil, or [placing] in his mouth a coin or pearl or other thing. Or who sing funeral dirges over him, or pour out the water from the pitchers and basins in the house of the deceased and in the neighbors' houses, saying that the soul of the deceased goes there to bathe, who eat sitting on the floor, behind their doors, fish and olives and not meat, from grief for the deceased, and do not leave their houses for a year in observance of that law. Or if they bury them in virgin soil or in the Jewish cemetery. Or if some of them have emigrated to revert to Judaism. Or if someone has said that the Law of Moses is as good as that of our Redeemer Jesus Christ. . . . [The document further lists customs of the Sect of Mohammed . . . Sect of Luther . . . Sect of the Illuminists[3] . . . and other diverse heresies[4]].

Or who have said or affirmed that there is no Paradise or Glory for the good nor hell for the bad. And that there is nothing more than living and dying. And have said "let me not suffer in this world, for thou won't see me suffer in the next," disbelieving in the last judgment. Or who have uttered heretical blasphemies such as "I do not believe" or "I disbelieve" or "I deny" God our Lord, or the virginity and purity of Our Lady the Virgin Mary, or who have denied her virginity, saying that our Lady the Virgin Mary was not virgin before, during and after giving birth, and that she did not conceive from the Holy Spirit. Or who have uttered heretical blasphemies against the saints in heaven. . . .

Given in the Holy Office of the Castle of Cuenca, March 15, 1624.

Dr. D. Pedro de Herrera y Guzmán

Dr. D. Pedro Pacheco y Girón

By order of the Holy Office: Julián Angel de Ibarrieta, Secretary.

## Notes

1. Jiménez Monteserín transcribed the Spanish of this text from the A. D. C. Inquisición, leg. 830 (1980, 503–37).
2. The conservative nature of the Edicts of Faith can be seen by the retention of clauses such as this one 130 years after the expulsion.
3. A mystical movement that flourished in Spain in the early years of the sixteenth century.
4. While this particular Edict of Faith does not tie these attitudes directly to Judaizing, in hundreds of trials they are considered to be essential parts of the crypto-Jewish belief system.

# ❦ Works Cited

Acosta, Uriel
    1901    *Espelho da vida humana.* Ed. Epiphanio da Silva. Lisboa: Lucas.

Adler, Cyrus
    1895    *Trial of Jorge de Almeida by the Inquisition in Mexico.* Baltimore: Friedenwald, 1937.
    1899    *Trial of Gabriel de Granada by the Inquisition in Mexico 1642–1645.* Publications of the American Jewish Historical Society 7. Baltimore: Friedenwald.

AGN
    *Archivo General de la Nación.* Mexico City: Sección Inquisición.

Alberro, Solange
    1988    *Inquisition et société au Mexique, 1571–1700.* Mexico City: Centre d'études mexicaines et centroaméricaines.

Amador de los Ríos, José
    1875    *Historia social, política y religiosa de los judíos de España y Portugal.* 2 vols. Madrid: Aguilar, 1973.

Angel, Marc Dwight
    1980    *The Jews of Rhodes: The History of a Sephardic Community.* New York: Sepher-Hermon.

Anonymous
    1989    "Additional Stories of Crypto-Jews." *Avotaynu: The International Review of Jewish Genealogy* 5.4: S5.

Aramón i Serra, R.
    1961    "Algunes poesies bilingües en cançoners catalans." *Estudis romànics* 9: 85–126.

Arbós Ayuso, Cristina
    1981    "Los cancioneros castellanos del siglo XV como fuente para la historia de los judíos españoles." *Jews and Conversos: Studies in Society and the Inquisition. Proceedings of the Eighth World Congress of Jewish Studies held at the Hebrew University of Jerusalem.* Ed. Yosef Kaplan. Jerusalem: Magnes. 74–82.

Asenjo González, María
    1986    *Segovia: la ciudad y su tierra a fines del medievo.* Segovia: Diputación Provincial.

Asensio, Eugenio
    1967    "La peculiaridad literaria de los conversos." *Anuario de estudios medievales* 4: 327–51.

Ashtor, Eliyahu
    1984    *The Jews of Moslem Spain.* 3 vols. Philadelphia: Jewish Publication Society.

Assis, Yom Tov
    1988    "Sexual Behavior in Medieval Hispano-Jewish Society." *Jewish History: Essays in Honour of Chimen Abramsky.* Ed. Ada Rapoport-Alpert and Steven J. Zipperstein. London: Peter Halban. 25–59.

Atienza, Juan García de
    1978    *Guía judía de España.* Madrid: Altalena.

Autoridades
    1726    *Diccionario de autoridades.* 3 vols. Madrid: Gredos, 1976.

Azevedo, João Lúcio d'
    1921    *História dos cristãos novos portugueses.* Lisboa: Teixeira, 1975.
    1955    "A evolução do Sebastianismo." *Arquivo histórico português* 10: 379–480.

Azevedo, Pedro A. d'
    1910    "O bocarro francês e os judeus de Cochim e Hamburgo." *Arquivo histórico português* 8: 15–20, 185–98.

Azevedo Mea, Elvira Cunha de
    1981    "Orações judaicas na Inquisição portuguesa—século XVI." *Jews and Conversos: Studies in Society and the Inquisition. Proceedings of the Eighth World Congress of Jewish Studies held at the Hebrew University of Jerusalem.* Ed. Yosef Kaplan. Jerusalem: Magnes. 149–78.
    1982    *Sentenças da Inquisição de Coimbra em metropolitanos de D. Frei Bartolomeu dos Mártires (1567–1582).* Cartôrio Dominicano Português Século XVI 17. Oporto: Arquivo Histórico Dominicano Português.

Baena, Juan Alfonso de
    1966    *Cancionero de Juan Alfonso de Baena.* Ed. J. M. Azáceta. Madrid: Consejo Superior de Investigaciones Científicas.

Baer, Yitzhak
    1936    *Die Jüden im christlichen Spanien.* Berlin: Schocken.
    1966    *A History of the Jews in Christian Spain.* 2 vols. Philadelphia: Jewish Publication Society.

Baião, Antonio
    1921    *A Inquisição em Portugal e no Brasil: Subsidios para a sua história.* Lisboa: Arquivo Historico Português.
    1938–53    *Episódios dramáticos da Inquisição portuguesa.* 3 vols. Lisboa: Seara Nova, 1972.

Baron, Salo
    1965    *A Social and Religious History of the Jews.* Vol. 10: *On the Empire's Periphery.* Philadelphia: Jewish Publication Society.
    1969    *A Social and Religious History of the Jews.* Vol. 13: *Inquisition, Renaissance, and Reformation.* Philadelphia: Jewish Publication Society.

Barros Basto, Artur Carlos de [Ben-rosh]
    1928a    "A lenda dos abafadores." *Ha-Lapid* 2.13: 2.
    1928b    "Tradições Cripto-Judaicas." *Ha-Lapid* 2.10: 4–8; 2.11: 6–8; 2.12: 4–6; 3.17: 1.

Bataillon, Marcel
    1937    *Erasmo y España.* Mexico City: Fondo de Cultura Económica, 1966.

Beinart, Haim
    1961    "The Judaizing Movement in the Order of San Jeronimo in Castile." *Scripta Hierosolymitana* 7: 167–92.
    1971    "The Converso Community in 15th Century Spain." *The Sephardi Heritage.* Ed. Richard David Barnett. Hoboken, N. J.: Ktav. 1: 425–56.
    1974    *Records of the Trials of the Spanish Inquisition in Ciudad Real.* 1: *1483–1485.* Jerusalem: Israel National Academy of Sciences and Humanities.
    1975    "Judíos y conversos en Casarrubios del Monte." *Homenaje a Juan Prado: miscelánea de estudios bíblicos y hebraicos.* Ed. L. Alvarez Verdes. Madrid: Consejo Superior de Investigaciones Científicas. 645–59.
    1977a    *Records of the Trials of the Spanish Inquisition in Ciudad Real.* 2: *1494–1512.* Jerusalem: Israel National Academy of Sciences and Humanities.

1977b   "The Jews in the Canary Islands: A Re-evaluation." *Transactions of the Jewish Historical Society of England* 25: 48–86.
1980   *Trujillo: A Jewish Community in Extremadura on the Eve of the Expulsion from Spain.* Jerusalem: Magnes.
1981a   *Conversos on Trial: The Inquisition in Ciudad Real.* Jerusalem: Magnes.
1981b   *Records of the Trials of the Spanish Inquisition in Ciudad Real.* 3: 1512–1527. Jerusalem: Israel National Academy of Sciences and Humanities.
1983   *Los conversos ante el Tribunal de la Inquisición.* Barcelona: Riopiedras.
1986   *Andalucía y sus judíos.* Córdoba: Monte de Piedad y Caja de Ahorros de Córdoba.

Bel Bravo, Maria Antonia
1988   *El auto de fe de 1593: los conversos granadinos de origen judío.* Granada: U de Granada.

Beller, Jacob
1969   *Jews in Latin America.* New York: Jonathan David.

Benito Ruano, Eloy
1957   "El memorial contra los conversos del bachiller Marcos García de Mora (Marquillos de Mazarambroz)." *Sefarad* 7: 314–51.
1972   "Del problema judío al problema converso." *Simposio "Toledo judaico."* Toledo: Centro Universitario de Toledo de la U Complutense. 2: 7–28.
1987   "Otros cristianos: conversos en España, siglo XV." *Encuentros en Sefarad: Actas del congreso internacional "Los judíos en la historia de España."* Ed. Francisco Ruiz Gómez and Manuel Espadas Burgos. Ciudad Real: Instituto de Estudios Manchegos. 253–64.

Bernáldez, Andrés
1962   *Memorias del reinado de los Reyes Católicos.* Ed. Manuel Gómez Moreno and Juan de Carriazao. Madrid: Real Academia de la Historia.

Blázquez Miguel, Juan
1984   "Almagro y la Inquisición." *Segunda semana de historia de Almagro.* Ciudad Real: Diputación de Ciudad Real. 5–38.
1985a   "Criptojudaísmo en Albacete: procesos de la Inquisición de Cuenca." *Congreso de Historia de Albacete*, Albacete, 1983. Albacete: Instituto de Estudios Albacetenses. 3: 57–69.
1985b   *La Inquisición en Albacete.* Albacete: Instituto de Estudios Albacetenses.
1986a   *La Inquisición en Castilla-La Mancha.* U de Córdoba Monografías 86. Madrid: Librería Anticuaria Jerez.
1986b   *El tribunal de la Inquisición en Murcia.* Murcia: Caja de Ahorros de Murcia.
1987   *Huete y su tierra: un enclave inquisitorial conquense.* Huete: Ayuntamiento; Madrid: Librería Anticuaria Jerez.
1988   *Inquisición y criptojudaísmo.* Madrid: Kaydeda.
1989   *Toledot: Historia del Toledo judío.* Toledo: Arcano.
1990   *Madrid: judíos, herejes y brujas. El Tribunal de la Corte (1650–1820).* Toledo: Arcano.

Bloom, Herbert Ivan
1937: rpt. 1969   *The Economic Impact of the Jews of Amsterdam in the Seventeenth and Eighteenth Centuries.* Port Washington, N.Y./London: Kennikat Press.

Bofarull y Sans, Francisco de Asís de
1910   *Los judíos en el territorio de Barcelona (siglos X al XIII).* Barcelona: Francisco J. Altés.

    1911–2    "Los judíos malsines." *Boletín de la Real Academia de Buenas Letras de Barcelona* 6: 207–16.

Böhm, Gunter
    1963    *Nuevos antecedentes para una historia de los judíos en Chile colonial.* Santiago de Chile: Universitaria.
    1984    *Historia de los judíos en Chile.* Santiago de Chile: Andrés Bello.

Braunstein, Baruch
    1936    *The Chuetas of Majorca: Conversos and the Inquisition of Majorca.* Oriental Series 28. New York: Columbia UP.

Bromberg, Rachel Mizrahi
    1984    *A Inquisição no Brasil: um capitão-mor judaizante.* São Paulo: USP-Centro de Estudos Judaicos.

Brookes, Reuben S.
    1959    *A Dictionary of Judaism.* London: Shapiro Vallentine.

Bujanda, Jesús M. de
    1991    "Recent Historiography of the Spanish Inquisition (1977–88): Balance and Perspective." *Cultural Encounters: The Impact of the Inquisition in Spain and the New World.* Ed. Mary Elizabeth Perry and Anne J. Cruz. Berkeley: U of California P. 221–47.

Bujanda/Cantera Burgos
    1947    "De cómo han de jurar los judíos." Fernando Bujanda and Francisco Cantera Burgos. *Sefarad* 7: 145–7.

Cabezudo Astraín, José
    1950    "Los conversos aragoneses según los procesos de la Inquisición." *Sefarad* 18: 272–82.
    1963    "Los conversos de Barbastro y el apellido 'Santángel'." *Sefarad* 23: 265–84.
    1970    "La expulsión de los judíos de Ejea de los Caballeros." *Sefarad* 30: 349–63.

Canelo, David Augusto
    1987    *Os últimos criptojudeus em Portugal.* Belmonte: Centro de Cultura Pedro Alvares Cabral.
    1990    *The Last Crypto-Jews of Portugal.* Trans. Werner Talmon-l'Armée. N.p.: Privately printed.

Cantera Burgos, Francisco
    1933    *La conversión del célebre talmudista Salomón Levi.* Santander: F. Fons.
    1944    "Fernando de Pulgar and the *conversos*." *Sefarad* 4: 295–348.
    1952    *Alvar García de Santa María: Historia de la judería de Burgos y de sus conversos más ilustres.* Madrid: Real Academia de la Historia.
    1970    "Los judíos expulsados de San Martín de Valdeiglesias." *Primer simposio de estudios sefardíes.* Madrid: Consejo Superior de Investigaciones Científicas, 1964. 23–32.
    1971    *Pedrarias Dávila y Cota: Capitán General y Gobernador de Castilla de Oro y Nicaragua. Sus antecedentes judíos.* Madrid: U de Madrid.

Cantera/Carrete
    1971    "La Judería de Hita." Francisco Cantera Burgos and Carlos Carrete Parrondo. *Sefarad* 32: 249–305.
    1975    *Las juderías medievales en la provincia de Guadalajara.* Francisco Cantera Burgos and Carlos Carrete Parrondo. Madrid: Viuda de C. Bermejo.

Cantera Montenegro, Enrique
    1982a    "Judeoconversos de Torrelaguna (Madrid) a fines del siglo XV." *Anales del Instituto de estudios madrileños* 19: 23–40.

1982b   "Algunos judeoconversos de Laguardia (Alava) penitenciados por el Tribunal de la Inquisición en el siglo XVI." *El Olivo* 16: 53–62.

1985   "Solemnidades, ritos y costumbres de los judaizantes de Molina de Aragón a fines de la Edad Media." *Actas del II congreso internacional "Encuentro de las tres culturas."* Toledo, October 2–6, 1983. Toledo: Ayuntamiento de Toledo. 59–88.

1987   "Relaciones judeocristianas en la diócesis de Osma en el último tercio del siglo XV." *Encuentros en Sefarad: Actas del congreso internacional "Los judíos en la historia de España."* Ed. Francisco Ruiz Gómez and Manuel Espadas Burgos. Ciudad Real: Instituto de Estudios Manchegos. 103–55.

Cardoza, Anne
    1989   "I am a Marrano." *Avotaynu: The International Review of Jewish Genealogy* 5.4: S2–3.

Caro Baroja, Julio
    1961   *Los judíos en la España moderna y contemporánea.* Madrid: Ariel.

Carrete Parrondo, Carlos
    1972   "La conversión de la comunidad hebrea de Maqueda en el siglo XV." *Sefarad* 32: 141–7.

    1977a   "Cobeña: aljama castellana en los albores de la expulsión." *Proceedings of the Sixth World Congress of Jewish Studies.* 1973. Jerusalem: World Union of Jewish Studies 2: 71–6.

    1977b   "Convivencia judeo-cristiana en Castilla antes de 1492." *El Olivo* 2: 29–34.

    1978   "Fraternization between Jews and Christians in Spain before 1492." *American Sephardi* 9: 15–21.

    1979   "La Inquisición y los clérigos judaizantes de Cuenca (1489–1491)." *Helmántica* 30: 51–61.

    1980   "Mesianismo e Inquisición en las juderías de Castilla la Nueva." *Helmántica* 31: 251–6.

    1985a   *El Tribunal de la Inquisición en el Obispado de Soria (1486–1502).* Fontes iudaeorum regni castellae 2. Salamanca: U Pontificia de Salamanca, U de Granada.

    1985b   "Los judaizantes de Cuenca procesadas por la Inquisición en 1490." *Actas del II congreso internacional "Encuentro de las tres culturas."* Toledo, October 2–6, 1983. Toledo: Ayuntamiento de Toledo. 97–104.

    1986   *Proceso inquisitorial contra los Arias Dávila segovianos: un enfrentamiento social entre judíos y conversos.* Fontes iudaeorum regni castellae 3. Salamanca: U Pontificia de Salamanca, U de Granada.

    1989   "Dos ejemplos del primitivo criptojudaísmo en Cuenca." *El Olivo* 29–30: 63–9.

    1990   "Los judaizantes de Uclés, 1490–1492." *Proceedings of the Tenth World Congress of Jewish Studies, Division B.* Ed. David Assaf. Jerusalem: World Union of Jewish Studies. 2: 167–74.

Carrete/Fraile
    1987   *Los judeoconversos de Almazán 1501–5: Origen familiar de los Laínez.* Carlos Carrete Parrondo and Carolina Fraile Conde. Fontes iudaeorum regni castellae 4. Salamanca: U Pontificia de Salamanca, U de Granada.

Carvajal, Miguel de
    1872   "Las Cortes de la Muerte." *Romancero y cancionero sagrados: Colección de poesías cristianas, orales y divinas.* Ed. Justo de Sancha. Biblioteca de Autores Españoles 35. Madrid: Rivadeneyra. 1–41.

    1932   *Tragedia Josephina.* Ed. Joseph Gillet. Princeton: Princeton UP.

Cascales Ramos, Antonio
    1986    *La Inquisición en Andalucía: Resistencia de los conversos a su implantación*. Barcelona: Biblioteca de la Cultura Andaluza.

Castañeda/Hernández
    1989    *El tribunal de la Inquisición de Lima, 1570–1635*. Paulino Castañeda Delgado and Pilar Hernández Aparicio. Madrid: Ceimos.

Castillo, Hernando del
    1882    *Cancionero general de Hernando de Castillo*. Madrid: Sociedad de Bibliófilos Españoles.

Castro, Américo
    1948    *España en su historia*. Buenos Aires: Losada.
    1954a   *La realidad histórica de España*. Mexico City: Porrúa.
    1954b   *The Structure of Spanish History*. Trans. Edmund L. King. Princeton: Princeton UP.
    1959    *El origen, ser y existir de los españoles*. Madrid: Taurus.
    1963    *De la edad conflictiva*. 2nd ed. Madrid: Taurus.
    1965    *Los españoles y cómo llegaron a serlo*. Madrid: Taurus.
    1971    *The Spaniards: An Introduction to Their History*. Trans. Willard F. King and Selma Margaretten. Princeton: Princeton UP.

Cervantes Saavedra, Miguel de
    1962    *Obras completas*. Ed. Angel Valbuena Prat. Madrid: Aguilar.

Chinchilla Aguilar, Ernesto
    1953    *La Inquisición en Guatemala*. Guatemala: Ministro de Educación Pública.

Cirac Estropañán, Sebastián
    1942    *Los procesos contra hechicería en la Inquisición de Castilla la Nueva*. Madrid: Consejo Superior de Investigaciones Científicas.

Coelho, António Borges
    1987    *Inquisição de Évora (Dos primórdios a 1668)*. Lisboa: Caminho.

Cohen, Gerson David
    1967    "Review of B. Netanyahu's *The Marranos of Spain*." *Jewish Social Studies* 29: 178– 84.

Cohen, Martin A.
    1965    [See Usque.]
    1968    "The Religion of Luis Rodríguez Carvajal." *American Jewish Archives* 20: 33–62.
    1972    "Some Misconceptions About the Crypto-Jews in Colonial Mexico." *American Jewish Historical Quarterly* 61: 277–93.
    1973    *The Martyr Luis de Carvajal: The Story of a Secret Jew and the Mexican Inquisition in the Sixteenth Century*. Philadelphia: Jewish Publication Society.
    1982    "Toward a New Comprehension of the Marranos." *Hispania Judaica: Studies on the History, Language and Literature of the Jews in the Hispanic World*. Ed. Josep M. Solà-Solé et al. Barcelona: Puvill. 1: 23–35.

Contreras, Jaime
    1982    *El Santo Oficio de la Inquisición de Galicia, 1560–1700: Poder, sociedad y cultura*. Madrid: Akal.
    1991    "Family and Patronage: The Judeo-Converso Minority in Spain." *Cultural Encounters: The Impact of the Inquisition in Spain and the New World*. Ed. Mary Elizabeth Perry and Anne J. Cruz. Berkeley: U of California P. 127–45.

Conway, George R. G.
    1928    "Hernando Alonso, a Jewish Conquistador with Cortés in Mexico." *Publications of the American Jewish Historical Society* 31: 9–31.

Coronas Tejada, Luis
    1988    *Conversos and Inquisition in Jaen.* Jerusalem: Magnes.

Cortes i Cortes, Gabriel
    1985    *Historia de los judíos mallorquines y de sus descendientes cristianos.* 2 vols. Palma de Mallorca: La Rodella.

Covarrubias, Sebastián de
    1611    *Tesoro de la lengua castellana.* Ed. Martín de Riquer. Madrid: Turner, 1977.

Cuervo, Justo
    1889    "Fray Luis de Granada y la Inquisición." *Homenaje a Menéndez y Pelayo.* Ed. Juan Valera. Madrid: V. Suárez. 1: 733–43.

da Cunha e Freitas, Eugénio de Andrea
    1952    "Tradições judio-portuguesas." *Douro-Litoral: Boletim da Comissão Provincial de Etnografia e História* 4th ser., 5–6: 17–22.
    1954    "Tradições judio-portuguesas: novos subsídios." *Douro-Litoral: Boletim da Comissão Provincial de Etnografia e História* 6th. ser., 1–2: 145–9.

Dánvila, Francisco
    1886    "El robo de la judería de Valencia en 1391." *Boletín de la Real Academia de la Historia* 8: 370–1.

Dedieu, Jean-Pierre
    1978    "Les causes de foi de l'Inquisition de Tolède (1483–1820): essai statistique." *Mélanges de la Casa de Velázquez* 14: 143–71.

Delicado, Francisco
    1528    *Retrato de la Lozana andaluza.* Ed. Claude Allaigre. Madrid: Cátedra, 1985.

Despina, Marie
    1979    "Las acusaciones de crimen ritual en España." *El Olivo* 9: 48–70.

Dillard, Heath
    1984    *Daughters of the Reconquest: Women in Castilian Town Society, 1100–1300.* Cambridge: Cambridge UP.

Dobrinsky, Herbert C.
    1986    *A Treasury of Sephardic Laws and Customs.* Hoboken, N. J.: Ktav.

Domínguez Ortiz, Antonio
    1955a    *Los conversos de origen judío después de la expulsión (La clase social de los conversos en Castilla en la edad moderna).* Madrid: Consejo Superior de Investigaciones Científicas.
    1955b    "El proceso inquisitorial de Juan Núñez Saravia, banquero de Felipe IV." *Hispania* (Madrid) 61: 559–81.
    1965    "Historical research on Spanish conversos in the last 15 years." *Collected Studies in Honour of Américo Castro's Eightieth Year.* Ed. Marcel Paul Hornik. Oxford: Lincombe Lodge Research Library. 63–82.
    1971    *Los judeoconversos en España y América.* Madrid: Istmo.
    1981    "Judíos en la España de los Austrias." *Nueva revista de filología hispánica* 30.2: 609–16.
    1991    *Los judeoconversos en la España moderna.* Madrid: Mapfre.

Edwards, John
    1984a    "Jewish Testimony to the Spanish Inquisition: Teruel, 1484–7." *Revue des études juives* 143: 333–50.
    1984b    "Elijah and the Inquisition: Messianic Prophecy among *Conversos* in Spain, c. 1500." *Nottingham Medieval Studies* 28: 79–94.
    1985    "The Conversos: A Theological Approach." *Bulletin of Hispanic Studies* 62: 39–49.

1988 "Religious Faith and Doubt in Late Medieval Spain: Soria, circa 1450–1500." *Past and Present* 20 (Aug.): 3–25.

Eimeric, Nicolau (1367) /Peña, Francisco (1578)
1973 *El manual de los inquisidores.* Ed. and trans. Latin to French, Luis Sala-Molins. Trans. French to Spanish, Francisco Martín. Barcelona: Muchnik.

Enc. Jud.
1972 *Enciclopedia Judaica.* 16 vols. New York: Macmillan.

Espinosa, Aurelio M.
1930 "Origen oriental y desarrollo histórico del cuento de las doce palabras retornadas." *Revista de filología española* 17: 390–413.

Falbel, Nachman
1974 *Estudos sobre a comunidade judaica no Brasil.* São Paulo: Federação Israelita do São Paulo.

Farinelli, Arturo
1925 *Marrano, Storia de un vituperio.* Biblioteca dell' "Archivum romanicum" ser. 2. 10. Geneva: L. S. Olschki. 36.

Faur, José
1990 "Four Classes of Conversos: A Typological Study." *Revue des études juives* 149: 113–24.
1992 *In the Shadow of History: Jews and Conversos at the Dawn of Modernity.* Albany: State U of New York P.

Fierman, Floyd S.
1987 *Roots and Boots: From Crypto-Jew in New Spain to Community Leader in the American Southwest.* Hoboken, N. J.: Ktav.

Fita y Colomé, Fidel
1884 "Un canónigo judaizante quemado en Córdoba (28 febrero 1484)." *Boletín de la Real Academia de la Historia* 5: 401–4.
1887 "La verdad sobre el martirio del santo Niño de la Guardia, o sea el proceso y quema (16 noviembre 1491) del judío Jucé Franco en Avila." *Boletín de la Real Academia de la Historia* 11: 7–134.
1892 "La Inquisición de Ciudad Real en 1483–1485. Documentos inéditos." *Boletín de la Real Academia de la Historia* 20: 462–520.
1893 "La Inquisición en Guadalupe." *Boletín de la Real Academia de la Historia* 23: 283–343.

Floriano Cumbreño, Antonio Cristino
1924 "El tribunal del Santo Oficio en Aragón. Establecimiento de la Inquisición en Teruel." *Boletín de la Real Academia de la Historia* 86: 544–605; 87 (1925): 173–206.

Fontes, Manuel da Costa
1992 "Mais orações criptojudias de Rebordelo." *Revista da Universidade de Coimbra* 37: 457–69.
1993 "Four Portuguese Crypto-Jewish Prayers and Their 'Inquisitorial' Counterparts." *Mediterranean Language Review* 6–7: 67–104.

Forteza, Miguel
1966 *Els descendents dels jueus conversos de Mallorca.* 3rd ed. Mallorca: Moll.

Foulché-Delbosc, Raymond
1915 *Cancionero castellano del siglo XV.* Ed. Raymond Foulché-Delbosc. Nueva Biblioteca de Autores Españoles 22. Madrid: Bailly-Bailliere.

Freehof, Solomon Bennett
  1964  "Home Rituals and the Spanish Synagogue." *Studies and Essays in Honor of Abraham A. Neuman.* Ed. Meir ben-Horin et al. Leiden: Brill. 215–27.
  1973  *The Responsa Literature and A Treasury of Responsa.* New York: Ktav.
Fuentes Estañol, María José
  1978  "Los juramentos de los judíos en la España medieval." *El Olivo* 5–6: 42–50.
Furtado de Mendoça, Heitor
  1925  *Primera visitação do Santo Officio ás partes do Brasil: Denunciações da Bahia 1591–3.* São Paulo: Paulo Prado.
  1929  *Denunciações de Pernambuco: Primeira visitação do Santo Officio as Partes do Brasil. Pel liçenciado Heitor Furtado de Mendoça. Capellão fidalgo del rey nossa Senhor e do seu desembargo, deputado do Santo Officio. Denunciações de Pernambuco 1593–5.* São Paulo: Paulo Prado.
  1935  *Primeira Visitação do Santo Officio ás partes do Brasil: Confissões da Bahia 1591–92.* Sociedade Capistrano de Abreu. Rio de Janeiro: Briguiet.
Galanes, Adriana Lewis
  1988  "Fray Luis de Granada y los *anuzim* novohispanos a fines del siglo XVI." *Américo Castro: The Impact of His Thought. Essays to Mark the Centenary of His Birth.* Ed. Ronald Surtz et al. Madison, Wisc.: Hispanic Seminary of Medieval Studies. 163–72.
Gampel, Benjamin R.
  1989  *The Last Jews on Iberian Soil: Navarrese Jewery, 1479–1498.* Berkeley: U of California P.
Gaon, Solomon
  1990  *Minhath Shelomo: A Commentary on the Book of Prayer of the Spanish and Portuguese Jews.* New York: Union of Sephardic Congregations.
García, Angelina
  1987  *Els Vives: una familia de jueus valencians.* Valencia: Eliseu Climent.
García, Genaro
  1910  *Autos de fe de la Inquisición de México con extractos de sus causas, 1646–48.* Documentos inéditos o muy raros para la historia de México 28. Mexico City: Viuda de Charles Bouret.
García Cárcel, Ricardo
  1980  *Heregía y sociedad en el siglo XVI: La Inquisición en Valencia 1530–1609.* Barcelona: Península.
  1985  *Orígenes de la Inquisición española: el Tribunal de Valencia 1478–1530.* 2nd ed. Barcelona: Península.
García Casar, María Fuencisla
  1989  "Pleito de unos judeo-conversos de Arévalo. La *ketubbah* de Torrelobatón, 1480." *El Olivo* 29–30: 91–103.
  1990  "Judíos castellanos colaboradores con el Tribunal de la Inquisición del distrito Cuenca-Sigüenza." *Proceedings of the Tenth World Congress of Jewish Studies, Division B.* Jerusalem. 2: 175–82.
García de Proodian, Lucía
  1966  *Los judíos en América: Sus actividades en los Virreinatos de Nueva Castilla y Nueva Granada S. XVII.* Madrid: Consejo Superior de Investigaciones Científicas.
García Fuentes, José María
  1981  *La Inquisición en Granada en el siglo XVI: Fuentes para su estudio.* Granada: Departamento de Historia de la U de Granada, Diputación Provincial.

Gilman, Stephen
    1972    *The Spain of Fernando de Rojas*. Princeton: Princeton UP.

Gitlitz, David M.
    1969    "Cervantes y el valor del hombre." *Humanidades* (Pontificia U Católica del Perú) 3: 69–83.
    1972    "Conversos and the Fusion of Worlds in Micael de Carvajal's *Tragedia Josephina*." *Hispanic Review* 40: 260–70.
    1974    "La actitud cristiano-nueva en *Las Cortes de la Muerte*." *Segismundo* 9: 141–64.
    1992    "Hybrid *Converso*s in the 'Libro llamado el Alborayque'." *Hispanic Review* 60: 1– 17.
    1993a    "Divided Families in *Converso* Spain." *Shofar* 11.3: 1–19.
    1993b    "The Book Called *Alboraique*." *Mediterranean Language Review* 6–7: 121–43.
    1996    *Los Arias Dávila de Segovia: entre la iglesia y la sinagoga* Bethesda, Md.: International Scholars Press.

Gómez Mampaso, María Valentina
    1980    "Profesiones de los judaizantes españoles en tiempos de los Reyes Católicos, según los legajos del Archivo Histórico Nacional de Madrid." *La Inquisición española: nueva visión, nuevos horizontes*. Ed. Joaquín Pérez Villanueva. Madrid: Siglo XXI. 671–87.

Gómez-Martínez, José Luis
    1975    *Américo Castro y el origen de los españoles: historia de una polémica*. Madrid: Gredos.

Gómez-Menor Fuentes, José Carlos
    1970    *Cristianos nuevos y mercaderes de Toledo*. Toledo: Librería Gómez Menor.
    1973    "Un judeoconverso de 1492: Diego Gómez de Toledo (Semuel Abolafia) y su proceso inquisitorial." *Sefarad* 33: 45–110.

González Simancas, Manuel
    1929    *Las sinagogas de Toledo y el baño litúrgico judío*. Toledo: Oficina Tipográfica Regina.

Gracia Boix, Rafael
    1982    *Colección de documentos para la historia de la Inquisición de Córdoba*. Córdoba: Monte de Piedad y Caja de Ahorros de Córdoba.
    1983    *Autos de fe y causas de la Inquisición de Córdoba*. Córdoba: Diputación Provincial.

Greenleaf, Richard E.
    1991    "Historiography of the Mexican Inquisition: Evolution and Interpretations and Methodologies." *Cultural Encounters: The Impact of the Inquisition in Spain and the New World*. Ed. Mary Elizabeth Perry and Anne J. Cruz. Berkeley: U of California P. 248–76.

Gutiérrez Nieto, Juan Ignacio
    1964    "Los conversos y el movimiento comunero." *Hispania* (Madrid) 94: 237–61.

Gutwirth, Eleazar
    1981    "Elementos étnicos e históricos en las relaciones judeo-conversas en Segovia." *Jews and Conversos: Studies in Society and the Inquisition. Proceedings of the Eighth World Congress of Jewish Studies held at the Hebrew University of Jerusalem*. Ed. Yosef Kaplan. Jerusalem: Magnes. 83–102.

Haliczer, Stephen
    1987    "The First Holocaust: The Inquisition and the Converted Jews of Spain and Portugal." *Inquisition and Society in Early Modern Europe*. Ed. Stephen Haliczer. London: Croom Helm. 7–18.
    1990    *Inquisition and Society in the Kingdom of Valencia: 1478–1834*. Berkeley: U of California P.

Halkin, Abraham S.
    1953    "A *Contra christianos* by a Marrano." *Mordecai M. Kaplan. Jubilee Volume on the Occasion of His Seventieth Birthday. English Section.* New York: Jewish Theological Seminary of America. 399–416.

Hayamson, Albert
    1951    *The Sephardim of England.* London: Methuen.

Henningsen, Gustav
    1977    "El banco de datos del Santo Oficio: Las relaciones de causas de la Inquisición española (1550–1700)." *Boletín de la Real Academia de la Historia* 174.3: 547–70.

Herculano, Alexandre de Carvalho e Aráujo
    1854–9    *Da origem e estabelecimento da Inquisição em Portugal.* 3 vols. Lisboa: Imprensa Nacional.

Hernando de Talavera
    [See Márquez Villanueva 1961.]

Hinojosa Montalvo, José
    1993    *The Jews of the Kingdom of Valencia: From Persecution to Expulsion, 1391–1492.* Hispania Judaica 9. Jerusalem: Magnes.

Holzberg, Carol S.
    1987    *Minorities and Power in a Black Society: The Jewish Community of Jamaica.* Latham, Md.: North-South.

Hordes, Stanley Mark
    1980    *The Crypto-Jewish Community of New Spain: 1620–49: A Collective Biography.* Diss., New Orleans: Tulane U.
    1991    "The Inquisition and the Crypto-Jewish Community in Colonial New Spain and New Mexico." *Cultural Encounters: The Impact of the Inquisition in Spain and the New World.* Ed. Mary Elizabeth Perry and Anne J. Cruz. Berkeley: U of California P. 207–17.

Huisman, Piet H.
    1986    *Sephardim: The Spirit That Has Withstood the Times.* Son, Netherlands: Huisman Editions.

Israel, Jonathan I.
    1970    *Race, Class and Politics in Colonial Mexico (1610–1670).* Oxford: Oxford UP.
    1990    *Empires and Entrepots: The Dutch, the Spanish Monarchy and the Jews, 1585–1713.* London: Habledon.

Jarval, Lily Jean
    1929    "Em Bragança entre os Marranos." *Ha-Lapid* 4.24: 1–4.

Jiménez Lozano, José
    1984    "Supervivencia de cultemas islamo-hebraicos en la sociedad española o el fracaso histórico de la Inquisición." *Inquisición española y mentalidad inquisitorial: Ponencias del simposio internacional sobre Inquisición.* New York, 1983. Barcelona: Ariel. 353–72.

Jiménez Monteserín, Miguel
    1980    *Introducción a la Inquisición española. Documentos básicos para el estudio del Santo Oficio.* Madrid: Nacional.

Kamen, Henry
    1965    *The Spanish Inquisition.* New York: Mentor.
    1985    *Inquisition and Society in Spain in the Sixteenth and Seventeenth Centuries.* Bloomington: Indiana UP.

Kaplan, Yosef
    1985    "The Travels of Portuguese Jews from Amsterdam to the 'Lands of Idolatry' (1644–1724)." *Jews and Conversos: Studies in Society and the Inquisition. Proceedings of the Eighth World Congress of Jewish Studies held at the Hebrew University of Jerusalem.* Ed. Yosef Kaplan. Jerusalem: Magnes. 197–211.
    1991    "The Portuguese Community of Amsterdam in the 17th Century Between Tradition and Change." *Society and Community: Proceedings of the Second International Congress for Research of the Sephardi and Oriental Jewish Heritage.* Ed. Abraham Haim. 1984. Jerusalem: Misgav. 141–71.

Karner, Francis P.
    1969    *The Sephardis of Curaçao.* Assen: Van Gorcum.

Kaufman, Tamar
    1992    "Hidden Jew Ventures out of the Closet—600 Years Later." *Northern California Jewish Bulletin* July 24: 19.

Kaufmann, David
    1895–6    "Jewish Informers in the Middle Ages." *Jewish Quarterly Review* 8: 217–38; 527–8.

Kayserling, Meyer
    1890    *Biblioteca española-portuguesa-judaica.* New York: Ktav, 1979.
    1894    *Christopher Columbus and the Participation of the Jews in the Spanish and Portuguese Discoveries.* New York: Hermon, 1968.
    1898  "Notes sur l'histoire de l'Inquisition et des judaisants d'Espagne." *Revue des études juives* 37: 266–73.

Klausner, Joseph
    1955    *The Messianic Idea in Israel.* Trans. W. F. Stinespring. New York: Macmillan.

Kohut, George Alexander
    1904    "Jewish Heretics in the Philippines in the Sixteenth and Seventeenth Century." *Publications of the American Jewish Historical Society* 12: 149–56.

Kurzweil, Arthur
    1980    *From Generation to Generation.* New York: William Morrow.

Ladero Quesada, Miguel Angel
    1984    "Judeoconversos andaluces en el siglo XV." *Actas del III Coloquio de Historia Medieval Andaluza. La sociedad medieval andaluza: Grupos no privilegiados.* Jaen, 1982. Jaen: Diputación Provincial de Jaen. 27–55.

Lazar, Moshe
    1991    "Scorched Parchments and Tortured Memories: The 'Jewishness' of the Anussim (Crypto-Jews)." *Cultural Encounters: The Impact of the Inquisition in Spain and the New World.* Ed. Mary Elizabeth Perry and Anne J. Cruz. Berkeley: U of California P. 176–206.

Lea, Henry Charles
    1906–8    *A History of the Inquisition of Spain.* New York: Macmillan.
    1983    *Historia de la Inquisición española.* Trans. Angel Alcalá and Jesús Tobío. Madrid: Fundación Universitaria Española.

Léon, Henry
    1907    "Les juifs espagnols de Saint-Esprit: chansons et prières." *Bulletin hispanique* 9: 277–85.

León Tello, Pilar
    1972    "Costumbres, fiestas y ritos de los judíos toledanos afines del siglo XV." *Simposio "Toledo judaico."* Toledo: Centro Universitario de Toledo de la U Complutense. 2: 67–90.

Lera García, Rafael de
    1987    "La última gran persecución inquisitorial contra el criptojudaísmo: el Tribunal de Cuenca 1718–1725." *Sefarad* 47: 87–137.

Levi, Moisés Orfali
    1982    *Los conversos españoles en la literatura rabínica. Problemas jurídicos y opiniones legales durante los siglos XII-XVI.* Salamanca: U Pontificia de Salamanca, U de Granada, Federación Sefardí de España.

Levy, Rebecca Amasto
    1987    *I remember Rhodes.* New York: Sepher-Hermon.

Lewin, Boleslao
    1939    *El judío en la época colonial: un aspecto de la historia rioplatense.* Buenos Aires: Colegio Libre de Estudios Superiores.
    1946    *Los Marranos, un intento de definición: contribución al estudio de los orígenes americanos y argentinos.* Buenos Aires: Colegio Libre de Estudios Superiores.
    1954    *Mártires y conquistadores judíos en la América Hispana.* Buenos Aires: Candelabro.
    1971    *La Inquisición en México: racismo inquisitorial. El singular caso de María de Zárate.* Puebla: José M. Cajica.
    1975    *Confidencias de dos criptojudíos en las cárceles del Santo Oficio (Mexico, 1645–6).* Buenos Aires: Julio Kaufman.
    1977    *Singular proceso de Salamón Machorro (Juan de León), Israelita liornés condenado por la Inquisición (México, 1650).* Buenos Aires: Julio Kaufman.
    1987    *Los criptojudíos: un fenómeno religioso y social.* Buenos Aires: Milá.

*Libro llamado del Alborayque*
    [See López Martínez 1954.]

Liebman, Seymour B.
    1964    *A Guide to Jewish References in the Mexican Colonial Era: 1521–1821.* Philadelphia: U of Pennsylvania P.
    1967    *The Enlightened: The Writings of Luis de Carvajal, el Mozo.* Coral Gables: U of Miami P.
    1970    *The Jews in New Spain.* Coral Gables: U of Miami P.
    1974    *Jews and the Inquisition of Mexico: The Great Auto de Fe of 1649.* Lawrence, Kan.: Coronado.
    1975    *The Inquisitors and the Jews in the New World: Summaries of Procesos, 1500–1810, and Bibliographic Guide.* Coral Gables: U of Miami P.
    1982    *New World Jewry, 1493–1825: Requiem for the Forgotten.* New York: Ktav.

Lipiner, Elias
    1969    *Os judaizantes nas capitanias de cima: Estudos sôbre os cristãos-novos do Brasil nos séculos XVI e XVII.* São Paulo: Brasiliense.
    1977    *Santa Inquisição: terror e linguagem.* Rio de Janeiro: Documentário.

Llamas, José
    1944    "La antigua biblia castellana de los judíos españoles." *Sefarad* 4: 219–44.

Llorca, Bernardino
    1935    "La Inquisición española en Valencia." *Analecta sacra tarraconensia* 11: 37–61.
    1939    "La Inquisición española incipiente." *Gregorianum* 20: 101–42; 507–34.
    1942    "La Inquisición española y los conversos judíos o 'marranos'." *Sefarad* 2: 113–51.
    1948    "Los conversos judíos y la Inquisición española." *Sefarad* 8: 357–89.

Llorente, Juan Antonio
    1817    *Historia crítica de la Inquisición de España*. Madrid: Hiperion, 1980.

López Martínez, Nicolás
    1954    "*Libro llamado el Alboraique*." *Los judaizantes castellanos y la Inquisición en tiempo de Isabel la Católica*. Ed. Nicolás López Martínez. Burgos: Seminario metropolitano de Burgos. 391–404.

Lorence, Bruce A.
    1982    "The Inquisition and the New Christians in the Iberian Peninsula—Main Historiographic Issues and Controversies." *The Sepharadi and Oriental Jewish Heritage*. Ed. Assachar Ben-Ami. Jerusalem: Magnes. 13–72.
    1991    "António Homem—A Portrait in New Christian Communal Leadership in Seventeenth-Century Portugal." *Society and Community: Proceedings of the Second International Congress for Research of the Sephardi and Oriental Jewish Heritage*. Ed. Abraham Haim. 1984. Jerusalem: Misgav. 91–101.

Machado, Casimiro de Morais
    1952    "Subsídios para a história de Mogadouro: os Marranos de Vilarinho dos Galegos." *Douro-Litoral: Boletim da Comissão Provincial de Etnografia e História* 1–2: 17–49.

Madariaga, Salvador de
    1940    *Vida del muy magnífico señor don Cristóbal Colón*. Mexico City: Hermes, 1952.

Malkiel, Yakov
    1948    "Hispano-Arabic *marrano* and Its Hispano-Latin Homophone." *Journal of the American Oriental Society* 68: 175–84.

Marcu, Valeriu
    1935    *The Expulsion of the Jews from Spain*. New York: Viking.

Marcus, Jacob R.
    1960    *The Jew in the Medieval World*. Philadelphia: Jewish Publication Society.

Marín Padilla, Encarnación
    1977    "La Inquisición en Barbastro y la Ermita de San Salvador." *Homenaje a Don José María Lacarra de Miguel en su jubilación del profesorado*. Estudios medievales 4. Zaragoza: U de Zaragoza. 213–33.
    1980    "Notas sobre la familia Lupiel de Calatayud (1482–1488)." *Aragón en la edad media: estudios de economía y sociedad (siglos XII al XV)*. Zaragoza: U de Zaragoza. 3: 227–62.
    1981–2    "Relación judeoconversa durante la segunda mitad del siglo XV en Aragón: nacimientos, hadas, circuncisiones." *Sefarad* 41: 273–300; 42 (1982): 59–77.
    1982    "Relación judeoconversa durante la segunda mitad del siglo XV en Aragón: matrimonio." *Sefarad* 42: 243–98.
    1983a    "Notas sobre la familia Constantín de Calatayud (1482–1488)." *Aragón en la edad media: estudios de economía y sociedad (siglos XII al XV)*. Zaragoza: U de Zaragoza. 5: 219–54.
    1983b    "Relación judeoconversa durante la segunda mitad del siglo XV en Aragón: enfermedades y muertes." *Sefarad* 43: 251–343.
    1988    *Relación judeo-conversa durante la segunda mitad del siglo XV en Aragón: La Ley*. Madrid: Privately published.

Marks, Copeland
    1992    *Sephardic Cooking*. New York: Donald Fine.

Marques, António Henrique R. de Oliveira
   1972    *History of Portugal*. 2 vols. New York: Columbia UP.

Márquez Villanueva, Francisco
   1960    *Investigaciones sobre Juan Alvarez Gato. Contribución a la literatura castellana del siglo XV*. Madrid: Real Academia Española.
   1961    ["Introduction."] Hernando de Talavera. *Católica impugnación*. Ed. Francisco Martín Hernández. Barcelona: Juan Flors.
   1965    "The *Converso* Problem: An Assessment." *Collected Studies in Honour of Américo Castro's Eightieth Year*. Ed. Marcel Paul Hornik. Oxford: Lincombe Lodge Research Library. 317–34.
   1980    "El problema de los conversos: cuatro puntos cardinales." *Hispania Judaica: Studies on the History, Language, and Literature of the Jews in the Hispanic World*. Ed. Josep M. Solà-Solé et al. Barcelona: Puvill. 1: 51–75.

Martín Gaite, Carmen
   1970    *El proceso de Macanaz: Historia de un empapelamiento*. Madrid: Moneda y Crédito.

Martínez Millán, José
   1989    "La persecución inquisitorial contra los criptojudíos a principio del siglo XVIII: el Tribunal de Murcia (1715–25)." *Sefarad* 49: 307–63.

Marx, Alexander
   1908    "The Expulsion of the Jews from Spain: Two New Accounts." *Jewish Quarterly Review* os 20: 240–71; ns 2 (1911–12): 257–8.

McGaha, Michael
   1991    "Who was a Jew in Seventeenth-Century Spain?" Unpublished Paper.

Medina, José Toribio de
   1887    *Historia del Tribunal del Santo Oficio de la Inquisición de Lima (1596–1820)*. 2 vols. Santiago de Chile: Gutenberg.
   1890    *Historia del Tribunal del Santo Oficio en Chile*. Santiago de Chile: Ercilla.
   1899a    *El Tribunal del Santo Oficio de la Inquisición en las Provincias del Plata*. Santiago de Chile: Elzeviriana.
   1899b    *Historia del Tribunal de la Inquisición en Cartagena de Indias*. Bogotá: Carlos Valencia, 1978.

Melammed, Renée Levine
   1985    "The Ultimate Challenge: Safeguarding the Crypto-Jewish Heritage." *Proceedings of the American Academy for Jewish Research* 53: 91–109.
   1991a    "Sephardi Women in the Medieval and Early Modern Period." *Jewish Women in Historical Perspective*. Ed. Judith R. Baskin. Detroit: Wayne State UP. 115–34.
   1991b    "Some Death and Mourning Customs of Castilian *Conversas*." *Exilio y diáspora: Estudios sobre la historia del pueblo judío en homenaje al Profesor Haim Beinart*. Eds. Aharon Mirsky et al. Jerusalem: Ben Zvi Institute. 157–67.
   1992    "Women in (Post 1492) Spanish Crypto-Jewish Society: Conversos and the Perpetuation and Preservation of Observances Associated with Judaism." *Judaism* 41.2: 156–68.

Menéndez Pelayo, Marcelino
   1880–1    *Historia de los heterodoxos españoles*. Buenos Aires: Librería Perlado, 1945–6.

Millás y Vallicrosa, José María
   1965    "Descubrimiento de una *miqwah* en la población de Besalú." *Sefarad* 25: 67–9.

Millgram, Abraham E.
    1971    *Jewish Worship*. Philadelphia: Jewish Publication Society.

Molho, Michael
    1950    *Usos y costumbres de los sefardíes de Salonica*. Madrid: Consejo Superior de Investigaciones Científicas.

Monsalvo Antón, José María
    1983    "Antisemitismo en Castilla durante la Edad Media. Aproximación histórico-metodolíca a un conflicto social." *El Olivo* 7: 49–99.
    1984    "Heregía conversa y contestación religiosa a fines de la Edad Media: Las denuncias a la Inquisición en el obispado de Osma." *Studia historica* 2.2: 109–38.

Monter, William
    1990    *Frontiers of Heresy: The Spanish Inquisition from the Basque Lands to Sicily*. Cambridge: Cambridge UP.

Montoro, Antón de
    1990    *Poesía completa*. Ed. Marithelma Costa. Cleveland: Cleveland State UP.

Moore, Kenneth
    1976    *Those of the Street: The Catholic-Jews of Mallorca*. Notre Dame, Ind.: Notre Dame UP.

Moreno, Humberto Baquero
    1985    "Movimentos sociais anti-judaicos em Portugal no século XV." *Jews and Conversos: Studies in Society and the Inquisition. Proceedings of the Eighth World Congress of Jewish Studies held at the Hebrew University of Jerusalem*. Jerusalem: Magnes. 62–73.

Moreno Koch, Yolanda
    1977    "La comunidad judaizante de Castillo de Garcimuñoz: 1489–1492." *Sefarad* 37: 351–71.
    1987    *Las Taqqanot de Valladolid de 1432: un estatuto comunal renovador*. Fontes iudaeorum regni castellae 5. Salamanca: U Pontificia de Salamanca, U de Granada.

Moses ben Maimon
    1949    *[Yad. 14] The Code of Maimonides: Book Fourteen, The Book of Judges*. Trans. Abraham M. Hershman. New Haven: Yale UP.
    1954    *[Yad. 10] The Code of Maimonides: Book Ten, The Book of Cleanness*. Trans. Herbert Danby. New Haven: Yale UP.
    1961    *[Yad. 3] The Code of Maimonides: Book Three, The Book of Seasons*. Trans. Solomon Gandz and Hyman Klein. New Haven: Yale UP.

Motis Dolader, Miguel Angel
    1985    *La expulsión de los judíos de Zaragoza*. Temas de historia aragonesa 4. Zaragoza: Diputación General de Aragón.
    1987    "La conversión de judíos aragoneses a raiz del edicto de Expulsión." *Encuentros en Sefarad. Actas del congreso internacional "Los judíos en la historia de España."* Ed. Francisco Ruiz Gómez and Manuel Espadas Burgos. Ciudad Real: Instituto de Estudios Manchegos. 221–52.

Muñoz de la Peña, Arsenio
    1970    "Los judíos en Extremadura: Hervás y el proceso del año 1519 contra el sacrilegio de los judíos." *Revista de estudios extremeños* 26: 373–82.

Nahon, Gérard
    1973    "Les sephardim, les marranes, les Inquisitions péninsulaires et leurs archives dans les travaux récents de I. S. Révah." *Revue des études juives* 132: 5–48.

1977 "Les marranes espagnols et portugais et les communautés juives issues du marranisme dans l'historiographie récente (1960–1975)." *Revue des études juives* 136: 297–331.

Narkiss, Bezalel
 1988 "The Gerona Hanukkah Lamp: Fact and Fiction." *Jewish Art* 14: 6–15.

Nehama, Joseph
 1977 *Dictionnaire du Judéo-Espagnol*. Madrid: Consejo Superior de Investigaciones Científicas.

Netanyahu, Benzion
 1966 *The Marranos of Spain, From the Late XIVth Century, According to Contemporary Hebrew Sources*. New York: American Academy for Jewish Research.
 1976 "Alonso de Espina: Was He a New Christian?" *Proceedings of the American Academy for Jewish Research* 43: 107–65.

Neuman, Abraham M.
 1942 *The Jews in Spain: Their Social, Political and Cultural Life During the Middle Ages*. 2 vols. Philadelphia: Jewish Publication Society.

New Cath. Enc.
 1967–79 *New Catholic Encyclopedia*. 16 vols. New York: McGraw Hill.

Nidel, David S.
 1984 "Modern Descendants of Conversos in New Mexico." *Western States Jewish Historical Quarterly* 16: 249–62.

Novinsky, Anita
 1972a "A Historical Bias: The New Christian Collaboration with the Dutch Invaders of Brazil (17th Century)." *Proceedings of the Fifth World Congress of Jewish Studies*. Jerusalem: World Union of Jewish Studies. 2: 141–54.
 1972b *Cristãos novos na Bahía*. São Paulo: Perspectiva.
 1982 "Some Theoretical Considerations About the New Christian Problem." *The Sepharadi and Oriental Jewish Heritage*. Ed. Issachar Ben-Ami. Jerusalem: Magnes. 3–11.

Nunemaker, J. Horace
 1946 *The Trial of Simon de León, 1647. Inquisition Papers of Mexico*. Research Studies of the State College of Washington 14. Pullman, Wash.: Washington State College P.

Oelman, Timothy
 1982 *Marrano Poets of the Seventeenth Century*. East Brunswick, N.J.: Associated U Presses.

Ollero Pina, José Antonio
 1988 "Una familia de conversos sevillanos en los orígenes de la Inquisición: los Benadeva." *Hispania sacra* 40: 45–105.

Ortega, Manuel L.
 1919 *Los hebreos en Marruecos*. Madrid: Hispano Africana.

Osorio Osorio, Alberto
 1980 *Judaísmo e Inquisición en Panamá Colonial*. Panamá: Instituto Cultural Panamá-Israel.

Palacios López, Antonio
 1957 *La disputa de Tortosa*. 2 vols. Madrid: Consejo Superior de Investigaciones Científicas.

Patai
 1989 *The Myth of the Jewish Race*. Raphael Patai and Jennifer Patai. Detroit: Wayne State UP.

Paulo, Amílcar
  1947  "Reminiscências judaico-trasmontanas." *Ha-Lapid* 21.137: 8.
  1970  *Os cripto-judeus.* Porto: Athena.
  1981  "O ritual dos criptojudeus portugueses (Algumas reflexões sobre os seus ritos)." *Jews and Conversos: Studies in Society and the Inquisition. Proceedings of the Eighth World Congress of Jewish Studies held at the Hebrew University of Jerusalem.* Ed. Yosef Kaplan. Jerusalem: Magnes. 139–48.
  1985  *Os judeus secretos em Portugal.* Lisboa: Labirinto.
Pereira, Isaías da Rosa
  1979  "A inquisição nos Açores: subsídios para a sua história." *Arquipélago* 1: 181– 201.
Pérez, Lorenzo (Llorenç)
  1974  *Anales judaicos de Mallorca.* Palma de Mallorca: Luis Ripoll.
  1986  *El Tribunal de la Inquisición en Mallorca: relación de causas de fe 1578–1806.* Lorenzo Pérez, Mateu Lleonard Muntaner, and Mateu Colom. Palma de Mallorca: M. Font.
Pérez/Escandell
  1993  *Historia de la Inquisición en España y América.* Joaquín Pérez Villanueva and Bartolomé Escandell Bonet. Estudios Inquisitoriales. Madrid: Biblioteca de Autores Cristianos.
Pimenta Ferro Tavares, Maria José
  1970  *Os Judeus em Portugal no século XIV.* Lisboa: Guimarães.
  1982  *Os Judeus em Portugal no século XV.* Lisboa: Universidade Nova de Lisboa: Facultade de Ciências Sociais e Humanas.
  1987  *Judaísmo e Inquisição: Estudos.* Lisboa: Presença.
Pinta Llorente, Miguel de la
  1953–8  *La Inquisición española y los problemas de la cultura y de la intolerancia.* 2 vols. Madrid: Cultura Hispánica.
Prinz, Joachim
  1973  *The Secret Jews.* New York: Random House.
Pulgar, Hernando del
  1943  *Crónica de los Reyes Católicos.* Ed. Juan de la Mata Carriazo. Madrid: Espasa Calpe.
Pullan, Brian
  1983  *The Jews of Europe and the Inquisition of Venice, 1550–1670.* Totowa, N.J.: Barnes and Noble.
Rábade Obradó, María del Pilar
  1990a  *Los judeo conversos en la Corte y en la época de los Reyes Católicos.* Madrid: U Complutense: Departamento de Historia Medieval.
  1990b  "Expresiones de la religiosidad cristiana en los procesos contra los judaizantes del tribunal de Ciudad Real/Toledo 1483–1507." *En la España medieval* 13: 303–30.
Raphael, David
  1992  *The Expulsion 1492 Chronicles.* North Hollywood, Calif.: Carmi House.
Reguera, Iñaki
  1984  *La Inquisición española en el Pais Vasco.* San Sebastián: Txertoa.
Represa, Amando
  1987  "Una carta de esponsales y otras prescripciones sobre el matrimonio entre judíos y conversos castellanos." *Encuentros en Sefarad. Actas del congreso internacional "Los judíos en la historia de España."* Ed. Francisco Ruiz Gómez and Manuel Espadas Burgos. Ciudad Real: Instituto de Estudios Manchegos. 33–9.

Révah, I. S.
    1959–60    "Les marranes." *Revue des études juives* 118: 29–77.
    1968    "L'hérésie marrane dans l'Europe catholique du 15e au 18e siècle." *Hérésies et sociétés dans l'Europe pré-industrielle: 11e–18e siècles.* Ed. Jacques Le Goff. Paris: Mouton. 328–39.

Riera i Sans, Jaume
    1971–5    "Un recull d'oracions en catalá dels conversos jueus (segle xv)." *Estudis romanics* 16: 49–97.
    1975    "Oracions en catalá dels conversos jueus: notes bibliográficas i textos." *Anuario de filología* 1: 345–67.

Rivkin, Ellis
    1957–8    "The Utilization of Non-Jewish Sources for the Reconstruction of Jewish History." *Jewish Quarterly Review* 48: 183–203.
    1971    *The Shaping of Jewish History: A Radical New Interpretation.* New York: Charles Scribner's Sons.
    1980    "How Jewish Were the New Christians?" *Hispania Judaica: Studies on the History, Language, and Literature of the Jews in the Hispanic World.* Ed. Josep M. Solà-Solé et al. Barcelona: Puvill. 1: 105–15.

Rodrigues, Samuel
    1937    "Mensagem do resgate." *Ha-Lapid* 11.80: 3–4.

Rodríguez Puértolas, Julio
    1968    *Poesía de protesta en la edad media castellana.* Madrid: Gredos.

Rojas, Fernando de
    1968    *La Celestina.* Ed. Julio Cejador y Frauca. Clásicos Castellanos. Madrid: Gredos.

Rojas, Ricardo
    1937    "Los conversos de Córdoba [Argentina]." *Judaica* 5: 194–6.

Rose, Constance Hubbard
    1971    "Spanish Renaissance Translators." *Revue de littérature comparée* 45: 554–72.
    1987    "The Marranos of the Seventeenth Century and the Case of the Merchant Writer Antonio Enríquez Gómez." *The Spanish Inquisition and the Inquisitorial Mind.* Ed. Angel Alcalá. New York: Columbia UP. 53–71.

Roth, Cecil
    1931–2    "The Religion of the Marranos." *Jewish Quarterly Review* 22: 1–33.
    1932a    *A History of the Marranos.* Philadelphia: Jewish Publication Society.
    1932b    "Immanuel Aboab's Proselitization of the Marranos." *Jewish Quarterly Review* 23: 121–62.
    1943–4    "The Strange Case of Hector Mendes Bravo." *Hebrew Union College Annual* 28: 221–45.
    1946    *Historia de los marranos.* Trans. Aarón Spivak. Buenos Aires: Israel.
    1947    *The House of Nasi: Doña Gracia.* Philadelphia: Jewish Publication Society.
    1948    *The House of Nasi: The Duke of Naxos.* Philadelphia: Jewish Publication Society.

Roth, Norman
    1992    "Anti-*Converso* Riots of the Fifteenth Century, Pulgar, and the Inquisition." *En la España medieval* 15: 367–94.

Saban, Mario Javier
    1991    *Judíos conversos II: Los hebreos nuestros hermanos mayores.* Buenos Aires: Distal.

Salomon, Herman Prinz
 1970 "Midrash, Messianism and Heresy in Two Spanish-Hebrew Hymns." *Studia Rosenthaliana*: 4: 169–80.
 1982 *Portrait of a New-Christian, Fernão Alvares Melo, 1569–1632*. Paris: Funcação Calouste Gulbenkian.
Sanabria Sierra, María del Carmen
 1984 "Los judeoconversos de la Baja Extremadura a finales del siglo XV." *El Olivo*: 157–201.
Sánchez Albornoz, Claudio
 1975 *Spain, A Historical Enigma*. Trans. Colette Joly Dees, and David Sven Reher. 2 vols. Madrid: Fundación Universitaria Española.
Sánchez Moya, Manuel
 1958 "La Inquisición de Teruel y sus judaizantes en el siglo XV." *Teruel* 20: 145–200.
 1966 "El ayuno del Yom Kippur entre los judaizantes turolenses del siglo XV." *Sefarad* 26: 273–304.
Sánchez Moya/Monasterio Aspiri
 1972 "Los judaizante turolenses en el siglo XV." Manuel Sánchez Moya and Jasone Monasterio Aspiri. *Sefarad* 32: 105–40; 33 (1973): 111–43; 325–56.
Santa María, Ramón
 1893a "La Inquisición de Ciudad-Real: Proceso original del difunto Juan González Escogido (8 agosto 1484–15 marzo 1485)." *Boletín de la Real Academia de la Historia* 22: 189–204.
 1893b "La Inquisición de Ciudad-Real; Proceso original del difunto Juan Martínez de los Olivos (6 septiembre 1484–15 marzo 1485)." *Boletín de la Real Academia de la Historia* 22: 355–72.
 1893c "Ritos y costumbres de los hebreos españoles." *Boletín de la Real Academia de la Historia* 22: 181–8.
Saraiva, António José
 1969 *Inquisição e Cristãos-Novos*. 5th ed. Lisboa: Estampa, 1985.
Schechter, Frank Isaac
 1917 "An Unfamiliar Aspect of Anglo-Jewish History." *Publications of the American Jewish Historical Society* 25: 63–74.
Scholberg, Kenneth R.
 1971 *Sátira e invectiva en la España medieval*. Madrid: Gredos.
Scholem, Gershom
 1971 *The Messianic Idea in Judaism*. New York: Schocken.
 1973 *Sabbatai Sevi: The Mystical Messiah*. Princeton: Princeton UP.
Schrire, T. Theodore
 1966 *Hebrew Amulets: Their Decipherment and Interpretation*. London: Routledge and Kegan Paul.
Schwartz, Barry D.
 1966 "The Hidden Synagogue of the Azores." *Jewish Digest* (Aug.): 66–8.
Schwarz, Samuel
 1925 *Os Cristãos-novos em Portugal no século XX*. Lisboa: Associção dos Arqueólogos Portuguêses.
Selke de Sánchez, Angela
 1972 *Los Chuetas y la Inquisición: Vida y muerte en el ghetto de Mallorca*. Madrid: Taurus.

1980 "El iluminismo de los conversos y la Inquisición. Cristianismo interior de los alumbrados: resentimiento y sublimación." *La Inquisición española: nueva visión, nuevos horizontes.* Ed. Joaquín Pérez Villanueva. Madrid: Siglo XXI. 617–36.

1986 *The Conversos of Mallorca.* Jerusalem: Magnes.

Sephardic Sisterhood
    1971 *Cooking the Sephardic Way.* Los Angeles: Sephardic Sisterhood, Temple Tifereth Israel.

Sephiha, Haim Vidal
    1970 "Bibles judéo-espagnoles: littératisme et commentateurs." *Ibero-Romania* 2: 56–90.

Serrano, Luciano
    1942 *Los conversos Pablo de Santa María y Alfonso de Cartagena.* Madrid: C. Bermejo.

Shapiro, Benjamin
    1989 "The Hidden Jews of New Mexico." *Avotaynu: The International Review of Jewish Genealogy* 5.4: S4.

Shepard, Sanford
    1982 *Lost Lexicon: Secret Meanings in the Vocabulary of Spanish Literature During the Inquisition.* Miami: Universal.

Shilstone, Eustace M.
    1956 *Monumental Inscriptions in the Burial Ground of the Jewish Synagogue at Bridgetown, Barbados.* N.p.: n.p.

Sicroff, Albert A.
    1960 *Les controverses des statuts de "pureté de sang" en Espagne du XVe au XVIIe siècle.* Paris: Didier.
    1965 "Clandestine Judaism in the Hieronymite Monastery of Nuestra Señora de Guadalupe." *Studies in Honor of M. J. Benardete.* Ed. Izaak A. Langnas and Barton Sholod. New York: Las Américas. 89–125.

Sierra Corella, Antonio
    1947 *La censura de libros y papeles en España y los Indices y catálogos españoles de los prohibidos y expurgados.* Madrid: Cuerpo Facultativo de Archiveros, Bibliotecarios y Arqueólogos.

Sierro Malmierca, Feliciano
    1990 *Judíos, moriscos e Inquisición en Ciudad Rodrigo.* Salamanca: Diputación de Salamanca.

[Silva]
    1896 "Translado do Processo feito pela Inquisição de Lisboa contra Antonio Joze da Silva poeta brasileiro." *Revista trimestral do Instituto historico e geographico brasileiro* 59: 5–51.

Silver, Abba Hillel
    1927 *A History of Messianic Speculation in Israel.* Boston: Beacon Press, 1959.

Silverman, Joseph H.
    1991 "On Knowing Other People's Lives, Inquisitorially and Artistically." *Cultural Encounters: The Impact of the Inquisition in Spain and the New World.* Ed. Mary Elizabeth Perry and Anne J. Cruz. Berkeley: U of California P. 157–75.

Simón Díaz, José
    1946 "La Inquisición de Logroño (1570–1580)." *Berceo: Boletín del Instituto de estudios riojanos* 1.1: 89–119.

Singerman, Robert
    1975 *The Jews in Spain and Portugal: A Bibliography.* New York: Garland.

1993 *Spanish and Portuguese Jewry: A Classified Bibliography.* Westport, Conn.: Greenwood.

Siqueira, Sonia
1978 *A Inquisição portuguesa e a sociedade colonial: a açao do Santo Oficio na Bahia e em Pernambuco na epoca das visitações.* Col. Ensaios 56. São Paulo: Atica.

Snyder, Patricia Giniger
1992 "The Long Road Back." *Hadassah Magazine* (Jan.): 18–20.

Solá-Solé/Rose
1976 "Judíos y conversos en la poesía cortesana del siglo XV: el estilo políglota de Fray Diego de Valencia." Josep Solá-Solé and Stanley Rose. *Hispanic Review* 44: 371–85.

Sperling, Abraham Isaac
1968 *Reasons for Jewish Customs and Traditions.* New York: Block.

Stavroulakis, Nicholas
1986 *Cookbook of the Jews of Greece.* Port Jefferson, N. Y.: Cadmus.

Suárez Fernández, Luis
1964 *Documentos acerca de la expulsión de los judíos.* Valladolid: Aldecoa.
1980 *Judíos españoles en la edad media.* Madrid: Rialp.
1991 *La expulsión de los judíos de España.* Madrid: Mapfre.

Szajkowski, Zosa
1960 "Trade Relations of Marranos in France with the Iberian Peninsula in the Sixteenth and Seventeenth Centuries." *Jewish Quarterly Review* 50: 69–78.

Tejado Fernández, Manuel
1950 "Un foco de judaísmo en Cartagena de Indias durante el seiscientos." *Bulletin hispanique* 52: 55–72.

Teyssier, Paul
1959 *La langue de Gil Vicente.* Paris: Klincksieck.

Tobias, Henry J.
1991 *A History of the Jews in New Mexico.* Albuquerque: U of New Mexico P.

Toro, Alfonso
1932 *Los judíos en la Nueva España.* Mexico City: Publicaciones del Archivo General de la Nación, 1982.

Torres Balbas, Leopoldo
1956 "La judería de Zaragoza y su baño." *Al-Andalus* 21: 172–90.

Tradições
1927 "Tradições Cripto-Judaicas." *Ha-Lapid (Porto, Portugal):* 8; 2.9 (1928): 8; 2.10 (1928): 4–8; 2.11 (1928): 6–8; 2.12 (1928): 4–8; 3.5 (1928): 8; 3.18 (1929): 4–6; 3.21 (1929): 6–8; 3.22 (1929): 6–8; 7.51 (1932): 2–4; 9.67 (1934): 3–5; 9.68 (1934): 6; 10.72 (1935): 2–4; 11.80 (1937): 7–8.

Uchmany, Eva Alexandra
1977 "The Crypto-Jews in New Spain During the First Years of Colonial Life." *Proceedings of the Sixth World Congress of Jewish Studies.* 1973. Jerusalem: World Union of Jewish Studies. 2: 95–109.
1982 "Criptojudíos y cristianos nuevos en las Filipinas durante el siglo XVI." *The Sephardi and Oriental Jewish Heritage.* Ed. Issachar Ben-Ami. Jerusalem: Magnes. 85–104.
1991 "El judaísmo de los cristianos nuevos de origen portugués en la Nueva España." *Society and Community: Proceedings of the Second International Congress for Research of the Sephardi and Oriental Jewish Heritage.* Ed. Abraham Haim. 1984. Jerusalem: Misgav. 119–37.

Usque, Samuel
   1965   *Consolation for the Tribulations of Israel.* Ed. and trans. Martin A. Cohen. Philadelphia: Jewish Publication Society.
Valbuena Prat, Angel
   1962   *La novela picaresca española.* Madrid: Aguilar.
Van der Vekene, E.
   1982–3   *Bibliotheca bibliographica historiae Sanctae Inquisitionis.* 2 vols. Vaduz: Topos.
Vasconcelos, José Leite de
   1958   "Cristãos-Novos do nosso tempo em Trás-os-Montes e na Beira: suas práticas judaicas." *Etnografia portuguesa. Tentame de sistematização.* Lisboa: Nacional. 4: 153–255.
Vicente, Gil
   1984   *Copilaçam de todas las obras de Gil Vicente.* Ed. Maria Leona Carvalhão Buescu. Lisboa: Imprente Nacional, Casa do Moeda.
Webster, Wentworth
   1889   "Hebraizantes portugueses de San Juan de Luz en 1619." *Boletín de la Real Academia de la Historia* 15: 347–60.
Willemse, David
   1974   *Un "Portugués" entre los castellanos: el primero proceso inquisitorial contra Gonzalo Báez de Paiba 1645–1657.* Paris: Funcação Calouste Gulbenkian.
Wiznitzer, Arnold
   1960   *Jews in Colonial Brazil.* New York: Columbia UP.
   1962a   "Crypto-Jews in Mexico During the Seventeenth Century." *American Jewish Historical Quarterly* 51: 222–68.
   1962b   "Crypto-Jews in Mexico During the Sixteenth Century." *American Jewish Historical Quarterly* 51: 168–214.
Wolf, Lucien
   1893–4   "Crypto-Jews Under the Commonwealth." *Transactions of the Jewish Historical Society of England* 1: 55–75.
   1926   *Jews in the Canary Islands.* London: Jewish Historical Society of England.
Wolff
   1987   *Judeus, judaizantes e seus escravos.* Egon Wolff and Frieda Wolff. Rio de Janeiro: Instituto histórico e geográfico brasileiro.
Yerushalmi, Yosef Hayim
   1971   *From Spanish Court to Italian Ghetto: Isaac Cardoso: A Study in Seventeenth-Century Marranism and Jewish Apologetics.* New York: Columbia UP.
   1980   *The Re-education of Marranos in the Seventeenth Century: The Third Annual Rabbi Louis Feinberg Memorial Lecture in Judaic Studies.* Cincinnati: Jewish Studies Program.
   1982   *Assimilation and Racial Anti-Semitism: The Iberian and German Models.* Leo Baeck Memorial Lecture 26. New York: Leo Baeck Memorial Institute.

# ❧ Index

Abarbanel. *See* Abravanel
Abravanel Dormido, David (England), 202
Abbas, Martín de (France), 151
Abcatar, Acat (Calatayud), 287, 300
Abella, Pedro (Barbastro), 321, 478, 550, 589–591
Aben Pando, David (Toledo), 357
Aben Xuxen, Mose (Molina de Aragón), 588
Abenatar Melo, David, 489
Abenpesat, Mayr (Calatayud), 291
Abençuçan, Jacob (Zaragoza, 255, 567
Abner of Burgos, *See* Valladolid, Alfonso de
Aboab, Immanuel, 335
Aboab, Isaac, 434, 522
Abravanel family, 13, 17
Abravanel, Isaac, 54
absolution, 154
Abudarme, Bachelor (Ciudad Real), 294, 302, 515
Abulafia, Samuel, 17
Acevedo, Rodríguez de (Peru), 149, 164
Acosta, Beatriz de (Galicia), 150
Acosta, Francisco de (Mexico), 150
Acosta, Manuel de (Mexico), 220, 248
Acuña de Noronha, Juan (Argentina), 465
Acuña, Manuel de (Jaen), 155, 252
*adafina*, *See* food; Sabbath, foods
*Adonai*, 433, 476, 477
Adret, Mosse Aninay (Aranda), 565
adultery, 261
afterlife, 110–115, 627
agnosticism, 137
Aguila, Ana de (Almazán), 537
Aguila, Francisco de (Aranda), 478, 616
Aguila, Isabel (Atienza), 462
Aguilar, Ana de (Granada), 579
Aires, Beatriz (Lisbon), 400
Alarcón, Beatriz de (Granada), 243
Alazar, Mosé (Teruel), 296
*Alboraycos*, 612. *See also Libro del Alboraique*
Alcalá, Hernando de (Calatañazor), 462, 475
Alcobaça, João de, 31
Alcofarada, Ana (Brazil), 502

Alconada, Gonzalo de (Soria), 600
Aldahuesca, Felipe (Teruel), 359
Aldonza (Frías), 162
Alemán, Mateo, 86, 596, 612
Alfaro, José (Valencia), 147
Alfonso V, Aragon, 12, 28, 32
Alfonso IX, Castile, 437
Alfonso X, Castile, 532
Alfonso XI, Castile, 6
Alfonso, Catalina (Huete), 463, 467
Alfonso, Pedro (Huesca), 27
Alfonso, Pedro (Valencia), 475
Alfonso, prince of Castile, 15
Alfonso, Rodrigo (Guadalupe), 463
*aljamas*, separation of, 8, 11, 18, 25, 38, 587
Almanza, Ana de (Mexico), 366
Almanza, Diego de (Mexico), 366
Almazán, Miguel de (Almazán), 18, 161
Almazán, Pedro de (Almazán), 166
Almeida, Antón de (Toledo), 333
Almeida, Catherina (Brazil), 250
Almeida, Jorge de (Mexico), 391, 434
Alonso (Almazán), 260
Alonso Membreque, Martín (Cordoba), 228, 334, 596
Alonso, Blanca (Huete), 154
Alonso, butcher (Soria), 112
Alonso, Hernando de (Mexico), 54, 160, 274
Alonso, Ysabel (Roa), 154
Alonso, Marcos (Ciudad Real), 388
Alonso, María (Huete), 427, 588
Alonso, Martín (Cordoba), 108
Alonso, Pedro (Roa), 154
Alumbrados. *See* Illuminism
Alvares, Brites (Evora), 149
Alvares, Catarina (Brazil), 163
Alvares, Diogo (Beja), 453, 517
Alvares, Francisco (Lisbon), 599
Alvares, Isabel (Torre de Moncorvo), 104, 106, 115, 158
Alvares, María (Brazil), 302
Alvares, Pedro (Lisbon), 468
Alvares, Simão (Oporto), 361
Alvarez de Alarcón, Catalina (Toledo), 135

Alvarez de Arellano, Manuel (Mexico), 279
Alvarez de Herrera, Inés (Granada), 298
Alvarez Gato, Juan, 85
Alvarez, Alfonso (Castile), 287
Alvarez, Elvira (Ciudad Real), 450
Alvarez, Ferrand (Aranda), 450, 473, 477, 538, 541, 572
Alvarez, Francisco (Galicia), 222, 225, 227
Alvarez, Inés (Toledo), 526
Alvarez, Jorge (Laguardia), 149
Alvarez, Leonor (Ciudad Real), 116, 220
Alvarez, Luis (Granada), 568
Alvares, Mari (Soria), 325
Alvarez, María, 576
Alvarez, María (Almazán), 477, 547, 551, 553
Alvarez, María (Granada), 123
Alvarez, María (Guadalajara), 393
Alvarez, María (Herrera), 105
Alvarez, María (Toledo), 254, 256, 453, 546
Alvarez, Mayor (Toledo), 41
Alvarez, Violante (Galicia), 224, 366
Alves, Antonio de (Almazán), 572
Alves, Catalina de (Almazán), 572
Alves, Elvira de (Almazán), 472, 473
Amidah. *See* prayers, Amidah
Amorós, Isabel (Valencia), 188, 470
Amsterdam, 517, 605
amulets, 40, 183, 186–187, 193, 528, 572, 627
Annes, Catharina (Lisbon), 330
Anes, Pedro (Lisbon), 510
Angola, Juan (Mexico), 319
Anriques, Pero (Brazil), 431
anti-Semitic propaganda, 14, 15, 23–25, 26, 52, 85, 117, 161, 168
Antichrist, 106
Antónia, Luísa (Coimbra), 448
Antunes, Beatriz (Brazil), 278, 283
Antunes, Diego (Mexico), 285
Antunes, Heitor (Brazil), 291, 300, 502
Antunes, Violante (Brazil), 298, 300
*anusim*, definition, 13
Aranda, Francisco de (Aranda), 251
Aranda, Gabriel de (Ciudad Real), 111
Aranda, Juan de (Soria), 112
Arbués, Pedro de (Aragon), 23
Arévalo, Juan de (Ciudad Real), 427
Argentina, 59
Arias Dávila, Diego (Segovia), 14, 272, 328, 333, 346, 368, 385, 427, 460, 508, 511, 514, 524, 543, 575–577, 591–592
Arias Dávila, Isabel (Segovia), 32, 378
Arias Dávila, Juan (Segovia), 617
Arias Dávila, Pedro (Nicaragua), 54
Arias Dávila, Pedro (Segovia), 14
Arias de Maldonado, Pedro (Mexico), 365, 527
Arias Montano, Benito, 85
Arriaga, Lope de (Almazán), 102
Assunção, Diogo da (Portugal), 601
Astorga, Juan de (Mexico), 164
Astori, Vidal, 17
Astoriano, Antonia (Aranda), 427
astrology, 184
atheism 112
*autos de fe*, 21, 45, 52, 158, 233, 516, 578, 598
Avayut, Jehuda (Calatayud), 255
Avayut, Salamon (Aragon), 207
Avayut, Sento (Calatayud), 255
Avelar, André de (Portugal), 371
Avendavit, Asser (Calatayud), 288
Averroism, 10, 90, 112, 114, 564
Avila, Alonso de (Mexico), 162
Avila, Antonio de (Segovia), 378
Avila, Cristobal de (Ciudad Real), 139
Avila, Hernando de (Ecija), 138, 163
Avila, Juan de, 66, 85
Avila, Marina de (Granada), 151, 243
Avila, Mencia de (Granada), 537
Avila, Rodrigo de (Peru), 147
Avila, Teresa de, 85, 86
Axalón, Juan (Aragon), 253
Axequo, Solomon (Calatayud), 279
Ayala, Diego de (Hita), 185
Ayala, Elvira de (Hita), 185
Ayllón, Fernando de (San Martín de Trevejo), 478, 594–595
Ayllón, Gómez de (Huete), 145, 152
d'Aça, Françisca (Almazán), 575
Azevedo, Branca de (Coimbra), 122, 570
Azores, 519

Bacanegra, 419
Báez de Paiba, Gonzalo (France), 205
ballads, 257
Baltanás, Domingo de, 66
Bancalera, Jamila la (Teruel), 462
baptism, 147
   adaptation of, 148
   disparagement of, 148

parody of, 160
removal of chrism, 88, 148, 202, 203, 627
Baptista, João (Lisbon), 434
Bar Mitzvah, 223
Barbados, 62
Barbas, Garçía (Ciudad Real), 542
Barbas, Gonçalo de (Sigüenza), 115
Barcellos, Antão de (Lisbon), 604
Barrera, Fernando de la (Cuenca), 475, 542, 587–589
Barrientos, Lope de, 86
Barrionuevo, Hernando de (Cordoba), 108
Barrios, Gaspar de (Brazil), 165
Barrios, Miguel de, 619
Barros, Manuel de (Bragança), 518
Baruh Louzada, Moseh (England), 202
Barzana, Leonor de (Toledo), 191, 192, 193
Basto, Artur Carlos de Barros (Portugal), 47, 292, 327
bathhouse. *See* mikvah
Bautista, Joam (Brazil), 599
Belenguer, Juan (Almazán), 161
Bellida, Sol (Ciudad Real), 208
Bello, Isabel de (Zaragoza), 192
bells, 152, 427
Belluga, Francisco (Teruel), 385
Belmonte, Diego (Cuenca), 186
Beltrán, Diego (Almazán), 526
Beltrán, Juan (Brihuega), 139
Benedict XIII, Pope, 5, 11–12, 28, 499
Benrosh, Thomas (USA), 528
Benveniste, Abraham (Granada), 231
Benveniste, Abraham (Soria), 12
Benveniste, Oropesa (Granada), 231
Bernal, Mestre (Almazán), 54, 338, 437, 550
Bernáldez, Andrés, 12, 18, 33, 65, 74, 337, 536
Besalú, 272
Besant, Pedro (Valencia), 89, 122
Besante, Brianda (Teruel), 122, 400, 475, 509, 522, 591
Besante, Donosa (Teruel), 192
Besante, Rita (Teruel), 338, 378, 379
Bible, the, 183, 232, 233
Bible substitutes, 429–432
Bibles
   Hebrew, 218, 425, 426–427, 517
   Latin, 40, 124, 427
   Spanish, 427
Billa (Majorca), 139

Binimelis, Ventura (Majorca), 164
Blanca, Clara (Mexico), 228
Blanca, Isabel (Mexico), 228
Blanca, Margarita (Mexico), 228
Blanca, María (Mexico), 228
Blasco, Juan (Calatayud), 260
blasphemy, 137, 627
blessing(s), 148, 155, 444, 452–455, 477, 626
blood libel, 5, 14, 23, 24, 136, 161, 190
Bonaboya, Michel de (Zaragoza), 426
Bonjorna (Teruel), 374
Bosque, Juan Baptista del (Mexico), 262
Bosque, Juana del (Mexico), 262
Bosque, María del (Mexico), 262
Botello, Francisco (Mexico), 400, 402, 434, 449, 464, 474, 575, 598, 600, 607
Bras, Manoel (Brazil), 511, 514
Brazil, 44, 54, 60, 61–62, 64, 517. *See also* remnant crypto-Jews, Brazil
bread. *See* dietary laws and customs, baking
Briuiesca, Fernando de (Guadalupe), 121
Buena Vida, Yucé (Calatayud), 258
Buendía, Juan de (Calatayud), 111, 151
Bueno (Alfaro), 324
Bugalho, Gil Vaz (Lisbon), 148, 429, 537
Buitrago, Juan de (Ayllón), 123
Burgos, Diego de (Ciudad Real), 151, 333, 566
Burgos, Francisco de (Guadalupe), 535
Burgos, Paul of, 564
burial customs. *See* funeral customs

Caballería family (Aragon), 11, 14, 16, 17, 18, 161
Caballería, Alonso de la (Aragon), 187, 426, 565
Caballería, Jaime de la (Aragon), 426, 573, 590
Caballería, Pedro de la (Aragon), 30, 85, 338, 566
Caballero, Lezar (Aranda), 543
Cabezas, Pedro Martins (Lisbon), 165
Cabra, de la (Calatayud), 612
Cáceres, Beatriz de (Lisbon), 510
Cáceres, Francisco de (Toledo), 565
Cáceres, Guiomar de (Coimbra), 394
Cáceres, Leonor de (Mexico), 452, 466
Çaçon, Esdra (Cordoba), 356
Caja, Jorge Dias de (Brazil), 513
Calatayud, Violante de (Aragon), 185
Calderón, Francisco (Gumiel), 164

calendars, 53, 356, 392, 444
Calle, Alonso de la, 54
Camargo, Alonso de (Ciudad Real), 144
Cambila, Francisco (Ejea de los Caballeros), 258
Campos, Branca (Coimbra), 455
Campuzam, Juan (Canary Islands), 512
*cancioneros*, 479
canopy. *See* marriage, canopy
Canto, Juan del (Soria), 535
Cardosa, Antonia (Lisbon), 116
Cardosa, Filipa (Coimbra), 361, 398
Cardosa, Guiomar (Fonte Arcada), 472
Cardosa, Luzia (Montemor-o-Velho), 41
Cardoso, Antonio (Barajas), 381, 384
Cardoso, Juan (Mexico), 525
Cardoso, Sebastián (Mexico), 431
Cardoza, Anne (Gerona), 223, 251, 327, 340, 612
Cardozo, Isaac (Italy), 207
Carlos V, Spain, 42
Carmona, Clemente (USA), 107, 223, 372, 377, 378, 419, 455, 494, 510, 518, 525
Carneira, Violante (Brazil), 191
Carneiro, Luiz (Bragança), 518
Carranza, António de Sá (Coimbra), 447, 465
Carrasco, Manuel (Mexico), 193
Carretero, Pedro (America), 164
Cartagena, Alonso de, 30
Carvajal family (Mexico), 324, 325, 326, 330, 395, 473, 474
Carvajal, Baltazar (Mexico), 330
Carvajal, Gaspar de (Mexico), 117, 232, 398, 570
Carvajal, Guiomar de (Mexico), 102, 221
Carvajal, Isabel de (Mexico), 394, 570
Carvajal, Luis de [elder] (Mexico), 56, 231
Carvajal, Luis de [younger] (Mexico), 56, 57, 102, 108, 115, 117, 150, 154, 221, 231, 281, 330, 367, 380, 383, 386, 387, 391, 404, 435, 444, 463, 468, 517, 534, 539, 546
Carvajal, Mariana de (Mexico), 391
Carvajal, Miguel de, 66, 85, 102, 596, 617
Carvalha, Lianor (Brazil), 512
Carvalho, João (Goa), 534
Casal, Isabel do (Brazil), 534
Casal, Lorenzo (Soria), 138
Castanho, Diogo (Brazil), 163

Castellano, Francisco (Toledo), 427
Castellano, Jacob (Medina del Campo), 329, 577
Castil, Juan (Cordoba), 108
Castillo (Canary Islands), 167
Castillo, Juan del (Cifuentes), 188
Castillo, Lope de (Aranda), 603
Castro, Antam de (Brazil), 599
Castro, Isaac de (Brazil), 234
Castro, Leonor de (Cuenca), 603
Castro, María de (Peru), 398, 528
Castro, María de (Soria), 567
Castro, Rodrigo de (Huete), 385
Cava, Sancho de la (Toledo), 427
Cavalcanti, Felipe (Brazil), 369
Cavallero, Sancho (Canary Islands), 550
*Celestina*. *See* Rojas, Fernando de,
celibacy, Jewish attitude toward, 243
Celma, Joan (Valencia), 462
Central America, 58
Cervantes, Miguel de, 86, 499, 617, 624
Cerveira (Portugal), 143
Cerveyra, Cristóvão (Brazil), 599
Chanukah, 137
charity, 507, 508, 588–589, 608–609
Chaves, Diego de (Galicia), 547
childbirth, 199–200, 627
    prayers, 200
Chile, 54
Chillón, Rodrigo de (Ciudad Real), 319
Chinchilla, Alfonso de (Almagro), 301
Chinchilla, Gomes de (Ciudad Real), 332
Chinchilla, Juan de (Ciudad Real), 294
Chinillo, Azarías (Calatayud), 252
chocolate, 57, 363, 398
Christianity
    disparagement of, 88, 100, 118, 135, 136, 137, 139, 141, 158, 166, 329, 516, 627
    plot against the Jews, 140, 166
Christians, disparagement of, 158, 159, 502
*chuetas*, 45, 47
churches, avoidance of, 147
circumcision, 51, 58, 59, 124, 147, 202–207, 233, 235, 255, 592, 627
    adult, 203, 204, 206
    mohel, 64, 203, 205, 207
    substitutes for, 206
Ciudad, Juana de (Ciudad Real), 208
Ciudad, Sancho de (Ciudad Real), 272, 333, 450, 474, 477, 511, 513, 514
clergy, disparagement of, 156

Climent, Francisco (Aragon), 261
Coca, Marina de (Ciudad Real), 301
Coelho, Gaspar (Brazil), 151
Coen Gonsales, Abraham (England), 202
Cofer, Yeuda (Granada), 567
Colombia, 59
Columbus, Christopher, 54
Comunidades war, 42
Concepción, María de la (Mexico), 281
Conchillos, Lope de, 18
confession, 154
Contreras, Sancho de (Segovia), 328
conversion
  attitudes toward, 39, 119, 571–578
  Christian policy toward, 9
  forced, 7–8, 49, 115, 565
  grounds for divorce, 252
  Jewish policy toward, 8
  on marriage, 249, 262
  reasons for, 4, 6, 10, 11, 26, 37, 50, 115, 245, 564–567
conversos
  chronology, 36–48
  demography, 76
  intellectual activity, 42–43, 85–86
  self-concept as Jews, 46, 83
  types, 22, 35, 37, 38, 83–90
Cordero, Antonio (Chile), 332
Córdoba Membreque, Alonso de (Cordoba), 93, 107, 324, 334, 451, 452, 514
Córdoba Membreque, Juan de (Cordoba), 475, 514–515
Córdoba, Abraham de (Guadalupe), 26
Córdoba, Gabriel de (Cuenca), 204
Córdoba, Gonçalo de (Canary Islands), 512
Córdoba, Gonzalo de (Sevilla), 579
Córdoba, Juan de (Guadix), 160
Coronel, Cristóvão (Monção), 163, 524
Corral, Isaac (Cuéllar), 566
Correi, Grácia Dias (Castela), 534
Cortés de Alfonso, Augustín (Majorca), 599
Cortés de Alfonso, Rafael (Majorca), 246
Cortés de Alonso (Majorca), 607
Cortés, Ana (Majorca), 104, 106, 226, 260, 293, 318, 361, 372, 379, 381, 394, 466
Cortés, Antonio (Majorca), 363
Cortés, Isabel (Majorca), 164, 469, 471
Cortés, Josef (Majorca), 104, 106, 226, 260, 293, 318, 372, 379, 394, 466
Cortés, Miguel (Majorca), 363

Cortés, Pedro Onofre (Majorca), 139, 143, 220, 447, 516, 535, 544, 580, 601, 607
Cortés, Rafael (Majorca), 102
Costa, Domingo de (Colombia), 156
Costa, Francisco da (Lisbon), 604
Costa, Uriel da, 563
Cota, Rodrigo, 85, 102, 478, 504, 533, 550
Council of Elvira, 532
Council of Trent, 400
Coutinha, Leonor (Vila Flor), 444, 589
credibility of evidence, 161, 165
Crescas, Hasdai, 10
Crespo, Catalina (Ubeda), 600
Crespo, Juan (Las Palmas), 163
crossing oneself, disparagement of, 155, 626
crucifixes, mistreatment of, 24, 88, 136, 161, 162, 163
Cruillas, Pedro (La Cedacería), 297
Cruz, Diogo Fernandes da (Lisbon), 476
crypto-Judaism, general characteristics, 81
Cuba. See remnant crypto-Jews, Cuba
Çuçen (Ciudad Real), 294
Cuéllar, Fernando de, 575
Cuéllar, Juan de (Segovia), 374, 573–574
Cuéllar, Yuda de (Cuéllar), 566
Cuenca, Tomás de (Ciudad Real), 286
Cunha, Maria José da (Brazil), 257
Curaçao, 62
cures, 191

d'Oliveira, Antonia (Brazil), 400
d'Oliveira, Margarida (Lisbon), 146
d'Olivera, Ana (Toledo), 150
da Gama, Isabel (Elvas), 429
Dalegre, Catharina Alvares (Lisbon), 326
dancing, 208, 247, 255, 259
Daniel, 470
Daroca, Pablo de (Calatayud), 279
David, Rabbi (Segovia), 433
Dávila, Juan (Ciudad Real), 321
Daza, Juan (Ciudad Real), 369
death. See also funeral customs
  asphyxiation, 278
  facing the wall, 277, 280, 627
  visiting the dying, 278–279
Delgado, Diego (Aranda), 297
Deli, Aldonza (Teruel), 364
Delicado, Francisco, 86, 553, 607, 624
demography, 73–76
Desfar, Johanna (Valencia), 433
Deza, Diego de, 19, 85, 594

Dias Enriquez, Duarte (Brazil), 150
Dias, Beatriz (Caminha), 144, 472
Dias, Branca (Brazil), 117, 150, 321, 336
Dias, Branca (Coimbra), 451
Dias, Christovão (Lisbon), 400
Dias, Diogo (Brazil), 291
Dias, Gaspar (Brazil), 120
Dias, Gonçalo (Lisbon), 604
Dias, Guiomar (Santa Marinha), 380
Dias, Luis (Setúbal), 109
Díaz Doncel, Juan (Ciudad Real), 533
Díaz Laínez, Rodrigo (Almazán), 427, 511
Díaz Márquez, Antonio (Mexico), 375
Díaz Martaraña, Amaro (Mexico), 399
Díaz Nieto, Diego (Mexico), 103, 109, 138, 381, 451, 461, 463, 502
Díaz Nieto, Ruy (Mexico), 141, 148, 319, 324, 332, 333, 338, 357, 361, 363, 375, 397, 445, 473, 522, 535, 536, 541, 544, 545, 604, 609, 611
Díaz, Alfonso (Ciudad Real), 286
Díaz, Alfonso (Huete), 284
Díaz, Alvar (Ciudad Real), 503
Díaz, Ana (Toledo), 514
Díaz, Antonio (Philippines), 60
Díaz, Juan (Ciudad Real), 159, 329, 425, 432, 453, 466
Díaz, Leonor (Mexico), 375
Díaz, María (Ciudad Real), 186, 254, 257 319, 320, 332, 377, 382, 383, 384, 433, 450, 473, 511, 527, 542, 604
Díaz, Ruy (Almazán), 386, 603
Diego, doctor (Soria), 595
dietary laws and customs, 43, 531–549
　baking, 548–549, 629
　blood, 53, 544–547, 626
　fat, 547
　fish, 228, 534
　forbidden foods, 533–542
　hindquarters of meat, 540
　koshering, 224
　porging, 58, 547, 626
　pork, 44, 53, 55, 62, 120, 137, 167, 224, 227, 363, 389, 532, 534, 540
　separate dishes, 540
　slaughtering, 51, 533, 542, 546, 626
　utensils, 541
　wine, 549
Dió, 102
disputations, 9–12, 37, 105, 115, 117
divorce, 251–253
Domingo (Barbastro), 254

Domínguez, Catalina (Canary Islands), 279
Dominicans, 4, 19, 24
dowry. *See* marriage
dreams, 190
drops, ceremony of, 192
Duarte, Blanca (Ciudad Rodrigo), 535
Duarte, Isabel (Mexico), 148, 243, 285, 401
Duarte, Sebastián (Peru), 601
Durán, Diego de, 55
Duran, Profet, 10

Ecija Zayas, Francisco de (Baeza), 571, 611
economics, 12, 13, 14, 16, 41–42, 55, 258, 587
　networks, 13, 39, 57, 232
　reason for marriage, 246
edicts of grace, 19, 22, 40, 57, 77, 80, 81, 82, 83, 112, 191, 208, 233, 274, 277, 280, 294, 296, 319, 323, 332, 333, 356, 363, 373, 377, 392, 477, 524, 526, 532, 549, 568, 578, 594, 625
education
　age at, 228
　books, 224
　coercive, 220
　from abroad, 56, 64, 100, 233, 434, 444, 525
　in divided families, 219, 222, 228
　methods of, 223, 224–225, 226, 233
　obligation of parents, 218
　of children, 222, 223, 425
　of spouses, 220
　teachers, 228
　while traveling, 224, 225
education of children, 220
Ejea, Pedro de (Aragon), 190
Eimeric, Nicolau, 586
Elijah, 107, 108, 613
emigration
　dreams of, 602–605
　prohibition of, 55, 63
　reasons against, 26, 63, 245, 566, 568, 602–603
　reasons for, 22, 26, 44, 49, 63, 106, 118, 252–253, 578, 594–595, 627
Encina, Juan de la, 85
endogamy, 39, 47, 58, 79, 82, 230, 245, 246, 251, 262
　prohibition of, 50, 245, 246
　reasons for, 219, 244, 246, 247
England, 27, 63
Enrique II, Castile, 6, 28

Enrique III, Castile, 7
Enrique IV, Castile, 12, 15, 30
Enríquez Gómez, Antonio, 72, 619
Enríquez Villanueva, Diego (Andalucía), 536, 545
Enríquez, Ana (Mexico), 188
Enríquez, Beatriz (Mexico), 401, 517
Enríquez, Blanca (Mexico), 109, 141, 149, 219, 243, 247, 282, 285, 286, 293, 302, 323, 401
Enríquez, Catalina (Mexico), 219, 319, 381, 411, 476
Enríquez, Diego (Toledo), 337
Enríquez, Duarte (Coimbra), 234
Enríquez, Duarte (Peru), 430
Enríquez, Gaspar (Mexico), 323
Enríquez, Gaspar (Toledo), 330
Enríquez, Isabel (Mexico), 399
Enríquez, Juana (Mexico), 58, 117, 332, 369, 470, 606
Enríquez, Manuel (Mexico), 381, 411
Enríquez, Micaela (Mexico), 270, 293, 298, 326, 368, 386
Enríquez, Rafael (Mexico), 270, 296
Enríquez, Rafaela (Mexico), 219, 247, 273, 281, 285, 293, 300, 362, 597, 616
Erasmus, 86, 428
Escobar, Clara (Calatayud), 279, 287
Escobar, Sol (Calatayud), 287
Escogido, Juan (Ciudad Real), 155, 542, 543
Esperança (Brazil), 261
Esperanza, Gerónima (Mexico), 109
Espina, Alonso de, 23, 24, 31
Espina, Alvaro de (Segovia), 15
Espinosa, Manoel Dias (Brazil), 601
Espinosa, Pedro de (Mexico), 286, 397, 599
Esplugas, Gracia de (Zaragoza), 296
Esplugues (Valencia), 187
Esteban, Inés (Herrera del Duque), 109
Estella, Diego de, 66, 85
Esther, 116–117, 429, 470
Esther scroll. *See* Purim
Estíbares (Soria), 160
eucharist, 598
   avoidance of, 151
   disbelief in, 88, 150, 278
exogamy. *See* intermarriage
Expulsion decree, 25, 230, 231
Expulsion from Portugal, 49
Expulsion from Spain, 105, 112, 115

Falcón, Alonso (Ciudad Real), 300
Falcón, Fernando (Toledo), 610
Falcón, Isabel (Ciudad Real), 300
Falcón, Juan (Ciudad Real), 113, 144, 145, 261, 453, 511, 544
Faria, Inez de (Portugal), 148
Farque, Isaac (Holland), 72, 205
Fast of *Bordón del alma*, 394
Fast of *Bredos*, 394
Fast of Elijah, 394
Fast of Esther. *See* Purim
Fast of Gedaliah, 392
Fast of Judith, 394
Fast of lentils, 394
Fast of Moses, 394
Fast of *Natalinho*, 395
Fast of the Newborn, 384
Fast of the seventeenth of Tammuz, 391
fasting, 43, 55, 191, 224, 225, 228, 355, 391–402, 515, 570, 608, 611
   dissemblance, 396, 398–399
   exemptions from, 397
   for Sabbath, 321
   on weekdays, 396, 628
   paying others to fast, 399, 400
   prayers, 395, 396
   reasons for, 399, 507–508
Felipe III, Spain, 44
Felipe III, Navarre, 6
Felipe IV, Spain, 44
Fernandes family (Brazil), 338, 339
Fernandes, Ana (Coimbra), 190, 245, 249, 280, 340
Fernandes, António (Oporto), 144
Fernandes, Belchior (Coimbra), 233
Fernandes, Catarina (Coimbra), 325, 552
Fernandes, Clara (Brazil), 163
Fernandes, Diego (Canary Islands), 188, 511
Fernandes, Diogo (Brazil), 601
Fernandes, Filipa (Seia), 105, 163, 326, 384, 546
Fernandes, Francisco (Coimbra), 338
Fernandes, Gomes (Brazil), 609
Fernandes, Guiomar (Brazil), 534
Fernandes, Guiomar (Lisbon), 112
Fernandes, Inés (Brazil), 336
Fernandes, Isabel (Lisbon), 281, 291
Fernandes, Juan (Canary Islands), 476
Fernandes, Luis (Evora), 149
Fernandes, María (Lisbon), 162
Fernandes, Simão (Lisbon), 118

Fernandes, Victoria (Coimbra), 535
Fernandes, Violante (Lisbon), 275
Fernández. *See also* Hernández
Fernández Cachito, Martín (Herrera), 292
Fernández Correa, Rodrigo (Mexico), 435
Fernández de Aguilar, Alonso (Ecija), 101, 146
Fernández de Alcaudete, Pedro (Cordoba), 400
Fernández de la Isla, García (Soria), 566
Fernández de Luz, Juan (Garcimuñoz), 526
Fernández Juan (Molina de Aragón), 453
Fernández Tristán, Luis (Mexico), 251, 453
Fernández, Blanca (Garcimuñoz), 288
Fernández, Catalina (Ciudad Real), 511
Fernández, Diego (Soria), 511
Fernández, Francisca (Guadalupe), 148
Fernández, Isabel (Cuenca), 252
Fernández, Isabel (Tembleque), 283
Fernández, Juana (Guadalupe), 148, 334
Fernández, Lucas, 66, 85
Fernández, Lucía (Ciudad Real), 318, 322, 333, 336, 339
Fernández, Luis (Ciudad Real), 462, 466
Fernández, Marina (Toledo), 154
Fernández, Violante (Guadalajara), 595
Fernando I, Aragon, 11, 12, 28
Fernando II, Aragon, 16–18, 41
Fernando III, Castile, 3
Ferrán, Gramel (Canary Islands), 476
Ferrandes, Alfonso (Castile), 287
Ferrandes, Antonio (Maqueda), 119
Ferreira, João Antonio (Bragança), 363, 518, 525
Ferrer, Antona (Aragón), 188
Ferrer, Jaime (Valencia), 525
Ferrer, Vicente, 10–12, 578
Fez, Juan de (Ciudad Real), 333, 502
Figueiredo, Inofre de (Bragança), 472
Figueredo, Caterina de (Brazil), 319
Figueroa, Nuño de (Mexico), 145
Flanders, 27
Flores, González (Mexico), 536
Fonseca, Aboab de (Brazil), 517
Fonseca, Estevan de Ares de (Madrid), 64, 234
Fonseca, Gaspar de (Mexico), 109
Fonseca, Hector de (Mexico), 375, 544
Fonseca, Manuel (Peru), 204
Fonseca, Manuel de (Colombia), 69, 463
Fonseca, Maria de (Aveiro), 472

Fonseca, Miguel Fernández de (Portugal), 234
Fonseca, Pedro de (Mexico), 539
food, 356
    *adafina*, 258, 337–338, 594
    at wedding, 255
    gifts of, 590, 594
    honey, 208, 259
    to sustain tradition, 247, 592
foretelling the future, 184, 186, 192
forgiving, 359
fornication. *See* sex, outside of marriage
*Fortalitium fidei. See* Espina, Alonso de
Forteza, Diego (Majorca), 429
Forteza, Isabel (Majorca), 363
fortune, 115–116
Franca, Ana (Brazil), 163
France, 27, 71, 434
Francês, Antonio Bocarro (Goa), 102
Francés, Yuçá (Soria), 511, 574
Franciscans, 4, 24, 30, 92
Francisco, maestre (Medina del Campo), 576
Franco, Alonso (Avila), 203, 575
Franco, Francisco, 48
Franco, García (Toledo), 611
Franco, Luis (Colombia), 604
Franco, Luis (Mexico), 568
Franco, Pero (Ciudad Real), 545
Franco, Yucé (La Guardia), 24
fraternization of Jews and Christians, 192, 258, 261, 588
    prohibition of, 11
fraternization of Jews and *conversos*, 13, 218, 230, 279, 287, 328, 508, 572, 573, 587–593
    prohibition of, 9, 16, 38
Fuente, Alonso de la (Calatañazor), 478
Fuente, Francisco de la (Almazán), 160
Fuente, Juana de la (Almazán), 386
Fuente, Pedro de la (Las Palmas), 157
funeral customs
    attending the corpse, 280
    cemeteries, 277, 290–292, 627
    charity, 303–304
    clothing the corpse, 277, 280, 283–284, 291, 593
    dirges, 277, 287, 299, 627
    fasting, 289, 295, 296, 298, 299, 303
    food, 292–295, 303
        eggs, 293, 295, 296, 302, 303
        fish, 277, 294, 295, 296, 627

no meat, 277, 293, 295, 296, 627
olives, 277, 627
funerals, 287–288
lamps, 280, 296, 300
mourning, 592
abstention from prayer, 299
abstention from sex, 298
covering mirrors, 297
nakedness, 297, 298, 300
not bathing, 297
rend clothing, 297
mourning period, 277, 295–297, 302, 303, 627
offerings,
coins, 277, 284, 285, 286, 287, 627
food, 285, 286
pearls, 277, 285, 627
professional mourners, 299–300
purification after death, 298
shaving the corpse, 277, 280, 627
shrouds, 279, 280, 282, 283, 627
sitting on floor, 277, 294, 627
virgin soil, 277, 290, 627
pillow, 277, 292, 595, 627
washing the corpse, 58, 277, 280–282, 627
water, 277, 300–303, 627
Fuster, Enrique de (Valencia), 147

Gabiría, Gracia de (Logroño), 119
Gallego, Juan (Molina de Aragón), 588
Gama, Izabel da (Elvas), 249, 607
Gaona (Soria), 596
García (Calatayud), 291
García Costello, Diego (Aranda), 339
García de Alonso Arias, Pedro (Segovia), 381, 503
García family (Casarrubios), 294
García Serrano, Ruy (Toledo), 373
García, Alonso (Guadalajara), 572
García, Benito (La Guardia), 24
García, Diego (Soria), 539, 549
García, Graça (Vila Real), 604
García, Inés (Guadalajara), 596
García, Inés (Guadalupe), 334
García, Isabel (Hita), 300
García, Juan (Aranda), 118, 458
García, Juan (Soria), 589
García, Juana (Ciudad Real), 294, 296, 300, 302, 545
García, Lope (Almazán), 121, 451, 572
García, Luis (Talavera), 158, 367

García, Martín (Coruña del Conde), 426
García, Pascual (Viana)s, 336
García, Pedro (Almazán), 151
García, Ruy (Soria), 186, 508
García, Santos (Maqueda), 119
Garreta, Aldonza (Lérida), 590
Garzas, Juan de (Almazán), 121
Gaspar, Moisés Abraão (Rebordelo), 435
Gencor, Castellana (Teruel), 273
general pardon of 1604, 44
*get. See* divorce
Gil de la Guarda, Manuel (Philippines), 60
Gil Rodríguez, Rafael Crisanto (Mexico), 59, 204
Gil Ruiz, Gil de (Teruel), 542
Gil, Manuel (Mexico), 148, 319, 338, 397, 430, 535, 536, 539, 541, 544
Gil, Miguel (Mexico), 547
*Gloria patri. See* prayers, *gloria patri*
Gome, David (Medina del Campo), 577
Gomes, António (Coimbra), 334
Gomes, Beatriz (Evora), 319
Gomes, Branca (Montemor-o-Velho), 41
Gomes, Diego (Toledo), 158
Gomes, Ferrand (Soria), 247, 542
Gomes, Gaspar (Brazil), 469
Gomes, Isabel (Lisbon), 162, 378, 388
Gomes, Isabel (Trancoso), 383
Gomes, João (Evora), 149
Gomes, Margarida (Lisbon), 103
Gomes, Ruy (Brazil), 332
Gomes, Violante (Seia), 395
Gómez Navarro, Manuel (Mexico), 139, 150
Gómez sisters (Ciudad Rodrigo), 357, 387, 390, 392
Gómez, Aldonza (Ocaña), 470
Gómez, Ana (Ciudad Rodrigo), 294
Gómez, Ana (Mexico), 150
Gómez, Catalina (Ciudad Rodrigo), 294
Gómez, Catalina (Ocaña), 470
Gómez, Costanza (Huete), 187
Gómez, Diego (Toledo), 321, 324, 336
Gómez, Esperanza (Canary Islands), 340
Gómez, Fernando (Turkey), 517
Gómez, Iñigo (Toledo), 336
Gómez, María (Mexico), 58, 227, 601
Gómez, Tomás (Mexico), 434
Gómez, Tomé (Mexico), 597
Gonán, Martín de (Soria), 333
Gonçalves, Beatriz (Chacim), 295, 540, 546

Gonçález de la Oz, Alonço (Segovia), 589
Gonçález, Ruy (Canary Islands), 550
Gonçalves, Simão (Coimbra), 597
Góngora, Luis de, 85
Gonsalves, Irmelina (USA), 528
González Aserrafe, Alonso (Ciudad Real), 297
González Daza, Juan (Ciudad Real), 103, 295, 516, 611
González de la Higuera, Alvaro (Ciudad Real), 324
González de la Rueda, Inés (Soria), 477
González de Pozuelo, Buena Pero (Atienza), 328
González de Santistéban, Juan (Ciudad Real), 301
González Escogido, Juan (Ciudad Real), 324, 516
González Husillo, Fernando (Toledo), 201
González Panpán, Juan (Ciudad Real), 516
González sisters (Ciudad Real), 147, 334, 534
González, Aldonza (Segovia), 433
González, Alonso (Ciudad Real), 454
González, Alvar (Azores), 163
González, Alvaro (Canary Islands), 116, 119, 140, 158, 185, 510, 514, 602
Gonçález, Ana (Las Palmas), 250
González, Antonio (Las Palmas), 150
González, Bartolomé (Guadalajara), 502
González, Beatriz (Ciudad Real), 324, 541, 542, 554
González, Catalina (Ciudad Real), 155, 284, 286
González, Diego (Ciudad Real), 385
González, Diego (Guadalupe), 283
González, Elvira (Ciudad Real), 330, 388
González, Elvira (Segovia), 272, 368, 385, 386, 437, 576, 591–592
González, Inés, 163
González, Isabel (Ciudad Real), 272, 324, 330, 338, 541
González, Juan (Casarrubios), 157, 292, 297
González, Juan (Toledo), 145, 297
González, Juana (Ciudad Real), 190, 455, 541
González, Leonor (Ciudad Real), 143, 324, 330, 382, 477, 541
González, Manuel (Guadalajara), 278
González, Manuel (Guadalupe), 468, 570, 609

González, Margarita (Las Palmas), 165
González, María (Ciudad Real), 111, 155, 164, 190, 200, 210, 220, 272, 274, 297, 319, 322, 325, 326, 336, 338, 363, 385, 396, 397, 455, 461, 513, 601, 610
González, Marina (Ciudad Real), 293, 473, 476
González, Mayor (Ciudad Real), 190, 533, 540
González, Mencía (Guadalajara), 190
González, Pedro (Las Palmas), 140
González, Pedro (Madrid), 357
González, Pero (Las Palmas), 378
González, Polonia (Canary Islands), 279
González, Silvestre (Las Palmas), 250
González, Violante (Garcimuñoz), 548
Gonzalves, Gregorio (Brazil), 163
Gonzalves, Manuel (Evora), 468
Gonzálvez, Beatriz (Evora), 105
Gonzalvo Ruiz, Gil de (Albarracín), 192
Goserán, Charles (Aragon), 568
Gracia (Burgos), 451
Gracia (Sigüenza), 121, 290
Grajal, Gaspar de, 65
Granada, Gabriel de (Granada), 205
Granada, Gabriel de (Mexico), 72, 206, 225, 285, 293, 295, 298, 303, 360, 362, 363, 367, 527
Granada, Isabel de (Mexico), 189
Granada, Luis de, 431, 435
Granada, Manuel de (Mexico), 295, 298
Granada, Rafael de (Mexico), 110, 191, 288, 527, 534
Grande, Juan (Ciudad Real), 432
Grande, Pedro (Calatañazor), 201
Guadalajara, Pedro de (Almazán), 110, 288, 477
Guarda, Simão Lopes da (Coimbra), 446, 463
Guardian Angel, 449, 471
Guatemala, 58, 194, 510
*guayas*, 370, 371, 477. See also funeral customs
Guernica, Fernando de (Aranda), 38, 113
Guerra, Nicolás de (Canary Islands), 300
Guillem, Felipe (Brazil), 155
Guiote, Antonio (France), 205
Gumiel de Mercado, Bernaldino (Soria), 479
Gurrea, Francisco (Aragon), 18
Gutiérrez, Catalina (Baeza), 107

Gutiérrez, Elvira (Baeza), 302
Gutiérrez, Leonor (Hita), 165, 477
Guzmán, Domingo (Ocaña), 189
Guzmán, Gaspar de, 44

Habacuc, 471
*hadas*, 207–209, 627. *See also* naming ceremony
Hadida, Isaac (Toledo), 231
Hagiz, Moses, 321
hair, 191, 274, 275, 319, 626
HaKohen, David (Greece), 288
halakhah, 43, 82, 101, 137
Haleví, Judah, 471
Haleví, Samuel (Toledo), 6
Halevi, Solomon. *See* Santa María, Pablo de
*halishah*. *See* divorce
*Hallel*. *See* prayers, *Hallel*
Halorki, Joshua. *See* Santa Fe, Jerónimo de
Hanukkah, 40, 376–377, 626
hat. *See kipah*
Heaven, 111–114, 627
head covering. *See kipah*
Hebreo, León, 435
Hebrew, knowledge, of 425, 475–479, 502, 576
Hell, 111–115, 627
Henriques, Beatriz (Oliveira do Conde), 400, 455
Henriques, Brites (Lisbon), 446, 447, 470
Henriques, Catherina (Portugal), 231
Henríquez de Fonseca, Rodrigo (Málaga), 544
Henríquez, Beatriz (Mexico), 257
Henríquez, Catalina (Mexico), 463
Henríquez, Clara (Granada), 449
Heredia, Juan de (Canary Islands), 606
Heredia, Luis de (Calatayud), 201, 207
Hernandes, Beatriz (Oliveira do Conde), 400
Hernandes, Pedro (Las Palmas), 250
Hernández. *See also* Fernández
Hernández de Diego Sánchez, Francisco (Soria), 111
Hernández de los Palacios, Diego (Soria), 546
Hernández, Beatriz (Canary Islands), 527
Hernández, Beatriz (Granada), 224
Hernández, Bernardina (Granada), 224
Hernández, Josefa (Cuenca), 252
Hernández, Marina (Granada), 146, 568
Herrera, Cristobal de (Mexico), 139, 140

Herrera, Juan de (Ciudad Real), 272
Herrera, María Alfonso de (Toledo), 273, 274
High Holy Days. *See* Yom Kippur, Rosh Hashanah
Higuera, Alvaro de la (Ciudad Real), 291
Higuera, Inés de la (Ciudad Real), 324
Higuera, Inés de la (Teruel), 192
Higuera, María de la (Ciudad Real), 291
Higuera, María de la (Teruel), 375
Higueras, Pedro de (Ciudad Real), 323
Hita, Isabel de (Hita), 477
Holland, 59, 63, 100, 234, 604–605
Holy Child of La Guardia. *See* La Guardia, Holy Child
Holy Days. *See* Yom Kippur, Rosh Hashanah
Homem, Ant. nio (Coimbra), 124, 335, 370–371, 377, 478, 517, 601
Homem, Pedro (Brazil), 149
homosexuality. *See* sex, homosexuality
Honduras, 510
honey. *See* food, honey
Horosco, Marina de (Almazán), 511
Hoshanna Rabba, 412
host desecration, 14, 24, 88, 136, 161
Hoyo, Juan del (Ciudad Real), 135
Huerta, Alvaro (Garcimuñoz), 208
*huppah*. *See* marriage
Hurtado, Diego (Almazán), 157
Hurtado, Enrique (Almazán), 334
Husillo, Fernando (Toledo), 294

Ibáñez, Gracia (Soria), 153
idolatry, 146, 162
Ilhoa, Diogo Lopes (Brazil), 511, 514
Illuminism, 86
images
  avoidance of, 146, 278, 512
  disparagement of, 62, 88, 102, 146, 156, 157, 160, 576
  Jewish, 100, 117, 187, 370
  mistreatment of, 88, 136, 161, 162–166, 167
  power of, 229
impure state. *See niddah*
Inburgo, Martín de (Soria), 138
indulgences, disparagement of, 158
informer. *See malsín*
Iniesta, Alfonso (Alfaro), 324, 325
Iñigo (Aranda), 572
Inquisition
  *autos de fe*. *See autos de fe*

Inquisition (*continued*)
   confiscations, 19, 21, 46, 51, 52, 77, 595, 598–600
   edicts of faith. *See* edicts of grace
   establishment of, 18, 105, 115
   jurisdiction, 19
   opposition to, 23, 52, 594
   Portuguese, 50, 51, 52, 61
   precursors of, 5, 15, 16
   prisons, 20, 595
   procedures, 18, 22, 77, 217, 355
   quantitative data, 22, 32, 46, 55, 62, 67–70, 75–76
   sentences, 21–22
   spies, 19, 45
   torture, 20, 599
intermarriage
   annulment for conversion, 244
   choice of mate, 251
   disparagement of, 244, 245, 249, 250
   mourning for, 250
   prohibition against, 244
   reasons against, 244, 246, 247, 248
   reasons for, 244, 245
   regret at, 245
   to old-Christians, 13, 37, 51, 61, 244, 335
Isaac, 471
Isabel (Garcimuñoz), 210
Isabel, queen of Castile, 15, 16–18, 69
Israel, Menasseh ben, 341
Italy, 63, 100, 604

Jaén, F. de (Toledo), 457
Jaena, Magdalena la (Almazán), 572
Jaime (Calatayud), 291
Jaime I, Aragon, 4, 426
Jaime II, Aragon, 5, 6
Jamaica, 62
Jarada, Gonzalo (Trujillo), 258
Jarval, Lily Jean, 327, 510, 612
Jerez, Diego de (Canary Islands), 275
Jerez, Hernando (Las Palmas), 165
Jeronymites, 87, 151, 325, 625
Jerusalem, 104, 105, 603, 604
Jesuits, 222
Jesus
   as a Jew, 139
   avoidance of, 141, 142, 611
   disbelief in, 138, 139, 167
   disparagement of, 156, 566
   euphemisms for, 139, 141
   folklore about, 140
Jew-badge, 8, 11, 16, 48
Jewish communities. *See* aljamas
Jewish missionaries, 234
Jews
   definition, 82–83, 137, 167
   Portuguese as synonym, 219
   professions, See economics,
   role models for conversos, 217
   stereotypes ,136
Jímenez, Juan (Albarracín), 192
Joan I, Aragon, 6
Joanna (Lisbon), 326
João II, Portugal, 49
Jonah, 470
Josep, maestre (Segovia), 576
Joseph, 470, 611
Josephus, 193, 413, 429
Joshua, 470
Juan I, Castile, 7
Juan II, Castile, 11, 12, 15, 28, 30
Juana (Garcimuñoz), 210
Juárez de Espinosa, Simón (Mexico), 220, 248, 579, 601
Juárez de Figueroa, Diego (Mexico), 124, 189, 261, 274, 284, 302, 332, 527, 611
Juárez, Ana (Mexico), 598
Juárez, Blanca (Mexico), 58, 394
Juárez, Violante (Mexico), 608
Judaism, superiority of, 118–120
Judaizing
   reasons for, 227
   reasons to start, 220, 229
   reasons to stop, 229, 245, 568, 570
Judith, 431, 470, 494
Jurada, Beatriz (Toledo), 193
Justianiano, Juan de (Canary Islands), 188

Kabbala, 5
*Kaddish*. *See* prayers, *Kaddish*
kashruth. *See* dietary laws and customs
*Kedushah*. *See* prayers, *Kedushah*
*Ketubbah*. *See* marriage, nuptial agreements
*Kiddush*. *See* prayers, *Kiddush*
kipah, 256, 523, 527–528
kosher. *See* dietary laws and customs

*La Celestina*. *See* Rojas, Fernando de
La Guardia, Holy Child, 24–25, 136
Laço, Fernand (Miranda de Ebro), 476
Lagarto, Jacobo (Brazil), 517

Lagarto, Juan (Sigüenza), 156
Laguna, Catalina de (Granada), 446
Laínez, Aldonza (Almazán), 112, 427, 511, 538, 547
Laínez, Alonso (Almazán), 260
Laínez, Ana (Almazán), 537
Laínez, Antonio (Almazán), 152
Laínez, Beatriz (Almazán), 550
Laínez, Catalina (Almazán), 152, 538, 554
Laínez, Diego (Almazán), 301
Laínez, Francisco (Almazán), 427, 511
Laínez, Gregorio (Almazán), 121
Laínez, Isabel (Almazán), 149
Laínez, Pedro (Almazán), 148, 166, 511, 526, 529, 543
lamps, 367
last rites, 153, 277, 278
  parody of, 160
Lateran Council, 4
*Lazarillo de Tormes*, 86, 350, 612, 624
Leal, Antonio (Peru), 464
Leão, Graça de (Coimbra), 325
Lemos, Esteban de (Mexico), 332, 547
Lent, violation of, 157, 626
León Carvajal, Ana de (Mexico), 398, 401
León Jaramillo, Duarte de (Mexico), 158, 166, 206, 226, 319, 515
León Jaramillo, Francisco (Mexico), 595, 597
León Jaramillo, Juan de (Mexico), 140, 143, 153, 154, 156, 163, 168, 186, 202, 205, 211, 213, 222, 228, 233, 243, 249, 255, 273, 286, 299, 307, 332, 348, 361–63, 368, 372, 383, 386, 387, 398–402, 463, 474, 517, 525, 527, 543, 544, 575, 597, 601, 605, 607
León, Alonso de (San Mertín de Trevejo), 478
León, Angelina de (Almazán), 551
León, Antonia de (Mexico), 397
León, Cristóbal de (Almazán), 386
León, Jorge de (Mexico), 320
León, Juan de (Aranda), 478, 600, 616, 620
León, Luis de, 65–6, 85–86, 436, 497, 615
León, Pancho (Mexico), 205
León, Simón de (Mexico), 158, 165, 205, 206, 226, 273, 319, 320, 397, 533, 540, 557
Leonor (Cifuentes), 188
Leredi, Abraham (Villanueva), 590
Leví, Biuas (Soria), 209

Leví, Salomón (Soria), 209, 374
Lianor, Dona (Brazil), 502, 545
*Libro del Alboraique*, 93, 96, 150, 478, 617
Lillo, Lucía de (Ciudad Real), 325
*limpieza de sangre*. See purity of blood laws
Livinyana, Joan (Orihuela), 105, 121
Lloreynte (Navapalos), 153
Lobo, Antonio Costa (Evora), 599
Lobo, Heitor (Lamego), 369
Loperuelo, Juan de (Aragon), 296
Lopes, Alonso (Aranda), 119
Lopes, Ana (Lisbon), 156
Lopes, Branca (Lisbon), 510
Lopes, Brianda (Lisbon), 281
Lopes, Cristovão (Evora), 387
Lopes, Diego (Ciudad Real), 302
Lopes, Diogo (Evora), 149
Lopes, Duarte (Evora), 469
Lopes, Fernão (Azores), 302, 396, 401, 533
Lopes, Francisco (Brazil), 428
Lopes, García (Aranda), 575
Lopes, Gracia (Coimbra), 463
Lopes, Gracia (Lisbon), 604
Lopes, Guiomar (Grajal), 476
Lopes, Henrique (Elvas), 429
Lopes, Isabel (Coimbra), 41
Lopes, Isabel (Duas Igrejas), 146
Lopes, Isabel (Evora), 321
Lopes, Isabel (Miranda do Douro), 455, 470
Lopes, Isabel (Vila Flor), 105, 156, 377
Lopes, João (Lisbon), 143
Lopes, Juana (Garcimuñoz), 477
Lopes, Leonor (Pinhanços), 397, 400
Lopes, Manuel (Lisbon), 325
Lopes, Manuel (Viseu), 249, 433
Lópes, Mari (Ciudad Real), 503
Lopes, María (Azores), 449, 461
Lopes, María (Brazil), 151, 533, 548
Lopes, Thomaz (Brazil), 328, 508, 520
López Blandón, Francisco, 57
López Cocodrillo, Gonçalo (Segovia), 589
López Coscolla, Juan (Calatayud), 288
López de Armenia, Juan (Toledo), 447
López de Arnedo, Gonzalo (Soria), 139, 142
López de Arroyo, Alvar (Ciudad Real), 224
López de Fonseca, Francisco (Mexico), 394
López de Hituero, Pedro (Viana), 336, 572
López de Montforte, Tomás (Mexico), 609
López de Morales Pedro (Mexico), 599
López Díaz, Francisco (Mexico), 368, 516, 528, 595, 597, 599, 608, 614

López Enríquez, Francisco (Mexico), 56
López Morales, Pedro (Mexico), 57, 256, 259, 262
López Villareal, Nicolás (Oporto), 234
López, Alonso (Burgo de Osma), 472
López, Alvaro (Brazil), 160
López, Antón (Ciudad Real), 542
López, Antonio (Mexico), 375
López, Beatriz (Hita), 322
López, Catalina (Ciudad Real), 154, 374
López, Costanza (Calatayud), 255, 259
López, Costanza (Molina de Aragón), 191
López, Diego (Colombia), 515
López, Diego (Garcimuñoz), 111, 152, 427
López, Franco (France), 205
López, García (Aranda), 157, 574
López, Guiomar (Soria), 288
López, Inés (Ciudad Real), 142, 283, 336
López, Juan (Aranda), 139
López, Juan (Mexico), 375
López, Juana (Garcimuñoz), 281, 282, 470
López, Manuel (Burgos), 465
López, María (Almazán), 588
López, María (Calatayud), 193
López, Pedro (Almazán), 140
López, Pedro (Cuenca), 150, 151
López, Pero (Cornago), 374
López, Pero (Toledo), 526
López, Ramiro (Almazán), 511
López, Teresa (Ciudad Real), 154
Lozano, Cristobal, 429
Lucena, Fernando de (Toledo), 249
Lucena, Juan de (Soria), 388, 446
Lucero. *See* Rodríguez, Diego
Luis, Francisco (Mexico), 363
Luis, Gracia (Brazil), 163
Luiz, Izabel (Lisbon), 106
Luján, Diego de (Almazán), 149, 573
Luna, Alvaro de (Almazán), 538
Luna, Alvaro de (Castile), 14

ma'ariv. *See* prayers, ma'ariv
Machorro, Salomón. *See* León Jaramillo, Juan de
Madeira, Pedralvares (Brazil), 163
Madrid, Diego de (Garcimuñoz), 120, 142
Madrid, Fernando de (Palos de Moguer), 103, 104, 106, 119, 426, 501
Madrid, Fernando de (Toledo), 502
Madrid, Gonzalo de (Guadalupe), 221
Madrid, Juan de (Segovia), 95, 142, 363, 589, 602, 609, 620

Maestre, María (Quintana del Pidio), 596
Maimonides, 104, 183, 436, 437, 603
Majorca, 45, 47. *See also chuetas*
Maldonado de Silva, Francisco (Chile), 59, 102, 105, 106, 139, 140, 143, 146, 155, 166, 206, 237, 318, 358, 363, 366, 398, 434, 444, 463, 465, 474, 503, 579–580, 602, 608, 611
Maldonado de Silva, Isabel (Peru), 105, 146, 608
Maldonado, Diego (Zaragoza), 590
*malsín*, 19, 251, 478, 596
mandrake, 185
Manoel I, Portugal, 49, 50
Manuel, João (Portugal), 151
Manzana, María la (Almazán), 511
Marcos, Alonso (Ciudad Real), 225, 449, 461, 462, 473, 539
Mardoqueo (Canary Islands), 188
Mariana, Juan de, 32
Marín, Rodrigo (Ciudad Real), 154, 157, 374, 503
Marina, María (Valdecuendes), 145
Marques, Filipa (Lisbon), 106
Marques, Manoel (Lisbon), 400
marranos. *See* crypto-Judaism
marriage. *See also* intermarriage
 age at, 251
 blessings, 254, 257
 break glass, 256
 canopy, 254
 Catholic, 254
 ceremony, 253, 254, 255, 256, 627
 choice of mate, 243, 248, 609
 dowry, 254, 255, 256
 endogamy. *See* endogamy
 exogamy, 262
 fasting before, 257, 259
 festivities, 258, 259, 588–590
 gifts, 258
 joining hands, 256, 257
 levirate, 252
 music, 254, 257
 nuptial agreements, 253, 255, 256
 preparations, 254
 requirement to marry, 243
 requirement to procreate, 219, 243, 247
 rings, 254, 255, 256–257
 wine, 256, 257, 258, 259
Martí, Balthazar (Majorca), 363
Martí, Leonor (Majorca), 537
Martí, Margarita (Majorca), 363

Martín (Soria), 260
Martin V, Pope, 28
Martín, Catalina (Ciudad Real), 147, 334, 534, 541
Martín, Francisco (Calatayud), 255
Martín, Marina (Almazán), 427
Martínez de Cantalapiedra, Martín, 497
Martínez de los Olivos, Juan (Ciudad Real), 368, 503
Martínez de Santángel, Jaime (Teruel), 111
Martínez del Abad, Juan (Aranda), 119
Mártinez, Antonio (Alburquerque), 565
Martínez, Blanca (Toledo), 360
Martínez, Catalina (Almazán), 189, 572
Martínez, Catalina (Ciudad Real), 321
Martínez, Ferrand (Sevilla), 6
Martínez, Herrand (Soria), 572
Martínez, Francisco (Soria), 433, 574, 584, 603
Martínez, Jorge (Aranda), 466
Martínez, Juana (Cuenca), 274
Martínez, Leonor (Mexico), 366, 448, 540, 612
Martínez, Luis (Mexico), 334
Martínez, Luisa (Mexico), 366
Martínez, Rica (Teruel), 190
Martínez, Ruy (Soria), 591
Martins, Catarina (Evora), 149
Martins, Lianor (Brazil), 185
martyrdom, 229, 600–602
martyrologies, 64, 370, 594, 601
Mary
 as a Jewess, 142
 disbelief in, 142, 167, 627
 disparagement of, 142, 144, 164, 167
mass
 avoidance of, 148
 disparagement o,f 124, 148, 574
Matheu, Violante (Aragon), 284
Matos, María de (Avila), 446
matza, 193, 259, 374, 383–387, 549, 611
 distribution of, 385
 names for, 380, 384
 preparation of, 385, 389
 substitutes for, 57, 386
Mayor, Jorge de, 86
Mayrena (Canary Islands), 536
Medina, Ana de (Galicia), 539
Medina, Fernando de (Mexico), 110, 120, 434
Medina, One-eyed (Mexico), 156
Medrano, Andrés (Genevilla), 157, 516

Melamed, Jacob (Segovia), 386, 591
Melamed, Meir, 17, 26
Meléndez, Antonio (Guadalajara), 610
Meléndez, Mayor (Guadalajara), 537
Mellia, Juana de (Granada), 604
Mello, Manuel (Mexico), 358, 510
Memé, Abrahán (Segovia), 32, 478
Mena, Alonso de (Burgo de Osma), 291
Mendes d'Abreu, Garcia (Lisbon), 143
Mendes, Antónia Candida (Oporto), 434
Mendes, Antonio (Brazil), 429
Mendes, Branca (Portugal), 158
Mendes, Duarte (Brazil), 601
Mendes, Filipa (Vinhais), 455
Mendes, João (Tancoso), 116
Mendes, Lionel (Brazil), 595
Mendes, Luis (Almazán), 503
Mendes, Luis (Brazil), 148
Mendes, Pedro (Almazán), 114, 158
Mendes, Violante (Brazil), 429
Mendesia, Gracia, 64
Méndez Bravo, Hector (Madrid), 376, 393, 525, 527
Méndez Chaves, Luis (America), 436
Méndez de Ayala, María (Granada), 232
Méndez de Dueñas, Garci (Peru), 120, 333, 606
Méndez de Villaviciosa, Juan (Mexico), 118, 300, 595
Méndez, Antonio (Mexico), 296, 319, 336, 429, 430, 445
Mendez, Beatriz (Lisbon), 103
Méndez, Diego (Almazán), 572
Méndez, Juan (Mexico), 220, 579
Méndez, Justa (Mexico), 109, 311, 465
Meneses, Marcos (Canary Islands), 188, 527
menstruation, 223, 271, 274, 405
Mercado, Marina de (Granada), 116, 232
Mercado, Pedro (Mexico), 332
Mérida, Inés de (Ciudad Real), 274, 333, 334
Mesa, Periáñez de (Ecija), 89, 123, 231, 570
*meshumadim*, definition, 13
Mesquita, Felipa de (Vila Real), 476, 546
messianism, 43, 58, 82, 100, 103–110, 114, 115, 117, 136, 227, 470, 626
Mexías, Diego (Soria), 113
Mexico 44, 53, 54, 55–58. *See also* remnant crypto-Jews, Mexico
mezuzzahs, 40, 51, 321, 523, 528
Migues, João, 64

*mikvah*, 209, 272. *See also tebilah*
Miranda (Cuenca), 248
Miranda, Francisco de (Madrid), 399
Miranda, Isabel de (Madrid), 364, 401
Miró, Juana (Majorca), 220
miscegination. *See* sex, between races
Mishnah, 40
*mizraḥ*, 529
Mohejo, Mosé (Toledo) 457
*mohel. See* circumcision
Molina, Fernando de (Ciudad Real), 610
Molina, Juan (Huete), 393, 588
Moneda, de la (Soria), 451
Moniz, Violante (Brazil), 297, 511
monotheism, 43, 82, 100, 101–103, 136, 151, 224, 226, 227, 367
Montalbán, Bernardina (Granada), 228, 568
Montalván, Leonor (Granada), 224
Monteiro, André (Brazil), 325
Montero, Simón (Mexico), 394, 517, 525
Montesa, Jaime de (Calatayud), 255, 259
Montilla, Isabel de (Granada), 334, 464
Montoro, Antón de (Cordoba), 85, 321, 367, 374, 451, 477, 478, 521, 538, 544, 555
Montoya family (Mexico), 385
Mora, Diego (Quintanar de la Orden), 372, 383, 387, 545
Mora, Elvira de (Alcázar), 393
Mora, Sancho de (Ciudad Real), 386
Morales, Gonzalo de (Mexico), 54
Moreno, Pedro de (Valdecuendes), 145
Morera, Margarita de (Mexico), 513
Morocco, 39, 418, 604
Mortera, rabbi (Amsterdam), 235
Moses
  belief in, 43, 89, 100, 106, 111, 116–117, 123, 158
  worship of, 117, 187, 227, 370, 453, 470
Moses, Master (France), 205
mourning. *See* funeral customs
Moya, Juan de (Cuenca), 105, 604
Muñiz, Mencia (Granada), 397
Múñoz, Catalina (Ciudad Real), 286
Münzer, Hieronymus, 610
Murcia, Francisco de (Castile), 509
music, 208, 259, 336, 576. *See also* marriage, music

Nachmanides, 4
Nadal, Antonio (Teruel), 292
Nadal, Pedro (Teruel), 292

nails, 189, 193, 274, 280, 319, 626
names
  converso, 201–202
  Jewish, 62, 201, 202, 233, 627
naming ceremony, 148, 200. *See also guayas*
Navarre, 27
Navarro, Gabriel Gomes (Lisbon), 303, 365, 366, 452, 453
Navarro, Juan (Soria), 260
Nebrija, Antonio de, 435
Netherlands. *See* Holland
Nevárez, José (Mexico), 327
New Mexico. *See* remnant crypto-Jews, USA
new moorn. *See* Rosh Hodesh
New Testament, disparagement of, 158
Nicaragua, 58, 510, 597
Nicholas V, Pope, 29, 30
Nicolas of Lyra, 436
*niddah*, 271, 273
  activities forbidden during, 209–210, 273, 627
North Africa, 63
Nunes, Bacharel Simão (Lisbon), 478
Nunes, Clara (Trancoso), 457
Nunes, Duarte (Lisbon), 599
Nunes, Felipe (Trancoso), 464
Nunes, Fernão (Lisbon), 478
Nunes, Gregorio (Brazil), 163
Nunes, Isabel (Lisbon), 116
Nunes, João (Brazil), 163
Nunes, Leonor (Coimbra), 41
Nunes, Luisa (Coimbra), 247
Núñez de Navarro, Francisco (Mexico), 598
Núñez de Peralta, Tomás (Mexico), 257, 539
Núñez de Santafé, Pedro (Aranda), 251, 566
Núñez de Silva, Diego (Argentina), 227, 241, 358, 436
Núñez Franco, Pedro (Ciudad Real), 363
Núñez Pérez, Luis (Mexico), 205, 224
Núñez, Alonso (Soria), 540
Núñez, Ana (Mexico), 109, 116, 125, 165, 206, 219, 227, 470
Núñez, Ana (Murcia), 300
Núñez, Antonia (Mexico), 206, 474
Núñez, Beatriz (Ciudad Real), 220, 338
Núñez, Beatriz (Guadalupe), 148, 283, 334, 338, 536

Núñez, Catalina (Canary Islands), 535
Núñez, Clara (Mexico), 394
Núñez, Ferrant (Albuquerque), 565
Núñez, Francisca (Mexico), 300
Núñez, Isabel (Ciudad Rodrigo), 141, 187, 321, 357, 364, 366, 394
Núñez, Isabel (Mexico), 206, 280, 322, 445, 473, 544, 545
Núñez, Jorge (Peru), 611
Núñez, Juana (Ciudad Real), 318, 322, 333, 336, 339, 363
Núñez, Leonor (Mexico), 282, 401, 598
Núñez, Luis (Mexico), 189, 191
Núñez, Manuel (Mexico), 399
Núñez, María (Ciudad Real), 514
Núñez, Pedro (Coruña del Conde), 139
Núñez, Pedro (Santafé), 251, 566
Núñez, Pedro (Soria), 453
Núñez, Urraca (Ciudad Real), 610
nuptial agreements. *See* marriage

oaths, 501–503
Ocaña, García de (Toledo), 221
Oleaster, Jerome, 436
Oliva, Leonor de la (Ciudad Real), 323
Olivares, Count Duke. *See* Guzmán, Gaspar de
Oliveira, Antonia de (Brazil), 318
Oliveira, Blanca (Galicia), 282, 364
Olivera, Beatriz de (Logroño), 163
Olivera, Matias Rodrigues de (Mexico), 187
Olivos, Isabel de los (Ciudad Real), 323, 328, 433
Onofre Cortés, Pedro (Majorca), 102, 430, 607
Oropesa, Alfonso de (Castile), 15, 66
Oroz, Pedro de (Mexico), 435
Orozco, Juan de, 436
Ortigas (Almazán), 161
Osorio, Simón de (Ecuador), 358

Pablo Christiani, 4
Pacheco de León, Juan (Mexico), 207, 397
Pacheco, Alvaro (Brazil), 398
Pacheco, Antonio Rodrigues (France), 205
Pacheco, Juan (Mexico), 362, 413, 445, 522, 543
Paiva, Gaspar de (Canary Islands), 473
Paiva, María de (Brazil), 534
Palencia, Diego de (Aranda), 427
Palençuela, María de (Canary Islands), 535

Palma, María de (Granada), 146, 568
Panama, 609
Papudo (Burgos), 381
Paraguay, 59
Paredes, Conde de, 102, 524, 550
Paredes, Luis Lopes (Brazil), 508
Passover, 44, 355, 379–390, 588, 592. *See also* Matza
   calendar, 380
   fasting, 384, 388, 389
   foods, 382, 386, 388, 626
      Paschal lamb, 387
   Haggadah, 382
   names for, 379
   prayers, 389, 390
   preparation for, 384, 388
   search for leaven, 383
   seder, 382, 383
   separate dishes, 383
Paul V, Pope, 44
Paz Pinto, Blas de (Colombia), 515
Paz, João de (Brazil), 144
Paz, Jorge Díaz de (Brazil), 431
Pedro I, Castile, 6, 28
Pedro, Master (Cordoba), 108
Peixoto, Manoel (Lisbon), 123
Peixotto, Moses (Brazil), 517
Pelligero, Miguel (Soria), 453
Peña, Mencia de la (Escalona), 599
Pena, Sebastían de la (Mexico), 320
Peñafiel (Segovia), 381
Peñafiel, Alonso de (Guadalupe), 570
Peñafiel, Fernando de (Cerezo de Río Tirón), 362
Peñafiel, Lope de (Guadalupe), 570
penitential garments. *See sambenitos*
Peraile, Juan (Bordonales), 158
Peralta, María de (Brazil), 163
Pereira, Diogo (Lisbon), 165
Pereira, Inés (Mexico), 58, 109
Pereira, Sebastião (Lisbon), 604
Pérez de Almazán, Miguel, 18
Pérez de Ariza, Juan (Aragon), 258
Pérez de Gijón (Burgo de Osma), 291
Pérez Jarada, Gonzalo (Trujillo), 588, 591
Pérez Roldán, Luis (Mexico), 322
Pérez, Agustín (Valladolid), 572
Pérez, Ana (Canary Islands), 279
Pérez, Beatriz (Granada), 448, 537
Pérez, Diego (Peru), 149, 158, 165
Pérez, Juan (Soria), 186
Pérez, Juana (Aranda), 193

Pérez, Manuel Bautista (Anzan), 522, 601
Pérez, Ruy (Philippines), 147, 536, 539
Pérez, Sebastián (Ciudad Rodrigo), 165
Periáñez de Mesa, doctor (Ecija), 570
Pero Gonçález, Buena de (Agreda), 590
Peru, 53, 54, 59, 619. *See also* remnant crypto-Jews, Peru
Pesach. *See* Passover
Peso, Luis del (Almazán), 572
Philippines, 59
phylacteries. *See* tefillin
Picardo, João (Brazil), 332
pilgrimages, disparagement of, 156
Pimentel, Salvador (Bragança), 465
Piña, Fernão da (Lisbon), 154
Pineda, Juan de, 430
Pintado, Juan (Ciudad Real), 601
Pinto, Fernán (Canary Islands), 300, 606
Pinto, Josepe (Extremadura), 597, 595
Pires, Fernão (Brazil), 160, 250
Pisa, María de (Zaragoza), 252, 261
Platero, Antonio (Roa), 148
Poeta, Juan, 102
Pomar, Gerónima (Majorca), 220
Pope, disparagement of, 158
population. *See* Jews, demography; *conversos*, demography
Portugal, 27, 36, 38, 48–53, 74, 76, 81
  immigration to, 49
Portuguese as synonym for Jews, 44, 52
Portuguese diffusion, 44, 46, 52, 56, 76, 232
potions, 191, 192
Prado, Alvaro de (Soria), 596, 600
prayer books, 40, 51, 218, 279, 329–330, 425, 432, 435
prayer shawl. *See* tallit
prayers
  *Amidah*, 40, 434, 462, 472
  call to, 328
  chanting, 474
  Christian, 139, 225, 226, 279, 468–471, 611
  daily, 445–450
  eating, 452, 453
  facing east, 473, 515
  facing wall, 472, 473, 626
  fasting, 224
  funeral, 285
  Gloria Patri, 464, 626
  *Hallel*, 411
  illness, 229
  *Kaddish*, 40, 118, 286, 287, 288, 451, 460, 462
  *Kedushah*, 434
  *Kiddush*, 256, 257, 453, 454, 477
  kneeling, 474, 515
  *ma'ariv*, 448–450
  movements during, 329, 471, 515, 626
  petitions, 455–459
  Psalms, 40, 329, 330, 370, 371, 428, 431–432, 434, 444, 445, 446, 462–464, 473
  quantitative, 155, 465
  *shaḥarit*, 446, 448
  *Shema*, 40, 57, 101, 218, 225, 330, 434, 444, 461, 515
  slaughtering, 545
  superstitious, 188
  the star, 224, 367, 448
  washing, 450, 452
priests' powers, disbelief in, 154
processions
  disparagement of, 156
  Jewish, 369, 375, 425, 427, 573, 588
proselytizing
  converso, 231
  Jewish, 231
Psalms. *See* prayers, Psalms
Puigdorfila, Antonio de (Majorca), 535
Puigmija, Manuel de (Valencia), 149, 503
Puigmija, Violante (Valencia), 149
Pulgar, Hernando de, 18, 84, 85
Purgatory, 111–115, 612
Purificação Prada, Beatriz da (Carção), 120
Purim, 137, 355, 356, 377–379
  calendar, 378
  Fast of Esther, 43, 44, 378, 379, 400, 626
  foods, 379
  Megillah, 377
  prayers, 378
purity-of-blood laws, 15, 16, 38, 41, 43, 45, 49, 51, 52, 61, 81, 82, 83, 119, 244, 245, 579, 596
Puxmija, Clara de (Teruel), 192, 338, 477, 538
Puxmija, Francés de (Teruel), 301, 368, 433, 463
Puxmija, Manuel de, 503
Puxmija, Tolosana (Teruel), 292

Quevedo, Francisco de, 612

rabbis, 331, 516–518, 591
  clothing, 371, 383, 514, 524–525
  women, 516
Rabinuça, Yudá (Burgos), 381
Raphael, Pedro Fernandes (Brazil), 508
Ram, Fernando (Teruel), 589
Ram, Juan (Teruel), 547
Ramírez de Montilla, Jorge (Mexico), 595
Ramírez, Blanca (Toledo), 338, 514, 546, 558, 589
Ramírez, Juan (Ciudad Real), 110, 147, 153, 329, 387, 427, 461, 462, 478, 610
Ramírez, Juan (Soria), 118
Ramírez, Leonor (Soria), 595
Ramírez, Luisa (Granada), 273, 537
Ramón y Zamora, Jerónimo, 430
Raymond of Peñafort, 4
Reed, Ruth Flores (Mexico), 187
reliability of evidence, 76–80
relics, 158, 165
remnant crypto-Jews, 89, 101, 138, 246, 247, 525
  Brazil, 528
  Cuba, 327, 498, 547
  Mexico, 327
  Peru, 327
  Portugal, 47, 53, 114, 152, 208, 210, 238, 240, 247, 266, 275, 278, 281, 405–6, 408–9, 434, 518, 520, 528
    birth customs, 200–210
    dietary laws and customs, 120, 340, 363, 534, 547, 549, 551
    funeral customs, 285, 296, 299, 303, 304, 312
    holidays, 361, 362, 365, 366, 367, 369, 377, 379, 380, 388, 390, 395
    marriage customs, 251, 257, 259
    prayers, 102, 151, 200, 201, 279, 288, 290, 396, 415, 419, 444, 446, 447–448, 449, 452, 453, 455, 458–459, 465, 466, 469, 471, 476, 510
    Sabbath customs, 325, 327, 331, 340, 344, 525
    saints, 117, 378, 471
  Spain, 223, 251, 327, 340, 620
  USA, 47, 107, 174–5, 177–8, 181, 223, 372, 377, 378, 414, 418–9, 455, 485, 494, 510, 518, 528
Reubeni, David, 105
Rhodes, 269, 315

Ribadaneyra, Pedro de, 430, 435
Ribas, Bernardo de (Calatayud), 255
Ribeira, Beatriz (Coimbra), 540
Ribeiro, Gaspar (Italy), 89
Rimoch, Astruc (Fraga), 9
rings. See marriage
Ríos Matos, Francisco (Mexico), 108
Ríos, Antón de (Soria), 549
riots against conversos, 14, 15, 16, 51
riots against Jews, 6–9, 37, 48, 105, 115
Ripoll, Pedro de (Albarracín), 121, 569
Riquel, Diego (Canary Islands), 162
ritual bath. See mikvah
ritual murder. See blood libel
Rivera, Catalina de (Mexico), 281, 283, 285, 286, 368, 380, 399, 401, 527
Rivera, Clara de (Mexico), 147, 158
Rivera, Isabel de (Mexico), 155, 262, 273, 278, 294, 296, 534
Rivera, Margarita de (Mexico), 58, 114, 189, 191, 225, 261, 281, 328, 608
Rivera, María de (Mexico), 225, 289, 399, 455–457
Roa, Diego de (Soria), 599
Robles, Juan de (Cuenca), 604
Rocha, Fernão da (Lisbon), 600
Rodrigo, alcalde (Ciudad real), 383
Rodrigues, Alonso (Maqueda), 150
Rodrigues, Alvaro (Lisbon), 233
Rodrigues, Beatriz (Lamego), 548
Rodrigues, Bernardo (Bragança), 395, 458, 545
Rodrigues, Gracia (Oporto), 156, 472
Rodrigues, Ines (Brazil), 160
Rodrigues, Isabel (Evora), 283
Rodrigues, Jerónimo (Coimbra), 464
Rodrigues, Leonor (Coimbra), 369
Rodrigues, Manuel (Huete), 587
Rodrigues, Manuel (Linhares), 89, 122
Rodrigues, Margarida (Lisbon), 400
Rodrigues, María (Lamego), 445
Rodrigues, Paulo (Coimbra), 470
Rodrigues, Pero (Lamego), 158
Rodríguez Arias, Antonio (Mexico), 247, 522
Rodriguez Arias, Diego (Canary Islands), 537
Rodríguez de Matos, Francisco (Mexico), 57, 284, 302, 497, 522
Rodríguez de Medina, Mencía (Guadalajara), 121, 184

Rodríguez de Montalvo, Garcia, 86
Rodríguez de Olivera, Matías (Mexico), 361, 363
Rodríguez family (Mexico), 336
Rodríguez Feijoso, Simón (La Roda), 291
Rodríguez López, Melchor (Mexico), 159
Rodríguez Lucero, Diego, 91
Rodríguez Maroto, Simón (Jumilla), 157
Rodríguez Tabara, Jorge (Mexico), 365
Rodríguez Tejoso, Duarte (Mexico), 510
Rodríguez, Alonso (Ciudad Real), 323, 340
Rodríguez, Ana (Brazil), 278, 285, 299, 300
Rodríguez, Ana (Soria), 209
Rodríguez, Antón (Tembleque), 281, 292
Rodríguez, Antonio (Cuenca), 252
Rodríguez, Baltasar (Brazil), 221
Rodríguez, Baltazar (Mexico), 117, 232
Rodríguez, Blanca (Huete), 588
Rodríguez, Blanca (Mexico), 399
Rodríguez, Blasco (Soria), 154
Rodríguez, Catalina (Mexico), 262
Rodríguez, Clara (Yepes), 280
Rodríguez, Costanza (Mexico), 375, 597
Rodríguez, Diego (Canary Islands), 164, 537, 540
Rodríguez, Duarte (Mexico), 320, 324, 430, 510, 536, 541, 545, 547, 597
Rodríguez, Esperanza (Mexico), 57, 262, 598
Rodríguez, Fernando (Mexico), 57, 399, 609
Rodríguez, Gonçalo (Canary Islands), 540, 544
Rodríguez, Isabel (Mexico), 320, 375, 535
Rodríguez, Isabel (Toledo), 364, 401
Rodríguez, Juan (Atienza), 287
Rodríguez, Juan (Tajaguerce), 475
Rodríguez, Juana (Granada), 399
Rodríguez, Juana (Mexico), 303
Rodríguez, Lucina (Canary Islands), 146, 535, 540
Rodríguez, Manuel (Granada), 232
Rodríguez, Manuel (Huete), 587, 590
Rodríguez, María (Valencia), 250
Rodríguez, Mariana (Mexico), 117
Rodríguez, Marina (Ciudad Real), 542
Rodríguez, Micaela (Mexico), 259
Rodríguez, Pedro (Ciudad Real), 140
Rodríguez, Pedro (Guadalupe), 468
Rodríguez, Perpetua (Canary Islands), 146, 156, 540
Rodríguez, Sebastián (Mexico), 375, 597, 607
Rodríguez, Simón (Mexico), 375
Rodríguez, Violante (Mexico), 547
Rofos, Rodrigo (Toledo), 541, 543
Roiz, Branca (Brazil), 318
Roiz, Gaspar (Zaragoza), 535
Roiz, Guiomar (Evora), 301
Rojas, Catalina de (Granada), 116, 122, 191, 232
Rojas, Fernando de, 66, 86, 191, 200, 617
Rojas, Juana de (Granada), 123, 570
Rojas, Leonor de (Granada), 123, 570
Rojas, Leonor de (Mexico), 368
Rojas, Rodrigo de (Toledo), 297
Román (Castile), 321, 367, 374
Román, Sebastián (Mexico), 109
Romeiro, Salvador (Brazil), 262
Romo, Pedro el (Soria), 474
Rosa, Pero Fernandes da (Coimbra), 446
rosaries, 155, 612
   disparagement of, 167
   mistreatment of, 165
Rosh Hodesh, 393
Rosh Hashanah, 137, 184, 356–357
Roza, Domingos Nunes da (Brazil), 609
Ruiz, Aldonza (Teruel), 254
Ruiz, Antón (Teruel), 192, 296, 297
Ruiz, Bartolomé (Soria), 469
Ruiz, Catalina (Ciudad Real), 286
Ruiz, Catalina (Huete), 294
Ruiz, Donosa (Teruel), 101, 146, 149, 157, 201, 591
Ruiz, Felipa (Galicia), 547
Ruiz, Francisco (Medina del Campo), 577
Ruiz, Gonzalvo (Teruel), 113, 457, 462, 507
Ruiz, Gracia (Teruel), 334
Ruiz, Josefa (Mexico), 262
Ruiz, Lucía (Ciudad Real), 142
Ruiz, María (Ciudad Real), 141
Ruiz, Martín (Teruel), 374
Ruiz, Rernand (Aranda), 203

Sa'adia ben Danan, 177
Sabbath, 43, 44, 317–341, 626
   avoiding work on, 62, 124, 158, 190, 318, 331–337, 340, 626
   bathing for, 319, 322
   calendar, 318, 322
   candles, 53, 318, 323–328
   clean clothes, 319–320, 626

clean table linen, 190, 321, 626
cleaning for, 318, 320–321
foods, 337–340, 549. *See also adafina*
goy, 334
*havdala*, 336
*Kiddush*, 318
prayers, 322–323, 325, 327, 329, 330–331, 576–577
Sambatyon, 340
visiting, 335–336, 515
sacraments, 147. *See also* baptism, eucharist, etc.
sacrilege, 137, 159, 160, 161, 167
Sahagún, Bernardino de, 55
saints
  disparagement of, 145, 157, 164, 627
  Jewish, 100, 116–117, 187, 331, 378, 379, 470
Salcedo, Juan de (Aranda), 38, 113, 140, 157, 297, 427, 450, 466, 473, 503, 527, 539, 542, 543, 595, 619
Salcedo, Pedro de (Almazán), 565
Salonica, 208
Salvador, Esperandeu (Zaragoza), 462
Salvador, Martín (Aragon), 261
salvation, 5, 21, 43, 89, 100, 106, 110–111, 113, 121, 167, 207, 220, 221, 225, 227, 229, 235, 278, 329, 363, 378, 383, 399, 569–570, 611
*sambenitos*, 21, 282, 598, 619
San Jordi, Francisco de, 11
San Juan, Bernardina de (Baeza), 154, 187, 209, 247, 273, 280, 283, 301, 380, 400, 514
San Juan, Diego de (Baeza), 187
San Juan, doctor (Baeza), 569
San Juan, doctor (Cordoba), 229
San Juan, Elvira de (Baeza), 143, 154, 187, 571
San Juan, Isabel de (Baeza), 187, 571
San Juan, Juan de (Baeza), 358
San Juan, Juana de (Baeza), 101
San Juan, Leonor de (Baeza), 279
San Juan, María de (Baeza), 101, 332, 397, 569
San Juan, sisters (Cordoba), 222, 229
San Pedro, Diego de, 85, 86
Sanbrana, Catharina (Lisbon), 283
Sanches, Alvaro (Brazil), 165
Sánchez Caballero, Gonzalo (Soria), 373
Sánchez Castro, Hernand (Uclés), 573
Sánchez de Badajoz, Diego, 66, 85
Sánchez de Calatayud, Juan, 6
Sánchez de Castro, Juana (Frías), 162
Sánchez de Guadalupe, Gonzalo (Talavera), 160
Sánchez de las Cosillas, Garci (Cifuentes), 458
Sánchez de Salarena, Martín (Covarrubias), 508
Sánchez de San Pedro, Diego (Ocaña), 587
Sánchez de Segovia, Rodrigo, 54
Sánchez de Tapia, Catalina (Calatañazor), 201
Sánchez de Tapia, Pedro (Calatañazor), 201
Sánchez Exarch, Juan (Teruel), 157, 323, 337, 368, 374, 392
Sánchez Exarch, Violante (Teruel), 385
Sánchez family (Aragon), 17
Sánchez, Alonso (Badajoz), 476
Sánchez, Alonso (Ciudad Real), 153, 323, 329, 433
Sánchez, Ana (Mexico), 366
Sánchez, Antón (Ciudad Real), 603
Sánchez, Elvira (Garcimuñoz), 548
Sánchez, Fernand (Soria), 112
Sánchez, Gonzalo (Soria), 589
Sánchez, Isabel (Cuenca), 151
Sánchez, José (Mexico), 394
Sánchez, Juan (Antequera), 112, 116
Sánchez, Juan (Granada), 337
Sánchez, Juan de Juan (Almazán), 161
Sánchez, Juan de Pedro (Almazán), 161
Sánchez, Juana (Garcimuñoz), 326, 533
Sánchez, Lope (Garcimuñoz), 299
Sánchez, Luis (Soria), 143, 426, 428
Sánchez, Mari (Cifuentes), 188
Sánchez, María (Ciudad Real), 515
Sánchez, María (Garcimuñoz), 163, 379
Sánchez, María (Guadalupe), 339
Sánchez, Marina (Soria), 185
Sánchez, Ruy (Soria), 386
Sánchez, Teresa (Garcimuñoz), 155, 185, 533, 538
Sancho, Teresa (Almazán), 280
Sandoval, Prudencio, 93
Sant Joan, Pedro de (Aragon), 566
Santa Clara, Jaime de (Aragón), 185
Santa Clara, Juan de (Toledo), 357
Santa Clara, Simón de (Calatayud), 121
Santa Cruz, Alonso de (Calatayud), 258
Santa Cruz, Graciana (Soria), 317

Santa Fe, Jerónimo de, 10, 11, 85, 385, 615
Santa María, Gonzalo García de (Almazán), 161
Santa María, Pablo de, 5, 10, 11, 30, 85, 563, 580, 615
Santaclara, Simón de (Calatayud), 375
Santacruz (Soria), 141
Santacruz, Catalina de (Granada), 119, 603
Santángel family (Aragon), 18, 54, 161
Santángel, Alba de (Teruel), 334
Santángel, Angelina de (Barbastro), 254
Santángel, Brianda (Teruel), 222, 245, 334, 542, 567
Santángel, Gracia (Teruel), 156
Santángel, Isabel de (Tarazona), 113
Santángel, Jaime de (Teruel), 511
Santángel, Leonardo (Calatayud), 261
Santángel, Leonor (Teruel), 374
Santángel, Rita (Teruel), 589
Santángel, Speraindeo de (Barbastro), 509
Santángel, Violante (Teruel), 156, 359, 374, 589
Santo Fimia, Elvira de (Granada), 116
São Tomé Islands, 39, 49
Saravia, María de (Soria), 152, 479
Saravia, Marzal (Galicia), 226
Sarmiento, Pedro (Toledo), 15
Sastre, Nicolau (Majorca), 142
Schwarz, Samuel, 47, 53
Sebastão, Portugal, 52, 105
secrecy, 220, 226
Segovia, Diego de (Guadalupe), 534
Segovia, Juan de, 105
Segueta, Juan de (Mexico), 280
Sem Tob, 430
Seneor, Abraham, 13, 17, 26, 54, 139, 374, 573, 613
Serrano, Juan (Zaragoza), 590
Serrano, Mazaltó (Soria), 546
Serrano, Pedro (Puebla de Montalbán), 104
Serrano, Ysaque (Soria), 546
Setevi, Isaac (Soria), 186
Sevilla, Juan de (Toledo), 149, 603
sex
    between Jews and Christians, 261
    between races, 57, 61, 262
    homosexuality, 261, 262
    on Sabbath, 322
    outside of marriage, 260, 261
    to commit sacrilege, 162
*shaharit. See* prayers, *shaharit*
Shavuot, 390–391
*Shema. See* prayers, Shema
*Shemini atzeret,* 375
Shemtob, Joseph ibn, 12
*shiva. See* funeral customs, mourning period
*shofar,* 356, 359, 370, 371, 588
shrouds. *See* funeral customs, shrouds
*siddur. See* prayer books
Sierra, Juan de la (CIudad Real), 118, 224, 225, 324, 330, 449, 461, 473, 541, 603
Sierra, Rodrigo de la (Ciudad Real), 320
Silbeira y Cardoso, Antonio (Mexico), 142, 156, 157
Siltón, Gento (Aragon), 573
Silva, Catalina (Murcia), 163
Silva, Diego de (Argentina), 227
Silva, Elena de (Mexico), 287, 293, 368
Silva, José da (Brazil), 221, 261, 318, 319, 444, 469, 608
Silva, Juan de (Atienza), 287, 477
Silva, Leonor de (Granada), 537
Silva, Pedro da (Brazil), 62
Silveira y Cardoso, Antonio (Mexico), 432
Simḥat Torah, 375–376
Simancas, Diego de (Seville), 103
Simoél, rabbi (Segovia), 576
Simuel, rabbi (Teruel), 359, 363, 364
Sixtus IV, Pope, 18
Soares, Helena (Bragança), 472
Soares, Manuel (Lisbon), 156, 330
Sobremonte, Tomás de (Mexico), 225, 510, 605
Soeiro, Fernão (Brazil), 152
Sol (Aragon), 279
Soler, Pedro (Almazán), 565
Solomon's seal, 188
Soria, Diego de (Soria), 152
Soria, Hernando de (Sigüenza), 339
Soria, Yñigo de (Aranda), 503
Sosa y Prado, Manuel de (Mexico), 120, 142, 145, 156, 157, 429, 432, 435, 599
spells, 187, 192
Suárez, Francisco (Soria), 386
Suárez, Gaspar (Mexico), 281, 282
Suárez, Mencia (Ocaña), 470
Sukkot, 51, 355, 357, 369, 371–375, 574, 588

booths, 373, 375, 626
calendar, 372
four fruits, 372
prayers, 373
visiting, 374, 375, 626
Sundays, violation of, 157
superstitions, 183–193, 210, 357, 390, 405
Surinam, 62
synagogues, 508–513
    clandestine, 328, 334, 381, 509–513
    outdoor, 511
syncretism, 118, 121–123, 569

*Takkanot* of Valladolid, 507
Talavera, Hernando de, 85, 173, 563, 580, 615
tallit, 51, 184, 474, 523–525
Talmud, 40, 425–426
Tapiazo, Antón (Aranda), 527, 535
Tardajos, Rodrigo de (Soria), 501
Teba, Hernando de (Ciudad Real), 369, 524
*tebilah*, 272, 507
    after childbirth, 209, 255, 272
    after menstruation, 224, 272, 273
    prior to festivals, 272, 273, 274, 360–361
    prior to Sabbath, 272, 592
    prior to wedding, 254
tefillin, 446, 523, 526–527
Teixeira, Bento (Brazil), 138, 142, 332, 428
Teixeira, Leonor (Coimbra), 539
Teresa de Avila, 66, 615
Terra, Luiz (Lisbon), 608
Teva, Diego de (Ciudad Real), 396
Teva, Gracia de (Ciudad Real), 111
Teva, Juan de (Ciudad Real), 141, 159, 318, 336
Texedor, Alfonso (Osma), 112
Texedor, Francisco (Aranda), 204
Texoso, Beatriz (Mexico), 614
Texoso, Francisca (Mexico), 165, 560
Texoso, Francisco Gómez (Mexico), 201
Texoso, Isabel (Mexico), 431, 468
Thomaz, Diogo (Lisbon), 142
Thomaz, João (Lisbon), 608
Tinoco, Catalina (Mexico), 220
Tinoco, Diego (Mexico), 220, 248
Tinoco, Juana (Mexico), 248
Tinoco, Miguel (Mexico), 58

Tinoco, Pedro (Mexico), 362, 382, 393, 398
Tinoco, Rodrigo (Mexico), 385
Tirguero, Antonio (Soria), 426
Tisha b'Av, 392–393, 413, 626
Tobit, 331, 431
Toledo, Alfonso de (Toledo), 118, 392, 429, 502, 594, 602
Toledo, Francisco de (Guadalupe), 535
Toledo, Juan de (Toledo), 435
Tomas, Heitor (Evora), 534
Torah, 218, 425
Torahs, 40, 51
Toriel, Juçe (Aragon), 207
Torquemada, Juan de, 30–1, 615
Torquemada, Tomás de, 19, 24, 85, 594
Torre, Catalina de la (Granada), 570
Torrejoncillo, Francisco de, 92
Torrellas, Berenguer (Aragon), 284
Torrellas, Fernando (Calatayud), 255
Torres Naharro, Bartolomé de, 66, 85
Torres, Alonso de las (Casarrubios del Monte), 261, 544
Torres, Catalina de (Garcimuñoz), 281
Torres, Diego de (Canary Islands), 536
Torres, Duarte de (Mexico), 262
Torres, Fernando de (Toledo), 610, 623
Torres, Francisco de (La Almunia), 245, 567, 574
Torres, Inés de (Granada), 273, 274
Torres, Juan de (Ciudad Real), 113
Torres, Luis de, 54
Torres, Rodrigo de (Ciudad Real), 386
Torrijos, Gonzalo de (Toledo), 121
Tortosa. *See* disputations
*toura*, 513. *See also* amulets
Treviño de Sobremonte, Rafael (Mexico), 144, 204, 225, 226, 227, 397, 448, 605
Treviño de Sobremonte, Tomás (Mexico), 58, 114, 120, 144, 190, 204, 227, 256, 259, 326, 333, 360, 361, 365, 366, 397, 401, 431, 444, 445, 447, 450, 451, 462, 474, 510, 517, 524, 543, 545, 605
Tribulet (Zaragoza), 259
Trinity, 5, 226
    disbelief in, 101, 138, 468, 501
Trujillo, Fernando de (Ciudad Real), 186, 254, 377, 516, 542
Tudela, Antonia de (Madrid), 158, 162
Turkey, 27, 63, 100, 109, 604

*tzitzit*, 514, 523, 525–526, 626

Uruguay, 59

Váez Sevilla, Gaspar (Mexico), 109, 117, 221, 222, 226, 368
Váez Sevilla, Leonor (Mexico), 287, 598
Váez Sevilla, Simón (Mexico), 57, 186, 399, 402, 510, 517
Váez Tirado, Antonio (Mexico), 298, 517
Váez, Antonio (Mexico), 57
Váez, Gonzalo (Granada), 103, 106, 114, 141, 158, 379, 380, 464
Váez, Gonzalo (Mexico), 430
Váez, Simón (Mexico), 609
Valdeolivas, Juana de (Garcimuñoz), 294, 301
Valdés, Alfonso de, 85, 86
Valdés, Juan de, 85, 86
Valença, Antônio (Mogadouro), 377
Valenci, Samuel (Toledo), 231
Valencia, Antonia de (Mexico), 166, 228
Valencia, Clara de (Mexico), 166, 228
Valencia, Francisco de (Mexico), 166, 228
Valencia, Luis de (Mexico), 225, 322, 597
Valencia, Simón de (Mexico), 116, 166, 167, 225, 227, 568
Valero, Francisco (Toledo), 138
Valladolid, Alfonso de, 4–5, 30
Valladolid, Juan de, 85, 524, 550
Valle, Antón del (Almazán), 573
Valle, Jerónimo de (Mexico), 162
Valle, Luisa del (Madrid), 158, 162
Valls, Rafael (Majorca), 249, 429, 430, 434, 516
Varca, María (Almazán), 110
Vaz Cordilha, Alfonso (Portugal), 393
Vaz de Azevedo, Sebastián de (Mexico), 399
Vaz, Alfonso (Lisbon), 432
Vaz, Antónia (Matosinhos), 119, 604
Vaz, Enrique (Brazil), 473
Vaz, Francisca (Lisbon), 358, 368
Vaz, Gonzalo (Portugal), 152
Vaz, Heitor (Coimbra), 604
Vaz, Joana (Aveiro), 138
Vaz, Pêro (Evora), 534
Vaz, Simão (Lisbon), 138
Vaz, Violante (Evora), 321
Vázquez, Costanza (Granada), 224, 228

Vecinho, Joseph, 54
Vega, Lope de, 71, 168, 195, 436, 616
Veigua, Manoel da (Brazil), 256
Velacha, Beatriz (Almazán), 151
Velacha, Martín de (Almazán), 151
Velasco, Sancho de (Viana), 336
Vélez, Antonio (Almazán), 146
Vélez, Luis (Almazán), 294
Vélez, Pedro (Almazán), 280
Vellida (Toledo), 392
Vellida (Trujillo), 261
Venezuela, 59
Vera, García de (Garcimuñoz), 385
Verga, Shlomo ibn, 435, 553
Vergara, Francisco de (Peru), 398, 607
Vergara, Juan de, 85
Vicente, Gil, 66, 85, 102, 486, 498–9
Victoria, João de (Lisbon), 233
Victoria, Juan de (Soria), 373
Vidigueira, Gaspar Dias (Brazil), 210
Villa, Catalina de la (Ciudad Real), 190, 540
Villalpando, María de (Soria), 288
Villanueva, Blanca de (Quintanar), 285
Villa Real, Lope de (Ciudad Real), 511
Villarreal, Pedro de (Ciudad Real), 333
Villarubia, Rodrigo de (Ciudad Real), 139
Villegas Selvago, Alonso, 430
Violante, Catalina de (Soria), 185
Vives, Luis, 508
Vives, Miquel (Valencia), 381, 510

washing, 272, 274, 626
    hands, 259, 275, 323, 451, 514, 525, 626
water, pouring out, 190, 191. *See also* funeral customs
"Wedding of Rodrigo Cota," 141
wet nurse, 209
wine, 626. *See also* dietary laws and customs
witches, 186, 188, 189, 191, 200
women, 37, 39, 53

Xeteui, doctor (Soria), 566
Xuet, Acach (Calatayud), 111

Yáñez, Rodrigo, 437
*yarmulke. See kipah*
Yom Kippur, 43, 44, 137, 167, 224, 227, 355, 357–371, 514, 603
    activities prohibited during, 359, 362, 626

blessing, 369, 371, 626
calendar, 357–359, 366
charity, 369
confession, 367
dissemblance, 362, 363, 369, 399
fasting, 359, 360, 362–365, 400, 626
foods, 360, 361, 363, 364–365
forgiving, 360, 361, 368–369, 626
lamps, 360, 361–362, 367, 368, 369, 370
physical mortification, 360, 365–366
prayers, 360, 365, 366–368, 369, 525
preparations for, 360–361, 363, 370
Yom Kippur Katan, 393

Zacuto, Abraham, 54
Zahalon, Yom Tob (Venice), 245, 250, 568
Zahara (Teruel), 400
Zamora, Catalina de (Ciudad Real), 144, 254, 299, 599, 610
Zamora, Diego de (Ciudad Real), 319
Zapata, García (Toledo), 374
Zapatero, Fernán (Soria), 600
Zaporta, Saloman (Sagunto), 231
Zaragoza, Isaac (Segovia), 478
Zaragoza, Juan de (Aragon), 259
Zaragoza, Judá (Segovia), 576, 577
Zaragoza, Mosé (Segovia), 478
Zárate, María de (Mexico), 117, 123, 142, 145, 146, 156, 164, 219, 252, 340, 380, 384, 400, 403, 420, 432, 445, 446, 463, 464, 603, 610, 618, 619
Zarco, Fernando el (Cuenca), 151
Zayas, Juan de (Calatayud), 111, 121
Zúñiga, María de (Mexico), 281, 282
Zvi, Shebtai, 109